THE WORD

THE WORD

The Dictionary that Reveals the Hebrew Sources of English

Isaac E. Mozeson

JASON ARONSON INC.
Northvale, New Jersey
London

First Jason Aronson Inc. Edition—1995

Copyright © 1995, 1989 Isaac E. Mozeson

10 9 8 7 6 5 4 3 2 1

For a lively slide presentation for any audience, for available video or audio cassettes, disks, foreign-language lists, a booklet with the many new discoveries since 1989, or to contribute additions or corrections to a future publication—please contact the author at: 693 Chestnut Avenue, Teaneck, NJ 07666, Tel. 201/836-3410 or 25/6 Yehoshua Bin Nun, Jerusalem, Israel, Tel. 02/638-851.

Library of Congress Cataloging-in-Publication Data

Mozeson, Isaac.
    The word : the dictionary that reveals the Hebrew source of
English / by Isaac E. Mozeson. — 1st ed.
        p.   cm.
    Includes bibliographical references and index.
    ISBN 1-56821-615-7 (alk. paper)
    1. English language — Foreign elements — Hebrew.   2. English
language — Etymology — Dictionaries.   3. Hebrew language — Influence on
English — Dictionaries.   I. Title.
PE1582.H4M69   1995
422'.4924'03—dc20   95-17239
                                                                      CIP

Manufactured in the United States of America.
Jason Aronson Inc. offers books and cassettes. For information and catalog write to Jason Aronson Inc., 230 Livingston Street, Northvale, New Jersey 07647.

ACKNOWLEDGMENTS

I thank my nurturing parents, Rabbi Leon Mozeson and Bernice Tunis Mozeson, and my kind in-laws, Elliott and Ruth Stavsky. While my teachers at Maimonides School (Brookline, Mass.) and Yeshiva University gave me the tools, I credit the Bible commentary of Samson Raphael Hirsch (1808–1888) for introducing me to the miracle of Hebrew.

The following people allowed me to add to the English, Hebrew or foreign language data in THE WORD: Alex Bacalau, Mordechai Bachar, Dr. Joshua Backon, Reverend Larry Baker, Howard Beck, Aaron Bulman, Dr. Samuel Climo, Yair Davidy, Gilbert Davidowitz, Joseph Eidelberg, Dr. Louis Feldman, Ruth Freedman, Rabbi Matityahu Glazerson, Suri Granek, Dr. Judith Hauptman, David Jankelowitz, Miriam J. Kaplan, Dr. Samuel Karp, Rabbi Dr. Leon Kassin, Sara Katz, Dan Klein, Sid Knopp, Rabbi Dr. Reuben Koolyk, Ron Lane, Dr. Israel Levavi, Jonathan Lowell, Rabbi Bensyon Man-of-Jerusalem, Bernice Mozeson, Rabbi Yonatan Mozeson, Gil Muzquiz, Menachem Nerenberg, David Newman, Howard Novak, Tim O'Callaghan, Joginder K. Pahuja, Rabbi Dov Richter, Daniel Santacruz, Dr. Michael Shapira, Sholomo Sherman, Avram Shuchatowitz, Rabbi David Shwarcz, Stephen Silin, Lois Stavsky, Rachel Stillman, Rabbi Pinchas Stolper, Barbara and Ben Strudler, Faina Tsipenyuk, Spencer Weisbard, Rabbi Israel Wohlgelernter, Fikrat Zabtciaglu, David Zaslow, and Givon Zirkund.

The massive index problems were solved by the computing genius of Barry Obut.

My thanks to Ann Cassouto for her help, to Arthur Kurzweil and Muriel Jorgensen at Jason Aronson, Inc., and to Aryeh Gallin and Lt. Col. Martin Gallin, who made republication possible.

*My sincere condolences to my dictionary widow
of these past dozen years,
Lois Stavsky.
My beloved wife, along with our children,
Daniel Reyes and Sara Ching,
have too often wished that I had more words for them.*

CONTENTS

CONTENTS

"I will restore to the peoples a pure language, that they may all call upon the name of the Lord, to serve Him with one consent."
— Zephaniah 3:9

FORE-WORD

In the beginning were these words. Come with me on an archeological dig. Let us remove the sands of millennia. We are deep in the valley of Shinar, reconstructing the Tower of Babel—one brick, one word at a time. Together we will change the way we speak about the way we speak.

Put away your dictionaries—with their charming, old-fashioned myths of standardized spelling and pronounciation, with their superstitious, tribal need to create a new language ("Indo-European") out of ignorance of the ancient one. Take out, instead, your Bible—and a pair of human ears.

The Word speaks to you. Don't worry if you've never read anything on language, or if you've never heard a Hebrew word. You will soon know that you've never heard a word that *wasn't* Hebrew.

Let the language of Eden echo in your soul like the sound of your mother's voice in a dream. . .calling you home from far away and long ago.

Yes, I began from the Biblical given that Hebrew is the Mother tongue (*Genesis,* chapter 11). It seems to me that I have begun to prove that "all the earth was of one speech, with a unified vocabulary." (The more words have changed, the more they have remained the same.) The "coincidence" criers cannot be happy with the mathematical odds of my having compiled all this data. Hebrew vocabulary has as much affinity with English as it has with Arabic. More English words can be clearly linked to Biblical Hebrew than to Latin, Greek or French. Most known English words or roots are treated in this book. Check the index, and note the many prefixes and suffixes covered as well.

With all my idol-breaking, I have remained too true to conservative linguistic rules to be iconoclastic. I am grateful for my brief training in linguistics, and for the century of research into Indo-European roots that often made my discoveries possible. I stand on the shoulders of giants—though the linguists wish I'd get off their backs.

In search of an honorable ancestor for the Aryan race, the linguists developed a theoretical, prototype language that could even claim Sanskrit as a child. And so, for the past several decades, Western historical linguists have been the proud Dr. Frankenstein creators of a proto "Indo-European" language that curiously favors the Germanic element. Who would research Hebrew as the root language when even the Ph.D.'s in Semitics hung Hebrew out on a limb called West Semitic? Nobody uncovered a clay tablet of Proto-Semitic, but surely, the argument went, Hebrew evolved from older, more cumbersome languages. The de-evolution of words, and the ongoing corruption of humankind, was simply not considered.

The logic was consistent with the Bible criticism. If the Babylonians and other peoples (including American Indians) all have a flood myth, then the Biblical flood must also be a myth borrowed from an older source (or a coincidental contrivance invented to explain a natural phenomenon). It was out of the question to think that Noah's flood was a fact, and that only the God-given Bible got the facts right, uncolored by cultural corruption over the generations.

Returning to language, the Hebrews are not the only people said to have "invented the myth" of a primordial tongue. They are the only surviving human entity, however, to preserve that language and to study its boundless, superhuman profundity and engineering with lifelong joy. Hebrew was spoken long before there was a Judea or an Abraham, but Hebrew was too much associated with Jews to be tolerated.

The last group of Westerners to take up the lost paradise of Hebrew included 17th-century Englishmen like John Milton and his Puritan counterparts in colonial America.

This book has roots in my own history in Plymouth, Massachusetts. As a child I would take Sabbath morning walks to places where I read the Hebrew tombstones and diaries of pilgrims like William Bradford. Governor Bradford was a new Hebrew in the "Promised Land" of America. (He reverently desired to study God's word in its original tongue; I don't know why so many Christians and Jews have settled for less.) The curriculum of Harvard was full of Hebrew, and an early graduate thesis at Harvard concerned Hebrew as the Mother tongue. Noah Webster's etymologies (discredited for 200 years now) were full of English words traced to "Shemitic" sources. Most significant of all, if a vote in the Continental Congress had gone the other way, America, and much of today's world, would now be speaking Hebrew.

Decades of reconstructing theoretical common ancestors of the Germans, Slavs, Italics, Hellenics, Indo-Iranians, etc. have ironically legitimized what Noah Webster and the Bible would call "Japhetic" language. The third son of Noah, Ham, is behind the generic term for African languages, and white gentiles in the linguistic community have no trouble with the evidence of a related Hamito-Semitic language family. Let the Blacks and Jews share the ghetto, whisper the professors, as long as Indo-European remains lily white.

It was a little bird that first whispered to me the obsessive dream that this book would be for me. (And the nightmare that *The Word* must be for anti-Semiticists.) That bird was the sparrow, whose Indo-European root, *sper*, represents the oldest generic word for "bird" in Western languages.

I knew a TSEE – PORE (Hebrew generic term for bird) when I saw one. I promptly left graduate school and began treating the dictionary as though it were compiled by fallible human beings. I was, in the next decade, to learn things about Hebrew that, sadly, are never taught.

Like physics or biology, language (Hebrew) is another divine creation that dazzles the puny human mind with its complex simplicity and ordered chaos. The three-letter Hebrew root is a chemical element composed of and charged by the dance of a pair of two-letter roots exchanging electrons. Only the dynamics of Hebrew, with its built-in synonym and antonym system, explains whey LeaF and FoLio (LF=FL) mean the same, and why BAD and BET(TER) are similar-sounding opposites. Only the vocabulary of Biblical Hebrew contains the common denominators of otherwise unlinkable words— both within and without the traditional language families. Only after mastering Hebrew can a person fully understand words in English, Basque, or Swahili.

Because the majesty of Hebrew is only faintly visible in its off-spring, it is no wonder that intelligent men can still maintain that most words are arbitrary and meaningless, or that language is the result of cavemen grunting. Of course, some of these same brilliant academi-cians will insist that a chimp at a typewriter will come up with a Shakespearian sonnet if given enough time (about eight billion years).

As far back as Biblical times the tribe of Ephraim (linked by some Christian theologians to the British royalty) pronounced Hebrew *SH*IBBOLETH as *S*iboleth. After *THE WORD* gets around it will no longer seem odd that Hebrew SHIM-SHONE came to be spelled Samson.

You no longer have to be drunk to read SOURCE as "SHORE— ESH" (the Hebrew word for root or source). You need only be intoxicated with the truth, and to read *The Word* with a clear, unbiased mind.

To the 1995 reprint I add that the linguistic community has recently come closer to accepting the Biblical thesis that all human languages are derived from a single Mother Tongue. Proponents of an Indo-European Mother Tongue and ancestral homeland must contend with developing linguistic "superfamilies" whose ultimate family trees take in Indo-European as just another branch of a universal, primal tongue called "Proto-World." Several cover stories in national maga-zines took up this controversial topic, notably the April 1991 *Scientific American* and *Atlantic Monthly.*

While the concept of monogenesis of language (all languages coming from a single original source) has moved rapidly toward respectability, the academic world remains in the dark about the unique molecular dynamism of Hebrew's two-letter roots, which makes "Proto-Semitic" the most logical candidate for the original human tongue. As the data gains in quantity and consistency, it shall soon be impossible to miss the fact that the diversity of the world's words is tied to the versatility of rendering ancient Hebrew's economical roots.

Geneticists were not afraid to refer to "Eve" in their recent experiments that indicate a single ultimate mother for the entire diverse population of humanity. The archaeologists, too, were helpful to the Genesis scenario when the oldest human skeleton with the hyoid bone for speech was found in a cave near Haifa, Israel. The burden of proof now rests on everyone who claims that the first human language was NOT an ancestor of Modern Hebrew.

All the necessary "proofs" lie within the primordial Hebrew vocabulary itself. If, for instance, the connection between the ear and our sense of balance is a relatively recent discovery, then why does only Hebrew have the same root for both terms? Many more questions and answers await the curious reader who explores the wondrous letters, roots and words that spill forth from Hebrew's innate neurological keyboard.

INTRODUCTION

It will soon be obvious that Greek and Latin are merely grandfathers, while Hebrew is the patriarch. How does a concept as logical as monogenesis of language get buried or resisted for so long? The same way that the ultra-orthodox, scientific mind rejected the "theory" that Earth's continents were once one united land mass. Although any child cutting up an atlas can put the peices together, the university-trained professors required the oceanographic technology of the 1950's before they could concede that all the earth was once an island. (The continental breakup is referred to in *Genesis 10:25*.)

Exactly when the continents or the language families broke up is another matter. Geologists, botanists, zoologists, or linguists might find many problems solved by moving up the dates of these global upheavals, and conceding that the rates of evolution (or de-evolution) were drastically higher in antiquity.

It is not my wish to reverse the Divine "punishment" meted out at Babel. *Viva les differences!* But it wouldn't hurt if we all had a second language which was a key to all the rest. With knowledge of Hebrew, foreign language acquisition is suddenly easy. *The Word* should spawn scores of dictionaries wherein sound-alike cognates replace mere definitions. Moreover, a computerized, universal translation device should now be possible. Hebrew is the central station on the Metro from which one may transfer to any other stop in the system.

The language teachers and the universalists should be pleased by the possiblilities presented in *The Word*, even if they reject any spiritual and Biblical underpinnings. The hard-core, tenured secularists have prejudged the thesis here, and will busily seek out a few bad drops of bathwater with which to ditch the baby. But even they will have to concede that this book greatly adds to the number of English words influenced by Semitic.

The religous reader, I pray, tingles at the romantic brush with the Great Other, that extra-terrestrial who endowed humans with the ability to reason, abstract, and form all human words. The original computing language in our random-access memories has been scrambled in the output stage by the Master Programmer. Whether you speak English or Arabic, you are still thinking Hebrew. The tongue of God, the kiss of our Creator, remains within our lips.

Whether we call the Creator of synonyms and antonyms the ALL, ALLAH or EL, let all the children of Noah know that we are all in the same boat, that we are all cognates with Biblical roots.

The classical Bible commentator of 12th century France, Rabbi Simon ben Yitshak or "Rashi," set down the laws of letter interchange in his commentary at Leviticus 19:16. His interchangable lip letters, throat letters, etc., are almost identical to the accepted rules of sound shifts. While the spelling of Biblical words is highly significant, much meaning is lost to those who ignore the many musical entendres and puns available through sound-alike letter substitution. (This is only one aspect of Biblical craft lost in translation to Greek, Latin or English.)

Only conventional, conservative forms of letter shifting are used here to trace all human words back to their Hebrew etymon (earliest form). Grimm's Laws, established by the same Jakob Grimm (d. 1863) who brought us those grim and bloodthirsty fairy tales, allow linguists to compare and historically link all letters formed by the same part of the mouth. D and T are called *dentals* because the tongue must touch the teeth in order to make the sound. Just as M and N are interchangeable *nasals* or sounds made in the nose, so D, T and TH may be considered the "same" letter.

Let us observe the little flea, and the Hebrew פרעוש / PHĀRŌSH (flea). Since the FLEA is universal, nobody had to borrow this term from the Hebrew Bible (*I Samuel 24:15*). In the millennia after Babel, the essential elements of the world's words for FLEA have not changed that much. Our review of Grimm's Laws continues as we examine the chart below.

Hebrew	Pharosh or PHaRGHoS (פרעוש) ParosSCH or PaRKHoS(H)
Arabic	BaRGHouTS
Czech	BLeCHa
Russian	BLoKHa
Hungarian	BoLHa
English	FLea
German	FLoH
Yiddish	FLoy
Swahili	KiRoBoTo
Finnish	KiRPpu
Scandinavian	LoPpa/e
Polish	PCHLa
Turkish	PiRe
Indo-European root	PLou
English (Greek)	PSYLla
Modern Greek	PSi'LoS
French	PuCe
Italian	PuLCe
Span., Portuguese	PuLGa
Rumanian	PuRiCe
Dutch	VLo

The Hebrew פ is pronounced P or PH. The letter resembles a pair of pressing lips, as does the less "pressing" ב (B, BH or V). As you go down the list of words for FLEA, you'll notice the whole spectrum of lip or *labial* sounds. Nine FLEA terms retain the initial P of the Hebrew, but there are four B's, three F's and a V.

Vowels are certainly interchangeable, and ought to be largely ignored when comparing words from different languages. In effect,

Biblical Hebrew has no vowels; the vowel letters in English (A, E, I, O, and U) are chaotic contrivances that help to make English a nightmare to spell.

The next consonant in the primordial (Hebrew) term for FLEA is an R. Only five of the listed languages keep the R, while most have shifted to the other *liquid* sound – the L. Orientals confuse L's and R's for good biological and historical reasons. The Hebrew ר (R) looks much like the ל (L), but the latter depicts the tip-of-the-tongue pressure on the roof of the mouth needed to produce the L.

The third Hebrew element is the ע. It is rendered as a guttural (G – H – K – Q) in the FLEA terms of Arabic, Czech, Russian, Hungarian, German, Spanish and Portuguese. Both Spanish and Arabic take a G; the historical ties between these two tongues are often reinforced in *The Word*. Just as Hebrews from Germanic lands have lost the guttural ע, German softens the ע to H while Yiddish bends it to a Y. FLEA and perhaps FLY can be linked to an F–L–G (or P–R–K) etymon by the same process tha (Germanic) WAY and WEIGHT and (Latin) FOY and VIA are traced by the *American Heritage Dictionary* (AHD) to the Indo-European (IE) root *wegh*.

The fourth element of the original FLEA word is a whistling fricative (soft C, CH, S, SH, ST, TS, ro Z). The Arabic is expected to echo the Hebrew, and even to slide an S or SH to a TS. (Aramaic, an ancient Semitic language, consistently renders the Hebrew ש (SH) as a T – see the "TAURUS" entry. Rumanian has no ties to Semitic, as compared with Turkish or Persian, yet the similarity between the Rumanian and the Hebrew here is striking.

The Italian is merely the Rumanian with an R→L change. The French has simply dropped the L of the Italian.

If the whistling *fricative* ש (CH, SH or S) is the final element of the original Hebrew, then what is it doing in the #2 slot in the Polish or Greek? There has simply been a *metathesis* or letter switch of adjoining letters of syllables. The Hungarian FLEA is closer to the Russian when you realize that "lo" is simply inverted to "ol." In the same way, millions of Americans say "aks" when they mean "ask."

This is why the Scandinavian FLEA term is relevant here. The Danish, Norwegian and Swedish LP term is an inversion of the German FL, the Dutch VL and the reconstructed (and woefully inadequate) Indo-European (IE) root *plou*.

The intriguingly similar Swahili and Finnish terms may represent a full, three-letter inversion of the P–R–K available in the Hebrew etymon. (Otherwise, these flea terms may relate to the crab – see "CRAB.")

The Word is full of Hebrew terms and IE ones that seem to relate with each other only when noting 1) a Grimm's Law letter change, 2) added letters (extra N's or M's, *nasalization*, is common), 3) metathesis or 4) inversions of the full three-letter root.

Only with Biblical Hebrew can we restore full meaning to language. Only with the logical Biblical premise of a single primordial vocabulary can we explore the how's and why's of our planet's divergent dialects and grammars. Because the language disk in our brain is formatted for language, a unique neurological disturbance may be behind Babel. Perhaps this phenomenon allows multiple personality patients and people who speak in tongues a mysterious facility with unlearned languages.

With your help, a Whole Earth Dictionary will one day be compiled. *The Word* is but the edge of the key to that uniquely human miracle of language.

THE HEBREW ALPHABET AND THREE DERIVATIVES

(Read from right to left; rotate letters when necessary. Many of these foreign letters will look familiar after viewing them through a mirror)

	th,t	sh	r	q	tz	p	o/u	s	n	m	l	c/k	i/y/c	t	h	z	r/v	h	d	g/j	b	a
1																						
2																						
3																						
4																						
5																						
ENGLISH	b,t	S	r	Q	Z	P	q,u	s	n	m	L	c,k	y,i	t,o	H	Z	f	(E)	D,T	J,K	b	A
GREEK		Ψ	Ρ		Σ	Φ	ου	εο	ν	μ	λ,λ	K	ι		H,η	3		(E)	Δ	Γ	B	A
OLD JAPANESE					Z																	

KEY

1. Hebrew-Phoenecian: about 8th century B.C.
2. Hebrew-Aramaic: 6th-4th century B.C.
3. Dead-Sea scrolls: about 1st century B.C.
4. Modern Print Letters.
5. Modern cursive letters.

> Hebrew letters are also numbers. The 4th letter in the alphabet (aleph - bet) is the <u>daled</u> (delta). Therefore, if you'd like to know why we have both a triangular #4 and a four that resembles an upside-down <u>h</u> check the "d" column above.

Key to pronunciation of the Hebrew

Hebrew		English
א		Vowel
ב		B (BH, F, V)
ג		G (K, KH, J)
ד		D (DT, T)
ה		H
ו		Vowel, BH, V, W, (R)
ז		Z (S)
ח		KH (H, Q)
ט		T (D, DT)
י		Y (J, vowel)
כ, *ך		K, KH, hard C
ל		L (R)
מ, *ם		M (N)
נ, *ן		N (M)
ס		S
ע		Vowel, G, KH, K
פ, *ף		P (F, PH, V)
צ, *ץ		TS (S, ST, T)
ק		K (Q, H)
ר		R (L, WR)
ש		S, SH (CH)
ת		T (S, TH)

* How the letter appears at the end of a word.

The Bible has no vowel marks in the original, handwritten parchment form. Only oral tradition allows the scribe or public Torah reader to read a ב as a B rather than a V, or vice versa. The ת is only pronounced as a T in standard Israeli pronunciation, a recent and unhistoric development. Variants in pronunciation emerge when noting the spoken Hebrew among Jews from Yemen, Iraq, Italy and elsewhere. Variations in spelling, also along the lines of Grimm's Laws, are common enough in the Bible to encourage the reader to hear—rather than see—the examined words in this book.

Classic Bible commentaries encourage variant readings of standard Hebrew words because alternative, intended multiple meanings emerge. Only the uninitiated do not treat a word from the Hebrew Bible as an infinitely open formula.

Key to pronunciation of English letters

Symbol	Key words
Ā	make, cane
A, Ä	mar, balm
E	sell, debt
Ē	queen, key
I	fill, rift
Ī	fine, kind
O	politics, mop
Ō	coat, cope
OO	food, fool
U	umpire, cuff

HOW TO READ "THE WORD"

The captioned (first) term atop each entry is chosen for its proximity to the Hebrew term. The given pronunciation of the captioned Hebrew term need not be the standard Israeli pronunciation. It is an available pronunciation, however, given the number of different ways Hebrew letters can be pronounced. Only the flexibility of pronunciation enjoyed by the Hebrew alphabet has made this book possible.

The Hebrew term immediately following is related etymologically (historically) to the captioned English term.

The bracketed English letters represent the root letters of the Hebrew word. In addition, if there is a letter change from the Hebrew term to the English word (e.g., from T to D, as Hebrew SHELET turns to English SHIELD), it is also seen within the brackets (e.g. SH−L−T→SH−L−D).

Any English word in capital letters (e.g. SLATE) is related to the Hebrew etymon (SHELET) and to the English entry word (SHIELD).

Transliteration or pronunciation guides to the Hebrew word(s) are capitalized; definitions (within parentheses) immediately follow.

Each entry has a ROOTS and BRANCHES section. In the ROOTS section, the Indo-European (IE) root of the considerd term is given (if available). Other historical information, as given in other dictionaries, is offered when relevant. The IE "base" of an entry word is *Webster's New World Dictionary's* equivalent of the IE "root" given by the *American Heritage Dictionary*. Following this, the author presents the word from the Hebrew Bible's perspective – that the ultimate source of any word is Hebrew.

Throughout the entry, those words most clearly related to the entry word appear first.

The BRANCHES section presents an elaboration and expansion of the material in the ROOTS section. Less directly related words, in which the reader is asked to apply alternate pronounciations or to reposition letters (like changing the first and second letters), will usually be found further along in the BRANCHES section.

Cognates, or words attributed to the same source, are often listed in this section. The author will present words that ought to be attributed to the same etymon (original word), both from English and from "foreign" languages.

Abbreviations

The only abbreviations or acronyms used here that are not easily found in a pocket dictionary are the following:

AHD = American Heritage Dictionary
IE = Indo-European
JPS = Bible of the Jewish Publication Society
KJ = King James version of the Bible

ABASH/בִּיֵשׁ
BEE-YAYSH   [B-SH]

ROOTS: ABASH means "to put to shame," and בִּישׁ/BĒ-YASH is to embarrass. The Old English term *baschen* is not an old enough etymon, so the rootless, Hebrewless dictionaries fumble with the Old French term *esbahir* (to astonish), which they trace to Latin *ex* (from) + *bah* (interjection of surprise).

בּוֹשׁ/BŌSH is "to be ashamed"; בּוּשָׁה/BOOSHÄ means "blush" or "shame"; and הֵבִישׁ/HAVĒSH is "to embarrass."

> **BRANCHES:** Related English words include: ABASHED, ABASHMENT, BASE, BASHFUL, DEBASE and EMBARRASS. Non-English cousins include *ws(tyd)* and *pah shiou*, the Polish and Chinese words for shame. Hebrew branches of similar sound and meaning include בשש/BŌSHES (to tarry). בזיון / *BEZÄYON* (shame), and פשע/PESHU (guilt). לבוש/L'VOOSH literally means "for shame," but is usually the term for clothes (which cover up our shame). The Indo-European (IE) root for WEAR (to clothe) is *wes*. The IE root for BARE is *bhoso* (naked).
> לבוש/L'VOOSH (clothes) is to בּוּשָׁה/BOOSHÄ (shame) what *wes* (source of VESTMENTS) is to *bhoso* (lack of clothes). If you go back far enough, to the IE roots and their Hebrew counterparts, even English displays a wonderful symmetry of sense and sound.
> For the first Biblical mention of shame, before clothes, see the Biblical verse below:
> "Both of them were naked, the man and his wife, but they felt no *shame*." יתבששו.–*Genesis*: 2:25
> See "VEST"

ABBO(T)/אַבָּא
AB-BAH   [ABA]

ROOTS: The Greek word *abbas* is the source for the title ABBOT, father superior of a monastery. Scholars prefer to pin paternity on the Aramaic word for father, אַבָּא/ÄBBÄ, rather than on the Biblical Hebrew term אב/ÄV or ABH.

> **BRANCHES:** Beyond Westminister ABBEY one finds ABBA as ministerial father of the Coptic church; ABBE is the French equivalent. An ABBESS is a "female father" heading an ABBACY. Note that PA and PAPA backwards is AV and ABBA (B or V=P). The venerated papa of the Catholic church is the POPE, from the Greek word for father – *pappas*. From the Romans come English words like ATAVISM, as *avus* means grandfather or ancestor in Latin. *Bpoo* is the grandfather term in Thailand.
> A sampling of "fathers" 'round the globe includes: *abu* (Arabic), *babbo* (Italian), *baba* (Javanese, Turkish and Swahili), *bà* and *fù* (Chinese), *apa* (Hungarian), *paw* (Thai) and *pa* (Vietnamese). Rather than seeing all these "father words" as chips off the old Hebrew block, linguists feel that these P and B sounds (bilabials) are easy for babies to say. "Mama" is easy too, which is the official reason why M's dominate the world's words for mother. (See "MAMA.") The linquists haven't explained, however, why at least 40% of all languages don't call fathers "mama" and mothers "papa." Scholars may be attributing too many words to the mouths of babes...and cavemen.
> "Is he not your *father*. . .?" אביך –*Deuteronomy* 32:6
> See "BABY."

ABERRA(TION)/עֲבִירָה
AH-VEY-RAH'   [A-BH-R]

ROOTS: An aberration is an abnormality; a transgression in Hebrew is an עבירה/ABHÄRA. Latin words *ab* (from) and *errare* (to wander) form the etymology of ABERRATION.

> **BRANCHES:** The word עבירה/AVÄRA itself is merely a first century term, but it's no sin to teach English and Hebrew speakers a common foreign word in such an easy way. Besides, the root verb עבר/ÄVOR means to *overstep* one's bounds by violating a norm or disobeying a rule. In *Joshua 7:11* Israel "transgressed" the covenant, while Mordecai the Jew in *Esther 3:3* would not bend to Haman and "disobeyed" the king's order.
> When he wanders and doesn't wander from the path, the עברי/IVRI or "Hebrew" is the eternal deviate. Abraham was not the first Hebrew speaker, but he was the first iconoclast, "othersider" or Hebrew.
> Why did Abraham cross Mesopotamia? To get to (or from) the Other Side.
> For sound-alike words that "cross-over" time and space see: "FERRY," "OVER," "PARA(SITE)" and "VEER."

ABRACADABRA/הַבְּרָכָה דִּבְּרָה
HABRAKHA DIBRA   [BRK + DBR]

ROOTS: With a puff of hocus-pocus the dictionaries attribute this to non-existent Latin or Greek words like *abracadabra*, vaguely defined by the AHD as "a magic word." Abracadabra is subsequently defined as 1) a word held to possess supernatural powers and 2) jargon or gibberish.

There is no prooftext to pull out of a hat. A first guess is the Hebrew phrase הברכה דברה/*HABRAKHA DIBRA*, meaning "the formula (blessing) is uttered." A second attempt is an Aramaic phrase אברא כדברא/ABRA K'DIVRA or "I will create as has been spoken."

[AC]CEL[ERATE]/קל
KULL   [KL]

ROOTS: קל/KULL is swift or fast in Hebrew, as well as light and easy. CELERITY and ACCELERATE are from Latin *celer* (swift).*

> **BRANCHES:** A מקל/(MA)KÄL (walking stick) allows for easier, accelerated walking. A קללה/KILALA (curse) is usually uttered in haste. Haste makes waste; קלקל/KILKELL is to spoil or damage. Ease and speed require a wheel or גלגל/GULGUL. קלח/KELAKH is a jet of water or a stream (KL speed plus LK wetness–see "LIQUID").
> CURRENT only requires the usual L to R change to fit these last two Hebrew words of "running." Besides CURRENT, the IE root *kers* (to run) includes CORRIDOR, COURSE, CURSIVE, CONCOURSE, CONCUR, DISCOURSE, EXCURSION, HUSSAR, INTERCOURSE, OCCUR, INCUR, PRECURSOR, RECUR, SUCCOR, CAR, CAREER, CARGO, CARICATURE, CARRY, CHARGE, CHARIOT, CARPENTER, and more.

גרה/GERÄ is an "accelerating" verb meaning to excite, stir up, and provoke. The IE root for ACCELERATE is *kel* (to drive, set in swift motion). The AHD lists cognates like HOLD, HALT, AVAST, CELEBRATE, and CELEBRITY.

The Rumanian horse, *cal*, might be an accelerator with four-feet drive. Reverse to *lekas* for "quick" in Indonesian, or to *lyokh'kee* for "easy" in Russian. Swift is *holo* in Hawaiian.

LIGHT, LIGHTEN and LIGHTER all come from the IE root *legwh* (light, having little weight) – a reversal of קל/KÄL (light). Other listed cognates include ALLEVIATE, CARNIVAL, ELEVATE, LEPRECHAUN, LEAVEN, LEVER, LEVITY, LUNG and RELIEVE.

Finnish *vikkela* (agile, brisk), English AGILE (swift and easy of movement) and Latin *agilis* are better traced back to קל/KÄL than to Latin *agere* (to act, do) and the IE root *ag* (to drive).

Isaiah 5:26 "come *with speed* swiftly" קל. *Ecclesiastes 9:11* "the race is not won by the *swift*" קל.

ACCOUT(ERMENTS)/חוט
KHOOT   [KH-T]

ROOTS: ACCOUTERMENTS means clothes and, more recently, equipment. *Webster's* offers Latin *consuere* (to sew), and the *American Heritage Dictionary* (AHD) presents the IE root *syu* (to bind, sew).

They have the right idea, but their etymons are a far cry from the K-D or K-T sewing term seen in French *couodre* (to sew).

Just as a COUTURIER(E) is a tailor or seamstress, so a חיט/KHÄYÄT or KH-Y-D(T) is a tailor. The Biblical "thread" is the חוט/KHOOT (*Genesis 14:23*).

BRANCHES: ACCOUTER, ACCOUTRE, COUTURE and more all tied together by the same thread. For other words traced to the IE root *syu* – see "SEAM." For more words from חוט/KHOOT, see "CHAETA" and "GUT."

Arabic *chayt* (thread) is unraveled further to *ata* (the Rumanian thread) and *ito* (the Japanese thread).

ACME/קומה
COMA   [KM]

ROOTS: ACME in Greek means the highest point, the top, or the age of maturity. The AHD traces the root of ACME to the IE *ak* (sharp); ACME is said to be a cognate of HEAVEN, VINEGAR and OXYGEN. (These *ak* terms are better linked to עקץ/ÖKETS (point, sting).

Instead of discarding the M of ACME, consider Hebrew words like קומה/KŌMÄ (height – *I Kings 6:2*) and קמה/KAMA (standing grain – *Judges 15:5*).

BRANCHES: קום/KOOM is to rise. Those little uprisings called ACNE (officially linked to ACME) aren't sharp. More at "CAMERA."

K-M antonyms include קמט/KAMAT (to contract) and נכמר/[NI]KHMAR (to shrink). ACME as "mature" is seen in כמר/KOMAR (to ripen).

Reverse KM to MK for *maki*, a hill in Finnish. (Remember that Finnish and Hungarian are not Indo-European languages.)

ACUMEN/חָכְמָה
HAKH-MAH   [H-KH-M]

ROOTS: ACUMEN is a Latin word meaning mental acuteness as well as a point and a sting. The IE root is *ak*, signifying sharpness. חכמה/HÄKH'MÄ means intelligence and skill, a word of mental acuity with many sharp branches.

BRANCHES: To sting is עקץ/OKUTZ or הכיש/HĒKĒSH. חוח/HOÄKH is a briar or thorn, while English COG is a tooth. חכה/HÄKU is a fish hook and חכה/HÄKA is to angle (for fish) or to wait.

The כמ/KM element of חכמה/HAKHMA recalls the objects of wisdom: the כמה/KUMA (how much), the כמו/KIMO (in common) and the כמוס/KAMOOS (hidden, concealed).

Long missing links include the term CHACMA, the (intelligent) baboon's name among the Hottentots of southern Africa, and *akamai*, smart, clever or skilled in Hawaiian.

Psalms 111:10: At the head of *wisdom* is awe for God. חכמה

ACUTE/חַד
KHUDT   [KHD→KH-T]

ROOTS: חד/KHUDT is defined as "acute, sharp, shrill" in the Ben-Yehuda dictionary. The term is translated "sharp" or "whetted" in *Proverbs 27:17* and *Ezekiel 21:14-15*.

Latin *acutus* has its T cut off, as the reference books cite Latin *acuere* (to sharpen) and the IE root *ak* (sharp). Other Latin words like *acidus* (sour) are similarly bereaved of their dental (D or T) and dumped with the IE root *ak*.

ACUTE, ACUITY, ACETATE (+ 40), ACID etc. are all cognates of W*HET* – also from חד/HUT or KHUDT (sharp). WHET has been filed under a different IE root called *kwed* (to sharpen).

BRANCHES: The sharpmindedness of ACUTE, ACUITY and CUTE are nicely matched with חדד/KHUTUT or KHUDUD (to be sharp, keen) and חד/KHUDT (to propose a riddle or enigma). Like-sounding "sharp" words include: חץ/KHÄTS (arrow), חדק/KHEDEK (thorn, brier), קוץ/KŌTS (thorn), עקץ/ÖKETS (point, sting, prick) and חוט/KHOOT (thread). Reverse K-D to D-K to get דק/DUK (thin) or even דג/DUG (the streamlined fish). כד/KUD (blunt) is a KD antonym, whence כדור/KADOOR (ball, globe).

The ACANTHUS, from Greek *akantha* and also aligned with the IE root *ak*, is a thorn whose name is credited to "Mediterranean origin." Another look at the Hebrew thorns above will show that the N was added on to this K-T root. (Extra N's are a common phenomenon called nasalization.)

Reverse חד/KHŌD (edge, point, apex) for the pointed meaning of the DG root, and reverse words like גדה/GÄDÄ (river bank – *Joshua 3:15*) or קצה/KÄTSEH (edge, extremity) for the "border" connotation of EDGE. CANT (corner, edge), CANTEEN, CANTON and Australian Aborigine *kandi* (cant, edge) are nasalized KD or KT relatives.

The acute angle of a street *corner* is *kado* in Japanese. *Haito* is the inner knife hand move in karate, while *toha* (חד/HUT reversed) denotes the sword edge hand thrust. In Russia, few women are interested in *khoodet'* (to get thin). To the Andrade Quileute Indians of Washington state, *t'cod* is the term for the point of an arrow.

To make the point more sharply, see the following entries: "ACACIA," "CATECHISM" (Appendix A), "CUT" and "GOAD."

ADD/עוֹד
ODE [OD]

ROOTS: ADD is to increase or state further; עוֹד/ŌD means still, yet, again and furthermore. The dictionary traces ADD to the Latin *ad* (to) + *dare* (to give). ADD is akin to the adverb עוֹד/ŌD which infers increasing and continuing. In *ADDITION*, וְעוֹד/V'OD is the common connective used when a writer wants to say "and furthermore." The epitome of furtherance is found in the word עַד/AD (eternity).

> **BRANCHES:** עֹדֶף/ŌDEF (surplus, excess) and תּוּ/TOO (again) may be added to the family. This last term, that reverses the dental-vowel order, is an Aramaic word that may link up to the adverb TOO. IT(EM) means also; IT(ERATE) means (do) again in Latin.
>
> The conjunction AND might be a nasalization (extra N thrown in); "and," in Old High German, is *unti*. The original Hebrew ODT sounds more like the French *et* (and) and the Japanese *to* (and).* The Japanese could be a typical reversal of עוֹד/ŌD or from the Aramaic תּוּ/TOO mentioned above. If it's wrong to extract the N from AND, then it, along with AN (2) and AN (1) (meaning "if" or "and") could come from אָם/IM (if) or עָם/IM (with).
>
> "Also" is Arabic is *aydan*, a metathesis away from AND. עוֹד/ŌD and עַד/ĂD mean 1) yet . . . more; 2) further and 3) more in *Exodus 11:1, Esther 9:12* and *Malachi 3:10*.
> *Da* is "also" in Turkish.
> See "TOO."

A(D)MIRAL/אָמִיר
AH-MEAR [AMR]

ROOTS: This term for the top naval commander comes to English from the Old French version (*amiral*) of the Arabic term *amir al, amir* meaning a ruler. The extra "D" added to this official borrowing was influenced by the word "admirable."

> **BRANCHES:** אמר / AMAR is to command in Hebrew (*Deuteronomy 26:17*) and in Aramaic. The naval commander is named for Arabic *amar* (commanded). עמר/ĂMĂR is a tyrant.* The verb התעמר/(HIT)ĂMER is to deal tyrannically – *Deuteronomy 21:14; 24:7*, and is often translated "to enslave." The Arab EMIRATES continue to name their form of government after this term.
>
> An alternative etymon for ADMIRAL may be the Aramaic title for the Temple administrator, the אמרכל/ĂMĂRKOL.**
>
> אמיר/ĂMER (*Isaiah 17:6, 9*) is the top or head of something, thus a chief or head of state. The עמר ĂMĂR (tyrant) orders עמל/ĂMĂL (labor, trouble – see "AMERICA.").

ADOLESC(ENT)/דָלַק
DOLL-LUCK [DLK]

ROOTS: This adjective or noun meaning teenager or youthful is from the Latin word *adolesc(ere)*, to come to maturity, burn, or be kindled. דלק/DOLĂK is to kindle or burn.*

If you have raised, taught, or been a teenager, the fiery part of this etymology is self-explanatory. If you prefer the "maturity" side of the Latin root, Joseph T. Shipley's *Origins*

of English Words groups ADOLESCENT with words like ADULT, ATTITUDE and EXALT. These words are all thought to derive from the IE root *al* meaning "to nourish, hence grow." עלה/ĂLĂ means to go up, rise, spring up and grow. Whichever etymological route or root you choose, ADOLESCENCE is recalled by our oldest surviving language, Hebrew.

> **BRANCHES:** Words like TORCH (T = D, R = L, CH = K) might also connect to DOLAK. להט/LUHUT, an anagram of the same elements in DOLAK, infers a blaze, heat or flame. LIGHT comes from LUHUT as well as from an anagram of DOLAK. (Remember, the Germans pronounce "light" as "likt").
> *"Kindling* the fire" is in *Ezekiel 24:10*.

ADONIS/אֲדוֹן
ah-DOAN [ADON]

ROOTS: It is not the aim of this book to include the multitude of names that derive from Hebrew. An ADONIS is more than a name from Greek myth in that it is synonymous with a handsome young man. The reference books somehow attribute the word to the Phoenician term for lord (*adōn*), rather than to the identical Hebrew term. In Hebrew אֲדוֹן/ADON means lord or Lord – (*Exodus 23:17*).

> **BRANCHES:** The Norse god ODIN appears to be another form of ADON. If Teutonic god *Woden* is related, then WEDNESDAY is an old German version of the Lord's day. Biblical Joseph, whose ADONIC good looks were legendary, was the אֲדוֹן/ADON "*ruler*" over all the land of Egypt" *Genesis 45:9*.
>
> *Taane* (T and D are interchangeable) is a god and a husband or man in ProtoEastern Polynesian. אדם/ĂDĂM (Adam, man) was the earth's lord and master – at least until Eve arrived.
>
> See "DAMN" and "MADONNA."

ADORE/הָדַר
HOD-ARE [HDR]

ROOTS: Failing to see the connection between ADORATION and ADULATION (R=L), the dictionaries were even less likely to ADORN their etymologies here with the HDR Hebrew term which connotes both esteem and embellishment. Instead, for ADORE, the texts give us *ad-* (the Latin prepositon "to") plus *oris* (mouth). Don't mistake mouthing for the essence of tribute.

הדר/HADUR means to honor or adorn.*

> **BRANCHES:** אדיר/ADER infers nobility and respectability. *Adal* is "nobility" in Gothic, whence names like ADELE and ADOLF. הדר/HEDER is "splendid" and "ornament." *Eder* is "beautiful" in Basque, the language with no known affinities.
>
> DEAR, DARLING and other terms of ENDEARMENT mean "worthy of admiration" and are also related to אדיר/ADER.
>
> Spotlighting the first element of *HDR*, הוד/HŌD means glory and splendor. הודה/HŌDA (to praise) is the source of ODE. הודאה/HŌDA'U is that noblest praise, thanksgiving.
>
> JUDAH and Jew are related to this last term, whose root is

ידה/YDH (to five thanks, to praise). תודה/(T)ODAH is "thanks." Rabbi Joseph Soloveitchik's one-word definition for *JUDAISM* or *YIDDISHKEIT* is gratitude. Ingratitude is a form of heresy.

*HADUR/הדר means to glorify in *Proverbs 25:6.* "You shall *honor* (HADAR) the presence of the sage, as you should have awe for your God." *Leviticus 19:32.*

AFFIDAVIT/עבטיט
AV-TEET' [A-V-DT]

ROOTS: AFFIDAVIT is said to come from "he has made oath" in Middle Latin, deriving from *ad* (to) + *fidere* (to trust). *Fidere* should be linked to Latin *vadis* (a pledge), to German *wetten* (to pledge, wager) and to Anglo Saxon *weddian* (to pledge, engage). WED and WEDDING are traced back to an IE root *wadh* (a pledge). WADSET, *wad* in Scottish, is a mortgage, a pledged security for a debt.

Consider a like-sounding Biblical noun and verb of guarantee, of pledging to repay a debt by leaving a valuable item as security. The three-letter root is עבט/AVT or A-BH-T, the likely source of the word BET. A BET, like AVT, refers to the pledged item (see *Deuteronomy 24:10).*

BRANCHES: CONFIDE, FEDERAL and FAITH are cognates of AFFIDAVIT at the IE root *bheidh* (to confide). The two-letter root here is VT or BT. Merely place a guttural after the VT, instead of before it and you'll see עבט/ABHOT or KHAVOT (pledge), become בטח/BETAKH (confidence) and בטחון / BETAKHON (guarantee, insurance). A pledged item is also called a PAWN. The early Frisian term *pand* (pledge) may be a nasalized (extra N thrown in) PD word, fitting all the labial-dental terms above as well as ודאי / VADAY (certainty).

For more labial-dental words of trust, like conFiDent and FIDelity, see "FAITH," as well as "BET" and "VOTE."

Deuteronomy 15:8 "lend him sufficient" (under obligation) והעבט תעביטנו; "that ladeth himself with many *pledges*" עבטיט *Habakkuk 2:6.*

AFTER/בתר
VA-TAR [BH-T-R]

ROOTS: AFTER can only be traced to the Anglo-Saxon *aefter* and Old High German term *aftur* (after). Both AFTER and POST- (afterward) are linked to the IE root *apo* or *ap* (off, away). For OFF see "AVIATE."

The Biblical Aramaic term בתר/VTR or BSR is commonly translated "after."

BRANCHES: AFT, FURTHER (switch TH and R) and, more remotely, the prefix POST- may also derive from בתרא/BASRA—meaning "the latest" in Aramaic. The city Basra is the last, the furthermost city in southern Iraq. Only Norwegian *etter* (after) prefers the אתר/ATTAR variant of בתר/VTR. The chart below illustrates what may have happened after Babel to "after."

	1	2	3
Hebrew-Aramaic	ב	ת	ר
Arabic	B	aaD	
Swahili	B	aaDa	
English	aF	T	eR
Danish, Swedish	eF	T	R
Russian, Serbo-Croatian	Po	S	Le
French	aP	R	eS

In column # 1 all remain labials (B, F, P). Column # 2 shows a Russian violation of Grimm's Laws (S is not a D-T dental), but the Hebrew ת may be a T or an S. Column #3 features liquids L and R dropping out, as they often do, at the end of words. For the French term, letters #2 and #3 swap positions.

Placed as cognates of AFTER and POST- are two dozen words like APPOSITE, COMPONENT, COMPOSE, COMPOUND, DEPOSIT, DISPOSE, EXPOUND, IMPOSE, OPPOSE, POSITION, POSITIVE, POST, POSTURE, PROVOST and REPOSIT. These words are all to derive from a pre-Latin combination *po-sinere* and a verb *sinere* (to leave, let; of obscure origin). חן / SAN is to place or to allow. Recalling פה / PO (here) is Russian *po* (next to). PS terms of coming after or too late include פסס / PASAS (to be gone) and פסד / PASADT (to be spoiled, to lose).

AGONY/יגון
YAH-GOAN [YGN]

ROOTS: The given etymology for AGONY has nothing to do with painful emotions. The etymons include Greek terms for an assembly, a contest, and, ultimately, the verb *agein* (to lead).*

AG is the root of the Greek etymon and הג/HG is the two-letter root of words like נהג/NAHAG (to lead, drive, conduct) and הגה/HEGEH (ship's rudder). See "NAG."

נהג/NEEHAG means not only to lead, but also to wail. This leads us to the definitions of AGONY, such as great mental or physical pain, death throes, and sudden strong emotion.

My choice Hebrew etymon is יגון/YAGON, defined by lexicographer Eben Shoshan as 1) great pain, 2) deep sadness, and 3) grief. Jacob fears eternal "sorrow" over the loss of Joseph in *Genesis 42:38.* The verb form for יגון / YAGON in *Lamentations 1:12* ("pain...wherewith the Lord hath *afflicted* me) is הוגה/HOGA; the infinitive is יגה/YAGA.

BRANCHES: Related terms include ענמה/AGMA (grief), הגה / HAGA (to moan), יגע/YAGA (exertion), and עקה/AKA (oppression). The word ACHE may fit somewhere here.

Back to AGONY from יגון/YAGON:
While the Hebrew letter Yod י/Y is more likely to take an I/i in Greek, the Yod takes an A in AEON as well as in AGONY. Any theological agony over the geological age of the earth is unnecessary, as יום/YOM ("day"–*Genesis 1:5)* is better translated as AEON (an age). יום/YOM is the term used in phrases like "ancient times" and "the Middle *Ages.*" *Juma* is a week in Swahili; יום/YOM can infer any period of time.

*Other words from Greek *agein* (to lead) include DEMAGOGUE, PEDAGOGUE, and SYNAGOGUE.

AGRI(CULTURALIST)/אכר
EE-CORE [EKR]

ROOTS: A field of AGRICULTURAL words has been

harvested, processed and distilled to the IE root *AGRO*. *Agros* (field) is Greek; *aecer* (field or ACRE) is Old English.

BRANCHES: אכר/ĒKĀR is to farm; קרקע/KĀRKÄ is land. In Aramaic, Hebrew's closest relative, ארעה/ARGÄ is land and חקל/ḤĀKĀL is a field. Remembering that L→R, חקלאות / HAKLA[OOT] is a well chosen Modern Hebrew term for AGRI CULTURE. A related two-letter root is reduced to GR, as גרש / GERESH is yield or produce, and (M)'*GRUSH*/(מ)גרש is a plot of land. עקר/ĀKAR (to uproot) is related.

אכרים "*Farmers* and vinedressers" (or *husbandmen* in older translations) are referred to in *II Chronicles 26:10*.

ALBINO/הַלְבָּנָה
HULL-BUN-AH   [LB(N)]

ROOTS: The ALBINO is white. לבן / LĀVÄN is white in Hebrew; הלבנה/HĀLBÄNÄ means whitening.* Just white out the vowels and there's a perfect match. Unfortunately, the N got washed out too in the Latin *albus* (white). The IE root *albho* (white) likewise has no N, despite names like Alban and Albania. ALBUMIN or egg white is חלבון/HALBŌN in Hebrew. חלב/HALAV (milk) indicates that the two-letter root in Hebrew for whiteness is just LB or LV.

BRANCHES: The Bible's LV(N) is a verb of whitening and bleaching. Therefore, some 20 words from Latin *lavare* (to wash) should be tossed in the hamper, such as LAVA, *LAVATORY*, LAVE, *LAVER* and *LAVISH*. Spanish *lavanderia* is laundry.

There are L-V reversals like Malay (Gani dialect) *wulan* (white) and Fijian *vula-vula* (white). Finnish white is *valkean; vaalea* means light or pale. Welsh *bal* (white spot) gives us BALD. The Malay is a purer white in that it swaps #1-#2 letters but remains closer to LVN than BLOND, BLAND, BLEND, BLIND, BLINK (milk), BLANCH and BLANK. The scholars feel that ALBUM, ALFRED, ALPINE, AUBURN, ELF, LAUNDRY and OLIVER all descended from the theoretical word *albho*. The Fijian term above reverses the LV in the same way the Russian (byeli) and Polish (BIALY) words for white do. The Irish white, *fionn*, may have lost an initial L. The name ALVAH is traced to Hebrew.

Equivalent to "Whitey" is the Biblical לבן/LĀVÄN (always Anglicized Laban). לבנה/LEVŌNÄ (frankincense) may be behind the aromatic but troubled history of the word LAVENDER.

*". . .though your sins be as scarlet, they shall be as *white* as snow (ילבינו/yaLBeNoo), *Isaiah 1:18*.

See: "BRIGHT" and "LUNAR."

(AL)COVE/קָבָּה
KOO-BAH   [KBH]

ROOTS: ALCOVE is from Arabic *al-gobbah* (the arch, vault, dome). The Hebrew כפה/KĒPÄ means arch, doorway, sky and skullcap, but קבה/KOOBÄ (compartment, hut, tent, brothel) connotes an ALCOVE (a secluded bower) as well. "He followed the Israelite into *the chamber* הקבה, *Numbers 25:8*.

BRANCHES: A CUPOLA is a rounded roof or dome. A CHAPEL

is a recessed, separate room in a church; a COPE is a canopy, a vault, or the sky.

HIVE is possibly related (ק/K→H). Hebrew branches include חפה/KHOOPÄ (canopy), יקב/YEKEV (wine celler) and כף/CĀF (cave, vault).

A COVE is also a sheltered nook. It is linked to German *koben* (poor room, pigsty), like קבה/KOOBÄ above. As a recess in cliffs, COVE resembles נקב/(NE)KEV (hole).

The Hopi Indian prayer alcove is the *kiva*.

See "CAVITY" and "CUBBY."

(AL)GEBRA/חבּוּר
KHEE-BOOR   [KH-B-R]

ROOTS: ALGEBRA is officially borrowed from Arabic *al* (the) + *jabara* (to reunite). In Hebrew there's חבור/KHEEBOOR (connection), חבר/KHÄVÄR (to unite), and חבֵר/KHÄVÄR (partner, friend). "*united* as one man" (חברום), *Judges 20:11*.

BRANCHES: A Finnish friend is a *kaveli*; Swahili reverses KH-V-R to *rafiki*.

Unifying tie-ins to חבר/KH-V-R include חבל/KHEVEL (rope, band), כבל/KEVEL (chain, cable) and קרב/KĀRÄV (to befriend). See "CABLE."

(AL)KALI/קלי
KALL-EE   [KLY]

ROOTS: Like many AL- words, this is officially borrowed from the Arabic: *al* (the) + *galay* (to roast in a pan). קלה / KÄLÄ is to roast, parch, toast (*Jeremiah 29:22*); קלי/KALĒ is "roasted grain" (JPS) or "parched corn" (KJ), the unbuttered popcorn Ruth ate in *Ruth 2:14*.

BRANCHES: The (מ)קלה/(MI)KLEH is the roasting place or hearth. Linked to Arabic *qaliy* (the ashes of saltwort) are 18 words like ALKALOID.

From IE root *kela* (warm) come words like CALENTURE, CAL-DRON, CALENTURE, CALORIE, CAUDLE, NON*CHAL*ANT and RECALESCENCE. *Caliente* is a hot Spanish relative. In Australian Aborigine *kalla* is fire and *kullu* is heat. *Cald* is Italian and Rumanian for hot, no matter how much it sounds like cold. The irony stems from Hebrew words like קר/KAR (cold) which are antonyms to toasty warm words like קלי/KÄLE. *Harr* in Arabic means "warm."

Many words included under this IE root require additional twists of imagination, such as LEE, CHOWDER and CHAFE.* (S)CAL(D) and *LUKE*(WARM) are cognates that do fit methods used here. See "CALDRON" and "CHAR."

*If this hot etymon for CHAFE (to rub) rubs you the wrong way, both שף/SHĀF and חפף/KHĀF(ÄF) mean rub in Hebrew.

See "CHAFE."

ALL/כָּל
KOLL   [(K)OL]

ROOTS: The IE root *al* means "all," and includes ALSO. IE root *kailo* means whole. כל/KOL or KHOL means all, whole, every. Many words in English that begin with a vowel may be traced to a guttural (G,K) root word. The Hebrew K of KOL or KHOL begins to soften as the Polish *caly* (whole, entire) moves westward to the Dutch *geheel* (all).

The Hebrew root expands to terms like כליל/KÄLIL (whole, complete), כלל/KLÄL (total, sum) and כולל/KŌLEL (general, universal, and community).

> **BRANCHES:** Under IE root *kailo* (whole, uninjured, of good omen) are terms like HAIL, HALE, HEAL(TH), and WHOLE-(SOME). Nothing combines wholeness and inclusiveness more than the ALL-powerful ALMIGHTY. A Hebrew ÄL term for the deity, as found in BethEL or DaniEL, corresponds to ALLAH in Arabic and the HALLOWED HOLY One in English. Words like HOLIDAY are traced to Anglo-Saxon *hal* (sound, whole), while the IE root of CELIBATE – *quai-lo* (hale, whole) – sounds even closer to כל/KOL. See "HEALTH."
>
> Other words via Greek *holos* (whole) include CATHOLIC and HOLOCAUST. J.T. Shipley indicates that HOLOCAUST meant a sacrifice whose victim was wholly burnt. The original Jewish HOLOCAUST was the עולה/KHŌLÄ or ŌLÄ (*Exodus 29:18*).
>
> The word WHOLE itself links back to כל/KOL just as WHELP (young dog) does to כלב/KELEV (dog). In both cases, drop the W and restore the H to a K.
>
> The Maya Indians of Central America have terms for ALL such as *tulakal* and *lah*. One seems to include KOL, and the other's an "inverted" ALL.
>
> See "CULL," "ELECT" and "HAIL."

ALLEY/עָלָה
AL-LAH   [ALH,KLH]

ROOTS: ALLEY is traced to French *aller* (to go) via Old French *alee* (a going, passage). עלה/ALH means going up, immigration, pilgrimage, a passing or progressing.

> **BRANCHES:** על/EL or KEL means towards, while reversing to L-K links לך/LÄKH (to go) and הלך/HOLÄKH (to walk, go) to עלה/ALH, KLH. There is no ascending, only going, in *II Kings 12:19* when King Joash "*went away* from Jerusalem."
>
> To (S)CALE is to ascend or go up. Angels on a ladder are ascending, עולים/KHŌL(ĒM) in *Genesis 28:12*. Very often the S must drop before a hard C. SCALE is from Latin *scala* (stairs, ladder), whence the musical SCALE. The ע/Ayin is usually rendered a guttural (C,G,K) via Latin or Greek, so no need to ES-CALATE your curiosity when you hear that SCALE and ESCA-LATE are from עלה/KÄLÄ. Adding the prefix מ/M, a מעלה/M'KÄLEH is the stairway of *Exodus 20:23*. Return to the vowel "ע" for AL words like *AL*TAR and *AL*TITUDE.
>
> LADDER, from Old English *hloeder* and the IE root *Klei* (to lean), might better link up with this Hebrew K-L term of *CLI*MBING up.
>
> To rise is *ala ae*, and a path is *ala* in Hawaiian. *Holo holo* is to go for a walk, while "to go" in Hawaiian is *hele*. To come in Chinese is *lai*, to rise up is *lî*.
>
> Current wisdom links WALK with the IE root *wel* (to turn, roll) – see "BALL." But the L-K in WA*L*K might link up with the Hebrew terms above, with R to L changes from רגל/R-G-L (leg; to tour by "legging" it on foot), or from דרך/(D)R-KH (to tread). Listen to the footfalls of Japanese *aruku* (to walk), Maidu Indian *wilek* (to go fast), Chinese *likai* (to depart), Fijian *lako* (to go) and Malay dialect *laka* (to go). *Alaku* is "went" in Assyro-Babylonian.

ALPHABET/אָלֶף-בֵּית
ÄLEPH-BET   [ALF-BYT]

ROOTS: It's as simple as A, B, C. Greek ALPHA is from Hebrew's primary letter א/ALEPH. There are ALPHA RAYS, particles, etc. See "BETA" for words from Hebrew's number two letter.

> **BRANCHES:** An *ABACE*DARIAN is learning the ABC's. One may learn numbers on an *ABACUS*, as the Hebrew ABC's or letters are also the 1,2,3's or numbers. Greek *abax* (counting board) doesn't sound like *ABC* due to the old confusion that turned Hebrew's 3rd letter/number, Gimmel/ג, into a soft C. The ג/Gimmel loooks like a reversed K, and should have remained sounding like a K or a hard G.
>
> Forms of אלף/ALEPH also mean large cattle, training and taming animals, friend and chief – all of which suggest the ELEPHANT (*elephas* in Greek).
>
> See "ELEVEN."

ALUM[NI]/עַלְמ(וֹת)
ALM(OS)   [ALM]

ROOTS: ALUMNUS in Latin doesn't only mean a pupil – graduating or not – but a foster son. The feminine counterpart is ALUMNA. Similarly, עלם/ÄLEM (young man, as in *I Samuel 17:56*) is countered by the better known term עלמה/ÄLMÄ (young woman, as in *Canticles* or *Songs 6:8*). ALME, listed in some English dictionaries, is an Arabic term for a dancing girl. It is derived from *alimah* (learned), implying that the young ladies are ALUMNI from a dance academy.

> **BRANCHES:** עלמות/ALMOOS is youth or vigor; עולל/ŌLEL is a child; נער/NA'ÄR is a boy or youth. *Marya* is a youth in Sanskrit, *Malchik* in Russian. Rescramble NA'AR back to ALM (L = R; M = N), then gutturalize the ע to get GLM and the Turkish word for boy, *oglan*.
>
> UHLAN, a mounted soldier in the Polish or German army, is traced to Turkish *oghlan* (youth).
>
> ALUMNI or ALUMNUS is placed at the IE root *al* (to grow, nourish). The listed cognates at this root include ABOLISH, AD-OLESCENT, ADULT, ALIMENT, ALIMONY, ALTITUDE, CO-ALESCE, ELDER, ENHANCE, HAUGHTY, OLD and PROLIFIC.

AMBER/עַנְבָּר
UN-BAR   [ANBR→AMBR]

ROOTS: The AMBER (yellow-brown) of America's waves of grain is originally Semitic. AMBER is an acknowledged borrowing from Arabic *'anbar* (ambergris). ענבר/ANBER is amber in Modern Hebrew.

> **BRANCHES:** The בר/BAR element probably means "grain, prairie or field."
>
> See "BARLEY" and "BARRIO."

AMEN(ABLE)/אָמֵן
AH-MAIN'   [AMN]

ROOTS: No one doubts that the prayerful response AMEN comes from Hebrew אמן/AMAN (so be it; it is true and certain). The very next entry after "Amen" in the dictionary is AMENABLE 1.) answerable, 2.) willing to believe and submit, and 3.) it is verifiable. The authorities trace AMEN-ABLE to Latin *minari* (to threaten) rather than to AMEN.

Related terms include: אמונה/EMUNÄH (faith, confidence); האמין/HE'EMIN (to trust, believe in); נאמן/NE'EMÄN (true, faithful) and אמנם/ÄMNÄM (truly, verily).*

BRANCHES: We expect our memory to be true and faithful, the means to verify all knowledge. Therefore M-N words from the Greek *mnasthai* (to remember), like AMNESTY and AMNESIA, may derive from the above M-N Hebrew words of verity and belief. All the many terms of (RE)MINISCENCE via Latin, may be long forgotten echoes of one resounding AMEN – see "SAMURAI."

Man himself, as our history sadly indicates, may be the believer more than the thinker and rememberer. The dictionaries posit that MAN is "probably" from the theoretical IE word *men* (to think).

Genuine in Japanese is *hummono*; faith in Polynesian is *mana*.

*"And all the people shall respond, *Amen.*" אמן *Deuteronomy 27:15.*

AMENITY is not related. It is from Latin *amoenlus* (pleasant), a reversal of נעים/NÄEM (pleasant).

OMEN is related; see "OMEN."

AMERICA/עָמָל
AH-MULL   [AM→AMR]

ROOTS: Place names are reserved for a later book, but for America an exception will be made. AMERICA means work. The New World was named for Italian navigator Amerigo Vespucci, whose Latinized first name is *Americus.* Related names like EMERY, AMELIA, MILLICENT and perhaps EMIL(Y) are linked to the Germanic root *amal* (work, trouble).

עמל/ÄMÄL is work, labor, trouble in both Hebrew and Arabic.

BRANCHES: EMULATE and CALAMITY might be related terms of striving and trouble, while התעמר/[HIT]AMÄR (treat as a slave) and the hard-working CAMEL/גמל are Hebrew relations. In Vietnamese, reverse עמל/ÄMÄL to *lam* (to work).

". . . I applied myself to understand this, but it seemed a *hopeless task* till I entered God's sanctuary . . ." עמל *Psalms 73:16.*

EMERITUS, like DEMERIT and MERIT, may be related since Latin *emereri* is to earn by service.

AMITY/עָמִית
UM-EET   [UMT]

ROOTS: עמית/AMIT is a friend or associate (*Leviticus 5:21*).

AMITY means friendship, derived from French *amitie* and Latin *amare* (to love) and *amo* (passionate love). Hebrew terms of friendly association like עם/EEM (with, close to) and עם/UM (nation) connect to חמד/HEMED (lust, desire) and חם/HUM (passion, heat).

BRANCHES: AMATEUR is from Latin *amator* (lover). Other AMATIVE or AMATORY terms include AMI(E), AMIABLE, AMICABLE, AMIGO, AMOROUS, ENAMOR, ENEMY, and INIMICAL. The IE root *amma* links these amatory terms to those of motherhood. In Hebrew there is: אם/EM (mother, womb), אם/ÖM (people, nation, race), and אמץ/IMATS (to adopt as one's child).

Returning to guttural terms like חם/KHUM (warmth, passion) and חמוד/KHUMOOD (lovable), reveals a better etymon for CHUM (intimate friend) than "probably a slang abbreviation of *chamber.*" COMRADE is dismissed as a roommate the same way – see "CAMERA."

A more intense friendship charges the word KAMA (desire, love, god of love), found in Sanskrit terms like KAMA SUTRA. The Sanscrit, Hindi's venerable ancestor, links up to Hebrew words like כמה/KAMA (to desire eagerly) and כמיהה/KIMEHA (yearning).

Japanese *Kami* is the Shinto deity in the word KAMIKAZE. While a universal God of Love fits the Judeo-Christian tradition, a word of desirous passion (חם/KHUM) is deemed less appropriate than a term of broad warmth. רחב/RHV (broad) and חם/HM (warmth) combine to form רחם/RHM – the word for womb and mercy. הרחמן/HÄ'*RÄKHÄ*MÄN is the Merciful One and womb of the world. God is a comforting mother in *Isaiah 66:13.*

Love for the Maya Indians (*yakuna*) similarly relates to heat. *Qin,* the Maya sun, resembles חמה/KHAMA (sun). *Cauma* means "heat of the sun" in Latin – see "Calm."

Chinese amity is *ho mu.* Emotional and solar warmth both emerge from Vietnamese *cam* (1. to fall in love with, 2. to suffer sunstroke). Vietnamese *am* is lukewarm; *ham* is to warm up.

To boil in Swahili is *chemsa*; for the Maidu Indians of California boiling is *hom.* To burn in Swahili is *choma*; in Spanish and Portugese the terms are *quemar* and *queimar.* כמר/KAMAR and חמר/KHAMAR in Hebrew also mean "to burn."

Perhaps *haima* means blood in Greek (whence HEMOPHILIA, HEMORRHAGE and HEMORRHOID) because of blood's warmth – see "ANEMIC." HUMID is traced, perhaps mistakenly, to the IE root *wegw* (wet) instead of an HM root of warmth. "Humid" in Thai is *cheun*; warm is *oon.*

The KM term of desire is reversed and doubled in Hawaiian (*makemake*), although *ho'omahana* does mean "to heat or warm."

ANCIENT/נוֹשָׁן
NO-SHUN   [(N)-SH-N]

ROOTS: The Old French *ancien* is inexplicably traced to the vulgar Latin *anteanus* (going before), from Latin *ante* (before).

נושן/NOSHUN (old, ancient) is rendered "long kept" in *Leviticus 28:10,* while נושנת/NOSHENET is "old" in *Leviticus 13:11.*

BRANCHES: Few languages pick up שן/S(H)-N for words of old age. Scandinavian tongues, for instance, use *gammal* (old). גמל/GAMMAL means to ripen, wean, come of age.

See "SENILE."

AN(EMIC)/אַיִן
AINE   [AYN]

ROOTS: Greek *a-* or *an-* means not or without. This is like Hebrew's אִין/ĀN (not) and prefix אִי/EE- (not, without).

אִי/EE-KHAVOD ("Ichabod") of *I Samuel 4:21* means *without honor*, or *"glory is departed"*; אִין/ĀYNE in *Jeremiah 8:19* appears in the phrase, "Is *not* the Lord in Zion?"

> **BRANCHES:** Other negative prefixes like IM-, IN- and Un- join A- and AN- in linking to Hebrew negatives like אִין/ÄYIN (nothing, not, no). Other AN- words include *ANARCHY*, *ANOMALOUS* and *ANONYMOUS*. Polynesian and Japanese have similar forms, see "NO."
>
> ANEMIC itself means without blood. The Hebrew source of Greek *haima* (blood) might be חם/HAM (warm) or חמר/HĀMER (wine). *Hamu* (red) in Malay might link up with Arabic *hinna* – the source of HENNA (a reddish brown dye).
>
> חמוץ/HAMOOTS (scarlet – *Isaiah 63:1*) as the source of Greek *haima* and English words like HEMATIC and HEMOPHILLIAC is taken up at "SANGRIA."

A(N)KLE/עָקוּל
EE-KOOL   [AKL]

ROOTS: The ANKLE was made to ANGLE, slant or bend. Old English *ancleow* and Old Norse *ankula* are connected to several other *ank* (the IE root) words: ANGLE, ANGLO-Saxon, ANKLE and ENGLAND. The IE root *ank* (to bend) is a nasalized form (anned N) of a two-letter Hebrew root – עק/AK. The root is noted in terms like עקף/AKĒF (roundabout), עקל/ĒKĀL (to bend), twist, pervert), עקם/AKAM (to curve, make crooked) and עקש/ĀKĀSH (to make crooked).

In this family of עק/AK (bending) words in Hebrew, עקל/EE-KOOL (crookedness) is closest to ANKLE in sound, while עקב/Ä-KĀV (heel) is closest in meaning. Jacob is named for the heel in *Genesis 25:26*; the pet name for יעקב/Y'ĀKOVH is "Yankle," as European Jews also nasalize in their pronounciation.

> **BRANCHES:** YANKEE, whether related to the Dutch name *Janke* or to ENGLISH nationality, should eventually derive from Y'AKOV (Jacob), AKĀV (heel), or עק/AK (root for bending words).
>
> ANKLE in Arabic is *coulchal*; עקלקל/ĀKULKUL is a longer (reduplicated) word of crookedness in Biblical Hebrew. In Japanese heel is *kakato*, while the ankle is *kurubushi*. Bend the AKL (Hebrew ANGLE) a bit to get קער/KÄER (curve, concavity). The German ankle is a fuss*KnoCK*le or foot knuckle. The KNUCKLE allows us to crook our fingers. See KNUCKLE AT "CROOK." the double guttural terms in Japanese and German may derive from rnedering the עק/AK as KK; the ע is often read as a guttural G, K or Q.
>
> Other body benders include the ANCON or elbow, from Greek *ankos* (a bend).
>
> The ANCHOR, bu its hook or crook, is connected to Greek *ankos* (a bend). It might relate to אנך/ÄNOKH (plummet, plumbline) or be a letter flip of עגן/ŌGAN (anchor in Aramaic).

ANNOY(AN)CE/עֲנוּת
EN-NOOSE   [E-N]

ROOTS: The suffix -ANCE (French – *ance*, Latin *antin*) forms nouns from verbs or adjectives as does וּת-/-OOS or OOT in Hebrew. The extra N (nasalization) of the suffix -ance is a common nuisance.

ANNOY is from the Old French *anoier* or *annoier*. The dictionary might have linked ANNOY to the Hebrew עני/EE-NOY (torture, affliction) rather than to the Latin *in odio* (at enmity). The definitions of ANNOY grow from irritating, vexing and bothering to harming, injuring and molesting. Similarly with the ענ/EN term, the mild self-affliction of *Genesis 31:42* or *Numbers 29:7* increases to a deadly molestation in *Deuteronomy 22:29* and *Judges 20:5* –"my consort they *ravished*, so that she died." ענו (University of Chicago's Bible translation). ענות / ENOOS means affliction.

> **BRANCHES:** ענות/EN-NOOS is thus related to אנס/ŌN-NESS (force, rape). For the guttural version of the ע in the ענ root, note the influence of עני/GANĒ (afflicted; pauper) on the word GAUNT.
>
> The ע to H permutation appears in the Hawaiian word for pauper and poor – *hune*. Hawaiian *inea* means hardship and suffering; its Proto Polynesian counterpart is said to be *ingo* (to abuse, persecute).

A(N)TIQUE/עָתִיק
AH-TEEK   [ATK]

ROOTS: The third definition of ANTIQUE is "of ancient Greece." ATTICA was a state of ancient Greece. ANTIQUE's extra N (nasalization) does not disguise the sense of quaintness and culture found in ATTICISM, though ANTIQUITY is not linked with ATTIC FAITH.

עתיק/ATEEK means ancient; עתיקות/ATEEKŌS are ANTIQUITIES (*I Chronicles 4:22* and the Aramaic of *Daniel 7:9*).

> **BRANCHES:** ALONG, ANCIENT, ANTE, ANTE-, ANTERIOR, ADVANCE, ANTI–, END and UNTIL are all considered cognates of ANTIQUE at the IE root *ant* (front, forehead). This IE root resembles the Hebrew brow or forehead – מצח/MET-(SAH).
>
> TK words might otherwise go back to קדם/KOD[EM] (before). קדים/ KADTOOM means ancient.
>
> The opposite of קדם/KODEM (before) is קדמה/KIDMA (front, progress). The opposite of our featured word עתיק/ATEEK (ancient, antique) is עתיד/ATEED (future). The two-letter word that ties all four terms together is עת/ĀTE or KHATE (time). ETESIAN is from the Greek *etos* (year). Old for the Dutch is *oud*, for the Japanese *oita*, and for the Turks *eski*. (ת is S or T.) "Ancient" for the venerable Chinese is *ku tai (te)*; reverse *tik* (old) among the Salishan languages of America's Northwestern Indians.

ARBO(R)/עֲרָבָה
AH-RAH-VAH   [A-R-BH]

ROOTS: ARBOR and eleven related words are from this Latin word for tree. All the Romance languages use the word, but the Portugese pronounce it *arVore*.

עֲרבה/ÄRÄBHÄ (willow) is a leafy tree worthy of an AR-BORETUM, as seen in *Leviticus 23:40*, "take . . . boughs of leafy trees, and *willows* of the brook." Following the Biblical command, traditional Jews include עֲרבות/ÄRÄVOT (willow branches) in their celebration of Sukkot or Tabernacles.

The weeping willow is not named because weeping is inherent in its graceful drooping. It is the immortal lines of *Psalms 137:1-2* that made all willows weep: "By the rivers of Babylon, there we sat down, yea, we wept, when we re-membered Zion. We hanged our harps upon the *willows* in the midst thereof." The quote here is from the King James version, which generations of English speakers grew up on. The newer translations (University of Chicago, JPS) render the same tree as a poplar, making עֲרבה/ÄRÄBHÄ the more appropriate etymon for a wider, generic tree word like ARBOR.

BRANCHES: TREE likewise derives from a Hebrew word for a particular tree. The תרזה/TIRZA of *Isaiah 44:14* has been trans-lated holm, oak, lime tree and linden tree. The Polish tree, *drzewo*, retains the Z that is weakened in Greek *drys* and which is pruned off the Russian (*dyerevo*), Danish (*trae*), and Anglo-Saxon (*treow*) trees. DRIAD, TRAY, and TROUGH, via the IE base, are all branches.

(ARCHI)PELAGO/פֶּלֶג
PELEG   [PLG]

ROOTS: Greek *pelagos* is the open sea (currents), away from the calmer coastal waters.

פלג/PELEG is a stream, channel, river or current (*Psalms 1:3* or *65:10*).

BRANCHES: An ARCHIPELAGO is a sea with many islands; PELAGIC means of the sea. Both the *pelagos* (stork in Greek) and the PELICAN (from Greek *pelekan*) ought to relate to פלג/PLG or פלח/PLK as either water birds or as water ploughers (to honor the given etymon). See "BREAK" and "PLOUGH."

הפליג/[HI]PHLEG is to sail or embark; יובל/[YOO]BHÄL is a stream (*Jeremiah 17:8*); מבול/[MA]BOOL is a flood (*Genesis 6:17*). אבל/OOBHAL is a river or canal (*Daniel 8:2*). The two-letter root for flowing, then, is P-L or BH-L. The corresponding IE root is *pleu* (to flow). It includes all manner of flotsam such as FREE, FLEET, FLIGHT, FLOAT, FLOOD, FLOTSAM, FLOW, FLUCTUATE, FLY, PLUTO, PLUVIAL, PNEUMONIA and PULMONARY.

Another IE root just downstream is *bhleu* (overflow, etc.). Polish *plukaé* is to rinse or wash.

Only פלג/P(F)-L(R)-G(K) could link the F-L river words of French (*fleuve*), German (*Fluss*), or Scandinavian (*flod*), with the R-K river terms in Slavic (like Russian *reka*).

If *reka* isn't from (P)-L-G turned to R-K, then it could be from ריק/RĒK (to empty, pour out). For more BL or VL flowing terms, see "WELT." For BRK relatives see "BROOK."

ARCHI(TECT)/עוֹרֵךְ
OR-EKH   [A-R-KH]

ROOTS: The ARCHIVIST and ARCHITECT derive from IE root *arkhein* (to begin, command, rule), a Greek verb of "unknown origin." The above mentioned professions involve organizing, arranging, and setting in order more than giving orders.

The Mishnaic word ארכיון/ÄREKĒON (archive) is borrowed from the Greek, but it has roots, of course, in the Hebrew Bible. ערך/ÄRECH is "order," "arrangement," and even "a dictionary entry"; ערוך/ÄROOKH is "prepared," "put in order," "edited." The Greek *archos* (chief) is the עורך/ŌRAKH, an administrative term that Israelis now reserve for an editor. Prefixed (-מ/M-) extensions of ARKH mean "row," "order," and "rank." "And he *set* a row of bread *in order*" ויערך (*Exodus 40:23*).

BRANCHES: All arch, -ARCH, ARCHAO- words are related, including ARCHBISHOP, ARCHON, and MONARCHY. REX and REICH might be regal relatives. Nature's great architect is the *ARACH*NID (spider).

Related terms of continuity to fill out this ARCHIVE include ארך/ÄRACH (to be long, continue) and אורחה/ŌRKHÄ (procedure, caravan).

See: "ARACHNID,"(A) "ORGAN," "REGAL."

AREA/אַרְעָא
ARE-AH   [AREA]

ROOTS: AREA is Latin for an open space or piece of land. The word implies a region, tract, measured surface, range or extent.

ארעא/ÄRÄ is Aramiac for land, region, earth and country. Found in the Aramiac parts of the Hebrew Bible (see *Jeremiah* below), it is equivalent to ארץ/ÄRETZ – see "EARTH."

BRANCHES: Supporting Hebrew terms include ארך/ŌREKH (length, dimension) and ארק/ARAK (the earth – *Jeremiah 10:11*). *Ara* is a field in Latvian.

(A)RITHM(ETIC)/רְשׁוּם
REE–SHOOM   [R–SH→TH–M]

ROOTS: Middle English *arsm(etic)* may derive from Greek *arithmein* (to count) and *arithm(os)* (a number). A number or an account is a notation, a mark, a sign or a registra-tion – the given definitions of רשום / RESHOOM ["record(ed)"] in *Daniel 10:21*.

BRANCHES: LOGARITHM is one of several words from the Greek etymon. The "log" prefix is from Greek *logos* (proportion, ratio). LOG-, along with GILL and GALLON (both liquid measures), may relate to לג / LŌG (a liquid measure).

The IE root for ARITHM(ETIC) is *ar* (to fit together), fitting together such so-called cognates as ARITHMETIC, ARM, ALARM, INERT, ARTHRO-, ARISTOCRACY, ADORN and RITE.

Hebrew ש / SH often leads to a Greek TH. CATHARTIC is from Greek *kathar(os)* (pure), from כשר / KÄSHER (kosher); *THANATOS* (death) is from שנה / SHĀNÄ (sleep); *THECA*, from *thēkē* (a case), is a SAC or שק / SUK (sack).

This TH / ש correspondence is clearer in Swahili where *thelathini* and שלשים / SHELŌSHIM mean thirty, *themanimi* and SHEMŌNIM mean eighty, and *thelugi* and שלג / SHELEG mean show.

ARK/אֲרְגָּז
ARGUZ   [ARGZ]

ROOTS: The IE root *arek* (to hold, contain, guard) is said to be the source of Latin *arca*, whence ARK. The term for an ark or chest in Hebrew is ארגז/ARGUZ. "Take the ark of the Lord . . . and put next to it in a *chest* the gold objects." [וב]ארגז—*I Samuel 6:8*.

> **BRANCHES:** A term of containment or guarding is less likely to become a ship term, like Noah's ARK and Jason's mythic ARGO.
> Connected to the mythic IE root *arek* are words like ARCANE, AUTARKY, COERCE, and EXERCISE.

A[R]M/אַמָּה
AMAH   [AMH]

ROOTS: If ARM may derive from IE root *ar* (to join, fit together), then it certainly could derive from אמה/ÄMÄ (forearm, arm-length, cubit – *Genesis 6:15*). (New Englanders hear no R in ARM.)

> **BRANCHES:** מ / MĀ can mean "from out of," "besides" or "part of." אמה / AMA is also a base, pedestal or servant.

ARSEN(AL)/דּיר זַיִן
(D)EER SZAYIN   [DYR + ZYN]

ROOTS: ARSENAL is officially borrowed from Arabic *dar as sina'ah* (workshop, house of skill or trade). Notice how the initial D was dropped.

The Hebrew is much closer to the way an ARSENAL is used, as a place for storing or making weapons. דיר/DEER is a shed and זין/ZAYIN is a weapon or armor.

ARYA(N)/אַרְיֵה
ARE-YAY   [ARI]

ROOTS: ARYAN is the term used before "Indo-European" for the hypothetical, prehistoric people who spoke the parent language of the European, Sanskrit, and Iranian languages. The term fell out of favor in the Nazi era when

Aryan came to mean any Caucasian of non-Jewish descent.

ARYAN comes from a tribal name in Sanskrit (*arya*) and in Old Persian (*ariya*). In *II Kings 15:25* "men from Argob and *Arieh*" help Pekah overthrow King Pekahiah of Israel — אריה. These "Aryans" were likely a fierce mercenary band with no sympathies for the northern kingdom of Israel. An old Persian connection may be seen in the sons of Haman, three of whom had names beginning with A-R-I. The אריה/ÄRYĀ or ארי/ARĒ (lion) is not only the symbol of the tribe of Judah, but a persistant symbol of Iran.

ASH/אֵש
AISH   [A-S(H)]

ROOTS: The ASH or ASHES left after a fire is traced to Old English *asce* and the IE root *as* (to burn, glow).

Germanic root *urjon* (to burn) is traced to the IE root *eus* (to burn).

The original flame that ignited these roots is the Hebrew אש/ĀSH (fire; fever).

"The bush was consumed with *fire*, and the bush was not consumed."– *Exodus 3:2*.

> **BRANCHES:** Where there's fire there's עשן/ÄSHÄN (smoke) – not אשון/ESHOON (darkness). Where there are ASHES or ASH cans, there may be an אשפה/ÄSHPÄ (garbage dump).
> Cognates of ASH at IE root *as* include ARID, ARDENT, ARDOR, ARSON and AZALEA.
> Cognates listed at IE root *eus* include ADJUST, COMBUSTION, EMBER, EURUS, UREDO and URN.
> Several of these terms from Latin *urere* (to burn) might also be traced to אור/OOR (fire) or אור/ŌR (light, shine).
> Reverse אש/ĀSH for Chinese *shau* (to burn).

ASH(TREE)/אֵשֶׁל
AISH(EL)   [A-SH-(l)]

ROOTS: From Old English *oesc*, the ASH tree is leafy and sturdy. אשל/ĀSHEL is a Biblical shade tree (*Genesis 21:33*) usually mistranslated as a tamarisk (which is a date palm – see "TAMARISK.") In *I Samuel 22:6* the אשל/ĀSHEL is "on the height" like a mountain ASH tree.

> **BRANCHES:** עץ/ĀZE or ĀTS is a tree, wood or timber; אשוח/ASHOOAH is a fir tree.
> The אשל/ĀSHEL that Abraham planted in *Genesis 21:33* grew, against all odds, to be a mightier tree or empire than ASSYRIA— אשור/ASHUR being their god of empire and symbol of expansiveness. The region was full of sacred trees or אשרה/ĀSHERÄ worship. (Fundamentalist Christians are right to disdain the Christmas tree as a pagan object of veneration.)
> Abraham's grandson ASHER (good fortune) has the tribal symbol of a wide, spreading tree.
> Reverse to *shu* for tree in Chinese.

ASHAMED/אָשֵׁם
USH-um   [A-SH-M]

ROOTS: Anglo-Saxon *ascamian* infers feeling shame and guilt, which are the primary meanings of SHAME as well. But then SHAME is traced to IE root (s)*kam* (to hide, cover), making SHAME a cognate of SHAM, CAMISADO, and CHEMISE.

אשם/ÄSHÄM is to be guilty or to bear punishment.*

    BRANCHES: The three-letter root is derived by adding the negative prefix אי/EE (A-) to שם/SHEM (fame, reputation) to get the *de*famation and *dis*repute that comes with SHAME.

    שמץ/SHEMETS (derision) is practiced to evoke SHAME. שמע/SHÄMÄ means hearing, report, fame and sound.

    To no people have both shame and renown been more significant than to the *SEMITES*, the sons of שם / SHEM.

    German *schanden* and the Yiddish *shander* (shame, disgrace) may relate to אשם/ÄSHÄM as well as to שמץ/SHEMETS. Arabic *sana'a* means "he was ashamed."

    שכם/SHEKHEM (*Genesis 34*), the rapist of Dinah and the scene of a shameful SCAM or SHAM by Shimon (Simon) and Levi, and the Hebrew terms above may offer better etymons for words like *SCANDAL*.

    *" . . . if the anointed priest should sin so as *to bring guilt* on the people . . ." לאשמת–*Leviticus 4:3*.

    See: "SMUT."

ASIA/אֵשׁ
AYSH   [A-SH]

ROOTS: ASIA is pronounced much like the Hebrew term אש/ÄSH (fire – *Deuteronomy 4:24*). Dr. Shipley's *Dictionary of Word Origins* (p. 144) cites an ancient Assyrian marker inscribed *Asu*, "land of the rising sun." We call this land mass ASIA, and the direction of the fiery sunrise we name EAST.

    BRANCHES: Christians celebrate the rising Son at EASTER. *Us* is fire in Basque; *shāo* is to burn, bake or roast in Chinese. In Japan, another "land of the rising sun," *asa* is morning. *EOSINE* is red dye; COMB*US*TION is traced to the IE root *eus* (to burn). For other links to אש/ÄSH see "ASH."

    For the redness of morning see "DAWN."

    For the land of the setting sun see "EUROPE."

ASIN(INE)/אָתוֹן
AH-SONE   [ASN]

ROOTS: Not to make the dictionary look ASININE (stupid as a donkey), but this term has been attributed to Celtic *assan*, Old Irish *asan* and Latin *asinus*, but never with a mention of אתון/ÄSON or ÄTON (donkey, ass).

No one makes a bigger ASS of himself than Balaam in *Numbers 22*. The verses below may have fed several nuances of the term in question.

(28) "Then the Lord opened the ASS's mouth . . .

(29) "Balaam said to the ASS, 'You have made a mockery of me!'"

(30) "The ASS said to Balaam, 'Look, I am the ASS that you have been riding all along . . . !'"

    BRANCHES: Hebrew doesn't denigrate the donkey's mulish intransigence in the face of cruel and impatient humans. Instead, related איתן/ÄSSON or ÄTON means strong, steadfast. See "TONE."

    Rumanian and Serbo-Croatian are among the few IE languages that don't have a form of ASN or ASL for donkey. Their term, MGR, is a #1-#2 letter flip of חמור/KHÄMOR (donkey).

    Greek *onos*, source of ONAGER (wild ass) is a #2-#3 metathesis of אתון/ÄSON (ass).

    GANTRY comes from Greek [k]a[n]thon (pack ass), which may be an אתון/ATHON (ass) loaded down with a nasalization and other common variations.

ASP/צֶפַע
(T)SEP(H)-A   [TS-PH-A→SP]

ROOTS: The ASP, from Greek *aspis*, is a poisonous snake with a horned variety.

    צפע/(T)SEP(H)A is an ASP in *Isaiah 14:29*. צפעני/TSI-PH(ONE) is an adder in *Isaiah 11:8*.

    The שפיפון/SHIPHÉPHON (viper, etc.) is the poisonous horned snake in *Genesis 49:17*. (Remember that שפ may be read as SH – PH or like the S-P of ASP.)

    The עכשוב/ÄKH-SHOOBH (viper) of *Psalms 140:4* is similar. (Just drop the עכ/AKH prefix found in the Hebrew words for the spider, rat and mouse.)

    There's also the פתן/PESEN (poisonous snake). It is rendered "asp" in *Isaiah 11:8* of the King James version –"and the suckling child shall play on the hole of the *asp* . . ."

All the snakes above contain the S and P of ASP, or variations like SH, TS, PH or BH.

    BRANCHES: The S-P root raises its venomous head in words like ANTI – SEPTIC, SEPTIC TANK and SEPSIS. All these are attributed to (Greek) *SEPS*, a poisonous snake common in classical literature.

    Snake in Arabic is *tsouban*. Polish *waz* (snake) reverses the S-P/BH. Snake is *savha* in Malay:Bouton.

    See "PYTHON" and "SERPENT."

ASPHAL(T)/שְׁפֵלָה
SHIH-PHALE-AH   [S(H)-PH-L]

ROOTS: The dictionaries don't stop at the Greek *asphaltos*, but go on to state "probably of Semitic origin."

The etymons for what was originally a tarlike bitumen should include שפל/SHÄPHEL (low, ebb tide, depression) and שפלה/SH'FÄLÄ (lowland; the low, coastal plain of Israel). This region of Israel where ASPHALT was first developed, is referred to in *Joshua 11:16*.

    BRANCHES: Back to the tarlike substance that made up early A*SP*HALT, *SLOPPY* primarily meant muddy. (Switch letters 2 and 3.) The same #2-#3 metathesis renders SLOPE.

    SLOPE, too, is defined as falling ground, a slant, and land that drains into an ocean.

SLOB, *slab* in Irish, is mud or any sloppy, SLIPPERY surface. Sloppier yet is זבל/ZEVEL or SEBHEL (dung, manure). ··

Other SH-P relatives include: שפע/SHÄFÄ (to flow or slope), (ה)שפיע/(HI)SHPEÄ (to make slant), שפך/SHEPHEKH (pouring out, place of pouring out, SPOUTING, and שפה/SHÄPHÄ (to incline, tilt). These S-P(H) words suggest etymons for SUPINE (sloping backwards), SPILE (spigot), SPILL (flow, drain), SPILLWAY (passageway for excess water) and, further down, for SUB. (*Asfal* is down and bottom in Arabic; שפולים/SHÊPOOLIM refers to bottom or lower parts.)

שפי/SHIPHÊ (hill, height), צבר/TSÄBÄR (to heap up), and צפת/TSEPHET (top of a pillar) are S-P(H) antonyms.

You might hear VALLEY in the second, פל/PH-L element of שפלה/SHIPHÄLA (lowland).

The root פל/PH-L indicates spilling or falling – see "FALL."
See "WALLOW" for the given etymon of VALLEY.
See "SEEP," "SOFA," "SPILL" and "SUPER."

ASPIRE/שֶׁבֶר
SAH-BHAR   [SBR]

ROOTS: Only at the Latin root of DESPAIR – *spes, speres* (hope) – could one justify a Hebrew etymon for ASPIRE (to long for or seek after). Instead of listing Latin *sperare* (to hope) as the source of ASPIRE, the dictionaries offer Latin *ad* (to) + *spirare* (to breathe).

Longing and seeking after involves looking hard, not breathing hard. צפיה/TSEPEÄ (hope) is an extension of צפה/TSEPHÄ (to look, expect).

Forgetting the Latin *spes* (hope) but retaining the R of ASPIRE are closer Hebrew etymons like שבר/SABHER or סבר/SÄVER ("hope"– *Psalms 146:5*) and שבר/SÊBER (to wait, hope).*

BRANCHES: The IE roots *spei* and *spe* link DESPAIR, ESPERANCE and PROSPER. *The Word* provides the key to international language, one of the ASPIRATIONS of ESPERANTO.

Now, back to the confusion of ASPIRE with SP words of RESPIRATION – which might include WHISPER and GASP. The SP two-letter root of breathing is established in Hebrew by שאף/SHAUPH (to pant, gasp, aspire) and the synonyms נשף/[NE]SHÄPH (to breathe, exhale), נפש/NEPHESH (breath, SPIRIT, character), נשב/NÄSHAV (to blow) and the blowing סופה/SOOFÄ (storm). PASSION may be a reversal of the S(H)-P.

*"The eyes of all *look to* you *expectantly.*" ישברו– *Psalms 145:15.* Reverse SB or SP for the IE root *bhes* (to breathe), source of PSYCHE, PSYCHIC and PSYCHO-.

ASSASS(IN)/חָשָׁשׁ
HASH-ASH   [H-S(H)-S(H)]

ROOTS: Political ASSASS(INS) and drugged up killers were common to the Middle East long before Anwar Sadat and Lebanese car bombs. ASSASSINS and their source of inspiration, HASHISH, are officially borrowed from the Arabic term *hashish* (dried hemp, grass).

חשש/HASHASH means dry grass, chaff or hay.
Isaiah 5:24 "Assuredly, as straw is consumed by a tongue of fire and *hay* (חשש) shrivels as it burns . . ."

BRANCHES: The "straw" of the above verse is קש/KÄSH, a

harder sound and feel than hay or חשש/HASHÄSH. קשה/KÄSHEH is hard; עשב/KHÄSEV is grass.

KASHA or KASZA is a Russian and Polish dish of hulled, crushed, coarse buckwheat that they still feed to humans. *Kusa* is grass in Japanese. CASSAVA, starchy plant food, is from Haitian *kasabi.* HASSOCK is from Anglo-Saxon *hass* (coarse grass). COHOSH is an herb named by the Algonquian Indians. Reverse K-S for other hay words like *SACATON* or *ZACATON* (from Aztec). HASH might resemble a clump of hay or חשש/HASH(ASH). HASH is currently linked to the IE rot *skep* (to cut, scrape, hack).

ASSUME/שׁוּם
SHUME   [S(H)-M]

ROOTS: Another awkward etymology would have ASSUME derive from Latin *ad* (to) + *sumere* (to take). PRESUMPTION guides these hodgepodge Latin etymons.

Hebrew שום/SHOOM (to value, estimate, assess) and Aramaic שומא/SHOOMA (assessment, estimate) make for sounder ASSUMPTIONS. שמא/SHEM-Ä (perhaps) and an idiom like ברי ושמא/BÄRE V'SHEMÄ (the evident and the *probable*) reinforce the sense of PRESUMING in Aramaic.

BRANCHES: שם/SUM (to appoint) and שם/SHAM (name, reputation) – see "SYMBOL"– speak to the #2 definition of ASSUME, "to take on, adopt."

ASSUME also means to undertake something PRESUMPTUOUSLY. Absalom the usurper ASSUMES the role of his sister's avenger: "This has been *decided* by Absalom ever since his sister Tamar was violated." שומה *II Samuel 13:32.*

Swahili "th" corresponds the the Hebrew ש; *thamani* is "value" in Swahili.

AT/עד
UDT   [AD]

ROOTS: AT means to, by, toward, on or close to a time. עד/ÄDT means until, up to or as far as. The Latin and IE roots of AT are both *AD* (to, near, at).*

BRANCHES: This entry could have been named after AD words like *ADEPT, ADHERE,* etc. AD NAUSEAM, but AT is more easily recognized, and the ד (dalet) to T correspondence is clearly established. The term *AD* INFINITUM echoes with the other, opposite meaning of עד/ÄD, eternity. Similarly, עוד/ŌD (see ADD) means not stopping AT someplace but going on further.

Whether this preposition refers to a point in time or in space, it is clear that AD-, AT, TO, and ADO all go back to עד/ÄD.

עת/ÄT is time; את/ÄT is the definitive accusative.

The final syllable in MASSACHUS*ETTS* is a locative meaning "AT." אתר/ÄTHÄR is a place or size; אתר/ÊTER is to localize.

TO is from IE root *de*, a reversal of עד/ÄD or AT (up TO).
*"and they came *unto* Haran" עד/ÄD – *Genesis 11:31.*

ATLA(S)/תלה
TALAH   [TL(H)]

ROOTS: ATLAS is a legendary giant supporting the heavens on his shoulders or, in Homer, a god in charge of the pillars of heaven. Latin *tollere* is to lift, while the IE root for ATLANTA, ATLANTIC or the ATLAS MTS. is *tela* (to lift, support, weigh). An ATLAS or book of maps derives from the legendary figure.

Lifting, supporting and weighing clearly point to hanging, suspending and affixing – the definitions of תלה / TÄLÄH. Hoisting a weight aloft is not the issue. Statues of Atlas with the earth on his shoulders infer suspension – not weight lifting. The pagan Atlas image leaps out of *Job 26:7* where the Lord is extolled for having "*suspended* earth over emptiness." תלה / TÄLÄH means "hanging" in *Genesis 40:19* or *Esther 7:10*.

> **BRANCHES:** נטל /(NÄ)TÄL is to lift; נטל / (NÄ)TEL is weight, burden or "heavy" in *Psalms 27:3*.
> Suspension and weights meet in the scales or balance – *tula* in Sanskrit or *talanton* in greek.
> Money and taxes are weighed, so TAEL, TALENT and DOLL(AR) are related to TOLL and *tala* (Samoan currency).
> Beyond the תלוי / TILÖY (handle) or תלי / TILÈ (quiver for arrows – *Genesis 27:3*), תלה / TÄLÄH also means to leave in suspense or doubt.
> This explains the T/D-L root of DALLY, DAWDLE (from Old French *dalier*), DELAY, and perhaps DANDLE and DANGLE. TANTALIZE and the mythic TANTALUS are official cognates of TOLL(HOUSE) at the IE root *tela*. Other listed cognates include ABLATION, COLLATE, DILATORY, ELATE, EXTOL, ILLATION, LEGISLATOR, OBLATE, PHILATELY, PRELATE, PROLATE, RELATE, RETALIATE, SUPERLATIVE, TALION, TELAMON, THOLE, TOLA, TOLERATE and TRANSLATE.
> The ear is a hanging, affixed handle. *Toli* and *telinga*, therefore, are ear terms in Malay.

AUS(CULATE)/אֹזֶן
OS-(EN)   [A-SZ-N]

ROOTS: *Aus* and *cultare* are two elements in the Latinate term AUSCULATE (to listen). The term is now used in medicine (as well as in Rumanian).

אזן / OS-EN is an ear.*

אזן / ÈSOON is listening. "*Give ear*, ye heavens . . . and let the earth hear" – *Deuteronomy 32:1* (האזינו).

> **BRANCHES:** Listen to the Hebrew A-S-N in both the Gothic term for ear, *auso*, and the Basque term for hearing, *e(n)tzun*. (The experts insist that Basque has "no known linguistic affinities.")
> Arabic hears the word differently and renders it *udhn*. (The Hebrew ז / Z is often hardened to a "d" in Arabic and Aramaic; Hebrew Ezra became Greek Esdras.) The Arabic ear term allows us a link with all the AUDIO words like AUDIBLE, AUDIENCE, and AUDITORIUM (from Latin *audire* to hear). OTOLOGY, the medical study of the ear, derives from Greek ear words like *ous* and *otos*.
> For the many S-N words of AUDIBILITY, see "SOUND."
> The Creator of Hebrew knew the profound connection between human audio equipment and the sense of balance. אזן / ÈZAN is also to poise or balance. The wind balancing osprey or hawk is the עזניה / ÄZNÈÄ.
> Now hear this: *(muv)azene* is balance in Turkish; *(t)ezina* is weight in Serbo-Croatian. *Sikin* is ear in Maya (switching the first two letters of אזן / KHOZEN (ear) or the last two letters of שמע / SH-M-KH (hear).

The second definition of אזן / ÖSEN is handle. An ANSATE jug is one with handles (or looping ears). The Indo-European root *ans* and Latin *ansa* means handle or loop.

Ears they have but hear not/(אזנים) – *Psalms 115:6*.

See "SOUND."

AUXIL(IARY)/עוֹזֵר
AU – ZAIR   [AZR→AXL]

ROOTS: Latin *auxilior* is to help or assist. A simple L/ R change from Grimm's Laws recalls עזר / OS – ZUR (to "help" – *Isaiah 41:6*). Eve was to be an עזר / ÄZER ("fitting helper" – *Genesis 2:18*) or an AUXILIARY. She was not to be but an A(N)CILLARY (maidservant; helper). The two 2-letter roots behind עזר / OZR are עז / OZ (strength) and זר / ZÄR (foreign). Assistance means outside strength.

> **BRANCHES:** ASSIST is more likely from עזר / ASSR than from Latin *ad* (to) + *sistere* (to make stand). SUCCOR, to help or aid, requires flipping letters #1 and #2 of the Hebrew etymon, and employing the gutteral ע / KH.
> AXILLA (armpit), AXIL (upper angle between twig and stem) and AXLE relate to אציל / ATSEEL (armpit, elbow, joint – *Jeremiah 28:12*) and ציר / TSEER (axle, axis, pivot, hinge). Relating to all the XL terms here are אזר / AZUR (to fortify) and זרוע / ZIROA (arm, strength).

AVA(RICE)/אָבָה
AVAH   [AVH]

ROOTS: AVARICE and AVID are from Latin *avere* (to desire). אבה / ÄVÄ means desire, as does אוה / ÈVÄ (*Numbers 1:4, Deuteronomy 12:2*).

> **BRANCHES:** Love, אהבה / ÄHÄVÄ, is only an "ah" away. איבה / ÄVÄ (hate) lurks on the flip side. תאוה / TA'AVA is lust, but תועבה / TÖÄVÄ is abomination.
> "Want to" in Fujian is *via*, AV backwards.

AVERAGE/עֲבֵרָה
A-VAY-RA   [AVR]

ROOTS: AVERAGE is officially borrowed from the Arabic *awar* (damaged gods) via the French *avarie*. Taking the AVERAGE meant figuring out the numerical results of a trading voyage by considering the various charges and items lost in transit.

Transition, passage, crossing, etc., are all implicit in עברה / ÄVÄRÄ (ford, transition) and עבר / OVÄR (to pass, be finished).

See "FERRY" and "OVER."

AV(IATE)/עָף
UFF   [UPH→UV]

ROOTS: To *AVIATE* is to fly, from Latin *avis* (bird). עָף /
APH or UF is to fly, to get UP and OFF the ground. עוֹף /
OAF is a bird or fowl.*

BRANCHES: There's no AVIATION without wings. אבר / ĀVER
is a wing; האביר / HE'EVEER is to wing, to fly, to soar. AVIATE
is a better rendition than "soar" in *Job* 39:26 – "Doth the hawk *soar*
by thy wisdom?" (אבר).

Hebrew AVR (VR→VL) may have influenced Latin *volare* (to
fly) and thus VOLANT, VOLATILE, VOLCANO, VOLLEY, etc. A
VOLARY is an AVIARY.

In the Hebrew aviary is the אוז / ĀVĀZ (goose), the first
international AVIATOR.

APIAN and APICAL are from nature's smaller, domestic
fliers – *apis* in Latin is a bee. The KIWI can't fly, but if this Maori
word is not echoic of the bird's cry then it may derive from עוֹף
/ KHOF (fowl). The gutteral ע offers more edible birds like the
CAPON, CAPERCAILLE and the Dutch *kip* (chicken).

OFF is dismissed as a variant of "of," but this adverb of removal
and distance deserves better than to be lumped together with
"after," "ebb" and "post" under the IE root *apo*.

An extension of עָף / U-P is תועפה / (TU)UPHĀ (eminence,
heights). The *UPPERMOST* typographical feature is a mountain,
and *avi* means "mountain" in the name MOHAVE (tribe of Yuman
Indians). עפל / ŌPHEL is a hill – see "METROPOLIS."

If UP relates to the Hebrew aviators of this entry, then IE root
UPO (under, over) did well to include ABOVE and EAVES as
cognates. "EAVES" and "TOPMOST" are two meanings of Chinese
wu, a typical reversal of עָף / UF.

Reversing Hebrew's AUP is the *PEACOCK*, from Latin *pauo*.
FUGUE, FUGITIVE, REFUGE(E), CENTRIFUGAL and
SUBTERFUGE, all via Latin *fuga* (flight), may be G-F or עָף
reversed.

PHOBIA is also from a BH – G IE root of fleeing.

The "bird" words in Germanic are all F-G or V-G terms. "Flying"
through dialects of Malay will sound like *Upena* and *gupu* (ע = G).
Khi-pe is "to fly off" in Kiowa (Indian); *fei* is to fly in Chinese; *phi*
or *bay* is the Vietnamese.

The Indo-European root *awi-* (bird) contains such alleged
cognates of AVIATE as AVIAN, AVICULTURE, AVIFAUNA, BUS-
TARD, COCKNEY, EGG, OCARINA, OSPREY, OSTRICH,
OVAL, OVARY, OVULE, OVUM and some twenty OO-words
known to students of OOLOGY (the science of birds' eggs).

*"Let *fowl fly* above the earth." (ועוף יעופף) – *Genesis* 1:20.

See "PEGASUS."

BABBLE/בָּבֶל
BUB(H)-ELL   [BBL]

ROOTS: A BABEL (confusion of voices, tumult) of
linguists take up the word BABBLE (inarticulate, confused
speech) and do not connect it back to BABEL. Dictionaries
will cite Swedish *babbeln* (to prattle), Latin *balbutire* (to
stammer) and Sanskrit *balbuthah* (stammerer), with no
mention of that monument to linguistic engineering – the
Tower of Babel.

The Oxford English Dictionary prefers to give BABBLE
an "origin unknown" designation. The OED states that "no
direct connection with Babel can be traced, though

association with that may have affected the senses." Were
the Tower of Babel a Celtic or a Norse myth, the dictionaries might insist on a Babel-BABBLE connection.

The scholars ignore the connection to Genesis 11:9 –
בבל /BABHEL) . . . Babel, because the Lord did there (בלל/
BĀLĀL) *confound* the language of all the earth." One BL
term doubles the L; the other the B. Babel may mean *bab*
(gate) *el* (of God) in Babylonian, but to Bible readers Babel
has always been associated with confused communication.
Those who have forgotten their Bible have forgotten that
the English-speaking world grew up on Scripture.

BRANCHES: בלבל /BĒLBĀL is to confuse; more at "BALL." A list
of English words from Hebrew proper nouns is found at
"RUTHLESS." For the BL link to BR terms of confusion like
BARBARIC see "GARBLE." BAFFLE (origin unknown) has
definitions (to perplex, to thwart) particularly suited to the
Biblical BABHEL or BAFEL.

BABY/בָּבָה
BOO-BAH   [BBH]

ROOTS: BABE and BABY are dismissed by most authorities as imitative of baby sounds. The "bow-wow" theory of
word origins is weak because we have no dog words that
sound like bow-wow, nor words for "infant" that sound like
"ga-ga."

בבה /BOOBĀ is a doll, derived from בבואה / BĀBHOO-
ĀH (a reflected, miniature image). Both terms may be
traced to בבה /BABHĀ which infers the pupil of the eye,
"apple of one's eye," or a small object of adoration and
delight – Zechariah 2:12.

BRANCHES: The double B or V BABY words around the world
are too numerous to mention, but Finnish babies prefer *vauva*
while North American Indians are partial to PAPOOSE.

אביב /ABĒBH or ABĒB is a green ear of corn or "baby"
corn. אב/ABH (youth, young sprout) became BABY just as אב/ ĀBH
(father) reversed and doubled to ABBOT and PAPA. The BA-
BOON (from Old French *babuin*) and *babah* (monkey in Malay:
Sian) may have been seen as delightful, childlike creatures, or as
miniature images of people.

Double B or P terms of prized miniatures include BUB, PUPA,
PUPIL, and PUPPY.

BOOB, BOOBY, and [NINCOM]POOP demonstrate our tend-
ency to call foolish people BABIES. BA(M)BINO (baby) is a compliment in Italian, but *bambo* (foolish, childish) is an insult. *Moro*
(baby) in Modern Greek is a cognate of MORON. A NINNY (fool)
can similarly be linked with baby words like Spanish *nene* (baby)
and *nino* (child), Chinese *nan* (child) or Malay *niana* (child) – all
of these are from Hebrew נין /NEEN (grandchild, offspring).

See "BAUBLE"

BAD/בָּדָאוּת
BUD(ADOS)   [B-D]

ROOTS: *Webster's* contends that Middle English *badde*

(bad, worthless) is from Anglo-Saxon *baddel* (hermaphrodite) – a bisexual imposter. BAD is defined as "not good, not as it should be, incorrect, immoral and not valid."

כראות/BÄD[ÄOOS] (deceit, fraud), כרא/BÄDÄ (to lie, concoct), and התברה/[HIT]BADA (to come to nothing) all form better etymons. BD is a "lying" term seen in *Nehemiah 6:8*; in *Isaiah 16:6* translators prefer "boastings" or "iniquity." The AHD links BAD to BIDE (trust), as in בטח/BODTAH (trust).

> **BRANCHES:** (שם) ברוי/(SHEM) BÄDOOY is a pseudonym. טוב/TOBH (good) reversed evokes "bad." באש/BA'ÄSH and ביש/BISH (Aramaic terms for BAD) also evoke "bad" since Aramaic SH and Hebrew dentals (T,D) interchange – see "TERZA RIMA."
>
> FAULT(Y), from French *faut*, and VICE, vicious and VITIATE from Latin *VITium* are possibly related. *FAITOUR* (an imposter), PER*FID*Y and *FUD*GE (a false story) have weak etymologies that might be upgraded with the Hebrew etymons here.
>
> For antonyms of FIDELITY see "FAITH."

BALL/בָּלַל
BALL-UL   [BLL]

ROOTS: The IE root of BALL is *bhel* (to blow, swell).

בלום/BALOOM (swollen) and בלט/BALAT (to protrude) point to a BL root of filling or expanding. Other Hebrew words match the rolling, mixed up sense of being all BALLED UP in a BALL of confusion. בלל/BALAL is to confound (*Genesis 11:9*), בלול/BALOOL is to mingle together (*Leviticus 2:5*) and בלבל/BILBOOL means confusion.

> **BRANCHES:** BALE, BALEEN, BALLET, BALLOT, BALOON, BOLL, BOULEVARD, BOWL, BULK, BULL, BULWARK, FOLLICLE, BOOL, PELLET, and PHALLUS are linked to IE root *bhel*. BOLUS is from a Greek word meaning "lump." Some of these recall בול/BOOL (lump – *Isaiah 44:19*).
>
> The פור/POOR (the round, pebble-like lots cast in *Esther 3:7*) resemble a Swahili *[m]pira* (ball), an Australian Aborigine *pula* or *boola* (ball, lump), a Tahitian *poro* (ball) or a Spanish *pelota* (ball). These BULLETS, PELLETS or BALLOTS were rolled or BOWLED or PELTED. To roll in Tibetan is *b'al*.
>
> To בלבל/BILBÄL (confuse) a consonant or syllable is to make it different (*mbalimbali* in Swahili). The common L to R change may account for the names of mixed race, mixed language peoples such as the BERBERS of North Africa and the BARBARIANS of Eurasia. "Together" is *beraber* in the richly mixed vocabulary of Turkish.
>
> See "BABBLE" for the BALLED UP sense of BL; see "WALLOW" for the rolling sense of BL and LB words; see "BLOAT," "BOULDER" and "VAULT" for the swollen sense of BL; see "BALE" for a tied-up ball.

BA(L)SAM/בֹּשֶׂם
BO-SEM   [BSM]

ROOTS: BALSAM is from Latin *balsamum*; it is a gummy plant resin used for perfume. BALSAMIC means fragrant.

בשם/BŌSEM is the term for the fragrant spices used in Temple worship. Spelled with a שׂ/s in *Exodus 30:23*, it is spelled with a ס/S elsewhere. Both spellings render words which mean perfume and the verb "to be fragrant."*

> **BRANCHES:** BALM is from Greek *balsamon* (balsam).
> * *Song of Songs 4:16* "Awake, O north wind, come, O south wind! Blow upon by garden, that its *perfume* may spread."

BAR/בַּר
BAR   [BR]

ROOTS: Old French *barre* and Latin *barra* are the given sources for bolt-like BARs and BARRIERs with which to BAR or BARRICADE the door. The preposition BAR in the Aramaic phrase בר מינן/*BÄR* MINÄN (*except* for him) corresponds to English phrases like "bar none."

Beyond the preposition are nouns of keeping out.

"All these were fortified cities with high walls, gates and *BARS*" – בריח/BÄRĒÄH (*II Chronicles 14:6*).

The more generic BAR infers a BOARD or בריח/BÄRĒÄH (translated "BAR" or "BOLT") common to Biblical construction sites (see *Exodus 36:33*).

> **BRANCHES:** The BARRAGE of BAR words includes BARKEEPER, BARREL, BARRETTE, BARRISTER and BARROOM. The WEIR (dam) bars water.
>
> The opposite of BAR as obstruction is seen in terms like בר/BÄR (open field) and ברור/BÄROOR (clear) – see "BARE" and "BARRIO".

BARE/בֵּעֵר
BEE-AIR   [BAR]

ROOTS: BARE cannot be traced with certainty beyond the Anglo-Saxon *baer*. The word means 1) uncovered, 2) cleared out, or 3) plain and simple. The BARE facts about all these connections are BARED below:

1) פרוע/PÄROOÄ is bareheaded (*Leviticus 13:45*).
2) בער/BEAR ("I have *cleared out* the consecrated portion" – *Deuteronomy 26:13*.
3) ברא/BÄRA (to cut down trees – "go up to the forest country and *clear* an area" – *Joshua 17:15*).
4) בר/BÄR (pure, clear) *Psalms 24:4*.
5) באר/BÄ-AIR (to expose, explain – *Deuteronomy 1:5*).
6) ברור/BÄROOR (evident, lucid, clear).
7) בהיר/BÄHĒR (clear).

> **BRANCHES:** Japanese *bareru* means to be exposed or found out. See "PURE"

BAR(LEY)/בַּר
BAR [BR]

ROOTS: BARLEY is from Anglo-Saxon *bere*; the IE root *bhares* (barley) ties in FARINA, FARRAGO, and BARN. בר/ BAR is grain or corn.

Genesis 42:3 "... Joseph's brothers went down to get *grain* rations in Egypt." בר

BRANCHES: As usual, the generic Hebrew term became specialized. *Farina* means flour in most Romance languages. Another IE root from BR is *puro* (grain) which includes FURZE and PYRENE.

BEER and BARM are from ברור/BIROOR (froth, lather, suds) and בר/BAR. בריה/BIR'YA (II Samuel 13:5) and ברות/BOROS (Ps. 69:22) are general food terms.

BERSEEM (fodder) is formally linked to Arabic.

Bras and *bira* are terms for rice among the dialects of Malay.

BAR(ON)/אַבִּיר
(A)-BEER [BR]

ROOTS: A BARON is a nobleman, powerful magnate, and even a double sirloin of beef.

אביר / ABER is an overseer, hero, knight, or "Mighty One" (in *Isaiah 1:24*). Saul's "chief" herdsman is an ABER / אביר in *I Samuel 21:8*. BARON is traced to Old High German *baro* (a man), though the etymon goes on to cite the IE base *bher* (to carry).

For the "CARRY" etymon see "FERRY."

BRANCHES: As for the "man" etymon, the BR root is seen in Hebrew words like (נ)בר / (GE)BHER (man, warrior).

Change the R to an L and you have the source of CABALL(ERO), CAVALIER and CHIVALRY. גבר /GEVER is a male, as well as the root for words of bravery and strength. This leads us to words like *VIRILE* and *WEREWOLF*. COVE is a man in British slang, adopted from Gypsy *covo*. Returning to more *BARONIAL* terms, גביר / GIBHEER is a lord, master or rich man.

Related to the BR words of power and VIRILITY (Latin *vir* is a man) is ברי / BAREE (healthy, vigorous). (הת)גבר / (HIT)GABAR means to overcome or (PRE)VAIL, but it also means to strengthen oneself. The R to L change renders dozens of more words via Latin *valere* (to be strong) – including: VALEDICTORIAN, VALENCE, VALENTINE, VALIANT, VALID, VALUE and VIRTUE. רפה / RAFA (weak) is the reverse of BR's macho. VIGOR, from Latin *vigere* (to be strong), may be a metathesis of גבורה / GVOORA (strength).

In Basque *aberats* is a rich man, recalling the ABER of our caption here. *Buru* is a head or chief in Basque.

See "VIRILE."

BARRIO/בַּר
BARR [BR]

ROOTS: Before inferring an Hispanic ghetto, BARRIO (from Latin *barra*) meant a suburb.

Suburb is the primary definition of בר / BARR, which also means a field or campus. It is rendered "open field" in *Job 39:4*, and, with help from Grimm's Laws, it aids אפר / APHOR (meadow, pasture) to give us words like *FIELD*, POLAND, *PRAIRIE*, PUR(LIEU) *VELT* and *WILD*. מדבר / MIDBAR (wilderness) is a stretch (MD) of open land (BR). ערבה / ARABHA (BR reversed) is a prairie or steppe.

BRANCHES: An extension and almost an antonym of בר/BARR is בירה / BEERA (capital city, castle, fort, sanctuary). A BOROUGH was a *buruh* (town, fortified place). בירה/BEERAH, as in *Nehemia 1:1*, is a fine etymon for words like BURG, BURGER, WEIR, BOURG (village near a castle), BOURGEOIS and BURH. Reverse B-R to get URB(AN).

בירנית/BERA(NET) is a palace, fortified castle or "fortress" in *II Chronicles 27:4*. Via the IE root *bhergh* (high), one may include BARROW, ICEBERG, BELFRY, BURGLAR, FORCE, FORT, FORTE, FORTITUDE, FORTRESS, COMFORT, EFFORT, ENFORCE, FORTIFY and REINFORCE. FORT might also be a #2-#3 letter flip of ביצור / B(H)-T(S)-R (fort).

VILLAGE need not come from the urban or suburban Hebrew etymons above, despite the fact that *Byr* is "village" in Old Norse, and *varos* is "town" in Hungarian. VILLAGE is supposed to mean a farm, via the Latin *villa*. כפר / (K)FAR (village – *I Samuel 6:18*) may be behind VILLAGE and FARM. כפרי / KOFRE is a farmer, as is the Scottish CROF(TER).

The city of SINGA*PORE* comes from the Sanskrit version of בירה / BERA (city). *Pur* merely changes the B to a P. Now change the R to an L and you have the IE root for (COSMO)*POLITAN* city words – *pele* (citadel, fortified high place). The primary Hebrew etymon is עפל / OP(H)EL (fortified hill).

See "METROPOLIS."
See "DELTA."

BASIL/בְּצָל
BEE-TSAIL [B-(T)S-L]

ROOTS: BASIL is an herb whose leaves are used as seasoning.

בצל / B-(T)S-L is to flavor or spice (as with onions). In *Numbers 11:5* the Jews cry over *not* having onions: "We remember the fish ... in Egypt ... and the leeks, and the *onions* and the garlic." (בצלים).

The Hebrew root implies vegetables like the onion and shallot. Onion in Arabic is *basal*. The dictionary offers the puzzling term *basileous* ("king" in Greek) as the source for BASIL.

BRANCHES: Onions almost peel themselves, thus the similarity between BE-TSAL / בצל and PE-TSAL / פצל, to peel or split.

Many tongues like the flavor of בצל / BE-TSAL. An easy #1-#2 letter flip (metathesis) of B/TS/L is TS/B/L. Here's the TSIBELE a Yiddishe mama cooks with, along with the CIPOLLA, ZWIEBEL, CEBULA, and SIPULI (onions all) that Italian, German, Polish, and Finnish mamas have cried over for centuries.

Tipula is an onion in Basque, the language with "no affinities." CHIVE is from Latin *cepa* (onion). *Sol* is an onion to Kiowa Indians.

BASIS/בָּסָם
BUS-US [BSS]

ROOTS: BASIS is the Greek and Latin term for a step or pedestal. Greek *pous* (foot) is closely related.

Hebrew offers בסס / BÄSUS (to step on), בם / BUS (to trample – *Zechariah 10:5*), and פסע / PUSÄ (to step), and פסת(רגל) / PĒSUS (REGEL) meaning "the sole (of the foot)."

BRANCHES: These words are the BASIS of many BASIC terms of BASE lowness, BASE tones, and moral ABASEMENT and DE BASEMENT. The IE root *bassus* (low) adds BAS-RELIEF, BASS[ET] and BASSO.

Definition #6 of BASE is "a center of operations, a headquarters." A military BASE is a kind of foundation, but the home BASE of BASEBALL might require a homier etymon. בית / BÄYIS (house, home, locale, family – *Genesis 12:1*) makes a fine home BASE.

Oboz is a camp in Polish; *bayuso* means place in Japanese; *vis* and *vastu* mean house in Sanskrit.

Some Israelis smirk at the European or Ashkenazic pronunciation of BÄYIS instead of BÄYIT. But Hebrew wasn't invented in the 20th century, and the shibbole*th* (from שבלת / SHIBOLE*T*) of divergent accents existed in Biblical days. The ancient Jewish community of Rome, which predated the Babylonian exile, is known to have pronounced the ת as an S (not a T). Those Israeli ears must surely wince at Americanized versions of ת as in *BETH*LEHEM (house of bread) or *BETH* ISRAEL (the Israelite house, family or community). Bethlehem can be mangled to Middle English *bedlam*, as London's St. Mary of Bethlehem mental hospital gave us the word BEDLAM (noisy confusion). ABODE (home) might also come from בית / BYT or B–Y–TH (house, home).

The Danes like TH from ת too, as a *both* – source of English BOOTH – means a dwelling in Old Danish. A BOOTH is a BASIC home when making a BASE camp overnight. בת / BHOTH means "spent the night" in *Daniel 6:19*.

Of course there are בית words that "correctly" sound like BAYIT. *Bydh* is a house in Welsh; *byt* is a Czech apartment; *batsu* means family in Japanese; *wat* is a Siamese temple.

בסים / BÄSĒS (BASIS, BASE) is the modern Hebrew term wrongly termed a "borrowing" from the Greek. A "re-borrowing" is more like it.

See "PACE."

BAT / בד
BUDT   [B(D)T]

ROOTS: The Anglo-Saxon and Celtic words for this stick, club or cudgel are traced all the way back to the source of WOOD (B = W, T = D), the IE root *vidhu* or *widhu* (tree).

We've all used a tree limb as a baseball BAT, and בד / BÄDT is a tree limb, wooden board, rod, staff or "stave" in *Exodus 25:13*.

BRANCHES: Branches or limbs of the same tree include: BATON, BATTEN, BOAT, FID, FIDDLE and WADDY (the BAT or cudgel of Australian aborigines). The royal *BATON* of a king or sire is שרביט / SÄR-*BH*ĒT or SHARVĒT; a שבט / SH*ABHET* is a rod or scepter.

Fid is an Old Irish tree; *ved* is Norwegian for wood; *Puuta* is wood or tree in Finnish. Reverse to *tupa* for a spear in Malay.

A BITT is a post on a ship's deck, the etymon given is Old Norse *biti* (a beam).

If the *pedon* (oar in Greek) belongs here, then its derivative PILOT should too.

For the verb BAT see "BEAT."

More at "LUTE."

BAUB(L)E / בבה
BAW-BHAH   [BBH]

ROOTS: Only one of the three terms for toy in Old French (*babel, baubel, belbel*) resembles a reduplication of Latin *bellus* (pretty), but the Latin term is credited. A BAUBLE is a showy trinket, a baby's toy or an ornamental item. This Babel of confusion results from scholars seeking out Greek and Latin *baubels* in a sea of Hebrew gems.

A בבה / BOBHÄ is a prized object, the apple of one's eye, and the pupil of the eye. *Zechariah 2:12* reads – "Whoever touches you [Zion] touches the *pupil* of his own eye." (בבת)

A BIBLEOT is a small, decorative and often rare object or trinket. This word, too, weakens the Latin etymon (*bel*) and favors the B-B term (with the -le diminutive suffix) from Biblical Hebrew.

BRANCHES: A little toying with P's and B's and one sees the etymon for PUPIL of the eye (that gem or BAUBLE in our eyes). PUPIL comes to English via Latin *pupilla* (a figure reflected in the eye). בבואה / BÄBHOOÄH is a reflected image. Other darling diminutives like POPPET, PUPPET and PUPIL (the student) are seen at the entry "BABY."

The apple of Eve's eye was the forbidden fruit. בבה / BÄBHÄ, rounded out by אפף / ÄPHÄPH (to surround, encircle), is a possible influence on words like APPLE, PAPAW and PAPAYA.

BE / בא
BAH   [BA]

ROOTS: This confusing "defective verb" in English sues several different etymons for paternity. One definition is "to come to," as in "peace BE with you."

בא / BÄ is to come or come to be. ". . . All he saith cometh surely to pass." בוא יבוא – *I Samuel 9:6*.

BE is also to exist, and הוה / HAVA is to BE, to exist. הוי /HEVEE is the imperative, as in "BE quiet!"

"*BE* lord over thy brethren" הוי – *Genesis 27:29*.

BRANCHES: BE, like WAS, is also linked to IE base *wes* (stay, remain). This resembles ישב / YOSHEV (dwell, sit), its S-V root reversed to V-S.

A different BE, the common prefix BE- in words like BENEATH or BETWEEN, means by, about, or near. The Hebrew prefix ב- / B- , B' or BIH also means BY, at or WITH.

BEAK[ER] / בק(בק)
BUCK-BOOK   [BK]

ROOTS: BEAKER is linked to Old Norse *bikarr* (a cup) and to Latin *bicarium (wine cup). In Yiddish there's bekher* (wine cup). The above terms, along with PITCHER, are traced to Greek *bikos* (a wine jar). Double the בק / B-K root of *vacuum* words (see "VACUUM") and you get בקבק / BUKBOOK, the jar, cruse or bottle of *I Kings 14:3*. Of the related B-K (bilabial-guttural) words in Hebrew, פך / PUKH (flask, vial) is closer to BEAKER size. See "BUCKET" for larger containers like the BAG and BOX. The "beaker" in *Isaiah 51:22* is קבעת / KOOB(Ä'S) – reverse the K-B root to get BEAK(ER).

BRANCHES: The spout of the BEAKER recalls a BEAK, a bird's mouth. Latin *bucca* (mouth) is the source of words like DEBOUCHE. פה / PEH (mouth) could be pronounced PECK (what a bird's mouth does) with a typical ה / H to K change. [Greek *herpein* is to Creep; shish Kebab is the Turkish and Arabic rendition of הכהב / HUBH HUBH (roast).]

For the piercing action of a beak see "PICK." בקעה / BIKĒÄ is a fissure, crack or cleft; פקע / POKÄ and בקע / BOKÄ both mean to split, crack or cleave.

A bottle in Chinese is *p'i[n]g*; the Chinese WOK might be another BK or VK receptacle.

BEAT/בָּעַט
BEE-ATE   [BUT]

ROOTS: The IE root of BEAT is said to be *bhau* (to strike). All the meanings of BEAT are covered by Hebrew soundalikes. BEAT is 1) to repeatedly strike, 2) to punish with flogging, 3) to tread upon or make flat, 4) to mix, as to BEAT eggs, 5) to outdo or defeat an opponent.

בעט / BĒÄT, and earlier BÄÄT in *Deuteronomy 32:15,* is to kick out at, trample and spurn. בטש / BÄTÄSH (Aramaic) is to beat or stamp, a relative of פטש / POTÄSH (to hammer out). Eben Shoshan's dictionary also states that the term means to conquer (beat) and to mix or stir (beat). Both פטיש / PATĒSH and BEETLE mean hammer. Repeated blows and strokes are implied by חבט / ḤABHAT, as in *Deuteronomy 24:20* "when you BEAT your olive tree" (תחבט / (TA)ḤBŌT).

BRANCHES: Beating a drum is only a PAT or TAP (PAT backwards)—תפף / TOPHÄF (strike lightly) is an extension of תף / TŌPH (drum). Besides פטש / POTÄSH above, words like BASH are linked to פחם / PÄḤÄS (to batter, beat out of shape).

The IE root *battuere* (to beat) is a "Latin verb of unknown origin." The following easily relate to the Hebrew terms above: ABATE, BAT (v.), BATTER, BATTERY, COMBAT, DEBATE, and REBATE. MORE at "BAT," "BOOT," and "BUTT."

BATTLE is traced to the IE root *battuere,* a Latin verb of unknown origin. פתל / PÄTÄL means "wrestled" (JPS Bible) or "struggled together" (*Hebrew-English Lexicon of the Bible*) in *Genesis 30:8.*

Listed cognates of BEAT include ABUT, BEETLE, BUSHEL, BUTT, BUTTOCK, BUTTON, BUTTRESS, HALIBUT, REBUT, REFUTE and SACKBUT. POU[N]D is a nasalized PT or PD word of striking.

BEHEMOTH/בְּהֵמוֹת
BIH-HAY-MOWTH   [BHMH]

ROOTS: BEHEMOTH (huge animal) is an acknowledged borrowing from Hebrew.

The singular is בהמה / BIHÄMÄ (animal, beast or "cattle"– *Genesis 1:25*). In *Job 40:15* the beast is assumed to be a hippopotamus. בהמות / BIHÄMŌT or BEHÄMŌTH means beasts or the hippopotamus.

BRANCHES: If the Caribbean islands were named for bestial cannibals (see "CARIBBEAN") perhaps בהמי / BAHAMĒ (brutish, animal-like) influenced the naming of the BAHAMAS.

BEMA/בָּמָה
BAH-MAH   [BMH]

ROOTS: BEMA (step, seat, raised platform in Greek) is not merely Greek, as במה / BÄMÄ is a high place, stage, mountain or altar (*I Samuel 9:12*).

The BEMA in a church or synagogue (where it is also called the בימה / BĒMÄ) is a chancel or enclosure around the (raised) altar or ritual staging area.

BRANCHES: A more defined structure and nasal sound is בניה / BĒNYA (building, structure).

BERRY/פְּרִי
PERRY   [PRY→BRY]

ROOTS: Any small fruit is a BERRY. The Anglo-Saxon *berie* (berry, grape) "may be" linked to the IE base *bha* (to gleam, shine) according to *Webster's,* even though many berries do not gleam or shine. The AHD is not sure either. They link BERRY to Germanic *bazja* (berry) with a "perhaps."

פרי / PIRĒY (fruit) is the more common pronunciation in the Bible, from *Genesis 1:29* on, but פרי / PERĒY is available too.*

BRANCHES: Where the English changes פ / P to B, the Sanskrit prefers to change the second letter of פרי / PRY. Berry in Sanskrit is *pippali.* The last syllable of the Hungarian strawberry, *foldiePER,* should mean berry.
*Ecclesiastes 2:5 –"I planted every kind of *fruit."*
More at "FRUIT."

BET/בָּטַח
BET-AH   [B-T]

ROOTS: To BET is to assert that one is בטח / BETÄH (surely, certainly) right about something. The reference books are "uncertain," guessing that BET is probably from ABET. ABET is from Old French *beter* (to harass with dogs).

BRANCHES: Do not BET that DEB(TOR) and DEB(IT) are "from Latin *de* (from) + *habere* (to have)" rather than from עבט / ÄBHŌT (a pledge to repay).

HYPOTHECATE is from Latin *hypotheca* (to pledge as security). To link this term with עבט / ÄBHOT is more than hypothetical since the ע to H change is documented in *Genesis 31:47* (שהד / SHÄHÄD in Aramaic and ער / ÄD mean witness). Furthermore, *hals* (neck in Old Norse and in Dutch RINGHALS) is from עול / ŌL (collar); and HEDONISM (Greek *hedone* means delight) is from ערנה / EDNÄ (delight).

ע to H changes occur in languages as close as Anglo-Saxon (*hræfen* and ערב / ORÄV mean raven), and in languages as exotic as Maidu (California Indians) where *hin* and עין / IYIN mean eye. At the same time, it is easy to hear הבטיח / HIVTĒÄH (to promise, to insure) in *hypotheca.*

More at "AFFIDAVIT," "FAITH," and "VOTE."

BETA/ בֵּית
BAIT   [BYT]

ROOTS: BETA is the second Greek letter, adopted from the "Phoenician" (read Hebrew) second letter. The Hebrew ב designates the number two and resembles the symbol 2.

BRANCHES: As usual, every available pronunciation of the Hebrew term has generated words.

All the BETA terms derived from pronouncing the ת as a T. BIS (twice – as in the musical direction to repeat) renders the ת as an S. BIGAMY is from Latin *bis* (twice) + Greek *gamos* (marriage).

The ת as TH (which gave us B*eth*esda, MD) allows us to see BOTH as meaning "the two." See "BOTH."

Finally, pronouncing just the letter ב/B, we get the BI- prefix of twoness seen in words like BIANNUAL or BIMONTHLY. As a BT term of twoness, BETA is the designed opposite of BT terms of exclusion like BUT (without, singled out – see "DIVIDED").

Ba is a plural prefix in Swahili; oba means "both" in Polish.

BIB(LE)/ בִּיב
BEEBH   [BYB]

ROOTS: Greek *biblia* (collection of writing) was done on *biblos* (papyrus bark) from the same Egyptian source of the word PAPER. The Egyptian reed, whose bark gives us PAPYRUS, is related to אבוב/ABOOBH (pipe, tube, knotgrass). In the BIBLE this reed is found in *Job 9:26* – אבה/ABEH (reed). ביב/BEB (pipe) is not a BIBLICAL term, but it's easy to follow the linguistic pipeline from a 1) hollow reed or pipe grass to 2) paper from that grass to 3) books or BIBLES from that paper. אבובא / ABOOBHA is read in Aramaic.

BRANCHES: Branches include BIBLIOGRAPHY and BIBLIO-PHILE. More at "BAMBOO," "FIFE" and "OBOE."

BID/ בטא
BADT-AH   [BT]

ROOTS: To BID is to command, declare, say or tell. In Middle English *beden* is to announce.*

בטא / BADA or VATTA is to proclaim or UTTER words; בטוי/BEDTOOY means "pronouncing" or "expression." Other connotations of BID are propositioning and inviting; פתה/PETA is to seduce with words.

*The IE root ascribed to BID, *bheudh* (making aware), doesn't infer commanding or inviting.

BRANCHES: בטאון/BE DTAON is a publication. A double BT/BD term is פטפט/PITPAT (chatter, idle talk). דבר/DABER (to speak, command) reverses the BD; a reversal of צו/T(S)AV (command) is similar.

BEADLE, BODE, BUDDHA, OM*BUD*SMAN and VER*BOT*EN are linked to BID by the IE root. BAIT (lure, entice) and *PA*TOIS (a dialect) may also be added. If Japanese *kotoba* (word)

doesn't relate to כתב/KITABH (letters, writing, script), reversing the Japanese term shows an affinity to בטה/BATAH (to utter words).

Latin *fatus* (to speak) appears in words like PREFACE. FATE, CONFESS and PROFESS are related. To cry out is *awat* in Maya Indian.

פיוט/PEOOT (POETRY, liturgical verse of piety) is a later mishnaic word, but links easily with the above Hebrew terms of expression and utterance. *Pyet* (to sing in Russian) doesn't support the current etymology of POET[RY] which cites Greek *poiein* (to make).

The IE root *wed* (to speak) is another derivative of בט/V-DT. The root speaks to words like COMEDY, MELODY, ODE, PAR-ODY, RHAPSODY and TRAGEDY.

Pidato is speech in Indonesian.

BISON/ בָּאשָׁן
BOS(H) – ON   [BAS(H)]

ROOTS: BISON have a Latin name traced to a root "of obscure origin" for strong-smelling animals.

באש / BAASH is to stink; באשן / BAASHON means "the stinker," and is today used for the skunk.

BRANCHES: The WEASEL is an official cognate of BISON. When dead and decayed the frogs of plague #2 made quite a "stink" (באש / BAS) in *Exodus 7:18*. יבש / YAVASH (dry) is related in that drying and rotting will lead to a fetid, putrid state. "Putrid" is a cognate of PUS, both from the IE root *pu* (to rot, decay). A sweet-smelling antonym is בשם / BOSEM (perfume, spice). The AHD offers the IE root *weis* (to flow) as a possible source of Germanic *wisunt* and Latin *bison* (bison). Germanic *wison* is the earlier form of Old English *wase* (mire, mud) and the source of OOZE (see "OOZE.") The definition of בצץ / BATSATS or VA(T)SA(T)S is to OOZE, trickle or drip. (For a backward synonym see "SEEP.") OOZE and mud are related in Hebrew, as בץ / BOTS is mud, mire (*Jeremiah 38:22* – see "PITCH") and בצה / BETSA is a swamp or marsh (*Job 40:21*). Swamps have the smell to fit the FETID and PUTRID things in this entry, and mud is a favorite medium for BISON or water buffalo. The cognates of BISON, OOZE and WEASEL at IE root *weis* are VIRUS, VISCID, VISCOUS and WISENT.

BIT/ בַּד
BUDT   [BD→BT]

ROOTS: Computer BITS and BITES help one to under-stand BIT and BITE as terms of separateness. The IE root is *bheid* (to split).

בדל/BOD[UL] or BOT[UL] is to separate, detach, isolate (*Genesis 1:6, 7*); בדד/BADTADT means solitary, alone (*Lamentations 1:1*). *Exodus 30:34* offers בד בבד/BADT B'VADT ("of each") – which implies BIT by BIT. לבד/ (LI)BHADT means alone, separate or only.

BRANCHES: בת/BUT (child, suburb) is a prefix of diminution which cuts a sound down to a בת קול/BUT KOL (echo) or a laugh down to a בת צחוק/BUT SHOK (smile). PETITE and PETTY re-late here as BT or PT terms of reduction.

בתור/BETOOR and בתק / BETAK are dissection and cutting off. A בתר/BET(ER) is a piece, part, or cut. The ברית/BRIT (pact, "brith") of the בתרים/BIT(ARIM) (bits, halves) is a covenant agreed upon or literally cut in *Genesis 15:10.*

    The IE root *bheid* includes ABET, BAIT, BATEAU, BEETLE, BITT, BITTER, BOAT, -FID, FISSION and FISSURE.

    More at: "BAT," "BUT," "PIECE" and "WIDOW".

BLAME /בִּלְעָם

BILL-UM   [BLAM]

ROOTS: It is difficult to accept the Greek word *blasphemein* as the source of BLAME. The original meaning of BLAME, a condemnation or expletive like "damned," doesn't match the profanation of the sacred originally inferred by BLASPHEMY.

    The Hebrew Bible records a long and humorous episode of a professional damner or curse-monger named בלעם/ BILAM (Balaam is the Anglicization). If fictional and real people can give us words like "malapropisms" and "spoonerisms," surely this memorable character in *Numbers 22-24* can offer a more satisfactory etymon for BLAME than the Greek source of blasphemy.

BLEAK/בָּלָק

BALL-LUCK   [BLK]

ROOTS: The "probable" etymon cited is Old Norse *bleikr* (pale). This would make BLEAK a synonym of "bleach" and an antonym of "black:" (see the L-B words of whiteness at "ALBINO"). BLEAK usually means desolate and gloomy, a topgraphical and emotional moonscape. בלק/BOLUK seems BLEAK enough in the verses below:

    "Behold the Lord maketh the earth *empty,* and maketh it waste . . ." (KJ) *Isaiah 24:1;* "she is empty and void and *waste*" (JPS) *Nahum 2:11.*

    BRANCHES: As a verb בלק/BÄLÄK (to lay waste) is akin to בלע/ BELA(KH) (to destroy). As a term of gloomy waste, בלק/BÄLÄK relates to אפל/ÄFÄL (dark, dim, gloomy) and אפר/ÄFER (ashes) – reversals and opposites of the L-B bleached pale words. BLACK is officially derived from IE *bhleg* (shine, gleam). ברקת/ BAREK(ET) is an emerald.

BLIST(ER)/יַבֶּלֶת

(YA)BELET   [BLT or BLS]

ROOTS: Old French *blestre* (blister) is thought to derive from the IE root *bhlei* (to blow, swell).

    יבלת/(YA)BELET or (YA)BELES is a wart (*Leviticus 22:22*), and is the source of WART and WELT as well as BLI(S)TER.

    BRANCHES: See entries like "BLOAT," "BOULDER," "VAULT," and "WELT" for בלט/BÖLÄT (to protrude) and other reinforcing terms.

BLOAT/בָּלַט

BOL-UT   [BLT]

ROOTS: BLOATED infers both fullness and flowing, just as its IE root, *bhleu,* means both to swell or well up and to overflow. יבלת/(YA)BELES (wart) (*Leviticus 22:22*), (*Jeremiah 17:8*), יבל/(YÄ)VÄL (stream – *Jeremiah 17:8*), מבול/ (MA)BOOL (flood – *Genesis 6:17*), בלום/BÄLOOM (swollen), and בלט/BOL-UT (protruding, prominent) all establish this B-L family of overflowings.

    BRANCHES: The official cognates fo BLOAT include AFFLUENT, BLOT, CONFLUENT, FLUCTUATE, FLUET, FLUID, FLUORIDE, FLUSH, FLUVIAL, FLUX, INFLUENCE, MELLIFLUOUS, PHLOEM and SUPERFLUOUS

    Other relevant terms are BEETLE (browed), BLADDER, BLEED (in printing, and possibly, as in flowing BLOOD), BOLT (as in bolthead), BULGE, FULLY, and perhaps POLLEX (thumb).

    See "BALL," "BLISTER," "VAULT" and "WELT".

    BOLD is traced to IE *bhel*[2] (to blow, swell), but like BLATANT, it recalls the prominence and standing our of בלט/BOLUT (to stand out, protrude, project). L→R changes allow us to consider בריא/BÄRE (translated as "fat" or "stout") and באר/B'ÄR (a "well of spring water" – *Genesis 26:19*).

    Just as the primary IE root combined swelling and flowing, we can see that to WELL up is akin to a flowing WELL of water. In other words, to FILL up is to FILL out and be FULL. Other possible connections include BULGE, FLOW, VAULTED (arched) and (S)WELL. See PL flowing terms at "ARCHIPELAGO."

    A like-sounding IE root, *bhle* (to blow), claims BLADDER and INFLATE, but they may relate to the BLOATED, BALOONING things in this entry.

BOBBY/וָו

VAWV   [VV]

ROOTS: It is guessed that the BOBBY pin was named for its use with bobbed hair. The metal hairpin and clasp is more likely related to one definition of a BOB (a small pendant object) and to BOBBIN (a small notched pin).

    A וו/VAWV or BHOBH is the small fastener pin or "hook" of *Exodus 27:10.* The letter ו/VAV means hook and serves as a hook or conjuction like the word "and." The ו also looks like a pin.

BONE (UP)/[הִתְ]בּוֹנֵ[ן]

(HIT)-BONE-(AIN)   [BN]

ROOTS: Like so may slang terms, there is no etymon available for BONING UP (studying hard). התבונן/HIS-BONÄN is to study; בינה/BENÄ is understanding; הבין/ HÄBHIN is to understand or teach; בן/BON is to discern – *Deuteronomy 32:10.*

    BRANCHES: נבון/(NA)BHON is wise or discriminating, as בין/

BĀN means between. As התבונן/HITBŌNAN also means to consider and reflect, OPINE (to think, suppose) and OPINIONS are possibly related. There's also a cerebral BEAN to consider.

BORE/בּוֹר
BORE   [BR]

ROOTS: One can BORE a hole or hollow out a BORE – from Old Norse *bora* (hole).

בר or בור / BORE is a hole in Hebrew too, as well as a pit or grave.*

BRANCHES: קבר/(KE)BHER is a *BUR*IAL hole or GRAVE (simply swap the V and R). More fully, a קבר/KEBHER was often a cave tomb – see "CAVITY" and *Genesis 23:9*. *Beorg* is cave and *byrgeles* is tomb in Old English. Nature provides many animals with a BURIN or BORER (from Old High German *boro*) with which to BURY themselves in a BURROW.

באר/B'AR and ביר/BAYIR mean a "well"; חפר/[HO]PHAR or KHOPHAR is to dig and פיר/PEER is a ditch. Therefore, *APER*TURE, *buraco* (hole in Portugese), FORAMEN, FURROW and PORE might all be related. Official cognates of BORE, listed at IE root *bher* (to cut, pierce, bore), include BARROW, BI*FORATE*, FORAMEN, PERORATE and *PHAR*YNX.

* "And if a man shall open a *pit*, or if a man shall dig a *pit* and not cover it..." 1. בור 2. בר. *Exodus 21:33*.

BOT(ANY)/נָבַט
(NA)BOT   [NBT]

ROOTS: BOTANY is from Greek *botane* (a plant or herb). *Nabat* in Arabic is a plant. The (N)BT root in Hebrew includes נבט/(NA)BHAT (sprout), both a noun and a verb of germinating and sprouting. בטן ∞ BOTEN are nuts in *Genesis 43:11*. An anagram of NBT is BTN; many such (Hebrew #1 to English #3) anagrams are seen in the appendix.

BRANCHES: Plant in Turkish is *nebat*; vegetable is *nabati* in Indonesian. נבג NEBH[EG] is a fungus – see "FUNGUS."

The initial נ/N of Hebrew roots often drops. See "VIDEO." A "sprout" is used, as is BUD, to infer a child. בת/BÄT (child, daughter, suburb) extends this B-T family of outgrowths – see "FETUS" and "PEDIATRICIAN." בטבט/BUTBAT is to swell and בטן/BETEN is the womb or belly. Reversing BT reveals the IE base *tubh* behind Latin *tuber* (swelling, lump) and English PROTUBERANCE, TRUFFLE and TUBER. פטם/PIT(OM) is another botanical protrusion, referring to the BUTTON or BUTT end of fruit – see "BUTTON."

Despite BT plants like בטן/BOTEN (NUTS) and Arabic *batatis* (potato), we're told that the Haitian term *batata* (sweet potato) gave us the POTATO.

The dictionary links BEETLE to BUD (a swelling) and then says that BUG is a confused form of Anglo-Saxon *budda* (beetle). One might link BUG with בקה/BUKHA (small insect). The term is Talmudic, but it may be seen as the reversal of the Biblical bug נוב/GOBH (locust). בד /BUDT is a tree limb – see "BAT" and "WEED."

BOT(H)/בֵּית
BET(H)   [B-Y-T-(H)]

ROOTS: The Greek BETA is the obvious borrowing from "Phoeneician" or Hebrew בית or ב/BET (the second letter; the number two). The original "B" has named our BETA rays and BETA Max. (See "BETA.")

English speakers render בית/BET (literally: a house – *Genesis 35:2*) like the first syllable in Bethlehem, Bethesda and BETHEL.

As ב/B signifies "two," BOTH means "the two."

BRANCHES: בית/BĀT or BĀS (two) relates to בת/BÄT or BÄS (child, daughter, suburb, extension – i.e. a second item like or related to the first). A בת-קול/BUS-KŌL (echo, second voice, or SUB-noise – BS reversed) reverberates with a sense of second best as well as with a sense of repetition. BIS means "twice" in musical directions. BIS(TORT) is Latin for twice (twisted).

The most common ב/B(2) is the BI – prefix of twoness that appears in scores of words like BILATERAL, BINARY or BISECTED.

BA – is the plural prefix in Swahili; "both" is *oba* in Polish.

Reading BAT like "VaTe" and reversing to T-V allows us to see the Swedish two (*tva*) and the many TWO words in Germanic and Slavic languages.

More at "ALPHABET," "DUO" and "TWIN"

BOULD(ER)/בּוֹלֵט
BOLE-AIDT   [BL(D)T]

ROOTS: A BOULDER is a large, "rounded stone" as seen in its Swedish etymon *bullersten*. Swedish *bulde* (a swelling) is a major component in the IE root *bhel* (to blow, swell). בולט/BOLĀDT means "protruding." A BL root of swelling may be seen in Hebrew: בלט/BOLUDT is to stand out, protrude, project; בלום/BÄLLOOM is swollen; בול/BOOL is increase; יבול/(YI)BHOOL is growth; and *[ge]bel* is a hill or mountain in Arabic. בול/BOOL is a lump or block (*Isaiah 44:19*).

BRANCHES: The many given cognates of BOULDER include BALE, BALOON, BAWD, BOLE, BOULVARD, BULK, BULL, FOOL, PALL-MALL, PHALLUS, and PHELOGEN.
More at "BALL," "BLOT," "VAULT" and "WELT."

BRASS/בַּרְזֶל
BAR-SZ(EL)   [BRZ(L)]

ROOTS: Old English *braes* (brass) is from the same "obscure source" (to quote the AHD) as the Latin noun and IE root *ferrum* (iron).

In (*Genesis 4:22*) Tubal-cain ushers in the Bronze Age (which preceded the Iron Age). The Hebrew term ברזל/BÄRZEL is translated "iron," but BRASS or BRO(N)ZE is more appropriate.

BRANCHES: A Biblical variant is פרזל/PÄRZEL or FÄRS[EL] (iron in Chaldean). BRASSY, BRAZEN, BRAZIER, FARRIER,

FERRI-, FERRO-FERROUS, FERRUGINOUS and FER-DE-LANCE are related.

BRASIL has the world's richest iron deposits. Speculation has attributed the name to Pre-Columbian Phoenician traders.

Perhaps COPPER can be linked to עפרת/KŌPHERES (usually translated "lead") and נחשת/NIKH[ŌSHET], the "brass" of *Genesis 4:22*, may link up to NICKEL.

BREACH/פְּרִיצָה
PREETZA   [P-R-TZ]

ROOTS: Derived from terms like Old High German *brecha*, a BREACH is specifically an opening made by breaking something. פרץ/PERETZ and פריצה/PREETZA are specifically defined as "breach,""break" and "opening."

"... Out [of the womb] came his brother; and she said, 'What a *breach* you have made for yourself!' So he was named *PEREZ*." פרצת, פרץ/ *Genesis 38:29*.

BRANCHES: (מ) ברץ/(MI) BHORATZ is "broken through," פצר/PÄTZER is "to urge or press," פצל/PÄTZEL is "to split," and פרישה/PREESHÄ is "stretching." More at "BURST," and "BREAK" and "PETARD."

To BROACH (make a hole, introduce) the subject of BRASH, the word BRASH means hasty and bold, a good quality for a BREACH-maker to have.

A more formal BREACH, and one closer to פרץ/P-R-T(S), is the opening we call a PORT, PORTAL, PORTCULLIS, PORTE-COCHERE, PORTHOLE, and PORTIERE.

מפרץ/(MI)PHRATZ is a bay; מפרץ/(MI)PHŌRAZ is open or militarily accessible.

BREAK/בְּרַח
B'RAKH   [BRK]

ROOTS: Germanic *brekan* is traced to the IE root *bhreg* (to break). In this large family of B/P + L/R + G/Kh words of breaking, ברח/BRAKH (flee! — as in *Genesis 27:43*) sems most appropriate for this entry because of its direct sound and meaning correspondence. One of the definitions for BREAK is "to dash off, run" and earlier "to begin, open or change suddenly."

To BREAK and run is to break one's previous posture, just as something FREAKY is a BREAK from normal behavior. פרע/P(H)-R-KH can mean a distrubance, riot, an unruly break out, or an outbreak of various kinds.

הפליג/(HI)PHLĒG (to depart, embark) is another relative of breaking as running away or fleeing. FLIGHT is a similar FLG term of breaking away. BREAK can also mean to plow up, see PLOUGH below.

BREAK is linked to Latin *frango* (to break); the Hebrew "breakers" offered below demand less letter changes.

BRANCHES: 1) ברג/BEREG. Preserved in Arabic, this cognate of BRACE and BRACKET now infers screw and bolt in Modern Hebrew. 2) ברק/BARAK. This is a bolt, *FLICKER* or broken line of lightning. 3) ברך/BEREKH. This is the knee, which BREAKs the length of the leg. (The verb from is in *Genesis 24:11*). BRACHY- words are from Greek *brachys* (short), while the arm's BRACHIUM is the Latin source of may arm-like words. These include BRACE, BRACELET, BRACHIO- (prefix for arm words), BRACKET (if not from the Arabic term above), BRA(N)CH and BREECHES. פרק/PEREK is a joint (bone). 4) פלג/PELEG. The FLOCK of words here includes BLOCK, BREAK, BRIGADE, FLAKE, FLUKE, FRACAS and PLUG.

Consider that *Genesisi 10:25* may refer to the break up of earth's single land mass into continents; otherwise Peleg was named for the tribal BLOCKs that took shape and migrated apart in his era. The same Hebrew term is the "divide" of "divide their tongue" in *Psalms 55:10*. פלגה/PILOOGA is a division (*II Chronicles 35:5*). The IE root *bhreg* (to break) includes BRACKEN, BRAKE, BRAH, BRAY, BREACH, BRECCIA, FRACAS, FRACTION, FRACTURE, FRAGILE, FRAIL, INFRACTION, INFRINGE, OSSIFRAGE, REFRACT, REFRAIN and SUFFRAGE. 5) פלח/FELAKH (piece, slice — *I Samuel 30:12*) is another FLAKE, FRACTION or FRAGMENT word. 6) פלח/POLUKH or FALAH (*Psalms 141:7*). This word refers to either the PLOUGH or the FELLOW who PLOWs. 7) פלך/PELEKH (*Nehemiah 3:9*). This spacial break off or partition means a district or PAROCHI(IAL) PLACE. 8) פרח/ PERAKH or FeRaKH. The BREAKING out here is the kind FRECKLES and PLAGUES might do. There's also the FLIGHT, spreading out and blossoming of birds, flora and FRAGRANCES. The budding sense comes from *Genesis 40:10*; spreading and "flourishing" is seen in *Proverbs 14:11*. Boils (perhaps bubonic plague) "breaks forth" in *Exodus 9:9*. אפרח/ EFRŌAKH is a baby bird; פרח/PORAKH is to blossom or flower. 9) פרכת/PAROKHES. The curtain of *Exodus 26:31*, this space breaker or partition is *pargodus* in Latin. Old Norse *balkr* (partition) is one of several terms attributed to IE root *bhelg*. Some of these include BALCONY, BALK, BULK, FULCRUM and PHALANX. 10) פרך/PORUKH. Appearing in *Exodus 1:13*, but more evident as a splitting word in Aramaic, it breaks up into English words like FLAKE, FLUKE and FREAK. 11) פרק/PEREK or PÄRUK (*Genesis 27:40*) The definitions of this word infer BREAKING OFF or PARKING in a text (a chapter) as well as removal words like FLECK, FLEECE, FLICK and PLUCK. Via IE root *plek* (to tear) one might add FLAY, FLESH, and FLETCH.

[BRETHR]EN/(אָח) ים
(AKH-)EEM   [YM→EN]

ROOTS: Traced only to Anglo-Saxon *-an*, the -EN plural suffix of words like (OX)EN and (CHILDR)EN matches the common Hebrew plural suffix ים-/EM.

BRANCHES: When writing the plural of CHERUB, borrowed from כרוב/KROOV (winged heavenly being — *Ezekiel 1:5-11*), both cherub*im* and cherub*in* appear in English translations of the Bible.

BRIG[ADE]/פְּרְקָה
PEER-KAH   [PRK]

ROOTS: BRIGADE is traced to Italian *brigare* (to brawl or fight).

פלינה/PLĒGÄ and פלונתא/PLOOG[TÄ] (argument and controversy) in Hebrew and Aramaic matches *briga* (strife, quarrel) in Late Latin. For an etymon that doesn't equate a BLOCK or faction of soldiers with factionalism, there's always פרקה/PĒRKÄ (a military division).

BRANCHES: For much more on פלג/PELEG (faction) and related terms see "BREAK."

BRIGH(T)/בָּרַק
BARUCK [BRK]

ROOTS: BRIGHT is from the IE root *bhereg* (to shine; bright, white), which also includes the BIRCH tree.

The sound connection to Hebrew's BRK is clear. To establish the meaning, ברק/BARUK is "glittering" in *Deuteronomy 32:41*, הבריק/[HI]BHRĒK is to shine; ברקאי / BĀRKĪ is the morning star; ברקת/BĀREKES is a gem (*Exodus 28:16*) and ברק/BĀRĀK is lightning (*Exodus 19:16*).

> **BRANCHES:** A related IE ROOT IS *bherek* (to shine, glitter). This takes in BRAE, BRAID, BREAM, BRIDLE, and UPBRAID. Even BLACK is attributed to an etymon meaning to shine or gleam. BLA(N)CH, BLEACH, BLEAK and BLIGHT may fit here as well.
>
> בהיר/BĀHĒR (bright) is a realted Hebrew term, as is בלח / BĀLĀKH (to flicker). The ה(H), ח(KH) and ק(k) are all look alike and sound-alike letters; they are merely set on different scales of intensity on the alphabetic Hebrew Keyboard.
>
> See "BLEAK," "FLICKER" and "(S)PARK."
>
> Arabic *bahir* (light-colored) matches the IE root *bher-* (bright, brown). Derivatives of *bher* include BEAR, BEAVER, BROWN, BRUIN, BRUNET and BURNISH.
>
> The BRK gem mentioned above, rendered "bareqeth" by *Webster's*, is the given source of Greek *maragdos*, Greek *smaragdos* (green beryl) and English EMERALD. See "ESMERELDA."

BROOK/בְּרֵכָה
BRAY-KHA [B-R-KH]

ROOTS: A BROOK is a small river or stream whose Anglo-Saxon root is presumed to be related to BREAK—see "BREAK." A ברכה / BRĀKHĀ (often translated as "pool") is a man-made irrigation canal that must be dug or BROKEN in to divert or split off natural water supplies.

Ecclesiastes (Kohelet) 2:6 reads: "I constructed *pools* of water, enough to irrigate a forest . . ." ברכות.

> **BRANCHES:** Another B/P-R/L-K/G in the BREAK family that is relevant here is פלג / PELEG (stream, river). See "ARCHIPELAGO."
>
> *Erreka* is a river in Basque; the Polish and Russian is *reka*; reverse the R/L-K to *kali* in Indonesian or the Japanese river term (*kawa*). If a K/G-R/L root seems to emerge from these and the Hebrew terms above, one should look further to works like נחל / NAKHĀL (stream), הגיר / HĒGĒR (to spill, pour out), הלך / HALEKH (flowing), קלח / KĀLĀKH (to stream, pour out), קל / KĀL (swift), עורק / ORĀKH or KHŌRAKH (vein), הריק / HĀREK (to empty, pour out) and קר / KĀR (to spring forth).
>
> See "CAR" and "CATSKILL."

BRUSH/בְּרֵשׁ
BAY-RUSH [B-R-SH]

ROOTS: BRUSH is from Old French *brosse* bush, brushwood), a related late Latin term *brustia*, and perhaps Old High german *brusta* (a bristle).

All of these, plus the Modern Hebrew verb and noun for BRUSH ברש / BĀRUSH and מברשת / MIBHRESHET, come from the Hebrew Bible's fir and pine tree – ברוש / BROSH. The source of BISTLE and FIR is seen in *Isaiah 60:13* or *II Samuel 6:5* . Pine needles, before boar bristles, were the stuff of hair brushes.

> **BRANCHES:** The needle-like BROACH and BROOCH are more easily linked to our Hebrew etymon than even BUSH or FOREST (that recall the pine and fir of ברוש / BROSH.)
>
> The IE root *bhar* (projection, bristle point) is the theoretical source of BASS, BRAD, BRISTLE, BORSCHT, EMBROIDER, FASTIDIOUS and more.
>
> A bristly relative of the IE root above is *bharda* (beard). This takes in BEARD, BARD and BARBER.

BUBB(L)E/בַּעֲבוּעַ
BUB-BOO-AH [BU]

ROOTS: The sixth plague of Egypt, boils, may have been the BUBONIC plague. Greek *bubon* is a swollen gland, and a boil or blister is a swollen BUBBLE under the skin.

In *Exodus 9:9* there's "an inflammation breaking out in *boils*." A BUBO (inflamed swelling) is a boil, and BUBONIC plague is a contagious disease with fever and BUBOES.

The Biblical אבעבועה / ĀBĀBOOĀ is a boil, blister, pimple or wart. בעבע/BUBOOĀ is a bubble; בעה/BO-OH is to bubble or boil as in "fire makes water *boil*"– *Isaiah 64:1*.

> **BRANCHES:** J.T. Shipley's IE root *va* (swelling) takes in WEN and WOUND. The AHD's root, *wen*, may be a nasalization (extra N) of בע / VA or BHA.
>
> Proto-Polynesian *fuafua* means pimples. *Ibo* is a wart in Japanese, while *awa* is a bubble.

BUCKAR[OO]/בָּקָר
BUCK-ARE [BKR]

ROOTS: BUCKAROO is the Spanish *vaquero* (cowboy) as pronounced by Gringos (foreigners or Americans). The cowboy tends his VACCA (cow in the lingo of the American Southwest), from Latin *vacca* (cow). VACCINE and VACCINATION come from that Latin term, while Latin *bacca* (cow) is the given etymon for BACHELOR and BACCALAUREATE. Latin *baccalarius* (young man) and BACHELOR might also have been influenced by בחור / BĀKHOOR (young or unmarried man – *I Samuel 8:16*). Back to cattle, Greek *boukolos* (herdsman) is the source of BUCOLIC. In Israel a cattleman or herdsman is a בקר / BUKAR or a בוקר / BŌKĀR (*Amos 7:14*). בקר / BAKAR is a generic term for domestic (herds of) cattle, cows, oxen, etc. In *Genesis 26:14* the term is pronounced VAKKAR, while the harder B, as in *bacca* above, is more common.

> **BRANCHES:** ALBACORE may sound like tuna fish, but it comes from Arabic *al* (the) *bukr* (young cow). The *paco* in ALPACA (llama) is the Peruvian Indian word for beast. *Pecus* (cattle) in Latin gives us PECULIAR, PECUNIARY and PECULATE. Also linked to Latin *peculium* (riches in cattle) via the IE root *peku* are

words like FEE, FELLOW, and FEUDAL. The meat of a buck or cow was called *baq* by Maya Indians. The Quechuan Indians named their domesticated, cud-chewing animal the VICUNA. *Wuha* is the native Australian cow.

BUCOLIC is given many cognates under the IE root *gwou* (ox, bull, cow). The root, like the word COW corralled within, is a reversal of the B(W) and K(C) of בק(ר) / BK(R). Similarly, a Thai buffalo is *kwy*.

BUGLE, BUCEPHALUS, GAUR, GAYAL and GORAL, along with BEEF, BOVINE, BUFFALO, BUTTER and BOTHER, are all traced to the IE root *gwou*.

BUCK(ET)/בַּקְבּוּק
BUCK-(BOOK)   [BK]

ROOTS: Anglo-Saxon *buc* is a pitcher or bucket. בקבוק / BUKBOOK is the "jug" of *I Kings 14:3*. In modern Hebrew the term means a bottle.

BRANCHES: BASIN comes from Latin *bacca* (bowl or water vessel). Just as a BASIN can mean a valley, בקעה / BIKÄ means valley or gorge. The large family of B/V + C/G/K of VAC(UUMS) and VAC(ANCIES) includes: BAG, BASINET, BEAKER, BIGGIN, BOX, BUCCAL, EVACUATE, VACATE, VAGABOND, VAGINA, VAGRANT and that temporary "valley" at the back of a moving ship – a WAKE.
בוקה / BOOKÄ is desolation, emptiness; בקיע / BIKEA is a crack. For P-K branches like POKE, POCKET and POX, see "PIT."
Reverse to K-V for the large family of CAVities seen at "CAVITY."

Also see "BEAKER" and "VACATE."

BULL(Y)/בָּעַל
BAW-ULL   [BUL]

ROOTS: Before it meant a tyrant or pimp, BULLY meant a lover. Dutch *boel* and Middle High German *buole* mean lover; in German the term is *buhle*.
בעל / BAAL is a husband, lord, owner or possessor, as seen in *Exodus 21:34* and *Proverbs 12:4*. The verb form means to marry or rule over – see *Deuteronomy 24:1* and *Isaiah 26:13*. A post-Biblical usage of the term infers sexual intercourse.

BRANCHES: If you recognize BAAL as a Canaanite deity (*Judges 4:13*) one more easily sees that to BULLY (from בעל) is to *lord* it over someone.
(Moving from BL to BR) אביר / ABEER can mean "bull," as well as "strong" and "mighty." See "BARON."
More on BULL, a cow's husband, at "HEIFER."

BUNT(ING)/אבְנֵט
UBH-NATE   [(A)BNT]

ROOTS: The dictionaries come closest at the third definition of BUNT (the bellying part of a square sail) when they cite Middle Dutch *bunt* (a binding bundle) and English BUND. More than baby clothes or World Series drapery, the essence of BUNTING may be seen in the BUNTLINE

(a rope to prevent a sail from bellying).
The cloth strip that BINDS or BUNDLES a person is a belt. אבנט / UBHNÄDT is the belt, girdle, or sash that the priests wear in *Exodus 29:9*.

BRANCHES: A BAND and a BANDAGE are related cloth BINDINGS. The CUMMER*BUND*, attributed to Hindi and Persian, is precisely this sash for the waist.
(CUMMER)BUND is tied in with BAND, BANANA, BEND, BOND, BUND and BUNDLE at the IE root *bhendh* (to bind). The Persian is *bando* and the Sanskrit is *baṅdha*. A FUND (ready money) is not from Latin *fundus* (bottom) but from פנדה / FOONDÄ (a "borrowing" from Latin in Talmudic Hebrew). The Latin term for a place to keep one's ready money is also the term for a belt, purse or money belt. The origin of this belt word, of course, is the אבנט / ÄBHNAD(T) or a nasalization of אפד / OFUD (to gird).
To arrive at BELT, affect a נ(N) →L change – see appendix B. The אבנט / [A]BNT keeps the בטן / BTN (belly) from bulging בלט) / BLT).
For the other kind of BUNTING at a baseball game see "BUTT."

BUR(N)/בֹּעֵר
BO-AIR   [BUR,BHUR]

ROOTS: IE base *bhreu* (to boil forth, well out) is cited as the source of BURN. Exodus 3:2 – "...behold, the bush *burned* with fire, and the bush was not consumed." בער / BOÄR (burn).

BRANCHES: The IE root for BURN is *g(w)her* (to heat, warm). This might resemble בער / VER and/or חרה / HORA or KHORÄ (to burn). This IE root takes in words like BRAND, BRANDY, BRANDISH, BRIMSTONE, BRINDLED, FORCEPS, FORNICATE, FURNACE, HYPOTHERMIA (-) THERM(Y), and THERMOMETER. The first element of *BAR*(BECUE) may belong here too.
The AHD uses *bhreu* as the IE root of BURN (a spring, stream or BOURN). This root springs forth from באר / B'AIR (a *well* of spring water – *Genesis 26:19*). The list of cognates that bubble forth from the IE root *bhreu* (to boil, bubble, effervesce, burn) includes: BRAISE, BRATWURST, BRAWN, BRAZE, BRAZIER, BARM(Y), BREAD, BREEZE, BREW, BREWIS, BROTH, FERMENT, FERVENT, FERVID, FERVOR, EFFERVESCE, IMBRUE, PHREATIC and SAUERBRATEN. WELL itself requires acceptable BH→W and R→L changes. *BERO* is hot in Basque; *wela* is hot in Hawaiian; *waru* is fire in Australian aborigine. *WAR[M]* is not far away; the IE root *wer* (to burn) is only linked to SAMO*VAR*.
See "FIRE."

BURRO/בְּעִיר
B'EER   [BUR]

ROOTS: A BURRO is from Spanish *burrico* and Latin *burricus* (small horse). Just as a BURRO (donkey) is a beast of burden, the בעיר / B'EER (beast) must be as well, as seen in *Genesis 45:17* – "lade *your beasts*." With the gutturalized ע, בעיר / B'EER is a clear relative of בקר / BÄKÄR (cattle). (Pronounced as BAKHAR, בעיר better fits the Latin etymon above.)

BRANCHES: Connected to the "small horse" of Latin *barri(cus)*, one should cite the German (*Pferd*) and Dutch (*paard*) words for horse. These are clearly bred from the פרד / PERED or PHERED – translated "mule" in *Zacharia 14:15*. פרד / PERRED is a close second choice as Hebrew source of BURRO, which is also a donkey in Portuguese.

Japanese typically reverses the term and drops the final letter in its donkey word *roba*. (Though רכב / ROKHABH is to ride). Swahili *punda* (donkey) may display a ר / R to N transformation [as seen in cognates paNth(er) and paRd].

Donkey terms like German *Esel* and Russian *asyol* are from the אתון / ASSON (donkey) one finds back at "ASSININE."

The Rumanian (*magar*) and Serbo-Croatian (*magarac*) donkeys are #1-#2 letter flips of חמור / KHAMOR (donkey – *Genesis 49:14*).

FILLY and FOAL may relate to the B/P + R(L) terms above.

The BOAR may connect with בעיר / B'EER (beast). The BOAR gave us words like PORK, *POR*CUPINE, *POR*POISE and AARD-*VAARK*. (The C or K may come from the gutturalized ע / KH).

Abere is a domesticated animal in Basque.

BURST/בָּרַץ
BORUTS　　　　　　　　　　　　　　　　　　　　　[B-R-TS]

ROOTS: Both the Hebrew and English terms above have different but related connotations – 1) bursting a hole and 2) expanding outward. The "BURSTING a hole" connotation is evident in terms like מברץ / (MI)BHORUTZ (broken through). The Biblical word פרץ / PERETZ (to burst or break through) is discussed at "BREACH." One IE root, *bhres*, means "to burst," while a second root (*bhreus*) is "to break." The latter root takes in BRUISE, BRUSH, and FRUSTULE.

The second connotation, too, is found in both ברץ / BARUTS (to fill to the brim) and the Biblical פרץ / PERETS as seen below.

Genesis 28:14 "And thy seed shall be as the dust of the earth, and thou shalt *spread abroad* to the west . . . east . . . north . . . and south. And in thee and in thy seed shall all the families of the earth be blessed." (The promise to Abraham has been largely fulfilled, as Jews, Christians and Moslems are blessed to be Abraham's heirs.)

BRANCHES: BLAZE is spreading abroad or publicizing. Spreading is sprouting, and a sprout is a *blastos* (Greek) in all the BLASTO- words. More on spreading out at places like "PLAZA."

The filling out of ברץ / BAYRUTS recalls the BREAST, which is listed at IE root *bhreus* (to swell) along with cognates BRISKET and BROWSE.

A BURST is also a BLAST or quick action. IE root *bheres* (quick) includes FESTINATE but not FAST. A BORZOI, the Russian wolfhound, comes from the Russian term for swift. PRESTO, and Yinglish PLOTZ and PLATZ (burst) might be mentioned here.

To explode, BURST and BLAST in Thai is *ra-but* (requiring a #1-#2 letter swap).

BUTT/בָּעַט
BA-UTT　　　　　　　　　　　　　　　　　　　　　[BUT]

ROOTS: One of several "butt's" in the reference books means to *ABUT* on or thrust against something, not only with the head.

בעט / BA'UT (to kick against) is not limited to physical striking out, nor is the Old French term *buter*.

"Jeshurun waxed fat and *kicked* / יבעט"– *Deuteronomy 32:15*.

BRANCHES: Strikingly similar words include חבט / HABHUT (to BEAT or ABATE). The Old French word *abattre* means to beat down, and פטיש / PUTESH is a hammer to BAT or BATTER with. BATTERY and possibly BAT (the animal) are also related.

To BUCK may be from בעט / BUKH(AT), gutturalize the ע and drop the final letter. BUNT and PUNT, hitting the ball in baseball and in football, may be nasalized (added N) forms of *BUTT*.

BUZZ(ARD)/בַּז
BUZZ　　　　　　　　　　　　　　　　　　　　　　[BZ]

ROOTS: The BUZZARD is a slow flying hawk, from Old French *busart*.

בז / BUZ is a hawk; בזיר / BUZIAR is a falconer. בז / BUZ is also loot or booty – the chief object of this scavenging carnivore. The double Z of BUZZARD is met by the double ז / z in בזז / BUZUZ (to spoil, plunder, "pillage"– *Jeremiah 3:37*.

BRANCHES: "Spoil" means "loot" or "to waste," just as בז / BUZ is spoils (of war) and בזבז / BIZBAZ is to squander, spoil or WASTE. Related terms like בזא / BAZA and בציעה / BITSEA (1. to divide, 2. to cut) refer to the ripping havoc (loot, waste) of hawks.

The American plains Indians (Kiowa) called a buzzard a *bosen*.

See "EM*BEZZLE*" and "BOOTY."

BY/-בּ
BEE　　　　　　　　　　　　　　　　　　　　　　　[B]

ROOTS: The versatile preposition BY was spelled *bi* and *be* in Middle English and Anglo-Saxon. It means near, beside, during, etc. and is also an adverb.

-בּ, the common prefix, is pronounced BIH, BAH, BAW, BEH and BEE and it means in, BY, at or WITH. We are to study and teach God's words even when we "walkest *by* the way." בדרך– *Deuteronomy 6:17*.

BRANCHES: Another form of BY (to the amount or degree) is seen in פי / PE. "*By* the number of" appears in *Genesis 47:12* as (ל)פי / (LI)PHEE. עלפי / ULL PE means according to or BY. Russian *po* means at, BY or next to, and Greek π/ pi relates to the proportional BY seen above. -EPI words like *EPI*DERMIS, *EPI*STLE or *EPH*EMERAL should be related.

-בּ / B' also means "in," as does *w* or *we* in Polish. Greek *epi* (at, on, upon, besides, etc.) is a spacial term, as are פה / POH (here, hither) and איפה / APHOH (where?).

POU STO is "a place to stand on," "a basis of operations." The words are directly from Greek, and a saying of Archimedes. Greek *pou* means "where," like Hebrew איפה / APHO (*Genesis 37:16*). Latin *ubi*, French *ou* (où) and Fijian *vei* all mean "where." AL*IBI* and *UBI*QUITOUS are from Latin *ubi* (where) and *ibi* (there).

CAB/קַבָּה
KOOB-AH　　　　　　　　　　　　　　　　　　　　[KB]

ROOTS: A taxi CAB is from French *cabriolet* (a horse carriage), whose etymon is traced back to Latin *caper* (he-goat). The CAB of a tractor or an air balloon, however, is the *compartment* for the passenger or operator.

קבה / KOOBÄ means compartment, alcove, tent, hut, or "chamber" (*Numbers 25:8*).

> **BRANCHES:** CABANA is from Late Latin *capanna* (hut), and CABARET is from Old French *cabaneret* (little hut). CABANE and CABIN are likely from the Hebrew hut word above. The CABOOSE (cabin house) of a train is another form of קבה / KOOBÄ (arched compartment). Even CABINET meant a small room before it meant the body of advisers who meet in a private alcove.
>
> נב / GOVE was the "den" of Daniel; חפה / KHOOPÄ (canopy), יקב / (YE)KEBH (wine cellar) and כף / KÄF (CAVE, vault) are more of the habitable K-BH cavities relevant here. French *cave* is a cellar. *Qabwe* in Arabic means compartment, as does *kupe* in both Swedish and Danish. *Kiva* in Hopi Indian is a large room or dwelling.
>
> COOP, HIVE and GABION are attributed to etymons that strongly resemble the second CAB in the dictionary—the Hebrew dry measure. This CAB is attributed to "*qab*, hollow vessel." Hebrew קב / KABH (*II Kings 6:25*) is related to a verb of hollowing out.
>
> See "ALCOVE," "CAVE" and "CUBBY."

CABLE/כֶּבֶל
KEBHEL   [KBL]

ROOTS: CABLE, the heavy rope, wire or chain, is linked to Old French and Late latin terms for cable and rope. The final etymons offered are Latin *capere* (to take hold) and the IE root *kap* (to grasp).

These KP etymons are covered at "CAPTURE," but Hebrew has a clear cable connection. כבל / KEBHEL is a chain or cable; כבל / KOBHUL is to chain or fetter. "Fetters" is a popular translation of כבל in *Psalms 105:18* or *149:8*.

> **BRANCHES:** חבל / KHEBEL is a rope; a human bond is a חבר / KHÄBER (friend). חבר / KHĒBER is to attach, couple or join— see "ALGEBRA."
>
> A chained procession of animals or slaves is a COFFLE, borrowed from Arabic *gafilah* (caravan). The dictionaries don't know where GYVE (fetter, shackle) comes from— but כבל / KEVEL (cable) should be the missing link. Anglo-Saxon *hefel* (weaving cord) is the source of HEDDLE.
>
> HOBBLE and HOPPLE and COUPLING are all links in the chain here. The שרשרת גבלות / SHÄRSHERES *GÄBHLOOS* ("*plaited* chains" of *Exodus 39:15*) adds one more twist to the GVL or KBL Hebrew connection. Predictably, as we linked three different gutturals to B-L, the meaning intensified as we moved up the alphabet: 1) נבל / GBL (plait), 2) חבל / HBL (rope), 3) כבל / KBL (cable).
>
> חבל / KHEVEL (rope)—*Job 18:10*) is made from many fibers being plaited or spun together—see "COUPLE." Welsh *gwlan* (wool) and the IE root for WOOL and *FLANNEL, wela* (wool), may derive from a hard and a soft way to pronounce חבל / KH-V-L or (HE)VEL.
>
> *Kavla* is cord or rope in Hawaiian; *Kupe'e* are fetters.

CAKE/כֵּכָּר
KEEK-(ARĒ)   [KK(R)]

ROOTS: The Anglo-Saxon *coecil* meant a little cake; the IE root suggests lumps and round things.

ככר / KĒKAR is a "loaf" in *Exodus 29:23*; the term designates a traffic circle in Israel today. רקיק / RIKĒK (a probable influence on CRACKER) is the small "cake" of *Exodus 29:2*—establishing KK as the two-letter root. Another double guttural "cake," in *Genesis 18:6*, is the עוגה / KHOOGA.

> **BRANCHES:** ענל / KHEGŌL is round—see "CIRCLE." The IE root *kak* (a round object, disk) puts CAKE, COOKY, COCKAIGNE, KUCHEN, and QUICHE in the same pan. Yiddish *KUGEL* may be added.
>
> Reverse עוגה / OOGÄ (cake) to approximate Chinese *gau* (cake).

CA(L)DRON/קִדְרָא
KID-RAH   [KDR]

ROOTS: CALDRON or CAULDRON, a large kettle or boiler, is traced to Latin *calidus* (warm). As a subdivision of IE root *kel* (warm) it is supposed to be a cognate of CHOWDER.

A better etymon is the קדרא / KIDRÄ or KIDARÄ (kettle, boiling pot)—and Aramaic word. Not to call the kettle black, but קדר / KÄDÄR (dark, black—*I Kings 18:45*) possible relates.

קלה / KALA and קלי / KALĒ are terms for heating and preparing food——see "ALKALI."

> **BRANCHES:** קלחת / KILAHAT (caldron—*Micah 3:3*) is a kettle word for those who don't want to dismiss the L of *calidus* and CALDRON. Exchanging the T and L of *kilahat* brings KETTLE into the picture. KETTLE is currently linked to Latin *catinus* (food container) which might be another כד / KÄDT (jug, container) word.
>
> See "CADDY" and "KIT."

CALI(BER)/קְלִפָּה
KAL-EE-PAH   [KLP→KLB]

ROOTS: Arabic *qalib*, a shell-like mold or last, is the official source for CALIBER, CALIBRATION, CALIPER and more; CALIBER refers to the size of a shell or bullet.

קלפה / KALĒPA is a shell, along with a rind, peel, husk and skin. קלופית / KILOPHĒT (outer skin) is from Aramaic. קלפין / KALPĒN (fish scales) is another Aramaic word for a hard, protective covering.

> **BRANCHES:** CALIPEE and CALIPASH are West Indian turtle shell delicacies. the dictionary speculates on a Spanish origin, as *carapacho*, from *caparacho*, is a shell. (Notice the letter transposition of P and R.) CARAPACE (the stuff of turtle shells, etc.) and probably CALABER (squirrel fur), CRAB, CREPE, KREPLACH (Yiddish *crepe*, or dish involving a shell or wrap of dough), CROP (tanned hide—just as קלף / KLÄPH means parchment) and (S)CORPION are all influenced by this versatile Semitic root.
>
> The anagramic letter play between KLP (to peel), PKL (to peel) and PRK (to remove) is seen at "(S)CALP" (which is also a noun and a verb of exteriors).
>
> Reverse קלף / KLP for Thai *bpleu-uk* (peel or rind). KLP reduces to LP in words like ילפה / (YA)LEPES. The word is defined as

"scab," but it is translated "scurvy" in *Leviticus 21:20*. Words like *LEPER* and *LEP*ROSY may be related.

The shelled oyster is an *elepo* in Hawaiian; *Kelapa* is the Indonesian coconut.

CALABASH is the shell of a gourd; this term is traced to the Persian melon (kharbus).

See "CARP," "CRAB," and "SCALLOP."

CALL/קוֹל
COAL   [KOL]

ROOTS: A call is a loud utterance or signal. קוֹל / KŌL (voice, sound) might better be rendered as signal or CRY in *Exodus 19:19* when the "voice" of the ram's horn blares. A companion term is קרא / KĀRĀ (call, proclaim, shout). It appears with קוֹל / KŌL in many verses such as *Isaiah 40:3*–"The *voice* of him that *crieth* in the wilderness"–קוֹרֵא .

Old Icelandic *kaller* is to call or cry; the IE base *gal* means to scream or shriek. Two relevant IE roots and their derivatives follow.

BRANCHES: 1) *gal* (to call, shout). CALL, CLATTER. 2) *kel* (to shout). ACCLAIM, CALENDAR, CLAIM, CLAIRVOYANCE, CLAMOR, CLASS, CLEAR, CONCILIATE, COUNCIL, DECLAIM, DECLARE, ECCLESIA(STES), ECLAIR, EXCLAIM, HALE, LOW, NOMENCLATURE, PROCLAIM, and RECLAIM.

CLAMOR does make a better translation for קוֹל / KŌL in *Exodus 32:17*–the "noise" or "cry" of war in the camp as heard from afar.

The CALLING in "name calling" best suits the קר / K-R word translated "appoint" in *Numbers 35:11* (והקריתם).

Many H words come from K etymons, so that HAIL, HALLOO, HELLO and HOLLER may belong here as well–see "HAIL."

To CURSE is to CALL down evil upon someone. If CURSE isn't from נער / GĀUR (curse), it may be from קלל / KĀLEL (curse)–which is the opposite of הלל / HĀLEL (to praise, HAIL, say HALLELUJAH). קלס / KĒLĀS is to praise. Other terms for "voice" (קוֹל / KOL) include *golos* in Russian, *hlas* in Czech and *koe* in Japanese (which has no "L"). Noise, another meaning of קוֹל / KOL, is *halas* in Polish. The common ק / K = H principle is evident, keeping in mind that graphically and audibly the ק / K is an extended ה / H.

ECLAT (from the French term for "noise" or "clap") may be influenced by קולות / KŌLOT (thunder). "Call" is *kalu* in Australian Aborigine.

See "CRY."

CA(L)M/חַם
KHUM   [KH-M]

ROOTS: We think of CALM as serenity, although it primarily is defined as a lack of wind. In Late Latin *cauma* means the heat of the sun; Greek *kauma* is heat. *Webster's* feels that the term designates the period of rest at midday, bringing *Genesis 18:1* to life: "And the Lord appeared unto [Abraham]. . .in the *heat* of the day" חם /KHOM. חם / KHAM means warm or hot.

BRANCHES: חמה / KHAMĀ is sun.
See "AMITY."

CALUM(NY)/כְּלִמָּה
KILL–EE–MA   [KLM]

ROOTS: CALUMNY is slander, that which hurts someone's reputation. The AHD links this word to Latin *calvire* (to deceive), a cognate of CHALLENGE at the IE root *kel* (to deceive, trick). כלמה / KALEEMA means insult or shame; הכלים is to offend, put to shame, CALUMNIATE (*Proverbs 28:7*).

BRANCHES: A related KLN etymon is קלון / KALON (shame – *Hosea 4:7*).

CAMEL/גָּמָל
GAMAL   [GML]

ROOTS: After citing Greek *Kamelos*, the dictionary concedes the obvious "Semitic origin" here. גמל / GAMAL is a camel (*Genesis 24:64*). The Hebrew ג (G) is often a K in Greek and other Western tongues (ג resembles a backwards K.)

BRANCHES: גמלון / GĀML(ŌN) is an arched gable; גלם / GŌLEM is a clump, lump or idiot (GML→GLM), ערמה / GHĀRĀMĀ is a pile or heap; קמר / KAMAR is to vault or arch (GML→KMR). Specifically regarding the camel's HUMP–the IE root is *qum-b*, based on a Sanskrit word beginning "k-u-m."

GAMMA rays are from גמל / GAMAL in that the third Greek letter is named for Hebrew's 3rd letter, the GIMEL, which is named for the GĀMĀL (camel).

The CAMEL is made for עמל / GAMAL or KHAMAL (work). CAMION (truck) might be a throwback to the camel or truck of the desert. The CAMELEOPARD is a giraffe. CAMLET is from Arabic *khamlat* (pile, plush) and CAMISE is from Arabic *qamis*–being cloth and clothes of camel hair. The dictionaries do not go on to link CAMISOLE, CHEMISE and possibly CAMOUFLAGE (a CAMEL-HAIR cover would hide one in the desert, not in France) to the CAMEL. For more English words from the CAMELBACK shape, see "CAMERA."

גמל / GĀMĀL (camel) backwards is just about LLAMA, the CAMELOID animal named by the Peruvian Indians. (L→R) רמך / RAMAKH (dromedary – *Esther 8:10*) and (reversing RM) אמרא / ĒMRĀ (sheep in Aramaic) are secondary etymons for LLAMA. LANOLIN (from Latin *lana* or wool) and צמר / (TSE)MER (wool) also come to mind. The GUANA(CO) is the Quechua Indian name for their *cameloid* animal.

For the CAMEL'S size and disposition, see "*MEGALO*MANIAC."

CAMERA/קָמַר
COME-ARE   [KMR]

ROOTS: From Greek *Kamara* (a vault), a CAMERA is named for the vaulted CHAMBER of its construction. The primary definition is a private office or small room, not a photographic device.

In Arabic and Turkish *qamera* is a cabin, and *qamar* is the crescent moon. קמר / KĀMĀR is to vault or arch; קימור / KĒMOOR is a semi-circle; and קמור / KOMOOR is bowed or convex. קם / KOOM means "rise up" (*Genesis 23:7*); מקום / (MA)KŌM can mean room or residence.

BRANCHES: The IE root *kamer* (to bend; a vault) is the given etymon for the following derivatives: CAMARILLA, CAMBER, BICAMERAL, CABARET, CAMERA, CHAMBER, COMRADE, CUMMERBUND and HEAVEN. HEAVEN is closer to חפה / HOOPÄ (canopy).

See "CAMEL" for several Hebrew terms of vaulted, piled up, humpy things. Pile on the term עמיר / KHÄMER (sheaf — but more like haystack in *Amos 2:13*) and one sees why ACCUMULATE, CUMULUS and CYME are related.

The R and M appear reversed in the Welsh word *crom* (bent). A CROMLECH is a circular, prehistoric tomb. While קום / KOOM is to rise; to rise up in Thai is *keun*.

See "ACME."

CAN(DY)/קָנֶה
CON-EH   [KNH]

ROOTS: CANDY is an acknowledged borrowing from Arabic *qandi* (candied). The word developed from the CANE of sugar cane or the קנה / KANE (stalk — *Genesis 41:5*).

See "CANE."

CANE/קָנֶה
CON-EH   [KNH]

ROOTS: The so-called IE root *kanna* (a reed) is admitted to be "of Semitic origin." Babylo-Assyrian *qanu* (pipe) is cited rather than קנה / KÄNEH (reed, tube, stem, the "stalk" of *Genesis 41:5*, the "shaft" of *Exodus 25:31*, and the "branch" of *Exodus 25:32*). כנה / KANAH is a stalk or root (*Psalms 80:16*) and כן / KAN is a base or foot (of a laver).

BRANCHES: Directly attributed to Greek *kanna* (reed, cane), the AHD only lists 7 cognates of CANE: CANAL, CANISTER, CANNELON, CANYON, CHANNEL, KENNEL, and (with Greek *kanon* meaning rod or rule) CANON — as in Biblical CANONIZATION. Most C-A-N- words in English derive from the versatile Hebrew etymon above. a CAN is a tubular container or CANISTER. קנקן / KANKAN means container, and is an Arabic extension of קנה / KÄNEH (tube). Longer and larger "cans" include the CANNIKIN, CANNON, CANNULA and CANOPICURN. Weaving the reed (KÄNEH) to larger containers will yield the CANASTA (basket, and later card game) and CANEPHOROS. Weaving rushes in wider, flatter shapes will produce a CANAPE, CANCEL (lattice, grating — thus a verb of crossing out), and CANOPY.

CANAPE and CANOPY also recall כנף / KÄNAF (extremity, wing) — a cousin of קנה / KÄNEH (branch, extension). Other possibilities include CANT HOOK, CANTEEN, CANTHUS, CANTINA, CANTILEVER, CANTLE, CANTO (angle, corner), and CANTON (a political branch).

For sugar CANE and CANE SUGAR return to קנה / KÄNEH (stalk, stem), reinforced by כן / KÄNE (base, post, upright). קנה / KÄNEH is a pipe too, and to pipe or produce shrill sounds with our widpipe, may be the KN source of all CANOROUS or CANTORIAL activity by a CHANTEUSE CHANTING a CHANSON — or that of a CANARY or CHANTICLEER (rooster). CAN-CAN and CHANTAGE involve the "singing'" of tattling and blackmailing. CANT is traced to the whining singsong of beggars. There's also the CANTATA, CANTICLE, CANTO, CANTUS, and CANZONE(T). For the IE root *kan* (to sing) and קינה / KÊNA (dirge) see "KEEN." Hungarian *enekel* (to sing) might be a reversed K-N singing term.

Returning to branches, bough in Polish is *konarm*. A canal (*kanat* in Arabic) is a *kanova* in Finnish.

See "CANDY," "CANOE," and "CINNAMON." See "OCEAN" for more on CAN or CANISTER.

A Chinese rod is a *kan*; the Thai equivalent is *kahn*. *Kano* in Hawaiian is a large, hard stem or a tool handle. קין / KAYIN is a cane-like spear (*II Samuel 21:16*); the Arabic קין / KEEN is a cane or spear.

CANVAS is from Latin *cannabis* (hemp) and the IE root *kannabis* (hemp — a late IE word borrowed from an unknown source). קנבוס / KÄNBOOS is an early post-Biblical term for hemp. Other Mishnaic variants sound like K'NOVES and KÄNÄVOS. The word HEMP is traced to Greek *kannabis* and Persian *kanab* (notice the K to H change, as well as the more common N→M and B→P Grimm's Law changes). The ultimate etymon is conceded by *Webster's* to be "a very early borrowing from a non-IE, possibly Semitic, language."

In seeking Semitic words related to קנבוס / KÄNÄVOS (hemp), consider Aramaic קנב / KENÄBH (to trim, prune — possible source of NIP and NIBBLE) and קנה / KÄNEH (stalk, stem, reed).

CANOE/קָנֶה
CON-EH   [KNH]

ROOTS: Spanish *canoa* is said to have originated in the Caribbean Indian word for a light boat. קנה / KÄNEH is a stem or reed. It ought to be the root of a boat word referring to either a hollowed out tree trunk (a "stem") or to reeds (the material of many small boats of antiquity).

See "CANE."

CAP/כִּפָּה
KEEP-AH   [KP]

ROOTS: CAP is flopped onto the IE root *kaput* (head).

Not to disturb traditionalists in Jerusalem or Rome, but the Arabic COIF, the כפיה / KAPHEÄ, should predate the כפה / KEEPÄ (skullcap, yarmulke). While not found in the Hebrew Bible, many terms cut from the same cloth. See the large family of concave K-BH/F/P words at "CAVE." One *chapeau* (hat in French) in the Bible is the קובע / KOBHÄ (helmet) worn by Saul in *I Samuel 17:38*.

BRANCHES: Other versions of the כובע / KOVÄ (hat) include the Arabic *qoubaa*, Swahili *kofia*, Italian *cappelo*, Portugese *chapeu* Polish *kapelusz* and the Modern Greek *kape'llo*.

Other KP coverings include חפה / KHOOPÄ (canopy), כפורת / KÄPORES (cover, curtain), קרקפת /[KÄR]KEPHET (skull, head) and עב / KHÄV (cloud).

CAPE, CHAPEL, CHAPERONE, CHAPLAIN and CHAPS are all covered here.

See "CAPITAL," "CAVE" and "HAT."

CAPITAL/כַּפְתּוֹר
KAPH-TOR   [K-PH-T-R→K-PH-T-L]

ROOTS: CAPITAL is traced to the IE root *kaput* (head). The first use of this versatile word is to designate any physical top or head that caps an object. A CAPITAL crime once called for DE*CAPIT*ATION. The CAPITAL of a pillar is CAPITATE, enlarged at the top. כפתור/KAPHT–ŌR is the CAPITAL of pillars in *Amos 9:1*. The term means "knob" in *Exodus 25:31*.

Aramaic קרקפת/[KAR]KEPHET (head, skull) is a specific Semitic counterpart for the IE root *kaput* (head). [The "KAR" element is from קרן/KEREN (horn, hard head covering) – see "UNICORN."]

BRANCHES: כפתור/KAFTŌ(R) is generally defined as a knob or button. Anything knoblike in anatomy or zoology, like the end of a joint bone, is a CAPITULUM. The Latin term *caput* (head) can work as the source for words like CAPITOL and CAPTION, but is less satisfactory when it comes to words like CAPSTAN (a spool-shaped cylinder aboard ship). The Hebrew term כפת/KEPHET (a button, knot, lump or block) is closer to the sense of CAPSTAN.

Words listed under IE root *kaput* (head) include: BICEPS, CABEZON, CADET, CAPE, CAPITULATE, CAPO, CAPRICE, CAPTAIN, CATTLE, CHAPTER, CHIEF(TAIN), HEAD, KERCHIEF, MISCHIEF, PRECIPITATE, and TRICEPS. They left out the CHEF (head of the kitchen). CAPE (headland) might link up with כף/KĀP[H] (rock, headland – *Job 30:6*).

For heads of state, see "HEAD" (Appendix A).

CAPIT(AL)ISM/חֵפֶץ
KHAY-FET(S)   [KH – PH –T(S)]

ROOTS: The financial senses of the word CAPITAL have nothing to with the Latin etymon *capitellum* (small head), but see כפת/KFT (button, knob, small head) at "CAPITAL."

חפץ/KHAFĀTZ or KHĀFETZ means wish, desire, object, matter, article, business, and affair: words of longing and belonging familiar to CaPiT(ALISTS).* CAPITAL – the money put down for investment, also recalls עבט/ABHŌT or KHABHŌT– see "AFFIDAVIT."

BRANCHES: Two other terms of desire with the gutturals (kh, c, k), plosives (f, p, v) and dentals (tz, t, d) of חֵפֶץ/KHĀFATZ (desire) are COVET and CUPID(ity). Read as [H]OPHĀTS, one might include OPTMISTIC, OPT and OPTION, as *optio* means to wish, desire in Latin.

CAPITAL infers assets, wealth, worth and investments, terms compatible with HAVE and HOPE. (Merely drop the end of HAPH(ATS)/חֵפֶץ, remembering that F is akin to V and P.)

כסף/KOSUF (to desire) is from the same root as כסף/KESEF (money). More hidden assets of חֵפֶץ/HĀFETZ include חפש/HĀPĀS (to seek), צפה/TĀZPĀH (hope, expectation), and קוה/KAVĀ (to hope).

CHAP, CHAPMAN and CHEAP, from Germanic *kaupaz* (trader) and IE *caupo* (small trader), are affiliates.

*I Kings 10:13 "and King Solomon gave the Queen of Shaba all she *desired*." חמצוה.

CAPRI[CORN]/עֹפֶר
KHO-PHERE   [KH-PH-R]

ROOTS: While Latin *caper* is a goat, the IE root of CAPRICORN, *kapro*, means buck or male deer as well as goat. Furthermore, CAPRIOLE is from Italian *capriulo* (a doe or a roe). KPR, then, is not specifically a goat word, and the IE root of HEIFER, *per* (young of animal) might lead us

to search for a more general [K]PR etymon.

Songs 2:8,9 offers עפר/KHOPHER, HŌPHER or ŌPHER (fawn or the young of hoofed ruminants).

BRANCHES: Linguists establish FARROW as a cognate of HEIFER, but they admit that the first element, the H of Heifer, is obscure. The first element of the proposed Hebrew etymon, ע, can lead to an *H* in English, but is more often guttural. Note the related term כפיר/KFĒR (young of lion, etc.). This term is an antonym, not synonym, as the כפיר/KPHER are the very lion or other cubs that prey upon their opposite numbers, the עפר/ŌPHER or KŌPHER (fawn). כפיר/K-P/B-(R) may be the source of CUB, (JA)GUAR, COUGAR and the "cat" words of Swahili (*paka*) and Malay (*boki*). נור/ GOOR or GVR is a lion's whelp.

The two Hebrew terms above reinforce the existence of a PR root meaning the young of animals (see IE root *per* above). Hebrew also offers the אפרח/EPHRŌĀKH (chick or young of birds). פרג/PRG is a sprout (young of plants), and פרח/PRKH is a youth, cadet or trainee (young of human).

פר/P-R is a popular element among Hebrew animals, from the little bird (צפור/TSĒPŌR– see "SPARROW") to the big bull (פר/PĀR). More relevant here is the צפיר/TSĀPHĒR (he-goat).

The IE root here, *kapro*, also gives us CABER, CABRILLA, CABRIOLET, CAPELLA, CAPRIFIG and CHEVRON.

CAR/כר
KHAR   [K-R]

ROOTS: Whether or not it's running, CAR is supposed to derive from Latin *currere* (to run), from the IE root *kers* (to run).

The CAR of an elevator or an air balloon doesn't run anywhere, but is the name of the riding compartment or cab. It is therefore quite possible that words like CAR, CHARIOT and CARGO originate from an ancient term for the CARGO or passenger area of a vehicle. Not to put the CART before the horse, camel riding and lading must have preceded even the crudest of CARRIAGES. Thus כר/KHĀR or KAR ("saddle pillow," "furniture") seems a good etymon for CAR. The poor translations of this term in *Genesis 31:34* have been updated. We can now picture Rachel stashing her CARGO of stolen idols in a palanquin, a saddle compartment with awnings and curtains set atop camels or elephants.

Double כר to get כרכרה/KIRKĀRA (carriage), translated "dromedary" in *Isaiah 66:20*. The dromedary is the fastest of camels.

BRANCHES: For running etymons, חרץ/KHĀRUTS ("bestir" in *II Samuel 5:24*) is a possibility. It is related to מהר/[MA]HĀR (hurry).

The Hebrew wheel (גלגל/GĀLGĀL) and cart (עגלה/ĀGĀLĀ) are merely Grimm's Law changes away from CAR. KR wheel-spinning etymons include: סחר/SĀKHĀR (to go around, circulate, reel) כרע/KERĀ (knee), כרך/KORAKH (to roll), כרכור / KĒRKOOR (whirl), circle) and כרכר/KĒRKOR (top, distaff, spindle).

Cognates of CAR not mentioned above include CAREER, CARICATURE, CARIOLE, CARRY, CORRIDOR, COURIER, COURSE, CURRENT, DISCOURSE, EXCURSION, HUSSAR, INCUR, INTERCOURSE, OCCUR, PRECURSOR, RECOURSE, RECUR and SUCCOR.

קרון / KARON is a wagon, street car or railroad car. Another Aramaic and Hebrew term to consider is גרר/GĀRAR (to pull). גררה / GIRĀRA is a snow CARRIAGE or sleigh.

See "ACCELERATE," "CYCLE" "HURRY," and "OCCUR."

CARAT/קְרָט
CAR-RUT [KRT]

ROOTS: CARAT, a 4 gram weight, is acknowledged to be from Arabic *qirat*. The equivalent Hebrew term is first recorded in the Jerusalem Talmud – קְרָט/KĀRĀT. Aramaic קרט/KŌRET is a particle, drop or small berry.

CARD/קְרַד
KAY-RUDD [KRD]

ROOTS: To CARD is to smooth out by scraping with a metal comb or wire brush. Late Latin *caritare* (to card) is pared down to Latin *carere* (to comb) and the IE root *kars* (to card).

Similarly, קרד/KĀRĀD (to scrape, curry) and נרד / GĀRĀD (to scrape, scratch – *Job 2:8*) have a shorter form in גרר/GĀRĀR (to scrape, plane – *I Kings 7:9*). קרצף/KĀRTS-ĀF is also to curry.

> **BRANCHES:** To CURRY a horse's back with a hard CURRY-COMB is so similar to CARDING cloth that it is surprising to see CURRY missing from the listed derivatives of IE *kars* (to card). Included are obscure terms like CARDOON, CARMINATIVE and CHARD. Even these plant words suggest the flat, stiff layers of papyrus that went into making a CARD, CARTON or CHART. It is common to name a product by the act of production, thus we add CARTOON, CARTIRIDGE, CARTOGRAM or CARTO-GRAPH to words like GRADE, CARTE-BLANCHE, and CARTEL.
> עדר/KHĀDĀR (to hoe) has reshuffled KRD to KDR.
> See GRADE, RAKE (K-R backwards), (S)CRATCH and more at "CHARACTER."

CARIB(BEAN)/כָּלֶב
KELEBH [K–L–BH→KRB]

ROOTS: The Carib Indians, their language, the CARIBBE-AN Sea, and CANNIBAL were all named for *caribales* (dogs) by Columbus – outraged at the man-eating natives then in Cuba and Haiti. The dictionary doesn't know why "dog" should sound like CARIB, so they add "as if from Latin *canis* (dog)."

It is now known that Columbus was a secret Jew. His first mate, Mendez, was brought along because a Jew who spoke Hebrew, (the acknowledged universal language or mother tongue), might be able to communicate with the alien peoples they would encounter. (See the turkey at "TOU-CAN" for Mendez' most enduring Hebrew coinage for a New World creature.) It is not clear where the slight L to R change originated, but dog in Hebrew is כלב/KELEBH.* For the harder B sound, כלבא / KĀLBĀ is the Aramaic term, *kalb* the Arabic.

> **BRANCHES:** The same L to R change may have given us CUR (mongrel dog), whose etymology is unknown. *Koira* is a Finnish dog. The COLLIE (sheepdog), too, has only a folk etymology. The Fijian term for dog is *koli*. Reverse to *luki* for fox in Basque.
> The dog-monster Scylla, from Greek *(s)kylax* (dog), remained a buried bone in the IE backyard.
> The wilder canines stress the back, not the front part, of כלב/KELEBH. See "LOBO." The Polish wolf, though, reverses K-L-V to *wilk*.

* *Proverbs 26:11*–"As a *dog* returns to his vomit, so a dullard repeats his folly." כלב.
The loyal, brave, emotional dog is כל לב/KAL LĀBH (all heart) – as was Biblical Caleb.

CAROB/חָרוּב
KHAR-OOBH [KH-R-BH]

ROOTS: The CAROB tree and seed pod are borrowed from the Arabic *kharrubah* (bean pod). The Hebrew for St. John's bread is חרוב/KHĀROOBH.

> **BRANCHES:** ערב/URĀBH or KHĀRĀBH means sweet.

CARP/חָרֵף
KHAR-UFF [KH-R-PH]

ROOTS: To talk in a CRABBY, complaining, accusatory and fault-finding way is the CARP intended here. The dictionary suggests Latin *carpere* (to pluck) as a possible etymon. חרף / KHĀRĀPH Is translated "reproach" in *Psalms 69:10*, and "to taunt" in *Isaiah 37:23*.

> **BRANCHES:** חריף / KHĀRĒF means sharp-tasting as well as reviling. A*CERB*ATE and EXA*CERB*ATE mean to make sour or bitter, and to irritate or vex. (Latin *acerbus* is bitter, harsh, and sour.) GRUFF (harsh) is traced to the IE root *kreup* (scab; encrusted).
> The CARP fish, from Slavic words meaning rough and scabby, could be a cognate of CARAPACE, and ultimately from words like קלפה / KLĒPĀ (shell, rind) and Aramaic קלפין / KULPIN (fish scales).
> The many CARP words from Greek *karpos* (fruit) may have something to do with קלפה / KLĒPĀ as shell, rind or peel. Terms like CARPOLOGY take in hard, covered seeds as well as many peel or rind-covered fruit.
> CARP backwards recalls Hebrew terms meaning to shell (פרק / P-R-K) and to bud, blossom and flower (פרח / P-R-KH).
> Speaking of backward synonyms, Latin *carpere* (like its definition "to pluck") is also a guttural (C,K)-liquid (l,r)-bilabial (p,b) term.
> *Carpere* is the etymon for CARPET, unless you prefer a "covering" term like קלפה / KLĒPĀ.
> See "BARK," "CALIBER," "CAROB" (encased in a pod), "CRAB" (encased in a shell) and "SCALP."

CARVE/חָרַב
KHER-EV [KH-R-BH]

ROOTS: The IE root given here is *gerebh* (to scratch), while German *kerben* is to notch. To CARVE is more than scratching, so consider חרב / KHEREV (sword, blade, plow – *Genesis 3:27*). The knife is a CARVER, as is a גלב / GĀLĀV (barber – *Ezekiel 5:1*). (The ג / G is often a K, and L = R.) גלף / GĀLĀPH is to carve, (S)CULPT, and (EN)GRAVE. קלף / KĀLĀPH is to skin or peel, and מגרפה / (MA)GRAPHA is a rake or (S)CRAPER. Other KR and GR roots are seen at "CARD."

> **BRANCHES:** CLAW (*chele* in Greek), CLEAVE, GLABROUS, GLYPH, GRAPH, -GRAPH, GRAVE (to carve), HARPOON, HARROW, KERF, (S)CRAWL, (S)CRIBE, (S)CRIBLE, (S)CRIPT, (S)CRIPTURE, (S)CRIVENER, (S)CROBICULATE, (S)CRUB, and (S)CULPTURE should all be cut in.
> The IE root *gerebh* included two from the list above. In the AHD's PARAGRAPH they did include CRAB, CRAWL, CRAY-

FISH, DIAGRAM, (-) GRAM, PROGRAM, TETRAGRAMMA-
TON and others that are linked here with alternate etymons.

See "GRAPHITE," where the IE root is subsequently (1985)
spelled "gerbh."

See "CLEAVER" and "HARROW."

CAST/קֶשֶׁת
KES(H)ET   [K-S(H)-T]

ROOTS: The reference books offer Old Norse *kasta* (to
throw) and Latin *gestare* (to bear, carry). The first definition
of cast is "to propel with haste or violence." This recalls קשת
/ KESHET (archer's bow *Genesis 27:3*) and חץ / KHĀTS
(arrow – *I Samuel 22:15*.) See "HASTE" AND "HASTATE"
(arrow or spear-shaped) to see why words for propelling,
haste, and violence ought to sound alike from their Hebrew
etymons.

BRANCHES: The CASTING of CAST IRON is supposed to
relate to the pouring process. If so, a reversal of צקת / TSEK(ES)
(cast – *Exodus 38:27*) or of יצק / (YA)TZĀK (to pour out, cast –
Genesis 28:8) is relevant. If hardness is at the core of CAST IRON,
however, terms like מקשה / (MI)KSHÄ (hard) are noteworthy.
CASTER, CASTOFF, FORECAST, OUTCAST, etc. are from the
same mold.

See "ENCASE."

CASTR(ATE)/קָצַר
CUTS-ARE   [K-TS-R → K-ST-R]

ROOTS: Latin *castr(are)* is to castrate or prune. קצר /
KĀTSĀR is to cut, reap, be short, be insufficient or power-
less. קיצור / KĒTSUR is shortening. Cut down to the K-TS
or K-ST two-letter root, there are terms like קצב / KĀTS(AV)
(to cut off), קצץ / KĒTS(OOTS) (chopping, cutting), קצע /
KĒTS(ĀA) (to trim) and קצה / KĒTSÄ (to cut off – see "CUT.")
The IE root, similarly, is *kes-* (to cut).

BRANCHES: Cognates of CASTRATE listed at this IE root
include CASTE, CASTIGATE, INCEST, and QUASH.
קצר / KĀTSĀR means short; the IE base of SHORT is *sqer* (to
cut). Switch the #1 and #2 root letters of the Hebrew etymon,
from K-(T)S-R to (T)S-K-R, to get the equivalent of *sqer*.
Reversing the K-TS or K-ST root of the term קציצה / *KITSETSA*
(a chopping off, a hamburger steak) produces the word STEAK.
כרת / KORAS is to cut off (switch root letters #2 and #3).
KS cutting terms appear in the etymology of AX. Old English
oecs is a pickax or hatchet, Germanic *akusi* and *ahhus* mean "ax,"
and Greek *axine* is an ax. These recall חצין / HATSĒN or
KHATSĒN (ax, חצב / *KHATS*AV or *KHAST*AV (to hew, cut), חצה
/ *KHATSA* or *KHASTA* (to divide) and חצי / *KHATSĒ* or *KHASTĒ*
(a half).

For SK cutting words see "SAXON."

CATCH/קוֹץ
COATS   [K-TS]

ROOTS: To CATCH is 1) to seize and hold and 2) to trap and
snare. One can be caught on a קוץ / KŌTS (thorn), and קש
/ KĀSH is to lay snares.

BRANCHES: קוץ / KŌTS might also be the source of HITCH.
HITCH is to catch as if entangled. (The ק / K to H change is
common – look up "head" or "heat."

See "ACACIA" (Appendix A).

Genesis 3:18 "*Thorns* also and thistles shall it bring forth
to thee." (There will aways be a CATCH in all our en-
deavors.) קוץ.
Isaiah 29:21 "Who cause men to lose their lawsuits, *laying
a snare* for the arbiter at the gate..." מוקש. קשין /
(MO)KĀSH is a snare.

After Middle English *catchen*, the given etymons get
caught up in words with different sounds (coming from
different Hebrew sources). Old Norman French *cacher* is
from קח / KĀKH (to take), while Latin *capere* (to take) and
the IE root *kap* (to grasp) are from חפן / KHÄPHÄN
(handful) and/or כף / KÄPH (hand).

(CATS)KILL/נַחַל
(NA)-KHULL   [N-KH-L]

ROOTS: Kill is a stream, channel, or creek term that
appears in placenames like the Catskill mountains and
Peekskill, NY. The Middle Dutch *kille* has no known origin.
נחל / (NÄ)KHÄL is a stream, ravine or "wadi" (*I Kings
17:7*). Almost a score of Biblical placenames include this
term.

BRANCHES: COULEE, CULVERT, GHYLL, GILL, GULCH
and GULLY may all relate. *Kali* means river in Indonesian; *kaeul*
is a stream in Korean.
Soften th נ / KH and substitue the L for an R for נחל / NHL to
reveal the closely related נהר / NÄHÄR (river, stream). Rivers
from the Nile to the Rhine now come into view (as NR becomes
NL or reverses its flow to become RN). Read NHR as NGR and
you may hear the ANGARA River in Siberia and the NIAGARA
River of New York and Ontario.
The CLOACA (sewer, urinary tract) may be from קלח /
KOLÄKH (to stream, to pour out). הלך / (HA)LEKH is flowing; לך
/ LAKH means "go!" פלג / (PE)LEG is a stream.
The given source of LEAK and LACK and one of the possible
sources of LAKE, IE root *leg* (to trickle), relates to Hebrew terms
like קלח / (KO)LAKH and לח / LAKH (moist). Otherwise,
LACUNA (ditch, hole, pool), LAGOON, LAKE and LOCH
connect to Hebrew words like לע / LOĀKH (crater), ריק / RĀKE
(empty) and (a reverse of) חלל / KHÄL(AL) (hollow).

CAUSE/עָשָׂה
KHASA   [KH-S-(H)]

ROOTS: The cited Latin etymon, *causa*, means purpose or
motive, but to CAUSE is to produce an effect or result.
עשה / KHÄSÄ or ÄSÄ is to make, do, or produce (*Genesis
2:2*).

BRANCHES: A CAUSE CELEBRÉ is close to a CAUSERIE, from
Latin *causari* (to dispute) or Provençal *causar* (to quarrel). These
are from עשק / KHÄS(EK) or ASEK (quarrel – *Genesis 26:20*"...
and he called the name...Esek, because they *contended* with
him"). A CAUSE also relates to עסק / KHÄSEK OR ĀSEK (con-

cern). CAUSALITY and CAUSATION are from Latin *causari*, which also means "to plead." Hebrew עתר / KHÄSAR is to pray or supplicate.

ESSAY is linked to a verb meaning "to do," but that verb is Latin *agere* rather than Hebrew עשיה / ASEYA (doing). The suffix -IZE (to cause, make into, etc.) should relate.

CAUT(ERIZE)/קָדַח
CO(D)T-AH   [KDH→KT]

ROOTS: To CAUTERIZE, to burn with a hot iron or needle, is traced to Greek *kauter* (burning or branding iron) and further to Greek *kaiein* (to burn). The given IE root is also melted down to *kai* (kai), although the extended form responsible for HEAT and HOT is *kaid.*

Hot HEBREW K-DT terms include קדח / KÄDATÄH (to kindle), יקד / (YA)KÄD (to burn), קדחת / KÄDT(ÄHÄT) (inflammation, fever), קטורת / KIT(ORET) (slow-burning incense) and מוקד / (MO)KÄDT (conflagration, hearth, bonfire). *Jeremiah 17:4* includes "flame" (קדחתם) and "burn" (תוקד).

> **BRANCHES:** Words like CAUSTIC, CAUTERY and (HOLO)-CAUST are placed with the IE root *keu* (to burn). The IE root *kand* (to shine) is related. It is merely a nasalized (extra N) KD or KT heat word.
>
> Add KINDLE to the following words, from IE *ka(n)d*, which directly come from Latin *ca(n)dere* (to shine): CANDENT, CANDID, CANDLE, CANDOR, INCANDESCENT, INCENDIARY and INCENSE. The AHD includes the incense SANDAL(WOOD), from Sanskrit *candanáh* – but consider קטורה / KITORÄ (incense – *Deuteronomy 33:10*)
>
> ODOR smells like it belongs here, as might AESTIVAL, ANNEAL, EDIFICE, EDIFY, ESTUARY, and ETHER – all from the IE root *aidh* (to burn).
>
> (S)CINTILLATE adds an unhistoric S to the already nasalized (added N) K-D root.
>
> Arabic fire is *qt'ya*. Hot in French is *chaud*, in Fujian it's *kata kata*. Reversing to T-K for Native American and Oriental languages: hot is *atatakai* (Japanese), *tuguou* (Korean) and *tsoko* (Mayan Indian).

CAV(ITY)/נָקֶב
(NEH)-KEV   [KV]

ROOTS: Latin *cavus* (hollow) is the etymon for many words of CONCAVITY. נקב / (NE)KEV (hole, perforation) is also the verb "to bore" (*II Kings 12:10* – נקבים). נקבה / (NI)KÄVÄ is female (*Genesis 1:27*), the receiving cavity in electronics terminology as well. נקבה / (NI)KVÄ is a tunnel or passage; קבה / KÄVÄ is a belly or womb; קבה / KÄVÄ is a stomach. כף / KAF is "hollow" in *Genesis 32:25*.

> **BRANCHES:** קבל / KÄB(EL) (to receive) is the source of words like (AC)*CEPT* and (RE)*CEIVE*. One affects (RE)*CEIP*T with the palm of the hand or the כף / KUFF (see "CUFF"). The source of COVE is Anglo-Saxon *cofa* (cave); a hollow rock or CAVE is a כף / KÄF in *Job 30:6*; כב / GOV is a den (*Daniel 6:8*); חוחים / KHÄ(AKHIM) are caves in *I Samuel 13:6*. יקב / (YE)KEV is a wine cellar; קבר / KEV(ER) is a grave; גב / GÄV is a pit. To EXCAVATE is חפר / KHÄPH(ÄR) (to dig – *Genesis 21:30*).

The IE root containing CAVE, CAVERN, CONCAVE, DECOY, EXCAVATE and GABION is *keu* or *keua* (so swell; vaul, hole).

Chippewa (American Indian) *ikwe* is woman; Dutch *kwabbe* is belly; Eskimo *naak* is belly (from NK[V]); French *cave* is cellar; Hawaiian *wahine* (woman) and Japanese *fugin* (lady) require reversals of NKV plus Grimms Law letter permutations.

The opposite of a curved CON*CAV*ITY is a קו / KAV (straight line). Reverse the K-V root and see "*VACATE.*"

Also see "ALCOVE," "CAB," "CAP," "CUP," "GAP," "GOBLET," "GOPHER," "GRAVE," "HAVEN," and "SCOOP."

CELL/כְּלֶא
KELL-EH   [KL]

ROOTS: The hard C is evident in the IE root *kel* (to conceal, to cover). A CELL is a small hut, a room in a prison, a small hollow cavity or compartment, etc.

The prison CELL is well covered by כלא / KELEH (dungeon – *II Kings 25:27*) or כלוא / KILOO (prison).

> **BRANCHES:** כלוב / KIL(OOV) is a cage. All the HL HOLES and HOLLOWS listed as cognates of CELL are more directly from חלל / KHÄLÄL (hole, space, vacuum) – see "HOLLOW." GAOL is an older British spelling of jail. Flip over the L of CELL to the Hebrew נ (N) for a KN cell word. קן / KAN (cell, little room, nest, board) is a better etymon for KENNEL than Latin *canis* (dog).
>
> See "INCARCERATE."

CENS(US)/עָנַשׁ
KHON-ES(H)   [KH-N-SH]

ROOTS: A CENSUS was taken by the Romans to assess tax potential; *censere* in Latin means "to tax" or "assess." קנס / KINUS (a fine) is a talmudic term, while ענש / KHONES(H) or ONESH in *II Kings 23:33* is the "fine," "indemnity," or tax imposed on Judea by Pharoah-necoh. ענש / KHONES(H) means "punishment" in common usage.

> **BRANCHES:** (S)CONCE is a term for a fine or punishment imposed at Oxford University for a breach of manners. Its origin is officially "unknown." (One must often drop the initial "S" in an SC word.) *Kuan shui* is customs in Chinese; *kanzei* is customs tax or duty in Japanese; Korean *kesan* (bill, account, check) may be another variant of guttural-nasal-fricative words of monies due. A Hebrew variant is מכס / MEKHES (tax), swap root letters #1 and #2 of K(H)-N-S to see the family likeness.
>
> The AHD lists CENSOR and RECENSION as cognates of CENSUS.
>
> Just as ענש / KNS is to punish, to CENS(URE) (condemn, blame) can also mean "to punish." *Censeo* is a judge in Latin, as his role was to mete out punishment (rather than justice).

CHAFE/שָׁף
SHAF   [SH-F]

ROOTS: To CHAFE is to rub. The given etymon, Latin *calere* (to be warm), attempts to link rubbing with warmth. Words like CHAFING DISH (a food warmer) and CHAUFFEUR (literally, an engine stoker) are allegedly cognates of

CHAFE. They do not infer rubbing and they, too, don't sound at all like *calere*.

שפשוף / SHIFSHOOF is to rub or polish. שף / SHÄF (*Genesis 3:15*) means to bruise, crush, grind (grain) rub and polish.

> **BRANCHES:** It is the Hebrew root שף / SH-F, not the IE root *kel* (to be warm), which speaks to words like CHAFER, CHAFE, CHEW, and COCKCHAFER. Reversing SF recalls IE root *bhes* (to rub) and derivatives EPSILON, SABULOUS, SAND and UPSILON. Greek *psen* is to rub or scrape.
>
> An alleged cognate of CHAFE, CHAUFFEUR, appears far closer to רחף / (DA)KHAF (to drive, hasten, incite – *Psalms 140:12*).
>
> (S)CUFFLE, from Old Norse *(s)kufa* (to push, shove), is ultimately from Hebrew terms like דחף / DÄKHUF (to push) and חפף / KHÄFÄF (to rub, comb, wash). The sea shore, חוף / KHOF, is where the sea CHAFES, rubs, grinds and cleans. These last three Hebrew words offer alternative KH-F etymons for CHAFE.
>
> American Indian words of rubbing clean include *cop(aiba)* (Tupi) and *cop(al)* (Nahuatl).

C(H)AISE/כּס
CASE   [KS]

ROOTS: A CHAISE, as in CHAISE LOUNGE ("long chair" in French), is not a Parisian French corruption of CHAIR as posited by *Webster's*. CHAISE demonstrates the typical CH softening by the French of a Hebrew K, in this case כס / KÄS or KHÄS (seat, throne – *Exodus 17:16*) The more common Hebrew term is כסא / KESÄ (chair, seat – *II Kings 4:10*).

> **BRANCHES:** CHAIR, Latin *cathedra*, CATHEDRAL, and SANHEDRIN are all linked to IE root *sed* (to sit), the source of EXEDRA. EXEDRA is understood to be from *ex* (out) plus Greek *hedra* (a seat). But the EXEDRA in ancient Greece was not merely outside seats, but an outdoor room, building or area containing seats and used for holding talks. An EXEDRA is an outdoor bench, but it originated in a word for room – חדר / HEDER (*Genesis 43:30*). The concordance uses the Latin term *conclave* (room) to define חדר / HEDER, again demonstrating the intimate association of חדר / HEDER with a conclave, boardroom or SANHEDRIN full of conference chairs.
>
> CHEDER is the Yiddish term for the one-room Jewish schools of Eastern Europe (where Hebrew was not taught).
>
> Rather than Latin *cathedra*, כר / KHAR (saddle, pillow, palanquin – *Genesis 31:34*) ought to be the source of Old French *chaiere* and English CHAIR.
>
> For the source of Latin *ex*, see "EXIT."
>
> A Japanese chair is an *isu*. For HUT and other חדר / HEDER derivatives, see "HOARD."

CHAN(G)E/שָׁנה
SHAN-AH   [SH-N]

ROOTS: Old French *changier* is said to come from Latin *cambire* (to exchange, barter). The IE roots offered are *skamb* or *kamb* (to curve or bend).

Yes, the S before a guttural is often expendable (*skamb* = *kamb*) and a French CH from a Latin hard C is common, but a G ("chan*g*e") coming from a B ("kam*b*") is not acceptable.

For the source of IE *kamb* see "CAMERA."

The Hebrew שנה / SHÄNÄH (to change, alter, be different) is the more logical etymon. "For I am the Lord – I have not *changed*") (שניתי) – *Malachi 3:6*. For the G of CHAN*G*E to come from an H (of SHANA*H*) is acceptable.

> **BRANCHES:** שנוי / SHENOOY is a change or difference; שניות / SHNEOOT is dualism or duality. The opposite of oneness, and the essence of difference, duality or otherness is captured in the number two. שנים / SHNÄ(YIM) is two and שני / SHÄNE means "second" (*Genesis 1:8*).
>
> The S(H)-N root above implies separation; so does the IE root *sen* or *seni* (apart, separate).
>
> These roots give us ASUNDER (apart), *sans* and *sine* ("apart" in French and Latin), SINECURE, and SUNDRY (diverse).
>
> Other S-N terms of change include שנה / SHÄNÄ (year) and שנה / SHÄNÄ (sleep) – which give us time to change. The ישן / (YÄ)SHÄN (old) shows that change. The שן / SHÄN (tooth) is a שנאי / SHÄNUY (transformer) which changes our food to a digestible state.
>
> זנה / ZÄNÄ (to go after strange gods or to have extramarital sex) infers aberrant or "changed" behavior and alienation from our (espoused) Lord or spouse. Such behavior is ZANY and a SIN.
>
> Infidelity in either realm is no mere SHENA(NIGAN). Perhaps SHENANIGAN (trickery) is from שנה נגון / SHÄNÄ NEGOON (changing one's tune); this word has no known origin.
>
> SINISTER (left-handed, evil) fits both connotations of S-N.
>
> Alienation leads to שנאה / SINÄH (hatred). The wife who is second (שני / SHÄNE) to a beloved, number-one wife is the שנואה / SINOOA (mistranslated "hated" in *Deuteronomy 21:14*). The S-N root of estrangement, of no longer being "as one," is clear in the Chinese term *sàn* (to dissolve partnership, to drop away, scatter, diffuse).
>
> Paradoxically, שנה / SHÄNÄ is to repeat and שמר / SHÄM(ÄR) is to preserve, to keep something SYN(ONYMOUS) or the SAME – see "SAMURAI" and "SIMILE." *Sahm* is "to repeat" in Thai.

CHAR/חָרה
KHAR-AH   [KH-R]

ROOTS: To CHAR or burn is dismissed as a back-formation of CHARCOAL. CHARCOAL is "probably" (read: origin unknown) from Old English *charren* (to turn). חרה / KHÄRÄ is to kindle, burn or be angry – *Numbers 11:33*. חרך / KHÄR(ÄKH) is to "roast" in *Proverbs 12:27*. The IE root *ker* means heat or fire; Shipley's equivalent root (*ker V*) means heat or burn – see "CERAMIC."

> **BRANCHES:** Related are כור / KOOR (smelting furnace), כיור / KEVOR (fire pot), and כירה / KEERÄ (stove, hearth). נחול / GÄKHOL (burning coal). קלי / KÄLE (roast) is found at "ALKALI."
>
> For antonyms there is the whole family of קר / KÄR words of cold, frost and freezing – yet ice burns, too.
>
> Perhaps red (hot) words like CHAR (the red trout) and CARROT connect to KR words like CARBON, CARBUNCLE, CERAMIC, CREMATE and HEARTH. *Harr* is warm in Arabic.
> Beef JERKY is from Spanish *charqui*, which is from Peruvian *ccharqui* (meat dried by CHARRING over a fire).
>
> The IE root *g(w)her* (to heat, warm) resembles חרה / KHÄRÄ (to burn); derivatives of this IE root include THERM terms like THERMAL and THERMOMETER. If the AHD is wrong about removing the T and the M from Greek *therme* (heat), דרומי / (D)TROME (southern) is a alternate etymon.
>
> See "COAL," "IRE," "(S)CAR," and "(S)CORCH."

CHARA(C)T(ER)/חָרוּת
KHAR-OOT [KH-R-T/S]

ROOTS: Greek *charakter* is a stamp derived from Greek *kharassein*, (to sharpen, notch, carve or cut).

The Ten Commandments are חרות / KHÄROOS or KHÄROOT ("graven") into the stone tablets in *Exodus 32:16*. חרט / KHERET is a writing style (*Isaiah 8:1*). חרט / KHÄRÄT is to engrave or chisel; the חרטמים / KHART(OOMÊM) or "magicians" of *Exodus 7:11* are masters of hieroglyphics or engraved CHARACTERS. חריצה / KHÄRETSÄ is sharpening; חרוץ / KHAROOTS is a thresher (*Isaiah 41:15*). A חריץ / KHÄRETZ is an incision; חרף / KHÄRÄPH is sharp, and חרש / KHÄRÄS(H) is to plow, engrave, or carve. The two-letter root is KH-R.

The IE root for CHARACTER is *gher* (to scrape, scratch). This matches up with גרד / GARAD (to "scrape"– as Job must do to his skin in *Job 2:8*). קרד / KARÄD is to scrape or curry.

> **BRANCHES:** One doesn't have to dig very deeply to see CARD, CURRY, (DE)GRADE, DEGREE, GRADE (to make level – גרר / GÄRAR is "smooth" in *I Kings :9*), GRATE, (S)CRAPE, (S)CRATCH and (S)HARP in the Hebrew words above.
>
> One does have to switch the KR to RK in order to see the source of RAKE (scraping and leveling tool) and RACC(OON) (literally "the hand scratcher" in Algonquian Indian).
>
> See "CARD," "HEARSE," "SCRAPER" and "SCRATCH."

CHASTE/חָסִיד
KHA-SEA(D)T [KH-S-DT]

ROOTS: CHASTE is from Latin *castus* (morally pure), the word meaning modest, abstaining (sexually), and unembellished. CHASTEN also means to restrain and be moderate.

חסיד / KHÄSED is a "pious" person or saint (*Micah 7:2*). The modest, retiring, unembellished "Jewish Amish," the Chassid(im) or Hassid(im), are the black-garbed pious Jews native to holy cities like Brooklyn, New York and Jerusalem.

חס / KHÄS is sparing, forebearance; חסם / KHÄSÄM is to muzzle, block or temper; חסך / KHÄSÄKH is to spare, withold, be without; and חסר / KHESER is to deprive. The two-letter root is חס / KH-S.

> **BRANCHES:** Related terms like HAUTEUR, from French *haut* (high, pious), might better relate to קרש / KODT(ESH) (set aside, sanctified. קרש / K-DT-S(H) is a "cut" word (see "CUT" and "CASTRATE") but an anagram (KST) resembles CHASTE.
>
> The IE root for CHASTE is *kes* (to cut). Listed cognates include CASHIER, CARET, CASTE, CASTIGATE, CASTRATE, CASTLE, INCEST and QUASH. See "CHASTISE" (Apendix A).

CHECKMATE/שֵׁיךְ מֵת
SHAYKH MATE [SH-Y-K + MT]

ROOTS: (1): Proclaiming CHECKMATE means that "the king is dead" and the chess game over. The term is an acknowldeged borrowing from Arabic, yet the dictionaries claim that the "check" of CHECKMATE (the Arabic ruler or SHEIK) derives from the Persian *shah* (king). *Shah* is to have evolved from the IE root *tke* (to take control of).

At stake in the contest for CHECKMATE are a dozen words like CHECK, CHECKING account, CHECK UP and CHESS (from French *eshec*, a version of Arabic SHEIK). Also at stake is a claim to the invention of CHESS.

שיך / SHAKH (sheik) relates to Aramiac שיך / SHAYAKH (own, possess), שוע / SHOOAKH (nobleman, wealthy man – *Job 34:19*) and perhaps זקן / ZAK(ÄN) (patriarchal leader, elder – *Leviticus 24:2*).

> **BRANCHES:** (1): זקן / ZAKAN may find parallels in the "chief" terms of the Algonquin Indians, SACHEM and SAGAM(ORE). Chief or elder in Chinese is *zhang* (a nasalized SHIEK, or a #2-#3 letter flip of זקן / ZAKAN or of סגן / SIGUN (army officer). SHOGUN is the Japanese (via Chinese) word for military commander.
>
> *Shoogo* is chess in Japanese; *saka* is Fijian for "sir."

ROOTS: (2): Now for the deathly second half of (CHECK)MATE: מת / MATE is to die (*Genesis 42:38*). The same MT root bears verbs of putting to death, killing and dying – *Deuteronomy 32:58*. The MATADOR (Spanish) is literally a killer, as *matar* is to kill. The second MAT in the dictionary is from an Old French term meaning defeated or "exhausted"; it is linked to Arabic *mat*.

> **BRANCHES:** Not officially linked to Semitic is NEED, from IE base *neu-ti* (to collapse with weariness). Gothic *naus*, like Hebrew MÄS (or MAT), means corpse. מזה / MOZEH is exhausted (*Deuteronomy 32:24*), מצה / METZA is to exhaust.
>
> MO(R)TAL, MO(R)TALITY, MO(R)TUARY and MU(R)DER are slightly butchered versions of Hebrew מות / MÄVET OR MWT (death). The ו / V is a vowel in verb forms of death (in phrases like מות תמות / MOT (TÄ)MOOT–"thou shalt surely die" of *Genesis 2:18*). But the consonant ו / V often slides over to W in Arabic (where *mawt* is death), and from there to the R of MORTGAGE, MORTICIAN, MORTIFY (from Latin *mortis*, death) or Russian *(s)myert* (death). This same ו / v to R change turns בושה / BOOSHÄ (shame) to (EM)BARRASS(MENT), תוך / TOKH (within, through) to THROUGH, or חומה / HOMÄ (wall) to the word for wall in Basque, *orma*.
>
> To better establish מת / MT or MS as the orignal death word, there is Malay *mate*, Fijian *mate* and Tongan *mate* – all words for death. Chinese *mou sha* is murder; Japanese *sinu* is to die, while *nete* is asleep. Recalling NEED and the death = exhaustion equation above, tired in Arabic is *mout(aab)*. In German, tired is *müde*. Again, to exhaust in Hebrew is מצה / MET(SÄ).
>
> Reverse MT to obtain תם / TOM (completion). Greek *thanatos* is death, whence THANATOPHOBIA (the fear of death).
>
> *Tuuna* is murder in Australian aborigine.

C(H)ER(ISH)/יָקָר
(YE)-CARE [YKR]

ROOTS: CHERISH is the word we use to describe holding something dear or valuing something highly. Old French *cher* and Latin *car(us)* mean "dear." A KR etymon is needed.

יקר / (YÄ)KAR) is dear, prized or valued. יקר / YEKAR is to honor, and יקר / (YI)KAR is honor or a precious thing. Updated translations of *Isaiah 43:4* will replace "honored" with CHERISHED: "Because you are precious to Me, and *honored*, and I love you." The concordance translates יקר / (YA)KAR with Latin *carus*. The translators get it right in *Jeremiah 31:20* where "Ephraim is a *dear* son."

BRANCHES: Official cognates include CARESS and CHARITY. The #3 definition of CARE, a liking or regard, is disregarded as it is believed that CARE derives from IE *gar* (to cry out).

Antonyms of the קר / KR Hebrew root include (KR→RK) ריקה / RĀKA (good for nothing), (KR→KL) קל / KUL (unimportant) and הקלה / (HĒ)KLÄ (to treat with contempt). HECKLE (to taunt a speaker) might better be linked to this last Hebrew term than to a Middle Dutch word for cleaning and dressing flax, etc.

Reversing רע / R-KH (friend), רק / RAK (only) and רחם / RAKH(AM) (to love) recall KR words that are near קרב / KR(BH)] and dear קרב / KĀRĀ(BH) is to befriend].

CHIN/טָחַן
(TAH)-KHUN   [(T)-KH-N]

ROOTS: Old English *cin* (chin) is from the IE root *genu* (jawbone, chin). טחן / (TĀ)KHĀN is to chew, mill or grind (*Exodus 32:20*). The jawbone is nature's טחון / (TI)KHŌN (millstone). *Tzaqn* is the Arabic chin.

BRANCHES: זקן / ZĀKĀN is a beard (for some chins). The given cognates of CHIN are CHAETOGNATH, GENIAL, GNATHIC, -GNATHOUS (Greek *gnathos* or jaw is an anagram of T-K/G-N) and HANUMAN (from the Sanskrit jaw, *hanu*). The initial dental (D,T) of T-KH-N is lost in the Sanskrit and Old English; it is pushed over to third place in the Greek.

Chin or jaw in Thai is *kahng*. The Turkish chin, *cene*, also favors the back of the Hebrew (DT)-K-N etymon; Indonesian *dagu* favors the front of DT-KH(N).

דקק / DÄKUK is to crush, make fine; הדק / (HĒ)DĀK is to press together or squeeze. TALC (from Arabic) and (reverse D/T-K) CUD are related.

See "GNAW."

CHORUS/כִּרְכֵּר
KIR – CARE   [KR]

ROOTS: Greek *choros* is to dance in a ring; CHOREA (a nervous disorder) is a Latin term that also means to dance in a ring.

The first recorded male CHOREOGRAPHER was also a fair singer-composer. King David's "dance" in *II Samuel 6:14* is subsequently translated "whirl"–because his כרכר / KERKAR (dancing, jumping around) was a circling motion. Reinforcing this link to the original sense of CHORUS is כרכור / KIRKOOR (to encircle).

See "CYLE."

BRANCHES: A KR to KH-L change leads one to the first female CHOREOGRAPHER, Miriam and her מחול / (MA)KHŌL (dance) in *Exodus 15:20*. התחולל / (HIT)KHOLEL is to whirl or turn around. More at "HULA." Another dance term, רקוד / RĒK(OOD), reverses the KR of CHORUS.

CAR(OL) and CHOIR were dance words before singing words. Musicologists trace the Greek chorus to the responsive singing of the Levites' choir at the Temple of Jerusalem.

See "SCURRILOUS."

CHROME/קְרוּם
KROOM   [KR]

ROOTS: The more than 80 CHROME words come from Greek *khroma* (skin, hence complexion and color).

קרום / KROOM is a Talmudic word for skin crust and membrane, related to קרם / KORUM (to cover with skin, crust or overlay – *Ezekiel 37:6, 8*). An Aramaic term used by Onkelos to define chrysolite in *Exodus 39:13* is כרום / KROOM; it matches the "yellow" sense of CHROME.

Greek *khros* (skin) and *kreas* (flesh), along with Latin COR[IUM] (hide, skin) and *caro* (flesh) indicate a KR family tailored by God in *Genesis 3:21*. Adam and Eve were no longer ערום / KÄROOM (naked) with their coats of עור / KHOR (hide).

BRANCHES: Related terms from Latin *caro* (flesh) include: CARCASS, CARNAGE, CARNAL, CARNATION, CARNIVAL, CARRION, CARNIVOROUS, CHARNEL, CORACLE, CORIACEOUS, CREATINE, CRONE, CURRIER, EXCORIATE and INCARNATE.

Change the KR root to KL for Hebrew קלף / KLUF (skin, parchment), English CALLOUS and Fijian *kuli* (skin). *Kulit* is skin or hide in Indonesian. See "CREAM."

עור / ŌR or KHŌR (skin) is spelled the same as עור / ĒVER or KHĒVER (blind – *Leviticus 19:14*). A #2-#3 root letter metathesis of EVER or EBHER resembles *orb* (blind in Rumanian). The connection between skin and blindness (skin covering the eyes) is clearer upon noting the primary definition of ORBIT (eye socket) and its zoological meaning (the skin around the eye of a bird). *(S)kora* is skin or leather in Polish. Chinese reverses עור / ŌR to *rou* (flesh).

Iro is color in Japanese.

See "GALYAK."

CHRYSANTH(EMUM)/נֵצָה + חָרוּץ
KHAROO(T)S + NEET(S)AH   [KHRTS + NTSH]

ROOTS: The first part of CHRYS(ANTHEMUM) is initially from the Greek *chrysos* (gold). This term is officially acknowledged to be borrowed from the Phoenecian-Hebrew חרוץ / KHÄROOTS (gold – *Zechariah 9:3*).

The second part of the word is from Greek *anthos* (flower). Flower in Hebrew is נצה / NĒTSÄH (*Isaiah 18:5*). The end צ / TS also takes a TH in ארץ / ÄRETS (earth).

BRANCHES: The two parts of CHRYSANTHEMUM appear in ten words like CHRYSALIS or CHRYSOLITE, and in sixteen words like ANTHER, ANTHOLOGY (literally, a league of flowers), -ANTHOUS, and ANTHOZOAN.

Aramaic *hara* (yellow) is related to the golden words of Greek (*chrysos*) and Hebrew חרוץ / HAR(OOTS). *Hari* is yellow in Sanskrit too, as seen in the word HART(AL). HARTAL shares the same IE root, the AHD's *ghel* (to shine), that is attributed to the word GOLD. If IE *ghel* can be the source of GOLD and HARTAL, then חרוץ / HÄROOT(S) or KHAROOTS (gold) can link up to GILD, GULDEN, GELT and ZLOTY as well. The Finnish (not Indo-European) word for gold is *kulta*; this seems to be a fine missing link from the KH-R-T(S) of the Hebrew to the G-L-D/T words in Germanic languages.

חרצית / KHÄRTSĒS is a CHRYSANTHEMUM in later Hebrew.

CINNAMON/קִנָּמוֹן
KIN-A-MOAN   [KN-MN]

ROOTS: CINNAMON is an acknowledged borrowing from Hebrew קנמון / KINĀMŌN (cinnamon – *Songs 4:14*). It is significant to note how the Latin *cinnamomum* took on a soft C (S) from its Greek source *kinnamomon*. The Hebrew may be from מין קנה / MĒN KĀNNE (a species of reed or cane).

> **BRANCHES:** Similar tree bark products include CINCHONA and QUININE.

CLEAVE/חֶלְבְּנָה
KHELVE-(INA)   [KH-L-V]

ROOTS: To CLEAVE is to adhere or cling to; it is traced to the IE base *gleibh*, where it connects to sticky things like CLAY, CLOVER (with a sticky sap) and GLUE.

חלבנה / KHELBHINĀ (galbanum) is the acknowledged source of Greek *chalbane* and English GALBANUM. Found in *Exodus 30:34*, this pungent spice ingredient is also defined as "gum," the principle glue of antiquity. The root of KHELBHINA is חלב / KHELEBH (fat), matching the IE base of CLEAVE (*gleibh*), while the extended form fits the German term *kleben*, an official cognate of CLEAVE.

> **BRANCHES:** CLEVIS, CLOVE, and GALE are related, the last two being pungent spices. LAVENDER has a sweeter aroma, and better fits another Biblical spice, לבנה / LEVONĀ (frankincense).
> The dictionary links CLAMMY to CLAY and GLUE, via a reduced IE base *glei* (to stick together). CLAMMY seems closer to חלמה / KHĀLMĀ (potter's clay) than to these KH-L-V words.
> More interpretively, to CLEAVE is to be faithful. At the name CALEB (כלב / KHĀLĀV in *Numbers 26:65*) the dictionary states, "Hebrew . . . , literally dog; hence, faithful." כלב / KĒLĀV is to baste together.
> קרבה / KĒRVĀ (contact, nearness and relationship) cleaves to this entry after an L to R change.
> More חלב / KHĀLEV (fat) and the IE root *leip* (to stick, adhere, fat) at "LIVER."

CLEAV(ER)/חַלָּף
KHAL-UFF   [KH-L-F]

ROOTS: Anglo-Saxon *cleofan* is the source of CLEAVE (to cut, slice); further etymons like IE base *gleubh* are more related to the cutting a barber (גלב / GĀLĀBH – *Ezekiel 5:8*) would do. חלף / KHĀLĀF is to pierce and חלף / KHĀLUF is the sharp butcher's knife best defined as a CLEAVER. See the "knives" of *Ezra 1:9*).

> **BRANCHES:** CLEFT, CLIP, CROP, CLAIVE (a sword) HALD and HALVE (which meant cut, divided) and the sharp (S)CALPEL are all related to terms like חלפית / KHĀPĒT (swordfish) and כלף / KĀLUF (ax).
> The shoulder blade, the (S)CAPULA, looks like the blade of a cleaver; to hear this relationship, reduce (S)CAPULA to KPL and switch the L and P. If you swap the S and K of כתף / KĀSĀPH (shoulder) you could also get SCAP(ULA).

Cognates of CLEAVE at IE *gleubh* (to cut, cleave) include: CLEVER, CLEVIS, CLOVE, GLYPH, HIEROGLYPHIC and KLOOF.

A ל / L to N change, might have allowed Anglo-Saxon *gnif* (source of KNIFE) to come from כלף / KLF or חלף / KH-L-F. *Gan-ib(et)* is a knife in Basque. *Kila* is a blade in Hawaiian.

See "CARVER" and "HARROW."

CLIM(ATE)/עוֹלָם
KHOLE-UM   [KLM]

ROOTS: CLIMATE comes from Greek *klima* (region, zone). The correct, guttural pronunciation of עולם / OLUM (world, eternity) is really KHŌLUM. Especially in the Aramaic עלמא / OLMA or KHOLMĀ (world), the sense is clearly the habitable region and not a planet. In Scripture the term infers time zones ("ages" in *Ecclesiastes 1:10*), while the rabbinic phrase עולם הבא / OLUM HĀBĀ (the world to come) suggests a twilight zone or afterlife beyond the realms of time and space. The antonym עלם / OLUM or KHOLUM (to disappear) is a spacial term, not a temporal one.

> **BRANCHES:** Perhaps REALM is related, if the R is unhistoric. REALM is currently linked with "regal."
> CLIME is another form of CLIMATE. As for the other CLIMB, as in INCLINE and CLIMAX, one might connect this word to סולם / SOOLUM (ladder) through the Greek *klimax* (ladder) and the hard C (K), soft C (S) confusion. The alleged Indo-European root of CLIMATE and LEAN (to rest) is *klei* (to lean). LEAN and LOUNGE (to loll – origin unknown) may link up with לון / LOON (to rest or stop for the night; to remain) and the LEAN –TO (hut) with the מלונה / [MI]LOONA (hut).

CLOT/קלוט
CULL-LOOT   [KLT]

ROOTS: A CLOT is a thick coagulated mass or semisolid lump. Anglo-Saxon *clott* is a round mass, related to Dutch *kloot* and German *klotz* (lump, block) via the Germanic base *klutto*. The etymology goes on to an IE base *gel* (to form into a ball . . .or coagulated lump).

קלוט / KĀLOOT means closed up. In the Talmud it specifically refers to an uncloven hoof, reminiscent of CLEAT (a wedge for the heel). In *Leviticus 22:23* it is rendered "contracted," while elsewhere the term refers to a limp. גלד / GELEDT in *Job 16:15* is translated "sore" (University of Chicago); the verb is defined as "growing skin over a wound." To cover CLEAT, גלדה / GILDĀ is a sole (of a shoe).

> **BRANCHES:** The bumbling blockhead or CLOD relates to several ways of rendering קלוט / KĀLOOT. The German KLUTZ or Yiddish KLOTZ is another such clumsy clod. Relevant words listed under IE root *gel* (to form into a ball) include CLOUD, CLOUT, CLUTCH, GLEET, GLUTEUS and GLUTINOUS. Other cognates massed under *gel* will be found at "CONGLOMERATE."
> Words like CLOSE, CLOSET and CLOISTER don't sound like they relate to קלוט / KĀLOODT until one notes their Latin source *claud(ere)* (to close).
> Latin *occludo* (to close up) opens up OCCULT for us. A ק / K to

H change reveals an HLD English word from קלט / KLT. To HOLD is to restrain, contain or close up in a HOLDING pen. קלט / KOLADT is to retain; criminals are HELD in cities of מקלט / (MI)KLAT (asylum) for rehabilitation according to Bibilical law. Translated as cities of "refuge" in *Numbers 35:11*, these are more precisely cities of detention.

קלט / KLT does contain echoes of asylum, as קל / KAL means swift and מלט / (MA)LÄT is to escape or "light out." To reinforce this entry, however, the antonymous restraint of the לט / L-DT phoneme is relevant. See "LID" (from HLD and KL etymons) for more containment and covering up. For an LT reversal, see "TILE."

COAL/נֶחָלֶ(ת)
GAH-KHELE(T)   [GHL→KL]

ROOTS: COAL is related to german *kohl* (charcoal) and Irish *gual* (charcoal), and is attributed to the IE root *g(e)ulo* (a glowing coal).

נחלי אש / GÄHÄLÄ (ÄSH) are the "glowing coals" of *Leviticus 16:12*. The singular נחלת / GÄHE(LET) is a glowing coal; נחל / GEHAL is a burning coal. All the G's in the etymology of COAL reinforce the contention that the √G often becomes a K (or hard C) in its IE permutations.

> **BRANCHES:** נחל / GAHAL (to burn – Arabic) and the IE root *ker* (heat, fire) are relevant.
> See "ALCOHOL," "ALKALI" and "CHAR."
> The engineered antonyms of G/K-L/R words like נחלת / GÄHELET (coal), קלי / KÄLE (toast), חרה / KHÄRÄ (kindle) and בור / KOOR (furnace) include קר / KÄR (cold) and קרח / KERAH (ice) – see "CRYOGENICS."
> Given cognates of COAL include CHOLLA, COLLIE and COLLIER.

COIF(FURE)/קוֹבַע
COVE-AH   [K-BH-A]

ROOTS: COIFFURE, a headdress or hairstyle, is an extension of COIF. COIF, a cap, is a French term traced to the late Latin word for helmet – *cofea*.

קובע / KOBHÄ is the "helmet" of *I Samuel 17:38*.

> **BRANCHES:** COIFFEUR is a hairdresser.
> See "CAP."

COIN/קָנָה
CONE-EH   [KN]

ROOTS: COIN is metallic money with a designated weight and value, and to COIN is to designate or name.

כנה / KEENÄ (to name – *Isaiah 45:4*) is thus an appropriate etymon.

Our dictionary attributes COIN to Latin *cuneus* (wedge or corner), a term cognate with QUOIN (exterior angle of a wall). QUOIN is pronounced "kwoin." COIN and QUOIN are from קרן / KEREN (corner – *Exodus 27:2*). [The R to W speech defect demonstrates how "kwoin" can come from KEREN. In the same way, WEAVE, WEFT, WOOF and Anglo-Saxon *owef* come from ערב / ÄREV (woof).]

Also consider a more monetary K-N term, קנה / KONÄ (to acquire, purchase) – a verb related to the COINAGE or name given to greedy CAIN in *Genesis 4:1*.

> **BRANCHES:** עֶרֶן / ÄYÄN or KEEÄN means to weigh – it might link up with the Japanese YEN. GAIN (to acquire) may be another derivative of קנה / KÄNÄ (to acquire, buy, possess). The opposite of possession is that have-not state of קנאה / KENÄ (envy).
> *Chin* and *ch'ien* are money and coin in Chinese.
> In Japanese *okane* is money and *kin* is gold. For the Eskimos *kinauyak* is coin and *akkinga* is price. *Kou mai* is purchase in Chinese.
> The קונה / KONEH is the possessor or owner, synonymous with husband or king in many cultures. *Kun* or *kina* is husband in several dialects of the Uto-Aztec Indians around Arizona. *Kane* is husband in Hawaiian, where the word for KING is *kini*.
> The root of מקנה / MIKNE (cattle, property) is קנה / KÄNÄ (to buy) because cattle or KINE were the KINETIC movable property used for COIN or currency.
> For the ICON or likeness on many coins, see "COMMON."

COLL(AR)/עֹל
KHOLE   [KL]

ROOTS: Latin *collare* is a band or chain for the neck: *collum* is neck.

על / KHOLE or ÖL is a collar or yoke, as in *Genesis 27:40*.

> **BRANCHES:** COLET and MACHICOLATE are from Latin *collum* but CARCANET reveals a French etymon – *carcan* (iron collar) – with a C-R instead of a C-L. This strengthens the case for Hebrew words like ערף / KHÖREF or OREF (neck), גרון / GÄRÖN (neck, throat), and גרגרת / GÄRGERET (windpipe).
> *Kall* is the word for neck in all dialects of the Maya Indians of Yucatan, Mexico. For the Chinese collar, reverse is *li(n)g. Kaulua* is a yoke in Hawaiian.
> ACCOLADE, ANCILLARY, COL and COLLET are cognates of COLLAR at the IE root *k(w)el* (to revolve, move around, sojourn, dwell).
> See "CYCLE," "GARCLE," "GIRAFFE" and "SCARF."

COLOSS(US)/גָּלְיָת
GOL-EOUS   [GLYS→KLOS]

ROOTS: The adjective COLOSSAL dates back at least to the giant *kolossos* (no known meaning) statue spanning Rhodes harbor. If an actual giant stood there it would be that most famous giant of the Bible – referring to *I Samuel 17:4* and גלית / GOLIOS (Goliath). The Greek pronunciation would sound like "kol-ios" – just as the גמל / GÄMÄL (camel) was rendered *kamelos*, and יעקב / YÄ'ÄKÖV (Jacob) was heard as *Iakobos*.

> **BRANCHES:** Whether or not Goliath founded (or sacked) the city of Colossae, *collosseus* got to mean gigantic by the time the Roman COLOSEUM was built.
> The COLLOSSUS was supposedly a statue of Apollo. Greek *apollyon* means "destroying." Were there marauding giants whom the Greeks subsequently deified? Such were Goliath's ancestors, the (N)ephilim who carried off "the daughters of man" (the stuff of many a Greek legend) and the same Anakim (race of giants)

who "were the heroes of old, the men of renown" (*Genesis 6:2-4*).

The root letters of נפלים / NEPHILIM (those who have landed, those who APPALL or make others FALL), like those of Apollo and the devilish Apollyon, are the letters P and L.

See "FALL" and "OGRE."

COMMO(N)/כְּמוֹ
KIM-O   [KM]

ROOTS: This COMMON word is from Latin *com* (together, with). French *comme* and Spanish *como* are even more COMPLETELY COMPARABLE with כמו / KIMO (as, like – *Genesis 41:39*), עם / KHIM or EEM (with – *Genesis 24:58*), and גם / GUM (also – *Genesis 3:6*). The essence of togetherness, of COMMUNITY, is the עם / KHUM or UM (nation).

BRANCHES: COM- and CON- are prolific prefixes. The *COMBINING* form within *COMPANY, COMPETE,* and a whole *COMPLEX* of *COM*PANION terms reduces down to the prefix CO-. Similarly -כ / K' is a prefix letter in Hebrew meaning "as," "like," or "approximately."

A CUM LAUDE (with praise) graduate owes that "with" to עם / KHIM (with). This term, along with גם / GÄM (also), relates to "together" words like GAM-, GAMETE, GEMINI, JAM and JOIN. *Cooma* means "together" in Australian Aborigine. The prefix in *COENOCYTE* is from Greek *koinos* (common). *CENOBITE* (a monk) is from the same Greek source.

The more COMMON prefix is the related HOMO-, from Greek *homos* (the same). Again, the Hebrew gutturals above prove to be HOMOGENEOUS with the English H. Hebrew offers insights into English HOMOGRAPHS, HOMONYMS AND HOMO-PHONES. HOMEOPATH displays a variant of HOMO-, while the Greek *homos* is almost invisile in ANOMALY.

The suffix *-kin* means "too", "also" and "likewise" in Finnish. AKIN and AGAIN may be distant kin.

The IE root *kom* (with, near, beside) is from עם / KHĒM (with, close to – *Genesis 24:58*). The root includes CO-, COENO- and COM- words, CON, CONTRA-, CONTRARY, COUNTER, COUNTRY (עם / KHUM is a nation), CUM, ENCOUNTER and ENOUGH.

Note the reversal of עם /ĒM in Indo-Pacific words for "with" – *me* (Hawaiian), *ma* (Tahitian and Samoan) – and the Japanese term for "together" (*mei*). *Kuma* is "together" in Australian Aborigine.

(CON)GLOM(ERATE)/גֹּלֶם
GOLEM   [GL]

ROOTS: Latin *conglomerare* is to roll together; *glomus* is a ball. גלם / GOLUM is to wrap, fold together – *II Kings 2:8*; גלל / GALAL is to roll (*Isaiah 34:4*). A big business CON-GLOMERATE may be a well-ordered operation, but a CONGLOMERATION in geology, for instance, means "clustered into a rounded mass." גלם / GOLEM is shapeless matter, a fetus or a lump (*Psalms 139:16*) – hence a term for clods or blockheads.

The IE root is *gel* (to form into a ball). In Hebrew there's: גלגל / GULGUL (wheel), גלגול / GILGOOL (rolling), גליל / GÄLEEL (spool, cylinder, and the *rolling* hills or the Galilee), גלל / GÄLÄL (dung) and גל / GULL (wave, pile). אגל / OGÄL (*Job 38:28*) is a collection or drop of material.

BRANCHES: The IE root is too much of an AGGLOMERATE, with cognates like CLOD and CLEAT which are found at "CLOT." Terms under *gel* that deserve mention are: CLUB, CLUMP, CLEW, CLOWN, CLUE, GLOBE, GLOBULE, CLAM, CLAMBER, CLAMP, CLIMB, CLENCH, CLINCH, CLING, CLUTCH, CLAY, GLEET, GLEY, GLUE and GLUTINOUS.

JUM(B)LE is more likely a jumble of גלם / GLM than a "merging of *jump* with *tumble, fumble,* etc." [*Webster's*].

(CON)SULT/שְׁאֵלְתָּה
S(H)'AIL-TAH   [S(H)-U-L]

ROOTS: Latin *consultare* is from *consulere* (to consider, deliberate, ask advice). Our CONSULT also means to seek information or to ask advice. The Latin term, however, is further broken down to *com* (with) plus a Gothic base related to "sell."

"To ask" in Hebrew is שאל / S(H)ÄUL (*Genesis 24:47, Exodus 13:4*). To retain the "T" of CONSULTATION, there is שאלתה / S(H)'ÄLTÄ (an official inquiry – from the Aramaic of *Daniel 4:14*).

BRANCHES: There is no IE root ascribed to CONSULT and it is unclear if CONSULAR, CONSULATE and COUNSELOR are related. These terms are also linked to SELL (to give up and deliver). Germanic *seljan* (to offer up, deliver), Old Norse *sola* (sale) and Anglo-Saxon *sellan* (to sell, deliver to) form the background to words like SELL, SALE and HANDSEL. The IE root of these three words is *sel* (to take).

שלל / S(H)ÄLÄL is to take. The Hebrew etymon best fitting the terms of "giving up" and "delivering" above is שלח / S(H)OLAH (to send off, extend, delegate – *Genesis 44:3, Genesis 32:4, II Kings 2:2*).

שליח / S(H)ÄLEÄH (delegate, agent) might also make a fine etymon for CONSUL (a nation's representative). השאיל / (HĒ)S(H)ÊL is to lend or LEASE (SL reversed). LEASE is now linked to "lax." The built-in antonym is seen in the noun שאלה / S(H)'ÄLÄ (loan, inquiry, problem).

Usul is a proposal in Indonesian.

COP/חֲפַן
KHAP-UN   [KH-P]

ROOTS: To COP is to seize; a COP is the fellow paid to seize those who COP (slang for steal). The given etymon is "probably" Latin *capere* (to take). חפן / KHÄPHÄN (to take a handful – *Exodus 9:8*) and כף / KUF (palm of the hand) point to a KH-P two-letter root. פח / PUKH (trap – *Ecclesiastes 9:12*) and הפח / HÄPHUKH (to ensnare) – reverse KH-P to P-KH. Related is GYPING or COPPING. קפח / KOPHAH is to steal, but it's not a Biblical word.

BRANCHES: While CAPABLE, CAPACIOUS and CAPACITY seem to belong with Latin *capere* and the Hebrew words of hand-CAPACITY, there are terms like CAPTIVATE, CAPTIVE, and CAPTURE that suggest a K-PT root. These KPT words, may relate, via metathesis, to חטף / KHÄTÄPH (to snatch) or חתף / KHÄTÄPH (to seize).

COPACETIC/הַכֹּל בְּצֶדֶק
(HA)-CA(LL) B'TSED-ECK   [K)L] + (T)S-(D)T-K]

ROOTS: COPACETIC means "all is well" in slang. The *Dictionary of American Slang* suggests הכל בסדר / (HA)KŌL B'SADER (everything is in order) or הכל בצדק / (HA)KŌL B'(T)SEDTEK (everything is just right or "squared away").

BRANCHES: A similar borrowing involves the word כשר / KÄSHER (ritually fit). A business deal can be KOSHER (o.k., "on the up and up," or legitimate).

CORAL/גּוֹרָל
GORE-ULL   [GRL→KRL]

ROOTS: Marine CORAL is traced beyond the Greek *korallion* to Hebrew גורל / GŌRÄL (pebble) and to Arabic *garal* (small stone). Such pebbles were used as lots to designate the scapegoat in *Leviticus 16:8.*

BRANCHES: גרעין / GÄREN is a stone or kernel; נרגר / GERGÄR is a berry or pill.
Again the Hebrew √G becomes an English K – see "CAMEL." CALCULATE, CALCULUS, and CROCODILE (Greek *kroke* is a pebble) are related. GRAVEL appears when one swaps letters #2 and #3 of גורל / G-V-R-L. GRAVEL might also be seen in the Aramaic term ערבל / KHERVÄL, a mixing term used for cement and concrete making.
CLERGYMEN and CLERKS owe their lot to גורל / GŌRÄL (lot). The Greek term for lot, *kleros*, gave rise to CLERIC and CLERK because members of the CLERGY were chosen by lot. Greek *klerikos* (clergyman, priest) is reduced to *clero* (clergy) in Spanish, Italian and Portuguese. C-L-R is but a #2-#3 letter flip from K-R-L or G-R-L in the Hebrew.

CORE/עקר
EE-CORE   [KR]

ROOTS: The CORE of fruit contains the seeds. עקר / ÄKER, in *Leviticus 25:47*, means seed or offspring. To CORE a fruit is to remove its seedcase. עקר / OKUR is to uproot (*Ecclesiastes 3:2*); עקרה / ÄKÄRÄ is barren (*Genesis 11:30*).
The textbook etymon is a "probably" for Latin *cor* (heart), making CORE and COURAGE to be cognates.
עקר / EKORE (root, principal, stump, nerve – *Leviticus 25:47, Daniel 4:12*) is the essence or CORE of a thing. Greek *kardia* (heart, stomach, orifice) implies a central pit in our anatomy. A pit or grape-stone is a חרצן / KHÄRTS(ÄN) or HÄRTS(ÄN). חריץ / KHÄRETS or HÄRETS is a trench.

BRANCHES: An extended form is מקור / MÄKORE (source, spring, origin). גרעין / GÄREEN is a fruit core or kernel, sharing a K-R core with חרצן / KHORZ(ON) – a grape kernel.
Corazon, center and heart in Spanish, might also link up with a #1-#2 letter flip of *markaz* in Arabic or מרכז / (ME)RKÄZ (center). Whether seen as seat of human emotions or of blood circulation, the heart is our רכזת / RÄKEZET (switchboard). חרצב / KHÄRTS(ŌV) or HART(ŌV) is pain (*Psalms 73:4*)
If IE *kerd* (heart) can be successfully linked to one of the Hebrew terms above, then words like ACCORD, CARDIAC, CARDIO-, CORDATE, CORDIAL, COURAGE, CREDENCE, CREDIBLE, CREDIT, CREDO, CREDULOUS, GRANT, HEART,

MISCREANT, PERICARDIUM, RECORD and RECREANT all belong here.
The Russian and Slavic word for "root" is *koren.*
A'kar is a root in Malay. Other forms of עקר / EKAR or GEKOR (root) include Hungarian *gyoker* and Finnish *juuri.* Reverse KR and change R to W for the Fijian root (*waka*); it links up with Malay: Teor *woki* (root) and (reversing letters) Malay: Mysol *aikowa* (root).
See "GRAIN."

CORN/גֹּרֶן
GO-REN   [GRN→KRN]

ROOTS: The IE root of CORN is *gra-no* (grain). גרן / GŌREN is "corn of the threshing floor" in *Job 39:12.* More at "GRAIN."

CORNER/קֶרֶן
CARE-EN   [KRN]

ROOTS: CORNER is from Latin *cornu,* a horn or projecting point. קרן / KEREN is a horn, corner or extending ray. Neither the holy altar nor Moses had horns coming out of them. For the "horns" given Moses by Michelangelo see "CORONA." In *Leviticus 27:2* –"make *horns* for it on its four corners"– it is a CORNICE (molding atop a wall or building) or a QUOIN (external corner of a building) that is meant by קרן / KEREN. (QUOIN is pronounced "kwoin," a slight corruption of KEREN.)

BRANCHES: GORE and GROIN are CORNICULATE terms or CORNER words. In the talmud, קרנות / K'RONŌS are street corners. Polish reverses to *rog,* which means "horn" and "corner" as well.
A corner is an extremity, extreme in Russian is *krainye.*
See "UNICORN" for animal horns.

CORN(ET)/קֶרֶן
KEREN   [KRN]

ROOTS: This trumpet or horn is from Latin *cornu* (a horn). CORNET and HORN are ultimately from קרן / KEREN (horn).
See "UNICORN."

CORNU(COPIA)/קֶרֶן
KEREN   [KRN]

ROOTS: Literally, a horn of plenty – see the previous entry and "UNICORN."

BRANCHES: The Assyrian horn is *qarnu.*

CORONA/קֶרֶן
COR-EN   [KRN]

ROOTS: Anything crown-like, such as the halo of light around the sun, is a CORONA. Latin *corona* is a crown, but the experts have erred in citing Greek *korone* (anything curved or bent, wreath – see "CURVE.").

Both CORONA and the CROWN are named for hornlike rays of extending light and not for any circle these rays might form. קרן / KEREN is a ray, extension, or horn. קרן / KOREN means shining and radiating (emitting a CORONA of light beams); "Moses' face was *radiant*" in *Exodus 34:29-30*. Michelangelo's statue of Moses shouldn't have included two horns on the head. He needed 7 or 8 extensions or rays of light to resemble the CORONA–CROWN on the Statue of Liberty. The original CROWNS were not bejeweled hats, like some CORONETS, but were raised spikes or horns connected by a band.

Habukuk 3:4 offers a resplendent CORONA which will help art historians understand the halos of light crowning saints, etc.:
"His splendor fills the earth. It is a brilliant light which gives off *rays* on every side – and therein His glory is enveloped." קרנים.

BRANCHES: A COROLLA or garland of flower petals (another example of Hebrew N/נ flipping over to an L) reinforces the picture of a CROWN as projectiles ringing a center rather than the CROWN as a ring or flat tiara. The KRL of COROLLA might also link up with כליל / K'LEEL (garland, crown).

Since קרן / KOREN is shining, other bright and beaming things to consider include the CARNATION, CORNEA, CRANBERRY, GERANIUM, GLANCE, GLEAM, GLIMPSE, GRAY (also from the IE root *gher* (to shine, glow), GREEN, KRONA (and other coin words).

See "CORNER," "CROWN," and "UNICORN."

COTTON/כֻּתָּן
KEY-TON   [KTN]

ROOTS: COTTON is acknowledged to be from Arabic *qutun*, coming to the West via Spanish.

Aramaic כתן / KETON is usually rendered as "flax" or "linen." כתנה / KOOTNÄ is the modern Hebrew word for cotton, while כתנת / KITONET (shirt, coat, garment) is the term used for Joseph's "coat" of many colors in *Genesis 37:3*.

Flax in Arabic is *kittan*; in Swahili it's *kitani*; the Turkish is *keten*.

BRANCHES: The Biblical Hebrew word above is credited as the source of CHITON (a tunic). TUNIC is an anagram of these KTN Semitic words. The Maya cloak is a *qetón*.

A TUNICLE is a clerical vestment much like a COTTA, a tunic in Late Latin. COTTA is linked to Germanic *kotta* (coarse cloth), but COTTA or COAT is not subsequently traced to כתן / KETON (linen).

COAT can otherwise be linked to עטה / KHÄTÄ and עטף / KHOTÄF (to wrap oneself). In *I Samuel 28:14* great Samuel's ghost is seen "wrapped" (עטה) in a coat. The Lord is "clothed. . .*wrapped* in a robe of light" in *Psalms 104:1-2*.

Both the עיט / KHÄYIT (vulture) and the עטלף / KHÄTÄLEF (bat) are uniquely wrapped or draped in their wings when in repose.

COAT is traced to Anglo-Saxon *kot* (a coarse outer garment); reverse KT for *takki* (coat in Finnish). The Roman TOGA might be derived from a similar reversal of עט / G-T or G-D. A *dogi* is a karate uniform in Japanese.

Swap the F and T of עטיפה / KHÄTEFÄ (a wrapping) to hear CAFTAN or KAFTAN (robe – from Turkish *qaftan*). The Hungarian *kabat* (coat) and Serbo-Croatian *kaput* (coat) are cut from the same cloth.

The Arabic coat, *mitaf*, uses the מ / M prefix and does not gutturalize the ע. The modern Hebrew term for cover, envelope or pillowcase is מעטפה / M'ÄTÄFÄ.

קדקד / KODKOD (crown of the head – see "HEAD") is another K-D/T protective word, so that HAT, HOOD, HIDE and COAT can ultimately fit into the same closet. The IE root *kadh* (to shelter, cover) includes HEED, HAT, and HOOD.

HIDE might also relate to חוץ / KHOOTS (outside, exterior – see "EXIT") or הדה / HADA (to stretch out).

For one more thread in this K-T entry that ties COTTON to COAT, consider that חוט / KHOOT is a "thread."

COUL(D)/יָכוֹל
(YAH)-KHOLE   [Y-KH-L]

ROOTS: COULD is the past of "can." Its etymology is very suspect, and no IE root is ventured. The *Oxford English Dictionary* speculates that the spelling was altered, influenced by "should" and "would."

All agree that the "D" is unhistoric; the "D" might be an "ed" past tense suffix added to the original CL or KL term. יכל / (YÄ)KHOL means "could." (*Genesis 45:1*)

BRANCHES: יכול / (YÄ)KHOL means "able to," "can" or "capable." It is used to speculate on what "could be."

יכלת / (YI)KHOL(ET) means "power" or "ability" – recalling the IE root *gal* (to be able, to have power). GALLIARD is a given cognate of Gallo-Roman *galia* (strength, power).

Gallu means "ability" in Cymric (Wales).

COUPLE/כָּפַל
COUGH-ULL   [K-P(H)-L]

ROOTS: The IE root of COUPLE is *ap* (to take, reach). COUPLE (from Latin *copula*) is seen as a cognate of CABLE and COPULATE.

כפל / KOPHUL is to double, multiply or fold; כפלים / KIPHL(ÄYIM) means twice as much; כפיל / KOPHEL is double or "spit and image"; מכפלה / (MA)CHPELAH in *Genesis 23:9* is the two-story burial cave of the ancestral COUPLES; קפל / KEPHEL is a fold or multiplication; קפל / KÄPHEL means double. First חבר / KHEBUR and then כפל / KOPHUL make a compatible twosome in *Exodus 26:9*–". . .you shalt *couple*. . .and you shalt *double* over. . ."

BRANCHES: Add to the above Hebrew term נבל / KÄVÄL (to plait – *Exodus 26:9*) and note that IE root *plek* (to plait) is an anagram of כפל / KPL. The more common words traced to *plek* include: APPLY, COMPLEX, COMPLICATE, DEPLOY, DISPLAY, DUPLEX, FLAX, DUPLICATE, GENUFLECT, INFLECTION, MULTIPLY, PERPLEX, PLEXUS, PLIANT, QUINTUPLE, REPLICA(TE), SUPPLE, and SUPPLICATE.

The Maya Indian word *u-ka-pul* (for the second time) and the Hawaiian word *palua* (couple) are two more COUPLINGS in the great chain of human languages.

The IE root *pel* (to fold) brings us FOLD as well as DECUPLE, DIPLOID and other -PLOID words, MANIFOLD and other - FOLD words, MULTIPLE, OCTUPLE, QUADRUPLE, SEPTUPLE, SEXTUPLE, and TRIPLE.

Polish terms like *falda* (fold, pleat, crease) are welcomed into the fold because they point back to the literal folding over of the Hebrew etymon. *Pelu* is to fold, hem or tuck in Hawaiian and Proto-Polynesian. *Kupola* is to roll, wrap up or curl up in Hawaiian. See "CABLE."

COURT/קַרְתָּא
CART-AH   [K-R-T]

ROOTS: Latin *cohors* and *cohortis* mean an enclosed place; the first definition of COURT is an uncovered space surrounded by walls or buildings. Keeping in mind that cities were walled, note Aramaic קרתא / KURTÄ [city] and קרת / KERET ("city" in *Proverbs 8:3*). COURT as royal palace is closer in meaning, however, to terms like קריה / KIRYÄ (town, center). The phrase *"city of the great king"* (קרית / KIRYAT) in *Psalms 48:3* is in the context of a "palace."

The law or basketball COURT refers to the walls which set off the court. קיר / KEER is a wall (*Leviticus 14:37*); the city wall was the traditional site of legal procedures.

The word that specifically means court, and a royal court in *Esther 1:5* is חצר / KHÄTSER. A metathesis of KH-TS-R to KH-R-T(S) will sound much like COURT. The given IE root of COURT is *gher* (to grasp, enclose); this resembles חגור / HAGOR (gird)—see "GIRDLE."

> **BRANCHES:** CHORUS, COHORT, and CURTAIN, HORTICULTURE and ORCHARD are from the IE root *gher* (to enclose—see"GIRDLE").
> Words like COURTEOUS and COURTLY are associated with COURT, but they may derive from a different Hebrew etymon —see "CURTSY."
> קרתה / KARTA or KARTHA was a town in the tribal province of Zebulun; perhaps CARTHAGE is a related place name.
> The IE root *carcer* (enclosure) ought to link up with COURT—See "INCARCERATE."

COVER/כָּפַר
CUFF-ARE   [K-PH]

ROOTS: The dictionary credits this to Latin *co* (intensifier + *operire* (to hide).

When Noah was told to *"cover* [the ark] inside and out with pitch" the word used was כפר / KOPHUR. חפא / KHÄPHÄ (cover, case), חפה / KHOOPÄ (canopy), חפיפה / KHÄPHEPHÄ (covering), קבע / KOBHÄ (helmet), קבר / KEBHER (grave), חבא or חבה / KHÄBHÄ (to hide) and כפרת / KÄPORES (covering on the holy ark) seem to cover the etymology more successfully.

> **BRANCHES:** יחף / YÄKHÄPH (barefoot) is an antonym.
> עפר / KEPAR means covered with dust.
> More at "CAB," "CAP," and "EVENING."

CRAB/עֲקְרָב
(AH)-CRUBH   [KRB]

ROOTS: The official etymology would have the CRAB mean "the scratcher," from Old High German *krebitz*, French *ecrevisse* (whence CRAYFISH), and the IE root *gerebh* (to scratch).

See "CARVER," "SCRAPER" and חרב / KHEREBH (knife, sharp tool) if you prefer the given source of CRAB.

Other Hebrew etymons appear to offer a fuller sense of the animal. עקרב / (Ä)KRÄBH is a "scorpion" (*I Kings 12:11*), but the term should be considered a generic term for similar hard-shelled crustaceans.

ערב / ÄROV or KHÄROBH signifies beetles and other hard-shelled arachnids—see "SCARAB."

The Greek word for crab is *kharkhinos* (hard-shelled creature). KR in Hebrew means hard, as seen in Aramaic קרקפתא / KÄRKÄFTÄ (skull) and קרן / KEREN (horn—see "UNICORN"). CANCER (crab) is from the IE root *kar* (hard).

> **BRANCHES:** Hard covered plants and animals in the KRB family may be seen at "CAROB" and "CARP."
> The קרב / KEREBH (animal innards—*Exodus 12:9*) lies exposed, beneath the CRAB's armor plating. This militaristic creature creeps or קרב / KORÄBH (approaches gradually, nears) for battle or קרב / KRÄBH (battle, warfare—*Psalms 144:1*) shielded by its CARAPACE or קליפה / KLEPÄ (shell—see "CALIPEE"). The crab, in short, is nature's CORVETTE (warship).
> The GRIBBLE (shrimp, crab) and the GRUB (the young of beetles), along with the CRAB and the CRAYFISH are diggers more than scratchers. A #2-#3 letter flip of חפר / KHOPHÄR (to dig) or קבר / KHOHÄR (to bury) ought to be considered here too. To GRUB is to dig or bore. GRUBBY (dirty) originally meant that maggots, etc. had infested or dug their way into something.
> Returning to CREEPY things that CRAW(L) with the belly, CRAW, or CROP near the ground, there's the עכבר / ÄKBÄR (mouse or rodent) and the COBRA to consider. Greek *herpein* (to crawl, creep) is allegedly a cognate of "serpent." *Kulipee* is to creep in Hawaiian.
> The modern Hebrew term for crab is סרטן/SÄRTÄN (the scratcher). Modern scholars went to the German model because they could not find a CRAB or crabness among Biblical Hebrew words.

CRACK/חֲרַק
KHAR-UCK   [KH-R-K]

ROOTS: A CRACK is a crevice, chink and "narrow opening as between boards" as well as a sudden, sharp noise. Only the noisy CRACK is assigned an IE root—*ger* (to cry out)—see "CRY" and "CREAK."

To fill the etymological CRACK or gap here, consider חרק / KHEREK (notch, incision). The "narrow openings between boards" sense of CRACK may be seen in *Songs 2:9*, where "cracks" is a far better translation than "lattice." (Lattice window construction is not found in the ancient Middle East.)

> **BRANCHES:** חרק / KHÄRÄK is an extension of חור / KHOR (hole); ריק / RÄK means empty. חלוקה / KHELOOKÄ is a partition or division; קרע / KORÄ or KORUKH is to rip.
> A crack implies an interval of space; רחוק / RAKHOK (distant) is derived by a #1-#2 letter swap.
> More at "SCORE."

CREAK/חָרַק
KHA-RUCK   [KH-R-K]

ROOTS: CREAK is dismissed as an echoic word, but the engineering of Hebrew suggests that even some imitative words were not merely spontaneous creations like "boom" or "clunk." חרק / KHÄRUK is the equivalent of CREAK, meaning the gnashing of teeth in *Job 16:9*

> **BRANCHES:** The same חרק / KH-R-K that is defined "squeak, gnash and grind" can also mean "insect." Insects do their share of creaking and chomping, and no insect is more famous for both than the חרגול / KHÄRG(OL) (locust). While the root is חרג / KHÄRUG (to spring or leap), the CROAKing CRICKET or locust is implied in sound and structure.
> צרימה / TSREEKHÄ (squeal) and שריקה / SHREEKÄ (whistle) resemble words like SHREIK, SQUAWK and SCREAK.

CREAM/קרום
KROOM   [KRM]

ROOTS: CREAM is said to be from Middle English *creme* and Late Latin *cramum* (cream).

As the hardened top layer of scum is the essence of CREAM, consider קרום / KROOM (crust, skin, membrane). קרם / KRM is a verb of casing or overlaying in *Ezekiel 37:6,8*.

The KR element means "hard"– see "UNICORN"; the RM element means "raised up"– see "RUM."

> **BRANCHES:** *RAMEKIN* [from German *rahm* (cream)], Finnish *kerma* (cream), and a reversal of Eskimo *amerk* (skin) all may unite only with the letters and meanings of קרום / KROOM.
> Related terms include קרוש / KÄR(OOSH) (curdled, congealed) and עור / KHOR (skin).
> CRUM meant a scraping from bread *crust*.
> Like most slang terms, CREAM (to defeat decisively) is not offered an etymon. החרים / (HE)KHREEM is to destroy; see "HARM."
> קום / KÖM (curd) may be rendered KRM; ו(vav) to R changes are listed at "CZAR."
> The yellowish foam of mild might also be named for the Aramaic yellow – כרום / KROOM.

CREASE/קרם
CORE-US   [KRS]

ROOTS: The dictionaries would have us believe that Old French *creste*, as in the crest or ridge of mountains, has something to do with folding or creasing.

קרם / KORUS (to bend – *Isaiah 46:2*) is the better etymon in sense and sound.

> **BRANCHES:** Go down one letter-number from the end ם / Samekh (60) to נ / Noon (50) to get the less intense bend word קרן / KEREN (corner, angle – see "CORNER." Add one number-letter on the alphabet scale to get קרע / KORU (to rend, tear), a stronger act of bending over.
> קער / KEÄR is to curve; כרע / KORÄ is to kneel, bow, or bend.
> See "CROSS" and "CURTSY."

CRECHE/ערש
KHAIR-ESS   [KH-R-S]

ROOTS: A CRECHE, as in a Christmas nativity display, is from the Old French *cresche* (crib).
ערש / ERES or KHERES is defined as a crib or divan. It is translated "bed" in *Psalms 41:4*, and as "couch" in *Amos 6:4*.

> **BRANCHES:** עריסה / ÄRESÄ or KHÄRESÄ is a child's crib; in *Numbers 15:20* it implies a kneeding trough. Aramaic ערסל / ÄRSOL or KHÄRSOL is a hammock.

CREED/חָרֵד
KHOH-RAID'   [KH-R-D]

ROOTS: CREED is said to be from Latin *credere* (to trust, believe). Searching for historical CREDENTIALS, the dictionary offers the INCREDULOUS etymology: "probably from IE base *kred* (heart) + *dhe* (to place, do)."

חרד / KHÄRÄD is defined as "God-fearing" and as "Orthodox" in different dictionaries. The Concordance offers "reverence." The more literal Bible translations prefer "tremble" for *Isaiah 66:5* –"hear the word of the Lord, ye that *tremble* at His word. . ." The 1978 JPS Bible renders the same phrase, "You who are *concerned* about His word." In both cases, a CREDO of reverential CREDENCE is the issue. The חרד / KH-R-D verb means "rallying to" or "following after" a leader from a sense of fear (*I Samuel 13:7*).

> **BRANCHES:** CREDIT, INCREDIBLE and (S)CARED are some of the more common branches. Godfearing at a lower level [ד (4) rolled back to ג (3)] is merely חרג / KHÄRÄG (to quake). At a higher level [ד (4) up to ה (5)] faith causes action – החרה / (HE)KHERÄH (to do with zeal).
> Wordplay with חרד renders רעד / RÄ-ÄD or RÄ-KHÄD (tremble), and ערץ / KHÄRÄTS (to fear, dread).
> DREAD is possibly related. The initial D might not belong on the IE base *dhredh* (to fear), and חרד can be read HÄRÄD.
> COWARD and Japanese *kowai* (afraid, scared) may ultimately link up.

CRIB/כלוב
KLOOBH   [KLB→KRB]

ROOTS: CRIB now infers a baby's bed with protective bars, but it used to mean a basket or an animal's cage – precisely the two meanings of כלוב / KLOOBH (*Amos 8:1*). Anglo-Saxon *cribb* meant an ox stall, but the dictionary describes the basic sense as "what is woven or plaited, basket."

To CRIB and to basket is old thieves' slang for stealing. Not CRIBBAGE, but CRIBWORK and CRIBIFORM give the basket weaving sense of כלוב / KLOOBH (basket, cage). Its next of kin is ערב / KHÄREBH (woof – *Leviticus 13:49*). While the L to R change is common, the Russian CRIB (*kalibyel*) remains KLB.

> **BRANCHES:** From interweaving terms and baskets like the CORF (Latin *corbis* is a wicker basket), we come to mixing words like GARBLE. GARBLE is credited to Arabic *gharbala*, but the

dictionary goes on to cite Latin *cribrum* (sieve) as the ultimate source.

ערבה/KHĀRĀBHH is a mixing trough, ערב/EREV or KHE-REBH is evening (the time of mixing dark and light), ערב / KHĀREBH is mixture or mixed company, and ערב/KHĀRBH or ĀRĀBH is Arabia. Like Barbary (see "BABBLE") and similar sounding place names, Arabia was named for its mixed race population. In this case, the ARAB people (Ishmael) descend from African royalty (Princess Hagar) and the Semitic Abraham.

Most of the so-called cognates listed under the IE root *ger* (curving, crooked) will be found later at "CURVE"—from קער/KĀER (to curve). CRAFT, CRIB, CROFT, CRA(M)P, CRIPPLE, CRI(M)P, CRU(M)PLE and CRU(M)PET all bend into place with etymons like ערב / KHĀREV (weave).

CRIM(SON)/כֶּרֶם
KERE – EM   [KRM]]

ROOTS: Both CRIMSON and CARMINE are official borrowings from Arabic *qirmizi* (scarlet).

If the Sanskrit *krmi* (insect) is any indication, the Arabic term might also derive from an insect or רמה/REEMĀ (vermin, see "WORM") which is used for a red dye.

II Chronicles 2:6 offers a more direct route with כרמיל/KĀRMĒL ("crimson"). Since ל/L to N changes are common (especially between Malayo-Polynesian languages and between the Cantonese and Mandarin dialects of Chinese), CARMINE (purple, crimson) is especially close to כרמיל / KĀRMEEL (crimson). For the purplish hue, or wine color, note the root word כרם/KEREM (vineyard and other wine words – *Genesis 9:20*). Joseph T. Shipley links this Hebrew term to CARMINE.

BRANCHES: As "vermin" came from רמה/REMĀ (vermin) so VERMILLION (vivid red) derived from כרמיל/(K)ĀRMĒL (crimson).

Hebrew relatives include חמר/KHĀMER or HĀMER (wine), קרן/KŌREN (shining, flaming), כלם/KELEM (to be red-faced or ashamed) and חומר/KHOMER (red clay).

CRANBERRY is linked to the same etymon as CRIMSON.

Red in Turkish is *kirmizi*, but the red-KRM connection fades to Serbo-Croatian *crven* and Malay dialect *kohor*. Russian *krasni* (red) may be switching the N/M and the S/Z from its Turkish counterpart above.

Arabic *ahmar* (red) and other MR red words may be seen at "MAROON."

CROSS/כֶּרֶם
KER-ESS   [KRS]

ROOTS: CROSS is linked to CURVE, to the IE base *(s)qreu-q* and to IE roots like *ger* (curing, crooked) which ignore the S's. See "CURVE" [from קער/KĀER (to curve)] but an etymon with an S added on to a similar קר/KR root would be most appropriate. The Old Norse cross (*kross*), as well as the Old Irish (*cros*) and Old French one (*cruis*), end in an S. Even the Latin crux or *crucis* (cross) encourages one to unearth the original CROSS with its S intact.

To quote the definition, a CROSS is an upright "beam," with another beam "fastened" horizontally, upon which the noble Romans would CRUCIFY convicted innocents. The *fastening* of boards and the *impaling* of hands and feet, as

well as the CROSS-WISE shape of a CROTCH or CROSS, all recall the term קרס/KERES (hook, clasp – *Exodus 26:11*). קרס/KORUS is to bow or bend (*Isaiah 46:2*). קרסל/KĀRSOL is a joint or ankle, and ערסל/KHIRSAL is to cross (one's legs). If a beam is crucial to a *CRUC*IFIX or any CRISS-CROSS shape, there is קרש/KERES(H) (board, plank – *Exodus 26:23*) to consider.

BRANCHES: Many of the following words are better linked to the Hebrew etymons above: ACROSS, CLASP, CREASE, CRESCENT, CRISP, CROCHET(Y), CRUISE, CRUSADE, CRUSADO, CRUX and LACROSSE.

See "CROUCH" and "CRUCIFIX."

CROUCH/כָּרַע
CAR – UKH   [K-R-K]

ROOTS: Old French *crochir* is to be bent; it is traced to the IE root *ger* (to curve, bend) seen at "CROSS" and "CURVE."

כרע/KORUKH is translated "crouch" in *Genesis 49:9*, corresponding to the #1 definition of CROUCH: to stoop low as an animal. The #2 definition of CROUCH is to bow humbly. The dictionary definition of כרע/KORUKH is to bend or kneel. הכריע/(HI)KHREĀKH is to subject or bend. קרס/KORUS is to bow or bend. קער/KEĀR is to curve.

BRANCHES: CREEK [from Old Norse *kriki* (a winding)], CRICK, CRICKET (the stick and the game), CROCHET CROOK(ED) and CROQUET all relate to the Hebrew etymon and its extensions like כרוכיה/KROOKEĀ (crane). CRICKET (the grasshopper) relates to כרע/KERĀKH ("jointed leg"– in *Leviticus 11:21* where crickets and grasshopers are discussed).

כרע/KERĀKH is a knee, while כרע/KORAKH is the verb of bending and kneeling. COWER, COWARD and COW should relate.

In Hawaiian (which has no *R*), *kuli* is a knee and *kulou* is to bow or bend.

CROW/עוֹרב
KHO-RAVE   [KH-R-V→CRW]

ROOTS: All the CORVINE (like a crow or raven) birds from Latin *corvus* (raven) are ultimately from ערב/ŌRĀV or KHŌRĀV (raven – *Genesis 8:7*).

BRANCHES: While Mediterranean tongues render ערב as KRV, an Anglo-Saxon would pronounce the same term *hræfn* (source of raven). To see why CROW is to CRAVE as RAVEN is to RAVENOUS, go straight (as the raven flies) to "RAVENOUS."

CROWN/קֶרֶן
KEREN   [KRN]

ROOTS: Linked to the IE root *(s)ker* (to turn, bend), the CROWN was inaccurately associated with roundness – as explained back at "CORONA." The IE scholars have a better root for CROWN – *ker* (horn, head . . . projecting parts) – but they failed to see the CROWN as a קרן/KEREN (horn, extending ray).

The old translations of *I Samuel 2:10* contained that puzzling phrase "horn of his anointed," as if the messiah (anointed king) had horns. The new JPS Bible renders the same קרן/KEREN as "'triumph." It's an improvement, but the word "crown" best expresses the regal splendor and kingly strength intended by this use of קרן/KEREN. The horns or antlers of many animals regally flaunt just this sense of dominant male of the herd.

BRANCHES: קרן/KEREN as animal horn appears in *Genesis 22:13*. CRANIUM and other hard-headed cognates may be seen at "UNICORN."

Other extensions of the CROWN of authority or the CROWN sitting atop the king's CROWN incude: CORONAL, CORONARY, CORONATION, CORONER, and CORONET. The ram's horn blown on coronation day (Rosh HaShana – the head or beginning of the year) calls forth another horn-crown connection of majesty and authority.

(CRUCI)FIX/ספח
(SU)F-UKH [(S)FK→FX]

ROOTS: For the first element of *CRUCI*FIX, see "CROSS." The SUF*FIX* is from Latin *figere* (to fasten, fix). ספח/(SÄ)FÄKH is to join or attach. This term is translated "cleave" in *Isaiah 14:1*, where the friendship of Christians and others is prophesied to be a FIXTURE of the repentant, revived Israel:

"But the Lord will pardon Jacob, and will again choose Israel, and will settle them on their own soil. And strangers shall join them and shall *cleave* to the House of Jacob."

דבק/(DA)BHÄK is to attach, glue or join. קבע/(KO)BHÄKH is to fix or drive in, the verb for fastening nails. This F/BH-KH two-letter root makes painfully clear what the FIX of CRUCI*FIX*ION refers to.

BRANCHES: תחב/(TÄ)KHÄBH (to insert, stick in) is a BH-KH reversal of the same meaning element.
The given IE root for FIX is *dhigw* (to stick, fix – see Hebrew word above.) Other derivatives of Latin *figere* include AFFIX, ANTEFIX, CRUCIFY, FIBULA, FICHU, FIXATE, FIXITY, INFIX, MICROFICHE, PREFIX and TRANSFIX.
Similar to Latin *figere* (to fasten) is Latin *pangere* (to fasten). *Pangere* is a nasalized (extra N) PG term, which is traced by the AHD to the IE root *pag* or *pak* (to fasten). Another derivative of this root is Old English *fegan* (to fit closely). The FG and PG words in this entry require a Hebrew פ/PAY or PHAY to bridge the P and PH(F) sounds.
A reversal of חב/KHABH, two-letter root of fastening, is also worth comparing to the IE root *pak* (to fasten).
חבט/KHEBH(ET) = fastening, buckle; חבל/KHEBH(EL) = a rope or region; חבק/KHABH(AK) = to embrace, clasp; חבק/KHEBH(EK) = saddle belt, garter; חבר/KHABH(AR) = to unite, be joined; חבש/KHABH(ASH) = to bind; חבת/KHEBH(ET) = a sandal strap.
The given derivatives of IE *pag* or *pak* are APPEASE, COMPACT, FANG, IMPINGE, PACE, PACIFIC, PACIFY, PAGAN, PAGE, PAGEANT, PAY, PEACE, PEASANT, PECTIN, POLE, TRAVEL and VANG.
For an alternative road to peace, see "PEACE."
Antonyms include בקע/BOKA (to cleave split) and פקע/POKA (to split).

CRUSH/כרסם
KIR-S(AME) [KRS]

ROOTS: CRUSH is from Old French *croiser* (to gnash, break). כרסם/KIRSÄM is to gnaw or devour (*Psalms 9:14*), an extension of that food crusher the כרס/KERES (stomach). A better Hebrew etymon, requiring but a G to K change, is גרם/GORUS (to crush, break – *Lamentations 3:16*).

BRANCHES: More words like CRU(N)CH and GRISLE at "GRIST."

CRUST/קרש
CAR-US(H) [K-R-S(H)]

ROOTS: Latin *crusta* and the IE root *kreus* (to begin to freeze, form a crust) link the hardening of CRUST to coldness.
Similarly, קרש/KÄRUSH (to clot, congeal, coagulate) is an extension of קר/KOR (cold – *Genesis 8:22*). קרש/KÄRESH is frozen; קרם/KORUM is to form crust; קרח/KERÄKH is frost.

BRANCHES: The official cognates of CRUST are CROUTON, CRUSTACEAN, CRUSTACEOUS, CRYSTAL(LINE) and CRYO-. See "CRYOGENICS" for other cold words.
GORE as clotted blood belongs here; see "GORE" for the less GORY connotation. Other related words like CRUD and CURD link up with Hebrew terms like קריד/KORED (crust of hardened sediment), קלוט/KÄLOODT (closed) and גלד/GELEDT (crust).
See "CLOT" and "CREAM."

CRY/קרא
CAR-AH [KRA]

ROOTS: Old French *quiritaire* (to raise a plaintive cry, wail or shriek) is cited, but the dictionary concludes that CRY is "probably of echoic origin."
קרא/KRÄ is to call out loudly, as in *Isaiah 58:1* – "*Cry* with full throat without restraint, raise your voice like a ram's horn!" Sanskrit *krosa* is a shout and קרא/KRA in *Judges 7:20* is rendered "shout." Elsewhere in Scripture, the verb קרא/KR fits the loud proclamation or recitation of the town CRIER.

BRANCHES: Via IE roots like *gar* (to call, cry), *ghel* (to call), *gera* (to call hoarsely) and *gher* (to call out) we may call on such related words as CARE, COR(MORANT), CRANE, CROAK, CROON, CROW, CUR, GARRULOUS, GERANIUM, GREET, (NIGHTING)GALE, QUAIL, SLOGAN, YELL and YELP. An appropriate GR etymon is גרון/GARON (throat) – see "GROAN."
קרקר/KÄRKER is to croak or shout; קול/KOL is a voice or call (R = L) – see "CALL."
CRY in Spanish or Portugese is *gritar* and in Russian *kritchat*.

CRYO(GEN)ICS/קָרַה
CORE-AH   [KR]

ROOTS: CRYOGENICS is the science of freezing things, from Greek *kryos* (cold, frost). קרה / KORÄ is the "icy cold" of *Psalms 147:17*. קר / KOR is cold (*Genesis 8:22*); קרח / KERAH is frost (*Genesis 31:40*.

Greek *kryos* is also the etymon for CRUST; see "CRUST" for the IE root of cryo-.

BRANCHES: Hebrew extensions of קר / KÄR (cold) include קרש / KÄRUSH (to clot, congeal, coagulate) and קרם / KORUM (to form a crust).

The usual R to L change brings words like CHILL, CONGEAL, COLD, COOL, GELATIN, GELID, GLACE, GLACIER, and JELLY—all of which are attributed to the IE root *gel* (cold, to freeze).

The GLD/T words recall the Talmudic term גליד / GELED (ice), a cognate of a congeal-clot term in *Job 16:15* (נלד / GELED – translated "sores" or "skin"). הנליד / (HI)GLED is to grow skin over a wound. The CLOTTING, CRUSTING and CRYSTALIZING of cells in the healing process is naturally akin to freezing. Swedish *gradde* (cream) and Italian *gelato* (ice cream) are two examples of this skin-cold-cream-GELATIN connection. The modern Hebrew word for ice cream, גלידה / GLEDÄ, is not a borrowing. In fact, it points to the Semitic origins of ice cream words like *glace* (French), *helado* (Spanish), and *jaatelo* (Finnish).

Galid is snow in Arabic. Reverse G-L-S to get שלג / SHELEG (snow). *Theluji* is Swahili snow.

Not only is the cold COOL from words like קרר / KÄRUR (to cool), but the "casual" cool is from קרי / KERÉ, as S. R. Hirsch renders the word in *Leviticus 26:21*.

Rumanian "cold" reverses to *rece*, while other COLD terms are closer to Hebrew קר / KÄR – such as Japanese *kareru* (to freze) and *kori* (ice). Maya *keel* is cold; *kelil* is winter. Cold in Swedish is *kall*, in Russian *khalodni*, and in Finnish *kylma*.

And just why is COLD *zimno* in Polish and *samui* in Japanese? And why are they so similar? Because צנן / ZINAN is to feel cold; צמרמרת / ZMÄRMORÉT is to shiver; and צם / ZM or (T)S-M is a root of (frozen) contraction as seen in צמצם / ZIMZEM (to compress, reduce) and צמק / ZÄMÄK or (T)SAMAK (to shrink). Yes, SMALL is related.

Latin *caldus* (warm) is the opposite of COLD because the original language (Hebrew) has built-in antonyms like קלי / KÄLÉ (toast). See "CHAR" for an antonym of קר / KR; see "CAUTERIZE" for Dutch *koud* (hot). Basque *hotz* (cold) is likely a GLD or KLT variation that dropped its middle L.

Note CHALAZA, from Greek *khalaza* (hailstone), for its IE root *gheled* (hail). Frozen rain, hail, is much like Arabic *galid* (snow). We also get, from the Greek-Semitic connection, a better etymon for HAIL than the given IE base *kaghlo* (small pebble.)

See "CLOT," "FROST," and "GLISSADE."

CUBBY/קָבָה
KOOB-BAH   [KBH]

ROOTS: A CUBBY or CUBBYHOLE is dismissed by *Webster's* as a children's word for a snug place to play. In British dialect, however, a CUB means a small shed or enclosed space. The AHD cites Germanic *kubon* (hut, shed) and Middle Dutch *cubbe* (pen, stall). קבה / KOOBÄH (compartment, tent, hut, brothel) appears in *Numbers 25:8*.

BRANCHES: HOVEL, COFFER, COFFIN and QUIVER all relate to a family of KB words like חבא / KHÄBÄ (to hide), חפא / KHÄPHÄ (case) and קפה / KOOPÄ (cash box, basket).

More at "ALCOVE" and "CAB."

CUBE/קְבִיה
KOOB-EE-YAH   [KBYH]

ROOTS: The geometric shape with six equal sides is said to come from the IE root *keu* (to bend). Greek *kybos* means a cube, die, or vertebra.

קביה / KOOBEÄ is Aramaic for dice or cubes. Arabic *ka'b* is a cube, as recorded in dictionaries under KAABA (the square Moslem shrine at Mecca). Arabid *k'aba* is to cube in mathematics; the Hebrew equivalent is עקב / EKÄBH. מעקב / (MI)OOKÄBH means CUBIC.

BRANCHES: קב / KABH is a Biblical measure; קו / KUV is a measuring line. The bending words that the AHD would link to CUBE via the root *keu* (to bend) are based on Hebrew words like חפת / KHÄPHET (to fold), כפף / KÄFÄF (to bend) and קבה / KÄBHÄ (stomach).

קבעת / KOOBÄT (cup) and קברת / KÉBORET (biceps) are related.

Another term relevant to the perfect square is הקביל / (HI)K'BEEL (to be opposite, parallel).

See "CUP."

CUCUM(BER) /קִיקָיוֹן
KEY-KAH-YONE   [KYKYN]

ROOTS: The Old French, with *cocombre,* had made the CUCUMBER more cumbersome than it was in the Latin *cucum(is)*.

קיקיון /KÉKÄYON, another double-gutteral-nasal, is the "gourd" or castor-oil plant in *Jonah 4:6*. Israelis order CUCUMBER with other words, but CUCUM(BER) is from a KKN Biblical term for vine-grown, gourd-like plants.

BRANCHES: The root קיק/KEEK may be the first element in Latin *cucurbita* (gourd); GOURD may come from Arabic *chiar* (cucumber).

קשות/KISHOOS (pumpkin) and קשוא/KISHOO (cucumber – *Numbers 11:8*) may have influenced (S)QUASH.

CUD/כַד
CUD   [K-D]

ROOTS: From Anglo-Saxon *cwundo*, an animal's ball of CUD is literally "what is rounded." The IE base cited is *geu-t* (to curve, bend).

כד/KUD means obtuse or blunt; the rounded pitcher is a כד/KUD (*Genesis 24:20*). כדור/KÄD(OOR) is the "ball" of *Isaiah 22:18*, or the "round about" in *Isaiah 29:3*.

BRANCHES: The round head is a קדקד/KŌDKŌD. The opposite of round, or KD backwards, is חד/KHUD [sharp – source of (A)CUTE]. CUDDY, CUDGEL and CUDWEED are round relatives.

The כד/KUD as pitcher is in our dictionary at ALBATROSS – acknowledged to be a corruption of Arabic al qadus (the water container). Greek kados, is a cask or jar, and CADDY (the tea container) is from an equivalent term in Malay. All CYTO- and -CYTE words are from Greek kutos (a hollow or vessel) which should draw from כד/KUDT.

The ALBATROSS and the canard (both a species of duck or a rounded airplane) suggest that DUCK is from כד/KUD backwards – the Arabs were not the only ones to notice the consistent curves in water fowl engineering. The obtuse etymology given to DUCKPINS (that the bowling pins were said to "fly like ducks") ignores the fact that these pins are rounded like a pitcher, duck, or kat(schke) – duck in Yiddish. Duck words in other languages (Turkish ordek, Russian utka, Indonesian itik) do not support the usual assumption that the bird was named for diving or ducking.

DUCKING may relate to the bird's constant קדה/KEEDÄ (head bowing) in its role as a דיג/DÄYUG (fisher).

The French elbow (coude) and Spanish elbow (codo) were seen as rounded.

CUFF/כף
CUFF   [KF]

ROOTS: Several uses of the word CUFF have no known origin. CUFF is a fold at the end of a sleeve or trouser leg. כפול/KUFFOOL is folded (see "COUPLE"); כפוף/KUF-FOOF is bent (Exodus 28:17; Psalms 145:14).

To CUFF (strike with an open hand), along with Middle English cuffe (mitten), makes the Hebrew etymon as clear as the front of one's hand. כף/KUF is the palm of the hand. Balaam strikes his hands together in Numbers 24:10. Both כף/KUF and קפה/KOFÄH are used in the sense of CAP(TURING). The latter term also means to strike (CUFF, COUP) and to steal or COP. CAPTURE is kobe for the Kiowa Indians; it's hopu in Hawaiian. קבץ/KOBH(ATS) is to gather; Arabic qabada is "he seized or clasped."

BRANCHES: GOLF means " to strike with the hand." שקף / (SHÄ)KUF, נקף/(NÄ)KUF and נגף/(NÄ)GUF all mean to strike or hit. If the L isn't historic then it's another כף/KUF word. COPE also meant to strike.

To BOX in a BOXING ring is a FISTICUFFS term with no known origin. Reverse BOX to a KB, throw in the Japanese fist (kobushi) and the Maya hand (gab), and כף/KUPH has got the scoop (see "SCOOP").

חב/KH-BH is shared by both חבט/KHOV(ÄT) (to thresh, beat) and חבל/KHOVÄL (to wound).

Kupapa'i is to grope, feel, or fight hand-to-hand in Hawaiian. Kapua'i is the sole of the foot or an animal's paw in Hawaiian – see "CAULK."

CUL(MINATE) / נל
GULL   [GL→KL]

ROOTS: TO CULMINATE (reach a highest point) is traced to the IE root kel (to be prominent; hill).

An equivalent term is Hebrew נל/GUL (wave; a prominent man-made "heap" – as seen in Genesis 31:46). Related Hebrew terms include עלה/ÄLÄ (or KHÄLÄ (to go up; to succeed) and הר/HÄR (hill, mountain) – GL→HR.

BRANCHES: The official cognates of CULMINATE are COLO-NEL, COLONNADE, COLOPHON, COLUMN, EXCEL, HILL and HOLM. (EX)CEL is better matched with עלה/KHÄLÄ (to succeed), while HILL is merely an L→R change away from הר/HÄR (hill).

CLIM[B] might have made an EXCELLENT cognate for CULMINATE, but CLIMB is linked to a related נל/GL term seen at "CONGLOMERATE."

To head for the hills, הרי אררט/HÄRÄ ÄRRÄT (the mountains of Ararat – Genesis 8:4) are the first subject of Biblical OROLOGY (the study of mountains). Oros is mountain in Greek. The common H→G change in Slavic allows the Russian mountain to be gora. Closest to the Hebrew is the Czech mountain – hora.

The double L in HILL or HILLOCK may derive from the variant הרר/HERER (mountain). Latin collis (hill) likewise doubles the liquid (L/R) at the end.

Whether or not the Harz Mountains of Germany relate to הר/HAR, the Galilee (hilly region of northern Israel) surely derives from נל/GÄL (mound, wave). The GALE (origin unknown), GALEON, GALLEY, and GULL may all be riding the same wave.

A CAIR[N] (Celtic; heap of stones as a monument) is identical to יגר / [YI]GAR in Genesis 31:41 (Chaldean). For the opposite of a HILL, see "HOLLOW."

CULPA(BLE)/חרפה
KHER-PAH   [KH-R-P→KLP]

ROOTS: CULAPABILITY is from Latin culpa (fault, blame, crime). חרפה/KHERPA is shame, outrage, abuse; חרף/KHÄRÄPH is to revile in Isaiah 37:23. The connection to CULPA is more חריף/KHÄRÄPH (sharp) if one keeps in mind that guilt evokes shame, and that blaming meant cursing and reviling. See "BLAME."

BRANCHES: After a #2-#3 letter swap, note that החפיר/(HE)-KHPĒR is to be ashamed, and כפור/KEPOOR means atonement or expiation. Yom Kippur offers forgiveness for the CULPABLE.

CUP/קבעת
KOOB-(A'US)   [K-B]

ROOTS: CUP has no direct etymon older than Anglo-Saxon cuppe to compete with קבעת / KOOOB(Ä'ÄS) (cup, goblet).

In Isaiah 51:22 there is "The cup of reeling, the bowl, the cup of my wrath." כפור / KIPH(ŌR) is a "bowl" in Ezra 1:10; גביע / GOBHEA is a GOBLET in Genesis 44:17 and a "cup" in Exodus 37:17; כפית / KUP(ĒS) is a spoon, similar to the "ladles" of Exodus 25:29 and similar to the Finnish cup (kuppi). Man's first drinking CUP was the CUP of his hand, the כף / KUPH (palm of hand, spoon – Genesis 40:11). The same term is used as a CUP of measurement in I Kings 17:12; the CUP of a sling appears in I Samuel 25:29.

The IE root is keu (to bend . . . whence a round or hollow object).

BRANCHES: The cognates include CAPSULE, CIBORIUM, COVEY, CUPBOARD, CUPOLA, CURULE, CYPSELA, HAWKER, HEAP, HIGH, HOOP, HUCKSTER, and HUNKER.

Latin *cupa* (tub) and the HOPPER evoke a Hebrew כלי קבול / (KLÄ) KEEB(OOL) (receptacle) of larger CAPacity—the חבית / KHÄBHĒS (barrel). A CUPEL is the bowl of weighing scales; reverse to *pei* for a similar cup in Chinese.

The "bend" of the IE root here is from K-P(H) benders and concavities like כפה / KĒPÄ (arch, cap) and כפיפה / KIPH(ĒPÄ) (bending, basket).

There is more at "CAVITY," "CUFF," "GOBLET," and "(S)COOP." The concave K-B(H) terms are reversed at "BEAKER"; convex antonyms are listed at "GIBBON."

CURB/כַּרְכֹּב
CAR-COVE   [K-R-(K)-BH]

ROOTS: French *courbe* is a curved object or horse's bit, whence (allegedly) the edging of a sidewalk or pavement. The dictionary offers Latin *curvus* as the etymon, making CURB a cognate of CURVE. The given IE root is *sker* or *ker* (to turn, bend). קער / KĒAR is to curve.

In the case of the Biblical CURB, כרכב/KURKŌBH, the word was bound to have been shortened over the years to KRB.

"And thou shalt put it under the *ledge* round the altar." כרכב – *Exodus 27:5*.

For curvature and turning, note that כרכב/KARKŌBH is also a rim and that כרכב/KĒRKÄBH means "to turn on a lathe."

BRANCHES: ערוב/ĀROOBH or KHĀROOBH can mean "limit;" ערב/EREBH or KHEREBH can mean "the eve of" or "the edge of" (night). Both ערב/KRB words speak to our other uses of CURB.

עבר/OVAR or KHOBHAR, a #2-#3 letter swap, means crossing over curbs, borders or limits—see "OVER."

CURT/כָּרַת
CORE-RUT   [KRT]

ROOTS: CURT is from Latin *curtus*, linked to the theroretical IE base *(s)qr-tus* (cut off). CURT (shortened) is the adjectival form of CURTAIL (to cut short). The IE root here is *sker'* or *ker* (to cut).

כרת/KORUT is to cut off, as in *Numbers 13:23*. Some interpret the divine punishment of כרת/KORĀT (*Leviticus 17:4*) as a curtailment of life. קרץ/KORUTS is to slice or cut, translated "nipped" in *Job 33:6*.

BRANCHES: Because SHORT and CURT are cognates, and *kurz* is short in German, we must consider a #2-#3 metathesis of קצר/K-TS-R. קצר/KOTSUR means "short" (*Isaiah 28:20*) as well as "to cut or harvest"(*Leviticus 23:10*). גרז/GORAZ means "cut off;" גרזן/GARZEN is an ax—see "GRAZE." CURTAL, CURTATE, CURTEL AX (a cutlass), CUTLASS, CUTLERY and CUTLET recall another K-R/L-D/T term, the קרדם/KURDT(ŌM) or ax. Other official cognates of CURT and SHORT include KIRTLE, SHIRT and SKIRT.

Japanese cutting terms like *kiru* and *kiri* are either curtailed cousins of words like *cortar* ("cut" in Spanish and Portuguese,) or they derive from KR cutters like קרע/KORÄ (to rend, tear).

See "CASTRATE" and "CUT."

CUR(VE)/קָעוּר
CAW-OORE   [K-R]

ROOTS: Latin *curvus* is bent, from the IE base *(s)quer* (to turn, bend) or the IE root *ger* (curving, crooked).

Hebrew offers קער/KEER (to curve), ענור/ÄGOOR (crane), קעור/KÄOOR (concave), קערה/KIARA (bowl— *Exodus 37:16*), כרוכית/KROOKĒT (roll), כרכור/KĒRKOOR (whirl, circle—*II Samuel 6:14*), כרע/KORÄ (to kneel, bow— *Genesis 49:9*) and הכריע/(HI)KHRĒÄ (to bend).

BRANCHES: CORRAL is from Spanish *corro* (a circle, ring). The dictionary goes on to attribute the Spanish term to Latin *currere* (to run).

The IE root *ger* (curving, crooked) includes: AGRAFFE, GRAPE, GRAPPLE, CARP, CART, CRADLE, CRAMP, CRANK, CRECHE, CREEK, CREEP, CRIB, CRINGE, CRINKLE, CRIPPLE, CROCK, CROFT, CROOK, CROP, CROUP, CRUM(PLE), CRUMPET, CRUSE, and CURL. CURVE itself is at IE *sker* (to turn, bend), where it is a cognate of CIRCLE.

To the CROCK above, add KIER (attributed to Old Norse *ker*, a tub). A KIER is just a larger קערה/KIÄRÄ or bowl. CORRIE is from an IE root *kwer* (something dish shaped).

To CRINGE, add COWER—from כרע/KORÄ (to kneel). COW(ARD) and QUAIL may surrender here too.

Also relevant is the HARP, from an IE base *(s)qereb(h)* (to bend, curve). A QUIRK is a related twist or turn. COIR (rope fiber) is from Tamil *kayaru* (to be twisted). *Coraat* is a word for "round" of the Luiseno Indians. *Kerek* is "round" in Hungarian; in Russian it's *krugli*. *Cor* is a circle in Irish. All the CIRCUM- words like CIRCUMFERENCE, fit here. *Kiwi* is curved in HAWAIIN.

The curved ARC or ARCH may simply be a backwards version of these KR words of CURVATURE.

See "CAR," "CROSS," "CROUCH," "CURB," "CYCLE," and "GRAPPLE."

CUT/כַּת
CUT   [K-T]

ROOTS: Icelandic *kuta* (to cut with a knife) represents one of the oldest KT cut words. There's Latin *caedere* (to cut), but somehow no IE root.

Hebrew has many K-T CUTTERS including: גדע/GODÄ or KOTÄ (to cut off), חטב/KHOTÄV (to cut, hew—*Deuteronomy 29:10*), חתך/KHOTÄKH (to cut), כת ∞ KUT (a sect, a cut from something), קצב/KOTSÄV (to cut off), קצה / KĒTSÄ (to cut off), קצע/KETSÄÄ (to trim), קצר/KÄTSER (cut down, harvest), חצה/KHÄT(S)Ä, (to halve—*Exodus 21: 35*).

BRANCHES: DEICIDE, HOMICIDE and SUICIDE are from Latin *caedere* (to cut down, kill). קטל/KATEL (to kill) is a "cut" word by family association. קדד/KODAD (to cut off) sounds closest to the Latin. (S)CYTHE and Chinese *t'ao k'o* (reversed KT, meaning to cut or carve) relate here.

CUTE, CUTICLE and ACUTE are elsewhere linked to sharp terms like חד/KHUD (sharp, thin), but they also relate to קט/KUT (tiny).

Writing once meant cutting into stone or clay, so that כתיבה/KITĒBHÄ (writing, manuscript) is an extension of CUT. A book is a KTB term in Arabic, Farsi, Indonesian, Swahili and Turkish. The Japanese *Kotoba* (word, language) is beyond the range of a borrowing from Semitic.

See "CURT," SAXON" and "SUICIDE."

CYCLE/עֲגוּל
KHEE-GOOL   [KH-G-L]

ROOTS: CYCLE is from Greek *kuklos* (circle); the IE root is *k(w)el* (to revolve, move around, sojourn, dwell). עגול/ĒGOOL or KHĒGOOL is a circle (*I Kings 7:23*). The IE root for CIRCLE, *sker* (to turn, bend), relates to the sound of סחר/SĀKHAR (to travel around), while the meanings of IE *k(w)el* match the GR word גור/GOOR (dwell, sojourn – *Genesis 32:5*).

Greek *kirkos* (a ring), Sanskrit *cakram* (circle), and Russian *krug* (circle) indicate that a double-guttural + liquid [K-K/G-L/R] is the more common axis to spin words of roundness on. Hebrew offers: גלגל/GULGUL (wheel), גלגל / GILGĀL (to roll, revolve, wander), חג/KHĀG (to make a cycle: a cyclical holy day), חגור/KHĀGOR (belt), כרכור/KIRKOOR (circle: to whirl), עגיל/ĀGEL or KHĀGEEL (earring) עגלה/KHĀGĀLĀ (cart, wagon), עגלגלת/ĀGOOLGELET (elliptic), and קערה/KĀKHĀRA (bowl).

BRANCHES: With a little turning, the whole family circle can fit into the Hebrew etymons above. Try words attributed to Greek *kirkinos* (circle) like CIRCLE, CIRCUIT, CIRCULATION, CIRCUMSTANCE, CIRCUMVENT, etc. Picadilly CIRCUS is a traffic circle. ככר/KĒKĀR means the same in modern Hebrew, while in *Exodus 29:23* it meant a round CAKE. COKE is from an IE base *gel-g* (rounded, ball-like).

CALENDAR and CYLINDER are from Greek *kylindein* (to roll); CALASH is from the many Slavic rollers like *kolo* (wheel). Czech, German and French also have KL wheel words from גלגל/ GULGUL or KUL(KUL) (wheel). BA*GEL*, CAREEN, CLEAN, GYRE, KUGEL, (S)KULL and more round out this family.

The *GYRATING HELIX* (Greek for spiral) of the EAGLE plummeting to its prey named this great bird (after circling terms like עגל/E-G-L). The Hebrew term for EAGLE, נשר/NESHER, likewise means both "eagle" and "dropping."

HELIX may have switched the #2 and #3 letters of עגל/(K)H-G(X)-L (round). A word like HELICOPTER is therefore from עגל plus a similar metathesis (letter swap) of פרד/PĀRĀDT (spread) to cover Greek *pter(on)* (wing). The HELICON (tuba) is bent into a circle (עגל), not a *helikos* (spiral).

See "CAR," "CHORUS," "CURVE" and "GYRE."

CYPRESS/גֹּפֶר
GO-FAIR   [G-PH-R]

ROOTS: The CYPRESS tree is attributed to Greek KYPARISSOS, while the similar גפר/GOPHER gopher tree or pitch pine – *Genesis 6:14*) is from Biblical Hebrew. ברוש/B'RŌSH is rendered "Cypress" in *Isaiah 55:13*. כברוש/KYBRŌS(H) would literally mean "like a pine or fir tree"– see "BRUSH,"

BRANCHES: The כפר/KŌPHER ("henna" or "CA(M)PHIRE" in *Canticles 1:14*) is rendered *cyprus* (Latin) in the Concordance.

Returning to *Genesis 6:14*, Noah was instructed to use the wood of the גפר/GOPHER or K-P(H)-R, and to line the ark with כפר/KOPHER (pitch) for waterproofing or denying moisture. כפירה/KIPHĒRA means denial.

CZAR/שַׂר
S + ARE   [SR]

ROOTS: Russian TSAR is supposed to be a contraction of *cesari*, via Gothic KAISAR and Latin CAESAR. Sara in Genesis, the first Jewish princess, introduces the word שר/SĀR as prince or officer. In *Jeremiah 17:25*, "King" and שר/SĀR are in the same breath. כתר/KESER means crown. עצר/ETSER or KETSER means authority and rule. זר/ZĀR is a crown or wreath.

BRANCHES: An עשיר/ĀSHĒR or KHĀS(H)ĒR is a wealthy man or CZAR of industry. A #2-#3 letter flip makes the עריץ/KHĀR-ĒTS (tyrant) sound like K-Z-R. CEASAR is said to mean "the hairy one." עשו/ESAU is literally "the hairy one" of antiquity whose kingdom, שעיר / SĀER or SKR (Seir), means hair (שער) and who is linked to Rome (of the Caesars).

עשו / ĀSĀV (Esau) is named for his hairiness in *Genesis 25:25* (akin to the Hebrew term עשב/ĀSEV or grass). As a twin who wanted to kill his brother Jacob, Esau is a likely source for the myth about the demigod Romulus who founded Rome and killed his twin. The initial ע of עשו/ĀSĀV (Esau) can certainly be read as a guttural. This leaves only the V/V,W to R change that would allow עשו to be prounounced KHĀSĀR *(Caesar)*. At "CHECK-MATE" the (ו) vav of מות/MĀVET (death) turned to a W in Arabic (*mawt*) and then made the easy W to R change to get MORT(AL). תוך/TŌKH or THŌKH (within, through) becomes "thRough" the same way. Similarly, the תוכי/TOOKĒ or TWKY (exotic bird) became TURKEY, and גוף/GOOF or G-W-PH (body) gave us CORPUS. Nobody doubts the link between Latin *serere* (to sow) and SOW(R = W). There is also a reason why Anglo-Saxon HORSE is a V→R change away from the Finnish *HoVose* (horse).

See "SHIRE" and "SIR."

DA(M)N/דָּן
DONE   [DN]

ROOTS: Latin *damnare* is to condemn or fine. דן/ DĀN is to punish or "judge" *(Genesis 15:14)*. דיין/ DĀYĀN is a judge *(Psalms 68:6)*. דין/ DEEN is law, judgment, justice, litigation and, in *Deuteronomy 17:18*, a legal plea as in to DUN. The theoretical IE root for DAMN, DAMAGE and CONDEMN is *dap* to apportion – in exchange). טעם / TAAM is a judgement or decree *(Jonah 3:7)*. DT–MN antonyms at "DUMB."

BRANCHES: DEEM is to judge; a DEEMSTER is a judge. REDEEM and REDEMPTION (to make amends, atone for guilt) relate to other DM terms like DAMAGE, Latin *damnum* (loss or injury), INDEMNITY, and INDEMNIFY (to make reparations). All these relate to דם / DAM ("bloodguilt"– *Exodus 22:1*).

To translate דם / DAM as literal blood makes for awkward translation in verses like *Leviticus 19:16* ("Do not profit by the *blood* of your neighbor"). The context clearly wants us to not profit by the *damnum* (Latin for injury or loss) of our fellow man. In many other verses the bloodthirsty translators failed to see דם/ DAM as a legal term of damages due, a relative of דמים/DĀMIM (value, cost), of דמי / DIMĀ (fee) and, of דין / DEEN (DOOM, judgment). טען / DT–N is to sue or claim.

CONDEMN, DEMON, DOOM are all judgmental terms. מדינה / (MI)DĒNA (province) literally means jurisdiction. As law implies jurisdiction, this D-N/M family has a bearing on words like DEMEAN, DOMINATE, (KING)DOM, etc.

See "MADONNA" and "ADONIS" for many D-N/M terms of mastery from אדון / ÄDŌN (master).

In Chinese *dian* is law or rule; *ding* is to pass judgment. *Tham* is to try or judge in Vietnamese.

DARK/דלח
DOLL-AKH   [DLK→DRK]

ROOTS: In Middle Low Germ *dork* is a place where dirt collects; DARK is traced to the IE root *dher* (to make muddy; darkness).

דלוח / DÄLOOÄKH is muddy, polluted; דלח / DÄLÄKH is "foul" in *Ezekiel 32:2.* (Foul is the opposite of "fair," and fair also means the opposite of dark.)

BRANCHES: קדר / KÄDÄR (dark) is an anagramic synonym (move letter #1 to the end of the word to get DARK). טלל / TILÄL or DILAL is Aramaic for shade. הדליק / (HI)DLĒK (to light, kindle) is a bright antonym of דלח / DALAK(H). דלק / DLK is the source of light (once pronounced LIKDT – affect another anagram). LIGHT and DARK both have a dental (D/T), liquid (L/R) and gutteral (GH/K) because their Hebrew etymons are designed antonyms. The given cognates of DARK include: DRAB, DREGS, DRIVEL, DROSS and TRACHEA.

Kotor is dirty in Indonesian; *hatoru* is night in Malay, Liang dialect. DOUGL(AS), dark in Celtic, is available from either Hebrew etymon with the help of letter swapping and Grimm's law of permutations.

DASH/דיש
DIE-YISH   [D-Y-SH]

ROOTS: Middle English *daschen* is to strike with violence. דיש / DAYISH is to thresh, beat or dash grain.

Employee benefits are divinely ordained in *Deuteronomy 25:4* – "You shall not muzzle an ox while it is *threshing.*" דש / DÄSH is to thresh, tread or trample.

The racing sense of a DASH or of DASHING OFF is from this treading and trampling, as well as from words like טש / DTASH (to fly, dart) – see "TOSS."

BRANCHES: אשד / ASHAD (he rushed) is a Biblical word preserved in Arabic. Reversed to D-SH it also recalls the running DASH. The root is spelled דוש / D-V-SH. With the ו / W to ו / R connection brought up at "CZAR" one can see why דרס / DÄRÄS (to tread, trample) is a close synonym.

Because of this connection, words like TARSUS (flat of the foot), THRASH, THRESH, THRESHOLD, and TROU(N)CE are more likely derivative of דרם / (D)TÄRÄS(H) than they are of their given etymons like IE root *ter* (to rub, turn).

דש / DÄS(H) is the ultimate source of DOUSE, which originally meant to hit forcefully. DOUSE is currently traced to Middle Dutch *dossen* (to beat noisily).

DAWN/אדם
(AH)-DUMB   [DM→DN]

ROOTS: Middle English *dawn(en)* is not treated by the dictionary, because there is no available history of the term. Instead, the etymology curiously concerns Anglo-Saxon

dagian (to become day) – as if *dagian* lost its "g" and became "dawn." The alleged IE root for DAWN is *agh* (a day).

אדם / ADÄM is to be red or grow red (*Isaiah 1:18*). אדמדם / ADÄMDAM means very red or glowing (*Leviticus13:42*).

BRANCHES: Not only does *dàn* mean DAWN in Chinese, but several Slavic terms for "day" (*dan*: Serbo-Croatian, *den*:Czech, *dyen*: Russian) suggest a dental (T,D) + nasal (M,N) term for DAWN. *Dimineata* is morning in Rumanian. Add to this words like MATIN and MATINEE, from French *matin* (morning) and Latin *Matuta* (goddess of the dawn), which are merely T-M reversed.

The rising-sun terms here ought to derive from אדם / ADÄM (to be red). An alternative etymon might be נצץ / NAT(SATS) (glittering – *Ezekiel 1:7*) or הנץ / (HÄ)NÄT(S) (to shine – NT→DN – הנץ החמה (shining of the sun) is a term for dawn. While דם / DAM is blood and אדום / ADŌM is red in Hebrew, reverse to *mada* for "blood" and "red" in Australian Aborigine. *Daang* is red in Thai.

Foliage would indicate that AUTUM(N) is the season for the color אדם / ADTŌM (red); Latin *autumnus* has no known etymon or meaning.

See "ASIA" and "SANGRIA."

DE(BRIS)/די
DEE   [DY]

ROOTS: The BRS element in DEBRIS means broken – see "BURST."

The DE element in DEBRIS and so many other English words means "from" or "of." DEBRIS results *from* something being *broken.* Latin *de,* French *de* and Old Irish *de* all mean "from" or "of."

די / DÄ means "from" (*I Samuel 7:16*). די / DE is Biblical Aramaic for "of, like the *de* of the Modern European languages" according to the *Hebrew-English Lexicon of the Bible.*

BRANCHES: A few examples of the many English words with this DE element are DEBRIEF, DECEIVE, DECIDE and DECLARE.

DECAY/דחי
DE-KHEE   [D-KH-Y]

ROOTS: DECAY is traced to Latin *decidere* (to fall down, fall away). This term is from *de*(down) + *cadere* (to fall), and the IE root *kad* (to fall).

דחי / DIKHĒ means fall or ACCIDENT; דחי / DEKHĒ is translated "stumbling" in *Psalms 116:8.* The D and K don't reverse in all the "fall" words of English and Hebrew, as קדד / KOD(AD) is to bow down.

BRANCHES: Cognates of DECAY under IE *kad* (to fall) include ACCIDENT, CADAVER, CADENCE, CADENT, CASCADE, CASE, CHANCE, CHUTE, DECADENCE, DECIDUOUS, ESCHEAT, INCIDENT, OCCASION and RECIDIVISM.

Greek *kata* (down) should link up with the Hebrew terms above, as well as with תחת / TÄKHÄT (under, below – TK→KT). This would yield the many CATA- words, from CATABOLIC and CATACLYSM to CATHODE and CATHOLIC. At CATHOLIC the dictionary reveals a second meaning for greek *kata* – completely. This recalls ÄKHAT HĒ (it is *all one and the same*).

(DE)CIPHER/סָפַר
SAPH-ARE [S-PH-R]

ROOTS: A CIPHER refers to any Arabic numeral; Late Latin *cifra* is an acknowledged borrowing from Arabic. Arabic *sifr* or *sefr* (a cipher; nothing) is the given source of ZERO (via Italian and French).

"Zero" or "nothingness" does not imply the decoding or deciphering of secret markings. Hebrew סָפַר / SÄPHÄR (to count, number) and סָפַר / SÉPÄR (to count, tell) does imply DECIPHERING symbols (letters or numbers). Semitic numbers and letters were a strange secret code to centuries of illiterate Western traders. Hebrew letters can disguise numbers or words; there is a vast science in numerological interpretations of decoded words in the Hebrew Bible.

> **BRANCHES:** To "recount" or give an "account" is an echo of the meanings of ספר / SÉPÄR (to count, to tell) – *Genesis 24:66*. If numbers and letters are DECIPHERED they will tell or SPELL out a ספור / SÉPOOR (SPIEL or story).
> See "GOSPEL" and "SPHERE."

DELTA/דֶּלֶת
DELET [DLT]

ROOTS: DELTA the fourth letter of the Greek alphabet, is from the fourth letter of the Hebrew alphabet – דלת / DELET (Daleth or "door"– *Proverbs 26:14*). DELTOID means triangular, and the old Daleth (ך) looked like a triangle (reverse D). The "door" of a tent is a triangular flap. תֶּרַע / TIRÄ (door, entrance) is a Chaldaic term listed in the *Hebrew-English Lexicon of the Bible*, and is another TR or DL word resembling DOOR.

> **BRANCHES:** If DOOR is related to Irish *duris* (door) and Polish *drz[wi]* (door), then Hebrew דלת / D-L(R)-S makes as good an etymon as the IE root *dhwer*. Related German words include *Tür* (door) and *Tor* (gate); נדר / GEDTER is a gate. The Japanese *to* (door) is as minimal as "door" pronounced in Alabama ("do"). אטר / ÄDTÄR is to close; דיר / DEER is a sheepfold.
> The IE root of DOOR, *dhwer* (door, doorway), orginally designated the entrance to the gate around the house itself. Arabic and Persian *dar*, as seen in DURBAR, means gate.
> The given cognates of DOOR include FOREIGN, FORENSIC, FOREST, FORUM and THYROID. Only THYROID is a D/T-R word. The others are traced to the mythic IE root *dhwer* via Latin *foras* (out of doors, outside). The F-R terms are better linked to בר / BÄR or BHÄR (field, outside – See "BARRIO").

DEMOCRAT/אֲדָמָה + עֲרִיץ
(A)DUMB-AH + CAR-EAT(S) [DM + KH-R-T-(S)]

ROOTS: Greek *demokratia* means rule (*kratein*) of the people or land (*demos*). The DM Greek term for land and people resembles אדם / ÄDÄM (Adam, man) and אדמה / ÄDÄMÄ (ground, country, region). Humankind is formed "of the dust of the *ground*" in *Genesis 2:7*. Greek *kratein* (rule) is a KRT term akin to עריצות / KHARÉT[SOOT] or ARÉTSOOT (tyranny – *Jeremiah 15:21*).

BRANCHES: The given IE root of AUTOCRACY, DEMOCRACY, or DEMOCRACY is *kar* (hard). Greek *kratos* (strength, might, power) and the IE root relate to קרן / KEREN (horn; power of men or states – see "CROWN" and the *Hebrew-English Lexicon of the Bible*).

While DEMOCRACY is listed at the IE root *da* (to divide) along with DEME, DEMOTIC, DEMAGOGUE, MEDIURGE, ENDEMIC, EPIDEMIC, and PANDEMIC, a better IE root for this "land" term might be *dan* (low ground). DANISH and DEN are traced to IE root *dan*.

Dan and אדמה / ÄDÄMÄ (earth, ground) ought to link up with words like *dam* (earth for the Kiowa Indians), *din* (ground in Thai), *tanah* (ground in Malay), *tian* (field in Chinese) and *timani* (mainland in Eskimo).

MUD might be an MD reversal of the Hebrew etymon.

(DE)VOUR/בָּרָה
VOR-AH [BH-R-H]

ROOTS: DEVOUR is from Latin *de* (an intensifier) and *vorare* (to swallow whole). ברה / BHÄRÄ is to "eat" (*II Samuel 12:17*); בלע / BOLÄ is to "devour." (*Isaiah 28:4*) or "swallow" (*Psalms 69:16*). בער / BHÉAR is a term of feeding, eating and consuming.

> **BRANCHES:** There are several related VR terms like CARNI*VORE* and *VORACIOUS*. Perhaps the "S" is unhistoric in (S)WALLOW and (S)WILL (to gulp) – connected to בלע / BOLÄ above.
> The IE root *g(w)ere* (to swallow) is the given source of DEVOUR. Derivatives like CRAW and REGURGITATE are hard to swallow. BR words like ABROSIA, BRONCHITIS and THEBROMINE are better cognates of DE*VOUR*. FRESS (to pig out or eat rapidly) is a Yiddish and German FR relative.
> בר / BAR is corn, בריה / BÉRYA is food, הבריא / (HÉ)VRÉ is to fatten and ברי / BIRÉ or בריא / BORÉ means fat. These BR terms recall Greek *barys* (heavy; source of BAR- and BARO- words like BAROMETER). The ברוז / BARVAZ (duck) and the BARB (domestic pigeon) are corn-fed or fattened for the eating.
> See "ABLATION."

(DIA)LECT/לָקַט + (דו)
DOO + LEK-ET [LKT]

ROOTS: The prefix DIA- (two) is from Aramaic דו / DOO (two) – see "DUO." Greek *dialektos* (discourse, discussion) is from *legein* (to choose, talk). The IE root is *leg* (to collect – with derivatives meaning to speak). Collecting and speaking deserve separate etymons: לקט / LEK[ET] is to choose, gather or glean (*Genesis 47:14*). להג / LÄHÄG means prattle, idle talk or DIALECT; the verb form means to speak or prattle.

> **BRANCHES:** Other liquid-guttural speaking terms include לחש / LÄKH[ÄSH] to (whisper), רחש / RÄKH[ÄSH] (to express), לעה / LÄKHÄH (to stutter), עלג / ÉLÄG (to stammer), לעז / LÄKHÄZ (to slander; speak a foreign tongue), רכיל / RÄK[HÉL] (to slander) and לגלג / LIGLÄG (to mock).
> Under various IE roots you'll find derivatives of Greek *legein* (to say, speak) and Latin *loqui* (to speak) such as DIALOGUE, ELOCUTION, ELOQUENT, LECTURE, LEXICAL, LEXICOGRAPHER and LOQUACIOUS.

LANGUAGE, LINGO and LINGUISTICS may be nasalized (added N) L-G words; the AHD files them under IE root *dnghu* (tongue). SOLILOQUY and VENTRILOQUISM have been placed at IE root *tolk* (to speak).

The slanderous Hebrew terms above connect to IE root *leugh* (to lie), the given source of BELIE, LIE and WARLOCK.

Greek *logos* (speech, word, reason), also similar to לקח / LEKÄKH (wisdom, knowledge, lesson), gave us ANALOGY, APOLOGY, DECALOGUE, LOGARITHM, LOGIC and PROLOGUE.

See "ELECT."

DIKE/דִּיְק
DA-YAKE   [DYK]

ROOTS: Old French *digue* is a dike; various embankments, causeways and walls are implied here beside the water walls of Holland.

דייק and דיק / DÄYÄK (of *II Kings 25:2* and *Jeremiah 52:4*) are poorly translated as "towers" or "forts," but are correctly defined in dictionaries as a siege-wall, bulwark or rampart.

BRANCHES: At the IE root *dhigw* (to stick, fix) DIG and DITCH are cognates of DIKE. The DOG, that prolific digger and bulwark of defence, may belong here as well. Relevant Hebrew words include תחח / TEKH[ÄKH] (to loosen soil by ploughing), דקר / DEK[ER] (pickax), and a reversal of D(T)K—כתל / KOT[EL] (wall). See "TACK."

DIL(UTE)/דָלַל
DUEL-(LULL)   [D-L]

ROOTS: To DILUTE is to thin down, weaken or reduce (a liquid). It is currently linked to Latin *diluere* (to wash away), where it is considered a cognate of "ablution," "lave" and "lye." See "ALBINO" and לבן / LÄVÄ(N) (to whiten, wash) for the Hebrew etymology of these words.

הדליל / (HE)DLEL is to dilute; דליל / DÄLEL means sparse or thin. דל / DUL (*Genesis 41:19*) means weak, thin or poor; Egypt's canals (דלל / DLL) "[di]minish" or "ebb" in *Isaiah 19:6*.

BRANCHES: דליחה / DILEHÄ is pollution. Samson's DELILAH (often translated "delicate") brought about the hero's weakening. Her name evokes words like הדלדל / (HE)DÄLDÄL (to be detached, be made limp; to be made thin, weak, reduced; to be humiliated).

DOLDRUMS, DOLT and DULL are DL terms that belong here, rather than with the IE root *dheu-* ("to rise in a cloud").

To DILATE (enlarge) is an antonym, linked to Hebrew terms like תלל / TELÄL (to pile or heap up)—see "TALL."

DIREC(TION)/דֶּרֶךְ
DER-EKH   [D-R-KH]

ROOTS: DIRECT is from Latin *di* or *dis* (apart, from) + *regere* (to keep straight, rule, control). With difficulty one can force "from rule" to mean a direction, but with ease one may be DIRECTED to the Hebrew דרך / DEREKH (road, way, journey, manner—*Genesis 16:7; Isaiah 43:16*). הדריך / (HI)DREEKH is to direct; הרגיל / (HI)RGEL is to lead or accustom.

The IE root *reg* (to move in a straight line) relates to רגיל / RÄGEL (regular), לך / LÄKH (go) and the back half of words like דרך / (DÄ)RÄKH (to march, step, tread).

The two parts of the given etymology are treated at "DEBRIS" and at "REGULAR."

As for the DR element טור / TOOR and תור / TOR (a line, row) relates to our etymon as a straight street.

BRANCHES: חרט / KHÄRÄD(T), the reversal of one's דרך / DRK (path, course), is to regret. Below is a chart of selected paths taken by דרך / DEREKH.

The second element, the liquid (L,R) plus guttural (G,K) element, is seen in moving flowing words—see "CATSKILL."

ADDRESS and DRESS are traced to Latin *directus*, while the noun DRESS might also have been influenced by אדרת /(Ä)DERES ("coat"–*Genesis 25:25* or "mantle" *I Kings 19:13*).

Also linked to DIRECT are DIRGE, ERRAND, ERRANT and WAY. See "REACH," "REICH," "REGULAR," and "TRACK."

Hebrew דֶּרֶךְ	(way, manner, journey, road)	De	Re	KH
Arabic	(highway, way)	Ta	Ri	Q
Australian	(paths)	Tu	Ri(n)	Gas
Aborigine	(straight, direct)	Thoo	R	Gool
Bouton: Malay	(road)	Da	Ra	
Chinese	(way)	Dau	Lu	
Czech	(track, way)	T	Ra	Ha
Finnish	(course, way)	To	La	
Gaelic	(journey)	Tu	Rus	
Indonesian	(direction)		aRa	H
Indonesian	(manner, way)	Tja	Ra	
Japanese	(journey)		Ryo	Ko
Japanese	(road)	Do	Ro	
Japanese	(street)	To	Ri	
Korean	(manner, way)		Ro	KHe
Korean	(reversal of *kil*, road, street)		Li	K
Latin	(to direct: source of DIRGE DIRIGIBLE)	Di	Ri	Gere
Polish	(course, track)	To	R	
Polish	(way)	D	Ro	Ga
Russian	(road, way)	Do	Ro	Ga
Spanish	(straight)	De	Re	Cho
Thai	(direct, straight)	Dt	Ro	Hng
English	(ROAD, reversed)	D	R	
	(ROUTE, ROUTINE and RUT reversed)	T	R	
(from Latin *iter*, journey)		iTine	Rary	
		Th	Rou	GH
		Tho	Rou	GHfare
		T	Ra	Ce
		T	Ra	CK
		T	Re	K
		T	Ru	dGe

(DIS)PERSE/פָּרַם
POR-US   [PRS]

ROOTS: Allegedly from Latin *dis* (apart) + *spargo* (to scatter, strew), Hebrew פרם / PÄRÄS (spread out—*Deuteronomy 14:7*), פרש / PÄRÄS(H) ("spread abroad"–*Zechariah 2:10*) or a #1-#2 metathesis of פצר / PÄSER (to scatter) are closer sounding etymons.*

The given IE root for DISPERSE is *(s)preg* (to jerk, scatter), which indicates that the S of Latin *spargo* is suspect.

BRANCHES: FRECKLE is one of the terms listed under IE *(s)preg* (to jerk, scatter). See "BREAK" for Hebrew etymons like פרוק / PÄROOK (dissolution, breaking up). PARC(EL) fits the dividing and distributing here, although it is linked to PART.

See "DIASPORA" for more SPR scattering; see "PART" for the PR 2-letter root.

*DISPERSE can mean "to distribute," a meaning shared by פרם / PÄRÄS and פרץ / PÄRÄ(T)S ("disperse"–*II Chronicles 11:23*).

dive

DIVE/טָבַל
DTOV-(UL) [T-BH-L→DV]

ROOTS: Anglo-Saxon *dyfan* is to immerse; Old Norse *dyfa* is to plunge. IE base *dheup* covers DEEP and DIP; IE root *dub* (to drop, dip) includes DI(M)P(LE), DOPE and DU(M)P. טבל / DTOGVAL is to dip or immerse –"So he went down and *immersed* himself in the Jordan . . ." (*II Kings 5:14*). In *Leviticus 9:9* and *Deuteronomy 33:24* the term is rendered "dip."

BRANCHES: טבע / DTOVÄ is to sink or drown; Polish *topic* (to drown) is related. DAB, DABBLE, DAP, DAPPLE, and perhaps DAUB, DAUPHIN, DOLPHIN, and both meanings of DOVE all fall in.

Other DT-P/V WET words include טפה / TEPA (drop) and דבש / DIV(ASH) honey and other liquids – *Deuteronomy 32:13*.

Manna fell like dew (*Exodus 16:31*) and tasted like honey (*Exodus 16:13*). Germanic *dauwaz*, the source of DEW, appears connected to דבש / DIVASH (honey, as in honeydew).

טפטף / TIPHTÄPH is to drip or drop.

The two-letter root טפ / TP (to drip) has probably influenced TIP (tilt) and TIPPLER. The mottled TABBY cat is from Arabic *attabi* (watered silk). The DIPPING and DAPPLING point to our TB or DP Hebrew etymon.

The DOPEY sense of DOPE is supposed to link up with a DIPPING and DABBLING into narcotics. Instead, DAFFY, DAFT, DEAF, DOPPESS, DUFFER, *FATUOUS*, *STUP*ID and TIPSY might be influenced by טפש / DTEPÄSH (stupid, thick).

(DI)VIDED/בָּדַד
VUD-UD [BH-D]

ROOTS: The IE root is *weidh* or *v(e)idh* (to divide, separate). בדל / BOD(ÄL) is to separate; לבד / (LI)VUD is apart, alone; only; בדד / BÄDÄD or VADAD is "solitary" or "alone" (*Lamentations 1:1*).

BRANCHES: BIT, BITE, BUT, DEVICE, DEVISE, DIVIDED and WIDOW keep company here. Those singular universalists, the Jews, are yet "a people that shall dwell *alone*. . .not reckoned among the nations" (*Numbers 23:9*). בדד.

The opposite of DIVIDE is found in the IE root *dhabh* (to fit together). DAFT, FABRIC and FORGE are fitted to this DB root which reverses the BD of בד.

A טבול / DTIVOOL (turban) or a תבה / DTÄVAH (box, word) is good if it is put together well. Something that is really "together" (good) is טוב / DTOV (good) – see "*DIVINE.*" The opposite of good, BAD, recalls our lonely or broken up BD Hebrew etymons.

See "PIECE."

DIV(INE)/טוב
D(T)OV [T-BH→DV]

ROOTS: Latin *divus* means divine or god. Latin *deus* is god, deity. The IE base *deiwos* (god) is related to the Germanic god *Tiwaz* and Old English *tiw* (god), source of TUESDAY. The Assyrian deity טבת / TEVES or TEVET (*Esther 2:16*) is used to name a month of the Jewish calendar. The IE root of DIVINE is said to be *deiw* (to shine).

Just as God is good (see "GOOD"), טוב / D(T)OV (good) is DIVINE. The term טוב / TOV or DOV is often used as a name and/or attribute of God. "Praise the Lord for He is good. טוב– *I Chronicles 16:34*.

BRANCHES: The opposite of good is bad, but IE *bhad* is good. Hebrew ט-ב / D-BH (good) is *bhad* reversed, and is the source of *dobry* (the Czech, Polish, etc., term for "good"). Derivatives of IE *bhad* (good) include BATTEN, BETTER, BEST and BOOT. Add APT and FIT as reversals of טוב / TOV. DAB and DABSTER infer good or expert skill. Sanskrit *DEVA* is the Hindu god or good spirit; *devah* means god, and *deva* is divine.

Tibil is good for the Maya Indians, while the Dakota Indians reverse to *wa(s)te*.

DIVES, from Latin *dives* (rich), recalls טוב / DTOV (prosperity, wealth).

The IE root *deiw* (to shine. . .sky, heaven, god) takes in ADIEU, DEICIDE, DEITY, DIAL, DIARY, DIET, DISMAL, DIVES, JOVE, JOURNAL, JOURNEY, JOVIAL, JULY , JUPITER, MERIDIAN and ZEUS – but why put faith in godless lexicography?

מטיב / (MÄ)TEBH is well-doing; היטיב / (HÄ)TEBH is to do well. These verb forms of T-B/טב resemble BEATIFIC and BEATIFY. Beauty is the fourth definition of טוב / TB. Reverse the TB again to see BEAUTY.

DOE/תאו
TOE [TO→DO]

ROOTS: A DOE is a female deer or antelope; a תאו / TO (*Deuteronomy 14:5*) is an antelope. Middle English *do* (doe) is elsewhere linked to the IE base *doma* (to make domestic).

DOLL/טָלֶה
DOLL-EH [TL→DL]

ROOTS: The dictionaries posit that DOLL is originally a pet name for Dorothy, but DOLL was originally a pet's name.

טלה / TOLLEH or DOLL-EH is a "suckling lamb" (*I Samuel 7:9*). When the primary language of the civilized world was Aramaic טליה / DOLLYÄ or TOLLYÄ was a common colloquial term for a young child. Both the Hebrew and the Aramaic word echo the second meaning of DOLL: a pretty (but dumb) young thing.

BRANCHES: Goodbye Dorothy, hello DOLLY – the etymology above is reinforced by the definitions of lambkin: 1. little lamb, 2. affectionate term for a young child.

DORM/רָדַם
ROD-UM [RDM→DRM]

ROOTS: *Dormire* is to sleep in Latin; DORM is to doze in Scottish.

רדם / RODUM is to sleep (*Jonah 1:5*); just flip the #1 and #2 root letters.

BRANCHES: A DORM or DORMITORY room is where college students often lie DORMANT, but seldom sleep. Adam was

[EN]TRAN[CED] before he met Eve, as God anesthetized him with a תרדמה / (TÄ)RDÄMÄ ("deep sleep"–*Genesis 2:21*). DOORMOUSE, DORMY, DREAM, TRANCE and DROWSE all relate.

רדם / RDM combines ירד / [Y]RD (to go down) with דמי / DM[Y] (rest, quiet).

חלום / HÄLLŌM (dream) is a possible source of HALLUCIN[ATION].

DRAW/דָלָה
DOLL-OH   [DLH→DRH]

ROOTS: Latin *trah(ere)* is to draw, pull.

דלה / DALAH is "to draw"–(*Exodus 2:19*) The Hebrew DLH easily slides over to the DHR of IE root *dhragh* (to draw) or to the TRH of Latin *trahere*.

BRANCHES: Cognates via IE *dhragh* (to draw) include DRAFT, DRAG and DRAY. IE root *tragh* (to draw, drag) will ATTRACT a dozen TRACT words besides PORTRAY, TRAIL and TRAIN.

T'o la is to pull in Chinese.

DRIP/דְלִיפָה
DIL-LEAP-AH   [DLP→DRP]

ROOTS: Anglo-Saxon *dreopan* (German *triefen*) is to drop or drip. The IE root that means "dripping" is *del*. Hebrew דלף / DOLL-UPH is to drip (*Ecclesiastes 10:18*). "An endless *dripping* on a rainy day and a contentious wife are alike." *Proverbs 27:15*.

BRANCHES: טל / TULL or DULL is dew; מטר / M(Ä)TÄR is rain; טוף / TOOF or DWOOP(H) is to drip. DABBLE, DIP, (DIS)TILL, DRAB, DRIB, DRIBBLE, DRIVEL, DROOP, DROP, (S)TAL(ACTITE) and TALLOW are related.

The IE root given for DREARY, DRIP, DRIZZLE, DROOP, DROP and DROWSE is *dhreu* (to fall, flow, drip, droop). This is probably a DR reversal of the RD root seen in ירד / (YO)RÄD (to go down), הוריד / (HO)RĒD (to bring down) and רדם / RODUM (to fall asleep–see "DORM".

The TEARDROP might better be listed with the TR and DR words here than at IE root *dakru* (tear).

DRIVE/דָרְבָן
DORV-(ON)   [D-R-BH]

ROOTS: IE root *dhreibh* is to drive, push, force on.

דרבן / DORVÄN is a verb and noun meaning spur or goad – (*I Samuel 13:21, Ecclesiastes 12:11*).

BRANCHES: Simon Perlman suggests a #1-#2 letter swap of רדף / RADUF (to chase after–*Genesis 44:4*), from RDF to DRF. Official cognates include DRIFT and DROVE. DRUB may also relate.

DRU(D)G(ERY)/טְרַח
TOR-AKH   [T-R-KH→DRG]

ROOTS: The origin of DRUDGE and DRUDGERY is listed

as "uncertain," but Anglo-Saxon *dreogan* is a person who does hard or unpleasant work. טרח / TORÄKH or DOR-AKH is "labor" or "endeavor," translated "cumbrance" or "trouble" in *Deuteronomy 1:12*.

BRANCHES: (IN)TRIC(ATE) and the slang DRAG may relate. Reducing to DR, the IE root *dere* (to work) takes in DRASTIC and DRAMA.

DUMB/דְמִי
DUMB-(EE)   [DM]

ROOTS: There's the Old English *dumb*, but for DUMB the dictionary offers the IE root *dheu* (to rise in a cloud...related to defective perception or wits). תמר / TĒMÄR or DĒM(ÄR) is to rise in a cloud–see "THYME."

DIM is traced to Old Norse *dimmr* (dark) and IE base *dhem* (smoky). Russian smoke is *dim*; in Turkish it is *duman*. Hebrew covers the silence and senselessness of DUMB. דמי / DUMMY, דמה / DOOMA (*Ezekiel 27:32*) and דממה / DIMAMA (*I Kings 19:12*) all mean silence. דמום / DUMOOM is silent. דם / DOM is to be dumb, while נדם / (NO)DUM is also defined as "dumb."

Dim perception is seen in words like דמדום / DIMDOOM ("dim light" and "blackout"–as in unconscious). טמום / D(T)UMOOM means stupid or senseless; טמטם / DTIMDTÄM is to make stupid; נטמה / (NI)DTMÄ (*Job 18:3*) is to be stupid; and תמה / TOMÄ is to be dumbfounded, astounded or in doubt (*Genesis 43:33*). (S)TUN is from this last term. טעם / DTOAM ("wise"–*Proverbs 26:16*) is an antonym.

BRANCHES: Old Norse *dimmr* (dark) and IE root *tema* (dark–source of TEMERITY) carry us from DM-TM words of physical darkness to terms of being "in the dark."

תם / TOM (a simpleton) may be behind words like TOMFOOL (stupid) and TOMMYROT (foolishness). DIM, the foolish DUMMY, MUTE and MUTTER (reverse the TM), and STAMMER (German *[s]tumm* means dumb) all are related. DUNCE and DUN(DERHEAD) are likely from these Hebrew roots, although the AHD offers the etymology "perhaps: one stunned by a thunderstroke." The opposite of DIM (quiet) is DIN. A loud antonym like DIN (clamor, uproar) relates to טען / DTÄ-UN (to argue, claim) and תאונים / TI-OON(ĒM) (complaint, grumble). DIM echoes of דמם / DTOMÄM are heard in Finnish *tyyni* (quiet) and Indonesian *tenang* (quiet).

See "STEM."

DUMMY/דְמֶה
DEM-EH   [D-M]

ROOTS: DUMMY is considered a derivative of DUMB – see previous entry. DUMMY as a mock-up, model or mannequin is not treated as a word with its own roots.

דמה / DEMEH is a decoy; דמה / DUMMÄ is to resemble (*Songs 7:8*); דמיון / DIM(YON) is a likeness (*Psalms 17:12*). Our human essence was made in the דמות / DIMOOS ("likeness"–*Genesis 1:26*) of our Creator.

BRANCHES: Reversing the MT root of IMITATE may reveal a cognate. If MODEL (representative) is not from MD measurement terms, then it is a DM (likeness) reversal.

If *DEMON* is not from אדון / ÄDŌN (lord) it may refer to a deified idol, image or likeness.

The TO*TEM* pole of American Indians contains deified likenesses. If דמ / D(T)-M (likeness) is not the etymon of TOTEM, then it may be דם / D(T)UM (blood, relations) which refers to the ancestor worship in totemic symbolism. We bear a likeness to our blood relations, thus the common DM root in these Hebrew words.

DUO/דו
DEW   [D-OO/V]

ROOTS: DUO is two in Latin; *di* is two in Greek. The IE root is *dwo* (two).

The Aramaic דו / DOO or DWOO means two. דו-שיח / DOO SEÄKH is a DUOLOGUE (DIALOGUE). To see the IE root *dwo* read the ו of דו as a consonant (V,W) instead of a vowel (oo).

BRANCHES: Cognates listed under IE root *dwo* include: All DI-, DIA-, or DIS- words, DEUCE, DEUTERONOMY, DICHOTOMY, DIPLOMA, DOUBLE, DOUBLET, DOUBLOON, DOUBT, DOZEN, DUBIOUS, DUAD, DUPLEX, DUPLICATE, TWELVE, TWENTY, TWICE, TWIG, TWILIGHT, TWILL, TWINE, TWIST, TWO and ZWIEBACK (from German *zwie*).
(See "CIRRUS.")

Words like TWAIN are discussed at "TWIN"– from תאום / TEŌM or TEWOM (twin– *Genesis 38:27*).

Malay *dua* (two) is not borrowed from French *deux* or Italian *due*.

DICAST is not another DI-word. It's from Greek *dike* (right, law, justice)– from צדק / (TSE)DEK (righteousness, justice).

Also losing the initial S might be the Japanese two, *ni*, from שני / (SHÄ)NĒ (second).

DINOSAUR, *DINO*THERE and DIRE, from IE root *dwei* (to fear) are related to IE root *dwo* (two) because the root for fear originally meant "to be in doubt, be of *two* minds."

DYE/דיו
D'YOE   [DYO]

ROOTS: DYE was spelled *die* or *deah* in Anglo-Saxon. Speculation links DYE with the Old German *tougal* (dark, secret).

Hebrew is a dark secret to most Westerners, so dictionaries could not cite the term דיו / DYŌ ("ink"– *Jeremiah 36:18*).

EACH/אחד
EKH-(UD)   [E-KH-(D)]

ROOTS: There is an *ech* version of EACH in Middle English, but the dictionaries present a combined Anglo Saxon term from *a* (ever) + *gelic* (alike). The IE root *lik* (body, form; like, same) would make EACH a cognate of "like" and "alike".

Both אחד / *EKHUD* (*Genesis 1:5*) and אחת /*EKHUS* 'or *EKHUT* mean "one". כל אחד / KOL EKHOD is "each," and אחד אחד / EKHOD EHKOD in *Isaiah 27:12* is "one by one." אח / AKH is an individual brother or countryman.

BRANCHES: אך / AKH means "but" or "only." אחה / ĒKHA is to put together. If EACH is ultimately from Hebrew, so should Japanese *ichi* (pronounced "each" and meaning number one), Hungarian *egy* (#1), Finnish *yski* (#1), and Chinese *ko ko* (each – reversing E K) and *ch'u* (but). אחת / AHAT or אחד / AHAD (one) is taken up by native (not from Chinese) Japanese *hit[otsu]* (#1), Korean *hit[ori]* (alone), Cantonese *yat* (#1), Fijian *dua* (#1– EHAD reversed), Arabic *[wa]hid* #1), and Thai *took* (each – reverse KT). Aramaic "one" is חד / KHAD. Polish and Czech *jed[en]* softens the KD to GD; the Russian is *ad[in]*.

Already at West Semitic, an N noses its way into ONE words such as Amharic *und*. Drop the end D and you get Greek *ein* (#1) or Latin *uni* (#1) (whence UNIT). Unit recalls the singularity of אין עוד / ÄN ŌDT (no other). It is also possible that UNITE was once יחד / YÄKHÄDT (unite), but the nasalization (N) nosed out the gutteral (KH). I(N)CH may be a missing link between EACH and ONE, as these words de-evolved from a primeval אח / EKH root of oneness. איש / EESH can mean EACH one or EACH thing (*Exodus 26:3*). See "Gather."

EARTH/אֶרֶץ
ERETZ   [A–R–T(S)]]

ROOTS: Middle Irish *ert* is ground; the IE base is *er–t*; the IE root is *er* (earth, ground). ארץ / ÄRET(S) or ERET(S) means ground, land, country, territory or "earth"– (*Genesis 1:1*).

BRANCHES: Related are AARDVARK and AARDWOLF via the Dutch *aerde* (earth).

Because land is *lad* in Polish, the N of LAND is probably a nasalized version of LD. LD is available in ארץ / (A)–R–T(S). Chinese *lu ti* (land) similarly makes the common R to L change, but holds onto the T of the original Hebrew. Reverse the RT to TR to get TERRAIN, TERRESTIAL or TERRITORY. Latin *terra* and *tellus* both mean earth. IE root *ter* (ground, etc.) includes DEAL, TALUS, TELURIC and TITLE.

AREA picks up the אר / AR first element. ארעה / ARAH is the earth in Biblical Aramaic; ארעית / ARĒT means bottom.

EBONY/הֶבְנִי
HAWV–NEE   [H–BH–N–Y]

ROOTS: The etymology traces Greek *ebenos* to Egyptian *hebni*. הבנים / HOBHN(ĒM) is "ebony" in *Ezekiel 27:15*.

BRANCHES: EBONITE, EBONIZE

EGRET/עָגוּר
UG–OOR   [UGOR]

ROOTS: French *aigrette* is a kind of heron, as is Old High German *haigiro*. עגור / UGOOR is the heron-like "crane" of *Isaiah 38:14* or *Jeremiah 8:7*.

BRANCHES: The EGRET is the GIR(AFFE) of the bird kingdom, sharing the GR neck root. נרגרה / GARGIRA means throat or front of the neck and נרון / GÄRON is the neck or throat – the most distinguishing feature of the CRANE or HERON. (G often becomes an H.)

More at "GARGLE" and "GROAN."

EIGHT/חֵית
KHET   [KH – T]

ROOTS: Anglo-Saxon *eahta*, German *acht*, Latin *octo* and IE base *okto/u)* all mean the number EIGHT.

The EIGHTH letter and the number eight in Hebrew is ח / HET or KHET.

BRANCHES: French *huit* (#8) sounds closer to the Hebrew than the Japanese *yattsu* (#8), the 8th Greek letter THETA or the Sula Island *gatahua* (#8).

Cognates via IE root *okto/u)* (eight) include OCTAVE, OCTOBER, OCTOGENARIAN, OCTOGON and OCTOPUS.

The -TH suffix of ordinal numbers (seven*th* or nin*th*) and fractions (one four*th*) is matched by the ת / TH,T suffix in Hebrew רביעית / RIVEYE*TH* (fourth)."Four" is taken up at "QUARTER."

Another -TH suffix, inferring the state or quality of being, occurs in words like steal*th* and weal*th*. A variant of this same suffix is the ending -T of words like heigh*t* or sleigh*t*. The same suffix in Hebrew turns עבד / EVED(servant) into עבדות / ÄVDOOT or ÄVDOO*TH* (servitude).

ELECT/לקוט
LEEK – OOT   [LKT]

ROOTS: Latin *electus* (a verb of picking and choosing) is traced to an IE root *leg* (to collect).

לקוט / LEKOOT is gleaning, picking; לקט / LOKUT is to gather, glean or pick –"gather" in *Genesis 31:46*. Choosing by casting lots is the לכד / LÄKÄDT of *Joshua 7:16*. התלכד / (HIT)LÄKÄDT is to unite.

BRANCHES: Cognates via IE *leg* include: ALLEGE, ANALOGY, APOLOGY, COLLECT, CATALOGUE, COLLEAGUE, COLLEGE, DELEGATE, DIALECT, DILIGENT, DIALOGUE, DECALOGUE, DSYLEXIA, ECLECTIC, ELIGIBLE, HOMOLOGOUS, INTELLIGENT, LECTERN, LECTURE, LEGEND, LEGIBLE, LEGION, LESSON, LEGAL, LEGISLATE, LEGITIMATE, LIGNEOUS, LOGARITHM, LEX, LOYAL, NEGLECT, PROLOGUE, PRIVILEGE, SACRILEGE, SELECT, SYLLOGISM and RELEGATE.

לקח / LEK(ÄKH) is a LESSON, wisdom, or that which is taken, gotten, or gathered in INTEL*LECT*UALLY. See "CULL" and "LEX."

EL(K)/איל
EYE – ULL   [EYL]

ROOTS: The ELK or large deer was spelled *elh* and *eolh* in Anglo-Saxon.The IE root is *el* (red, brown ...forming animal and tree names).

איל / ÄYEL is a stag or hart *(Isaiah 35:6)*; אילה / ÄYÄLÄH is a doe, gazelle or hind *(Genesis 49:21)*.

BRANCHES: The ELAND is an official cognate. Reverse to *lu* for a Chinese deer, the WAPITI might be from צבי / T(S)IV – VÈ (deer) backwards; *sibil*-keh, the Maya deer, better resembles צבי / (T)SIBHÈ (deer).

ELM/אילן
EE-LUN   [ELN→ELM]

ROOTS: Like the Hebrew אילן / ELN (tree), the ELM is a generic name for hardy shade trees. The stump of Latin *ulmus* (elm) is the IE root *el* (red, brown – see the previous entry). The *el* root corresponds to אלה /ÄLH (terebinth tree in *Genesis 35:4*). Four verses later, in *Genesis 35:8*, is the אלון / ÄLON(oak tree). אילם / ELIM (literally "terebinth trees" or "grove of oaks") is the name of the tree-filled oasis of *Exodus 15:27*.

BRANCHES: The Southern Israeli city of אילת / ÄLAT(Elat) is also a tree name. The IE root *el* only takes in the ALDER and ELDER trees. ULMACEOUS means of the Elm family. ULM, Germany is probably related, as is the ALAMO – from a Spanish term for the cottonwood or poplar tree.

ALMUG and ALGUM trees are official borrowings from Hebrew אלגום / ALGOOM. The ILANG-ILANG tree (Tagalog), the LINDE(N) and the LIME tree all relate. Hebrew branches include ארן / OREN (Pine, fir) and ערמון / URMON (chestnut tree). *Lin* is a forest in Chinese. *Lemn and legne* are the words for "wood" in Rumanian and Italian.

(ELM)HURST/חרש
(K)HOAR – ESH   [H – R – SH]

ROOTS: For the ELM of ELMHURST (a common place name), see the entry above.

A HORST meant a thicket and a HURST means a grove or small wood – mainly preserved in place names like PINEHURST.חרשא / HOORSHÄ is a forest in Aramaic, חרש / HORESH is "thicket," wood or bush in Hebrew *(Ezekiel 31:3)*. This HRS word is usually a place name in Scripture.

BRANCHES: HOLT is an archaic term for a grove or copse, akin to German *HOLZ* (wood) – note the HRS to HLS/T changes. RUSTIC and, more remotely, FOREST are related – see the RS element at "BRUSH." There is an IE root *hule* (forest, timber) from a Greek noun "of unknown origin."

It includes terms like HYLOZOISM and METHYLENE.

(EM)BEZZ(LE)/בזז
BUZ – UZ   [BZZ]

ROOTS: To (EM)BEZZLE is to steal, but the given etymon is Old French *besillier* (to destroy). Similarly, WASTE is from Latin *vastare* (to lay waste). Laying WASTE a conquered city involved constructive looting, not just destructive vandalism.

בז / BĀZ is spoil or plunder. Spoil and WASTE have both come to mean "ruin" instead of BOOTY. בזבוז / BĒZBOOZ or VĒSBHOOS is squandering, extravagance or WASTEFULNESS.

The verb is בזז / BĀZAZ or VĀSĀS(to plunder, pillage – *Jeremiah 3:37 or 50:37*). Hebrew's בזז / BZ etymon for EMBEZZLE implies both stealing and destroying.

BRANCHES: Cognates of WASTE at IE root *eu* are listed at "VACATE." Nature's looter, taking spoils after the battle, is the hawk or BUZZARD. *Bosen* is a buzzard for the Kiowa Indians. See "BUZZARD."

EMISSARY / מְסָר
MOSS–ARE   [MSR]

ROOTS: EMISSARY, EMISSION and EMIT are all said to have originated with Latin *missus*, a past perfect of *mittere* (to send).

The IE root is *(s)meit* (to throw); שמט / S(H)ĒMAT is to REMIT or "release"– *Deuteronomy 15:2*.

BRANCHES: מסר / MOSĀR is to deliver or transmit – EMISSARIES or representatives are "delivered" in *Numbers 31:4*. מסה / MĒSA is tribute or offering (*Deuteronomy 16:10*); נתן / (M)NOSUN or NOTUN is to give or deliver up (*Genesis 25:6*), and נדב / NO(D)TUV is to donate (See "ENDOW").

A cognate like MISSILE recalls מסלה / MISĒLA (way, path, orbit, course – *Isaiah 40:3*) in that a projectile has a trajectory (מסלול / MUSLOOL). Coursing through the skies are the heaven-sent constellations or מזלות / MĀZĀL(OS).

מטר / MATAR(to rain on, send down upon) recalls Latin *mittere* (to send).

EMISSARY'S official cognates include: ADMIT, COMMIT, DISMISS, (church) MASS, MESS, MESSAGE, MISSION, MISSIVE, OMIT, PERMIT, PREMISE, PROMISE, REMISSION, SUBMIT, SURMISE and TRANSMIT.

(EN)CASE / כָּסָה
CUSS–AH   [K–S–(H)]

ROOTS: The dictionaries hand us the Latin *capsa* (box) and IE root *kap* (to take, grasp, hold) as the source of CASE, ENCASE, CASEMENT, CAISSON and CASKET.

The *kap* above is from words like כף / KAPH (palm of the hand – see "CUFF").

Hebrew terms of encasement include כסה / KĀSĀ (to cover, conceal, encase – *Leviticus 13:13*), החסין / HĒKHS[ĒN] (to store up), חסוי / KHĒSOOY(shelter), and כים / KĒS (pocket, SLIPCASE, purse – *Proverbs 1:14*).

BRANCHES: Reverse to *saku* for the Indonesian pocket – see "SACK." קשקשת / KAS(H)KES(H)ET is the protective scales on fish or men (in armor).

CASCARA, CASING, CASK, CASQUE, CASSETTE, CASSOCK, CASTANETS (and perhaps CASTLE) are all covered here. See "HOUSE" and "MAGAZINE."

CHEST (the box) and CHEST (the breast) are both considered cognates of CIST and CISTERN at IE root *kista* (basket). The anatomical CHEST has Hebrew etymons to consider, such as חצן / KHATSAN or KHASTAN (bosom, chest – related to a word in *Nehemiah 5:13* and חשן / KHOSHEN (breastplate).

ENDOW / נָדַב
NOD – UV   [N – D – BH→NDW]

ROOTS: Middle English *endowen* or Old French *endouer* is allegedly a combination of *en* (in) and *douer* (to give) – from Latin *dotare* (to give). This etymology is suspect because of words like *nadawac*(to give) in Polish.

נדב / NODUV is to donate, נדבה / NIDOVĀ or NIDOWĀ is a donation, alms or the "freewill offering" of *Exodus 35:29*.

BRANCHES: DOWAGER and DOWRY are cognates.

DONATE, from Latin *dono* (to give), recalls the imperative תן / TĀN (give! – *Genesis 14:21*). Latin *donum* is a gift or DONATION; אתנן / ETNĀN (*Deuteronomy 23:19*), מתן / MĀTĀN (*Genesis 34:12*), and נדבה / NIDĀVĀ (the DN reversed are the Hebrew equivalents. תן / SĀN resembles *zona*(to give, present – in the extinct Venetic language of Northeast Italy).

Appearing in the name Isadore, Greek *doron* is a gift. דורון / DŌRON is a gift in Aramaic. Spanish, Portuguese, and Italian have "dar" giving terms.

There is also a double-dental dimension to giving terms, as seen in Latin *dotare*(to give – source of DATA), Greek *didonai*(to give – source of ANTIDOTE), or Russian *dat* (to give – source of SAMIZDAT). All these are prefigured by תת / TĀT or DTĀDT, rendered "to give" in *Genesis 29:19* or "to yield" in *Genesis 4:12*.

The IE root here is reduced all the way to *do* (to give). Cognates of ENDOW, DONOR and ANTIDOTE include ADD, ANECDOTE, APODOSIS, BETRAY, CONDONE, DACHA, DADO, DATE, DATIVE, DATUM, DIE(2), DOT(2), EDITION, EPIDOTE, GUERDON, PARDON, PERDITION, RENDER, RENT(1), SURRENDER, TRADITION, TRAITOR, TREASON and VEND.

T'an is to apportion in Chinese; *yuti* is to hand over or give in Arabic (יד / YĀDT is a hand in Hebrew); *ataeru* is to give in Japanese; *ad* is to give in Hungarian; *antaa* is the equivalent in Finnish, *toa* (like the IE root *do*) is giving in Swahili.

E(N)GL(ISH) / עָקַל
EE-KOOL   [EKL→ENGL]

ROOTS: The IE root of ANGLE and ENGLAND is *ank* (to bend). Latin *Angli* (the Angles) retains the L. The language of the Angles (and Saxons) is linked to עקל / ĒKĀL (to bend, twist, pervert – *Habakkuk 1:4*).

BRANCHES: Cognates and evidence of the nasalization (added N) of the Hebrew etymon may be seen at "ANKLE."

(EN)SCON(CE) / שָׁכַן
S(H)A-KUHN   [S(H)-KH-N]

ROOTS: To be ENSCONCED is to be placed somewhere safely, snugly and securely. No one could be better ensconced than Benjamin. "He *rests* securely beside Him . . .*rests* between His shoulders."– *Deuteronomy 33:12*. The Hebrew here is שכן / S(H)ĒKAN (caused to dwell, fixed) or שכן / S(H)ĀKHĀN (to settle down, abide, dwell.)

Just as ENSCONCE can mean to shelter and its Dutch source (*schans*) can mean a fortress. שכון / S(H)ĒKOON means housing, and שכונה / S(H)IKHOONĀ a settlement.

Under the same roof there's SCENE, from Greek *skene* (a covered place or tent). The Hebrew etymon appears in *Judges 8:11* to describe "tent dwellers." See "SCENE."

Dutch *schans* originally meant wickerwork, before SCONCE meant to shelter or screen and a hut or shed. סכך / SÄKHÄKH is to entangle (as wickerwork), to screen, and to cover – *Exodus 28:28*. סכה / SOOKÄ is a booth, shed or tabernacle (*Leviticus 23:42* – see "SHACK") and סכך / SIKHÄKH is the covering of tangled branches upon this SCO(N)CE or hut.

Added to the SK root of sheltering is a KN word like קן / KÄN (nest, dwelling). The two elements combine to make SKN sound cozy and safe.

BRANCHES: Joining the SCENE are SCENARIO and SCENERY, with other possibilities including (AB)SCOND (the equivalent of "to house" – a current slang term of stealing and hiding), ISCHIUM (from Greek *ischion* – the bone where the body rests when sitting), and SKIN (the protective covering we're ensconced in – a word credited to *sek*, an IE root that means to cut.)

(Ja)skinia is a cave in Polish, *song* is to live in Vietnamese (switch #2-#3).

See "HAUNT."

ESMER(ELDA)/שָׁמִיר
S(H)A-MEER   [S(H)-M-R]

ROOTS: Esmeralda the name, like the gem EMERALD, is traced from Middle French *esmeragde* or *esmeraude* to Latin *smaragdua* and Greek *smaragdos*.

שמיר / SHÄMÊR is a diamond, emery or "flint" in *Ezekiel 3:9*. One dictionary defines שמיר / SMR specifically as *smiris corundum*; EMERY is a hard corundum used in grinding and polishing (gem stones and other material). The IE base of EMERY is *smer*.

BRANCHES: *Webster's Third International Dictionary* does say that EMERALD is "probably of Semitic origin." See "BRIGHT."
ESMERALDA is also a region and language family in Ecuador.

ETYM(OLOGY)/אֱמֶת
EM-ET   [EMT→ETM]

ROOTS: ETYMON (from Greek) infers the literal sense of a word. The etymon of ETYMOLOGY is the Greek word *etymos* (true). The true etymon never lies in a language as late as Greek. Merely flip root letters #2 and #3 (ETM to EMT) to see אמת / EMET (true, truth, truly).

". . . the word of the Lord in thy mouth is *truth*."– אמת / *I Kings 17:24*.

BRANCHES: To form "truth" one takes the first (א) and last (ת) letters of the Hebrew alphabet, placing the middle letter (מ) between them. "TRUE" north refers to the earth's middle or axis, not her magnetic poles. The true path is the middle road. אמצע / EMTZÄ is middle.
Womb (אם / ÄM = mother) to tomb (מת / MÄT=death) is our abiding objective truth. Truth requires אמץ / ÕMETZ (courage) for overcoming human subjectivity.

"True" in Japanese is *honto*; reverse to *dina* for the Fijian. It isn't false to switch the M to an N and the T to a D. *Genesis 11* would have us think of these national and linguistic differences as God-given.

Maa-t is truth in the language of ancient Egypt.

EUROPE/מַעֲרָב
(MA)-ARE-OV   [U-R-B(H)→URP]

ROOTS: The dictionary doesn't know what EUROPE means. *Eurōpe* or EUROPA in Greek mythology was the Phoenician princess carried off to the West (Crete) by the bullish Zeus. A Phoenician-Hebrew etymon is not out of place here.

EUROPE is "the West," especially to a Middle-Easterner. In the Hebrew vernacular מערב / (MÄ)UROBH means "West," as in *Psalms 103:12*. The directional prefix מ / m is added to the root ערב / EREBH (evening), as West is the direction of twilight and the setting sun. Joseph T. Shipley cites Assyrian monuments presenting *Ereb* ("setting sun land") and *Asu* ("land of the rising sun"). These became known as "Europe" and "Asia." EUROPA's story may be yet another folk etymology in our reference books.

BRANCHES: An R→L change might allow us to see the natural connection between west [ערב / (A)RV] and LEF(T), from Latin *laevus* (left). There are also several LEVO- terms like LEVODUCTION.
Magharibi, Swahili's word for "west," retains the initial M of מערב / MÄURÄBH. The Arabic (also gutturalizing the ע to GH) is pared down to the Semitic root – (*gharb*).
Perhaps the expanse of EUROPE might be linked in part to EURY- (wide, broad in Greek). EURY's IE root *wer* (wide, broad) is a reversal of רוח / RV)w)H (wide, spread, space, interval) – a probable influence on words like FAR and ROVE.
See "ASIA."

EVE(NING)/הֶעֱיב
(HEY)–EVE   [EV]

ROOTS: Middle English *eve* meant EVENING, and may or may not have been shortened from EVEN (evening) or EVENING (twilight until fully dark). The given etymology is in the dark, groping with an Anglo-Saxon verb *aefnian* (to grow toward evening) and citing IE bases *epi* and *opi* which mean "after" and "later." (See "Over.")

העיב / (HÄ)EV is to darken or become cloudy. יעיב / (YÄ)EV in *Lamentations 2:1* means "covered with a cloud." The infinitive of this verb, עוב / E-(W)-BH or KH-(W)-BH, is a match for the IE root *kwep* (to smoke, etc.) and Greek *kap(nos)* (cloud, smoke) – the sources of VAPOR. עב / ÄV or KHÄV means thick, "thicket" (*Jeremiah 4:29*), or "cloud" as in: "the sky grew black with *clouds*"– *I Kings 18:45*.

BRANCHES: The darkening skies of twilight and its mixed light are also seen in Hebrew's principal word for EVE (the night before) or EVENING – ערב / EREV (*Genesis 1:5*). ערוב / ÄROOV is a mixture. Terms like חפה / HOOPA or KHOOPÄ (canopy) are seen at "COVER." Reverse עב / GV (cloud) to see FOG. Cognates of VAPOR at IE *kwep* include VAPID and EVAPORATE. Cloud words that hear עב / ÄV as a vowel with a bilabial (two-lip) consonant include *awan* (cloud in Indonesian) and *opun* (cloud in Hawaiian). There's *ufi* (to smoke) in Tongan. Reduce to *o* (cloud in Fijian); reverse to *wu* (fog in Chinese).

EVIL/עֲוֶל
AH-VELL   [EVL]

ROOTS: Despite Middle English forms of evil like *uvel*, dictionaries offer us the IE base *upo* (up from under) or the IE root *wep* (bad, evil) as the source of EVIL.

עול / UVEL is "iniquity" in *Deuteronomy 32:4*; עולה / UVLÄ is injustice or wrong.

BRANCHES: עוה / UVÄ (to sin, do wrong), עוון / UVŌN (sin), עון / ÄVEN (wickedness), עבירה / ÄVÄRÄ (sin), נבל / NÄVÄL ("a vile person"), בליעל / BILEAL (wickedness), נפל / (NA)PHAL (to fall) and אפילה / ÄPHÄLÄ (darkness) all ultimately relate.

English terms like BALE (evil), VILE and VILLAIN are better placed in the bad company above. DEVIL might feel at home with these, or with תפלה / TIFLÄ (unsavoriness, obscenity) rather than the given etymon: Greek *dia* (across) + *ballein* (to throw)...thus to slander.

Perhaps the colloquial AWFUl (very bad, ugly, unpleasant) is connected to these Hebrew terms. It may have been confused with the "full of awe" AWFUL which has opposite meanings like "worthy of reverence."

See "VILE."

EXIT/חוץ
KHOOTS   [KH-OO-T)S) → K-ST]

ROOTS: Exit is from *ex* plus *ire* (Latin: to go). Greek *exo* is "outside out." The IE root is *eghs* or *eks* (out). Latin and Greek *ex* mean out; חוץ / KHOO(T)S or HOOT(S) means the outside (*Genesis 24:31*) or exterior. The KS or HT root hinges on the צ / TS. צא / TSÄ means "go out!" (*Genesis 8:16*). הוציא / (HO)TSEE or HŌSTE is to bring out, to *EX*CLUDE, or to OUST.

BRANCHES: חוץ מין / KHOOTS or (H)OOTS (MIN) means EXCEPT. קצה / KÄTSEH is an EXTREMITY. The X or Xerxes, etc. demonstrates the X/S affinity. There are hundreds of words with OUT in it or with prefixes like ECTO-, EX-, and EXO-.

Bakate is "out" in Korean; בחוץ / (BÄ)KHOOTS is the outside. *Chut* is out in Cantonese. *Odchodzic* is to leave or go away in Polish.

Outgoing food material is צאה / TSÄÄ (EXCREMENT). Birth is an EXILE, and we have all been EXPELLED. צאצא / TSE-TSÄ means children or offspring. *Uzazi* is birth in Swahili; *zi* means children (and bullets) in Chinese.

In Cantonese *zŏu* is to come out or discharge; in Vietnamese *Xuat* is to export or send out.

יצא / YATSÄ is to go out, depart or expire. *YESTER*DAY, the departed day, is currently traced to the IE root *ghjes* (yesterday). יצא / Y-TS-Ä might be seen in the "yesterday" words of Dutch (*gister*), Serbo-Croatian (*juče*) and Japanese *sakujitsu*.

חוצה / HOOTSA (out – *Genesis 24:29*) ought to link up with Germanic and Old English *ut* (out). If so, the cognztes of OUT include ABOUT, AUSLANDER, BUT, CAROUSE, ERSATZ, HU(BRIS), ORT, OUTLAW, UTMOST and UTTER.

EYE/עין
EYE-IN   [EY(N)]

ROOTS: There are older EYE words in Middle English like *ein* and *eyne*. The Old Teutonic *augon* (eye) has gutturalized the ע to a G and switched places with the י / Y. The given IE root for EYE, *ok(w)* (to see), resembles neither עין / UYIN (eye – *Exodus 21:24*) nor a score of the cognates attributed to this theoretical root.

BRANCHES: The L of EYELET is from *oeil*, the French eye. OCUL(AR), (MON)OCLE and OGLE also display the ן/נ (N) to L change seen in the connection between ba*n*k and Old English ba*l*ca (bank), or that between ma*n* and ma*l*e. Reading סכל / SKL (to look at) as OKL or KL also renders LOOK, OCULAR, and OGLE.

It's not hard to see EYE to EYE with the following versions of עין which contain an ע (vowel, CH,G or K), a י (Y,J or H) and/or a נ (N, M or L):

Chinese *yan*, Eskimo *iye*, German *auge*, Italian *occhio*, Japanese *me*, Cantonese *ngaan*, Korean *nun*, Malaya: Galela *lako* (OCULAR reversed), Malay: Sula Island *hama*, Maidu (California Indians) *hin*, Portugese *ojho*, Spanish *ojo*, Swahili *jicho*, Welsh *llyg(ad)* Yoruba (Nigerian) *oju* and Tamil *kan*. Reverse to *mada*, the Hawaiian eye.

The Welsh term is a cognate of LOOK. (See the Malay *lako* above.) עין / KH-Y-(l) reveals that OCUL(IST) and LOOK are backwards cognates. עין / ÄYIN is also to eye or see. Unlike the noun above, Chinese for to EYE or LOOK is *k'an*.

עין / KYN renders CANNY, CONAN, CAN, CONNOSSEUR, CONNOTE, GAN(DER), IGNORE, IGNORANT, KEN, and KNOW, since seeing or perceiving is knowing.

Window is cognate with *okno* (window in Czech, Polish, and Russian) and *ikkuna* (the Finnish window). These are all from עין/KYN (the eye, or window of the soul).

FACUL(TY)/פעל
FAW-KUL   [PH-KH-L]

ROOTS: Latin *facere* is to make, do; פעל / POAL, PHOÄL or PHOKHÄL is to do, make, act, פעל / PHŌKHAL is "work" (of hands) in *Deuteronomy 33:11*. Latin *farious* (doing), French *faire* (to do) and *facere* above are all filed under the IE root *dhe* (to set, put). The Hebrew PH–L and PH–K terms better suit the etymons above.

הפיק / (HA)PHEK is defined as "to produce;" in *Proverbs 3:13* and *12:2* the verb is translated "to attain" and "to earn."

BRANCHES: AFFECTION, ARTIFICE, ARTIFACT, DIFFICULT, EFFECT, FACILE, FACT(ION), FACTOR(Y), MANUFACTURE, PERFECT, SACRIFICE, and much more are listed cognates of FACULTY.

See "FIGURE."

FADE/פיד
FEED   [FYD]

ROOTS: The 3rd definition of FADE is "to disappear slowly, die out." The *Hebrew-English Lexicon of the Bible* defines פיד / PED as "disappeared, died." In the Bible this term is most often pronounced פיד / FĒD.

The given etymology of FADE can only guess: "probably [from] Latin *vapidus* (stale); influenced by fatuous, foolish, silly."

> **BRANCHES:** Because the Biblical translations of פיד / FĒDT in *Proverbs 24:22* and *Job 30:24* favor "doom" and "calamity," we might consider (DE)FEAT a possible cognate.

FAG/פָּג
FUG   [PH-G]

ROOTS: FAG as fatigue or weariness is considered an earlier form of FLAG (to droop, decline, hang loosely). FLAG is traced only as far back as Middle English *flacken* (to flutter).

פג / PHUG is "faint" in *Genesis 45:26*, "slacked" in *Habakkuk 1:14* and "feeble" in *Psalms 38:8*.

פגר / P(H)GR is a term of sluggishness or exhaustion (*I Samuel 30:21*).

> **BRANCHES:** פגר / PEGER is a corpse, empty of life as well as of energy. For B-K terms of emptiness see "VACATE."

FAITH/בֶּטַח
VET-AH   [BH-T-Ḥ]

ROOTS: FAITH is believed to have originated with Latin *fides* (faith, trust), from the IE root *bheidh* (to persuade, compel or confide). Instead, have FAITH in the oldest and greatest body of writing and in words like בטחון / BHE(D)T(ÄHON) (faith, trust, CONFIDENCE). "But I *trust* in your faithfulness." בטחתי — *Psalms 13:6*.

> **BRANCHES:** עבט / AVODT (pledge) helps establish the two-letter root as B(H)-(D)T. Antonyms include בטל / BHÄDT(ÄL) (null, VOID). ABIDE, ABODE and BIDE, also somehow linked to IE *bheidh*, are more likely from בטל / BOTÄL (to stop, to be idle, to suspend).
> A BD antonym that recalls BAD, בדאות / BÄD(ÄOOT) (fraud, deceit) betrays CONFIDENCE and FAITH. A FAITOR is an imposter. *The IE root wegwh (to preach, speak solemnly) sounds like an imposter, and not like the true BH-T source of DEVOTE, DEVOUT or VOTIVE.*
> *FIANCE is also linked to the IE root bheidh.* The related IE root *wadh* (pledge) includes DEGAGE, ENGAGE, GAGE, MORTGAGE, WAGE, WAGER, WED, WEDDING, WEDLOCK and PRAEDIAL.
> The closest cognates to FAITH are FEALTY, FIDELITY, INFIDEL(ITY), and PERFIDY. Other cognates, and more data are seen at "AFFIDAVIT," "BET," and "VOTE."

FAKER/פָקִיר
FAH-KEER   [FKR]

ROOTS: There is no real etymon for FAKE and FAKER. FAKE had been spelled "feague" and "feake," and speculation leads to 17th century thieves' slang.

Unnoticed is the affinity with the non-IE word FAKIR. The theoretical "thieves" who gave us FAKER were probably alluding to their Near and Middle Eastern "colleagues"– the FAKIR or FAQIR. This Arabic term refers to India's class of holy beggars who display self-made infirmities and who are venerated as miracle workers. To Westerners the FAKIR is a beggar, con man and FAKER, but this Moslem or Hindu ascete is respected for pronouncing הפקיר / (HE)F'KEER (renouncing of all property). פקיר / FÄKER is the Hebrew term for FAKIR.

> **BRANCHES:** A #2-#3 letter exchange reveals the related verb פרק / PÄRÄK (to unload, throw off – *Genesis 27:40*). A #1-#2 letter swap offers כפר / KOFÄR or KIPPUR (to deny, to atone – *Leviticus 23:28*). The sincere FAKIR is living a long Yom Kippur of ascetic denial to win repentance. The insincere or FAKE FAKIR is showing off his self-made sorrow to win a few coins or a BAKSHEESH (gratuity).
> A BAKSHEESH in Hindi, Persian, Turkish and Egyptian is a tip, from the Arabic word for a gift or bribe. Whether it is the Indian FAKIR standing painfully on one leg or the bellhop at the Cairo Hilton, their "services" demand (with the full dignity of Eastern beggars) a BAKSHEESH – from בקשה / BÄKÄSHÄ (entreaty, request).
> If one hears BEG (or possibly BESEECH) in בקש / BÄKÄSH (to beg, pray for, ask – *Isaiah 1:12*) it is because this term links the sound of the word BEGGAR with that of FAKIR and FAKER.
> For begging in Thai, reverse to *kaw* (KW=GB). *Bak* is to ask in Coeur d'Alêne, a Sulishan Indian language of the Pacific NW.
> *Beggen* in Middle Dutch means to request urgently, but the etymon eludes the experts. In Holland of the 13th Century there thrived another lay brotherhood of BEGGARY called BEGHARD.
> BECK, BECKON and BEHEST have no known source earlier than Anglo-Saxon, and so they all may be influenced by בקש / BÄKESH (to ask, seek).
> הפגין / (HI)FGIN is to publicly demonstrate and cry out. הפגיע / (HI)FGEÄ (to beseech, entreat – *Genesis 23:8* or *Ruth 1:16*) is yet another like-sounding term of BECKONING and BEGGING.
> Finnish *parka* (poor, pitiable) may link up with FAKIR.

FALL/נָפַל
(NAW)-FUL   [PH-L]

ROOTS: Anglo-Saxon *feallan* and the IE root *phol* (to fall) have not FALLEN far from the Hebrew נפל / (NÄ)PHÄL (to FALL, to BEFALL). הפיל / (HE)PEEL is to FELL or TOPPLE (make fall). Falling into a pit is the נפל / (NÄ)FÄL of *Exodus 21:33*, while the FALL or DOWNFALL of a city recalls מפלה / (MÄ)PÄLLÄ (ruin, downfall, defeat).

> **BRANCHES:** APOLLYON the angel is from a Greek verb of ruining and destroying. The mysterious *Nephilim* (fallen ones – *Genesis 6:4*) may have landed like *nephele* (clouds – Greek source of NEBULA).
> Darkness and night FALL. אפל / APHAL is to set (as the sun); אפלה / APHÄLA is darkness. Official cognates of FALL include OFFAL, but not FAIL, FAUL(T), (reversing P-L) LAP(SE) or LABILE.
> The French and Rumanian "rain" words seem to have the PL root of falling.

FAN/נָפָה
NAWPH-ĀH]   [N – PH → FN]

ROOTS: FAN is from Latin *vannus* (winnowing device), linked to IE terms of blowing.

נפה / NĀPHĀ is a FAN; נפה / NĒPĀ is to winnow; הניף / (HĀ)NEEPH is to swing, wave or FAN – *Exodus 35:22*. As an etymon for FAN, נפח / NĀPHAH (to blow, swell, breathe – *Genesis 2:7*) is more than a match for IE root *pu* (to blow, swell), which is credited with EMPHYSEMA, PHYSO-, PREPUCE and PUSTULE. כנף / (K')NĀF (wing) literally means "like a fan."

BRANCHES: The same PN (NP, VN or WN) root appears in words like PNEUMA, PNEUMONIA, VENT(ILATE), WIND and WINNOW. Greek *pnein* and the IE root *pneu* is to breathe; Germanic root *fneu* is to sneeze.

The wind must have blown the word *pniw* (to blow) to the Klamath Indians of Oregon.

נפש / NEFESH is breath or soul (*Genesis 1:30*). *Nafas* is breath and *njawa* is soul in Indonesian (where J = S). "Breath" in Modern Greek is *anapnoe*, and in Swahili it is *pumzi* (akin to our PN terms).

FAT/פטם
FEET-(AĬM)   [P(H)-T-M]

ROOTS: Anglo-Saxon *faettian* is to fatten; פטם / FĒT(ĀM) is to fatten. Reversing to DP, ADEPS (Latin) is the scientific term for animal fat; פדר / PĀD(ER) is animal fat – *Leviticus 1:8*.

FAT is officially linked to the Germanic root *paid* and the IE root *pei* (to be fat, swell).

BRANCHES: פטם / PĒT(OM) is the knob, BUTTON or swelling on the ends of some fruit. (The word is Hebrew via Aramaic.) בטן / BET(EN) is the belly (too often a repository of bulging fat).

כטבט / BIDT(BEDT) is to swell; אבוס / ĀBHOOS is fattened; טפש / TOPH(USH) is to become fat; *fat/ima* is fat in Arabic.

The P(H)-T reverses in תפח / TEPH(ĀH) swelling and תפוח / TAPOOĀH (apple...*POTATO*). כבד / (KO)VEDT is heaviness.

English words like BUD, BUTT, BUTTER, BUTTOCKS, BUTTON, FEED, FODDER, PASTOR and PASTURE are possibly related. Arabic *al-fas-fasah* (good fodder) is the given source of ALFALFA.

See "BOTULISM," "OBESE," and "PAD."

FERRY/עֶבְרָה
(AH)–VARA   [U-BH-R]

ROOTS: Anglo-Saxon *ferian* is to convey or carry; Greek *pherein* is to carry.

One ought to hear the BH-R source of FERRY in this phrase from *II Samuel 19:19* – V'OVRAH Ha'AVARA La'AVEER ET BAT HaMELEKH / "And the ferry-boat passed to and fro to bring over the king's household" (JPS). עברה / ĀVĀRĀ or ĀBHĀRĀH is also rendered ford, transition and crossing. עבר.

BRANCHES: FERRY is traced to IE root *per* (to lead, pass over) which carries freight such as: COMPORT, DEPORT, EMPORIUM, EXPORT, FARE, FERE, FERN, FIRTH, FJORD, FORD, IMPORTUNE, OPPORTUNE, PERONEAL, PORT, PORTABLE, PORTAGE, PORTER, PORTFOLIO, PURPORT, RAPPORT, REPORT, SPORT, SUPPORT, TRANSPORT, WAYFARER, and WELFARE.

Faru in Anglo-Saxon is a journey; Arabic *(yous)afir* (travel) gave us SAFARI.

העביר / (HE')EVER is to bring over or cause to pass over; מעבר / (MĀ')ĀVĀR and מעברת / (MA')BORE(T) mean ferry and ferryboat; העברה / (HA)AVARA is a transfer; and מעברת / (MĀ')OOBER(ET) means pregnant or BEARING an עבר / OOBĀR E(M)BRYO).

The IE root *bher* (to carry; also to bear children) bears BEAR, FOREBEAR, BIER, BORE (a wave), BAIRN, (WHEEL)BARROW, BURDEN, BIRTH, BRING, -FER, FERTILE, CONFER, DEFER, DIFFER, INFER, OFFER, PREFER, PROFFER, REFER, SUFFER, TRANSFER, VOCIFERATE, FERRET, FERTIVE, -PHORE, AMPHORA, EUPHORIA, METAPHOR, PERIPHERY, PHEROMONE and PARAPHERNALIA.

See "SUFFER" for an alternate Hebrew source.

הוביל / (HŌ)BHĒL is to bring, lead, carry, and transport. אפריון / ĀPĒRĒON (*Songs 3:9*) is a litter for carrying or transporting royalty, etc.

Other English words that might relate include BARREN, FAR, VEHICLE and VEIN.

See "FUHRER" and "OVER."

FET(US)/בַּת
VUT   [BH-T]

ROOTS: Latin *fet(us)* means offspring or pregnancy.

בת / BUT or BHUT is a daughter (*Genesis 29:10*), a suburb (*Joshua 17:11*), and a term equivalent to the phrase "a native of."

BRANCHES: ביצה / BĀTSĀ is an egg in Hebrew; the Arabic is *bēd*. פעוט / PĀOT or FAOT is a minor or child, while טף / TUF (infant – *Jeremiah 40:7*) reverses to FT. *Poti'i* is a girl in Tahitian; Akkadian *buntu* (daughter) is a nasalized BT word.

BUD and BUDDY can mean a baby or child; (RAJ)PUT and FITZ(ROY) mean son of the king; *fata* is a girl in Rumanian.

EFFETE and FAWN are cognates of FETUS.

See "BOTANY" and "PED(IATRICIAN)."

FICK(LE)/הֲפַכְפַּךְ
(HA)-FUKH-(PUKH)   [(H)-PH-KH]

ROOTS: Old English *ficol* (treacherous, false) is traced to IE *peig* or *peik* (evil-minded, hostile).

הפוך / HEPOOKH or (HE)FOOKH is reversal or change. The root appears in *Genesis 3:24*, but a more relevant citation would be *Proverbs 17:28* – "who speaks *duplicity* falls into trouble." הפך / HĀFEKH is the opposite or contrary; הפכפך / HĀFĀKHPUKH (*Proverbs 21:5*) is defined in Hebrew dictionaries as "fickle" and "changeable."

BRANCHES: For other flip-flops, reverse to terms like כפה / KOPHĀ (to invert) and גב / GĀV (back).

See "HAVOC."

FIG/פַּג
FUG   [P(H)-G]

ROOTS: Latin *ficus* is the given source of FIG. "Her green figs"–פגיה / FUG(EHÄ) appears in *Songs 2:13*.
    The fig and unripe date or fruit is elsewhere rendered פגה / PUGÄH or PUG.

    BRANCHES: פגג / PAGUG is an unripe fig in Arabic.
      By Talmudic times a פגה / PUGÄ had come to mean an immature or young girl.
      Perhaps the immature or young of hogs came to be called *pigge* (Middle English) and later PIG.

FIGURE/פֶּגֶר
FEG-ERR   [PH-G-R]

ROOTS: Latin *figura* (shape, form) is the given source of words like FIGURE (outline, human form), FIGURINE and EFFIGY. The Latin, however, should originally mean "a result of kneading" and is supposed to derive from *fingere* (to shape) and the IE root *dheigh* (to form, build).
    פגר / PGR or FGR should mean body, not carcass. The dead פגרים / FIGÄR(ĒM) in *II Kings 19:35* are dead bodies, not (doubly) dead carcasses.

    BRANCHES: גופה / GOOPHA is a torso (FG reversed).
    German *Figuren* (puppets) was a common Nazi euphemism for corpses in the mass murder compounds.

FIN/חֹפֶן
(KHO)-FUN   [KH-PH-N]

ROOTS: The FIN as a slang term for the hand and for a five dollar bill is not given an etymon of its own in *Webster's*. The hand, of course, is a natural symbol of five, and חפן / (HŌ)FUN means a hand (*Exodus 9:8*).

    BRANCHES: IE root *penkwe* (five) is the given source of FIFTEEN, FIVE, CINQUE, FINGER, FIST, FOIST, KENO, PENTA-, PENTATEUCH, PENTECOST, PUNCH, PUNJAB, and QUINT(ET). FIFTY will sound more like HŌFUN or KHŌPHÄN (חפן) when you note its roots in German (*funf*=5) and Sanscrit (*pancha*=5).
    These PNK words are an anagram of חפן / KPN.
    French *poing* is a fist; Tagalog *kapit* is to hold or grasp – see "CAPTURE."
    PUNKA(H) (a fan – from Hindi) recalls an outspread hand – see "PANICLE." PUNISH and PUNK, along with PINCH and PENURIOUS (tightfisted or penny-pinching) all go hand in hand. See "QUINTET."

FIN/פנה
PHEEN-ÄH   [P(H)-N]]

ROOTS: The winglike limb of a fish, FIN, need not come from IE base *pet-na* (a wing or feather). פנה / PĒNÄ or PHĒNÄ is a corner or projecting point – see "PENGUIN."

BRANCHES: To get Darwinian and link the FIN with hand (also called a FIN) see the entry above.

FINICK(Y)/פָּנַק
P(H)A-NUCK   [P(H)-NK]

ROOTS: FINICKY is defined as "fussy," "hard to please" and "too dainty." The *American Heritage Dictionary* speculates that FINICKY is "probably ultimately from fine."
    מפנק / (MI)FOONAK means "spoiled" or "pampered."
    פנק / PANAK or PHANAK in *Proverbs 29:21* is translated as "pampered" (JPS) or "brought up delicately" (KJ).

    BRANCHES: FINICAL is related. The PINKIE finger may be named for its small, delicate size. PINK is of unknown origin; it can infer a carnation, a pale red, the "finest condition" or the highest degree of excellence ("in the pink of health"), or a verb of adornment.

FIRE/הֶבְעֵר
(HEH)-V'AIR   [B(H)-E-R]

ROOTS: The above term is Aramaic for fire; *Exodus 22:5* blames המבעיר את הבערה / (HÄMÄ)VEER et (HA)*BIARÄ* ("he who kindled the *fire*"). Old English fire is *fyr* ; Greek is *pyr* and the IE root is *pur*.

    BRANCHES: Official cognates of FIRE include EMPYREAL, PYRE, PYRETIC, PYRITES, PYROMANIAC, etc.
    SAMOVAR, from IE root *wer* (to burn), should be added. FRY comes via IE *bher* (to cook, bake).
    אור / OOR (fire) relates to the silent ע in בער/ VUÄR (to burn), while חרה / KHÄRÄ (to burn – see "CHAR") ties in to the guttural ע.
    Change the BR→BL to get BLAZE, FUEL, FLAME or Finnish *pala* (to burn). Switch the end L with the middle guttural to see FLAGRANT, CONFLAGRATION, EFFULGENT, PHLEGM, and PHLOX. These last six words, along with BLUE, FLAVIN, BLAZE, BLANK, BLUSH, BLACK, FLAME, FLAMINGO and more, all are credited to the IE root *bhel* (to shine, flash, burn). FURY is a FIERY emotion.
    Dutch *vuur* and German *Feuer* are FIRE words that easily come from בער / B(H)UR. Just as BAKE may come from (בער) / BAKE(R), Romance languages drop the end R (e.g. Italian *fuoco*). Slavic fire prefers חם / KHÄM (heat), as in Russian *agon*. Basque reverses the principle Hebrew fire term – using *su* instead of אש / ÄS(H). Arabic *nar* (fire) is related to נר / NÄR (light or lamp).
    See "BURN" and "LIGHT."

FLAG/פֶּלֶג
FEL-EG   [PH-L-G]

ROOTS: Not the banner, but the FLAKE or piece of stone found in FLAGSTONE derives from Old Norse *flaga* (slab or flake of stone). פלג / PELEG or PHELEG is a part, faction, division or stream.

    BRANCHES: BLOCK, BREAK, BRIGADE, FRACAS, PELAGO, and PLOUGH are all related. Much more at "BREAK," "FLAKE" and "PLOUGH."

Genesis 10:25 may refer to the פלג / PELEG or continental breakup that insured the growth and development of separate peoples and forked tongues.
See "PLUG."

FLAKE/פֶלַח
FEL-UKH   [PH-L-KH]

ROOTS: Middle English *flake* derives from Norwegian *flak* (a flat piece or flake).

פלח / PHELÄKH is precisely such a sliced or peeled off (flat) portion. In *I Samuel* King David's irregulars feed an Egyptian boy a פלח / PHELÄKH or "*piece* of pressed fig cake." (One can picture the dried fig sections peeling off FLAKE by FLAKE.) The King James version of *Songs 42:3* renders the word as a "*piece* of pomegranite" (which is being compared to a woman's brow). Section or FLAKE would make a better translation of פלח / FLK.

BRANCHES: Change FLK to FRK. A flower, פרח / PHERÄKH, may not only be analyzed as a פרי / PRE (fruit, botanical product) which has ריח / RÄÄKH (scent), but also as something with many a section, petal or flake (פלח / PHELÄKH).

The two letter root favors the harder liquid (R), as several פר / PR words mean spreading out and breaking up (see "PREACHER" and "SPREAD.") פרור / PÄROOR is a crumb or fragment, fitting with flakey terms like FRIABLE, FURFUR (dandruff flakes) and (Yiddish) FARFEL.

The official cognates of FLAKE include ARCHIPELAGO, COMPLACENT, IMPLACABLE, FLUKE, PELAGIC, PLACATE, PLACEBO, PLACENTA, PLACID, PLAGIARY, PLANCHET, PLANK, PLEA(D), PLEASANT and PLEASE.
More at "BREAK," "FLAG" and "PLOUGH."

FLEET/פָלַט
FALL-UT   [P(H)-L-T]

ROOTS: FLEET and FLIGHT needn't belong with FLOAT at the IE root *pleu* (to flow). Old English *flyht* (act of fleeing, escape) more simply and directly comes from פלט / PLT or PHOLUT (to escape, be saved – *Ezekiel 7:16*) and פליטה / FLÄTÄ ("escaped"– *Exodus 10:5*).

BRANCHES: FLEE, FLIT, FLUSTER and FLY are better off rescued from IE *pleu* (to flow) – see "FLUTTER."

BLEED (BLOOD) and FLOOD might also come from פלט / P-L-DT, as the Hebrew term can also mean to discharge, escape or vomit forth – see "BURST." The PL element in liquid gushings s found in Indo-European "rain" words.

A related LT root of hiding and concealment is seen at "LID."

To LIGHT OUT (escape) might be from the לט / LT back of this PLT 3-letter root. Twice a פלט / PO)LET (refugee), Abraham's nephew לוט / LOT had to רוץ / ROOT(S) (run) from war and God's wrath (LT→RT).

FLICK/פָרַק
FO-RAKE   [P(H)-R-K→FLK]

ROOTS: The dictionary offers a theory but no etymon for

FLICK (to remove): "Probably partly echoic and partly back-formation from FLICKER."

פרק / PORUK or PHORUK means to remove – *Genesis 27:40*.

BRANCHES: הפליג / (HI)FLEG is to depart.

As for FLICKER, הבליח / (HI)BHLEÄKH in the Jerusalem Talmud means to FLICKER. An older noun and verb of FLICKERING is ברק / BÄRÄK or BHÄRÄK (lightning – *Exodus 19:16*). ברקת / BHAREKES is the agate gem of *Exodus 23:17*; בלג / BHÄLÄG is to flash. EF*FLUGENT* and BLI(N)K relate to the FLICKERING of light, while FLECK and FLING are related to the throwing off of FLICK.

FLUTT(ER)/פָלַץ
FEL-ET(S)   [PH-L-T(S)]

ROOTS: The AHD feels that FLUTTER is from Old English *flotorian* (to float back and forth), but FLUTTER is to vibrate, tremble or quiver. פלץ / P(H)OLUTZ is to shake; פלצות / PÄLÄT(SOOT) quivers in the phrase "I *shudder* in panic" in *Isaiah 21:4*.

BRANCHES: Instead of *pleu* (to flow), a better IE root would have been *pol* (to touch, feel, shake). CATAPULT, FEEL, PALPABLE, PALPEBRAL, PALPITATE, POLLEX, PSALM and PSALTERY all tremble at IE root *pol*. Change PL to PR to note words like פרפור / PERPOOR (to twitch, jerk – *II Kings 15:13*) and פרפר / PÄRPÄR (the flutter-by or butterfly – see "PAPILLON"). See "PULSE."

FOR/עֲבוּר
AH-VOOR   [U-BH-O-R]

ROOTS: Old English *for* (on account of) is the source of one sense of FOR.

בעבור / (BÄ)ÄVOOR means "for," "for the sake of" or "in order that" (*Genesis 27:4*).

BRANCHES: FOR is placed at the prolific and badly jumbled IE root *per* (base of prepositions and preverbs). Latin *per* (through, for, by) connects to the BH-R Hebrew etymon above, giving us the Hebrew source of PER, PER-, PARAMOUNT, PARAMOUR, PRO, and PRO-.

While PARA- (beyond) is from עבר / OPHÄR or OBHÄR (passed over – see "OVER"), most of the listed prefixes at IE *per* mean "around" and "near." They derive from Hebrew terms like עבר / ÄVER (side), ערב / EREV (on the eve of) and קרוב / KÄROV (near).

The related English terms include BEFORE, FIRST, FORE, FORE-, FOREMOST, FORMER, FRO, FROM, FORWARD, PARADISE, PRE-, PRIOR, PRO-, PROTEIN, PROTOEROZOIC, PROTO-, PROTON, and PROW.

APPROACH, APPROXIMATE, and PROXIMITY are from Latin *prope* (near) and perhaps קרוב / KAROBH (near). [A ק→P change is also seen as SCOPE and SCOFF come from צחק / (T)SKOK (laugh, mock).]

The words for "because" in most IE languages have the various permutations of בר / VR seen above. In Danish and Norwegian "because" is *fordi*, in Czech *protoze*, in German *weil* and in Yiddish *veil*. The Italic languages add כי / KE (because) to form *parce que* (French) or *porque* (Spanish, Portuguese). טעם / TÄ'ÄM and סבה / SEBÄ (reason, motive) may form the "because" terms in Russian (*patamu shto*), Indonesian (*sebab*) and Swahili (*kwa sababu*).

FRAC(TION)/פְרֶק
FER-REK   [PH-R-K]

ROOTS: FRACTION is traced to the IE root *bhreg* (to break). Latin *fractus* (broken) corresponds to פרק / P(H)EREK and פרקה / PERKÄ (division), פריקה / PIREKÄ (breaking up), פרק / PARAK (fragment – *Isaiah 65:4*) and פריכה / PHIREKÄ (breaking, cracking, splitting).

> **BRANCHES:** Aramaic פלוגתא / PLOOGTÄ (PLG→PRG) is the split that arguments are made of. ANFRACTUOUS, FRACAS, FRACTED, FRAGILE, FRAGMENT, FRAIL, FRAY, and FRIABLE are among the connected FRACTIONS. AFFRICATE, DENTRIFRICE, BRISANCE, DEBRIS, FRICATIVE and FRACTION are all related to Latin *friare* (to crumble) and to פרר / PARAR or FARAR (to crumble).
>   Much more at "BREAK."

FREAK/(הִ)פְריג
(HI)-FREEG   [PH-R-G]

ROOTS: The dictionaries, in a FREAK (unusual) display of candor admit "origin unknown" for this one.

The Biblical Hebrew terms at "FREE" will do well to match the capricious, whimsical and disordered connotations of FREAK. Abnormal behavior, as in the slang phrase "to FREAK OUT," is precisely the kind of abrupt, emotional change of mood in the Aramaic verb הפרין / (HE)FREEG.

> לפרקים / (LI)FRÄK(ÈM) means "on rare occasions."
> See "BREAK" and "PERK."

FREE/פְרַע
FAR-OO-AH   [PH-R-U]

ROOTS: The IE root of FREE is *pri* (to love). Anglo-Saxon *freo* means not in bondage; פרע / PHÄROOÄ or PÄROOÄ is unrestrained or "broken loose" in *Exodus 32:25*. The term is rendered "threw off constraints" in *II Chronicles 28:19*.

> **BRANCHES:** פרע / FRE or PRK relates to both פרק / PÄRÄK (to free, untie, loosen, save) and פרא / PEREH (wild – *Genesis 16:12*). The פר / P(H)-R root indicates breaking out or spreading forth in scores of Hebrew words – see "FRUIT," "SPARROW," and "S(P)READ."

FRO(ST)/כְּפוֹר
(KIH)-FOR   [(K)-PH-R]

ROOTS: Old English *forst* (frost) is traced to IE *preus* (to freeze, burn).

Hebrew offers כפור / (K)FOR or(K)PR ("hoar-frost" – *Psalms 147:16*) and בער / VÄER (burn – see "BURN" and "FIRE").

> **BRANCHES:** ברד / VARADT is hail or frozen rain. For connections between words for frozen precipitation and cold, see "SANGFROID."
>   FREEZE and FROZEN are cognates of FROST.

FRUC(TIFY)/פְרַח
FAW-RUKH   [P(H)-R-KH]

ROOTS: FRUCTIFY (to bear or cause to bear fruit) is traced to the IE root *bhrug* (agricultural produce – cognate with BROOK and FRUGAL.)

Hebrew provides a better FR or PR etymon, פרי / PHIRE (fruit – see "FRUIT"). It also allows us to link Latin *frux* (fruit) with FRAGRANCE. פרח / PHÄRUKH (bud, blossom, flower – *Numbers 17:23*) is the combination of פרי / PHR(È) (fruit, agricultural product) and ריח / RÄUKH (smell, scent – see "REEK"). FRAGRANT and FLAIR are otherwise linked to IE root *bhrag* (to smell).

> **BRANCHES:** As a verb, פרח / PHORUKH (to flower) can also mean to BREAK OUT like a PLAGUE (see *Leviticus 13:12* and "BREAK"). *FRUC*TOSE is the sugar of fruit. פרג / PORUG is to sprout or germinate.
>   Latin *felix* (fruitful, fertile) shows an R to L change, showing us how to get FELICITY or INFELICITY from Hebrew fruit and flowering. No wonder we express FELICITATION (congratulation) with a FELICITOUS bouquet of flowers.

FRUIT/פְרוֹת
FAY-ROTE   [P(H)-R]

ROOTS: Latin *frux* is fruit; *fructus* is enjoyment. Both are contained in the IE root *bhrug*, the alleged source of FRUIT and other terms like BROOK, FRUCTIFY, FRUGAL, FRUITION and FRUMENTY.

Instead of this interpretive fruit-enjoyment equation, the Hebrew Bible presents a natural connection between FER(TILITY) and FRUIT. The Lord blessed all living things (including words) to *"be fruitful and multiply"* (פרו / PIROO or PHIROO – *Genesis 1:28*). The plural of פרי / FRE (*Genesis 1:29* – elsewhere pronounced PRE) is פרות / P(H)ÄROT (FRUIT).

The Old French is *fruit* or *fruict*. These FRC terms derive from פרח / P(H)ERÄKH (bud, blossom, flower – noun or verb – *Genesis 40:10*). פרת / PORÄT is fruitful (*Genesis 49:22*). PARADISE or an orchard of FRUIT is a פרדם / P(H)ÄRDT(ÄS) (*Ecclesiastes 2:5*); פרודה / PROODTÄ of *Joel 1:17* is translated "seed" or "grain."

> **BRANCHES:** PR FRUITS of the womb include the אפרה / EPHROÄH (PULLET or chick of *Deuteronomy 22:6*), the עפר / (O)PHER (fawn), כפיר / (K')FÈR (lion cub) and פרחה / PIRKHÄ ("BROOD" in *Job 30:12*). Relevant PR words in English include PROLAN, PROLETARIAN, PROLICIDE, PROLIFERATE, and PROLIFIC.
>   From Latin *proles* (offspring) we move to Latin *parere* (to beget, give birth) which delivers -PARA, PARENT, -PAROUS, VIPER and REPERTORY. These פר / PR terms also are FERTILE grounds for BREEDing BR terms like BAIRN (child), BEAR, BIRTH, BORE and BORN.
>   The IE root *virere* (to be green – "of unknown origin") and words like VERDANT fit here. בר / B(H)ÄR means field.
>   Children and the spawn of fish are called FRY; Old Norse *frio* meant seed or offspring. For R–F or R–PH offshoots see "TROPHY."
>   This entry ought to return to botanical produce like APRICOT,

APPLE, perhaps APRIL, FRUCTOSE, PEAR, PLUM, PRUNE, and (S)PROUT (the meaning of פרג / P(H)ORUG). PROGENY and other PRO- words ultimately relate.
See "BARLEY," "BERRY," "(S)PRIG," and "VIRGIN."

FUHR(ER)/מַעֲבִיר
(MA'AH)-VEER   [U-BH-R]

ROOTS: FUHRER is from German *fuhren* (to lead). The Indo-Aryan root was *per*; the IE root is *per* (to lead, pass over).
העביר / HE'EBHER is to cause to pass over (*Deuteronomy 18:9*).
There is much more at "FERRY," but the Hebrew origin of FUHRER deserved special handling.

FUL(FILL)/פלא
FUL-AYE   [PH-L-A]

ROOTS: Anglo-Saxon *fullfyllan* is less confused when noting *ple*, "a variant form" of the IE root *pel* (to fill). This "variant" contains the correct connotations of FULFILL, as it is seen as the source of ACCOMPLISH, COMPLETE, COMPLIMENT, COMPLY, EXPLETIVE, IMPLEMENT, REPLETE and SUPPLY.
פלא / FULA is to fulfill or pay a pledge, etc. (*Leviticus 22:21*).

BRANCHES: FILL and FULL are related.

FUNG(US)/נֶבֶג
NEVEG   [NVG→FNG]

ROOTS: FUNGUS is a mushroom or fungus in Latin.
Swap the F and N and hear that נבג / NEVEG and Aramaic נבגא / NIVGA is a FUNGUS.

BRANCHES: *Webster's* feels that Latin soaked up *fungus* from Greek *spongos* (SPONGE). *Ebhen Shoshan* lists ספוג / S'FOG (sponge) as being borrowed from the Greek. The Latin FNG, Greek (S)PNG and late Hebrew term should all be offshoots of a primeval NVG word fossilized in Aramaic *nivga* or *nibhga* (fungus).
More נב / B-BH plant words at "BOTANY."

GAG/גג
GUG   [GG]

ROOTS: Middle English *gaggen* has no known etymon; the dictionary concludes, "of echoic origin." A GAG is something put into or over the mouth to prevent speaking or etc. גג / GAG is the cover or roof of a house (to prevent rainwater or etc. from coming in – *Joshua 2:8*).

GALA/גילה
GEE–LAH   [GYL]

ROOTS: Old French *gale* (joy, enjoyment) is a fine source for GALA (festive; a festive occasion). The authorities go on to add that GALA is "probably from Middle Dutch *wale* (riches, wealth)." גיל / GEL and גילה / GELA mean joy and rejoicing – *Isaiah 65:18*. רגל /(RE)GEL is a pilgrimage holiday.

BRANCHES: GALLANT, GLEE, JOLLY and REGALE are all related. Hawaiian *hauoli* (glad) may relate. Reverse גל / GL to get ליג / LAUG (to jest, laugh at).

GALA(XY)/חַלְבִי
KHAL–AH(VEE)   [KH–L–BH]

ROOTS: The Milky Way named our GALAXY, from Greek *gala* (milk). This Greek term is such an INTERGALACTIC mystery to the scholars that it is included at the IE root *melg* (to rub, to milk) " to mark the unexplained fact that no common IE noun for milk can be reconstructed."
As usual, the answer is as distant and as near as Hebrew. חלב / KHALAV is milk – *Exodus 3:8;* milky is חלבי / KHALAVE.

BRANCHES: חלב / KHALEV is fat. GALACTOSE and GALALITH are among the words derived from Greek *gala* or *galaktos* (milk).
CLABBER, from Irish *clabar*, means sour or curdled milk. See "MILK", but also see "ALBINO" and "LIVER" for the LV element of the KH–L–V root.

GALBANUM/חֶלְבְּנָה
KHEL–BEN–AH   [KH–L–B+N]

ROOTS: This bitter Asiatic gum resin (Latin spelling) is from Greek *chalbane*, an acknowledged borrowing form חלבנה / KHELBENA (galbenum, gum – *Exodus 30:34*).

BRANCHES: חלב / KHALEV is fat or lard; GLIB (from a Dutch term for jelly) may be related.
See "LIVER".

GALL/גֹּעַל
GAW–UL   [GUL]

ROOTS: The bitterness of the GALBANUM entry might be relevant here, but the bitterness of spirit of GALL matches געל / GOUL (to loathe, abhor – *Leviticus 26:43*). Aside from rancor, the bitter fluid stored in the GALL bladder evokes געל / GOUL (nausea).
Greek *chole*(bile) is cited for GALL and CHOLERA.
חלא / KHALA is to be ill (*II Chronicles 16:12*). חולירע /

KHŌLĒRÄ (cholera) might well be a later term than CHOLERA, but it means "bad illness."

The given IE root of GALL is *ghel* (to shine), recalling terms like הלל / HOLUL (to shine) and נחל / GOHUL (glowing coal).

> **BRANCHES:** ACHOLIA, CHOLE- and MELANCHOLY are sensible cognates.
>
> A second GALL (a skin sore) infers vexation, like נעל / G – U – L, rather than "shining."
>
> The third GALL in our dictionary refers to a tumor or spherical growth. This GALL is probably from גל / GUL (wave, pile). See "HEALTH."

GAP/ גֶב
GAVE   [G – BH]

ROOTS: A GAP Is a hole or opening, cleft or ravine. The IE root is the wide open *ghai* (to yawn, gape). גב / GĀBH is a pit or "trench" (*II Kings 3:16*). כף / KĀPH is a cave, vault or hollow rock – see "CAVITY."

> **BRANCHES:** נף / GĀPH and אנף / ÄGĀPH are verbs of filling holes. קופא / KOOPÄ is Aramaic for the hole in an axehead or needle.
>
> Most of the cognates of GAP sound quite unrelated. These include CHASM, GILL, and YAWN. GILL (ravine) seems better linked to Hebrew terms found at "CATSKILL" and "HOLLOW." GAPE, from Old Norse *gapa* (to yawn, gape), does sound appropriate as a cognate of GAP.

GARBLE / עִרְבֵּל
GEER – BALE   [GRB]

ROOTS: The Italian *garbellare* is already linked to Arabic *gharbala*. The dictionaries cite Late Latin *cribellare* (to sift) and *cribrum* (a sieve), though GARBLE means to mix up or confuse. The Hebrew words GARBLED by Babel, the centuries, or both include ערבל / ERBAL or GERBAL (to sift, to mix, to confound), ערבל / GĀRBOL (concrete mixer, whirlpool, whirlwind), and the three letter root ערב / G – R – B(H) or A – R – BH which renders "mixed" (*Exodus 12:38*), "woof" (*Leviticus 13:49*), "evening" (or mixed light – *Genesis 1:5*) and "Arabian" (or mixed Hamito-Semitic race – *Nehemiah 2:19*).

> **BRANCHES:** CERTAIN, CRIMINAL, DISCRIMINATE, ENDOCRINE, SECRET, and RIDDLE are some of the alleged cognates of GARBLE under the IE root *krei* (to sieve, discriminate, distinguish). Other listed cognates include CONCERN, CRISIS, CRITIC, DECREE, DISCERN, EXCREMENT, and HYPOCRISY. The IE root is so much the opposite of GARBLE (to scramble) that it ultimately links up with Hebrew K – R terms like הכר / (HE)KĀR (recognition).
>
> An antonym for גבול / GĒBOOL (kneading) is גבול / GIBHOOL (boundary). Other related terms include CRIB, GRIFFE (mulatto), GRIFFIN, (UN)RAVEL and WARP. A #2-#3 root letter flip reveals GIBBER(ISH).

GARGLE/ גִּרְגֵּר
GIR – GAIR   [GRGR➡GRGL]

ROOTS: Latin *gurgulio* means a throat or windpipe; גרגרת /GĀRGERET is defined as windpipe, and translated as "throat" in *Proverbs 3:3*. גרגר / GIRGĀR (to gargle) is not in the Bible, but גרון / GĀRON (throat, neck) and ערף / ŌREF or GŌR[EF] (back of neck) are.

> **BRANCHES:** IE roots *g(w)er* and *gwel* both mean "to swallow." They include many terms that echo throat words like German *Kehle* or Italian *gola*. Some of these are GOLIARD, GORGE, GLUTTON (a גרגרן /GĀRGERÄN in Hebrew), GULLET, JOWL and KEEL.
>
> The IE roots do not include GARGANEY, GARGOYLE (a gurgling waterspout), GORGEOUS (formerly concerning neckwear), GULP, GURGLE and the mouthwash of academia – JARGON (from the Sanskrit word for gurgling).
>
> The Indonesian throat term begins with "ker"; *gorlo* is the Russian throat.
>
> More at "COLLAR," "GIRAFFE," and "GROAN."

GATHER/ גָּדַר
GE(D)T – ERE   [GDR→GTR]

ROOTS: In Middle English the word was pronounced *gaderen*; the IE root is *ghedh* (to unite, join, fit). גדר / GEDTER (gate) and גדר / GADTAR (to fence in) are chosen for sound correspondence, but other GD terms of gathering tie up the strong bond in meaning. אגד / ÄGUD or ĒGĀD is to unite, tie and bind together. אגדה /ÄGOODÄ is a "bunch" in *Exodus 12:22*; in *II Samuel 2:25* "the children of Benjamin gathered themselves together after Abner, and became one *band*." גדד / GĀDĀD is to gather troops; גדוד / GIDOOD is a troop or group – *I Kings 11:24*.

> **BRANCHES:** (S)QUAD and CADRE might be related. A גדר / GEDER (gate) corrals a גדר / GĀDER or עדה / GĀTÄ (gathering of people or animals), as does a GATE or a GHETTO. *Kado* is gate in Japanese.
>
> The only official cognates of GATHER are GOOD and TOGETHER, which are synonyms in 1960's lingo. Other gutteral-dentals of unification are עקד / ĀKAD (to bind) and אחד / EKHUD (one). Instead of reversing the "teg" of INTEGRATE and seeing it as a GT / D term of unification, the authorities say that INTEGER is from Latin *in* (not) + *tangere* (to touch). אחת /AKHAT is the form of "one" used in context of togetherness. COITUS means "meeting" in Latin. *Ugoda* is agreement in Polish. *Ikat* is a bundle or sheaf in Indonesian; it is the root of their word of tying and joining. *Kaatoa* is to get together in Proto-Polynesian.
>
> See "GOOD" and "JUXTAPOSE."

GAUDY/ חָדָה
KHAD – AH   [KH – D]

ROOTS: GAUDINESS, showy ornamentation, brings joy to most children and Americans. Latin *gaud(ere)* is to rejoice.

חדה / KHADA means rejoice (*Exodus 18:9*); חדוה / KHED(VÄ) means gladness and joy (*Nehemiah 8:10*).

BRANCHES: Somehow, ENJOY, JOY and REJOICE are listed as official cognates at the IE root *gau* (to rejoice). Cognate GANOID is from Greek *ganos* (brightness), a GN→NG link to נגה / NOGA (brightness).

    Looking now at the back "half" of חדוה / (KH)DVH, antonyms include דוה / DOVEH (sad) and ראבה / D'ÄVÄH (sorrow).

GAUZE/עזה
GAZA   [G–Z–H]

ROOTS: Those strips of light, open weave cotton were named after their place of origin – the Gaza Strip on the lower Israeli coastline. עזה / GÄZÄ was once peopled by the savage Philistines, lending little nobility to all who might call themselves Palestinians. Mentioned as early as *Genesis 10:4* and as late as *Zechariah 9:5*, עזה /AZA (Gaza) provides us with a powerful precedent for pronouncing the ע as a hard G. See "GONORRHEA".

GAZE/חזה
KHAZA   [KH–Z→GZ]

ROOTS: Middle English *gazen* is from an uncertain source; no IE root is available.

    חזה / KHÄZÄ is to perceive or behold; "star-GAZERS" are חוזה (בכוכבים) / KHŌZEH (BÄKŌKHÄVĒM) in *Isaiah 47:13*.

BRANCHES: חזה / KHŌZEH is a seer; חזיון /KHĒZÄYŌN is a vision. A vision in Old English was spelled *gesiht*. It is a cognate of SEE and SIGHT at the IE root *sek(w)* (to perceive, see). These all relate to reversals of חז / KH–S like סכה / SÄKHÄ (to see, look), סקר / SEKER (look), and שנח / S(H)ÄG(ÄKH) ("gaze"–*Songs 2:9*).

    For a synonym of חזה / KHZH that doesn't reverse the KH / G – S / Z there's always הצצה / HÄTSÄ(TSÄ) (glance).

    Beside GAZEHOUND, the only possible term to add here would be GAZEBO. For GAZEBO we quote the *Webster's New World Dictionary*: "said to be jocular formation (after Latin *videbo*, I shall see), replacing earlier *gazing room* but perhaps altered from an Oriental word."

    Speaking of Oriental words, *zhu*, (to gaze at) in Chinese, typically reverses the HZ of the Hebrew. The Indians of NW Washington State have a term *sey-a* (to see). To see is *seh(en)* in German, and *se* in Swedish, Danish and Norwegian.

GENI(US)/גאון
GA–OWN   [GAON]

ROOTS: Before גאון / GÄŌN came to mean a genius or rabbinic leader, it was used to describe the "excellence" or "triumph" of God when affecting human events– as in *Exodus 15:7*. Similarly, a JINNI in Moslem legend is a supernatural being that can influence human affairs. In the secular West, GENIUS came to mean an "inborn tutelary spirit."

Webster's gives the Latin etymon for GENIE and GENIUS, hoping that nobody checks the cross-reference

to the Arabic "JINNI" to discover that GENIUS is not exclusively Western. The AHD cites Latin *genius* (procreative divinity) and the Indo-European root *gen* (to give birth).

BRANCHES: קנה /KÄNEH is to create. עין / GYN can mean source or judgement.

    ENGINE, GIN (machine), INGENIUS and INGENUITY are related, as Latin *gignere* (to produce) is another attempt to bottle up the Semitic GENIE with Western etymons.

    Many Arabs and Jews from Arab lands render the ג / G as a J; the *jimmel* (ג) had been lost by the more far-flung Hebrew speaking communities.

    See "KIN" and "ORIGIN."

GERM/גרם
GORE–UM   [GRM]

ROOTS: Latin *germen* (sprig, offshoot, bud) is presumed to be from the IE root *gen* (to give birth, beget).

    No disappearing R trick is needed to link GERM to גרם / GORUM (to cause, bring about). גרה / GÄRA is to provoke or produce. גלם / GŌLEM (embryo, fetus – *Psalms 139:16*) is a GRM→GLM change away.

BRANCHES: גרעין / GÄRĒN is a seed or kernel. Switch letters #2 and #3 of גרם / GRM (to bring about) to get an antonym for GERMINATING – גמר / GOMAR (to finish, complete – *Psalms 12:2*).

    The GERMINAL figure of the German people might be Gomer or his son Togarmah (*Genesis 10:2-3*), the brother of Ashkenaz (Germany).

    For the origin of IE *gen* see "ORIGIN."

GIBBON/גבין
GUB–BEEN   [GB + N]

ROOTS: From French, the Gibbon is a slender ape with a large, bushy brow. גבין / GUBHĒN (eyebrow) is an extension of the Biblical eyebrow גבה / GUBÄ in *Leviticus 14:9*. GIBBOUS means humpbacked; גבן / GĒBÄ(N) is the hunchback of *Leviticus 21:10*. Latin *gibbus* or *gibba* is a hump, giving rise to words like GIBBOSE and GIBOSITY (a rounded swelling, a protuberance.) גבב / GÄBHUBH is to heap up and גבנון / GUBH(NOON) is a rounded peak of a mountain or etc. The common denominator connecting eyebrows with hunchbacks or the GIBBOUS (crescent) moon is convexity.

BRANCHES: A GABLE is a likely relative, as is the OGIVE (pointed arch, OGEE, *ojiva* in Spanish). *Gabal* is a mountain in Arabic; נבע / GEBHÄ is a hill in Hebrew. נבה / GOBHÄ is to be high in Hebrew; *goù* is high in Cantonese. Dutch dialect *kovel* (rounded hill) is linked to COBBLE.

    גב / GUBH is a back or hub – the possible source of HUB (G = H). Reverse to *puuk* for hill in Maya; *kow* is a hill in Thai.

    The Basque eyebrow is *bekaina* – (swap the B and K).

    HEAP, HOOP, HYPER- and HYPSO- (high) all fit here, further documenting the G→H change common in IE roots and in Germanic-Slavic cognates. (*H*itler is called *G*itler in Russia.)

Thus, (EP)*HEBUS* ("at early manhood" in Greek) is derived from גברות / *GUB*HROOS (adulthood); גמגם / GIMGĀM means to HEM (and haw); and גל / GUL is a HILL.

כפה / KĒPĀĀH also means tall or high; HIGH and HIVE are cognates at the IE root *keu* (to bend). כפף / KOFUF is to bend or curve. Reverse KP for *piko* (bent, arched) in Proto-Polynesian.

Getting back to back, גן / GĀN and גב / GUBH mean "back." *Kiw* or *kiu* is also "back" in Maidu (California Indians). BACK and BOUGH (from *bog* or shoulder in Scandinavian) are reversals of GB or KB.

Another GB reversal is BAGEL, from German *biegen* (to bend). BAGGY means swelled up, so it too relates back to GIBBOUS. For more G/K-PH/BH terms of hunched over things see "KYPHOS."

Monkeys like the GIBBON are hunched over, unlike erect Man.

For a more direct monkey term for GIBBON, there's always קוף / KŌPH (ape – *I Kings 10:22*). If COWHAGE is officially from Sanskrit *kapi* (monkey), then קוף / KŌPH can be the source of *kapi*, COWHAGE, GIBBON and APE. Conceded to be from an unknown, non-IE loan word, APE is from Sanskrit *kapi* and Hebrew KOPH just as "*amorous*" relates to Sanskrit *kama* (desire, love) and Hebrew KH-M terms – see "AMITY."

Other English *A* from Hebrew *Koph* (ק / K) words include AESTAS from קיץ / KĪTS (summer), AM from קים / KĪĀM (to exist) and ATROCIOUS from Latin *ater* (black) and Hebrew קדר / KĀDTĀR (dark).

גב / GĀV (pit) is an antonym of terms like גבנוני / GAV(NOONĒ) or CONVEX – see "CUP." Hawaiian *kewe* means CONVEX or CONCAVE.

For B/V-G/K antonyms see "VACATE."

GIR(DLE)/חגורה
(HA)-GORE-(AH) [HGR]

ROOTS: Old Norse *gjorth* is the source of words like GIRDLE and GIRTH. The IE root *gher* means to grasp or enclose, with derivatives meaning "enclosure."

חגר / (HĀ)GUR is to "gird" in *Exodus 29:9*. חגור / (HĀ)GŌR is a belt or girdle.

BRANCHES: סגר / (SĀ)GUR (to close, shut in, lock) establishes the Hebrew GR two-letter root which parallels the IE root. (It also may have influenced words like CIGAR(ETTE), SECRET and SECURE.) Similarly, אגרוף / EGROF is a closed hand or fist – an extension of אגר / OGUR (to gather, collect). דגר / DOGUR is a hatch.

Cognates of GIRD and GIRDLE at IE *gher* include CHOIR, CHORAL, CHORALE, CHORUS, COHORT, CORTEGE, COURT, COURTEOUS, COURTESAN, COURTESY, COURTIER, CURTSY, GARDEN, GARTH, HORTICULTURE, KINDERGARTEN, ORCHARD, and YARD.

As usual, checking the index here will lead you to alternative Hebrew etymons for some of these alleged cognates.

The GARTER belt, GARAGE, GARRET, GARROTTE and GIRDER are more GR possibilities.

HUG may be from חבק / HVK (to embrace). Otherwise, HUG, what a GIRDLE does, and HOG (an animal of GIRTH) may be from the HG first half of חגר / HGR. חג / HOG is to make a circle.

The belts of Germany (*Gurtel*) and Rumania (*curen*) certainly fit the Hebrew חגור / KHĀGOR (belt), but not as well as the Basque belt – *gerriko*. Guttural-liquid-guttural also appears in *kaliki*, the Hawaiian girdle.

GI(R)L/עוֹלֵל
GOAL–ALE [GLL]

ROOTS: GIRL is traced from a Middle English term for a youngster of either sex to a word for primrose blooms. GILL means girl, woman or sweetheart – as does GIRL – note how the double L of GILL supplants the RL of GIRL. This is reinforced with GILLIE and GILLY (Gaelic), meaning a lad or page. GAL, the short form or GIRL, also weakens the R of GIRL.

עולל / GOLAL or OLAL means child or "infant" in *I Samuel 15:3*. Both עולל / GOLAL and ערלה / GORLA infer young fruit, as found in the blooming etymology of GIRL.

BRANCHES: עלה / GOLEH or OLEH is a leaf; עלמ(ה) / GEL(EM / A) is a young male or female – see "ALUMNI."

GLAB(ROUS)/גלב
GUL–OBH [G–L–BH]

ROOTS: Latin *glaber* means smooth and bald; the object of the shaving גלב / GĀLOBH ("barber"– *Ezekiel 5:8*). The IE root, *gladh* (smooth), matches גלד / GELED ("skin"–*Job 16:15*).

BRANCHES: גילוף / GĒLOOPH is carving; קלף / KLĀPH is parchment (skin made smooth and bald).

Cognates of GLABROUS (without hair) at IE root *gladh* (smooth) are GABRO and GLABELLA. Other IE roots meaning baldness are *kelewo* and *klewo*, giving us CALVARIUM, CALVINIST, CALVARY and CALVITIES. GLABROUS deserves mention at IE root *gal* (bald, naked) along with CALLOW.

See "GALYAK(A)."

GLISS(ADE)/גלש
GALL–LUS(H) [GLS]

ROOTS: A GLISSADE is an intentional slide by a mountain climber or a ballet dancer. גלש / GOLĀS(H) is to slide, glide or ski. *Songs 6:5* should read:

Your hair is like a flock of goats
Glissading down from Gilead.

King James had the goats "appear;" different JPS versions had them "trail" or "stream."

גלש / GL(S) is an extension of גל / GL terms like גלגול / GILGOOL (rolling) and גלל / GALAL (to roll – *Isaiah 34:4*).

BRANCHES: The given IE root for GLISSADE is *ghel* (to shine; with derivatives referring to colors...yellow metal...bile or gall). The dictionary has slipped here, but they do cite Old High German *glitan* (to glide) and some relevant cognates likeGLASS, GLAZE, GLIDE, GLOSS and GLITCH, or GLITSH (originally a slide or skid, now a slip up or error). These words belong together for their slipperiness, not their shine. Add GLACIS, from Old French *glacier* (to slip), as well as GLACIER.

Let your לשון / LĀSHŌN (tongue) be a backwards גלשון / GĀLSHŌN (glider) and let's SLOG and גלש / GĀLOSH (slide) in our GALOSHES through the שלג / SHELEG (snow).

See "SLUDGE."

GNA(W)/טְחַן
(TAH)-KHUN   [(T)-KH-N]

ROOTS: English GNATHIC or Greek *gnathos* (the jaw) is traced to the IE root *ghen* (to GNAW).
The same GNH or KHN grinding and milling appears in טחן / (TÄ)KÄN (to mill, grind, pulverize, chew). Moses *"ground* the golden calf to powder" in *Exodus 32:20.*

BRANCHES: To GN(ASH) is to grind (the teeth) together.
Breaking down IE root *ghen* (gnaw), we get GNAT, NAG (GN reversed) and NOSH. Reverse German *nach*(en) (to eat on the sly) to get שֵׁן / SHEN (tooth; the legal term for food ruined by errant beasts).
The irritating GNAT also relates to כן / KÄN (louse – *Exodus 8:12*). Lousy bedfellows of this third plague of Egypt include the כנה / KENÄ (beetle), and so the *CANTHARIS* (blistering beetle or Spanish fly) and the *CIMEX*. A Polish gnat is *komar*. A louse in Eskimo is *komak*; in Malay:Galela the louse is a *gani*.
Retaining the dental (D,T) of our Hebrew etymon allows us to bite into the IE root *denk* (to bite), switching the #2 and #3 root letters of טחן / DTaKHaN (to chew). IE root *denk* gives us TANG, TONGS, TOUGH and ZINC.
The initial TK element of טחן recalls Old English *tux* (canine tooth) and its derivative TUSK. Rendering טחן as DHN we might move on to all the DENTAL words at IE *dent* (tooth – but traced to an earlier term that meant "to bite.")
German *zahn* (tooth), Tupi Indian *sainha* (tooth), Norwegian *tann* (tooth) and Swahili *jino* (tooth) all point to forms of שׁן / SHÄN (tooth) as well as to טחן / DT-H-N (chew, grind) for the roots of the world's teeth.
קטם / KOTAM (to chop), קטן / KÄTÄN (small) and דק / DUK (thin) are related to our DT-K-N etymon of pulverization. Speaking of KN words of ground down things, the IE root *keni* (dust, ashes) gave us words like INCINERATE and CONIDIUM. CINDER is not connected by the dictionaries, although French *cendre* means ashes.

GOAD/חֹד
KHOAD   [KH – D → GD]

ROOTS: A GOAD is a sharp, pointed stick used in driving oxen. Germanic *gaido* (goad, spear) is traced to the IE root *ghei* (to propel, prick).
חֹד / KHOD is an edge or point (*Proverbs 27:17*). חד / KHAD is sharp.

BRANCHES: עידוד / GEDOOD is encouragement, arousal. Sharp KD words include חץ / KHÄTS (arrow), קוֹץ / KOTS (thorn), עקץ / OKETS (prick, sting, point). A GADFLY provokes by biting, not (as stated) by gadding or roaming around. See "CUT", "HADDOCK" and "HASTATE."

GOAT/גְּדִי
GIDT–(EE)   [GD → GT]

ROOTS: The original D in GOAT is restored in the IE root *ghaido* (goat). גדי / GIDE is the KID of goats in *Genesis 38:17;* עתוד / GÄTOOD is a male goat in *Genesis 31:10.*

BRANCHES: History's scapegoat or גדיא / GUDYÄ (goat in Aramaic) is sung about at the Passover seder. The Arabic goat is a *gidye*, like the Danish *ged*.German *Ziege* seems unrelated to *koza* (goat in Slavic – similar to goat words in Turkish, Hungarian and Modern Greek), but ZG is merely the reverse of עז / GÄZ, KHÄZE or ÄZ (goat – *Genesis 38:17*).
AEGIS and perhaps GIDDY are also grandkids of these Hebrew etymons. Reverse גד / GD to get *digh* (she-goat), the Indo-European root of TYKE. Informally, a TYKE is a KID (small child) – yet another example of reversing words (TK → K – D / T). The root *digh*(she-goat) probably gave German *Tochter* ·and English DAUGH(TER). Indonesian *gadis* is a girl.

GOB(LET)/גְּבִיעַ
GOBH – EEYA   [G – BH – U]

ROOTS: Old French *gobelet* is from a Breton word *gob*. גביע / GOBHEA is the "goblet" of *Genesis 44:17.*

BRANCHES: קבעת / KOOBUÄS is a CUP or goblet. See "SCOOP."

GONORRHEA/עֲמֹרָה
GOMORRAH   [GMRH]

ROOTS: Sodom is the acknowledged source of the word sodomy. Its twin city, Gomorrah (*Genesis 19:24*), was also nuked to oblivion. In Joseph T. Shipley's book, *The Origins of English Words* (Johns Hopkins University Press, 1984), it is noted that GONORRHEA was spelled *gomoria* in the Sixteenth Century in the belief that the disease was an affliction of Sodom and Gomorrah. Gomorrah is from עמרה / ÄMORÄ or GÄMORÄ, indicating again that the ע is a guttural.
The etymon offered in most dictionaries, and the one which influences our current spelling of the term, is *gon* (semen) + *rhoia* (flow). These Greek words represent the mistaken notion that discharges of semen are involved, but the offered etymology may be an attempt to Hellenize an elusive, foreign term.

BRANCHES: The ע of another Biblical city is rendered as a G at "GAUZE."

GOOD/גַּד
GUD   [GD]

ROOTS: Anglo-Saxon *god* and German *got* go back to the IE root *ghedh* (to unite, join, fit). The IE root echoes גד / (O)GUD (to unite, fit together), but גד / GUD (fortune, success – *Genesis 30:11*) fits the common use of GOOD well enough. Good in Arabic is *gayid*.

BRANCHES: That GOD is GOOD (and really TOGETHER) ought to be implied by the similarity of these Germanic terms. The same גד / GUD (good fortune) above is the name of a deity mentioned in *Isaiah 65:11.* The given IE root for GOD is *Gheu(a)* (to call, invoke).
See "GATHER."

GOPHER/חוֹפֵר

KHO–PHERE   [KH–PH–R→G–PH–R]

ROOTS: GOPHER wood is a borrowing from Hebrew, see "CYPRESS." GOPHER, the burrowing rodent, has been linked to *gaufre* (French for honeycomb and waffle). WAFER, WAFFLE and (their etymon) *gaufre* are terms of pleating or crimping – not digging.

Wells are dug or EXCAVATED in *Genesis 21:30* – see "CAVITY." The Hebrew verb there is חפר / KHOPHÄR (to dig), recalling the GOPHER. Another famous digger is the mole. חפר-פרות / KHÄPHÄRPAROT, literally a hole-digger, is translated "mole" in *Isaiah 2:20*.

> **BRANCHES:** Moving from GPR to GRP, GRAVE is from Old English *grafan* (to dig) – see "GRAVE."
> A related rodent is the עכבר / AKHBÄR or ÄKHBHÄR (rendered "mouse" and placed alongside the mole in *Leviticus 11:29*).

GORE/חרא

KHOR–AH   [KH–R→GR]

ROOTS: While it now infers shed and clotted blood, GORE or *gor* meant dung and filth in Anglo-Saxon and Middle English. חרא / KHORÄ is excrement or "dung" in *II Kings 6:25*. חריונים / KHER–YONIM are bird droppings.

> **BRANCHES:** נלל / GÄLÄL is dung (L=R). There's a GORHEN and threee GORY adjectives of GORINESS.
> The bloody connotation of GORE may be from ערה / ÄRÄH or GÄRÄH (to pour out, to transfuse blood).
> *Ora'h* is blood in a Malay dialect.

(GO)SPEL/סְפוּר

SEE–POOR   [SPR→SPL]

ROOTS: Anglo-Saxon *godspel* originally meant "good spell, good story or good news." *Spel*, a story or history, is traced to the IE root *spel* (to say aloud, recite).

ספר / SEPÄR is to tell or recount (*Genesis 24:66*) as well as to count (*Genesis 15:5*). סְפוּר / SEPOOR is a story or narrative; ספר / SÄPHER is a book (*Deuteronomy 31:26*), scroll or letter (*II Samuel 11:14*). The common R to L change is all that is needed.

> **BRANCHES:** SPIEL is a talk, speech or a verb of speaking in colloquial English. The German *spiel* (play, game) is cited as the source, instead of linking SPIEL to GOSPEL and SPELL at the IE *spel* (root of recitation – whence a "play," dramatization, or game in the German and Yiddish sense).
> The AHD's links SPELL (signalling letters and reciting a magic formula) to terms like Gothic *spill* (recital, tale). Hebrew letters are also numbers. This is why an accounting or recounting is an extension of counting. See "DECIPHER."
> SYLLABUS (now thought to be a misprint of Greek *syttyba*) might be a scrambled cognate of SPELL or from שביל / S(H)IB(H)ÉL (path, course). The equally problematic etymology given for SYLLABLE suggests that we see SYLLABLE as a

SPELLING term, recalling that each Hebrew letter usually involves a whole SYLLABLE.

URSPRACHE (parent language) is from German *sprache*(language). Perhaps ספר / SPR or שפה / SAPHA (language) link up with the source of *spr(ache)*. A #1–#2 metathesis of SPR (to tell) resembles BSR or בשר / BÉSÄR (to bring tidings), a cousin of פרסום / PÉRS(OOM) (publicity, publication) and our SPR etymon. Hebrew BSR may be behind BUZZ, and SPR may have been retold as WHISPER. The IE root *swer* means "to buzz, whisper." IE *swer* (to speak, talk) is the given source of ANSWER and SWEAR. Besides ספר / SPR, these two terms may relate to השיב / (HÄ)SHÉV (to answer) and השביע / (HÉ)SHBÉA (to swear).

GOVE(R)N/כּוֵן

KEY-VANE   [KH-V-N]

ROOTS: GOVERN is from Latin *gubernare* and Greek *kybernan* (to steer, pilot, direct, guide). No IE root is available.

כון / KÉVÄN and כונן / KO(V)NÄN mean to direct or put in the right place – *Psalms 11:12*. כיון / KÉVOON means direction; כונת / KÄVENET is a guide or gunsight.

> **BRANCHES:** COMPOUND is attributed to Latin *com* (together) + *ponere* (to place). Only a few of the dozen meanings of COMPOUND have anything to do with putting things together. The etymology provides terms like Old French *componre* (to direct), which could be a nasalized (added M) form of כון / KÉVOON (to direct).
> A clearer example of the treachery of spelling involves the building COMPOUND. The dictionary acknowledges that the source is Malay *kampun* (enclosure) – see "HAVEN."
> A few of the meanings of COMPOUND (better reduced to KPN) may well derive from חפן / KHOPHÄN (to take a handful) and חפן / KHOPHEN (a handful, a measurement). The CMP of COMPOUND (to compute), the CMP of COMPUTE and the CMB of COMBINE could all be from a #2–#3 letter swap) of חפן / KH-PH-N. The connection between Hebrew "hand" terms and words of counting is established at entries like "MITT" and "QUINTET." Latin *ponere* can also mean to found or set up. COMPOUND, COMPONENT, EXPOUND and EXPONENT may be PN terms ultimately related to בנה / BANA (to build).

GRADE/גֶרד

GAY-RAID   [GRD]

ROOTS: The given etymology does not take up that sense of GRADE which means "to make level" or to GRATE (from Old French *grater*, to scrape). This sense derives from גרד / GÄRÄDT or GARAD (to scrape – *Job 2:8*).
See "CHARACTER."

> **BRANCHES:** Reversing GRD recalls DRAG, another forceful pulling term. גרר / GÄRAR is to scrape or plane. Not GRADE but GRATE is a cognate of SCRATCH at IE *grat* (to scratch). The related IE root *red* (to scrape, scratch, gnaw) lists ABRADE, ABRASION, ABRASIVE, CORRODE, CORROSION, CORROSIVE, ERASE, ERODE, RADULA, RASH, RODENT and ROSTRUM. A good match for Latin *corrodare* (to gnaw, corrode) is חלד / KH-L-D, an R→L cousin of גרד / GRD. חלדה / KHÄLOODÄ is rust, and חלדה / KHOOLDÄ is a rat. Hebrew

thereby links the animal and chemical forces that eat away at our goods – see "HALT." Now RODENT and ERODE make more sense as cognates, and now it is clear that RAT and RUST belong here beside RODENT and ROSTRUM.

Other GR chewing terms include גרה / GĀRĀ (cud – *Leviticus 11:7*).

And now to the GRADE (step, rank) that appears in DEGREE and DEGRADE. Latin *gradus* is a step or rank; the IE root is *ghredh* (to walk, go). Reverse GRD to DRK to hear דרך / DORAKH (to walk, step, tread).

The IE root's "to walk, go" is far too weak a connection to "rank," "degree," "grade," or "step." Dutch *rang*, Turkish *derece* and Arabic *daraga* are all words for "degree." These, along with RANK and RUNG suggest a (D)-R-G/K etymon. (RANK and RUNG have dropped the initial D and taken on an N via nasalization.) The true etymon ought to be versatile enough to reverse to GRADE, and to scramble to form the Swahili word for "degree"– *kadiri*.

Hebrew offers דרגה / DĀRGĀ (step, grade, rank) and מדרגה / (MĀ)DRĀGĀ (rung, scale, step, grade, or "steep place" in *Ezekiel 38:20*.

See "GRAVE."

GRAIN/גַרְעִין
GAR-EEN   [GRAYN]

ROOTS: Latin *granum* is a seed; Greek *karyon* is a nut or seed. גרעין / GĀREN is a kernel, stone or seed; מגורה / (MI)GORĀ is a "granary"– *Haggai 2:19* ; גרגר / GĀRGAR is a single berry, grape or grain – *Isaiah 17:6*.

BRANCHES: Cognates of GRAIN under IE root *gra-no* (grain) are CORN, FILIGREE, GARNER, GRAM, GRANADILLA, GRANARY, GRANGE, GRANITE, GRANULE, GRENADFE, and KERNEL.

גורל / GORĀL is a pebble (or lot); גרם / GEREM is bone or astral body; גרן / GOREN is the corn of the threshing floor or the granary itself – *Job 39:12, Joel 2:24*. כרמל / KĀRMEL (*Leviticus 2:14*) is defined as "fresh grains."

CARAWAY is supposed to be an Arabic borrowing from Greek *karon* (caraway). CARYOPSIS, and two other CARYO- words, along with KARYOTIN, and four other KARYO- words, are from Greek *karyon* (seed). This two-letter KR root recalls עקר / EKAR (root) and מקור / (MA)KOR (source) – see "CORE." The KR words complement many of the Hebrew גר / GR terms above.

GRAPE, from a GR IE root, should link up with גרגר / GĀRGAR above. CRUMB, GRIND and GROUND echo the grinding at the גרן / GOREN (granary) and that of גרם / GORUM (to crush bone – *Numbers 24:8*). See "GRADE."

GRANOLA, GRANULAR and POMEGRANITE are clear extensions of the AHD's cognate list.

MARGARIC, MARGARINE and MARGARITE are from Greek *margaron* (a pearl). This infers a *garon*, grain, granule, גרגר / GĀRGAR or גרעין / GĀREN from the *mare* or sea (see "MARINE").

Some of the many foreign GR terms that reinforce this entry are "grape" terms that belie the given etymolgy. The reference books move from Old High Germnan *krapfo* (hook – see "GRAPPLE") to Old French *graper* (to harvest grapes). Then, with a "back-formation" the dictionary comes up with "grape" from *graper*.

The foreign GR "grape" terms include Polish (*winogrono*), Serbo-Croatian (*grozdje*), Indonesian (*buah anggur* – the first element matches the Fijian word for seed) and Russian *vinagrat*.

Only a GR root, as seen in גרגר / GĀGAR (berry, grape, grain), holds them all together.

GRAPHITE/עוֹפֶרֶת
GO-PHER-ET   [G-PH-R→G-R-PH]

ROOTS: *Graphein* is to write in Greek – see "SCRAPER." The IE root is thought to be *gerbh* (to scratch). The essence of GRAPHITE, the soft, black form of carbon used in lead pencils, existed before writing. It is therefore more logical to assume that GRAPHICS or writing was named for the writing material and not vice versa.

The given etymology forgets that pencil lead is applied, not scratched into a surface. The term for lead in *Exodus 15:10*, עופרת / OFERES or GOPHER(ET), switches the #2 and #3 root letters to get GRAPHITE. A lead pencil is an עפרון / EPĀRON or GEPĀRON, as the root is עפר / OPHOR or GOPHOR (loose earth, dust).

See Malay *kapur* (chalk) at "CA(M)PHOR."

The suffix on both the Hebrew and the English captioned terms is identical in sound and sense. The same ת / T suffix of derivation appears in עברית / EVRET (Hebrew; lit *of* the Hebrews) or in the first word of the Hebrew Bible, בראשית / BERASHET (from the beginning *of*. . .). Beside the -ITE suffix in GRAPH*ITE,* dynam*ite* or Brooklyn*ite,* the ת / T or S suffix gave us the -ESE (of) suffix in "journal*ese* " and the -ITIOUS (of) suffix in "nutr*itious*."

> **BRANCHES:** *Genesis 18:27* musically relates עפר / ĀPHĀR (dust) and אפר / ĀPHER (ashes). The music is grave and mortal, as carbon we are and to carbon we shall return (to play on *Genesis 3:19*). CARBON, what GRAPHITE is made of, is possibly related – while its IE root *ker* (heat, fire), would tie it to חרה / KHĀRĀ (to burn).
>
> Greek *tephra* (ashes) is too close to אפר / ĀPHER (ashes) to not mention TEPHRITE. Greek *aspros* (white – source of DIAPER and ASPIRIN, a white powder) is close enough to אפר / ĀPHOR (gray) and אפר / ĀPHER (ashes) to consider.
>
> For the scratching, cutting words of writing see "CARVE"– an alleged cognate of GRAPHITE. For "engrave," see "GRAVE."

GRAP(PLE)/אֶגְרֹף
(EH)-GROP(HE)   [G-R-P(H)]

ROOTS: GRAPPLE is a hand grip or to wrestle; אגרף / EGROPH is a fist or to fist fight (*Exodus 21:18*). אגרף / EGRAF is to clench a fist.

The given etymology posits that GRAPPLE is from Old French *grape* (a hook), from the IE root *ger* (curving, crooked). This IE root should link to קער / KEER (to curve, see "CURVE").

> **BRANCHES:** AGRAFFE, CRA(M)P, CROP (originally a cluster) and GROUP, from the words credited to IE *ger*, belong here in that a fist is a group of connected fingers and because a clenched hand resembles a GRAPLIN(E), GRAPNEL or GRAPPLING HOOK ready to grab hold.
>
> GRAB, GRA(S)P, or GRIP are GRB or GRP terms that all involve the closed hand. Old English *gripa* (handful) is from the IE root *ghreib* (to grip). This root contains GRIP, GRIPE, GRIPPE and GROPE. GRAB and GRASP are found at the IE root *ghrebh* (to seize, reach).
>
> If CLAMP, CLIP and CLUMP do not belong at "CONGLOMERATE," then they might fit in with the tight

GROUP here – change CLP to GRP.

French *griffe* (claw) became *harpe*, whence our HARPOON.

Drop the end B, F or P and it is easy to see Greek *kheir* (hand) as another derivative of נרף / G(K)-R-(F). This would allow us to include a dozen CHIRO- words like CHIROPRACTOR, SUGERY and SURGEON.

In Chinese the words for "fist," "group," and "grip" are similar – reinforcing connections made above.

GRASS/גֶּרֶשׁ
GER-ES(H) [G-R-S(H)]

ROOTS: Old English *græs* is traced to an IE base *ghres* (plant growth) and the IE root *ghre* (to grow, become green – whence GREEN and GROW).

Likewise, גרש / GERES(H) is general agricultural yield or produce (*Deuteronomy 33:14*); גרש / GARUS(H) is to put forth or expel (plants are "driven out" of the soil as they grow).

Webster's definition of GRASS ("pastureland or lawn") is like מגרש / (MI)GRÄS(H), "pasture" *Numbers 35:3*).

BRANCHES: A relative of GRASS, CRESS, is traced to a Germanic term for fodder and the IE root *gras* (to devour).
חציר / KHÄ(T)SER (grass – *Isaiah 51:12*) requires a #2-#3 letter swap. חוץ / KHOOTS (outside) is the sense here too.
Only a folk etymology about a bed of grass attempts to explain the phrase GRASS WIDOW (discarded mistress).
גרושה / GROOS(H)Ä is a divorced woman (*Numbers 30:10*).
A better eytmon for GREEN might be רען / RGN and רענן / RÄÄNÄN or RÄGÄNÄN (verdant, fresh or "green" in the *Hebrew-English Lexicion of the Bible*). A #1-#2 letter swap allows RGN to be read GRN.
See "GRAZE" and "TROPHY."

GRAVE/גֶּרֶב
GORE-UV [G-R-BH]

ROOTS: Old English *grafan* (to bury) is traced to IE root *grebh* (to dig, bury, scratch).

גרב / GORABH is a Biblical root of scratching, related to גרב / GOROBH (scurf – see "SCURVY") and גרד / GORAD (to scratch – *Job 2:8* – see "GRADE"). An alternative Hebrew connection requires a #2-#3 letter switch, as קבר / KOVÄR is to bury and קבר / KEVER is a grave. Both noun and verb appear in *Genesis 23:6*.

BRANCHES: Cognates of GRAVE (the pit for burial) include ENGRAVE, GRABEN, GRAVURE, GREAVES, GROOVE, and GRUB.
More at "CAVITY," "CRAB" and "GOPHER."
The heavy GRAVE, and cognates AGGRAVATE, BARITONE, BLITZ*KRIEG*, BRUTE, GRAVITY, GRIEF, GRIEVE, GURU, ISOBAR and QUERN are traced to the IE root *gwera* (heavy). This theoretical reconstruction resembles words like גבר / GAVAR (to "prevail upon" – *Genesis 7:19*) and עפרת / GOFERES ("lead" – *Numbers 31:22*).

GRAZE/גֶּרֶז
GOR-UZ [GRZ]

ROOTS: There are two GRAZE words in English. The first GRAZE means "to feed on herbage"; the second is "to scrape." GRAZE is thought to derive from Old English *groes* (grass); the second GRAZE "probably" meant "to come close to the grass."

The common denominator in the two GRAZE words is the act of cutting; not the presence of grass. גרז / GARAZ is to cut (*Psalms 31:23*).

BRANCHES: Displaying metathesis in Hebrew synonyms is the word גזר / GAZAR (to cut). Further examples of this phenomenon include terms for breath (נפש / NEFESH and נשף / NASHAF), a lamb (כבש / KEVES and כשב / KESEV), and a dress (שמלה / SIMLA and שלמה / SALMA). Every Hebrew word contains the genetic code of its synonym and antonym, but more than a simple swap of letters is usually required.
גרזן / GARZEN is an ax.
See "GRADE" and "GRASS."

GRIS(T)/גֶּרֶשׁ
GER-ES [GRS]

ROOTS: Old High German *grist-grimmon* means to "gnash the teeth." The closest verb in English is to GRIT (grind the teeth), while Hebrew has גרס / GORUS (crush – "he has *broken* my teeth on gravel. . ." – *Lamentations 3:16*). See "CRUSH." As *gor grimmon*" or the related GRIN and GROMWELL, גרם / GEREM is bone and גרם / GORUM is to crush bone.

GRIST (ground grain) is from גרש / GERES (defined as "grist" but translated as "GROATS" and "GRITS" at *Leviticus 21:14*). The IE root for GRIST, GRIT and GROATS is *grendh* (to grind). See "GRAIN."

BRANCHES: גרום / GROS is a grist maker.
Greissen is "split" in German.
A chewy GR word of relevance here is גרה / GÄRA (cud).

GROAN/גֶּרוֹן
GA-ROAN [GRN]

ROOTS: Anglo-Saxon *granian* is supposed to connect with German *greinen* (to weep) and to GRIN. There is no non-Germanic cognate available, and no IE rot offered for GROAN.

גרון / GÄRON is a "neck" (*Ezekiel 16:11*) or throat –"cry with full *throat*" (*Isaiah 58:1*). This quote helps one hear the throat-groan connection, as Hebrew often links words to relevant parts of the body.

BRANCHES: רגן / ROGÄN (to grumble) is a related term and an anagram of גרון / GÄRON. In *Deuteronomy 1:27* the "murmuring" fits the 2nd definition of רגן / RGN – to "rebel." The apostasy in this context offers an alternative etymon for RENEGE nad RENEG(ADE) – switch RGN to RNG.
GRUMBLE, along with GRIM, GRIMACE, and POGROM, are

from IE root *ghrem* (angry). This root is from חרון / KHÄRON (anger – *Nehemiah 13:19*) or a #1–#2 letter swap of רעם / RÄÄM or RÄGÄM (to rage, rave or roar). Russian *grom* and Hebrew רעם / RUÄM both mean thunder.

Moving back from anger to the place we register the emotion, Greek *geranos* (crane) gives us GERANIUM. Also related to גרון / GÄRON are words like CRANE, CRANBERRY, CROON and CUR. These are cognates of GERANIUM at IE root *gera* (to cry hoarsely). GRUNT didn't make it here. CRANING the neck, the HERON and the CRANE are neck words, not cries.

"ANGER" and "NECK" are also linked at "HANG."
See "CRY," "GARGLE" and "NECK."

GROUND/גֹּרֶן
GORE-EN   [GRN]

ROOTS: Anglo-Saxon *grund* means sea bottom, and GROUND is originally to have meant the bottom of anything.

גרן / GOREN is a threshing floor; the King James Bible renders it just "floor" in *Joel 2:24*.

There is no known root for GROUND, but speculation points to the IE base *ghren* (to rub against).

גרר / GÄRÄR is to scrape or plane; גרידה / GIRÉDÄ is scratching.

More at "GRADE" and "GRAIN."

GUERR(ILLA)/גְּרָה
GUR-RAH   [GRH]

ROOTS: A GUERILLA is an irregular soldier (or a terrorist whose cause a news editor espouses). *Guerra* is skirmishing warfare in Spanish, Italian and Portugese; the French spell it *guerre*.

גר / GUR is to quarrel, as in *Deuteronomy 2:9* – "neither *contend* with them in battle." An extension of גרה / GURÄ ("strive" – *Jeremiah 50:24*) is תגרה / (TÉ)GRÄ (strife, contention, conflict).

BRANCHES: Like-sounding relatives of גרה / GÄRÄ (to provoke) include חרחור / KHÉRKHOOR (quarreling), חרחר / KHÉRKHÄR (to provoke strife); נחרה / NEKHÄRÄ (to contend – *Isaiah 41:11*), התחרה / (HÉT)KHÄRÄ (to compete, rival), קרב / KERÄV (battle – *Psalms 144:1*), חרב / KHEREV (sword, destruction) and חרום / KHÄROOM (state of war).

An R to L switch allows חיל / KHÄYÄL (soldier) and (reversing KH-L) לחם / LÖKHÄM (to wage war).

The sound of חרב / KHEREBH (sword; a figurative term for "war" – *Genesis 31:27*) rattles above the words for "war" in Arabic and Turkish (*harb*) as well as Hungarian *haboru* (switch B and R).

The AHD attempts to link "guerrilla" with WAR, LIVERWURST, WORSE, WORST and WURST at the IE root *wers* (to confuse, mix up). This confusion is a metathesis of ערוב / AROOV (mixture, confusion – RV→WR and harks back to the בלל / BÄLÄL (mix, confuse – BL→WR) back in *Genesis 11:9*. See "RIVALRY."

There are two paths to the etymology of QUARREL. First, there are the Hebrew etymons in this entry. Second, there is the given IE root *kwes* (to pant, wheeze).

The root doctors didn't completely miss out on a GR or KR term for "war." IE *koro* means war, war-band, host and army. חיל /

HÄYÉL or KHÄYÉL (KL→KR) means host and army as well; appearing alongside גרה / GURÄ in *Daniel 11:25*.

The words traced to IE *koro* include HARANGUE, HARBINGER, HARBOR, HARRY, HERALD, and HERIOT. Old English *here* is "army." Germanic *hild* (battle, war) gave us BRUNHILD, HILDA, HILDEBRAND and HILDEGARDE. (Hilda is nowhere linked to חלדה / KHOOLDÄ the prophetess of *II Chronicles 34:22*).

That bellicose ape, the GORILLA (a West African term), might relate to our GUERRILLA. GORILLA Might also relate to CHURL (a rude, rustic or ill-bred man), to Britonic *girlopp* (lout), and to CARL and its IE root *karlaz* (man). These terms all probably evolved from ערל / ÄRÄL or GORÄL. In *Leviticus 19:23* ערל / GRL infers that which is unripe, unsuitable and thus uncouth. By *I Samuel 17:27* the term is negative and condescending, referring to a Philistine as "uncircumsized" (thus unevolved and brutish). The word denotes stupidity in *Jeremiah 9:25*.

GUESS/חוש
KHOOS(H)   [KH-O-S(H)]

ROOTS: Middle English *gessen* is from Old Swedish *gissa* (to guess). The IE root offered for GUESS *ghend* or *ghed* (to take, seize). Hebrew offers נחש / (NÄ)KHÄS(H) (to guess or "divine" in *Genesis 44:5*); the KS root appears in חוש / KHOOS(H) (feeling, sense). כסס / KOSSUS (to reckon – *Exodus 12:4*) is another possibility; its double S is a plus.

BRANCHES: Middle Englsih *gessen* (to think) best fits חשב / KHOS(HÄBH) (to think, figure, or "reasoning" in *Ecclesiastes 7:29*).
See "MAGIC."

GUT/גיד
GEEDT   [GYD→GYT]

ROOTS: Gut is traced to the IE root *gheu* or *ghud* (to pour). Old English *guttas* means intestines. CATGUT is the dried intestines or GUTS or animals that were used for chords in musical instruments like *GUITARS*.

Greek *kithara* (lyre, lute) is only a bridge to גיד / GÉDT (chord, artery, tendon or "sinew" of *Genesis 32:32*). *Kithara* is said to the the source of קתרום / KITROS (stringed instrument or "zither" of *Daniel 3:5*), but the Aramaic term ought to be older.

BRANCHES: חוט / KHOOT is also a cord, sinew or thread; *chayt* is the Arabic.

After CHAETA and CHITTERLINGS, more GUITAR terms like the GITTERN, CITHARA and CITHER twang on our ears. They sound like the Japanese stringed instrument, the *koto*, and the mysterious נתית / GÉTÉS that accompanied Psalms (like #8) in antiquity.

GYRE/גַּלְגַּל
GULL-(GULL)   [GL→GR]

ROOTS: Greek *gyros* (circle, ring spiral) is but an R→L change from GL terms like גלגל / GUL(GUL) (wheel –

Ecclesiastes 12:6) and עגל / ÄGŌL (round).
קער / KÄER (curve, bend) כבר / KĒKÄR (traffic circle) and כרכר / KĒRKAR (top, spindle – from a KR word in *II Samuel 6:14*) also relate. כרע / KORA is to bend – see "CROUCH."

> **BRANCHES:** GYRE, GYRATE and GYRO- are from the IE root *geu* (go bend) . . ."more likely of unknown origin."
> WHEEL as well as COLONY, CULT(IVATE), CUTURE and SILVICOLOUS are traced to Latin *colere* (to till, cultivate, inhabit) and the IE root k/w/el (to revolve, move around, sojourn, dwell).
> These IE roots and Grimm's Laws point out the connection between גלגל / GULGUL (wheel) and the mobile, restless GYRATIONS of the גר / GÄR ("stranger," sojourner or alien – *Exodus 23:9*).
> The restless GULL might be named for GYRATIONS in the air or for prowess upon the round and bending גל / GUL (wave).
> The PAN*GOL*IN (scaly anteater) is able to roll into a ball. Malay *gulin* (to roll) is another form of גלגל / GIL-GÄL (to roll) or גלל / GÄLÄL (to roll).
> See "CYCLE."

(HA)DDOCK/דג
DUG   [DG→DK]

ROOTS: The HADDOCK is a food fish of the northern Atlantic that resembles its relative, the COD (DK reversed). Middle English *haddok* is the earliest known etymon.

Less well known are 16 ICHTHY– words from Greek *ikhthus* (fish) and from the IE root *dhghu* (fish). The same reversal involved in going from the KT Greek term to the DG of the IE root is required for most of the fishy words in this entry.

The generic term for "fish" in *Genesis 1:26* is דגה / DÄGÄH.

> **BRANCHES:** Fish, which are streamlined and חד / KHÄD (sharp) have the גד / GÄD (good fortune) to be prolific at דגה / DAGA– (multiplying – *Genesis 45:16*). דק / DUK is thin; *ohut* is thin in Finnish – see "ACUTE" and "DAGGER." נדוד / GIDOOD is a troop (as a school of fish).
> GADOID, from Greek *gados* (a kind of fish), is a large family of chiefly marine fishes. The COD and HADDOCK are in the GAD(OID) family; the DACE and SHAD (from Anglo-Saxon *[s]kadd*) are not.
> MOBY DICK, the most famous whale outside the book of Jonah, has a surname that might well echo the דג / DÄG (easily changed to DAK – translated "fish" in *Jonah 2:1*). A whale is a CETACEAN. *Cetus* is Latin for a large sea animal; the Greek is *ketos,* while the Russian whale is a *kit. Qwat/la)* is a whale for the Coeur d'Alêne Indians of British Columbia.
> The DUGONG (Malay term for the sea cow) has often been mistaken for mermaids or mermen; דגון / DÄGŌN is the half-man, half-fish deity of the Philistines in *I Samuel 5:2.*
> The Hamito-Semitic "fish" term preserved in Arabic *samak* and Swahili *samaki* is more popular among world languages. Note the following changes to SMK: The Japanese fish is *sakana* (#2-#3 swap and M→N); the Korean fish is *saengson* (M→N +K→G). In Malay *ikan* we have the Japanese fish missing the S; the Fijian and Tongan fish, *ika,* has lost the N; drop or move the I of this last fish to get *kai* (the fish of Maya Indians).
> More researh is required before PISCES (Latin source of FISH) could be linked to Hebrew terms like פסת רגל / *PĒSUS* REGEL

(the fish-like *sole* of the foot), פחום / PÄKHOOS (flat level), or פסח / POSUKH (to leap over).

HAGIO(GRAPHA)/חג
HUG   [HG]

ROOTS: HAGIOGRAPHA Is the third tier of books in the Hebrew Bible, containing non-legal, non-prophetic books like *Psalms.* The dozen HAGIO- words are form Greek *hagios* (holy) and "perhaps" from the IE root *yag* (to worship, reverence).

חג / HÄG is a holy day, holiday or (pilgrimage) festival; the noun and verb are found at *Exodus 23:14-15.* חגיני / HAGEGĒ is solemn, exalted or festive; חגינות / HÄGĒGOOT is solemnity.

> **BRANCHES:** חגא / HÄGÄ is "terror," but Ebhen Shoshan's dictionary adds that it implies a pagan holiday. Arabic *haji* is one who has made a holy pilgrimage; חנינה / HÄGĒGÄ is a pilgrimage.
> חג /HÄG is "to make a circle." The pilgrim is roundly hugged by circles and cycles, sacred places and holy days.

HAIL/הלל
HA–LAIL   [HLL]

ROOTS: To HAIL is to shout in greeting, to name by way of tribute, or to salute. Middle English *hailen* is to slaute. The etymology lapses to terms of health, such as IE root *kailo* (whole, uninjured, of good omen).

כל / KOL is all and חיל / KHAYIL or HAYIL is health; see "ALL" and "HEALTH." הלל / HĒLÄL is to praise (*Jeremiah 10:23*) ; הללו(ק)ה / HÄLILOOYÄ (HALLELUJAH) means "praise ye the Lord!" – *Psalms 146.*

> **BRANCHES:** HALLOW is from Old English *halgian* (to bless, consecrate). Instead of the pariseworthy Hebrew etymons above, HALLOW and HOLY are linked to IE *kailo* – where they are allegedly cognates of WHOLESOME and HEALTH. To HALLOO (shout) a HOLLER of HELLO or *heil* is to HAIL – see "CALL." קלם / KEL(ES) is praise, but הקל / (HÄ)KAL is to belittle and קלל / KĒLÄL is to curse.
> The HAIL of HAILSTONES is traced to Germanic *haglaz* and to the IE root *kaghlo* (pebble, hail). The English term *CHALAZA* is not cited as a cognate, although it is from Greek *chalaza* (hailstone). The IE root of CHALAZA and CHALAZION is *gheled* (hail). This takes us to Arabic *galid* (snow).
> For a KGL (or KLG) term to match IE *kaghlo* (pebble), there's קלע / KELÄG ("slingstones"– *Job 41:20*).

HALO/הלה
HEEL–AH   [HL]

ROOTS: A HALO is a ring of light often depicting splendor or glory. Ungloriously, dictionaries yoke HALO with Greek *halein* (to grind) because of the circular path made on a threshing floor.

הלה / HELA is a halo or sheen, as befitting the moon or a prophet's head. הלל / HOLUL is to shine, as in *Job 29:3*—"When His lamp *shone* over my head." Speaking of glory, הלל / HALEL is to glorify and HALLELUJAH means praise the Lord—see "HAIL."

BRANCHES: H and G are widely interchangeable in IE languages; [GAB may come from הבי / HUBHĪ (vain talk) and GIVE from הב / HUBH (give—*Genesis 30:1*)]. If HALO links up with the IE root *ghel* (to shine) as well as הלל / HÄLUL (to shine), then the following *ghel* derivatives are basking in the same glow: ACHOLIA, CHOLE–, CHOLERA, CHLOASMA, CHLORO–, FELON, GLAD, GLEAM, GLEE, GLISTEN, GLOAMING, GLOW, GOLD, GUILDER, GULDEN, MELANCHOLY, YELLOW and ZLOTY. Hawaiian glitter is *hulalali*; shining is *hulali*. See "COAL."

HAMS(TER)/חֲמָס
HUM–US   [HMS]

ROOTS: HAMSTER is a German word, deriving from Old High German *hamustro* and Slavic. As so often the case with animal names, we no longer know the intended meaning.

The language of Adam offers us חמסן / HÄMSUN (plunderer), from חמס / HÄMUS (plunder, "injustice" or "crime" in *Genesis 6:11*). Cute as they are, these ratlike raiders are distinguished by their capacity to carry off large cheekfuls of stolen grain.

BRANCHES: Destruction, rather than robbery, is the issue with the word חמס / HMS in *Proverbs 8:36*.

חמ / HM reinforcements for the stealing of these varmints include חמד / HOMUDT (to covet, desire) and especially חמרן / HÄMOTS (brigand).

If other characteristic activities went into the name, חמס / HEMÄS is to scratch.

"Ham," a bone word, should have no bearing on HAMSTER, although "ster" is possibly a suffix here.

HANG/חֲנָק
HEH–NECK   [HNK]

ROOTS: German *haenken* is to execute, but the etymology goes on to assume that strangulation, HANGING, is the same as HANGING up a coat (from Old English *hon*). IE *kenk* (to gird, bind) refers to the work of the HANGMAN, but not the given root of HANG—*konk* (to hang).

NICK, along with KNIGHT, KNIT and KNOT, is traced by *Webster's* to Old Norse *kneikja* (to squeeze, pinch) and the IE base *gneig* (to squeeze together). חנק /HENEK or KHENEK and HENÄK mean strangulation and to strangle (*Nahum 2:13*). ענק / ÄNÄK or GÄNÄK is a necklace or choker—*Proverbs 1:9*.

BRANCHES: One hears NECK in those Hebrew words—see "NECK" and "CINCTURE."

A HANGNAIL is not named for dangling or hanging; it is from Anglo-Saxon *ang*, which means tight and painful. *Cheken*, (to CHOKE) in Middle English, may have switched the N and K from חנק / KHENEK (to choke).

SPHINX, from Greeek, literally means the strangler. *QUINSY* is from Greek *anchein* (to choke). Latin *ango* (choke) gives us choking emotions like ANGER, ANGST, ANGUISH and ANXIETY.

See "HOOK."

HAREM/חֵרֶם
HAY–REM   [HRM]

ROOTS: Of course HAREM is borrowed from the Arabic, but *harim* means a prohibited place or thing—not simply a Moslem chieftan's wives and concubines or the seraglio where they live. The HAREM was so off-limits that only a eunuch was allowed inside. Arabic *harama* (to forbid) is precisely like חרם / HAREM (to ban, excommunicate, place in protective custody). The verb and noun חרם / HAREM forms appear in *Leviticus 27:28*—"a devoted thing...to devote." The least inaccurate translation of the same term in *Deuteronomy 13:18* is "declared taboo" in Aryeh Kaplan's *Living Torah*.

BRANCHES: Letter play allows חמור / HÄMOOR (strict) and קרום / KIROOM (skin, membrane, crust) to be seen as related words of protective custody.

HARM/חָרְמָה
HARM–AH   [HRM]

ROOTS: To HARM (damage) is traced to IE root *kormo* (pain, torment).

The sense is much closer to החרים / (HE)H'RÉM (to destroy—*Deuteronomy 13:16*); חרמה / HÄRMÄ is destruction or extermination.

BRANCHES: The ח may also be rendered as a KH. To CREAM is a slang version of "to destroy." Both CALAMITY and QUALM have etymons inferring injury, damage, death or disaster—but see "KILL" for destructive KL terms in Hebrew.

HARROW/חָרֵב
HERR–EV   [HRV → HRW]

ROOTS: HARROW Is a verb of plowing, cutting and tormenting; a HARROW is a plowing device. *Webster's* can only present a "probable" connection to Old Norse *hervi* and Danish *harv*, adding that the IE base is "possibly *(s)qer-* (to cut)."

חרב / HERREV is a sword, knife or blade of a plow—*Genesis 3:24*. החריב / HE)HERÉREV is to destroy. See "CARVER."

BRANCHES: See "HEARSE" for HARSH HR plowing words like חרש / HORUSH (to plow, engrave). Latin *hirpex* is a HARROW. חריף / HÄRÉF is sharp, acute; חרף / HOREF is the sharp and biting winter. חריצה / HÄRÉTSÄ is sharpening or cutting.

The HAR terms above explain why Latin *arare* means to plow. The Latin and IE root *ara* are the source of ARABLE. *Orac* in Polish is to plow. An R or L to N change is need for Basque *ganibet*, Scandinavian *kniv* and English KNIFE to tie in to חרב / KHEREV (knife) and חלף / KHÄLOF (very sharp knife). KNIFE might also derive from a #1-#2 letter swap of נקב / NAKAV (to pierce).
See "CARVE." and "CLEAVER."

HAST(ATE)/חֵץ
HATSE   [H–TS→HST]

ROOTS: A HASTATE leaf is spearlike; Latin *hasta* is a spear. The IE root *ghasto* (rod, staff) is the source of HASTATE, HASLET, GAD, and YARD. A similar IE root is *ghaiso* (a stick, spear); the cognates listed there include GARFISH, GARLIC, GORE and GYRFALCON.

חץ / HĀTS or KHĀTS (arrow – *II Samuel 22:15*) is the likely source of *hasta* (sticklike projectile of war).

BRANCHES: חצץ / HĀTSÄTS or KHĀTSÄTS is a noun (arrow) or verb (to partition or divide). A #1-#2 letter flip of חצץ / KH–(T)S–TS (arrow – *Proverbs 20:17*) gives us Latin *sagitta* (arrow) and SAGITTARIUS. *Gaida,* the Lombardic javelin, and other חד / KHÄDT or HÄDT (sharp) terms are found at "GOAD" and "ACACIA." Arrows are directed חוץ / KHOOTS (abroad).
Reversing from KT to TK, *toxon* is the Greek arrow – the source of TOXIC. *Tuku* is to discharge in Proto-Polynesian.
Another such reversal appears at ASAGAI (spear); the *zaghhayah* (slender spear) appears in Spanish, Portuguese, and Arabic, but is said to be of Berber origin.
The unhistoric initial "s" is common among the IE tongues. One might suspect that Old English *scytel* (a dart, missile) is from חץ / KHĀTS (arrow). *Scyt(el)* is the source of SHUTTLE, and cognates under IE root *skeud* (to shoot, chase, throw) include SCHUSS, SCOT, SCUTTLE, SCOUT, SHEET, SHOOT, SHOT, SHUT, and SKEET. SCATTER may relate. More Hebrew connections at "SHOOT."
Haetat is the arrow term for the Coeur d'Alêne Indians of British Columbia. Nearby, *K'it* was the arrow shot by the Andrade Quileute Indians of NW Washington State. The spear of the Andrade Quileute Indians is a *t'si*; a dart in Proto-Polynesian is an *ise.* Reverse to *dika* for a Malay spear, and soften the reversed חץ / HĀ(T)S for *shih* – the Chinese arrow. See "DAGGER" and "STICK."

HASTE/נְחִיצָה
(NIH)–HEETS–(AH)   [H–TS→HST]

ROOTS: Old French *haste* is believed to be from Germanic, but there is no IE root available for HASTE, HASTEN or HASTY. חץ / HĀTS the arrow (see "HASTATE") is named for its speed as well as its ability to split or cleave (חצב / HĀTSÄBH) its target. In other words, a dart (arrow) darts (flies with great haste and pressure).
נחיצה / (NI)HETSÄ is haste and pressure. לחץ / (LÄ)HĀTS means pressure – *Deuteronomy 26:7*. As נחץ / (NA)HĀTS means "to press or urge," so אץ / ÄTS is to urge, press or "hasten"– *Genesis 19:15*.

BRANCHES: The H–TS root may be softened to H–S(H), as חש / HÄS(H) is to make haste. The verb form of חיש / HĒSH (quickly, speedily) appears in *Isaiah 60:22* –"I the Lord will *hasten* it in its time."

HUSTLE (speed and pressure are implied) and HASENPFEFFER are probably related. The latter term comes from German *hase* (rabbit – that proverbial hustler).
An HS antonym is הסס / HĒSÄS (hesitate) – see "HESITATE." In Chinese, *ts'ui ts'u* is to hurry and *hsun su* is haste.
A reversal of HT appears in *touhu* (bustle, confusion in Finnish). תהו / TŌHOO is usually translated "unformed" when describing the world in *Genesis 1:2*; the Finnish term may offer a better rendition.

HATE/חַת
HUT   [HT]

ROOTS: The Middle English is *haten*; a related German term is *hassen*; the IE root is *kad* (sorrow, hatred). The primary meanings of HATE are "to loathe" or "shrink from." חתה / HĀTÄ is defined "to abhor;" חת / HĀT is fear (*Genesis 9:2*); קץ / KĀTS is to loathe or fear; קט / KĀDT is to loathe.

BRANCHES: The cognates of HATE are HATRED and HEINOUS. We fear and hate ghosts. The IE root for AGHAST, GHOST and POLTERGEIST is *gheis* (fear or amazement). חתת / KHÄSÄS means terror or dismay. ODIOUS (hateful) ought to be related.

HAUN(T)/חָנָה
HAUN–AH   [HNH]

ROOTS: Old French *hanter* is to frequent or resort to; a HAUNT is a place often visited or stayed in.
חנה / HÄNÄ or KHÄNÄ is to encamp, incline or settle (*Exodus 19:2*). מחנה / (MÄ)HÄNEH is a camp (*Genesis 32:22*); קן / KĀN is a nest, dwelling or chamber.

BRANCHES: The IE root for HAUNT is *kei* (to lie, bed, couch, night's lodging, home) or *tkei* (to settle, dwell, be home). The relevant terms listed at these loosely defined roots include BOHEMIAN, CEMETERY, HAME, HAMLET, INCUNABULA, and HOME. HOME is from Greek *keimai* (to lie down, rest) which recalls חנה / KHÄNÄ (to incline, settle down). Reverse to נח / NAKH for a word that means "to rest" or "to lie." COMA might be related.
Another KN "home" word is KENNEL, now thought to originate with Latin *cannis* (a dog).
A tent in Arabic is *chayma*, in Swahili it's *hema,* and in Indonesian *kemah*. *Huone* is a room in Finnish.
An antonym for these KN terms of settlement is נע / NÄ or NÄKH (to be unstable, to wander about).
Hawaiian *nohona* (a dwelling) and *hoho* (Hawaiian verb of dwelling, taking up residence and staying) relate to (a reversal of) חנה / HÄNÄ (to encamp, settle down).

HAVOC/הֲפֵכָה
HA–FAY–KHA   [H–PH–KH]

ROOTS: HAVOC means great destruction; it "probably" derives from Germanic terms like *haver* (to hook, take) or *heffen* (to lift up).

הפוך / HĀFOOKH is inverted – see "FICKLE."

הפכה / HAFĀKHA is destruction or an overthrow, best seen in *Genesis 19:21* to describe the leveling of Sodom and the five towns.

> **BRANCHES:** הוה / HŌVĀH is ruin or calamity (*Isaiah 47:11*); the opposite is הוה / HĒVĀH (to form).
>
> HEAVE may be related to the overturning above. HYPO- (under in Greek) may link up to the inversion and undermining here. Flip PH – K over to גב / GUV (back).
> See "FICKLE."

HAZE/חזיז
HA–ZEEZ   [HZYZ]

ROOTS: Here's the HAZY etymology from *Webster's* : "Connection with Anglo Saxon *hasu* (gray) is possible, but probably via Late German proverb *de hase brouet* (the hare is brewing) as applied to a mist." HAZE means fog or vagueness. חזיז / HĀZEZ is a cloud in mishnaic Hebrew; "bright cloud" is the rendition in *Zechariah 10:1* (KJ).

> **BRANCHES:** CHAOS, GAS and the second, (wind) element in Japanese (KAME)KAZE link up to the "vapor" and "confusion" in the definition of HAZE and to גו / GUZ [to change, move (in the wind)] – *Numbers 11:31; Psalms 90:1.*

HE/הוא
HOO   [HOA]

ROOTS: Anglo-Saxon *he* is the source of our pronoun HE. In Herew הוא / HOO is HE, and היא / HĒ is SHE.

> **BRANCHES:** ההוא / HĀHOO means "that one." הם / HĀ(M) is "they" (the ם/M is a plural suffix); *hie* is "they" in Anglo-Saxon. *Hij* is HE in Dutch; *ia* is he or she in Indonesian; *O* means he in Hungarian and Turkish. See "THEM."

HEAD/קדקד
COD–CODE   [KD→HD]

ROOTS: The given IE root for HEAD is *kaput* (head) – see קרקפת / (KAR)KEPHET (head) at "CAPITAL." If one would consider KPT as the ancestor of an HD term, why not prefer Hebrew קדקד / KAD – KŌD (head, crown of head – *Deuteronomy 33:16*)? After all, the ק (K) is merely a ה(H) with a longer stem.

To see more examples of English H words from Hebrew ק words, look up terms like HAND, HEAT or HEMP (from Greek *kannabis*, attributed to a Semitic origin). HORN is from Latin *cornu* and Hebrew *keren*. IE root *kad* is the given source of HATE, and IE *kadh* is the etymon listed for HAT, HEED and HOOD.

Franco was the political head or CAUD[ILLO] of post-war Spain. The word is officially borrowed from the Arabic; *akid* is a colonel in Arabic.

A Spanish commander, ALCAIDE, and a Spanish mayor, ALCALDE, are also from Arabic words like *qada* (to lead). LACKEY is said to be from Arabic *al-kaid* (the captain). The awaited Moslem *mahdi (messiah) is from hada* (to lead aright).

To lead is to head, as the head leads the body (or ought to). קדם / KĀDUM is to go forward or HEAD FOR something. קדם / KĒDĀM is to HEAD OFF or precede. קדימה / KĀDĒMĀ is AHEAD; קדמה / KIDMA is progress or HEADWAY.

Other HEADS of state, or of estates, carry KD titles like COU(N)T and (reversing to DK) DUKE. The DK terms under IE root *deuk* (to lead) include DUCHESS, (CON)DUCT and TUG.

The flip side of "HEADS" is "tails." KD or KT tail terms include קץ / KĀT(S) (end), קצה / KĀTSEH (edge, extremity) and תחת / (TĀ) KHĀT (rear end, under, below).

These give us CODA (tail), CAUDAD, CAUDAL, CAUDATE, HI(N)D (words of posteriority), QUEU and QUETZAL (from Latin and Nahuatl tail words). If not from Latin *cauda* (tail), QUEU (a line) may trace lineage to קו / KAV or QUOO (line). Greek *kata* (down) is found in many words like CATAPULT, CATARACT and CATHEDRAL.

קדה / KĀDĀ (bowing the head to KOW TOW or give KUDOS) is both a "head" word and a term of going downward.

Snipping off the initial S reveals more KT tails. (S)CUD and (S)CUT are from older words like *(s)kutt* (a fox tail in Icelandic). In Old Norse *(s)kot* is "something projecting," and *(s)kutr* is the stern of a boat.

Krut is "end" in Korean; reverse to *tidaq* in American Indian (NW Washington State). The IE root *dek* (horsetail, etc.) is a CODA (KD) reversed.

Back to the top of this entry, the crown or קדקד / KADKŌD infers the protective covering of the head. HAT, HEED, HOOD and HUT should all fit our HEAD. TOQUE, a cap, reverses to TK. *Oteq* means "head" in the Coeur d'Alêne tongue (Pacific NW). The IE root *kadh* is to shelter or cover. *Katto* is a Finnish roof or ceiling.

Other forms of קץ / KĀTS (end) and קצה / KĀTSE (edge) include Thai *ket* (boundary, border, limit). Reverse to *take* (border or edge) in Proto-Polynesian.

See "PRECEDE."

HEALTH/חלוץ
HEAL–OOTS   [HL]

ROOTS: Old Norse *heill* is healthy; the IE root is *kailo* (whole, uninjured, of good omen – cognate with "holy.") Both חלוץ / HĒLOOTS (*Isaiah 58:11*) and חיל / KHĀYEL or HĀYEL mean "vigor" and "strength." חלם / HĀLĀM is to be healthy or to heal.

> **BRANCHES:** CELIBATE, CURE, HALE, and HEAL are related. Antonyms like AIL(ING) and ILL are from sound-alike opposites such as חלה / HŌLE (sick) and חלי / HŌLE (ILLNESS) – see *Deuteronomy 29:21.* חלש / HĀLĀ(SH) means "weak" and חיל / HĒL is trembling.

CHOLE[RA] is mentioned at "GALL." *Ola* is health in Hawaiian; *ahul* is weak, feeble or debilitated in Basque.
See "ALL" and "HAIL."

HEARSE/חַרַשׁ
HOAR – US(H)   [HRS]

ROOTS: Middle English *herse* is said to have originated with Old French *herce* (a harrow or elaborate plow). See "HARROW."
חרש / HORĀS(H) is to plow (*Micah 3:12*) or engrave; מחרשה / (MÄ)HĀRĀS(H)Ä is a plow.

> **BRANCHES:** חרת / HORUS is to engrave; חרץ / HORĀTS is to cut into; נחרץ / (NE)HERĀTS is dug or plowed.
> The harsher pronunciation of חרש is KHARAS(H). HARSH is from the IE base *qars* (to scratch, comb); GASH is from Old French *garser* (to make a deep cut).
> See "CHARACTER."

HEDON(ISM)/עֶדֶן
EDEN   [EDN→HDN]

ROOTS: A HEDONIST seeks *hedoné*, Greek for pleasure or delight. עדנה / EDNÄ or KHEDNÄ is "pleasure"– *Genesis 13:12*; עדן / ĀDEN is delight, enjoyment and the name of the paradisic garden (Eden) where Biblical Adam named the animals with his innate (Hebrew) vocabulary – *Genesis 2:8*.

> **BRANCHES:** ANODYNE is from Greek *odyne* (pain) – a sound-alike antonym. Greek *hedos* (pleasure) is the source of AEDES. AEDES and HEDONISM are cognates of ASSUAGE, DISSUADE, PERSUADE, SWEET and SUAVE at the IE root *swad* (sweet, pleasant). *Edes* is sweet in Hungarian (not IE).
> IE *swad* is merely רבש / D'VAS(H) backwards. The term is usually translated "honey", but at *Leviticus 2:11* רבש / DVS is rendered '"sweet" in Aryeh Kaplan's translation. He cites classic Bible commentator Rashi, who sees the term including sweet things such as fruit extracts.
> A missing link to "sweet" is Arabic *atzb* (sweet), which is only a ZB reverse away from TBZ or רבש / D – BH – SH (honey, sweet). *Zoet* ("sweet" in Dutch; similar on other Scandinavian tongues) may be reversing the TZ of the Arabic.

HEG(EMONY)/הֶגֶה
HEG – EH   [HG]

ROOTS: Greek *hegemonia* is leadership; *hegemon* is a leader. Greek *hegeisthai* (to lead) is the source of EXEGESIS and HEGEMONY. The leadership root appears to be HG.
A twist on Greek *hegemon* (leader) is Hebrew מנהיג / MÄN*HEG* (leader). הגה / HEGE is a rudder or steering wheel (which leads the way). נהג / (NÄ)HÄG is to lead (*Exodus 3:1*). הגאי / HÄGĪ is a pilot.

> **BRANCHES:** Somehow the given IE root for HEGEMONY is *sag* (to seek out) rather than *ag* (to drive). IE *ag* includes ACT, AGENDA, AGENT, AGILE, AGITATE, ALLEGE, AMBIGUOUS, COGENT, ESSAY, EXAMINE, EXIGENT, FUMIGATE, INTRANSIGENT, LEVIGATE, LITIGATE, NAVIGATE,

PRODIGAL, RETROACTIVE, SQUAT and TRANSACT – all from Latin *agere* (to act, conduct, lead). Greek *agein* (to lead, drive) also lends cognates like AGONY, PEDAGOGUE, PROTAGONIST, STRATAGEM, and SYNAGOGUE.

HELD/חֶלֶד
HEL – E(D)T   [HLD]

ROOTS: Old English *healdan* (to hold, retain) and German *haltan* (to stop, hold back) are linked to IE *kel* (to drive, set in swift motion. "Hypothetical base of various loosely connected derivatives"). קל / KAL (swift) is a KL etymon – see "ACCELERATE."
Nothing is "loosely connected" in the Hebrew language. חדל / HĀDTÄL is to cease or stop (*Genesis 18:11*) and חדל / HEDTEL means cessation or the earth (where mortal man is HELD). The HDL→HLD anagram atop this entry is חלד / HELEDT (the span of life, the world). Stopping, containment (HOLDING) and temporality is the issue, as seen in *Psalms 39:6* –

> "You have made my life just handbreaths long; its *span* is as nothing in Your sight..."

> **BRANCHES:** HALT, HALTER and HALTING are related. The opposite of HALT or stop is to start. A slight rescrambling of the terms above produces תחל / THL, as in התחיל / (HĒ)THĒL (to begin). See "CLOT."

HEM/קֶמֶט
KEM – (ET)   [KM(T)→HM]

ROOTS: Old English *hem(m)* is a doubling over or a HEM; the IE root is *kem* (to compress). To compress in Hebrew is קמט / KOMUT (*Job 16:8*); קמט / KEMET is a fold, wrinkle or crease.

> **BRANCHES:** קמץ / KOMUTS is to compress the hand. IE root *ken* (pinching, closing tight) is the source of NAP, NIBBLE, and NIP. IE *ken* (to compress) is credited with KNACKER, NECK, NEWEL, NOCK, NOOK, NOUGAT, NUCLEUS and NUT. *Humu* is to sew, stitch or bind in Hawaiian. See חנק / KHENEK (strangulation) at "HANG."
> See "HEAD" for other K→H changes. The other HEM, in "hem and haw," recalls נמגם / GIMGÄM (stammer).

HERD/עֶדֶר
(K)HADE – ERE   [KH – D – R→(K)H – R – D]

ROOTS: Old Norse *hjord* (herd) opens with an H, but Sanscrit *cardha* (flock, herd, troop) and the IE root *kerdh* (row, herd) again establish a gutteral origin for an English H word. עֶדֶר / KHĀDER is a flock, herd or "drove" (*Genesis 32:17*); a metathesis of the #2 and #3 root letters allows KDR to be read KRD.

> **BRANCHES:** COWHERD, HERDSMAN, SHEPHERD and SWINEHERD all flock together.

Reading *Genesis 32* one sees why a "row" (orderly arrangement) is an appropriate second definition for the IE root of HERD. The word ORDER may ultimately relate to עדר / ĀDER (flock) and to סדר / SĀDER (order, arrangement). These two Hebrew terms are identical but for the initial letters – which are consecutive in the Hebrew alphabet. See "SIDEREAL." The DR or RD root here appears in טור / DTOOR (row, column).

Other possibly related English terms include HUDDLE (a crowd), CRO(W)D (the W is unhistoric), and CATTLE (presently thought to be from "head" terms like Latin *caput*).

עדר / ĀDER or GĀDER is dissectable into two menaing elements (as are all three-letter Hebrew roots) – עדה / ĀDĀ or GĀDĀ (assembly, community) and the DR root above. Both דיר / DEER and גדרה / GIDĀRĀ mean "sheepfold."

HERE/הֲרֵי
HURR–AY   [HRY]

ROOTS: Anglo-Saxon *her* and German *hier* are traced to thje IE root *ko* (this). See "THIS."
הרי / HĀRĀ is defined as "here is," and כה / KŌ is thus, so, or "here" in *Genesis 31:37*.

BRANCHES: Cognates of HERE listed at IE *ko* are BEHIND, ET CETERA, HE, HENCE, HER, HIND (see "CAUDILLO"), HINDER, HINTERLAND, and HITHER.
כאן / KUN means "here" or "now;" הלה / HULĀ and הללו / HULĀLOO mean "that one" and "these" and may have given us the LO in "lo and behold." הנה / HĀNĀ and הלם / HĀLŌM mean "here" too.
הנה / HĀNĀ (here) resembles Hawaiian *ianei* (here); Japanese doubles up with *koko* (here). Spanish and Portuguese prefer *aqui* (here).

HERES(Y)/חֵרוּת
HAY–ROOSE   [HROS]

ROOTS: Greek *hairesis* means "a taking, selection, school, sect and heresy." HERETIC is traced to Greek *hairetikos* (able to choose, heretical), from *hairen* (to choose).
בוחר / (BO)HAIR is to choose (*Deuteronomy 30:19*); חרות / HĀROOS or HĀROOT is freedom; חרר / HORUR is free (*Ecclesiastes 10:17*).

BRANCHES: הוראה / HŌRĀʾĀ is instruction; חרוף / HĀROOF is blasphemy.
The HR root of free and open choice takes on spatial terms at "HOLLOW."
Hiraita is "open" in Japanese.

HESITANT/הַסְסָן
HUH–SIS–UN   [HSS]

ROOTS: Latin *haesitare* is to stick fast or hesitate; the IE root is *ghais* (to adhere, hesitate).
הסס / HĒSAS is to hesitate; הסוס / HĒSOOS is hesitation. Both terms are Aramaic. הססן / HĀSISĀN is a hesitant or indecisive person.

BRANCHES: Reverse to שהה / SHĀHĀ (hesitate) for a synonym. הסה / HĒSĀ (to be silent or HUSHED) is related. For antonyms like חיש / HĒS(H) (haste) – see "HASTE." Thinking about consequences can make us HESITATE, so חשש / HĀS(H)ĀS(H) (apprehension, worry, fear) should be considered. Other HS terms to note include חת / HĀS (dismayed, discouraged) and חשה / HĀS(H)Ā (to be silent, inactive) – see "HUSH." HESITATION can be positive when it implies חם / HUS (forbearance, patience; compassion).

HOARD/חָרָד
HAR–UD   [HRD]

ROOTS: Anglo-Saxon *hord* is loosely traced to IE root *(s)keu* (to cover, conceal). The sense is good, but not the sound. A HOARD meant a storage place, then a secret place for treasure, etc. Similarly, a HOARDING implied a wooden fence. Like HURDLE, HOARDING and HOARD should rather be linked to Old French *hourde* (fence).
חרד / HARAD is a cupboard or closet. A #2-#3 letter swap uncovers הדר / HEDER or KHEDER (chamber, room – a place to hide in *I Kings 20:30*) and גדר / GEDER (fence – *Numerals 22:24*). They fit the sound and sense more successfully than *skeu*.

BRANCHES: גדרה / GIDĀRĀ is a sheepfold; חית / KHĀT is a fence. HUDDLE originally meant ot put out of sight or HIDE, akin to HOARD. אגר / OGAR (to hoard) might also be the source of an HR word for hoarding.

HOARSE/חָרֵשׁ
HOAR–US(H)   [HRS]

ROOTS: The dictionary has a question mark for the origin of Middle English *hors* and Germanic base *hairsa*. The dictionary understands the basic sense of HOARSE (husky voiced) as "dried out, hence rough." Therefore, IE base *qai* (heat) is the offered etymon.
חרישית / HARESH(ET) is the dry, hot (wind) of *Jonah 4:8*. For the HR sense of heat see "CHAR." Sounding HOARSE are התחרש / (HĒT)HORĀS(H) (to whisper – *Judges 16:2*) and חרישה / HĀRĒS(H)Ā (dumbness, silence). חרש / HORĀS(H) is to be silent (*Psalms 83:2*) or secretive.

BRANCHES: חרש / HĀRĀSH is a deaf person; התריש / (HĒ)H'RĒSH is to plot (with a hoarse whisper so that others are deaf to the scheme).

HOKUM/חָכְמָה
HOKH–MA   [HKM]

ROOTS: "Perhaps from hocus-pocus" states the AHD in presenting a possible source for HOKUM (nonsense, fakery).
חכם / HOKHUM is wise and חכמה / HOKHMA is wisdom. Much wisdom gets dismissed as nonsense and hokum. The Hebrew terms may be used sarcastically to describe the unwise or overly wise. See "ACUMEN."

HOLLOW/חָלַל
HOLL–OL   [HLL]

ROOTS: Old English *holh* is HOLLOW; *hol* is a HOLE. The IE root sounds fine, *kel*, but its meaning ("to cover, conceal, save") leaves a gaping logical rift.

חלול / KHĀLOOL or HĀLOOL and חלל / KHĀLĀL or HĀLĀL mean "hollow." The latter term means "space" and "vacuum" as well. חלל / KHOLĀL is "pierced" (*Psalms 109:22*), חלון / KHĀLŌN is a window (*Genesis 26:8*), חליל / KHĀLĒL is a flute (*I Kings 1:40*) and מחילה / (MI)KHĒLĀ is a cave (*Isaiah 2:19*) חלחל / KHĒLKHĀL is to perforate.

BRANCHES: חר / HŌR or KHŌR is a hole (L=R). A physical hole or vacuum is חרות / KHĀROOT (freedom) in spatial terms. Not linked to Hollow is Greek *koilos* (hollow), source of CEILING, -CELE, -COEL, and -COELE.

Of the many cognates of HOLLOW at IE *kel*, only CELL, CELLAR, COLEUS, HALL, HELL, HOLSTER, HULL and (VAL)HALLA might be relevant. Add the suffix -COELE, from Greek *koilos* (hollow). KL reversals like LAG(OON), LAKE and LOCH are large cavities in the earth that recall Hebrew words such as לע /LOĀKH (crater) and ריק / RĀK (empty).

The Finnish "hole", *reika*, similarly reverses KR. The CHEROKEE Indians are "cave people," so this Muskhogean word may relate. Japanese *horeru* is to be hollowed. An IE root that does mean "hole" and "cavity" is *aulo*. It gives us ALVEOLUS, CAROL and (HYDR)AULIC.

Another man-made HOLLOW, like HALL (large, covered room of a palace, etc.), is GALLERY (portico). Late Latin *galeria* has no known origin and may relate to היכל / HĀKHĀL (hall, "temple" in *Hosea 8:14*). The Temple in Jerusalem included just such a colonnade. *Kuil* is a temple in Indonesian. JACAL, from Nahuatl or Aztec, is also a large room of upright poles filled in with wicker. Perhaps the IGLOO is the HALL that an Eskimo builds with snow. The Assyro-Babylonian cognate for Hebrew HĀKHAL is *ekallu*. A related HOLLOW home is the אהל /OHEL (tent). A Hawaiian house or building is a *hale*. LEE and LEEWARD are from Old English *hleo* (shelter).

HOOF/עָקֵב
(AH)–CAVE   [UKV→HF]

ROOTS: The oldest HOOF terms are Sanscrit *capha* and the IE *kapho*. עקב / AKĀV is the heel (*Genesis 25:26*) or a hoof (*Judges 5:22*).

BRANCHES: Drop the L of Latin *calx* (heel – source of CALCAR, CAULK, and CALK) to hear a double guttural reading of עקב / KHAK(ĀV). *Cauquer* is to trample in Old French. Arabic drops the initial ע in its heel word *kaab*. Turkish *okce* and Japanese *kakato* drop the end ב. Polish reverses to *obcas*. The Hawaiian heel is *kapuai*; the ankle in Thai is *kaw(tao)*.

INCULCATE is another derivative of *calx* or *calcis* (heel), as teaching can resemble trampling underfoot. The bottom of the foot is a כף / KAPH (*Genesis 8:9*), and the ankle is a קרסל / KEPHETS. See "COVER" for K–PH and HF words that speak to the HOOF as a covering.

Shoe in Turkish (*ayakkabi*), as HOOF in English (from Sanscrit *capha*), comes from עקב / ĀKĀBH. *Kaupua'i* is the sole of the foot or an animal's paw in Hawaiian – see "CUFF."

The IE root for horse terms is *ekwo*, taking in EOHIPPUS, EQUESTRIAN and HIPPOPOTAMUS. Perhaps Latin *equus*

(horse) liked the sound of the עקבי סום / ĒKVĀ SOOS ("horses hooves"– *Judges 5:22*). The graphic influence of ק on the English Q is obvious. Other examples of English "qu" words from a Hebrew KV souurce might include AQUA – (water) from מקוה / (M)IKVĀ (ritual bath, resevoir, "gathering together" or pool in *Genesis 1:10*) and EQUAL, EQUI –, etc. frtom קו / KĀV (line, measuring line – *Psalms 19:5*). EQUATION, EQUATOR and EQUITY come to English from Hebrew by way of Latin *aequus* (plain, even, flat). Most "qu" words in English have GW or KW IE roots. See "ANKLE."

HOOK/חַכָּה
HUK–(AH)   [HKH]

ROOTS: *Old Norse haki* is a hook; the IE root is *keg* (hook). חכה / KHĀKĀ is a fishhook (*Job 40:25*).

BRANCHES: A companion to חכה / KHĀKĀ (hook) is חכה / KHĒKĀ (to fish, wait, or hope– in fishing or angling the connection is obvious). Official cognates of HOOK include HAKE, HARQUEBUS, HOOKER, HECKLE and HACK.

HA(N)KER (to long for) is so much like חכה / KHĀKĀ (await, hope) that its cognates (CUNCTATION, HANG, and HINGE) at IE *konk* (to hang) may be pinned on the same etymon.

The HOOK or the sharp COG may ultimately hook up to words like חח / KHĀKH or HĀKH (buckle, brooch – *Exodus 35:22*) and חוח / KHOAKH or HOAKH (briar, thorn).

HOOT/הֵד
HAYDT   [HD→HT]

ROOTS: The origin of HOOT is uncertain, but Swedish and Norwegian *huta* is similar.

To HOOT is to shout or cry out, and הד / HĀ(D)T is a shout or noise. In *Ezekiel 7:7* it is translated "joyful shouting."

BRANCHES: *HOITY*–TOITY is defined as noisy mirth. A *HOOT*[ENANNY] involves similar noise. In Finnish, *houta* and *huudan* mean to cry, call, exclaim or shout.

HORRID/חָרַד
HOR–RAID   [HRD]

ROOTS: HORRID is from Latin *horrere* (to shudder, be terrified); the IE root for HORROR and (AB)HOR is *ghers* (to bristle). חרד / HORRĀD is to tremble or to fear (*Genesis 27:33*); חרדה / HĀRĀDĀ is terror.

BRANCHES: HORRENDUS, HORRIBLE, HORRIFIC and HORRIFY are related. רעד / RAUD or RAKHUD (trembling) is a slight shakeup of חרד / KHARAD. ערץ / KHORĀT(S) is to frighten, fear or dread. See "SCARED" for more on the R–DT or DT–R root of terror and trembling.

HORUS/חֶרֶם
HER–ES   [HRS]

ROOTS: HORUS, the Egyptian sun god, is a Greek rendition of an ancient Egyptian word.

חרסה / HÄRSÄ or חרם / HERES in *Job 9:6* means "sun." חרה / HÄRÄ is to burn; חרב / HOREBH is heat or dryness.

> **BRANCHES:** Such HR sun terms offer alternative etymons for HOUR, HOROLOGY and HORO(SCOPE). They are thought to derive from the IE root *yer* (year, season). The direct source of HOUR is Greek *hora* (hour, time, period, season). More HR time words at "HURRY."
>
> A more difficult IE root linkage is seen with Greek *helios* (the sun). The IE root for this source of HELIOCENTRIC or HELIUM is not an HL or HR term but *sawel* (sun). The Semitic "Town of Heres" in Egypt (*Isaiah 19:8*) was renamed the Greek equivalent of Sun City – Heliopolis.

HOUSE/חַסוּת
HUS – OOSE   [HSH]

ROOTS: Old English *hus* is linked to the IE base *(s)qeu* (to cover, hide). The IE base recalls סכה / SOOKÄ (booth – see "SHACK"). Hebrew has enough HS and KS words of covering or shelter to meet terms like HOUSE, HOSE (socks or foot covers), *Casa* (house in Spanish) or CASINO.

These include חסות / HÄSOOS or KHÄSOOT (refuge – *Isaiah 30:3*), חסוי / HĒSOOY or KHĒSOOY (shelter, sanctuary) and חסה / HÄSÄ or KHÄSÄ (to seek refuge or "take shelter" in *Judges 9:15*).

> **BRANCHES:** מחסה / (MÄ)HÄSEH or (MÄ)KHÄSEH in *Isaiah 4:6* is a "pavilion." In *Psalms 104:18* it is a "refuge" for rock-badgers that might better be called a HUTCH. חסן / HÄSÄN or KHASAN is to store (see "MAGAZINE").
>
> חם / HUS or KHUS (to have compassion) is a covering term, a desire to shelter and house the stranger. IE root *ghos-ti* (stranger, guest, host) may therefore link up to these KH – S or HS terms. If so, we can add the cognates GUEST, HOST, HOSTAGE, HOSTEL, HOSTILE and HOSTLER along with HOSPICE, HOSPITAL and HOSPITALITY.
>
> *Ta hsia* is a Chinese mansion.
> See "ENSCONCE" and "SCENE."

HUBBUB/יבכה
YIBH – BUB – AH   [YBB]

ROOTS: HUBBUB, an uproar or tumult, is said to come from Irish *hooboobbes* (cry).

יבכ / YEBÄBH is to wail or sob (*Judges 1:28*);יבכה / YIBHÄBHÄ is sobbing.

> **BRANCHES:** BOBBERY, an Anglo-Indian term, means an exclamation of sorrow. WEEP is from Germanic *wopjan* (to wail) and the IE root *wab* (to cry, scream). Stoic reductions of this BB or WB sobbing word might include *wu* (a sob or whimper in Chinese) and *uwe* (a cry or howl in Hawaiian). See "WOE."

HULA/חָל
HULL   [HL]

ROOTS: The native Hawaiian dance, HULA – HULA, and other dances in the region do not require steps or partners. The dancers writhe and shake in place.

חל / HUL or KHUL is to dance, writhe or tremble. The מחולה / (MI)HŌLA or (MI)KHŌLÄ (dance) is an extension. At *Exodus 15:20* Miriam the prophetess and "all of the women" danced to praise the Lord after the splitting of the sea. The brazen dancing (same HL term) before the golden calf in *Exodus 32:19,* however, almost ended the Israelite mission.

> **BRANCHES:** חלחל / HILHÄL or KHILKHÄL is to shake; חלחלה / HULHULÄ or KHULKHULÄ is a convulsion. CHOREA is a nervous disorder of convulsions; the word initially derives from Greek *khorea* (choral dance). The convulsion-dance connection is established above. See "CHORUS." Related dance terms include התחולל / (HIT)KHŌLÄL (to whirl) and כרכר / KIRKÄR (to dance – *IISamuel 6:14*). (S)CURRY and the HORA (dance) ought to relate.

HURRY/מַהֵר
(MA)HAIR   [H – R]

ROOTS: There is no known source for HURRY. The best theory available is "probably from an echoic base seen in 'hurl.'" מהר / (MÄ)HER means "in a hurry;" מהר / (ME)HÄR is to hurry or "hasten" in *Genesis 18:6.* נהר / (NA)HUR is to flow or run (as a river); במהירה / (BE)MHÄRÄ is soon.

> **BRANCHES:** הרף / HER(EF) is a moment or instant. An הר / HR root of quickness emerges. Perhaps HOUR fits better here than at the IE root *yer* (year, season). The hustling HARE is currently linked to the IE root *kas* (gray). Thai reverses the HR of HURRY, as *reh-oh* means quick. [In Thai the hare or rabbit (*gradty*) doesn't hurry as much as jump, leap or hop (*gradoht*). These last two Thai words are reversals of דלוג / DTĒLOOG (skip, jump).] הר / HR is close to קל / KL; קל / KUL is swift – see "ACCELERATE." בהל / (BE)HÄL is to hasten or cause to hurry. As for HURL (see above), הרעל / HORUL is "were thrown" (said of javelins in *Nahum 2:4*). An HR antonym is אחר / ÄHAR (to delay, be late). מחר / [MA]HAR (later, afterwards; to morrow) is another HR temporal term – see "HORUS."

HUSH/חָשָׁה
HUSH – AH   [H – SH]

ROOTS: HUSH was *hussht* in Middle English, but the term is dismissed as imitative. חשה / HUSHÄ is to be silent; חשי / HUSHĪ is stillness or quiet. An extended form is החשה / HEHESHÄ (*Isaiah 42:14*). הם / HUS is defined as "hush;" Caleb "hushed" the people in *Numbers 13:30.*

> **BRANCHES:** HISS is akin to לחש /(LÄ)HUSH (to whisper). חרש / HORUSH means "to be silent." רעש / RAKHASH is noise.

HYSSOP/אֵזוֹב
AYE – ZOVE   [A – Z – B(H)→HSP]

ROOTS: The sound correspondence isn't very sharp, but HYSSOP is an official borrowing from the Hebrew אזוב / AZOV or ASOBH (*Exodus 12:22*). The Greeks rendered this aromatic plant as *hyssopos* or *hyssopon*; by the time Anglo-Saxon uses the word it is spelled *ysope*.

BRANCHES: It is not wrong to hear SOAP in the above terms, as the HYSSOP is sweet smelling and connected with ritual cleansing. See SOAP at "SEEP."

I(pronoun)/יְ
EE   [Y]

ROOTS: Old English *ic*, Latin *ego* and IE root *eg* all mean I (first person pronoun). These link up nicely with *aku*, the Indonesian "I," but we can not know for sure that "I" is a shortened form of *ic*.

1) Others have linked *ic* etc. to אחד / EKH(AD) (one). The I or EGO is number one to many.

2) The letter "I" (pronounced as "eye") is often pronounced EE overseas, and the EEY or Ē sound matches the first person element in Hebrew grammar. Eve declares in *Genesis 4:1* that "I have gained (קניתי / KĀNĒSĒ) a male child with the help of the Lord." The יְ / EE at the end of possessive constructs also forms the first person – בי / BEE is "by me." Similarly, לי / LEE means "to me." In future tense, the "I" element is א / A. אלך / ĀLĀKH means "*I* shall go."

BRANCHES: Russian *ya* (I) and Spanish *yo* (I) are reversals of this first person form. Fijian *au* (I) is also just a vowel sound; *ia'u* means "me" in Hawaiian. French *je*(I) conforms to the usual Hebrew י / Y to J pattern. Just as the י / ĒY suffix makes אני / ANĒ mean "me," the ו / OOW suffix makes אנו / ANOOW mean "we." Unlike French *nous* (we) which resembles the entire word אנו / ANOOW, English WE and Chinese *wŏ* (we, us) only pick up – and reverse – the ו / OOW element. See "ME." If *ic, ego* and/or I prove to be traceable to אחד / EKHA[D] (number one), then, conversely, number ONE may relate to first person terms like אני / ANĒ (I).

IBIS/אבו
EEB – OO   [ABO]

ROOTS: Latin and Greek *ibis* (heron) and the Aramaic אבו / EBOO (the targum's rendering of the "heron" in *Deuteronomy 14:18*) seem to be birds of a feather.

BRANCHES: אבר / ĀBHER (wing) might figure in the terms above and in the JABIRU (wood ibis named by the Tupi Indians of Brazil).

IDEA/ידיעה
(Y)ID – EE – ĀH   [D – E/A]

ROOTS: Greek *idea* means idea (as well as appearance and form – though these last two defintions may be confused with Greek *eidos*).

ידיעה / YIDĒÄ is knowledge or information; הודע / HODÄ means brought to one's knowledge – *Leviticus 4:23*; ידע / YODÄ is to know or be aware of something – *Genesis 31:32*.

The two letter root is דע / DÄ (which is "know!" in the imperative).

BRANCHES: Perhaps *da* ("yes" in Russian and Rumanian) is affirmation as דע / DA is acknowledgement.

See "IOTA" for another Greek I or i from a Hebrew י (Yod); the Greeks heard יעקב / YÄ – ĀKŌV (Jacob) as Iakobos.

See "ORTHODOX" and "VEDA."

IF/אף
UF   [AF]

ROOTS: IF has an "uncertain" history. IF can mean although, possibly and even though.

אף / UF is defined as "though" or "nevertheless." אפילו / ÄF(ĒLOO) means EVEN, EVEN THOUGH or IF.

BRANCHES: The IE root of IF, *i*, resembles אי / Ē ("if" in Aramaic).

(IN)CITE/הסית
(HE) – SEAT   [ST]

ROOTS: Latin *citare* is to set in motion or urge. The given IE root is *kei* (to set in motion). French *inciter* is an ST, not a KT word.

The Hebrew root is סת / ST, as seen in יסיתך / (YÄ) SĒT(KHÄ) – "entice (you)" at *Deuteronomy 13:7*. הסית / (HÄ)SĒT is defined "to incite, to instigate.

BRANCHES: The IE root *kei* takes in (BE)HEST, CITE, EXCITE, RESUSCITATE, and SOLICIT. Because the *kei* sound is so ill-defined, the root goes on to include words like "kinetic." ENTICE might be a TS reversal of this ST root. ENTICE is thought to derive from *in* + *titio* (a burning brand). אוד / OOD or OOT is a firebrand.

(I)NER(T)/נָהָר
NAHAR   [NHR]

ROOTS: INERT is said to be from Latin *in* (not) + *ars* or *artis* (skill, art). The IE root is *ar* (to fit together). A "lack of skill" or "not fitting together" has little to do with INERTIA (not moving, inactive).

The Polish word *nurt* (current) echoes the Hebrew נהר / NÄHUR (to flow). נהר / NÄHÄR is a river or stream *(Isaiah 6:12)*. רץ / RAT(S) is to run – see "ROTATE." In light of the NR or RT Hebrew etymons, INERT should mean "not running or moving."

BRANCHES: Reversing the NR of נהר / NaHaR is RUN – see "STREAM." One might also get the RHINE and RHONE rivers, which are no mere RUNNELS (rivulets). נחל / NÄHÄL or NÄKHÄL is a stream – see "CATSKILL." One might hear NILE in this word. Returning to our stream-flow-move formula, נחל / NŌHUL is a procedure (NL=NR).

A river in Arabic is *nahr*; in Turkish its *nehir*. The Indonesian river, *kali*, is from נחל / (NA)KHAL, as is COULEE, GHYLL, GILL and GULLY. קלח / KELAH is a stream. The initial IN-, the negative element of INERT, is from אין / ÄYN (not).

INSO(M)NIA/אֵין שֵׁנָה
AIN S(H)AIN–NAH — [AYN + SH–N–H]

ROOTS: Taking the prefix first, -IN is from the IE root *ne* (not). אַיִן / UYIN is "not" (*Genesis 30:1*); אֵין / ĀYN means "there is no" or "none"– *Genesis 37:24*. A shortened negative prefix is אִי / Ē (*I Samuel 4:21*).

The negatives listed at IE *ne* include A-, ABNEGATE, AN-, ANNUL, ANNIHILATE, DENY, NAUGHT, NAY, NEFARIOUS, NEGLECT, NEGLIGENT, NEGOTIATE, NEITHER, NEUTER, NEVER, NIHILISM, NIL, NIMIETY, NIS, NIX, NO, NON-, NONE, NOR, NOT, NOTHING, NULLIFY, RENEGADE, RENEGE, and UN-. Note the ease with which these negatives swing from vowel-N words to N-vowel words. More at "NO."

Latin *somnus* (sleep) is the immediate source of words like SOMNAMBULENT and SOMNOLENT. Somehow, the given IE root is *swep* (sleep), which takes in such different sounding terms as SOPORIFIC, SOMNUS, and HYPNOSIS.

The first recorded man is already asleep by *Genesis 2:21*. The noun שֵׁנָה / S(H)ĀNÄ (sleep) appears in *Genesis 31:40*, where Jacob has lost sleep from counting too many sheep.

BRANCHES: If one needs an SN sleep term that includes the M of SOMNI-, there's תְּנוּמָה / SINOOMA ("slumber"– *Proverbs 6:4*). SLUM(BER) is a נ (N) to L change away from תְּנוּמָה / SINOOMA. שַׁאֲנָן / SHÄ ÄNÄN is "tranquil" or "to be at ease"; see "CHANGE" for more nuances of human sleep. Polish *sen* is dream or sleep; *senny* means sleepy. Eskimo sleep, *sinikpok*, begins with SN. Korean *chim* (sleep) makes one consider COMA a possible cognate. *Shin* is to go to bed in Japanese. Sleep seems to have been abbreviated to *shui* in Chinese and to *si'e* among Indians of Washington State. More sleep words are available at "DORM" and "NUMB."

(IN)STALL/שָׁתַל
S(H)A–TEAL — [STL]

ROOTS: Medieval Latin *stallum* gave us STALL and INSTALL, while Old High German *stellen* is the source of GESTALT. The IE root is *stel* (to put, stand), but most significant is STOLON, from Latin *stolo* (branch, shoot). In botany, a STOLON is "a trailing branch or shoot that takes root at the tip to form a new plant." שָׁתִיל / S(H)ÄTĒL is a shoot or sapling (*Psalms 128:3*); שָׁתַל / S(H)ÄTÄL is to plant or transplant (*Jeremiah 17:8, Psalms 1:3*).

BRANCHES: The shoots or runners of IE *stel* include APOSTLE, DIASTOLE, EPISTLE, FORESTALL, INSTALLMENT, PEDESTAL, PERISTALSIS, STALK, STALL, STALLION, STELE, STILL, STILT, STOLE (garment), STOLLEN, STOUT, STULTIFY and STOUT.

SET and SETTLE might belong here, but the AHD files them under IE root *sed* (to sit). SETTLE does mean to plant firmly in a place or to migrate – fitting the planting and transplanting above. שָׁת / S(H)ÄT is to put, place, SET or station.

See "SEAT" and "SET."

IOTA/יוֹד
YO(D)T — [YOD →IOT]

ROOTS: IOTA is the ninth letter of the Greek alphabet. The tenth letter of the Hebrew alphabet is יוֹד / YODT. The lower case IOTA is as small as the Hebrew YOD (י / Y) – which is why IOTA means a small quantity or a jot.

BRANCHES: The source of JOT (very small thing) is traced to IOTA, but not all the way back to יוד / YŌDT or JŌDT. The Hebrew י / Y is most often rendered I: *Israel* is *Ysrael* in Hebrew, and *Ionia* is יון / YAVÄN or YÄON (*Genesis 10:2* – *where the Greek brother of Media, Moscow and Thrace is rendered Javan in English Bibles*). יד / YÄD is a hand or peg (*Exodus 26:17*). More examples of י / Y taking an *i*, *I* in Greek at "JINX."

IRE/חָרָה
HUR–AH — [HR]

ROOTS: IRE (anger) is from Latin *ira* (wrath). The given IE root is *eis* (root for words denoting passion). חָרָה / HÄRÄ is to be angry (*Genesis 4:6; Deuteronomy 29:23*). The same Hebrew term means to burn or kindle – see "CHAR."

BRANCHES: Another fire-fury, burning mad connection is seen with רָתַח / RETÄKH (to boil), רִתְחָה / RITKHÄ (anger – Aramaic) and רָתְחָן / RÄTKHÄN or RASKHAN (IRASCIBLE). Here is an RSK etymon for IRASCIBILITY, also traced to IE *eis*.

IRATE, though, should belong with IRE and terms like חֲרִי / HÄRĒ or KHÄRĒ (burning anger).

An extension, חָרוֹן / KHÄRŌN (wrath – *Nehemiah 13:18*), should be behind the IE root *ghrem* (angry). This root is the source for GRIM, GRIMACE, GRUMBLE and POGROM. אָרָה / ÄRÄ is to curse (*Numbers 23:7*). *Jaru* is furious in Old Slavic. In Japanese, *hara* is anger and *kirau* is hate. *Haragos*, angry in Hungarian, is probably not from חָרָה / HÄRÄ but רֹגֶז / ROGEZ (RAGE).

IS/יֵשׁ
(Y)AIS(H) — [Y–S(H)]

ROOTS: IS, the third person present of "to be," is traced to Greek *es-ti*, Sanskrit *as-ti*, and the IE root *es* (to be). יֵשׁ / YÄS(H) means "there IS…," "All the earth shall know that *there is* a God in Israel."– (*I Samuel 17:46*). (See "IOTA" for the י / Y=I equation.) הֱיוֹת / HEYOS means "to be" in *Genesis 2:18*.

BRANCHES: Aramaic's related הֲוָת / HÄVÄS evokes WAS. Aramaic אֲרָא / ÄRÄ (was) may be the source of ARE; Hebrew אֵלֶּה / ĀLE (these are) is another possibility. Cognates of IS at IE *es* include ABSENT, AM, ENTITY, ESSENCE, IMPROVE, INTEREST, -ONT, ONTO-, PROUD, QUINTESSENCE, REPRESENT, SIN, SOOTH, SOOTHE, SUTTEE, SWASTIKA, and YES. יֵשׁ / YES(H) means property as well as existance, so HAS may derive from יֵשׁ / Y–S(H) or from אָחַז / AHAS (to hold, possess).

As the Spanish and Italian YES reverses to *si*, so Chinese *shi* (yes, am, are, is) reverses IS. *Hsi* and *shih* are also forms of "to be."

אֵת / AS is Biblical Aramaic for "the same," recalling both IS and AS. היות / HEYŌS (whereas) and שׁ / S(H)E (because) also contribute to the uses of AS.

See "LESS" and "BE."

IT/אֶת
ET   [AT]

ROOTS: The pronoun IT is from Anglo-Saxon *hit*; the basic sense is "this one." The IE root cited is *ko* (this, etc.). אֶת / ET and ĀT is the sign of the definite accusative (*Genesis 1:1*). אוֹתוֹ / OTŌ and אוֹתה / OTÄ may be rendered "it." אוֹת / OT means sign or symbol.

> **BRANCHES:** For the sense of "this one," the Hebrew (אחת / ÄHUT) and Aramaic (חד / HUDT) words for "one" are worth mentioning. The suffix -ITE should relate. *Yat* is one in Cantonese; *do* means "same" in Japanese. An extension of אֶת / ET is אותו / OTŌ (self or him), a likely source of Greek *autos* (self), English AUTO—, AUTOMOBILE and 50 other such words.

JACK/יַעֲקֹב
YA–AH–COVE (or JACOB)   [Y–A–K–BH→JAK]

ROOTS: Several words come from the name Jack, from Jacob or יעקב / YÄ'ÄKOBH. In *Genesis* Jacob is named the Hebrew term which means heel, to supplant, to overreach, and to deceive (see *Genesis 27:36*).

> **BRANCHES:** Jake's career begins as a younger twin baby who grabs Esau by the heel and who, using deceit, supplants his undeserving brother as the privileged firstborn.
> To JOCKEY means to cheat, swindle, and maneuver for position or advantage. An unrefined Bible reader would consider Jacob a JACK (knave) who cheated his brother Esau out of his inheritance or JACKPOT with his JOCULAR brand of JUGGLING.
> And why might this maligned patriarch be the inspiration for JACKDAWS, JACKRABBITS and a dozen other male birds, beasts and fish? It might be because, after much jockeying and financial juggling with Laban, he hits the jackpot with some magical tricks of animal breeding. In addition, after some juggling and jockeying of wives, Jacob ended up with four wives and at least thirteen children.

JAN(UARY)/הַגֵּן
(HEY)–JANE   [GN→JN]

ROOTS: JANUARY honors the pagan deity Janus. This vigilant deity was known as the guardian of portals. Historically, a JANITOR was a doorkeeper. Latin *ianus* is a covered arcade or a door; *ianua* is an outer door. The sense here is protection, not a piece of wood that swings on a hinge. גנן / GÄNÄN or JANAN is to cover over or defend (*Isaiah 37:35*); גנונה / GINŌNÄ or JINŌNA is an awning; הגן / HÄGÄN or HÄJÄN is to defend or protect.

> **BRANCHES:** A protected place was the first home of our Biblical ancestors – גן עדן / GÄN ÄDEN (the *garden* of Eden). The Hebrew ג can be a G or J, just as Geoffry is pronounced like

Jeffrey. The opposite of a JANITOR (guardsman) is the גנב / GÄN(Ä**U**) (thief–*Exodus 21:37*) who breaks into doors–see "KNAVE." גנז / GÄNÄZ is to hide: גנזך / GINZÄKH is a treasury. *Yin ni* is to conceal in Chinese; *ginza* (treasury) is Toyko's financial center. גנזה / GINĒZA is a storehouse.

JASPE(R)/יָשְׁפֵה
JOS(H)–P(H)AY   [Y–SH–PH →JSP]

ROOTS: Greek *iaspis* is traced to Arabic *yashb* (jasper) rather than to ישפה / YÄSHPHÄ or JÄSPÄ ("jasper"–*Exodus 39:13*).

> **BRANCHES:** JASPER is an opaque quartz gem. ספיר / SÄPHĒR (SAPPHIRE–*Exodus 39:11*) and כסף / (KE)SEPH (silver–*Exodus 22:24*) lend further sound and sense. Perhaps names like Caspar and the Caspian Sea relate to silvery qualities.
> Other J words borrowed from Arabic are harder to trace ot Hebrew. JASMINE (from Arabic *yasamin*) might come from ישימון / YIS(H)ĒMŌN (wilderness–*Deuteronomy 32:10*). JAR, from Arabic *jarrah* (earthenware vessel) might connect to חרם / KHERE(S) (earthenware).

JERK/ירק
JAH–RUK   [YRK→JRK]

ROOTS: JERK has no known origin according to the AHD. *Webster's* offers: "a variation of archaic YERK"– and YERK (a jerk, blow; to beat, lash) is "of obscure origin." JERK (to pull at, twist, push, thrust or throw with a sudden, sharp movement") may be influenced bvy terms like ירק / YORÄK or JORÄK (to expectorate or spit out–*Numbers 12:14*) and ירה / YÄRÄ (throw or cast–*Exodus 15:4*).

> **BRANCHES:** ירך / YEREKH is the thigh (the muscular system's biggest jerk); זרק / (ZÄ)RÄK is to throw; לקה / LÄKÄ is to flog. יריעה / YIRĒA or JIRĒAKH is a strap (see the lashing above) or a strip (as in the Peruvian Indian source of JERKED beef).
> See "JET."

JET/ירה
JEE–(D)TAH   [YD →JT]

ROOTS: JET (to spurt forth or emit in a stream) is said to be from Latin *jactare*, a frequentive of *jacere* (to throw). Latin *jacere*, after a #2-#3 letter swap, is a ringer for ירק / YORÄK or (Anglicized) JORÄK (to throw–see "JERK.") Much simpler etymons are available for JET, however, such as ידה / YEDÄ or JĒ(D)TÄ (to "cast"–*Lamentations 3:53*) and ירה / YÄDÄ or JÄ(D)TÄ (to "shoot"–*Jeremiah 50:14*).

JET PLANE, JETSAM, JETTISON, JETTY (pier), JUT and perhaps JUTES (if this Germanic tribe were named for propelled weapons) relate to the Hebrew terms above as well as to יד / YÄD or JÄ(D)T (hand, handle, tenon), יצא / YÄTSÄ or JÄT(S)A (to go out) and יצק / JÄT(S)ÄK or YÄT(S)AK (to cast, to pour out).

The AHD traces JET back to the IE root *ye*(to throw). The listed cognates of JET include ABJECT, ADJACENT,

ADJECTIVE, AMICE, CATHETER, CONJECTURE,
DEJECT, DIESIS, EASE, EJACULATE, EJECT, ENEMA,
GIST, INJECT, INTERJECT, OBJECT, PARESIS, PARGET,
PROJECT, REJECT, SUBJACENT, SUBJECT, SYNESIS and
TRAJECTORY.

JINX/יוֹנָה
JONAH   [YNH→JNX]

ROOTS: Nobody knows where the word JINX came from. But this hoodoo person or thing that is supposed to bring bad luck sounds much like what we call a JONAH. יונה / YŌNÄ (Jonah) caused a near shipwreck until he was tossed overboard. There are several ways to explain the *X* at the end of JINX, but perhaps no better way to explain the term.

    BRANCHES: *Webster's* theorizes that JINX may relate to Greek *iynx*, a bird used in incantations and charms. This may be the same peeping bird that appears in the first half of Swahili *njiwa* (pigeon) or the 2nd half of Late Latin *(pip)ionis*, Old French *(pi)jon* Italian *(picc)ione* and English (PI)GEON. יון, יונה / ION, YON or JŌN(AH) means dove and pigeon (*Genesis 8:11*).
    The Greek penchant for pronouncing the י / Y as an I is seen in names like JOHN (from Greek *Ioannes* and Hebrew יוחנן / YŌHANAN).
    See "'IOTA." The AHD links JINX with JUBILATE – see "JUBILANT."
    An example of guttural deriving from an H (as Jonah became JINX) involves the word BAKE. [BAKE is from the IE root *bhe*. Polish *piec* (bake) and Thai *ohp* (bake) are variations of אפה / ÄPHÄH (to bake – *Genesis 40:17*). Akkadian *epū* is to bake.]

JOVIA(L)/יקוק
JEHOVAH   [JHVH]

ROOTS: JOVIAL (jolly) is from Latin *Jovis* (Jupiter); JOVE is the chief deity in the Indo-European pantheon of gods. יקוק (using a ק instead of a ה) / YHVH or JHVH (Anglicized as JEHOVÄH – *Genesis 2:4*) is the principle Hebrew name for God. This name infers God as the Eternal, and connotes the divine modality of love, mercy (and perhaps JOVIALITY).

    BRANCHES: Biblical Jubal (see "JUBILANT") might have been deified by those who associate the source of musical joy with the source of life.
    JULY and JUPITER are official cognates in much the same way that the first syllable of Jehoram or Jehosaphat is from the JH element of deity.
    More godliness at "DIVINE;" more jollity at "JUBILANT."

JUBIL(ANT)/יוֹבֵל
YO–BHAIL   [Y–BH–L→JBL]

ROOTS: Just as "amenable" is not linked to "amen" (see "AMENABLE"), JUBILEE is overlooked as the source of JUBILANCE. Latin *jubilare* is to exult, to raise a shout of joy. The IE root is *yu* (outcry of exultation). JUBILEE is an acknowledged borrowing from יובל / YŌBHÄL or JŌBÄL (the Jubilee year of spiritual and economic regeneration – *Leviticus 25:8-17*). Only at JUBILEE does the dictionary cite the characteristic cry, the joyous, blaring call of the Jubilee – the יבל / YŌBHÄL or JŌBÄL (ram's horn – *Exodus 19:13*).

    BRANCHES: This horn sounds like a *jubilum* (Latin for "wild shout"). People (especially debtors) waited 49 years to JUBILATE with great JUBILATION, adding their own shouts of joy to the blast of the ram's horn which signalled the JUBILEE. Another official cognate is JINX; see "JINX." יובל / YOOBHÄL or "JUBAL" is the name of Cain's great-great-great-grandson who invented musical wind instruments (*Genesis 4:21*).

JU(N)GLE/יַעַר
JUG–ARE   [Y–GR→JGL]

ROOTS: JUNGLE Is from Hindi *jangal* (desert, forest, jungle), which came from Sanskrit *jangala* (wasteland, desert). יער / YÄ'ÄR or JÄGÄR means wilderness or "forest" (*Deuteronomy 19:5*). As most *J* words in IE, the Hebrew original was a י / Y. Before a guttural, like the ע / G, a nasalization (extra N) is common. Lastly, the R + L change is a universal principle in linguistics.

    BRANCHES: If the second element in *juaguarondi* or *yaguarundi* means anything like "cat," then the JGR or YGR element of this Tupi word should mean "jungle." The Tupi Indians live in the jungles of Brazil; the Portuguese conveyed to us this native term for the JAGUAR (wildcat of the jungle).

JURIS(DICTION)/יֹשֶׁר
JO–S(H)ERE   [Y–SH–R→JRS]

ROOTS: Words like JURIS(PRUDENCE) derive from Latin *jus* or *juris* (right, law). The IE root is *yewes* (law). ישר / YŌS(H)ER or JŌS(H)ER (right, equity, "uprightness"– *I Kings 9:4*) is the only word with the genes to parent *jus, juris* (swap letters #2 and #3) and *yewes* (keep the original Y, swap the smae two letters, but pronounce the R as a W)
    The equation of "right" = "law" is sharper in Hebrew. "Right" means "in a straight line, " and ישר / YÄSHÄR is "straight," "even" or "honest" in *I Samuel 29:6*. ישרה / YISHRÄ is "integrity" in *I Kings 3:6*.

    BRANCHES: שורה / SHOORÄ (line, row) and other straight terms may be seen at "SERIES." The people who are kept in line when they do not act as the keepers of God's JURISPRUDENCE (law) are called ישרון / YESH OOROON or JESHURUN (the Jewish people – *Isaiah 44:2*) or ישראל / (Y)ISRÄEL. Read one way, Israel (YSR + EL) means honest-to-God or "straight to God."
    The cognates of IE JURISDICTION at *yewes* include ADJUDICATE, ABJURE, ADJURE, CONJURE, INJURY, JUDGE, JURAL, JURIST, JURY, JURIDICAL, JUST, PERJURY, and PREJUDICE.
    A less crooked path to JUDGE might involve JUDAH. The state of JUDAH's greatest export was Judean law, both in the era of kings and when JEWS (a short form for "Judean") were in exile. JUDAH himself (the son of Jacob) was so famous a judge, that one of the great moments in American literature is drawn from Judah's trials in *Genesis 38*. Just as Judah presides over the

adultery trial of Tamar, Nathaniel Hawthorne has Reverend Dimmesdale judging Hester in *The Scarlet Letter.* Both judges are the guilty males in the adultery cases.

Returning to ישר / YASHAR (straight), "all right" is *yoroshi* and "straight-backed" is *ushiro* in Japanese. *Suora* is straight, upright and candid in Finnish.

JUXT(APOSE)/יַחַד
JUKH – U(D)T   [Y–KH–D→JKT]

ROOTS: Latin *iuxta* means "together;" Latin *juxta* is "near" or "beside." IE root *yeug* (to join) links JUXTAPOSE to YOKE. יחד / YOKHU(D)T is to unite (*Genesis 49:6*) or to be together (*Genesis 22:8*). יחד / YÄKHÄ(D)T is together.

"How good and pleasant it is that brothers dwell *together*– יחד–*Psalms 133:1.*

> **BRANCHES:** יחוד / YĒKHOOD means "union with God"– akin to YOGA, an official cognate of JUXTAPOSITION. Other cognates include ADJOINING, ADJUST, CONJOIN, CONJUGAL, CONJUGATE, CONJUNCTION, ENJOIN, INJUNCTION, JOIN, JOUST, JUGULAR, JUGUM, JUNCTION, JU(N)CTURE, JUNTA, YOKE, ZEUGMA, ZYGOTE, -ZYGOUS. For these ZG terms see "ZYGOTE."
> Back to YKT, *ikut* is to join in Indonesian. In Cantonese, *yihkdov* is "also, too, as well;" *yatchai* is together; *yhta* or *yhden* is "one" in Finnish. "Together" in Finnish is *yhdesse*; in Hungarian it's *egyutt.* חד / KHAD is "one" in Aramaic; אחד / EKHAD is the Hebrew counterpart.

KAISER/כֶּתֶר
KES – ERE   [K–S–R]

ROOTS: כתר / KESER means crown, authority or rulership – see "CZAR."

KARATE/יַד רֵיק
KARE + (D)TUY   [Y–DT + RK → KR + T(Y)]

ROOTS: This form of Japanese martial arts is pronounced kah-rah-tay. This weaponless discipline is named *kara* (empty) + *te* (hand). Oriental words are more likely to reverse the Hebrew.

"Tay" backwards is יד / YÄ(D)T (hand –*Genesis 27:22*); *kara* backwards is ריק / RĀK (empty –*Genesis 37:24*).

> **BRANCHES:** For the Hebrew "hand" see "JET." The verb "to hand" is *ti* in Chinese. Hand, the noun, is *t'ai* for the Indians of Northwestern Washington State. Perhaps the Eskimo hand, *ad[gak]*, relates too.
> A RAKE is a dissolute, profligate and wasted man. The human extensions of ריק / RĀK (empty) involve "men of low character" (*Judges 11:3*) and "worthless and reckless fellows" in *Judges 9:4*. These ריקים / RĀK(IM) or RAKES are akin to the ריקא / RĀKÄ (good for nothing).
> RK and KR relatives of ריק include רוח / REVAKH (space, interval), חור / KHŌR (hole, cave), קרח / KĀRĀAKH (bald). עקרה / AKARA (barren) and ערה / KHĀRA (to pour out, make empty), resembling הריק / [HĀ]RĒK (to empty, pour out).

KEEN/קינה
KEEN – AH   [KN]

ROOTS: For that KEEN which infers "sharpness" or "agreeable" there is חכם / (HÄ)KHÄM (smart – see "ACUMEN"), סכין / (SÄ)KEEN (knife) and חנית / KHÄN[ĒT] (javelin), כן / KĀN (yes) and חן / KHĀN (charm, grace, favor).

KEEN is wailing for the dead, from the Irish *caoine* (lament). קינה / KEENÄ is also a "lament" (*Jeremiah 7:29*) or stylized wailing for the dead. In *II Samuel 1:17* "David intoned this *dirge* over Saul and his son Jonathan." While *Jeremiah 9:9* places the קינה / KĒNÄ in the context of "weeping and wailing," the reference to מקוננות / (MI)KŌN(INŌT) or "dirge-singers" in verse 17 assures us that the KEENING of Israelites (as of the Irish) is singing – not merely crying.

> **BRANCHES:** While the Japanese reverse KN (*naku* means " to cry") and remove song from the sense, the IE root *kan* (to sing) has lost the sense of elegy.
> קנה / KONEH (throat, windpipe – see "CANE"), however, would justify a KN term of piping (singing) divorced from any connotation of a mornful dirge. Moreover, ענה / KHANA is to sing (*Exodus 32:18*). IE *kan*, related to both Hebrew KN terms, gives us ACCENT, CANT, CANTICLE, CANTILATE, CANTO, CANTOR, CANZONE, CHANT, CHARM (which seems to link up with KEEN above), ENCHANTED, INCANTATION, INCENTIVE, OSCINE and RECANT.
> *Kūmākena* is to lament, bewail or mourn loudly for the dead in Hawaiian. *Chang* is to sing in Chinese.

KERNEL / כַּרְמֶל
CAR – MEL   [KRML→KRNL]

ROOTS: Old English *cyrnel* (seed) and IE root *gra-no* (grain) match גרעין / GĀRĒN (kernel, seed) and גרגר / GĀRGÄR (grain, etc.). See "GRAIN."

Added here is כרמל / KĀRMEL (rendered "kernel" in *Leviticus 2:14*).

> **BRANCHES:** Of the cognates already cited at "GRAIN," GRAM is most suited to an alternative etymon containing an *M*.

KHAN /כֹּהֵן
KO – HANE   [KHN]

ROOTS: The title KHAN (lord, prince) given to Genghis Khan and his successors (or to Riza*khan* Pahlavi, the former Shah of Iran) is said to be a native Turkish term from the Ural – Altaic languages. That would make KHAN an Indo-European term, not a Semitic one. TYCOON is from Chinese *kiun* (prince). Indo-European has lost exclusive claims to KN "prince" words.

Whether or not he ruled a KHANATE, Moses' father-in-law Jethro was the כהן / KŌHĀN of Midian (*Exodus 2:16*). The usual trnslation is "priest"– as the term applies to the descendants of Levi – but classical Bible commentators like Rashi render כהן / KHN here as a "chief." Aryeh Kaplan's

1981 translation prefers "sheik."

In *II Samuel 8:18* King David's sons (not Levites) are called כהנים / KOHAN(EM). The translation "priests" is foolish; the context calls for a military "commander."

> **BRANCHES:** Named for קנין / *KIN*YAN (possession), קין / KAYIN or Cain was the ruler of Biblical Man's first city (*Genesis 4:17*). The city was named for Cain's son Khanokh. These KN terms might have influenced princely words like KING. KHN as priest appears as the *koyane* of Japan, the *kachinas* (Hopi Indian), the *kohuna* (priest or minister) of Hawaii, the Mayan *h-qin* and perhaps (again switching G/Q and H) the Haitian *houngan*.

KIBITZ/קפץ
KOP(H)–AHTZ [K–PH–TZ→K–B–TZ]

ROOTS: Entering English via Yiddish, German *kiebitzen* is to meddle, (to jump in) and to look on (as at a card game).

A קפצן / KÄPTS(ÄN) is just such an "impetuous person," literally a jumper. קפץ / KEPATZ is the "leaping'" in *Songs 2:8*, where the KIBITZING of a lover is like the (ES)CAPADES of a gazelle.

> **BRANCHES:** HOP, (S)KIP and perhaps HIPPO — (*hippos* is the Greek horse) are one small leap from the Hebrew etymon. קפץ / K–PH–(T)S (to jump, leap, bounce) might also have bred the Finnish horse, *hovoss*. Keep in mind that the ק / K is only a harsher version of the ה / H. The hopping frog is a *gohp* in Thai.

KIBOSH /כבוש
KEY–BUSH [K–B–SH]

ROOTS: To "put the KIBOSH on" something is to squelch, veto or put an end to it. This slang term is of uncertain origin, though *Webster's* suspects a Yiddish version of Germanic *keibe* (carrion).

In *Genesis 1:28* כבש / KOBHUSH is rendered "to master" or "subdue." כבוש / KEBOOSH, the noun form, means "conquest."

> **BRANCHES:** Related K–BH terms include חבש /KHOBHUSH (to imprison) and גבר / GOBH(ÄR) (to conquer).
> Reverse K–BH for the IE root *weik* (to conquer, to fight) – the source of (CON)VINCE, EVICT, INVINCIBLE, VANQUISH, VICTOR and WIGHT.
> IE root *gwes* is the source of ASBESTOS; the root means "to extinguish." *Ko fu* is to conquer in Chinese.
> See "QUASH" and "VICTOR(ﬀ)."

KILL/קלקל
KULL–KALE [KL]

ROOTS: Middle English *killen* is to kill, from the IE root *gwel* (to pierce).
חלל / KHELAL is to pierce or "slay" in *Ezekiel 28:9*. חלל / KHÄLÄL is a corpse (*Deuteronomy 21:2*) – the root infers piercing a hole – see "HOLLOW."
Several other usages of KILL involve wasting time, exercising a veto or spoiling. קלקל / KILKAL is to spoil, damage or destroy.

> **BRANCHES:** QUELL and BELONEPHOBIA are the given cognates of KILL. כלה / KELÄ is to annihilate; כליון / KEL(ÄYON) is destruction (*Isaiah 10:22*). נחר / (NÄ)KHÄR is to kill by stabbing in the throat. כלה / KÄLÄ is to finish; reverse to *luhk* for "finish" in Thai.

KIN/קנה
KON–EH [KN]

ROOTS: Old English *cyn(n)* means "race, family [or] KIN." The IE root given is *gena* or *gen* (to give birth, beget).
קנה / KONEH may be the source of KINDRED or KINFOLK since it means both to "create" (*Genesis 14:9* – where Cain is named) and a "branch" (of a candelabra – *Exodus 25:32*).
קן / KÄN is a "nest," but the term infers the brood or family in *Deuteronomy 32:11*. עם / UM or KHAM is a nation or people; עם / EEM or KHEEM means with or close to.

> **BRANCHES:** More creative KN terms are available at "GENIUS" (גאון / GÄON is a genius) and "ORIGIN" (עין / ÄYIN, KHIIN or GIIN is a source or spring).
> Words officially AKIN to KIN include KING, KIND, -GEN(Y) and GEN- words, GONAD, ENGINE and GERMAN.

KISS/נשקה
(NIH)–S(H)EEK–AH [S(H)–K→KS]

ROOTS: Old English *cyssan* is to kiss; Germanic *kussaz* is a kiss; and the IE root *kus* means "a kiss."
In *Genesis 27:27* Isaac tells Jacob נשה / GISHÄ ("come near") and שקה / S(H)IKÄ ("kiss"). KISS appears to be a reverse of the Hebrew kiss – the extended noun is נשקה / (NI)S(H)EKÄ), and related to השיק / (HE)SHEK (to touch), השיג / (HE)SEG (to reach), and נישה / GESHÄ (approach, copulation).

> **BRANCHES:** The best kisses include the Hungarian *csok* and the Luiseno Indian *chu(n)gi*.
> Japanese *seppum* (kiss), (and reversing SP to BS) Swahili *busu*, Turkish *buse*, Russian *patselui*, Spanish *beso* and English BUSS (kiss) are from שפה / SÄP(H)Ä (lip). Kissing forms a bridge נשר / GES(HER). SG antonyms at "SAG."

KIT/כד
KU(D)T [KD→KT]

ROOTS: A KIT originally meant a bucket or small tub, as seen in the Middle Dutch term *kitte* (a container, akin to the KID).כד / KÄDT is a pitcher in *Genesis 24:19*.
The ALBATROSS is the Portuguese version of Arabic *al* (the) *qadus* (bucket). Greek *kados* (cask, jar) is "probably of Semitic origin" according to *Webster's*.

> **BRANCHES:** The CADDY (container), KETTLE and (S)CUTTLE all fit in the same tub – see"CADDY." Greek *kutos* (a vessel) is the source of -CYTE and CYTO- words. A bottle is *koo-ut* in Thai.

KITE/עיט
KHAH–YIT   [KH–Y–T]

ROOTS: The Old English *cyta* was a hawk before it meant a toy that could glide (like a hawk or falcon) in the wind. עיט / ÄYIT or KHÄYIT is a "bird of prey" in *Genesis 15:11*.

> **BRANCHES:** Arabic *chada* and Greek *iktinos* are birds of prey cited by Bible commentators discussing the ראה / KÄ'ÄH ("kite" of *Leviticus 11:14*).
>
> The Swahili eagle is a *tai*; in Modern Greek it is *aetos*; the Finnish is *kotka*. The CONDOR (from *cuntu(r)* in Peruvian Indian) is a nasalized (N added) עיט / KYT or KITE.

KITTEN/קטן
KUTT–UN   [KTN]

ROOTS: A KITTEN (young cat) may not be a CAT after all. The term had been applied to the young of other animals, and the given IE base *qat* (to bear young) has no feline connotations. CADELLE (beetle larva) is from Latin *catella* (a puppy or whelp).
קט / KÄT means "small" (*Ezekiel 16:47*); קטן / KÄTÄN is small, young (*Genesis 44:12*) or a child. גדי / GIDTE is the KID of goats – see "GOAT." Reversing to DT–K, דק / DTAK is small. The largest housecat is a miniature or CUT-down version of a lion. See "CUT" for other KT *chiquitos* (little ones in Spanish).

> **BRANCHES:** CHIT is from Anglo-Saxon *cith* (shoot, sprout); the term means a child. The first element in *KIND*ERGARTEN is the German kid or child, the *Ki(n)d*. Similarly, the first element of *CHAUT*AUQUA (a Seneca Indian word) means child.
>
> TK reversals are seen in the Sanscrit child (*takman*) and in *tek-no* the Germanic source of THANE. Both terms might be using the N of קטן / KTN or of an anagramic sibling תינוק / TENOK (infant). Perhaps this last term influenced the Dutch diminutive suffix seen in (MANI)*KIN*. Reversing to *neko*, we have the Japanese cat.
>
> Of all the CAT terms, Indonesian *kutjing* sounds most like קטן / KÄTÄN; small in Indonesian is *ketjil*. It is unlikely that Arabic *qit* (cat) is a borrowing from the French *chat*, Spanish *gato* or Scandinavian *kat(t)*. חתול / KHÄTOOL (cat) is not in the Bible, but is found in Aramaic. The GENETTE is a small wildcat said to be from Arabic *jarnayt*. GENETTE might be a scrambled version of KTN/ קטן. קטן / KTN (youth, small) and its antonym, גדול / GÄDOL (adult, large), both have a gutteral (G/K), dental (D/T) and an L/N;(the LN relationship is documented often here). For a Thai child or KID, reverse to *dek*. *Tama*, a child in Proto Polynesian, may take up the TN end of K–T–N.
> See "SCANT."

KNAVE/גנב
GUN–OV   [GNV→KNV]

ROOTS: KNAVE is said to come from Old English *cnafa*, which may mean either a boy or a servant.
A KNAVE (dishonest person) is a גנב / GÄNÄV (thief – *Jeremiah 20:26*). The noun and verb form of גנב / GNV or KNV are seen at *Exodus 21:37 + 22:1*.
Webster's traces KNAVE to IE base *gnobh* (a stick, piece

of wood). ענף /ÄNÄPH or GÄNÄF is branch or bough (*Ezekiel 17:23*).

> **BRANCHES:** Given נ / N=L, Greek *kleptes* (thief) and KLEPTOMANIAC may be related to גנב / K–N–BH. GRAB may be more distantly related, while FINAG[LE] (to cheat) requires a reversal of גנב / GNF.
>
> The opposite of a KNAVE is a KNIGHT, yet the given etymon for "Knight" is similar – Anglo-Saxon *cniht* (boy, retainer, servant). Simon Perlman's Hebrew etymon for KNIGHT is the youthful but more dignified חניך / KHÄNEKH (pupil, apprentice). The verb "to knight" may be heard in Hebrew words like חנך / KHÄNÄKH (to educate, inaugerate) and התחנך / (HET)KHÄNÄKH (to be dedicated). The IE base of KNIGHT is said to be "*gen*, as in kinfe." חנית / KHÄN[ET] is a dagger.

KNOCK/נכה
NOKH–AH   [N–KH–H]

ROOTS: KNOCK and KNUCKLE are said to be from Anglo-Saxon *cyncled* (bent, crooked) and the IE root *gen* (to press together). עקל / KHAKAL is crooked and חנק / KHANAK is to squeeze or strangle. נכה / NOKHÄ is a root meaning "to beat" or "strike" (*II Samuel 11:15*). הכה / HEKÄ and מכה / MÄKÄH are more familiar forms. To KNOCK is to strike.

> **BRANCHES:** נקישה / NIK(ESHÄ) and נקיפה / NIK(EFÄ) both mean KNOCKING. נגע / NOGÄ or NOGÄKH is to strike. HACK, HOCKEY, and (TOMA)HAWK may link up with הכה / HEKA (to strike). נגד / NG(D) and נגר / NG(R) are striking and hammering terms preserved in Aramaic and Syriac.

KYPH(OS)/כפוף
CUFF–OOF   [K–PH–PH]

ROOTS: Greek *kyphos* is a hump or hunch; *kuphos* means "bent." כפוף / KÄPHOOPH is "bent"–"The Lord... makes *all who are bent* stand straight" (*Psalms 145:14*).

> **BRANCHES:** CUBIT and HASP are related – see "GIBBON." זקוף / ZÄKOOPH (upright, erect) is an antonym. Reverse to *piko* for bent or arched in Proto-Polynesian. *Kupou* is to bend far forward in Hawaiian. Greek *kampulos* is listed at the IE root *kamp* (to bend). If not a KM bending word (covered at "CAMERA") *kamp* is a nasalized (extra M) KP word. Words listed at IE *kamp* include GAMBIT, GAMBOL, GAMMON and JAMB.

LAD/ילד
(YEH)–LED   [LD]

ROOTS: The *Oxford English Dictionary* states "of obscure origin" for LAD. Noah Webster's 18th Century dictionary, scorned by the O.E.D. and the linguistic establishment, cites Chaldaic and Syriac sources for LAD.
ילד / (YE)LED is a boy (*Genesis 21:8*); ולד / V'LAD is an infant or child. *Walad* is a boy in Arabic. לד / LD is the root, as seen in לדה / LÄDÄ (birth).

BRANCHES: .מולדת (MŌ)*LEDE*T means progeny, offspring, ande birthplace. Adding an M to LD in Serbo-Croatian (*mlad*) or Russian (*malaadoy*) gives us words for "young." The word for boy in Basque, *mutil*, requires only a #2-#3 root letter metathesis and a D to T change. *Maulidi* means "birthday" in Swahili. OLD, ELDER, and ALDERMAN more likely relate to this לד / LD root than to its given IE root, *al* (to grow, nourish). The LD or LT root might also be seen in LITTER (to give birth; a group of offspring) and, more remotely, in words like LITT(LE) and (CH)ILD.

LATE/לָאַט
LI'UTT   [LAT]

ROOTS: *Webster's* cities Anglo-Saxon *laet* (slow, sluggish, tardy). Dutch *lant* and German *lass* (slow, lazy) are related; the IE base is *leid*. The AHD reduces the IE root for LATE down to *le*. לאט / LIÄT is slow or sluggish (*Isaiah 8:6*).

BRANCHES: לאות / LĀOOT or LĀOOS is weariness or exhaustion; LASSITUDE (weariness) is from Latin *lassus*(faint) – LAZY is ultimately related. Cognates of LASSITUDE and LATE at IE *le* (to let go, slacken) include: ALAS, LAST-, LATTER, LENIENT, LET- and LIEGE.

A nasalization (extra N) of לאת / LIÄT (slow, slowly) gives us Rumanian *lent* (slowly) and French *lentement* (slowly). "Slowly" in Hungarian is *lassan*. Antonyms of the captioned term include רהוט / RÄHOOT (quick). For LS words of LOOSE LASSITUDE see "LOOSE." עצל / ATSÁL ("lazy," "idle"–*Judges 18:9, Proverbs 6:6*) is a reversed LS or LT term.

LAUG(H)/לָעַג
LAH–UG   [LUG]

ROOTS: LAUGH is from Anglo-Saxon *hleahhan*; akin to German *lachen*. The IE base is *gleg*; the IE root is *kleg*. Both are to mean "to cry out, sound."

קול / KŌL (L–K/G reversed) is a sound or call – see "CALL."

A better etymon is לעג / LÄÄG (to jest, to laugh at or "to mock"). In *Proverbs 17:5* the term is parallel to the verb "rejoice."

BRANCHES: Since L=R, it is possible that the slang RAG (to tease –"origin uncertain") is from the captioned term or לגלג / LÉGLÁG (to jeer, make fun of).

Reversing to GL renders גיל / GÉL (rejoice) – see "GALA." LA(R)K (a prank) may derive from לעג / L–U–G. LARK and (WED)LOCK, however, are officially traced to the IE root *leig* (to leap, tremble). דילוג / (DE)LOOG is to jump, while (G–L reversed) חל / KHÄL is to tremble.

LAVA/לְהָבָה
L'HAVA   [L–H–BH]

ROOTS: The given source is Latin *lavare* (to wash). להבה / LEHÄVÄ (flame) and לבה / LÄBÄ ("flame" in *Exodus 3:2*) are more satisfactory etymons.

BRANCHES: לבן / LÉBÁ[N] (to wash) is the source of Latin *lavare*. The *Alkalay Hebrew Dictionary* offers לבה / LABA for

LAVA, calling it a borrowing from the Latin.

For clean, hot and passionate LB and BR terms, see "ALBINO," "BURN," and "LOVE."

LEEC(H)/עלוקה
AH–LUKE–ÄH   [ULK]

ROOTS: This parasitic worm is attributed to various theoretical sources, including Gothic *lekeis* (healer) and the IE root *leg* (to collect). The עלוקה / ÄLOOKÄH (leech) of *Proverbs 30:15* offers a straightforward etymon.

BRANCHES: Covering the given sources, לקט / LOK[AT] is to collect and חיל / KHAYIL is vigor – see "ELECT" and "HEALTH."

LEOPARD /לְבִיא-בָּרֹד
LA(V)EE–BAROD   [LVY + BRD]

ROOTS: LEO and PARD must be dealt with separately. To understand PARD, note Old Celtic *brith* (varicolored) and Cornish *Bruit* (speckled). In *Genesis 31:10* Jacob dreams about sheep that are ברד / BÄRŌD (spotted, mottled or grizzled). It is now easier to see the spotted LEOPARD or PARD, like the BLOT (spot) or BLOTCH (skin discoloration), as a form of ברוד / BÄRŌD (spotted) rather than a meaningless animal name from the Greek *pardos* (panther). (Greek *panther*, with no IE root, may be a PARD that was nasalized and had its T and R switched.) The post-Biblical term for PANTHER, ברדלם / BARDILOS, should not be seen as a Hebrew borrowing from Greek. It is likely a combination of ברד / BRD (spotted) and ליש / LAYIS[H] (lion).

Now for LEO (Latin) the LION. LEO obviously relates to the following lion words: *leao* (Portuguese), *leu* (Rumanian), *Lowe* (German), *leeuw* (Dutch), *love* (Danish and Norwegian) and *lev, lav*, and *lyef* in Czech, Serbo-Croatian and Russian. More obviously, all these leonine words are from לביא / LÄVIE (lion – *Genesis 49:9*).

BRANCHES: Reverse the L–V/F to get *felis* (cat in Latin), the source of FELINE.

ארי / ÄRIE (lion) may also be behind LEO and ERIE (the cat term in Huron Indian which named a lake, canal and town).

LEX/הלכה
(HA)–LÄKH–(AH)   [L–KH]

ROOTS: LEX (law in Latin) is traced to IE root *leg-* (to collect). See "ELECT" if one pursues this path to LEX and LEGAL. הלכה / (HÄ)LÄKHÄ is law. Literally, it means "the way to go," as לך / LAKH is "go" in *Genesis 12:1*. "Behave" is meant by this verb in *I Kings 15:26*.

BRANCHES: DELEGATE and RELEGATE are cognates of LEX (LEGISLATE, LEGITIMATE, LOYAL and PRIVILEGE), yet Latin *legare* (to depute, commission, charge) is no "collect" word. The AHD lamely offers "? 'collection of rules.'" A deputy or agent is a

אלאך / (MÄ)LÄKH (messenger, angel – literally "one made to go").
מלך / (ME)LEKH (king – is chief LEGISLATOR, and "the one who makes others go").

The LEX/LEGAL problem is solved via Hebrew as is the REX/REGAL one. These RG terms are taken up at "DIRECTION" and "REGULAR."

LICK/לָחַךְ
LAH – UCK   [LHK]

ROOTS: LICK is said to be from Greek *leikhein* and the IE root *leigh* (to lick).

A better reason for the double guttural (C and K) might be found in לחך / LÄHÄKH or LÄKHÄKH (to lick – *Numbers 22:4*. לֵחַ / LÄÄKH means moisture and חך / HÄKH or KHÄKH means "palate."

> **BRANCHES:** לקק / LOKÄK is to lick (*I Kings 21:19*) and עלע / ÄLÄK or KHELÄK is to lap or swallow.
> Cognates of LICK include ANILINGUS, ELECTUARY, and LECHER. Although Latin *lingere* ("to lick") is mentioned here, Latin's *lingua* (tongue) words such as LANGUAGE, LINGUIST, etc. are listed instead at the tongue-twisted IE root *dnghu*.
> The IE root may link up with טעם / DT – GH – M (to taste). See "LIQUID" and "SLANG."

LID/לאט
LAH – UDT   [L – A – (D)T]

ROOTS: LID is said to be from Old English *hlid* (cover), from a Germanic root meaning "that which bends over." The IE root is somehow *klei* (to lean).

For an etymon that doesn't bend over backwards, try לאט / LÄ'ÄD(T) (to cover – *II Samuel 19:5*) or לוט / LODT (a covering).

> **BRANCHES:** בלאט / (BÄ)LÄT is secretly or, literally "under cover." Reverse LT for more "cover" terms at "TILE." The HLD and KL etymons from our dictionaries point to קלט / KOLAT or HOLADT (to retain, hold – see "CLOT").
> LID should join LATENT and LETHARGY at IE root *ladh* (to be hidden) in linking up with words like לט / LAT or LADT (covert), לוטה / LOOTA(concealed) and לוט / LOT (veil, covering – *Isaiah 25:7*). Akkadian *litu* is a curtain.

LIGHT/לַהַט
LAH – HUT   [LHT]

ROOTS: Stopping at Old English *leoht* or *liht* (light), we could easily trace the source of LIGHT to להט / LÄHÄT ("flaming," "fiery" – *Genesis 3:24*). With German *licht* (light) and the IE root *leuk* (light, brightness), an etymon with a K seems better.

> **BRANCHES:** דלק / DOLÄK (to burn), הדליק / (HÄ)DLÄK (to light, kindle) and Aramaic דליקתא / DILÄKTÄ (fire) require a #1 → #3 letter shift to match *licht*, but the LK element should light the way to LUCID and ELECTRIC. (Greek *Elektra* means shining one.)

A נ / N → L change might allow נגה / NOGÄ (to shine, be bright) to reinforce IE root *leuk*.

The listed cognates of LIGHT include ELUCIDATE, ILLUMINATE, ILLUSTRATE, LUCIFER, LUMINARY, LUMINOUS, LUNA(TIC), LUSTER, PELLUCID and TRANSLUCENT. *Ild* is fire in Danish; reverse to *tuli* for Finnish fire.
See "FIRE."

LILAC/לִילָה
LIE – LAH   [LYL]

ROOTS: LILAC is traced to Arabic *laylak* and *lilak*, but our proudly Indo-Aryan dictionaries go on to offer Sanscrit *nila* (indigo) and the IE root *nei* (to be excited, to shine). Arabic *layla* and Hebrew לילה / LILÄ mean night (and its purple or dark blue hue). "And the darkness He called *night*" – לילה – *Genesis 1:5*.

> **BRANCHES:** LILITH, the she-demon of myth, is from Assyrian-Babylonian *lilitu* (of the night). Lilith harks back to the לילית / LELET (screech owl – *Isaiah 34:14*).

LIQU(ID)/לַח
LUKH   [L – KH]

ROOTS: Latin *liquere* is "to be liquid;" the IE root is *wleik* (to flow, run). לח / LÄKH is soggy or moist; (at *Numbers 6:3* it infers the opposite of "dry"). לחלח / LEKHLÄKH is to moisten or dampen; לחך / LÄKHÄKH is to lick – see "LICK." לח / LÄKH is the term used in the phrase "liquid measure;" לג / LOG is a Biblical liquid measure. See "LEX" for LK terms of movement.

> **BRANCHES:** זלח / ZOLÄKH is to be wet.
> IRRIGATE is from IE *reg* (moist); R = L. IE root *leg* (to dribble, trickle – source of LEECH and LEAK) may link up with (a reversed) נחל / (NÄ)KHAL (stream), with ברכה / B'RÄKHÄ (pool) or with ברח / BÄRÄKH (to run, flee). The AHD lumps LIQUOR together with Latin *lixa* (lye) and Latin *prolixus* (stretched out). *Loka* is mud or dirt in Finnish; לכלוך / LEKHLOOKH is dirt. *Kale*, watery in Hawaiian, is an LK reversal.

LIV(ER)/חֶלֶב
(HAY) – LEV   [(H) – L – BH]

ROOTS: Middle English *livre* is traced to Greek *lipos* (fat) and to the IE root *leip* (to stick, adhere, fat).
חלב / HÄLEV is fat (*Leviticus 10:15*) or lard; an extension means "gum" – (see "GALBANUM"). Hebrew's LV "fat" word best remembers LIV[ER].

> **BRANCHES:** The given cognates of LIVER are ALIPHATIC, LEAVE, LIFE, LIPO-, LIVELY, and SYNALEPHA. IE root *leip* (to adhere) matches לוה / LOVA (to adhere – see "LOVE"). See "GALAXY" for חלב / KHÄLÄV (milk). Basque appears to use חלב / KH – L – BH for "liver" as well, though *gibela* demonstrates a #2-#3 root letter swap.

The ear LOBE and the LIP are collections of fat. The IE root of LIP is *leb* (lip), taking in LABIAL, LABIUM, LABELLUM, LABRET and LABRUM. LUBRICATE and LUBRICATION may get its slipperyness from חלב / (HĀ)LEBH fat or fatty oils. *Lihava* is fat and fleshy in Finnish. See "BALL" for rolly polly BL relatives of this LB root.

LOBO/כֶּלֶב
(KEH)–LEB(H)   [(K)–L–BH]

ROOTS: LOBO, from Spanish and latin *lupus* (wolf), is the timber wolf of the American West. *Webster's* maintains an IE base *wlp* or *lup* for voracious animals of prey, citing Latin *volpes* (fox).

לביא / LĀBHĒ is a lion (see "LEOPARD"); כלב / KELEBH (dog – *Exodus 11:7*) could be understood to mean כ / K' (like) + לביא / LĀVĒ (lion). The courageous, loyal and emotional dog is כל / KOL (all) + לב / LĀV (heart) or "all heart." The L-BH root points to lionheartedness.

This entry centers on the back 2/3 of (K)–L–BH, just as "CARIB" will give you the canine implications of K–L–(BH) at the head of the Hebrew etymon. For a harder B, there's Aramaic כלבא / KĀLBĀ (dog).

BRANCHES: With a #1 → #3 anagram, KLB would be LBK. This recalls the ALOPECIA, from Greek *alopex* (fox). A cognate is VULPINE at the IE root *wlp-e* (fox).

The IE root of LOBO is *wlkwo* (wolf). Replace or drop that initial W, and you are a mere metathesis away from the Aramaic *klwo* or *klbo*.

Gilbert Davidowitz, who worked to establish IE-Semitic unity at Columbia University, proposed a progression from Semitic *kalbu* to IE *kwelb* and *hwelp*, to Old Norse *huelpr* to Old High German *hwelf* and Old English *hwelp* (source of WHELP).

The cognates of LOBO and WOLF include AARDWOLF, ADOLPH, LOUP-GAROU, LOUVRE (the French museum), LUPINE, LYCANTHORPE (from *lukos*, the Greek wolf), RALPH, WOLFRAM, and WOLVERINE.

LOT(US)/לוֹט
LOTE   [LOT]

ROOTS: The Greek LOTUS was an opium-like plant. לוט / LOT or LOD is rendered LAUDANIUM in *Genesis 37:25*; it is a spice and an herbal opium preparation. Etymologist Ernest Klein links Greek *lotos* to Hebrew לוט / LOT (LADANUM).

BRANCHES: Greek *ledon* (rock-rose) and LABDANUM are related variants.

LOVE/לוה
LEAVE–(ĀH)   [LVH]

ROOTS: Old English *lufu* is love; *leuf* means "beloved." Latin *libido* is desire; the IE root of LOVE is *leubh* (to care, desire; love).

In *Genesis 29:34*, after establishing that Jacob loves

Rachel more than Leah, Scripture quotes Leah after the birth of Levi: "Now this time *will* my husband *be joined unto me*." The newer JPS Bible renders ילוה / (YĒ)LOVEH as "will become attached." Two verses earlier, after the birth of Reuben, Leah had also said "now my husband will love me" (using a different verb in Hebrew).

Another prooftext to show that לוה / LĒVĀ can mean emotional attachment (and not mere accompaniment) is in *Isaiah 56:6*. There a parallel is established between the נלוים / NĒ)LVE(M) – the aliens "that join themselves to the Lord" and to those who "love the Name of the Lord."

A second link to LOVE involves לב / LĀV and לבה / LĒBĀH (heart – *Genesis 8:21; Ezekiel 16:30*). לבב / LEBĀV is defined as a verb of encouragement and fascination. Instead of using the word "love," the translators render לבבתני / LĒBĀV(TĀNĒ) in *Songs 4:9*, "you have ravished my heart" or "captured my heart."

BRANCHES: A reversal of לב / LB (heart) is בל / BAL (heart – the Aramaic of *Daniel 6:15*). Getting warmer, לבה / LĒBĀH is to set ablaze or kindle, and להבה / LEHĀVĀ is a flame.

German *Liebe* and Russian *lyubof* sound like the Hebrew terms above, but the "love" word of Rumanian, *iub(ire)*, prefers אהב / ĀHUBH (to love) and חבה / HĒBĀH (love).

The official cognates of LOVE include BELIEF, BELIEVE (see the *Isaiah* quote above), FURLOUGH, LEAVE, LIBIDO, and LIEF. IE *bhilo* (dear, familiar) – is the reverse of our LB etymons. This root bears cognates like PAM, -PHILE, -PHILIA, PHILOSEMITE, PHILOSOPHY, -PHILOUS and PHILTER. *Pili* is to cling, join, associate or a close relationship in Hawaiian and Proto-Polynesian; reversing to *alofa* (love) bears the reconstructed ancestor of Hawaiian *aloha* (love).

(L)UTE/אוד
OODT   [O–O–(D)T]

ROOTS: Old French *leut* and Spanish *laud* are official borrowings from Arabic *al'ud* – literally "the wood." אוד / OOD is a firebrand or a piece of wood (*Isaiah 7:4*), but in Arabic it means wood more generally.

BRANCHES: The Hebrew branches of this wood word include עץ / ĀTZ (wood, tree – *Genesis 2:9*). A T or TS to D change is common; the Hebrew צב / TSĀB (lizard) is identical to the Arabic *dab*. בד / BUD or VUD is a tree limb. This source of *FIDDLE* (see "BAT") should link up with the LUTE (a form of guitar).

The *outh* (wood) of VERMOUTH is from German *wermut* (worm*wood*). The *ut* in ORANG*UTAN* might also be cut from the Hebrew tree (עץ / ĀTS), as *utan* is a forest in Malay. A stick in Arabic is *asa*, while in Japanese it is *tsue*. Also reversing עץ /ETS or ETZ is *zhu* – the Chinese tree trunk.

CAUDEX is Latin for the trunk of a tree. CODE might be a typically gutturalized עץ or KĀT(S). GUIT[AR] might fit here too, if the GT root refers to wood rather than to its gut-made strings – see "GUITAR." Reversing to TK yields tree words in Japanese (where *take* is bamboo) and Malayalan (where *tekka* is the source of TEAK wood).

The IE root of WOOD is either *widhu* (AHD) or *vidhu* (Shipley); Norwegian wood is *ved*, while *fid* is an Old Irish tree. To derive WOOD from אוד / A-V/W–D, simply drop the initial A and treat the ו as a consonant V or W (rather than as the vowel OO). Also see בד / VUD above.

MACABRE/מַקְבִּי
MUCK–AH–BEE   [MKBY]

ROOTS: Dictionaries trace this term for "gruesome" to the historical Maccabees of Judea. They cite Aramaic *maqqaba* (hammer) as the source of Judas Machabaeus' surname, although the Hebrew appears in *Isaiah 44:12*. מקבת / MAKEBHET is a hammer or mallet; the word is likely an extension of מכה / MÄKÄH (blow, strike – *Judges 15:8*) or of נקב / NKB (to pierce, bore).

    BRANCHES: A MACE is a club with a metal head. It strikes of the MK Hebrew terms, though it is somehow traced to Late Latin *mattea* (a club). In any case, מטה / MÄTEH is a rod.
    The MACHETE (heavy knife) is from Spanish *macho* (an ax or hammer). The older term is said to be Latin *marcus* (hammer) – but moving or striking off the R better links *marcus* to מכה / MÄKEH (to beat) and to Provençal *macar* (to beat), source of MACHICOLATE.

MACHINE/מְכוֹנָה
MIKH–OWN–AH   [M–KH–N]

ROOTS: Greek *makhana* is a device; earlier, the term meant "that which enables." The theoretical IE root is *magh-* (to be able, have power). מכונה / MIKHŌNÄ is a machine in Modern Hebrew. The Biblical word, identical in spelling, is a "base" with an elaborate structure that included wheels – see *I Kings 7:27-35*. In Mishnaic Hebrew מוכני / MOOKHNĒ is a wheel-work or derrick. These early machines were MECHANICAL preparations. מוכן / MOOKHÄN and נכון / NAKHON mean ready, prepared, fixed. כן / KÄN is a base.

    BRANCHES: GAINLY is from Middle English *gein* (convenient, ready). Other words from the MACHINE shop include MECHANIC, MECHANISM and MECHANO-. Other cognates include MAIN, MIGHT, DISMAY and MAY. The contingency use of MAY, seen in MAYBE and MAYST, could link up with אם / ÉM (if, whether, or), *ama* ("maybe" in Korean), and *'ina* ("if" in Hawaiian).

(M)ADONNA/אֲדוֹן
AH–DOAN   [ADON]

ROOTS: MADONNA means "my lady" in Italian; *ma* (my – from Latin *mea*) + *donna* (lady). The title "lady" is the feminine of "lord." The title DAN is from Old French *dan* (master, sir); thought to have originated with Latin *dominus* (master, lord). Instead of a DN root of mastery, the Latin-DOMINATED reference books trace MADONNA and DAN to the IE root *deme-* (house, household).
    As usual, Hebrew has a clear etymon that requires no manipulation of sense. אדון / ÄDON means sir, mister (i.e. master), or lord in *Genesis 24:18*, while in *Genesis 45:9* the same term means Lord (i.e. God). אדון / ÄDON plus י / AI (my – adding up to "my Lord") is the most common name of God.

BRANCHES: דן / DÄN means judge (noun and verb), and law is the DOMINANT principle in the Hebrew Bible's DOMINION. Greek *daimon* means deity, not "household." The word DEMON, therefore, is probably a DM or DN word of lordship and mastery. DON JUAN is just a variation of אדון יוחנן / ÄDON YOHÄNÄN (Mister YOHANON).
    IE *deme-* (to constrain, force) infers the INDOMITABLE PREDOMINANCE of the דין / DEEN (law) which the אדון / ADŌN (lord or Lord) gave us to TAME or DOMESTICATE us. ADAMANT and DIAMOND are also cognates of DAUNT at IE *deme-* (to force). מדינה / (MI)DĒNÄ is a state. A successful political DOMAIN or KINGDOM should display a CONDOMINIUM of power, where no single DON, DEAN, DAM, DAME or MADAME DOMINEERS. DYNASTY belongs with the DN words here, too. See "ADONIS" and "DAMN."

MAGAZINE/מַחְסָן
MAKH–SON   [M + KH–S + N]

ROOTS: MAGAZINE (a store or a storage area for bullets or essays) is an official borrowing from Arabic *makhzan* (storehouse). מחסן / MÄKHSÄN (storage area) is an extension of words like מחסה / MÄKHÄSEH ("pavilion" in *Isaiah 4:6*) and חסה / KHÄSÄ ("to take shelter" in *Judges 9:15*).

    BRANCHES: A long lost relative might be the MOCCASIN (shoe or foot covering) of the American Indians (Massachusett and Narragansett). More on the KH–S root at "ENCASE" and "HOUSE."

MAG(IC)/מַג
MUG   [MG]

ROOTS: Greek *magos* is traced to Old Persian *magu* (member of priestly caste, magician).
    The מג / MAG of *Jeremiah 39:3* means magician according to most translators and lexicographers.

    BRANCHES: The MAGI, wise men of the East, derive from the Latin *magus* (sorcerer).

MAIM/מום
MOOM   [MIM]

ROOTS: MAIM is said to derive from Old French *mahaigner* (to maim); cognates are MANGLE and MAYHEM.
    Middle English *maime* echoes מום / MOOM (a "defect" in *Leviticus 21:17* – such as being lame or hunchbacked). The noun MAIM means a crippling or a mutation. הומם / (HOO)MÄM is to become deformed or crippled.

    BRANCHES: The given IE root for MAIM is *mai-* (to cut). A more defined etymon would be the IE *mend* (physical defect), source of (A)MEND.

MAL(IGN)/מָעַל
MAH – ULL   [MAL]

ROOTS: Both Latin *malus* (bad) and *male* (ill) are traced to the root *mel* (bad).

The "ill" meaning of MAL- words like MALADY should link up to אמלה / AMOOLA (sick – *Ezekiel 16:30*), while the MALICIOUS and MALEVOLENT MAL- terms belong with מעל / MÄ'ÄL (wrongdoing – a verb and noun in *Leviticus 5:15*).

> **BRANCHES:** Other MAL- terms like MALIGN and MALEDICTION seem to favor another meaning of מעל / MÄ'ÄL (fraud, treachery).
>
> Other cognates include DISMAL, MALICE, MALEFACTOR, and MANILLA. IE root *mel-* (to miss, deceive) fits here, but it only adds MALLEMUCK to English.

MAMA/אִמָּא
EEM – MAH   [AM → MA]

ROOTS: Whether or not she raised Cain, Eve was the *mother* of all – אם / EM (*Genesis 3:20*). אמה / EMA means MOM or MOMMA.

The IE root for MA, MAMA, MAMMAL(IA), and MOM(MY) is *ma-* (mother). MA reverses אם / EM (mother) just as PA reverses אב / ÄBH (father).

The *American Heritage Dictionary* declares, when presenting the Indo-European root, that MA is "an imitative root derived from the child's cry for the breast (a linguistic near-universal...)."

> **BRANCHES:** Pre-verbal children do not cry "ma" any more than they cry "wa," yet there are no "mother" terms named for the "wa" or "ba" of a baby crying to press lips (with a B or W pout) to a breast. More importantly, all the usual non-"imitative" changes occur to the "ma" root, becoming "am," "an" and "na."
>
> There is nothing wrong with Hebrew, Arabic, Korean or Basque infants who call out for their *ēma, oum, oma* or *ama*. A cry should end in a vowel, not begin with one. No one cries with an N sound, but vowel-N or N-vowel "mother" terms constitute about 40% of the total. A scientific linguist should conclude that Eskimo (*ananak*), Hungarian (*anya*) and Turkish (*ana*) are "mama" terms reflecting a non-echoic or non-imitative original "mother" word (in this case אם / EM) which underwent as many permutations as possible.
>
> IE root *nana* is similarly dismissed as a "child's word for a nurse or female adult other than its mother." Don't tell an Aztec child that his dear *nan* (mom) is other than his mother. NANNA, NANNY and NUN are listed at IE *nana*. AUNT is listed at IE *amma*, along with AMAH (*amma* meant mother in Medieval Latin) and AMOUR. See "AMAH" and "AMITY."
>
> MAY, MATER(IAL), METRO-, MOTHER, MATERNAL, MATRIX, MATTER, etc. are "based ultimately on ...*ma-*אם / ÄM also means womb or origin. אמה / OOMA is a nation or "mother country." אמנה / AMNA means education or nursing; אמץ / EMÄTS is to adopt. -מ / MĒ or MÄ means "from" or "of;" a more biological M word of origins is מיא / MAYA (water – Aramaic). In Sumerian, *ma* means both water and origin.

MAN/מאן
MÄ – UN   [MAN]

ROOTS: Old English *man(n)* is traced to an IE root spelled *man-* or *mon* (man).

In Aramaic מאן / MÄ'ÄN means someone or anyone. MANKIND might also be named for "kind" or specie מין / MĒN – *Genesis 1:21*) as though to say "our own kind."

> **BRANCHES:** Cognates include LANDSMAN, MANIKIN, MANNEQUIN and MEN.
>
> אנוש / ENNŌSH (man, human) recalls MAN in Turkish, *insan*; in Malay it's *manesh, mon,* or *omani*. This last term echoes a fine alternative etymon for MAN – אמן / ÄMÄN (craftsman, artisan – *Songs 7:2*). אמון / ÄMŌN is an artificer or builder. Sounding even more like HUMAN is Assyro-Babylonian *ummanu* (artist). See "MOON" for Man the thinker. *Nan* is man in Chinese; *namja* is the Korean.
>
> HUMAN and MONKEY are primates who share the use of a hand. Not only does אמנות / ŌMÄN(OOT) mean the characteristic *handi*craft or *handi*work of MAN, but ימין / (YA)MEEN is the right hand and the right hand side. Latin *manus* (hand) links up COMMAND, COMMEND, COUNTERMAND, DEMAND, EMANCIPATE, MAINTAIN, MANACLE, MANAGE, MANDATE, MANEUVER, MANICURE, MANIFEST, MANIPULATE, MANNER, MANUAL, MANUFACTURE, MANUSCRIPT, MANURE, REMAND and RECOMMEND, with words like מנה / MÄNÄ)to appoint, mandate, assign, count and hand out).

MANN(ER)/מין
MEAN   [MYN]

ROOTS: Latin *manuarius* (of the hand) and IE root *man* (hand) do not clearly address the archaic usage of MANNER (kind or sort).

מין / MĒN is a kind, variety or specie.

> **BRANCHES:** The Hebrew etymon first appears in *Genesis 1:12* referring to the many "kinds" of birds. The variety of birds in the South Pacific is so remarkable, that מין / MĒN might well be the source of the bird term (*manu*) in Hawaiian, Malay and Tahitian. *Manumanu* means animal or bird in Fijian. NAME (MN → NM) is related to specie classification.
>
> See "MAN."

MANY/הָמוֹן
(HA) – MOAN   [(H)MON]

ROOTS: Old English *manig* (many) is traced to the IE root *menegh* (copious).

המון / (HÄ)MON means abundance or multitude. Abraham is promised to be "the father of a *multitude* of nations" in *Genesis 17:4*. A variation is אמון / AMŌN (*Jeremiah 52:15*).

> **BRANCHES:** מנה / MÄNÄ is to count or number. Much (many) is *megen* (Dutch and Norwegian), *mnoho* in Czech, and *mnogo* in Russian and Serbo-Croatian. *Mone* is many in Finnish. MEAN (low in amount) is an antonym from מן / MEEN (out of) – see "MINUS." For synonyms see "MONEY" and "NUMBER." *Mani* is plenty in Korean; *mano* and *manoa* mean "numerous" in Hawaiian.
>
> MILLION ought to have and MULTITUDE has an ML root; נ (N) to L changes may have occcured here. Otherwise, מלא / MÄLÄ means full. The Fijians live fully without MILLIMETERS, MILLENNIUM or MULTIPLICATION tables. "Full" in Fijian settles for the number five. *Lima* (5) is the reverse of מלא / MÄLÄ (full), as five is a full hand's worth of fingers.

MAP/מַפָּה
MUP–AH   [MPH]

ROOTS: MAP is from *mappa* (napkin, towel, cloth). This Latin noun is said by Quintilian to be of Carthaginian origin. Since Carthage was founded by Phoenicians, the Semitic origin of the talmudic word מפה / MÄPÄ (tablecloth, map, flag) needn't be suspect. Etymologist Ernest Klein cites מנפה / MINAPHA (streaming cloth, banner) and נוף / NOPH (to swing) as the Hebrew-Punic source of MAP.

> **BRANCHES:** Cognates are APRON, MOP, NAPERY, NAPKIN and NAPPE.

MAR(INE)/מר
MAR   [MR]

ROOTS: The English derivatives of מר / MÄR (bitter) are revealed when noting that MARASCHINO cherry comes from Latin *amarus* (bitter tasting). מריר / MIRÉRE ("bitter" in *Deuteronomy 32:24*) is rendered *amarus* by the Latin concordance. MARINADE and MARINATE leads one to MARINE words of the briny sea, as these food-soaking terms are from Spanish *marino* (briny and marine).

The "bitter" water of the Bible can now be understood to mean unsweet, undrinkable, saline or sea water.

> **BRANCHES:** MR salt water brings us to the first desalinization plant in recorded history—the tree cast into the "bitter" (מרים / MÄRÉM) waters of Marah to make them "sweet"–*Exodus 15:23-25*.
> מרים / MIRIAM is Moses' sister. Her name, which gave us names like MARY and nouns like MARIONETTE and MARIGOLD, translates as "briny sea."
> The IE root *mori* (body of water...sea) takes in MARE, MARINARA, MARINA, MARINE, MARITIME, MARSH, MEERSCHAUM, MERE, MERMAID, ORMER and SUBMARINE. MORELLO is another "bitter" term from Latin *amarus* (bitter). MORULA, MURREY and MULBERRY are cognates at IE root *moro* (blackberry). מר / MAR (bitter) should be the ultimate etymon.
> *Hamar* is poured water in Arabic; related to an MR term rendered "torrents" or "floods" or "watery pit" in *Psalms 140:11*.
> MOOR (marsh) is not traced to IE *mori*. It is linked instead to the IE root *ma* (damp). This and another IE root, *meu* (damp–given source of LITMUS, MIRE, MOSS, MUST and MUSTARD), are related to מיא / MÄYÄ (water–Aramaic), מים / MÄY(IM) (waters–*Genesis 1:2*) and מי / MÄ (the waters of). Reverse to ים / YÄM (ocean), while מר / MÄR means "drop" in *Isaiah 40:15*. *Umi* is sea in Japanese; *mu yu* is bath in Chinese; *yam* is a drink in Cantonese.
> MARGARET and MARGUERITE ("pearl" words of uncertain origin) can now be understood to mean a גרגיר / GARGÉR (berry, pill) from the MR (sea). See "GRAIN" for a breakdown of MARGARINE.
> See "MYRRH."

MARK/מְכָּר
MOO–KAR   [MKR → MRK]

ROOTS: Old English *mearc* is a boundary, landmark, sign or trace. A MARK is a visible identification; to MARK is to pay attention to. The IE root is *merg* (boundary, border). מכר / MOOKÄR is recognized or known; מכר / MÄKÄR is an acquaintance (*II Kings 12:6*). The three-letter root is נכר / NKR (to recognize); the two-letter root is KR. הכיר / [HÉ]KÉR is to acknowledge, distinguish or be acquainted with.

> **BRANCHES:** Even the antonyms נכר / NÄKHÄR (strangeness), נכר / NÉKÄR (to ignore) and נכרי / NOKHRÉ (foreign) address the concepts of recognition, paying attention, and the border marking foreign territory.
> Cognates worth MARKING include DEMARCATION, MARCH, MARCHIONESS, MARK (German money), MARKKA (Swedish money), MARQUEE, MARQUIS, MARGIN and REMARK.

MARK(ET)/מְכַּר
MAH–KHAR   [M–KH–R → M–R–KH]

ROOTS: Latin *merx* (merchandise) and *mercari* (to trade) are traced to the "Italic root" *merk* (aspects of commerce).
Latin *merces* (pay, reward, price) matches up with מחיר / MIKHÉR (pay, "price" in *II Samuel 24:24*). מכר /MEKHER is a price or sale; מכר / MOCHÄR is to sell (*Genesis 37:36*) and מוכר / MOKHÄR is a merchant.

> **BRANCHES:** The *merk* root gives us COMMERCE, MARKET, MART, MERCANTILE, MERCENARY, MERCER, MERCHANT, MERCURY and MERCY.
> It is all the better that a #2-#3 root letter exchange is required; this way the very mercantile terms most expected to be borrowed from Hebrew, Phoenician or Arabic are harder to dismiss as mere borrowings.

MAR(OON)/חֲמָר
(HEH)–MERR   [HMR]

ROOTS: MAROON (dark, brownish red) is from French *marron* (chestnut) and Italian *marrone* (dark brownish red). Arabic *ahmar* is red. חמר / HEMER is wine or clay, a good term to infer a wine color. חמרמר / HOMÄRMÄR is "red" in *Job 16:16*. חמר / HÄMÄR is also to burn.

> **BRANCHES:** The יחמור / [YAH]MOOR is a brown goat or gazelle.
> ALHAMBRA, from Arabic *al hamra*, means the red (house). *Merah* is red in Malay.
> The red planet, MARS, is also an MR term; MARCH, MARITAL and MARTIAN are related. See "CRIMSON."

MAS(CULINE)/מת
MUS   [MS]

ROOTS: The IE root and Latin *mas* (male) is "of unknown origin." מת / MÄS is defined as a man or a person; in *Deuteronomy 3:6* the phrase "men (מת / MÄS), women and children" would encourage a connotation of adult males.

BRANCHES: Cognates of MASCULINE include EMASCULATE, MACHO and MALE. Russian *muzh* (man) gives us MUZHIK (peasant); Polish *mezczyzna* means "man." Aramaic מר / MAR (master, sir) and Arabic *imru* (man) may have given us MALE (MR→ML).

מות / MŌS or MŌT (death) is to מתי / MISĀ or MITĀ (men) as אנש / ONASH (mortal) is to אנוש / ENŌSH (man).

Given the Greek propensity to render the ת / T or ש / S as a TH, some 40 ANTH[ROPO]- words from *anthropos* (man, human) must be related to the Hebrew MS ro NS words above. Moving from ANTHROPOLOGY to Adam (man or "earthling" in Hebrew), Greek *andros* (man, male) — as in ANDROID — is either a harder version of ANTHRO-, or a #2-#3 letter flip of ארם / ĀDĀM (Adam, man).

The M and N are interchangeable. Swahili "man" is *mtu*, while *ntu* means "man" in "Bantu."

See "MAN" for other MS (German *Mensch*, Indonesian *manusi*) or NS (Turkish *insan*) terms that could be nasalized forms of מת / MĀS.

The shortest "man" terms around (Rumanian *om* or Ainu *ainu*) all seem to have the M or N element of ארם / ĀDĀM (man), אנוש / ENŌSH (mankind) and מת / MĀS or MĀT (man, person). Gaelic *duine* or Fijian *tamata* (person) makes a fine Adam. Also consider *tahambis* ("man" – Uto-Aztecan Indian), *otona* ("adult" – Japanese), *nan tzu* and *nan hsing* ("male" – Chinese), *namja* ("man" – Korean), and *anishinabe* ("man, human" – Chippewa Indian's אנש / ENŌSH).

The IE root for HUMAN, *dhghem* (earth), does have a DM. It therefore might ultimately link up with ארם / ADAM (human) and ארמה / ADAMA (earth).

MASK/מַסֵכָה
MAS – AYKH – (AH)   [M – S – KH]

ROOTS: French *masque* is from Italian *mascara* (a mask), which is an acknowledged borrowing from Arabic *maskharah* (bufoon).

The bufoonery is expendable since מסכה / MĀSĀKHĀ is a mask or covering and מסך / MĀSĀKH is a curtain, screen or diaphragm (*Exodus 26:36*). מסכת / MĀSEKHES is a woven web (*Judges 16:13*).

BRANCHES: To separate the elements in the molecule MSKH, there is the MS of מסוה / MĀSVEH (veil, mask – *Exodus 34:33*) and S – KH terms like סכך / SĀKHUKH (to screen, cover) and סך / SĀKH (visor).

MASCARA, MASCOT, MASQUE and MASQUERADE are all linked to MASK. One of the distant cousins of M – S – KH is (T)S – N – KH (#1-#2 letter switch). הצניע / (HĒ)TZNĒĀKH is to be modest or to hide – see "SNEAK."

MASS/מַצָּה
MA(T)S – (AH)   [M – (T)S]

ROOTS: Old French *masse* is from Latin *massa* (a lump or mass). The earliest term is Greek *maza* (barley cake).

A barley cake is poor man's bread, and "poor man's bread" is another name for מצה / MĀ(T)ZĀ (MATZOH) – the unleavened bread eaten by the Hebrew slaves in Egypt.

The AHD calls Greek *maza* a kneaded lump. Just as MASSAGE is from Portuguese *amassar* (to knead) and

Greek *massein* (to knead), so מצה / MEE(T)SĀ is to wring and squeeze out. מץ / MĀ(T)S is to churn or beat.

BRANCHES: MASS generally means "a large quantity." The Mass. of Boston, Mass. has a similar meaning, as *massa* means "big" in the Algonquin language of the *MASSA*CHUSETT Indians.

Official cognates of MASS include AMASS and *MAZA*EDIUM. MASSIVE is the adjective form. MASSIF is the central MASS of a mountain ridge. Reversing to צם / TS – M, צמצם / TSIMTSĀM is to confine and צמק / TSAM[AK] is to shrink. Other Hebrew MS terms of mass or bulk include משא / MĀSĀ (burden) and עמם / ŌMES (load, burden). IE root *en-es* (burden) carries ONUS, ONEROUS and EXONERATE.

The Greek *massein* (to knead), and thus the Hebrew terms above, link up with MACERATION. An alternative etymon for MACERATE (to soften by soaking in liquid) would be משרה / MĒSRĀ (a liquid term in *Numbers 6:3*). The word is translated "maceratio" in the Latin concordance. Given מצוי / MĒTSOOY (squeezing, wringing out) in a food context, consider connections to MASSETER, MASTIC, MASTICATE, MOUTH and MOUSTACHE as well as MASTERBATE, MASTODON and MASTOIDECTOMY.

The above Hebrew "squeeze" term may realte to NASTIC – from Greek *nastos* (pressed close). The opposite of מץ / MĒTS (juice extract – source of MOIST) is צמא / TSĀMĀ (thirsty, dry). The reverse of מצה / MĀTZĀ (unleavened bread which must not get wet) is חמץ / HĀMĀTS (leavened grain) – see "ZYME."

MAT/מִטָּה
MEAT – (AH)   [MTH]

ROOTS: Late Latin *matta* is a MAT. A MAT is "a flat, coarse fabric of woven hemp... as a floor covering... doormat." מטוה / MĀT(VEH) (yarn, web – *Exodus 35:25*), מטה / MĒTĀ (couch, "bed" – *Genesis 48:2*) and מטה / MĀTĀH (down, below, under – *Deuteronomy 28:43*) are offered from Hebrew.

Old French *meteres* and English MATTRESS are already attributed to Arabic *matrah* (throw cushion).

BRANCHES: A second MAT is from Arabic *mat*, exhausted – see "CHECKMATE." Throughout human history the "bed" was more often a MATTED MATTE (mat of rushes). The מט / M-DT words above are officially linked to נטה / NADTA (to stretch, incline, lower). Many words for down, under and beneath have an N-DT root to match the M-DT of מטה / MĀTĀH (down, below, under). IE root *ndher* (under) includes INFERIOR, INFERNAL, INFERNO, INFRA- and U*NDER*. IE root *ni* (down) takes in BENEATH, NEST, NETHER, and U*NDER*NEATH. *NADIR* (now linked to Arabic) and *NOTORNIS* (Greek *notos* is south) are also related. For "down" see "UNDULATE."

ME/אֲנִי
(AH) – NEE   [ANY→MY]

ROOTS: ME, the objective case of the first person pronoun, is also *me* in Latin. The IE root *me* includes MINE, MY and MYSELF.

אני / ĀNĒ is the first person pronoun in Hebrew; the only difference is that אני / ĀNĒ is the "I" or subjective case.*

BRANCHES: AM and AINT contain the element *mi* (Anglo-Saxon) which is a first-person pronoun. *Nous*, the French first person plural pronoun ("we") sounds like אנו / ÄNOO (we). *Im* is a first person suffix in Irish; *n* is the "my" prefix in Piro (an Arawakan language of Peru).

Seven more versions of "I" around the world that echo the Hebrew first person are: *emi* (Yoruba), *mi* (Gaelic), *na* (Korean), *ngo* (Cantonese), *ngi* (Australian Aborigine), *ni* (Basque), *ni* (Uto-Aztecan languages), *nin* (Chippewa Indian), and *noo* (Luiseno Indian).

See "I."

*In the famous words of King David, "My God, my God, why hast Thou forsaken *me*" (*Psalms 22:2*), the "me" (the usual first-person objective pronoun suffix) is ני / -NĒ.

MEAN(ING)/מַעַן
MA'AN   [MUN]

ROOTS: To MEAN is to intend, purpose or indicate an intended meaning. The IE root is *mei-no* (opinion, intention).

מען / MÄ'ÄN is a purpose, address or answer. The common term למען / (LI)MÄ;ÄN (*Exodus 1:11*) means "for the sake of" or "with the purpose of."

> **BRANCHES:** Cognates of MEANING include BEMOAN and MOAN. Given the activity of all this "intending," perhaps IE root *men* (to think) is related. If so, scores of words like ADMINISTER, MEMENTO, MIND and MONEY would be relevant here. While NAME is MN reversed, the "address" definition of מען / MÄ'ÄN is synonymous with NAME. מנה / MĒNÄ (to appoint) is seen at "MINISTER."

MEASURE/מְשׁוּרָה
MIH–SOOR–AH   [MSURH]

ROOTS: Latin *mitiri* (to measure) and IE root *mē* (to measure) are the given sources of MEASURE.

משורה / MISOORÄ ("measure"– *Leviticus 19:35*) offers a superior etymon.

> **BRANCHES:** See "METER" and "MOON" for better etymons for these alleged cognates of MEASURE.

MEEK/מַךְ
MUCKH   [M–KH]

ROOTS: Old Norse *mjukr* (soft) and IE root *meug* (slimy, slippery) are the given etymons for MEEK (humble, submissive).

מך / MÄKH is lowly or depressed; מכך / MOKHÄKH is to sink, fall or be humiliated; מג / MÄG is to melt; מוגג / MOGÄG is to soften and התמונג / (HIT)MOGÄG is to become soft, to melt away or to flow. MUCILAGE, MUCO-, and MUCUS are cognates of MEEK. The best picture of MEEKNESS using the MG of מוג לב / MOOG LÄV (of a *cowardly* heart) is in *Exodus 15:5* where the Canaanite enemy are so submissive that they are "melted away."

> **BRANCHES:** MEECH, an archaic verb, is to cringe or be falsely humble. Cognates of MEEK not mentioned above include

EMUNCTORY, MATCH, MOIST, MUGGY, MUSTY, -MYCETE, MYCO-, SCHMUCK, SMOCK, SMUG, SMUGGLE and STREPTOMYCIN.

See "MUCK."

Just as the MG Hebrew etymons fit MEEK (an MK term from an MG root), MEAGER goes better with מך / MÄKH (poor – *Leviticus 27:8*). KM synonyms include קמט / KOM[UT] (to bow down, to compress, to contract); KM antonyms include קם / KAM (to rise).

MEET/מוֹעֵד
MO–AI(D)T   [MOED → MOET]

ROOTS: Old English *metan* (to meet) is from the IE root *mod* (to meet, assemble).

מועדה / MOÄ(D)TÄ is a meeting place. The tent of מועד / MOÄ(D)T ("meeting"– *Exodus 30:26*) and a מועד / MOÄ(D)T (fixed time, holiday or festival) are points in space and time to MEET the Lord. מצא / MÄT(S)Ä is to meet, come upon or discover.

> **BRANCHES:** The official cognates of MEET include FOLKMOTE, GEMOT, MOOT and WITENAGEMOT. MAIL is also listed here, but see "MELODRAMA."

MELO(DRAMA)/מִלָּה
MEEL–AH   [MLH]

ROOTS: The AHD's IE root for MELODRAMA, MELODY and MELISMA is *mel* (a limb). Greek *melos* is a limb, "hence a musical member or phrase, hence music, song, melody." A better etymon would be Old High German *meldon* (to proclaim, reveal – source of MELD). Its IE root is *meldh* (to pray, speak words to a deity). MELODY and MELODRAMA resulted from human exercises in prayer or religious proclamations.

מלה / MELÄH is a speech or word, a rhetorical "byword" in *Job 30:9*. מלל / MELAL is to utter or proclaim, reinforcing the ML root of heightened, MELODRAMATIC speech. Echoed by MELIS(MA), a מליץ / MÄLETS is a rhetorician or advocate. The term is also used to mean someone who prays to God on one's behalf.

מליצה / MILETSÄ is flowery speech or a metaphor; poetry is wedded to song (*melos* in Greek). MELIC (of poetry; lyric) is also from Greek *melos* (song).

> **BRANCHES:** *Mele* is a poem, hymn or song in Hawaiian. *Melissa* is a bee in Greek; *meli* is a bee and honey in Hawaiian. *MELLIFLUOUS* (sweetly flowing) speech might be better traced to the ML of מליצה / MILETSÄ (flowery speech) than to the *mellis* (honey in Greek) made by the chanting, buzzing bees.
>
> ML is a root of talking in Slavic too, as *zamolchite* in Russian means not saying anything.

METER/מִדָּה
MEEDT–AH   [MD → MT]

ROOTS: Old English *metan* (to measure out), Lajtin *metiri* (to measure) and Greek *metron* (measure, rule, length, proportion) are the topsoil roots of words like METE,

METER, MEDIATE, and MODE.

The given IE roots are *me* (to measure) and *med* (to take appropriate measures). The deeper M-DT Hebrew roots include מד / MUDT (measure – *Job 11:9*) and מדה / MĒDTÄ (measure, size, characteristic – *Exodus 26:2*).

> **BRANCHES:** מדד / MODTÄDT is to measure; מדד / MĒDTÄDT is to survey; and מדד / MEDTEDT is a measurement. Cognates of METER at IE root *me* include COMMENSURATE, DIAMETER, DIMENSION, GEOMETRY, IMMENSE, ISOMETRIC, MAHOUT (from Sanscrit), MEAL, MENOPAUSE, METER, -METER, -METRY, METRONOME, MONTH, MOON, PIECEMEAL, SEMESTER, and TRIMESTER. (See "MOON" and "MONEY" for Hebrew MN words of counting and measuring.)
>
> The following words are attributed to IE root *med:* ACCOMODATE, COMMODE, EMPTY, IMMODERATE, IMMODEST, MEDIAL, MEDICATE, MEDICINE, MEDICO, MEDITATE, METHEGLIN, MODAL, MODE, MODEL, MODERN, MODEST, MODICUM, MODIFY, MODULATE, MODULE, MOLD-, MOOD-, MOTE-, MODIOLUS, MUST, MUTCHKIN, and REMEDY.
> See "MODE."

(METRO)POL(IS)/עֹפֶל
O – P(H)EL [O – P(H) – l]

ROOTS: Greek *polis* is a city; the IE root is *pel* (citadel, fortified high place).

עפל / ŌP(H)EL is defined as a "fortified mound, hill;" it is translated "citadel" in *Isaiah 32:14*.

> **BRANCHES:** The cognates of POLIS are ACROPOLIS, COSMOPOLITAN, MEGALOPOLIS, METROPOLIS, NECROPOLIS, POLICLINIC, POLICY, POLITICS, POLITY and SINGAPORE (Sanskrit *pur* is a city). בירה / BĒRÄ is a city, see "BARRIO."
>
> Latin *villa* (country house – source of VILLA, VILLAGE and VILLAIN) is currently linked to IE root *weik* (clan). עפל / OPHEL or KHOPHEL and its cousin כפר / KŌFER or K'FÄR (village – *I Samuel 6:18*) offer better etymons.
>
> כפרי / K'FORĒ is a farmer; so is a CROFT(ER) – switch the positions of the R and F.

MIGHT /מאֹד
MIH – O(D)TE [MOD→MOT]

ROOTS: Anglo-Saxon *miht* (power) may or may not derive from IE root *magh* (to be able, to have power).

If it doesn't, one possibility is מאֹד / MIŌ(D)T (force, strength or "might" in *Deuteronomy 6:5*).

> **BRANCHES:** MIGHT is allegedly a cognate of MAY and MAIN. See alternative Hebrew etymons at "MACHINE" and "MAGIC"– two other terms listed as cognates at IE root *magh*.

MILK/מָלַק
MA – LUCK [MLK]

ROOTS: Old English *meolc* or *melk* is traced to IE root *melg* (to press out, to milk).

מלק / MÄLÄK is defined as "to wring off" and is translated in *Leviticus 1:15* as "to pinch off." Both the progressive pressing of the sacrificial bird's neck and the MILKING of a cow's udders require similar action.

> **BRANCHES:** MILCH and MILCHIG (Germanic) are cognates as surely as Russian *malako* is . LACTATE, LACTO- and LETTUCE are listed too, coming to English from Latin *lac* (milk). Reversing *lac*, one can hear Greek *gala* (milk) – which is also listed at IE root *melg* as a cognate. Both the LACTIC and GALACTIC words may be better linked to חלב / KHÄLÄBH (milk – see "GALAXY").
>
> EMULSION is another cognate of MILK that prefers the ML of MLK, not the LK. Another ML term relevant to the action of milking is מלל / MÄLÄL (to rub, squeeze).
>
> BONNY CLABBER (thickly curdled milk) begins with Irish *bainne* (milk). This BN milk term should come from לבן / LÄBHÄN (white – see "ALBINO"), which also contains the L – BH heart of חלב / HÄLÄBH (milk). *Laban* in Arabic means milk, and Finnish *luu* (milk) might also be an L – BH milk-white word.
>
> Irish *bainne*, as a "white" word, recalls the other BONNY (Scottish for pretty) and the blond=fair=beautiful=good equation. BONNY has no known origin, but Europeans associate "white" with "good" and "dark" or "black" with "evil." Perhaps a BONUS, BONANZA or BON BON are "good" words (Latin *bonus* is good) for the same reason that BONE (only in Germanic) is a BN word – they come from לבן / (L)BN (white).
> See "BONNY."

MILL/מָלַל
MA – LULL [MLL]

ROOTS: Latin *molere* is to grind. The IE root is *mela* or *mel* (to crush, grind) and one of its derivatives is MOLDER (crumble, rot). מלל / MÄLÄL also means the breaking down of a substance by either an abrasive rubbing and scraping or by a melting (*Job 18:6*) and withering (*Psalms 37:2*).

> **BRANCHES:** קמל / (KO)*MAL* is withered. The cognates of MILL include BLINI, BLINTZ, BLITE, IMMOLATE, MALLET, MALLEABLE, MALLEUS, MALM (crumble), MAUL, MEALIE, MEAL, MILIUM, MILLET, MOLAR, MOLD, MOLE-, MOULIN, MULL, MULLER, MYLONITE and PALL-MALL.
>
> Another cognate, MAELSRROM, recalls the other MILL of MILLING around. מלל / MÄLÄL is "shuffles (with his feet)" in the University of Chicago translation of *Proverbs 6:13*.
>
> Cognates MEALIES (maize) and MILLET (grass with edible seeds) fit closer to מלילה / MILELÄ (ripe corn or "ears" in *Deuteronomy 23:26*). IE root *mel-* is soft and *mel-* is a soft material – wool. מולת / MÄLÄS is a mishnaic word for wool; there is no indicaiton that the word was borrowed from Greek *mallos* (wool). Reverse ML to LM, and shift to LN, to get LANOLIN (from Latin *lana*, wool).
>
> At IE root *mel-* (soft) are several terms that warrant inclusion here. מלל / MÄLÄL means to melt, and MELT, SMELT and MULCH are logical derivatives. MALT, MILT, MOIL, MOLLIFY, MOLLUSK, EMOLLIENT, ENAMEL, MILD and MALTHA are *mel-* derivatives that are also relevant to the Hebrew words here.
>
> Alternate etymons for cognates SCHMALTZ and MUTTON are in order, as Old High German *smalz* (animal fat) is not made soft or broken down in the characteristic way for these ML words. Fat is soft, of course, but it is also greasy. שמן / SHEMEN means fat, oil and grease – the N →L change is taken up in an appendix. As for Old French *moton* , source of MUTTON, it may

be a reversal of the TS-N or TM in צאן / TSŌN (sheep; other small cattle).

Perhaps the closest IE root to מלל / MÄLÄL (rub, wither) is *mer-* (to rub away, harm). The sense connection is so good, we can forgive the minor L→R change. Listed cognates of MORTAR and MARASMUS (from a Greek word meaning "to wither or waste away") include AMARANTH, NIGHTMARE, MORDANT, MORSEL, REMORSE, MURDER, MORT(AL), MORIBUND, MURRAIN, and MANTICORE. The AHD considers the painful SMART an extension of this same root.

All Germanic languages use ML relatives of MEAL for their term for flour. The Japanese don't tamper with the original flour, as *komugiko* is only an additive away from קמח / KEMÄKH (flour). Swahili changes KMK to *unga* (flour), while KMK becomes *muka* (flour) in Russian.

The MEAL or repast is currently traced to the IE root *me-* (to measure). The true etymon might be a reversal of לחם / LEHEM ("meal" in *I Samuel 20:27*). Similarly, MELEE might be a reversal of לחם / LOHEM (war, battle); current etymological theory links MELEE to "meddle" and "mix." לחם means both meat, bread or meat (Arabic) and waging war, because most wars are economic struggles.

MINI(STER)/מן
MEAN   [MN]

ROOTS: MINISTER and DIMINISH are from Latin *minuere* (to reduce, diminish) and the IE root *mei-* (small). With מן / MEN ("from," "of"– *Genesis 2:6,7*) the sense is a small part of a larger whole.

> **BRANCHES:** MEIOSIS is from Greek *meion* (less, lesser). Cognates include MENU, MINCE, MINUTE, MINESTRONE, MYSTERY and MENSHEVIK. Latin *minister* (inferior, servant) shows that the MINISTRY ought to be a humble service profession.
> MONAD, MONASTERY, MONK, and MONO- are traced to the related IE root *men-* (small, isolated).
> See "MEANING" and "MINUS."

MINUS/מנת
MIN–US   [MNS]

ROOTS: Latin *minor* (less, lesser, smaller) is traced to IE root *mei* (small – see "MINISTER"). Latin *munus* is a portion. Along with מן / MEN (from, out of), there is מנת / MINUS (part, portion – *Jeremiah 13:25*) – another term denoting a smaller piece of something.

> **BRANCHES:** Cognates of MINUS are MINI-, MINIMUM, MINOR, MINUSCLUE, MINUTE and MIS-.
> For related MN words see "MINISTER" and "MONEY." For antonyms see "MANY." *Mun-ne* means "some" or "part of" in Australian Aborigine; *mehen* is "small" in Maya Indian.

MIRRO(R)/מראה
MAR–RAW   [MRAH]

ROOTS: MIRROR is from Late Latin *mirare* (to look at). The given IE root is *smei* (to laugh, smile – see "SMIRK"). מראה / MÄRÄH is a mirror (*Exodus 38:8*) and מראה / MÄREH is a sight, image, view or vision.

> **BRANCHES:** נראה / NIRÄH is to appear; ראה / RÄ ÄH is to see.
> Cognates of MIRROR that fit these Hebrew words are ADMIRE, MARVEL, MIRACLE and MIRAGE (a vision).

MIS(ANTHROPE)/מאס
MA–US   [MAS]

ROOTS: Greek *miso* is from the verb *misein* (to hate). A MISANTHROPE hates people, and a MISOGYNIST hates women. מאס / MÄUS is defined "to despise," and is most often translated as a term of disgusted rejection. In *Amos 5:21* ("SÄNÄSE MÄUSTE," "I loathe, I spurn,"), the Hebrew hisses with an SN word (שונא / SONÄ is to hate) and then (reversing) our MS term of disgust.

> **BRANCHES:** MISOGAMIST (marriage hater) is another MISO-term.

MISS/מוש
MOOS(H)   [MIS]

ROOTS: Old English *mis* and *missan* (to miss) are traced to the IE root *mei-* (to change, go, move).
מוש / MOOS(H) or מש / MÄS(H) is to remove, withdraw or "depart" in *Exodus 13:22*. To paraphrase from this verse, the column of smoke was never MISSED.
משה / MÄS(H)Ä(H), to pull out (of water) is the Biblical etymology for Moses' name (*Exodus 2:10*).

> **BRANCHES:** The opposite of "miss" is "hit;" משש / MÄS(H)ÄS(H) is to touch or feel.
> The clearer cognates of MISS include AMISS, MIS- and MISTAKE.

MITE/מיעוט
ME–OOT   [MUT]

ROOTS: Middle Dutch *mite* is a small insect, small object or small coin; the IE root is *mai* (to cut).
מעט / MOOÄT is small; מעט / MIÄT is a small number, a few (*Deuteronomy 26:5*); מיעוט / MEOOT is a minority.

> **BRANCHES:** Becuase מעט / MOOÄT can also be pronounced MOOKAT, the MITE, MAGGOT, EMMET (an ANT), MIDGE and perhaps MOTH can all be connected.
> *Webster's* links MAD to the IE base *mait* (to cut down); מעט / MEÄT is to reduce, make small. If the Hebrew etymon reduces to עט / vowel plus T, it would link up with ITTY (as in "itty bitty) and Proto-Polynesian *iti* (small, little). Reversing to T(S)-M, צמצום / T(S)M –T(S)OOM is shrinkage.

MITT/קמץ
(KO)MUT(S)   [(K) – M – T(S)]

ROOTS: A MITT is a fingerless glove or slang for a hand. *Webster's* considers MITT a short form of MITTEN. Old French *mitaine* is cited, but the etymon is uncertain.

Webster's goes on to speculate that MITTEN is from Late Latin *mi* (pet name for a kitten). A less strained but unconvincing etymon for MITTEN is Latin *medius* (middle, half) – offered by the *American Heritage Dictionary*.

Respecting slang, see the MITT as a hand and consider קמץ / (KO)MUTS (hand, closed fist – *Leviticus 6:8*). Initial K's very often soften to an H, where they might easily drop away altogether.

> **BRANCHES:** HAND softened the ק / K and shifted the MT(S) of קמץ to ND. Malay's word for "hand" in Gani dialect, *komud*, is much truer to the original קמץ / KOMUT(S).
>
> The verb קמץ / KOMUTS is to take a handful (note the sense of a measurement or count) or to compress the hand. קמצץ / KUMTSOOTS is to pinch, and קמט / KEMEDT is a fold, wrinkle or crease. Aramaic קמט / KIMAT means "he seized."
>
> All this hand closing or folding reinforces our image of a MITTEN, and depicts the way people used to do their COUNTING and COMPUTING. Arabic *qabada* is "he seized or clasped."
>
> As popular as the word HAND is among Germanic languages, there are no IE bases or roots available. One guess is that HAND is from Gothic *hinthan* (to seize). The seize=hand equation is fine. אחז / ÄKHÄZ (to seize, grasp) is behind the "hand" word of Hungarian (*kez*), Finnish (*kasi*) and (reversing KS) Basque (*esku*). See "CATCH" and "SHAG" for more seizing terms. *Cam* is to take hold of in Vietnamese, returning to קמץ / KM(TS). A relevant anagram is נקט / NÄKÄT (to hold, take, seize).
>
> As alluded to above, K–M–T(S) influenced words of hand measuring and counting such as COUNT, COM(P)OU(N)D, and COMPUTE. Old French *conter* (to count) need not come from Latin *computare*. The CNT and CMT in COUNTER and COM(P)UTER are directly from קמץ / KOMÄT(S). A numerical cousin of K–M–TS is חמש / KHÄMÄSH (five). If human hands had four fingers each, counting words would correspond to Hebrew's "four" words, and we'd have number and money systems based on the number eight.
>
> The number TEN is from Germanic *tehun*, a modification of Latin *decem* (ten). Words like DECEMBER, DECIMAL, DECIMATE and DUODECIMAL are a DKM anagram (#1 → #3) of Latin *-ginta* (ten times) or Greek *-konta* (ten times). These Greek and Latin terms are seen as aberrations from the IE root *dekm* (ten). It may be proven, however, that KMT is the original ten or counting root (from קמץ).
>
> The Latin GNT gives us words like OCTOGENARIAN and SEPTUAGINT, while the Greek KNT is behind PENTECOST(AL).
>
> Other derivatives of IE root *dekm* that point instead to קמץ / KMT are words like HUNDRED and CENT. Old English *hundred* had the Germanic ancestor *kmtom* according to the AHD. Latin *centum* (hundred) is close enough to KMT to feel that CENTAVO, CENTENARY, CENTI-, CENTURY, CENTENNIAL, PER CENT and PERCENTAGE are in the grasp of our Hebrew etymon. Some cognates of CENT at IE *dekm* include DIME, DOZEN, DENARIUS, HECTO- and SATEM.
>
> More KMT (KNT) counting terms are at "QUINTET," where the focus is on one hand (five). If not happy with QUANTITY (amount, number) deriving from Latin *quantus* (how great) and *quam* (to what a degree), see the Hebrew etymon offered at "QUANTITY" or see it as going hand in hand with COUNT.

MIX/מֶסֶךְ
MESS–EKH   [M–S–KH → M–KH–S]

ROOTS: MIX, from Latin *misceo*, is traced to IE root *meik* (to mix).

מסך / MOSÄKH is to mix (*Proverbs 9:2*). The mixing of the MSK to (the easier) MKS resembles the way "ask" has lapsed to "aks" for many native New Yorkers.

> **BRANCHES:** מסכת / MÄSEKES is a web (*Judges 16:13*) – a fine source for MESH. MESH is linked to IE root *mezg* (to knit); מזג / MÄZEG is a mixed or blended drink in *Songs 7:3*.
>
> Cognates of MIX include APOMIXIS, ADMIX, COMMIX, IMMIX, MEDDLE, MEDLEY, MELANGE, MESTIZO, MISCELLANEOUS, MISCEGENATION, MIXTURE, PELL–MELL and PROMISCUOUS. MASH, from Old English *masc*, is listed as a possible cognate.
>
> Other possibillities might be MISHMASH, MUSIC (mixed sounds) and MUSTANG (linked to Latin *miscere*, to mix).
>
> *Massak* in Eskimo means mixed snow and water; Japanese *issho ni* (together) may be from MSK too. "Together" in Modern Greek is *mazi*.

MOAT/מוט
MOAT   [MOT]

ROOTS: Having no IE root, the scholars guess that MOAT(a ditch dug to obstruct entry) is from Old French *mote* (hill). מוט / MOT is an obstruction (*Psalms 66:9*); מעד / MOÄDT is to slip.

> **BRANCHES:** Arabic *māta* is "he deviated from right course." עמד / ŌMÄDT (to stand) is an anagramic antonym.

MOCK/מוק
MOOK   [MOK]

ROOTS: Old French *moquer* is to mock (jeer). מוק / MOOK is to mock, insult or "scoff" in *Psalms 73:8*.

> **BRANCHES:** No IE root or cognates in English are available. מוקיון / MOOK[YŌN] (jester, clown) is traced to Greek *mokos* (mocker –"of uncertain origin") by those who mock the antiquity of Hebrew.

MODE/מד
MUD   [MD]

ROOTS: Latin *modus* (mode, manner) is from the IE root *med* (to take appropriate measures). MODE has come to imply fashion and dress; MODEL infers uniformity. מד / MÄD is a measure, garment or uniform (*Job 11:9*); מדה / MEDÄ (*Exodus 26:2*) means measure, size or characteristic.

> **BRANCHES:** For cognates see "METE;" for DM terms of llikeness see "DUMMY."

MOLAR/מלל
MOLL–ULL   [MLL→MLR]

ROOTS: The MOLAR teeth are the body's MILLSTONES. Latin *moler* (to grind) and *mola* (a millsone, mill) are from IE root *mel* (to crush, grind).

מלל / MOLÄL is to rub, scrape and soften. Much more at "MILL."

MONEY/מְנֶה
MOAN – EH   [MNH]

ROOTS: MONEY is said to come from Old French *muneie*, Latin *moneta* (a mint), Latin *monere* (to remind, warn, advise) and the IE root *men* (to think). Greek and Latin *mina* (weight) is not cited, perhaps because it is linked to Semitic along with MAUND. MAUND, *mana* in Sanscrit, is a unit of weight in India, Turkey and Iran.

מנה / MONE is a weight or coin (*Ezekiel 45:12*); מנה / MÄNÄ is to count or number, as in *"counted* the money" (*II Kings 12:11*). מנא / MINÄ is to number, to quote from the Aramaic of the handwriting on the wall (*Daniel 5:25*).

ממון / MÄMON Is money; *Webster's* traces MAMMON from Greek to Aramaic *mamona* (riches), and from *ma'mon* (that which is made secure or deposited) to *'aman* (to trust). For the Hebrew source of MAMMON (and perhaps of MONEY) see "AMENABLE."

> **BRANCHES:** Latin *munero* (to give) relates to מנה / MÄNÄ (portion – *Leviticus 7:33*). Latin *nummulus* (little coin) suggests that some NM or MN money terms relate to NAME (as in naming or assigning value). מנה / MÄNÄ Is to appoint. מין / MÉN is a specie or kind; another NAME (MN reversed) for coin is specie.
> The given cognates of MONEY, such as MUSTER or MONSTER, do not have any MONETARY sense, with the exception of MINT. Similarly, the IE root *men* (to project) is the given source of AMOUNT instead of superior etymons like מנין / MÉNYÄN (quorum, "number"– *Ezra 6:17*).
> MANDATE (to entrust, order) is placed with IE root *man* (hand), but it smacks of אמון / ÄMOON (trust) or מנה / MÉNÄ (to appoint). ENUMERATE and NUMBER are verbs placed at IE root *nem* (to assign, allot) – they are not linked to any of the MN terms above.
> Latin *moneta* (mint, money) is conjectured to be from Phoenician origin by etymologist Ernest Klein.
> See "NUMBER," "MOON" and "MANNER."

MOON/מוֹנֶה
MOAN – EH   [MONH]

ROOTS: Old English *mona* and Greek *mene* mean MOON. Greek *mene* is a MONTH; the IE root for MOON and MONTH is *me* (to measure).

Many moons ago there was a universal counting word like מנה / MÄNÄ (to count, number – *Genesis 13:16*). מונה / MONEH is a time or occasion (*Genesis 31:41*). Moons number our months; the Divine Astronomer "determines" or "reckons" the number of stars (and moons) and names them in *Psalms 147:4* (מונה /MNH). מנין / MIN(YAN) is a number (*Ezra 6:17*).

> **BRANCHES:** First, the relevant cognates of MOON and MONTH include AMENORRHEA, MENARCH, MENOPAUSE, MENSES, MENSTRUATE, SEMESTER and TRIMESTER.
> The Hawaiian moon, *mahina*, is similarly an MN counting

word rather than a term of whiteness or brightness. מונה / MONEH as a verb of reckoning and calculation brings MIND to MIND. Cognates of MIND at IE root *men* (to think) include DEMENTED, MENTAL, MENTION, AUTOMATIC, AHRIMAN, MEMENTO, COMMENT, REMINISCENT, MINERVA, EUMENIDES, MENTOR, MANIA, MANIAC -MANCY, MANTIC, MANTIS, MANDARIN, MANTRA, MINT, MONEY (see "MONEY"), MONITOR, MONSTER, MONUMENT, MUSTER, ADMONISH, DEMONSTRATE, PREMONITION, SUMMON, MOSAIC, MUSE, MUSEUM, MUSIC, AMNESIA, AMNESTY, and MNEMONIC.

אמן / ÉMÄN is to train or teach; Mordechai was Esther's MENTOR or אמן / OMÄN (*Esther 2:7*). An extension of IE *men* might be *mendh* (to learn), which allows us to link MN reckoning with Greek *manthanein* and English MATHEMATICS. (Otherwise, the MND and MNT terms are nasalized forms of למד / [L]MD, to learn).

If the MOON was Man's heavenly calculator, his hand (see "MITT") or *manus* (Latin for hand) was his earthly one. MN hand words at IE *man* (hand) include MANACLE, MANAGE, MANNER, MANUAL, MAINTAIN, MANEUVER, MANICURE, MANIFEST, MANIPULATE, MANUFACTURE, MANURE, MANUSCRIPT, MASTIFF, EMANCIPATE, MANDATE, COMMAND and DEMAND.

If hand=calculator, then perhpas MAN the thinking, reckoning animal was given an MN name for the same reason. MAN is from the IE root *man* (man). An alternative spelling for the root in the AHD is *mon*.

See "MASCULINE," "MOON" and "NUMBER."

MOR(ON)/נַעַר
NO – ARE   [NOR → MOR]

ROOTS: Greek *moron* is a form of *moros* (foolish), which relates to *moro* (baby in Modern Greek). A MORON is childish, officially rated to have the intellect of an 8-12 year old. נער / NOÄR is youth; נער / NÄ'UR means boy, lad, youth (*Exodus 2:6*); נערות / NÄUROOT is puerility, foolishness or immaturity.

> **BRANCHES:** *Marya* is youth in Sanskrit.
> From the IE root *mo(u)ro* (foolish) we add OXYMORON. The IE root *mari* (young woman) is only an M→N change from נערה / NA'ARA (young woman). MARITAL and MARRY are traced to IE *mari*.
> See "NEW."

MORT(AR)/מֶלֶט
MEL – ET   [MLT→ MRT]

ROOTS: Latin *mortarium* (mortar) is "probably" from IE root *mer* (to rub away, harm) states the AHD. MORTAR means a mixture of cement.

מלט / MELET (mortar, cement – *Jeremiah 43:9*) is but an L→R change away. מלל / MALAL (to rub, wither) matches the meanings of IE *mer*.

MUCK/מק
MUCK   [MK]

ROOTS: *Webster's* would trace MUCK and Old Norse *myki* (dung) to MUCUS and MEEK (see "MEEK"). MUCK is defined as black earth containing decaying matter, so it is best traced to מק / MUK (decay, "rottenness" or "rot"– *Isaiah 5:24*).

> **BRANCHES:** Aramaic *miqaq* means "it rotted or decayed." Reversing to KM, קמל / KOM[UL] is to wither or become decayed.

MUSC(LE)/מְשַׁךְ
MUH–S(H)UKH   [M–S(H)–KH]

ROOTS: Latin *mus* and Greek *mus* mean "mouse." The IE root for "mouse" and MUSCLE is *mus*, "from the resemblance of a flexing muscle to movements of a mouse."

Rather than flexing rats, consider משך / MOS(H)ÄKH (to pull, extend, lengthen, drag, or "draw up" in *Jeremiah 38:13*).

> **BRANCHES:** Arabic *masaka* is "he grasped and held;" Ethiopic *masaka* means "he bent the bow."

MUSK/מָתוֹק
MAH–SOAK   [MSK]

ROOTS: Still fixated on mice from the previous entry ("MUSCLE") *Webster's* feels that a diminutive of *mus* (mouse) inspired the Sanskrit word *mushka* (testicle) which gave rise to MUSK. The MUSK of perfumes can originate from an abdominal sac of the male MUSK DEER, but the MUSK MELON, MUSK OX, MUSKRAT, MUSK ROSE and all other MUSKY things do not.

The AHD offers Persian *muskh* to claim an Indo-Aryan origin for MUSK (a strong, sweet smelling substance). After Greek *moschos*, *Webster's* does list Arabic *mushk* and *musk* (musk). With this acknowledged Semitic connection, we move on to מתוק / MÄSOK or MÄTOK (sweet, soft, pleasant, juicy – *Songs 2:3*).

> **BRANCHES:** מתיקה / MISEKÄ or MITEKÄ are sweetmeats; מגד / MEGED is something sweet or delicious; מיץ / METS is juice; תמד / TEMED is to moisten and mead; רמע / DOMÄKH is juice; דם / DÄM is wine – (*Genesis 49:11*); תמר / TÄM(ÄR) means a date; טעם / TÄ'ÄM or TÄKHÄM is flavor; and an anagramic antonym is חמץ / KHÄMETS (sour).
>
> The above configurations of M–S/T/D–K can be sweetly tasted in the words below: The IE root *medhyo* (honey, mead) yields MEAD (honey wine); AMETHYST and METHYLENE (from Greek *methu*, wine); DOUCEUR (*doux* and *doce* are sweet in French and Portuguese); *madu* (honey in Malay); *makeata* (sweet in Finnish); MAST, MEAT, *med* (honey in Russian); MESCALINE; MESQUITE (Aztec: a sweet plant food); *mitsu* (honey, nectar in Japanese); MOIST; MOSCHATE(L); MOUSSE; MUSCAT (grapes); MUSCATEL (sweet wine); MUSACEOUS; MUSCADEL; MUSCADINE; MUSCOVADO (raw sugar); MUSH(Y); MUSIC; MUSK ROSE; MUSKEG (Ojibway American Indians: bog of decaying vegetable matter); MUSQUASH (Algonquin Indian name for the muskrat); *muxika* (a peach in Basque); and TOKAY (a sweet Hungarian wine).
>
> Reverse to -*tamu* for sweet in Swahili (but see טעם / TÄ'ÄM above). The SK element may be tasted in SACCHARIN and SUGAR. The SK in Persian *persicus*, source of PEACH, should mean "sweet." That leaves PR to mean "fruit," as seen at "FRUIT."

MYR(TLE)/מר
MORE   [MR]

ROOTS: For MYRRH, Arabic *murr* (bitter, myrrh) is cited. The Hebrew is left for a cross-reference, even though מור / MOR (myrrh – *Exodus 30:23*, *Psalms 45:8*) is a separate term from מר / MÄR (bitter). MYRRH is a fragrant, bitter-tasting shrub like the MYRTLE, which is traced to Greek *myrtos* (myrtle).

> **BRANCHES:** MYRTACEOUS is the MYRTLE's family of shrubs and trees; the name MYRON is from Greek *myron* (ointment, perfume) and also bears the fragrance of MYRRH. Biblical MYRRH was used in anointing oil as well as in perfume.

MYSTER(Y)/מִסְתָּר
ME–STAR   [STR]

ROOTS: Greek *mysterion* is the secret worship of a deity or a secret thing. With blind faith we are then to believe that the source of MYSTERY goes back to Greek *muein* (to close the eyes), and before that to an IE root *mu* ("imitative of inarticulate sounds").

There is an alternative to this pagan, voodoo linguistics. מסתר / MESTÄR is a "secret place" (*Jeremiah 13:17*), while במסתר / (BI)MESTÄR means "secretly" (*Psalms 10:9*). מסתר / MISOOTÄR is "secret" (*Proverbs 27:5*); the root is סתר / SÄTER (secret).*

> **BRANCHES:** Given cognates of MYSTERY are MIOSIS, MYOPIA and MYSTIC – but ESOTERIC is filed under IE root *en* (in). An eye-closing verb closer to MYSTERY is מצמץ / JMETSMÄTS (to wink the eyes).
>
> *"The *secret things* belong unto the Lord our God; but the things that are revealed belong unto us and to our children for ever..."– *Deuteronomy 29:28* נסתרות / NISTÄROS
>
> Latin and Greek Astarte is linked to Semitic cults and mystery religions involving Ashtoreth (Phoenician, Syrian) and Ishtar (Babylonian, Assyrian) which are mentioned in the Bible. The ancient Tibetan *Stanzas of Dzyan* refer to Ashtar (the highest magical knowledge).

NAG/נָהַג
NA–HUG   [NHG]

ROOTS: There is a natural connection between NAG (to urge on with constant scolding) and NAG (a saddle horse – who might need constant cajoling). Dutch *negghe*, source of NAG, is not linked to the questionable source of NAG – Old Norse *gnaga* (to bite) and the IE root *ghen* (to gnaw – see "GNAW").

נהג / NÄHÄG is to drive, conduct or lead. Moses "drives" his flock in *Exodus 3:1*; a cart is "driven" in *I Chronicles 13:7*.

> **BRANCHES:** Other possibilities for NAG include the נקה / NÄKA or נאקה / NÄ'ÄKÄ (she-camel). To supplement NAG there are synonyms such as נחה / NÄKHÄ (to lead, guide, conduct) and נחץ / NÄKHÄTS (to press, urge).
> See "HEGEMONY."

NAVY/נֶבֶךְ
NAVE – (EKH)   [N – BH]

ROOTS: There is something in common between a NAVAL fleet (of ships) and the NAVEL depression in mid-abdomen. A boat or ship, *navis* in Latin, is also hollowed out.

נבוב / NÄV(OOV) is hollow (*Jeremiah 52:21*), while נבך / NÄV(EKH) MEANS "depth (of the sea)"–*Job 38:16.*

BRANCHES: This last Hebrew etymon better explains NAVIG(ATE) and NAVIG(ABLE)–"wide or deep enough to navigate."

Of course, two separate IE roots are given to NAVEL and NAVAL. IE root *nobh*, the root for NAVEL, is defined as a "central knob"–just the opposite of the "point of depression" we also find on the NAVEL ORANGE. (Perhaps the lexicographer has an "outsy" rather than an "insy" belly button.)

The IE root for NAVY is *nau* (boat)–remember this U=V principle. Appropriately enough for land lubbers, NAUSEA is a cognate of NAVIGATE. Other cognates listed are AERONAUT, AQUANAUT, ARGONAUT, ASTRONAUT, COSMONAUT, NACELLE, NAUTICAL, NAUTILUS, NAVICULAR and NOISE.

The NAVE of a church is the main space (or hollow) between the aisles. The Old French source of NAVE is shanghaied to serve aboard the Latin *navis* (ship).

NECK /חֶנֶק
(HEH) – NECK   [(H) – N – K]

ROOTS: Old English *hnecca* (neck) is from the Germanic root *hnekk* (neck–a narrow or compressed part). The IE root is *ken* ("something compressed").

A fine etymon for the sound and sense of NECK and *hnekk* is the Hebrew חנק / HENEK (strangulation, hanging by the neck, suffocation). חנק / HENÄK is to "strangle" in *Nahum 2:13*. There also is ענק / ÄNOK or KHÄNOK (necklace–*Songs 4:9*). ענק / ÄNUK or HÄNUK is to put on the neck.

BRANCHES: Another NK link between choke (strangle) and choker (necklace) is שנק / SHENÄK (to strangle). Much like the Swahili neck, *shingo*, these last terms suggest connections with strangling SNAKES and with CHOKE (with an N having dropped out).

נאק / NÄ'ÄK is a groan, moan, or heavy sigh (*Exodus 2:24*; אנחה / ÄNÄKHÄ means precisely the same (*Exodus 2:23*). These are neck-made sounds, just as "groan" is from the Hebrew word for throat–see "GROAN."

A necktie in Arabic is [*roubat al-ou*] *noug*; *inko* is the Japanese throat.

Official cognates of NECK include KNACKER, NEWEL, NOCK, NOOK, NOUGAT, NUCELLUS and NUCLEUS.

Many more related words are to be found at "CINCTURE" and "HANG."

NEW/נוב
NOVE   [NWV]

ROOTS: Latin *novus* (new) appears akin to נוב / NŌV (to spring forth, to bear fruit – *Psalms 92:15*).

Old English *niwe* (new) appears related to Old Norse *nyr*

(new). The W=R connection is reinforced at the IE root *newo* (new) where the AHD establishes that Greek *nearos* (young, fresh) is related to Greek *newos* or *neos* (new).

The Hebrew source of Greek *nearos* (young, fresh) is both נער / NOÄR (youth – *Psalms 88:16*) and the NR reversal רענן / RÄÄNÄN (fresh – *Deutereronomy 12:2*). נער / NOÄR (*I Samuel 1:24*) and נעורים / NIOOREM (*Isaiah 54:6*) also mean the state of being young; baby Moses is a נער / NÄÄR (young child) in *Exodus 2:6*.

BRANCHES: Related to the נב / N – BH Hebrew etymon is נבט / NEV[ET] (sprout), ענף / ANAF (branch), ענב / ANABH (grape) and (reversing to BN) בן / BEN (son, child). Related to the Greek etymons above are words like NEO-, NEON, NEOTERIC and MISONEISM. From the Latin term *novus* (new) we may add cognates INNOVATE, NOVA, NOVATION, NOVEL, NOVELTY, NOVICE and RENOVATE.

The AHD feels that NOW is related as well; see "NOW." *Nawa* in Australian aborigine means newborn babe or infant. Finnish *nuorehko* (youthful) is closer to the NR Hebrew etymon.

See "MORON."

The common speech defect ("You cwazy wabbit!") and the linguistic phenomenon of R becoming a W (or V) may also be seen in the following word pairs where the Hebrew ר / R shall be rendered WR or W(R): AWE from יראה / YIW[R]Ä (reverential fear), BOV[INE] from פר / PÄW[R] (bull: source of BULL too – change P to B and R to L), DOVE from תור / D[T]OW[R] (turtledove), SOW (pig) from חזיר / [HÄ]ZEW[R] (pig), SOW (seed) from זרע / ZOW [R]Ä (to sow), TWO from תרי / TW[R]Ä (two in Aramaic), VEIL from רעלה / W[R]IÄLÄ (veil), VITALITY (French *vite* means quick) from רהוט / W[R]EHOOT (quick), WASH from רחץ / W[R]ÄHÄ[T]S (wash), WEAK from רך / W[R]ÄKH (soft, timid, tender), WET from רטב / W[R]ÄTÄV (moist), WOOF (WEAVE and WEFT) from ערב / ÄW[R]EBH (woof), WORM from רמה / WREMÄ (worm), and WRO[N]G from רע / WRÄ or WRÄG (bad, evil). רצה / W[R]ÄTSÄH (to wish, desire) may provide a better etymon for WA(N)T and WISH than the IE roots *eu* (lacking, empty) or *wen* (to desire, strive for – the given root for WISH). Changing רצה / RÄTSÄH (desire) to LÄ(T)SÄH might offer a more desirable etymon for LECHERY. Currently, Old French *lechier* is traced to the IE root *leigh* (to lick).

Also see "WOMAN" and "SAW."

NEXT/נֶגֶד
NEG – E(D)T   [NGD→NXT]

ROOTS: נגד / NEGEDT is translated "before" in *Joshua 5:13* and as "in front of" in *Exodus 19:2*. NEXT can also mean "just before" (in space, in time, or in rank). The IE root is *hehw-iz* (near).

The 2-letter Hebrew root נג / NG is akin to NIGH. This root appears in words like נגע / NOGÄ (to approach, touch) and נגש / NEG(USH) (to near).

BRANCHES: NEAR and NEIGHBOR are cognates of NEXT, whose original guttural sound is better preserved in the German *nächst* (next).

The opposite of NEXT TO or NEAR is seen in the translation of the same נגד / NEGEDT in *Deuteronomy 32:52* ("afar off"). The "opposition" sense of נגד / NGD has encouraged some to see ANTI- in its counterpart נגד / NE(G)E(D)T (against, opposed). The IE root of ANTE- and ANTI- is *ant* (front, forehead), which shares effrontery with מצח / MÄT(SH)ÄH ("forehead"–*Jeremiah 3:3*).

NIB/נִיב
NEEBH   [N–Y–BH]

ROOTS: A NEB or NIB (end of anything sharp) is from Old English *nebb* and the IE root *nabja* (both mean "bird's beak"). נִיב / NĒBH is a canine tooth in Aramaic and Arabic; נבר / NĀBHĀR is to dig with the snout.

> **BRANCHES:** NIPPLE is an official cognate, though NIBBLE and NIP are more sharply connected. Reversing the N–BH allows one to see the pointed kinship with words like FAN(G), FIN(CH), PEN and PIN – see "PENGUIN."
> More at "NIP."

NICK/נָגַע
NUH–G(KH)A or NOG–AH   [N–G–KH]

ROOTS: Both NICK and KNOCK are words of striking that are linked to words of squeezing like "knot," "knit" and "knuckle." Old English terms like *cnocian* (might) are said to derive from the IE base *gen* ("to squeeze together").

NICK (to strike, catch or hit) is better linked to words like נגע / NOGĀ or NOGKHĀ (to strike, reach or "touch" in *Genesis 32:32* when Jacob is injured in the thigh.

> **BRANCHES:** IE root *nek* (to reach) is the source of ENOUGH and ONCOLOGY. Other terms that match this particular meaning to an NK sound include נקף / NOKUF (to knock, strike, bruise), נקד / NOKUD (to prick), נגף / NOGUF (to strike – *Exodus 21:12*) and נגח / NUGĀKH (to butt, gore – *Exodus 21:28*).
> Relevant Latin words include *nocere* (to injure, harm) and *noxa* (injury, hurt, damage). They gave us English words like INNOCENT, INNOCUOUS and NUISANCE, plus NOXIOUS and OBNOXIOUS.
> See "NOXIOUS."

NIP/קָנַב
(KA)–NUBH   [(K)NB→NP]

ROOTS: Middle English *nippen* is linked to an IE base *qneib* and subsequently to the IE base *qen* (to scratch, rub) or to the (AHD's) IE root *ken* (pinching...closing eyes). The IE base *qneib* best speaks to the severing, clipping and biting of NIP and NIPPY (biting). A NIPPER is a tool to sever wire. קנב / KONĀBH is to trim or prune; the term is non-Biblical but Aramaic and Arabic.

> **BRANCHES:** A NIPPER is also the incisor tooth of a horse; נִיב / NĒBH is a canine tooth in Aramaic and Arabic. Reverse to *fahn* for the Thai tooth; English PIN also reverses NP. To NIP is to steal in slang, possibly from גנב / (GO)NĀBH (to steal). NAP and NIPPLE are considered cognates; more at "NIB."
> A small drink of liquor is also a NIP. This could refer to a small amount (as a bite) or to the biting quality of the liquor. The liquor called NIPA is a Malay word, as the sap from this feathery leafed palm goes into NIPA. נוף / NŌPH (boughs of a tree) may be behind the Malay term.
> See "NIB," (reversing NP) "PENGUIN" and "POIN(T)."

NITRO(GEN)/נֶתֶר
NET–ERE   [NTR]

ROOTS: NITER (the stuff of NITRATES) is traced to Greek *nitron* (native soda, NATRON), then to Hebrew *nether* (sic). The etymology concludes, "probably from Egyptian *ntrj*." נתר / NETER is the better pronouncing of the "NATRON" (cleaning material) in *Jeremiah 2:22*, but the Anglicized "nether" better hides Hebrew's contribution to English.

> **BRANCHES:** About 55 words use NITRIC, NITRO- and NITROUS.
> NITON, from Latin *nitere* (to shine), is seen in נצץ / NĀTSĀTS (to shine).

NO/נוא
NOO   [NOA]

ROOTS: Old English *ne* is traced to the IE root *ne* (not). הניא / (HĀ)NĒ and יניא / (YĀ)NĒ are verbs translated "disallow" in *Numbers 30:6* and *30:9*, where a vow is annulled or "said NO to." The infinitive is rendered נוא / NOO.

> **BRANCHES:** The many cognates of NO and other Hebrew words like אין / AN (not or no – NO reversed) are seen at "INSOMNIA."
> While N negatives dominate the IE family, "no" is *ma* in Maya and *my* in Thai.
> The Salishan Indians of the American Northwest refuse by saying *lu* (no). לא / LŌ is the primary Hebrew "no;" English N's from Hebrew L's are documented in an appendix.
> The "no" of Germany (*nein*) and Hungary (*nem*) recall מאן / MĀAN (to refuse).

NOD/נד
NOD   [ND]

ROOTS: Middle English *nodden*, "in basic sense 'to shake the head,' " is akin to German *notten* (t move about). *Webster's* and the AHD go on, however, to trace NOD to theoretical base words of knocking, scratching and rubbing, or to the IE root *ken* (pinching, closing eyes...).

"(They)...will be appalled and will *shake* their heads." In this quote from *Jeremiah 18:16*, the word "shake" is הניד / (HĀ)NĒD. Similar to the rocking and shaking of נדד / NĀDĀD is נוד / NĒD (movement, swing –"sway like a reed" in *I Kings 14:15*).

INNUENDO, NUMEN and NUTATION are traced to the IE root *neu* (to nod). They, too, may relate to נט / NĀT (to shake, move) and מוט / MOT (to shake, tooter) and נדד / NĀDĀD (to wander about, to flee). עמד / OMĀD (to stand) is antonymous. Given the interchangeability of M and N, we should consider MT movement words like COMMOTION, EMOTION, MOMENT(OUS), MOMENTUM, MOTIF, MOTION, MOTIVE, MOTOR, PROMOTE and REMOTE. All these words and more are listed cognates at the IE root *meue* (to push away).

נדח / NĀDĀH means push away, expel, move away or slip away (*II Samuel 14:14*). A #2-#3 letter flip of נדח /

NADTAKH (to drive away, expel) may reveal the source of Greek *nektos* (swimming) and English NEKTON. In swimming not only is water מנד / (MOO)NADT (expelled), but we are נוד / NOODT (moving back and forth). The N – DT word of swimming or *NAT*ATION in Latin is *natare*. *Nadar* is to swim in Spanish and Portuguese.

See "UNDULATE" and "WANDER."

NOOK/נקק
NOK – (UCK)   [NK]

ROOTS: NOOK is linked to words meaning "hook," "to drive back," "the neck," and, on the IE base and root level, "something compressed." A NOOK, however, is a small recess, a secluded retreat.

God shields Moses in a "cleft of the rock" in *Exodus 33:22*; נקרה / NI[RÄ] is defined as a crevice or hole. נקור / NĒK(OOR) is chiseling. Even closer to NOOK in the family of NK perforation and NICKING words is נקיק / NÄKĒK (cleft, crevice). A "cleft of the rock" is a hiding place or NOOK in *Jeremiah 13:4*.

> **BRANCHES:** NICHE is related, but Hawaiian *nakakaka* (a crack) and *naka* (to crack) are even closer. Reversing to KN in Hawaiian, *kj'ono* is a nook; *ho'okuno* is to indent.
> נקבה / NIKÄVÄ (female – *Genesis 1:27*) and נקב / NEKEV (perforation) are obviously extensions of the נק / NK root of cavities and concavities. After a 1→3 anagram of נקב [NQV→QVN] one can see how the Hebrew term for female gave us English words like QUEEN. QUEAN is from Old English *cwene* (woman, prostitute, wife). In Hebrew, a woman, wife, or queen is the feminine of terms for a human, spouse, or king – not merely a man's receptacle. Arthur's queen, *GUINEVERE*, was Lancelot's *cwene*. Cognates of QUEEN at the IE root *gwen* (woman) include BANSHEE, GYNECOLOGY, MISOGYNIST, POLYGYNY and ZENANA.

NOS(TALGIA)/נם
NASE   [NS]

ROOTS: Greek *nostos* (a return home) is linked to the IE root *nes* (to return safely home).

נם / NAS or the infinitive נוס / NOOS means to "flee" (*Numbers 10:35*) or to escape (danger and return safely).

> **BRANCHES:** HARNESS is a cognate of NOSTALGIA; it is said to link up with Old Norse *nest* (food for a journey). NEST is possibly related.

NOTARY/נוטר
NOTE – AIR   [NT]

ROOTS: Old French *notaire* and Latin *notarius* is the immediate source of NOTARY (a legal witness). נוטריון / NŌTÄR(YŌN) is a NOTARY PUBLIC in Modern Hebrew because נוטר / NŌTÄR is a watchman (*Songs 1:6*).

> **BRANCHES:** The cognate verb to NOTE or NOTICE (now linked to IE *gno*, to know) relates to another NT watch word, as נוצר / NŌT(S)ÄR is also a guard or watchman. נוצרי / NŌTSRE is a Christian, as vigilance is inherent in the name of the town Nazereth (נצרת). נצח / NĒTSÄH is to superintend.

NO(W)/נא
NUH   [NU]

ROOTS: The IE base and root of NOW is *nu* (now). While it is often meant the same way as the NOW in "come NOW, you can't be serious"–the Biblical נא / NÄ of *Genesis 12:11*, *18:21* or *27:2* is often translated "now." The NOW meaning "at this moment" is better represented by הנה / HÄNÄ (translated "now" in places like *Judges 16:13*).

> **BRANCHES:** *Nu* in Hittite is now. Norwegian *na* (now) is the reverse of Arabic (*il*)*an* (now). Japanese *ima* (now), Dutch *nu* (now), English NOO (now – an adverb) are all related.
> See "NEW."

NOXIOU(S)/נכה
NOH – KHUH   [N – KH – H]

ROOTS: Latin *noxa* (injury, hurt, damage) is traced to IE root *nek* (death).

נכה / NÄKÄ (the root of הכה / HĒCÄ) means "to kill" (*II Samuel 11:15*) as well as to defeat, beat or strike.

> **BRANCHES:** Cognates include INNOCENT, INNOCUOUS, INTERNECINE, NECRO-, NECROMANCY, NECTAR, NECTARINE, NOYADE, NUISANCE, OBNOXIOUS and PERNICIOUS.
> נכא / NOKÄ is smitten or afflicted; ננף / NOG[AF] is to smite, injure or plague; נגף / NEG[EF] is a stumbling block; and נגע / NOGA is to strike or afflict. These Hebrew terms better match up to Latin *nocere* (to injure, hurt) than does the given IE root. See "NICK."

NOZZLE/נוזל
NO – ZALE   [NZL]

ROOTS: A NOZZLE is a spout; נוזל / NŌZÄL is to spout (or flow). NOZZLE is considered a shortened form of NOSE, whose IE root is *nas* (nose). נזם / NEZEM is a nose ring (*Genesis 24:22*); נוזלת / NŌZELET is a head cold.

> **BRANCHES:** The NZ in צנור / [T]ZEN[ŌR] (pipe) and the reversed ZN in זנק / ZÄNÄK (spurt) offer possible links to SNEEZE and NOSE. Cognates of NOSE include NASAL, NASO-, NOSTRIL, NUZZLE and PINCE – NEZ.
> See "SNORKEL."

NUMB/נם
NUMB   [NM]

ROOTS: NUMB (insensible, deadened) is somehow linked to Old English *niman* (to take, seize) and the IE root *nem* (to assign, allot, take). נם / NUM (the root is נום / NOOM) means to "drowse" (*Isaiah 56:10*), or to "slumber"–"Behold, the watcher of Israel neither *slumbers* nor sleeps"– *Psalms 121:4*.

> **BRANCHES:** An extended form תנומה / S'NOOMÄ (slumber) may have influenced SLUMBER and SOMN(AMBULIST) – see "INSOMNIA." Hebrew's influence reached beyond Arabic *yanam* (sleep) to the Orient. Japanese *nemui* means sleepy; *nemuru* is sleep. Reverse to *mania* (inactive, sleepy) in Hawaiian. To sleep in Tahi is *nawn*; in Maxaki (Brazil) it is *non*.

NUM(BER)/מָנָה
MUN–AH   [MN→NM]

ROOTS: Latin *numerus* is a number or division; the IE root is *nem* (to assign, allot; take). מנה / MÄNÄ is to number; מיון / MEOON is a classification; מנה / MÄNÄ is to "appoint" in *Daniel 1:11.*

> **BRANCHES:** מנין / MIN[YAN] is a number (*Ezra 6:17*), counting or quorum; מנה / MANA is a part or portion. See "MAN," "MONEY," and "MOON."

NUTS/נָאַץ
NUH–UTS   [N–U–TS]

ROOTS: Because it's slang, NUTS is not taken up seriously. NUTS! is an exclamation of disgust, scorn or angry refusal. נאץ / NÄUTS (to condemn, spurn, be wrathful) is in *Proverbs 1:30* and *16:5*. נאץ / NEÄTS is to curse or insult; נאצה / NIÄTSÄ is contempt or blasphemy in *Isaiah 37:3.*

OATH/אוֹת
OATH   [A–O–T(H)]

ROOTS: Old English *ath* is akin to German *eid*, from the IE root *oito* (an oath). An OATH is a ritualistic declaration of ongoing faith in God. An אות / OT or OTH (*Genesis 9:13, Isaiah 37:30*) is the mark of a divine promise.

> **BRANCHES:** The divine אות / OT serves as an עד / AD (witness) to a future עת / AT (time).

OBEDIE(N)CE/עֲבָדוּת
UBH–DOOSE   [O–BH–D+OS]

ROOTS: This entry would not only suggest a connection between Latin *obed[iens]* (submission) and עבד / OBHUD (to serve, be a slave to – *Genesis 29:18*), but also between the noun-forming suffix of both OBEDIE(N)CE and עבדות / ÄBHDOOS (servitude).

OBESE/אָבַם
OBHUS   [OBS]

ROOTS: Latin *obesus* is said to derive from *obedere* (to devour) and the IE root *ed* (to eat; originally meaning to bite). אבם / OBHUS is to fatten, stuff; אבוס / UBHOOS is "fatted" in *I Kings 5:3*; and עבה / OBHEH is thick or fat. *Deuteronomy 32:15*–"You grew fat and *gross* and coarse." עבה.

> **BRANCHES:** Reversing עב(א) / A–BH (fat, to fatten) resembles IE root *pa* (to protect, feed) whose derivatives include FODDER,

FOOD, FOSTER, PASTOR and REPAST. The IE root *pap* (food – baby-talk root) seems to be a doubled form of *pa*. At this root we find that PA(M)PER meant to cram with food. POPPYCOCK is listed here.
  A third possibly relevant IE root is *pei* (to be fat, swell). Some listed cognates here include FAT, PIP, PITUITARY and *Iwer-iu* (the prehistoric Celtic name for IRELAND).
    See "FAT."

OBI/אוֹב
OVE   [O–I–BH]

ROOTS: OBI or OBEAH is a West African name for a brand of witchcraft or magic practiced in parts of Africa and the West Indies.
  The term אוב / OBH is defined as magic, necromancy and (for the rationalists) ventriloquism. In *Leviticus 19:31* it is translated as "ghost" or (KJ) "familiar spirit."

OBIT(UARY)/אָבַד
OBH–U(D)T   [O–BH–DT]

ROOTS: OBIT means he or she died, as Latin *obitus* is death. The alleged breakdown of this death term is *ob* (totally) + *ire* (to go).
  אבד / OBHU(D)T is to be lost, to perish; התאבד / (HIT)ÄBÄ(D)T is to commit suicide; and אבדה / ÄBHA(D)TÄ is a casualty. ABADDON (hell) is a Hebraicism, as אבדון / ABHÄDON is the place where the dead body decays – *Proverbs 15:11*. The slain Jew-haters in *Esther 9:6* are אבד / ABÄD ("exterminated" or "destroyed"). See "BAD."

OBOE/אָבֶה
AY–BHEH   [O–BH–H]

ROOTS: The OBOE is a reed or wind instrument said to derive from English hautboy, Old French *bois* (wood), and the IE root *busk* (a bush). אבה / ÄBHE is a reed (*Job 9:26*); אבוב / ÄBOOBH is a tube, PIPE, and the wind instrument played at the Temple in Jerusalem.

> **BRANCHES:** The doubled B, F or P of BOOB, FIFE and PIPE can also carry a tune from words like נבוב / (NI)BHOOBH (hollow – *Exodus 27:8*). The pipe between our eyes, the אף / UPH (nose) also has a reduplicated counterpart in a term like אפף / ÄPHÄPH (encircle).
> *Popoe* is round and *pōai* is a circle in Hawaiian. The Maya pipe is a *hobon*; reverse to *wei* for a reed or rush in Chinese. As BA(M)BOO takes an extra M, so does the tubular PU(M)P.
>   See "BAMBOO" and "BIBLE."
>   Nasalization is evident in Semitic daughters of Mother Hebrew such as Akkadian *imbubu* (flute, pipe) and Arabic *inbub* (pipe, tube).

(OB)SCURE/שָׁחֹר
S(H)Ä–KHORE   [S(H)–KH]

ROOTS: Latin *obscurus* is from *ob* (toward) + the IE root *(s)keu* (to cover, conceal). (OB)SCURE means dark and murky as well as vague and unclear. The connection to SKR and SK Hebrew terms should never have been obscured. שחר / S(H)ÄKHŌR is dark or "black" (*Leviticus 13:31*); שחק(ים) / SHIKHĀK(IM) means clouds, heaven or "skies" (*Deuteronomy 33:26*), and סכך / SÄKHÄKH is to screen or cover over.

> **BRANCHES:** The connection is clearer when considering that SKY, from Germanic *skeu-jam* (cloud), is a cognate. many of the listed cognates of OBSCURE, like KISHKE, relate to KS terms like כסה / CÄSÄ (to cover) or כים / KĒS (slipCASE, pocket). Also relevant is חשך / KHŌSHEKH (darkness).
>
> The IE root *kers* (dark, dirty) is an anagram of שחור / SHAHŌR (*Lamentations 4:8*) – which may be be pronounced SHÄHVŌR or SHWR (with the vowel ו as the consonant V or W). This would explain why Arabic *aswad* (black) resembles IE base *swordo* (dirty, black). Dutch and Norwegian "black" is *zwart*; German is *schwarz.*. The English cognates here are SWARTHY and SORDID.
>
> The basic שחר / SH – KH – R is elsewhere preferred for "black": *chorni* (Russian), *cuk*(Papayo Indians), *czarny* (Polish), *kara* (Turkish), *kuroi* (Japanese), and *shih hei* (Chinese). Some words for "night", like Swahili *usiku* and Hungarian *ejszaka*, ought to be from חשך / HŌSHEKH (darkness – *Genesis 1:2*) and/or שחר / SHÄKHŌR (black). שחר / SHAKHAR means light in *Isaiah 8:20*.
>
> Mental blacking out or being in the dark is evoked by שכור / SHÄKHOOR (drunk, intoxicated) and שכחה / SHĒKHIKHÄ (forgetfulness). *Su hu* is negligence in Chinese.

OCCUR/קְרָא
CAR–AH   [KRA]

ROOTS: OCCUR (to happen) is said to be a combination of Latin *ob* (towards) plus *currere* (to run). Such a term should be pronounced "obcur," and it would not come to mean "happen."

Meanwhile קרא or קרה / KÄRÄ means to befall, meet up with or happen – see *Genesis 42:29*, *Genesis 49:1*, *Deuteronomy 22:6* and *Deuteronomy 25:18* for a series of chance OCCURANCES and purposeful happenings.

> **BRANCHES:** Read קורות / KOROS (history, literally: happenings) to see patterns REOCCUR. עראי / KHÄRĒ means incidental. Noncoincidentally, *okoru* is to happen in Japanese.

OG[RE]/עוֹג
OAG   [OG]

ROOTS: An OGRE is a hideous monster or giant; mighty עוג / OG, King of Bashan, was the last of the giants of Scripture (*Numbers 21:33, Deuteronomy 3:11*). Judging from the Bible illiteracy in graduate literature classes, the fellows who wrote that OGRE was probably coined by French fairy tale writer Charles Perrault (d. 1703) had probably never heard of Og. The Frenchman explains the "re" suffix added to Og's name.

> **BRANCHES:** In not pronouncing the Hebrew *ayin* (ע) like a G or K, remember that the French OGRE would take the voiceless European (Ashkenazic) accent. And is there a Mediterranean (Sephardic), guttural KG or GG version of a giant? Joseph P.

Shipley lists the Indo-European root *gigas* which begat the Greek and Latin *gigas* and *gigantos*, bearing offspring like GIANT and GIGANTIC.

The illiterate Greeks, who clumsily borrowed an alphabet from the Semites, probably paganized the stuff of many Biblical epics. One of these was the account of mighty Og and the Anakim (Nephilim) battling God's army for the rights to settle Canaan. Gigas (Og) is a major figure in their mythic battle between the Titans and the gods. As for Og's wife, note the Old Norse term for ogress, *gygr*. This is the given source for the Scottish word for an evil spirit or ogre, GYRE (2). For other English words from Hebrew names see "RUTHLESS."

A synonym for GIGANTIC, HUGE is actually a cognate; עו can be rendered HG (see "HONEY" in Section II). HUGE is traced to Old French *ahoge* (of uncertain origin, but considered a possible relative of HIGH).

OMEN/אָמֵן
O – MEN   [AMN]

ROOTS: Latin *omen*, a prognostic sign, is traced to an IE root meaning "to believe, hold as true." אמונה אמן / EMOONA ŌMEN is translated "faithfulness and truth" in *Isaiah 25:1*. The אמן / AMN verb of believing appears first in *Genesis 45:26*.

> **BRANCHES:** AMMON In Greek and English is a form of *Amen*, the ancient Egyptian name for Zeus or Jupiter.
> See "AMENABLE" and "SEMANTIC."

OOZE/עָסִים
OS – EESE   [OSYS]

ROOTS: An OOZE is a gentle flow; to OOZE is to exude a fluid. Anglo-Saxon *wos* (sap, juice) and IE root *wes* (wet) are the given etymons. It is notable that *wos* is "sap" backwards (W=P), but a vowel plus S would make a juicier etymon still. עסים / ÄSĒS is juice (*Songs 8:2*); עסה / ĒSÄ is to squeeze or press.

> **BRANCHES:** To treat IE *wes* (wet), רבש / (DI)VÄS(H) is dew or honey and יבש / (YA)VÄS(H) means dry.
> See "BISON," "SAP" and "SAUCE."

OPAQUE/קְפָאוֹן
QEY – PAH – (OWN)   [QPA→P–Q]

ROOTS: OPAQUE (impenetrably dense) is allegedly from Latin *opacus* (shady). קפאון / KĒP(ÄON) is translated "dark" or "thick" in *Zechariah 14:6* –"There shall not be light, but heavy clouds and *thick*..."

OR/אוֹ
OWE   [OW→OWR]

ROOTS: One can either accept the given source of this conjunction (Anglo-Saxon *othth* – a form of "OTHER") *OR* the Hebrew אוֹ / O or ŌW (or). In New England the R in OR is merely pronounced as a weak W.

> **BRANCHES:** Other וֹ / Ō, V, W to R changes are documented at "CHECKMATE" and elsewhere. Reverse *reu* for "or" in Thai. The Dutch "or" is closer to אוֹ / ŌV; the Spanish "or" is also *o*.

ORCHE(S)T(RA)/ רָקַד
ROCK – U(D)T   [R – K – DT]

ROOTS: Greek *orkheisthai* is to dance; רקד / ROKUDT is to dance – as David does in *I Chronicles 15:29*. To ORCHESTRATE (before the term got associated with music) must have resembled the verb in *Psalms 29:6* הרקיד / (HĒ)RKĒD ("to make skip" or dance).

> **BRANCHES:** The ORC (Latin *orca* is a dolphin whale) is nature's dancer on the seas; ARCTIC(S), Greek *arktikos* means "of the bear", represents the most accomplished dancer among land animals. Bear in Modern Greek is *arkou'da*.
> The ORCHID is named for its resemblance to male reproductive equipment. The verb ROCK (from IE base *reg* – to push with a pole), the ROCKET, ROCK N' Roll, and the ROCKETTES all attest to the sexuality which the West associates with dance.

ORGAN/ אִרְגּוּן
EAR – GOON   [ARG]

ROOTS: Latin *organum* and Greek *organon* are terms that mean instrument, implement or engine. The IE root is *werg* (to do).

Man's first real ORGAN or ORGANIZED machine was the loom or shuttle (ארג / EREG). The first "machines" in America, for instance, were spinning wheels. The weaver (אורג / ŌRĀG or AVRG) was emblematic of the craftsman, and weaving (ארג / ORĀG) became synonymous with manufacturing in Indo-European languages.

ארג / ORĀG is seen in *Judges 16:13* or *Isaish 59:13*.

> **BRANCHES:** ארגון / ĒRGOON is an ORGANIZATION. See "ARCHITECT" for related terms of arrangement. Cognates of ORGAN include ALLERGY, ARGON, BOULEVARD, BULWARK, CHOLINERGIC, DEMIURGE, ENERGY, EXERGUE, EXOERGIC, GEORGIC, LITURGY, METALLURGY, ORGANON, ORGY, SURGERY, SYNERGISM, THAUMATURGE, WORK, WRIGHT and WROUGHT.

OR(IENTATION)/ עָר
OR   [OR]

ROOTS: Latin *oriens* (direction of the rising sun) is from Latin *oriri* (to arise) and the IE root *er* (to move, set in motion).

Similarly, עורר / ŌRĀR is to "wield" (a sword in *II Samuel 23:18*) or be roused. עור / OR (the infinitive) means "to rouse oneself" or "to awake." The common denominator is to stir

(move or rise from sleep). העיר / (HĀ)ĒR is to stir up; ער / AR is "awake" (*Songs 5:2*).

> **BRANCHES:** The official cognates of ORIENT are ABORT, ARE, ART, EARNEST, ORIGIN and ORIGINAL. GREGORY and GREGORIAN are from Greek *egeirein* (to awaken) – from the gutteral, ORIENTAL way of pronouncing ער / GĀR.
> Being awake and aware involves being in touch with one's senses. Therefore עור / ŌR (skin – see "CHROME"), the most extensive organ of touch and sensation, is related. The antonym spelled exactly the same as the words for "arising," "arousal" and "skin" is עור / EVER (blind). Pronouncing the ו of our term עור / ĀVŌR or ĀWOR (awake) leads us to AWARE – see "TARIFF."
> עיר / EER or GEER is a watcher or GUARD (*Daniel 4:10*). To guide one's ORIENTATION to terms of awareness that arose from עור / OR, AVR or AWR, presented here are the cognates of "aware" at IE root *wer* (to perceive, watch out for): ARCTURUS (Greek *ouros* is a guard), AWARENESS, EPHOR, FIELDFARE, GUARD, PANORAMA, REARWARD, REVERE, REWARD, STEWARD, WARD, WARDEN, WARDER, WARDROBE, WARE and WARY.
> YARE (ready, active), from Anglo-Saxon *gearo*, should be related. The R→L change brings up the verb עלה / ĀLĀ (to go up, ascend) – see "ALLEY." ORIENTALS in China use the term *li* when saying "to rise up." *Heree* is awake in Finnish; *ara* is to awake in Proto-Polynesian.

(ORI)GIN/ עַיִן
GA – YIN   [GYN]

ROOTS: IE root *gen* (to give birth, beget) is the given source of ORIGIN. In the entry "ORIENTATION," the "ORI" half of ORIGIN was discussed. It is the ORiental languages that help one to see the origin of *GEN*ERATE and ORI*GIN*. In Chinese, as in Hebrew, the words for eye, source and spring are similar (*yan/yuan*). Pronouncing the ע as a G (Hebrew's Eastern pronounciation), Chinese helps one think of עין / ĀYIN or GĀYIN (source, spring) in terms of ORIGINATING and not merely as a wellspring GENERATING water. עין / GYN is translated "fountain" in *Deuteronomy 8:7*; מעין / (M)Ā'YĀN or (MA)GAYAN is a fountain or source.

> **BRANCHES:** Alternative ties to words like GENESIS are קנה / KĀNĀ (to create – *Genesis 14:19*), קנה / KONEH (stalk, stem – *Genesis 41:5*) or קן / KĀN (nest – *Deuteronomy 22:6*). The IE root *gena* or *gen* (to give birth, beget...) has extensive branches. From Old Englilsh comes KIN, KINDRED and KING. A Germanic source offers KIND, KIND, KINDERGARTEN, KRISS and KRINGLE. From Latin there's CONGENIAL, GENDER, GENERAL, GENERATIVE, GENERATION, GENERIC GENEROUS, GENRE, GENUS, DEGENERATE, ENGENDER and MISCEGENATION. A Greek term bears -GEN, GENEALOGY, GENOCIDE, GENOTYPE, -GENY, and HETEROGENEOUS. Latin ingenuity came with ENGINE, INDIGENOUS, INGENIOUS, INGENUOUS, GERM, GERMAN, GERMANE, GERMINAL and GERMINATE. GENESIS and -GENESIS are Greek. Latin *gignere* begot GENITAL, GENETIVE, GENITOR, GENT, GINGERLY, CONGENITAL, PRIMOGENITURE, PROGENITOR and PROGENY. Latin also bore AGNATE, BENIGN, COGNATE, CONNATE, ENATE, INNATE, MALIGN, NAIVE, NASCENT, NATAL, NATION, NATIVE, NATURE, NÉE, NOEL, PUNY and RENAISSANCE. The final segment of the AHD's entry cites EPIGONE, GONAD and GONO- from Greek.
> See "GENIUS" and "KIN."

OR(IOLE)/אוֹר
ORE   [AUR]

ROOTS: ORIOLE, the brightly colored bird, is linked to the IE root *aurum* (gold). French *or* (gold) is related. An AUREOLE is a halo of radiance or a band of light, as around the sun. Latin *aureus* also appears in AUREATE: the AURORA borealis are the northern lights. Aurora is the Roman godess of dawn and *aurum* is gold.

Three verses into the Hebrew Bible we get the creation-command, "Let there be *light*"– אוֹר / OR (light, fire, shine). *Genesis 1:4* opens with the verb of seeing, ראה / R–A–H, echoing the word for light. Only the primordial language links light and vision. The אורים / UR(IM) of the Yale motto and of *Exodus 28:30* are oracular gems (which might have influenced the word ORA(CLE).

Jonathan's eyes "lit up"–ארו / OROO in *I Samuel 14:29*. חרוץ / HÄR[OOTS] is gold; the Aramaic term for yellow or gold, *hara*, more closely resembles Latin *aur(um)* or gold. חרה / HÄRÄ is to burn or kindle – see "IRE."

> **BRANCHES:** The candelabra of lit up branches here includes ORIODE, URANIUM and URN (from Latin *urere*, to burn). LIGHT is what wakes us; אור / ORE (light) therefore sounds like ער / ERE (awake). The ו of אור functions as a vowel like O or as a consonant like V. The latter rendition brings two antonyms to light: 1) אפל / ÄFÄL (dark) and 2) עור / ÉVER (blind). Reverse the AUR of our Hebrew etymon and get RA the Egyptian sun god. In Chinese, sun is *ri*. Hawaiian has no R; its word for sun and day is *la*. Malay dialects also have vowel-liquid sun terms.
> (מ)אור(מ) / (MA)ORE is a luminary, especially the sun (*Genesis 1:16*). *Mahira* is the sun in the oldest recorded Indo-European language (Sanskrit). *Haeru* is to shine in Japanese.

OR(OLOGY)/הָר
HOR   [HR]

ROOTS: OROLOGY, the study of mountains, is from Greek *oros* (mountain).
הר / HÄR (*Genesis 8:4*) is a mountain or hill. HILL or Old English *hyll* (hill) should get its double L from the double liquid (L or R) of הרר / HERER (mountain).

> **BRANCHES:** ORO- is a combining form for mountain words like OROGENESIS, OROGENY, OROGRAPHY and OROMETER. Latin and Greek ORESTES is from the same source. Dropping the H in favor of a vowel goes all the way back to ARARAT of Noah's time. There may be no place name on earth in longer continuous use than this Turkish mountain range named from הררי / HERERE (mountainous). Between הר / HÄR and נל / GAL (mound) we find the usual G–H–K interchanges with terms like Spanish *colina* or *cerro* (hill), Russian and Polish *gora* (mountain) and Czech *hora* (mountain – closest to הר / HÄR).
> The Geologist-Linguist who made הר / HÄR made opposites like חר / HOR (hole) and חלל / KHÄLÄL or HÄLÄL (hollow).
> The Harz mountains of Germany are recalled. נל / GAL is also a wave; *kleun* is the Thai wave.

(ORTHO)DOX/דֵעַ
DAY–AKH   [D–KH]

ROOTS: Latin *docere* (to teach) is a match for הורע /

(HO)DÄKH (to inform, make known – *Leviticus 4:23*), while Greek *dokein* (to think) parallels דע / DÄKHÄ (opinion, knowledge, wisdom – *Job 32:10, Isaiah 28:9*).
דעת / DÄKHÄS is knowledge in *Exodus 31:3*; מדע / (MÄ)DÄKH is science or knowledge. Related is דק / DÄK (to scrutinize) and דקדקן / DUKDIKÄN (pedant, grammarian). A דעתן / DUKHTÄN (obstinate person) is too ORTHO*DOX*.

> **BRANCHES:** From the Latin and Greek above come DOCENT, DOCILE, DOCTOR, DOCTRINE and DOCUMENT along with DOGMA(TIC), HETERODOX and PARADOX.
> THA(N)K, THI(N)K and THOUGHT, from IE *tong* (think), are related.

OSTEOM(A)/עֶצֶם
ETZ–EM   [O–TS–M→O–ST–M]

ROOTS: OSTEOMA is a bone tissure tumor; Greek *OSTEON* IS A BONE. Of the 36 words of bone to pick (OSPREY to OSTEOTOMY), OSTEOMA is chosen for the heading because of its resemblance to the Hebrew עצם / ETZEM (bone) in SOUND. Most often, only *OSSIS* or *OS* is cited for the Greek term. "This is now *bone* of my *bones*..." *Genesis 2:23* עצם

> **BRANCHES:** Connected to words like ENDOSTEUM and PERIOSTEM at IE root *OST* (bone) is the OYSTER.
> Perhaps STEM belongs here, especially when considering that עץ / ÄTS is a tree (trunk).
> Other ע-צ-ם / O–TS–M words mean body, substance, independence, power and essence – giving us the essence of bone-ness. Other cognates of OSTEOMA include OSSEIN, OSSUARY, OSSIFRAGE, OSSIFY, OSTRACIZE, PERIOSTEM and TELEOST.
> Slavic prefers the harder pronunciation of עצם / K–TS–M as *kost* is a bone in Russian, Czech and Serbo-Croatian. The Hungarian, *csont*, has more of the original linguistic marrow. Favoring the back of עצם / K–(T)Z–M is Chinese *zhōng* (backbone).
> עצם / ÖTZEM means might.

OVER/עָבַר
OV–ARE   [O–BH–R]

ROOTS: OVER as a temporal word has no known origin; עבר / OVAR is past (in time or grammar). All the spacial connotations of OVER were already (כבר / K'VÄR means already, long ago) taken up at "ABERRATION" and "FERRY."

> **BRANCHES:** The past has happened BE*FORE* (Middle English *fore* means before), at some PRIMAL time (Latin *primus* means first or former). The עברי / IVRE (Hebrew) is a miraculously preserved member of a PRIMORDIAL people, speaking עברית / IVRIT (Hebrew), the PREMIER and FOREMOST language. An antonymous link to עבר / AVR or KHVR and כבר / KVR is עבר / OOBÄR (fetus, embryo). קבר / KOVAR (to bury) is rather synonymous. English terms cognate with those FR and PR words mentioned above include FORE-, FIRN, FIRST, FORMER, PRIME, PRIMITIVE and PROW. *PRE*CEDING the son, בר / BAR in Aramaic, is the *pere* (father in French). The prehistoric name for Ireland is *Iveriu*; *owari* is an end or termination in Japanese.

OVIS / כֶּבֶשׂ
(K)EV–ES   [(K)–BH–S]

ROOTS: Latin *ovis* is a sheep; the IE root is sheared down to *owi* (sheep – whence EWE, OVINE and OVIBOS). כבש / (K)EVES is a lamb or sheep (*Genesis 30:40*).

> **BRANCHES:** To get SHEEP, let the third Hebrew letter (S) jump back over the KV of KVS (sheep) to the #1 position. The SKV will recall Anglo-Saxon *sceap* (source of SHEEP). Easier still is a #1–#2 letter switch of כשב / KESEBH (lamb – *Genesis 30:32*) to get *sceap* and SHEEP. Yiddish often retains archaic elements from German. Sheep in Yiddish, *scheps*, may be keeping an end -s dropped in Dutch *schaap*. The initial *S* before the *C*, as usual, may be unhistoric. Norwegian *sav* (sheep) is from either כשב / KESEV (lamb – notice the resemblance to KEVES) or שה / SEH (lamb). Finnish *lammas* (sheep) recalls the llama of South America. Arabaic *souf* is a sheep's wool.

PACE / פָּשַׂע
POS–AH   [PSE]

ROOTS: Latin *passus* means step, stride, pace; פשׂע / PÄSÄ is to march or "step" (*Isaiah 27:4*). PACE is currently traced to the IE root *peta* (to spread).

> **BRANCHES:** פתה / PÄTÄ is to open wide – see "PATIO." For the step that resembles a pedestal, see "BASIS."

PACK / פָּקִיעַ
PICK–(EE–AH)   [PKE]

ROOTS: *Pakke* is Middle English; a Middle Latin equivalent is *paccus*. PACK, like PACKET and PECK, meant a bundle. פקיע / PIKEÄ is a bundle or bunch (of sheaves), related to the פקע / PEKA (ball-shaped ornament) of *I Kings 6:18*.

> **BRANCHES:** The opposite of that which is packed like a פקעת / PIKAS (coil, ball of thread) is inherent in הפקיע / [HE]PHIKEA (to split, unravel). פקק / PIKAK is a cork, stopper or BU[N]G; פקח / POKAKH is to open.

PAD / פֶּדֶר
PUD–(AIR)   [PD(R)]

ROOTS: The dictionary can only guess that PAD is "probably" related to the IE base *bu* or *bhu*, to blow out, swell, inflate. פדר / PÄD(ER) is animal fat (*Leviticus 8:20*) or "suet" padding the kidneys, etc.

> **BRANCHES:** רפד / [RE]PÄD is to PAD or upholster (*Job 17:13*); מרבד / MARBHAD is a rug. See "FAT."

PALL / אָפֵל
(AH)-P(H)AIL   [A–P(H)–L]

ROOTS: Greek *pelios* is dark; PALL is a dark or gloomy

covering – as a pall of smoke.

אפל / (Ä)P(H)ÄL means darkness or gloom; the 9th plague (darkness) employs an extended form of PL in *Exodus 10:23*.

> **BRANCHES:** אפר / ÄPHER is ashes; אפר / ÄPHÄR is an eye mask. אפר / ÄPHOR is grey. For related antonyms see "ALBINO." Cognates with Greek *pelios* at IE root *pel* (pale) include APPALL, FALCON, FALLOW DEER, PALE, PALOMINO, PALLOR, and PELOPS. מאפל / MÄ'ÄPHÄL (darkness – *Joshua 24:7*) might have influenced Greek *nephele* (cloud), the source of NEBULA and NEBULOUS.
> OFFAL, FOUL, VEIL and VIOLET are more distant possibilities. As distant as Hawaii is from Greece and Israel, Hawaiian for dark or black is *poeleele*; the term for black or Negro is *pa'ele*. Hawaiian and Proto-Polynesian *pelapela* means *FILTHY*, dirty and obscene.

PA(L)M / פַּעַם
PA–UM   [PUM]

ROOTS: The PALM of the hand (or foot) was once spelled like *paume* (from the Old French). The L stepped in from the Latin *palma* (linked to IE root *pel*, which means flat or spread). Old French *paume* is the more authentic etymon. The "feet" in *Isaiah 37:25* demonstrate that פעם / PÄUM means foot as well as a step or beat. The ball of the foot, not the flat of it, is intended.

> **BRANCHES:** פעם / PÄUM also means time, and an extended term that beats musical time or metrical feet is the bell or פעמון / PÄUMON. Just as a bell is bulb-shaped, a פעמון / PÄUM(ON) resembles a POM POM, POMPON, POME (Latin *pomum* means apple or fruit) or POMMEL (a round knob). פימה / PEMÄ is fat (*Job 15:27*).
> Via IE root *pomum* (apple – Latin noun of unknown origin) one could add cognates POMACE and POMADE. It is appropriate to see פעמון / PÄUM(ON) as a POME[GRANITE]-shaped thing because it is linked to a gold רמון / REMON ("pomengranite") in the decorative items mentioned in *Exodus 28:34* and elsewhere. *Song 8:2* suggests that the RMN is a juice fruit, more likely a citrus fruit than a pomegranite. "POM" terms in Polish include the orange and tomato; limiting *pomme* (French) to apple is wrong.
> רמון / REMON is not to be limited to a single fruit specie either; it is the probable source of LEMON. (R to L change). The word LEMON is currently believed to have come to Europe via the Arabic *laimun*. Correctly treating LMN or RMN as a generic fruit term, the Arabs call a grapefruit *laimun hindi*. MELON and ORANGE [from Arabic *naran(ji)*] are simply two more ways to slice a רמון / R/L – M/N – N. Lime, the fruit, is currently traced to Arabic *limah*. *Omena* is the Finnish apple.

PANE / פָּנִים
PUN–(EEM)   [PN]

ROOTS: A PANE is a flat piece of material, the flat side of something that has many sides. Similarly, a PANEL is a flat piece of wood, etc. that forms a surface.

The second verse in the Bible has the Creator hovering over the "face" or the "surface of" the waters. The Hebrew is פני / PINÄ. פנים / PÄN(EM) means face, countenance, front and surface (*Genesis 43:31*). As a verb, פנה / PÄNÄ is to face (*Genesis 18:22*). Our reference books can only offer

Latin *pannus* (piece of cloth, rag) and the IE root *pan* (fabric) as the source of PANE, PANEL, VANE (which points out or faces wind direction) and PANICLE (see "PANIC").

BRANCHES: דפן / (DŌ)PHEN is a board or partition, another PANEL. A VN surface word like VENEER is currently attributed to Old French *fournir* (to furnish). PAINT (allegedly from Latin *pingere*) is another PN term of surfacing.

Showing the face or appearance is the sense of Greek *phainesthai* and therefore of DIAPHONOUS, EMPHASIS, EPIPHANY, FANTASY, HIEROPHANT, PANT, PHANEROGAM, PHANTASM, PHANTASMAGORIA, PHANTOM, PHASE, PHENO-, PHENOMENON, PHOSPHENE, SYCOPHANT, THEOPHANY and TIFFANY. To VANISH is to never show one's face. As our face precedes us, so לפני / (LĒ)PHINĀ (before, in the face of , in front of) was before Old French *avant* (before) in allowing the development of words like VANGUARD, VAM(P), ADVANCE and (AD)VANTAGE. Learning Hebrew is AVANT–GARDE. (The T in words like AVAUNT is not pronounced.)

Other entries will PAN out over the wide *PANORAMA* of BN, FN, VN or WN words of direction that are WINDING to all four WINDS. See פנים / PINĒM (interior) and the POINTING inward at "*PENETRATION*."

PANIC/פָּנַג
PUN–UG   [PNG→PNK]

ROOTS: PANIC, from PANICLE and Latin *panicula*, originally referred to disordered, irregularly shaped food grasses. פנג / PĀNĀG or PHĀNĀG (*Ezekiel 27:17*) are plants (perhaps balsam) with irregular, scattering flowers. The *Lexicon* cites PANIC, a kind of millet, in defining פנג / PĀNĀG.

BRANCHES: As פנג / PĀNĀG is also a pastry or honey cake, it is possible that PANIC(LE) and פנג / PĀNĀG relate to Latin *panis* (bread) as well as to PANOCHA and PANOCHE (Mexican fudge candy). As the balsam flower bursts and scatters seeds when ripe, so a group of people scatters with hysteria or PANIC. Our dictionary credits Pan the Greek faun with (emotional) PANIC – with the flimsy notion that Pan inspired sudden fear.

A disorderly PANICLE or flower cluster appears on the corn stalk of another plant from which bread is made. Corn PONE is an Algonquin Indian word for corn bread or cake. The Indians of Virginia called bread *apân*. Pan isn't just bread in Spanish (with variations throughout IE); *pan* is also bread in Japanese – (the Korean variation is *ppang*). The AHD links PANICLE to Old English *fana* (flag, banner) at IE root *pan* (fabric). The waving tassels atop corn and other grain stalks do resemble the PANACHE of BANNERS or PENNANTS atop castle towers or lances. An NP→PN reversal of הניף / (HĀ)NĒPH (to shake, FAN) and נוף / NŌPH (boughs of a tree), along with פנה / PĀNĀ (turning to and/or away), also contributes to the literal and figurative sense of plant and human PANIC. People clear out when PANIC sets in; פנה / PĒNĀ is to clear out (*Genesis 24:31*). See PAN at "POINT" (another term of outwardness), and more pointing at "PANE."

PARK/פָּרֶק
PAR–UK   [PRK]

ROOTS: From Old French *parc*, a PARK is an enclosed area set aside (or broken off) for special use. PARKING a car is not placing something in a *parc* (enclosure) but breaking off from one's traveling. פרק / PEREK is just such a break or "section." פרקה / PERKĀ is a division; פריקה /PIRĒKĀ is

breaking up; פרק / PĀRĀK is to free or save; and פרק / PĀRUK is to sever, break or remove (*Genesis 27:40*).

BRANCHES: פרכת / PĀRŌKH(ET) is a curtain (*Exodus 26:31*); a similar space breaker is Greek *phragma* (fence – source of DIAPHRAGM). Cognates of DIAPHRAGM at IE root *bhrekw* (to cram together) are FARCE, FARCI FARCY, FREQUENT and INFARCT. Closer relatives of your neighborhood PARK are PARCEL and PARQUET.
Much more at "*BREAK*."

PART/פְּרָט
PRUT   [PRT]

ROOTS: PART is said to come from Latin *pars* and the IE root *pera* (to grant, allot).

פרט / P'RĀT is a PARTICULAR or detail; פרט / PĀRĀT is to specify or be PARTICULAR; פרטי / PIRĀTE means private, single or SEPARATE. פרט / PERET in *Leviticus 19:10* infers "individual" neglected grapes (as translated by Aryeh Kaplan). פטר / PATAR is to separate (*I Samuel 19:10*); פטר / PETER is that which separates.

BRANCHES: פרידה / P'RĒDĀ is a PARTICLE; פרוד / PĀROODT is SEPARATE or APART; and פרוד / PĀROODT is SEPARATION or DEPARTING. The IE root spearates PART from APART and DEPART; the only like-sounding cognates listed are BIPARTITE, COMPART(MENT), and IMPART.

FRATERNITY sounds akin to פרט / PRT or PH – R – T. Perhaps a *PATRIARCHAL* society named the FATHER and BROTHER for the male members who IMPART or split up (בתר / BOTĀR or BHOTHĀR is to cut up or PART) the inheritance, and for those BRATS who receive the בתר / BETER (piece, part – *Genesis 15:10*).

If there is a connection between Latin *pater* (father) and the ("unknown origin") source of PETRO-, PETRIFY and PETER, it may be that a *petros* (rock, stone in Greek) is but a PART or piece of a larger geological whole. פרור / PĀROOR (crumb, fragment) best demonstrates the fractional sense of these פר / PR words. FRITTER (a small piece, fragment) is related. See "PATRON."

(PATCH)OULI/עָלֶה
OL–EH   [OLH]

ROOTS: It is not a household word, but this East Indian plant that produces a fragrant oil is in *Webster's* . The second element is the Tamil (Southern India) word *ilai* (leaf). עלה / OLEH is a leaf; Jonah's dove plucks an olive *leaf* in *Genesis 8:11*.

BRANCHES: Leaves that bear oil make one suspect an influence of עלה / OLEH on OIL – see "SESAME." *La* is a Vietnamese leaf; it is *lav* in Hawaiian and Tongan, and *le* in Maya. More leaves at "TROPHY."

PATE/פֹּת
POTE   [PT]

ROOTS: The dictionaries all agree on this one – the origin is "unknown." PATE means the head. פת / PŌT is translated "head" in *Isaiah 3:17* (JPS, 1978).

BRANCHES: פרחת / PĀDT(ĀHĀT) is the forehead. PT backwards is "top," and PATE often refers to the top of the head. See "TOP."

PATIO/פָּתָה
PA–TAH   [PTH]

ROOTS: Latin *patere* is to open; the IE root is *pet* to (spread). פתה / PÄTÄ is to open wide; פתח / PÄTÄH is to open (*Genesis 7:11*); פצה / PÄTSÄ is to open a mouth or to set free (*Genesis 4:11*); פצח / PÄTSÄH is to burst or open.

    BRANCHES: פצל / PĒTSÄL (to divide, split, branch off) is especially suited to PETAL. Cognates of PETAL at the IE root above include FATHOM, EXPAND, PACE, PAS, PASS, PAN, PATEN, PATENT, PATINA and PATULOUS. Our entry, PATIO, is linked to Latin *patere* (to lie open). PATELLA is also traced to *patere*, and a word like PATH ought to get an opening here beside PACE and PASS. PT and BT words for door (פתח / PETÄH is a doorway, entrance or opening) in dialects of Malay include *bata*, *pi(n)to* and *yebuteh*. A mountain PASS, linked to Latin *passus* (stretched out), might be linked to פסה / PASA (to spread, be extended) and פשה / PASHA (to spread out) as well.

    Related to the PT words here are PS terms from Latin *fissus* (split) like FISSION, FISSURE and FISTULA.

    A TRESS*PASS* may link up with פשיעה / PISHĒA (tresspass, crime of negligence). This PS term is a moral opening or gap, just as a PAUSE is an opening in time. PAUSE recalls פסח / PASAH (to PASS or skip over) and פסק / PASAK (to pause, interrupt). SKIP might be an anagram of these last two Hebrew words.

PATR(ON)/פָּטַר
PA–TERE   [PTR]

ROOTS: A PATRON of ancient Rome was one who freed a slave; the AHD's IE root is *pater* (father). פטר / PÄTAR is to set free or "dismiss" (*II Chronicle 23:8*).

    A פזרן / PÄSRON is generous; the מפזר / [MI]FAZÄR of *Proverbs 11:24* is "one who gives freely."

    The FATHER also cuts up (בתר / BHÄTÄR – *Genesis 15:10*) the family's food.

    BRANCHES: A family itself is a cut or detail פרט / P'RAT – see "PART") from the larger tribe. Family is *patria* in Latin. The PATRICIAN (aristocrat, administrator) evokes PRT terms like פרתם / PÄRTÄM (elder, leader – *Esther 1:3*) and פריץ / PÄRETS (nobleman – see "PROTOTYPE"). Cognates of PATRON not mentioned above include EXPATRIATE, FOREFATHER, PADRE, PATRIARCH, PATRICIDE, PATRILINEAL, PATRIOT, PATRIMONY, PATRONIZE, PATRONYMIC, PATROON and SYMPATRIC.

PAUCITY/פָּחוּת
PA–KHOOT   [P–KH–T]

ROOTS: PAUCITY (fewness, scarcity) is from French *paocite*, Latin *paucus* (few) and the IE root *pau* (few, little). פחות /PÄKHOOS means less, minus or inferior; פחת / POKHUS is to lessen or diminish; פחיתות / PIKHĒSOOS or פחת / PIKHÄT means diminution; פחתת / PIKHESES is a fret (threadbare, decay of fabric – *Leviticus 13:55*). פחיתה / PIKHĒSÄ is crushing or flattening.

    BRANCHES: Cognates of PAUCITY include CATCHPOLE, ENCYCLOPEDIA, FEW, FILLY, FOAL, PAGE, PARAFFIN, PAUPER, PEDO-, POCO, POOR, PONY, POOL, POVERTY, PULLET and PUSILLANIMOUS. PICA, PICAYUNE, PICCOLO and PICOT may belong here too. פעט / POKHUT is to decrease or diminish; see next entry. *Pooku* means little (said of money) in Yoruba (Hamitic).

PED(IATRICIAN)/פָּעוֹט
PA–OD(T)   [PET→PED]

ROOTS: The PED of PEDIATRICIAN, PEDANTIC, PEDAGOGUE and PEDERAST is from Greek *paidos* (child). In talmudic Hebrew פעוט / PÄODT is a child or minor; פעוט / PÄOODT means small or young. בת / BÄT is a daughter (*Genesis 29:10*) or a generic term for children (*Isaiah 62:11*).

    BRANCHES: Reverse the captioned term to get טף / TÄPH or DÄPH (children – *Jeremiah 40:7*). Arabic uses *tifl* for "child." "Daughter" in Indonesian is *puteri*; in Tahitian it's *poti'i*; and in Swahili *bi(n)ti*. *Putra* means son in Sanskrit; RAJ*PUT* is a member of a ruling caste of northern India. Other PT terms of littleness include PET, PETIT(E), PETTICOAT, PETTIFOY and PETTY. See "PAUCITY."

PEEK/פָּקַח
PEEK–AY–AH   [PKH]

ROOTS: PEEK (glance or look) is from Middle English *piken*, but the scholars cannot find an earlier source. They should have taken a PEEK–A–BOO at the Hebrew Bible. In *Exodus 23:8* ("a gift blindeth *them that have sight*") a sighted person is a פקח / PĒKÄÄH. Earlier, at *Exodus 4:11*, the term is rendered "seeing:"

      "And the Lord said unto [Moses]:
      Who hath made Man's mouth?
      or who maketh a man dumb, or deaf,
      or *seeing*, or blind?
      Is it not I the Lord?"

    BRANCHES: פקח / PAKOH is an inspector. Arabic *faqqaha* means "he opened the eyes."

(PEGA)SUS/עָף + סוּם
(GAPH)–SOOS   [GP+ SS→PGSS]

ROOTS: The "pega" element in the winged horse of Greek mythology parallels Latin *fuga* (flight). Back at "AVIATE" there are several such reversals of Hebrew עף / UF or (with the typical Greek rendering of the ע) GUPH (to fly – *Genesis 1:20*. G–PH flew over to PG in Pegasus.

    The "sus" is no suffix (as "*us*" in Latin), but is an ancient "horse" term from the Middle East. סוס / SOOS is a horse (*Genesis 47:17*). The Akkadian is *sisū*.

    BRANCHES: זז / ZOOZ means "move," what horses do best. The word SYCE in India is a horse groom, officially borrowed from Arabic *sus* (to tend a horse). The more travelled Hebrew horse is the רכש / REKHESH (fast mount, steed – *I Kings 5:8*). Switch the (K)H and the R to get HORSE. In one German horse word, *Ross*, the (K)H retained in Old High German *hros* is lost altogether. A second German horse is the *Pferd* – straight from פרד / PERED (mule – *Zechariah 14:15*).

    In *Exodus 14:23* is found both the רכב / REKHEBH (rider or chariot – from a similar verb of riding) and the פרש / PÄRÄSH (horseman). Swahili prefers the latter, as *farasi* is their horse word. The former term may be preferred by the Japanese. Japanese keeps the R and B, as *roba* is a donkey. Then, keeping the K and B of רכב / R–KH–BH, *kiba* means horseback.

    The MULE is easily (R→L change) from the חמור / (HÄ)MŌR (ass – *Genesis 22:3*). The MARE might be riding alongside. The

Chinese *ma* and Japanese *uma* are "horse" words that could also come from the MR word רמך / RÄMÄKH (race horse). See "KIBITZ."

PEN(CHANT)/פְּנִיָּה
PIN – EE –YAH   [PN]

ROOTS: PENCHANT infers a strong inclination or liking. The etymology shold have stopped with French *pencher* (to incline), but it goes on to cite Latin *pendere* (to hang). We naturally incline or point towards that which we desire. פניה / PINĒYÄ (inclination, design, motive) is a natural extension of פנה / PÄNÄ (to turn). One cannot literally "turn to" prayers or to other gods, so that the PN turning verbs in *I Kings 8:28* or *Deuteronomy 31:18* might better be rendered "incline towards" and "venerate."

לפנות / (LĒ)PHIN(ŌS) means "toward" in *Genesis 24:63* – see "POINT."

> BRANCHES: IE root *wen* (to desire, strive for) lists many varieties of our PN etymon of inclination. A few of these are BANIAN, VENERATE, VENERY, VENEREAL, VENOM, VENUS, WIN and WON(T).
> Chinese *pan* is to long for.

PENE(TRATE)/פְּנִים
PIN – (EEM)   [PN(M)]

ROOTS: Latin *PENITUS* is inward; *penus* means inmost. פנימה / PIN(ĒMÄ) is within (*Leviticus 10:18*); פנימי / PIN(ĒMĒ) is inner (*I Kings 6:27*) and פנים / PIN(ĒM) means interior. Ugaritic *pnm* is "into."

> BRANCHES: For PN words of exteriority see פנים / PÄN[ĒM] (face, surface) at "PANE." Related insiders include: BEN (inner room), BIN, DEFENSE, FENCE, FENCING, FENDER, IMPOUND, PAN (*panzi* is a dish in Chinese), PEN, PENATES, PENT, PINFOLD, POND (retainer for fish), POUND (retainer for dogs), and PUND. POND (whose given IE base is *pan* – slime or mire) is otherwise joined as a derivative of יון / (YÄ)VAN ("mire"– *Psalms 69:3*). The AHD places POND at the IE root *bend* (protruding point) along with IMPOUND, etc. They would then relate to the writing PEN (pointing out), not the pig PEN (holding in) – see "POINT."
> *Pin* means "into" in Maidu (California Indian); reverse to *nei pu* for the Chinese word for inside. *Ane* means "in" in Korean, so it is quite possible that IN is a clipped version of the original PN preposition of interiority. Reverse to *ny* for "in" in Thai. *Bin* is a bottle in Japanese.
> What is more "interior" than a pearl encased within an oyster? פנינה / PINĒNÄ is a pearl (*Lamentations 4:7* or *Proverbs 8:11*). A pearl in Samoan is *penina* too.

PEN(GUIN)/פְּנָה
PEEN–AH   [PN]

ROOTS: PENGUIN is said to derive from Welsh *pen* (head) and *gwyn* (white). White in Irish is *fionn*, so that *(g)wyn*, too, is possibly linked to לבן / (LÄ)BHÄN (white – see "ALBINO.") The Welsh head (*pen*) also appears in *PENDRAGON* (the title of the supreme leader in ancient Britain). פנות / PĒN(ŌT) are also the heads and leaders of ancient Israel as seen in *I Samuel 14:38*. Physically, the head is a high extension. פנה / PĒNÄ is also a parapet.

BRANCHES: פנה / PĒNÄ is usually translated corner. The concordance's primary Latin translation is *pinna* (wing, feather, arrow and battlement atop a wall). All of these tie in with "head" and "corner" because they are narrow projections extending from a larger body. פנה / PĒNÄ is a "high tower" in *Zephania 1:16*.

The famous rejected stone of *Psalms 118:22* is predicted to become the ראש פנה / RŌSH PĒNÄ (head pēnä). It might better be described as becoming the keystone (highest and most significant) rather than the "chief cornerstone" (which is awkward and redundant). A BEN, from Scottish and Irish, is a mountain peak. Among the sharp PN terms we get from פנה / PĒNÄ are APPENDAGE, APPENDIX, FANG, FIN, FINCH, FINGER, PAIN, PANG, PEN, PENCIL, PENIS, PINCER, PINEAPPLE, PINE, PINION, POIGNANT, POINT (the noun), PONIARD, PONTIFF, PORCUPINE, PUNCTUAL, PUNCTURE, and SPINE. Left out are the given IE roots because it is hard to see PENCIL deriving from *pes* (penis), or PINNATE and PINNULE coming from IE *pet* (to fly, rush). Reversing פן / PN offers more sharp things.

See "NIB," "NIP," and "POINT."

PEN(ULTIMATE)/פָּנָה
PAN –AH   [PN]

ROOTS: The PEN- of PENULT(IMATE), PENUMBRA and PENNINSULA is from Latin *paene* (almost).

פנה / PÄNÄ is facing; פנים / PÄNĒ(M) is front or surface; and לפנות / (LĒ)PHIN(ŌS) means close to or near (*Judges 19:26*). These terms imply proximity.

> BRANCHES: לפני / (LĒ)PHINÄ is "before," as is a Punic PN term.
> See "PANE."

PEPPER/פִּלְפֵּל
PILL – POOL   [P(L)PL→PPR]

ROOTS: Greek *peperi* is a pepper, but the Sanskrit *pippali* (pepper) is "a noun of unknown origin." *Pippali* is the IE root. פלפל / PĒLPÄL (pepper) is a talmudic word, but the Aramaic פלפלתא / PĒLPÄLTÄ is even older. Arabic pepper is *filfil*, the source of FALAFEL. Swahili pepper, *pilipili*, also prefers L to R.

> BRANCHES: The listed cognates of PEPPER are PEEPUL and PIMPERNEL, but PAPRIKA and PEPPERCORN should be included. The AHD defines Sanskrit *pippali* as "berry." See "BERRY." The PL of the pepper plant might be named for a resemblance to the פלך / PELEH (spindle – *Proverbs 31:19*).

PERK/פְּרַע
PERR – UCK   [P–R–KH]

ROOTS: The dictionaries don't know where PERK came from, but one theory is "probably from Old Norman French *perquer* (to perch)." Perching is too sedentary for the PERKY (spirited, jaunty) senses of the word. PERK is "to raise, as the head, briskly or spiritedly."

פרע / PERÄKH is a verb of spirited behavior, rendered "broken loose" in *Exodus 32:25*. It literally (and thus figuratively) means letting the hair down in *Ezekiel 44:20* or "unrestrained" in *II Chronicles 28:19*.

> BRANCHES: פרק / PÄRÄK (to throw off, free) and even פרח / PERÄKH (flower) are related.
> See "FREE" and "FREAK."

PERSIMMON/אֲפַרְסְמוֹן
AH – PHAR – SIM – MOAN   [PR+SMN]

ROOTS: This tree with plumlike fruit is traced to *pasimenan*, Algonquin and Cree Indian terms meaning "dried fruit." אפרסמון / ÄPHÄRSIMŌN (balsam, persimmon) is a Talmudic word, but a clear combination of פרי / PRĒ (fruit) and סמים / SÄMIM ("spices"–*Exodus 25:6*).

> **BRANCHES:** BALSAM, the other defintion of אפרסמון / (Ä)PÄRSIM(ŌN) and a possible corruption of this term, could also be an extended form of בשם / BŌSEM (perfume, spice – *Exodus 35:28*). The dictionary insists that both BA(L)SAM and BALM are from Greek *balsamon* (an aromatic mint or fragrance). APRICOT is another PR fruit, not attributed to אפרסק / APÄRSÄK (peach) or to פרי / PRĒ (fruit – see "BERRY" and "FRUIT").

PESTER/פָּצַר
PA – TSUR   [P–TS–R→P–ST–R]

ROOTS: To PESTER (annoy repeatedly) is said to derive from Latin *pastus* (to feed), but "influenced by" Latin *pestis* (a plague). פצר / PÄTSÄR is to press or urge (*Genesis 19:3* – "urged greatly").

PET(ARD)/פָּצַץ
PA – T(SUTS)   [P–T(S)–TS]

ROOTS: PETARD (an explosive to force an opening in a wall) is traced to Latin *pedere* and the IE root *pezd* (to break wind). פצץ / PÄTSÄTS is to explode (*Jeremiah 23:29; Job 15:12*).

> **BRANCHES:** פרץ / PÄRÄTZ is to burst, break through, breach – a #2-#3 root letter swap resembles PETAR(D). See "BREACH" and "BURST."

PHON(ETICS)/נִיב
NEEV   [N–BH→PH–N]

ROOTS: The (TELE)PHONE we speak with and the PHONOGRAPH we hear are from Greek *phōnē* (voice) and *phanai* (to speak). The highly inclusive IE root is *bha* (to speak). . פה / PEH (mouth) can mean "word;" פוח / POOAH is "uttered;" פום / POOM is a mouth (Aramaic). -PHASIA and PROPHET are traced to Greek *phanai*; reverse the PH – N to N – PH or N – BH and נביא / NÄBHĒ is a prophet. נבא / NĒBHÄ is to prophecy (*Numbers 11:25*). ניב / NĒBH means idiom, speech or dialect; נב / NÄBH is to utter. נבע / NÄBHÄ is to voice; נבח / NÄBHÄH is to bark (*Isaiah 56:10*).

> **BRANCHES:** Cognates of PHONETICS include BAN(ISH) BOON, CACOPHONY, EUPHONY, (DE)FAME, (IN)FAMOUS, EUPHEMISM, ANTHEM, PHONEME, PHONETIC, PHONO-, -PHONY, and SYMPHONY.

Latin *fari* (to speak) is also a listed cognate; דבר / (DA)BHÄR is to speak. Other words at this root are found at "BID." One figurative citation for ניב / NĒBH in *Isaiah 57:19* might be said to contain much of the message of this book: "Peace, peace, to...far...and near, saith the Lord that createth the fruit of the lips."

PHOS(PHORUS)/פָּז
PUSZ   [PZ]

ROOTS: PHOSPHORESCENT materials glow; PHOSPHORUS becomes yellow when exposed to light. Greek *phos* means light and the IE root is said to be *bha* (to shine). פז / PÄZ or PHAZ is fine gold in *Psalms 19:11*; מופז / (MOO)PHÄZ is similar in *I Kings 10:18*. הפז / HÄPHÄZ is to shine.

> **BRANCHES:** There are over 20 words like PHOSPHATE, and over 150 related PHOTO- terms like PHOTOGRAPHY and PHOTOELECTRIC. See "TOPAZ."

PHRASE/מִפֹרֶשׁ
(MIH) – PHOR – AS(H)   [P–R–SH]

ROOTS: PHRASE is from Greek *phrazein* (to point out, show). מפרש / (MI)PHŌRÄSH means explained; פרש / PÄRÄSH is to clarify, explain or interpret. Greek *phrazein* can simply mean "to declare;" לפרש / (LĒ)PHRŌSH in *Leviticus 24:12* is "to declare."

> **BRANCHES:** Cognates of PHRASE include HOLOPHRASTIC, METAPHRASE, PARAPHRASE and PERIPHRASIS. See "PREACH."

PICK /פָּקַע
PUCK – AH   [PKU]

ROOTS: To PICK is to break up, as with a PICK or sharp instrument; it also means selecting or choosing – PICKING ON or PICKING OUT. The AHD lumps the two PICKs together with the etymology, "probably from Latin *picus* (woodpecker)." The PICK of selection is from פקד / POK(ÄD) – to assign or "appoint" in *Genesis 39:4*. בחר / BOKH(ÄR) is to choose. For the PICK of a PICKAX, *Webster's* came closer suggesting the influence of Old French *piquer* (to pierce). פקע / PÄKÄ is to burst or split; פקע / PEKÄ is a crack; בקע / BÄKÄ is to cleave or split (*Genesis 22:3*). פכר / PÄKÄR is break in Aramaic.

> **BRANCHES:** פקח / PÄKÄH is to open wide (*Genesis 3:7*). *Pekac* is to split, burst or break in Polish. A dimple is not as deep as a POCKET and is more attractive than a POCKMARK. A Chinese dimple is a *wa ch'u*. As בקיה / BĒKÄH is a valley or gorge (perhaps riven by a river), so *bekan* is a river in Maya Indian. PECK and various PIKEs may relate. More PK or BK *cavities* at "VACATE."

PIECE/פְּתִית
PA–CEASE   [PSS]

ROOTS: There is no IE root available for PIECE, but suggestions for an etymon include Old French *pece*, Late Latin *pettia* and a Celtic source seen in Welsh *peth* (little). פתית / PÄSĒS, PÄTHĒS or PÄTĒT is a crumb, fragment, bit or "piece" in *Leviticus 2:6*. פסה / PĒSÄ is a piece or slice; in *Genesis 37:3* it means PATCHES in the quiltlike coat of many colors.

> **BRANCHES:** פתת / PÄSÄS or PÄTÄT is to crumble or break up (in the same *Leviticus 2:6* as above). There are PIECE words like פת / PÄS or PÄT ("morsel"– *Genesis 18:5*) and פסג / PĒSÄG (to split or sever).
> בתר / BS(R) or BT(R) is both a verb and noun of pieces and of cutting into pieces – see Abraham's piecemaking at *Genesis 15:10*. בצר / BÄTÄR is to dissect, בתק /BĒTÄK is to cut and בדל / BODTAL is to separate. These BT and BD BITS are listed at IE root *bheid* (to split). Cognates of BIT and BITE include ABET, BAIT, BATEAU, BEETLE, BITTER, BOAT, BOATSWAIN, -FID, FIDDLE, FISSI-, FISSILE, FISSION and FISSURE. See "DIVIDED."

PILE/פְּרַע
PERE–AH   [PR→PL]

ROOTS: PILE carpeting is related to PILOSITY (hairiness). Latin *pilus* and the IE root *pilo* means hair. פרע / PERÄ means hair (*Numbers 6:5; Ezekiel 44:20*) – a common R to L change is required. פרוה / PÄRVÄ is fur.

> **BRANCHES:** Listed cognates of the hariy PILE are CATERPILLAR, DEPILATE, PELAGE, PILAR, PILEUS, PILLAGE, PILOCARPINE, PILOSE, PILUS, PLUCK, PLUSH and POLLU. Not listed were PILEATE, PILIFEROUS, and PILIFORM. PELT, PILLION (a cushion made of furry hide) and PILLOW may be related. Switching to FL may lead to more loose threads like FELT, FILAMENT, FILTER and FILIUM. The פרעש / PÄRŌSH (FLEA– *I Samuel 24:15*) is a lousy (louse-like) parasite that might also be rooted in these hairy PR, FR, FL, PL terms. WOOL and *FLEECE* may be related, as Proto-Polynesian *fulu* means FUR, wool or fleece. Arabic פרוה / PÄRVÄ or FÄRVÄ (fur) is a better etymon for FUR than Old French *fuerre* (sheath).
> FELT is currently traced to the Indo-European root *pel* (to thrust, strike, drive) and is not seen as a derivative of Arabic *libd* (felt– LBD→FLT). The Semitic LB may be turning over to BL in the same way that *BLOOM* and *BLOSSOM* link to Aramaic and Hebrew לבלב / LABHLÄBH (it bloomed, blossomed) or *BLAZE* links up to לבה /LABA (flame – *Exodus 3:2*).

PION(EER)/פָּנָה
PEA–NAH   [P–N]

ROOTS: PIONEER is from *pionnier* and Old French *peonier* (foot soldier). The first sense of the term is that of a military engineer who precedes the troops. PIONEER then meant anyone who goes before and prepares the way for others. The obsolete meaning of PIONEER, a digger or minor, fits the Hebrew etymon below even better.

In *Genesis 24:31* Laban tells Abraham's steward, "Come in, ... I have *cleared* the house, and made room for the camels." The verb used is פנה / PĒNÄ (to remove, empty); the sense is "to clear the way for later use." *Webster's* defines

PIONEER (the verb) as "to prepare or open (a way, etc.)."

> **BRANCHES:** פנוי / PĒNOOY means emptying or clearing. PEON and PAWN (the chessman) are cognates. See "VAIN."

PIRATE/פָּרִיץ
PAR–EAT(S)   [P–R–T(S)]

ROOTS: PIRATE is from Greek *peirates* (pirate); the theoretical IE root is *per* (to try, risk... lead over or press forward). פריץ / PÄRĒT(S) is "a vicious, violent man" in the dictionary. *Jeremiah 7:11* and *Ezekiel 18:10* specify "robbers" in context of "a shedder of blood."

To match the IE root, there's פצר / POTSÄR (to press, urge – swap the R and TS), פרץ / PORÄTS (to press, urge), and פריץ / PHIRĒTS ("ferocious"– *Isaiah 35:9*). See "FERRY" for a PR root of leading over.

> **BRANCHES:** Cognates of PIRATE and PIRACY are FEAR, PERIL, EXPERIENCE, EXPERIMENT, EXPERT and EMPIRE, as listed at IE root *per*. Corresponding to many world leaders, פריץ / PÄRĒTS means not only a vicious man but a "nobleman" and a "prince." The N of PRI(N)CE is unhistoric, a nasalization; the Hebrew is easy to hear after dropping the N. *Prestu* is a nobleman in Basque as well; *Furst* is a German prince. PREDATOR and PREDATORY (living by or characterized by plundering or robbing) are probably PRD, PRT words related to our etymon. Too many rulers or PRINCES have been PREDATROY PIRATES. *BRU*TAL (savage, cruel) is better linked to פריץ / PRT (ferocious) than to its given IE root – *gwer* (heavy).

PIT/פַּחַת
PA–HUT   [PHT]

ROOTS: PIT is traced to Old Norse *pyttr* and to Latin *puteus* (a well).

פחת / PÄHÄT is a cavity or "pit" (*II Samuel 18:17*). פתח / PETÄH is an opening; פתה / POTÄ is a socket.

> **BRANCHES:** English has a PITFALL, PITMAN, PIT SAW and PITTED (pock-marked) surfaces. Read with a hard, gutteral ח / KH, פחת / PÄKHÄT fits with פח / PÄKH (pitfall, can), פך / PÄKH (flast) and בקבוק / BÄKBOOK (bottle – see "BEAKER") as PK or BK words of hollowed containers. English words in this phonetic BOX include POCK, POCKET, POKE, POUCH and POX. These, in turn, are related to KP or KV cavities or concavities found at entries like "CAVE." The noun and verb of opening is *wete* in Proto-Polynesian, and *weka* in the Hawaiian variant. *Bput* is to open or be open in Thai.

PITA/פִּתָּה
PITA   [PTH]

ROOTS: PITA is the Mideastern "pocket" bread. פתה / PĒTÄ is an Aramaic word; it may relate to the פת / PÄT or PÄS eaten in *Genesis 18:5* ("morsel of bread") or *II Samuel 12:3*.

> **BRANCHES:** *BIS*CUIT (originally a hard bread), PIZZA (named for the breadlike crust) and PASTA are possibly related. Considering biscuit as more of a *dough*nut, בצק / BÄTSÄK means dough. PASTE primarily means dough. PASTA is flour PASTE; PASTEL is from PASTE. See "PITCH" for a similar B→P change.

PITCH/זֶפֶת
BOATS   [B–TS→P–TS]

ROOTS: PITCH is said to derive from Middle English *pich* and Latin *pix* or *picis* (pitch). PITCH is the black, sticky substance formed in the distillation of coal tar, etc. בץ / BOTS is mud or mire (*Jeremiah 38:22*); בצה / BĒTSÄ is a marsh or swamp (*Job 40:21*).

> **BRANCHES:** BIT(UMEN) originally meant mineral PITCH; BITUMINOUS coal yields PITCH or tar when it burns. זפת / ZEPHET means pitch; ZPT can be scrambled as PTZ. See "BISON" and "PITA" for similar development.

PIV(OT)/פִּיפִיָה
PEEF–EE–YÄ   [PYFYH]

ROOTS: A PIVOT is the "point, shaft or pin on which something turns."
פיפיה / PĒPHEYÄ is a tooth, prong or edge of a sword – *Isaiah 41:15*.

> **BRANCHES:** Italian *pivolo* is a peg; Old Provencal *pua* (or P–V–A) means the tooth of a flax comb – much like the use of the Hebrew etymon in *Isaiah*.

PIZAZZ/פָּזַז
PEA–ZAYZ   [PZZ]

ROOTS: PIZAZZ rates an "origin unknown" or is dismissed as expressive slang by various dictionaries. PIZAZZ means exuberance, pep, dashing style, flamboyance, zest or flair. פזז / PĒZAZ is to leap, jump or dance (*II Samuel 6:16*), as King David displayed lots of PIZAZZ when rejoicing boisterously before the Lord.

> **BRANCHES:** פזז / PÄZÄZ or FSS is to be agile or quick; פזיז / PÄZĒZ means haste in Aramaic. These words are fine etymons for FAST (rapid), which had been forced to share an etymology with the "firm, stable" FAST. FAST also means "reckless, wild, dissipated and promiscuous." These recall FS words like הפיץ / (HĀ)FĒTS (to scatter) and פתע / FESA (suddenly).

PLAT(OON)/פְּרָט
PRUTT   [PRT→PLT]

ROOTS: A PLATOON of soldiers is a subdivision, a unit or a detail. All these terms precisely define פרט / PRÄT (change R to L). The attempt at a non-Hebrew etymon involves *pelote*, the French term for ball. The thinking behind this is that a ball may be seen as a bunch of units clumped together. See "PART."

PLAZA/פְּרָזָה
PEER–ZA   [PRZ→PLZ]

ROOTS: PLAZA is said to derive from Greek *platus* (flat, broad) and the IE root *plat* (to spread). Effect another ר / R to L change, noting that פרץ / PÄRÄT(S) is to "spread abroad" (*Genesis 28:14*). Closer to PLAZA is פרוז / PÄROOZ (open, unwalled) and פרזה / PĒRZÄ (open or unwalled villages – *Ezekiel 38:11*).

> **BRANCHES:** Cognates of PLAZA at IE *plat* include FLAT, FLATTER and FLOUNDER from Germanic sources; CLAN, FLAN, PLAN, PLANT, PLANTAIN, PLANTAR, PLANTIGRADE and SUPPLANT from Latin; and PIAZZA, PLACE, PLANE, PLATE, PLATEAU, PLATITUDE, PLATY, and PLATYPUS from the Greek. Not included were BLI(N)TZ (a pancake – via Ukranian), BROAD, PLATFORM, and PLATTER. *Platz* in German is an open area; PEL[VIS] is also a dish word.

PLEA/פָּלַל
PEAL–ALE   [PLL]

ROOTS: A PLEA (appeal, entreaty) is from Old French *plai* (a suit or plea). The search for older etymons brings in Latin *placitus* (an opinion) and Latin *placere* (to please, be agreeable). This last term is traced to IE root *plak* (to be flat). פלל / PĒLAL is to entreaty (*Psalms 106:30*). It is defined as "to intercede" as well as "to think, judge." התפלל / (HIT)PÄLÄL is to pray.

> **BRANCHES:** BAILIFF (magistrate), PLEAD and PRAY(ER) should all be related. (PRAY requires and L→R change.) Since lawyers think up PLOYS (origin unknown) to intercede for clients, PLOY is a possible cognate of PLEA. APPEAL and APPELATE, initially from Latin *appellare* (to entreat), belong here rather with the given Indo-European root *pel* (to thrust, strike, drive).

PLOUGH/פָּלַח
POL–UKH   [P–L–KH]

ROOTS: PLOUGH and PLOW are traced to Late Anglo-Saxon *ploh*, which is "akin to German *pflug*...probably a borrowing from non-Indo-European." Arabic פלח / PÄLÄKH or PÄLÄH is a farmer or PLOWBOY; פלחה / PHÄLKHÄ is agriculture. Hebrew פלח / PÄLÄKH is to "cleave" (the earth) in *Psalm 141:7*. In *II Kings 4:39* it is rendered to "slice." The dictionary defines this verb as to till or split.

> **BRANCHES:** Reverse פלח / P–L–KH to get חלף / KHÄLÄPH (to pierce). חרב / KHEREBH is the blade (of a plow). קלף / KÄLÄPH is to remove a surface. פלחן / POOLKHÄN is service or worship; פעל / PÄKHÄL (swap KH and L) is to act or do. WORK and PLUG (work doggedly) are distantly related.
> See "FELLAH" and "BREAK."

PLUCK/פָּרַק
POR–UCK   [PRK→PLK]

ROOTS: PLUCK (to pull off or out) is from Old English *pluccian*, which is "thought by some to be from Latin *pilus* (hair)." (See "PILE.") Simply pronounce פרק / PÄRÄK as a Japanese would. The term means "to remove," "to take out" or "to unload" – *Genesis 27:40* or *Exodus 32:2*.

> **BRANCHES:** Chicken feathers are PLUCKED, FLICKED or FLECKED, and the skinning of animals takes similar sounding terms. FLAY (to strip skin), FLECK, FLESH and FLITCH are traced to the IE root *plek* (to tear). A PELT (animal skin) may be related. Returning to PRK, a PARKA (heavy jacket) is traced by the AHD to the Russian word for pelt. *Webster's* traces the same word to the Aleutian (Alaskan) Indian term for a heavy shirt. In either case, the word should link up with פרקת / PHÄRKÄS (shirt) and Arabic פרוה / PHÄRVÄH (pelt). The Arabic provides

a better etymon for FUR, FURRIER and FURRY than the Old French *fueere* (sheath). More PRK removable skins or jackets include the FROCK, the Spanish *abrigo* (coat) and the Basque *berokia* (coat). FILM is a cognate of PELT listed at IE root *pel* (skin, hide). PLAGIARIZE, from Latin *plagium* (kidnapping), may be another removal term from פרק / PÄRÄK. See "BREAK."

FLEECE and PLU[ME] are cognates at the Indo-European root *pleus* (to pluck).

PLUG/פלג
PEL–EG   [PLG]

ROOTS: A PLUG is a wedge or a piece of tobacco, among other things. The given source is Middle Dutch *plugge* (a BUNGE, plug or BLOCK).

Aramaic פלינ / PLEG (division) and Hebrew פלגה / PÄLGÄ (a BLOCK of people – *Judges 5:15*) lend this word a bit more antiquity. פלג / PELEG is a piece or stream (that has FORKED off from a larger whole or river). For the verb form there's פלג / PELÄG and *Psalms 55:10*, which echoes the belief that God can split language into dialects: "Destroy, O Lord, and *divide* their tongue [speech]...."

> **BRANCHES:** פלח / PHELÄKH is a slice (*Songs 4:3*). FLUGELHORN, from German *flugel* (wing), may relate in the "division" sense of wing. FLUKE, FLOCK, FOLK and many other break-offs are available at "FLAG," "FLAKE" and "BREAK."

POIN(T)/פנה
PON–AH   [PN]

ROOTS: The dictionaries only address the sharp "point" (taken up here at "PENGUIN"), but not the verb of aiming or directing attention to a specific place. Another way to point somewhere is "to face" it; פנים / PÄN(EM) is a face. פנה / PÄNÄ is to turn, to face or to direct attention (*Exodus 2:12*). לפנות / (LE)PHNOS is "toward" in *Genesis 24:63*; פנה / PHÄNÄ can mean WANE, POINT downward or "decline" (*Jeremiah 6:4*).

> **BRANCHES:** The closest IE root is *wendh* (to turn, wind, weave). Its cognates include WANDER, WANDERLUST, VANDAL, WEND, WENTLETRAP, WIND, and WINDLASS. The four WINDS mean the four directions (see "FAN"). צפון / (TSÄ)PHONE means north. *Pina* is "he turned" in Syriac.
> *Peny* is "to bend" in Maidu Indian. BEND and WINCE are verbs of turning inward, while Latin *defendere* means turning away or warding off. From this Latin word we get DEFEND, DEFENCE, FENCE, OFFEND and OFFENSE. FEND, FIND and WENT are direction words that go outward, like BOUND or VANE. For WANTING and other emotional aiming see "PENCHANT." For PN POINTERS that turn inward see "PENETRATE." Pointing every which way recalls the PAN- of PAN-AMERICAN or PANCREAS – see "PANIC" and "PANE."

PORE/פיר
PEER   [PYR]

ROOTS: The last word on PORE (an opening) is Greek *poros* (passage). Aramaic פירא / PERÄ is a ditch; the Hebrew is פיר /PER. חפור / HÄPHOR is to excavate or make holes, passages or channels. פער / PÄUR is a space or gap; פעור / PÄOOR is wide open; and פער / PÄUR is to open wide (*Isaiah 5:14*).

> **BRANCHES:** בור / BOR is a pit – see "BORE." PR openings such as OPPORTUNITY, PORCH, POROUS, PORT and PRY should all be related – see "BREACH."
> Switching to PL, PYLON is from IE *pulē* (gate –"Greek noun of obscure origin.") A RAVINE, RIFT or RIP is merely the reverse of the PR root here – see "TROPHY."

POUT/פטר
POT–(ARE)   [PTR]

ROOTS: POUTING is thrusting out the lips, as in sullenness. After Middle English *pouten*, the dictionary pouts, "probably from Old Norse *puta* (to swell)." For PT swellings see "FAT." But for POUT see פטר / POT[ÄR] (to pout) and *Psalms 22:8* –"all who see me mock me; they *curl* their lips, they shake their heads." The note on this verse in the JPS adds "they open wide with a lip."

> **BRANCHES:** For openers see "PART," "PATRON" and "PIT."

PREACH/פרש
PAW–RUSH   [P–R–SH]

ROOTS: *Prechen* and *precher* of Middle English and Old French are dismissed, as usual, in the search for a classical etymon. The reference books come up with Latin *praedicare* (source of "predict"). *Prae* means before, and *dicere* is to say. To foretell or predict, however, has nothing to do with the expounding or proclaiming of a PREACHER. Moreover, the difference in sound between the Latin etymon and PREACH is significant.

Hebrew suggests פרש / PÄRÄSH (to comment on text, to "take apart" a text by expounding upon it). A פרשן / PARSH(AN) or מפרש / (MI)PHORUSH is an exegete, commentator, or teacher of texts – see "PHRASE." Akkadian *parāshu* is to explain or decide as a judge.

> **BRANCHES:** The splitting and spreading apart of a text is to obtain a פתירה / PISÄRÄ (solution, unraveling) or a פתרון / PISÄR[ON] or *PITARON* (*INTERPRETATION*) – swap #2 and #3 root letters). A פשר / PÄSHER (interpretation, solution) is another unraveling required for a פשל /PÄSHÄL (knot) or פתיל / PISÉL (twisted cord). Knotty questions are PUZZLES that are POSED. See "FUSE." To cover the oratorical rather than the analytical craft of the PREACHER, פרש and פרס / PÄRÄS mean "to spread." בפרוש / (BI)PHÄROOSH is explicit and פרסם / PERSÄM is to publish. A PREACHER is thus a divine publicist. To see English or Old French CH from another ש / SH term in Hebrew, see "BUTCHER."

(PRE)CEDE/קדם
KEED–(AIM)   [KD→CD]

ROOTS: PRECEDE, from Latin *praecedere*, is a combining of *prae* (before) + *cedere* (to move). To PRECEDE is 1) to be or to go before in time or place 2) to introduce with prefatory remarks.

קדם / KED(ÄM) means to PRECEDE, go forward, to greet or to welcome (*Psalms 88:14; 95:2*). The two-letter Hebrew root קד / KD is seen in that part of the body which (should) always take PRECEDENCE, the קדקד / KOD–KOD (the head – *Deuteronomy 33:16* – which goes "ahead" or קדימה / KĀDĒMĀ). See 'CAUDILLO. The hard C we need here is confirmed by the IE root *ked* (to go, yield).

> **BRANCHES:** The "yield" recalls קדד / KODĀD (to bow – both a yielding and a greeting). Cognates of such yielding, such as DECEASE and RETROCEDE (both filed under IE *ked*), recall דחי / KIKHĒ (fall, stumble) – a DK antonym of KD advancement. More on these last two Hebrew words at "DECAY."
> Other cognates of PRECEDE at IE *ked* include: ABSCESS, ACCEDE, ANCESTOR, ANTECEDE, CEASE, CEDE, CESSION, CONCEDE, CONCESSION, DECEASE, EXCEED, INTERCEDE, NECESSARY, PRECEDENT, PREDECESSOR, PROCEED, RECEDE, SECEDE and SUCCEED.

(PRE)PARE / פְּרָא
PARA   [PRA]

ROOTS: PREPARE is traced to a Latin verb *parere* and an IE root *pera* that mean "to produce." פרה / PĀRĀ is to bear fruit; פרא / PĀRĀ is to be "fruitful" (*Hosea 13:15*). בר / BĀR is a son and פרי / PRĒ is a fruit – see "FRUIT."

> **BRANCHES:** Cognates of PREPARE include APPARATUS, APPAREL, DISPARATE, EMPEROR, IMPERATIVE, IMPERIAL, PARACHUTE, PARASOL, PREPARATORY, PREPPY, -PARA, PARENT, -PAROUS, RAMPART, REPAIR, REPERTORY, SEPARATE, SEVER, and SEVERAL.

PRESS / פְּרָץ
PAR – U(T)S   [P–R–(T)S]

ROOTS: PRESS is said to be a frequentive of Latin *premere* (to press). The IE root is *per* (to strike). Both פרץ / PORĀTS and פצר / POTSĀR mean "to press, urge" – see "PESTER" and "BREACH."

> **BRANCHES:** Cognates of PRESS include COMPRESS, DEPRESS, EXPRESS, IMPRESS, IMPRINT, OPPRESS, PREGNANT, PRESSURE, PRINT, REPRESS, REPRIMAND, and SUPPRESS.
> *Purista* is to press in Finnish.

PRIZE / פְּרָס
PRUSS   [PRS]

ROOTS: PRIZE is from Middle English *pris* (value, price). This is traced to Latin *prendre* (to take) and the IE root *ghend* (to seize, take). APPRISE and APPRAISE are covered, but PRIZE as a reward is simply ignored. פרס / PRĀS in Aramaic is a reward, prize or gift. פרס / PĀRĀS is to "deal" or give out in *Isaiah 58:7*.

PROSTITUTE / פְּרִיצוּת
PREETS – UTE   [P–R–TS→P–R–ST]

ROOTS: PROSTITUTE is from Latin *prostituere* (to expose publicly, to prostitute). The etymology procedes to break down as the Latin is broken down to *pro* (before) plus *statuere* (to cause to stand). The IE root then is *sta* (to stand) – nothing one could get arrested for. פריצות / PRETSOOT means obscenity or licentiousness; פרץ / PĀROOTS is immodest – the sense of impetuous behavior is seen in *Genesis 38:29* or at "PIRATE." פרוז / PĀROOZ is open.

> **BRANCHES:** Antonyms include פרישות / PRESHOOS (abstinence, celibacy, piety, restriction). For IE root *sta* see "STABLE." PRESS, BRASH and BRAZEN may be related to פרסום / PĒRSOOM (publicity) and the "PR" words above.

PROTO(TYPE) / פֶּטֶר
PET – ERE   [PTR ➡ PRT]

ROOTS: PROTO- is from Greek *protos* (first).

פטר / PETER is the firstborn or "firstling" in *Exodus 34:19-20*. פטר / PETER means beginning or opening; פרץ / PORATS is to burst forth. In birth, the פטר / PETER is the FIRST to BURST the womb, the *PROTO*TYPE of the siblings to come.

In *Genesis 38:29* "Peretz" is so named for the "breach" he makes in order to be born first, before his twin brother. (See "BREACH" and "BURST.")

As a firstborn, PERETZ is destined to be a *proteios* (prime or chief in Greek) or a פרץ / PORĒTZ (prince, nobleman – PRINCE appears at "PIRATE"). The Latin etymon for PRINCE, *princeps*, means "he who takes first place." Since the BURST – FIRST – PRI(N)CE association has already been BROACHED (introduced), it is notable that a German prince is a *furst*.

> **BRANCHES:** A brief selection of relevant PROT- words includes: PROTAGONIST, PROTEIN, PROTOCOL, PROTON, PROTOPLASM and PROTOZOA. The IE root of PROTO-, *per*, stakes a claim on dozens of words meaning: forward, through, in front of, before, early, first, chief, toward, against, near, at and around. For a Hebrew root to match the many meanings of IE root *per*, there is עבר / (A)BH – R (went beyond, passed through, side, towards, opposite to, forwards [*Ezekiel 1:9*] and ford). See "FERRY" and "OVER."

PSALM / זְמֶר
SZEM – (ERE)   [ZMR]

ROOTS: PSALM may be treated the way it sounds (SM) or the way it is spelled (or percieved). The Middle English etymons include both *psalme* and *salm* or *saume*. Going back to the Greek, there is only *psalmos* (song sung to the harp), from the harp-twanging verb *psallein* (to twitch). The clearest sense of PSALM is that of a *SONG, SONNET* or *SONOROUS SONATA*. These SN or SM words (recalling Middle English *saume*) echo words like זמר / ZEMER (song, tune), זמירה / ZMĒRĀ (psalm, hym) and זמר / ZĒMER (to sing; to play a musical instrument). See "SOUND." As for the PSL terms for harp playing, there's פתיל / PSĒL (cord, thread), פתילה / PSELĀ (twisted cord – see "FUSE"), פתל / POSĀL (to twist) and פתלתל / PSĀLTOL (twisted – *Deuteronomy 32:5*). Twisting נ / N to L (see appendix), פסנתרין / PSĀNTĀR[ĒN] in *Daniel 5:3* is a PSALTERY.

> **BRANCHES:** PSALTERY is one of the cognates of PSALM listed at IE root *pol* (to touch, feel, shake). Other cognates, CATAPULT, PALPABLE, PALPITATE and PALPEBRAL, suggest a Hebrew source like פלץ / POL[ATS] (shook, trembled – *Job 9:6*). Etymons for PSA(L)M that require no twitching include פזם / PĒSAM (to sing) and פזמה / PISMA (song with a refrain) – both via Aramaic.

PUER(ILE)/פֶּרַח
PER – (AH)   [PR]

ROOTS: PUERILE (childish) is from Latin *puer* (child), traced to the IE root *pau* (few, little – see "PAUCITY"). פרחה / PERHAH is a youth (*Job 30:12*); התפרחח / (HET)PÄRHÄH is to become puerile or infantile. אפרוח / EPHROÄH is a chick or birdling; פרח / PERÄH is a youth, cadet or trainee; עפר / ŌPHER is a young of deer; כפיר / K'PHEER is a young lion; and פרג / PORÄG is a sprout.

> **BRANCHES:** Switching to BR from PR, עבר / OOBÄR is a fetus and בר / BÄR is a son. The more sensible cognates of PUERILE are FOAL (colt), FILLY, PONY, PUERPERAL, and PULLET. Not listed was FILS (son or youth – from French) or AFFILIATE (Middle Latin *affiliare* is to "take to oneself as a son"). Perhaps a more obvious omission is PARR (the young of fish). A Maya Indian dad called his son *pal* (son); reverse PL for *lapsi* (a Finnish child). Greek *pallax* is a youth. See "CAPRICORN."

PUGN(ACIOUS)/חֹפֶן
KHO – P(H)UN   [KH – P(H) – N→PGN]

ROOTS: Latin *pugillus* is a handful, while *pugnus* is a fist. חפן / KHOPHÄN is a handful (*Exodus 9:8*) and a closed hand. כף / KUPH is an open hand – see "CUFF." In either case a sleight of hand, switching the פ / P(H) and the ח or כ / KH, brings the PG Latin fist into focus.

> **BRANCHES:** פגע / POGÄ is to strike or touch. "To punch, strike" is the first sense of PUG. Cognates of PUGNACIOUS (given to fighting) at IE root *peuk* (to prick) include IMPUGN, PONIARD, PUGILISM, PUGIL STICK, and REPUGNANT, BUNG, COMPUNCTION, POUNCE, PUNCTUATE, PUNCHEON and PUNCTUATE; and lastly, PYGMY (from the Greek fist or *pugmē*). Despite all thes fists flying, the AHD did not include PUNCH.

PUTSCH/פֶּצַע
PETS – AH   [P – TS – U]

ROOTS: From German and Swiss dialect, a PUTSCH is a push or blow (and thus a political uprising). פצע / PETSÄ is a bruise or wound; פצע / PÄTSÄ is to bruise or wound (*Genesis 4:23; Exodus 21:25*).

> **BRANCHES:** After a #1-#2 letter swap, there's also טפח / TOPHÄKH (to strike, push). PATCH or PETCH is Yiddish for a swift application of child psychology to the cheek or buttocks.

PUZZLE/פְּתִיל
PIS – SEAL   [PSL]

ROOTS: A FUSE (as on dynamite) is from Italian *fuso* (a cord). The less common term, PIZZLE (a whip), is from *pese* (Middle Dutch for a sinew or bowstring). פתילה / P'SELÄ is a twisted cord or wick (fuse); פתיל / PISEL or PITEL is translated "cord" or "thread" in *Numbers 15:38*. פתיל / PÄSEL means twisted or tied up; its antonym is פתירה / PISERÄ (solution, unraveling). PUZZLE is from Middle English *poselet* (bewilder, confuse), tied in with the knotty words above.

> **BRANCHES:** פתלתל / P'TÄLTÄL is crooked or twisted (*Deuteronomy 32:5*); תלתל / TÄLTÄL is a curl (*Songs 5:11*). תלתל / TILTÄL is to curl or CONTORT. Simply twist the L to an R for the source of DISTORT, EXTORT, TORSION, TORT, TORTOISE, TORTUOUS, TORTURE and TURTLE.

PYTHON/פֶּתֶן
PETH – EN   [P–TH – N]

ROOTS: The PYTHON, a large snake that twists around and strangles its victims, is said to be from Greek Pythian and (earlier) Pytho (older names for Delphi). Apollo is the patron of the Delphic oracle (at Pytho), and Apollo was to have slain a snake at Mount Parnassus. This is a classic folk etymology, eluding any sense of lexical meaning. פתן / PETHEN (one way to pronounce PESEN or PETEN) is a deadly snake. *Isaiah 14:29* proclaims that when the Messiah comes "a babe shall play over a *viper's* hole." See "ASP."

> **BRANCHES:** In the etymology Greek *ophites* and *ophis* (snake – source of OPHITE and OPHITIC) were not mentioned.
> The PYTHON, a twisting constrictor, should relate to פתל / PÄTÄL or PÄTHÄL (to twist) and its antonym פתירה / PITERÄ or PITHERÄ (unraveling) since the ל / L or ר / R can be bent to an N. See "PUZZLE."

QUAR(TER)/רֶבַע
REV – AKH   [RVQ→QVR]

ROOTS: Given the fact that the Europeans borrowed "Arabic" numerals from Semites whose letters went from right to left, some confusion was inevitable. The Hebrew for one fourth (¼) is רבע / REVÄKH (*Exodus 29:40*). Dutch *kwart* (¼), Polish *cwierc* (¼), and Latin *quartus* (pronounced "kvortus") require a full inversion of Hebrew's R – V – KH or RVQ. The reconstructed IE root for "four" is the strange concoction *kwetwer*.

Four (4) in Hebrew is ארבע / ÄRBÄKH or ÄRBÄ (*Genesis 23:16*). QUARTER (¼) in Arabic (*rouba*) and Swahili (*robo*) do not have the gutteral K or Q here, leaving Hebrew as the most logical source for all forms of FOUR, like QUA(T)R[AIN] or (S)QUARE.

> **BRANCHES:** Other examples of a 123→321 reversal include STACK from גדיש / GÄDESH or KTS (stack of sheaves – *Judges 15:5*), SWEET from דבש / DIVASH or TVS (honey, etc.) and *SLOG, SLEIGH* or *SL*EDGE from גלש / GALAS[H] (to ski – see "GLISSADE").
> Some of the FORTY cognates of QUARTER at IE root *kwetwer* include CADRE, CAHIER, CARILLON, CARNET, FARTHING, FIRKIN, FOUR, FOURTEEN, QUADRANT, QUADRATE, QUADRILLE, QUADROON, QUARANTINE, QUART, QUARTO, QUARREL, QUARRY, and SQUAD. For the RV root's meaning see "RIFE."

QUASH/כָּבַש
KAV – USH   [Q–V–SH]

ROOTS: To QUASH is to put down or suppress forcibly and completely. QUASH is thought to derive from Latin *cassus* (empty) and the IE root *kes* (to cut). כבש / KOVASH is to master, force or subdue (*Genesis 1:28*).

> **BRANCHES:** Most "qu" words are attributed to KW roots in IE. *Ko fu* is to conquer in Chinese. See "KIBOSH" and "VICTOR(Y)."

QUERY/חֵקֶר
(HAY) – QERE   [H – K – R]

ROOTS: QUERY is from Latin *quaerere* (to seek); the IE root is this same "Latin verb of unknown origin." In *Deuteronomy 13:15* חקר / HĀKĀR is to investigate, explore or study. The translation reads, "you shall investigate and *INQUIRE* and interrogate thoroughly." חקר / HĀKER is an inquiry.

> **BRANCHES:** Cognates of QUERY include ACQUIRE, CONQUER, EXQUISITE, INQUIRY, INQUISITION, PERQUISITE, QUAESTOR, QUERIST, QUEST, QUESTION, and REQUIRE. Related words not listed by the AHD include SCOUR (see "SCOUR") CURIO, CURIOSITY and perhaps QUARRY. A synonymous word is שחר / SHĀKHAR (to seek); an anagramic of חקר / KH – K – R is רחק / RĀKHĀK or RĀHĀK (to be distant).

QUIET/שֶׁקֶט
(SHEH) – QET   [(SH) – K – T]

ROOTS: Both Latin *quies* and *quietas* (quiet, calm, retiring) suggest either a KT or KS etymon. The IE root for QUIET is *k(w)eia* (to rest, be quiet) – whence ACQUIESCE, COY and REQUIEM. Hebrew covers all three routes to the root of QUIET. שקט / SHEKET is quiet, connoting "rest" in *Ruth 3:18*, and "calm" in *Isaiah 7:4*. A synonym and anagram of this is שתק / SHOTUK or SHOSUK (to be silent, quiet, or to "calm down" – *Jonah 1:12*). Various combinations of K's, S's and T's are shared by these two Hebrew terms. As for the KW or KV in the IE root or in QUIET, שכב / [SHA]KHAV is to rest and כבש / KOV(ĀSH) is subdue.

> **BRANCHES:** ACQUIT, QUIET and ACQUIESCE are silent partners of the Latin terms above. Latin *tacere* and IE root *tak* mean "to be silent." This brings in TACET, TACIT and RETICENT. שתקנות / SHUTKĀNOOT is *TACITURNITY*; notice also the identical suffix of each (ות / -OOT and -ITY). Japanese *szuka* (quiet) and Russian *tee'khee* (quiet) prefer שתק / SH – S – K or (SH) – T – K.
> The opposite of the inactivity of שקט / SH – K – T is seen in שקידה / SHIKĒDĀ (bustling diligence – see "SCOOT.") An antonym favoring SH – K is שקשק / SHIKSHĀK (to make much noise). Reinforcements for KT silencers include הקטין / (HĒ)KTĒN (to reduce), קטל / KOTUL (to kill) and קץ / KĀTS (finish). All these are שק / SH – K (noise) stoppers that add up to make שקט / SH – K – T (quiet).
> For נחת / (NĀ)KHĀT (quietness, repose, rest) – see "NIGHT."

QUINT(ET)/קָמֵץ
COME – MUTTS   [Q – M – TS → QNT]

ROOTS: Latin *quintus* (fifth) is somehow placed at the IE root *penkwe* (five – see "FIN" and "PUGNACIOUS" for this root). קמץ / KOMĀT(S) means hand and hand measurement (*Leviticus 6:8*). The sense development from "hand" to "five" and "ten" words, and to related counting terms are discussed at "MITT." חמש / KHĀMESH (five – *Genesis 1:23*) is really the chief etymon here, as ש / SH to T changes are standard between Hebrew and Aramaic. [Hebrew שור / SHOR (ox, bullock) is תור / TOR in Aramaic – giving us TAURUS the bull.] Either Hebrew etymon provides a KMT or QNT handle to QUINT(ET).

> **BRANCHES:** KANTAR (Egyptian equivalent of a hundredweight) is from Arabic *qintar*, borrowed (says *Webster's*) from Latin *quintarius* (containing five).
> HAND (another KMT term) in Malay: Gani is *komud*, and a fist in Chinese is *quantou*. Chen is the Chinese five. There are so many links between HAND and COUNTING (KNT) terms, that even the jumbled IE root *penkwe* lists FIST and FINGER.
> The IE root *wikmti* (twenty) is a compound of *wi* (two) plus *kmt-i* (decade – a form of IE root *dekm*). *Wikmti* is ultimately a compound of ב / VE (two – see "BOTH") plus קמץ / KOMAT(S) (hand, thus ten). Cognates of QUINTET include CINQUE, KENO, QUINATE, QUINDECENNIAL, QUINQUAGENARIAN, QUINT, QUINTAIN, QUINTILE, QUINTESSENCE, QUINTILLION and QUINTUPLET. Basque (with "no linguistic affinities") has an H – N/M word for "ten," *ham(ar)* – fitting קמץ / KM(TS) and HAN(D), and a FIST look-alike for "five" – *bost*. Bost and FIST were influenced by תפש / TOFĀS (to seize, grasp – *Deuteronomy 21:19*). This is why five (5) in Finnish is *viisi*, in Turkish is *bes*, and in Slavic there are various PT "five" terms.

RACK/רָקַע
RUCK – (AH)   [R – K – KH]

ROOTS: Middle Dutch *recken* is to stretch, as in torturing as infidel on the RACK. The noun RACK is from Middle Dutch *rakke* (framework). The IE root is *reg* (to move in a straight line, with derivatives meaning to direct, lead, rule). רקע / RĀKĀ is to stretch (*Isaiah 42:25*). In *Isaiah*, as in *Genesis 1:6*, we have the Lord stretching out the רקיע / RĀKEĀ (firmament, heaven – the RACK or framework of the world).

הדרך / [HĒD]RĒKH is to direct or lead – see "DIRECTION."

> **BRANCHES:** Rumanian *cer* (sky) may be an RK reversal, leading us to the Italian and Spanish "sky" term, *cielo*, and our CEILING. That which we stretch out and straighten out in order to move us is the leg or רגל / REG(EL). More related terms from Hebrew at "REACH." At IE root *reg* the Greek stretching term *oregein* gives us ANORECTIC and ANOREXIA. Latin *rogare* (ask) means "stretching out the hand." The English words that reach us from this source include ABROGATE, ARROGATE, CORVEE, DEROGATE, INTEROGATIVE, PREROGATIVE, and SUBROGATE. Old English *reccan* (to extend, stretch out) gave us RECK and RECKLESS. Some of the other alleged cognates of RACK at this IE root are presented here even if they are linked to better Hebrew etymons elsewhere: RIGHT from Germanic; REALM, RECTITUDE, RECTOR, RECTUM, REGENT, REGIME, REGIMENT, REGION, CORRECT, DIRECT (see "DIRECTION"), ERECT, RECTANGLE, RECTIFY, and SURGE from Latin; RICH from Old English; REAL, REGAL, REIGN, ROYAL, REGICIDE and VICEROY from Latin; MAHARAJAH, MAHARANI, RAJ, RAJAH, RANI and RYE from Sanskrit; RAIL, REGULAR (see "REGULAR"), REGULATE and RULE from Latin; RAKE, RECKON, RANK from Germanic. An R to L change away, Hawaiian *'ilikai* means "the surface of the sea" or "horizontal."

RAKE/שָׂרִיק
(SAH) – REEK   [(S)RK]

ROOTS: A garden RAKE is used to "gather, smooth, loosen, or scrape with." The AHD places RAKE and Old English *raca* at IE root *reg* (to move in a straight line). The explanation for this placement is that a RAKE is an "implement with straight pieces of wood." שריק / (SÄ)RĒK is the combing and carding of *Isaiah 19:9.* סרק / (S)ÄRĀK is to comb hair, RAKE flesh, or comb an area in searching. מסרק / (MÄS)RĀK is a comb; רחת / RÄKH(ÄT) is a winnowing fork (*Isaiah 30:24*).

> **BRANCHES:** קרד / *KÄR*ĀD (to scrape, curry) contains an RK reversal, and indicates that CURRY (KR) is ultimately related to RAKE. *RAK*ING is scraping because the *RAC*COON in Algonquin Indian is literally "the hand scratcher." *Arahkun* combines our RK RAKE or scratch element with the KN "hand" element found at "QUINTET" and "MITT." The IE root *Reg* (to move in a straight line) is taken up at "RACK." For RAKE (the dissolute profligate or bum) see "KARATE."

RAID/רְדָה
ROD–(AH)   [RD]

ROOTS: A RAID is an attack for pillage and looting, but the etymology ends with the RIDE to the victim's camp. The IE root for RAID is *reidh* (to ride), with cognates like ROAD and READY. Even רד / RĀD (to roam) is a more worthy etymon for the activity of predatory humans, but more relevant to looting is רדה / RODÄ (to take out, remove – *Judges 14:9*). The same verb appears in *Genesis 1:26* where Man is charged with "rule" or "dominion over" the fish of the sea. A literal understanding of ruling over fish is ludicrous, except for the sense of (OVER)RIDING or domineering with RAIDING privileges. Man was allowed to RIDE (tyrannize, control) the seven seas, to ROOT out, ROUT and LOOT the denizens of the deep. Another use of רדה / R–DT in Scripture involves waging war upon a city "until it is *reduced*" (*Deuteronomy 20:20*). The verse might better read "until it is ROUTED."

> **BRANCHES:** ROUT and LOOT are somehow filed under the IE root *reup* (to snatch). RID and RIDDANCE shouldn't be cognates with "rod" at IE *reudh* (to clear land); they are both form רדה / RD. As רודן / RŌD(ÄN) is a tyrant or dictator, so is an עריץ / ÄRĒT(S). (Reverse the RT to get TYR(ANT) – a word whose Greek meaning similarly combines sovereignty with usurping.) Other RD terms include רדוי / RĒDOOY (conquest) and רדף / ROD(UPH) (to pursue, hunt, persecute).

RAM/רְאֵם
R'AIM   [RAM]

ROOTS: The RAM is thought to derive from a Germanic root *rama* and an Old Norse term *rammr* which means "sharp, bitter...with reference to the strong smell in the mating season." Whether or not this etymology smells good, this "bitter" term *rama* is merely a reversal of מר / MÄR (bitter – see "MARINE"). Other RM or RN "bitter" smelling terms include RANCID, RANCOR and RANK. Hebrew etymons for RAM (male sheep) include אמרא / IMRÄ (sheep in Aramaic – another RM reversal) and ראם / R'ÄM ("wild-ox"– *Deuteronomy 33:17*). The same term is defined "reindeer," but this male animal is known for butting or goring as seen in the Biblical citation. As dominant male of the flock, the RAM is רם / RÄM (exalted).

> **BRANCHES:** In defense of *REIN*DEER as a derivative of ראם / R'ÄM there is the Old Norse etymon *hreinn* and the "lofty horns"

of this unknown beast in *Numbers 23:22. Hreinn* might also be from קרן / KEREN (horn – source of HORN, as seen at "UNICORN"). The RN of HORN and קרן / KEREN is a welcome sound-sense element here. RUNT is linked to Dutch *rund* (ox), but also to sword names. The charging RAM as a hurled (רמה / RÄMÄ) lance (רמח / RŌMÄH) recalls the verbs RAM and CRAM. The אמרא / IMRA (sheep) might link up with LM words like LLAMA – see "CAMEL."

RATT(LE)/רָטַט
RET–TET   [RTT]

ROOTS: The Germanic etymon *rattelen* might infer the cause of the RATTLE, the vibration, more than the clatter or noise. To RATTLE can also mean to cause something to RATTLE (by shaking). רטט / RETET is "trembling" in *Jeremiah 49:24;* רתח / RÄTÄT also gets down to shake, rattle and roll.

> **BRANCHES:** There's the child's RATTLE and the RATTLESNAKE. רעד / RÄUDT and חרדה / HÄRÄDTÄ mean fearful trembling; רתח / RÄTÄH is to boil.
> Reverse these fearful RT terms to experience TERR(OR). See "IRATE" and "SCARE."

RAVE/רָהַב
RA–(H)UV   [R–H–BH]

ROOTS: From Old French *rever* (to rave, revel), to RAVE also means to "talk with excessive enthusiasm about someone or something." רהב / RÄHÄV is to boast or be haughty; it is translated "encourage" in *Psalms 138:3.*

> **BRANCHES:** הרהיב / (HĒ)RHĒV is to exalt or to confuse, the latter meaning relating to the wildness of RAVING. Because "rant and rave" is a twosome, note that רטן / RÄTÄN (to grumble – switch the T and N) may have influenced RANT.

RAVE(N)/עוֹרֵב
OH–RÄVE   [O–R–BH]

ROOTS: The Old English *hraefn* (raven) is a cognate of the Latin *corvus* (raven) at the IE root *ker* (echoic root of loud noises or birds). The ideal root would allow for the HRF of the Germanic RAVEN as well as the KRV of the Mediterranean pronunciation (see "HEDONISM"). The true etymon would be more than merely immitative of caws – whether or not crows crow and grackles cackle. The עורב / ŌRÄV, HŌRÄV or KHŌRÄV (raven) sent by Noah in *Genesis 8:7* – source of CORVUS, CROW, *hraef(n)* and RAVE(N) – is related to more than just KR terms like קרא / KÄRÄ (to shout, call) and קורא / KŌRÄ (partridge).

> **BRANCHES:** Several meaningful connections are listed in the next entry, "RAVENOUS," which, not surprisingly, the authorities do not link to "raven." See "RAVENOUS." The entire *CORV*INE or *corvidae* family of RAVENS and CROWS derives from עורב / KŌRÄV (raven). The CORBEL and CORBINA are included. A GRAB (ship – a possible source of CRAFT as a ship) is from the Arabic raven, the *ghurab.* The Greek *korax* and Irish *bra(n)* are ravens of the same feather.

RAVE(NOUS)/רָעֵב
RA-AVE   [R–A–BH]

ROOTS: The verb to RAVEN means to devour greedily, to seize, and to prowl hungrily. The adjective RAVENOUS is traced to Old French *ravener*, Latin *rapere* (to seize) and the IE root *rep* (to snatch – see "TROPHY"). The primary meaning of RAVENOUS, hungry, is sidestepped because רעב / RAAV (hungry – *Proverbs 25:21*) and רעב / RAAV (famine – *Genesis 26:1*) are unknown or irrelevant to most linguists.

BRANCHES: That rapacious bird the RAVEN (see previous entry) is also ignored, even though the ערב / ŌRĀV (raven) of Scripture is consistently associated with hunger. In *Genesis 8:7* Noah sends this voracious bird out, knowing that it would vigorously seek out food. In *I Kings 17:4-6* God sends out ravens to feed Elijah. The association is further feathered by the following verse:

> Who provideth for the RAVEN his prey,
> when his young ones cry unto God,
> and wander for lack of food – *Job 38:41*

The קרב / KEREV (animal stomach) tells the animal of prey (טרף / [TE]REPH is food or prey) to vigilantly maintain the ארב / ĀRĀV (lying in wait or ambush). Humans CRAVE (wrongly linked to "craft" and strength) foods that are sweet (ערב / ĀRAV or KĀRĀV – *Songs 2:14*). Delicious is *ah-rawy* in Thai. Upgrade all these ערב / ORV or KH–R–V terms on the alphabet scale (ב to ג or letter 2 to letter 3) and we get ערג / ORĀG or KHORAG ("crave"– *Psalms 42:2*). CRAVE or K–R–V is merely a #1-#2 letter swap from רעב / R–K–V or RAKHAV (hungry). See "URGE."

REACH/אֹרֶךְ
(O)–REKH   [O–R–KH]

ROOTS: Anglo-Saxon *raecan* (to stretch out, reach) is traced to the IE root *reig* (to reach, stretch out) where it is cognate with RIGID and RIGOR. רקע / REKĀ is to stretch or spread (*Isaiah 42:5*); אֹרֶךְ / ŌREKH means length (*Genesis 6:15*), matching the #3 defintion of REACH: "the distance or extent covered in stretching."

ערכו / ERK(OO) means "range (yourselves)" in *Jeremiah 50:14;* ארח / ĀRĀKH is to travel. רחב / ROKH(AV) means breadth.

BRANCHES: REACH primarily means extending the hand, and *ruka* is a hand in Russian and Serbo-Croatian. Reversing to *chir* for the Greek "hand" gives us CHIROPRACTOR and SURGERY. *Ruka* is also an arm in Serbo-Croat.; reverse to *kar* for the Hungarian arm.

The Indonesian arm, *lengan*, is an R→L bridge to related terms like LENGTH and LONG. The N here is unhistoric; LEG is from the IE base *leq* (limb). RA(N)GE is another R/L–G/K term of far reaching connotations. *Lokihi* is long in Proto-Eastern Polynesian; in Tibetan it is *rinqu.* זרוע / (Z)RŌĀKH is an arm; רגל / REG(EL) is a LEG; לך / LĀKH is to go. Go to "RACK" and "DIRECTION" for more long, straight terms.

RED/וֶרֶד
(VA)–RODE   [VRD]

ROOTS: RED is akin to German *rot* and Scandinavian *rod*. The IE base is *reudh*, corresponding to the IE root *reudh*

(red, ruddy). Terms like RHODA and RHODODENDRON, from the Greek rose or *rhodon*, are traced to the IE root *wrod* (rose – of unknown origin). ורד / VERED is a rose and ורד / VĀRŌD is rosy red in Mishnaic Hebrew. ורדינון / VĀRD(ENON) is rose oil in the Jerusalem Talmud. The term is not in the Bible, but there is no indication that the term is borrowed from a non-Semitic source. Aramaic *varda* is a rose.

BRANCHES: וריד / VĀRED is a vein, and may have influenced BLEED and BLOOD. Finnish and Hungarian "blood" is *ver(i)*.

Words traced to the IE roots above include CORROBORATE, ERYTHEMA, JULEP, RAMBUNCTIOUS, ROBUS, ROBUST, ROWEN, ROUGE, RUBELLA, RUBRIC, RUBY, RUDDY, RUSSET, and RUST.

REEK/רֵיחַ
RAY–UKH   [R–Y–KH]

ROOTS: Old English *reocan* (to smoke, reek) is akin to German *rauch* and the IE root *reug* (to vomit, belch, smoke, cloud). REEK means smoke or a strong, (unpleasant) smell, and the verb of exuding the same.

ריח / RĀUKH is a smell and to smell; God "*smelled* the pleasing *odor*" of Noah's sacrifice in *Genesis 8:21.* סרח / (SĀ)RĀKH is to smell bad or "go stale" in *Jeremiah 49:7;* רקח / RĀKĀH is perfume (*Exodus 30:25*) as is זלח / (ZE)LĀKH. רקב / REK(EV) is rot, decay; רקב / RĀK(UV) is to rot or decay.

BRANCHES: The vaporous sense of REEK is partially met by רוח / ROOĀKH (breath, spirit, ghost – *Genesis 1:2*) reverse to *kiri* for Japanese "fog." Linked to BRACH and FLAIR at IE root *bhrag* (to smell), FRAG(RANT) recalls פרח / PHERĀKH (flower; a verb of spreading out). To spread out the PR and RK elements see "FRUCTIFY."

ERUCT is cognate with REEK; *wech* is a Polish smell. RA(N)CID, RA(N)COR and RA(N)K (stinking) should relate. Dutch *reuk* is to smell; the Scandinavian languages switch to LK terms. OL(FACTORY), from Latin *olere* (to smell), may be a softer ריח / RYH.

REEVE/עֶרֶב
(AY)–REV   [ERV]

ROOTS: REEVE is a nautical term of rope fastening. The etymology reads, "probably Dutch *reven* (to reef or tie down a sail)."

W and R interchange in the "Elmer Fudd rule" ("You cwazy wabbit" instead of "You crazy rabbit"). WOOF, therefore, originating from Anglo-Saxon *owef*, should link up with RV terms of tied ropes or threads like REEVE.

Not *owef* but ערב / ĀREV is the "woof" of *Leviticus 13:49.* Just as WARP and WOOF threads intermingle in WEAVING, ערב / ĀREV means "mixture." טרוף / (TĀ)ROOF is confusion.

BRANCHES: ROVE, WEB, WEBSTER, WEFT, WHARF, WHARP and WHARVE (originally a spinning term) should all relate. *Orv* is to weave in Japanese. See "CRIB" and "RHAPSODY."

REFUSE/רֶפֶשׁ
REF–ES(H)   [R–PH–S(H)]

ROOTS: The given etymology credits Laitn *refundare* (to pour back) and the IE root *gheu* (to pour). REFUSE (trash) might be a throw back to רפם / RÄFÄS (to foul, pollute – *Ezekiel 32:2*) and רפש / RÄFÄSH (to make filthy or dirty – *Ezekiel 34:18*).

> **BRANCHES:** RUBBISH, from Anglo-French *rubbous*, might also have been influenced by רפש / REFESH or RPS (dirt).

(RE)GRET/חָרַט
KHAR–UT   [KH–R–T]

ROOTS: REGRET (sorrow, remorse) is derived "probably from a Germanic base seen in Anglo-Saxon *gretan* (to weep, lament)." חרטה / KHÄRÄTÄ Is repentance or regret; חרדה / KHÄRÄDTÄ is fear, anxiety or "trouble" in *II Kings 4:13*.

> **BRANCHES:** GUILT, from Anglo-Saxon *gylt*, is only two Grimm's Law changes away from חרט / KH–R–T (KH→G, R→L). The R→W change allows Japanese *kowai* (afraid) to come from חרד / KHORÄD (to fear). The Japanese gives one the courage to suggest that COW, COWER and COWARD are from this same KH–(W)R Hebrew term. Akin to regret are several meanings of חרץ / KHÄRÄT(S) (was courageous, was determined; punishment). Descending one letter on the alphabet scale, חרף / KHARAF is to reproach.

REGUL(AR)/רָגִיל
RUG–EEL   [RGL]

ROOTS: Latin *regula* (a straight piece of wood) and the IE root *reg* (to move in a straight line) only speak to spacial REGULARITIES.

See "RACK" and "REACH" for the many Hebrew "straight" terms with RK or RG. רגל / *REGEL* (the anatomical LEG) can also mean the straight wooden LEG of a table (*Exodus 37:13*). The dimension of time is present in the Hebrew, but not in the IE etymon. REGULAR intervals are not "straight" ones. רגיל / RÄGEL means usual, normal or habitual (REGULAR), as רגל / REGEL means a "time" or occasion in *Numbers 22:28*.

> **BRANCHES:** רגל / REGEL is also one of the REGULARLY occurring pilgrimage holidays with all their attendant REGULATIONS. The walk to Jerusalem on the רגלים / RIGÄLEM (festivals) required use of the רגלים / RÄGLÄEM (legs), which may keep a REGULAR beat, marching like army REGULARS רגלי / RÄGLE – *Exodus 12:37*). See "DIRECTION."

REICH/רִיכָא
REE–KHAH   [R–Y–KH–(A)]

ROOTS: The linguistic roots of this German word for empire follow Anglo-Saxon *rice* to Latin *rex* (king) and back to the IE root *reg* (straight...to direct – see "RACK"). ריכא / REKHÄ is a noble (Aramaic); אברך or "Abrech" is the Egyptian title given to Joseph the viceroy (*Genesis 41:43*); הדריך / (HED)REKH is to lead, guide, direct (see "DIRECTION"); רועה / ROEH or ROKHE is a shepherd or leader of the flock; ערך / ÄRÄKH is to set in order; מלך / *MELEKH* (king) is literally the one who makes things לך / LÄKH (go! – pronounced RÄKH after an L→R change).

> **BRANCHES:** R–KH rulership terms not listed at IE *reg* include the Welsh (or KKK) DRAGON (leader), RAGNAROK and Old Norse *regin* (god), and Greek *arkhein* (to rule, command) as seen in MONARCHY. *Errege* is a king in Basque; *ariki* is a chief or king in Proto-Polynesian.

RESIDUE/שָׂרִיד
SAH–REED   [SRD→RSD]

ROOTS: RESIDE and RESIDENCE are said to come from Latin *re* (back) plus *sedere* (to sit). "Sitting back" may or may not infer RESIDENCY, but RESIDUE (what is left over) is another matter. Old French *residere* (remainder, rest) has nothing to do with occupation, so the linkage of RESIDENTIAL to RESIDUAL ought to be suspect. Hebrew offers an SRD etymon which could well have given rise to RSD words like *residere*, RESIDUARY, and RESIDUUM. שריד / SÄRED is a remnant or survivor (*Numbers 21:35; Job 18:19*). שרד / SÄRÄD is to leave over.

> **BRANCHES:** The SR element is seen in שאר / S(H)IÄR and שארית / S(H)IÄRET; both mean a remnant or a remainder. The sense of human survivor is kept alive in the Polish word for orphan – *sierota*. REST (remainder) ought to be related; the Latin etymon here is *restare* (to remain). RESTING (dormancy), RESTIVE and RESTLESS are more distantly related.

RESUMÉ/רְשִׁימָה
RIS(H)–EE–MA   [RSM]

ROOTS: A written RESUMÉ or record is from the French. The word is allegedly related to the verb "resume," although nothing is taken up again or necessarily resumed in a written record. רשימה / RIS(H)EMA is a list or register. רשם / RAS(H)AM is to record (*Daniel 10:21*).

RHAPSODY/רַפְסוֹדָה
RHUP–SODA   [RPSODH]

ROOTS: A RHAPSODY once meant a miscellany; it now infers an improvised musical composition which is free and irregular.

This sense of hodge-podge is captured in רפסודה / RÄPSODÄ (raft – *II Chronicles 2:15*). Probably a combination of רפס / REPHES (junk – see "REFUSE") and יסוד / YISOD (compilation), the raft of odd logs is an irregular miscellany.

The given etymon for RHAPSODY is Greek *oide* (song – see "ODE") plus *rhaptein* (to stitch together). Reverse the RPT of the Greek to get תפר / TAPHAR (to sew together – *Genesis 3:7*).

> **BRANCHES:** The RP Greek etymon should relate to ערב / ÄREV (woof – see "REEVE") and ערוב / ÄROOBH (mixture, confusion). RAFT, RAFTER, RIB, RIBAND, RIBBON, and ROOF may relate to these RF terms of stitching, weaving or jumbling together. טרף / TÄRÄF (rip) is an antonym; רפואה / RIPHOOÄ (healing) is an RP term of putting together. REEF (1) and REEF (2) are cognates of RIB at IE root *rebh* (to roof over). ROOFS were thatched or woven together, much like the tied-together RAFT above. The IE base for ROOF is *krapo*, fitting the hard pronunciation of ערב / KHÄREBH or KRB. Another approach to the RAFT or "float" (*I Kings 5:23*) is to reverse דברה / DTOBHR[ÄH]. See "ROOF."

RIBO(FLAVIN)/עֲרָב
(AH)–ROB(H)   [U–R–BH]

ROOTS: RIBOFLAVIN, a vitamin in milk, is from Latin *Arabicus*. *Arabicus* means "Arabic," and ARABIA and ARAB are Biblical, Semitic designations. ערבי / ÄRBHE means "Arab"– (*Nehemiah 2:19*).

> **BRANCHES:** RIBOSE is a cognate. ערב / ARABH is Arabic; ערבה / ARABHA means desert.

RICE/אֹרֶז
OH–REZ   [ORZ→RS]

ROOTS: Latin *oryza* and Greek *oryzon* are "of Oriental origin." ארז / OREZ (rice) appears in first century literature, but the tie-in to Biblical Hebrew is ארז / ORÄZ (to pack, bundle – *Ezekiel 27:24*). The grains of the RICE plant are densely packed.

> **BRANCHES:** אזר / AZAR is also to bind (ARZ=AZR).
> Despite the "of Oriental origin" designation cited above, Chinese *mi* and Japanese *kome* did not give us "rice." [These terms are probably from קמה / KÄMÄ (standing corn or grain).] Closest to all the RS rice terms in the IE and Finno-Ugric languages is Korean *sal* (rice – reverse SL and change L to R). The Spanish and Portuguese *arroz* is close to the Hebrew and to Arabic *ourz*.

RICHES/רְכוּש
RIKH–OOS(H)   [R–KH–SH]

ROOTS: RICH is thought to be a royal term, cognate with Latin *rex* (king – see "REICH"). RICHES is a singular noun because Old French *richesse* is from רכוש / RIKHOOSH (wealth, property – *Genesis 15:14*).

> **BRANCHES:** עשר / OSHER or KHOSHER (an anagramic synonym of R–KH–SH) means wealth. *Rikas* is rich in Finnish. רש / RÄSH means impoverished, dispossessed, or a poor man; in *Deuteronomy 2:31* it is an imperative verb meaning "possess" or "inherit." For other related words with R and S see "SIR."

RIFE/רַב
RUV   [R–BH]

ROOTS: RIFE means prevalent, abundant; רב / RÄV is "abundant" in *Exodus 34:6*. רב / ROV means multitude or majority; רבה / RÄVÄ is to increase or multiply; רבים / RÄB(EM) means plural, majority, or many. Anglo-Saxon *rife*, however, is linked to "reap," "ripe" and other harvest terms at the IE base *rei* (to tear off). To pursue the given etymon, see טרף / (TÄ)RÄF (to tear) at "TROPHY."

> **BRANCHES:** The AHD's cognate list for RIFE includes ARRIVE, REAP, RIFT, RIGATONI, RIMOSE, RIPARIAN, RIPE, RIPPLE, RIVAGE, RIVE, RIVER and ROPE. Consider the Hebrew RV etymon that fits the meaning and possible cognates like RAFT (a large number or quantity), French *(t)rop* (many) and VERY (an RV reversal that infers quantity more than truth).
> With an R→L change we can see רב / RV in Fijian *levu* (great) and Hawaiian *lau* (many). Reversing LV or LF bears FULL, 100 words beginning with POLY- (much, many) and the words for "much" in German (*viel*) and Finnish (*paljo*). RV reversals go back to ancient Egyptian as well, as *wr* is "great" in that venerable tongue. רוה / RAVA is filled or satiated with.

RISE/זָרַח
ZAR–(AH)   [ZRH→RS]

ROOTS: German *reisen* means rise (of the sun). RISE (pronounced "rize" is a #1-#2 metathesis of זרח / ZAR(ÄH) (to rise, as the sun). "The sun *rises* and the sun sets"– *Ecclesiastes 1:5*.

> **BRANCHES:** IE root *risan* (to rise) takes in ARISE and RAISE. (A)ROUSE, ROUST and ROOSTER ought to relate. מזרה / (MI)ZRÄH or (MI)SRAQ is East, where the sun RISES. East in Arabic is *sharq*, source of SIROCCO. שחר / SHÄHÄR is to rise early, as well as a noun meaning early morning. זהר / ZHR is not to rise but to shine.

RIV(ALRY)/ריב
REEVE   [R–Y–BH]

ROOTS: Latin *rivus* (brook) is the given folk etymology for RIVAL, as water rights may cause a RIVALRY. *Webster's* is honest enough to add "but influenced from another unknown source." Going to the Source, there is a ריב / REV (quarrel, dispute or "STRIFE") in *Genesis 13:7*. רב / RÄV is to (ST)RIVE.

BRANCHES: מריבה / (MI)RÉVÄ is (ST)RIFE (*Numbers 20:13*); קרב / (K')RÄV is battle (*Psalms 144:1*). For antonyms see "RHAPSODY." A ROW is a (SC)RAP or violent RIFT. Reverse רב / RAV or RAW to get WAR. *Werra* is strife in Old High German. Rivalry in Polish is *rywal[izacja]*.

ROC/רָחָם
ROKH–(OM)   [R–KH–M]

ROOTS: The ROC is a huge bird of prey in Arabian and Persian legend. Arabic *rukhkh* and Persian (Indo-European) *rukh* are the given etymons. Not cited is the רחם / RÄKHÄM, a bird in the eagle family that is translated "vulture" in *Leviticus 11:18*. A bird of prey may רחם / RKM (have mercy on) its own young, but elsewhere is skilled at חרם / KRM (destruction).

    BRANCHES: רחוף / RÄKHOOF means soaring or hovering (*Genesis 1:2*). The ROOKERY for ROOKS (crows) may have been influenced by רחם / R–KH–(M). See KR birds at "CROW."

ROCK/רָגַע
ROG–AKH   [R–G–KH]

ROOTS: Old English *rocc* and Middle Latin *rocca* have no known antecedents. ROCK (stone) may link up with רגם / ROGUM (to stone) or with millstone terms like רכב / REKH[EV] and רחים / RÄKHÄ[YIM]. This entry is primarily concerned with the other ROCK (to shake, cause to tremble). The shaky ROCK is "probably akin to German *rucken* (to pull, push)" and the IE base *req* (pole, to push with a pole).

    רגע / ROGÄ or ROGÄKH is to set in motion, disturb or "stir" as in "I am the Lord thy God, who *stirreth* up the sea" (*Isaiah 51:15*). The same רגע / R–G–KH also means to be at rest. Trembling relatives include רחף / RAKH[AF] (to shake), רעש / RÄKHÄSH (tremble, earthquake), and רעד / RÄKHÄD (trembling, tremor).

    BRANCHES: The shaky given etymology lists no cognates, but WAG (W=R) is linked to Swedish *vagga* (to rock).

ROOF/עֲרִיף
(AH)–REEF   [(U)–R–Y–PH]

ROOTS: Old English *hrof* (roof) is traced to an IE root *kropo* (roof).

    As seen at "RHAPSODY," ערב / ÄREV or KHÄREBH (woof) may provide the underpinnings of ROOF. (See "RAVEN" for a similar Hebrew etymon becoming an HRF term in Old English and a harder sound elsewhere.) As ROOF can mean the top or peak of anything we add ערף / ÖREF (scruff) to עריף / ÄREF (sky, clouds – *Isaiah 5:30*) and ערפל / ÄRÄFEL ("heaven" – *I Kings 8:12*).

ROOT/רָד
RODT   [RD→RT]

ROOTS: To ROOT (scream, or cheer for one's team) is a slang term of uncertain origin that may ultimately link up with *reden* (to talk in German) and to READ (proclaim). רד / RÄDT is to scream, wail or sigh (*Psalms 55:3*). The ROOT of plants and words grew form Latin *radix* (root) and the IE root *wrad* (branch, root).

    Arabic JEREED (found in English dictionaries) is a Turkish or Arabic javelin deriving from Arabic *jerid* or *jarid* (rod, shaft, javelin). A ROD or shaft is akin to a branch or root. The Arabic *jarid* sounds like ירד / YÄRÄDT (to go down – *Genesis 38:1*). The root is רד / R–DT, and ROOTS grow downward.

    BRANCHES: ROOD and ROD are from an IE base *ret* or *rot* (a pole, thin branch). Similarly, the root of ROD and RID is *reudh* (to clear land), and to ROOT is to dig up. The immediate source of ROD, as listed at IE root *reudh*, is Old English *rodd* (stick).

    Another R–D/T term that helps link ROOT to shaft and branch words (remember that the root of ROOT means "branch") is the REED. The IE root of REED is *kreut*, as Old English *hreod* (reed) is traced to Germanic *hreuda*. These terms sound much like a #2-#3 letter swap of חטר / (HO)TER (branch, stick) or Aramaic חטרא / KHOOTRÄ or HOODTRÄ (stick, rod). The official cognates of ROOT are ERADICATE, RACE, RADICAL, RADISH, RADIX, and RUTABAGA. תרד / (TE)REDT is a beetroot. For a Semitic etymon with a W or V (as in the IE root of ROOT, *wrad*), there is also שרביט / (SHÄ)RVÉDT (baton, shoot, twig – swap the R and W of *wrad*). רבד / RAVAD is to spread (*Proverbs 7:16*).

ROTA(TE)/רָצָא
ROT(S)–AH   [R–T(S)–A]

ROOTS: ROTARY and ROTATE are from Latin *rota* (wheel), which has been traced to the IE root *ret* (to run, roll). רצא / RÄT(S)Ä is to run (*Genesis 24:29*).

    BRANCHES: TORY, a cognate of ROTATE and a reversal of the RT, is from Old Irish *toir* (pursuit). רדף / RODT(ÄF) is to pursue or run after (*Genesis 44:4*). Other cognates of ROTATE are CONTROL, PRUNE, RODEO, ROLL, ROTA, ROTIFORM, ROTOGRAVURE, ROTOR, ROTUND, ROTUNDA, ROULETTE, ROUND, and ROWEL. Running alongside are terms like דהר / DTÄHÄR (to gallop), דור / DTOOR (rim of a wheel – see "TIRE"), and רהוט / RÄHOOT or W(R)ÄHOOT (quick – a possible influence on *vite*, "quick" in French). Like the French term, *witi-witi* is quick in Proto-Eastern Polynesian. Closer to the Hebrew is *joraat* (quickly) in Maya. רץ / RÄ(T)S (to run) has probably given rise to RACE and RUSH. RACE is from Old Norse *ras* (rushing) and the IE root *ers* (to be in motion). Cognates include ERR, ERRATIC, ERRATUM, ERRONEOUS, ERROR and ABERRATION (but see "ABERRATION"). A form of רץ / RÄ(T)S in *Genesis 41:4* is to "rush;" a מרץ / (MÄ)RÖ(T)S is a running race. Haste does make waste and error but we RUSH for a REASON. רצא / RÄTSÄ (to run) is motivated by רצה / RÄTSÄH (to wish, desire), and the motivation of רצון / RÄTSON (will, wish, desire) gave us REASON and RATION(ALE).

    The given etymon for RATIONALIZATION and other words from Latin *ratio* (reason, plan) is the IE root *ar* (to fit, join). רצוף / RÄTSOOF is joined.

    Running, will, desire, and RATIONALIZATION are most intensely involved when ready to commit רצח / RETSÄH (murder). For LUST, change the R–TS etymon to L–ST.

ROVE/רֹוֶה
ROVE – EH   [R – BH]

ROOTS: The verb to ROVE (set free, unloose) is originally an archery term based on Anglo-Saxon *arafian*. The ROVER Ishmael is the רבה קשת / RŌVEH (KASHUT) (bow shooter or "archer" of *Genesis 21:20*). רכב / ROVUV is to shoot; רובה / RŌVEH is a rifle in modern Hebrew.

    BRANCHES: For ROVER as a pirate, see words of like sound and sense such as RAPE, RAVEN and ROB. RIFLE (the verb) is from Dutch *rijffelen* (to plunder); RIFLE the noun is linked to French *rifler* (to scrape) instead of the R – BH Hebrew etymon above. For the ROVE in weaving see "REEVE."

RUCKUS/רֵעַשׁ
RAH – KHUS(H)   [R – KH – S(H)]

ROOTS: RUCKUS has "no known origin." Well known to Jewish liturgy is *Ezekiel 3:12* with its noise, commotion or "*roaring sound*" of angels' wings – רעש / RUKHUS(H) or RÄUSH.

    BRANCHES: *Räusch* is noise in German.
    RACKET, RUCKUS (tumult, noisy commotion), or RUCTION are louder, gutturalized forms of רעש / RKS. (BULL)RUSHES and RASPBERRIES make a RASPING RUSTLE too. This softer noise is covered by רחש / RUHUSH (whisper) – akin to לחש / LUHUSH (whisper) as well as to רעש / RUKHUS(H) (noise). For an antonym there's the anagramic counterpart חרש / KHARUSH (to be silent). Slanderous whisper is a derisive RAZZ or RASPBERRY (slang); לעז / LÄUZ is slander (L→R). רעשן / RAKHSHUN is a rattle; רגז / RŌGEZ is agitation. קרקש / (KĒ)RKÄSH is to rattle.

RUG/אֶרֶג
(EH) – REG   [ARG]

ROOTS: RUG is linked to Old Norse *rogg* (woven tuft of wool). Instead of tracing this to the IE root *ruk* (fabric, spun yarn), the AHD traces RUG and RAG to IE *reu* (to smash, knock down, tear out, uproot). ארג / EREG is a woven cloth, along with a loom or shuttle. אריג / ÄREG is woven cloth, material or stuff. While CARPET and WEB are probably from ערב / ĀREBH, ĀW(R)EB or KHĀREB (woof – see "REEVE"), ארג / EREG is often translated "web" in Scripture. Perhaps the most unfortunate use of "web" instead of RUG is in *Isaiah 38:12* – "my life is rolled up like a *web*."

    BRANCHES: Words attributed to IE *ruk* include RATCHET, ROCAMBOLE, ROCHET and ROCKET.

RUM/רם
RUM   [RM]

ROOTS: RUM, now obsolete, meant great or excellent. RUMMER is a glass to raise a public toast with; it derives from Dutch *roemen* (to praise). רם / RUM means high and exalted (*Isaiah 2:13-14; Isaiah 6:1*). רמה / RÄMÄ means flagrantly or publicly exalted (*Exodus 14:8; Numbers 15:30*).

BRANCHES: רם / RÄM (exalted) is often used in the context of the Almighty; RAMA (Sanskrit) is a Hindu deity. IRMA is also associated with a deity; perhaps RAMSES and ROME are too. מרא / MARĀ (an RM reversal) means "Lord" in Aramaic.
    The hills of ROME may be echoed in רמת / RÄMŌT (heights, high ground – *I Kings 22:3*). RAMP, RAMPAGE, RAMPANT and ROAM are all words of rising, climbing up and rearing up. הרם / (HĀ)RĒM is to raise, lift or exalt; הרם / HÄRĀM is a pyramid; רמה / RÄMÄ is a height or hill. ROMP and RIM refer to the public and to the raised connotations of רם / RM. A RAM (pump) raises water.
    Reversing to MR we get MORRO and MORAINE, terms for a hill, bluff or projecting rock. MORE and CLAYMORE are from Old English and Gaelic words for "great."
    Antonyms for all this RM greatness, blatant ROMPING and high climbing include רמה / RĒMÄ (worm), רמיה / RIMĒÄ (stealth, deceit), רמש / ROMAS (to crawl, creep) and רמיסה / RIMĒSÄ (trampling). *Lani* (R=L and M=N) means heaven and majesty in Hawaiian.

RUM(BLE)/רָעַם
RA – UM   [RUM]

ROOTS: RUMBLE (a heavy, rolling sound) is from Middle Dutch *rommelen*.
    רעם / RÄUM is to rave, rage, roar or thunder (*I Samuel 7:1; Psalms 96:11*).

    BRANCHES: Both רעם / RÄUM and נהם / NÄHUM (roar) might ultimately echo the liquid (L/R)-nasal (M/N) of LION (from Greek *leōn* – see "LEOPARD").

RUNE/רן
RUN   [RN]

ROOTS: Possibly related to RUNIC writings, a RUNE in its fourth sense is a poetic term for a song or poem. The word is traced to Finnish *runo* (poem, canto). רן / RUN is to sing or chant (*Psalms 32:7*); רנה / RĒNÄ is song, joy, or prayerful chant (*Psalms 126:2, Jeremiah 7:16*, and *Psalms 61:2*).

    BRANCHES: *Rana* is a frog in Italian and Spanish; Hebrew רן / RN lets us know that the creature sang for his reputation. The bird or *ornis* (Greek) is known for its singing – thus the RN in ORNITHOLOGY. CORONACH, from Irish *ranach*, is a dirge for bagpipes. רנה / RĒNÄ also means rumor; רמשית / RÄMSHES is a serenade. RUMOR, RIME and RYHME may be related. Yoruba *erin* means laughter; *oran* is song in Gaelic. Reversing RN for Oriental terms, *norae* is a song in Korean and *inori* is prayer in Japanese.

RUTH(LESS)/רות
RUTH   [RT→R–TH]

ROOTS: The Biblical Book of Ruth is significant because Ruth's son is King David's grandfather. The heroine and her story are marked by grief, sorrow, pity and, above all, compassion. The four terms above are precisely the definitions listed for the archaic word RUTH. Pity and compassion are antonyms of RUTHLESS. RUTHFUL means showing or arousing pity or sorrow. The dictionaries would sidestep the Biblical ancestor of the Messiah and link the word RUTH to Middle English *reuthe*, which derives from Old English *hreowan* (to rue). The word "rue", also from *hreowan*, means regret or repent, and is traced to the IE base *qreu* (matted blood, raw flesh...basic sense "to shudder with horror.")

See "GORE" and "SCARE."

While Ruth's name is a Moabite one, רות / ROOT or RUTH may connect to terms like רתת / R–T(H)–T(H) (to shake, as with awe – see "RATTLE") or רעות / RÁOOT(H) (friendship).

BRANCHES: Other English words linked to Hebrew names elsewhere in this book include: BABLE (Babel), BLAME (Balaam), COLLOSUS (Goliath), GONORRHEA (Gomorrah), JACK and JOCKEY (Jacob), perhaps JUDGE – and certainly JEW – (Judah), JINX (Jonah), JOVIAL (Jehova), MACABRE (Maccabee), OGRE (Og), and SODIUM (Sodom). To speculate further: JILT might relate to Jael; JORDAN (a chamber pot) ought to come from the river; JOHN (noun) and ZANY (adjective) originate with the name Yohannon; JORUM (a bowl) should be from King Jorum (*II Samuel 8:10*); a JOSEPH is a coat; *RIBALD* (linked to a theoretical name and to Middle Dutch *ribe* – a whore) may come from Rahab the prostitute in *Joshua 2-6*; and SCAM, SCAMP and SCANDAL might have been influenced by the ploy, the rogue and the disgrace of Shechem in *Genesis 34*. SIMONY is ultimately derived from the Biblical שמעון / SHIMON (Simeon).

SABOT(AGE)/שבוט
S(H)E–BOOT   [S(H)–B–O–T]

ROOTS: SABOT (the shoe, the boat or the piece of military projectile) is officially traced to *sabbât* (sandal in Arabic). שבוטא / SHĒBOOTÄ in Aramaic or שבוט / S(H)ĒBOOT in Hebrew is the flat flounder fish or the sole, resembling the sole of the foot. The destructive act of SABOTAGE (French *saboter* is to damage) comes from the practice of ruining machinery with these sturdy wooden shoes.

BRANCHES: A SABOTEUR in Spain wears *zapatos* on his feet. A shoe in Portugal is *sapato*, and in Indonesia *sepatu*. For the Turkish shoe, *ayakkabi*, see עקב / ÄKĀBH (heel, hoof) at "CAULK." While BOAT is only a possibility, BOOT is more likely related to the Semitic terms here. (*But* is a shoe in Polish.) See "BOOT."

SACK/שק
SUCK   [SK]

ROOTS: Linguists concede that SACK is a universal word, yet they do not explain why SK should sound like a pouch or bag. Greek *sakkos* and Latin *saccus* are acknowledged derivatives of שק / SUK (in *Leviticus 11:32* a "SACK," bag; SACKCLOTH in *Genesis 37:34*). The Germanic *zack* in words like KNAP*SACK* is from the related term צקלן / ZĒKLON (sack – *II Kings 4:42*).

BRANCHES: Reversing to KS bears similar containers like CASE or CYST.

כסה / KÄSÄ is to conceal; כים / KĒS is a pocket or purse. CYST and ASC(USO) are from Greek *kystis* and *askos* – both of which mean SAC or bladder.

After SACCULE, SACHET and SATCHEL, the wearable SACKS include the SACK coat, SACK dress, SACQUE (jacket) and those bags on our feet – SOCKS. While SK words for SOCKS are popular in Germanic languages, Indonesian reverses to *kaus*. The Arabic sock, *gawrab*, is shared by Hebrew (גרב / GEREV), Rumanian (*ciorapi*), Serbo-Croat. (*carape*), Turkish (*cora*) and Polish and Yiddish (*skarpetki*). To SACK (pillage, ruin) is linked to the looter's SACK or grab bag, but שכל / S(H)ÄK[ŌL] (to believe, "rob" in *Leviticus 26:22*) ought to be considered as well as הזיק / [HĒ]ZĒK (to damage). See "CASE."

SACK/צחיח
(T)SAKH – (ĒĒ – UKH)   [(T)S – KH]

ROOTS: A dry SACK, dry white wine, is from Latin *Siccus* (dry). The theoretical IE root for SACK is *seik(w)* (to flow). צחה / (T)SĒKH(ÄH) means thirsty or parched. Extensions of the צח / (T)S – KH root are seen in terms for arid places in *Isaiah 58:11* or *Psalms 68:7*.

BRANCHES: The IE root *seik(w)* (to flow) seems related to the SK antonym צחצוח /(T)SÄKHÄKH (to flow). צחצוח /(T)SÄKH – (T)SŌÄKH is a droplet. For other antonyms see "SOAK." נסך / (NA)SAKH is to pour; סחיטה / SIKHĒTA means squeezing out. Official cognates of SACK are DESICCATE. EXSICCATE, SECCO and SICCATIVE. An extended IE root *skel* (to parch, wither) yields SKELETON. SKELETON more likely links up to שלד / SHELED or SC(H)ELET (skeleton), preserved in Syriac *shilada* (skeleton). See SHIELD."

Suchy is dry in Polish and Czech. *Saka* is dry, and *seca* is to be dry for the Dakota Indians. *Sec* is dry in French; the Rumanian is *uscat*. חרב / KHURAV (to be dry) is the Hebrew behind "dry" words like Turkish *kuru* and Indonesian *kering*. The middle R may have dropped out in Finnish *kuiva*, Swahili *-kavu*, Japanese *kawaitu* and (the more distant) Arabic *gaaf*.

SAFFR(ON)/שרף
SAR–UF   [SRF→SFR]

ROOTS: SAFFRON, the orange-yellow color and plant, is officially borrowed from Arabic *za'faran*. This should be a typical #2-#3 letter flip (metathesis) of Hebrew שרף / SÄRUF (to burn) and שרפה / SRÄFÄ (fire – *Genesis 11:3*).

BRANCHES: For a similar metathesis, Arabic *zarâfah* (giraffe) came from Hebrew צואר / TSÄVÄR (neck) – see "GIRAFFE." See "SERPENT."

SAG/שַׁח
S(H)AKH   [S(H) – KH]

ROOTS: To SAG is linked to Swedish *sacka* (to sink), Danish *Sakke* (to drop astern) and Middle Dutch *zakken* (to subside). The IE root for SAG and SINK is *seng(w)* (to sink). שׁח / S(H)AKH is to sink or bow down (*Isaiah 51:23*), and שׁקע / S(H)ÄKKÄ is to sink, dip, subside or "abate" (*Numbers 11:2*).

> **BRANCHES:** שׁחת / S(H)UKHUT means pit (a SUNKEN place); שׁקע / S(H)EKKÄ is a SOCKET. שׁכך / S(H)AKHUKH also means to abate.
> שׂנא / S(H)ÄGÄ (to grow) and שׂנה / S(H)ÄGÄH (to increase) are SG antonyms. The N of SINK and of the IE root *se(n)gw* is a nasalization (N added), while שׁכב / S(H)ÄKHÄV (to lie down) might explain the W in *sengw* – see "SUCCUBUS." השׁיג / [HE]SEG is to move back; נשׁוג / [NÄ]SOG is to turn back. Reversing to GS, נגשׁ / [NÄ]GÄSH is to recede (like sagging). It also means to draw near or approach. More GS antonyms at "KISS."

SAGA/שׂיח
SEE – AKH   [S – Y – KH]

ROOTS: The IE root *sek(w)* (to say, utter) is the source of SAGA as well as SAW (a saying), SAY and SCOLD. SAGA (a narrative) is echoed by שׂיח / SEÄKH (talk, tell, "recite" in *Psalms 145:5*). שׂיחה / SEKHÄ is a speech, talk or oration.

> **BRANCHES:** סח / SÄKH is to talk or tell; שׂגר / S(H)OG[ÄR] means to speak fluently or to flow. Reverse SH – G for the source of GUSH.
> The teller of SAGAS was often a SAGE, though the savants trace SAGE to Latin *sapere* (to know, taste) – see "SAVOIR – FAIRE").

SAKE/זָקֶה
ZEEK – AH   [AK→SK]

ROOTS: Anglo-Saxon *sacu* is a cause, lawsuit, or contention; the meanings of SAKE include: motive, purpose, end, cause, advantage, behalf, benefit and account. The IE root is *sag* (to seek out). עשׂק / (Ä)SEK means contention – *Genesis 26:20* – see "COSSACK." Several ז–כ/ק (Z/S – K) terms added nuances of meaning to SAKE: זכה / ZEKÄH (to bestow, to credit), זקה / ZEKAH (relevance, debt, obligation, tie), זקוק / ZSÄKOOK (tied to, dependent on), זכיה / SZIKHEÄ (claim, merit) and זכות / ZSIKH(OOS) (merit, privilege, credit).

> **BRANCHES:** Since the IE root for SAKE, *säg* (to seek out), considers SEEK to be a cognate, see "SEEK." SAKE (SÄKE), the alcoholic beverage from Japan, may well relate to שׁכר / S(H)ÄK(HÄR) (intoxicating drink, beer) – the probable SK water element in WHISKY as well – see "SOAK." CIDER is an acknowledged borrowing from שׁכר / S(H)ÄKHÄR. Not acknowledged is the fact that Arabic *iksir* is a #1-#2 letter swap of שׁכר / S – K – R. *Al iksir* is the immediate source of ELIXIR.

SALVA(TION)/שַׁלְוָה
S(H)AL – VAH   [S(H) – L – V]

ROOTS: Latin *salvus* means whole, safe, healthy and uninjured; the IE root is *sol* (whole). שׁלוה / S(H)ÄLVÄ is peace, quiet and ease; its SL roommate at *Psalms 122:7* is שׁלם / S(H)ÄL(OM) (peace). Her twin sister is שׁלם / S(H)ÄL(ÄM) (whole, healthy, uninjured). שׁל / SL is the two-letter root – see "SLAM."

> **BRANCHES:** Listed cognates at IE root *sol* include CONSOLIDATE, SAFE, SAGE, SALUBRIOUS, SALUTE, SALUTORY, SALVAGE, SALVO, SAVE, SOLEMN and SOLID. See "SALUTE" and "SOLEMN."
> El *SALVADOR* and JERU*SAL*EM are linked to *SALVATION*. שׁבה / S(H)ÄVÄ is to take capture during war (*Deuteronomy 21:10*). Capturing a prisoner or an object in war is to SAVE or to SALVAGE that person or thing from certain destruction. If hoarding or SAVING loot does not evoke a spiritual SAVIOR, שׁב / S(H)ÄV also means to repent, to return, to restore and to redeem. SAFE might also be influenced by ספן / *SAF*(AN) (covered, secured – *Deuteronomy 33:21*), a variant of צפן / *TSAF*OON (hidden).

SAMURAI/שׁוֹמֵר
S(H)OAM – AIR   [S(H) – M – R]

ROOTS: A SAMURAI was the Japanese royal guard. A שׁומר / S(H)OMER is a guard or "watchman" – *Songs 3:3*. שׁמורה / S(H)IMOORÄ is a trigger guard.

> **BRANCHES:** שׁמור / S(H)ÄMOOR is watched, guarded or preserved. This term is interchangeable with זכור / ZÄKHOR ("remember" – see the 4th of the Ten Commandments at *Exodus 20:8* and *Deuteronomy 5:12*). The IE root *smer* (to remember) is another form of preserving or keeping. The "S" of *smer* was subsequently forgotten, but its legacy includes MEMORIAL(IZE), MEMORY and MOURN. Germanic *scrim* (a guard, protection) and German *schirm* (screen, protection) are but a RM→MR letter flip away from שׁמר / SH – M – R. SCREEN, SCRIMMAGE, and SKIRMISH are therefore related. In Chinese, *zhen* is to guard and *shenlu (te)* is prudent. The samurai's code of honor is the *Bushido*. In Japanese 1)*bu* is military, 2)*shi* is man and 3)*dō* is a code. In Hebrew צבא / [TSA]BHU is military, 2)אישׁ / EESH is man and 3)עד / ÄD or KHÄD is a CODE or law.

SANDAL/סַנְדָּל
SUN – DULL   [S – N – D – L]

ROOTS: Some dictionaries stop at Greek *sandalon* for the shoe, and *sandanon* for the SANDALWOOD tree. Others claim Sanskrit *Candana* as the (Aryan) source, but do concede that Arabic *çandal* (SUN – DULL) is a term for the open shoe and for the wood its sole was made from. A סנדלר / SÄNDLÄR (shoemaker) was a profession and a surname in Mishnaic times. (Note the similar -ÄR or -ER suffix designating the maker.)

> **BRANCHES:** סאן / SÄON is a shoe or sandal (*Isaiah 9:4*) in the E Shoshan dictionary. סנדל / SÄNDÄL could therefore mean the shoe of a דל / DUL (poor man).

(SANG)FROID/בָּרָד
BHA–RUD   [BRD→FRD]

ROOTS: SANGFROID means cold-blooded – see "SANGRIA" for the first element. *Froid* is cold in French; *freddo* is the Italian cognate. The FRD terms are given the cold shoulder by reference books, even Latin *frigidus* (cold, cool) is traced to the IE root *srig* (cold).

This SRG root is from שלג / S(H)ELEG (snow – *Jeremiah 18:14*), and the source of the FRD terms above is also from a Hebrew word for frozen rain – ברד / BÄRÄD or VÄRÄD (hail – *Exodus 9:18*). "Cold" in Arabic is *barid*; in Swahili it's *baridi*.

BRANCHES: The frozen-rain-equals-freezing-cold equation allows SNOW (*snieg* in Russian) to come from צנה / (T)SENÄ (cold). Polish *zimny* already means cold and winter. The Biblical citaiton for צנה / (T)SENÄ puts this ice-cold equation on ice: "Like the *coldness* of snow" – *Proverbs 25:13*.
Japanese cold is *tsum(etai)*; Korean is *ch'an*. Cold in Chinese is *shang han*.
In Malay: (Massaratty) cold is *(da)bridi*. Cold in Cantonese is *don*; winter in Chinese is *tung*.
FRIGID and REFRIGERATOR might also be BH–R–D terms. Otherwise, the IE root of Latin *frigus* (cold) is also *srig* (cold) – suggesting that FRIGIDITY, too, is linked to שלג / S(H)ELEG (snow – SLG→SRG). See "FROST."

SANG(RIA)/נֶצַח
NE(T)S–UKH   [N–(T)S–KH→SNG]

ROOTS: SANGRIA, the Spanish wine, literally means bleeding. Latin *sanguis* is blood. There is no IE root.

The word is a metathesis from the original Hebrew. It is hard to say נצח / NETSÄH (blood – *Isaiah 63:3*), so letters #1 and #2 got swapped (NSK to SNK) to get terms like *singe* (blood in Rumanian).

BRANCHES: Hamites and Semites kill in passion and zeal, but Japhetics can murder with SANG-FROID (French – cold blooded composure.) SANGUINE is blood colored, ruddy or cheerful. The context with נצח / NETSÄKH ("blood") in *Isaiah 63:3* is clearly painting a picture with the redness of blood. This bright redness is evident in terms like נצח / NOTSÄKH (to shine) and הנץ / HÄNETS (shining). The shine is a crimson one, as הנץ החמה / HÄNETS HÄHÄMÄ means "shining of the sun" or dawn.
חמה / HÄMÄ (sun, heat, glow) has the warmth and the redness to be at the root of HEMOGLOBIN and 50 words from Greek *haima* (blood) – HEMATAL (of blood) and HEMATEIN (reddish dye) recall an anagram of נצח / N–TS–H – חמוץ / HAMOOT(S((scarlet – *Isaiah 63:1*). This (H)M–T(S) term, with our captioned N–T(S) two-letter root of shining red, may color dawn and morning terms in English such as *MATIN* and *MATINEE*. They derive from Latin *Matuta* (goddess of the dawn). Reinforcing this etymology are D/T–M/N terms like אדם / ÄDOM (red) and דם / DÄM (blood in Hebrew, Arabic and Swahili). See "ANEMIC", "DAWN," and "RED." נצח / NETSÄKH also means to be victorious. Remove the N for Gothic *sigis* (victory – source of SIGMUND); remove the TS for NIKE (victory – a Greek noun and IE root "of unknown origin").

SAPPHIRE/סַפִּיר
SAP(H)–EAR   [SPYR]

ROOTS: Greek *sappheiras* is the source cited by the AHD. *Webster's* admits to the existence of Hebrew ספיר / SÄPER or SÄPHER ("sapphire" – *Exodus 39:11*), but covers up with "from Sanscrit *Sanipriya*, literally, dear to Saturn."

BRANCHES: SAPPHIRA the feminine name is admitted to be from Aramaic, but akin to Greek *sappir* (beautiful). Even Aramaic שפרא / SHOOFRÄ (elegance, glory) is from שפר / SHEPHER (beauty, goodliness – *Genesis 49:21*). SPLENDID and RESPLENDENT, from IE root *spel* (to shine, glow) ought to relate (SPR→SPL). שפל / S(H)–P(H)–L renders antonyms of humiliation and depression – see "ASPHALT." *Szep* is beautiful in Hungarian. Anyone named Shifra Shapiro ought to be doubly beautiful. See "JASPER" + "SUPER."

SAR(CASTIC)/שְׁאָר
S(H)ÄIR   [S(H)–A–R]

ROOTS: SARCASM literally infers tearing flesh or *Sarx* in Greek.
שאר / S(H)'ÄR is defined as meat (*Psalms 78:20*), flesh or food (*Exodus 21:10*).

BRANCHES: SARCOPHAGUS, SARCOMA and ANASARCA are among the related words which have somehow been traced to the IE root *twerk* (to cut). Perhaps טבח / TÄBHÄKH (slaughter, butcher) is what *twerk* was influenced by. בשר / (BÄ)SÄR is the common Biblical term for flesh or meat. See "BUTCHER".

SASH/שֵׁשׁ
S(H)AYSH   [S(H)–SH]

ROOTS: SASH, an ornamental band, is borrowed from Arabic *sash* (turban). The turban or "mitre of fine linen" of *Exodus 28:39* ought to explain why the Arabic turban was named for שש / SHASH ("fine linen").

BRANCHES: The fine fibers of this venerable Mid-Eastern hat of nobility might have been silk as well as fine linen. SYCEE is from the Cantonese (Chinese) *hsi ssu* (fine silk) which sounds like שש / SH–SH. שש ומשי / SHASH–(OO)MESHE ("fine linen and silk") are yoked by proximity in *Ezekiel 16:13*. SISAL means linen of fine plant fiber, yet it is supposedly named for its places of origin. SISAL is a Maya term from the Yucatan (Mexico).

SAT(ISFY)/סָעַד
SAW–UDT   [SAD→SAT]

ROOTS: Latin *satis* means enough, gratification and contentment. SATED is from Latin *satur* (full of food), the source for SATIRE and SATURATE as well. ASSET, SAD and SATIATE all tie in at IE root *sa* (to satisfy), while many ST words mean food in Latin and Greek. Abraham wants to "sustain" or "refresh" his guests with food in *Genesis 18:5* / סעד / SÄUDT. A meal is a סעדה / S'OODTA. ציד / (T)S–Y–DT is a verb of supplying, or a noun meaning provision, food or game (*Genesis 27:7*).

BRANCHES: *Syotta* is feed in Finnish; שד / S(H)OD is nutrition from mother's breast (*Isaiah 60:16*). See "PARASITE."

SATR(AP)/שׁוֹטֵר
S(H)O–TEAR [S(H)–T–R]

ROOTS: A SATRAP evokes a Near Eastern ruler, but the word is claimed for the Indo-Aryans with the Greek *satrapes* and the Old Persian *shathrapauan* ("protector of the land"). Policemen are protectors, and a policeman or an "officer" (*Deuteronomy 16:18*) is a שׁוֹטֵר / SHOTÄR.

BRANCHES: Add the prefix מ / M for משטר / MIS(H)TÄR (executive power, regime) and you get the (BURGO)MASTER, the mayor or head MAGISTRATE of a German town. Biblical judges or magistrates were also political leaders. We no longer lend MAJESTY (not from Latin *magnus*) to magistrates and mayors, nor to the many people called MASTER and MISTER. משטר / (ME)S(H)TÄR is to rule and to regiment, related to סדר / SODÄR or SOTÄR (to arrange, put in order). There's also שדרה / S(H)IDTÄRÄ (a row or regiment of soldiers; an avenue – see "STREET") and שדרה / S(H)EDTRÄ (the spinal column). MAESTRO and MISTRESS, like MISTER and MASTER, are credited to the IE root *meg* (great).

The starry aspect of STELLAR is taken up at "SIDEREAL," while the other STELLAR (leading, chief) may relate better to the organizing and ordering of a SATRAP or a STEERING committee. To STEER not only means to guide by a rudder, but to direct, oversee and control. STEER and STERN (of a boat) are from Old Norse *styra* (to steer), but are lumped together with 100 loosely connected words at IE root *sta* (to stand) – see "STABLE."

SENTRY, of uncertain origin, could well be a nasalized (+N) שטר / STR (policeman, protector). שלטון / SHILTON (authority, government) is an STR→SLT relative – see "SULTAN."

SAUCE/עָסִים
AH–CEASE [USYS]

ROOTS: Old French *sause* had a variant spelled *Saulse*. This allows etymology-seekers to link SAUCE (mashed or stewed fruit) with Late Latin *salsa* and Latin *sal* (salt). SALSA is apparently borrowed from Arabic *salsa* (gravy), and SAUCE has no L in its past. These statements can be made from analyzing the "gravy" entry in Bergman's 26 language dictionary. Only Turkish and Spanish have SLS words for gravy, indicating the usual Arabic connection. The Italian, French, Rumanian, Germanic and Slavic terms are all forms of SAUCE (mashed or stewed fruit). עסים / (Ä)SES is the fruit juice in *Songs 8:2*; עסם / ÄSUS or KHÄSUS is to mash, press or squeeze.

BRANCHES: The reduced form, עסה / ESÄ or KHESÄ (to squeeze, press), is the source of (S)QUEEZE, (S)QUASH and (S)QUISH. Backups include שחט / SHÄKUT (to press, as grapes – *Genesis 40:11*), סחוט / SÄKHOOT (squeezed dry), כבש / KOBHUSH (to press) and כתוש or כתות / KÄSOOS or KÄSOOSH (crushed). (S)QUEEZE is initially from Anglo-Saxon *cwys(an)* (to crush – and a possible source of CRUSH), which favors כבש / KOVÄSH as its etymon. The Dutch word for gravy did not fit any other language mentioned above. Dutch *jus* does, however, indicate that JUICE too is an extract of עסים / KHÄS(ES), GUS(ES), or (ÄS)JES. Indonesian milk is *susu* (a liquid which comes from squeezing). Polish sauce is *sos*, but juice is *sok* עס / KH – S reversed). Latin *sucus* (juice) gives us SUCCULENT (see "SOAK"). A SAUCER is not a plate for (salty) flavorings or dressings, but a receptacle to "catch any spilled liquid" (*Webster's*). עסיסי / ÄSESEY is JUICY; notice the similar adjectival suffices (EY and Y). See "OOZE."

SAVANNA/שׁוְיוֹן
S(H)EAVE–YONE [S(H)–V–H]

ROOTS: השוה / (HE)S(H)VÄ is to smooth or level; שוה / S(H)ÄVÄ is plain; שׁוְיוֹן / S(H)IVYON is equality. These terms gave rise to the Carib Indian word for a flat, level plain or SAVANNA. In Swahili, a Hamitic language, *sawa* means flat.

BRANCHES: SEWAN, in an English dictionary, is the Algonquin Indian word for shells used as money. שוי / S(H)ÄWE is price or worth; שוה / S(H)ÄVÄ means equivalent to or worthwhile – both excellent connotations for legal tender. שוה / S(H)OWEH is equal or worth. "It *profiteth* not the king to suffer them"– *Esther 3:8*. "For wisdom is better than rubies; no good can *equal* her"– *Proverbs 8:11*. "Likewise" and "also" are equivalent terms. ALSO is from Anglo-Saxon *eal* (all) + *swa* (likewise), much like our Hebrew root here.

SAVOIR – (FAIRE)/סָבַר
SOV–ARE [S–BH–R]

ROOTS: SAVOIR – FAIRE, a French term borrowed by English, means skill, tact or literally "to know how to do." We are concerned with only the "*savoir*" here, which is a cousin of SAVVY. The latter term is from Spanish *saber* (to know); the Spanish and French words are both linked to Latin *sapere* (to have taste, to be wise). סבר / SOVÄR or SÄBHÄR in Aramaic means to understand or think.

BRANCHES: Other intelligent SV terms include שעף / SÄÄPH (thought – *Job 4:13*) and חשב / (HA)S(H)ÄV (to think, calculate, design with skill – *Exodus 31:4*). The term means "considered as" or "deemed to be" in *Proverb 17:28* –"Even a fool, if he keeps silent, is *deemed* wise." Cognates of SAVVY at IE root *sep* (to taste, perceive) include SAGE, SAPID, SAPIENT, SAPOR, SAVANT and SAVOR. Greek *sophia* (skill, intelligence, wisdom) should be related. That would take in PHILOSPHY and other -SOPHY terms like SOPHISM, SOPHISTICATED, SOPHISTRY and SOPHOMORE. An equivalent of SAVANT was the title סבורא / SÄVORÄ, conferred in the Babylonian era when the Talmud was compiled.

SAW/מִשּׂוֹר
(MA)SOAR [SWR]

ROOTS: The dictionaries do not explain how Middle English *saw* (the cutting tool) came from Anglo-Saxon *saga*. They merely go on to connect *saga* and German *sage* to Latin *secare* (to cut) and the IE base *seq* (to cut). See "SAXON" for covering this etymological route.

The SAW of the Bible is משור / (MÄ)SOR or (M)SUR – *Isaiah 10:15*. A synonym is מסור / (MÄ)SWOR (saw). The מ / M prefix is a common feature with implements. Examples include the מגן / (MÄ)GÄN (shield) and the מגרד / (MÄ)GRÄDT (grater). Either the ו is rendered as a V or W, or the ר / R of an SR root is pronounced as a W.

BRANCHES: An SR root is suggested by שרט or סרט / SORUT (to incise or scratch) and the סרטן / SÄRTUN (crab) with its saw-like pincers or tail. נסר / (NA)SAR is to saw or plane. See "SERRATED" and "SHIVER."

SAXON/סכין
SUCK–IN   [SKYN]

ROOTS: ZAX is from Anglo-Saxon *seax* (a knife), the weapon which probably gave its name to the horde of barbarians known as Anglo-Saxons. SAXON is traced to IE root *sek* (to cut – see "SKILL"). סכין / SÄKÉN is a knife; שכין / SAKÉN is the spelling of this knife term in *Proverbs 23:2*. Also related are the many KS cutting words like קצה / KÉTSÄ (to peel, cut off, scrape) seen at "CUT." Still reversing to KS, there are more cutters like גזז / GÄ Z(ÄZ) (to cut, shear – *Genesis 31:19*) and כסוח / KÄSOOÄH (to cut off – *Isaiah 32:12*). A sharper knife connection to סכין / SÄKÉN (knife) is seen with SKEAN. SKEAN is from Old Irish *scian* (knife), traced to IE root *skei* (to cut, split). סכן / SKN is linked to sharp danger or סכנה / SÄKÄNÄ in *Ecclesiastes 10:9*.

BRANCHES: Hebrew offers SK terms of cutting off that are more subtle. These include שך / SUKH (to fence up... and thus cut off an area), שכבה / S(H)IKÄVÄ (layer, stratum), שכל / S(H)IKÖL (bereavement...cut off from loved ones) and שכח / S(H)OKHUKH (to forget...cut off from consciousness).

IE *skei* takes in 30 words including CONSCIENCE, CONSCIOUS, ESQUIRE, NICE, OMNISCIENT, PRESCIENT, SCHEDULE, SCHISM, SCIENCE, SCHIZO and SHIN. SICKLE and SCYTHE are the most relevant cutters at IE root *sek*. Other terms there include DISSECT, INSECT, INTERSECT, NOTCH, RISK, SAW, SECTION, SECTOR, SEDGE, SEGMENT and SKIN. שחין / S(H)KHÉN is a *skin* affliction, see the SK Hebrew words above which speak to the layers and divisions of SKIN. Since NICE (cut fine) is listed here, we include the anagramic relative of סכין / SKN, נתח / N–S–KH (surgical slice). IE root *nsi* (sword) gives us ENSIFORM. The second chemical element in our SKN molecule is KN. It may mean "sharp" or KEEN (see "KEEN") as seen in words like חנית / KHÄNÉT (dagger) and *cheni* (a knife in Mysol dialect of Malay). Reversing to IE root *nogh* (nail, clew), we might scratch in NAIL.

Returning to the SK element of our root, the AHD cites several IE roots as extensions of IE *sek* (to cut). Some relevant terms from IE roots like *sker*, *skeri*, *skeru*, and *sked* include: ASCRIBE, CERTAIN, CIRCUMSCRIBE, CONSCRIPT, CORTEX, CRISIS, CRITIC, DESCRIBE, DISCERN, ESCROW, SCABBORD, SCAR, SCATO-, SCORE, SCRABBLE, SCRAP(E), SCREEN, SCREW, SCRIBBLE, SCRIBE, SCRIPTURE, SCROLL, SCRUB, SHARD, SHARE, SHARP, SHATTER, SHEAR, SHINGLE, SHIRT, SHORT, SHRED, SHREW, SHRIVEL, SHROUD, SKIRMISH and SKIRT. Many of these SK terms are really KR terms, the initial "S" being non-historic. See "CASTRATE" and "CURT." שחט / SHAKHUT (to slaughter with a knife) involves the שח / SK two-letter root of flattening down and the KT two-letter root of cutting – see "CUT." שכה / SOOKA is a spear (*Job 40:31*), שכים / SÉK(ÉM) are thorns (*Numbers 33:55*) and שך / SOKH is a fence (*Lamentations 2:6*). These sharp, divisive SK terms may link IE *sek* (to cut) with IE *sak* (to sanctify) in that holy things are cut off or sectioned off from the profane. If so, CONSECRATE, EXECRATE, SACRED, SACROSANCT, SAINT and SA(N)CTITY are related to SK cutting terms here. The Hebrew word for SA(N)CTITY, קדושה / KIDT(OOSHA), is a KT cutting term.

SCAB/שכבה
S(H)IH–K(H)AB(H)–AH   [SKB(H)]

ROOTS: The dictionary suggests, "probably influenced by Latin *scabies* (roughness, itch)." A scab is not an itch. Note the Hebrew term for a thin, natural protective covering – שכבה / SKB (translated "layer" in *Exodus 16:13*).

BRANCHES: Flip root letters #2 and #3 of ספחת / SÄPÄKH(US) (scab) to scratch out a related term.

SCABB(LE)/קצב
CO(T)S–ABH   [K(T)SB→(T)SKB]

ROOTS: SCABBLE is from IE root *skep* (to cut, hack etc.). קצב / KO(T)SÄBH is "to cut off" in *II Kings 6:6*; its defintion includes "to stipulate" and "to determine." The next of kin is קצב / KE(T)SEBH (shape, cut or "proportions") in *I Kings 6:25*. Put the two together to get the kind of SHAVING or SHAPING that a (LAND)SCAPER or gardener does.

BRANCHES: קצה / KÉTSÄ is to cut off; קצה / KOTSEH is an extremity or edge; קצע / KÉTSÄÄ is to trim. Cognates like SHAPE, SHAVE and SHIP help to document the ק / K to ה / H change that is common from Hebrew (and IE roots) to English. Doubtless, this is why the *koph* (ק) looks like an extended *hey* (ה). Other cognates listed at IE *skep* include BATHYSCAPE, CAPON, SAPSAGO, SCAB(ROUS), SCAPHOID, SCAPULA (this shoulder term also resembles the Hebrew shoulder, the כתף / KOSÄPH or KOTÄPH), SCOOP (minus the S it resembles the cuplike כף / KUPH or palm of the hand), SHABBY, SHAFT, and SHIP. SHIPSHAPE is one of thirty SHIP words, not counting related terms like (FRIEND)SHIP or (SPORTSMAN)SHIP. SKIFF and SKIPPER belong in the same boat. Chinese only pronounces letters 2 and 3 of קצב / K–TS–BH as a cut (style) is a *ts'ai fa*. See "SHABBY" and "SYNCOPATION."

SCALE/שקל
S(H)OCK–ULL   [SH–K–L→SKL]

ROOTS: To SCALE is to weigh; שקל / S(H)ÄKÄL (to weigh) is how Abraham "weighed" the 400 SHEKELS of silver in *Genesis 23:16* when purchasing Hebron. The Aramaic תקל / TEKEL (weighed) from the handwriting on the wall (*Daniel 5:25*) displays the usual SH→T variation from the Hebrew. Ignoring patriarchal title deeds and prophetic graffiti, SCALE, as in ESCALATE or ECHELON, is credited to Latin *scala* (stairs, ladder) and the IE root *skand* (to leap, climb). For the Hebrew source of the Latin and IE SK terms, add an nonhistoric S to a couple of guttural (K) words – a phenomenon very common here in the "SC" part of this dictionary. First add an S to קום / KOOM (to rise) to see words like SCAMPER. Then, add the S to עלה / ÄLÄ or KÄLÄ (to go up) to bring ESCALATOR into view. מעלה / [MÄ]ÄLÄH or [MÄ]KHÄLÄ means steps or stairs in *Exodus 20:23*.

BRANCHES: For the SCALE connected to SCALL and SHELL see "CALIBER." Hebrew connections to שקל / SHÄKÄL (to weigh, ponder) include שכל / SÄKHUL (to be wise), שער / SHEKHÄR or SHÉÄR (to measure) and שער / SHÄÄR or SHÄKHÄR (market, price, value). The Scandinavian *SKILLING* and English *SHILLING* are small coins whose etymology weighs heavily upon the שקל / SHEKEL. One third of a SHEKEL (coin) is a פים / PÉM (*I Samuel 13:21*), a possible influence on the word PENNY.

SCALLION/אַשְׁכְּלָן
USH – KEL – ON   [SKL]

ROOTS: Latin (*caepa*) *Ascalonia* is officially borrowed from the name of a town in Israel – אשכלן / ÄSHKELON.

> **BRANCHES:** The SHALLOT is from French *eshalotte*, from Old French *eschaloign.* This last term is described as "a city in Philistia," the same Israeli city as above.

(S)CALLOP/קְלִיפָה
KILL – LEAP– (AH)   [KLP]

ROOTS: As usual, the S before a C is nonhistoric, often originating from the Old French habit of prefixing words with *es.* Old French *escalope* is the given etymon for SCALLOP (the shelled mollusk or its shells). Old French *escale* (husk, shell) is the source of the scaly SCALE, whose IE root is listed as *skel* or *kel* (to cut). The S-less variant is common for SK IE roots. קלפה / KILĒPÄ is a shell or to shell, to peel – see "CALIPEE." קלפין / KÄLP(ĒN) are fish scales in Aramaic.

> **BRANCHES:** Cognates at IE root *SKEL* include SHALE, SHELL, SHIELD, and SKOAL. The ELAPID, from Greek *elops* (a fish with scales), swims without the C of SCALLOP. Ōlepe is an oyster, and *kulepe* is to shell or split open in Hawaiian. See "SCALP" and "SHIELD."

(S)CALP/קְלִפָּה
KILEE – PAH   [KLP]

ROOTS: The IE root is *skel* or *kel* (to cut), and one Hebrew etymon is קלף / KOLUP(H) to skin, peel (or SCALP) – see "(S)CALLOP." קלף / KLAP[H] is parchment. Other Hebrew terms to consider include קרח / KÄRÄ – ÄH (bald – *Leviticus 13:40*), גלב / GÄLOB (barber – *Ezekiel 5:1*), גליפה / GILĒPHÄ (carving, engraving) and גלגלת / GILGŌLET (skull, head – *Exodus 16:16*).

> **BRANCHES:** SCALL (old Norse *skalli* is a bald head), SCALPEL and SCULPTURE are official cognates. Consider adding CALLOW, CALVARY, CALVINISM, CALYPTRA, CARVE, CLIP, CREPE, GOLGOTHA, (reversing to) PEEL, PILL(AGE) and PARCH(MENT). Drop the ק to get the source of IE root *lep* (to peel) and LEPER, LEPIDO, LEPROSY, etc. Russian *galava* is a head. See "CALIPEE", "GALYAK", "GLYPH", and "SKULL".

(S)CANTINESS /קַטְנוּת
CUT – NOOSE   [KTN → KNT]

ROOTS: SCANT means inadequate in size or amount. The given IE root is *kem* (hornless) wherein SCANTY and

"HIND" are seen as cognates. *Webster's* offers the "capon" as a cognate. The first thing to do with many an SC word is to drop the initial S. A common #2-#3 root letter flip then reveals etymons like קטן / KÄTON (little, to be small) and קטנות / KÄTNOOS (paltriness). קטן / KITÄN- is a prefix meaning "short of" or "lacking." קטע / KUTÄ is to cut off or amputate; see "CUT". קטן / KTN means "little" in *II Samuel 12:3* and "unworthy" in *Genesis 32:11*. Note the similar suffices in the captioned terms.

> **BRANCHES:** SCANTILY and SCANTLING are related. When considering the ל = נ (L=N) equation, קטן / KTN (small, tiny) is much like its antonym גדול / G – DT– L (great, large). See "KITTEN."

(S)CAR/כִּירָה
KEER – AH   [KYRH]

ROOTS: A SCAR is the mark of a flesh wound, etc. The dictionary traces the term to Greek *eschara* (fireplace, mark of a burn). The root should be KR as seen at "CHAR". כירה / KĒRÄ is a HEARTH; כור / KOOR (*Deuteronomy 4:20*) or כור / KHOOR (*Isaiah 48:10*) both mean "furnace." See "SCORCH."

> **BRANCHES:** For an etymon that speaks to other aspects of a SCAR (mark, impression) try זכר / ZÄKHER (remembrance, memory – *Exodus 17:14*) or זכרון / SĒKÄR[ON] (memorial, record – *Exodus 13:9*). The second SCAR in our dictionary is said to derive from old Norse *sker* (a low reef). Because the word is filed under IE *sker* (to cut) see "CURT." A rockier etymon appears at "SILICON."

(S)CARAB/עָרֹב
[KH]AR – ROVE   [KH – R – BH → KRB]

ROOTS: This beetle is *scarabeus* in Latin, but *karabos* (beetle) in Greek. Once again, almost every *S* before a *C* is nonhistoric.

The SCARAB, the black winged dung beetle, was historically deified and sculpted on tombs and jewelry by the ancient Egyptians. Precisely because of this beetlemania, M.M. Kolisch (British Bible commentator, 1828-1885) is correct to translate the fourth plague of Egypt (ערב / ÄROV or KHÄRŌBH – *Exodus 8:17*) as "beetles" instead of a "swarm of flies". (All ten plagues ruined gods of Egypt, whether the Nile, the sun-god or cattle.)

> **BRANCHES:** CARBINE (the rifle) is from the French beetle, the *(s)carabée.* The Italian cockroach is a *(s)caraf(aggio).* Other creatures dressed for (S)CRAPPING or for קרב / KRÄBH (battle) like the shelled scorpion (עקרב / ÄKRÄBH) may be seen at "CRAB". קליפה / KILĒPÄ is a shell (KLP=KRB). A GRUB is the worm-like larva of insects, "especially of a beetle"– (*Webster's*).

SCARE/שָׂעַר
SAW–(C)AR   [S–KH–R]

ROOTS: *Webster's* believes that SCARE is "probably" from an Indo-European base *(s)quer-* (to jump about) – see "SCURRILOUS." The AHD links SCARE with Old Norse *skjarr* (shy, timid). Hebrew offers שער / SO–ÄR or SOKHÄR (dread, shudder – *Deuteronomy 32:17*). שעיר / SÄER or SÄKHĒR is a demon in *Leviticus 17:7*.

BRANCHES: Lop off the S of [S]CARED (so often necessary with SC words) and one can see חרד / KHORÄD (afraid, timid, trembling – *Genesis 27:33; Numbers 33:24*). Anagrams of this KH–R/L–D/T term include ערץ / KHORÄTS (to dread), רעד / ROKHUD (trembling), רעץ / RÄKHÄTS (to fear) and דחיל / DIKHĒL (fear – *Daniel 4:2*). This last term reduces to חיל / KHĒL (anguish, trembling). Add הרטיט / [HĒ]RTĒT (to terrorize) and רטט / RĒTÄT (to vibrate) and an RT root of fear and TREMBLING emerges. Non-coincidently, three of six TR roots in the AHD mean "TREMBLING." TREMENDOUS, TREMOR and TREMULOUS come from IE root *trem*; TREPIDATION and INTREPID are linked to IE root *trep*; and DETER, TERRIBLE, TERRIFIC and TERROR are traced to IE *tres*. DREAD belongs with these DT–R and R–DT words as well. See "RATTLE."

(S)CARF/עֹרֶף
KHO–REF   [KH–R–F]

ROOTS: Old French *escreppe* meant a purse suspended around the neck; a SCARF now indicates any neckerchief, especially those worn for warmth. There is no IE root available for SCARF or CRAV[AT] (necktie). [S]CARF and *[es]creppe* should lose the initial "ES" or "S" added to so many guttural (K,C) roots. The KRP root here is ערף / KHŌREPH or ŌREF (neck – *Leviticus 5:8*).

BRANCHES: If the Russian scarf (*sharf*) suggests a different origin, there's always Arabic *isharb* (scarf) for a softer Semitic etymon. The dictionary lapses to folk etymology in trying to trace the CRAVAT to the scarves worn by Croatian (*Krawat* in German dialect) soldiers. A necktie in Serbo-Croatian is a *Kravata*; the Spanish is *corbata* and the Portuguese *gravata*.
Just as Arabic *raqaba* (neck) is a #1-#2 letter flip of ערף / KH–R–PH (neck), Serbo-Croatian *vrat* (neck) is a #1-#2 metathesis of רבד / RIVĒDT (collar, necklace – *Genesis 41:42*). רבד / R–V–DT is a secondary etymon for CRAVAT; כרבד / KIRVĒDT could mean "like a necklace or collar." Serbo-Croat (*ovratnik*) and Russian (*varatnik*) are terms for "collar" that came from רבד / RIBHĒD, as did Dutch *boord* (collar). See "GIRAFFE" and "SCRUFF".

SCAR(LET)/סָקַר
SAW–CAR   [SKR]

ROOTS: SCARLET is officially from Persian *saqalat* or Arabic *siquillat*. סקרה / SIKRÄ (bright red paint – via Aramaic) gave rise to the verb סקר / SAKAR (to paint red). These terms are a metathesis (a #2-#3 root letter flip) of terms like שרק / SÄRŌQ (red – *Zechariah 1:8*).

BRANCHES: More remotely, there's תלע / SOOLÄKH (to be dressed in scarlet). סקר / SKR and שרק / SRK may have

influenced the CR(KR) "red" terms in Slavic, and perhaps the RS ROSE-like terms for red in Italian and Rumanian. Shifting KR to GR, *gorria* is red in Basque (the reverse of Spanish *rojo* or our ROUGE). See "RED".

SCATH(ING)/שָׁחַת
S(H)E–KHATHE   [SH–KH–T→S–K–TH]

ROOTS: SCATHE is from Old Norse *skadha* (to harm); IE root *sket* is to injure. The great flood was a SCATHING (blasting, withering) act of de-creation for re-creation. The term there at *Genesis 9:11* is שחת / S(H)ĒHAS or S(H)ĒKHÄTH ("destroy") – but the verb is also defined as "to ruin, to harm".

BRANCHES: The only listed cognate of SCATHE in English is SCHADENFRUDE, from German *Schaden* (harm, injury, damage). Related words include שחת / SHÄKHÄT (pit, grave), the source of SKOTIA (a deep concave molding), שחט / SHÄKHÄT (to slaughter) and שד / SHÄD (demon).

SCAUP/שַׂחַף
S(H)A–KHUPH   [SH–KH–PH→SKP]

ROOTS: The SCAUP is a general term for wild ducks that includes such species as the canvasback and the red head. An "obsolete variation of *scalp*" is the best the dictionary can offer in terms of etymology. The שחף / S(H)ÄKHUPH is a non-kosher seagull or "sea-mew" mentioned in *Leviticus 11:16* and *Deuteronomy 14:15*. שחה / S(H)AKHA is to bow or stoop (or duck); חוף / KHŌPH is the shore. Add SK and KP for an SKP bird that ducks for food at the beach.

BRANCHES: This generic water bird might also be a scavenger, due to the sound of its name – see "SCAVENGER" from שקף / S(H)ÄKUPH (to look out). It is a wild bird since kosher (Biblically edible) birds can all be domesticated and fed only grains, etc. (as opposed to fish and insects).

SCAV(ENGE)/שָׁקַף
S(H)AH–CUFF   [S(H)–K–PH]

ROOTS: To SCAVENGE is to look for food; SCAVENGERS in the animal kingdom eat refuse and decaying organic matter – Old English *sceawian* is to look at: Old Norman French *escauwer* is to inspect. The Hebrew term for "looking out at" is שקף / S(H)ÄKUF – (*Genesis 26:8*).
See "SCOPE".

BRANCHES: The שחף / S(H)ÄKHUF (seagull – *Leviticus 11:16*) is a SCAVENGER whose supermarket is likely to be a garbage dump. See "SCAUP". The following cognates of SCAVENGER are listed at IE root *keu* (to perceive, see, hear): ACOUSTIC, HEAR, HEARKEN, SCONE, SHEEN and SHOW (also from Old English *sceawian*). An anagramic relative of שקף / SH–K–F is קשב / KASHUV (to listen, regard – *Isaiah 32:3*).

SCENE/שְׁכִינָה
S(H)K(H)EEN–AH   [S(H) – K(H) – N]

ROOTS: A SCENE is a setting or locale; the given etymon is Greek *skene* (a tent, covered place, stage). No IE root is available. שכן / S(H)ĒKOON is housing; משכן / (MĒ)S(H)KUN is a "dwelling" or the abode in *Numbers 16:24* which specifically included tents (verse 26). שכני באהלים / *S(H)ĒKOONĀ B'OHĀLĒM* ("tent *dwellers*") appears in *Judges 8:11*. A SCONCE is a shelter or hut. See "ENSCONCE". In dissecting SKN, SK means "covered" and KN means "place."

> **BRANCHES:** To understand the SK half of the SKN etymon, see "SHACK". for the KN latter half there are terms like חניה / KHĀNĀYĀ (encampment) and קן / KUN (nest – see "HAUNT." The verb שכן / SHĀKHUN (to dwell) appears in *Exodus 25:8* –"And let them make me a sanctuary that I may *dwell* among them."

S(C)EPT(ER)/שֵׁבֶט
S(H)AY–VĒT   [S(H) – BH – T→SPT]

ROOTS: Middle English and Old French *ceptre* (scepter) are closest to שבט / S(H)ĀBHET which, like SCEPTER, can mean a rod or staff (*Isaiah 28:27*), or royal authority –"the *SCEPTER* shall not depart from Judah"(*Genesis 49:10*). The given etymon, however, is the Greek *skeptron* (staff to lean on) which influenced our spelling (the C), but not our pronunciation. The Greek term is based on *skeptesthai* (to lean on something). A royal SCEPTER is wielded, not leaned on. The Greek SKP word is more likely from שכב / S(H)ĀKHĀBH (to lie on – see "SUCCUBUS") or סעפה / SIĀPĀ or SIKĀPĀ (a short branch or bough – *Isaiah 17:6*).

> **BRANCHES:** The שרביט / SHĀRVĒT (scepter, baton, twig – *Esther 4:11*) is a שבט / SHĀVET (rod) for a שר / SAR (officer, noble), thus SR + BT. See "BAT."
> שוט / SHŌT or S(H)VŌT is a whip or thin rod – see "SWITCH". STAFF may be a #2-#3 letter flip of terms like שבט / S(H)ĀVET (staff). Its given etymons – Sanskrit *stabhnati* (he supports) and the IE base *stabh* (post, pole) are from "pillar" and "stabilizer" terms – see "STABLE". For a figurative branch (a tribe) of this branch term, see "SEPT".

SCHER(ZO)/סְחַרְחַר
SIKHAR – (KHAR)   [S – KH – R]

ROOTS: SCHERZO, from Middle High German *scherzen* (to leap with joy), is a lively, playful movement in 3/4 musical time. The IE root is *sker* (to leap, jump about). The cognate of SCHERZO, CORUSCATE, primarily means to vibrate. סחרחר / SIKHĀR (KHĀR) is defined as palpitating. It is translated at *Psalms 38:11* by two different JPS editions, first as "my heart *fluttereth*" and later as "my mind *reels*". If the S is unhistoric, the preferred etymon is כרר / KORAR (to leap about, dance – *II Samuel 6:14*).

> **BRANCHES:** סחרר / SIKHRĀR is to make dizzy; סחרחרה / SIKHĀRKHĀRĀ is a carousel. The core of these terms may be seen at KR entries like "CURVE".

SCHOOL/אֶשְׁכּוֹל
ES(H) – COAL   [A – SH – K – L]

ROOTS: A group or SCHOOL of fish is said to derive from Middle Low German *schole* (troop), from Germanic *skulō* (a division). The IE root would be *skel* or *kel* (to cut). One of the cognates of SCHOOL (group) at this root is SKILL. Hebrew also connects שכל / SĀKHEL (understanding, skill) with a cutting off term like שכל / SHIKŌL (bereavement; loss of children). Latin *singulus* (alone) and SI(N)GLE may be a nasalization of שכל / SKL. Bereavement is specifically a loss from the group, and so the related SKL word for a cluster or bunch – אשכול / ESHKŌL (*Numbers 13:23*) – makes a fine, more direct etymon for SCHOOL.

> **BRANCHES:** אשכול / ESHKŌL is associated with a "cluster" of grapes (*Genesis 40:10*), figs (*Micah 7:1*) or henna (*Songs 1;14*). The term shouldn't be restricted to botanical groups; for example, a "pod" (seedcase of peas, beans, etc.) is also used for groups of birds and whales. A second SKL "group" word from Semitic is *sugullo* (a "herd" in Akkadian).

SCHWA/שְׁוָא
SHVAH   [SH – V – A]

ROOTS: This (German) lingusitics term is an acknowledged borrowing from the Hebrew vowel שוא / SHVĀ. It infers, according to *Webster's*, the unstressed, central vowel sound of most unstressed syllables in English.

> **BRANCHES:** שוא / SHĀV means nothingness or "in vain" (*Exodus 20:7*).

(S)CISS(ORS)/גְּזַז
GAUZE – UZ   [GZZ→KSS]

ROOTS: The etymology of SCISSORS could use a good KS cutting word so that words like S*CISS*ORS and EX*CISE* (to cut out or away) needn't depend on a past perfect form of Latin *caedere* (to cut) or the loosely connected IE root *kae-id* (to strike). See "CUT." Greek does have *schizein* (to cleave, cut), the source of SCHISM and SCHIZOPHRENIA. Not trimming off the initial S, however, these are all traced to IE root *skei* (to cut, split). See "SAXON". Hebrew provides גזז / GĀZĀZ (to shear, clip – *Genesis 31:19*), קצר / KO[T]SAR (to cut – *Job 24:6*), גזר / GĀZĀR (to cut – *II Kings 6:4*), קצץ / KOTSĀTS (to sever, chop – *Deuteronomy 25:12*), and כסוח / KĀSOOĀH (to cut off, trim – *Isaiah 33:12*). כרת / KORĀS is to cut off; it is a #2-#3 letter flip away from KSR.

> **BRANCHES:** Cognates of SCISSORS and EXCISE include ABSCISE, CAESURA, CIRCUMCISE, CONCISE, INCISE, PRECISE and RECISION. A *caesura* in Latin is a cutting. A CAESAREAN operation or section is another precise KSR cutting; the "Caesar" connection bit is probably a folk etymology – see "KAISER." All of the above, especially "circumcision," are precise cuttings – not terms of "striking" as the IE root insists. IE root *kes* (to cut) is the given source of CASHIER, CASTE, CASTLE, CASTIGATE, CASTRATE, INCEST and QUASH. See "CASTRATE."

(S)COOP/כַּף
CUFF   [K–P(H)]

ROOTS: Middle Dutch *schope* is a bailing vessel; *schoppe* is a shovel. A SCUPPER (opening in a ship's deck) is from Old French *escope* (bailing scoop). The initial S of SCOOP therefore, should be seen as a late development via the Old French prefix form *"es."* The AHD agrees. They trace SCOOP back to IE root *skep*, but concede that the root may also be *kep*. The כף / KUPH in *Numbers 7:14* is translated "ladle," while the dictionary definition is "spoon." The primary human SCOOP or trowel is the כף / KUPH (palm of the hand – *Genesis 20:5*).

> **BRANCHES:** The כף / KUPH ("hollow") of Jacob's thigh in *Genesis 32:36* recalls the (S)CAPULA or shoulder blade (a hollowed bone used for scraping). COPE(POD) is from Greek *kope* (oar), that which scoops or shovels water.
> Words from the IE root *skeubh* like SCUFF(LE), SHOVE and SHUFFLE, may connect to דחף / (DÄ)HÄF or (DÄ)KHÄF (to push; walk hurriedly – *Esther 6:12*). SHOVEL may fit here better than at IE root *skeuabh* (to shove).
> גבים / GÄV(ĒM) are diggers in *II Kings 25:12*. גביע / GUBHĒÄ is a goblet; כפה / KÄPHÄ is to invert. CYPSELA is a hollow vessel. SCOOP relates to all manner of concavities. See "CAVITY," "CUP" and "GOPHER."

SCOOT/שָׁקַד
S(H)OCK–ŪDT   [SH–K–D→SKT]

ROOTS: To SCOOT is to go quickly or to dart. The dictionary guesses that SCOOT is "probably via dialect" and is traceable to the Old Norse *skiota* (to shoot). The noun SCOOT means "a scurrying off". שקד / S(H)OKÄDT is to hurry – *Jeremiah 1:12*. שקדים / SHIKÄDEM are almonds (*Genesis 43:11*) because they are the quickest to bloom.

> **BRANCHES:** שקידה / SHIKĒDÄ is diligence. If the initial S of SCOOT proves unhistoric, we aim for words like חץ / KHÄTS (arrow – see "HASTATE"). שקט / S(H)ÄKÄT (calm – *Isaiah 7:4*) is antonymical. SCAT, SKIDADDLE, SKIDDOO – and possibly SKETCH – are fast friends. See "SHOOT."

SCOPE/שָׁקַף
S(H)KOP(H)   [SH–K–PH→SKP]

ROOTS: A SCOPE is one's field of vision or "aim," as in Rumanian *scop* or Italian *scopo*. The TELESCOPE too is from IE base *seqw* (to see). The IE base of -SCOPY, SKEPTIC and SCOPE, however, switches the SKP to SPK. IE root *spek* is to observe. The IE root *sekw* (to perceive, see) includes only SEE and SIGHT. *Skopein* means "to look" in Greek. שקף /S(H)KUPH is to face, to be seen, or "to look out at" *Genesis 26:8*. השקיף / (HĒ)SHKEPH is to observe or contemplate (source of *SPECULATE*). The CP of SCOPE is also reversed for PERS*PEC*TIVE, a fair translation of השקפה / (HÄ)SHKÄPHÄ (view, observation, outlook, point of view).

BRANCHES: שקף / S(H)ĒKÄPH is to cause to be seen, to depict or portray. שקיפות / S(H)KĒPHOOS is transparence, clearness. Cognates listed at the IE root *spek* (to observe) include: ASPECT, AUSPICE, BISHOP, CIRCUMSPECT, CONSPICUOUS, DESPICABLE, DESPISE, (DE)SPITE (but see "SPATE"), EPISCOPAL, ESPECIAL, ESPIONAGE, ESPY, EXPECT, FRONTSPIECE, HOROSCOPE, INSPECT, INTROSPECT, PERSPECTIVE, PROSPECT, RESPECT, RESPITE, RETROSPECT, SPECIES, SPECIMEN, SPECIOUS, SPECTACLE, SPECTRUM, SPECULATE, SPY and SUSPECT. A Polish spy is a *szpieg* – see "SPY." More SK SIGHT words at "SCAVENGE" and "SEEK."

(S)CORCH/חָרַךְ
KHOR–UKH   [KH–R–KH]

ROOTS: To SCORCH (burn slightly, discolor the surface, to parch by heat) is linked to Old French *escorcher* (to flay, take skin off) and to ON *skorpna* (to shrink, be shriveled). The IE roots are *skerbh* and *sker* (to turn, bend). For a warmer etymon consider חרך / KHORÄKH (to "roast" – *Proverbs 12:23*). Related "hot" terms appear at "CHAR" and "SCAR."

> **BRANCHES:** To cover other approaches, there is שחור / S(H)ÄKHOR (black – see "OBSCURE"), גלח / GOLÄKH (to shave off – *Leviticus 14:8*) and כרע / KORÄ (to bend, bow).

SCORE/שָׂכַר
SOKH–ORE   [S–KH–R]

ROOTS: All the meanings of SCORE are linked, as usual, to the one available etymon. Old Norse *skor* is a notch, tally or twenty (20). The given etymons, IE roots *sker* and *ker* (to cut), take us to cognates SCAR, SHEAR, SHORT, and CURT.
Hebrew has KR cutting words like חרר / KHORUR (to bore), חור / KHOR (hole – *II Kings 12:10*), חרץ / KHORÄTS (to cut into), חרט / KHORÄT (to engrave, chisel), חרק / KHORÄK (crack – see "CRACK"), כרת / KORUT (to cut) and קצר / KO(T)SÄR (to cut, reap, to be short – see "CURT").
Kiri is a cutting or cut in Japanese. As for the Old Norse sense of twenty (20), the core of the Hebrew twenty – עשר / KH–S–R (ten) – is a #1-#2 root letter swap away from *skor* (tally, twenty). עשר / KHASUR is to decimate or tithe.

> **BRANCHES:** SCORE doesn't mean a "notch" in usage, so supplemental Hebrew etymons are noteworthy for the word's other connotations. SCORE is an "account" or a "sum due," "anything offered as a reason or motive" (*Webster's*). שכר / SOKHOR is reward, hire; שכירות / S'KHĒ (ROOT) means salary, wages or rent. שער / S(H)ÄKHÄR is a price; שכר / SOKHOR (profit) fits the 9th definition of SCORE, "to achieve credit or success." There is a connection between keeping SCORE in one's mind (remembering) and making a notch. Science shows that זכר / SÄKHOR (to remember) is literally to make an impression, to notch a groove in the floppy disk of our brain. שער / S(H)AAR or S(H)AKHAR (valve, measure – *Genesis 26:12*) might have influenced both SCORE and SHARE.

SCOUR/שָׁחַר
S(H)OKH–ARÉ   [SH – KH – R→SCR]

ROOTS: SCOUR, to range over or through as in search of something, is "probably from Old French *escourre* (to run forth)"– and from Latin *currere* (to run). See "CAR." The given IE root is *kewero* (north, north wind); the AHD also sees SCOUR (to range over) as a cognate of Old English *scur* (shower, storm) – see "SHOWER."

שָׁחַר / S(H)ÄKHÄR is to SEARCH for or SEEK (*Psalms 78:34, Hosea 5:15*).

סַעַר / SAKHAR is a verb and noun of tempestuous wind (*Jonah 1:11*).

> **BRANCHES:** סחר / SÄKHÄR is to travel or go around (*Genesis 42:34*). חקר / (HÄ)KUR is to investigate, explore, study – see "QUERY."

(S)CRAPE(R)/(מֶ)גְרֵפָה
(MA) – GRAYF–AH   [G – R – PH→KRP]

ROOTS: Old Norse *skrapa* (to scratch) is traced to IE root *sker* or *ker* (to cut). See "SCORE."

A garden rake is a scraper and a (S)CRAPER is a "hoe" or מגרפה / (MI)GRÄPHÄH (*Joel 1:17*). The word is elsewhere rendered "furrow."

> **BRANCHES:** נלב / GOLABH is to scrape or shave; חרב / KHEREV is a sword or blade.
>
> One can hear GRAPH in the captioned Hebrew term, even if one doesn't have a Texas drawl. Cognates of GRAPH at IE root *gerbh* (to scratch) include AGRAPHA, CARVE, CRAB, CRAWL, CRAYFISH, DIAGRAM, EPIGRAM, EPIGRAPH, GRAFFITTI, GRAM, -GRAM, GRAMMAR, -GRAPH, GRAPHITE, ICONOGRAPHY, PARAGRAPH, PROGRAM, PSEUDEPIGRAPHA, TETRAGRAMMATON, and TOPOGRAPHY. חפר / KHOPHAR (to dig) is akin to a KRP cutting term – see "GOPHER." See "CARVER," "CRAB," "GRADE," and "GRAPHITE."

(S)CRATCH/קָרֵד
KAY – RAID(T)   [K – R – (D)T]

ROOTS: SCRATCH is "said to be from Middle English *scratten*, fused with *cracchen* (to scratch) – from Middle Dutch *cratsen* (to scratch)." The IE root is *grat* or *krat* (to scratch).

חרט / KHORÄT is to engrave, חרש / KHORÄSH is to plow or engrave; חרת / KHORÄT is to engrave or inscribe. קרד / KÄRA(D)T is to scrape or curry, קרדם / KÄRDŌM is a hatchet (*Judges 9:48*), חריץ / KHÄRET[S] is an incision or slice (*I Samuel 17:18*).

> **BRANCHES:** GRATE, a cognate of SCRATCH, is from גרד / GEREDT (to scratch, "to scrape"– *Job 2:8*). This matches the IE root *grat* (to scratch). If keeping the initial S of SCRATCH, consider שרט or סרט / SORÄT (scratch – see "SERRATED.") חרץ / KHÄRUTS also means to be diligent. (S)CRUTINY is linked to IE root *skreu* (to cut, cutting tool). SCRUTINY'S cognates are SCREED, SCROTUM, SHRED and SHREW. *Garuk* is to scratch in Indonesian. See "CHARACTER" and "GRADE."

(S)CRUFF/עֹרֶף
KHOR – EFF   [KH – R – PH]

ROOTS: The SCRUFF is the back or nape of the neck. *Webster's* links SCRUFF to Old Norse *skopt* or to the IE base *sque-p*, which mean hair or a tuft. The AHD serenely declares "origin unknown." Decapitate the S before the C, as usual, to expose the ערף / ŌREF or KHŌREF (neck – *Leviticus 5:8*). In *Jeremiah 2;27*, the (new) JPS rendition is "to Me they turned their *backs*, not their faces." The back of the head is clearly the intent here with ערף / KRF.

> **BRANCHES:** The antonymical variation of the same root is ערף / ORUF or KHORUF (to decapitate or break the neck – *Deuteronomy 21:4*). Farmers don't decapitate CROPS, but to CROP off anything is to chop it off near the top. A bird's CROP is an enlargement on its neck. (S)CROFULA is from Latin *scrofulae* (swellings of the neck glands). The 2-letter root bottlenecks down to G/K–R/L (guttural-liquid) as גרגרת / GÄRGERET is the windpipe and עול / KHŌL is a yoke or collar. Most IE words for NECK are CL, HL or KR terms, but Arabic *raqaba* is a #1-#2 letter flip of ערף / K–R–PH. Basque has neck word to fit ערף / ŌREPH, *lepo*(R→L). צואר / TZÄ(V)ÄR (front of the neck) is *eztarri* in Basque. See "CRAVAT," "GIRAFFE," and "SCARF."

(S)CULLE(RY)/כֶּלִי
KELLY   [KLY]

ROOTS: The SCULLERY is the kitchen room for pots and pans or kitchen work. No IE root is available, but KL should mean "utensil" in the French etymon. *Escuelerie* is the care of dishes of kitchen utensils in Old French.

While כלי / KÄLEE is a general term meaning "utensil," כלי / KELE is specifically a "vessel" for liquid (*Numbers 19:17*) or "vessels" of clay or brass (*Leviticus 6:21*) for storage or cooking.

> **BRANCHES:** A (S)CULLION is one who does kitchen work. Other כל / KL terms of containment include כלא / KELE (prison) and כלוב / KLOOV (cage, basket). *Kuali* is a pen (cage) in Indonesian.

(S)CURRILOUS/כְּרְכֵּר
KEY'R – CARE   [KR]

ROOTS: *Webster's* feels that SCARE and SCURRILOUS are from the IE base *(s)quer* (to jump about), as in Latin *scurra* (buffoon).

"To jump around" is the defintion of כרכר / KĒRKÄR. In *II Samuel 6:14*, David's whirling, public dance before the Lord is described by this term. Princess Michal haughtily despised what she felt was David's SCURRILOUS buffoonery. (SCURRILOUS now largely refers to coarse language.)

> **BRANCHES:** SCURRY is conjectured to be a combination of "SCOUR" and "HURRY." סחר / SÄKHÄR (to go around) and סחרחרה / SIKHÄR–KHÄRÄ (carousel) might serve as SKR etymons for SCURRY or for the buffoon's dizzy SCURRILITY. For more guttural-liquid (KR/L) dancing terms, see "CHORUS," "HULA," and "ORCHESTRA."

S(C)URVY/נֶרֶב
GORE – OV   [GRV→KRV]

ROOTS: SCURVY was originally spelled SCURFY. SCURF, from Scandinavian terms like Danish *skurv*, means dry scales shed by the skin (like dandruff) or any scaly coating. נרב / GÄRÄV is defined as a "SCAB" (a scaly covering or "boil scar") but it is in the exact context of "SCURVY" at *Leviticus 22:22*. קלף / KLP means skin, parchment, bark or shell – see "CALIBUR" and "CALIPEE."

    BRANCHES: Dandruff is itchy. For נרב / GORAV (to scratch) see "GRAVE." Greek *skariphos* (scratching) might also be related – see "SCRAPER."

SEAM/צֶמָה
(T)SUM – AH   [TS – M→SM]

ROOTS: A SEAM is any line formed by the joining of separate materials. Anglo-Saxon *seam* is said to be tied up with COUTURE, HYMEN, KAMASUTRA, SEW and SUTURE at the IE root *syu* (to bind, sew). The Germanic root *saumaz* (seam) offers more defintion. צמה / (T)SŌMES is a juncture; צמד / (T)SÄMÄD is to attach or join. The root is (T)S – M, as צמה / (T)SÄMÄ is a braid (*Songs 4:1*).

    BRANCHES: SEAMSTRESS and SEAMY are related – see "SEAMY." See "ACCOUTERMENT" for a better source of "COUTURE." *Sumu* is a seam or stitch in Proto-Eastern Polynesian.

SEAMY/זְמֹה
SZEE – MA   [ZMH→SM]

ROOTS: SEAMY (degraded, sordid, vile) is said to be an extensioin of SEAMY (showing the unattractive, unfinished underside of a garment where the *seams* show – see "SEAM"). זמה / SZEMA ("lewdness"– *Leviticus 18:17*) suggests a different and direct etymon for the harsher sense of SEAMY.

    BRANCHES: זנות / ZINOOS means fornication; SIN may be related. צניע / (T)SINEA (modest, chaste) may be an S – MN antonym.

SEAR/שָׂרֹף
SAR – (UF)   [S – R – (PH)]

ROOTS: To SEAR is 1) to dry up, wither or 2) to scorch or burn. Anglo-Saxon *searian* is said to come from the IE root *saus* (dry). שרף / SÄR(ÄPH) is to burn (*Leviticus 4:12*) and שרב / S(H)ÄR(ÄV) means burning heat or parched ground – *Isaiah 49:10*. The 2-letter root is SR.

    BRANCHES: The cognates of SEAR at IE *saus* (dry) that do sound relevant are AUSTERE, SERE, SORREL and

SURMULLET. The angelic SERAPH (a Hebrew borrowing) is a fiery creature. It is not known if Serbia was named for dryness; but *Webster's* has a startlingly Biblical definition for SERBONIAN –"of Lake Serbonis in ancient Egypt, a bog, now dry, in which whole armies were said to have sunk." *Szaraz* is dry in Hungarian. *Xeros*, dry in Greek, gives us 6 words from XERODERMA (dry skin) to XEROSIS (an abnormal dryness). PSORIASIS and 5 other terms are related. For SRB and SRP antonyms, see "SYRUP."

SEAT/שֵׁת
S(H)ATE   [S(H) –T]

ROOTS: Old English *sittan* (to sit) and Latin *sedere* (to sit) are linked to IE root *sed* (to sit). Man was given a SEAT, שת / S(H)ÄT (buttocks – *Isaiah 20:4*), on which to SIT or to שת / S(H)ÄT (place, station, set – *Genesis 41:35*) himself. שת / S(H)ÄT is a foundation or basis, and so is a יסוד / (YI)SŌDT (*Leviticus 4:7*).

    BRANCHES: The cognates of SEAT listed at IE root *sed* include: ASSESS, ASSIDUOUS, DISSIDENT, ERSATZ, HOSTAGE, OBSESSION, POSSESS, PRESIDE, RESIDE, SADDLE, SEANCE, SEDATE, SEDENTARY, SEDILIA, SEDIMENT, SEE, SESSION, SETTLE, SEWER, SIEGE, SITZBATH, SOIL, SOOT, SUBSIDE, SUBSIDY, SUPERCEDE and SYNIZESIS. See "CHAISE," "INSTALL" and "SET."

(SE)CRET/כֶּרֶת
CORE – ATE   [KRT]

ROOTS: SECRET (secluded) is from Latin *secretus* (separate, set apart) and the IE root *krei* (to sieve, discriminate, distinguish). The SECRET Hebrew etymon is closer to the Latin and to the sense of the English term. כרת / KHÄRÄT is to cut off an object (*Numbers 13:23*) or to "cut off" a person from one's place (*Jeremiah 4:19*).

    BRANCHES: KR terms of discrimination include בחר / [BA]KHAR (to choose). To SECRETE or to EXCRETE (to separate out a substance) has the Hebrew sense of extraction, not the IE root's sense of discernment. In the following sampling from the AHD's cognates for SECRET, remember that כרת / KRT can also be pronounced KRS: CERTAIN, CONCERN, CRIME, CRISIS, CRITIC, CRITERION, DECREE, DIACRITICAL, DISCERN, DISCRIMINATE, EXCREMENT, HEMATOCRIT, HYPOCRISY, INCERTITUDE, and RIDDLE. See "CURT."

SECURE/סְנוּר
SUG – OOR   [SGR→SCR]

ROOTS: To SECURE is to make firm, fast or tight. This may or may not derive form Latin *securus*, a combination of *se* (apart from) and *cura* (care). If one cares to pursue this etymology, see the Hebrew source of "CARE" at "CHERISH." Alternative etymons include סגר / SAGUR (to close, lock seclude – *Leviticus 13:5, 14:38*) and סכר / SAKUR (to close, dam).

    BRANCHES: שער / S(H)ÄAR or S(H)ÄKHÄR is a gate. Perhaps the CIGAR and CIGARETTE (rolled up tobacco) were influenced by terms like סנור / SIGŌR (enclosure, encasement). See "SIEGE."

seduce

(SE)DUCE/דָחָה
DUKH – (AH) [D – KH]

ROOTS: Latin *seducere* (to lead apart) is from *se* (apart) + *ducere* (to lead). The IE root is *deuk* (to lead). דחה / DUKHÄ is to push, drive, urge on to fall, or impel, or defer (*Psalms 118:13*); ידח / (YĒ)DUKH or נדח / (NĒ)DUKH is to be seduced. מדוחים / (MÄ)DOOKH(ĒM) is "seduction" in *Lamentations 2:14*. מדיח / (MÄ)DĒÄKH is a seducer.

> **BRANCHES:** דחי / DIKHĒ is impulse. נדח / [NA]DAKH is INDUCED to an action (*Proverbs 7:21*). דחף / DÄKH(ÄF) is to push or drive; דחיפה / DIKHĒFÄ is pushing or incitement. Cognates of "SEDUCE" at IE root *deuk* (to lead) include ABDUCT, ADDUCE, CONDUCE, CONDUCT, DEDUCE, DEDUCT, DOCK (of the bay), DOGE, DOUCHE, DUCAL, DUCAT, DUCHESS, DUCHY, DUCTILE, DUKE, EDUCATE, INDUCE, INTRODUCE, PRODUCE, REDOUBT, REDUCE, SUBDUCTION, SUBDUE, TEAM, TEEM, TIE, TRADUCE, TRANSDUCER, TUG, and WANTON. See "CAUDILLO" for human conductors (DK reversed) and "DOUCHE."

SEEK/סְכּוּי
SEEK – (OOŸ) [SK]

ROOTS: To SEEK is to search for, to try, or to attempt. Old English *secan* (to seek) is traced to the IE root *sag* (to seek out). שקק / S(H)OKUK is to long for, to rush about – *Isaiah 33:4*; סכוי / SEKOOY means prospect or expectation; סכה / SOKHÄH is to see or look; שקד / S(H)EKED is diligence; שקר / SĒKER means to ogle; and שקף / S(H)OKUF is to look at – see "SCOPE."

> **BRANCHES:** Official cognates of SEEK include BESEECH, EXEGESIS, FORSAKE, HEGEMONY, PRESAGE, RANSACK, SAGACIOUS, SAKE and SEEK. The opposite of CHASE (see "CATCH") but the fulfillment of SEEK is השיג / HĒSĒG (to overtake, reach, attain – see "SHAG"). To SEEK in Polish is *szukac*. Motivating the seeking here are SK terms like חשק / HÄS(H)EK (desire, pleasure) and תשוקה / TES(H)OOKÄ (longing, desire – *Genesis 3:16*). These appear to link up with Japanese *suki na* (fond of) and *utsukushii* (beautiful). ASK would appear to be a related SK term; the IE root of ASK is thought to be *ais* (to wish, desire, seek out). Besides the SK Hebrew terms above, consider KS words like קשיה / KOOSHIA (objection, question) and בקש / BĒKÄSH (to seek, search, desire, ask). A strong-armed form of ASKING is עשק / AS(H)AK (to extort).

SEEP/זָב
SOBH [Z – BH→SP]

ROOTS: Old English *sypian* (to drip, seep) is traced to the IE root *seib* (to pour out, sieve, drip, trickle). זב / ZABH or SABH is to ooze or flow out as in "a land *flowing* milk and honey"– זב(ת) (*Exodus 13:5*).

> **BRANCHES:** Cognates of SEEP at IE *seib* are SAPONATE, SAPONITE, SIEVE, SIFT and SOAP. Hebrew can now wash its hands of a "borrowing" (from Latin) like סבון / SÄBON (SOAP). SAP (from a tree) belongs here too. SOAP and Greek *hyssopon* (hyssop) relate to the cleansing אזוב / ĀSŌBH (hyssop – see

"HYSSOP"). Some unsweet SEEPAGE involves the person with an "issue" or flow (*Leviticus 15:33*) called a זב / ZÄV or SABH. זבל / ZEBHEL or SEVEL (dung) may provide a better etymon for SWILL, SEWER, and *SYPH*ILIS.

SEEP and SIP are opposites because שאב / S(H)OÄBH (to draw, absorb, suck in) is an SB antonym of זב / S – BH . שפע / S(H)ÄPHÄ is to flow; שפך / S(H)ÄPHÄKH is to pour. French *suer* or *sver* (to sweat) leads one to believe that German *schweissen*, Yiddish *shvitz* and English SWEAT is another bodily liquid issuing from זב / S – BH or S – V. *Suupee* is (running) nasal mucus in Proto-Eastern Polynesian. See "BISON."

SEET[HE]/זיד
SEEDT [SZ – DT→ST]

ROOTS: SEETHE is from Old English *seothan* (to boil) and the IE root *seut* (to seethe, boil). זיד / ZEED or SEET is to boil or SEETHE –"and Jacob SOD pottage" (*Genesis 25:29*).

> **BRANCHES:** נזיד / [NA]ZEEDT is Jacob's "pottage" or any boiled preparation. זוד / ZOODT is to swell or behave insolently (*Deuteronomy 17:13*), as when SEETHING with indignation. זידון / ZÄDŌN or SÄD[ŌN] is overflowing (*Psalms 124:5*). SUDS is an official cognate of SEETHE.

SEIZE/שָׂסָה
S(H)AH – SAH [S(H) – S]

ROOTS: To SEIZE is to grab suddenly or to legally confiscate or assume possession. There may be competing meanings and etymons here, as Old French *siesir* (seize) is made a cognate of SAKE (lawsuit) at the IE root *sag* (to seek out). The common use of SEIZE is covered by S(H) – S terms like שסה / S(H)ÄSÄ (*I Samuel 23:1*) and שסס / S(H)ÄSÄS (*I Samuel 17:53*) which mean "to steal, rob, plunder." To satisfy the alleged link to an SG sound and a possessive sense, there is השיג / (HĒ)SĒG (to attain, obtain – *Leviticus 14:21*) and (reversing to KH – S) אחז / ÄKHÄZ (to seize, grasp, take legal holdings of property, etc.– *Genesis 22:13; Genesis 23:4*). אחז / AKHAZ is a SEIZURE or fit in *Job 21:6* –"my body is SEIZED with shuddering."

> **BRANCHES:** SEISE, SEISIN and SEIZIN are variations of SEIZE.

SELL/שָׁלַח
S(H)EEL – (AH) [S(H) – L – (H)]

ROOTS: At the etymology for COUNSEL one discovers that Anglo-Saxon *sellan* meant to sell or deliver. SELL primarily means to give up and deliver an item. The Germanic base is *saljan* (to offer up, deliver). שלח / S(H)ÄLÄH is to send away (*Genesis 44:3*), to abandon, sell out (*Isaiah 27:10*) or to send a representative or COUNSELOR (*II Kings 2:2*).

> **BRANCHES:** The given IE root of SELL is *sel* (to take, grasp) which may relate to שלל / S(H)ÄLÄL (plunder). Cognates are SALE and HANDSEL. שלם / S(H)ÄLÄM is to pay; סלא / SĒLÄ is to weigh or value. סחר / SÄHÄR is to trade; שער / S(H)Ä'ÄR is a price or value.

SEMAN(TIC)/סִימָן
SEE–MUN   [SM]

ROOTS: French *semantique* is that branch of linguistics that is concerned with the meanings of speech forms. Greek *semantikos* means "significant." Greek *semainein* is to show, while Greek *sema* is a sign. As if to mock SEMANTICS, the given IE root of SEMANTIC is *dhei* (to see, look), while SEEM is attributed to the IE root *sem* (one, as one).

סימן / SĒMĀN (mark, sign, symptom) is a borrowing from the Greeks. The following terms show just where the Greek terms originated: סימה / SĒMĀ (Arabic) is a sign, as תמונה / TIMOONA or SIMOONA is a picture or "image" (*Deuteronomy 4:16*). ציון / (T)SĒYOON (signpost, monument, mark – *II Kings 23:17*). ציון / TSĒON is Zion (*Isaiah 1:27*), so true Zionists must strive to be "signposts" in the Lord's Public Relations department.

A third Semitic source for SEMANTIC is the source of SEMITIC. שם / SHEM, Noah's son who stayed in the middle ground when the Hamites went down to Africa and the Japhetics went up to Europe, has a name that means "name"– *Genesis 2:11*. As Greek *semantikos* means "significant," so a שם / S(H)ĀM (name) is a signification. שם / S(H)ĀM is better rendered "fame" or "repute," and the term is translated "renown" in *Genesis 6:4*. Ill repute involves אשם / ASHAM (guilt – see "ASHAMED.") An OMEN may be a related sign. OMEN in earlier Latin was *osmen*. See "OMEN."

PSYCHOSOMATIC, SEMAPHORE, SEMATIC, SEMIOLOGY, SEMIOTIC, and ZEN are among the cognates of SEMANTIC. A SENNET is an audible sign – see "SOUND." See "SIGN" and "SIMULATION."

SEN(ILE)/יָשֵׁן
(YA)–S(H)UN   [SN]

ROOTS: SENILE and SENILITY are from Latin *senex* and *senis* (old, aged). (The connection between cognates SENATOR and SENILE is demonstrated all too often.) The IE root is *sen* (old). ישן / (YĀ)S(H)ĀN is old; יושן / (YŌ)S(H)EN is oldness. נושן / (NŌ)S(H)UN is old or inveterate – see "ANCIENT."

BRANCHES: Growing old and full of sleep (שנה / S(H)ĀNĀ – see "INSOMNIA") is a time of maturity and change (שנה / S(H)ĀNĀ – see "CHANGE.") In time, all things become שונה / S(H)ŌNEH (different). Cognates of SENILE at IE root *sen* (old) include (MON)SEIGNIOR, SENATE, SENECTITUDE, SENESCENT, SENIOR, SENOPIA, SIGNORY, SIR, SIRE, and SURLY. *SHAN*TY is from an "old" term in Old Irish. *Sempai* is a senior in Japanese.

SEPIA/צֶבַע
(T)SEBH–AH   [TS–BH→SP]

ROOTS: Greek *sepia* is a cuttlefish noted for its inky fluid.

SEPIA is thus a dark brown pigment or color. צבע / (T)SĀBH means color or dye.

BRANCHES: To consider the shell of the cuttlefish, we add the term צב / (T)SABH (tortoise, covered wagon – see "TOP"). The helmeted tortoise and the colors of flags and armies connect these two TS – BH Hebrew terms to צבא / (T)SĀBHĀ (army, military service – *Numbers 1:20*). Here is the source of SEPOY (a native of India serving in a European army). The given etymology cites the Hindi and Persian word *sipah* (army). SPAHI and SPAHEE are related army terms in Turkish and Persian.

SEPT/שֵׁבֶט
S(H)EBH–ĒT   [SH–BH–T→SPT]

ROOTS: A SEPT is an "old Irish clan or tribe ruled by a patriarch" or any similar group. The term is linked to Old French *septe* and is guessed to be a variant of "sect." שבט / S(H)ĀBHET is a "tribe" (*Numbers 24:2*) or a branch.

BRANCHES: The SWAT people of East India may be named for a lost cognate of SEPT. The verb SWAT is similar for good reason – see "SWITCH." SIBLING, SIB and GOSSIP are from Old English *sibb* (relative). Perhaps *sibb* is a clipped form of שבט / S(H)ĀB(H) – B(H)ET.

SERF/שָׂרַף
SUH–RUF   [SRF]

ROOTS: SERF and SERVANT are from Latin *servus* (a slave). God's celestial servant is the שרף / SĀRĀF (Seraph, attendant angel). A tyrant treats his footmen like footstools; שרפרף / SIRĀFRĀF is a footstool.

BRANCHES: SERVE, SERVER and SERVICE are among 20 such SRV terms. An R→L change summons SLAVE. The AHD lists CONCIERGE, DESERVE, SERGEANT, SERVILE and SERVITUDE at its IE root *servus* (slave –"Latin noun of unknown origin"). The SHERIFF is a hireling seen at "SHIRE." See "SIR" for SR antonyms of mastery; שרת / S(H)ĀR[ĀT] (to serve) is an SR synonym. סרב / SEREV (mutiny) is an SRV antonym.

SERIES/שׁוּרה
SHOOR–AH   [S(H)–R]

ROOTS: Latin *serere* means to arrange; the IE root is *ser* (to line up). שורה / S(H)OORĀ is a row or line (*Job 24:11*); ישר / [YA]S[H]AR means straight (*Proverbs 4:25*); שור / S(H)OOR is a wall in *II Samuel 22:30*. Latin *serere* also means "to bind;" צרר / SORUR is bound up or straightened (*Joshua 9:4*). The Arabic is similar.

BRANCHES: To SHIRR is to gather fabric into parallel rows – the origin of the word is listed as "unknown". The line at the sea's SHORE might also relate. The official cognates of SERIAL, SERIATE or SERIES include ASSERT, ASSORT, CONSORT, DESERT, DISSERTATION, EXPERT, INSERT, SEAR, SERMON, SERRIED, and SORCERER. שרך / SAR[AKH] means going everywhere but in a straight line (*Jeremiah 2:23*). For more antonyms see "SWERVE."

SERP(ENT)/שָׂרָף
SUR–UPH   [S–R–PH]

ROOTS: SERPENT may not derive from a past perfect of Latin *serpere* (to creep). *Serpere* is suspect because Greek *herpein* (to crawl, creep) is probably the older and more correct term. The Greek is more correct for its correspondence with CREEP and with the Hebrew etymons found at "CRAB," "CRAW," and "SCORPION." Crabs and scorpions creep, but legless serpents and snakes slither and sidewind. The IE root for SERPENT, SERPIGO, HERPES and HERPETOLOGY shouldn't be *serp* (to crawl, creep). Greek *herpein* is cited as the immediate source of the two HRP words. No such SERPENTNE derivations are required. שרף / SĀRĀP[H] is the second "serpent" in *Isaiah 14:29* –

>...out of the serpents's root
>shall come forth a basilisk,
>and his fruit shall be a flying *serpent*.

This "flying serpent" (perhaps a leaping or spitting cobra) appears beside a viper in *Isaiah 30:6*. These snakes may be related to the "fiery" (שרפים / *SERAPH*EM) serpents of *Numbers 21:6-8* who gave us the medical symbol of the snake on a pole.

> **BRANCHES:** שרף / SĀRĀPH is to burn (FREEZE and BLAZE backwards), and snake venom can sting or burn. So it is with the sting of the *syrphos* (Greek for gnat) – source of the SYRPHUS FLY. A more formidable foe from a fiery setting would be SERAPIS, the Egyptian, Greek and Roman god of the lower world.
>   ZAFFER or ZAFFRE is traced to Arabic *sufr* (yellow copper, brass). Along with 50 SULFUR words, these yellow substances are likely from שרף / SĀRĀPH (to burn – *Leviticus 4:12*). Swap #2-#3 letters for the Arabic; change R to L for Latin SULPHUR. The curing snake of *Numbers 21:9* was also copper and yellowish. See "SAFFRON."

SERRATE(D)/שָׂרַט
SORE–RUT   [SRT]

ROOTS: SERRATED leaves have sawlike notches along their edge. Latin *serratus* is an extension of *serra* (saw). שרט / SARĀT is a verb and noun in *Leviticus 21:5*, a verse which forbids making "cuttings" or "gashes" in the skin.

> **BRANCHES:** סרט / SĀRĀT (to incise or scratch) is a non-Biblical variation of the same term. The R – D/T element is shared by גרד / GĀRAD and קרד / KĀRĀD (to scrape) and also by חרט / KHĀRĀT (to engrave, inscribe). The sharp-toothed RAT and RODENT may be related. SLIT (straight cut) and SLAT (narrow strip) are R→L changes away from SRT.

SERUM/זרם
SZOR–UM   [ZRM→SRM]

ROOTS: Latin *serum* is whey, but the word can mean any animal or vegetable fluids – especially blood SERUM. The IE root *ser* means "to flow." זרם / ZĀRĀM or SZĀRĀM is to flood, pour down or stream; זרם / SZEREM is a flow, stream or current (*Psalms 77:18; Isaiah 28:2*). The Hebrew sub-root is clearly ZR as demonstrated by זורר / ZŌRĀR (to sneeze – *II Kings 4:35*), זרק / ZEREK (serum), זריר / ZĀRZĒR (rain shower – *Psalms 32:6*) and זרב / ZŌRĀBH (to spill forth or "thaw"–*Job 6:17*).

> **BRANCHES:** Cognates of SERUM at IE root *ser* are SAMSARA (from Sanskrit), SERAC and STRUDEL (from a Middle High German word for whirlpool). This S to St change happened back in Old High German, and it helps us see how STREAM belongs here with זרם / SZEREM (stream). There is also an IE root, *sreu*, that means "to flow." Here we not only find STREAM and MAELSTROM, but also several words that seem to have picked up the RM second half of זרם / ZRM. These cognates of STREAM are CATARRH, DIARRHEA, HEMORRHOID, RHEO-, RHYME, RHYTHM, RHYOLITE and -RRHEA.
>   When the dictionaries can link Greek *rhein* (to flow) and Greek *rheuma* (stream) to an *sreu* root, surely we can rejoin SR and RM words to their Hebrew mother ZRM.

(SE)SAME/שֶׁמֶן
S(H)EM–(EN)   [S(H)–M(N)]

ROOTS: The Modern Hebrew term for SESAME (a plant whose seeds yield oil) is שמשם / SHOOMSHOOM. The Modern Hebrew is said to derive form Latin *sesama* and *sesamum*, which, in turn, is from Greek *sesame* and *sesamon*.

This oldest SSMN term retains the SMN of the original Hebrew etymon – שמן / S(H)EMEN (oil, fat, grease). שמן / SHEMEN is oil in *Exodus 30:24-25*, and שמשם / SHIMSHOOM may be a reduplicated form.

> **BRANCHES:** *Minyak* is oil in Indonesian; *maslo* is the Russian (switch the S and M, and note the נ / N to L changes in the appendix). Russian *maslo* is close to the Serbo-Croatian (and Rumanian) word for olive, *maslina*. Olives and oil, like SESAME and oil, are terms that are bound to intertwine.
>   Like Portuguese, Turkish, Indonesian and Swahili, Arabic uses the Hebrew word for olive. The Arabic term for oil, *zayt*, is even closer to Hebrew זית / ZĀYIT (olive – same verse as above) than is Arabic *zaytoun* (olive). French oil, *huille*, (and thus English OIL) may be from חלב / HAL[EBH] (fat), just as Japanese oil, *abura*, might be.(Reverse the Hebrew word, changing L to R).
>   The fat=oil=grease equation inherent in שמן / SHEMEN may allow us to slide over to SCHMEER, SEMEN, SLIME and SMEAR. SMEAR is from the IE root *(s)mer* (grease, fat). SLIME was *schleim* in German; the word is traced to the greasy coating of various animals. One greasy animal is the שממית / SIMĀMĒT ("lizard"– *Proverbs 30:28*). The שמיר / SHĀMĒR worm emitted an acidic slime that was said to have cut the Temple stones.
>   שמנת / S(H)ĀMENET is cream and שמן / S(H)ĒMĀN is to oil or grease. SEMEN has the consistency of these Hebrew etymons, while it is attributed to Latin *semen* (seed). Seed and oil are interchangeable, as established above.
>   Having divinity students studying in a "seed plot" or SEMINARY is too strained a sense development. A SEMINAR, whether or not it is SEMINAL, may be better related to זמן / ZMN (whose meanings include all the appointments, preparedness and designation of SEMINARIANS and seeds). See "SUMMON." IE root *sme* (to smear) is the given source of MEASLES, MICRO- and SMITE. שמנמן / SHIMĀNMÄN is fattish; *manoanoa* means thick in Hawaiian. The common element in three Thai words for oil, grease and lard is *mahn*. Returning to SCUMMY fluids and to the first part of שמן / SHEMEN, SCUM is from German *schaum* (foam, scum). Although it can be useful, שמנת / SHĀM[ENET] or cream is the SCUM of milk. See "DENSE." The opposite of שמן / SH–M–N (rich, fertile, resinous) is שמם / SHAMĀM (desolate, laid waste) and אשמנים / ASHMAN[ĒM] (desolate places – *Isaiah 59:10*).

SET/שֵׁת
S(H)UT   [S(H)T]

ROOTS: Old English *sittan* is to sit, while *settan* is to set. The given IE root is *sed* (to sit), while an etymon of placing is preferable. (We can SET our rear end on a chair, but we cannot SEAT a watch, stage, condition or price.) שת / S(H)ÄT is to set; Joseph is appointed or set as a viceroy of Egypt with this term in *Genesis 41:35.* שתת / S(H)ÄTÄT is to place; לתית / (LÄ)TÄT or (LÄ)SÄT is "to give" (appearing twice in *Nehemiah 9:8*). For anyone set on a sitting etymon there's שת / SHÄS or S(H)ÄT (buttock, bottom – *Isaiah 20:4*).

BRANCHES: Turning to the settings of gems or cornerstones, יסד / (YÄ)SÄDT is found, establish or set; יסוד / (YI)SŌD is a base or principle. סדר / SÄDT(ÄR) is to SETTLE, arrange, set (a watch); סדר / SĒDTÄR is to set type. Many cognates of SIT and SET are found at "SEAT."

SEVEN/שִׁבְעָנָה
S(H)IV–AH–NAH   [S(H)–V–E–(N)]

ROOTS: One can accept the IE root *septm* (seven) as the source of Old English *seofan* and our SEVEN, or one can trust the Biblical SEVEN or שבענה / S(H)EVÄNÄ ("seven"– *Job 42:13*). The prevalent "seven" is the shorter שבע / S(H)EVÄ or SHEBHÄ – as in the city of BEER–SHEBA ("seven wells"). Unlike Dutch *zeven* or Danish *syv*, German *sieben* prefers the harder B of Arabic *sabaa* and Swahili *saba* – (all words for #7).

BRANCHES: שבע / SHÄVOOÄ is a week or heptad, and שבת / SHÄBBÄT means SABBATH or week – cycles which always שב / SHÄV (return). The week is a radical, Biblical concept that does not correspond to cycles of the moon or sun. It is therefore possible that the Biblical שבת / S(H)ÄBÄT (Sabbath or week) influenced the French *sept* and Latin *septem* (seven). A theory that carries weekends and S–BH seven words along cultural or trading routes may not suffice to explain why *zazpi* is seven in Basque, why *shuu* (U=V) is "week" in Japanese, why *vitu* (reverse; S→T) is seven in Fijian or why "week" is *sahp-dah* in Thai.

The number seven, too, has a meaning in the meaningful universe of Hebrew. שבע / SÄVÄ means plenty, abundance, as the number so often signifies in Scripture. More at "SUFFICE" and "SWASTIKA." Cognates of SEVEN include SEPTEMBER, SEPTENNIAL, SEPTET, SEPTI-, SEPTUAGINT, SEPTUPLE and SEPTENTRION. The AHD also lists HEBDOMAD, HEPTA- and HEPTAD from Greek *hepta* (seven). At least Hebrew שבת / SHÄBBÄT has the H retained by the Greek.

The *septm* root demands that Russians dropped a P and a T in their *syem* (seven). Hebrew שבענה / S(H)EVÄNÄ could allow for the Russians merely sliding a V over to a Y. Swedish "seven" is similarly pared down to *sju*. WEEK may derive from שבע / (SH)EVÄ (seven) pronounced the guttural way – (SHE)VÄKH. German *Woche* (week) is less harsh back in Old High German *wehha*. Words for week include the Dutch *week*, Norwegian *uke*, Finnish *viikko*, Yiddish *voch* and Indonesian *peka(n)*. The IE root for WEEK is *weik*- (to bend, wind) which may be an inversion of כפה / KÄPHÄ (to invert) or קפל / KÄPHÄL (to fold, roll up). The French *semaine*, Spanish and Portuguese *samana* and Hungarian *het* are terms for WEEK that add up to eight with inclusive

counting. שמונה / S(H)IMŌNÄ means "eight," while ח / HET is the number 8. African culture does not value dividing time into numbers like seven (or eight). The Swahili week is *juma*, echoing the Hebrew יום / YŌM (day, period of time, EON – see "AGONY"). Rumanian *saptamina* (week) may demonstrate where the French and Spanish WEEK terms came from. In either case, the Rumanian could be a combined term like שבת -ימים / S(H)ÄBBÄT-(Y)ÄMIM (a week of days or a stop in days – see "STOP").

SHABBY/סֵחֲבָה
SIH–HABH–ÄH   [S–H–BH]

ROOTS: The given etymon is the Old English *sceabb* (a scab or scratch) and the IE root *skep* (to cut, scrape, hack, etc.). SHABBY means "worn, ragged, threadbare (said of clothes)". For a less SHABBY etymon, turn to *Jeremiah 38:11* and the phrase "worn *cloths* and rags." סחבה / SIHÄBHÄ or SIKHÄBHÄ is there defined as a "rag" or "shabby garment."

BRANCHES: סחב / SÄHÄBH or SÄKHÄB is to drag, an action that quickly cuts clothes into shabby rags. The alleged cognates are listed at "SCABBLE."

SHACK/סֻכָּה
SOO–KAH   [SKH]

ROOTS: The dictionaries are not sure where SHACK (crude cabin, shanty) came from, but they gamely offer "said to be a contraction of Mexican *jacal*, from Aztec *xacalli* (wooden hut)." שך / SŌKH (which may be read SHOKH) is a booth, pavillion or "tabernacle" in *Lamentations 2:6.* סך / SŌKH is a booth (*Psalms 27:5*), and the more common סכה / SOOKÄ is a booth or tabernacle. *Leviticus 23:42* charges Israelites to "live in booths" for seven days on the Festival of Booths or Tabernacles.

BRANCHES: שך / SŌKH is also an enclosure; סך / SŌKH can also mean a thicket. סכך / SÄKHÄKH is to screen or cover. See "ENSCONCE" and "SCENE" for extensions of these SK cover-shelter-housing terms; see "HOUSE" for KS reversals of same.

SHACK(LE)/זִק
ZAKE   [ZK]

ROOTS: A SHACKLE is a metal fastening, usually one of a linked pair. Dutch *schakel* is a chain link, but the hypothetical IE base is *(s)kenk* (to gird or bind). *Webster's* also suggests an influence from *sceacan* (to shake). The etymology should have stopped at Anglo-Saxon *sceacul* (shackle), with SK as the root. זק / ZÄK is a fetter (*Nahum 3:10*); זקים / ZĒK(ĒM) are shackles or "chains" in *Psalms 149:8*.

BRANCHES: Connected links in the chain include terms like זקה / ZĒKÄ (tie, obligation), זקק / ZÄKŌK (tied to, dependent on), סגר / SEGER (lock, chain) and חזק / HÄZÄK (strong). Chinese *zhi* means fetters or shackles (Hebrew ק / K often softens to H). See "SECURE."

SHADE/שֵׁד
SHADE   [SH – D]

ROOTS: The eighth definition of SHADE is a phantom, ghost, or spirit. The IE root only addresses that SHADE which means darkness, and *skot* is the given IE root of SHADOW and SCOTOMA. שד / SHĀD is an evil spirit or demon (*Deuteronomy 32:17*).

> **BRANCHES:** BANSHEE is a ghostly informer from Gaelic (*bean*) *sidhe*, meaning "(woman) of the fairies." The Polish ghost or spirit, *duch*, might be a reversal of SH – D. SCOTIA is not listed at the IE root *skot* (dark, shade). SCOTIA is from Greek *skotia*; *Webster's* etymology reads "literally, darkness: so called from the shadow within the cavity." A SCOTIA is a deep concave molding at the base of a column. A "concavity=dark shadow" equation emerges, suggesting שחת / SHĀKHĀT (pit, grave, abode of the dead – *Isaiah 51:14*). The grave is the darkest of places, and long associated with SHADY, harmful characters. שחת / SHĒKHĀT is to destroy and שדוד / SHĀDOOD is translated "dead" or "destroyed" in *Judges 5:27*. (Here is a possible influence on DEAD). Dis is the Roman god of the lower world of Hades. DIS may be a reversal of S(H) – D here. The prefix DIS- (negation, reversal) and the prefix DYS- (the later traced to IE root *dus*, bad or evil) may there relate to שוד / S(H)ŌD (ruin, violence). DYSGENIC (*deterioration* of hereditary qualities) echoes this ruination more clearly than terms like DYSENTERY or DYSFUNCTION.

SHAG/הִשִׂיג
(HE) – SEEG   [SG]

ROOTS: To SHAG after baseballs is to chase after and catch them. The term is older than the game of baseball which preserved this verb. SHAG is of unknown origin. השיג / (HE)SEG precisely means to overtake and catch up to (*Genesis 44:4*) or to reach (*Leviticus 5:11*) or obtain.

> **BRANCHES:** Polish *siega* (to reach) should link up, as might the term for "hand" in Basque, *esku*. The Finnish (*kasi*) and Hungarian (*kez*) either reverse this Hebrew term or take their cue from אחז / ĀKHĀZ (to seize, grasp, hold). An antonym with more precise correspondence to our captioned term is הסיג / (HE)SEG (to move back, retreat). Another slang word of chasing after is SICK. A farmer might SICK his dog on a varmint to pursue and attack the intruder.
> Two IE roots seem related to השיג / (HE)SEG (to chase and overtake or to reach, attain, obtain). The first is IE *sek(w)* (to follow), which includes words like ASSOCIATE, INTRINSIC, SECOND, SIGN and SOCIAL. Derivatives of Latin *sequi* (to follow) include CONSEQUENT, ENSUE, EXECUTE, OBSEQUIOUS, PERSECUTE, PROSECUTE, PURSUE, SECT, SEGUE, SEGUIDILLA, SEQUACIOUS, SEQUEL, SEQUENCE, SUBSEQUENT, SUE and SUITOR. המשך / [HEM]SHĀKH is a follow-through. The second root, tuned into the second meaning of השיג / (HE)SEG, is *segh* (to hold). Relevant cognate terms here include EPOCH, HECTIC, SCHEME, SCHOLASTIC, SCHOOL and EUNUCH.

SHAG(GY)/זָקָן
SZUK–(UN)   [ZK(N)→SG]

ROOTS: SHAGGY, covered with long, coarse hair, is linked to Old Norse *skegg* (a beard).

זקן / ZĀK – K(ĀN) or SZUKĀN is a beard (*Leviticus 14:9*); שער / SĀKH(ĀR) or *SHĀGHĀR* means hairy (*Genesis 25:25*).

> **BRANCHES:** שיח / SĒAKH is a bush.
> There are SHAG rugs and SHAGGY dogs, but SCRAGGLY beards might be related. *Szakall* is a beard in Hungarian (N=L).
> Beard owners are often זקן / ZĀKĀN (old); *sukun* is "older brother" in Maya Indian.

SHAM(BLES)/שְׁמָמָה
SHIM – (UM – AH)   [SH – M]

ROOTS: If the place is a SHAMBLES, it is a scene of great disorder or destruction. The etymonlogy follows Anglo-Saxon *scamel* (a bench) and Latin *scamnum* (a bench) to presume that the word evolves from the scene of carnage on work benches in butcher shops. The given IE root is *skabh* (to prop up, support). Similar sounding etymons for such a work bench include שכב / SHEKHEBH (lower millstone) and שכב / SHOKHĀBH (to lie...be stretched across), and שכם / SHEKHEM (shoulder, back – where we prop up and support weights). Directly influencing our usage of SHAMBLES, though, may be words like שממה / SHIMĀMĀ (waste, desolation, horror) and נשם / (NĀ)SHĀM (to be destroyed, to be appalled – *Ezekiel 36:35*; *Jeremiah 4:9*).

> **BRANCHES:** SHAMO is the Chinese word for that desolate wasteland, the Gobi desert.
> See SH – M antonyms at "SESAME."

SHA(N)K/שׁוֹק
SHOAK   [SH – O – K]

ROOTS: The SHANK is the leg, the knee to the ankle, or the upper foreleg (as a cut of beef). Anglo-Saxon *scanc* is akin to the base of German *Schenkel* (thigh). The hypothetical IE base and root are *squeng* (to squat, stoop, bend) and *skeng* (crooked).

שחח / S[H]AKHAKH is bowed or stooped. שוק / SHŌK is a leg or foreleg (*Leviticus 7:33*). The extra N of SHANK is a common nasalization.

> **BRANCHES:** Arabic *saq* is a leg; reverse to *koshi* for the Japanese hip. CUISSE is a thigh protector (armor), so maintain an SK→KS reversal for Old French *cuisse* (thigh), Latin *coxa* (hip), Old High German *hahsa* (shin) and Old Irish *coss* (foot). At all these terms the extra N was not present; nasalization usually adds an N before a guttural like K . The European words for "ham" are almost all SNK terms. German *Schinken* (ham) is clearly akin to *Schenkel* (thigh) above. Even the Modern Hebrew for "ham" is שוק חזיר / SHŌK HĀZER (*leg* of swine). HAM and SHIN resemble the many S–(H)–I–N–(K) terms for "ham" among Scandinavian, Slavic and Finno-Ugric languages. The given IE root for SHIN is *skei* (to cut, split), and for HAM it's *konamo* (shinbone, bone).

SHED/אֶשֶׁד
(EH) – SHED   [E – SH – D]

ROOTS: The verb SHED is "to pour out, or to cause to flow in a stream or fall in drops."
אשד / ESHED is a waterfall (*Numbers 21:15*).
Words like WATERSHED are said to be from Anglo-Saxon *sceadan* (to separate) and the IE base *sqei* (to cut).

> **BRANCHES:** The AHD offers no IE root for this SHED; for a storage SHED see "SHADE." For ST words of liquid input (drinking) and output (urination) – see "SOT."

SHEER/יָשָׁר
(YAH) – SHAR   [SH – R]

ROOTS: SHEER the adjective has a third definition meaning "absolute, downright, unqualified" as well as "perpendicular" or straight and steep as a cliff wall.
ישר / YÄSHÄR means both kinds of uprightness as well: honest and straightforward (*I Samuel 29:6*); even and straight (*I Samuel 6:12*). *Webster's* only offers Old Norse *skiaer* (bright, pure) as an etymon for the other meanings of SHEER. The AHD has no IE root.

> **BRANCHES:** The SH – R is the root, as seen in שורה / SHOORÄ (line). Straight is *suroaam* in Finnish. See "STRETCH" and the following entry.

SHEER(ING)/סור
SOOR   [SR→SH – R]

ROOTS: To SHEER is to turn aside from a course or to deviate, precisely the opposite of SHEER and ישר / (YÄ)SHAR (to go straight – *I Samuel 6:12*) in the entry above. The given source of SHEERING is "a form of 'shear', " probably influenced by a cognate of Late German *scheren* (to cut). Again the AHD has no IE root.
סור / SOOR (pronounced SEER in some communities) is to "turn off" to the right or left (*Deuteronomy 2:27*).

> **BRANCHES:** See "SWERVE," which also came from סור / SOOR or SVR. שרך / SARAKH or SHAR[AKH] is to wander in all directions – *Jeremiah 2:23*. More SR words of being in line or deviating from a course at "SERIES" and "SERF."

SHIELD/שלט
SHEL – EDT   [SH – L – DT]

ROOTS: Old English *scield* (shield) is said to derive from the IE root *skel* (to cut). שלט / SHELEDT is a "shield" in *II Samuel 8:7* and *II Chronicles 23:9*.

> **BRANCHES:** An LT/לט root of defensive words emerges when considering לוט / LOOT (cover, conceal), פלט / (PÄ)LÄT (to be saved, to escape), פליט / (PÄ)LËT (refugee, fugitive, escapee) and לוט / LÖT (veil, covering; Abraham's nephew). Lot is rescued from the Biblical world war (*Genesis 14*) and is shielded from the destruction of Sodom (*Genesis 18*).

We then get the source of "to LIGHT OUT" (to depart suddenly), and perhaps of PELTAST and PELTATE (from Greek *pelte*, a light shield). One escapes blows with one's shield. A SHIELD also bore the sign of one's allegiance; שלט / SHELEDT also means a sign. Polish *szyld* is a sign-board, so that the SHIELD may be behind SLATE as an item to draw on or to list contestants with. A knight or thane would always have his emblazoned SHIELD when vying in an "election" or joust. SLATE as fine-grained rock might be from a different soruce – see "SILICON." See "LID." Human organs are carefully shielded by the שלד / SHELED (skeleton – see "SACK" #2).

SHIRE/שכיר
SAH – KHEER   [S – (K)H – R]

ROOTS: SHIRE is from Anglo-Saxon *scire* (office or chare). Old High German *scira* means "official charge." No older etymons are known. SHIRE as county may derive from the domain of the SHERIFF. A שכיר / SÄKHER is a paid employee (*Deuteronomy 24:14*); "that is hired" in *Isaiah 7:20* refers to paid soldiers (or peacekeepers). Assyro-Babylonian *sharru* (chief, captain) is a form of שר / SAR. See the SR root of high office at "CZAR" and "SIR."

> **BRANCHES:** To avoid seeing the SHERIFF as just a hired gun or civil servant (see "SERF"), consider Arabic SHARIF (chief magistrate of Mecca). A CHARWOMAN does CHORES or CHARE (housework for pay). The origin of Anglo-Saxon *hyr* (wages – source of HIRE) is unknown. Consider the (K)H – R element shared by שכר / (SÄ)KHÄR (to hire), כרה / KÄRÄ or KHÄRÄ (to hire, buy), מכר / (MÄ)KHÄR (to sell), מחיר / (MI)HËR (price, pay) and מהר / (MÖ)HÄR (bride price, dowry).

(SHISH)KEBAB/הַבְהֹב
HABH – HOBH   [HB→KB]

ROOTS: Turkish *shish* is said to mean "skewer," though it may refer to שש / SHÄSH (six) pieces of meat on the spit. The *kebab* or *kebap* (*Funk & Wagnall's* spelling) means roast meat in Turkish.
CABOBS, from Arabic *kabab*, means roast meat in India and elsewhere in the Far East. The Arabic is a guttural hardening of הבהב / HÄBH – HÄBH, a roast meat offering in *Hosea 8:13*. הבהב / HËBH – HÄBH is to roast.

> **BRANCHES:** להבה / (LE)HÄBHÄ is a flame.

SHIVER/שֶׁבֶר
SHEVER   [SH – BH – R]

ROOTS: To SHIVER is to break into pieces. Middle English *schiveren* is to break.
שבר / SHOVUR is to break – as Moses did to the tablets of Law in *Exodus 32:19*. The English and Hebrew both have noun forms meaning a fragment or splinter.

> **BRANCHES:** Of the many cognates listed under IE root *skei* (to cut, split), only SHEAVE and SHELF seemed related to SHIVE and שבר / SH–V–R. To SEVER (break) is obviously related; SEVERE and SEVERITY may relate to שבר / S(H)EVER (calamity). *Swer* is an IE root of cutting. It is the given source of SWORD, but not of SEVER and SHIVER – see "SAW." See "SAXON" for SK cutting words.

SHOOT/שׁוט
SHOOT   [SH–T]

ROOTS: Anglo-Saxon *sceotan* is traced to the IE base *(s)qeud* (to throw, cast) or the IE root *skeud* (to shoot, chase, throw). One shooting term with the SKT is קשת / KASHOT (archer – *Genesis 21:20*). A SHOOT (sprout) is matched by שתיל / SHÄTEL (shoot, sapling – *Psalms 148:3*).

To SHOOT the rapids ("to pass swiftly over") may be countered by שוט / SHOOT (to roam, float or row – *Numbers 11:8; Ezekiel 27:26*). The "pour or empty out" definition of SHOOT is met by שטף / SHOTÄF (bursting forth, flooding – see "SPOUT") and שתן / SHETEN (to urinate – *I Kings 16:11*). The "darting," "quickly painful" and "twig" senses of this versatile word may also relate to שוט / SHOT (whip or twig – *Proverbs 26:3*). For the casting and chasing of a turkey SHOOT, there's צד / TSÄDT (to hunt, shoot). See "STUDY."

> **BRANCHES:** The #1 definition of SHOOT, "passing swiftly over," also recalls שקד / SHÄKÄDT (to do something with urgency and speed – *Jeremiah 1:12*) and English words like SCAT, SKETCH, SKIDADLE and SKIDOO.
>
> חץ / KHATZ (arrow) and שך / SHÄKH (dart) may relate to old English *scytel* (a dart, missile), the source of SHUTTLE. Cognates of SHOOT, beside SHUTTLE, include SCHUSS, SCOT, SCOUT, SHEET, SHOT and SKEET. *Ckut* means "shoot" in Salish (Indians of Northwestern Washington State). See "SCOOT."

SHOWER/שׂעיר
SIH–EAR   [S–KH–R]

ROOTS: Anglo-Saxon *scur* is akin to German *Schauer* (shower, squall). The IE base is believed to be *(s)qeu*, to cover over; the given IE root is *kewero* (north, north wind – as in SCOUR). שעיר / SIER, SHIER or SIKHER is a "shower" (*Deuteronomy 32:2*). For SK cover terms see "SHACK."

> **BRANCHES:** For something stronger see סער / SÄUR or SÄKHÄR (storm, tempest – *Jonah 1:12*) at "SQUALL." זרזיף / ZÄR(ZEF) is a shower in *Psalms 42:6*. שקה / SHAKA is to water – see "SOAK."

SHRIEK/שׁריקה
SHRIEK–AH   [SH–R–K]

ROOTS: Old Norse *skrika* is to cry; the IE base and root is *ker* (loud noses of birds). The dictionaries say that SHRIEK, SCREAK, SCREAM, SCREECH and SHRIKE are all echoic relatives of Latin *corvus* (ravine), but there is much meaning available at "RAVEN" and "CROW."

A high-pitched sound that fits SHRIEK is שריקה / SHREKÄ (whistling, derisive hooting – *I Kings 9:8*). צרח / TSÄRÄKH is a shout, cry, scream or SQUEAL (*Isaiah 42:13; Zephania 1:14*).

> **BRANCHES:** Cognates of SCREECH not mentioned above include RING and RETCH.
>
> An SH–R–K whistle is a tune without lyrics or a שיר / SHEER (song) + ריק / RÄK (empty). Crying and shouting terms without an ר / R include זעק / ZÄUK, צעק / TSAUK, and שאג / SHÄUG (lion roar) and שוע / SHEVÄKH (to hue and cry). The flip side of crying is צחק / TSÄHUK (to laugh). To cry in Indonesian is *teriak*; the Sioux Indian crow is *(av)sarek*.

SICK/צוק
(T)SOAK   [(T)S–I–K]

ROOTS: SICK means to be troubled or grieved; the American usage stresses ill health. Anglo-Saxon *seoc* is traced to the IE base *seug* (distressed); no IE root is offered. צוק / (T)SOK and צוקה / (T)SOOKÄ mean distress and affliction (*Isaiah 30:6; Proverbs 1:27*). The verb הציק / (HÄT)SEK is "to torment" (*Deuteronomy 25:55*).

> **BRANCHES:** צעק / TSÄUK (cry) and שקם / SHEKÄM (to rehabilitate) are among the related words.
>
> *Tsuku* is anguish or pain in Japanese; *sakit* means both sick or pain in Indonesian. Dutch(*ziek*), Swedish (*sjuk*) and Norwegian (*syk*) "sick" terms support an SK or ZK etymon, not an SG one.

SIDE/צד
TSUD   [(T)S–D]

ROOTS: Old English *side* is "probably from the base of Anglo-Saxon *sid* (ample, broad)"; the IE base is guessed to be *sei* (to stretch out). The AHD suggests a Germanic root *sido* (long surface or part) and the IE root *se* (long, late). צד / (T)SÄD means "side" (*Exodus 25:33*). In Aramaic, סטר / SITÄR or SIDT[AR] and סתרא / SITRÄ mean a physical and a philosophical SIDE or position. CITRA is from Latin *citra* (on thsi side of) and *citer* (hither). *Shatt* is side in Arabic.

> **BRANCHES:** צדד / TSEDÄD is to turn sideways or to SIDE with.
>
> ZEST is from French *zeste* (a partition membrane in a nut); *zid* is a wall in Serbo-Croatian. "Front" is *forside* in Danish and Norwegian, and *przod* in Polish.
>
> The eskimo ear, *siut*, may be related. In Thai, direction (of a compass) is *tit*.

SIDERE(AL)/סֶדֶר
SEE – DARE　　　　　　　　　　　　　　　　[SDR]

ROOTS: SUTURE is the line on which sewing is done; סדר / SĀDTER is a row or arrangement. SUTRA is a thread in Sanskrit, and is the term used for the scriptural narratives in Buddhism. Aramaic סדרא / SIDTRĀ is a series, and סדרה / SIDRĀ means a portion in the Hebrew scriptural narrative. Considering the S – DT – R terms above, SIDEREAL (of the stars or constellations) would suggest that Latin *sideris* (star) is a constellation, arrangement or row (of stars). For further proof that *sideris* infers a constellation and not an individual star, note the IE root for SIDEREAL. Although some define IE *sweid* as "shine," the derivatives CONSIDER (which meant "observe stars carefully") and DESIRE (which meant "to await from the stars" according to the AHD) have astrological connotations. Astrological CONSIDERATIONS involve the סדור / SĒDTOOR (order, arrangement) of stars, clusters and their סדיר / SĀDER (regular, orderly) STELLAR movements.

> **BRANCHES:** STAR is then influenced by סדר / SDTR, by שדרה / SHIDTĀRĀ (row) and by other more astrologically charged terms like סתר / SĀTER (hidden; related to ESTHER), עשתרת / ĀSHTŌRETH (*I Kings 11:5* – ASTARTE worship), משטר / (MĒ)SHTĀR (to rule – see "SATRAP") and שלט / SHĀLĀT (to rule – see "SULTAN"). These last two terms recall the ancient error that the STARS STEER us, rather than our steering by the stars. Greek *aster* (star) gives us ASTERISK, ASTEROID, ASTRAL, and many ASTRO- words from ASTRONAUT and ASTRONOMY to ASTROPHYSICS.

SIEGE/סִיג
SEE – AIG　　　　　　　　　　　　　　　　[SYG]

ROOTS: A SIEGE involves the surrounding of a town or fortress in order to starve them out and take over. A SIEGE can last a long time, and so SIEGE came to mean a long period of time as well. The dictionaries somehow trace SIEGE to Latin *seder* (to sit) and the IE root *sed* (to sit). (Equally puzzling is the unacceptable D to G change.)

To LAY SIEGE and a SIEGE WALL are terms of encirclement and blockade – not of seats or sitting. סיג / SĒYĀG or SĒĀJ is to fence in (*Songs 7:3*); סיג / SIYĀG or SEĀJ is a fence or hedge. סגר / SOGĀR or SOJ(ĀR) is to lock, imprison or close – see "SECURE."

> **BRANCHES:** Both הסיך / (HĀ)SĒKH and שך / SŌKH mean fencing or hedging about and shutting in.

SIGN/צִיון
(T)SEE – OON　　　　　　　　　　　　[(T)S – Y – N → S(G)N]

ROOTS: SIGN (pronounced sīn) is allegedly from Latin *signum* (mark, sign) and the IE root *sek(w)* (to follow) – see "SHAG". The linguists posit that a SIGN meant "standard that one follows." Look to the Bible and to words like ציון / (T)SĒOON or SĒYOON (mark, *sign*post – *II Kings 23:17*). The word also means SION or ZION. The י / Y most often rendered J, is hardened to a G here with SIGNET or SIGNIFY. In the same way, OGLE and Old Teutonic *augon* (eye) came from עין / EYN (eye).

> **BRANCHES:** Turn over a word like נס / NĀS (sign, standard, signal) to see SN or SIGN. *Seun* (a letter in Cantonese) is one of many SN or SM "sign" terms – see "SEMANTICS." צנה / (T)ZĒNĀ is a shield; see "SHIELD" for the shield = sign equation.

SILIC(ON)/סֶלַע
SELL – AKH　　　　　　　　　　　　　　　[S – L – KH]

ROOTS: SILICON is from Latin *silex* or *silicis* (flint – a rock), צור / (T)SŌR is flint (see "STYLE"), but a better SLK etymon is סלע / SELĀKH (rock – *Judges 6:20*).

> **BRANCHES:** סקל / SĒKĀL is to stone and also to clear away stones – *Exodus 19:13*.
> SAXATILE is from Latin *saxum* (rock, stone). SILEX, SILICA, SILICATE, SCAR (a projecting rock), SHALE (a rock said to derive from *scealu*, Old English for a husk or shell), SLATE, CROMLECH (flat stone) and KILLICK (anchor stone) might all be related. See "ROCK" for the LK → RK shift.
> סלול / SĀLOOL (paved) may relate to the SL element of crushing rock to a *SIL*ICEOUS, *SIL*ICIFEROUS form. After סלה / SELĀ (trampling), these quartz-like SILICON rocks can resemble *SAL*T, *SIL*T (from Middle English *cylte*, gravel) or סלת / SOLET (fine flour – *Genesis 18:6*).

SILL/שׁוּל
S(H)OOL　　　　　　　　　　　　　　　　[S(H) – L]

ROOTS: A window SILL is the window's support or bottom frame. Old English *syll* and German *Schwelle* are traced to IE root *swel* (post, board). שול / S(H)OOL or SH – W – L is a rim, margin, hem – (*Exodus 28:33*).

> **BRANCHES:** צלע / (T)SELĀ is a side or rib.

SILO/שְׁאול
S(H)IH – OLE　　　　　　　　　　　[SH – O – L → SLO]

ROOTS: The roots of SILO are underground. Latin *sirus* and Greek *siros* are pits, like missile SILOS, to store fodder. An SR etymon is less direct than שאול / S(H)EOL (pit, grave – *Genesis 37:35; Jonah 2:3*).

Swap the L and O of שאול / SIOL to get SILO.

> **BRANCHES:** The Greek SR etymon may derive from סרה / SĒRA (a well or tank – *II Samuel 3:26*) or סיר / SEER (pot, vessel).

SIMUL(ATION)/סֵמֶל
SEM – EL   [SML]

ROOTS: To SIMULATE (to look like or RESEMBLE) and SIMULTANEOUS (at the SAME time) are both from Latin *simul* (together with, likewise). SAME, SEEM and SIMILAR are all ASSEMBLED at IE root *sem* (one, as one) . A סמל / SEMEL (image, likeness, SYMBOL, logos) is a SIMULATION. *Deuteronomy 4:16* prohibits limiting God by depiction in an "*image* in any *likeness* whatever, having the form of a man or a woman." "Likeness" was the translation of סמל / SEMEL, while "image" was a rendering of תמונה / TIMOONA or SIMOONA (picture – see "SEMANTICS"). Biblical verses often yoke like-sounding SYNONYMS (SML=SMN).

Any variation of SML bears a likeness: שמלה / SIMLÄ is a guise or dress; שלמה / SÄLMÄ is a garment. [SIMAR and CYMAR are related garments, attributed to Arabic *sammur* (sable).] צלם / (T)SELEM is an image, likeness or idol – see "TALISMAN."

Reverse to a liquid-nasal-fricative (SML→RMZ) to get רמז / REMEZ (hint, indication). A #1-#2 letter flip of SML reveals משל / MÄS(H)ÄL (parable, allegory, comparison, metaphor, SIMILE). משל / MŌSHEL is resemblance. An SM likeness term is שם / S(H)ĀME (name, fame association), as a name is "as one" with the thing it names. A סמלון / SIMLŌN (yoke), like a SIMILE, yokes two things together of a peculiar זן / ZÄN (sort, kind). זן / SZAN in Aramaic means "same," according to the *lexicon*.

BRANCHES: An antonym for the SM sub-root of SAMENESS is שונה / SHŌNEH (different) – see "CHANGE." Some cognates of SAME not mentioned earlier include:ANOMALOUS, ASSIMILATE, ENSEMBLE, HAMADRYAD, HAPLOID, HENOTHEISM, HOMEO-, HOMO-, [but note כמו / KIMŌ (like)] HOMILY, SAMSARA, SANSKRIT, SEEMLY, SIMPLE, SINGLE (Latin from *semel*), SIMPLICITY and SOVIET. To the AHD's list add SYMPTON and scores of SYM- and SYN- words; Greek *syn* means "with"– see "SYNOD." SHAM and SHAMANISM relate here as well. No creature is more SIMILAR to man than the SIMIAN; Latin *simia* means "ape." Perhaps the SENSES, like SMELL, stimulate associative SIMULATIONS, and we should be SENTIENT of relatives in the SM families of SEEMING and SIMILARITY.

In Chinese, *zhen* is a symptom and *su miao* is a drawing. Name in Chinese is *xing*, while in Cantonese a surname is *sing*.

SIN/זָנָה
SZAN – (AH)   [ZN→SN]

ROOTS: Old English *synn* has no known source; *Webster's* creates an IE base called *snta* to fill the gap. Others suggest Latin *sons* (guilty), which resembles אשם / [A]SHAM (was guilty, sinned – see "ASHAMED"). זנה / ZÄNÄ or SÄNÄ is to go astray or to fornicate (*Exodus 34:15; Genesis 38:24*).

BRANCHES: Abnormal behavior is often SINFUL (see "ABERRATION" for the sense of going off the straight path). SINE, a wave, is from Latin *sinus* (bend, curve, fold). The SN similarity would INSINUATE a link between the deviation in terms like SINUS and INSINUOUS and the deviant behavior that we call SINISTER or SINFUL. שונה / S(H)ONEH is different; this is the SN verb used when David "*changed* his behavior" and acted ZANY (*Psalms 34:1*). See "CHANGE."

SIP/שְׂפָה
SAPH – [AH]   [S – P(H)]

ROOTS: SIP and SIPHON are neighbors in the dictionary, but these two terms of sucking in liquids are not seen to be connected. SIPHON is from Latin *sipho* or Greek *siphon* (a tube). SIP is traced to Middle English *sippen* and "possibly" the IE root *seu* (to take liquid).

An SP element is shared by שפה / SÄPHÄ (lip – *I Samuel 1:13*) and סף / SUPH (cup, goblet – *Jeremiah 52:19*). The lips form a siphon to סבא / SÄBHÄ (drink) or שאב / S(H)ÄUBH (draw liquid – *Genesis 24:13*).

BRANCHES: סף / SAP(H) or ספל / SEPH(EL) is a mug or cup with which to SIP or SUP a SUPPER of SOUP. צפחת / TSÄPÄHÄT is a mug; אזוב / ÄZŌBH (hyssop) is used as a sponge or absorbant in *Exodus 12:22*. More synonyms and antonyms at "SEEP."

Seppun is a Japanese kiss. Perhaps *Bilo*, the Fijian cup, prefers the back half of ספל / (SE)PHEL (cup). VASE and VESS(EL) may be a reversal of the S – PH. See "SUPPER."

SIR/שַׂר
SAR   [SR]

ROOTS: SIR, SIRE and SURLY are traced to French *messieur*, Old French *sieur* (a master) and somehow on to Latin *senior* and the IE root *sen* (old – see SENILE").

שר / SÄR is a chief, leader, captain, minister or ruler ("officer" in *Jeremiah 17:25*). שררה / SÄRÄR is to rule; שררה / SIRÄRÄ is dominion; שרת / S(H)ÄRÄT is to minister.

BRANCHES: The last element in Balshazzar is from Babylonian *usar* (king). *Sar* means lord in Hittite, an ancient Indo-European language. The loftiest position in human anatomy is SR reversed, as ראש / RŌS(H) means "head." *Sar* is head in Persian, as found in English words like SARABAND and SIRDAR. כתר / KESER is a crown; זר / ZÄR is a crown or wreath. See "CZAR."

The SIRE (lord) is usually עשיר / [A]SHEER (rich) and no רש / RAS[H] (poor person). See "SERF" for SR antonyms.

SIRE(N)/שִׁיר
SHEER   [S(H) – R]

ROOTS: The deadly singer of myth, the SIREN, is traced from Greek *seiren* to the IE root *twer* (to grasp, hold; hard – making SIREN a cognate of QUARTZ). אסר / ÄSÄR is to tie or bind (*Genesis 46:29*), and צרור / TSÄROOR is bound or tied up. Yet a SIREN is more than "she who enthralls." We'd prefer an SR singing etymon to match the SERIN (a singing canary-like finch). שיר / S(H)ÄR is to sing (*Exodus 15:1*); שיר / SHER is song or poetry.

BRANCHES: *SERENADE* is possibly from שר / SHÄR. The given source of SERENADE (a vocal or musical performance) is Latin *serenus* (clear, serene). Singing is piping and צנור / (T)SENOR is a pipe; SNR is one note off from SRN. See "SNORKEL." *Shr* is poetry, and *shrren* is poet in Chinese. CHEER and CHARADE might be distantly related to שר / SHÄR (chant).

SIX/שֵׁש
SHAYSH   [S(H) – S(H)]

ROOTS: Latin *sex* (#6) and the IE root *s(w)eks* do dominate the Germanic languages, but note how the Hebrew six, שש / S(H)ĀS(H) – *Genesis 1:31*, fared in the table below:

	Six – #6
Arabic and Swahili – *sit(t)a*	
Basque – *sei*	
Chinese – *sz'*	
Czech and Serbo-Croatian – *sest*	
Dutch – *zes*	
French – *sis*	
Gothic – *saihs*	
German – *sechs*	
Greek – *hex*	
Italian – *sei*	
Norwegian and Danish – *seks*	
Polish – *szesc*	
Portuguese and Spanish – *seis*	
Rumanian – *sase*	
Russian – *shest*	
Swedish – *sex*	

שש / SHĀSH did quite well, especially when considering how conservative a hard K sound tends to be. (X and S are not so far apart. BORAX, for instance, is initially from Old French *boras* and ultimately from ברית / BORĒS.)

BRANCHES: Cognates of SIX at IE root *s(w)eks* include: HEXA-, HEXAD, SEICENTO, SEMESTER, SESTER, SESTINA, SEX-, SEXT(AN), SEXTANT, SEXTILE and SEXTODECIMO. The Hebrew SIX is related to שש / SAS (to be happy) and ששון / SASŌN (rejoicing) – see "SEVEN."

SKEP(TIC)/סָעֵף
SAY– KHAPHE   [S – K(H)P(H)]

ROOTS: Greek *skeptesthai* is to examine, an etymology that takes us back to השקיף / (HĒ)SHKĒPH (to observe, contemplate) and "SCOPE." Other Hebrew etymons however, may be precisely guiding the sense of doubting, questioning and denying behind SKEPTICISM as we use it. סעף / SĀ – ĀPH or SĀ – KĀPH is a doubter (*Psalms 119:113*).

BRANCHES: Aramaic ספקא / SPHĀKA allows for Hebrew ספק / SĀPHĀK (doubt) and ספקנות / SĀPHKĀNOOT (skepticism). A #2-#3 letter change is required to get SKEPTICAL from these terms, yet the given IE root of SKEPTIC is *spek* (to observe) which requires a similar letter swap.

SKILL/שֵׂכֶל
SAY– KHELL   [S – K(H) – L]

ROOTS: Old Norse *skil* (reason, discernment) is akin to *skilja* (to cut apart, separate). Both are traced to the IE root *skel* (to cut). Hebrew does not demand that thinking came from cutting, while it does maintain the link between understanding (שכל / SĀKHEL – *Genesis 3:6*) and separation or bereavement (שכל / S(H)ĀKOL – *Genesis 27:45*). סכין / SĀKĒN (knife) and other literal cutting terms are found at "SAXON."

BRANCHES: Hebrew adds to the idea of SKILL as mental discrimination, with a link to שקל / SHĀKĀL (weighing, pondering – see "SCALE"). Judgement, as well as dissection, serves a SCHOLAR in SCHOOL. שכלות / SĒKHLOOT (folly) and the סכל / SĀKHĀL (fool) are, hopefully, antonyms of SCHOLARSHIP and the SCHOLAR.

*SKULL*DUGGERY (deceptive skill) has an "unknown origin." The opposite of cutting away and separation is the אשכול / ESHKOL (cluster – see "SCHOOL"). Latin *scire* (to know) is related. CONSCIOUS, CONSCIENCE and SCIENCE are given cognates, but so are SCIOLISM (surface knowledge) and a 4-letter word for defecation (at the IE root *skei*, to cut or split). סעף / SĀKH[ĀF] to divide and שסע / [SHA]SAKH (to divide, cleave – *Judges 14:6*) present another SK cutting root.

SKIRT/מִסְגֶּרֶת
(ME) – S'GERET   [SGR]

ROOTS: To SKIRT is to move along the border or edge. The OUTSKIRTS of a city, for instance, need not be related to the SKIRT or SHIRT we wear. The "border" SKIRT is nonetheless lumped together with the "cloth" SKIRT, so that the etymons are old Norse *skyrta* (shirt) and IE *sker* or *ker* (to cut).

קרע / KORA is to rend and כרת / KORĀT (to cut off) is taken up at "CURT."

To offer an etymon for the SKIRT which means edge or fringe מסגרת / (MĒ)SGERET is a border or rim (*Exodus 25:25*).

BRANCHES: "Enclosure" is the literal sense; see "SECURE."

(S)KULL/גֻּלְגֹּלֶת
GHOUL – (GOAL – ET)   [GL→KL]

ROOTS: Forgetting that an S before a C or K in English is suspect, the scholars did not go to *GOLG*OTHA (Calvary; "place of a SKULL") for the source of SKULL.

Middle English *skulle* is presently linked to Norwegian dialect terms for the shell of an egg or nut. A GL or KL etymon was beckoning, as Latin *calvaria* means SKULL, and CHOLLA (a cactus) is from a Spanish term for SKULL or head. גלגלת / GOOLGOLET (skull, head – *Exodus 16:16*) is named for its shape. סגלגל / SGULGUL is elliptical or oval; עגל / ĀGŌL means round; גל / GUL is a wave or pile.

BRANCHES: (S)KULL is, therefore, more closely related to "hill" and "wheel" (both linked to GL Hebrew terms) than to "shell." Entries like "CALIPEE," "SCALP" and "UNICORN" will lead one to KL and KR terms that relate to shells and the cranium. גלגל / GULGUL is a wheel and גלגל / GĒLGĀL is to roll.

Too often, man has proven that "heads will roll." For ג / G becoming other gutturals like a C or Q, see "*ficus*" at "FIG" and "quarrel" at "GUERRILLA."

SKUN(K)/צחַנָה
TSAH – KHUN – AH   [(T)S – KH – N]

ROOTS: Nature's stinker is a North American animal with an American Indian etymon. Algonquin *seganka* or *segonku* is cited, along with Massachuset *squnck*.

צחן / (T)SÄKHUN is to stink (*Joel 2:20*). צחנה / TSÄKÄNÄH is a smell or STENCH.

זנח / SZANUKH is defined as "stank" in the *Lexicon; JPS* translates it "turn foul" at *Isaiah 19:6*.

> **BRANCHES:** Switch #2 and #3 letters of the Hebrew TS – K – N or ST – K – N for Anglo-Saxon *stenc* and *stincan* (sources of STENCH and to STINK). The AHD has no IE root for STINK, while *Webster's* offers: "probably from IE base *steu* (to push), in the basic sense 'to rise up, rise up like dust.' "
>
> A SCANDAL is a *shtunk* in German and Yiddish, people making a big *stink* about something. Also linking olfactory offenses to moral offense, it may be better tying SCAN(DAL) to צחן / TSÄKHÄN rather than to Greek *skandalon* (a snare) and Latin *scandere* (to climb). There's nothing rotten in Denmark; the SCAN + NAVIA in SCANDINAVIA are probably from שכונה / SHKOONÄ (settlement, colony) + נאוה / NÄVEH (beautiful). Things smell and rot when they dry, see SACK (the dry sack). *Hauna* or *hohono*, stench in Hawaiian, is combined with their "dog" term to say "skunk."

SLALOM/סולָם
SOOL – LUM   [SLM]

ROOTS: SLALOM is a noun or verb of skiing in a zigzag, downhill race. The word is Norwegian; no IE base or root is available. SLANT is from Norwegian *slenta* (a slope), so that an SLN or SLM etymon of sloping up or down is needed. סולם or סלם /SOOLÄM is the ladder, ramp or stairway in Jacob's dream – *Genesis 28:12*.

For the SL connotations of SLALOM, סוללה / SŌLILÄ is a ramp, סלול / SÄLOOL is paved (macadamized), and סלסל / SILSÄL is to curl. Put these together for the sense of balance and engineering necessary in downhill racing or uphill road building.

> **BRANCHES:** SWARM is to climb. סלם / SOOLÄM may be read SVLM or SWLM, then only an L→R shift away from SWRM. Somewhere behind the confusion of the soft C (S) and the hard C (K) may lie a connection between SLALOM, SLANT and the HARD C *CLIMBING* words. Latin *clinare* (to lean) and Greek *klimax* (ladder) are among the etymons that gave us the following possible derivatives of סלם / soft C – L – M: ACCLIVITY, CLIENT, CLINIC, -CLINO, CLIMATE, CLIMAX, DECLINE, INCLINE, LEAN, PROCLIVITY.
>
> If completing a race gave SLALOM its SLM, see "SLAM."

SLAM/שלֵם
S(H)A – LAME   [S(H) – L – M]

ROOTS: SLAM is a term in card games, "with reference to its *finality*." The more familiar SLAM involves shutting a door with noise and force. Both SLAMs earn the rare "origin unknown" designation from most dictionaries. *Webster's* offers, "probably from Old Norse...compare Norwegian dialect *slemma*."

The finality, completion or fullness of the GRAND SLAM is inherent in שלם / SHÄLÄM (full, complete, finished – *Deuteronomy 25:15; I Kings 7:51*). The term means whole and healthy in *Genesis 33:18* and *Job 9:4*. Completing a financial transaction or paying remunerative damages involves שלם / SHELÄM (paying up or paying back – *Exodus 22:5*). The familiar שלום / SHALOM (peace) is an appropriate "hello" or "goodbye" if the two parties will be or have been completing something peaceably.

> **BRANCHES:** *Zahlen* is to pay in German; *chieh lun* means conclusion in Chinese. The list of Indo-European roots attached to the *American Heritage Dictionary* includes an *slm* root that does not appear in the 1985 edition of IE roots (published separately). Under "*slm* (to be whole) – Semitic root" are found words like ISLAM, [MOSLEM], MUSLIM, SALAAM, SALOME (Greek *Salome* means "peace"), SHALOM and SOLOMON. The etymons cited are Arabic *salama* (he was safe), Arabic *salam* (peace) and Hebrew *shalom* (peace).
>
> The new AHD listing contains שלם / S(H) – L – M words too, but under the IE root *sol* (whole). Cognates listed here include CATHOLIC, CONSOLIDATE, HOLO- (as in HOLOCAUST), SAFE, SALUBRIOUS, SALUTATION, SALUTE, SALVAGE, [SALVATION], SAVE, SOLEMN, SOLICITOUS and SOLID. SERENE (L→R) and SILENCE (M→N) may be influenced by שלום / SHÄLOM (peace). שלום / SHÄLOM (goodbye) might have been corrupted to SO LONG! (goodbye – origin unknown).

SLAN(G)/לָשׁון
LAH – S(H)ONE   [LSN→SLN]

ROOTS: SLANG is non-standard speech or street language; it has no known etymon or IE root. Norwegian shares the term with English, in that *slengjeord* is a "slang term" and *slangjenamn* is a "nickname."

Slang would be called "mother's tongue" or "native tongue" in various cultures, especially those who lived under the linguistic domination of an occupying power. לשון / LÄSHŌN (*Genesis 10:32*) means tongue or language; a #1-#2 letter swap allows SLAN(G) to be heard.

> **BRANCHES:** Another SLN term from Hebrew LSN is SLANDER, from לשן / LÄSHUN (to slander – *Proverbs 30:10*).
>
> German *zunge* (tongue) and Yiddish *tsung* may indicate that TONGUE was an SN term long ago – see "SOUND."
>
> LOZENGE, from Old French *losenge*, is a candy named for its diamond shape – or perhaps by the Hebrew לשון / LSN (tongue) and its shape.
>
> Among the words for "language" only Turkish *lisan* is clearly form לשן / LÄSHŌN (language). The Arabic (*lougha*) and Swahili (*lugha*) are noteworthy because LANGUAGE (*langue* in French) is merely a nasalization (added N) of the LG term in Hamito-Semitic. Reversing LG evokes Finnish *kieli* (language), which allows us to hear קול / KŌL (voice – *Genesis 27:22*). Perhaps the Finnish enables us to trace LA(N)G(UAGE) all the way back to קול / KŌL. If SLANG is linked to LANG(UAGE), we still have it covered by a Hebrew etymon. See "LICK" for an LK Hebrew etymon that also might lead us to words like *LINGUISTICS*.

SLOUGH/שָׁלַח
S(H)A–LUKH   [S(H)–L–KH]

ROOTS: Dictionaries spell the Middle English version either *slouh* or *slughe*, but SLOUGH means to cast off, discard or shed. *Webster's* cites German *schluach* (a skin bag) and suggests the IE base *sleug* (to glide, slip).

שלח / SHÄLÄH or SHÄLÄKH is to send off, send away or set free. When Moses demands, *"Let my people go"* (*Exodus 7:16*) – the verb is שלח / S(H)LÄKH. To match the German skin term and the SLOUGH (skin that is shed) of a snake, שלח / S(H)ELÄKH means hide or untanned skin in Aramaic.

BRANCHES: SLI(N)G may be an SLK term with the N SLUNG or thrown in (nasalization). To SLOUGH (pronounced sluf) is to SLIP off. שלף / S(H)ÄLÄPH is the verb of removing things like shoes (*Ruth 4:2*). SLIPPER and SLIPPERY are related. שלה / SHÄLÄH (to draw out, pull out) links SLIP and SLOUGH, and favors the *slouh* spelling at the source of SLOUGH. זרב / ZEREBH is a slipper or lining.

The opposite of taking off is שלב / SHĒLÄV (to join, put together). SLEEVE should come from here and from related terms like שרווּל / SHÄRVOOL (sleeve – Mishnaic Hebrew) or סניף / SNĒPH (attachment, branch). SLEEVE is presently traced to IE root *sleubh* (to slide, slip).

If SLICE is unrelated (a SLICE bar loosens coals), it may link up to שלש / S(H)ĒLÄSH – (to divide into three parts – *Deuteronomy 19:3*). There is no verb for cutting into fourths.

SLU(D)GE/שֶׁלֶג
S(H)ELL–EGG   [S(H)–L–G]

ROOTS: SLUDGE has a #2 definition meaning "a slush of snow" or finely broken drift ice. Middle English *slike*, Dutch *slijk*, German *schleich* and the IE base *sleug* (to slip, glide) all dispatch of the D in SLUDGE, whether or not they are good etymons. שלג / S(H)ELEG is snow (*Jeremiah 18:14*).

BRANCHES: Swahili snow is *theluji*, a typical Swahili rendering of the Hebrew ש / SH and ג / G. Indonesian snow is *sladju*, a variant of שלג / SHELEG whose DJ parallels the D of SLUDGE. In both cases the D simply makes the ג / G into a J or *jimmel* (the soft ג / G, as in Giovanni). The same L→N change that brought us NO from לא /LO (no), CANNIB(AL) from כלב / KELEBH (dog – see "CARIBBEAN") or Slavic *nem* (mute) from עלם / ĒLÄM (mute), allowed שלג / SHELEG to become *snijeg* in Serbo-Croatian and *snieg* (snow) in Polish.

The French drop the S in their *neige* (snow). In German and Yiddish the SNG or SNK (Russian snow is *snyek*) is softened, and letters #2 and #3 are swapped to get *Schnee* (snow). We SLOG through the snows of Siberia to Kilimanjaro to get to the English SNOW. The IE root of SNOW is *sneig(w)h*.

An alternate SN etymon is צנה / (T)SENÄH (cold), as in "the coldness of snow" (*Proverbs 25:13*). Polish *zimny* means cold and winter. SLUSH and SLEET appear at IE root *sleu* (no definition given) where they are cognates of SLUG and SLUGGARD. SLEIGH, the snow vehicle, will SLOG by with more ease if one turns to "GLISSADE." Reversing the S(H)–L–G of שלג / SHELEG (snow) reveals גלש / GALUSH (to glide, slide, ski) – identical to the SLG base of SLUDGE listed above.

SMASH/צָמַת
(T)SAH–MUS   [(T)S–M–S]

ROOTS: SMASH, to ruin completely or break into pieces, is matched by צמת / (T)SÄMÄS (to destroy, smash or make smaller – *Laments 3:53*). *Webster's* offers, "perhaps from MASH," while the AHD comes up with, "perhaps a blend of 'smack' and 'crash.'"

BRANCHES: צמק / TSÄMÄK is to shrink or wither; the opposite is צמח / TSÄMÄKH (to sprout or spring up). The TS–M root of making smaller is best seen with צמצום / TSIMTSOOM (condensing, confining, contraction).

SMALL deserves a better IE root than *melo* or *smelo* (small animal). Enlarging the TS-M family is צנום / TSÄNOOM (shrunken, meager). SKIM, linked to Old Norse *skemma* (to shorten) may be a #2-#3 letter swap of צמק / TSÄMÄK (to shrink). נשם / (NA)SHAM is to be destroyed. For more destructive SM terms, see "SMITE."

SMITE/הִשְׁמִיד
(HE)–S(H)MEEDT   [S(H)–M–(D)T]

ROOTS: To SMITE (destroy, kill, punish, strike hard) or SMIT is identical to the Hebrew השמיד / (HĒ)SHMĒDT (to destroy, exterminate).

Breaking into SMITHEREENS is destructive (Irish *smidirin* means broken bits), but the work of a SMITH (German *schmid*) is constructive. SMITH is linked to IE root *smi* (to cut, work with a sharp instrument) while SMITE is sloppily filed under *sme* (to smear – see "SESAME").

Both SMITE and SMITH belong to שמד / S(H)–M–D(T) (to destroy, cut off – *Genesis 34:30*). צמת / (T)SAMAT is to destroy – see "SMASH."

BRANCHES: Both SMASH and SHMATA (rag in Yiddish) are cousins of the SMITHS. Hebrew ASHMODAI is the given source of Greek and Latin ASMODEUS (demon of destruction) and ought to be the source of *Samedi*, the voodoo god of death in Haiti. The SCIMITAR or SCIMITER sword is believed to mean "the smiter."

SMUG/שָׂמַח
SOME–AKH   [S–M–KH]

ROOTS: To be SMUG is to be happy with oneself. The dictionary smugly offers Germanic *smuck* (neat) and the IE root *meug* (slimy, slippery) as etymons.

שמח / SÄMÄUKH is a joyful satisfaction (*Deuteronomy 16:15*).

BRANCHES: SMIRK and Anglo-Saxon *smercian* (to smile) are from the same base as SMILE. The IE base is *smei* (to smile, be astonished); the IE root is *smei* (to laugh, smile). The Bible has no SMILE term, but שמח / SÄMÄH or SÄMÄKH is to rejoice or be glad (*Proverbs 17:5*). If, as *Webster's* suggests, astonishment (as well as happiness) brings a smile to our lips, consider ישם / (YĒ)SOM ("shall be astonished"–*Jeremiah 49:17*). שמה / SHÄMÄ means horror. תמה / TOMÄ, THOMA or SOMA is to be astounded or amazed or to wonder. THAUMATOLOGY is from Greek *thauma* (a miracle, a wonder), but this term is not linked to SMILE as "admire," "miracle" and "marvel" are. Hebrew happiness is shared because Polish *usmiech* is a smile and Cantonese *some* is happy.

SMUT/שֶׁמֶץ
S(H)EM – ET(S)   [S(H) – M –T(S)]

ROOTS: English SMUT is linked to German *schmutz* (dirt); no older etymons are known. The term is defined as "sooty matter, a *particle* of this," a soiled spot and something obscene.

שמץ / SHEMETS is likewise defined as a "particle"– (*Job 4:12*), but also as an object of shame and derision. שמצה / SHIMTSÄ is in *Exodus 32:25*.

> **BRANCHES:** Yiddish *smutz* also has both meanings; Yiddish *samd* (sand) may be a clue that those particles of soil we call SAND may be related (M=N; T=D). Related words should include SMIDGE, SMUDGE, SMUTCH and perhaps SMI(R)TCH and BESMIRCH. מץ / MÖTS (chaff) links up with one element of SMT.

SNAKE/שָׁנָק
S(H)E – NAKE   [S(H) – N – K]

ROOTS: SNAKE is from Anglo-Saxon *snaca* and, perhaps, the given IE root *sneg* (to creep; creeping thing). It is not entirely accurate to describe a SNAKE as a creeper (see "SERPENT"), and to make the SNAKE a cognate of SNAIL. The SNAKE can be a strangler; שנק / S(H)NAK is to strangle in Aramaic. The SNAKE also squirts (venom) and can leap forth – the definitions of זנק / ZENAK (*Deuteronomy 33:22*).

זנב / ZÄNÄV (tail) and שן / S(H)EN (tooth...fang) are relevant SN terms as well.

Another etymon for SNAKE is נחש / NÄKHÄSH (snake – *Genesis 3:1*). Yes, the end S of נחש / NKS has to snake its way to the front of the word, but one sees many examples of this Hebrew letter #3 to English letter #1 phenomenon.

> **BRANCHES:** The NK element in world SNAKE words is striking. The Indo-European root *ang(w)hi* (snake, eel) includes ANGUINE and ANGUILLIFORM from Latin *anguis* (snake). ECHINO-, ECHINODERM, ECHINUS and ECHIDA are at this root thanks to Greek *ekhis* (snake – which has only lost the initial N of נחש / NÄKHÄSH).
>
> The ANACONDA (python-like snake) is an NK snake term from Singalese or Ceylonese that stresses the constriction seen at "HANG;" חנק / HENEK and שנק / SHENAK both mean the kind of strangulation that boa constrictors do for a living.
>
> To SNIGGLE is to catch SNIGS (eels in English dialect). The least subtle נחש / NÄHÄSH (snake) is the Hawaiian *nahesi* (snake). More SNAKE words include the Amazon Indian *kana*, Arabic *hanash* (eel – #1-#2 letter swap), Hawaiian *kuna* (eel – NK reversed), Japanese *unagi* (eel), Kiowa Indian *sane* (K drops out; Russian *smeya* is similar), Maya Indian *kana*, Indonesian *ikan belut* (eel), *noso*, *niha* and *katoun* in various Malay dialects, Swahili *nyoka* and Thai *ngoo*.
>
> Reversing [N]HS to Chinese *she* (snake) recalls נחוש / (NE)HOOSH or NEKHOOSH (divination, magic). Snake handling is long associated with magic, from snake charmers in Bombay to medicine men among the American Indians. American medicine men with M.D.'s show the sign of the snake on a pole because of *Numbers 21:9*. The healing "brass serpent" is admired by copperheads everywhere. (נחושה / NIHOSH(ET), or brass, is *nossoe* in Korean).

Taking up serpents is one of the five signs of believers saved from damnation at the end of the gospel of *Mark*. Whether one sees the SNAKE as a healing or as a satanic figure, these creatures have taken a נשיכה / NIS(H)EKHÄ (bite) out of Man's consciousness. Snakes are biting in *Numbers 21:6*; a #1-#2 letter swap of נשך / NSK will also get one back to SNAKE. See "ASP" and "SNEAK."

SNAP/זְנַב
ZEE – NAYBH   [Z – N – BH→SNP]

ROOTS: Middle Dutch *snappen* is from the Germanic base *snab*.

To SNAP off, to SNIP, various definitions of SNUFF (to trim off), and SNUB (to stop a rope) are all from זנב / ZENABH (to trim, to cut off the tail, to attack – *Joshua 10:19*). SNAP can mean a sudden movement, not just a breaking off, a biting or a verbal attack. Recalling this smart, sudden motion is the סנפיר / SNÄPER (fin of a fish – *Leviticus 11;9*).

> **BRANCHES:** While the SNAPPER fish may be named for its biting, rather than for its fin, the SPINNAKER (a large triangular sail on racing yachts) may be named for the fish's dorsal fin. Fins do not only "sail" or stabilize aquatic propulsion, they can be used to SPANK (another #2-#3 letter swap) the water to generate propulsion. See "SPANK." The AHD sees SNIP, SNAP, SNUB and SNUFF as "words connected to the nose," and places them at the IE root *snu*. See "NOZZLE."
>
> The flip side of SNIPPING off the tail is זנב / ZÄNÄBH (tail, stump – *Deuteronomy 28:24*). Fins and tails work together, so naturally they sound alike in Hebrew. The SLAP of a fin may connect to the SNP Hebrew terms above or to צליפה / (T)SLEPÄ (whip, beat, lash) – only an L to R change away from STRAFE, STRAP and STRIPE (lash). Current wisdom makes SLAP a cognate of COLLAPSE, ELAPSE, LABEL, RELAPSE and SLAVER at the IE root *leb* ("hanging loosely"). These loosely hung terms might relate to words like רפה / RÄFÄ (to be loose – RF→LB) and to a reversal of נפל(ו) / (NA)FÄL (to fall – see "FALL").
>
> For a more binding Hebrew etymon for STRAP (Greek *stroppos* is a band or cord), consider a #1-#2 letter flip of רצף / R–TS–P (to join closely) and its cousin צרף / TS–R–P or ST–R–P (to join).

SNEAK/זְנִיקָה
ZIN – EEK – (AH)   [ZNK]

ROOTS: SNEAK is from Anglo-Saxon *snican*, thought to be related to "snail" at IE base *sneq* (to creep). זנק / ZENAK is the furtive and quick leaping after prey attributed to lions who sneak-attack in *Deuteronomy 33:22*. SNEAK is defined as moving quickly and stealthily, qualities that only a dictionary could associate with snails.

> **BRANCHES:** The secrecy inherent in SNEAK is echoed by הצניע / (HET)SNEÄKH (to be modest, to hide). To hide oneself in chinese is *tzu ni*.

SNOR[KEL]/צִנּוֹר

(T)SEE – NORE   [(T)S – N – R]

ROOTS: SNORKEL is a breathing tube, and Hebrew has a word like צנור / (T)SĒNŌR (pipe, drain – *Psalms 42:8*). Nonetheless we are offered German *snarchen* (to snore) as an etymon. The IE root is *sner* ("expressive root of various verbs for making noises).

BRANCHES: The first of the given cognates is SCHNORRER (a beggar in Yiddish). The AHD traces SCHNORRER to Middle High German *snurren* (to hum, whirr). Other cognates of SNORKEL are SNARL, SNEER, SNORE and SNORT. All these sounds are made in the natural SNORKEL or breathing tube we call the nose.

There is an IE root *srenk* (to snore) that includes RHONCHUS and Greek *rhunkhos* (snout). Neglected were all the RHINO-words from Greek *rhinos* (nose) – a reversal of צנור / (T)SĒNŌR and נחיר / NIHĒR (nostril).

The IE root *srenk* is a #2-#3 letter swap from צנור / (T)S – N – R; allow slight shift to T(S) – N – R and we can discover TRN and TRM words from the same Hebrew pipeline. The TRUNK of a tree is the stem or main pipe, while the TRUNK of the elephant is a SNORKEL that belongs with all the nasal SNORTING here. Besides a food and water pipe, the elephant's TRUN(K) [now linked to IE root *ter* (to cross over, overcome)] is the world's first *TRUMPET* or *TROMBONE*. Old Norse *trumba* is a tube.

If words like SNOUT, SCHNAUZER (snarling dog) or SCHNOZZLE (nose) do not belong here, perhaps they could fit back at "NOZZLE." One has to be in love to equate SNORING with a SERENADE, but a #2-#3 letter swap of צנור / (T)S – N – R echoes piping sounds like the SIREN. See "SIREN" and "SOUND." A similar transposition makes the Gaelic nose, *sron*, more familiar.

SO/זוֹ

ZO   [ZO→SO]

ROOTS: Middle English *so* or *swo* is from the IE root *swo* (so). SO means "in such a way" or "likewise." זו / ZŌ or ZWŌ (*Psalms 132:12*) means "the same"; the Hebrew can be read SWŌ as well. Another term that means "equal" (*Proverbs 8:11*) and that matches the IE root is שוה / S(H)ÄVEH or S(H)ÄWE.

BRANCHES: Cognates of SO include NISI, QUASI and SUCH. See "THIS."

SOAK/סָךְ

SOKH   [S – KH]

ROOTS: SOAK is from Anglo-Saxon *socian*, an IE base *sucan* and the IE root *seue* (to take liquid). To SOAK is to make thoroughly or excessively wet.

סך / SOKH is to anoint (*Ruth 3:3*); יצק / (YÄ)TSŌK is to pour liquid and משח / (MÄ)S(H)ÄKH (source of MESSIAH) is to anoint (both appear in *Leviticus 8:12*). שקה / S(H)AKA is to water or irrigate; שקע / S(H)ÄKÄ is to dip, sink or immerse.

BRANCHES: שקת / S(H)ŌKES is a watering trough; שקוי / S(H)ĒKOOY is a drink; שכור / S(H)ĒKOOR is a drunk, an intoxicated person or a SOAK.

Cognates of SOAK include SUCCULENT, SUCK and SUCTION; *Webster's* links SOGGY to SOAK as well. See

"SHOWER" and "SQUALL." *Teng* is the IE root that means "SOAK." If SK became TG with a nasalization (extra N) thrown in, then cognates DUNK, TAINT, TINCT, TINGE and TINT ultimately relate to our SK or T(S) – K Hebrew etymons.

SOB/שְׁאַב

S(H)AW – UB(H)   [SH – A – BH→SOB]

ROOTS: A SOB is a gasping breath taken when crying, etc. Anglo-Saxon *sobbian* is linked to IE base words of swallowing and sucking in.

To suck in, absorb or draw (water) is שאב / S(H)OÄB(H) (*Genesis 24:13*).

BRANCHES: SIP, SIPHON, SOP (to absorb) and SUP relate. For synonyms see "SIP," for antonyms see "SEEP."

SOD/שָׂדֶה

SOD – EH   [SDH]

ROOTS: SOD means turf or lawn; here the dictionaries can only guess that SOD is "probably" related to SODDEN (soaked).

שדה / SODEH (field, land) is one Hebrew etymon for SOD. It appears in *Genesis 4:8*. Primarily, the term indicates irrigated (SODDEN) and cultivated land. This is evident in Polish *sad* (orchard).

To see the roots of SOD, turn it upside down to DS. דשא / DÄSHÄ is to sprout or grow grass; דשא / DESHE is the "grass" or lawn of *Genesis 1:11*.

BRANCHES: DASYURE and TUSSOCK are related to דשא / DESHE or TESHE. DASHEEN, the edible sprouts of the taro, has no known etymon. One theory in *Webster's* is *de* ("of" in French) + *Chine* (China).

Returning to SD earth words, שיד / SĒD is lime and יסור / (YI)SŌD is "foundation"– (*I Kings 6:37*). SODA, from Italian *sodo* (firm), should be related. SODA is officially linked to Latin *solidus*, whose source is taken up at "SLAM." SODDEN might relate to ST water terms, see "SOT."

SODIUM/סְרֹם

S'DOME   [SDM]

ROOTS: SODIUM is commonly associated with salt, though SODIUM is supposed to derive from SODA (see "SOD"). Linking it to the Biblical source of SODOMY, סרם / SIDŌM (Sodom – *Genesis 18:20*), is an alternative.

The entire region of Sodom was to have been turned into a wasteland of "sulphur and salt" (*Deuteronomy 29:22*). The Dead Sea near Sodom is so saline that it makes Utah's Great Salt Lake look like a watering hole for animals on a low SODIUM diet. Lot's wife, who turns back toward the city, becomes a pillar of salt. The Arabs have named a mound of salt *Jebel Usdum*. To further spice the SODIUM/Sodom equation, note that "salt of Sodom" was common tablefare in the Near East according to first century Talmudic literature. The "ium" suffix and spelling might, therefore, be the work of lexicographers rather than representative of the actual SDM salt word as it developed historically.

SODOMY/סְדֹם
S'DOME   [SDM]

ROOTS: SODOMY and SODOMITE are borrowed from סדם / S'DOM (Sodom) the sinful city of *Genesis 18-19*. The fact that sexually aberrant behavior is not specifically mentioned in the Sodom story reinforces the point that even suggestions and connotations from Biblical place names or people names made their way into the English language.

    BRANCHES: See "RUTH" and "SODIUM."

SOFA/סְפָּה
SUP-AH   [SP→SF]

ROOTS: A SOFA or SOFA BED is an acknowledged borrowing from Arabic *suffah* (a saddle cushion) or from Arabic *sufah* (dais). סְפה / SÄPÄH or SÄPHÄ in *II Samuel 17:28* is understood to mean a couch or a rug by most translators.

    שפה / S(H)ÄFÄ is to incline, tilt, be at ease; שופי / S(H)OFÉ is ease; שפל / S(H)ÄFÄL is to recline or get down low. שב / S(H)ÄV is to sit (imperative); שובה / S(H)oovä is rest or retirement. The king's sofa or *"couch"* is the מסב / (MOO)SABH in *Songs 1:12.* הסב / (HÄ)SÄV is to recline (at table); the nobility ate while *SUP*INE or reclining on SOFAS.

    BRANCHES: SOPOR, a Latin sleep term, and SOPORIFIC are likely relatives. HYPNOSIS and other HYPNO- words are cognates of SOPOR at IE root *swep* (to sleep). SUB- and SUPPLE are cognates of SUPINE. See "ASPHALT."
    · To sit is *sekba* in Maya Indian, relating to S–BH words here or to שכב / S(H)ÄKHÄBH or S(H)ÄHÄV (to lie down, to sleep – see "SUCCUBUS").

SOLE/שַׁעַל
S(H)A–ULL   [S(H)–U–L]

ROOTS: The SOLE of the foot is traced to Latin *solea* (a sandal) and Latin *solum* (bottom, foundation). The IE root is *sel* (human settlement) in the AHD's belief that SALON, SALOON and SOLUM are cognates of SOLE. See "SOLEMN." שעל / S(H)ÄÄL is a footstep (*I Kings 20:10*); משעול / (MI)S(H)ÖL is a footpath (*Numbers 22:24*). סלה / SELÄ is to trample. שעל / S(H)ÖAL is the "hollow of the hand" (*Isaiah 40:12*), so that the palm or sole of the foot may be an extension of this term.

    BRANCHES: The SOLE fish is probably named for its resemblance to the SOLE of the human foot.
    For the lonely SOLE see "SOLITARY."

SOLEMN/שָׁלֵם
S(H)A–LAME   [S(H)–L–M]

ROOTS: SOLEMN is traced to Latin *sollemnis* (yearly, annual, hence religious, solemn) and to the IE root *sol* (whole).
    SOLEMN and Latin *sollus* (all) are from שלום / SHALOM (peace) and שלם / S(H)ÄLAM (complete – see "SLAM").

    BRANCHES: Visitors to a mosque are greeted with *salaam* (the Arabic שלום / SHALOM or greeting) in the *selamlik* (reception room). The Semitic SLM reception room provides a better etymon for SALON and SALOON than offered above at "SOLE."

SOLIT(ARY)/זוּלַת
ZOO–LUTT   [ZLT→SLT]

ROOTS: SOLITARY AND SOLE are from Latin *solus* (by oneself, alone).
    זולת / ZOOLUS or ZOOLAT means "except" or "save only." The adverb form in *Deuteronomy 1:36* or *Deuteronomy 4:12* ("exclusively;" "nothing but") is זולתי / ZOOLÄTE. סלה / SELÄH ("selah") may be a musical note or instruction indicating a SOLO of sorts. It otherwise infers being beyond time.

    BRANCHES: DESOLATE, SOLILOQUY, SOLITAIRE, SOLITUDE and SULLEN are cognates of SOLE and SOLITARY.
    של / S(H)EL (belonging to) is also a term of exclusivity.

SOLVE/שָׁלַף
S(H)ALAF   [S(H)–L–F]

ROOTS: Latin *solvere* is to loosen, untie. שלף / S(H)ÄLÄF is the loosening, untying or unbuckling done when removing shoes (*Ruth 4:7*). The words for shoe, bolt and lock are the same in Hebrew.

    BRANCHES: The Hebrew key to ABSOLVE, DISSOLVE, SOLUTION, and RESOLVED are more fully unlocked at "LOOSE" (an SL reversal).

SOME/שׁוּם
S(H)OOM   [S(H)–O–M]

ROOTS: SOME (certain unspecified ones) is from Anglo-Saxon *sum* (a certain one) and the IE root *sem* (one). The Aramaic שום / S(H)OOM means "anything" or "any."

    BRANCHES: שם / S(H)ÄM (a name) is how we refer to "a certain one."
    See "SIMULATION."

SO(N)/צֶאֱצָא
(T)SEH – (TSÄH)   [(T)S – E]

ROOTS: Old English *sunu* (son) is traced to the IE root *seu* (to give birth).

A reduplicated form of צא / (T)SÄ ("go forth!"– *Genesis 8:16*) is צאצא / (T)SE(T)SÄ (children, offspring, creature, produce – *Isaiah 61:9*).

> **BRANCHES:** Chinese confirms this sound and meaning with *zi* (children, offspring, bullet). A child is more than a "bullet" that goes forth from us, and womb fruit should never be treated like mere צאה / (T)ZÄÄ (excrement – *Deuteronomy 23:14*). Hebrew has many less anatomical terms for children, such as נין / NĒN (descendant, great grandchild – source of Spanish *niño* or child).
> *Sun* is a Chinese grandson or grandchild, and *sonyon* is a boy in Korean. One Semitic SN "son" or "child" word is Egyptian *mes* or *messu* (child, son).

SORE/צר
(T)S+ ARE   [(T)S – R]

ROOTS: Old English *sar* is painful or SORE; Germanic *sairaz* (suffering, sick, ill) reduces to the IE root *sai* (suffering). צרה / (T)SÄRÄ is distress or "anguish" (*Genesis 42:21*); צר / (T)SÄR is an adversary; צער / (T)SÄÄR is pain, sorrow or trouble.

> **BRANCHES:** צרות / (T)SÄRŌS, a plural form meaning "pressing troubles," is a fine parallel for STRESS (and DISTRESS) as צר / (T)SÄR means "narrow" and "tight" as well as DISTRESS.
> The world identifies with the exodus from מצרים / MIZRÄYIM (Egypt) because מצר / (MÄT)SÄR means DISTRESS as well as isthmus. A SORRY Biblical ailment is צרעת / (T)SORÄÄS (mistranslated "leprosy"). This word, and not Greek *psora* (an itch) is the probable source of PSORIASIS and PSOROSIS (a scaly plant disease). The antonym and antidote for all this SORE pain is צרי / (T)SÄRĒ (balm – *Genesis 43:11*). יסור / [YĒ]SOOR is suffering. *Szorit* is hurt or press in Hungarian; *sorta* is oppress in Finnish. See "STRAIT" and "STRESS."

SORGH(UM)/שְׂעוֹרָה
S'GORE – AH   [SGR→SRG]

ROOTS: SORGHUM, cereal grasses grown for grain or fodder, is Modern Latin. Italian *sorgo* is said to come from Latin *syricas* (Syrian), so that SORGHUM means Syrian grasses.

Syria has the Semitic name of אשור / ÄSHOOR (ASSYRIA – *Laments 5:6*), but an SRG etymon would be more satisfactory. שעורה / S'ŌRÄH or S'GŌRÄH (*Deuteronomy 8:8*) means barley or cereal grass – a #2-#3 letter swap is needed to get SRGH.

> **BRANCHES:** שורה / SŌRÄH is barley in *Isaiah 28:25*.

SOT/שֹׁט
SOT   [ST]

ROOTS: A SOT is a habitual drunkard; Late Latin *sottus* (stupid) is the given etymon. Two Hebrew etymons shall have to cover SOT. First, to cover the "stupidity," there is

Aramaic שטיא / S(H)OTĒÄ and שוטה / S(H)OTE (fool, idiot). שטות / SHTOOS means foolishness. The Biblical Hebrew connection involves שט / SĒT (*Hosea 8:2*), שט / SÄT and (*Numbers 5:12*) שטה / SÄTÄ (verbs of deviating and rebelling). סט / SÄT is a transgressor or rebel, just as the שטן / SÄTÄN (Satan) is that force of deviation and rebellion that obstructs our spiritual progress and can lead to foolish sin. The sinner and fool are equated by classical Bible commentators.

Directly addressing the sense of SOT as drunkard are words like שתה / S(H)ÄTÄ (to drink – *Deuteronomy 9:9*), שתוי / S(H)ATOOY (drunk) and שתין / S(H)ATYAN (a drunkard). These words can also be read with two S's and SOUSE means to make or become intoxicated. Demon rum is the common denominator in these two approaches to SOT.

> **BRANCHES:** שטוף / S(H)ATOOF (flooded) came to mean "addicted to." SATURATE and SODDEN may be related.
> The opposite of drinking is שתן / SHÄTÄN (to urinate – *I Kings 16:11*). See "SHED." SATIRE is currently thought to be a cognate of SAD at the IE root *sā* (to satisfy). It might better be linked to the ST folly terms above. The Syriac term *shita* (he went wrong, played the fool, was out of his wits) links up with Arabic *shatt* (side) – a word of spacial deviation. See "SIDE."

SOUN(D)/שָׁאוֹן
S(H)A – OWN   [SN]

ROOTS: Latin *sonare* is "to sound;" the Indo-European root is *swen* (to sound).

שאון / S'ON or S'WŌN is noise or tumult; שאון / S(H)AŌN is "noise" (*Isaiah 24:8*). שאן / S(H)AAN is to make noise.

> **BRANCHES:** The ear and "to hear" are אזן / AZN – see "AUSCULATE." From SN and ZN we move to שמע / SHAMA (to listen) and שמע / SHÄMA (a sound or report). זמר / ZEM(ER(is the sweet sound of SONG; זמירה / Z'MĒRA is a (P)SA(L)M; זמזם / ZĒMZÄM is to buzz or hum – akin to ZOOM. The SINGING of a cat, שונרא / SHOON(RA) in Aramaic, can be less than *SONOROUS* at 3:00 A.M.
> The SN antonym is שאנן / S(H)AANAN (quiet) – *tenang* is quiet in Indonesian.
> Cognates of SOUND include ASSONANCE, CONSONANT, DISSONANT, RESOUND, SONANT, SONATA, SONE, SONIC, SONNET, SWAN and UNISON.
> French *chanter* sounds most like שאון / SHAON, while Dutch *zingen* (to sing) best resembles זמר / ZĒMÄR (to sing). CHANT is considered a KN word – see "CANE." Sound or noise is *see-ung* in Thai; *chang* is to sing in Chinese. *Seinn* is to sing in Gaelic. *Shum* is noise in Russian.
> צנור / (T)SĒNŌR is a pipe, and piping is singing or sounding through a reed instrument or the NOSE – see "SNORKEL." Another זמ / ZM term essential to musical sound is זמן / ZMAN (time).
> שם / SHÄM (name, reputation) is a most significant human sound and object of reportage. NOISE is presently thought to derive from Latin *nausea* and the IE root *nau* (boat). NOISE means "loud sound" or, formerly, "a bad report." Rather than making NOISE a cognate of "astronaut" and "nausea," reverse the SN root of שמע / SHAMA (report) and שאן / S'ON (noise). This entry and book would establish that sound is sense, and that the sequence and spelling of those basic, universal sounds is less important.
> MUSIC is מתוק / MASŌK (sweet), but it might also be an NS or MS cognate of NOISE and SOUND.

SOUTH/תחת
SUH – UTH   [S – H – T(H)]

ROOTS: Anglo-Saxon *suth* (south) is weakly linked to theoretical Germanic terms like *sunthaz* (sun-side) and to the IE root *sawel* (the sun). To pursue the given etymological direction see שמש / S(H)EMESH (sun) at the "SUN" entry.

The better etymon appears to be is תחת / TUKHUT or SUHÄTH (below, under, beneath). "Let the waters *under* the heaven be gathered..."– *Genesis 1:9*. The Anglo-Saxon rendering of ת as TH is seen elsewhere at "BOTH", "OATH" and "THOU." שת / SHÄT or SÄTH (posteriors) relates to Semitic ST terms that mean lowest part or bottom.

> **BRANCHES:** The ת is a harder T in French (and English) *SOUT*ANE (tunic worn by Roman Catholic priests), deriving from Italian *sotto* (under). French *sous* (under) is like the Latin prefix *sus* (under) that appears in words like *SUS*CEPTIBLE, *SUS*PECT, *SUS*PEND, *SUS*PENSE, *SUS*PIRE and possibly *SUS*SEX (a southern British kingdom). These are all available because תחת can also be read SUHS. The dictionary claims that Latin *subtus* (under) is the source of *sotto* and *sus*.
>
> Aramaic pronounces the ת as a T both times and drops the ה / H altogether. תת / TÄT (under) is thus the modern hebrew equivalent of the prefix sub-. Pronounced SUS, we have another source of Latin *sus*. The Arabic is *taht* (under).
>
> Perhaps TAHITI (originally *otaheite*), the South Sea island, was named THT for being SOUTHERN. "Under" in Japanese is *shita(ni)*; in Chinese it is *zai xia* or *zay shiah*. Turning to the harder KT element in תחת / [SA]KHAT, the Greek prefix *kata* (down) of *CATA*COMB, etc. may relate. "Below" is *sat'* for the Andrade Quileute Indians of northwestern Washington state. Japanese *soko* means "bottom."

(SO)VIET/ועד
VAH – UDT   [VD→VT]

ROOTS: The term SOVIET is from *su* (together) + *vetu* (council).

ועד / VÄÄT or VÄ'ÄD is a committee, an extension of עדה / ÄDTÄ (assembly, community – *Judges 20:1*).

> **BRANCHES:** (SO)VIET is linked to the IE root *weit(e)* (to speak, adjudge), which recalls בטא / VETÄ or BÉTÄ (to pronounce) and בטא / B(H)OTOH (to utter). בטרי / BÉTOOY or VÉTOOY means uttering, pronouncing or expression. For the *su* of the given etymology consider את / ÄS (with) and see "SO."

SOW/זרה
SAWR – AH   [ZR→SW]

ROOTS: SOW is traced to Old English *sāwan* (to sow) and the IE root *sē-* (to sow). The scholars do not link SOW to Latin *serere* (to sow), but they insist that SEASON and INSERT are from *serere*.

זרה / ZÄRÄ or SAW[R]A (to disperse) is rendered "scatter" in *Ezekiel 5:2* and "strawed" in *Exodus 32:30* -KJ. זרע / ZORÄ is "sowed," or scattered or dispersed (*Exekiel 36:9*; *Zechariah 10:9*).

BRANCHES: פזר / (PÉ)ZÄR is to disperse or scatter; זרק / ZÄRÄK is to sprinkle or throw; סער / SÄUR is to hurl away.

IE *stere* (to spread) is the root of the verb STREW. Official cognates of STREW include: CONSTERNATE, CONSTRUCT, DESTROY, INSTRUCT, OBSTRUCT, STERNUM, STRAIN, STRATAGEM, STRATH, STRAW, STROMA and SUBSTRATUM. If the extra T in STREW is bothersome, "strudel" with its T is traced to the IE root *ser*. The ר / R to W change has come up before (see "weave" at "REEVE"), so that SOW (scatter, plant, spread abroad) easily relates to our ZR etymons here.

THROW may be linked here with STREW; its given IE root is *ter* (to rub, turn).

SPACE/שבת
S(H)UB – US   [S(H) – B – S→SPC]

ROOTS: SPACE is from Old French *espace* and Latin *spatium*.

Just as a SPACE is an interval of area or of time, the familiar שבת / S(H)ABOS or SBT (sabbath – *Exodus 20:8*) break in time is supplemented by תשבית / (SÄ)SHBHES ("leave out"– *Leviticus 2:13*) a break in the realm of space.

> **BRANCHES:** *Sobota* is Saturday in Polish, even though Sunday is the SABBATH day in this largely Catholic country. See SABBATICAL at "STOP."

SPA(N)K/ספק
SOPH – UCK   [S – P(H) – K]

ROOTS: SPANK is dismissed as "echoic" and not treated etymologically. SPANK means "to strike with something flat, as with the open hand."

ספק / SOP(H)ÄK is to strike or clap; hands are clapped in *Numbers 24:10*. The N is extra in SPA(N)K, as the *Hebrew-English Lexicon of the Bible* defines ספק / SPK as "smote upon the thigh."

> **BRANCHES:** Another approach to SPANK is seen at "SNAP."

SPARE/מספר
(MI)S – PAR   [SPR]

ROOTS: Only the merciful sense of SPARE, of leaving unharmed, relates to the Anglo Saxon word *sparian*. As an adjective SPARE also means meager and scanty.

מספר / [MI]SPAR or (M)SPR is an adjective of scantiness as seen in *Numbers 9:20* –"the cloud rested over the tabernacle for BUT A FEW days..."

> **BRANCHES:** SPAR(SE) might have originally meant few in number. It now infers scattered and widely spaced, and is linked by most dictionaries to the word "spark." The מ / M of מספר / *MISPAR* is a prefix.
>
> Other ספר / SPR words here are seen at "GOSPEL" and "SPHERE."

SPARR(OW)/צִפּוֹר
(T)SEE – PORE   [(T)S – P – R]

ROOTS: The SPARROW was a *spearwa* in Old English, a *sporr* in Old Norse and a *sporgilos* in Greek. The IE root is *sper* (bird's name, sparrow). צִפּוֹר / (T)SĒPŌR is the generic word for bird in Hebrew (*Deuteronomy 4:17*), the right word to name the most common of birds, the SPARROW. The *Hebrew-English Lexicon of the Bible* offers "specially, a sparrow" at its צפור / SPR entry.

BRANCHES: Only the language of creation fully depicts birdness: צפר / (T)SĀPHĀR is to rise early, whistle or sound an alarm. The צפצוף / TSIPHTSOOPH (twitter, whistle, CHIRP) is heard in the צפירה / TSIFĒRA (morning – *King James Version* at *Ezekiel 7:7, 10*) or צפרא / (T)SĀPHRĀ (morning – Aramaic). Just as morning is "bird time," the Aramaic for night time is רמשא / RĀMSĀ ("worm time"). Only the early bird catches the night crawler (worm). For the PR element linking birds with butterflies see "*PYRALIDID(A).*"
   Birds seem to צף / TSĀPH (float) to the צפת /TSEPHET (top) of trees where they are צפון / TSĀPHOON (hidden) in foliage and צפה / TSOOPĀ (covered) in feathers. From above they צפה / TSĀPHĀ (keep watch, observe, waylay), catching prey with their צפורן / TSĒPOREN (talon).
   PASSERLINE, from Latin *passer* (sparrow), requires a #1-#2 root letter swap. *Passaro* and *pasare* are the "bird" words in Portuguese and Rumanian. Arabic *asfour* (bird) is closer to the BR element of Indonesian *burung* (bird) or of English BIRD. פרידה / PIRĒDĀ (Mishnaic Hebrew for a dove or pigeon) is closest to the Old English *bridd* (source of BIRD). The PARROT and PETREL might also be related.
   ALTAIR is from another Arabic bird word, *ta'ir*. It seems similar to Japanese *tori* (bird) and Basque *tixori* (bird). Perhaps these are T(S) – P – R words without the P, just as the "bird" of Malay (*tuwi*), Russian (*ptitsa*) and Maya Indian (*tsits*) dispense with the R. The CHIRP is OB*STREP*EROUS, as is the noisy צפרדע / TSPHARDĀA (frog). The IE root *strep* means "to make a noise." The root is considered "imitative," but, swapping letters #2 and #3, the Hebrew TS–P–(R) sounds more like a chirp.

SPATE/שָׁטַף
S(H)AH – TŪPH   [S(H) – T – P(H) → SPT]

ROOTS: SPATE is a flash flood, a sudden heavy rain or a large pouring out of words. The source is "said to be from Old French *espoit*, from a Germanic base seen in SPOUT." שטף / S(H)ĀTĀP(H) is to rinse, wash off, flood, run, flow or burst forth. "Overflow" is the translation in *Psalms 78:20*. A #2-#3 letter flip of SPT brings a SPATE of words like SPATTER, SPIT and SPU(R)T.

BRANCHES: שצף / S(H)ET(S)EP(H) is a flood; קצף / S(H)ĀT(S)ĀP(H) is to be angry. A SPATE of words may burst out in a SPITE[FUL] SPAT. SPEED got momentum from the "run" definition, while SPOUT is from the flowing forth of שטף / S(H)ĀTĀP(H).

SPELT/שִׁבּוֹלֶת
S(H)E – BOLE – ET   [SBLT→SPLT]

ROOTS: From Late Latin *spelta*, SPELT is a hard-grained wheat. שבולת / S(H)ĒBOLET is an ear of corn (*Genesis 41:5*). An extended term means "oats," while שבר / S(H)EBHER is "grain" (*Genesis 42:1*).

BRANCHES: שבר / S(H)EBHER (provisions) may have influenced Latin *cibare* (to feed), the given source of SABADILLA (a flower named for its resemblance to barley). See SHIBBOLETH at "SPILL."

SPHERES/סְפִירוֹת
SPHERE – OSE   [S – PH – R]

ROOTS: A SPHERE, any round figure or planet, is said to derive from Greek *sphaira*. Ancient astronomy had a system of hypothetical, SPHERICAL orbits, domains or SPHERES where the planets ranged. These astrological-astronomical SPHERES of influence were carefully plotted and counted. (How else would these scientist-mystics know where "seventh heaven" was?) SPHERE is thus intimately related to counting words like ספר / SIPHOR (enumeration, number, boundary) and the verb of counting in *Leviticus 23:15*.
   Arabic *sifr* (zero) is SPHEROID, and the Semitic numbers we use are SPHEROIDAL – unlike Roman numerals. ספרה / SIFRĀ means a number (via Arabic); SPHERE as domain echoes Aramaic ספר / SPHĀR (boundary). The ספירות / SPHĒROS (celestial SPHERES) are common terms in Cabala, but one need only turn to *Genesis 15:5* to see the counting-astronomy connection. Abraham is taken on a space walk (12th Century Rashi refers to the vacuum of outer space) to ספר / SFR "count" the stars, and to know that the Lord is above any astrological predictions of Abraham's childlessness.

BRANCHES: Round numbers, like letters and planets, SPELL out a whole SPIEL – see "DECIPHER," "GOSPEL" and "SPIRAL."
   The SPHERE, like mathematics, presents a paradox of eternal beginnings and ends, of finiteness and infinity. Before T.S. Elliot, the circular scroll or ספר / SĀPHER of the Hebrew Bible presented the end in its beginning, and a beginning in its end or סוף / SŌPH.
   The two-letter root of this entry is the ס-פ / S – PH of both הסיף / (HĀ)SĒPH (to make an end of) and הוסיף / (HŌ)SĒPH (to add, to continue). The SPHERE perched between the plus and minus realms is an ס-פ / S – P reversal, אפס / EPHES (zero). See "SPIRAL."

SPILL/שִׁבֹּלֶת
S(H)E – BOLE – (ET)   [SH – B – L→SPL]

ROOTS: A SPILLWAY is a channel to carry off excess water. A SPILL is a run, flow or shedding (as of blood). This flowing is nowhere in the given etymology of SPILL: from Old English *spillan* (to spill, destroy) and the IE root *spil* (to split, break off). Look up the word SHIBBOLETH and one sees a term for a password or test word which is borrowed from the Hebrew word for a stream or flood, שבלת / SHĒBOLET or S(H)ĒBŌLES (*Psalms 69:3*).

The "password" meaning comes from the episode in *Judges 12:6* where Ephraimites could not pronounce the SH of SHIBBOLETH. Even though a tribe in ancient Israel rendered each שׁ / SH as an S, there are those who challenge similar conservative sound shifts (TS to T or S, PH to P, etc) that make this book possible.

> **BRANCHES:** The SPL word of splitting and breaking that the AHD cites as the source of DESPOIL, SPELT, SPILL, and SPOIL might be related to שבר / S(H)EBHER (to break into pieces – *Genesis 19:20*) – change SBR to SPL. SPOILED also shows the influence of פסול / PĀSOOL (unfit, defective – a #1-#2 letter swap). The antonym here is בתולה / BHISSOL(Ä), translated "virgin" in *I Kings 1:2*.
>
> A second etymon for SPILL (upend) is שפל / S(H)ĀP(H)ĀL (to become low). With the connotations of slumping down and inactivity (שפלות / SHIPHLOOS in *Ecclesiastes 10:18*), this SPL term may have influenced SYPHILIS, SLEEP and LAPSE. The PL element of נפל / (NÄ)PHÄL (FALL) and the SP element of lowness are seen in the following words: שפה / S(H)ĀP(H)Ä is to incline or tilt, שפע / S(H)ĒPOOÄ is to slant or slope, שפך / S(H)ĀP(H)ÄH is to pour or SPILL out and שפע / SHAPHA is to flow, to be abundant and to slope. An SP antonym is שפי / S(H)EP(H)Ē (hill, height) – also see "SUPER."

SPIRA(L)/צְפִירָה
(T)SP(H)EER – AH   [TS – PH – R→SPR]

ROOTS: Latin *spira* (a coil) is from Greek *speira*.

Just as the SPIRAEA or SPIREA (meadowsweet and other shrubs in the rose family) is named for its botanical SPIRALING, so צפירה / (T)SPHĒRÄ is both a turn and a wreath (*Isaiah 28:5*).

> **BRANCHES:** The צפור / TSĒPŌR (bird) spirals in flight; the horns of the צפיר / TSIPHĒR (he goat) spiral; and the uncut צפורן / TSĒPŌREN (fingernail) of humans grows in spirals. A ספר / SÄPHER (book, but originally a scroll) is rolled or coiled with turns and twists. The IE root *sper* (to turn, twist) lists only SPIRE and ESPARTO as cognates. See "SPHERES."

SPIRE/צָבַר
(T)SA – BHAR   [(T)S – BHR→SPR]

ROOTS: Old English *spir* (slender stalk) and the IE root *spei* (sharp point) are given etymons which do not address all the meanings of SPIRE. To SPIRE is to extend upward or to rise, just as to ASPIRE used to mean "to rise high" or "to tower." These meanings are covered by צבר / TSÄBHÄR (to heap up) and צבר / (T)SEBHER (pile, heap – *Genesis 41:49*), even while the Arabic צבר / (T)SÄBÄR and Hebrew צבר / (T)SÄBHÄR (cactus, SABRA) indicate the "sharp point" of the *spei* root.

To make this point sharper add אצבע / E(T)SBÄ (finger – *Exodus 8:15*) and הצביע / (HĒT)SBEÄ or (HĒT)SBEÄKH (to point). This last term sounds like SPIKE, while צבט / (T)SÄBHÄT (to seize or pinch the skin) echoes STAB after a #2-#3 letter swap.

> **BRANCHES:** Cognates of SPIRE and SPIKE at IE root *spei* include ACROSPIRE, ASPIC, PORCUPINE, SPARLING, SPICA, SPICULUM, SPILE, SPILL, SPINE, SPINEL, SPINNEY, SPIT, SPITZ and SPOKE. See "SPIT."

SPIR(IT)/צָפַר
(T)SA – P(H)AR   [(T)S – P(H) – R]

ROOTS: A SPIRACLE is an air hole or blow hole by which a whale blows out air (with a whistling sound). SPIRANTS are sounds produced by passing breath through partly closed lips (as in whistling). ASPIRANT comes from Latin *spirare* to breathe or to blow. The IE root *spirare* ("to breathe: Latin word of unknown origin") leaves out the whistling and blowing which appear to important meaning elements in the SPR words above. צפר / (T)SÄP(H)ÄR is to whistle. צפירה / (T)S'P(H)ĒRÄ (whistling) returns to Hebrew via Arabic, while Biblical Hebrew retains the whistling, chirping animals like the צפור / (T)SĒPŌR (bird – see "SPARROW") and the צפרדע / (T)S'P(H)ÄRDÄÄ (frog).

> **BRANCHES:** Latin *spiritus* meant "the breath of a god," linking SPIRIT with the whistling "wind" of God that we encounter in Scripture. God doesn't "breathe," but we can hear the presence of the Lord in the blowing wind – especially if we've just eaten a forbidden fruit.
>
> The given cognates of SPIRIT include CESSPOOL, CONSPIRE, EXPIRE, INSPIRE, PERSPIRE, RESPIRATION, SUSPIRE and TRANSPIRE. The two-letter root of צפר / (T)S – P(H) – R is צף / (T)S – P(H). צפצף / TSIPHTSÄPH is to chirp. Hope is breathless – see "ASPIRE."

SPIT/שִׁפּוּד
S(H)A – POO(D)T   [SH – P – D→SPT]

ROOTS: A SPIT is a thin rod or bar on which meat is impaled and held for roasting. The Anglo-Saxon etymon is *spitu*, and the given IE root, *spei* (a point), is seen at "SPIRE." שפוד / S(H)ÄPOODT is precisely a SPIT or skewer. שפודא / S(H)ÄPOODÄ is the Aramaic term. שבט / S(H)ÄBHET (a rod) is related – see "SWITCH."

> **BRANCHES:** While the given cognates are listed at "SPIRE," other related words might include SPADE, SPATULA, SPRIT (a pole, as in BOWSPRIT), SPUD and SPUDDER. Danish *spyd* (a spear) is the probable source of these last two sharp implements. For the wet SPIT, see "SPATE."

(S)PREAD/פָּרַד
PA–RADE   [PRD]

ROOTS: Because there is no older term than Old English *sproedan* (to spread), the S of SPREAD may have gotten tacked on by association with SPR words like SPORE and SPROUT. These are listed as cognates of SPREAD at the IE root *sper* (to strew) – see "DIASPORA." SPREADING and strewing are not the same, however, and the PRD root of SPREAD is better yoked with FAR, ABROAD, APART and BROAD.

The Hebrew etymon for these would be פרד / PÄRÄD (to spread apart, divide, separate – *Genesis 13:9*).

BRANCHES: Closely allied with פרט / PÄRÄT (see "PART"), הפריד / (HĒ)PHRĒD means to SEPARATE or PART. פרד / PRÄD is the Modern Hebrew word for atom. PARADISE is from פרדס /PÄRDÄS (park, enclosure – *Songs 4:13*) because it is SEPARATED land (just as a "park" is a "broken off" piece of land – see "PARK"). BREED may join BRITTLE and BROTHEL at IE root *bhreu* (to break up), as all three BRD or BRT terms could come from פרד / PÄRÄDT.

To INTER*PRET* a text is to SPREAD it apart, but פתר / PÄTÄR (to interpret) is the better etymon (despite the #2-#3 letter swap). Such a letter swap plus an R to L change may allow us to spread out to Greek *petalos* (outspread), the source of PETAL. Greek *ptero* (wing) is another spreader, so we may have just bagged a *PTERO*DACTYL. A FIORD or FJORD could refer to geological spreading. פרץ / PERET[Z] (fissure, crack, cleft) relates to this kind of spreading out. FAR relates to these פר / PH–R terms and to the פלא / PH–L term equivalent to "distant" in *Deuteronomy 30:11*. The 1960's phrase "far out"(marvelous) allows us to link נפלא / (NI)PHLÄ (wonderful) to FAR.

SPY/צָפָה
(T)SEE–PAH   [(T)S–P]

ROOTS: Old High German *spehon* is to search out, examine or investigate; the IE root is *spek* (to observe).

צפה / (T)SĒPÄ is to look; צפה / (T)SÄPHÄ is to keep watch or observe (*Proverbs 15:3; 31:27*); צופה / (T)SŌPHEH is a scout (whose duties might include ESPIONAGE). If one prefers the harder SPK of the IE root, note שקף / S(H)'KÄPH (to look out – swap letters #2-#3. See "SCOPE.").

BRANCHES: The צפור / (T)SEPŌR (bird) likes to ESPY and to הבט / (HĒ)BĒT (watch – BT is T(S) – P reversed). Knowledge and vision terms always intersect, so צפ / (T)S – PH may have influenced Greek *sophos* (wise) and thus SOPHISTICATION, SOPHISM, PHILOSOPHY and more.

A Polish spy is a *szpieg*. Reverse the eye words of Maya Indian (*wits*), Hopi Indian (*poosi*) and Greek (*ops*) for more צפ / TS – P(H) words. Extensions of the Greek term give us AUTOPSY, IODOSPIN, MYOPIA, -OPIA, -OPSIS, -OPSY, OPTHALMIC, OPTHALMOLOGY, OPTIC, OPTOMETRY, SYNOPSIS, etc.

SQUALL/סָעַר
S'CAR   [S–KH–R→SQL]

ROOTS: The dictionaries can only offer "probably of Scandinavian origin." SQUALL, a violent wind storm usually with rain, fits סער / S–KH–R (shifted to SQL) in *Jonah 1:4*..."But the Lord cast a mighty wind upon the sea, and such a great *tempest* came upon the sea that the ship was in danger of breaking up." Three verses down the term is rendered "storm."

BRANCHES: שעירים / S'KHĒR[ĒM] (light rain) might be more of an antonym than a synonym – (*Deuteronomy 32:2*). See "SHOWER" and "SOAK."

SQUAT/שָׁחַט
SA–KHUT   [S–KH–T]

ROOTS: Both SQUASH and SQUAT are allegedly from Latin *quatir* (to press flat). SQUAT is somehow traced to IE root *ag* (to drive). סחיטה / SIKHĒTÄ (squeezing) is from שחט / S–KH–T in *Genesis 40:11*, where grapes are "pressed" into Pharoah's cup.

BRANCHES: If SQUEEZE cannot be squeezed in here, its IE base *gwei* (to overpower, press strongly) might fit the גבר / GV[R] term of weighty overpowering when the flood "waters *prevailed* וינברו upon the earth" in *Genesis 7:24*. גבורה / GIV[OORA] is power. The KT element recalls חד / KHADT (sharp), דכא / DAKHA (beat small) and דקק / DAKAK (ground small) – see "HADDOCK." See "JUICE" and "OOZE." The SK element of SKT recalls שחוח / SHAKH [OOAH] (bent down) and שחוק / SHAKH[OOK] (crushed). See "SAG."

STAB(LE)/הָצֵב
(HOO)–TSABH   [TS–BH→STB]

ROOTS: Latin *stabilis* means standing firm, source of STABLE and ESTABLISH. The overly inclusive IE root is *sta* (to stand).

הצב / HOOTSÄBH means set up or established; הציב / HĒTSĒBH is to ESTABLISH (*Psalms 74:17*). The TS–BH verb of "setting up" or STABILIZING a "monument" or a STABLE, free-standing pillar is found in *Genesis 35:20*. נצבה / [NĒ]TSBHÄ is steadfastness – see "STUBBORN".

BRANCHES: Instead of the IE root *steu* (to push, stick, knock, beat) consider a church STEEP[LE] (tower) akin to the pillar or מצבה / (MÄ)TSÄBHÄ put up by Jacob in *Genesis 35:20*. But see "MASTABA" for a discussion of the actual shape of such "pillars." In Polish, *staw[iac]* is to stand up or erect; *[pod]staw* is a base or foundation. Jacob's ladder was מצב / (MOO)TSÄV (based or set upon) the ground – *Genesis 28:12*.

Arabic *istabl*, Spanish *establo*, Portuguese *estavel*, Rumanian *staul* and Hungarian *istallo* infer that STALL as well as STABLE originated in the land of the Arabian horse.

STAGE/הַצִיג
(HE)–TSEEG [TS–G→ST–G]

ROOTS: To STAGE is to present, represent or exhibit. Old French *estage* is the last point in the given etymology where this sense or sound remains at all intact. The given IE root is *sta* (to stand). יצג / (YĒ)TSAG is to represent; הַצִיג / (HĒ)TSEG is to introduce or present. Joseph displays or STAGES his brothers in *Genesis 47:2*. This verb is rendered "set up" when the ark of the covenant is brought to David's tent; "set up" is a definition of Latin *stare*, the older etymon provided for STAGE.

> **BRANCHES:** German *zeigen* is to show. Latin *stagnare* (to cause to stand) may allow words like STAGNANT and STAGNATE to relate here. The opposite of STAGING or propping up is to STAGGER (from Old Norse *staka*, to push, cause to stumble). תעה / TA'AH or TAGA (staggered) and דחה / DTAKA (to push or urge on to fall) are likely influences on STAGGER.

STALK/צָלַע
TSAL–UKH [TS–L–K→ST–L–K]

ROOTS: STALK can mean "a slow, stiff step or gait"– this from Anglo-Saxon *stealcian*. צלע / TSĀLĀKH is to limp, as Jacob does in *Genesis 32:32*.

> **BRANCHES:** Another STALK is the botanical stem or main axis. This should relate to the צלע / TSĀLĀKH or TSĀLĀ (rib – *Genesis 2:21-22*). The senses of "rib" are met in the definitions of Polish *dzial* (part, section, branch, column).
> In IE root *stel* (to put, stand) are a few terms that relate to either the stiff-legged gait of the first Hebrew term or the straight, stiff support column inferred by the second Hebrew term. There's PEDESTAL, STOLON (a branch), STOLID, STOLLEN (post), STELE (pillar), STALK and STILT (from a word for crutch and a verb for strutting). שתל / SHĀTĀL (to plant) reinforces the STL sense of putting or standing in place. See "STULTIFY."

STEAL/הַצִיל
(HE)–TSEAL [TS–L→ST–L]

ROOTS: Anglo-Saxon *staelan* is linked to the IE root *ster-* (to rob, steal). STEAL means to take secretly or just to move surreptitiously.
הציל / (HĒ)TSEL means "taken away" in *Genesis 31:16*. Unable to sue for a few hundred years back pay, the freed slaves "*spoil* the Egyptians" or loot them in *Exodus 3:22*. Paradoxically, נצל / [NĒ]TSAL means "save," "strip" or "spoil." The two letter root for this stealing is צל / TS–L; appropriately, these letters spell the word for "shadow."
Another shadowy activity is hiding or "stealing away." The verb for this is סתר / SĀTER (to hide – *Isaiah 16:3* or *I Samuel 23:19*). The STR of this etymon matches the IE root.

> **BRANCHES:** IE root *ster-* (to rob, steal) is also the given source for STEALTH and STALK (as in hunting). צול / TSOOL means "lay hid" in Arabic. See "MYSTERY."

STEIN/צִנְצֶנֶת
TSEEN – (TSENET) [TS–N→ST–N]

ROOTS: A large mug or STEIN is "probably from German *steingut* (stoneware, earthenware)"– see "STONE."
צנצנת / TSĒNTSENET is a flask or jar (*Exodus 16:33*). TS–N or ST–N is the root.

> **BRANCHES:** צנור / (T)SENŌR and צנתר / TSĀNTĀR mean a tube or pipe (*Zechariah 4:12*). See "SNORKEL."

STEM/סָתַם
SOT–UM [STM]

ROOTS: To STEM is to stop, check, dam up (as a river) or plug. Middle English *stem* is believed to be from the hypothetical IE root *stam* (to push, stutter, stammer).
סתם / SOTĀM is to stop up, shut, fill or clog. Wells are filled or stopped up with this verb in *Genesis 26:15*. סתום / SĀTOOM (closed, clogged, vague) appears in *Ezekiel 28:3* and *Daniel 12:9*. עצם / ĀTSĀM is to shut (the eye) – *Isaiah 33:15*.

> **BRANCHES:** An antonym is שתם / S(H)ĀTĀM (to unseal, open, uncork). SHUT is an antonym of this term. The IE root would make STAMMER, STUM (Dutch *stom* is mute) and STUMBLE cognates of STEM.
> סתום / SĀTOOM means vague and indefinite as well as clogged, and סתמי / S'TĀMĒ also infers incoherence. All the Germanic and Romance languages have ST–M or MT words for MUTE – see "DUMB." The Arabic for MUTE is *samit*.
> Because STEM was spelled *tam* in Middle High German, we close up this part of the entry with DAM. אטם / (O)DTĀM means shut up or closed; "stop up" in *Proverbs 21:13*. See "DAM." The nouns STEM and STUMP may be influenced by סרן / SĀDTĀN (tree trunk, tree stump... hence anvil). סרנא / SĀDTĀNĀ is the Aramaic form. See "STYMIE" and "STOMACH."

STICK/עֹקֶץ
(EE)–KATĒS [K–TS→ST–K]

ROOTS: The IE root that means a pole or STICK is *steg*. IE root *stegh* means "to STICK, prick; pointed." Although one must flip these Hebrew words over from K–TS to ST–K, the Hebrew etymons ultimately stick closer to the meanings and spelling of STICK: עקץ / ĀKATS is to sting: עקץ / ŌKETS is a sting, point, prick or STALK (of plants – as in a stick of wood). קוץ / KŌTS is a sticking thorn (*Genesis 3:18* – see "ACACIA"). עץ / KHĀTZ is a "stick" (of wood) in *Ezekiel 37:16*.

> **BRANCHES:** תקע / TOKĀ (to stick in) doesn't have to be reversed, but an S has to be stuck on the front – see "TACK."
> THISTLE is traced to IE base *(s)teig* (a point), and is linked to Sanskrit *tig-ma-h* (pointed, sharp). Notice the expendable S.
> Cognates at IE root *steg* include ATTACH, ATTACK, STACK, STAGGER, STAKE and STOCKADE. Derivatives of IE root *stegh* indlude STAG, STI(N)G and STOCHASTIC. DT–K and K–DT sharp points are made at "ACUTE."

STOM(ACH)/שְׁתֻם
S(H)TOOM   [S(H)−T−M]

ROOTS: STOMACH is traced to Greek *stoma* (mouth) and to IE roots like the AHD's *stamen* (various body parts and orifices) or J.T. Shipley's *stoman* (an opening, receptacle).

שתום / S(H)TOOM means "open" in *Numbers 24:3*; the open body part here is the eye. שתם / S(H)ETEM is a hole. For antonyms see "STEM" and "STYMIE."

> **BRANCHES:** Cognates of STOMACH include ANASTOMOSIS, ANCYLOSTOMIASIS (hookworms), STOMATO-, STOMATOUS, -STOMY, etc.

STONE/צוּנָם
TSOON−(UM)   [TS−N→ST−N]

ROOTS: STONE is from Old English *stan*; Old Norse *steinn* (stone) has a double nasal (M or N). The given IE root is *stei* (stone). צונם / TSOONÄM means rock, granite or flint; צונמא / TSOON(MÄ) is the Aramaic form.

> **BRANCHES:** עצם / ETSEM (bone) might ultimately relate. The listed cognates are STEENBOK, STEIN and TUNGSTEN.

STOP/שָׁבַת
S(H)ABH−AT   [S(H)−BH−T→STP]

ROOTS: SABBATICAL is a borrowing from Hebrew שבת / SHÄBBÄT (SABBATH – *Exodus 20:8*). (Here is another proof that Hebrew SH is regularly rendered as an S in English.) As common as these terms of rest and cessation are, the dictionaries leave us with questionable etymons for RESPITE and STOP.

(RE)SPITE is a delay, postponement or rest. שבת / S(H)ÄBHÄT is to "cease" in *Genesis 8:22*; השבית / (HĒ)S(H)BĒT is to "make rest" or "cease" in *Exodus 5:5*; שבת / S(H)EBHET is "tarried" in *Deuteronomy 1:6*.

RESPITE, *respit* in Old French, is currently traced to IE *spek* (to observe). STOP is merely a #2-#3 letter swap away. Nonetheless, the authorities trace STOP to Late Latin *stuppare* (to stop up, stuff), which is from Latin *stuppa* and Greek *stuppe* (to tow). The AHD attributes STOP to IE root *steu* (to push, knock, beat).

> **BRANCHES:** An all too common word in Israeli Hebrew is שביתה / S(H)IBHĒTÄ (strike or work STOPPAGE). The Bible was the first union document, legislating that we might periodically שב / S(H)ÄBH (sit! rest! and return!...to being more human and less "productive"). The opposite of all this SPT stopping is שטף / S(H)ÄTÄPH (to run,flow – see "SPATE"). BUSTLE (#1-#2 letter swap of SBT) fits better here as well, rather than linked to "busk." A BUST can also mean a decline in activity.

STORE/אוֹצָר
OATS−ARE   [TS−R→ST−R]

ROOTS: STORE is said to derive from Old French *estorer* (to erect, furnish, equip) and Latin *instauare* (to repair, restore, equip). The AHD falls back on their favorite IE root, *sta* (to stand).

אוצר / OTSÄR is a storehouse or treasury (*Proverbs 21:20*). אצר / OTSÄR is to store; אצירה / ÄTSĒRÄ is STORING or hoarding. עצור / ÄTSOOR means closed up.

> **BRANCHES:** THESAUR(US) is from Greek *thesauros* (treasure). TREASURE is TSR→TRS letter swap of the Greek and Hebrew terms above. An anatomical storehouse might be the UTERUS; Greek *hustera* (womb) gives us HYSTERIC and HYSTERO- words. For an alternative Hebrew etymon, see "STYLE."

STOR(Y)/סֵדֶר
SAY−DERE   [S−DT−R]

ROOTS: Latin *historia* is the telling of a connected HISTORY or series of happenings. The dictionary follows an unconnected path to Greek *eldenai* (to know) and the IE root *weid* (to see) – see "VIDEO".

Narration of the Egyptian exodus STORY is סדר / SÄDTÄR (set) into a formulated סדר / SÄDER (arrangement) during the Passover *Seder*.

סדר עולם / SÄDER OLÄM (The *Order* of the World) was an ancient HISTORY text known in the First Century.

סדרה / SIDRÄ (a section of text) is Aramaic. Beside the "order" and "arrangement" senses of סדר / SDR, the chronology of a STORY or a HISTORY also fits the sense of "row" (line-up of connected things) seen at "STREET."

> **BRANCHES:** HISTORY is too often related to HISTRIONICS (theatrics). Latin *histrio* (an actor) may be one who studies his סדר / SEDER (order) of speeches. Linking HYSTERIA to אי סדר / Ē− SÄDER (disorder) provides a less misogynous etymon than linking HYSTERIA to Greek *hystera* (the uterus) – see "STORE" and "STYLE" for alternative etymons. See "SIDEREAL."

STRAIT/צָרוֹת
TSAR–OOT　　　　　　　　　[TS–R→ST–R]

ROOTS: STRAIT is from Middle English *streit* and Old French *estreit*. Convinced that all roads must lead to Rome, the dictionaries take us on a circuitous route to Latin *strictus*, the past perfect of *stringere* (to draw tight or to bind tightly).

צָרוּר / TSÄROOR is tied up or bound (*Exodus 12;34*). STRAIT or STRAITS is a narrow strip of land or מֵצַר / (MÄ)TSÄR (isthmus). מֵצַר / (MÄ)TSÄR also means DISTRESS; STRESS is a fine definition for צָרוֹת / TSÄROS or STAROT (pressing troubles). The emotional tight squeezes are taken up at "SORE," but here we are concerned with צָרוֹת / TSÄROOT (narrowness). צַר / TSÄR is narrow; it forms the two-letter Hebrew root, and it clarifies most IE roots with an STR. The IE root of STRAIT is *streig* (to stroke, rub, press).

BRANCHES: The irrelevant meaning of the given IE root notwithstanding, many of the cognate words listed here concern straightness and narrowness. On the same string as STRAIT, from Latin *stringere*, are ASTRINGE, CONSTRAIN, DISTRAIN, PRESTIGE, RESTRICT, STRICT, STRIGIL, and STRINGENT. The next root over is *strenk* (tight, narrow). Listed here are STRANGLE, STRANGULATE, STRENGTH, STRING and STRONG. *Webster's* IE base *ster* (to be stiff, rigid) includes STRETCH and STRIDE, terms not included in the AHD's similar IE root mentioned at "STREET." See "STRESS" and "STRETCH."

STRE(ET)/שְׂדֵרָה
S'DTAIR–(ÄH)　　　　　　　[SDR→STR]

ROOTS: The scattered etymology traces Latin *strata* (road) to Latin *sternere* (to strew, scatter...hence pave...hence road). Rumanian *strada* and Dutch *straat*, "street" words, are thus linked to the given IE root *ster-* (to spread) and made a cognate of "strew."

שׂדרה / S'DTÄRÄ is defined as an avenue, boulevard or row (of men). In *II Chronicles 23:14* the translations render this term as "ranks" or "ranges," but it is clear in the context that wicked Athalia is killed in the STREET. The concordance considers שׂדרה / S'DTÄRÄ akin to סדר / SÄDER (row, order, arrangement – another SD/TR etymon for both STREET and STRAIGHT).

Al Sirat (swap the T and R) means "the road" in Arabic.

BRANCHES: Echoing IE root *ster-* (to spread) is שׂדר / S(H)ÄEDÄR (to broadcast). Another Aramaic term, one that recalls IE root *ster* (stiff), is שׂדרא / S(H)IDTRÄ (spinal column). This twin of our captioned term relates to Greek *sterizein* (to support – source of STERIGMA) as well as to the "columns" we call STREETS. STARK, STERE, STEREO, STERN, STORK and STRUT are all cognates of STERIGMA at IE root *ster-*. These words follow the straight path from "straightness" to "stiffness" or "firmness." To stray from the straight and narrow – see "SWERVE." See "SERIES" for SR straight rows.
The DT–R element of straightness and of ROADS (DR reversed) is seen at "DIRECTION." See "STRAIT" and "STREAK" for more STRATA of meaning in STR words.

STRESS/צָרוֹת
TSÄR–OSE　　　　　　　　　[TS–R→ST–R]

ROOTS: צָרוֹת / TSÄROS means anguish, DISTRESS or STRESS. See "SORE" and "STRAIT." The given etymon is Laitn *strictus* (strict). It is thought that STRESS is a contraction of DISTRESS, but from the צר / TS–R root of narrowness and oppression it is more likely that DISTRESS is an extenion of STRESS.

BRANCHES: *Osaeru* in Japanese is to push down, keep down, repress. Stress and distress result from repressed desire. זור / ZOOR means compressed or squeezed, but like סור / SOOR, זור / ZR can mean the opposite – receded, made separate.

STRE(T)CH/הִשְׂתָּרַע
(HE)–STAR–AKH　　　　　　[S–R–KH]

ROOTS: Old English *streccan* is to STRETCH. *Webster's* cites IE base *ster* (to be stiff, rigid). See "STREET."

שׂרוע / SÄROOÄKH is stretched out, extended, long-limbed. הִשְׂתָּרַע / (HE)STÄRÄKH is to stretch oneself out (*Isaiah 28:20*). סרוח / SÄROOÄKH is stretched out (*Amos 6:4*); זרוע / ZIROÄKH is the arm, forearm, and by extension, other reaching, stretching things (*Exodus 6:6*). Lastly, שׂטוח / S(H)ÄTOOÄKH is flat or stretched out (*Psalms 88:10*).

BRANCHES: Other relevant Hebrew terms include שׂדרא / SHEDTRÄ (spinal column) – see "STREET." STRAKE, STREAK, STREW and STRIATE are all related extensions. A STRETCH word with שׂר / SR that is not יָשָׁר / [YA]SHAR (straight) is שׂרך / SARAKH (wandering in all directions – *Jeremiah 2:23*). See "SHEER."

S(T)RIKE/זָרַק
ZÄRAK　　　　　　　　　　[ZRK→ST–R–K]

ROOTS: For a source of STRIKE, *Webster's* offers *striken* in Middle English (to proceed or to flow). STRIKING after the elusive source of STRIKE from a different angle, the AHD suggests the IE root *streig* (to stroke, rub, press).
The primary definition of STRIKE is to take off, take away, or to strike off by or as by a blow. The fourth definition is to dash, cast; another definition is to send down or put forth (roots).
The STRIKING correspondence here is with זרק / ZÄRÄK (to throw, toss, sprinkle – *Numbers 19:13*). Middle English *striken* (to flow) is most like זרק / ZEREK (serum).

BRANCHES: One can make a #2-#3 letter flip of זרק / ZARAK to זקר / ZÄKÄR (to throw, fling). The Polish words *zrzucac* (to throw, cast down or off), *rzuacac* (throw, fling) and *rzut* (throw) are natural spinoffs from זרק / ZÄRÄK and זרע / ZÄRÄ or ZÄRÄKH (to sow, scatter).
For a similar English ST from the Hebrew ז / Z, see "strew" at "SOW."

STUB(BORN)/נִצְבָּה
(NEE)TSIB – BAH   [TS – B→ST– B]

ROOTS: The dictionaries have enough trouble with STUB and STUBBLE, which they connect to the IE root *(s)teu* (to push, stick, knock, beat) in the sense of "stubbing" one's toe. Middle English *stoborne* (stubborn) ought to connect to STUB, but the authorities are not sure how.

A ticket STUB and STUBBLE in the field is that which STUBBORNLY remains firm after cutting or harvesting. The STUBBORN Hebrews have a two-letter root צב / TS – B (standing firm) as seen in נצב / (NĒ)TSÄBH (standing – *Genesis 18:2*), נצב / (NĒ)TSUBH (handle, hilt – *Judges 3:22*), נציב / (NÄ)TSEBH (pillar, column), נצבה / (NĒ)TSBÄH (resoluteness, steadfastness) and יתיצב / (YISYÄ)TSÄBH (to "stand up to" someone or stubbornly oppose them – *Deuteronomy 7:24*).

> **BRANCHES:** Latin *stabilis* (standing firm) and *stipula* (stalk, stem) – note their Hebrew counterparts above – are related. STIFF and STU(M)P are also related.
> See "MASTABA" and "STABLE".

STUD(Y)/צָעַד
TSA – UD   [TS – U – D→ST– U – D]

ROOTS: STUDY is from Latin *studere* (to be diligent), but the verb's original meaning is "to be pressing forward" according to the AHD.

"Moved forward" is the translation of צעדו / TSA'UD(OO) in *II Samuel 6:13*. צעד / TSA'UD is defined as "to advance," "to step," "to march" or "to progress."

> **BRANCHES:** STUPID and SHTICK are cognates of STUDENT at the theroetical IE root *(s)teu* (to push, etc). A good STUDENT likes צד / TSUD (to hunt) for truth.
> *(Lah) Saht* is to hunt in Thai.

STYLE/צורה
TSOOR – AH   [TS – R→ST– L]

ROOTS: Three definitions of Latin *stilus* are 1) a sharp, slender pointed instrument used in writing; 2) a pen, needle, and 3) an engraving tool. The AHD offers no root, but J.T. Shipley's IE root, *steig*, means stick, prick; pointed, sharp. The Hebrew צר or צור / TSOR (flint) was a sharp enough object for Moses' wife, Zipporah, to use in the circumcision of her son (*Exodus 4:25*). The TS – R of צור / TSOR easily becomes the ST – L of the sharp STILO (dagger), STILETO, and STYLUS.

צורה / TSOOR – ÄH means form, pattern, image, shape, figure, the counterpart of STYLE. ציור / TSEYOOR is a drawing, image or sketch. צלם / TSEL[EM] is also an image, though not as STYLISH.

> **BRANCHES:** In *Jeremiah 1:5* is the statement "Before I *formed* thee in the belly, I knew thee". יצר / YÄTSÄR is to form or create.

This term combines צורה (see above) with יצא / YÄTSÄ (to go out, come forth). HYSTERECTOMY, HYSTERIA and HYSTERICAL are a sexist threesome from Greek *hystera* (uterus, womb). UTERUS and HYSTERO- should fit here since the womb is the יצרן / YÄTSRÄN (producer). יצר / Y–TS – R (to form, create) could be read YOSTÄR. Far from denigrating the womb or the woman, Hebrew associates יוצר / YŌTSER (creator) with the צור / TSOOR (God, rock of refuge) as well as with ציר / TSĒR (birth pang). See "STORE."

Returning to the compensatory artistry of wombless males, יצר / Y–TS – R or J–TS – [R] may be behind Japanese JU*JITSU* (art). *Yi shu* is art in Chinese.

STYMIE/סָתוּם
SAH – TOOM   [STM]

ROOTS: STYMIE is a verb or noun of blocking or hindering. The ditionaries are rather STYMIED (thwarted, blocked) here, offering "perhaps from Scottish *stymie* (a person with poor eyesight)."

A visionary whom the Bible makes an ass (donkey) of is Balaam (see "BLAME"). Balaam refers to himself as שתום / S(H)ITOOM (open-eyed, of a penetrating eye – *Numbers 24:3*). But it was the ass of the seer who saw the שטן / SÄTÄN (*obstructing* angel – *Numbers 22:32*), while Balaam remained סתום / SÄTOOM (clogged, closed) or blind to the phenomenon.

> **BRANCHES:** סתומה / STOOMÄ is vague; סתמי / SITÄMĒ means undefined or indefinite. שטן / SÄTÄN is better rendered "to STYMIE" in *Numbers 22:22*. שטן / STN means "to oppose" (*Psalms 71:13*).
> STUMP (to keep others unaware), STUM (dumb), STUMBLE and STUN should join STYMIE as derivatives of these Hebrew words – see "STEM." For the antonym of openness – see "STOMACH."

SUC(CEED)/תחת
SUKH – (US)   [S – KH – (S)]

ROOTS: SUCCESS means not going under, but the given etymon of SUCCESS is Latin *sub* (under) + *cedere* (to go). *Succedere* is "going beneath." The KD "going" term is from קדם / KODUM (to go forward). Latin *succedere* also means "following after," and SUCCESS can depend upon whom we replace or inherit. It is difficult ot see how the prefix SUC- (which means "under" in words like SUCCINCT and SUCCOR) or SUS- (a prefix meaning "under" in words like SUSPECT) is a variation of Latin *sub* (under) – why not drop the B of "sub" if "sub-ceed" or "sub-cor" were so hard to pronounce? The Hebrew "sub" may be underneath all of this. תחת / SUKHUS, TUKHUS or SUHUS is "under" in *Genesis 1:7*. Elsewhere the term means "in place of" (as in a SUCCESSOR). An abbreviated form used in prefixes is תת / SUS, TUT or SUT.

> **BRANCHES:** In Chinese, the adverb and preposition "under" is *tsai hsia*. In Japanese, *soko* is bottom, while *shita* means under. *Sat* is "below" for the Andrade Quileute Indians.
> The standard Ashkenazic pronounciation of תחת / TUKHUS (buttocks) gives Yiddish and "Yinglish" its TOCHIS or TUCHIS (as spelled by Leo Rosten in *The Joys of Yiddish*).

SUCCUBUS/שְׁכָבְת
S(H)OKH – KHEBH – ES   [S(H) – K(H) – B(H)]

ROOTS: Latin *succuba* is a strumpet. *Succubare* (to lie under) is said to derive from *sub* (under) + *cubare* (to lie). SUCCUBUS is a mythical female demon who seduces sleeping men. Just as this myth is akin to the extra-Biblical legends about Lilith (Adam's original, disobedient wife), the term SUCCUBUS is probably a form of שכבת / S(H)IKHŌBES (copulation – *Leviticus 18:20*). שכבת / SHOKHEBHES can literally mean "she sleeps," as in a strumpet who "sleeps around." Potiphar's wife commands Joseph *SHIKHBHA ĒTĒ* ("*lie with me!*"–*Genesis 39:7* and *39:12*). The verb primarily means lying down, sleeping and even dying.

The elements in the compound SH – KH – BH include the S(H) – K terms of sinking and bowing found at "SAG," coupled with the KH – BH/PH of "folding over" seen at "COUPLE." The IE root for SUCCUBUS is *keu-* (to bend), better rendered K – BH or KV.

> **BRANCHES:** At the above root, the AHD lists the English words from Latin *cubare* (to lie down on). Listed after *cubare* are CONCUBINE, COUVADE, COVEY, CUBICLE, INCUBATE and SUCCUBUS.
>
> שכב / SHOKHĀBH clarifies the meaning of CONCUBINE, the American Indian term SQUAW (woman, wife) may be a related SKV or SQW term. SQUAW and CONCUBINE are sexist terms as it is, but leaving out the Hebrew etymon turns concubines into mattresses for "lying down on" rather than partners for cohabitation.
>
> Also at IE root *keu* is Latin *cumbere* (to lie down, recline). This is another form of שכב / (SHA)KHABH, as nasalization has placed an extra M between the K and the B. Bedfellows of RECUMBENT here include ACCUMBENT, DECUMBENT, INCUMBENT, PROCUMBENT and SUCCUMB. Like שכב / SHĀKHĀBH, SUCCUMB can mean dying. Sleep in Polish is *spac*, a possible #2-#3 letter swap of שכב / S(H) – K(H) – BH ("lay down to sleep"–*Genesis 28:11*). We often sleep in our SKIVVIES (undergarments) – a word with no known origin.

SUFFER/סוֹבֵר
SO – BHAR   [SVR → SFR]

ROOTS: Yet another difficult combination in our given etymologies is BORNE by the word SUFFER. Latin *suffero* is said to come from *sub* (beneath) + *fero* (to bear). To BEAR already means to suffer or endure under the weight of a burden. Similarly, סבל / SOVĀL means to suffer, endure or bear (*Lamentations 5:7*; *Genesis 49:15*). סבל / SĀVEL is a physical burden or load; סבל / SĀBĀL is a porter (*I Kings 5:29*). SLAVE, now thought to come from Slav, might be a #2-#3 root letter swap of סבל / SVL.

The Aramaic counterpart is found in the targum or translation of *Deuteronomy 1:12*, where "how *will I bear*... the burden" is אסובר / [Ā]SOVĀR.

BRANCHES: סבלנות / *SĀLVLĀNOOT* (patience, tolerance) results from סבר or שבר / SĀVER (hope, expectation). FORE*BEAR*ANCE is the theme. METAPHOR and TRANSFER are among the many cognates of BEAR that one finds listed at "FERRY." The IE root of SUFFER and BEAR is *bher* (to carry); העביר / [HE]BHĒR is to bring over or transport.

SUFFICE/סָפַק
SUPH – UCK   [S – PH – K]

ROOTS: Latin *sufficere* is to provide or suffice. Not finding this etymon SUFFICIENT, the scholars go on to break down SUFFICE into *sub* (under) + *facere* (to make), this last element traced to the IE root *dhe-* (to set, put).

No "make under" contortions are necessary to link SUFFICE with ספק / SOPHUK (to be sufficient) and ספק / SĀPHEK (SUFFICIENCY). שפק / SEPHEK is the Biblical spelling of nouns and verbs of sufficiency, providing and abounding (*I Kings 20:10, Isaiah 2:6, Job 20:22* and *36:18*). ספק / SĒPAK (to supply) recalls the unbroken Latin etymon.

> **BRANCHES:** שפק / SEPHEK can also mean abundance and affluence. שפע / SHOPHĀ or SHOPHĀKH is to be abundant. שבע / SĀVĀĀ or SĀBHĀĀKH means satisfied or satiated – see "SEVEN" and "SWASTIKA." The S – PH root of abundance is seen in הוסיף / (HŌ)SĒPH (to add, increase), הוספה / (HŌ)SĀPHĀ (supplement) and the name יוסף / [YŌ]SĀPH (Joseph). SP terms like *SUPPLEMENT*, *SUPPLY*, PRO*SP*ER and *SUFFIX* may ultimately relate. נספח / (NI)SPĀKH (appendix, addition) also recalls SUFFIX. ספח / SOFFĀKH is to join or attach – see "CRUCIFIX."

SUICIDE/קָטַל[ן] + תוֹ-
SOW + CUDT   [S – O/V + K – DT]

ROOTS: The first half of the word is from Latin *sui* (of oneself). The IE root *s(w)e* is a pronoun of the third person, a refective which refers back to the subject of the sentence. This is precisely the suffix תו- as seen in אדמתו / ĀDMĀSOW (land of [his/theirs] – *Deuteronomy 32:43*). The second half of the term is from Latin *caedre* (to cut down, strike mortally, kill). Connected to the many words seen at "CUT," קטיעה / KIDT(ĒĀ) (amputation) קטב / KODT(UV) (to annihilate) and קט[ו]ל / KODT(ĀL) (to kill – *Job 24:14*) are the most deadly of the Hebrew cutting words.

> **BRANCHES:** Cognates under IE root *s(w)e* include: DESOLATE, ETHNIC, ETHOS, GOSSIP, IDIOM, IDIOT, PER SE, SECEDE, SECLUDE, SECRET, SECURE, SEGREGATE, SELECT, SELF, SEPARATE, SIBLING, SOBER, SOLE, SOLILOQUY, SOLIPSISM, SOLITARY, SULLUN, SWAIN and SWAMI. See "AUTO".
>
> Other -CIDE terms include DEICIDE, HOMICIDE and REGICIDE. The deadly CUTLASS might be more directly related to קטל / KTL than to Latin *culter* (knife).

SUIT/סות
SUIT   [ST]

ROOTS: Your reference book states that Old French *sieute* (suit, suite) is from Latin *sequi* (to follow). The Hebrew Bible offers סות / SOOT (garment, suit – *Genesis 49:11*).

> **BRANCHES:** An extended form is כסות / K'SOOT (garment – *Deuteronomy 22:12*). שית / S(H)ĒT is a "garment" in *Psalms 73:6*. See "VEST."

SULTAN/שִׁלְטוֹן
S(H)IL–TONE   [S(H)–L–T]

ROOTS: SULTAN is from Arabic *sultan* (victorious; a ruler or prince). The dictionaries do not add that שלטון / S(H)ILTŌN in Hebrew means rule, power, government or authority (*Ecclesisastes 8:4*). The verb form is שלט / S(H)ÄLÄT. Notice how Arabic too changes a Hebrew SH to an S. שליט / S(H)ALĒT is a ruler. שרת / S(H)ÄRÄT is a ministry.

> **BRANCHES:** רדה / RÄDTÄ is to rule (LT→RD); סדר / SÄDER is to order (add a #2-#3 letter swap and see "SIDEREAL"). Since the LT element of S(H)–L–T seems to be taking charge, note that LEAD, LEADER, and *LEIT*MOTIF are traced to Old High German *leiten* (to lead). Other L/R–D/T possibilities include LORD, RIDDEN, RIDE, ROUT and TYR(ANT). The Polish "government," *rzad*, has all the right components, but needs a switch in root letters. For an STR relative, see "SATRAP."

SUMAC/צֶמַח
(T)SEM–UKH   [(T)S–M–KH]

ROOTS: SUMAC refers to a number of related plants with red fruit. The dictionaries give us Arabic *summaq*, from *sumaka* (to be tall). Much is lost by not giving the Hebrew etymons. צמח / (T)SÄMÄKH is to spring up (*Genesis 2:5*) and צמח / (T)SEMÄKH means plant, growth, sprouting and vegetation. צמיחה / (T)S'MĒKHÄ is growth, while צמיקה / (T)S'MĒKÄ means shrinkage. Other antonyms include צמצום / (T)SIMTSOOM (contraction – see "small" at "SMASH") and צנח / (T)SÄNÄKH (to descend).

SUMMIT/צָמֶרֶת
(T)SUM–(ER)–ET   [(T)S–M]

ROOTS: SUMMIT and SUM are said to derive from Latin *summus* (highest, topmost). The Latin is traced to the IE root *uper* (over) by the topmost historical linguists of our day. See "OVER."

צמרת / (T)SUM(ER)ET is defined as "summit," and is translated as "top" in *Ezekiel 17:3, 22* and *31:3, 10*. SM terms of tallness and smallness are nearby at "SUMAC."

> **BRANCHES:** ZENITH (high point, summit) is a sound-alike synonym. It is attributed to Arabic *semt-ar-ras* (way of the head), with *semt* to derive from Latin *semita* (path, way). AZIMUTH is a related term from Arabic, and from measured arcs in astronomy. If SUMMIT is not related to these SMT words, perhaps שמש / S(H)EMES(H), or SMT with an S→T change, is. S(H)EMESH means sun; שמים / S(H)ÄM(ÄYIM) is heaven.

The red SUMAC fruit may relate to סמק / SŌMÄK (red, redness). Indonesian *semak* is a bush. Nahuatl (Aztec Indian) *tomatl* gives us that tall-sprouting T(S)–M vegetable plant we call the TOMATO.

See "SYCAMORE" for a #2-#3 reversal of our SMK etymon. See "SUMMIT" for more tall SM words. SCION, a shoot, requires a #2-#3 letter swap and an M→N change, but the given etymology reads "probably from Latin *sectio* (a cut)." For TM growth words see "VENTRICLE."

SUMMON/זְמַן
ZEE–MAIN   [SZ–M–N]

ROOTS: SUMMON is said to derive from Latin *summonere* (to remind privily). Latin *sub* is "under" or "secretly," which is to be combined (dropping the B) with *monere* (to advise, warn). The given IE root is *men* (to think).

זמן / SZEMÄN (to invite) is an extension of זמן / Z'MAN (appointed time – *Ecclesiastes 3:1*).

שמע / S(H)ĒMÄ is to assemble or announce (*I Samuel 23:8*), fitting the definitions of SUMMON which include "to call together," "to issue a SUMMONS" and to "call forth." שמע / S(H)ÄMÄ is a report; שם / S(H)ÄM is a name.

> **BRANCHES:** The MN element of זמן / ZMN is seen in מנה / MŌNEH (time) and מנה / MOONA (to be appointed). See "MONEY" for the IE root given here.

SUN/שָׁנָה
S(H)UN–ÄH   [S(H) – N – H]

ROOTS: The dictionary would have us believe that SUN is from the same IE root (*sawel*) as SOUTH and HELIUM. (see "HORUS"). The scholars cannot see the natural progression from SHEMESH (sun in Hebrew) to *shams* (Arabic) to Russian *sontse* or Serbo-Croatian *sunce* and, finally, down to the Anglo-Saxon *sunne*. The sixth definition of SUN is a year – just as months are moons. שנה / S(H)UNÄ is a year (*Deuteronomy 11:12*), as well as the verb of repetition and change. The SUN repeats its heavenly circuits to age (ישן / [YA]SHUN is old, see "SENILE") and to change the plum of youth into a wizened prune.

שמש / S(H)EMESH is the sun (*Deuteronomy 4:41*). It can be broken down to שם אש / SHUM ÄSH (fire is there), and it relates to terms like שמש / SHÄMÄSH (servant). (Some idolaters merely worship the Lord's sexton – the sun).

> **BRANCHES:** SHIMMER is not traced to שמש / SHEMMESH but to IE *skeai* (to gleam). This theoretical root, and not שחר / S(H) – KH – R (dawn, light; dark, black; seek), is also the given source of SQUIRREL. An R to L change allows one to link SOL(AR) to שחר / SHAHAR (dawn, light).
>
> SHIMMER, SHINE and SUMMER might find a spot under the Hebrew sun, or with gems like שהם / SHOHUM (onyx) and שמיר / SHÄMER (diamond).
>
> Changing the נ / N of שנה to an L (mirror reversals of each other) might bring SOLAR words into view. SOL (sun in Latin) might also connect with מסלה / (MI)SELÄ (orbit or course). הנץ / (HA)NE(T)s (shining – see "DAWN") is an SN term reversed. Perhaps Latin *annus* (year) has reversed שנה / S(H)ANNA (year) or has dropped its initial SH. (Super is traced to the IE root *uper*.) If so ANNALS, ANNUAL, ANNUITY, ANNIVERSARY, MILLENNIUM, PERENNIAL and more all relate. These words are currently linked to the IE root *at* (to go). עת / ÄT is a time or season.

SUPER/שַׁפִּיר
S(H)UH–PEER   [S(H) – P – R]

ROOTS: SUPERB is from Latin *suberbus* (proud, delicate), and it means extremely fine, excellent. SUPER, however, is traced to Latin *super* (above) and the IE root *uper* (over) as if height, rather than SUPERIORITY were the issue. See "up" at "AVIATE" and see "OVER."

שפר / S(H)OP(H)ÄR (*Psalms 16:6*) and שפר / S(H)EP(H)ER (*Genesis 49:21*) are both translated "goodly." שפרה / SHIFRÄ (*Exodus 1:15*) was named for her goodness or FAIR (beautiful) qualities, not for any towering height. שפיר / S(H)ÄPER (whence Shapiro and SAPPHIRE) means handsome, elegant, fine or good. שפור / S(H)EPOOR means improvement, upgrading something to a SUPERIOR position. שופרא / S(H)OOP(H)RÄ in Aramaic means the best or the most INSUPERABLE.

> **BRANCHES:** Derivatives of Latin *super* include, SOPRANO, SOUBRETTE, SOVEREIGN, dozens of SUPER- words;

SUPERNAL, SUPRA-, SUPREMACY, SUPREME, and SUPREMO. SUFFRAGE, from Latin *suffragari* (to favor) may be related. Hungarian *szep* (beautiful) is clearly related.

Greek *huper*, English HYPER-, and the IE root *uper* (over), are linked to Latin *super* (above) – see "OVER." Two SP "above" terms are שפי / SHIPHE (height) and שפריר / S(H)ÄP(H)RER (canopy – *Jeremiah 33:10*). A lowly antonym is שפל / SHÄPHÄL (low – see "SPILL"). See "SAPPHIRE."

SUPPE(R)/סְפָה
SUP(H)–AH   [S – P(H)]

ROOTS: SUPPER and SUP are traced to Anglo-Saxon *supan* (to sup, drink), the IE base *seu* (something damp and soft, sap) and the IE root *seua* (to take liquid). The drinking part of the etymology is taken up at "SIP;" SUP also means to eat or prepare SUPPER. ספה / SUP(H)Ä is to feed; ספי / SIP(H)Ä is the Aramaic counterpart. ספיה / SIP(H)EÄ and מספוא / (MI)S'PO mean animal food or fodder (*Genesis 24:25*).

> **BRANCHES:** Several SP terms of supplying are seen at "SUFFICE." מסיבה / (MI)SEBÄ is a banquet. One may SIP or SUP from a סף / SUPH or SUP (goblet, bowl). צפחת / TSAPAHAT is a dish or vessel; צפיחית / TSAPEHET is a cake.

SUPPLE/שָׁפֵל
S(H)UH–P(H)AIL   [SH – PH – L→SPL]

ROOTS: Latin *supplex* means humble, submissive. These same connotations apply for שפל / S(H)ÄP(H)ÄL (humble, lowly – *Isaiah 2:9, 13:11* and *57:15*).

> **BRANCHES:** The word is often considered to mean "folding under." See "SOFA" for the SP initial element. The etymology goes on to trace the PL of SUPPLE to Latin *plicare* (to fold, double up). The "pliant" connotations are taken up at "COUPLE."

SURF/סוּף
SOOWF   [SWF→SRF]

ROOTS: SURF has no known origin. *Suff* was an earlier form of SURF, which fits the name of the sea, (סוף / SOOF – *Exodus 13:18*) which is split for the Israelites. This sea, rendered "the Red Sea" or the Sea of Reeds, might have been The Surf Sea. Pronouncing the ו / V or W as a consonant allows us to pronounce the term SVF or SOOWF (which is closer to SURF).

> **BRANCHES:** Seaside SURF is suggested by סוף / SOF (the end), שפה / SÄFÄ (river bank), סור / SÄVÄR (longshoreman), סור / SVÄR (pile...akin to a wave), סער / SÄÄR (to storm, tempest), סף / SÄF (to come to an end – *Ecclesiastes 7:2*) and סף / SÄF (sill, threshold). רציף / RÄ[T]SEF is a quay or dock; a #1-#2 letter swap might bring SURF (offshore waters) into view.

SUR(PASS)/יֶתֶר
(YEH)–SERE   [(Y)SR]

ROOTS: To *SURPASS* is to exceed; to *SURCHARGE* is to overcharge. The issue is excessiveness, not necessarily "over" or "above." Nonetheless, the SUR- of *SURFEIT* (an excess) is somehow traced from Old French *sur-* or *sour-* to Latin *super* or *supra* (over, above) and to the same IE root *uper* (over) discussed at "SUPER."

יתר / (YE)SER means "exceeding" in *Genesis 49:3*; it is also defined as rest, remainder, or what is "left over." יותר / (YŌ)SĀR is defined as "more" or "too much;" *Ecclesiastes 7:16* advises us not to be "OVERwise" or " the wise man *to excess*."

> **BRANCHES:** *SUR*NAME and *SUR*PLUS infer "extra" more than "above." Having extra implies עשר / [Ō]SHER or ŌSER (wealth). *SURCEASE* is from Old French *surseoir* (to pause, delay, leave off). These connotations are met by סור / SOOR (to leave off, turn aside) and the antonymical שאר / S(H)ĀAR (to remain), שרד / SĀRĀD (to leave over) and שריד / SĀRĒD (a SURVIVOR).
> *Sierota* is an orphan in Polish.

SWALL(OW)/שְׂלָו
SLAV   [SLW→SWL]

ROOTS: The SWALLOW is a small bird known for its regular migrations. Anglo-Saxon *swalewe* is traced to IE base *swol-wi* (a bird name), but it is also linked to Russian *solovej* and Czech *slavik* (a nightingale, etc.). Notice how effortlessly the etymon slid from SWL to SLV. Likewise, the Bible's migratory bird eaten by the Israelites is a שלו / SLĀV or SLW (usually translated "quail"– *Exodus 16:13*).

> **BRANCHES:** Migratory animals follow an instinctive שביל / S(H)VĒL (path, course, lane) and שב / SHĀV (return) annually. If not named for their use as "slaves" by the Romans, the SLAVS might be named for their migrations. The surname SOLOV[EITCHIK] appropriately infers a rare and migratory nightingale. For the "SWALLOW" of the Adam's apple – see "DEVOUR."

SWA(STIKA)/שֶׁבַע
SOV–AYE–(AH)   [SVA→SWA]

ROOTS: The notorious SWASTIKA symbol of the Nazis was originally neither an Aryan symbol nor a bent cross. Not exclusive to the Aryans of Persia, it is a mystical symbol found in ancient Japan, and among the Indians of Asia and America. Moreover, the symbol represents a seven (7) pointing in all four directions, the four sevens joined at a central axis.

Sanskrit *svasti*, the root of SWASTIKA, means "well being," "good luck" or "living in good condition." The IE root is *su* (well, good) – and is better pronounced "suv."

Abraham is שבע / SĀVĀA ("contented") in *Genesis 25:8*; שבע / SĀVĀ is plenty or abundance. What might number seven have to do with satiety and good fortune? שבע / S(H)EVĀ is seven in Biblical Hebrew, the proverbial number of plenty. The ancients did not arbitrarily associate SEVEN with good luck; they displayed the symbol to the four winds in an appeal for abundance.

> **BRANCHES:** Indonesian reverses to *puas* (satisfied). *Sa-by* is happy or comfortable in Thai. See "SEVEN" and "SUFFICE."

SWELL/צָבַר
(T)SOV–ARE   [(T)S–V–R→SWL]

ROOTS: Anglo-Saxon *swellan* is traced to the theoretical IE base *swel*. No IE root is available. צבר / (T)SĀVĀR is to heap up (*Genesis 41:49* – R→L change). צבה / (T)SĀVĀ is to "swell" (*Numbers 5:21*).

> **BRANCHES:** צבר / TZEBHER is a pile or heap. Polish *zbior* is a collection or crop; *zabierajc* is to gather or collect.
> *Tap* in Vietnamese is to pile or gather. See the WL element of WELLING up at "WELT."

SWERVE/סור
SVOOR   [SVR]

ROOTS: From the IE root *swerbh* (to turn, wipe off), SWERVE means to turn aside from a straight line or course. סור / SOOR, SWOOR or SVOOR means to turn aside precisely this way.

Deuteronomy 2:27: "I will keep strictly to the highway, *turning off* neither to the right nor to the left." The "wiping off" in the IE root is from הסיר / (HEY)SEER (to remove, put aside), related to the same SR Hebrew root. זור / ZVR also means "to turn away."

> **BRANCHES:** סורר / SŌRER is perverted, rebellious (*Deuteronomy 21:18*). שור / SOOR also means to turn aside or depart; its antonymic counterpart is שורה / S(H)OORĀ (line, row – see "SERIES"). A שביל / SHVEEL or SWL (lane, path) is something to SWERVE from.
> Pronouncing the vowel ו/ Ō or OO as the ו/ V or W consonant also allows one to see AWARE in עור / AWR (usually pronounced OOR – to awake, to rouse oneself), to see DWELL in דור / DWR (usually pronounced DOOR – to dwell, live), or to see SWARTHY in שחור / SHWR (usually pronounced SHAKHOR – dark, black). See "SHEERING" and "SWIVEL;" for antonyms see "STRESS." Reverse SR for Old French *ruser* (to detour), source of RUSE (a trick, strategem).

SWIT(CH)/שֵׁבֶט
S(H)AVE–ET   [S(H)–V–T]

ROOTS: The oldest and best etymons available for SWITCH are Late German *zwuske* (long thin rod) and Middle Dutch *swick* (a whip). SWITCH is defined as a flexible twig, rod or stick for whipping.

שבט / S(H)ĀVET is a rod (*Isaiah 28:27*) or staff; a whipping rod is the implication in *Proverbs 10:13.* שוט / S(H)ŌT, SWT or S(H)–V–T is a "whip" (*Proverbs 26:3*).

BRANCHES: SWAT is easily related, while STAFF and STAVE require a #2-#3 letter switch. See "SCEPTER." For a human branch, or S–BH–T tribe word–see "SEPT."

SWIV(EL)/סְבִיבוֹן
S'VIV–(OWN)   [SVV→SWV]

ROOTS: Old English *swifan* (to revolve) is traced to the IE root *swei* (to bend, turn).

סבב / SOVÄV is to turn around (*Joshua 6:4*) or to turn away (*Genesis 42:24*). נסב / (NÄ)SÄV is to surround (*Genesis 19:4*). הסב / (HÄ)SÄV is to turn something roundabout (*Exodus 13:18*); it means to turn over (control) to another in *I Chronicles 10:14.* סב / SV is the two-letter root.

BRANCHES: שב / S(H)ÄV is to turn back. סביבון / SIVÉVŌN is a toy top. Cognates of SWIVEL include SWAP, SWAY, SWEEP, SWIFT, SWITCH, SWIM, and SWOOP. Under IE root *sweng* (to swing, turn) are related terms like SWAG, SWANK and SWING.

Consider SPIDER, SPIN and SPINDLE, along with SWERVE and SWIRL, as SP or SW associates. סבה / SÉBHÄ is a turn of events or a pivotal reason. "Because" is *sebab* in Indonesian, and *kwa sababu* in Swahili. The circling fly or bee is the זבוב / ZIVOOV.

SYCAMORE/שִׁקְמָה
S(H)IEK–MAW   [S(H)–K–M]

ROOTS: Unlike the American buttonwood, this tree of Asia Minor has figlike fruit. The SYCAMINE tree of *Luke 17:6* may be an SKM tree that was not altered in spelling like the SYCAMORE. SYCAMORE is said to be from *sykon* (Greek for fig) plus *moron* (black mulberry).

שקמה / S(H)IKMÄ is a sycamore (*I Kings 10:27*).

BRANCHES: Related words include: SYCONIUM, SYCOPHANT (a flatterer, literally: one who shows figs), SYCOSIS (a disease of the outside of the head).

The SMK words for fig in Rumanian (*smochina*), Serbo-Croatian and Russian (*smokva*) are a #2-#3 letter flip of S(H)IEKMAW. See "FIG" and "SUMAC." For the SK root of sweetness see "MUSK."

SYNCOPAT(ION)/שֵׁנִי + קְפַר
S(H)YN–AY + KEY–PAID   [S(H)–N] + [KPD]

ROOTS: The many SYN- and SYM- words are from Greek *syn* (with) – the Hebrew sources are at "SYNOD," but note that שני / S(H)ÄNÉ is second. For SYNCOPATION (shortening words or shifting musical accents) it is more relevant to add that שנה / S(H)ÄNÄ is to repeat.

Greek *koptein* (to cut) gives us the KPT heart of our entry, coming from קפד / KÉPA(D)T (to cut off, shorten – *Isaiah 38:12*). A close synonym is קצב / KOTSUBH (to cut off – *II Kings 6:6*). קצב / (KET)SEB(H) is a shape, rhythm or cut (as of clothes – *I Kings 6:25*). This is noteworthy because SHAPE and -SHIP (as in relation*ship*) are official cognates of SYNCOPATION at the IE root *skep* (also designated *kep* – meaning "to cut or hack.")

BRANCHES: קפדה / KIPÄDÄ is annihilation; קפח / KOPHÄH is to strike. Both קפץ / KOPHÄTS (to CHOP– attributed to Greek) and קפנדריא / KÄPENDÄRYÄ (shortcut – borrowed by Hebrew from Latin) might be considered "reborrowings." Other cognates of (SYN)COPAT(ION) include CAPON (castrated chicken), KOPECK (via Russian *kopat* – to hack), and SARCOPTIC MANGE. KP cut-offs to consider include CHIP, COUPÉ (a shortened car) and COUPON. See "CUT", "SCABBLE" and "TEAM".

SY(N)DIC(ATE)/צֶדֶק
(T)SED–ECK   [(T)S–D–K]

ROOTS: SYNDIC and SYNDICATION are from Greek *synikos* (judge's advocate, judge). Mistaken for a combination of *syn* (together) + *dike* (justice), SY(N)DIC is merely a nasalized (extra N) form of צדק / (T)SEDEK (justice – *Deuteronomy 16:20*).

BRANCHES: סנדק / SÄNDÄK (godfather) is Late Hebrew, coming from Greek and from Hebrew צדק / SDK. DICAST, EURYDICE and THEODILY are also from Greek *dike* (justice, right, court case). The IE root here is *deik* (to show, pronounce solemnly), which includes ADDICT, BENEDICTION, CONTRADICT, DICTATE, DICTION, DICTUM, INDICT, JUDGE, JUDICIAL, JURIDICAL, JURISDICTION, PREDICATE, PREJUDICE, VERDICT, and VINDICATE. These DK words may connect to the verb צדק / (TSE)DÄK (to "justify"– *Exodus 23:7* or to "declare (someone in the) right"– *Deuteronomy 25:1*). הודיע / (HŌ)DEKHÄ (to inform, make known) and הודעה / (HŌ)DÄKHÄH (announcement) also must be heard from. Because צ / TS may take a J on occasion (e.g. JADE via Spanish *ijada* (side) from צד / TSÄD (side) or JOKE from צחק / TSHŌK (joke)], JUDGE, JUDICIAL and JUSTICE might come from all three letters of צדק / TS→J–D–K→C. As J words more often come from a Hebrew י / Y, consider another possible source for JUDGE. *Judex* means JUDGE in Latin, while Judah, Judea and Judaism have always been synonymous with things JUDICIAL. All the "jud" words in English involve JUDICIOUS things or Judean ones.

Judah happens to be the first judge in recorded history. The courtroom drama of Judah judging his own daughter-in-law for adultery is striking. It is so striking, in fact, that *Genesis 38* gave American literature one its greatest moments. Arthur Dimmesdale publicly condemns the adulterous mother of his own child in Hawthorne's *The Scarlet Letter*. Tamar, too, stands trial for adultery as the mother of Judah's own twin boys.

Judah's progeny take up their dad's law practice as Solomonic judges and kings, and Judean legal principles are noted by the early Greeks and Romans before anyone fully employs the term *judex* or JUDGE.

SYNOD/צֶמֶד
(T)SEM–ED   [(T)S–M–D→SND]

ROOTS: SYNOD, an assembly, is said to be from Greek *syn-* (together) + *hodos* (way). There may be no second element behind SYNOD as נצמד / (T)SEMED is a team, couple, yoke or "pair" (*Judges 19:10*). צמד / (NĒT)SMÄD means "joined up with" in *Numbers 25:3*. The two-letter root is (T)S–M as seen by צמה / (T)SÄMÄ (braid) *Songs 4:1*.

BRANCHES: Backing up the concept of an SM or SN root of togetherness are words like תאום / S'ŌM (twin – *Genesis 25:24*), תאמות / S'ĒMOOT (SYMMETRY), תאם / SÄUM (to join, combine) and שני / S(H)ÄNĒ (second – *Genesis 1:8*). Two in Thai is *sawng*.

The SYM- words (SYMBOL, SYMPATHY, SYMPHONY, etc.) may be direct from the Hebrew, rather than a variation of SYN- (as is now believed). The SYN- words (SYNAGOGUE, SYNONYM, SYNTHESIS, etc.) are also too numerous to mention.

SYRUP/שְׂרַף
SUR–UP(H)   [S–R–P(H)]

ROOTS: SYRUP or SIRUP is officially borrowed from Arabic *shariba* (to drink). שרף / SÄRUPH (to swallow, drink in) is the better etymon from Aramaic and Arabic. שרב / S(H)EREBH is the term used in Israel today for syrup.

BRANCHES: SHERBET is the English term more directly descended from Arabic *sharbah* (a drink). SHRUB (a drink) is related. These Semitic terms easily absorb the IE root *srebh* (to suck, absorb). Cognates of ABSORB include ADSORB, RESORB, and SLURP. Whole armies are said to have been sucked down in ancient Egypt's Lake Serbonis. The name *Serbonis* is Greek. שרף / SIRUPH (gum, resin) isn't far from SIRUP.

שרף / SÄRUPH (to burn) and שרב / S(H)ÄRÄBH (parched ground – *Isaiah 49:10*) are the motives for all the drinking – see "SEAR."

TAB/תָו
TUBH   [T–BH]

ROOTS: A TAB can mean a record or a reckoning, thus the TAB or bill to pay at a restaurant. The etymology is "unknown" to the AHD, while *Webster's* suggests a corruption of "tablet" or "tag." תו / TÄBH is a mark, sign or musical note (*Ezekiel 9:4*).

BRANCHES: דבה / DĒBÄ or DTĒBÄ is a "report" in *Genesis 37:2* or *Exodus 13:32*.

TABOO/תּוֹעֵבָה
TOE–AYE–BHA   [T–A–B(H)]

ROOTS: תועבה / TŌÄBHÄ is translated "abomination." But it couldn't be that "every sherperd is an *abomination* unto the Egyptians" (*Genesis 46:34*), or that the "*abomination* of the Egyptians" is to be sacrificed to God in *Exodus 8:22*. The new JPS Bible's rendition, "untouchable," is far better. "Untouchable" is the basic meaning of the Tongan word TABOO. Sheep were TABOO to the Egyptians, and various misdeeds in Biblical law are TABOO – off limits, but not outrageous or abhorrent. The "off-limits" sense of תועבה / TŌÄBHÄ is best seen in *Deuteronomy 7:26* where it is compared to a חרם / KHÄREM ("devoted thing," "proscribed" thing – see "HAREM").

BRANCHES: TABOO is spelled *tabu* in Polynsian; *tapu* means consecrated. While תאב / TÄ–ÄBH is to loathe, תאב / TOÄBH is to desire or long for. To Eve, the forbidden fruit was a תאוה / TÄÄBHÄ (lust, passion or "delight"– *Genesis 3:6*). Hebrew thus captures the psychological complexity of TABOOS like incest, simultaneously revolting but desirous.

TACK/תָּקַע
TOCK–AH   [TKU]

ROOTS: To TACK is to ATTACH with a nail. Nonetheless, two different etymons are ATTACHED to these terms. Old French *tache* (fastening, nail) is traced to the IE rot *dek* (a fringe, lock of hair or horsetail). תקע / TÄKÄ (or T–K–KH, which explains the C and K of TACK) means to drive or stick in. The translation in *Genesis 31:25* is "pitch" (to implant), but STAKING a tent might be the better term. תקוע / TÄKOOÄ means STUCK in or attached.

BRANCHES: דקר / DTÄK(ÄR) is to pierce; שך / SÄKH is a thorn. Reversing D/T–K lets us tack on קוץ / KŌTS (thorn), חץ / KHÄTS (arrow), and חד / KHÄDT (sharp).

A TICK is a sharp, flat insect that ATTACKS by ATTACHING itself to the skin of its host.

Since V's tend to blend into U's, note that דבק / DTÄVÄK is to be ATTACHED or STUCK together. עתק / ÄTÄK (to remove – *Genesis 12:8*) is an antonym (and an anagram) of תקע – see "TAKE." The given cognates of TACK are SHAKO, TACH, TAG and TAIL. Relevant IE roots include the following three, which are not linked to IE *dek* or to one another: 1)*steg* (pole, stick): ATTACH, ATTACK, STACK, STAGE, STAKE and STOCKADE. 2)*stegh* (to stick, prick; pointed): STAG, STI(N)G and STOCHASTIC. 3) *steig* (to stick; pointed): ASTIGMATISM, DISTINGUISH, ETIQUETTE, EXTINGUISH, INSTIGATE, INSTINCT, STEAK, STICKLEBACK, STIGMA, STITCH, TICKET and TIGER. IF something sticks, it TAKES – see "TAKE." *Tao kou* is a barb in Chinese.

TACTIC(IAN)/(מִ)דַקְדֵק
(MI)DTUK – DTAKE   [DK]

ROOTS: TACTICS, historically, are matters of arrangement. Greek *taktikos* means fit for arranging. תכן / TOKH(ÄN) is defined as "arranged or set in order;" the term is translated "measured" in *I Samuel 2:3*. תכן / TOKHÄN also means to regulate or to formulate a program (or TACTIC).

   Another master of arrangement is the מדקדק / (MI)DÄKDÄK (grammarian, pedant). Like a true TACTITIAN he will דקדק / DÄKDÄK (see to details), דיק / DĒYÄK (be precise – Aramaic) and דק / DÄK (scrutinize). דק / DTÄK is fine, as in fine points or details.

> **BRANCHES:** Cognates of TACTICS at IE root *tāg* (to set in order) include ATAXIA, HYPOTAXIS, PARATAXIS, SYNTAX, TAXIS and TAXO-.
>   TACT and TAX relate to תכן / TOKH(ÄN) as "measure." Latin *taxare* is to assess. TACTFUL in Russian is *takteech'(nee)*. See "ORTHODOX" and "TECHNICAL." TALC or TALCUM powder is from Arabic *talq*, related to Arabic *daqiq* (flour). These derive from דק / DTÄK (fine, minute; a "mote" in *Isaiah 40:15*) and טחן / DTÄKHÄN (to grind – *Exodus 32:20*). The *taixi*, an ant in Tupi Indian (Brazil), may be a related TK term of small size and precise arrangement. For KT words see "KITTEN."

TAG/תָּג
TUG   [TG]

ROOTS: TAG is considered a cognate of TACK and TAIL – see "TACK" or "TAIL." One meaning of a TAG is a decorative flourish or stroke in writing. A תג / TÄG is an ornamental crownlet on the scribal letters of Hebrew Scripture.

> **BRANCHES:** תג / TÄG can also be pronounced TAJ. The TAJ of Taj Mahal means "crown" in Persian. תג / TÄJ is an Arabic word for crown; the Aramaic is תנא / TÄGÄ (crown, crownlet of scribal arts). The anatomical crown קדקד / KÄDKŌD reverses the T/D – G/K of TAG. See "CAUDILLO." כתר / KET[ER] is a diadem or crown.

TAIL/תַּלְתַּל
TUL – TUL   [TL]

ROOTS: Anglo-Saxon *tagel*, akin to German *zagel*, is traced to the IE root *dek-* (a fringe, lock of hair, horsetail). In Arabic, *tzayl* is a tail. תלתל / TÄLTÄL or SÄLSÄL is a curl (*Songs 5:11*), as is a סלסול / SELSOOL. דלה / DTÄLÄ is a lock of hair (*Songs 7:6*) and דלדל / DOOLDÄL is to hang limp – perhaps the source of DILLY – DALLY.
   תלה / TÄLÄ means hung, suspended (*Genesis 40:19, Deuteronomy 21:23*).

> **BRANCHES:** A טלית / *TÄLĒT* is the set of ritual fringes worn by observant Jewish men. CYNOSURE (dog's tail) is from Greek *soura* (tail) – an L→R change from the SL etymon above.

TAKE/הִתִּיק
(HE) – TEAK   [T–K]

ROOTS: Old Norse *taka* (to take) is linked to an IE base *deg* (to lay hold of) and the IE root *tak* (to take). עתק / ÄTÄK is to "remove" in *Genesis 12:8*. התיק / HETEK is to "draw away" in *Joshua 8:6*; the removal sense of TAKE is best seen in נתק / (NÄ)TÄK (to tear away or draw away).

> **BRANCHES:** The only cognate listed for TAKE is WAPENTAKE. The ATTACK sense of TAKE is better attributed to תקף / TOK(UPH) (to attack). For antonyms see "TACK." Reversing TK, קת / KAT is a hand in Assyrian and a handle in Hebrew.

TALC(UM POWDER)/דַק
DUCK   [DK→T(L)K]

ROOTS: Middle Latin *talcum* is officially linked with Arabic *talq*. TALC and TALCUM POWDER are likely from דק / DTUK (minute; a tiny particle) as in *Isaiah 40:15* –"The isles are as a *mote* in weight."

> **BRANCHES:** Arabic uses דק / DUK in its word for "flour," *daqiq*. For other flour terms see "MILL". For relatives of דק / DK see טחן / T–KH–(N) (to grind, chew) at "GNAW". The KT root of cute, cut-off or otherwise small things is seen at "KITTEN."
>   We might go from the mote (speck) to the mite (tiny insect) in considering the Brazilian Indian (Tupi) name for ant – *taixi*.
>   Antonyms for the TK reduction here include טחה / TAKHA (to expand).

TALISM[AN]/צֶלֶם
TSEL – EM   [TS–L–M→TLSM]

ROOTS: The dictionary lists Arabic *tilasm* and *tilsam* (magic figure) for this word that means a good luck charm (with an engraved figure upon it). Engraved צלם / TS–L–M "figures" in *Ezekiel 23:14* created in the צלם / TS–L–M "image" of God (*Genesis 1:26*) try to evoke a Deity beyond time and space in the confines of a tangible figure or image. The Hebrew term in both verses above is צלם / TSELEM (image, idol, likeness) – simply switch the S and L in the Arabic words above.

> **BRANCHES:** The dictionary goes on to assert that the Arabic term derives from the Greek *telesma* (payment), from *telein* (to complete). שלם / SLM or TL(M) is to pay or complete – see "SLAM" and "telic."

TALL/תָּלוּל
TALL – OOL   [TLL]

ROOTS: Falling short once again, the best our dictionary can offer for TALL (high in stature) is Middle English *tal* (dexterous, seemly) and Anglo-Saxon *getoel* (swift, prompt). תָּלוּל / TÄLOOL is "towering" in the "tall towering mountain" of *Ezekiel 17:22*. תל / TAL is a height, hill or heap (*Deuteronomy 13:17*). Tel Aviv means "the hill of spring."

> **BRANCHES:** TALL in Arabic is *tawil*. Reverse TL for Latin *altus* (high), source of ALTITUDE and ALTO. דל / DAL (low, lowly) and ירד / [YA]RAD (to go down) are related antonyms.

TAP/תֹף
TOP[H]E   [T–P[H]]

ROOTS: TAP, from Old French *taper*, is dismissed as an echoic word. Playing TAPS originally involved a drum signal. תף / TŌP(H) is a hand-drum, *"TAMBREL" or "TABRET"* (*Genesis 31:27*). תפף / TŌP(H)AP(H) is to TAP a drum (*Psalms 68:26*)

> **BRANCHES:** דפק / DTAP(HÄK) is to rap or TAP (*Judges 19:22*). Other small tapping drums include the TABOR (attributed to Persian *tabirah*) and the TA(M)BOURINE, credited to Arabic *ta(n)bur*. TUP is a striking and a hammer term. TYPING derives from Greek *typos* (a blow) and *typtein* (to beat, strike). A certain TYPE of TYPOGRAPHY or TYPOLOGY might be TYPICAL, as though (S)TA(M)PED from the same mold.
>
> טפוס / DT'PHOOS (printing press, form, mold) is not so much a borrowing from Greek as an extension of טפיחה / DTIPHĒHA (striking). STAMP and STAMPEDE are said to come from the IE base *stebh* (a post, pole). They are more likely beating or pounding terms stretched from a TP root with a nasalization (added M). Similarly, Greek *tympanon* (a drum) gives us TYMPAN, the TYMPANIC membrane (eardrum), and TYMPANY (bombast, conceit).

TARIFF/תַּעֲרִיף
TAH – AH – REEF   [TRF]

ROOTS: TARIFF is a listing of import and export taxes. Officially borrowed from Arabic *ta'rif* (information, explanation), this word is from Arabic *'arafa* (to know). Hebrew תעריף / TÄ'ÄRĒF is also "borrowed" from Arabic, but Arabic *'arafa* should be a typical #2-#3 letter swap from עור / AVR, the root of ער / ER ("awake"– *Songs 5:2*). The עור / AVR root gives us AWARE (see "ORIENTATION") – the "knowing" counterpart of *'arafa*.

> **BRANCHES:** עור / AVR or AWR means AWARE, just as עור / ĒVAR means "blind" or unaware (*Deuteronomy 28:29*).

TAUR(US)/תּוֹר
TORE   [TOR]

ROOTS: The IE root and the Greek *tauro* (bull) is the given source of Latin *taurus* (bull).

Aramaic תור / TŌR (bull) shows a typical Aramaic T from Hebrew SH change, as the Hebrew bull is a שׁוֹר / SHŌR (*Deuteronomy 33:17*). More on the SH to T change at "TERZA (RIMA)."

> **BRANCHES:** Cognates in the bullpen with IE *tauro* (bull) include: MINOTAUR, TAURINE, TAURO, and TOREADOR. It's more likely that the STEER belongs here than with IE *sta* (to stand). If one likes the steadiness of associating "stand" with the bull or ox, Hebrew offers שור / SHOOR (wall), שאר / SHÄER (to remain) and, relevant to the consistency of this plough-dragger, שורה / SHOORÄ (line, row).
>
> Perhaps the best way to brand STEER "Semitic" is via the Arabic ox – *tsor* – swap #1-#2 letters. Bambara (Hamitic) has a word for bull that sounds like *toro*.

TEAL/צָלַל
TSUL – UL   [T(S)–L–L]

ROOTS: From Middle English *tele*, a TEAL is a duck. צלל / T(S)ALAL (to dive, sink – *Exodus 15:10*) makes a fine etymon for a duck. Diving in the water, or ducking in it, is why ducks are called ducks.

> **BRANCHES:** *Toloa* is a duck in Proto-Polynesian (the granddaddy of Hawaiian and Samoan). The SEAL might be another diver from this (T)S – &L root.

TEAM/תְּאוֹם
TIH – OME   [TAM]

ROOTS: For TEAM, the dictionaries cite Old English *team* (descendant, family, race). (The source of this word is probably דם / DTÄM (family, "blood"– *Numbers 35:19*). Team is then somehow traced to the IE root *deuk* (to lead), as a TEAM of oxen might be said to be "leading" a wagon or plow. Hebrew offers the TM root of "two together" as seen in תאום / TIŌM or TVM (twin – *Genesis 25:24*) and צמד / T(S)EMED (couple, yoke or "a pair"– *Judges 19:10*). צמד / T(S)ÄM(ÄD) is to attach, join, couple or harness.

> **BRANCHES:** Any old TEAMSTER (person driving two draft animals in TANDEM) will tell you that TEAMWORK is required (BE)TWEEN one animal and its TEAMMATE. Traditional yokes were for TWO or TWIN animals – and never the TWAIN shall part. The vowel ו / O of the etymon doubles for a consonant pronounced like a V or W.
>
> Only the M to N (Grimm's Law) change is required for many of these words. More TM togetherness at "SYNOD." All THOMAS words, TOMBOY and TOMCAT included, are from תאום / TIŌM (twin).

TEAT/דד
DUD   [DT–DT]

ROOTS: Old French *tete* is the given etymon for TEAT, the protuberance on a breast or UDDER. Although T and D are officially interchangeable, Latin *uber* (udder) is cited as a source for UDDER. The double dental (D or T) etymon for TEAT and UDDER is דד / DTÄDT (breast, nipple – *Ezekiel 23:8 ; Proverbs 5:19*).

BRANCHES: TITILLATE and KITTLE are cognates at the IE root *tit* (to tickle...expressive root). TICKLE should be related – see "TOOTS." Baby mammals TITILLATE to receive mother's milk.

A TITTLE is a DOT; both may relate to Norwegian *titta* (little girl), to DAUGHTER (from Sanskrit *duhitar*), to TOT (small child, perhaps the sense was "suckling") and to the little TITMOUSE. *Doot* is to suck in Thai; *dada* is a breast in Indonesian.

TECHNI(CAL)/תקון
TEA–COON   [TKN]

ROOTS: TECHNOLOGY is credited to the Greek *tekhne* (art, skill); the IE root is *teks* (to weave...fabricate). תך / TÄKH is a stitch, and perhaps the source of (S)TITCH. תך / TEKH means craft according to the *Hebrew-English Lexicon of the Bible*. תקן / TÄKÄN is to make straight, repair or TINKER (*Ecclesiastes 1:15; 7:13*). To TINKER (repair – TKN→TNK) has no known origin. *Txukun(du)* is to fix in Basque, the language with "no known affinities."

תכונה / T'KHOONÄ means arrangement, order, structure, preparation or astronomy. תכן / TÄKHÄN is to regulate, measure, formulate a program (*II Kings 12:12 ; Isaiah 40:2, 3*). תכן / TOKHEN is measurement or content (*Exodus 5:18*). תכנית / TÄKHNET is a measurement, plan, program or TEQHNIQUE. The ARCHITECT's plan is the sense in *Ezekiel 43:10*.

BRANCHES: תחם / TÄKHÄM is to set limits. The IE root makes the TECHNICIAN a cognate of the DACHSHUND. Other cognates listed at IE root *teks* are CONTEXT, PRETEXT, SUBTLE, TECHNICAL, TECTONIC, TILLER, and TOIL.

TEXTILE is an extension of TEXT. The Greek *tekton* (carpenter, builder) does not weave, but does all the planning and measuring (and repairing) seen in the Hebrew etymons above. See "TACTITIAN."

TELE(VISION)/המיל
(HE)–TEEL   [TYL]

ROOTS: The TELE- prefix in TELEGRAPH, TELEPHONE and TELEVISION is said to come from Greek *tele* (far off, at a distance). The given IE root is *k/w)el* (far). *Tele* is not linked to an IE root like *tela* (to lift, support, weigh) because

the original sense of being thrown to a distance or cast from afar was lost.

The "lift" sense of the IE root is in נטל / (NÄ)TÄL (to raise – *Isaiah 63:9*). Also see "ATLAS." הטיל / (HE)TEL is to throw (*Jonah 1:12*). TELEVISION is a video signal that is thrown or TELECAST from afar, not a "far-off vision." טלטול / TELTOOL is moving; טיול / TEYOOL is a far walk or hike. טיל / TEL is a rocket or long-distance missile, just as Latin *telum* is a dart.

BRANCHES: טרי / DTIRÄ (to throw in Aramaic) may be the source for DART and THROW. טלטל / TELTAL is to move back and forth (*Isaiah 22:17*) and מטלטלת / (MI)TOOLTELET is a pendulum. Along with נטיל / (NÄ)TEL (laden, burdened), these Hebrew words closely match the "support, weigh" sense of IE root *tela* as well. The cognates listed here include TELAMON (from Greek *telamon*, bearer), again why TELE- words relate here. For VISION see "VIDEO."

TELIC/תכלית
TUKH–L(EET)   [T–KH–L→TLK]

ROOTS: TELIC means directed towards an end, or purposeful; Greek *telikos* is traced to Greek *telos* (an end). תכלה / TEKHLÄ is also a purpose or end (*Psalms 119:99*). תכליתי / TÄKHLETE is purposeful; a #2-#3 letter flip is required. תכלית / TÄKHLET (end, purpose, completeness, perfection – *Nehemiah 3:21; Job 26:10*) also matches the "completion" definition of Greek *telos*.

BRANCHES: TELIC and TELO- words like TELOPHASE are somehow placed at the IE root *k(w)el* (to revolve, sojourn) which echoes גור / GOOR or GWR (to sojourn) and גל / GÄL (to revolve, roll). Cognates of TELIC include ENTELECHY, TALISMAN, TELEOLOGY, TELEOST, and TELIUM. See "TALISMAN." An antonym is תחילה / TIKHELÄ (beginning). See "TERM." Greek *telesma* (payment) is from the verb *telein* (to complete). שלם / SLM or TL(M) is to pay or complete – see "SLAM."

TERM/טרם
TERR–EM   [TRM]

ROOTS: Latin *terminus* is a boundary. IE root *ter* is the base of various boundary terms. טרם / TEREM is a boundary in time, rather than space. It means "not yet" or "before" (*Genesis 24:15*). It infers just before or at the edge of a DETERMINING TERMINUS in time.

BRANCHES: Related TERMS include DETERMINE, EXTERMINATE, TERMINATE and perhaps THRUM. A hardened שלם / SHÄLEM (complete) would be TLM; see "TELIC." טור / TOOR and תור / TOR mean a row or a range.

TERZA (RIMA)/תֵּלַת
TILL–US   [TLS→TRS]

ROOTS: TERZA RIMA is an Italian verse form. Latin *tres* is three, as is Sanskrit *tri* and Greek *trias*. The IE root for three (3) is *trei*.

תלת / TILÄS (three – *Daniel 7:20*) is Aramaic, merely an L to R change away. תלתא / T'LÄSÄ is the targum's Aramaic translation of שלשה / SHILŌSHÄ (three) in *Genesis 6:10* and elsewhere. In Aramaic, the Hebrew ש / SH is consistently rendered as a ת / T (see "TAURUS").

> **BRANCHES:** Cognates from Germanic include THREE, THRICE, THIRTY and THIRTEEN; from Latin TREY, TRIO, TRAMMEL, TRECENTO, TREPHINE, TRIUMVIRATE and TROCAR; THIRD and RIDING are from Old English and Old Norse; TRI- as in TRICOLOR and TRIPLE are also from Latin; Greek also has a TRI-, along with TRICLINIUM, TRIDACTYL, TRITONE and more; TRIMURTI is from Sanskrit; more Greek 3's are TRIAD, TRICHOTOMY, TRIERARCH, TRITIUM, etc; Latin adds ATTEST, CONTEST, DETEST, OBTEST, PROTEST, TESTAMENT, TESTIMONY, and TESTIFY; SITAR is from a Persian three; TRINE and TRINITY are from Latin *trini* (three each); and Russian adds TROIKA.
>
> Arabic turns שלשה / SHILOSHA into *tsalatsa*. Fijian *tolu* or *dolu* was not borrowed. Chinese and Japanese *san* (three) may represent an ל / L to N change, a permutation taken up in an appendix.
>
> Another example of a ש / SH to T change from Hebrew to IE is seen in the word for "there", *tam*, in Slavic languages. שם / SHÄM is "there" in Hebrew.

THEM/אוֹתָם
O–THUM   [A–O–T(H)–M]

ROOTS: The pronoun THEM was *theim* in Old Norse. אותם / ŌTHÄM is likewise the 3rd person objective pronoun. *Genesis 1:27* makes clear that Man and Woman were created equal: "male and female created He *them*." אותם.

> **BRANCHES:** One form of THEM was *hem* in Middle English, recalling הם / HÄM (they – 3rd person subjective pronoun). While the IE root of THEM is *to* (demonstrative pronoun), the Biblical Aramaic pronoun for "this" and "that" is דן / DÄN. (THEM is pronounced "dem" in Brooklyn; many "th" words derive form "d" terms.) See "THOU."

T(H)ERAPY/תְּרוּפָה
TIROO–PHAH   [T(H)–R–PH]

ROOTS: THERAPY is from Greek *therapeuein* (to nurse, treat medically).

Herbal THERAPEUTICS is described in *Ezekiel 47:12* – "the fruit thereof shall be for food, and the leaf thereof for *healing*"– תרופה / TIROOPHA or THIROOPA.

רפואה / REFOOÄ is healing or THERAPY; רפא / RÄPHÄ is to heal or cure – (*Exodus 15:26*).

> **BRANCHES:** A leaf, טרף / TEREPH, rustles with the TRP sound of THERAPY. Antonyms include תרפה / TOORPÄ (weakness – see "TORPID") and רפה / RÄPHÄ (weak).

THIN/צָנוּם
TSUN–(OOM)   [T(S)–N–(M)]

ROOTS: Anglo-Saxon *thynne* is traced to the IE root *ten* (to stretch).

The stretching terms at this root may be linked to נטה / NÄTÄ (to extend – reverse TN – see "EXTEND"). צנום / T(S)ÄN(OOM) is lean, THIN or meager (*Genesis 41:23*). צנע / TSÄNÄ means austere.

> **BRANCHES:** צמצם / TSIMTSÄM is to limit, compress or reduce; צמק / TSÄM[ÄK] is to shrink, wither or shrivel. קטן / [KA]TAN is small. See "SMASH." טחן / THN means ground down.

THIS/זֹאת
ZOWSE   [ZAS]

ROOTS: Old English *this* is traced to an IE root for most any pronoun beginning with a T– *to* (demonstrative pronoun). זאת / ZŌS means THIS (*Genesis 34:15; II Kings 5:4* renders it "thus"). THUS is related.

> **BRANCHES:** זו / ZO can mean "this one" or SO.
> Polish *az* (until) is a match for אז / ÄZ (then, at that time, in this case or therefore). Finnish *siis* is "thus." THIS in Chinese is *zhe*.

THOU/אַתָּה
AH–T(H)AH   [A–T(H)–H]

ROOTS: THOU (you) is *thu* in Old English; the IE root of this second-person singular pronoun is *tu*. אתה / ÄTU or ATHA is "you" or THEE or THOU (*Genesis 23:6*).

> **BRANCHES:** Cognates include THY and THINE. The second-person suffix form in the past tense is ת / TA or THA. *Teh* is "you" in Nahautl (Aztec Indian); *tah(n)* is the Thai "you." *Taau* means "yours" in Proto Nuclear Polynesian.

T(H)YME/תֶּמֶר
TEAM–(AIR)   [TM(R)]

ROOTS: Old French *tim* and Greek *thymon* are traced to a theoretical term *dhumo* (smoke) and the IE root *dheu* (to rise in a cloud). Ben-Yehuda defines תמר / TĒMAR or THĒM[ÄR] as "to rise up (smoke)." תמרוק / SUMROOK or THUM(ROOK) means perfume in *Esther 2:12*. The rising aromatic clouds of THYME scent are most apparent in *Songs 3:6* –

> "Who is she that comes up from the desert like *columns* of smoke, in clouds of myrrh and frankincense . . . " תימרות.

> **BRANCHES:** PERFUME, FUME and THIONINE (sulphur, brimstone) are official cognates of THYME, but so are DUMB, ENTHYMENE, DEER, DOWN, DUSK, TYPHUS, DEAF, DOVE, DWELL, DRUMS, DOCK, DULL and DOLT.
>
> The initial S of STEAM is suspect because it only appears in West Germanic languages. See "DUMB".

TIARA/עֲטָרָה
ATARA   [UTR]

ROOTS: Greek *tiara* is "probably of oriental origin" to *Webster's* . The AHD feels that this crown term is from a Greek word for turban, but no IE root is offered.

עטרה / ÄTÄRÄ is a crown (*Songs 3:11*). עטר / ÄTÄR is to surround.

BRANCHES: תור / TÖR is a circlet; דור / DTOOR is the rim of a wheel – see "TIRE". Because עטרה / ÄTÄRÄ can also be read KHATÄRÄ, the כתר / KETER (crown) is closely related. See TIER for straight TR antonyms. Catharine, Kathy, Kate, Catarina and Kathleen are thought to come from Greek *katharos* (pure), but עטרה / KHÄTÄRÄ is a regally feminine Hebrew name.

K–TH may infer pure in Hebrew as כתם / KETH[EM] is pure gold and כתית / KATH[ET] is pure oil.

TICK(LE)/דִגְדֵג
DIG – (DAIG)   [DG→TK]

ROOTS: Middle English *tikelen* is linked to Old Norse *kitla* (to tickle) – see "TEAT." An easier etymon is דגדג / DIGDÄG or TIKTÄK (to TICKLE, titillate), from Arabic דעידע / (D)TAKH – (D)TAKH.

BRANCHES: Reverse TK for antonyms like עקץ / ÖKETS (sting). *Gatal* is itch in Indonesian (reverse the G – DT). See "TOUCH."

TIER/טור
TOUR   [TIR]

ROOTS: TIER is from Old French *tire* (order, rank, row). טור / TOOR is a row, line or column (*Exodus 28:17*).

BRANCHES: תור / TÖR is a line, row or turn. The DR or TR element of straightness in דרך / DEREKH (see "DIRECTION") links up with שורה / SHOORÄ (row, line) because of the ש / SH = ת / T connection. Each generation or דור / DTÖR forms a kind of row or line. The ו (vav) of טור and דור / TVR is also a consonant, thus תפר / TEPHER (stitch) is a related line or row. See "TIARA" for round TR antonyms, and "TOWER" for vertical ones.

TILE/טלא
TEE – LAY   [TLA]

ROOTS: Anglo-Saxon *tigele* and Latin *tegere* (to cover) are said to be the sources of TILE. The IE root is *(s)teg* (to cover). טלל / TELÄL is to cover or roof – *Nehemiah 3:15*. טלא / TELÄ is to patch.

BRANCHES: מטלית / MÄTLES is a patch, extending from the TL root. This word may have given rise to MOTLEY and MOTTLED. Latin *tela* (a web, woven material) may link up with these patchy Hebrew words. If so, TOIL and TOILET are connected to bathroom TILES and other such patchwork coverings.

Perhaps a TAIL[OR] can be seen as a "patcher" as well. The TG words of covering at IE *(s)teg* (DECK, DETECT, PROTECT, THATCH, THUG, TILE and TOGA) as well as words like SHTICK and STUCCO (now traced to Old High German *stukki*, crust, covering) are better linked to words like טוח / TOOAKH (plaster, paint, overlay – *Leviticus 14:43*).

TALIPES is a clubfoot. The word is presumably a combination of Latin *talus* (ankle) plus *pes* (foot). טלף / TELEPH (hoof) is a single term for the hoof or ankle-foot (of feetless, toeless animals). The TALUS is the ankle bone or entire ankle, also resembling the טלף / TELEF (hoof). As the hoof is a horny covering on the feet, the טל / TL two-letter Hebrew root here is found in טלל / TLL (to cover over, to TILE). The horny TALON is also from Hebrew TL, via Latin *talus* (ankle). In Sanscrit, too, the word for "hoof" also means "claw."

TIM(B)ER/תָּמָר
TUM – ARE   [TMR]

ROOTS: No etymology keeps the "B" in Old English *timber* (building material, lumber). The term is traced to German *Zimmer* (room), Latin *domus* (house) and finally to the IE root *dem* (house, household).

Consider the pillar-like royal palm tree and note that TIMBER means trees or wooded land, especially in words like TIMBERLAND, TIMBERLINE and TIMBERWOLF. A TIMBER is also a sturdy beam. תמר / TAMAR is a palm or date tree (*Songs 7:9*). תמיר / TAMEER is tall, upright; תמר / TEEMÄR is to rise straight up, תמרור / TAMROOR or TMRVR means "column" (*Jeremiah 31:21*), and תימרה / TEMARA is a "pillar" (*Songs 3:6*).

There's no problem linking the TAMARIND (date tree of India) or the TAMARISK (an evergreen shrub) to Hebrew תמר / TÄMÄR (date – *Leviticus 23:40*). They are already considered borrowings form Arabic *tamr* (date).

BRANCHES: The TAMARACK (an Algonquin Indian term for this swamp tree) also branches off from the same Semitic trunk.

Perhaps the TAMARIN was named form this same primieval tree term, TAMARIN being a Carib name in Guiana for tree-dwelling marmosets.

If Latin *domus* (house) derives from תמר / TM[R], then DOME, DOMESTIC, DOMICILE and TAME are related too. A DN Hebrew etymon for terms of *"dominion"* is seen at "MADONNA."

The Arabic name for the multi-ribbed fruit of the date tree is not *tamr* but *tarich*. *Tarich* seems to have changed from צלע / T(S)ALAKH (rib, side plank – R = L). Add DA to TLK to get *datulja* (the Serbo-Croatian date) or *datolya* (the Hungarian date). German reduces this to *Dattel* (date), and English reduces it all the way down to DATE.

Take the Hebrew TLK and flip the K toward the front of the word to get Greek *(da)ktylos* and Polish *daktyl* (date). DACTYL is related to DIGIT, as Greek *daktylos* means finger. The "fingers" we are pointing to are the appendages, ribs, side planks or sections of the date fruit.

TIME/תֶם
TUM   [TM]

ROOTS: Anglo-Saxon *tima* (time) is traced to the Ie base *dei* (to part, divide up) and the IE root *da* (to divide). Reversing *da* does recall עת / ĀDT (time – *Ecclesiastes 3:1*). Pronounced עת / KHĀT, it too is a CUTTING term. There is a range of TM TIME words in Hebrew. תם / TUM is to be finished, to be destroyed, to cease, or to be "spent" in *Numbers 26:20*. Reversing this term brings מת / MĀT (to die) and מתי / MATĪ (when?). תמול / TIM(ŌL) is "formerly" or "yesterday"– *Genesis 31:2*. On the contrary, תמיד / TĀM(ĒD) means "always" and "continuity" (*Exodus 28:29*).

> **BRANCHES:** צמית / T(S)ĀM(ĒT) means perpetual or final. תחום / T'HOOM is a limit. מרה / MĀDTÄ (measurement) reversed is a DT–M term.
> More distant connections to TIME and TEMPO may be seen at "CHANGE," "SUN" and "TERM." *Tuma* is a period of time in Bambara (Hamitic). *Tihng* is a stop or pause in Cantonese.

TIM(ID)/תֶמַה
TAME–AH   [TMH]

ROOTS: TIMID is from Latin *timere* (to fear), a cognate of TIMOROUS (lacking self-confidence). There is no IE root, but TM is the core.
תמה / TOMÄ is to be in doubt; תמהון / TIMÄ(HŌN) is "dismay" *Deuteronomy 28:28*.

> **BRANCHES:** Affecting a T→SH change evokes שממה / SHIMÄMÄ (horror).

TIN/טני
TIN–(ĒĒ)   [TN(Y)]

ROOTS: Anglo-Saxon *tin* has no known etymon, or relatives outside of Germanic. A TIN can mean a can, pot or pan of TIN, so that an implement may have named the material (rather than the reverse).
טני / TINĒ is a metal bin or tray used to collect fat from the Temple altar. The word is post-Biblical, but with no evidence of borrowing.

> **BRANCHES:** טנא / TENE is a basket or other receptacle (*Deuteronomy 26:2*).

TINE/צֶן
T(S)ANE   [T(S)–N]

ROOTS: Old English *tind* is the farthest back anyone could trace TINE. A TINE is a sharp, projecting point, a spike or a prong. *SNAG's* Old Norse and Norwegian roots are defined in much the same way, so a TN or SN etymon of sharpness is needed.

צן / TSĀN is a barb, thorn or briar (*Proverbs 22:5*); צנין / TSĀN(ĒN) is a thorn or prick (*Numbers 33:55*). In this last Biblical verse the Canaanites are called "*thorns* in your sides"– the "obstacle, difficulty" sense mentioned at SNAG. סנה / SNEH is a thornbush (*Exodus 3:2*); שן / SHEN is a tooth (*Exodus 21:24*). A *SNAG* is also a broken or irregular tooth, otherwise known as a SNAGGLETOOTH. The toothy PIRANHA fish has a Tupi Indian (Brazil) name, half of it based on the term *sainha* (tooth).

> **BRANCHES:** Because the S in שן / SHEN can become a T (see "TAURUS"), TINE, TENON, TENACITY, TENACULUM (hooked instrument) and TANG (prong) are all related. TANG and TONGS are cognates at the IE root *denk* (to bite). IE root *dent* (tooth) is the source of DENTAL, INDENT, -ODON, TOOTH and TUSK German *zinko* (spike, prong) helps fit ZINC (with a salty "bite") into the picture. צנורה / TSINORA (hook, needle) helps us latch onto "ten" terms like TENTACLE. שנינה / SHINĒNÄ is a "sharp word" or "taunt." TAUNT, using words that STIN[G], is another TN term that ultimately belongs here.
> *Tama* is a tooth for the Comanche and Hopi Indians, providing another distant TN relative for words like DEN(TIST). Reversing צן / TSN bears נעץ / NOÄTS (to prick, puncture, stick in). נעץ / NOÄTS or NOGÄT(S) is an alternative etymon for GNAT– (see "GNAW"), while נעצוץ / NAATSOOTS (thornbush – *Isaiah 7:19*) seems a likely source of *NETTLE* and perhaps NEEDLE and NASTY (dangerous – origin unknown).

TIRE/תוֹר
TORE   [TIR]

ROOTS: Middle English *tyre* is thought to be short for "attire" (equipment). A primary choice for Hebrew etymon is דור/DOOR or TOOR (rim of a wheel). תור / TŌR (circlet, turn) is a close second. עטרה/ATARA is a crown (Songs 3:11); עטר/ATAR is to surround – see "TIARA."

> **BRANCHES:** The Biblical source for דור/DTOOR is Isa. 29:3 –"And I will encamp against thee *round about*." כדור This prefixed כדור/KÄDŌR (like a rim, thus "round about") gave rise to כדור/KÄDOOR (ball, globe). Related to Arabic, דרדור / DTARDTOOR means "that which is rolled."
> תאר/TÄUR is "curved" (Josh. 18:14).
> In Arabic, *itar* is a TIRE, and *daira* is a circle.
> For a reversed, RT term, see "ROTATE."
> For TR antonyms of straightness, see "TIER."

TIT(ILLATE)/דוֹדים
DODE-(EEM)   [DID→TIT]

ROOTS: The IE root is *tit* (to tickle.)
דודים/(D)TŌ(D)T(ĒM) means "lovemaking" in Ezekiel 23:17.

> **BRANCHES:** See "Teat" and "TOOTS"

TITTIE/דּוֹדָה
TOE-TAH or DOE-DAH   [DT-I-DT]

ROOTS: TITTIE or TITTY means sister in Scottish; *titta* is a little girl in Norwegian. דוֹדה/TŌTÄ or DŌDÄ is an aunt, or sister of a parent – Exodus 6:20

> **BRANCHES:** The etymon for AUNT is suspect – Latin *amita* (which, like דוֹדה/DTŌDTÄ, can mean female friend). A look at Czech *teta* (aunt) or Russian *tyotya* confirms that the *tante* (aunt) of French, German, Dutch, Danish and Norwegian is a nasalization (extra N) of a TT aunt term. In English, AUNT is a T[N]T word that has lost its initial T.
> See "TOOTS."

TOBACCO/טַבַּק
TABAK   [TBK]

ROOTS: This modern Hebrew word relates to Arabic *tabaq* (a euphoria-causing herb). This cancer-causing herb was previously traced to the West Indian term for a pipe, but the *American Heritage Dictionary* is probably right in favoring the well-traveled Spanish-from-Arabic route for so many English words.

TOIL/תִּלְאָה
TIL-A-AH   [TLAH]

ROOTS: The dictionaries cite Latin *tudes* (hammer) and the IE root *(s)teu* (to push, stick, knock, beat) as the sources of TOIL.

Hebrew offers תלאה/TILÄ-ÄH (hardship, weariness, trouble – Numbers 20:14) as an alternative.

TOLL/צְלָצֵל
TSIL-TSAIL   [T(S)-L]

ROOTS: Middle English *tollen* is to pull; TOLL means the act or the sound of ringing a bell.

If the act gave us TOLL, there is דלה/DTOLLO (to draw – as in pulling up water in a bucket by rope – Exodus 2:19). If the sound of the tolling bell is the issue, צלצל/T(S)IL-T(S)ÄL (to ring) is a doubled form of צלל/T(S)OLUL or T(S)LL (to "tingle" – II Kings 21:12).

> **BRANCHES:** Related to דלה/DOLOH (to draw) are derivatives of IE roots *dhragh* and *dhreg* (both mean "to draw") such as: DRAFT, DRAG, DRAW, DRAY, DRENCH, DRINK, and DROWN.

TON/טָעַן
TAW-UN   [TUN]

ROOTS: TON used to mean "loaded to capacity"; טען/TÄUN means to be laden – Gen. 45:17. It is said that Anglo-Saxon *tunne* is a 17th century variation of TUN. Anglo-Saxon *tonne* is a large cask and a liquid measure.

To fit this etymon, טנא/TENE is a large produce basket – Deut. 26:2. This large basketful might have given rise to the weight we call a TON.

> **BRANCHES:** Swedish *tung* means weighty, with no specific TONNAGE in mind.
> The TUNNY and TUNA fish might have been named for their great bulk and weight – see "TUNA."

TON(IC)/אֵיתָן
(AH)-TON   [ATN]

ROOTS: TONIC is from Greek *tonikos* and from the IE root *ten* (to stretch) – see "EXTEND."

TONIC is a medicine that invigorates; the resiliency of TONE also implies strength.

Similarly, איתן/ÄTÄN means strong and perpetual, "enduring" in Jer. 5:15. אתן/ETÄN is to recuperate, and TONIC in Modern Hebrew is אתן/ÄTÄN.

> **BRANCHES:** Many TN words are better linked to an etymon of strength and steadfastness.
> The אתן/ATŌN (donkey – see "ASININE") is an enduring pack animal known for her TENDENCY to keep an even TENOR, persevering with TENACITY throughout its TENURE of service.
> For the sense of holding fast that is behind words like TENANT, TEND, TENNIS, TENON and TENTACLE even a word like צנין/T(S)INEN (thorn, prick – Numbers 33:55) is a better etymon than the *ten* root of stretching.

TOO/תּוּ
TOO   [T-OO]

ROOTS: There is no attempt to link TOO with ADD or TWO. The given etymon for TOO (in addition) and the preposition TO is a theoretical root *de* (base of prepositions and adverbs). This IE root has only one other adverb or preposition with a D or T listed.

Like TOO, Aramaic תו/TOO means "further," "more" or "again."

> **BRANCHES:** Aramaic תו/DTOO is two; עוד/ŌDT means "more" or "further." תאום/T'ō[M] is a twin.
> *Do* means "same" in Japanese; TOO is *t'ai* in Chinese, and *taai* in Cantonese. *Doo-ay* is TOO or "also" in Thai.
> See "ADD" and "DUO."

TOOT(S)/דוֹד
DODE [DOD→T-OO-T]

ROOTS: TOOTS and TOOTSY are slang terms of endearment, terms beneath the attention of etymologists.

As TOOTS means "darling" or "dear," דוֹד/DTŌDT is a friend or lover – Songs 6:3. דודים/DTŌDTĒM means lovemaking; see "TEAT" and "TITILLATION."

ידיד/YIDTĒDT is a beloved friend (Deut. 33:12).

BRANCHES: David loved God and vice versa; דוד/DÄVĒD (David) means "beloved." A nickname for David is DOODY, which is a near relation to TOOTSY. Near relations like uncle and aunt are called דוד/DTŌDT and דודה/DTŌDTÄ. The TT "aunt" word in Russian (tyóta), Finnish (tati), Czech (teta) and Serbo-Croatian (tetka) gets nasalized (extra N) in French, German, Dutch, Danish and Norwegian (tante).

DAD or DADDY is the close, beloved relative or lover of English-speaking households. ידד/(YÄ)DÄD (loved one) is a Biblical variant.

DAUGHTER might also be a DT-DT term from this same source, as Sanskrit duhitar (daughter) resembles Norwegian titta (little girl).

A group of friends or associates acting as one forms a נדוד/(GI)DTOODT (troop). Here is another Hebrew DT-DT term to match IE root deuta (tribe), the source of DEUTSCHLAND, DUTCH, TEUTON and TEUTONIC. The Teutons might also be the דדנים/DTŌDTÄNIM of Gen. 10:4.

TOP/צָפָה
T(S)EEP-AH [TS-P]

ROOTS: Anglo-Saxon top, akin to German zopf, is traced to the IE root tap whose definition reads like this: "Germanic base of various loosely related derivatives; 'plug, wad, small compact object, projecting part; to plug, strike lightly.' " For "striking lightly" see "TAP," but let us leave theoretical IE roots for some real words. German zopf, cited above, means a TUFT of hair or a summit. Sufit is a ceiling in Polish. STUPA, from Sanskrit, is a mound covering a shrine. Now an S(T)-P(H) root word of TOPS and TOPPING is beginning to appear.

צפה/TSĒPÄ is a cover or TOP (Exodus 26:29), צפוי/TSĒPOOY is covering over or plating (Exodus 38:17), צפון/TSÄPHŌN is north or the TOP of the compass (Gen. 13:14), צף/TSÄPH is to float (atop), צפירה / TSIPHĒRA is a crown (Isaiah 28:15), צפת/TSEPHES is the capital or TOP of a pillar (II Chron. 3:15), and תועפה/TOÄPHÄ is a height or eminence (Psalms 95:4).

BRANCHES: The TOUPEE, a cognate of TOP and TUFT, is clearly a צפוי/T(S)ĒPOOY (covering).

טפל/TOPH(AL) is to lay on, lay over, cover or conceal.

Topi is a hat in Indonesian; txap(ela) is a cap in Basque. Reverse FT for the futa, a lid or cover in Japanese. The teepee is paralleled by the Amazon Indian tapiy (hut, shelter). To put on top of or to overlay is tahp in Thai.

For given cognate TIP (end) one should note a more distantly related word such as סוף/SŌPH (end).

(TO)PAZ/פָּז
PUZZ [PZ]

ROOTS: From Greek topazos, TOPAZ is a yellow crystal gem stone. It is also a bird with green and gold plumage, and a brownish-gold color.

פז/PÄZ is gold (Psalms 19:11); מופז/(MOO)PHÄZ is "refined gold" in I Kings 10:18.

BRANCHES: הפז/(HÄ)PHÄZ is to shine. See "PHOSPHORUS."

TORPID/תַּרְפָּה
TOOR-PAH [TRP]

ROOTS: From Latin torpere (numb), TORPID means dormant, sluggish and losing the power of motion.

This is exactly what happens to angels' wings in Ezekiel 1:24 – "when they stood still, they would let their wings droop." תרפינה

תרפה/TOORPÄ, defined as "weakness," is the adjectival form of the verb above. The term is an extension of רפה/RÄPHÄ (to be weak). רפה/ROPHEH means slack, loose and weak.

BRANCHES: The antonym of the RP term above is רפא/RÄPHÄ (to heal, cure); the opposite of our captioned word is תרופה/TIROOPHÄ or THIROOP(H)Ä (healing – see "THERAPY").

TORPOR and TORPEDO come from the same Latin etymon as TORPID. The cognates of TORPID at IE root ster (stiff) do not include the word DROOP.

TOSS/טוּש
TOOS [TS]

ROOTS: TOSS (to throw or be thrown; to move around vigorously) is of unknown origin. It should link up with טוש/TOOS (to fly swiftly – Job 9:26).

BRANCHES: טיסה/TĒSA (fly) and יתוש/(YA)TOOSH (gnat, mosquito) recall the African (Bantu) TSETSE fly and the Chinese tsao (flea). To DASH (sudden movement) is like the variant טש/DTASH (to fly, dart). See "DASH."

The opposite of flying swiftly is שט/SHAT (to float).

TOUCAN/תּוּכִּי
TOO – KEY [T(V)KY]

ROOTS: The large-billed and brightly colored bird has a Tupi (Brazilian Indian) name, *tucana*.

The exotic תוכיים/TOOKEEM of I Kings 10:22 or II Chronicles 9:21 are understood to mean parrots or peacocks.

> **BRANCHES:** The male TURKEY has a fan-tail that, according to some, inspired Luis de Torres to name the bird after the תוכי/TOOKEY (peacock). Luis de Torres, Columbus' first mate, was not a secret Jew like Columbus. Aside from seeking a haven for persecuted Spanish Jewry, the first mate was aboard to speak Hebrew (the acknowledged mother tongue) to any New World natives the expedition might encounter.
>
> A second theory links the TURKEY to the guinea fowl, which may have been imported by the country Turkey. A TK element is prominent in the Greek parrot, *psittakos*, source of PSITTACOSIS.

TOUCH/דָחָה
DTUHK-AH [D-KH→T-CH]

ROOTS: Old French *tochier* and Late Latin *toccare* are traced to an IE base "of echoic origin" called *tok* (a light blow).

Hebrew's DT-KH "light blow" words also recall those definitions of TOUCH that mean provoking, motivating and TOUCHING OFF.

דחה/DTÄKHÄ is to push (Psalms 36:13; 62:4; 118:13). רחף/DTÄKHÄPH is to push or drive (Esther 6:12); and דחק/DTÄKH(ÄK) is to press (Joel 2:8).

> **BRANCHES:** דגדג/DTÊGDTÄG is to TICKLE; the Arabic is רעידע/DTÄKHDTÄKH.

TOUR/תּוּר
TOUR [T-OO-R]

ROOTS: TOUR, to take a sightseeing trip, is from Old French *tourner* (to turn).

The TOURIST sense is far sharper in the Biblical Hebrew where תור/TOOR is to "explore" the land (Numbers 13:2).

> **BRANCHES:** תור/TÔR (line, row or TURN) covers the TOUR of duty sense. תיר/TÄYÄR is a TOURIST in Modern Hebrew.
> See "TIER" and "TURN."

TOWEL/טְבוּל
TIV-OOL [T-BH-L]

ROOTS: TOWEL in Old High German was spelled *dwahila*, close to the Middle English *towaille*. The Old High German term is said to be from the Germanic word *dwahan* (to wash). A washing Hebrew etymon could be terms like טבל/TOBHUL or DOWHÄL (to dip, immerse – see "DIVE"). This word clearly implies cleansing in II Kings 5:14.

A preferred Hebrew etymon is טבול/TIVOOL, the long, rectangular cloth worn in the ancient Near East and translated "flowing *turbans*" in Ezekiel 23:15.

> **BRANCHES:** Focusing on the fabric of the towel allows us to link TOW to TOWEL. Old English *towhus* is a *spinning* house; טוה/TÄVÄ or TOWÄH is to spin cloth etc. (Exodus 35:26).
>
> To weave in other TV or T-PH terms, טפיט/TÄPHET (rug, carpet, tapestry) and earlier תפר/TOPHÄR (to sew – Genesis 3:7) are the sources of words like TAFFETA (via Persian *taftan* – to weave, spin, twist), TAPA (a native Polynesian name for an unwoven cloth), TAPE (woven strips of cotton), TAPESTRY (the Greek word for carpet, *tapes*, inferred a hand-woven, heavy cloth), TWEED, TWIDDLE, TWILL, TWIRL, and TWIST.
>
> Cognates of TOW at IE *taw* (to make, manufacture) include TAW and TOOL.

TOWER/טִירָה
TEE-RAH [TR]

ROOTS: TOWER is from Old English *tur* and Latin *turris* (tower). Anglo Saxon *torr* is a tower or rock.

טירה/TÊRÄ is a TURRET, a fortified town, village or enclosure (Numbers 31:20). צור/T(S)OOR is a rock of refuge (II Sam. 22:3); בצר/(BÄ)TSÄR is to fortify; מבצר/(MIBH)TSÄR is a fortress or stronghold (Numbers 32:36).

> **BRANCHES:** צור/T(S)ÔR is a flint (Exodus 4:25), and צור/T(S)OOR is a large rock (Exodus 33:21). טורה/TOORA (a mountain) is Aramaic (Daniel 2:35).
>
> The English word TOR means a tower, rock or high rocky hill. The TURTLE may be better understood as nature's TURRET or fortification.
>
> The ancient city of צור/TSÔR (TYRE) is surely related; TR cities like Tours, Troy, Troyes, and Turin might also have been named as fortifications.
>
> While TR mountains and towers are rising and vertical, טירה/TÊRÄ is a horizontal row (see "TIER") and רד/RÄDT means "go down." Related TL words at "TALL."

TRACK/דֶרֶךְ
DOR-AKH   [(D)T-R-K(H)]

ROOTS: The noun TRACK as a route or way is covered at "DIRECTION." The verb TRACK (to tread) is traced by *Webster's* to IE base *dreg* (to pluck); the AHD offers no IE root.

See Joshua 1:3 where דרך/DTORÄKH is rendered "tread." The Hebrew dictionaries add "to step," "march" and "walk." The IE root *der* means to run, walk, or step.

> **BRANCHES:** IE root *der* includes – DROM, DROMEDARY, TEETER, TRADE, TRAMP(OLINE), TRAP, TREAD, and TROT. TRUDGE and TRAIPSE should have been included. IE root *dhreg* is to run – see DRAG.
>
> דרם/DTORUS is another verb of treading and trampling underfoot. The flat of the foot, the TARSUS (Greek *tarsos*), may relate, along with THRASH, THRESH(OLD) and TROU(N)CE. See "DIRECTION."
>
> If TRACE (a trail or to trail) is a TRK word it belongs here; if it is a TRS word it recalls דרש/DTARAS(H) (to seek, investigate – Deuteronomy 13:15). דורש / DŌRASH or DVRSH is a seeker, inquirer or demander – the source of Persian *darvish* (beggar) and English DERVISH.

TRAMMEL/תַּרְמִיל
TAR-MEAL   [TRMYL]

ROOTS: The AHD traces TRAMMEL to Late Latin *tremaculum,* a combination of IE root *trei* (three) and IE root *macula* (spot, blemish). Old French *tramail* is the better etymon for this word of confining and restraining. A TRAM is a frame used for carrying, or the basket or car of an overhead conveyer.

תרמיל/TÄRMEL is Aramaic for knapsack, bag, seedbag, pod or capsule.

> **BRANCHES:** TRAMROAD, TRAMWAY.

TREK/דֶרֶךְ
(D)TER-EKH   [D – R-KH→TRK]

ROOTS: TREK is South African Dutch, from a Dutch term *trekken* (to draw, as a wagon).

To tread is דרך/DTÄRÄKH (Josh. 1:3); a TREK or way is דרך/DEREKH – see "DIRECTION" and "DRAG."

TROPHY/טֶרֶף
TER-EPH   [T-R-PH]

ROOTS: טֶרֶף/T-R-PH means to tear, rip, feed, food, prey and leaf. These words seem unrelated if one doesn't follow them as the natural, animal process of getting nourishment. טרף/TOROF is "plucked off" in Genesis 8:11 and "torn" in Genesis 37:33.

TR words TEAR, TORE and TORN are traced to the IE root *der* (to split off). Related R-P(H) words are RIP, RIVE, RIFT and RUPTURE. The TR and RP pieces can only fit the puzzle with a DT-R-PH root of predatory tearing.

The lion is not after RAPID RAP(INE) or a mere TROPHY of conquest – his prey is his food. TROPHY is from Greek *trephein* (to nourish), a twin of הטריף/(HI)TRÊPH (to feed – Proverbs 30:8). The woman of valor in Proverbs 31:15 brings טרף/TEREF to her family. This means nourishment, not *treif* (unkosher food; literally, animals that have been torn apart). A providing parent doesn't let the family ATROPHY (Greek *atrophos* is ill-nourished). (PREDATORY animals, T-R-P(H) reversed, are unkosher.)

> **BRANCHES:** At the base of the food chain, nothing provides nourishment more than the טרף/TEREF (leaf). Only the Hebrew root explains the link between one RAPE (predatory trapping, seizing) and the other RAPE (plant of the mustard family whose leaves are used for fodder). The (T)R-PH of טרף is only an R to L change away from לפת/LEPHET [Rape and other ROUGH(AGE)]. Backwards or forwards, *FOLIO* or *LEAF,* one sees this pattern in many leaf words. *BLADE* (leaf), *FRO(N)D* and PHYLL (Greek leaf) are cognates. TALIPOT (Bengali) is linked to Sanscrit *pattra* (leaf). In Russian, where grass is *trava, list* (leaf) resembles Maya *leh tse* (leaf) and Finnish *lehti.* Leaf is *ailow* in Malay, *drau* in Fijian. RAPHE (from Greek *rhaptein* – to stitch together) is a like-sounding antonym of RIP, just as צרוף/TSAROOPH (joining together) is an antonym of טרף/T-R-PH (rip).
>
> To TEAR and RE(N)D (cognate of RIND) are TR or DR (reversed) links to טרף/DTOR(APH) (to tear apart). Treating TEAR and RIP as nouns, note how טרף/DTEREP(H) stacks up against the words for "hole" in several related languages.

| | טרף | |
	D/T	R P(H)
Czech, Russian	Di	Ra
French	T	Rou
Modern Greek	T	Ri' Pa
Polish	Dziu	Ra
Serb-Croatian	u	Ru Pa

> Returning to plant nourishment, "grass" (pasturage) in Russian and other Slavic languages is *trava.* The RB or RV in the "grass" words of the 5 Romance languages makes one suspect that טרף/(T)-R-PH (leaf, nourishment) is behind words like HERB as well.
>
> The AHD does not link IE root *rep* (to snatch) with IE root *reup* (to snatch). Cognates at the former inclde RAPACIOUS, RAPE, RAPID, RAPT, RAVEN (see "RAVENOUS"), RAVISH and SURREPTITIOUS. Cognates at the latter include ABRUPT, BANKRUPT, BEREAVE, CORRUPT, DISRUPT, ERUPT, INTERRUPT, IRRUPT, LOOT, REAVE, RIP, ROB, ROBE and ROVER. The RIP-OFF artist or thief is a *dorobo* in Japanese.
>
> For the PR element of predators and their prey, the כפיר/KFÊR (young lion) and the עפר/ŌFER (fawn – PH-R terms) – see "CAPRICORN."
>
> טרף/TARAPH (to tear apart), ערף/ARAPH (to behead) and, reversing to PR, פער/PAUR (to open wide – see PORE) establish an R-P(H) root of *RIPPING* seen in RIFT and RIVE. Old Norse *rifa* (to tear) appears in the AHD's IE root *rei* (to scratch, tear, cut) as a cognate of ARRIVE, REAP, RIFT, RIPARIAN, RIPE, RIPPLE, RIVAGE, RIVE, RIVER, and ROPE.
>
> The IE root *orbh* (to put asunder, separate) is the given source of ORPHAN. ORPHAN ought to be a distant relative of RIP, and, ultimately, of TROPHY.

TRU(D)GE/דָּרַךְ
DTOR-ÄKH   [(D)T-R-KH]

ROOTS: TRUDGE is to walk laboriously. For a source *Webster's* suggests Anglo-Saxon *trucian* (to fail, run short) and Middle Low German *truggelen* (to beg) from the IE base *dreug*.

The Bible suggests דרך/DTÄRÄKH (to tread – Josh. 1:3). See "DIRECTION" and "DRAG."

TUCKET/תְּקִיעָה
TICK-EEYAH   [TKYUH]

ROOTS: TUCKET, an archaic word, means a flourish on a trumpet. The suggested etymon is "tuck" (to beat a drum). תְּקִיעָה/TIKĒÄ is a blast or blowing of a horn – Ezekiel 7:14.

TUNA/תַּנִין
TUN-EEN   [TN]

ROOTS: TUNA and TUNNY are traced to Greek *thynnos*, "of non-Indo-European origin – akin to the source of Hebrew *tannin* (serpent, sea monster)."
תנין/TÄNĒN (serpent, large marine animal) appears in Genesis 1:21.

BRANCHES: An eel of New Zealand is called TUNA, a Maori name given by a Polynesian people. *Tuna* is an eel in Proto-Polynesian.

TN words can infer large bulk – see "TON." The TN might also allude to the toothiness of the tuna fish – see "TINE."

TURN/תּוֹר
TORE   [TR]

ROOTS: Old French *turner* is from Latin *tornare* (to turn in a lathe) and from Greek *tornos* (a lathe). The IE root is *tera* (to rub, turn).
תור/TŌR (a circlet, line or turn – Esther 2:15) covers both the circling and the "opportunity" sense of TURN.

BRANCHES: Relevant cognates include CONTOUR, DETOUR AND RETURN. More related terms at "TIER" and "TOUR."

TUR(TLEDOVE)/תּוֹר
TORE   [TR]

ROOTS: The "turtle" in TURTLEDOVE is from Latin *turtur*. The name is dismissed as "of echoic origin" despite the echoes of Gen. 15:9 – תר/TŌR (turtledove).

BRANCHES: דרור/DTRŌR is a swallow or wild pigeon (Psalms 84:4). תור/TOOR is to tour or seek out. Flight patterns are also evident in תר/TR words that mean circles or straight lines. תאר/TOAR means "turned, made a circuit."
צוצל/TSOTSÄL is a name for the TURTLEDOVE recorded in the Jerusalem Talmud.
דרר/DTORAR (whose Biblical meaning is preserved in Arabic) means "flew, went round" according to the *Lexicon*.
See "DIRECTION," "TOUR" and "TURN" to home in on the direct, round-trip flights of these birds.

TW(IST)/טָוָה
TUV-VUH   [TWH]

ROOTS: TWIST is said to come from Germanic *twis* and the IE root *dwo* (two) – see "DUO."
TAFFETA, a cloth term, is traced to Old French *taffetas* and the Persian *taftan* (to weave, spin, twist).
For a non-Indo-Aryan etymon note TW and TF words like טוה/TÄWÄ or TAVA (to spin, twist fibres – Exodus 35:25,26), תפר/TÄPHÄR (sew – Gen. 3:7) and טפיט/TÄPHĒT (rug, carpet, TAPESTRY – perhaps a borrowing).

BRANCHES: Spin-offs include TAPA (a native Polynesian name for an unwoven cloth), TAPE (woven strips of linen, etc.), TAPIS (TAPESTRY used as a tablecloth, etc.), TIE, TOW (a spinning term), TOWEL, TWIDDLE, TWEED, TWILL, TWINE, and perhaps TWIRL.
We don't think of TURF as a weaving word, but the etymon is IE base *derbh* (to twist together) so that it intertwines with a rewoven תפר/TPR→DBR→DRB (to sew). טרף/DTÄRÄPH (to beat, confuse, mix together) also fits the pattern.

ULUL(ATION)/יְלָלָה
YIH – LUL – UH   [YLLH]

ROOTS: To ULULATE is to howl, wail or lament loudly. Latin *ululare* (to howl) is traced to an IE root *ul* (to howl). יללה / YILÄLÄ is howling or wailing; ילל / YILÄL is the adjective "howling" in *Deuteronomy 32:10*. The verb איליה / ALĒLÄ occurs in *Micah 1:8*.

BRANCHES: הלל / HÄLÄL (praise!) and HALLELUJAH are antonymical interjections or joyful shouts. Official cognates of ULULANT and ULULATION are HOWL, OWL, OWLET and OWLISH. See "WAIL" and "YELL."

UNDU(LATION)/נָדַד
NAD–UD   [ND]

ROOTS: To UNDULATE is to move or cause to move in a wavelike motion; Latin *unda* means "wave." נד / NĀD is a mound or hill (*Isaiah 17:11*), an earthen "wave" if you will. נדד / NADAD is to shake or move. In *II Samuel 23:6* the verb means "driven about" or "agitated." One who has ridden the waves knows why נדנד / NĒDNĀD is to shake, rock or swing and why נדנדה / NADNĀDA is the term for rocking chair.

BRANCHES: Instead of an ND root of billowing and swaying, the AHD offers the IE root *wed* (water, wet). The immediate cognates of UNDULATE are ABOUND, INUNDATE, REDOUND, REDUNDANT, SURROUND and UNDINE.

Reversing the ND "wave" root, we get that sandy wave, the DUNE. DOWN, the direction, is from a term that meant "from the hill" or dune. If one prefers to link DOWN to the many ND Germanic words for "down"–see "MAT." DOWNS the topographical term (as in Suffolk Downs) is from the same DN hill word.

(UNI)CORN/קֶרֶן
KER–EN   [KRN]

ROOTS: Latin *cornu* means horn, as does קרן / KEREN ("horn"–*Deuteronomy 33:17*). The IE root *ker* means horn and head, as Greek *kranion* (skull) extends the sense of this term to various HORNY or hard aspects of the head or CRANIUM.

BRANCHES: Cognates include: ACORN, CAPRICORN, CARAT, CARROT, CEREBELLUM, CEREBRAL, CERVIX, CORN, CREST, GORE, HARD, HART, HORN, HORNET, KARYO-, KERNEL, KERATIN, KERATO-, MIGRAIN, REINDEER, RHINOCEROS, RINDEPEST, RUNT, and TRI*CERA*TOPS.

קרנא / KĀRNĀ is a musical horn in *Daniel 3:5*.

Other Hebrew KR terms that relate include קרם / KORUM (to form a crust), קרוש / KAR(OOSH) (congealed), גרם / GORUM (bone) and גלגלת / GOOL–GŌL–ET (skull).

KAROO (dry tableland) is from a Hottentot word for hard– *Karusa*.

CARIBOU might be the Algonquin KR equivalent of a *REINDEER* or HART. CARABAO (water buffalo) is from Malay *karbau*; Malay *kras* means hard, and *uruka* is head in related dialects. *Kiwi* means "horn of an animal" in Hawaiian. *Kurr-ân* is "hard" in Australian Aborigine. The Amazon Indian term *kran* (head) is anything but an amazing coincidence. קרקפת / KĀRKEPHET (head, skull) is an Aramaic combination of קר / KĀR (which should mean HORNY or HARD) plus קפת / KEPHET (head–see "CAPITAL").

The IE root *kar* (hard) gives us CANCER, CANKER, CARCINOGEN, CAREEN, CHANCRE, CARINA, CARYOTE, (DEMO)CRACY, GILLYFLOWER, HARD(Y), STANDARD and SYNKARON. Softening a bit to IE root *kal* (hard), we get CALLOSE, CALLOUS, CALLUS and EX*CALIBUR*. [S]CORN, from Old French *escorner* (to disgrace), is supposed to literally mean "to unhorn." The alternative to קרן / KRN for this etymology might be חרון / KHARŌN (anger). See "CORNER", "CORNONA", "CREAM" and "CROWN."

URGE/עֶרְגָה
ERR–GAH   [URGH]

ROOTS: URGE, URGENCY and URGENT involve pleading and a strong, impulsive need. The given etymon is Latin *urgere* (to urge, drive, press hard) and the hypothetical IE root is *wreg* (to push, shove, drive)–see "WRECK." ערג / ERGĀ is a longing and craving. ערג / ĀRUG is defined as "to long for, crave" and it is translated "cry for" and "pant after."

"As the hart panteth after the water brooks, so *panteth* my soul *after* Thee, O God."– *Psalms 42:2*

BRANCHES: The cognates of URGE at IE root *wreg* include GASKET, RACK, WRACK, WREAK, WRECK, and WRETCH.

The "entreaty" sense of URGE appears in the Latin *rogare* (to ask), whose RG offshoots include ABROGATE, ARROGANT, ARROGATE, DEROGATE, INTERROGATE, INTERROGATIVE, PREROGATIVE, SUBROGATE and SUPEREROGATE.

Words related to the Hebrew URGE should sound more compelling. ער / ĀR is aroused; עור / ŌR means skin; ערטל / ER(TĀL) is to strip naked; ערום / ĀRŌM is naked; ערוה / ERVĀ means genitals, pudenda or nakedness; and, reversing the ער two-letter root, רעב / RĀĀV is hungry or craving–see "RAVENOUS."

USE/עֲשִׂיָה
US–EE–AH   [USH]

ROOTS: USE is so confused with different meanings that no IE base or root could be concocted. As it is, the Latin "etymon" *usus*, a past perfect of *uti* (to use), doesn't fit most of the USAGES of USE.

Meaning #1 of USE is to employ. Middle Latin *usagium*, source of USAGE, leads us to העסיק / (HE')ESEK (to employ). עסק / ĀSĀK is to be busy or occupied, just as a machine can be IN USE. עסוק / ESOOK (occupation; business) is from Aramaic.

To USE judgement is to "do" the right thing or to "behave" properly. עשה / ĀSĀ is to do, act or behave (*Genesis 24:12* – "*deal* graciously") as well as to make or produce. עשיה / ĀSEYĀ is doing or acting.

To USE UP one's batteries recalls עשש / ĀS(H)ĀS(H) (to waste away– *Psalms 31:10*).

In law, USE can mean profit, benefit or advantage in a real estate context. עשק / ĀS(HĀK) is to extort and oppress financially (*Leviticus 19:13*); יתרון / YISRON means profit, gain, advantage and surplus– see "SURPASS."

BRANCHES: One can hear USURY (charging excessive interest) in those last two Hebrew words. Latin *usura* is linked to USE. Old French *ues* (gain) is cited at the "use" entry of *Webster's*. USANCE used to mean interest for the USE of money.

Some of the more USABLE cognates here include ABUSE, USEFUL, USER, USUAL(LY), USUFRUCT, USURIOUS, and USURP.

ABUSE is perhaps better traced to בוז / BOOZ (mockery, contempt); בזבוז / BEZBOOZ is squandering.

Because (B)USY and (B)USINESS are unique to one branch of Germanic, we could dismiss the initial B and consider the etymons above. *(B)ysig* and *(b)isig* (occupied) are the Anglo-Saxon forms of BUSY.

VAC[ATE]/בָּקַק
VUCK–UCK   [BK→VK]

ROOTS: Latin *vacare* is to be empty; *vacuus* means empty. בקעה / VIKÄ or BIKÄ is a valley (*Deuteronomy 11;11*); בקק / BOKÄK or VOKÄK is to empty (*Isaiah 24:1*); בוקק / BOKÄK or VOKÄK is empty; בוקה / BOOKÄ or VOOKA is emptiness and desolation (*Nahum 2:11*). A verb of *VACATING* and E*VACUATION* is seen in *Isaiah 19:3* –"And the spirit of Egypt shall be *made empty. . ."* – ונבקה / (VENI)V'KÄ. Aramaic בוק / BOOK and Hebrew בקבק / BÄKBOOK (*I Kings 14:3*) is a jar, cruse, bottle, etc. – see "BEAKER" and "BUCKET."

> **BRANCHES:** The given IE root is *eu* (lacking, empty). Cognates of VACATE at IE root *eu* include EVACUATE, VACANT, VACATE, VACATION, (VACUITY), VACUUM, VAIN, VANISH, VANITY, VAUNT, VOID; (AVOID), (DEVOID), WANE, WANT and WASTE. The VN words above should derive from a VN Hebrew etymon and are seen at "VAIN." The cognate list would have been less VACUOUS if it considered Grimm's Law variations of BK emptiness to include words like BAG, BOX, POCK(ET), POKE(Y), VAGINATE (like a sheath) and WAKE (the valley or water-groove that follows a ship).
>
> *Fa(n)ga* is a valley or gulch in Proto-Polynesian. See "GIBBEN" for antonyms that reverse BK or BG.
>
> Variants of the Hebrew root include בועה / BOOKHÄ (bubble), פגר / POGÄR (empty of energy, exhausted – *I Samuel 30:21*) and פגרה / PÄGRÄ (Aramaic term for free time or a VACATION). These last two terms may help form a better etymon for VAGABOND, VAGARY, VAGRANCY and VAGUE.
>
> Reverse the BK root for the many holes seen at "CAVITY." *Ipuka* in Hawaiian is a hole in the wall for air or light. A Chinese dimple is a *wa ch'u.*

VAIN/אָוֶן
OVEN   [AVN]

ROOTS: VAIN, VANITY and VANISH are from Latin *vanus* (empty) and the IE root *eu* (lacking, empty).

1) און / AVEN is "nothingness" or vanity in *Isaiah 41:29*.

2) פנוי / PÄNOOY or PHÄNOOY means empty, unoccupied. פנה / PENÄ or PHENÄ is to empty or clear away – *Genesis 24:31*. To WANE and VANISH recall פנה / PHÄNÄ (to turn from, to "decline" (JPS) or "to go away" (King James Version) – *Jeremiah 6:4*.

VAMOOSE, from Spanish *vamos* (let us go) favors the "going away" translation. FINISH and (the anatomical) FIN are similar because they mean an end in time or an extremity in space, and because they derive form פנה / PHÄNÄ and פנה / PENÄ or FENÄ (a corner).

A FAINEANT (idler) has פנאי / PINI or PHINI (leisure, free time).

> **BRANCHES:** Cognates of VAIN at IE root *eu* are listed at "VACATE." Cognates of FINISH include FINAL(E) and FINANCE. Accounts are ended, completed and cleared away just as שלם /SH–L–M can mean completion or payment.
>
> *Hopena* is final in Hawaiian. In Chinese, *wan* is finished and *wǎng* is "in vain." *Wahng* means free, at leisure or vacant in Thai.

VAN[DYKE]/בֶּן
VEN   [BH–N]

ROOTS: A VANDYKE, can refer to a collar, a beard or a shade of brown used by Anthony Van Dyck. The VAN in Rip VAN Winkle or in President Martin VAN Buren is a Dutch term meaning "of" or "from." בן / BAN or VAN means offspring (*Leviticus 4:3*), son or branch (i.e. a derivative). Just as VAN indicates place of origin in Dutch names, a בן ירושלים / BHEN YEROOSHÄLIEM is a citizen *of* Jerusalem.

> **BRANCHES:** A בן–אבות / BHEN – ÄVOS (Aramaic) is a man "*of* good ancestry." A בן בית / BHEN – BAYIS is "*from* home," a homeboy or intimate friend. A בן–זוג / BHEN ZOOG is a partner, spouse or, literally, "*from* a couple."
>
> "From" in Dutch (*van*) shifts to *von* in German and *fun* in Yiddish. Variants of בן / BAN (son, child) include *abinō-dji* (child in Chippewa Indian), *panik* (daughter in Eskimo) and *wana* (child in Malay).
>
> One builds, בנה / BNH, with children; בנין / BIN[YAN] is a building. *Bahn* is a house in Thai; *bygning* is a building in Danish and Norwegian. The Scottish equivalent of VAN is MAC or MC, from a term meaning "son." MAC, like NIECE (now traced to Latin *neptis*), may derive from נכד / NEKH[ED], a Biblical term for descendant.

VAT/חָבִית
(HA)VEET   [(H)VT]

ROOTS: A VAT is a large tank tub or cask. Anglo-Saxon *faet* (cask, vessel) is thought to derive from the IE base *ped* or *pod* (to seize, hold) and linked to German *fassen* (to hold, grasp). The given IE root is *ped* (container). חבית / HÄVET or [HA]BET is a barrel or cask (Aramaic).

> **BRANCHES:** The BH–T element may be behind BODY (originally a cask term), BOTTLE, POT and (reversing BH–T) TUB. Cognates of VAT at *ped* include FETTLE and FRITTER. The KH–B first element of חבית / KHÄBH[ET] relates to החביא / (HE)KHEBE (to hide, cover – see "COVER") and חביונה / KHEBHYONÄ (small barrel, cask). The Latin vat, *cupa*, relates here; COWL is traced to *cupa*.
>
> A HOPPER is a tank for liquid; reverse to *pahu* for the Hawaiian barrel. Japanese *chibusa* (woman's breast) is not related to חבית / KHÄBES (jug) as much as to חב / KHOBH (bosom – *Job 31:33*).

VEER/עָבַר
AH–VORE   [AVR]

ROOTS: French *virer* is to turn around. VEER means to change directions or sides. עבר / OVÄR is to pass over from one עבר / ÄVER (side) to another. In *I Samuel 14:4* "Jonathan sought *to go over* unto the Philistine's garrison"– עבר / ÄVOR.

> **BRANCHES:** VEERING from the straight path morally is an עברה / ÄVARÄ (sin). EN*VIRONS* and EN*VIRONMENT* are related. The AHD lists words like FAR, FURTHER, PARA[DISE], PER- and PERI- as cognates of VEER. See "ABERRATION," "FERRY" and "OVER."

VENT(RICLE)/בֶּטֶן
VET–EN   [B(H)–T–N→VNT]

ROOTS: Latin *venter* is the belly. The given IE root is *udero*, as the root doctors magically link the VENTER (womb) to the uterus by way of "taboo deformation." בטן / BETEN or VETEN means womb (*Genesis 30:2*), belly, bowels or "bulge" (in a non-anatomical usage in *I Kings 7:20*). בטבט / BHUTBHAT is to swell.

The VNT of VENTER (abdomen, belly or womb) is simply a #2-#3 letter swap of the Hebrew VTN. VENTRAL, VENTRICLE, VENTRICOSE and VENTRILOQUISM (speaking from the belly) are all cognates.

BRANCHES: Latin A*BDOMEN*, minus the "en" ending, is a slightly disguised בטן / BEDTEN. The PUDEN(DUM) may be an extension of בטן / B–DT–N too, while פה / POT (secret parts) could also have been an influence. Scottish *pud* (belly) gave us the bulge-belly adjective PUDGY.

Shifting over to the T–N(M) second element, we find the often TUMID (bulging) TUMMY. The scholars who consider the Swahili stomach (*tumbo*) irrelevant, have dismissed TUMMY as "a child's word." Latin *tumere* (to swell, bulge) has also given us TUMEFACTION, TUMEFY, TUMESCENCE, TUMIDITY and TUMOR. Antonyms at "SMASH." *Tum* is a belly for the Amazon Indians as well. *Wutan* is a belly in Javanese (Malay). Woman is a womb-man in many cultures. *Wanita* is a woman in Indonesian; a wife is a *watan* for the Maya Indians. See "WOMAN." For SM growth words see "SUMAC."

VES(T)/לְבוּשׁ
(LI)VOOS(H)   [(L)–V–S(H)]

ROOTS: Latin *vestire* is to clothe. The IE root drops the unhistoric T, as *wes-* is to clothe. בוש / BOSH or VOS(H) is to be ashamed (or ABASHED), and clothes are ל / LI (for) the בושה / BOOSHA (shame) of nakedness – see "ABASH."

לבוש / (LI)VOOS(H) is "clothing" in *Job 24:7* and "apparel" in *Esther 6:8* . The verb לבש / [L]VS "to clothe" appears first in *Genesis 3:21*, where God sets a precedent in clothing the naked.

BRANCHES: Cognates of VEST at IE root *wes* include DEVEST, INVEST, REVEST, TRAVESTY and WEAR. VESTED, VESTEE, VESTIARY, VESTING, VESTMENT, VESTRY (perhaps VESTIBULE, like VESTRY, is a room to put clothes on), and VESTURE are also related.

The IE root *bhoso* (naked) links up with the BASHFUL, clothes-less sense development discussed above. The root is also a fine antonym for its echo of בשר / BAS[AR] (flesh). Derivatives of this root are BARE and BALLAST. פשט / PASHAT (to remove, as clothes) is an antonym of the VS clothes root as well. Dress is *elbise* in Turkish. Change the L to R and the Turkish derivative of לבוש / LIBHOOSH will resemble Russian and French clothes words like *rubashka* and *robe*. The French term gives us BATHROBE, DISROBE and ROBE.

VET(ERAN)/וָתִיק
VUT(EEK)   [VT[K]]

ROOTS: VETERAN is from Latin *vetus* or *veteris* (old) and the IE root *wet* (year).

ותיק / VATEK means VETERAN, long-time or steady. The word is non-Biblical, but Semitic, occuring in *Ben Sira 36:20* and the *Talmud*.

BRANCHES: עתי / ETE also means steady, periodic, ready or usual. Like עתון / ETON (periodical, newspaper), it is from עת / AT (time). עת / AT means season in *Leviticus 26:4*, and year in *Genesis 18:14*.

Greek *etos* is a year, whence ETESIAN – a cognate of VETERAN. (VT=ET). The many Hebrew ע to English B, V, W permutations recall the familiar U=V formula; note the similarity between Latin *vit[ulus] [yearling]* and Greek *et[os]* (year).

ותיק / VAT(EK) and עת / AT are closely related because a VETERAN is seasoned.

Cognates of VETERAN at IE root *wet* include ETESIAN, INVETERATE, VEAL, VETERINARY and VITELLUS.

VATIC (prophet) and VATICAN may be more closely related to words like בטה /BATA or VATAH (to utter words).

"Year" in Finnish is *vousi*. The Russian ע is pronounced the guttural way, so that their עת (year) is not AS or AT but *got*. עתיק / ATEEK means ancient (*1 Chronicles 4:22*). –See "ANTIQUE."

VETO/בטל
VEET–(ALE)   [BH–T–(L)]

ROOTS: VETO is said to be from Latin *vetare* (to forbid). VETO shares most of the meanings of בטל / BATAL or VATAL (to stop – *Ecclesiastes 12:3*) and בטל / BETAL or VETAL (to suspend, abolish, cancel).

BRANCHES: Like VETO, VOID and VITIATE (to legally invalidate), בטל / BH–T–L is largely a legal term. See "VOTE" for antonyms. ABATE may derive from the sense of stopping here.

We may have to VETO or VOID blurted promises or lies. התבדה / (HET)BADTA is to be caught lying or to come to nothing. בטה / BATA is to speak rashly. The unknown source of BLOT (to cancel or erase) might be בטל / BTL with a #2-#3 letter swap. See "BAD."

VIA/בָּה
VAH   [BH–H]

ROOTS: The Latin *via* means a way; בא / BA is to come or enter. The two words part ways, so that VIATORS are wayfarers in English and באים / BA(IM) are those who have arrived in Hebrew.

ובה / (OO)VA (ADA) is translated "*thereby* shall I know" in *Genesis 24:14*, but it might also be rendered "by way of this shall I know." בו / BO also means "by," "of," or "by means of."

BRANCHES: Beside the many BY and WAY words and phrases, English retains Latinate terms like VIA, MEDIA and VIATICUM.

An extension of בוא / VO or BO is הביא / HA–VE (to bring in, lead in). This could lead us to the IE root *wegh* (to draw, to go). Some of the many English words cognate to VIA via this root include: ALWAYS, AWAY, CONVEX, DEVIOUS, ENVOY, FOY, HEAVE, INVEIGH, OBVIOUS, PREVIOUS, TRIVIA, VECTOR, VEHICLE, VEX, VOGUE, VOYAGE, WAG, WAGON, WAIN, WAVE, WEIGH and WIGGLE. Another cognate is CONVEY; Cain and Abel CONVEY or "bring" offerings to God in *Genesis 4:3,4* –(ו)יבא / (VAYA)VA, (ה)ביא / (HA)VE.

VIDEO/נבט
(NA)–VADT [BH–T→VD]

ROOTS: Latin *videre* and the IE root *weid* both mean "to see." הבט / (HÄ)BEDT or (HÄ)VEDT means "look!" (*Genesis 15:5*); הביט / (HĒ)BÈDT is to look; the three-letter root is נבט / NAVADT; and נבט / (NĒ)BÄDT is to have a vision (*Isaiah 5:30*). The two-letter root reduces to בט / BH –T or VD.

BRANCHES: Cognates of VIDE and VIDEO at IE root *weid* include TWIT, GUIDE, WITE, WISE, WISDOM, WISEACRE, DISGUISE, GUISE, EIDETIC, EIDOLON, IDOL, IDYLL, -OID, KALEIDOSCOPE, HADAL, HADES, WIT, UNWITTING, WITTY, IWIS, VIEW, VISA, VISAGE, VISION, VISTA, VOYEUR, ADVICE, ADVISE, BELVEDERE, CLAIRVOYANCE, ENVY, EVIDENCE, EVIDENT, INTERVIEW, PREVISE, PROVIDE, REVIEW, SUPERVISE, SURVEY, and VEDA.
מבט / [MA]BAT is expectation or hope (*Isaiah 20:5*). Add BUDDHISM, WAIT, WATCH and WI*T*NESS to the cognate list. *Wits* is an eye in Maya. In Polish, *widok* means sight or view; *widz* is a spectator and *zwiedzac* is to visit, see or tour.

VILE/נבל
(NAH)VULL [(N)VL]

ROOTS: VILE is said to come from Old French *vil* and Latin *vilis* (cheap, base). There is no IE root available for VILE (wicked, sinful, depraved), but the vile VILLAIN is traced to Latin *villa* (farm) and the IE root *weik* (clan).
Isaiah 32:5 is rendered, "The VILE person shall no more be called liberal" or "no more shall a VILLAIN be called noble." The words "vile" and "villain" here are translations of נבל / (NÄ)VÄL.

BRANCHES: The cheap and base sense of Latin *vilis* may derive form בלוי / BÄLOOY (shabby) and בלה / BÄLÄ (worn out; decay). Both BL words may be read VL. FOUL, FILTH and DEFILE are linked to Old English *ful* (unclean, rotten). נול / NĒVÄL is to disfigure or make ugly. מנול / (MINOO)VÄL is repulsive or despicable, perhaps why MANAVELINS is a nautical term for leftovers. MANAVELINS also means to steal ("origin unknown"), and VILLAINY is the dominant theme in Hebrew VL terms. עול / ÄVEL means injustice or wrong – see "EVIL" and "iniquity" in *Deuteronomy 32:4*.
To VILIFY (use abusive language) is a verbal evil. נבול פה / (NĒ)*VOOL* PEH means lascivious speech, obscenity, or, literally, "VILE-mouthed." תפלה / (TI)PHLÄ also means unsavoriness and obscenity. See "PALL" for the color of VILE.

VINE/גפן
(GE)FEN [(G)–PH–N→VN]

ROOTS: Latin *vinea* (vine) is related to Greek *oine* (vine). The IE root is *vinum* (wine). The AHD adds, "Latin noun, related to Greek *oinos* (wine). Probably from a

Mediterranean word *win* or *woin* meaning 'wine.' " The "Mediterranean" is the closest some Western scholars can get to admitting that a word is Semitic. The WINE term behind Greek *oin* words is יין / YÄYIN or IIN (wine – *Genesis 9:21*). The Biblical Hebrew VINE is גפן / (GE)PHEN or (GE)FEN – *Deuteronomy 8:8*.

BRANCHES: Cognates of VINE at IE root *vinum* include OENOLOGY, OENOMEL, VINACEOUS, VINEGAR, VINI- and WINE. Reverse the FN or VN for ענב / ÄNÄV (grape, berry) and ענף / ÄNÄF (branch, bough). Also relevant to the VN of VINE are בן / BÄN (branch) and אפון / ÄPHOON (pea – a possible FN relative of the BEAN and of *VAN*ILLA). Spanish *vaina* is the podlike capsule of the VAN(ILLA) BEAN.
The "grape" or "bean" of the sea is the oyster's pearl. פנינה / PINĒNÄ (pearl – *Laments 4:7* ; *Proverbs 8:11*) is strikingly like the Samoan pearl, *penina*.
Old English *ifig*, source of IVY, may be a reversal of the GF in גפן / GFN. (*Tao)wahn* is a vine in Thai. Gaelic wine is *fion*. See "PANIC" for another פנ / PN or FN botanical term.

VIR(ILE)/גבר
(GE)VER [(G)VR]

ROOTS: Latin *vir* is a man; the IE root is *wiro* (man). גבר / (GE)VER is a man, as in "gird up thy loins like a *man*" (*Job 38:3*). גברי / (G)ÄVRĒ means male-like or manly; גבורה / (G')VOORÄ is strength, might or heroism. גביר / (G)VĒR is a lord or master.

BRANCHES: גבר / (GÄ)VÄR is to be strong or to conquer. CABALLERO (a Spanish gentleman or knight) and CAVALIER may be related, as גבר / (G)EVER also means a warrior. Various nuances of CAVALIER (haughty, carefree, gallant) appear in the Hawaiian גבור / GĒBOR (hero). *Kupu'eu* means hero, wondrous one, scamp and rascal.
Cognates of VIRILE at IE root *wiro* include LOUP-GAROU, TRIUMVIRATE, VIRAGO, VIRTUE, VIRTUOSO, WEREWOLF, WERGELD and WORLD. See "BARON."

VIV(ID)/אביב
A–VEEV [AVV]

ROOTS: VIVID (animated, lifelike) is traced to Latin *vivus* (living, alive) and the IE root *g(w)ei* (to live).
VIVACIOUS (animated, sprightly) is a match for אביבי / AVĒVĒ (spring-like) as אביב / AVĒV means the springtime (*Exodus 13:4*) and botanical VIVIFICATION (*Exodus 9:31*; *Leviticus 2:14*).

BRANCHES: אב / ÄV means greenness or freshness in Hebrew. One life-giver is the אב / AV (father) – see "ABBOT." A deathly AV antonym is אבד / AVAD (perished) – see "OBITUARY." Given cognates of VIVID include AEROBIC, AMPHIBIOUS, BIO-, CONVIVIAL, MICROBE, REVIVE, SURVIVE, VIABLE, VIAND, VICTUAL, VITAL, VITAMIN, VIVA and VIVI.
VIVIAN, a name which long predated the modern Tel-Aviv (hill of spring), celebrates the spring-like qualities of like – not merely life as the absence of death.

VOC(ALIZE)/בכה
VOKH – EH   [BH – KH→VC]

ROOTS: Latin *vocare* is to call (cry out); the hypothetical IE root is *wek-w* (to speak).

בכה / BŌKHE or VŌKHE is to be crying; baby Moses is VOCALIZING in *Exodus 2:6*. The term is often translated "wept," as though tears were the issue rather than audible crying.

Verses like *Genesis 27:38* make it clear that בכה / BĀKHÄ (to cry) is an exercise of the VOICE, not of the tear ducts: "Esau lifted up his voice and *wept*."

> **BRANCHES:** הביע / (HĒ)BĒÄ or (HĒ)BĒKHÄ is to utter, express – *Psalms 78:2*. נבח / (NÄ)VÄKH is to bark. שוע / (SHE)VAKH is a cry for help (*Psalms 5:3*). התופח / (HĒTVÄ)PÄKH is to cry out bitterly; פעה / PÄKHÄ is to groan, cry or bleat (*Isaiah 42:14*).
> Cognates of VOCAL at IE root *wek(w)* include ADVOCATE, AVOCATION, CALLIOPE, CONVOKE, EPIC, EPOS, EQUIVOCAL, EVOKE, INVOKE, PROVOKE, REVOKE, UNIVOCAL, VOCABLE, VOCATION, VOICE, VOUCH and VOWEL.
> A בקשה / BÄKÄSHÄ (request) is another BK vocal term. To cry in Latin is *vagire*, in Serbo-Croatian *vik(ati)*, and in Turkish *bag(irmak)*.

VOTE/עבט
AH – VOTE   [(U)VT]

ROOTS: Latin *votum* is a vow; the given IE root is *wegh(w)h* ("to preach or speak solemnly").

The Hebrew עבט / ÄVOT (to give or take a pledge – *Deuteronomy 24:10*) returns us to the Latin vow or promise. A VOTIVE is "given or dedicated in fulfillment of a vow or pledge." עבוט / ÄVOT (pledge) is the noun form.

> **BRANCHES:** הבטחה / (HÄ)V'TÄHÄ (promise, assurance) and בטח / VETÄH (security) are closely related – see "AFFIDAVIT," "BET," "FAITH" and "WED." Cognates of VOTE at IE root *weg(w)h* include DEVOTE, (DEVOUT), VOTARY, (VOTIVE) and VOW
> See "VETO" for antonyms.

WAIL/אבל
AH – VAIL   [A – BH – L→WL]

ROOTS: Old Norse *vala* is to lament; the IE root is *wai* (alas!).

The IE root is covered by אבו / ÄVO (WOE! alas! – *Proverbs 23:29* – see "WOE"). WAIL is matched with אבל / ÄVĀL (mournful), אבל / AVEL (mourning, sorrow) and התאבל / (HĒTÄ)BÄL (to mourn, lament). The *Hebrew English Lexicon of the Bible* translates the term to mean "grief, howling."

> **BRANCHES:** The familiar אוי / OY can be read as AVI or AWY. Cognates of WAIL at IE root *wai* include WELLAWAY and WOE. HOWL and OWL may ultimately link up – see "ULULATION."

(W)ALK/הלך
(HAW) – LUKH   [(H) – L – KH]

ROOTS: WALK is said to come from Anglo-Saxon *wealcan* (to roll, journey); the IE base is *walg*. The IE root is *wel* (to roll).

For the BH – L rolling terms see בלל / BÄLÄL (to ball up, mix up, roll together) at "BALL." Humans wiggle but do not roll when they walk, so return to the IE base *walg*. Several times here we have seen a W derive from a Hebrew ר / R. Now switch the #2 and #3 letters of the IE base *walg* and WLG can be rearranged as R – G – L. רגל / REGÄL is a LEG (*Leviticus 11:42*), but "legging it," walking, touring and spying out an area is the sense of רגל / RĒGÄL in *Joshua 6:25* and elsewhere. WGL or (W)RGL also recalls the WIGGLE in our WALK.

Rather than the WL beginning of WALK, see the LK second element as more significant. לך / LÄKH means "go!" (*Genesis 12:1*). הלך / HOLÄKH (to walk) and four variants of the LK "going" root appear in *Judges 4:8*.

> **BRANCHES:** דרך / DÄRÄKH is to tread; דלג / DOLÄG is to skip or jump; גלגול / GĒLGOOL is rolling, revolving. An LG two letter root emerges here, giving WALK many a Hebrew LEG to stand on. עלה / ÄLÄ (to go, go up – see "ALLEY") can be read GL (L – G reversed). An L→R change can also recall Latin *ire* (to go).
> Latin *gradi* (to step, walk) reverses דרך / D – R – KH above. Chinese *li kai* is to leave or depart; Fijian *lako* means go; Maidu Indian *wilek* and *ylek* mean going fast; Malay *laka* is to go; and Japanese *aruku* is to walk. More RK traveling at "DIRECTION."

WALLOW/בלל
VOLL – ULL   [VLL]

ROOTS: Old English *wealwian* is to roll (in mud); the IE root is *wel* (to turn, roll).

בלל / BÄLÄL or VÄLÄL is to mix, confuse, stir or knead (*Genesis 11:9*). בליל / BILĒL or VILĒL is a mixture. See "BALL."

> **BRANCHES:** Cognates of WALLOW at IE root *wel* include DEVOLVE, EVOLVE, HELIX, INVOLVE, OBVOLUTE, REVOLVE, VALLEY, VALVE, VAULT, (VOLT), VOLUBLE, VOLUME, VOLUTE, VOLUTIN, VOLVOX, VOUSSOIR, WALK, WALTZ, WELL and WELTER.

WAND(ER)/נוד
NOWD   [NWD→WND]

ROOTS: WANDER is from Anglo-Saxon *wandrian* and the IE root is *wendh* (to turn, wind, weave).

Because Cain couldn't share half a world with his brother he was cursed to be a landless WANDERER or נוד / NÄVÄD or NÄWÄD (a mere #1-#2 letter swap away) from WND. נוד / NOD, NVD or NWD is wandering (*Genesis 4:12*), and is the official Hebrew root.

> **BRANCHES:** A WN or PN turning word that may link up with WINDING or WENT is פנה / PANA (turn oneself to go away – see "POINT"). Cognates of WANDER at IE root *wendh* include VANDAL, WAND, WANDER, WANDERLUST, WENTLETRAP, WIND, and WINDLASS.
> ANDANTE (moderately slow) is from Italian *andare* (to walk). *Enda* is to go in Swahili. These two terms help one dismiss or move the W of WANDER and WEND. נדד / NÄDÄD is to wander about, to flee, to shake (whence NOD), and to move. See "NOD."

WEAK/רַךְ
W(R)AKH   [R–KH→WK]

ROOTS: The AHD's IE root, *weik* (to bend, wind), is linked to Old Norse *vikja* (to bend). German *weich* (tender) is the etymon cited by *Webster's*.

1)Not VK but KV or כפף / KOFAF is to bend (*Isaiah 58:5*).

2) רך / RÄKH or WÄKH (with an R→W change seen several times here) means "soft" or "tender" or "weak" as different Bible translators picture Leah's eyes in *Genesis 29:17*. The term implies weak-(hearted) or faint-(hearted) in *Deuteronomy 20:8*; in *Deuteronomy 28:54* רך / RÄKH or WÄKH is "tender." The ר / R to L shift explains why Finnish *lauha* means mild, gentle and soft.

> **BRANCHES:** Cognates of WEAK at IE root *weik* include VETCH, VICAR, (VICARIOUS), VICE, VICISSITUDE, WEAKFISH, WEEK, WICKER and WYCH ELM. An extension of רך / R–KH might be מרך / MŌREKH ("faintness"–*Leviticus 26:36*). Also defined "cowardice" and "timidity," מרך / M–R–KH might link up with IE root *mera* (to delay). DEMUR, MORATORIUM, MORATORY and REMORA are all traced to Latin *morari* (to delay). מרי / MIRĒ (obstinate, resistant) might also be influencing the words attributed to the IE root *mera*.

WED/וַדאי
VUD–(EYE)   [VD→WD]

ROOTS: Latin *vadis* is a pledge; the IE root *wadh* is a pledge or to pledge.

עבט / ÄVŌT or ÄWŌD(T) is a noun and verb of pledging (*Deuteronomy 24:10*). Better still for the sense of a WEDDING, יעוד / YEOOD or YĒWOOD is a betrothal (*Exodus 21:8, 9*).

For the caption there is a non-Biblical relative of these words, ודאי / VÄDĪ or WÄDĪ (certainly), because it needs little sound change, because it is common among Hebrew speakers, and because it is more likely to encourage marriage than the source of BET. See "AFFIDAVIT," "BET," "FAITH" and "VOTE."

> **BRANCHES:** Cognates of WED at IE root *wadh* include DEGAGE, ENGAGE, GAGE, MORTGAGE, PRAEDIAL, WAGE, WAGER and WEDLOCK.

WEED/בַד
VUD   [BH–D]

ROOTS: Old English *wæd* is a garment or cloth; Old High German *wat* is a linen term; and the IE root *au* is to weave. These terms are cited as the background of WEED (clothing; widow's mourning clothes). בד / BHUD, VUD or WUD is the linen clothes of the priest in *Leviticus 16:4*. See "BATISTE."

> **BRANCHES:** Cognates of WEED at IE root *au* include WATTLE. The botanical WEED may derive from נבט / [NE]VEDT

(sprout–see "BOTANY"). WEED might also link up with בד / BUD or WUD (limb of a tree – *Exodus 25:13*). בדל / BODÄL or WOD(ÄL) is to separate or WEED OUT. See "BAT," "BUT," and "DIVIDED."

WELT/יבלת
(YA)BEL–ET   [YBLT→WLT]

ROOTS:WELT is "probably from the base of *wealtan* (to roll) or the base of English *wale* (ridge)." Old English *walu* (streak on the skin, WEAL, WELT or WALE) is cited at IE root *wel* (to turn, roll). See "BALL" for a BL Hebrew etymon of rolling or turning.

יבלת / (YÄ)BELET or (YÄ)WELET is a small lump or growth on the skin, such as a WART, WELT or BLIST(ER) – see *Leviticus 22:22*. בלט / BÄLÄT or WÄLÄT is to stand out or protrude.

> **BRANCHES:** An IE root only an L→R change away is *wer* (high, raised spot). It includes VARICOSE and VERRUCA; (Latin *verruca* is a WART). See "BLISTER" and "VAULT."
>
> All raised marks on the skin involve bodily FLUIDS such as pus or BLOOD. These FLD and BLD terms relate to WELT (WLT) as words of flowing (rather than rolling or turning). יבלת / [YA]BELET is therefore defined as an issue, not merely a bump. יבל / [YA]VAL is a stream, יבל / [YA]VUL is to carry or bring, מבול / [MA]BOOL is a flood and אבל / OOVAL is a river or canal (*Daniel 8:2*). The BL or VL root recalls words like BEAR, BLOOD, BORNE, FLOAT, FLOOD, FLOW and WELL [a watery cognate of WALTZ and WELTER at IE root *wel* (to turn, roll)]. For a PL flowing root see "ARCHIPELAGO."

WET/רָטֹב
W(R)ATT–OVE   [RT(V)→WT]

ROOTS: Anglo-Saxon *waet* is traced to the IE root *wed* (water, wet).

רטב / RÄTŌV or W(R)ÄT(ŌV) means moist or wet, especially like the moisture of "green" plants (*Job 8:16*). The Rt root recalls the IE base *lat* (wet), the source of LATEX, which likewise refers to the moisture of plants. The common R→L change is not needed for another Hebrew word of moistening and dampening – לחת / LÄTÄT.

> **BRANCHES:** Reversing the TV element of רטב / RTV will also resemble WET. Hebrew rain words like טל / TÄL (dew) and מטר / MÄTÄR (rain) prefer the RT or LT element. Cognates of WET at IE root *wed* include DROPSY, HYDATHODE, HYDRA, HYDRANT, HYDRO, (HYDROUS), NUTRIA, OTTER, VODKA, WASH, WATER and WINTER.
>
> The WET WATER of green plants is dripping with VERDURE and green words like VERDIGRIS, VERDITER and VERT. To get *vert* (green in French) take the third letter of רטב / RTV and flip it to the front of the word. See an appendix for more #3–#1 flips. The IE root *virere* (green . . . Latin verb of unknown origin) includes BILIVERDIN, TERRE–VERTE, VERDANT, VIRESCENT and VIRID.
>
> And what happened to the standard Hebrew water word – מים / MÄYEM or MÄEM? For example, there is *mom* (water) in Maidu Indian, and *nahm* (water) in Thai. Native Floridians named the MIAMI RIVER for a term that means drinkable water.

(W)HEAT/חִטָּה
HEAT–AH   [H–T–H]

ROOTS: Traced to *kweit* (white), the IE root for WHEAT retains the guttural of the Hebrew etymon. "For the Lord brings you to a good land...a land of *wheat* and barley...." חטה / HETÄ or KHEETÄ – *Deuteronomy 8:8.*

    BRANCHES: WHITE and WHITING are cognates of WHEAT under the same IE root *kweit* (white; to shine).

WHEN/בְּן
BHEEN   [BN→WN]

ROOTS: Old English *hwanne* (when) is traced to the widely inclusive IE root *kwo* (stem of relative and interrogative pronouns) – see "WHO."
    One sense of WHEN is echoed in בֶּן-לילה / BĒN or BHĒN LÄYLÄ (*during* the night – *Jonah 4:10*). בין / BĀN or VĀN is also defined as "during."

(W)HO/הוּא
WHO   [HVO]

ROOTS: Germanic *hwa* and *hwi* gave us personal pronouns like WHO, WHOSE and WHOM.
    הוא / HOO and היא / HĒ are also personal pronouns that connect subject to predicate. They are translated as "he," "she," "it," "this" and "the same," but "who" is a smoother rendition for the הוא / HOO (he) in verses like *Genesis 4:20, 21.*

    BRANCHES: EITHER, HOW, NEITHER, WHAT, WHEN, WHENCE, WHITHER, WHERE and WHETHER are considered cognates of WHO at the IE roots *kwo* and *kwi* (stems of relative and interrogative pronouns). See "HE" and "WHEN."

WOE/אֲבוֹ
(AH)–VOE   [A–BH–O]

ROOTS: WOE and WOES are traced to the IE root *wai* (alas! – interjection). אבו / ABHO or AVO is the precise equivalent – *Proverbs 23:29* .

    BRANCHES: The listed cognates of WOE at IE root *wai* are WAIL and WELLAWAY. Alas! in Chinese is *wu*. See "WAIL."

WOM(AN)/רֶחֶם
W(R)EH–HEM   [RHM→WM]

ROOTS: The only etymology offered for WOMAN is Anglo-Saxon *wif* (female) + *mann* (a human being, man).

רחם / WREHEM can mean a woman or "damsel"(*Judges 5:30*). Elsewhere, רחם / W(R)EHEM means *WOM*(B) (*Genesis 29:31*).

    BRANCHES: *Webster's* links Latin *venter* (belly) to "womb" via the IE base *wend-ri*. If they are right, WOM(B), too, is from בטן / BEDTEN (belly, womb – see "VENTRICLE") Otherwise, the German *wamme* (womb) points to רחם / W(R)ÄHÄM (womb – *Genesis 49:25*). See "CLEMENCY."

(W)ORM/רְמָה
REAM–AH   [RMH]

ROOTS: Latin *vermis* (worm) is traced to IE root *wer* (to turn, bend).
    רמה / REMÄ or WRĒMÄ is a (W)ORM (*Isaiah 14:11*). רמש / ROMÄS is to creep or crawl; Aramaic רמשא / RÄMSÄ is evening. These add up to the fact that worms are night crawlers.

    BRANCHES: The Sanscrit worm is *krmi*. Cognates of this term at the IE root *kwrmi* are CRIMSON and KERMES.
    Another Biblical worm (also in *Isaiah 14:11*) is the תולעה / TŌLÄÄH or SŌLÄKHA. This worm and cloth term may provide the source of SILK. Cognates of WORM at IE root *wer* include VERMEIL, VERMI, and VERMIN. For the opposite of the lowly worm, see "RUM."

WRA(TH)/עֶבְרָה
(E)VRAH   [VR]

ROOTS: WRATH (raging anger) is from Anglo-Saxon *wraeth* and the IE root *wer* (to turn, bend). עברה / (E)VRÄH is translated "wrath" in *Isaiah 14:6.*

    BRANCHES: WROTH is an official cognate; an FR term like FURY should ultimately link up through the burning mad terms seen at "BURN."

WRECK/הִבְרִיחַ
[HE]–VREE–AKH   [V–R–KH→WRK]

ROOTS: To WRECK is to demolish, recalling BRK breaking words like פרך / PARAKH (to crush, demolish – Aramaic; *Exodus 1:13*) – see "BREAK." Historically, however, WRECK is linked to breaking away, fleeing and expelling. WRECK and WREAK are traced to Old Norse *vrek*, Germanic *wrakjon* (pursuer, one pursued) and Old English *wrecan* (to drive, expel).
    הבריח / [HE]VREEAKH is to cause to flee or "put to flight" (*I Chronicles 8:13*). ברח / B–R–KH is to flee (*Genesis 31:22*). בריח / BAREEAKH (a fugitive) is echoed by Frankish *wrakjo* (an exile).

    BRANCHES: Listed cognates of WRECK include URGE (see "URGE"), WRACK and WRETCH. FLIGHT (FLG), FUGITIVE (from FGR etymons), and פרח / PARAKH (to fly) are more distantly related.

WRO[N]G/רַע
RVG   [RG→WR–G]

ROOTS: WRONG is said to derive from Old Norse *rangr* (crooked, wrong) and the IE root *wer* (to turn, bend).

WRONG may be a nasalized רע / RA, WRUG or RUG (translated "bad" or "evil," although the tree in *Genesis 2:17* is better rendered "the tree of the knowledge of right and *wrong.*"

> **BRANCHES:** A BRK(→WRG) bending term is ברך / BEREKH (knee).
> See "BREAK" and "FREAK."

XENO(PHOBIA)/שׂונֵא
SONE–AY   [S(H)–N–H]

ROOTS: XENOPHOBIA is a fear or hatred of strangers or foreigners, (a major reason why a universal dictionary wasn't compiled centuries ago). Greek *xenos* (also the given IE root) means strange or foreign.

שׂנה / S(H)ÄNÄ is to change or be different. שׂני / S(H)ÄNÉ is a second, an "other." שׂנא / SÄNÄ is to hate; שׂונֵא / SONÄ is a foe or enemy – *Proverbs 25:21.* Leah was not "hated," שׂנואה / SNOOÄ (*Genesis 29:33*), as much as feeling second-best and thus estranged. The SN theme of being different, strange and hated emerges from all these terms.

> **BRANCHES:** Strange cognates of XENO- at IE root *xenos* include EUXENITE, PYROXENE and XENON. The Greek X is a soft *xi* or *si*, not a hard *eks* sound. See "CHANGE."

XIPH(OID)/סַיִף
SIGH–IF   [S–Y–PH]

ROOTS: XIPHOID (sword-shaped) is from Greek *xiphos* (a sword).

סיפא / SÄYÄPHÄ is to fence with a sword in Aramaic; סיף / SÄYIPH is a sword. סיף / SEÄPH is to destroy or put an end to something; סף / SOPH means the same in *Psalms 73:19.* סוף / SOPH is a temporal end (*Ecclesiastes 7:2*) or a physical end (*II Chronicles 20:16*).

A sword is named for an "end" or "extremity" word here, just as a *pin* or *poniard* (dagger) is named for the פינה / PENÄ (corner). Many arrow or thorn terms (see "ACACIA" and "HASTATE") are extensions of קצה / KÄTSEH (edge, extremity).

> **BRANCHES:** XIPHOSURAN is an obviously related term, but EPEE (from Old French *espee*) is a sword word not linked to *xiphos*. Similarly, the SPADE is from Latin *spatha* (which also can mean a sword). *Sai* is a sword in Japanese karate terminology. Reverse SP for *pisau* (a sword in Malay:Isowa), and for *pi-shou* (a dagger in Chinese).

YELL/יְלַל
YIL–ALE   [YLL]

ROOTS: YELL is traced to Old English *giellan* and the IE root *ghel* (to call).

קול / KOL is a call (*Exodus 19:19*). More directly, there's ילל / YILÄL ("howl" in *Deuteronomy 32:10*) and אילילה / ÄLELÄ ("wail" in *Micah 1:8*).

> **BRANCHES:** See "CALL," "ULULATE" and "WAIL."

YEN/עָנָן
UN–UN   [UN(N)]

ROOTS: A YEN, a deep longing or desire, comes from the Chinese term for opium smoke. Smoke is *yen* and cloud is *yun* in Chinese.

One may link *yun* to עָנָן / UN(UN) ("cloud"– *Genesis 9:14*) just as other Chinese Y from Hebrew ע changes are seen at "EYE" and "ORIGIN."

> **BRANCHES:** The Hebrew ע is gutturalized in the Japanese *Kumo* (cloud) and French *nuage* (cloud – reversed ענ / KH–N or GN).

YES/הָיוֹת
(HEH)–YOSE   [(H)YOS]

ROOTS: Anglo-Saxon *gese* or *gise* (yes) is traced to the IE root *es* (to be).

היות / (HE)YOS is "to be" (*Genesis 2:18*). Other like-sounding words that speak to the affirmative sense of YES include יש / YÄSH (there is – see "is"), יאות / YÄOOS (properly, rightly) and ישר / YÄSHÄR (straight, even, right, correct – see "JURISDICTION").

> **BRANCHES:** Cognates of YES at IE root *es* include ABSENT, AM, ENTITY, ESSENCE, IMPROVE, INTEREST, QUINTESSENCE, PRESENT, PROUD, REPRESENT, SOOTH, SOOTHE and SWA*STIKA.*
>
> Cognates of YES listed at IE root *i* include ID, IDEM, IDENTICAL, IDENTIFY, IDENTITY, ILK, ITEM, ITERATE, REITERATE, YEA, YET, YON, and YONDER.
>
> A YS antonym of negativity is יאוש / YÄOOS[H] (despair – *Ecclesiastes 2:20*). Spanish and Italian reverse *es* or YES to *si.* Portuguese *sim* (yes) may be a reversal of אמת / EMES (true).
>
> Czech *ano* and Hungarian *igen* pick up Hebrew YES terms אין / ÄN and כן / KÄN (yes; honest). *Jing* is true in Thai.

(Y)ET/עוֹד
ODE   [ED→ET]

ROOTS: Middle English *yete* was *giet* (still) in Anglo-Saxon, and is related to Old Frisian *ieta*.

עוד / ŌD or GŌDT means "still" or "yet." One of the meanings of YET fits the "time" sense of עת / ĀT (a time – see "VETERAN").

עדי / ĀDĒ or GĀTĒ means YET as in "not yet." עד / ĀDT is "until a certain time." YET as a conjunction is more like עוד / ŌDT (moreover – see "ADD").

BRANCHES: Cognates of YET are listed under IE root *i* – see "YES." English DAY, Spanish and Portuguese *dia*, German *tag* and Rumanian *zi*, like the many words for "time" around the globe, all appear to link up with Arabic *id* and Hebrew עת / ĀDT or ĀS or GĀT (or a reversal of these words). Similarly, ETESIAN is from Greek *etos* (year), while *got* is a year in Russian.

ETHOS and CACOETHES are from Greek *ethos* (habit, custom), recalling עתי / ĒTĒ or ĒTHĒ (periodic).

YOKE/יחד
YUKH – (ŪD)   [Y–KH–(D)]

ROOTS: Middle English *yok*, Old English *geoc* and IE base *jeug* (to yoke) are traced to the IE root *yeug* (to join). יחד / YŌKH(ĀD) is to join (*Genesis 49:6*); יחד / YĀKH(ĀD) is together (*Genesis 22:8*). Two draft animals are YOKED together in a YOKE or collar-like frame. Arabic *yaqa* is a collar.

BRANCHES: Cognates of YOKE are listed at "JUXTAPOSE." Together is *yi qi* in Chinese. In Cantonese *yatchai* is together and *yuhdou* is to meet. *Ikut* is to join in Indonesian.

YOLK/ירוֹק
YOUR–OAK   [YRK→YLK]

ROOTS: Middle English *yelke* is linked to YELLOW and to terms like Latin *galbinus* (greenish yellow). This green-yellow connection links YOLK with ירוק / YĀRŌK or (with an R→L change) YĀLŌK (green or greenish – *Job 39:8; Leviticus 14:37*).

BRANCHES: Latin *galbus* (yellow) and German *gelb* (yellow) are possibly linked to the Hebrew חלב / KHĀLEBH (animal fat). *Ki'iroi* (yellow) is a Japanese reversal of ירוק / YĀRŌK. The Fijian word for green, *drokadroka*, is close enough to ירקרק / YIRAKRAK (greenish – *Leviticus 14:37*).

YOUNG/יוֹנֵק
YO–NAKE   [YNK]

ROOTS: YOUNG is linked to German *jung* and to a theoretical IE root *yeu* (vital force, youthful vigor).

Hebrew offers an etymon that fits both English YOUNG and Latin *juvenc[us]* and *juvenis* (source of JUVENILE). The Hebrew י / Y is often rendered as a J (יואל / YŌĀL becomes Joel). The Hebrew ו is versatile enough to allow Latin and

the Romance languages to get a V, while Germanic tongues may read it as the vowel O. The remaining N and K of the captioned Hebrew term pose no problem.

יונק / YŌNĀK or JŌVNĀ(K) is a "suckling child" in *Numbers 11:12*. As such, the child is ינק / YĀNĀK (sucking or YANKING away) while the mother is הניק / HĀNĒK (suckling – *Genesis 21:7*).

BRANCHES: Cognates of YOUNG at IE root *yeu* include GALLOWGLASS, JUNIOR, JUNKER, JUVENOCRACY, REJUVENATE and YOUTH. YOUNKER and JUNKER (from "young" terms in Dutch and Polish) are closer to the original Hebrew than YOUNGSTER. YOUNKER (a young lord) is not a bad etymon for those privileged babes of history, the YANKEES (Americans). There is no known origin for YANKEE.

The Hebrew י / Y also reappears as a G or a vowel. A child is a *gye(r)mek* in Hungarian, and an *anak* in Indonesian.

ZEALOUS/זָרִיז
ZAH – REEZ   [ZRZ→ZLS]

ROOTS: ZEALOUS (enthusiastic, diligent) is from Late Latin *zelas* and Greek *zelos* (ardor, fervor).

זריז / ZĀRĒZ (quick, alert) is a Mishnaic word only an R→L change away. זרז / ZĀRAZ is to stimulate or urge; זרזין / ZĀRĒZ(ĒN) are ZEALOTS or fervently pious people; נזדרז / (NĒ)ZDĀRĀZ means "to be alert, to be ZEALOUS, conscientious."

BRANCHES: ZEAL and ZEALOTRY might dance to a SALSA beat. Latin *salis* or SALT may be a stimulant related to זרז / ZRZ or SLS. Otherwise SALT, SILT and Middle English *cylte* (fine sand) might be influenced by סלת / SOLET or SOLES (fine flour) and סלת / SĒLĀT (to make fine flour). סלה / SĒLĀ (to trample) might also relate to making salt (IE root *sal*) or other powdery substances. The AHD links ZEAL(OUS) to "JEALOUS" at IE root *ya*.

ZIRCON/זרְחָן
ZAR–KHON   [Z–R–KH–(N)]

ROOTS: The mineral ZIRCON is said to be a French term borrowed from the Arabic *zarqun* (cinnabar), which Indo-Aryan scholars believe was borrowed from Persian *zargun* (gold-colored). Persian *zar* (gold) is thus the oldest acknowledged source for ZIRCON.

זרחן / ZĀRKHON is the modern Hebrew for phosphorus, but only because זרח / ZĀRĀKH (to shine) is in the Bible (*Psalms 112:4*). זהר / ZŌHĀR (splendor) and הזהיר / (HĒ)ZHĒR (to radiate, shine – *Daniel 12:3*) are closely related as are ZRH and ZHR.

BRANCHES: Hungarian *sarga* (yellow) is ultimately from זרח / ZĀRĀKH, as are ZIRCONATE, ZIRCONIA, ZIRCONIC and ZIRCONIUM.

SIROCCO is an Italian borrowing from Arabic *sharaqa* (to rise . . . as the sun). זרח / ZĀRĀKH (to rise . . . as the sun) figures in *Ecclesiastes 4:1* – "the sun also *rises*."

The *Lexicon* adds "be white" to the definitions of זרח / SRH. *Shiroi* is white in Japanese.

ZODIAC/צֶדֶק
(T)ZED – EK [ZDK]

ROOTS: ZODIAC (an astrological belt in the heavens) is not (as claimed) from Greek *zoion* (animal) + *kyklos* (circle). It's ZODIAK, not "zoklos," and the ZODIAC (without animals for the most part) was employed centuries before the Greek isles were settled.

צדק / (T)ZEDEK means justice (*Leviticus 19:16*), prosperity and ascendancy (*Isaiah 46:13*), theological or mathematical justification, and the planet Jupiter.

> **BRANCHES:** For the etymons to the given etymology, see "ZOO" and "CYCLE." "Just" can also mean "exact" or "accurate," and both sides of a text or of a legal case must be "justified." צדק / TZEDEK (justice) is a combination of צד / TSAD (side) and דיק / DĒĀK (exact).

ZOO/זוע
ZOO – AH [ZOU]

ROOTS: In zoos or biological gardens one finds many a *zoion*, animal in Greek. They are so named because they are ZOOID, capable of moving. זח / ZĀH, זוז / ZOOZ and זיע / ZĒÄ all mean movement. "Mordecai did not rise or even *stir* on [Haman's] account . . ." זע / ZU – *Esther 5:9*. If ZOON or *zoion* derives from a generic animal term, consider צאן / (T)ZŌN (small cattle, sheep, goats, etc. – *Genesis 4:2*).

> **BRANCHES:** There are over 60 words beginning or ending with the Greek root. זעזע / ZĀZĀU or SĀKH – SĀKH means to shake, and is the source of SHAKE. זחל / ZĀHĀL or ZĀKHĀL is to crawl. *The American Heritage Dictionary* maintains that ZOO may be traced to the Indo-European root *g(w)ei*)to live). Thrown in the same menagerie with ZOO are so-called cognates like AMPHIBIAN, BIOLOGY, HYGIENE, MICROBE, QUICK, REVIVE, SURVIVE and VIVID. חי / KHĪ is life; the verb form is similar. חיה / KHAYA is a beast or creature. *Kai* means life force in Japanese.

ZYG(OTE)/זוג
ZOOG [ZUG]

ROOTS: Greek *zygon* (yoke) is traced to the IE root *yeug* (to join) seen at "JUXTAPOSE" and "YOKE." זוג / ZOOG is also a yoke. There is no evidence of borrowing from a non-Semitic source, although the term is post-Biblical. זוג / ZOOG also means a pair or even numbers; זוג / ZĒVĀG is to join. We all originated in a ZYGOTE, a cell formed by the union of two gametes.

> **BRANCHES:** AZYGOUS precedes a dozen other ZYGO- terms. The cognates of ZYGOTE at IE root *yeug* are listed at "JUXTAPOSE." *Zawg* is a husband in Arabic; בן-זוג / [BEN]-ZOOG is a spouse in Hebrew. One's marital partner is a *zivig* in Yiddish; a husband in Modern Greek is *si'zigos*. Arabic *jauza* (twins) reverses the ZG root.

ZYME/חָמֵץ
(HÄ) – MAYTZ [MZ→ZM]

ROOTS: A ZYME is a ferment or ENZYME, from Greek *zyme* (a leaven). חמץ / [HÄ]MĀTZ is to leaven (*Exodus 12:34*); חמץ / HĀMĀTZ is leavened or soured bread or grains. The given IE root is *yeu* (to blend, mix food), taking in -ZYME and ZYMO- words.

> **BRANCHES:** יזם / YĀZĀM is to initiate. Reversing ZM is צמח / TZĀMĀH (to grow upwards). Antonyms include צמצום / TZĒMTZOOM (condensing, contraction). The most significant opposite of חמץ / HĀMĀTZ is מצה / MĀTZĀ (unleavened bread). See "MASS."

APPENDIX A

Entries are placed in this secondary listing for any of several reasons: 1) The English entry word is uncommon. 2) The Hebrew word is not Biblical and may be "borrowed." 3) More than one standard linguistic shift is required to relate the Hebrew to the English word. For example, an L must be shifted to R *plus* a second and third root letter must swap positions. 4) The linkage of the English and Hebrew word requires a speculative shift in meaning or usage.

While the format of "roots" to "branches" continues here, the symbol = will set off a definition, and the symbol < will mean "derives from" or "is thought to derive from."

ABLA[TION]/בָּלָה BALL-AH [BL]

ROOTS: Latin *ablatius* < past perfect of *auferre* (carried away). 1) הֶעֱבִיר/[HE]EVEER = to transfer, remove. See FERRY." 2) The second definition of ABLATION is a geological term of wearing or wasting away. בלה/BALA = to decay, wear out, consume (*Deuteronomy 29:4*).

BRANCHES: בלע/BEELA = to [DE]VOUR, swallow or BOL[T] down food, destroy. נבל/[NA]BHAL = to fade, shrivel, wither, decay. ברה/BARA = to eat. בער/BEEAR = to burn, consume, remove.

ABOUT/בַּעַד B'UDT [BUD → BUT]

ROOTS: ABOUT = 1. concerning, 2. close or near to. ABOUT < Anglo-Saxon *onbutan* (combination of "on," "by" and "out"). בעד/BUUDT = through, ABOUT (*Genesis 26:8*), for, on behalf of (*I Samuel 7:9*), behind (*Songs 4:1*).

ABYSS/אֶפֶס EPH-ESS [APS→ABS]

ROOTS: ABYSS (primeval chaos, bottomless pit, immeasurable depths or void) < 1. Sumerian *apsu* 2. Greek *a* (without) + *byssos* (bottom – see "BASE"). אפס/EPHES = non-existence, naught, zero, end, outer limits (*Genesis 47:16, Isaiah 45:6, Deuteronomy 33:17*).

BRANCHES: אפע/EPHA = nothing; פסס/POSAS = to fail, be gone. פסה/PASA = to be extended; סוף/SOPH = end. Cognate: ABYSMAL.

ACACIA/קוֹץ COATS [K-TS]

ROOTS: ACACIA (a-KAY-sha) = thorny tree < Greek *ake* (a point). קוֹץ/KOTS = thorn (*Genesis 3:18*); עקץ/OKETS or KOKETS = point, prick; קץ/KATS = extremity; חץ/KHATS = arrow.

BRANCHES: חד/KHADT = sharp; שך/SAKH = thorn; סך/SOKH = thicket; שיח/SEEAKH = bush, shrub. OXYGEN < Greek *oxus* (sharp). Latin *acus* = needle. CACTUS < Greek *kaktos* (a kind of plant – see KOKETS above). *Qasil* = sagebrush in Uto-Aztecan languages. See "ACUTE," "CUT," "SAGEBRUSH," "STICK," and "TACK."

ADOL(PH)/אַדִיר AH-DEER [ADR → ADL]

ROOTS: ADOLPH < Gothic *adal*, Old High German *edili* = nobility. אדיר/ADEER = noble (*Jeremiah 14:3 – R → L*). See "ADONIS" and "ADORE."

AIR/רוח ROOAH [RI(H) → IR]

ROOTS: Both AIR and אויר/AVER (air) < Greek *aer* (air, mist). *Definitions of AIR: Hebrew -/R-H words:* 1. gases, atmosphere ריח/RAYAH (scent); 2. sky, space above earth רוח/ROOAH (quarter of heaven), רוח/REVAH (space); 3. wind, breeze רוח/ROOAH (wind, air); 4. general appearance, airs רוח/ROOAH (mood); 5. to publicize רוח/RAVAH (to spread) רוח/ROOAH = wind or "spirit" (*Genesis 1:2*), as AURA in Greek = AIR or breeze. אור/OR = light; על/AL = height.

BRANCHES: העביר/[HE]EVEER = to soar; אבר/AVER = wing. AERIAL, AERO-, AIR, AORTA, ARIA, ARTERY, AURA and MALARIA < IE root *wer* (to raise, lift, hold suspended). Arabic *ria* = lung. Avestan *ahura* = spirit.

ALCOHOL/כֹּהַל CO-HULL [KHL]

ROOTS: Acknowledged borrowing < Arabic *al kohl* (powder of antimony). Biblical Hebrew cognate uncertain – see "COAL."

ALOES/אֲהָלוֹת A-HULL-OSE [AHL]

ROOTS: ALOES (a bitter African lilly) < Greek *aloe*. צוֹלְדִרְהַךְ∞אהלות ("חעלא,,, עץ טנאלפ" *Songs 4:14*) is a companion to the bitter myrrh.

AMAH/אָמָה AM-AH [AMH]

ROOTS: Anglo-Indian AMAH (maidservant) < Portugese *ama*. In the Orient, including China, a woman servant, nurse, nursemaid or MAMMY is called an AMAH. אמה/AMAH = maidservant (*Genesis 30:3*). אם/AM = mother.

BRANCHES: AUNT, AMITY, and AMAH < IE root *amma* ("nursery word"). See "AMITY" and "MAMA."

ANGEL/מַלְאָךְ MA-LAKH [MLK → NKL]

ROOTS: Greek *angelos* (angel, messenger) < "unknown Oriental source." Perhaps an-gel was corrupted from am-gel, ma-leg or מלאך/MALAKH (angel, messenger – *Genesis 22:11*). Ethiopic לאך/LOAKH = he sent, ministered; מלאכות/MALAKH[OOT] = message, embassy (*Haggai 1:13*).

BRANCHES: The prophet Malachi, then, may relate to words like EVANGELICAL and LOS ANGELES.

ANIMUS/נְשָׁמָה NIS(H)-AMA [N-S(H)-M → NMS]

ROOTS: Greek *anemos* = wind; Latin *anima* = soul, air. נשמה/NIS(H)AMA = breath (*Genesis 2:7*), soul (*Joshua 11:11*); the *Lexicon* adds "anger" and "wind." Aramaic *nishma* = breath, life (*Daniel 5:2 3*).

BRANCHES: ANEMO-, ANIMATE, ANIMISM, ANIMOSITY, EQUANIMITY, PUSILAIMOUS, UNANIMOUS. PNEUMONIA < Greek *pneuma* (breath). Korean *sum* = breath; Tagalog *simoy* = breeze.

ANON/אֵינוּן EE-NOON [ANON]

ROOTS: ANON = 1. in a little while, 2. at another time. ANNON < Anglo-Saxon *on an* (in one) or Old English *onan* (soon). Aramaic אינון/EENOON = then; "and it came to pass *in those days*" (rendition of *Exodus 2:11*). מאן/[MA]AN = whence.

ARACH(NID)/אוֹרֵג ORE-EGG [ARG]

ROOTS: Greek *arachne* = spider. אורג/ORAG = weaver ("they ...*weave* spider webs" – *Isaiah 59:5*.)

BRANCHES: ARGYLE may relate to ארג/EREG (a woven cloth). See "ORGAN" and "RUG."

ARIES/אַיִל EYE-ALL [AYL → AR]

ROOTS: Latin *aries* (ram) < IE root *er* (root for domestic horned animals). איל/AYAL = ram (*Deuteronomy 14:5*).

BRANCHES: ARIEL (gazelle) < Arabic *aryal*. אילה/AYALA = gazelle or doe. Chinese *lu* = deer. See "ELK."

BALA(N)CE/פֶּלֶס PEEL-ACE [PLS → BLS]

ROOTS: BALANCE (equilibrium) < Latin *bis* (twice) + *lanx* (dish). פלס/PEELAS = to balance, level (*Psalms 78:50*); פלס/PELES = a balnce, scales (*Isaiah 40:12*).

BRANCHES: Consider BALLAST (used to stabilize ships or to level railroad ties) < Dutch *barlast* (*bar* = waste + *last* = load).

BALE/חֲבִילָה (HA)-BHEEL-AH [HBL]

ROOTS: BALE < Old High German *balla* (package, ball). חבילה/HABHEELA = BALE, parcel, bundle; חבל/HEBHEL = rope, band, binding (*Zechariah 11:7*). See "BALL."

BALE[FUL]/בְּלִי BILL-LEE [BL]

ROOTS: BALE and BALEFUL (harmful, evil, malignant, woeful) < Old English *bealu* (harm, ruin) < IE root *bhelu* (to harm). בלהה/BALAHA = calamity, terror (*Job 18:14*); בלי/BILEE = corruption, annihilation (*Isaiah 38:17*); בלע/BELA = destruction.
  BRANCHES: אבל/ABHAL = desolate, ruined; חבל/HABHAL = wound, destroy; בלה/BOLA = harassing (*Ezra 4:4*). See "EVIL," "VILE."

BALLOON/כְּלוּם BALL-OOM [BLM → BLN]

ROOTS: BALLOON < Italian *pallone* < IE base *bhel* (to swell up). בלום/BALOOM = swollen (Mishnaic Hebrew) < בל/BL root of בלט/BOLAT = to protrude (see "BLOAT").
  BRANCHES: PULM[ONARY] < Latin *pulmo* (lung). בלימה/BILEEMA (restraint, nothingness) is an antonym of BLM and perhaps of BULIMIA (< Greek *limos* = famine).

BA(M)BOO/אבוב AB-BOOBH [ABOB]

ROOTS: BAMBOO < Malay *bambu* = a hollow, treelike grass with jointed stems. (Similar nasalization in Italian *bambino* + baby.) אבוב/ABOOBH = hollow pipe or tube derived from jointed reeds or knotgrass, an extension of אבה/ABHE (reed – *Job 9:26*). .
  BRANCHES: נבוב/[NI]BHOOBH is hollow (*Exodus 27:8*) See BIBLE, FIFE, and PIPE at "OBOE."

BARK/פָּרֵק PA-RAKE [PRK → BRK]

ROOTS: Tree BARK < German *borke*. To BARK = remove bark, skin. פרק/PARAK = to remove, break off, unload (*Genesis 27:40*).
  BRANCHES: To DEBARK or DISEMBARK = to unload goods or passengers. EMBARK recalls הפליג/[HEE]PHLEEG (to embark, sail away). For PLG root see "ARCHIPELAGO" and "BREAK." פורקת/POREK[ET] = barge; *fulk* = Arabic ship; *bachira* = Arabic boat. Related boats include: BARK, BARKENTINE, BARGE, FELUCCA (West Indian log canoe) FRIGATE, PIRAGUA (Spanish log canoe), and PIROGUE (Carib log canoe). FLITCH = strip from outer tree trunk < IE base *plik* (to tear off). PLUCK, PEEL and PARE may relate. פרק/PORAK (*Psalms 136:23*) and Aramaic פורקן/PORKAN = the breaking out of redemption (whence surname FARRAKHAN).

BASTE/שְׁבֵּץ (SHE)-BAITS [(SH)-B-TS → B-ST]

ROOTS: BASTE = to sew with long, loose stitches < Old French *bastire*. שבץ/[SHEE]BATS = knitting; "weaving in checkerwork" (*Exodus 28:39*).
  BRANCHES: BASTION and BASTLILLE < Germanic *bastjan* (to make or build with bast or thatch. Perhaps PATCH is related.

BATISTE/בוץ BOOTS [B-O-TS]

ROOTS: BATISTE (fine linen) < so called from the supposed maker, Baptiste of Cambrai." בוץ/BOOTS = fine linen (*I Chronicles 15:27*).
  BRANCHES: בד/BU(D)T = white linen. BAST = a fine plant fiber. BYSSUS (fine linen cloth) < Greek < Semitic. Polish *wata* = cotton wool; Finnish *vaate* = cloth or garment.

BAZOOKA/בָּזָק BA-ZAK [BZK]

ROOTS: BAZOOKA (portable rocket launcher) < "echoic term." בזק/BAZAK = lightning flash (*Ezekiel 1:14*); זיק/ZAK = spark.

BEAM/בֵּן BANE [BN → BM]

ROOTS: BEAM = 1. a long, thick piece of wood, metal or stone, used in building, 2. a ship's maximum breadth, 5. the crossbar of a balance, 6. the balance, 9. main shaft of a deer's antlers. BEAM is linked to the Anglo-Saxon. בן/BAN = branch; בנה/BANA = to build (*Genesis 11:4*), לבנה/[LI]BHANA = brick, stone slab (*Genesis 11:3*), בין/BAN = between (*Genesis 1:4*).

BEAR/בָּהִיר BAH-HERE [BHR]

ROOTS: BEAR, BRUIN, and BROWN < IE root *bher* (bright, brown). בהיר/BAHEER = bright, clear (*Job 37:21*); בהרת/BAHER[ET] = freckle or bright spot on the skin (*Leviticus 13:2*).
  BRANCHES: בר/BAR = clear; Arabic *bounni* = brown. Related are BEAVER, BRONZE, BRUNET and BURNISH.

BEAUTY/פִּיוּתָא PUY-OO-TA [PYT → BYT]

ROOTS: BEAUTY < Latin *bellus* (pretty) < IE root *deu* (to do, perform, revere, show favor). Aramaic פיותא/PAYOOTA (beauty) and Syriac פאיות/PAAYOOT reverse the יפ/YP root of יפי/YOPHE (beauty – *Proverbs 31:30*).
  BRANCHES: טוב/TOBH = beautiful; צבי/TSIBHE = beautiful (*Isaiah 28:5*). Hungarian *szep* = beauty. BEATITUDE < Latin *beare* (to make blessed); ברוך/BAROO[KH] = blessed (*Genesis 22:18*).

[BE]STOW/זָבַד SOVADT [ZVD → STW]

ROOTS: BESTOW (to give as a gift) < Middle English *bestowen* < *be* + *stow* (a place). זבד/ZOVAD or SOVAT = to give a gift; זבד/SZEVEDT = "bestowal," a gift (*Genesis 30:20*).
  BRANCHES: Swahili *zawadi* = gift.

BICKER/בִּקֵּר BEE-CARE [BKR]

ROOTS: BICKER (to quarrel, squabble) < Middle English *bikeren* (to attack). בקר/BEKAR = to criticize, censure; בקרת/BIKOR[ET] = chastisement (*Leviticus 19:20*). וכוח/VEEKOOAKH = debate.

BIG/בָּנַר BOG-(ARE) [BG(R)]

ROOTS: BIG < Germanic base *bugjn* (swollen, thick, big) and IE root *bhu* (to blow out). 1. בנר/BOGAR = to grow up; בגרות/BUG[ROOT] = maturity. 2. גבה/GAB[HOA] = tall, high (*Genesis 7:19*), significant (*Ecclesiastes 5:7*) – BG reversal. גבר/GEBH[ER] = grown man. 3. נפך/[NE]PAKH = to blow out, swell up (*Job 20:26*).
  BRANCHES: Turkish *buyuk* = large; Swahili *kubwa* = large; Thai *gow* = old; Malay *bakeh, bagewa*, and *bagut* = large; Norwegian *bugge* = a big man. Antonyms include בחור/BAKHOOR (young man) and פג/PUG (unripe fruit, immaturity).

BOLSH[EVIK]/בָּשֵׁל BOSH-ALE [BSL → BLS]

ROOTS: BOLSHEVIK (pre-revolutionary political party in Russia; any radical) < Russian *bolshe* (the larger, the majority). בשל/BOSHAL = fully grown, ripe, having reached majority (*Joel 4:13*). בסר/BOSAR (unripe fruit) is a BSR antonym.
  BRANCHES: Malay *besar* = large; Russian *bolshoy* = large.

BONNY/נָאוֶה NOBH-EH [N-BH → BN]

ROOTS: BONNY (Scottish and English dialect term for beautiful) has no known origin. נאוה/NOBH[EH] = nice, pretty, comely (*Songs 1:5*; reverse N-BH).
  BRANCHES: לבן/[LA]BHAN (white – see "ALBINO") may link up to the following BN words of fairness (pale, beautiful or good): BONA FIDE, BONANZA, BONBON, BONUS, and FINE. Malay *phien* = good; Chinese *wan* = beautiful.
See "DIVINE" and "MILK."

BOOR/בור BOOR [BUR]

ROOTS: BOOR (a rude, uncultivated person) < Dutch *bouwen* (to build, cultivate). בור/BOOR = uncultured, boorish; בער/BAAR = boor, ignorant person; "brutish" (*Psalms 92:7*). בר/BAR = to be empty, uncultivated, to lie fallow.
  BRANCHES: בר/BAR = field; בר/BOR = innocence. For BORING or BOREDOM see "BORE."

BOOT/בָּעַט BA-UTT [BUT]

ROOTS: BOOT < Old French *bote* = a high shoe, a kick, or to kick out. בעט/BAUT is to kick or spurn (*Deuteronomy 32:15*). Aramaic שבוט/[SHEE]BOOT and Arabic *sabot* (sandal) are shoe words – see "SABOTAGE." For the boot-foot connection see "OCTOPUS."

BOOTY/בֶּצַע   BET(S)-AH   [B-T(S)-U]

ROOTS: BOOTY < Middle German *bute*. Obsolete BOOT in "to boot" = advantage, profit. בצע/BET(S)A = profit, "unjust gain" (*Exodus 18:21*). בזה/BEEZA and בז/BUZZ = booty, plunder – see "BUZZARD."

BORAGE/פֶּרַג   PERE - AGH   [PRG → BRG]

ROOTS: BORAGE (plant with hairy leaves) < probably from Latin *burra* (coarse hair). פרע/ PERA or PERAGH = hair, unruly hair; thicket (*Numbers 6:5*).

   BRANCHES: פרעוש/PAROSH or PARGOSH = FLEA (see Introduction).

BORAX/בֹּרִית   BORE - EES   [BR]

ROOTS: BORAX (a crystalline compound used to make detergents, etc.) < Arabic *buraq*. Old French *boras* is more directly from בֹּרִית/BOREES (lye, alkali, soap (*Malachi 3:2*). בר/BOR = lye (*Isaiah 1:25*).

   BRANCHES: BORACITE, BORATE, BORIC [ACID], BORIDE, BORON.

BOT[ULISM]/בֶּטֶן   BET - EN   [BT(N)]

ROOTS: BOTULISM (food poisoning) < Latin *botulus* (sausage) < IE root *gwet* (intestine). 1. בטן/BETEN = belly, womb (*Numbers 5:21*), bowels (Ben-Yehuda), *venter* (stomach in Latin; via the concordance). 2. בטל/BOTAL = to abolish, remove, vacate, VENT. In both these Hebrew etymons, consider the L = N formula taken up in a later appendix.

   BRANCHES: BOWEL is a cognate at IE *gwet* (intestine), which may derive from כבד/KOVADT = liver (*Exodus 29:13*). כבד/KOVEDT (abundance) and כבד/KOVADT (weighty) fit the large intestine better than the liver. The intestines, not the liver, appears to be a better rendition of כבד/KOVADT in *Lamentations 2:11* and *Ezekiel 21:26*. The K-V-DT words above may link up with ABU(N)D(ANCE) and WEIGHT (switch positions of GH and W). See "VENTRICLE."

BRIO/בְּרִיאוּת   BREE-OOT   [BRY]

ROOTS: BRIO (Italian) = animation, vivacity and zest. Given IE root = *gwer* (heavy). בריאות/BREEOOT, בריא/BAREE (*Genesis 41:2*) and בריא/BOREE = health, fitness. בריה/BIREEA = creature or animal.

   BRANCHES: פרוע/PAROOA = wild. For בר/BR wildness see "BARRIO." IE root *gwer* (heavy) recalls גבר/GOVAR (was powerful – *Psalms 12:5*) and floodwaters "swelling" in *Genesis 7:17*. Arabic *Allah akbar* = God is powerful or great. בריא/BOREE (fat) recalls Greek *barus* (heavy) and *baros* (weight), which are linked to IE *gwer*. Listed cognates include AGGRAVATE, BARITONE, BARIUM, BAROMETER, BRUTE, GRAVE, GRAVITY, GRIEF, GRIEVE and ISOBAR. Another cognate, GURU (venerable, heavy), recalls גביר/GVEER (master, lord).

BRIT/בָּרֹד   BA - RODT   [BRD → BRT]

ROOTS: BRIT (young of herring and other fish) < Old Celtic *brith* (varicolored) and akin to Cornish *bruit* (speckled). ברד/BARODT = spotted, "mottled" (*Genesis 31:10*).

   BRANCHES: The BLOT[CH], [LEO]PARD, PA[N]THER (switch the R and T), and ברדלס/BARD[ILAS] (panther; "borrowed" from Greek) all display the B-R-DT of the Hebrew etymon.

BROOD/וָלָד   VA - LAD   [VLD → BRD]

ROOTS: BROOD (offspring) < Old English *brod* (offspring). Given IE root is *bhreu* (to boil, burn – see "BURN"). ולד/VALAD or BHLOD = child (*Genesis 11:30*); Arabic *walid* = baby; see "LAD" for LD root of giving birth.

   BRANCHES: See "PART" for alternative links to BRAT, BREED, etc.

BULL[ETIN]/בּוּל   BOOL   [BUL]

ROOTS: BULL (edict from the Pope, etc.) < Latin *bulla* (a knob or seal), as all documents were sealed with an official BULLA. Arabic *bool* = postage stamp; the word is now used in Modern Hebrew. The knoblike lump of lead resembling the medical BULLA < בּוּל/BOOL ("block"– *Isaiah 44:19*). יבלת/[YA]BEL[ES] = blister or boil; בלט/BOL[AT] = protrude – see "BALL" and "BLOAT."

   BRANCHES: BILL, BOIL, BOUILLON, BOWL, BULLET, BULLETIN and BULLY are cognates at the IE root *beu* (to swell).

BURR/בַּרְקָן   BAR-(KON)   [BR(K)]

ROOTS: BURR (rough outgrowth on tree) < Middle English *burre*. BRIAR or BRIER (thorny plant) < Old English *broer*. ברקן/BAR[KAN] = thistle, brier; sharp-toothed threshing wagon (*Judges 8:7*). ברוש/BIR[OSH] = FIR tree (*II Samuel 6:5*).

   BRANCHES: Latin *burra* = coarse hair. BARB and BEARD < IE root *bharda* (beard). BRAD and BRISTLE < IE root *bhar* (projection, bristle, point). BRAMBLE, BRIM and BROOM < IE root *bhrem* (to project; a point, spike, an edge). See "BRUSH."

BURS[AR]/בָּשָׂר   BUS-ARE   [BSR → BRS]

ROOTS: BURSAR (treasurer) < IE root *bursa* (hide, wineskin – "Greek noun of unknown origin"). בשר/BASAR = "flesh," skin or "body" (*Leviticus 14:9; I Kings 21:27* – BRS → BSR).

   BRANCHES: Cognates include BOURSE, BURSA, BURSITIS, DISBURSE, PURSE, PURSER, REIMBURSE and SPURRAN. ברסה/BOORSA (stock exchange) in Arabic and Hebrew was "borrowed." VALISE, a larger leather purse, is linked to Arabic by *Webster's*.

BUTCHER/בָּשָׂר   BUS-ARE   [BSR → BCHR]

ROOTS: BUTCHER < Old French *bouchier*. IE root = *bhugo* (male animal). 1. בשר/BASAR = meat or "flesh " (*Genesis 2:21*). 2. בתר/BASAR or BATAR = to cut or divide (as the pieces of animal flesh in *Genesis 15:10*).

   BRANCHES: טבח/TABAKH = to slaughter (T-B-KH → B-T-CH). שאר/SH'AR = meat, flesh – see "SARCASTIC and "BURSAR."

BUTTON/פִּטָּם   PEA-TOME   [PTM → BTN]

ROOTS: BUTTON < Old French *buton* (button, knob). IE root = *bhau* (to strike, push). 1. פטם/PEETOM (from Aramaic) = protuberance or nipple on fruit. 2. בעט/BAUT = to kick out, push away, spurn (*Deuteronomy 35:15*).

   BRANCHES: פטם/PEETAM = to fatten (see "FAT"); בטן /BOTEN = nuts (*Genesis 43:11* – see "BOTANY")./ חבט/HOBHAT = to beat (see "BEAT"). Cognates of BUTTON = ABUT, BUTT, BUTTOCK, BUTTRESS, HALIBUT, REBUTTAL, REFUTE, and SACKBUT.

CABAL/קַבָּלָה   KAB-A-LA   [KBL]

ROOTS: CABAL (small group of schemers) formerly linked to French, now acknowledged (AHD) < Hebrew קבלה/KABALA (tradition; literally that which is received). קבל/KABAL = undertake (*Esther 9:23*).

   BRANCHES: ACCEP[T], KEEP, CABLE and [RE]CEIVE are further links in the KB[L] chain – see "ALCOVE" and "CABLE."

CALAM[US]/קָלָם   CULL-UM   [KLM]

ROOTS: CALAMUS (a quill pen) < Greek *kalamos* (a stalk or reed) < IE root *kolem* (grass, reed). Arabic *qalam* = stalk or reed. קלח/KELAH is a stalk or stem – see "CANE."

   BRANCHES: חלל/KHALAL = empty space (see "HOLLOW"), חליל/KHALEEL = (reed) flute. CALUMET, CARAMEL and HAULM are cognates.

CAL[F]/עֵגֶל   (AYE)-GEL   [AGL → KL]

ROOTS: Both the baby cow CALF and CALF of the leg are traced to the IE base *gelebh* (to swell out; hence swelling, fetus, offspring). עֵגֶל/ĀGEL is the golden CALF of *Exodus 32:8*; עָגֹל/AGŌL (round – *I Kings 7:23*) matches the rounded גל/GUL (wave, heap) at the CALF of the leg.

BRANCHES: The Greek CALF (young cow) is also a GL term.

CA[M]PHOR/כְּפָרִים KIPH-ARE-(EEM)   [K-PH-R]

ROOTS: CAMPHOR (strong-smelling crystalline compound used in insect repellent) < Malay *kapur* (chalk) and/or Arabic *kafur*. כפרים/KIPHAR[EEM] is translated "henna" (*Song of Songs 4:13*); it is the given source of CAMPHIRE (*Funk & Wagnall's*).

BRANCHES: כפר/KOPHAR is to deny. A CAMPHOR BALL is a moth ball.

CANOPY/כָּנָף   KIN-UPH   [K-N-P(H)]

ROOTS: CANOPY (protective covering) < Greek *konopion* mosquito net. For KN GNA[T] and mosquito terms see "GNAW." כנף/KINAP(H) = "skirt," covering, bed covering (*Leviticus 23:1*) or (protective) wing (*Ruth 3:9*).

BRANCHES: כנף/KNP is a verb of hiding (*Isaiah 30:20*).

CAPO[N]/קָפַד   KEEP-AID   [KP(D)]

ROOTS: CAPON (castrated rooster) < Latin *capo* < Greek *koptein* (to cut). 1. קפד/KEEPĀDT = to cut off (*Isaiah 38:12*). 2. עוף/KHOPH = bird, chicken – see "AVIATE."

BRANCHES: KP cut terms include CHOP, COUPE and COUPON.

CARR[ACK]/אָחוֹר   AH-KHORE   [A-KH-R]

ROOTS: CARRACK (galleon or ship) < Greek *kerkos* (tail) + *oura* (tail, rear). אחור/AKHOR = rear, buttocks, back (*Ezekiel 8:16*). Arabic *qurqur* (a merchant ship) is not considered the etymon.

BRANCHES: URAEUS (snake figure) < Greek *oura* (tail); Indonesian *ekor* = tail. אחור/EEKHOOR (lateness) recalls Japanese *okur[eru]* = to become late or to become backward. אחורה/AKHORA = backwards. ARCHAIC, ARCAEOLOGY and ARCHE[TYPE] may be AKR → ARK terms of backwardness. אחר/AKHAR (after – *Genesis 9:28*) and אחורה/AKHŌRA (backwards) may link up to the prefixes RE- and UR- (primitive) as well as to URAEUS, URINE, URO- and UROLOGY. The antonym of חר/KH-R or [H]UR retrogression is seen in the RK element of progression at DIRECTION."

CASE[FY]/קָשָׁה   KOS(H)-EH   [KS]

ROOTS: To CASEFY or affect CASEATION is the process of hardening and drying CASEIN into CHEESE. Latin *caseus* = cheese; *caso* = curdled and coagulated. See "SACK" for KS/SK terms of dryness. קשה/KASHEH = hard (*Exodus 7:3*); קש/KASH = straw; קשקש/KASHKASH = scales of fish or scale armor (*I Samuel 17:5*).

BRANCHES: קשה/KOSHEH also means the difficult hard." The "hard CAUSES" or difficult law CASES were to be brought to Moses in *Exodus 18:26*. CASE = "a question or problem (definition ff16). קשי/KŌSHEE = difficulty; קשיה/KOOS[HEA] = objection, question; הקשה/[HEE]KSHA = to ask a difficult question. QUESTION and ACCUSATION may relate – see "QUERY" and "SEEK" (KS reversed). Japanese *kosei* = hardness; *koshi* = examination.

CASSIA/קְצִיעָה   KIT-TSEE- AH   [K-TS-A]

ROOTS: CASSIA (bark, pods or pulp) is an acknowledged Greek borrowing from Hebrew קציעה/KITSEEA (cassia, dried fig). קצה/KEETSA = to strip off bark, peel or scrape.

BRANCHES: TEAK may be a metathesis of קציצה/KITS[EETSA] (a chopping off; hamburger steak). כסח/KHASAH = to cut off, trim; חסוי/KHISOOY (covering – see "ENCASE") matches the bark and pod sense of CASSIA.

CAT[ECHISM]/חַד   KHADT   [KH-D → CT]

ROOTS: CATECHISM (didactic drilling with questions) < Greek *catachein* = to teach < *kata* (thoroughly) + *e khe* (to sound) < IE root *(s)wagh* (to resound – source of ECHO). 1. חד/KHADT = to propose a riddle (*Daniel 5:12*); חדחד/KHADT = sharp; חדחד/KHADTADT = sharpening. 2. חד/KHADT and אחד/EKHADT = one (Aramaic and Hebrew) + ענב/OOG[AV] = pipe or organ (*Genesis 4:21* – reversal of W-GH or VG of the IR root above).

BRANCHES: דק/DAK = to scrutinize; דקדוק/DIKDOOK = detail, grammar; דע/DĀA or DĀKHA = knowledge. An Antonym of K-DT sharpness is כד/KUDT (round, blunt, obtuse or THICK). DICTATE, DIDACTIC, DIGIT, DOCENT (teacher), DOCILE, DOCTOR, DOCTRINE, DOCUMENT and TEACH (K-DT reversed) may relate. See "ACUTE" and TACTITIAN."

CATHAR[TIC]/כָּשֵׁר   KASH-AIR   [K-SH-R → K-TH-R]

ROOTS: CATHARTIC (purgative) < Greek *katharos* (pure). כשרות/KASHR[OOT] = purity; כשר/KASHĀR = ritually fit, wholesome; acceptable (*Esther 8:5*). See "ARITHMETIC."

BRANCHES: CATHARSIS, CATHERINE, KATE, KATHLEEN, and KITTY.

CERAM[IC]/חֹמֶר   KHOME-AIR   [KH-M-R → KRM]

ROOTS: CERAMIC < Greek *keramikos* < *keramos* or *kheramos* (potter's clay). IE root is *ker* (heat, burn, fire). 1. חמר/KHŌMER or HŌMER = clay (*Jeremiah 18:6*); חמרה/KHAMRA or HAMRA = red earth, clay. 2. חרה/KHARA = to burn (see "CHAR").

BRANCHES: HM cognates at IE root *(d)hghem* (earth): from Anglo-Saxon *clam* (clay): CLAMMY; from Greek *khamai* (on the ground): CHAMELEON, CHAMOMILE, GERMANDER; from Latin *humus* (earth): EXUME, HUMBLE, HUMILIATE, HUMUS; from Latin *homo* (human being): HOMAGE, HOMBRE, HOMICIDE, HOMINID, HOMO-, HUMAN.

CHAETA/חוּט   KHOOT   [KH-T]

ROOTS: CHAETA (bristle, thread) < Greek *chaite* (hair). חוט/KHOOT = thread (*Genesis 14:23*).

BRANCHES: גיד/GEEDT = sinew; קוצה/KVOOTSA or KOOTSA = curl, lock of hair (*Songs 5:2*); IE root *ghait* = curly, wavy hair. Perhaps CADDIS, CAT (*chat* in French), CATERPILLAR and Yiddish *sheitle* (wig) relate. Arabic *chayt* = thread; Rumanian *ata* = thread; Japanese *ito* = thread. Hair = *hutu* (3 Malay dialects); reverse to *tukka* in Finnish. Japanese *keito* = wool. See "ACCOUTERMENTS" and "GUT."

CHALICE/כְּלִי   KAY-LEE   [KL(Y)]

ROOTS: CHALICE < Latin *calix* (cup) and Greek *kalux* (seed – vessel) < IE root *kal* (cup). כלי/KĀLEE = vessel (*Numbers 19:17* – see "SCULLERY").

BRANCHES: CALIX, CALYX and KYLIX are cognates.

CHASTISE/חָסַד   KHEES-AID   [KH-S-D → CH-S-T]

ROOTS: CHASTEN (to criticize severely) < Latin *castigare* (to correct, punish). CHASTE (morally pure, sexually abstaining) is considered unrelated. חסד/KHEESADT = to reproach, to accuse of baseness and impiety (*Proverbs 25:10*). חסיד/KHASEEDT = pious man, saint; חסית/KHASEET = sparing, saving. קדוש/KADTOS[H] (holy, removed) also recalls CHASTE – see "CHASTE."

CHESS/קש   KASH   [KS]
ROOTS: CHESS (brome grass, weedy grain grass) ? < "variety of chase" (a groove). קש/KASH = straw (*Exodus 5:12*).

CHUCK[LE]/צָחק   TSA-KHUK   [TS-H-K → CH-K]
ROOTS: CHUCKLE (to laugh softly) < hen's call; imitative. צחק/TSAHUK = to laugh (*Genesis 17:17*).
BRANCHES: צחוק/TSIHOK = joke, sport or laughter; CHUCK (to pat playfully), JOCULAR, JOKE, SCOFF and SCOP (entertainer) may relate. Maya *tsek* = laugh; Chin. *shiaw*, Hawaiian *ho'aka* = laugh. צעצע/TSAHTSOOAHK = toy, plaything; שעשע/SHAKHSHAKH = played, fondled (*Isaiah 11:8, 66:12*). Yiddish *chatchka, tchotchke,* or *tsatska* = toy < Slavic. German *zeug* and Rumanian *juc[arie]* = toy. TOY, like the Hebrew etymons, meant amorous behavior. Antonyms include זעק/ZAUK and צעק/TSAUK = to cry.

CINC[TURE]/חנק   KHAN-AK   [KH-N-K → CNC]
ROOTS: CINCTURE < Latin *cinctura* (girdle) < IE root *kenk* (to gird, bind). חנק/KHANAK = to strangle, hang (execute – *II Samuel 17:23*).
BRANCHES: CINCH, PRECINCT, SHINGLES and SUCCINCT are cognates; Perh. HANG, HANKER and HUNGER. See "GIRDLE," "HANG" and "NECK."

CIRR[US]/שריג   SAR-(EEG)   [SR(G)]
ROOTS: CIRRUS (pro. sir'us) = a plant tendril < Latin *cirrus* (tendril, lock, curl). שריג/SAR[EEG] = tendril, curling branch of grape vine (*Genesis 40:10, Joel 1:7*); שער/SAAR = hair (*Genesis 27:11*).
BRANCHES: זרד/ZERED or SER[ED] = shoot, young sprout; זר/ZAR = wreath; סלסלה/SALSEELA (*Jeremiah 6:9*) and זלזל/SALSAL (*Isaiah 18:5*) = tendril (SL → SR). CIRRIPEDS and CIRRO-CUMULUS relate.

CLAM/עלם   KHA-LAM   [KH-L-M]
ROOTS: The CLAM and CLAMSHELL < clamping action of the shell – see "CONGLOMERATE." Consider עלם/KH-L-M to hide, be concealed (*Deuteronomy 22:1*) or עלמים /KHALOOM[EEM] (hidden things – *Psalms 90:8*).

CLEM[ENCY]/חמל   KHOM-ULL   [KH-M-L → KLM]
ROOTS: CLEMENCY < Latin *clemens* (merciful). חמל/KHOMAL = to spare, have pity (*Deuteronomy 13:9*); חמלה/KHEMLA = pity, compassion.
BRANCHES: Anagramic synonyms are מחל/MAKHOL (to pardon, forgive, grant CLEMENCY) and רחם/RAKHAM (have pity – L = R). Swahili mercy = *huruma*. CLEMENT, INCLEMENT and MERCY relate.

CLIM[ATE]/עולם   KHO-LUM   [KH-L-M]
ROOTS: CLIMATE < Greek *klima* (region, zone). עולם/OLAM or KHOLAM = world; eternity (*Genesis 9:12*). See "CLAM" above to reinforce the spacial view of עלם/KLM.

COATI/חטם   KHOAT- (EM)   [KH-T-(M)]
ROOTS: COATI (a racoon-like animal with a long snout) < Tupi (Brazilian Indian) *cua* (cincture) + *tim* (nose). חטם/KHOTEM or [HO]TEM = nose, snout (*Isaiah 48:9*). The KH-T element is seen in חטר/KHOT[ER] (branch; the TM element in the Hebrew nose word appears in טעם/TAAM (flavor).
BRANCHES: Indonesian *hidung* = nose; Modern Greek *miti* = nose (TM reversed); Maya *kitam* = boar. HUNT and HOUND are possibilities.

COCKROA[CH]/עקרב   KAK-IH-RAV   [KH-K-R-BH]
ROOTS: COCKROACH < Spanish *cucaracha* (wood louse), the "roach influenced by a fish name." The Italian *[s]carafaggio* and French *cafard* (both mean cockroach) indicate a KRF etymon. ערב/AROV or KHAROBH = beetle – see "SCARAB." עקרב/AKRAV or KHAKIRABH = "scorpion" (*I Kings 12:11*) – this generic term for hard-shelled insects is the source of [S]CORPION. For KR terms of hardness and related animal words – see "CRAB."
BRANCHES: עקרבות/KHAKRABH[OOS] = spider. The Dutch, Scandinavian, and Polish COCKROACH are all KKR terms.

COG/חוח   KHOKH   [KH-O-KH]
ROOTS: COG (tooth, notch) < Middle English *cogge*. חוח/KHOKH = thorn, briar (*Songs 2:2*).
BRANCHES: COGON is a tall coarse grass of the Philippines, the name is from native Tagalog. See "ACUMEN."

COLL[EEN]/כלה   CULL-AH   [KLH]
ROOTS: COLLEEN < Irish, diminutive form of *caile* (girl). כלה/KALA = bride, daughter-in-law (*Ruth 2:22*) or pet name for young woman (*Songs 4:9* – and Hittite usage). Australian Aborigine *kurri* = girl.

COMB/קומה   COMB-AH   [KM]
ROOTS: COMB #5 (the high crest of a wave, helmet or rooster) is of uncertain origin. קומה/KOMA = height, stature" (*I Samuel 16:7*). קמה/KAMA = standing corn (which waves and wears a tuft). קום/KOOM = rise up (*Leviticus 19:32*).
BRANCHES: KAME = hill or ridge. CYMO[GRAPH] < Greek *kyma* (wave). A COOMB and a *comb* in Breton = valley or ravine; reverse KM for the opposite of a hill in Hebrew – עמק/AMEK (valley). To COME to be or that which CAME up links less with קום/KOOM (to arise) than with קים/KAYAM (existing, lasting).

[CON]TAMI[NATE]/טמא   TEE-MAY   [TMA]
ROOTS: The TM part of CONTAMINATE is said to relate to Latin *tangere* (to touch) and the IE root *tag* (to touch). טמא/TEEMA = to pollute, defile (*Deuteronomy 24:4*); טמא/TAMA = impure, unclean.

COSMOS/נשמיות   GUSH-ME-(YOOS)   [GSM]
ROOTS: COSMOS < Greek *kosmos* (universe, order, world). נגשמיות/GAS[H]M[EEOOS] = corporeality, גשמי/GASHMEE = of the physical, material realm; גשם/GEESHAM = to execute a plan; גשם/GESHEM = regular, ordered rains (*Leviticus 26:4*).
BRANCHES: Joseph set up his brothers in the land of Goshen, a GSN or GSM term inferring material order and plenty. COSMETICS and the COSMO- words are related.

COSSACK/עשק   CASE-SACK   [KH-S-K]
ROOTS: COSSACK < Russian *kosak* or Turkish *qazaq* (irregular soldier or fighter). עשק/ASEK or KHASEK = fight or quarrel (*Genesis 26:20*).
BRANCHES: עשק/OSHEK or KHOSHEK = extortion, oppression. Polish *ucisk* = oppression. Turkish *asker* and Swahili *askari* = fighter. The law CASE or CAUSE < Provençal *causer* might relate.

CRAW/קֵרֶב KER-EV [K-R-BH → CRW]

ROOTS: CRAW (animal stomach) < Middle-English *crawe*.
קרב/KEREV = animal innards, intestines (*Leviticus 8:21*).

BRANCHES: CROP = bird's stomach, similar to the sources of GARB[AGE] and GIBL[ET]. IE root *ghera* (gut, entrail) links CHORD, CORDON, HERNIA, HARU[SPEX] and YARN to our etymon. קרב/KEREV = inner part, resembling IE root *k(w)erp* (body). Terms listed there include CORPORAL, CORPORATE, CORPS(E), CORPULENCE, CORPUSCLE, CORSET, and LEPRECHAUN. MIDRIFF < Old English *hrif* (belly), another form of KRV. Japanese belly = *hara*, as in HARI-KARI (disembowelment). Turkish *karin* and Modern Greek *kilia* = belly. Australian Aborigine *huli* = abdomen.

CROC[US]/כַּרְכֹּם CAR-COMB [KRK(M)]

ROOTS: The CROCUS flower and color are acknowledged borrowings from Hebrew כרכם/KARKOM (saffron – *Songs 4:14*), Arabic *kurkum*, and Aramaic *kurkama* (safron, crocus).

BRANCHES: CURCUMA = tropical plant of the ginger family.

CULL/עָלַל KHUL-ULL [KH-L-L]

ROOTS: Old French *cuillir* = to pick, slect, gather. עלל/OLUL or KHOLUL = to pick or glean (*Leviticus 19:10*); קהל/KOHULL = to assemble (*Leviticus 8:3,4*).

BRANCHES: קהלה/KIHEELA (congregation), מכלה/[MI]KHLA (corral), and מכללה/[MI]KHLALA (college) evoke COLLEGE – see "ALL" and "ELECT." IE root *ger* (to gather) resembles the KL root here. Listed cognates there include AGORA, ALLEGORY, CATEGORY, CRAM, CONGREGATION, EGREGRIOUS, GREGARIOUS, and PANEGYRIC. Hawaiian *kaiaulu* = community.

CURTSY/עָרִיץ KHAR-EATS [KH-R-TS]

ROOTS: CURTSY (respectful bow) is thought to be a cognate of COURT < IE root *gher* (to grasp, enclose). 1. חגר/HAGAR (to gird) – see "COURT" and "GIRDLE." 2. כרס/KORUS (to bend, bow) – see "CREASE." 3. הֶעֱרִיץ/[HE]EREETS or [HE]KHEREETS = to venerate (*Isaiah 29:23*).

BRANCHES: עריץ/KHOREETS = tyrant; ערץ/KHERETS = power. ARISTOCRAT, AUTOCRAT and DEMOCRAT < Greek *kratos* (power or rule).

DAIS/טָס DTAS [TS → DS]

ROOTS: DAIS < Old French *deis* (raised table in dining hall) < Latin *discus* (platter). Aramaic טס/TAS or DAS = metal plate or serving tray.

BRANCHES: DESK, DISCUS, DISH, and DISK. German *Tisch* and Yiddish *tish* = table.

DAM[P]/דָם DUMB [DM]

ROOTS: DAMP (wet)? < Middle English term for poison gas. דם/DAM = liquid, especially blood (*Genesis 4:10*) or wine (*Genesis 49:11*). דמעה/DEEMA = juice (*Exodus 22:28*) or teardrop (*Jeremiah 31:15*).

BRANCHES: MEAD and other wet DM reversals relate to terms like מיץ/MEETS (juice) and מטר/MATAR (rain – an alternative etymon for WATER). טנן/DTEENAN = to dampen or moisten.

DA[N]CE/דָץ DO(T)S [D-TS → DNS]

ROOTS: DANCE (to move to music or to leap) < Old French *danser*; no IE root is known. דץ/DAT[S] = to leap (*Job 41:14*); the N of DANCE was added.

BRANCHES: Russian and Yiddish *tants* (dance) retains a TS ending.

DATA/תֵת TATE [TT → DD]

ROOTS: Latin terms of giving include *datus*, *dotare*, and *dare*. Greek *didonai* = to give; the IE root is *do* (to give). תת/TAT = "give" (*Genesis 29:19*); the infinitive נתן/NOTAN = to give. נתון/NATOON = give or DATUM.

BRANCHES: Cognates at IE *do* include ADD, ANECDOTE, ANTIDOTE, BETRAY, CONDONE, DATE, DONATE, DONOR, DOWRY, EDITION, ENDOW, PARDON, PERDITION, RENDER, RENT, SAMIZDAT, SURRENDER, TRADITION, TRAITOR, TREASURE and VEND. See "ENDOW." Swahili *toa*, Hungarian *ad*, and Russian *dat* = to give.

DAUB/טָבַל DTABH-[AL] [T-BH-(L) → DB]

ROOTS: DAUB (to paint crudely) < Latin *dealbare* (to whitewash) < IE root *albho* (white). 1. For this etymology see "ALBINO." 2. טבל/DTABH[AL] = to dip, plunge (*II Kings 5:14*); to stain, dye. 3. צבע/T(S)ABHA = to paint, dye, dip (Heb., Aram., Arabic).

BRANCHES: DAB, DAPPLE, TABBY (borrowed from Arabic) and TABLEAU may be related – see "DIVE."

DELIC[ACY]/דֶקֶל DECK-EL [DKL → DLK]

ROOTS: DELICACY < Latin *delicere* (to delight – no IE root is known). DOLCE < Latin *dulcis* (sweet) < IE root *dlk-u* (sweet). דקל/DEKEL (DLK after metathesis) = date palm or its sweet fruit (Talmudic Hebrew, related to חדקל/HEEDEKEL of *Genesis 2:14*). A relevant DK or TK word is מתוק/[MA]TOK (sweet).

BRANCHES: DELICATE[ESSEN], DELICIOUS, DELIGHT, DULET, DULCIFY, DULCIMER, GLUCOSE, GLYCERIN and LICORICE.

DENSE/דֶשֶׁן DES[H]-EN [DSN → DNS]

ROOTS: DENSE < Latin *densus* (thick) and IE root *dens* (thick). דשן/DES[H]EN = fat; דשן/DAS[H]AN = "waxen fat" (*Deuteronomy 31:20*; DNS after metathesis).

BRANCHES: Listed cognates include CONDENSE, DENSITY and DASYURE.

[DE]STROY/צוּר TSOOR [TS-R → ST-R]

ROOTS: DESTROY < Latin *destruere* < *de* (down) + *struere* (to build). צור/TSOOR or STOOR = to "fashion" (*Exodus 32:4*) or "form – see "STYLE." מצור/[MA]TSOR = citadel.

BRANCHES: סדר/SADTAR = to order or arrange. Cognates of DESTROY include CONSTRUCT, INSTRUCT, OBSTRUCT and STRUCTURE.

DEX[TROUS]/דֵעַ DAY-KHA [D-KH]

ROOTS: DEXTROUS < Latin *dexter* (skillful; right-hand side) < IE root *deks*. ידע/YODAA or [YO]DAKHA = "skilled" (*I Samuel 16:18*). דע/DAKHA or דעת/DAKHAS = knowledge, wisdom.

BRANCHES: AMBIDEXTROUS, DEXEDRINE, DEXTERITY.

[DIA]SPORA/פְּזֻר PA-SARE [PSR → SPR]

ROOTS: DIASPORA < Greek *sporas* (scattered, dispersed) < IE root *sper* (to strew). פזר/PEEZAR or PEESAR = disperse, scatter (*Esther 3:8*).

BRANCHES: פרוס/PAROOS and פרוש/PAROOSH = spread. הפיץ/[HA]FEETS (to scatter) probably influenced Old English *fesian* (to drive off), the source of FAZE. תפוצה/[TI]FOOTSA = diaspora, dispersion. Cognates of DIASPORA include BOWSPRIT, SPRAWL, SPERM, SPIT, SPREAD, SPORADIC, SPORE, SPROUT, and SPURT. Consider DISPERSE, INTERSPERSE, SPARSE, SPRAY and SPRY. See "SPREAD."

DIK-DIK/דקדוק   DIK-DOOK   [DK]

ROOTS: DIK-DIK = native Ethiopic name for the foot-tall miniature deer. דק/DUK = fine, very small (*Exodus 16:14*); דקדוק/DIKDOOK = detail, minuteness; grammar. See "TALCUM."

DILEMMA/דלמא   DILL-MA   [D = LMH]

ROOTS: DILEMMA (perplexing situation) < Greek *di* (two) + *lemma* (proposition or assumption). Aramaic דלמא/DILMA = perhaps, what if. Aramaic דו/DOO = two (see "DUO"); למה/LAMA = why, wherefore (*Genesis 24:31*).

BRANCHES: LEMMA = assumed premise.

DIN[GO]/תן   TON   [TN → DN]

ROOTS: DINGO is the native name for the Australian wild dog. תן/TAN = jackal (*Isaiah 34:13*).

BRANCHES: Japanese *tanuki* = fox, racoon-dog; Maya *tsamak* = fox; Indonesian *andjing* = dog. MUTT reversed may be a TM variant of a TN etymon; it is currently linked to the epithet "muttonhead."

[DINO]SAUR/שרץ   SHERR-[ETS]   [S-R-(TS)]

ROOTS: [DINO]SAUR < Greek *sauros* (lizard). שרץ/S(H)ERE(T)S = reptile (*Genesis 1:20*). The Hebrew S-R-TS etymon infers swarming; the R-TS element is רץ/RUTS (to run).

BRANCHES: [LI]ZARD is a cognate of DINOSAUR. The prefix *deinos* (monstrous) recalls the תנינים/TANEEN[EEM], the "sea monsters" of *Genesis 1:21*. Elsewhere the TN (DN) term is rendered "crocodile." See "TUNA."

DIVAN/דחון   DAH-VAHN   [DHVN]

ROOTS: DIVAN (a large, low sofa or a council room in the Orient) < Turkish and Persian. DEWAN (a government official in India), however, is linked to Arabic. דחון/DAHVAN = a long, low coffee table (as set up in Near-Eastern offices) appears in the Biblical Aramaic of *Daniel 6:19*.

DOODLE/דדה   DEE-DAH   [DD]

ROOTS: DOODLE (to scribble , move aimlessly, dawdle) < English dialect term for wasting time. The IE root of DODDER and DOTE is *dud* (to shake), while the IE base *dheudh* combines moving confusedly with shaking. נדד/[NA]DAD = to wander (*Proverbs 27:8*) and to shake (*Psalms 64:9*). דדה/DEEDA = to walk like a baby or to go "softly" or slowly" (*Isaiah 38:15, Psalms 42:5*).

BRANCHES: DAWDLE (origin unknown), TEETER, TOT, TODDLE and TOTTER should all relate here.

DOUCHE/דוח   DOO-UKH   [D-O-KH]

ROOTS: DOUCHE (French; a jet of liquid used in bathing) < Latin *ductio* (a leading away) and *ducere* (to lead) < IE root *deuk* (to lead). הדיח/[HA]DEEAKH = to rinse or flush. The genital cleansing of DOUCHE is apparent in *Isaiah 4:4* –"When my Lord has *washed away* the filth of the daughters of Zion." נדח/[NA]DUKH or ידח/[YEE]DUKH = to thrust away, expel.

BRANCHES: CONDUCT, DOCK, DUCT – see "SEDUCE."

DOXY/תחת   TUKH-US   [T-KH-(S) → DX]

ROOTS: DOXY (slang for beggar's mistress) < obsolete English term *docke* (rump). תחת/TAKHAS or TAKHAT = under, beneath (*Genesis 18:4*); rump, buttocks – as in Yiddish *tochis* or *tukhis*.

BRANCHES: Reverse to KT for Greek *cata* (down), source of CATA-words like CATARACT.

DUNE/נד   NADE   [ND → DN]

ROOTS: DUNE < Old English *dun* and Germanic *dunaz* (hill). נד/NAD = mound, "heap" (*Exodus 15:8*).

BRANCHES: MOTTE (clump, hillock), NODE. The ANDES mountains derive from Quechua Indian *andi* (high crest). See "UNDULATE."

DUR[IAN]/דרדר   DAR-DAR   [DR]

ROOTS: DURIAN (prickly fruit) < Malay *duri* (thorn, prickle). We all encounter "thorns and *thistles*" (דרדר/DARDAR – *Genesis 3:18*) when working our fields of endeavor.

BRANCHES: THORN, akin to Germanic *dorn*, is related. The IE root for prickly plants is *(s)ter*.

DUR[UM]/אטריה   IDT-REE-YAH   [TR → DR]

ROOTS: DURUM (hard wheat used for spaghetti) < Latin *durus* (hard). DURRA or DOURAH (grain producing sorghum) < Arabic *dhurah*. Aramaic אטריה/ID(T)REEAH = spaghetti, noodle, vermicelli.

EDDY/אד   AID   [ED]

ROOTS: EDDY (current of air or water; whirlpool) < Middle English *ydy* < Old Norse *idha* (an eddy, whirlpool). אד/AD = "flow" or "flood" (*Genesis 2:6*).

BRANCHES: EDDY and ET CETERA are cognates at IE root *eti* (above, beyond) – see "ADD." If Latin *unda* (wave) is a nasalization of an AD root of effluence, then INUNDATE, SURROUND and UNDULATE also relate.

EFFULGE[NT]/בלג   VOL-UG   [BH-L-G]

ROOTS: Latin *effulgere* = to shine out; EFFULGENCE infers figurative luster and radience as well. בלג/BHALUG = "flash" (*Amos 5:9*) or "good cheer" (*Job 9:27*); בלג/BALUG = shine in Arabic.

BRANCHES: Harden the G to see the flashing FLICK[ER]; harden the liquid (L to R) to see ברק/BARAK (the flash of lightning).

ESPAL[IER]/סבל   SA-BALL   [SBL → SPL]

ROOTS: ESPALIER (trellis) < Italian *spalla* (shoulder, support). סבל/SABOL = porter; סבל/SABHAL = to carry, bear, or shoulder (*Psalms 144:14*).

ESTRO[GEN]/צרעה   TSEER-UH   [TS-R-U → ST-R-U]

ROOTS: ESTRUS and ESTROGEN are terms of female desire < Greek *oistros* (gadfly, sting). צרעה/TSEERAH = hornet (*Exodus 23:28*). צר/TSUR = distress.

BRANCHES: צריך/TSOREE[KH] = desire; reverse TS-R for רצה/RATSA (to want, desire). RUT, EROTIC[ISM] from Greek *erotos* and LUST (R to L change) may be related.

[EX]TEN[D]/נטה   NOT-UH   [NT → TN]

ROOTS: EXTEND < IE root *ten* (to stretch). נטה/NATA = to extend or "stretch out" (*Exodus 10:12* – NT→TN).

BRANCHES: Cognates include ABSTAIN, ATTENUATE, CONTAIN, CONTEND, CONTINUE, DETAIN, DISTEND, ENTERTAIN, EXTENSION, INTEND, LIEUTENANT, MAINTAIN, OBTAIN, OSTENSIBLE, PERTAIN, PRETEND, RETAIN, SITAR, SUSTAIN, TENABLE TENACIOUS, TENANT, TENDER (see "ENDOW"), TENEMENT, TENET, TENDRIL, TENON, TENOR, TENUOUS, TENURE, and THIN. For a TN antonym: צנום/T[S]AN[OOM] = meager, shrunken.

[E]XULT/סלד　　　SEAL-AIDT　　　[SLD → SLT]

ROOTS: EXULT < Latin *exsultare* < *saltare* (to leap up). סלד/SEELÄDT = (to spring, jump, leap up, exult (*Job 6:10*).

BRANCHES: Cognates include SALIENCE, SALIENT, SALLY, SALMON (the leaping fish), SALTANT, SALTARELLO, SALTATORY, and SALTIGRADE. סלד/SEELADT also means to praise, so that SALUTE (a leaping as well as a SALUTARY gesture), and LAUD may relate.

FAIL/נפל　　　(NA)-FAL　　　[PH-L]

ROOTS: FAIL (to be unsuccessful, to decline) < Latin *fallere* (to deceive). נפל/[NA]PHAL = to fall or "fail" (*I Kings 8:56*). הפיל/[HEE]PEEL or [HEE]FEEL = to defeat.

BRANCHES: FAULT is a cognate. See "FALL."

FATUITY/פתיות　　　FIT-EYE-OOT　　　[FT]

ROOTS: FATUITY (stupidity, foolishness) < Latin *fatuus* (foolish). FATUOUS = foolish. פתיות/PITAYOOT or FITAYOOS = foolishness. The PT or FT root appears twice in *Proverbs 1:22* – "How long, you *simpletons*, will you prefer *ignorance*?" Note the English suffixes -UITY and -OUS that echo the Hebrew יות/YOOT or YOOS.

BRANCHES: טפש/TEEPÄSH or DEEPÄSH = stupid person; תפל/TOPFUL = to be silly; טף/TUF = infant. FT = FD; BEFUDDLE, FUDDLE and FUDDY-DUDDY are related. Reversing FD or PD reveals DAFF (Scottish – to act the part of a fool), DAFFY, DAFT, DOPE (see "DIVE"), DOPPESS (Yiddish) and DUFFER. DEAF and STUPID may be more remotely connected.

FEAGUE/פגע　　　FEG-AH　　　[P(H)-G-U]

ROOTS: FEAGUE (to whip – now obsolete) < uncertain origin. פגע/P(H)AGA = to attack, meet, or "strike" (*II Samuel 1:15*).

BRANCHES: FIGHT, currently linked to IE root *pek* (to pluck, comb or fleece hair), might better be traced to the P(H)-G root above or to אבק/AVÄK (to wrestle – *Genesis 32:24*).

FEAR/פלח　　　FALL-(AKH)　　　[FL(H) → FR]

ROOTS: FEAR < Old English *faer* (sudden calamity) akin to Latin *periculum* (danger) < IE root *per* (to try, risk). פלח/P(H)ALAKH or FALAH = fear (Aramaic and Assyrian). בהלה/B(H)IHALA = sudden haste or terror (L = R).

BRANCHES: PERIL is a cognate of FEAR. Spanish *peligro* (danger) echoes our PL(K) etymon. Hawaiian *weli* and Proto Eastern Polynesian *weliweli* = fear, terror (P = W).

FELLAH/פלח　　　PHUL-LUH　　　[P(H)-L-H]

ROOTS: FELLAH = a laborer, peasant or commoner in Arabic countries < Arabic *felaha* (to plow). פלח/FOLAH or POLAKH = to break up earth or plow (*Psalms 141:7*). Aramaic פלחן/FOOLKHAN or POOLKHAN = service, temple worship.

BRANCHES: The common FELLOW or PLOUGH[MAN], plain FOLK who are VULGAR (Latin *vulgus* = common people) might derive from the FL(K) or PLK root above – see "BREAK" and "PLOUGH." The hard work of PLK appears in Rumanian *plic[ticos]* (tedious). IE root *bhlagh* is the source of Sanskrit *brah[ma]* (prayer, priest). This may link up to the PLH prayer service term or to the possible source of BRAHMA, BRAHMANISM and the BRAHMIN – אברהם/ABHRAHAM (Abraham). Abraham is to have sent monotheism to the East according to commentaries on *Genesis 25:6*.

FEN[WAY]/יון　　　(YA)-VEIN　　　[(Y)VN]

ROOTS: Boston's FENWAY was built on boggs; FEN = a marsh < Germanic *pon-yo* and Gothic *fani* (mud) < IE root *pen* (swamp). יון/[YA]VÄN = mud, mire (*Psalms 69:3*).

BRANCHES: FENNY is the adj. Chinese *juan ni* = mire (ju < יו/YV).

FERO[CIOUS]/פרא　　　FERR-EH　　　[PH-R-E]

ROOTS: FEROCIOUS < Latin *ferus* (wild or fierce). פרא/PHERE = savage or wild, applying to man (*Genesis 16:12*) or beast (*Jeremiah 14:6*).

BRANCHES: Related are words like FERAL, FERINE, FIERCE and FREE. The given IE root of FEROCIOUS is *ghwer* (wild beast), which recalls כפיר/K'FEER (young lion or predator – see "CAPRICORN"). בר/BAR = wild; the BR element combines to form words like מדבר/MIDBAR (wilderness) – see "BARIO." The WL of WILD may relate to the FR or BR root, as *weliweli* = fierce in Hawaiian. See "FREE."

FORAY/פרע　　　FOR-AH　　　[P(H)-R-U]

ROOTS: Old French *forrier* = to plunder or forage. פרע/FORA, FORAG or PORAG = to plunder, rob or pillage (*Judges 5:2*). Lack of restraint is the meaning in *Exodus 32:25*.

BRANCHES: PILLAGE is an L to R change away. FORAGE, POGROM, and PREY may be related. פרעוש/PAROSH or FARGOSH (flea) is a tiny pillager, foraging on living tissue. See "FREAK" and "FREE."

FORK/פרק　　　FER-EK　　　[P(H)-R-K]

ROOTS: Latin *furka* = hayfork; *furcatus* = cloven. פרק/PEREK or FEREK = body joint; fork in the road or crossway" (*Obadiah 14*). ברק/BHARAK = (forked) lightning.

BRANCHES: BIFURCATION, FURCATE and FURCULUM. See "BREAK."

GAD[ABOUT]/עדה　　　GADA　　　[GDH]

ROOTS: To GAD, the action of a GADABOUT, is to roam abroad idly or to ramble. Origin unknown. עדה/ADA or GADA = "to pass by," as a lion does in *Job 28:8*.

BRANCHES: To walk in Czech = *chod[iti]*; in Fijian its *gade*.

GALYAK/גלוח　　　GEEL-OO-AKH　　　[G-L-KH]

ROOTS: GALYAK (premature lamb) < Russian *golyak* (bare, naked). The IE root *gal* and Russian *golyi* = bald or naked. גלוח/GEELOOAKH = shaving; נגלח/GEELAKH = to shave off hair (*Leviticus 14:8*); נגלוי/GALOOY = uncovered (*Numbers 24:4*); נגלה/GALAH = to reveal, uncover, lay bare or naked (*I Sam. 9:15*).

BRANCHES: קרח/KORAH = bald (*Leviticus 13:41, 42*). CALLOW = bald. German *kahl* and Rumanian *chel* = bald. Chinese *ch'ih lo[te]* and Hawaiian *holowale* = naked. See "GLABROUS."

GEN[OCIDE]/עם　　　GUM　　　[GM → GN]

ROOTS: GENOCIDE (ordered mass murder of a recognizable racial or other group) < Greek *genos* and *genea* (race, family) < IE root *gen* ("to give birth . . ."). 1. עם/UM or GUM = people or nation (*Numbers 23:10*). 2. The first recorded birth involves the verb קנה/KANA (to create, acquire – *Genesis 4:1*). Cain was the progenitor of the first recognizable tribe. קנה/KONEH = branch.

BRANCHES: GENEALOGY, GENTEEL, GENTILE, NATION, etc. see "KIN."

GES[TURE]/עָשָׂה   GUS-AH   [GSH]

ROOTS: GESTURE < Latin *gestus* (gesture) < "verb of unknown origin" [AHD] meaning to carry, carry on, act or do. The earliest form of this verb is ascertained to be *ges*. עשה/GASA or ASA = to do (*Genesis 2:2*), behave (*Genesis 20:9*) or "deal with" (*Genesis 24:12*).

BRANCHES: Given cognates include BELLIGERENT, CONGEST, DIGEST, GERUND, GEST[E], GESTATION, GESTICULATE, INJEST, REGISTER, SUGGEST, and VELIGER. More ע as G at "GAUZE" and GONORRHEA."

GHERK[IN]/יָרָק   JER-EK   [JRK → GH-R-K]

ROOTS: GHERKIN < Dutch *agurkje* (cucumber). ירק/YEREK or JEREK = vegetable (*Exodus 10:15*); ירוק/YAROK or JAROK = green — see "YOLK."

BRANCHES: "Gemini" derives from the IE root *yem*, so G words may have Y roots. Similarly, ten of the first fifteen Y words indexed in the AHD derive from G roots. Another English G from Hebrew י/Y, J might be GET from יד/YAD or JADT (hand — *Genesis 16:12*) [via the IE root *ghed* (to seize, take)]. A given cognate of GET, however, is GUESS — suggesting a Hebrew etymon like אחז/[O]KHAZ (to seize, grasp, get legally).

GIAOUR/גֵר   GAIR   [GR]

ROOTS: GIAOUR = a non-Moslem < Turkish *giaur* or Persian *gaurigabri*. (Both given etymons are non-Semitic languages.) גר/GAR = stranger (*Exodus 2:22*).

GILL/נַחַל   (NA)-KHAL   [(N)-KH-L → GL]

ROOTS: GILL #4 = a river or stream < Old Norse *gil* (ravine). נחל/[NA]KHAL = ravine, stream (*Leviticus 23:40*).

BRANCHES: GHYLL is a stream or ravine. The GILA MONSTER (lizard) was named after the Gila River in Arizona. See "CATSKILL." GILL #1 (respiratory organ of fish) < IE root *ghel-[una]* (jaw); CHIL[OPOD] is a cognate. לחי/LEKHEE (KH-L reversed) = jaw or cheek; לחה/LAKHA = cheekbone in Arabic. GILL #2 (a liquid measure < Latin *gillo* (cooling vessel). לג/LOG (GL reversed) is a Biblical liquid measure — see "LIQUID." כלי/KALEE = vessel — see "SCULLERY." GILL #3 (girl) is related to JILL (sweetheart), GILLIE (lad) and names like GILLIAM and JULIEN. ילד/YELED or JEL[ED] = boy; YALDA or JAL[DA] = girl; עלם/ELEM or GEL[EM] = young man; עלמה/ALMA or GAL[MA] = young woman or GAL. See "ALUMNI."

GIPO[N]/גוּפִיָּה   GOOP(H-EE-AH)   [G-P(H)]

ROOTS: GIPON (tunic worn under armor) < Old French. גופיה/GOOP(HEEA) = undershirt; גוף/GOOP(H) = body (*I Chronicles 10:12*).

GIVE/הַב   HAV   [H-BH → GV]

ROOTS: GIVE < IE root *ghabh* (to give or receive). הב/HAV = give (*Genesis 29:21*). See "HAVE" and "HAVEN."

BRANCHES: יהב/YAHAV or JAHAV = to give. חב/KHOV = a debt (*Ezekiel 18:7*). It is the possible source of GIVE and of the following given cognates of GIVE: DEBIT, DEBT, DEVOIR, DUE, DUTY, and ENDEAVOR. Other cognates listed at *ghabh* include ABLE, BINNACLE, COHABIT, FORGIVE, GAVEL, GIFT, HABIT, EXHIBIT, INHABIT, INHIBIT, PROHIBIT and PROVENDER. Chinese *kap* and Hawaiian *haawi* = to give.

GUZZLE/חָסַל   KHA-SAL   [KH-S-L → GZL]

ROOTS: GUZZLE (to drink greedily) < origin unknown. חסל/KHASAL = to devour (*Deuteronomy 28:38*).

BRANCHES: חסיל/KHASEEL = locust; חסול/KHEESOOL = liquidation; גזל/GOZAL = to steal.

HAND[SOME]/חָמוּד   HA-MOOD   [HMD → HND]

ROOTS: HANDSOME (good looking) < Middle English *handsom* = easy to handle. חמוד/HAMOOD = noble, lovely and חמד/HEMED = "handsome" (*Ezekiel 23:6*). חן/HAN = grace and charm.

HA[T]CH/חֵיק   HAKE   [HYK]

ROOTS: HATCH (to bring forth young by applying warmth) < Middle English *hacchen* (probably unrecorded Anglo-Saxon term for rearing young or for genitalia). חיק/HAK = bosom or lap. "...Carry them in your *bosom* as a nurse carries an infant..."– *Numbers 11:12*.

HAVEN/חֹפֶן   HO-FUN   [H-PH-N]

ROOTS: HAVEN (sheltered place, harbor) < German *hafen* < IE base with basic sense "that holds" < IE root *kap* (to grasp). חפן/HOPHAN or KHOFAN = to take a fistful; חפן/HOPHAN or KHOFAN = a fistful (*Ecclesiastes 4:6*); כף/KAPH = palm of hand.

BRANCHES: חפה/HAFA or KHAFA = to cover; חפה/HOOPA or KHOOPA = a canopy; חבה/HABHA or KHABHA = to conceal. קבל/KAB[AL] = receive. ACCEPT, CAPSULE, COOP, COVE, COVER, HEAVEN, HOVEL, KEEP are related HV or KP terms — see "CAVITY," "CUBBY," and "CUFF." Thai *gep* = to hold or keep. Malay *ka[m]pun* = enclosure.

HEAD/קָדְקֹד   COD-CODE   [KD → HD]

ROOTS: HEAD < IE root *kadh* (to protect). קדקד/KODKOD = crown of the head (*Deuteronomy 33:20*); קדד/KADAD = to bow the head *Genesis 24:48*); קדם/KOD[EM] = [A]HEAD; קדם/KOD[UM] = to HEAD for.

BRANCHES: Arabic *kaid* = captain or head; CAUDILLO is a leader or head (Spanish < Arabic). HAT and HEED are listed cognates of HAT; the CHUDDAR (< Hindi *cadar* or shawl), the HOOD and the TOQUE (KT reversed) should be related headgear. CODA is an antonym.

HONES[T]/כֵּנוּת   KHANE-OOS   [(K)H-N]

ROOTS: Almost every H word is traced to a K etymon, but the etymology of HONEST (true) stops at Latin *honos* (honor). הן/HAN = yes; כן/KAN = yes, honest, upright (*Genesis 42:11*); כנות/KHANOOS = honesty; נכון/[NA]KHON = correct.

BRANCHES: HONOR and *honos* might relate to הון/HON (wealth). Korean *choun* = good.

HONEY/עֹנֶג   (K)HO-NEG   [KH-N-G → HNY]

ROOTS: HONEY < Old English *hunig* < IE root *keneko* (yellow, golden — no known English cognates). ענג/ONEG or KHONEG = pleasure, enjoyment, "delight" (*Isaiah 58:3*). הנאה/HANA'AH = pleasure. עוני/(K)HENOOY = pain — an antonym.

BRANCHES: ענב/(K)HANA[V] = (sweet) grape, berry.

HOOT/הֵד   HADE   [HD → HT]

ROOTS: HOOT (shout, hollow sound) < Middle English *houten* (to utter the exclaimation "hoot!"); ? < Old Norse. הד/HĀDT = echo, noise, shout or "joyful shout (*Ezekiel 7:7*).

BRANCHES: HOITY-[TOITY] = noisy mirth; HOOT OWL, HOOTENANY and perhaps (S)HOUT. הו/HŌ is an exclamation like English HO.

HO[W]/הֵיךְ   HEYKH   [H-Y-KH]

ROOTS: HOW < Old English *hu* < IE root *k(w)o*. היך/HEYKH = "how" (*I Chronicles 13:12*). איך/ĀYKH and איכה/ĀYKHA = how.

BRANCHES: Polish *jak* = how (preserving Hebrew's Y-KH).

HUG/חָגַר   HUG-(ARE)   [HG(R)]

ROOTS: HUG (to clasp, embrace) "probably" < Old Norse *hugga* (to console, comfort). 1. חגר/HOG[AR] = to gird, bind, clasp—see "GIRDLE." 2. חבק/HAVĀK = to embrace (*II Kings 4:16*—HVK = HUG).

BRANCHES: חוג/HOOG = circle. The HOG has a round girth.

HUM[US]/חֶמֶר   HAME-(AIR)   [HM(R)]

ROOTS: HUMUS (brown or black decomposed animal or vegetable matter) < Latin *humus* (earth). Greek *khamai* = on the ground. The reconstructed IE root is *dhghem* (earth—DM and GH-M combined. חמר/HŌM[ER] or KHŌM[ER] = earth, clay (*Jeremiah 15:6*); חמר/HĀME[R] or KHĀME[R] = pitch, bitumen, slime (*Genesis 11:3; Exodus 2:3*). חמיץ/HUMEE[TS] = fermented, decomposed silage; חום/KHOOM = brown. The DM of *dhghem* < אדמה/ADAMA (earth, ground) + אדם/ADAM = earthling, man—*Genesis 2:7*.

BRANCHES: Given cognates include BRIDEGROOM, CHAMELEON, CHAMOMILE, EXHUME, GERMANDER, HOMAGE, HOMBRE, HOMINID, HOMO, HUMAN, HUMANE, HUMBLE, HUMILIATE, ZAMINDAR (via Persian), and ZEMSTVO (via Russian). CERAM[IC] is a #2-#3 root letter metathesis of חמר/KHŌMER (clay). חמרי/HOMREE = material.

HYGIE[NE]/גֵהָה   GAY-HAH   [GH → HG]

ROOTS: Greek *hugies* = healthy < IE root *g(w) ei* = to live. גהה/GĀHA = "good health" (*Proverbs 17:22*); נהות/GAH[OOS] = hygiene. The IE root and cognates like QUI[CK] echo חי/KHI (to live; alive, active—*Genesis 3:22*); חיה/KHAYE = lively, strong (*Exodus 1:19*); חיוא/KHĀVA = living creature (Aramaic).

BRANCHES: Listed cognates include AEROBIC, AMPHIBIOUS, BIO-, BIOTIC, CENOBITE, MICROBE, REVIVE, SURVIVE, SYMBIOSIS, VIABLE, VIAND, VICTUAL, VITAL, VIVA, VIVACIOUS, VIVID, (consider אביב/AVEVE = springlike) and ZOO. Old Indic *ayu* = alive.

HYOS(CYAMINE)/חֲזִיר   HUS-(EAR)   [HS(R)]

ROOTS: Greek *hys* = pig. The IE root *su* =pig. חזיר/KHAZEER or HAS[EER] = pig (*Leviticus 11:7*).

BRANCHES: Listed cognates include HOG, HYENA, HYOSINE, SOW and SWINE. While the Arabic pig, *chanzir*, is merely a nasalization of the Hebrew KH-S-R, the Norwegian *gris* and the Modern Greek *chi'ros* swap #2 and #3 root letters (metathesis). The first two root letters are reversed in the pig words of Celtic (*sukko*), Chinese (*shi; chu* = hog), Finnish (*sika*), Malay: Tidore (*soho*), and Old English (*sugu* – sow).

IGN[ITION]/נָגַה   NO-GAH   [NG → GN]

ROOTS: Latin *ignis*, Sanskrit *agnih*, and IE root *egni* = fire. נגה/NOGA = to shine, be bright (*Isaiah 9:1*); brightness.

BRANCHES: Cognates include AGNI, IGNEOUS, IGNITE and IGNITRON. Rusian *agon* and Polish *ogien* = fire. Czech *ohen* recalls חם/HAM or KHAM (heat; sun).

IL[LEGAL]/אַל   ULL   [AL]

ROOTS: The negative prefix IL-, used in L words like ILLICIT, is said to be a variant of IN- (see "INSOMNIA"). אל/AL = no (*Genesis 19:17*), don't or naught (*Job 24:25*).

BRANCHES: Reverse vowel-L for לא/LŌ (no). The prefix ILL- (< Old Norse *illr*, bad) could relate to the etymons here or to terms like עול/AVEL (injustice, wrong).

[IN]CARCER[ATE]/קִר   KEER   [KR]

ROOTS: IE root *carcer* = barrier, enclosure, prison < "Latin noun, probably borrowed from an unidentified source." קר/KEER or קיר/KEEYR = a wall (*Leviticus 14:37*) or (walled) city (*Isaiah 15:1*). קרה/KĀRA = to board up or seal.

BRANCHES: קריה/KEERYA and עיר/KHEER = (walled) city. Cognates of INCARCERATE are CANCEL, CHANCEL, and CHANCELLOR. See "CELL" and "COURT."

INN/חָנָה   HUN-NAH   [HN]

ROOTS: INN (hotel; originally a dwelling or lodging) < Old English, akin to Old Norse *inne* (within). חנה/HANA or KHANA = to encamp, מחנה/[MA]HANE = a camp—see "HAUNT."

BRANCHES: אונה/AVNA or OONA = roadside inn (post–Biblical Hebrew). KHAN = inn in Turkey, etc.; Chinese *lukuan* = hotel.

I[SLAND]/אִי   EE   [EY]

ROOTS: ISLAND < Middle English *iland* < Anglo-Saxon *iegland* (island land) < Germanic *aujo* ("thing on the water"). אי/EEY or EEJ = island (*Isaiah 11:11*).

JIB/גַב   JAV   [G-BH → JB]

ROOTS: JIB (to move backwards) < French *regimber* (to kick back). גב/GABH or JABH = a back.

BRANCHES: Other JIBs = projecting arms of a crane or projecting sail. גב/GABH or JABH = towards.

JIFFY/יָעַף   JA-UFF   [YAF → JIF]

ROOTS: JIFF or JIFFY = a moment, an instant; "done in a JIFFY" < origin unknown. יעף/YAUF or JAUF = in a great hurry, swiftly (*Daniel 9:21*).

BRANCHES: עף/AF = to fly—see "AVIATE." Both יעף/YAĀF and עיף/AYĀF = weary, slowed by fatigue.

JOI[N]T/יַחַד   JA-HADT   [YHD → J(N)T]

ROOTS: JOINT and JOINTLY (together) < Old French *joi[n]d[re]* (to join). יחד/YAKHĀD or JAHADT = to join (*Genesis 22:8*)—see "JUXTAPOSE." The N of JOINT is added by nasalization.

BRANCHES: יחד/JUHA(D)T and Spanish *junto* = together.

KEN[NING]/כנוי   KEEN- OOY   [KN]

ROOTS: KENNING = 1. recognition in Scotish, 2. a metaphysical name < Old Norse *kennungar*. The IE root is *gno* (to know). כנוי/KEENOOY = surname, nickname, pronoun or pseudonym. כנה/KEENA = to name or give a title. כנה/KANA = to call by name (Biblical Hebrew and Syriac).

BRANCHES: כן/KAN = yes (term of acknowledgement); עין/EEYĀN or KEEYĀN = to see (and thus know). Many of the following cognates of KENNING should relate: ABNORMAL, ACQUAINT, ANNOTATE, CAN, COGNITION, COGNIZANCE, CON, CONNOISSEUR, CONNOTE, CUNNING, DIAGNOSIS, ENORMOUS, GNOME, GNOSIS, IGNORANT, IGNORE, KEN, KITH, KNOW, NARRATE, NOBLE, NORMAL, NOTE, NOTIFY, NOTION, NOTORIOUS, PHYSIOGNOMY, PROGNOSIS, QUAINT, and RECOGNIZE.

KIN[D]/חנון   KHAN-(OON)   [KH-N]

ROOTS: KIND (merciful) < Germanic *kundjaz* (natural, native) < IE root *gen* (to give birth). חנון/KHANOON = kind, merciful, gracious (*Exodus 22:26*), חן/KHĀN = grace, favor; חנן/KHANAN = to act kindly; תחנה/[TI]KHEENA = favor, mercy, prayer for mercy.

BRANCHES: נחם/NOKHAM = pity (*Hosea 13:14*). GEN[TLE] and [BE]NIGN are akin to "gentile" and "kind" (manner, genre).

KNEE[L]/כנע   KON-AH   [KNU]

ROOTS: KNEEL (bow down on knees) < Latin *genu* (knee) and IE root *genu* (knee, angle). כנע/KONA = to humble, bring down, subjugate (*Leviticus 26:41*); כנעה/KEENA = subjugation.

BRANCHES: קמט/KEM[ET] = to fold or crease; כנן/KEENĀN = to coil; כנס/KANAS = to gather. The concordance suggests a link between כנע/KONA and כרע/KORA (to kneel); כרע/KERA = knee. KNEE and GENUFLECT are given cognates; KNUCKLE is not – see "ANKLE." Amazon Indian *kon* = knee.

LAQUER/לכה   LUCK-AH   [LKH]

ROOTS: *LAQUER* (a clear varnish) < Hindi *lakh* and Sanskrit *laksha* (a resinous substance on trees used in making shellac). לכא/LAKA = laquer; לכה/LAKAH = a glaze, polish; לכה/LEEKAH = to stain wood. These words are Mishnaic, not Biblical Hebrew.

BRANCHES: LAC and SHELLAC are related. SHELLAC in slang = to whip. לקה/LOKOH = to flog or LICK (beat up).

LEAT[HER]/גלד   (GE)-LET   [GLD → LTH]

ROOTS: LEATHER akin to German *Leder* < IE root *letro* (leather). גלד/[GE]LED = skin (*Job 16:15*). לט/LADT = cover – see "LID."

BRANCHES: Arabic *gild* = skin; Indonesian *kulit* = skin, leather.

LESS/לית   LACE   [LYS]

ROOTS: LESS < IE root *leu* (to loosen, divide, cut apart). לית/LĀS = "there is not" (Aramaic); ? < לא/LŌ (no) + יש/[Y]ASH (there is).

BRANCHES: In words like PRICELESS and USELESS, the suffix -LESS = "there is no" price or use, not that either has been loosened, divided or cut apart. LOSS is a cognate. See "LOOSE" below.

LOCK/לכד   LEKH-(ED)   [LKD]

ROOTS: LOCK (to secure) < Anglo-Saxon *loc* (a bolt, bar, enclosure, prison) < IE root *leug* (to bend, turn, wind). לכד/LEKHED = to seize, catch or take (*Deuteronomy 2:35*); it also means a snare or trap (*Proverb 3:26*).

BRANCHES: LATCH < Middle English *lacchen* (to seize, catch hold of). Latin *laqueus* = a snare. לחי/LIKHEE (cheek, clamps of a vise); Finnish *leuka* = cheek. לקח/LOKAH = to take. Given cognates include GARLIC, LEEK, and LOCKET. For LOCH, LAKE and LK or KL holes – see "HOLLOW."

LOC[UST]/ילק   (YE)LEK   [(Y)LK]

ROOTS: Latin *locusta* < IE root *lek* (to leap, fly). ילק/(YE)LEK = a kind of locust (*Jer. 51:14; Joel 1:4*).

BRANCHES: דלג/(DA)LUG is to leap. LOBSTER is a given cognate.

LOOSE/שלה   S(H)OL-OH   [S(H)-L → LS]

ROOTS: LOOSE < Old Norse *lauss*, akin to Germanic *leusan* and Old English *leas* (loose, free from, without) < IE root *leu* (to loosen, divide, cut apart). שלה/S(H)ALA = to be at ease, negligent (*II Chronicles 29:11*), to draw out; שלה/S(H)ALAH = to set free or let loose (*Genesis 8:7*); שלף/S(H)ALAF = to draw out or draw off (by untying); שלשל/S(H)ILS(H)AL = to loosen (bowels). Beside SL reversals, there are RS → LS shifts to consider: רשל/REES(H)ĀL = to loosen, to weaken; רשול/REES(H)OOL = indolence, neglect; רשות/RIS(H)OOT = permission.

BRANCHES: SL antonyms infer the opposite of loose or divided: שלשלת/S(H)ALSHELES = a chain; שלל/S(H)ILAL = to baste or stitch; שלב/S(H)EELĀV = to fit together; שליבה/S(H)ILEEVA = a bow or knot; של/S(H)EL = belonging to. Cognates of LOOSE include ABSOLUTE, ABSOLVE, ANALYSIS, DIALYSIS, DISSOLVE, LEASE, -LESS, LOSE, LYSIS, LYSO-, -LYTE, -LYTIC, PARALYSIS, RESOLVE, SOLUBLE, SOLUTION, and SOLVE. LASSO and LEASH ought to relate, though LEASH is linked to LAX and Latin *laxus* (loose). The IE root for LAXATIVE, RELAX, and SLACK is an SL term for *sleg* (slack, languid). SLOUCH ("origin uncertain") ought to relate. See "LATE," "SLOUGH," and "SOLVE." LASSITUDE < Latin *lassus* (faint, weary) should link up with חלש/HALASH (weak) and רשיש/RAS[HEESH] (weak – L=R). רשלן/RASHLAN (sluggard) is is an RS relative of SL and LS words like עצל/ATSĀL (lazy – *Proverbs 6:6*), LAZY, SLAT[TERN], SLOTH, and SLUT. Hungarian *lusta* = lazy.

LOUT/ירד   (YA)-RUD   [RD → LD]

ROOTS: LOUT (akward, stupid person) < Old English *lutan* (to bend down) akin to Old Norse *luta* (to bend down < "to make small") < IE root *leud* (small). ירד/[YA]RAD = to go down; הוריד/[HŌ]REED = to bring down, to lower; ירוד/[YA]ROOD = degenerate. Reverse LD for דל/DUL = poor (or DULL) person; דלל/DALAL = to dwindle; ילד/[YE]LED = (small) boy; a DL antonym is גדול/[GA]DOL (great, large) – see DILUTE" and "LAD."

BRANCHES: Cognates of LOUT include LITTLE and LOITER.

LUCK/חלק   HEY-LECK   [HLK]

ROOTS: LUCK < Middle Dutch *luc*, akin to German *gluck* (fortune, good luck). Yiddish *glick* is related. 1. חלק/[HĀ]LEK or KHALEK = fate, share or portion in life (*Isaiah 17:14*). 2. צלח/[TSA]LUK = prosperity, success, luck (*Genesis 24:42*).

LUNA[R]/לְבָנָה L(IVE)-UN-AH   [LVN → LUN]

ROOTS: Latin *luna* (moon) < IE root *leuk* (light, brightness). 1. לבנה/LIVANA = moon (*Isaiah 24:23; Songs 6:10*) or white (*Leviticus 13:4*). לבן/LAVAN = white (*Genesis 30:35* — see "ALBINO." LVN → LUN, as LAUN(DRY) < Latin *lav[are]* < לבן/LVN. The LK IE root < דלק/[DA]LUK (to burn — see "LIGHT").

BRANCHES: LUNAR CAUSTIC (a silver nitrate) is silvery or white, not from the moon, bright, or light-giving. LUNA, LUNATE, LUNATIC and SUBLUNARY are true cognates of LUNAR, but not LEA, LIGHT, LUCIFER, LUMINOUS, LUSTER, LYNX and OUNCE (as the AHD suggests). "Moon" in various dialects of Malay employ Hebrew's LVN: *bulan, fhulan, phulan,* and *wulan.* Fijian *vulavula* = moon.

MAR[BLE]/מְרַח MAR-(AH)   [MRH]

ROOTS: MARBLE < Greek *maramaros* < IE base *mer* (to rub). מרח/MORAH or MORAKH = to rub, to smooth (*Isaiah 38:21*); מרק/MORA[K] = rubbed, polished, scoured (*Leviticus 6:21*).

BRANCHES: מלל/MALAL = rub; מלץ/MAL[ATZ] = smooth; מלטש/MIL[OOTASH] = polished. The smooth, polished pearl may relate to MARBLE.

MARGARINE and MARGARITE, < Greek *margaron* and IE root *margarites* (pearl), may link up with the MRK etymons here — otherwise see "MAR[INE]" + "GRAIN." IE root *mer* (to rub away, harm) is the given source of NIGHTMARE, MORBID, MORSEL, MORTAL, MORTAR, and MURDER. These negative MR words recall the mottled quality of MARBLE and the disfigurement of MAR. The MR, ML etymons above can also rub the wrong way — see "MILL." מילה/MEELA = circumcision. The luster of MARBLE and the PEARL, along with the "bright" definition of מרק/MARAK (*II Chronicles 4:16*) recalls the IE root *mer* (...dim illumination). This root is the given source of MORGEN, MORNING, MORROW and MURKY.

MARE/חֲמוֹר (HA)-MORE   [(H)MR]

ROOTS: MARE < Old English *mere*, Germanic *marhon* and the IE root *marko* (horse). 1. חמור/HAMOR or KHAMOR = donkey or "ass" *Genesis 22:3.* 2. רמך/RAMAKH = a fast horse (*Esther 8:10* — RMK → MRK).

BRANCHES: MARSHAL is the only listed cognate of MARE. Donkey and horse terms merge, as German *Pferd* and Dutch *paard* (horse) match the פרד/PERED or PHERED (mule — *I Kings 18:5*). The KM or KN of the Hebrew donkey appears in Slavic horse names; MOKE is slang for donkey (KM reversed).

MARJO[RAM]/מִרְקַחַת MEER-KAH-(UT)   [(M)RKH]

ROOTS: MARJORAM (fragrant mint plants) < Latin *amarcus* (marjoram) < Greek *amarkos.* מרקחת/MEERKAKHA[T] = aromatic ointment (*Exodus 30:25*); מרקח/MERKA[K]H = perfume.

MARRO[W]/מוֹחַ MOW-AKH   [MWH → MRH]

ROOTS: MARROW < Anglo-Saxon *mearh* < IE base *mozgho* (marrow, brains). מוח/MOAH or MOWAKH = marrow, brains (*Job 21:24*).

BRANCHES: מצח/MAZAKH = brow, forehead. מצוע/MEEZOOAKH = midst.

MARRY/נַעֲרָה NAH-AR-AH   [NR → MR]

ROOTS: MARRY < Latin *maritus* (married) < IE root *mari* (young woman). נערה/NA'ARA (young woman — *Genesis 24:14*).

BRANCHES: MARITAL is a cognate of MARRY. MAY < Old Norse *maer* (girl). נערות/NA'AR[OOT] = youth. נער/NU'AR = young man or boy. Greek *meirax* (boy), Sanskrit *marya* (youth) and Latin *maris* (a man) are the given etymons of MALE. Finnish *nuore* = young. Linguists working on reconstructing a proto language called Nostratic arrive at the root *majr* (young male). The Altaic (Japanese-Korean-Mongolian) counterpart is *miarra* (to marry a man), the Asiatic is *mjr, mr* (man). See "MORON."

MASTABAH/מַצֵּבָה MA-TSAY-BHA   [M-TS-B → MSTB]

ROOTS: MASTABAH = oblong tomb or mortuary chapel in Arabic; equivalent to the dolmen or cromlech (top stone laid across base stones) found in pre-historic burial sites throughout Eurasia. מצבה/MATSABHA = tombstone, monument. The MUSTABAH or dolmen that Jacob builds over Rachel's grave is wrongly translated "pillar" in *Genesis 35:20.* מצב/MOOTSABH = military post, elevation or monument; יצב/[YA]TSABH = to set up, stabilize.

BRANCHES: See "STABLE" and "STUBBORN."

MAT[HEMATICS]/לָמַד (LA)MADT   [MD → MT]

ROOTS: MATHEMATICS < Greek *mathema* (science) < IE root *mendh* (to learn). מדע/MADA or MATA = science, knowledge or mind (*II Chronicles 1:11*). למד/[LA]MADT = to learn (*Deuteronomy 17:14*); ממוד/MAMUDT, מודד/MADTADT and מד/MADT = measure.

BRANCHES: More MD or MT measure words at "METER." The N in MENTAL, MIND and the IE root *mendh* is likely a nasalization. Aztec *mati* = to know.

MATTO[CK]/מַטֶּה MUTT-EH   [MTH]

ROOTS: MATTOCK (long-handled tool) < Vulgar Latin *mattea* (club), Latin *mateola* (rod, club), Sanscrit *matya* (club) and IE root *mat* (a kind of tool). מטה/MATEH = long stick or "rod" (*Exodus 4:2*).

BRANCHES: Cognates of MATTOCK include MACE, MACHETE, MASON and MASSACRE. MAST < IE root *mazdo* (pole, rod, mast). IE base *mei-t* (post, stake) is the etymon for METE (boundry mark). MATRASS (long glass tube) < Gaulish *mataris* (javelin). MASHIE or MASHY (golf club) < Late Latin *mattiuca.*

MAW/מֵעִי M'EE   [MGY]

ROOTS: MAW (the stomach or its cavity; now used for gullet and mouth as well) < Old English *maga* (stomach) < IE root *mak* (leather bag). מעי/MIEE or MIGEE = intestine, entrails, "belly" (*Jonah 2:1*). The IE root's MK leather bag could also derive from a KM reversal of חמת/KHAM[ET] (water skin or bag — *Genesis 21:14*).

BRANCHES: Dutch *maag*, Finnish *maha*, German *Magen*, Hungarian *gyomor* (reversing MG), Norwegian and Swedish *mage*, and Yiddish *mogen* all mean stomach.

MAZA[RD]/מֵצַח MAY-TZAH   [M-(T)Z-H]

ROOTS: MAZARD (now obsolete) = head, skull or face < IE root *ant* (front, forehead). מצח/MA[T]ZAH or MAT[ZAH] = brow or forehead (*Jeremiah 3:3*).

BRANCHES: Cognates of MAZARD include ADVANCE, ANCIENT, ANTE, ANTERIOR, ANTI-, ANTIC, ANTIQUE, UNTIL and VEDANTA. The AHD links the following words to *ant*: AMBI-, AMBIDEXTROUS, AMBIENCE, AMBIGUOUS, AMBITION, AMBIVALENCE, AMPHI-, AMPHIBIAN, AMPHITHEATER, AMPUTATE, BE-, BESET, BEDAZZLE, BEDECK, BEJEWEL, BEWHISKERED, BIVOUAC, OMBUDSMAN and UMLAUT.

MEAT/מֵצָה   [OO]MIT[SA]   [(A)M-T(S)-H]

ROOTS: MEAT akin to Sanskrit *madana* (delightful) < IE root *mad* (moist). מעדן/MA'ADAN = tidbit, "dainty" food (*Genesis 49:20*). עדן/ĀDEN = delight, Eden. אמצה/OOMT[SA] = meat, beefsteak; תמד/TEMED = to moisten.

BRANCHES: Cognates include MATE and MYNA.

MEGALO[MANIAC]/גָּמָל   GAMAL   [GML → MGL]

ROOTS: Greek *megalo* = great < IE root *meg* (great). גמל/GAMAL = to ripen, mature, wean, grow large (*Genesis 21:8*). The largest animal in the Middle East is the גמל/GAMAL (camel). גמר/GAMAR = to complete; גמר/GIMAR = complete, learned (intellectual greatness or mastery – Aramaic of *Ezra 7:12*).

BRANCHES: The many cognates of MEGALO- and MEGA- words include: MAESTRO, MAGISTERIAL, MAGISTRATE, MAGNATE, MAGNITUDE, MAGNUM, MAGNANIMOUS, MAGNIFICENT, MAGNIFY, MAGNILOQUENT, MAHATMA, MAHARAJAH, MAJOR, MASTER, MISTER, MAXIMUM, MAY (month), MICKLE (from Old Norse *mikill*, great), MUCH and OMEGA. MACRO- words are related; Greek *makros* and Australian Aborigine *murr-ka* = large.

METAL/מְטַל   MA-TAL   [MTL]

ROOTS: METAL < Greek *metallon* (mine, quarry). מטל/MATAL = Arabic "forged iron: hence the English word METAL" (citing from *The Hebrew-English Lexicon of the Bible*.

BRANCHES: מטיל/MITEEL and מוטה/MOTA = iron bars (*Leviticus 26:13; Job 40:18*).

MEZZA[NINE]/אֶמְצָע   EM(T)Z-AH   [M-(T)Z-A]

ROOTS: MEZZANINE (lower balcony or sub-story in a building) < Italian *mezzo* (half, medium, moderate and middle). MESO-/ Greek *mesos* (middle) < IE root *medhyo* (middle). אמצע/EMT(Z)A or EM(T)SA = middle; מציעא/MI(T)ZEEA or MIT(S)EEYA = middle, midst or average in Aramaic.

BRANCHES: Arabic *nisf* and Swahili *nusu* = half (NS = MS). מזוזה/MIZOOZA (doorpost or MEZUZAH) refers to the Scriptural passage placed in the middle of the doorposts, which were in the middle of each home. Reversing to ZM, עצם/ETZEM = bone, body, substance, ESSENCE and probably "middle part." The term in *Exodus 12:41* should not be translated "on that *selfsame* day," but "at midday" – as also evidenced by the similar Chinese term *zhong* (center, middle, neutron, core, middle finger, backbone, noon and midday). See OSTEOMA." Cognates and related words should include: AMID, INTERMEDIATE, MEAN, MEDIAL, MEDIAN, MEDIATE, MEDIEVAL, MEDIOCRE, MEDITERRANEAN, MEDIUM, MERIDIAN, MESO-, MESOLITHIC, MESOSPHERE, MEZZO-, MIZZEN, MIZZENMAST, MIDDLE, MILIEU, and MITTEN. From Greek *meta* (between) comes words like METATARSUS and METATHESIS. **See "METER."**

MOLE (3)/מִלּוֹא   ME-LO   [ML]

ROOTS: editMOLE (3) = a barrier, breakwater, massive jetty < Latin *moles* = a mass, heavy bulk, dam, mole, massive structure. מלוא/MEELŌ = low wall, fortified building, "Millo citadel (*II Samuel 5:9; I Kings 9:15*). מלו/MILŌ = filling matter; מלא/MALĀ = to be full, to fill; מלל/MELEL = border; מול/MOOL = facing.

BRANCHES: Cognates of MOLE (3) are DEMOLISH, MOLECULE and MOLEST. A MULLION is a dividing structure, and MURAL (wall) is an R→L change away. Latin *murus* < IE root *mei* (to build fences or fortifications).

MOSAIC/מַשְׂכִּית   MUSK-EES   [MSK]

ROOTS: MOSAIC (design made by setting colored tiles or etc.) < Greek *mouseios* (of the Muses) < IE root *men* (to think). משכית/MUSKEES = picture, mosaic, "figured stones (*Lev. 26:1*).

MOTHER/מוֹתָר   MO-THAR   [M-T(H)-R]

ROOTS: MOTHER (2) = the dregs of a container, or the slimy substance on the surface of fermenting liquids. *Webster's* suggests a link to "mud," "probably by folk etymology" via the Middle Dutch *moeder*. מותר/MŌSAR or MŌTHAR and נותר/NŌSAR or NŌTHAR = remainder, left over (*Ecclesiastes 3:19; Exodus 12:10*).

MOUCH[OIR]/מָחָה   MOKH-AH   [M-KH → M-CH]

ROOTS: MOUCHOIR = handkerchief < French *moucher* (to wipe). מחה/MAKHA = to wipe out, excise, or clean; "blot out or "erase" in *Exodus 32:33*).

BRANCHES: מחט/MOKHAT = to wipe or blow the nose. נקה/NEEKA = to cleanse, clear. Chinese *mo ch'u* = to erase.

MULLIGAN/מָרָק   MARAK   [MRK → MLG]

ROOTS: MULLIGAN = stew, "probably" from a personal name. MULLIGATAWNY < Tamil *milagitannir* (meat soup). מרק/MARAK = soup, broth (*Judges 6:19*).

MUN[IFICENT]/מִנְחָה   MIN-[HA]   [MN]

ROOTS: MUNIFICENT (generous) < Latin *munus* gift. מנחה/MIN[HA] = gift, offering (*Genesis 4:3*); מנה/MANA and מן/MAN = portion, manna, share for distribution (*I Samuel 1:5*).

BRANCHES: Latin *communis* (common, public) is linked to *munus* at the IE root *mei* (to change, go move). *Communis* recalls MN relatives like המון/HAMŌN (multitude – *Genesis 17:4* – see "MANY"). Both Latin words provide cognates like COMMON, COMMUNE, COMMUNICATE, COMMUNISM, DEMEAN, IMMUNE, MEAN, MUNICIPAL, and REMUNERATE. The opposite of MUNIFICENCE is seen in MN antonyms like MINCE (see "MINUS") and מנע/MONA (to withhold). One's lot or portion in life is one's מני/MINEE (fate, fortune, "destiny" – *Isaiah 65:11*). Polynesian *mana* = luck, the supernatural force of good fortune.

MURMUR/הִתְמַרְמֵר   (HIT)MAR-MERE   [MR]

ROOTS: MURMUR = muttering; a mumbled or muttered complaint – of echoic origin. מלמל/MILMAL = to mumble, indistinctly slander; התמרמר/[HIT]MURMĀR = to complain bitterly; ממרים/MUMR[EEM] = complainers (*Deuteronomy 31:27*).

BRANCHES: ממר/MEMER = bitterness (*Proverbs 17:25*). מימר/MĀMAR = to say (Aramaic).

MU[S]T/מֻתָּר   MOOT-(ARE)   [MT(R)]

ROOTS: MUST and MOTE (it is permitted) < Old English *motan* (to be allowed or permitted). מתר/MOOTAR = permissable, set free, loosened (*Psalms 146:7*); נתר/NOSAR or NOTAR = to permit.

NET[HER]/מַטָּה   MAT-AH   [MT → NT]

ROOTS: NETHER (below or under) akin to German *niedar* (down) and Sanskrit *nitaram* (lower) < Germanic *nitero* (lower). מטה/MATA or MADA = down, below, under (*Deuteronomy 28:43*).

BRANCHES: נחת/NAHAT = to descend. See IE root *ndher* (under) at "MAT" – although it is not cited for BENEATH, NETHERWORLD, NETHERLANDS, or UNDERNEATH. DOWN (an ND word in other IE tongues), NOTORNIS (Greek *notos* = south), NEST, NICHE, NIDUS, and UNDER should all be related ND and NT terms.

NIGHT/נחת   NA-KHUT   [NHT]

ROOTS: NIGHT < Anglo-Saxon *neaht* < Latin *noctis* < IE base *noqt* or IE root *nek(w)t* (night). נחת/NAHAT or NAKHAT = repose, rest, or "quiet" (*Isaiah 30:15*); it is also a verb of encampment (*II Kings 6:9*). נחה/NAKH = to rest, to lie down.

BRANCHES: Cognates include EQUINOX, NOCTI-, NOCTURNAL, and NYX. IE cognates include German *nocht*, Russian *noch*, and Spanish *noche*. Reverse to KN for night, *keun*, in Thai. חנה/KHANA = to encamp, incline, settle down. Hungarian *ejszaka* (night) and Japanese *usiku* (night) may derive from חשך/KHOSHEKH or [H]OS[H]EK[H] (darkness).

NOON/נון   NOON   [NWN]

ROOTS: NOON = midday, highest point. Germanic *niwun*, Latin *novem* (nine) and *nonus* (ninth), Greek *ennea* (nine) < IE root *newn* (nine)./נון/NOON or NWN = letter Nun; number 50 – the midpoint to 100; drawn out: "while the sun *lasts*, may his name endure" (*Psalms 72:17*).

BRANCHES: נין/NEEN = descendant; נון/NEEVAN = to deteriorate. Cognates of NOON include ENNEAD, NINE, NONA-, NOVEMBER, and NOVENA. See "EIGHT."

NOUS/משש   MAS(H-USH)   [M-S(H) → NS]

ROOTS: NOUS = understanding < Greek *noos* < IE root *nous* (sense, intellect ..."of unknown origin." משש/MAS[HASH] = to feel, touch, grope (*Deut. 28:29*); המיש/[HA]MEES[H] = to cause to feel, to feel in order to discern (*Genesis 27:21, 22*).

BRANCHES: NOESIS, NOUMENON, PARANOIA. ממש/MAMASH = actual.

NUISAN[CE]/נסיון   NEE-SA-(YONE)   [NS]

ROOTS: NUISANCE = anything causing trouble < Old French *nuis[ir]* < IE root *nek* (death – see "NOXIOUS"). נסיון/NEESAYON = a trial, test, difficult or trying experience. נסה/NASA = to test, vex, try (*Deuteronomy 6:16*).

BRANCHES: נשואה/NISOOA = burden (*Isaiah 46:1*). NISUS = an effort, endeavor, striving./נסה/NASA = to attempt.

NY[M]PHET/נאפת   NO-EPH-ET   [N-A-PH]

ROOTS: NYMPH (minor nature goddesses, lovely young woman) and NYMPHET (sexually attractive girl) < Greek *numphe* (nymph,, bride) < IE root *sneubh* (to marry). נאוף/NEEOOPH (adultery, idolatry – *Hosea 2:4; Jeremiah 3:9*); נאף/NOAPH and נאפת/NOEPHET = male and female adulterer or harlot (*Leviticus 20:10*). נאוה/NAVAH = beautiful (*Jeremiah 6:2*), woman (*Psalms 68:13*).

BRANCHES: Given cognates include CONNUBIAL, NUBILE and NUPTIAL. Note the identical feminine suffix, -ET and ת/ET in the captioned terms. NYMPHOMANIA (excessive sexual desire in women) infers a less pristine etymon than the Greek bride.

OCEAN/אגן   O-GEN   [OGN → OKN]

ROOTS: OCEAN < Greek *okeanos* (the outer stream of water that encircles the earth). To the Greeks, the sea beyond the Mediterranean was the world's encircling rim deified as the god Okeanos. 1. אגן/OGEN or OKEN = a rim (of a bucket), brim, border or edge. אגן/AGON = "basin (*Exodus 24:6*); אגנה/AGANA = a hopper (CAN and CANISTER may relate – see "CANE"). 2. אגם/AGAM or AKA(M)N = lake (*Psalms 107:35*).

BRANCHES: SEA < IE base *se[i]* (to drip, wet). The salt SEA and ZEE (from the Dutch) may relate to זעה/ZAA (sweat). ים/YAM (ocean) and מים/MAYIM (water) are terms not used in IE languages. American Indian water words include American rivers such as the MAUMEE (Indiana), MIAMI (Florida), and MIANUS (New York); Maidu Indian (California) *mom* = water. Cantonese *yam* = drink; Chinese *mu yu* = bath; Japanese *umi* = sea.

OCHLO[CRACY]/קהל   KOHOL   [KHL]

ROOTS: OCHLO[CRACY] (mob rule) < Greek *okholos* (a mob, populace). קהל/KOHOL = a multitude or assemblage (*Exodus 12:6*). קהלה/KIHEELA = congregation or assembly (*Deuteronomy 33:4*).

BRANCHES: OCHLOCRAT, OCHLOPHOBIA. See "CULL."

OF/אב   AV   [A-BH]

ROOTS: OF (preposition: from) < Old English *aef* < IE root *ap[o]* (off, away). אב/ABH or AV = originator, source, *Genesis 17:15; Deut. 32:6*), father, ancestor – see ABBOT."

BRANCHES: Complements of אב/ABH include ב/B' (in, by, at) and בא/BA (to come). OF should be closer to PA (father) and words of belonging to and originating from, rather than to words like OFF and away. OFF may be closer to removal words like UP – see "AVIATE." A "source word like OVA or OVARY may belong here. UNCLE, traced to IE root *awo* (male relative), surely relates. Listed cognates of OF include AB-, AFTER, AWKWARD, OFFAL, PREPOSTEROUS, PO[GROM], POST – and the many words like COMPOUND and POSITION from Latin *ponere* (to place). The -OV suffix in Slavic names like Molotov (father of the MOLOTOV COCKTAIL) means of or from. Similar locative suffixes include -OF, -OFF and -OW.

OPIN[ION]/בינה   BEAN-AH   [BN → PN]

ROOTS: OPINION < Latin *opinari* (to think). בינה/BEENA = understanding, reason (*Proverbs 1:2*); התבונן/[HEET]BONAN = to consider, reflect, survey" (*Job 38:18*). בין/BEEYAN = to interpolate; בין/BAN = between.

BRANCHES: The last BN terms above recall decision making, and the IE root for OPT, OPINE, and OPINION is *op* (to choose). Other cognates include ADOPT and CO-OPT.

OPU[S]/עבד   OBH-[UD]   [OBD]

ROOTS: OPUS = a work in Latin < IE root *op* (to work, produce in abundance). עבד/OBHUD = to work, serve, be a slave to (*Genesis 29:18*); עבודה/ABHODA = work or service.

BRANCHES: Cognates of OPUS include COOPERATE, COPIOUS, [CORNU]COPIA, INURE, MANEUVER, MANURE, OPERA, OPERATE, OPTIMUM and OPULENT. [R]OBOT (from a Slavic "work" term) might be related. See "OBEDIENCE."

OVE[N]/אפה   OFF-AW   [A-PH-H]

ROOTS: OVEN < Anglo-Saxon *ofen* < IE root *augw* (cooking pot). 1. אפה/OPHAH .= to bake; אפה/OPHEH = baker (*Genesis 40:5*). 2. כבשן/KIV[SHAN] = furnace (*Genesis 19:28*); see KV terms at "CAVITY." BRANCHES: Perhaps PIE and BAKE (< IE root *bhe*) link up to the PH Hebrew baking word. Thai *ohp* = bake. Ovens were hollowed rocks; אבן/OVEN = rock (*Genesis 31:45*). Finnish *kiven* = rock.

PACKET/פקעת   PICK-AH-UT   [PKK]

ROOTS: PACK, PACKAGE, PACKET and PECK are words of bundling or cramming together. The earliest etymon is Middle Low German *pak*. פקעת/PIKA'AT or PIKAKHAT = coil, ball of thread; פקעים/PIKA[EEM] = globular ornaments (*I Kings 6:18*); פקיע/PIKEEA = bundle, bunch (of sheaves).

BRANCHES: פקקת/PAKEKET = clot. פגג/PAGAG = to coagulate.

PALTER/התפתל   (HIT)PA-TAIL   [PTL → PLT]

ROOTS: PALTER = to deal crookedly. ? < PALT (rag) < origin unknown. התפתל/[HIT]PATAL = to deal torturously; פתלתל/PITALTOL = crooked, perverse (*Deuteronomy 32:5*); פתל/PATAL = to twist; פתיל/PATEEL = cloth for covering (*Numbers 19:15*). פסולת/PISOLET = refuse, worthless matter.

BRANCHES: PALTRY (worthless).

[PARA]SITE/סָעַד   SAH-UDT   [SUD → SIT]

ROOTS: PARA- (beside) < Greek and IE root *per*–see "OVER."
עבר/ĀBHER = the sides of (*Exodus 32:15*)–see VEER." The second half
of PARASITE < Greek *sitos* (food). ציד/(T)SAYIDT = provision, food,
game (*Genesis 27:7*); צע/SAUDT = eat (*Genesis 8:5*)–see "SATISFY."

   BRANCHES: Finnish *syoda* = eat; Czech *jisti* = to eat. An
alternative etymon for PARASITE is פרעוש/PAROS[H] (flea–*I Samuel
24:15*). FLEA and PSYLLA may derive from the PRS or FLS Hebrew
etymon. The parasitic LOUSE might also be involved.
פרעוש/FAROS[H] (louse, flea) might be broken down to פרע/PERA
(hair) + עש/USH (moth or other insect).

PEWT[ER]/בַּעַץ   BA-AAT[Z]   [B-U-TZ → PUT]

ROOTS: PEWTER (an alloy with tin) < Old French *peautre*.
בעץ/BAAT[Z] = pewter, tin; אבצן/EEBHTZ[AN] = shining one (a name
in *Judges 12:10*). אבץ/ABHATZ = zinc.

POKE/פָּנַע   POG-AH   [PG → PK]

ROOTS: To POKE (jab, thrust) < Middle English *poken*. פגע/POGA
= to strike, attack (*I Samuel 1:15*); פגע/PEGA = contact;
פגיון/PIG[YON] =dagger.

   BRANCHES: BUCK, PECK, the sharp PICK, and PUG[ILIST] may
relate–see "FEAGUE." The POKE that relates to a POCK, POKEY (jail)
or POUCH links up with פחת/PAKHAT (container, pit–*Proverbs 22:5*)
and other PK or BK container words seen at "PIT" and "BUCKET."

PULSE/פָּלְסָא   POOL-SA   [PLS]

ROOTS: PULSE < Latin *pulsare* (to beat) < IE root *pel* (to thrust,
drive, strike). פלסא/POOLSA = a blow or lash (Aramaic).

   BRANCHES: Cognates of PULSE include ANVIL, APPEAL,
COMPEL, DISPEL, EXPEL, FELT, FILTER, IMPEL, INTERPOLATE,
PROPEL, PULSATE and PUSH. A heavier PL striker is the
פלח/PELAH (millstone). A subtler etymon for PULSE might be
פלץ/POLA(T)S (to shudder–*Isaiah 21:4*). Austral. Aborigine *boola* =
pulse. See "FLUTTER."

PULVER[IZE]/פָּרַר   PAIR-ARE   [PR → PL]

ROOTS: PULVERIZE < Latin *pulvis*(dust, powder) < IE root *pel*
(dust, flour). עפר/AP(H)AR = dust (*Genesis 18:27*). פרר/PARAR = to
crumble or pulverize something into small pieces.

   BRANCHES: Cognates of PULVERIZE include PAILLASSE,
PALEA, PALYNOLOGY, POLLEN, POULTICE, POWDER and PULSE
(2). A PR or FR flour term in Italian is *farina*; FARINA AND
FARINACEOUS (powdery) should therefore link up here. Likewise
the following "dust terms: *pil* (Spanish, Italian, Finnish and Russian),
prach (Czech), and *praf* (Rumanian). Arabic dust is *ghoubar*, a
gutteralized עפר/GAPHAR. CA[M]PHOR < Arabic *kafur* or Malay
kapur (chalk).

PYR[ALIDID]/פַּרְפַּר   PAR-PAR   [PR]

ROOTS: PYRALIDID (family of moths) < Greek *pyralis* < *pyr* (fire–
as moths were supposed to live in or on fire). See "BURN." The folk
etymology needn't detract from considering a PRPR etymon for PPL
butterfly words in Latin (*papilio*–source of PAPILLON) and in the
Morella dialect of Malay (*pepeul*). פרפר/PARPAR (butterfly) is post-
Biblical, but note פרפור/PERPOOR (twitching–*Job 16:12*) and the PR
reversal רפרוף/REPHROOPH (fluttering, hovering–*Job 26:11*).

   BRANCHES: צפור/[TSEE]POR = bird; פרעוש/PHAR[OSH] = flea.
The following words may link up with the PR-RP etymons above:
FEAR, FLAP, LAP[WING], PALPITATE, RAPID, RIFFLE, RUFFLE
and WHIR (to fly, vibrate). Nahuatl *papalo-[tl]* = butterfly; Australian
Aborigine *purraparrari* = tremble.

QUANT/חַנִית   KHAN-EAT   [KH-N-T]

ROOTS: QUANT (boat pole) < origin unknown. חנית/KHANEET =
spear, javelin (*II Samuel 23:7*).

   BRANCHES: GAUNT < Old Norse *gand[r]* (a thin pole). At IE root
kent (to prick, jab) are the cognates AMNIOCENTESIS, CENTER, and
ECCENTRIC. Chinese *gang* = pole. Chippewa Indian *anit* = spear.
Egyptian *chams* = lance; it is cited in reference to
חמשים/KHAMOOS[HEEM] ("armed"–*Exodus 13:18*). Japanese *nuk[ite]*
= spear (KN reversal).

QUAN[TITY]/כַּמָּה   KAMA   [KMH]

ROOTS: QUANTITY < Latin *quantas* (how great). = how many, how
much (*Genesis 47:8*), a QUANTITY, or a (large) amount (*I Kings 22:16;
Zechariah 7:3*).

   BRANCHES: Latin *quom* (when) and *quondam* may relate to כמה
עד/[AD] KAMA (until when). QUAN[DRY] is a term of doubt and
dilemma with no known origin. An alternative etymon for
QUANTITATIVE, QUANTITY and QUANTUM involves the
קמץ/KOMATZ (measured hand) used in calculations and amounts–
see "MITT" and "QUINTET."

QUIB[BLE]/עָקַב   AH-KUBH   [A-K-BH]

ROOTS: QUIBBLE (a cavil or evasion of truth) < perhaps from
obsolete *quib* (equivocation). עקב/AKABH = to deceive (*Genesis 27:36*),
to hold back, or restrain (*Job 37:4*).

   BRANCHES: עקבה/AKBHA = fraud, deceit (*II Kings 10:19*). Related
KV terms of deceit and/or holding back could include CAVIL.

RABBIT/אַרְנֶבֶת   AR[N]EBHET   [ARNBT]

ROOTS: RABBIT (hare) < Middle English *rabet*. Perhaps from the
name Robert, but this may be a folk etymology. ארנבת/ARNEBHET
= hare (*Leviticus 11:6*).

   BRANCHES: Arabic *arnab* = rabbit. ניב/NEEBH = (canine)
tooth–see "NIB." A נ to L change would allow for LEPUS and
LEPO[ORID] (the hare or rabbit family). The LP root may link up with
other RB terms. The GERBIL is traced to Arabic *yerbo* (JERBOA–a
leaping rodent).

RAZZ/לָץ   LU[T]Z   [L-(T)Z → RZ]

ROOTS: RAZZ (to ridicule, deride) < raspberry (slang for
contemptuous, pasping sound). לץ/LA[T]Z = to mock, scorn (*Proverbs
9:12*). לזות/LIZ[OOT] = slander, evil talk; לעז/LAAZ = slander.

ROAM/רָמַשׂ   ROAM-ACE   [RM(S)]

ROOTS: ROAM (to move or travel) < Middle English *romen*.
רמש/ROM[AS] = to move as a quadruped, to creep or crawl (*Genesis
1:26*). רמס/ROM[AS] = to trample, tread (*Isaiah 28:3*).

   BRANCHES: RAMBLE, RAMP (to rush violently), and RAMPAGE,
like ROAM, have no IE roots. They may link up with the RM root
above.

ROCH[ET]/חוּר   KHOOR   [KH-R → R-CH]

ROOTS: ROCHET = linen vestment of bishops < Old French *roc*.
חור/KHOOR = white linen (*Isaiah 19:9*) or the fine linen of nobles
(*Esther 8:15*).

ROOK/צְרִיחַ   [TZIH]-REE-AKH   [(TS)-R-KH]

ROOTS: ROOK = the chess piece also known as the castle < Persian
rukh. צריח/(TS)IREEAKH = fortress, high tower (*Judges 9:46*). See
"ROCK" and "SILICON."

ROOM/אַרְמוֹן   ARM-[OWN]   [RM]

ROOTS: ROOM = (space, paritioned interior space, apartment) < Old English *rum* (space) < IE base *rewos* (wide, broad) < IE root *reue* (to open; space). 1. רוח/REVAKH or REWAH = space, interval (*Genesis 32:17*); רחב/RAKHABH or RAHAW = broad, opened (*Exodus 3:8*). 2. אַרְמוֹן/ARM[ON] = palace (*Jeremiah 9:20*).

    BRANCHES: Cognates of ROOM include RUMMAGE, RURAL and RUSTIC. RANSACK < Old Norse *rann* (a house). Malay *rumah* = house. Scandinavian tongues have RM room terms. ארון/ARON = closet. Old French *run* = ship's hold.

SAGE[BRUSH]/שִׂיחַ   SEE-AKH   [S-KH → SG]

ROOTS: SAGE (aromatic shrub) < Latin *salvia*. שִׂיחַ/SEEAKH = bush or "shrub" (*Genesis 2:5*).

    BRANCHES: שׂךְ/SAKH = thorn; סֹךְ/SOKH = thicket; שׂחיף/SAKH[EEF] = twig; שׂחת/SHAKH[AS] = corngrass; שׂנשׂג/SEEGSAG = to grow, blossom. SAGUARO, SEDGE < Old English *secg*, and SHAW (thicket) < Old Norse *skagi* may relate. See "ACACIA" and "SHAGGY."

SA[M]PAN/סְפִינָה   SIPH-EEN-AH   [SPN]

ROOTS: SAMPAN = flat-bottomed Oriental boat < 1. Chinese *san ban* [AHD]. 2. Chinese *san-pan* < Spanish *champan* (canoe) – probably of South American Indian origin [*Webster's*]. ספינה/SIP(H)EENA = boat (*Jonah 1:5*).

SCADS/שֹׁחַד   SHO-KHAD   [S(H)-K(H)-D]

ROOTS: SCADS = large amounts (of money) < Old English *sceat* (treasure, tribute, tax). SCOT = money assessed or paid, tax. שֹׁחַד/S(H)OKHAD = bribery (*Exodus 23:8*). (Tribute was bribery.)

    BRANCHES: SCAT was a synonym. סעד/SAKHAD = to support.

SCHIZO[POD]/שָׁסַע   SHAW-SAKH   [SH-S-KH → SKZ]

ROOTS: SCHISM and SCHIZO- words < Greek *skhizein* (to split) < IE root *skei* (to cut, split). SCHIZOPOD = lit., a split foot. שׁצע/SHASA or SHASAKH = to divide, split, cleave. The cloven hoof requirement for kosher animals is found in *Leviticus 11:3*.

    BRANCHES: SCHIZOPHRENIA = שׁסעת/SHISA'AS or S(H)ISAKHAS. SCHIST and SCHIZOID are cognates of CONSCIENCE, ESQUIRE, NICE, SCIENCE, SHEATH, SHED and SHIN at IE *skei*. See "SAXON" and "SCISSORS" for other Hebrew SK and KS cutters. Cognate SCIRE FACIAS < Latin *scire* (to know) may relate to זכור/ZAKHOR (to remember).

(S)CRA[M]BLE/עִרְבֵּל   KHEER-BALE   [KH-R-B]

ROOTS: SCRAMBLE (to mix, distort) < blend of obsolete SCAMBLE (to struggle for) + CRAMBLE (to crawl). עִרבּל/KHEERBAL = to mix, confound; ערוב/AROOV or KHAROOBH (mixture, confusion – *Exodus 12:38*). See "GARBLE."

SEECATCH/תַחַשׁ   SAH-KHASH   [S-KH-SH]

ROOTS: SEECATCH = seal, adult male of the Alaska fur seal < Russian *sekach*. תחשׁ/TAKHASH or SAKHASH = seal (*Exodus 25:5*). Translators unaware of seals in the Persian Gulf have rendered the term "dolphin" or "badger."

SEIS[MIC]/זְעֵזֵעַ   SEEIH-SAH   [ZA]

ROOTS: SEISMIC (of an earthquake) < Greek *seismos* (earthquake) < Greek *seiein* (to shake). זעזע/ZEEIZA or SEEISA and זע/ZA or SA = to tremble, shake (*Esther 5:9; Habakkuk 2:7*). שכשׁך/SHIKHSHOOKH = shaking.

    BRANCHES: SEISM, SEISMO- and SISTRUM are cognates at IE root *twei* (to agitate, shake, toss). SHAG (to shake), SHOCK and SEIZURE (convulsion) might also be related. סוס/SOOS = horse (a bumpy way to זוז/ZOOZ or move). See SHAKE at "ZOO." Kiowa Indian *za(n)ge* or *ca(n)ge* = shake. A זקן / ZAK [AN] (old person) might shake.

SER[OW]/שָׂעִיר   SAH-EAR   [SAR]

ROOTS: SEROW = goat antelope of Eastern Asia < native Tibet or Sikkim name. שעיר/SAEER = goat, "goat-demon" or "satyr" (*Isaiah 13:21*). שער/SAEER = hairy (*Genesis 27:11*).

SI[G]N/צִיוּן   [T]SEE-OON   [TS-Y-N → SIN]

ROOTS: SIGN < Middle English *sygne* < Latin *signum* (identifying mark, sign, "standard that one follows") < IE root *sikw* (to follow). ציון/[T]SEEOON = signpost, mark, monument, Zion (*II Kings 23:17*); ציּן/[T]SEEYAN = to mark, note.

    BRANCHES: SN reversed, נס/NAS = sign, signal, standard, banner (*Isaiah 11:10*). סים/SOOYAM = to mark, distinguish. Cognates of SIGN not pronounced with the GN of INSIGNIA include ASSIGN, CONSIGN, and DESIGN. Cantonese *seun* = letter. See "SIMULATION."

SILLY/כְּסִיל   K'SEEL   [(K)SL]

ROOTS: SILLY (foolish, imbecile) < Old English *gesaelig* (happy) < IE root *sel* (of good mood; to favor). כסיל/(K)SEEL = a fool; כסילות/K'SEELOOS = silliness; כסל/COSAL = to be a fool (*Jeremiah 10:8*).

SM[ELL]/סם   SUM   [SM]

ROOTS: SMELL < IE base *smul* (akin to SMOLDER – basic sense "to give off smoke"). OSMIUM and OSMATIC < Greek *osme* (odor). סם/SUM = spice. Both סמים/SUM[EEM] (sweet smelling [incense]) and בשם/[BO]SEM (spice) are in *Exodus 35:28*.

    BRANCHES: בסם/BOSEM = spice, perfume. זנח/ZANAH and צחן/[T]SAHAN can mean "stink." OZONE is a cognate of OSMIUM. The SM and ZN terms link up with SNIFF and SN words at "SNORKEL."

SMIL[AX]/שָׁמִיר   S(H)AH-MERE   [SMR → SML]

ROOTS: SMILAX (prickly, woody vines) < Greek *smilax* (bindweed). שמיר/S(H)AMEER = thistle (*Isaiah 5:6*). Thorns guard the plant; שמר/S(H)-M-R = to guard – see "SAMURAI."

SOUTACHE/צִיצָה   TSEETS-AH   [TS-TS-H → SSK]

ROOTS: SOUTACHE (a braid) < Hungarian *szuskak* (a pendant curl). ציצה/TSEETSAH = fringe; ציצת/TSEETSEET = tassel, lock of hair (*Ezekiel 8:3*), fringe (*Numbers 15:38*).

    BRANCHES: TASSEL and German *zotte* (tuft of hair) may relate.

[S]PARK/בָּרָק   BAR-UCK   [BRK → PRK]

ROOTS: SPARK < IE base *sp(h)er(e)-g* (to strew, sprinkle). ברק/BARAK = to flash lightning (*Exodus 19:16*); ברקת/BAREKES = emerald or agate gem (*Exodus 28:17*).

    BRANCHES: הבריק/[HEE]BHREEK = to glitter or SPARK[LE].

[S]PRIG/פָּרַג   PA-RUG   [PRG]

ROOTS: SPRIG = small twig or shoot of plant < Middle English *sprigge* – "probably from a base seen in 'spray' and 'spark.'" פרג/PARAG = to sprout, germinate. If the P rather than the S is unhistoric, there's שריג/SARIG (shoot, small branch – *Genesis 40:10*).

BRANCHES: PRG relatives include פרח/PERAKH (flower, bud, blossom – *Numbers 17:23* – see "FRUCTIFY." [AS]PARAG[US] has branchlets rather than leaves. VIRG[ATE] = having many twigs < Latin *virga* (twig) – akin to VIRGIN, VIRGO, VIRGULATE and VIRGULE (small rod). Latin *virgo* = young girl or maiden, just as a young boy is a "sprout" or a "stripling." "Virgo" also might link up to אפרח/EPHRŌAKH (chick – *Deuteronomy 22:6*), בנירה/BIGEERA (puberty, adolescence – swap root letters #2 and #3) and גבירה/GIVEERA (lady – an anagramic antonym). The VIRAGO (domineering woman) is a VRG antonym of VIRGIN – see BARON." See בר/VAR (pure) at "BORAX."

STAITH/שָׂטַח   S[H]ET-AH   [STH]

ROOTS: STAITH = stage, wharf, path along an embankment < Anglo-Saxon *staeth* (shore), IE base at "stand." שטח/S[H]ETAH = extent, surface area; משטח/[MI]SHTAH = place for spreading nets (*Ezekiel 26:5*).

S[T]ARE/שָׁר   S[H]AR   [SH-R → ST-R]

ROOTS: STARE < Old English *starian* < IE root *ster* (stiff). שר/S[H]AR = to see, observe, "behold" (*Numbers 23:9*). ישר/[YA]SHAR = straight; שורה/SHOORA = "row"; צר/TSAR (may be rendered as STAR) = narrow. Other "stiff" or straight STR etymons are seen at "SATRAP."

BRANCHES: תור/TOOR = to spy out – see "TOUR." Other ש/SH to ST permutations include BRISTLE < ברוש/B'ROSH (see "BRUSH"), HURST < חרשה/HOORSHA (see "ELMHURST") and STEER < שור/SHŌR (see "TAURUS").

STILL/סֵדֶר   SAY-DARE   [SDR → STL]

ROOTS: STILL (motionless) < Greek *stellein* (to put in order) < IE root *stel* (to put, stand). סדר/SODTAR = to set in order (Syriac); סדר/SĀDER or SĀDTER = order, orderly arrangement (*Job 10:22*); מסדרון/[MI]SDTIR[ON] = portico (*Judges 3:23*).

BRANCHES: Cognates of STILL include APOSTLE, EPISTLE, GESTALT, INSTALL, PEDESTAL, STALK, STELE, STILT, STOLE, STOLID, STOUT, STULTIFY, and STALLION. See "STREET."

STR[AND]/צְרוֹר   TSIR-ORE   [TS-R → ST-R]

ROOTS: STRAND (bundles of thread twisted together) < Old French *estran*. צרור/TSIRŌR = bundle, knot; צרר/TSORAR = to bind up (*Hosea 4:19*); צר/TSAR = narrow.

BRANCHES: STRING is related – see "STRAIT." For STRAND (shore) see "STREET" – צרטון/SARTŌN = sandbank. STRAP and STRIPE both mean a narrow band. These ST-R relatives are reinforced by other etymons such as רצף/TSARAPH and רצף/RATSAPH (to join), רצועה/RITSOOA (strap, STRIP – another TS-R reversal), שרט/SERET (long incision, as from whip), סרט/SERET (ribbon), and שרוך/SRŌKH (strap).

SUMM[ER]/שְׁכֶם   S[HIKH]-EM   [S-(KH)-M]

ROOTS: SUMMER = a large horizontal supporting beam, girder, or lintel < Latin and Greek *sagma* (pack saddle). שכם/S[H]IKHEM = shoulder, load (*Genesis 48:22*); שכמה/SHIKMA = shoulder blade (*Job 31:22*).

BRANCHES: SUMPTER = pack mule (sharing same etymology as above). If SUMMER (season) is not related to שמש/SHEMMESH (sun – see "SUN"), consider זמרה/ZIMRA or SIMRA ("choice fruits," cropping, ingathering of fruits – *Genesis 43:11*).

TAB[ES]/דּוּב   DTOOBH   [D-BH → TB]

ROOTS: TABES (any emaciation or consumption) < Latin *tabere* (wasting away) < IE root *ta* (to melt, dissolve) and its extended form *tabh*. דוב/DOOBH or TOOB = wasting, languishing (*Leviticus 26:16*); דוי/DIVUY = sickness, disease (*Psalms 40:4*).

BRANCHES: Cognates of TABES are THAW and EUTECTIC. The latter is from Greek *tekein* (to melt), recalling התך/[HOO]TAKH (to be melted – *Ezekiel 22:22*) or התוך/[HE]TOOKH (melting).

THEORY/תּוֹרָה   THORA   [TRH → TH-R]

ROOTS: THEORY = a set of rules or principles for the study or practice of an art or discipline < Greek *theoria*. (No IE root). תורה/TŌRAH or THŌRA = direction, law, instruction, Revelation (*Exodus 12:49;16:4*); way, manner (*I Chronicles 17:17*).

BRANCHES: תור/TOOR or THOOR = to direct aright (*Proverbs 12:26*) or to seek after the heart, go astray (*Numbers 15:39*). THEORUM (an idea demonstrably true) < Greek *theorein* (to look at) recalls תור/TOOR or THOOR (to search out – see "TOUR").

THES[IS]/לָתֶת   (LA)-THES   [TH-S]

ROOTS: THESIS (a premise or given) < Greek *thesis* (a placing, position, proposition) < Greek *tithenai* (to put, place). נתן/NATAN or [NA]THAN = to give, put, place. לתת/[LA]SES or [LA]THES = "[to] give" (*Genesis 15:7*); לתתן/[LI]TEETĀN or [LI]TEETHĀN = "[to] place" (*I Kings 6:19*).

BRANCHES: See "DATA" and "ENDOW."

TOIL/תְּלָאָה   TIL-AH-A   [TL]

ROOTS: TOIL = to work or proceed with painful effort < Anglo-French *toiler* (to strive, dispute); Latin *tudes* (mallet); or IE root *steu* (to push, knock, beat). תלאה/TILAAH = weariness, hardship, trouble, "travail" (*Numbers 20:14*).

BRANCHES: תועלת/TŌELET = utility. טרח/TŌRAKH = to take the trouble, make an effort; a variant is rendered "wearying" or "cumbrance" (*Deuteronomy 1:12*). TIRE and TIRED may relate, along with DRAMA and DRASTIC (derivatives of IE root *dere*, to work). Old French *travailler* is the source of TRAVAIL and TRAVEL.

TOMEN[TUM]/צֶמֶר   T[S]EM-ERE   [T(S)-M-(R)]

ROOTS: TOMENTUM = a growth of wooly hairs < Latin *tomentum* (a stuffing of wool or hair). TOMENTOSE = covered with wooly hair. צמר/T[S]EMER = wool (*Leviticus 13:47*) < צמ/T(S)-M of צמח/T(S)OMAH (to grow) + מר/MR of אמר/EEMAR (lamb).

BRANCHES: The MR element may link up with LAM[B] and LAN[OLIN] – see "RAM." See TM growth at "TUMOR" (Appendix A).

TOM[THUMB]/צָמַת   T(S)OM-AS   [T(S)-M]

ROOTS: TOM THUMB = a tiny hero of English legend or any dwarf. A TOMTIT in British dialect = a small bird, such as a wren. צמת/T[S]OM[AS] = to contract; צמצם/T[S]IMT[S]OOM and צמק/T[S]AMAK = to shrink. This last term also means dry (*Hosea 9:14*); צמוק/TSEEMOOK (dry grapes) echoes Italian *simmuki*.

BRANCHES: צנם/TSANAM = withered (*Genesis 41:23*). A צמ/TS-M antonym of growth appears in the entry above. TINY and TEENSY may relate – see "SMASH" for SM[ALL].

TOTE/דּוּדָא   DTOODTA   [DD → TT]

ROOTS: TOTE (to carry, haul) < origin unknown. דודא/DOODA or TOOTA = basket (*Jeremiah 24:1*).

TROUT/טרית TREAT [TRYT]

ROOTS: TROUT (fresh water fish) < Greek *troktes* (a seafish). טרית/TREET = a food fish in Talmudic Hebrew.

TUB/תֵּבָה TABHE-AH [T-BH]

ROOTS: TUB = a vessel for storing; a slow-moving clumsy ship or boat (colloq.); a bathtub < Middle English *tubbe*. תבה/TÁBHA = box, chest, "ark" or rectangular barge of Noah (*Genesis 6:15*). The nursery rhyme "rub-a-dub-dub, three men in a tub..." might be based on the three sons of Noah.

BRANCHES: כתב/KITABH = writing: The KT element infers cutting or ingraving; the T-BH element could mean box – like or rectangular (the shape of Hebrew letters). Japanese *kotoba* = word or language.

TUM[OR]/צָמַח T[S]AM-[AH] [T(S)-M]

ROOTS: TUMOR = a swelling in Latin; *tumere* = to swell. צמח/T[S]AMAH = to spring up, grow (*Genesis 2:*).

BRANCHES: See T[S]-M antonyms of shrinkage at "TOM THUMB" above. THUMB, along with THIMBLE, TOMB, TUMEFY, TUMID, TUMULUS (mound), and TUMULT are cognates of TUMOR at IE root *teue* (to swell). MOAT < Old French *mote* (a mound) may be an MT reversal. See TOMATO at SUMAC." SM cognates of TUMOR that confirm a TS-M etymon are SOMA, SOMATO- and -SOME, as in PSYCHOSOMATIC and CHROMOSOME. TUMMY and Amazon Indian *tum* (belly) relate here and to the TN element of בטן/BETEN (belly; the projecting part of the chapter of a column). VENTRICLE and VENTRILOQUISM, from Latin *venter* (belly), require a slight scrambling of בטן/VETEN. The swelling STOMACH sounds closest to צמח/STOMAKH.

ULCE[R]/לָקָה LUCK-AH [LK]

ROOTS: ULCER = any sore, lesion or festering condition < Latin *ulcis* (a sore) < IE root *elkos* (wound). לקה/LAKA = to be afflicted with disease; לקות/LIKOOS or לקוי/LEEKOOY = defect, blemish. The root appears in Aramaic.

UMBR[ELLA]/סַנְוֵרִים [S]UN-BHARE-[EEM] [SNBR → MBR]

ROOTS: UMBRELLA < Latin *umbra* (shadow) < IE root *undho* (blind, dark). סנורים/[S]UNBHÁR[EEM] = blindness (*Genesis 19:11*). עור/EEBHER = blind (*Leviticus 22:22*) + M (nasalization) = EMBHER or UMBR.

BRANCHES: ADUMBRATE, UMBEL, UMBRAGE. Antonyms of עור/EEVER or EOR are AWARE (see "ORIENTATION") and אור/ŌR or AVR (light).

UNI[QUE]/אֲנִי UN-EE [UN]

ROOTS: UNIQUE < Latin *unicus* < IE root *oi-no* (one, unique). 1. אני/ANEE = I, first person (see "ME"). 2. אנד/UNDT = one in Amharic, the Southern Semitic language of Ethiopia which commonly nasalizes Hebrew words like אחד/EHADT or EKHAS (one – see "EACH"). 3. IE *oi-no* might represent a word pair like עוד אין/ÁN Ō[D] (no other – see "ANEMIC").

BRANCHES: Cognates of ONE and UNIQUE include A, AN, ANY, ALONE, ANON, ATONE, ELEVEN, INCH, LONE[LY], NONE, ONCE, OUNCE, TRIUNE, UNI-, UNION, UNITE, UNITY, UNANIMOUS, UNICOM and UNIVERSE.

VAT[ICAN]/נָבַט [NA]-VUT [BH-T]

ROOTS: VATIC (of a prophet or seer) and VATICAN < Latin *vates* (prophet). 1. נבט/[NA]VAT = to look at – see VIDEO." 2. בטה/BATA = to utter words.

VERY/בָּרִי BA-REE [BR]

ROOTS: VERY < Latin *verus* (true) < IE root *wero* (true). ברי/BAREE or VAREE = certainly, surely; ברור/BAROOR or VAROOR = certain, evident; באר/BAER or VAER = to explain (*Deuteronomy 1:5*); בר/BAR or VAR = pure, clear (*Psalms 24:4*).

BRANCHES: VERY = extremely; רב/RAV (VR reversed) = much, many – see "RIFE." גבר/[GA]VAR = confirm (*Daniel 9:27*). Cognates of VERY include AVER, VERDICT, VERIFY, VERITY, VERISIMILAR, PERSEVERE and SEVERE. PER- = prefix of intensification.

VIAL/נֵבֶל [NAY]-VEL [(N)VL]

ROOTS: VIAL or PHIAL (small vessel or botle) < Greek *phiale*. נבל/[NĀ]VEL = leather or ceramic bottle or jug (*Jeremiah 13:12*).

BRANCHES: פרור/PAROOR or PHAR[OOR] = pot. PAIL, linked to Middle Latin *pagella* (a measure) might relate to פך/PAKH or PAH (flask, cruise).

VIC[TOR]/כָּבַשׁ CUV-[USH] [K-V-(SH) → VK]

ROOTS: VICTOR < Latin *vincere* (to conquer) < IE root *weik* (to fight, conquer). כבש/KOV[ASH] = to subdue, master (*Genesis 1:28*); military conquest is the meaning in *Joshua 18:1*. Reverse KV to VK to hear VIC[TORY]; the U of [CON]QUEST and [VAN]QUISH may be read as a V to hear KVS.

BRANCHES: גבר/GOVAR or KOVAR = to conquer; גבר/GEVER = warrior. Cognates of VICTOR include CONVINCE, EVICT, [IN]VINCIBLE, and VANQUISH. COW (2) is akin to an Old Norse term meaning "to subdue." Chinese *kofu* = conquer. See "KIBOSH" and "QUASH."

VILLA/חַוִּילָה [HA]-VEE-LA [HVL]

ROOTS: VILLA = large suburban residence < term for country seat or farm in Latin. חוילה/HAVEELA = villa (Mishnaic Hebrew – but no evidence of borrowing). See METROPOLIS."

BRANCHES: HOVEL may relate to the HVL etymon or to קבה/KOOBHA (brothel, hut, tent – see "ALCOVE").

VOL[UNTEER]/בָל VAL [VL]

ROOTS: VOLUTEER < Latin *velle* (to wish, will) < IE root *wel* (to wish, will). 1. בל/BAL or VAL = the heart, mind (*Daniel 6:15*) 2. לב/LĀV = heart, the seat of emotions and the mind – see "LOVE." 3. הואיל/HOEEL or [HŌ]VEEL = willing.

BRANCHES: RV and VR terms include Aram. רעוא/RA'AVA (will) and בחירה/BIHEERA or BHIHEERA (choice, free will). WALE = to choose. Cognates of VOLUNTEER include BENEVOLENT, GALLOP, MALEVOLENT, VOLITION, VOLUPTUOUS, WALLOP, WEALTH, WELL, WILL, and WILLING. Australian Aborigine *boola* = heart.

WAS[H]/כָּבֵס [KEY]-VAIS [(K)-V-S]

ROOTS: WASH < Old English *wascan* < IE root *wed* (wet, water). כבס/[KA]VAS = to wash, launder (*Leviticus 13:55*). The C of *wasc[an]* could come from the K of KVS. For an alternate etymon based on the IE root see "WET."

[WAR]LOCK/לחש   LOKH-[USH]   [L-KH-(SH)]

ROOTS: [WAR]LOCK < Old English *woerloga* (oath- breaker) < Germanic *lugiz* < IE root *leugh* (to tell a lie). לחש/LOKH[ASH] = to whisper (spells), to charm a snake; מלחש/[MI]LAKH[ASH] = pronouncer of charms, enchanter" (*Isaiah 3:3*). For an LG verb of lying there's לעז/LAGAZ = slander.

BRANCHES: BELIE and LIE may relate to the Hebrew as well as the Germanic LGZ etymon. נחש/NAKHASH = sorcery; snake (נ/N = L).

WEIGHTY/כבד   [KA]-VEIDTE   [(K)VD → WHT]

ROOTS: WEIGHTY (heavy, important) < Middle English *weiht* < Old English *gewiht* < IE root *wegh* (to go, transport in a vehicle). כבד/KAVĀD or KHAVĀT = weighty, heavy (*Exodus 5:9*), important.

BRANCHES: For the given IE root of WEIGH and WEIGHT– see CONVEY." גבר/GV[R] = to overcome; an important person – a possible link to GRAVITY (weight and importance).

WHE[RE]/איפה   AYE-FOE   [A-Y-PH-O]

ROOTS: WHERE < Anglo-Saxon *hwaer*, akin to Germanic *wo* and the base *hwa* < IE root *kwo* or *kwi* (stem of relative and interrogative pronouns). The R is unhistoric; a V or K persists. 1. איפה/ĀYPHŌ = where? (*Genesis 37:16*); פה/PŌ or פו/POW (*Job 38:11*) = here. 2. איפה/ĀYPHŌ = where (*II Kings 6:13*); איכה/AYEKAH = where art thou? (*Genesis 3:9*).

BRANCHES: 1. Germanic *wo* softens in Yiddish *vu* (where) or Swedish *vaar* (where), softening further in Modern Greek *pou'* (where). Latin *ubi* = where; *ibi* = there. 2. The guttural cognates of WHERE include QUA, QUIBBLE and QUORUM.

WIZ[EN]/יבש   [YA]-VAYS[H]   [(Y)VS]

ROOTS: WIZENED (shriveled) < Anglo-Saxon *wisnian* (to become dry) < Germanic *weis* or *wis* < IE root *wei* (to wither). יבש/[YA]VĀS[H] = dry, to become dry (*Genesis 8:14*); הוביש/[HO]VEES[H] = to dry up, make to wither.

BRANCHES: The IE root *wes* = wet; this VS antonym in Hebrew includes רבש/[D]VS (honey, honey dew, the watery camel's hump).

WREAK/ריק   REEK   [RYK]

ROOTS: WREAK (to inflict or express) < Old English *wrecan* (to drive, expel, vent) , IE root *wreg* (to push, shove, drive). ריק/REEK = emptied, "led forth" (*Genesis 14:14*).

BRANCHES: URGE, WRACK, WRECK, WRACK–see "URGE." הבריח/[HEE]VREEAKH = "put to flight" (*I Chronicles 8:13*).

WREST[LE]/רצץ   RATS-ATS   [R-TS → R-ST]

ROOTS: WRESTLE < Old English *wraestan* (to twist) < IE root *wer* (to turn, bend). *Webster's* cites Old Norse *reista* (twisting). For RV, RW words of twisting and striving see –"REEVE" and RIVALRY." רצץ/RATSATS = to oppress; התרוצץ/[HET]RŌTSĀTS = to struggle together, push one another (*Genesis 25:22*).

BRANCHES: Reverse RS for שר/SAR (to wrestle, tumble) or שרך/SARAKH (twisting its course – *Jeremiah 2:23*). שזר/SHAZAR = to twist.

XEROX/בצרת   [BA]-TSORE-ESS   [TS-R → XR]

ROOTS: XEROX (trademark) < XEROGRAPHY (a dry photocopying process transferring images via electric charges) < Greek *xeros* (dry) < IE *ksero* (dry). בצרון/[BĒ]TSAR[ŌN] and בצרת/[BA]TZŌR[ES] = drought (*Jeremiah 14:1*).

BRANCHES: זר/ZAR = to squeeze out; זרב/ZŌR[AV] = to be scorched; זרם/ZOR[AM] = to flood, pour out – see "SERUM; חסר/KHASĀR = lacking; צרב/TSAR[AV] = to scorch; צרבת/TSAR[EVET] = a scab; שרב/SARAV = parched ground. Listed cognates include ELIXIR, PHYLLOXERA, SERENE, and XERO-.

APPENDIX B

Beyond Grimm's Laws (see Introduction) there are letter permutations that offer more English-from-Hebrew connections.

One of the better documented permutations involves English L's from Hebrew ב/N's. Note how these two right-angle letters are mirror opposites, as though L were being written from right to left (the original, Hebrew way to write).

English SUN is a cognate of SOL (as in SOLAR); the dictionary traces COUL[D] from CAN. Latin *lutra* (otter) is the source of NUTRIA as well as Spanish *lutria*. LILAC is one of the few L- words in English attributed to an N- IE root.

Outside of the Indo-European family of languages are the common N/L switches between Mandarin Chinese and Cantonese. One says *Nay ho ma?* or *Lay ho ma?* (how are you?) depending on the dialect. My daughter (from Hong Kong) asked for the butter "life" instead of "knife." L's in Fijian, Hawaiian and Malay are typically rendered as an N in related Tongan.

Just as all of Grimm's Laws apply between Semitic tongues and between related (synonyms and antonyms) Hebrew words, the L/N phenomenon is found in Semitic as well. Assyrian *ablu* (son) matches Hebrew/בן/BEN (son, child). [Aramaic *bar* (son), Maya *pal* (boy), and English PAL and BROTHER are all likely offshoots of the primeval BN element whose NB reversal forms words of growth and sprouting.] Aramaic *nahama* (bread) echoes Hebrew/לחם/LEHEM (bread). Arabic *qalam* (reed) recalls קנה/KANE (reed).

Within Hebrew, both נחץ/LAHATZ and לחץ/NAHATZ mean "to press;" and both לוץ/LOOTS and נאץ/NA'ATS mean "to scorn." קטן/KATAN (small) and /GADOL (great) are related antonyms because guttural-dental-N matches gutteral—dental-L.

Below are several L from N cases to consider; consult a dictionary for the conventional etymologies.

BELT/אבנט	ABHNAT (belt)	BLT < BNT
BOTUL[ISM]/בטן	BETEN (bowels)	BTL < BTN
BUIL[D]/בנה	BONEH (build)	BL < BN
CELL/קן	KAN (cell)	KL < KN
CL[OUD]/ענן	KANAN (cloud)	KL < KN
CULEX/כנה	KEENA (gnat)	KL < KN
DHOLE/תן	DTAN (jackal)	DL < TN
ECCLESIA/כנסת	KINES[ET] (cong.)	KLS < KNS
KLEPTO-/גנב	GANABH (steal)	KLP < GNV
KUMMEL/כמן	KHOMUN (kummel)	KML < KMN
LAST(ING)/נצח	NETSAH (lasting)	LST < NTS
LEASE/נשי	NES(H)EE (loan)	LS < NS
LIB[ATION]/נבע	NABHU (gush out)	LB < NB
LIGULE/נעל	NAGUL (to strap)	LGL < NGL
LIVE/נוה	NAVAH (dwell)	LV < NV
OLIVE/ענב	ONAV (grape)	OLV < ONV
SCHMALTZ/שמן	SHEMEN (fat)	SML < SMN
SICKLE/סכין	SAKEEN (knife)	SKL < SKN
SLUMBER/תנומה	S'NOOMA (sleep)	SLM < SNM

The lesser known etymons of words provide more and better connections to the Hebrew source. The word EYELET, for example, derives from French *oeil* (eye), a L/נ change away from עין/OYIN. Moreover, LAY derives from Old English *licgan* and the IE root *legh* (to lie, lay). A fitting N-KH etymon is נח/NAKH (to rest) or הניח/[HA]NEEAKH (to lay, set at rest). A Russian version of THE WORD would note that *osyol* (donkey) is an L from נ/N derivative of אתון/ASON (donkey—see "ASININE"). Studies on other languages' ties to Hebrew would likewise document letter changes both within and without the Grimms' Laws perimeter.

AFTER-WORD

The polygenesis theory of language origin, that languages evolved independently, is a cherished icon of the high priests of voodoo linguistics and secular humanism. THE WORD would not sweep skeptics off their feet even if it were ten times as extensive. The best research is smugly dismissed with the cry of "coincidence," just as it a "coincidence" that the Maya, the Chinese, the Persians and the Greco-Romans have variations of the Hebrew Bible's Tower of Babel account. With THE WORD as a beginning, it is hoped that like-thinking professional researchers can find the kinds of regularities that linguistic science demands. In time, variations within the Indo-European languages will more often and more successfully be explained via a Hebrew etymon then through the theoretical Indo-European root.

My goals in this initial study are to prove the following:

1) "Borrowings" from Hebrew and Semitic are far more extensive than now conceded in etymological texts.

2) The number of sound-alike, mean-alike terms in Indo-European and Semitic far exceed the allowable number of borrowings or "coincidences."

3) Hebrew's extensively related synonyms and antonyms, along with its modular, reversible two-letter roots, reflects a uniquely profound system of language that resembles the organicism of natural science rather than the product of human development.

4) If there is an original language, one from which all other languages can ultimately be traced, it is the language of the Hebrew Bible. It is in this document of unequaled power and antiquity that we might search for the words spoken by the Noahs, Adams and Eves at the dawn of humankind.

KEY TO THE INDEX: The upper case English word in both the Hebrew and English Indexes indicates the entry where the word is listed. A parenthetical (A) or (B) indicates the word is listed in Appendix A or Appendix B.

RICE/	ארז
REACH/	ארח
ARYAN/IS/LEOPARD/	ארי
RUG/	אריג
ARYAN/	אריה
ARCHITECT/AREA/REACH/	ארך
ARCHITECT/	ארכיון
ROOM(A)/	ארמון
ELM/	ארן
AREA/	ארעא
AGRICULTURALIST/EARTH/	ארעה
EARTH/	ארעית
AREA/EARTH/	ארץ
AREA/	ארקא
CULMINATE/	ארט
ASH/ASIA/	אש
SHED/	אשד
SCALLION/	אשכלן
ASHTREE/	אשל
ASHAMED/	אשם
ASH/ASIA/COAL/FIRE/SUN/	אש
DASH/SHED/	אשד
ASHTREE/	אשוח
ASH/	אשון
ASHTREE/SORGHUM/	אשור
SKILL/	אשכול
SCALLION/	אשכלן
ASHTREE/	אשל
ASHAMED/SEMANTIC/SIN/	אשם
SESAME/	אשמנים
ASH/	אשפה
ASHTREE/	אשרה
THOU/	אתה
TONIC/	אתן
AT/IS/SOVIET/THIS/	את
THOU/	אתה
ASININE/BURRO/TONIC/	אתון
ASININE/	אתון
TONIC/	אתן
ENDOW/	אתנן
AFTER/AT/	אתר
BE/	בא
BISON/	באשן
BABY/	בבה
BAUBLE/	בבה
BABBLE/	בבל
BIG(A)/	בגר
BAT/BIT/	בד
BAD/	בדאות
BEAR(A)/	בהיר
BEHEMOTH/	בהמות
BULLETIN(A)/	בול
BATISTE(A)/	בוץ
BOOR(A)/	בור
BOULDER/	בולט
BORE/	בור
BUZZARD/	בז
EMBEZZLE/	בזז
BAZOOKA(A)/	בזק
BID/	בטא
BET/	בטח
BOTULISM(A)/	בטן
BIBLE/	ביב
OPINION(A)/	בינה
ABASH/	ביש
BETA/BOTH/	בית
BALLOON(A)/	בלום
BLOAT/	בלט
BALEFUL(A)/	בלי
AGRICULTURALIST/	אכר
AGRICULTURALIST/	אכר
AGRICULTURALIST/	אכרים
ILLEGAL(A)/	אל
ELM/	אלנום
ELM/IS/	אלה
ELM/	אלון
I pronoun/	אלך
ALPHABET/	אלת-בית
ALPHABET/	אלף
ADD/AMAH(A)/AMITY/ETYMOLOGY/MACHINE/MAMA/	אם
MAMA/	אמא
AMAH(A)/ARM/MAMA/	אמה
MAN/MANY/MONEY/	אמון
AMENABLE/	אמונה
ADMIRAL/	אמיר
MALIGN/	אמלה
AMENABLE/MAN/MOON/OMEN/	אמן
MAMA/	אמנה
MAN/	אמנות
AMENABLE/	אמנם
AMITY/ETYMOLOGY/MAMA/	אמץ
MEAT(A)/	אמצה
ETYMOLOGY/MEZZANINE(A)/	אמצע
ADMIRAL/TOMENTUM(A)/	אמר
CAMEL/RAM/	אמרא
ADMIRAL/	אמרכל
ETYMOLOGY/	אמת
UNIQUE(A)/	אנד
Ipronoun/ME/	אנו
MAN/MASCULINE/	אנוש
NECK/	אנחה
Ipronoun/ME/UNIQUE(A)/	אני
ANKLE/	אנך
ANNOYANCE/	אנס
MASCULINE/	אנש
SUFFER/	אסובר
SIREN/	אסר
IF/OBOE/	אף
BUNTING/	אפד
JINX/OVEN(A)/	אפה
EVIL/	אפילה
IF/	אפילו
BLEAK/FALL/ORIOLE/PALL/	אפל
FALL/	אפלה
ABYSS(A)/SPHERES/	אפס
ABYSS(A)/	אפע
BAUBLE/OBOE/	אפף
BARRIO/BLEAK/GRAPHITE/PALL/	אפר
PUERILE/	אפרוח
CAPRICORN/FRUIT/SPRIG(A)/	אפרח
FERRY/	אפריון
PERSIMMON/	אפרסמון
PERSIMMON/	אפרסמון
PERSIMMON/	אפרסק
HASTE/	אץ
SPIRE/	אצבע
AUXILIARY/	אציל
CHRYSANTHEMUM/EARTH/	אר
RAVENOUS/	ארב
QUARTER/	ארבע
ARACHNID(A)/ORGAN/RUG/	ארג
ORGAN/	ארגון
ORGAN/	ארגון
ARK/	ארגז
IRE/	ארה
ORIOLE/	ארו
ROOM(A)/	ארון

VACATE/	בוק
BUCKET/VACATE/	בוקה
VACATE/	בוקק
BUCKAROO/	בוקר
BOOR(A)/BORE/PORE/	בור
ABASH/VEST/	בוש
ABASH/CHECKMATE/VEST/	בושה
BOOTY(A)/BUZZARD/EMBEZZLE/	בז
BUZZARD/	בזא
EMBEZZLE/USE/	בזבז
BUZZARD/	בזבז
BOOTY(A)/	בזה
BUZZARD/EMBEZZLE/	בזז
ABASH/	בזיון
BUZZARD/	בזיר
BAZOOKA(A)/	בזק
EXIT/	בחוץ
BIG(A)/BUCKAROO/	בחור
VOLUNTEER(A)/	בחירה
PICK/SECRET/	בחר
BID/	בט
BID/SOVIET/	בטא
BID/	בטאון
BOTANY/FAT/VENTRICLE/	בטבט
BID/VATICAN(A)/VETERAN/VETO/	בטה
BID/	בטוי
AFFIDAVIT/BAD/BET/FAITH/	בטח
VOCALIZE/	
AFFIDAVIT/FAITH/	בטחון
BUNTING/	בטך
BOTULISM(A)/FAITH/VETO/	בטל
BOTANY/BOTULISM(A)/BUTTON(A)/	בטן
FAT/TUMOR(A)/VENTRICLE/WOMAN/	
SOVIET/	בטרי
Ipronoun/	בי
BEMA/	בימה
BEAM(A)/BONE/OPINION(A)/WHEN/	בין
BONE/OPINION(A)/	בינה
FETUS/	ביצה
BARRIO/	ביצור
BORE/	ביר
BARRIO/METROPOLIS/	בירה
BARRIO/	בירנית
ABASH/BAD/	ביש
BASIS/BOTH/VANDYKE/	בית
VOCALIZE/	בכה
GAZE/	בכוכבים
BALLOON(A)/LOVE/VOLUNTEER(A)/	בל
LID/	בלאט
BABBLE/BALL/	בלבל
EFFULGENT(A)/	בלג
FLICK/	בלג
ABLATION(A)/BALEFUL(A)/	בלה
BALEFUL(A)/	בלהה
BALL/	בלול
BALL/BALLOON(A)/BLOAT/	בלום
BOULDER/	
BALL/BALLOON(A)/BLISTER/	בלט
BOAT/BOULDER/BULLETIN(A)/	
BUNTING/WELT/	
BALEFUL(A)/	בלי
WALLOW/	בליל
EVIL/	בליעל
BABBLE/BALL/GUERRILLA/WALK/	בלל
WALLOW/	
ABLATION(A)/BALEFUL(A)/BLEAK/	בלע
DEVOUR/	
BLAME/	בלעם
BLEAK/	בלק

BALL/	בלל
BLAME/	בלעם
BLEAK/	בלק
BEMA/	במה
BEAM(A)/	בן
BASIS/	בסס
BUBBLE/	בעבוע
ABOUT(A)/	בעד
BOOT(A)/BUTT/	בעט
BURRO/	בעיר
BULLY/	בעל
BARE/	בער
PITCH/	בץ
COPACETIC/	בצדק
BASIL/	בצל
BOOTY(A)/	בצע
BUCKET/	בקבוק
BEAKER/	בקבק
BICKER(A)/BUCKAROO/	בקר
BAR/BARLEY/BARRIO/	בר
BRIT(A)/	ברד
BRASS/	ברזל
VERY(A)/	ברי
BRIO(A)/	בריאות
BORAX(A)/	ברית
BROOK/	ברכה
BURST/	ברץ
BURR(A)/	ברקן
BRUSH/	ברש
BOLSHEVIK(A)/	בשל
BURSAR(A)/BUTCHER(A)/	בשר
BE/CONVEY/OF(A)/VIA/	בא
CONVEY/	באה
VIA/	באים
BARE/BLOAT/BORE/BURN/VERY(A)/	באר
ARK/	בארנז
BAD/BISON/	באש
BISON/	באשן
BIT/	בבד
BABY/BAUBLE/	בבה
BABY/BAUBLE/	בבאה
BABBLE/	בבל
BAUBLE/	בבת
SPRIG(A)/	בגירה
BIG(A)/	בגר
BIG(A)/	בגרות
BAT/BATISTE(A)/BOTANY/DIVIDED/	בד
WEED/	
BAD/	בדא
BAD/FAITH/	בדאות
BIT/DIVIDED/	בדד
BAD/	בדוי
BIT/DIVIDED/PIECE/WEED/	בדל
VIA/	כה
BARE/BEAR(A)/	כהיר
HURRY/	בהל
FEAR(A)/	בהלה
BEHEMOTH/	בהמה
BEHEMOTH/	בהמות
BEHEMOTH/	בהמי
BEAR(A)/	בהרת
CONVEY/VIA/	בו
VIA/	בוא
USE/	בוז
HERESY/	בוחר
BALL/BOULDER/BULLETIN(A)/	בול
BOULDER/	בולט
VACATE/	בועה
BATISTE(A)/	בוץ

VERY(A)/
BRUSH/BURR(A)/CYPRESS/STARE(A)/ ברוש
BARLEY/ ברות
BRASS/ ברזל
LIQUID/WRECK/ ברח
BARON/BRIO(A)/DEVOUR/VERY(A)/ ברי
BLOAT/BRIO(A)/DEVOUR/ בריא
BRIO(A)/ בריאות
BARLEY/BRIO(A)/DEVOUR/ בריה
BAR/WRECK/ בריח
BIT/BORAX(A)/SIX/ ברית
WRONG/ ברך
BROOK/LIQUID/ ברכה
BURSAR(A)/ ברסה
BREACH/BURST/ ברץ
EFFULGENT(A)/FLICK/FORK(A)/SPARK(A)/ ברק
BURR(A)/ ברקן
BLEAK/FLICK/SPARK(A)/ ברקת
BRUSH/ ברש
BOLSHEVIK(A)/ בשל
BALSAM/BISON/PERSIMMON/SMELL(A)/ בשם
BALSAM/ בשמיו
BURSAR(A)/BUTCHER(A)/GOSPEL/SARCASTIC/VEST/ בשר
ABASH/ בשש
BOTH/ בת-קול
BASIS/BIT/BOTANY/BOTH/FETUS/PEDIATRICIAN/ בת
PART/ כתד
SPILL/ בתולה
BIT/ בתור
BIT/PIECE/ בתק
AFTER/BIT/BUTCHER(A)/PART/PATRON/PIECE/ בתר
AFTER/ בתרא
BIT/ בתרים
GENIUS/KIN/ גאון
GENIUS/ גאון
GIBBON/ גבין
CAB/CAVITY/FICKLE/GAP/GIBBON/HAVOC/JIB(A)/ גב
GIBBON/ גבב
BIG(A)/GIBBON/ גבה
GARBLE/ גבל
VIRILE/ גבור
BARON/SQUAT/VIRILE/ גבורה
SCOOP/ גבים
GIBBON/ גבין
CUP/GOBLET/SCOOP/ גביע
BARON/BRIO(A)/VIRILE/ גביר
SPRIG(A)/ גבירה
CABLE/COUPLE/ גבל
CABLE/ גבלות
GIBBON/ גבן
GIBBON/ גבנן
GIBBON/ גבנוני
GIBBON/ גבע
BARON/BIG(A)/BRIO(A)/GRAVE/KIBOSH/SQUAT/VICTOR(A)/VIRILE/ גבר
GIBBON/ גברות
VIRILE/ גברי
GAG/ גג
GOAT/GOOD/HADDOCK/ גד
GATHER/ גדד
ACUTE/ גדה

BEMA/ במה
HURRY/ במהירה
MYSTERY/ במסתר
VANDYKE/ בן-אבות
VANDYKE/ בן-זוג
WHEN/ בן-לילה
BEAM(A)/BONE/NEW/VANDYKE/WHEN/ בן
BEAM(A)/GOVERN/VANDYKE/BEMA/ בניה
VANDYKE/ בנין
BASIS/ בס
COPACETIC/ בסדר
BASIS/ בסים
BASIS/ בסם
BOLSHEVIK(A)/ בסר
BUBBLE/ בע
BUBBLE/ בעבע
FOR/ בעבור
ABOUT(A)/ בעד
BUBBLE/ בעה
BOOT(A)/BUTT/BUTTON(A)/ בעט
BURRO/ בעיר
BULLY/ בעל
PEWTER(A)/ בעץ
ABLATION(A)/BARE/BOOR(A)/BURN/DEVOUR/FIRE/FROST/ בער
PREACH/ בפרוש
BISON/PITCH/ בץ
COPACETIC/ בצדק
BISON/PITCH/ בצה
BUZZARD/ בציעה
BASIL/ בצל
BASIL/ בצלים
BOOTY(A)/ בצע
BISON/ בצץ
PITA/ בצק
PIECE/TOWER/ בצר
XEROX(A)/ בצרון
XEROX(A)/ בצרת
BEAKER/ בק
BUCKET/PIT/ בקבוק
BEAKER/VACATE/ בקבק
BOTANY/ בקה
PICK/ בקיה
BUCKET/ בקיע
BEAKER/CRUCIFIX/PICK/ בקע
BEAKER/BUCKET/VACATE/ בקעה
VACATE/ בקק
BICKER(A)/BUCKAROO/BURRO/ בקר
BICKER(A)/ בקרת
FAKER/SEEK/ בקש
FAKER/VOCALIZE/ בקשה
AMBER/BAR/BARE/BARLEY/BARON/ בר
BARRIO/BEAR(A)/BOOR(A)/BORAX(A)/BORE/BRIO(A)/DELTA/DEVOUR/FEROCIOUS(A)/FOR/FRUIT/OVER/PREPARE/PUERILE/SPRIG(A)/VERY(A)/
BARE/ ברא
GRAPHITE/ בראשית
BRIT(A)/FROST/LEOPARD/SANGFROID/ ברד
BRIT(A)/LEOPARD/ ברדלם
ABLATION(A)/DEVOUR/ ברה
LEOPARD/ ברוד
DEVOUR/ ברוז
BEAUTY(A)/ ברוך
BAR/BARE/BARLEY/BORAX(A)/ ברור

JANUARY/ — גניזה
JANUARY/ — גנן
GALL/ — גנל
CALL/ — גער
GAP/ — גף
CYPRESS/ — גפר
GIAOUR(A)/GRAIN/GUERRILLA/GYRE/ — גר
GRAVE/SACK/SCURVY/ — גרכ
MARINE/ — גרניר
CORAL/GARGLE/GRAIN/KERNEL/ — גרנר
EGRET/ — גרנרה
GARGLE/ — גרנרן
COLLAR/GARGLE/SCRUFF/ — גרנרת
CARD/CHARACTER/GRADE/GRAVE/SCRATCH/SERRATED/ — גרד
ACCELERATE/GERM/GRADE/GRIST/GUERRILLA/ — גרה
COLLAR/CRY/EGRET/GARGLE/GROAN/ — גרון
GRIST/ — גרום
GRASS/ — גרושה
GROAN/ — גרון
CURT/GRAZE/ — גרז
CURT/ — גרזן
GROUND/ — גרידה
GERM/GRAIN/GRIST/UNICORN/ — גרם
CORN/GRAIN/GROUND/ — גרן
CRUSH/GRIST/ — גרס
CORAL/CORE/GERM/GRAIN/KERNEL/ — גרעין
GRAPPLE/ — גרף
GRAZE/ — גרצן
CAR/CARD/CHARACTER/GRADE/GROUND/ — גרר
CAR/ — גררה
GROAN/ — גררן
GRASS/ — גרש
AGRICULTURALIST/GRASS/GRIST/ — גרש
GRIST/ — גרש
COSMOS(A)/ — גשמיות
KISS/ — גשה
COSMOS(A)/ — גשם
COSMOS(A)/ — גשמי
COSMOS(A)/ — גשמיות
KISS/ — גשר
GUT/ — גתת
GAUDY/ — דאבה
KITE/ — דאה
ABRACADABRA/ — דברה
TAB/ — רבה
CRUCIFIX/TACK/ — דבק
BID/PHONETICS/ — דבר
ABRACADABRA/RHAPSODY/ — דברה
DIVE/HEDONISM/OOZE/QUARTER/WIZEN(A)/ — דבש
ACUTE/HADDOCK/ — דג
TICKLE/TOUCH/ — דגדג
HADDOCK/ — דגה
HADDOCK/ — דגון
GIRDLE/ — דגר
TEAT/ — דד
DOODLE(A)/ — דדה
TOOTS/ — דדים
ROTATE/ — דהר
DIALECT/DUO/ — דו
DOUCHE(A)/ — דוח
DUO/ — דו-שיח

GATHER/HADDOCK/TOOTS/ — גדוד
LOUT(A)/SCANTINESS/ — גדול
GOAT/KITTEN/ — גדי
GOAT/ — גדיא
QUARTER/ — גדיש
DELTA/GATHER/HOARD/ — גדר
HERD/HOARD/ — גדרה
HYGIENE(A)/ — גהה
HYGIENE(A)/ — גהות
GIPON(A)/ — גופיה
BOTANY/ — גוב
CZAR/GIPON(A)/ — גוף
FIGURE/ — גופה
GIPON(A)/ — גופיה
CAPRICORN/CYCLE/TELIC/ — גור
CORAL/GRAIN/ — גורל
CORAL/ — גורל
HAZE/ — גז
SAXON/SCISSORS/ — גזז
GUZZLE(A)/ — גזל
GRAZE/SCISSORS/ — גזר
CHAR/ — נחול
COAL/GALL/ — נחל
COAL/ — נחלת
CHAETA(A)/GUT/ — גיד
GALA/LAUGH/ — גיל
GALA/ — גילה
GLABROUS/ — גילוף
KISS/ — גישה
CALF(A)/CONGLOMERATE/CULMINATE/GALA/GALL/GIBBON/GLISSADE/GYRE/OROLOGY/SKULL/TELIC/ — גל
CARVE/CLEAVER/GLABROUS/SCALP/SCRAPER/ — גלב
CONGLOMERATE/GLISSADE/WALK/ — גלגול
ACCELERATE/CAR/CONGLOMERATE/CYCLE/GYRE/SKULL/ — גלגל
SCALP/SKULL/UNICORN/ — גלגלת
CLOT/CRUST/CRYOGENICS/GLABROUS/LEATHER(A)/ — גלד
CLOT/ — גלדה
GALYAK(A)/ — גלה
GALYAK(A)/ — גלוח
GALYAK(A)/ — גלוח
GALYAK(A)/ — גלוי
GALYAK(A)/SCORCH/ — גלח
CRYOGENICS/ — גליד
CRYOGENICS/ — גלידה
CONGLOMERATE/ — גליל
SCALP/ — גליפה
COLOSSUS/ — גלית
CONGLOMERATE/GLISSADE/GORE/GYRE/ — גלל
CAMEL/CONGLOMERATE/GERM/ — גלם
CARVE/ — גלף
GLISSADE/QUARTER/SLUDGE/ — גלש
GLISSADE/ — גלשון
COMMON/ — גם
GIBBON/HEM/ — גמגם
AMERICA/ANCIENT/CAMEL/COLOSSUS/MEGALOMANIAC(A)/ — גמל
CAMEL/ — גמלון
GERM/MEGALOMANIAC(A)/ — גמר
GIBBON/ — גן
JANUARY/KNAVE/NIP/ — גנב
JANUARY/ — גנונה
JANUARY/ — גנן
JANUARY/ — גנך

ORTHODOX/	רעתן
PANE/	רפן
TAP/	רפק
DANCE(A)/	רץ
ACUTE/CATECHISM(A)/DIK-DIK(A)/	רק
GNAW/HADDOCK/KITTEN/ORTHODOX/ TACTICIAN/TALCUM/	
DIK-DIK(A)/	רקדוק
CATECHISM(A)/DIK-DIK(A)/	רקדוק
TACTICIAN/	רקדק
ORTHODOX/	רקדקן
DELICACY(A)/	רקל
CHIN/SQUAT/	רקק
DIKE/TACK/	רקר
DRIVE/	ררבן
GRADE/	ררנה
TIRE/	ררדור
DURIAN(A)/	ררדר
CHAR/	ררומי
TURTLEDOVE/	ררור
DIRECTION/DRAG/TRACK/TREK/ TRUDGE/	ררך
ALLEY/DIRECTION/DRAG/GRADE/ TIER/TRACK/TREK/TRUDGE/WALK/	ררך
DASH/TRACK/	ררם
TURTLEDOVE/	ררר
TRACK/	ררש
DENSE(A)/	רשן
DASH/	רש
SOD/	רשא
DENSE(A)/	רשן
AIR(A)/AVIATE/	האביר
AUSCULATE/	האוינו
AMENABLE/	האמין
GIVE(A)/HALO/	הב
CLIMATE/	הבא
BEAKER/SHISHKEBAB/	הבהב
VOCALIZE/	הבטחה
BET/	הבטיח
HALO/	הבי
CONVEY/VIA/	הביא
SPY/	הביט
BONE/	הבין
VOCALIZE/	הביע
ABASH/	הביש
FLICK/	הבליח
EBONY/	הבני
EBONY/	הבנים
FIRE/	הבער
FIRE/	הבערה
DEVOUR/	הבריא
WREAK(A)/WRECK/	הבריח
SPARK(A)/	הבריק
AGONY/	הג
HEGEMONY/	הנאי
AGONY/HEGEMONY/	הנה
BROOK/	הניר
CRYOGENICS/	הגליד
JANUARY/	הגן
HOOT/HOOT(A)/	הד
COTTON/	הדה
DOUCHE(A)/	הדיח
DILUTE/	הדלדל
DILUTE/	הדליל
DARK/LIGHT/	הדליק
CHIN/	הדק
ADORE/HOARD/	הדר
DIRECTION/REICH/	הדריך
RACK/	הדרך

DIALECT/DILEMMA(A)/DUO/	רו
TABES(A)/	רוב
TOOTS/	רור
TOTE(A)/	רודא
TITTIE/TOOTS/	רורה
TITILLATE/TOOTS/	רורים
GAUDY/	רוה
TABES(A)/	רוי
ROTATE/SWERVE/TIARA/TIER/TIRE/	רור
ENDOW/	רורון
TRACK/	רורש
DASH/	רוש
TOOTS/	רוד
TITTIE/	רוֹדה
TITILLATE/	רוֹדים
SEDUCE/TOUCH/	רחה
DIVAN(A)/	רחון
DECAY/PRECEDE/SEDUCE/	רחי
SCARE/	רחיל
SEDUCE/	רחיפה
DIVAN(A)/	רחן
CHAFE/SCOOP/SEDUCE/TOUCH/	רחף
TOUCH/	רחק
DEBRIS/	רי
CUD/	רין
DYE/	ריו
DYE/	ריו
DIKE/	רייק
LAUGH/	רילונ
DAMN/MADONNA/	רין
DIKE/TACTICIAN/	רייק
ARSENAL/DELTA/HERD/	ריר
DASH/	ריש
SQUAT/	רכא
DILUTE/LOUT(A)/SANDAL/TALL/	רל
DRAG/LOCUST(A)/WALK/	רלנ
TAIL/	רלדל
DRAW/TAIL/TOLL/	רלה
HURRY/	רלונ
DARK/	רלוח
DARK/	רלח
DILUTE/	רליחה
DILUTE/	רליל
DRIP/	רליפה
LIGHT/	רליקתא
DILUTE/LOUT(A)/	רלל
DILEMMA(A)/	רלמא
DRIP/	רלף
ADOLESCENT/DARK/LIGHT/	רלק
DELTA/	רלת
DAMN/DAMP(A)/DAWN/DUMB/ DUMMY/MUSK/SANGRIA/TEAM/	רם
DUMMY/	רמ
DUMB/	רמרום
DUMB/DUMMY/	רמה
DUMB/	רמום
DUMMY/	רמות
DAMN/DORM/DUMB/	רמי
DUMMY/	רמיון
DAMN/	רמים
DUMB/	רמם
DUMB/	רממה
MUSK/	רמע
DAMP(A)/	רמעה
DAMN/MADONNA/THEM/	רן
CATECHISM(A)/DEXTROUS(A)/IDEA/ ORTHODOX/	רע
TICKLE/TOUCH/	רעירע
DEXTROUS(A)/ORTHODOX/	רעת

DAWN/SANGRIA/SUN/	הנץ
HUSH/	הם
SOFA/SWIVEL/	הסב
HESITANT/	הסה
HESITANT/	הסום
SHAG/	הסיג
SIEGE/	הסיך
SPHERES/	הסיף
SWERVE/	הסיר
INCITE/	הסית
HASTE/HESITANT/	הסס
HESITANT/	הסן
ABLATION(A)/FERRY/FUHRER/ SUFFER/	העביר
FERRY/	העברה
EVENING/	העיב
ORIENTATION/	העיר
USE/	העסיק
CURTSY(A)/	העריץ
FAKER/	הפגין
FAKER/	הפגיע
FICKLE/HAVOC/	הפוך
PHOSPHORUS/TOPAZ/	הפז
COP/	הפח
FAIL(A)/FALL/	הפיל
DIASPORA(A)/PIZAZZ/	הפיץ
FACULTY/	הפיק
FICKLE/	הפך
HAVOC/	הפכה
FICKLE/	הפכפך
FICKLE/	הפכפך
ARCHIPELAGO/BARK(A)/FLICK/	הפליג
PACK/	הפקיע
FAKER/	הפקיר
FREAK/	הפריג
SPREAD/	הפריד
STABLE/	הצב
SPIRE/	הצביע
STABLE/	הציב
STEAL/	הציל
SICK/	הציק
MASK/SNEAK/	הצניע
GAZE/	הצצה
ALCOVE/	הקבה
CUBE/	הקביל
QUIET/	הקטין
HAIL/	הקל
CHERISH/	הקלה
CASEFY(A)/	הקשה
CULMINATE/HURRY/OROLOGY/	הר
DIRECTION/	הרניל
RAVE/	הרהיב
AMITY/	הרחמן
SCARE/	הרטיט
HERE/	הרי
BROOK/KARATE/	הריק
RUM/	הרם
HURRY/	הרעל
HURRY/	הרף
ORCHESTRA/	הרקיד
CULMINATE/OROLOGY/	הרר
OROLOGY/	הררי
SMITE/	השמיד
CONSULT/	השאיל
GOSPEL/	השביע
SAVANNA/	השוה
GOSPEL/	השיב
KISS/SAG/SEEK/SEIZE/SHAG/	השיג

HE/	ההוא
HE/WHO/	הוא
HOOT(A)/	הו
HE/WHO/	הוא
VOLUNTEER(A)/	הואיל
FERRY/	הוביל
WIZEN(A)/	הוביש
AGONY/	הוגה
ADORE/	הוד
ADORE/	הודאה
ADORE/	הודה
SYNDICATE/	הודיע
IDEA/ORTHODOX/	הודע
SYNDICATE/	הודעה
BE/HAVOC/	הוה
BE/	הוי
MAIM/	הומם
HONEST(A)/	הון
SPHERES/SUFFICE/	הוסיף
SUFFICE/	הוספה
EXIT/	הוציא
HERESY/	הוראה
DRIP/LOUT(A)/	הוריד
IS/	הות
SACK/	הזיק
VAT/	החביא
DAWN/SANGRIA/	החמה
ENCASE/	החסין
CULPABLE/	החפיר
CREED/	החרה
HARROW/	החריב
CREAM/HARM/	החרים
HUSH/	החשה
TELEVISION/	הטיל
TROPHY/	הטריף
HE/WHO/	היא
IS/	היות
DIVINE/	היטיב
HOW(A)/	היך
HOW(A)/	היך
HOLLOW/	היכל
KNOCK/NOXIOUS/	הכה
MARK/	הכיר
ACUMEN/	הכיש
CALUMNY/	הכלים
GARBLE/	הכר
CROUCH/CURVE/	הכריע
ALBINO/	הלבנה
ALBINO/	הלבנה
HALO/HERE/	הלה
WALK/	הלך
ALLEY/BROOK/CATSKILL/WALK/	הלך
LEX/	הלכה
CALL/GALL/HAIL/HALO/ ULULATION/	הלל
HERE/	הללו
HAIL/	הללוקה
HERE/	הלם
HE/THEM/	הם
MANY/	המון
MANY/	המון
NOUS(A)/	המיש
SHAG/	המשך
HONEST(A)/KHAN/	הן
HONEY(A)/	הנאה
HERE/NOW/	הנה
NO/	הניא
NOD/	הניד
FAN/PANIC/	הניף

SOLITARY/	זולת
SOLITARY/	זולתי
SWERVE/	זור
SERUM/	זורר
SNORKEL/THIS/	זו
JACKAL/	זחל
SEETHE/	זיד
SEETHE/	זידון
ARSENAL/	זין
BAZOOKA(A)/	זיק
SESAME/	זית
SAKE/	זכה
SAMURAI/SCHIZOPOD(A)/	זכור
SAKE/	זכות
SAKE/	זכיה
SCAR/SCORE/	זכר
SCAR/	זכרון
CIRRUS(A)/	זלזל
LIQUID/REEK/	זלח
SOUND/	זם
SOUND/	זמזם
PSALM/SOUND/	זמירה
SESAME/SOUND/SUMMON/	זמן
PSALM/SOUND/	זמר
SUMMER(A)/	זמרה
SIMULATION/	זן
SNAKE/SNAP/	זנב
CHANGE/SIN/	זנה
SKUNK/SMELL(A)/	זנח
SNEAK/	זניקה
NOZZLE/SNAKE/SNEAK/	זנק
SEISMIC(A)/	זע
SEISMIC(A)/	זעזע
CHUCKLE(A)/SHRIEK/	זעק
PITCH/	זפת
SHACKLE/	זק
SAKE/SHACKLE/	זקה
KYPHOS/	זקוף
SAKE/	זקוק
SHACKLE/	זקים
CHECKMATE/CHIN/SHAGGY/	זקן
SHACKLE/	זקק
STRIKE/	זקר
AUXILIARY/CIRRUS(A)/CZAR/SIR/	זר
SERUM/SLOUGH/XEROX(A)/	זרב
CIRRUS(A)/	זרד
SOW/	זרה
AUXILIARY/REACH/	זרוע
SHOWER/	זרויף
SERUM/	זרויר
RISE/	זרח
SERUM/XEROX(A)/	זרם
NEW/SOW/STRIKE/	זרע
JERK/SERUM/SOW/STRIKE/	זרק
ALGEBRA/	חפור
CRUCIFIX/CUFF/GIVE(A)/VAT/	חב
COVER/CUBBY/	חבא
COVER/HAVEN(A)/LOVE/	חבה
ALGEBRA/	חבור
BUTT/BUTTON(A)/CRUCIFIX/CUFF/	חבט
VAT/	חביונה
BALE(A)/	חבילה
CUP/VAT/	חבית
ALGEBRA/BALE(A)/BALEFUL(A)/ CABLE/CRUCIFIX/CUFF/	חבל
CRUCIFIX/GIRDLE/HUG(A)/	חבק
ALGEBRA/CABLE/COUPLE/ CRUCIFIX/	חבר
CRUCIFIX/KIBOSH/	חבש

KISS/	השיק
SMITE/	השמיד
SEEK/	השק
SCOPE/	השקוף
SKEPTIC/	השקיף
SCOPE/	השקפה
SHAG/	השינ
TAKE/	התיק
BARON/	הת
OBITUARY/	התאבד
WAIL/	התאבל
BONE/	התבונן
BAD/VETO/	התבדה
BONE/OPINION(A)/	התבונן
TABES(A)/	התוך
VOCALIZE/	התופח
CHORUS/HULA/	התחולל
HELD/	התחיל
KNAVE/	התחנך
GUERRILLA/	התחרה
HOARSE/	התחרש
TAKE/	התיק
TABES(A)/	התך
ELECT/	התלכד
MEEK/	התמונג
MURMUR(A)/	התמרמר
ADMIRAL/AMERICA/	התעמר
PLEA/	התפלל
PUERILE/	התפרחח
PALTER(A)/	התפתל
WRESTLE(A)/	התרוצץ
HOARSE/	התריש
ANNOYANCE/	ות
VIA/	וכה
AFFIDAVIT/WED/	ודאי
ROVE/	וה
BOBBY/	וו
SQUAT/	וינברו
ALLEY/	ויעל
ARCHITECT/	ויערך
BICKER(A)/	וכוח
BROOD(A)/LAD/	ולד
SASH/	ומשי
VACATE/	ונבקה
SOVIET/	ועד
ADD/	ועוד
CAPITAL/	ור
RED/	ורד
RED/	ורדינון
RED/	וריד
ASSUME/	ושמא
VETERAN/	ותיק
FATUITY(A)/QUIET/	ות
VETERAN/	ותיק
ALUMNI/	ות
JACKAL/	זאב
THIS/	זאת
SEEP/	זב
BESTOW(A)/	זבד
SWIVEL/	זבוב
ASPHALT/SEEP/	זבל
SEEP/	זבת
RISE/	זהר
SOLITARY/	זולת
SNORKEL/	זו
SEETHE/	זוד
PEGASUS/SEISMIC(A)/	זוז

ALBINO/CLEAVE/GALAXY/GALBANUM/LIVER/MILK/SESAME/	חלב
ALBINO/	חלבון
GALAXY/	חלבי
CLEAVE/GALBANUM/	חלבנה
GRADE/HELD/	חלד
GRADE/GUERRILLA/	חלדה
HEAD/	חלה
HEAD/	חלון
HOLLOW/	חלול
DORM/	חלום
HOLLOW/	חלון
HEAD/	חלון
CRACK/	חלוקה
HOLLOW/HULA/	חלחל
HULA/	חלחלה
HEAD/	חלי
CALAMUS(A)/HOLLOW/	חליל
CALAMUS(A)/CATSKILL/CELL/HOLLOW/KILL/OROLOGY/	חלל
HEAD/	חלם
CLEAVE/	חלמה
CLEAVER/HARROW/LOUGH/	חלף
CLEAVER/	חלפית
LUCK(A)/	חלק
HEAD/LOOSE(A)/	חלש
AMITY/ANEMIC/CALM/FIRE/IGNITION(A)/	חם
HAMSTER/	חמ
AMITY/HAMSTER/HANDSOME(A)/	חמד
AMITY/CALM/SANGRIA/	חמה
HANDSOME(A)/	חמוד
AMITY/HANDSOME(A)/	חמוד
ANEMIC/HAMSTER/SANGRIA/	חמיץ
ASININE/BURRO/HAREM/MARE(A)/PEGASUS/	חמור
MARE(A)/	חמור
HUMUS(A)/	חמיץ
CLEMENCY(A)/	חמל
CLEMENCY(A)/	חמלה
HAMSTER/	חמם
HAMSTER/	חמסן
MASS/MUSK/AMITY/ANEMIC/CERAMIC(A)/CRIMSON/HUMUS(A)/MAROON/	חמר
CERAMIC(A)/	חמרה
HUMUS(A)/	חמרי
MAROON/	חמרמר
MITT/QUINTET/	חמש
QUANT(A)/	חמשים
MAW(A)/	חמת
HANDSOME(A)/KEEN/KIND(A)/	חן
HAUNT/INN(A)/NIGHT(A)/	חנה
KIND(A)/	חנון
KNAVE/	חניך
KEEN/KNAVE/QUANT(A)/SAXON/	חנית
KNAVE/	חנך
KIND(A)/	חנן
CINCTURE(A)/HANG/HEM/KNOCK/NECK/SNAKE/	חנק
CHASTE/HESITANT/HOUSE/	חס
CHASTISE(A)/	חסד
HOUSE/MAGAZINE/	חסה
HOUSE/	חסות
CASSIA(A)/	חסוי
ENCASE/HOUSE/	חסוי
GUZZLE(A)/	חסול
HOUSE/	חסות
CRUCIFIX/	חבת
CYCLE/GIRDLE/HAGIOGRAPHA/	חג
HAGIOGRAPHA/	חגא
COURT/CYCLE/GIRDLE/	חגור
GIRDLE/	חגורה
HAGIOGRAPHA/	חגיגה
HAGIOGRAPHA/	חגיגות
HAGIOGRAPHA/	חגיני
CURTSY(A)/GIRDLE/HUG(A)/	חגר
ACACIA(A)/ACUTE/CATECHISM(A)/	חד
CUD/CUT/EACH/GOAD/HADDOCK/HASTATE/JUXTAPOSE/SQUAT/TACK/	
ACUTE/	חדד
GAUDY/	חדה
GAUDY/	חדוה
CATECHISM(A)/	חדחד
HELD/	חדל
ACUTE/	חדק
DELICACY(A)/	חדקל
CHAISE/	חדר
ACCOUTERMENTS/CHAETA(A)/	חוט
EXIT/	חוץ
ROCHET(A)/	חור
GUESS/	חוש
HUG(A)/	חוג
ACUMEN/COG(A)/HOOK/	חוח
CAVITY/	חוחים
ACCOUTERMENTS/ACUTE/CHAETA(A)/COTTON/GUT/	חוט
VILLA(A)/	חוילה
ILLEGAL(A)/	חולה
GALL/	חולירע
CHECKMATE/	חומה
CRIMSON/	חומר
CHAFE/SCAUP/	חוף
COTTON/EXIT/GRASS/HASTATE/	חוץ
EXIT/	חוצה
CRACK/KARATE/ROCHET(A)/SCORE/	חור
GUESS/	חוש
COG(A)/	חוח
GOPHER/	חופר
GAZE/	חז
GAZE/	חזה
GAZE/	חזיון
HAZE/	חזיז
HYOSCYAMINE(A)/NEW/SHANK/	חזיר
SHACKLE/	חזק
HOOK/	חח
CUT/	חטב
WHEAT/	חטה
CLIMATE(A)/	חטם
COP/	חטף
CLIMATE(A)/ROOT/	חטר
ROOT/	חטרא
HYGIENE(A)/	חי
HYGIENE(A)/	חייא
ACCOUTERMENTS/	חיט
GUERRILLA/HAIL/HEAD/LEECH/SCARE/	חיל
HATCH(A)/	חיק
HASTE/HESITANT/	חיש
EIGHT/HOARD/	חית
LICK/	חך
HOOK/ACUMEN/HOOK/	חכה
HOKUM/KEEN/	חכם
ACUMEN/HOKUM/	חכמה
HULA/LAUGH/	חל
GALL/	חלא
GALBANUM/	חלבנה

HOARSE/	חרישה
HOARSE/	חרישית
SCORCH/	חרך
CHAR/SCORCH/	חרך
HAREM/ROC/TABOO/	חרם
HARM/	חרמה
HORUS/JASPER/	חרס
HORUS/	חרסה
CARP/CHARACTER/CULPABLE/HARROW/REGRET/	חרף
CULPABLE/	חרפה
CULPABLE/	חרפה
CAR/HEARSE/REGRET/SCORE/SCRATCH/	חרץ
CORE/	חרצב
CHRYSANTHEMUM/	חרצית
CORE/	חרצן
CRACK/CREAK/SCORE/	חרק
HERESY/SCORE/	חרר
ELMHURST/HEARSE/HOARSE/	חרש
CHARACTER/ELMHURST/HARROW/HEARSE/HOARSE/HUSH/RUCKUS/SCRATCH/	חרש
ELMHURST/	חרשא
STARE(A)/	חרשה
HEARSE/SCRATCH/	חרת
HUSH/	חשה
ASSASSIN/	חשש
HASTE/	חש
GUESS/SAVOIR-FAIRE/	חשב
HESITANT/HUSH/	חשה
HUSH/	חשי
NIGHT(A)/OBSCURE/	חשך
ENCASE/	חשן
ASSASSIN/HESITANT/	חשש
HATE/HESITANT/	חת
HATE/	חתה
KITTEN/	חתול
CUT/	חתך
COP/	חתף
HATE/	חתת
TOBACCO/	טבק
DIVINE/	טב
TOWEL/	טבול
DIVIDED/TOWEL/	טבול
BUTCHER(A)/SARCASTIC/	טבח
DAUB(A)/DIVE/TOWEL/	טבל
DIVE/	טבע
DIVINE/	טבת
TIER/	טור
TOSS/	טוש
BAD/BEAUTY(A)/DIVIDED/DIVINE/	טוב
TOWEL/TWIST/	טוה
TILE/	טוח
DRIP/	טוף
DIRECTION/HERD/TERM/TIER/	טור
TOWER/	טורה
TOSS/	טוש
DIVINE/	טוב
TALCUM/	טחה
CHIN/	טחון
CHIN/GNAW/TACTICIAN/TALCUM/THIN/	טחן
TELEVISION/	טיול
TELEVISION/	טיל
TOSS/	טיסה
TOWER/	טירה
DRIP/TILE/WET/	טל
TILE/	טלא

CHASTE/CHASTISE(A)/	חסיד
GUZZLE(A)/	חסיל
CHASTISE(A)/	חסית
CHASTE/	חסן
GUZZLE(A)/	חסל
CHASTE/	חסם
HOUSE/	חסן
CHASTE/XEROX(A)/	חסר
COVER/CUBBY/	חפא
ALCOVE/CAB/CAMERA/CAP/COVER/EVENING/HAVEN(A)/	חפה
PORE/	חפור
COVER/	חפיפה
CATCH/COP/FIN/GOVERN/HAVEN(A)/PUGNACIOUS/	חפן
ALKALI/HAFE/	חפף
CAPITALISM/	חפץ
GOPHER/	חפר-פרות
BORE/CAVITY/CRAB/GOPHER/SCRAPER/	חפר
CAPITALISM/	חפש
CUBE/	חפת
ACACIA(A)/ACUTE/CAST/GOAD/HASTATE/HASTE/SCOOT/SHOOT/TACK	חץ
CASTRATE/HASTE/	חצב
CASTRATE/CUT/	חצה
CASTRATE/	חצי
CASTRATE/	חצין
GRASS/	חציר
ENCASE/	חצן
HASTATE/	חצץ
COURT/	חצר
AGRICULTURALIST/	חקל
AGRICULTURALIST/	חקלאות
QUERY/SCOUR/	חקר
CARRACK(A)/HOLLOW/OROLOGY/	חר
GORE/	חרא
CARVE/CLEAVER/CRAB/GUERRILLA/HARROW/HORUS/PLOUGH/SACK/SCRAPER	חרב
CREAK/CREED/	חרג
CREAK/	חרגול
CREED/HOARD/HORRID/REGRET/SCARE/	חרד
HORRID/RATTLE/REGRET/	חרדה
BURN/CERAMIC(A)/CHAR/COAL/FIRE/GRAPHITE/HORUS/IRE/ORIOLE/	חרה
CHRYSANTHEMUM/	חרוץ
CHARACTER/HERESY/	חרות
GUERRILLA/	חרום
GROAN/IRE/UNICORN/	חרון
HERESY/	חרוף
CHARACTER/CHRYSANTHEMUM/ORIOLE/	חריץ
CHARACTER/HERESY/HOLLOW/	חרות
GUERRILLA/	חרחור
GUERRILLA/	חרחר
CHARACTER/DIRECTION/REGRET/SCORE/SCRATCH/SERRATED/	חרט
REGRET/	חרטה
CHARACTER/	חרטמים
IRE/	חרי
GORE/	חריונים
CARP/CULPABLE/HARROW/	חריף
CHARACTER/CORE/SCRATCH/	חריץ
CHARACTER/HARROW/	חריצה

IOTA/	יוֹד
JINX/	יוֹנה
EACH/JOINT(A)/JUXTAPOSE/	יחד
JUXTAPOSE/	יחוד
MAROON/	יחמוּר
COVER/	יחף
COULD/	יכוֹל
COULD/	יכוֹל
COULD/	יכל
COULD/	יכלת
ALBINO/	ילבינוּ
GILL(A)/LAD/LOUT(A)/	ילד
LOVE/	ילוה
ULULATION/	ילל
ULULATION/	יללה
CALIBER/	ילפת
LOCUST(A)/	ילק
ALGEBRA/MARINE/OCEAN(A)/	ים
SEVEN/	ימים-
MAN/	ימין
NO/	יניא
SET/	יסד
RHAPSODY/SEAT/SET/SOD/	יסוד
SORE/	יסוֹר
INCITE/	יסיתך
WED/	יעוד
AVIATE/	יעוּפף
EVENING/	יעיב
JIFFY(A)/	יעף
ANKLE/COLOSSUS/IDEA/JACK/	יעקב
JUNGLE/	יער
BEAUTY(A)/	יפ
BEAUTY(A)/	יפי
EXIT/JET/STYLE/	יצא
MASTABAH(A)/	יצב
CAST/JET/SOAK/	יצק
STYLE/	יצר
STYLE/	יצרן
ALCOVE/CAB/CAVITY/	יקב
CAUTERIZE/	יקד
JOVIAL/	יקוֹק
CHERISH/	יקר
NEW/	יראה
DORM/DRIP/ROOT/TALL/	ירד
JERK/	ירה
LOUT(A)/	ירוד
GHERKKIN(A)/	ירוק
VANDYKE/	ירוּשלימבן
JERK/	יריעה
JERK/	ירך
GHERKKIN(A)/JERK/JET/	ירק
IS/	יש
SENILE/	ישׁן
JASPER/	ישׁפה
JURISDICTION/SHEER/	ישׁר
IS/	יש
BE/	ישׁב
ASPIRE/	ישׁברוּ
JASPER/	ישׁימון
SMUG/	ישׁם-
CHANGE/SENILE/SUN/	ישׁן
JASPER/	ישׁפה
JURISDICTION/SERIES/SHEER/ SHEERING/STARE(A)/	ישׁר
JURISDICTION/	ישׁראל
JURISDICTION/	ישׁרה
JURISDICTION/	ישׁרון
ABASH/	יתבששׁוּ
TOSS/	יתושׁ
DOLL/	טלה
TELEVISION/	טלטוּל
TELEVISION/	טלטל
DOLL/	טליה
TAIL/	טלית
DARK/TILE/	טלל
TILE/	טלף
CONTAMINATE(A)/	טמא
DUMB/	טמוּם
DUMB/	טמטם
TIN/TON/	טנא
TIN/	טני
DAMP(A)/	טנן
DAIS(A)/	טס
CLIMATE(A)/DAMN/DUMB/FOR/ LICK/MUSK/	טעם
DAMN/DUMB/TON/	טען
FATUITY(A)/FETUS/PEDIATRICIAN/	טף
DIVE/	טפ
DIVE/	טפה
TAP/	טפוּם
PUTSCH/	טפח
DIVE/	טפטף
TAP/	טפיחה
TOWEL/TWIST/	טפיט
TOP/	טפל
DIVE/FAT/FATUITY(A)/	טפשׁ
REEVE/	טרוּף
DRAG/DRUDGERY/TOIL(A)/	טרח
DRAG/	טרחה
TELEVISION/	טרי
TROUT(A)/	טרית
TERM/	טרם
RAVENOUS/RHAPSODY/RIFE/ THERAPY/TROPHY/TWIST/	טרף
DASH/TOSS/	טשׁ
BLISTER/WELT/	יבלת
HUBBUB/	יבב
HUBBUB/	יבבה
BOULDER/	יבוּל
BLOAT/JUBILANT/WELT/	יבל
BLISTER/BLOAT/BULLETIN(A)/ WELT/	יבלת
BISON/OOZE/WIZEN(A)/	יבשׁ
AGONY/	יגה
AGONY/	יגון
AGONY/	יגון
AGONY/	יגע
CULMINATE/	יגר
ENDOW/IOTA/JET/KARATE/	יד
TOOTS/	ידד
ADORE/JET/	ידה
DOUCHE(A)/SEDUCE/	ידח
TOOTS/	ידיד
IDEA/	ידיעה
DEXTROUS(A)/IDEA/	ידע
GIVE(A)/	יהב
FENWAY(A)/	יו
ARCHIPELAGO/JUBILANT/	יובל
IOTA/	יוד
JINX/MADONNA/	יוחנן
AGONY/SEVEN/	יום
FENWAY(A)/IOTA/JINX/PENETRATE/	יון
JINX/	יונה
SUFFICE/	יוסף
STYLE/	יוצר
SENILE/	יישׁן
SURPASS/	יותר
JUBILANT/	יוכל

FOR/	כי
GOVERN/	כיון
CHAR/	כיור
ENCASE/OBSCURE/SACK/	כיס
CHAR/SCAR/	כירה
CAKE/CYCLE/GYRE/	ככר
ALL/HAIL/LOBO/SCULLERY/	כל
CELL/SCULLERY/	כלא
ALL/CLEAVE/LOBO/SLUDGE/	כלב
LOBO/	כלבא
COLLEEN(A)/KILL/	כלה
CELL/	כלוא
CELL/CRIB/SCULLERY/	כלוב
CHALICE(A)/GILL(A)/SCULLERY/	כלי
KILL/	כליון
ALL/CORONA/	כליל
ALL/	כלל
CRIMSON/	כלם
CALUMNY/	כלמה
CLEAVER/	כלף
ACUMEN/	כמ
ACUMEN/AMITY/QUANTITY(A)/	כמה
ACUMEN/COMMON/SIMULATION/	כמו
ACUMEN/	כמום
AMITY/	כמיהה
ACME/AMITY/	כמר
CANE/GNAW/KEEN/KENNING(A)/ MACHINE/	כן
CANE/COIN/GNAW/KENNING(A)/	כנה
KENNING(A)/	כנוי
KNEEL(A)/	כנן
KNEEL(A)/	כנם
KNEEL(A)/	כנע
KNEEL(A)/	כנעה
CANE/CANOPY(A)/FAN/	כנף
CHAISE/	כס
CHAISE/	כסא
ENCASE/OBSCURE/SACK/	כסה
SAXON/SCISSORS/	כסוח
SUIT/	כסות
CASSIA(A)/	כסח
SILLY(A)/	כסיל
SILLY(A)/	כסילות
SILLY(A)/	כסל
GUESS/	כסם
CAPITALISM/JASPER/	כסף
ALCOVE/CAB/CATCH/CAVITY/ COP/CUFF/CUP/ENCASE/GAP/HOOF/ PUGNACIOUS/SCABBLE/SCOOP/	כף
CAPITAL/	כף
ALCOVE/CAP/CUP/FICKLE/SCOOP/ SEVEN/	כפה
CUFF/	כפול
CUFF/KYPHOS/	כפוף
CULPABLE/CUP/FROST/	כפור
CAP/	כפורת
GIBBON/	כפח
CAP/	כפיה
COUPLE/	כפיל
CUP/	כפיפה
CAPRICORN/FRUIT/PUERILE/ TROPHY/	כפיר
CYPRESS/	כפירה
CUP/	כפית
COUPLE/	כפל
COUPLE/	כפלים
CUBE/GIBBON/WEAK/	כפף
BARRIO/CAMPHOR(A)/COVER/ CYPRESS/FAKER/METROPOLIS/	כפר
STUBBORN/	יתיצב
SURPASS/	יתר
USE/	יתרון
KIBOSH/	כבוש
WEIGHTY(A)/	כבד
CABLE/	כבל
QUASH/VICTOR(A)/	כבש
OVIS/	כבש
CADDY/CUD/KIT/	כד
ALCOHOL(A)/	כהל
GOVERN/	כון
SCAR/	כירה
CAKE/	ככר
ALL/	כל
CELL/	כלא
LOBO/	כלב
COLLEEN(A)/	כלה
CRIB/	כלוב
CHALICE(A)/SCULLERY/	כלי
CALUMNY/	כלמה
COMMON/	כמו
KNEEL(A)/	כנע
CANOPY(A)/	כנף
CHAISE/	כס
ENCASE/	כסה
SILLY(A)/	כסיל
CUFF/SCOOP/	כף
CAP/	כפה
KYPHOS/	כפוף
FROST/	כפור
COUPLE/	כפל
COVER/	כפר
CAMPHOR(A)/	כפרים
CAPITAL/	כפתור
CURB/	כרכב
CROCUS(A)/	כרכם
CHORUS/SCURRILOUS/	כרכר
CRIMSON/	כרם
KERNEL/	כרמל
CRUSH/	כרסם
CROUCH/	כרע
CURT/SECRET/	כרת
CATHARTIC(A)/	כשר
COTTON/	כתן
CUT/	כת
KAISER/	כתר
HERE/	כאן
BOTULISM(A)/FAT/WEIGHTY(A)/	כבד
KIBOSH/	כבוש
ALGEBRA/CABLE/	כבל
WASH(A)/	כבם
OVER/	כבר
CYPRESS/	כברוש
GRAZE/KIBOSH/OVIS/QUASH/ QUIET/SAUCE/	כבש
OVEN(A)/	כבשן
ACUTE/CADDY/CALDRON/ CATECHISM(A)/CUD/KIT/	כד
ABRACADABRA/	כדברא
ACUTE/CUD/TIRE/	כדור
HERE/	כה
KHAN/	כהן
KHAN/	כהנים
CAP/	כובע
ALL/	כולל
GOVERN/	כון
GOVERN/	כונן
GOVERN/	כונת
CHAR/COAL/SCAR/	כור

LAVA/LOVE/SHISHKEBAB/	להבה
DIALECT/	להנ
ADOLESCENT/LIGHT/	להט
LIVER/LOVE/	לוה
FLEET/LID/LOTUS/SHIELD/	לוט
LID/	לוטה
CLIMATE/	לון
LOTUS/	לוט
RAZZ(A)/	לזות
CATSKILL/LICK/LIQUID/	לח
GILL(A)/	לחה
GILL(A)/LOCK(A)/	לחי
LICK/	לחך
LICK/LIQUID/	לחך
LIQUID/	לחלח
GUERRILLA/MILL/	לחם
HASTE/	לחץ
DIALECT/HUSH/RUCKUS/	לחש
WARLOCK(A)/	לחש
CLOT/FLEET/LEATHER(A)/LID/ SHIELD/	לט
I(pronoun)/	לי
GALA/	לינ
LILAC/	לילה
LILAC/	לילית
LEOPARD/	ליש
LESS(A)/	לית
ALLEY/CATSKILL/DIRECTION/LEX/ REACH/REICH/WALK/	לך
LAQUER(A)/	לכה
LAQUER(A)/	לכא
ELECT/LOCK(A)/	לכד
LAQUER(A)/	לכה
ALBINO/	לכו
LIQUID/	לכלוך
MATHEMATICS(A)/MOON/	למד
DILEMMA(A)/	למה
MEANING/	למען
CATSKILL/HOLLOW/	לע
LAUGH/	לענ
DIALECT/	לעה
DIALECT/RAZZ(A)/RUCKUS/ WARLOCK(A)/	לעז
BY/	לפי
PENCHANT/PENULTIMATE/ POINT/	לפנות
PANE/PENULTIMATE/	לפני
FREAK/	לפרקים
PHRASE/	לפרש
TROPHY/	לפת
RAZZ(A)/	לץ
JERK/ULCER(A)/	לקה
ELECT/	לקיט
ELECT/	לקוט
ULCER(A)/	לקוי
ULCER(A)/	לקות
DIALECT/ELECT/LOCK(A)/	לקח
DIALECT/ELECT/LEECH/	לקט
LICK/	לקק
SLANG/	לשון
GLISSADE/SLANG/	לישון
SLANG/	לשן
SPILL/	לת
SET/	לתית
THESIS(A)/WET/	לתת
THESIS(A)/	לתתן
MIGHT/	מאד
ORIOLE/	מאור
ANON(A)/MAN/NO/	מאן
BARRIO/METROPOLIS/	כפרי
CAMPHOR(A)/	כפרים
COVER/	כפרת
CAPITAL/CAPITALISM/	כפת
CAPITAL/	כפתור
CAR/CHAISE/	כר
SCARF/	כרבד
SHIRE/	כרה
CHROME/	כרודם
CROUCH/	כרוכיה
CURVE/	כרוכית
CHROME/CREAM/	כרום
CURB/	כרכב
CAR/CHORUS/CURVE/CYCLE/	כרכור
CROCUS(A)/	כרכם
CAR/CHORUS/GYRE/HULA/ SCURRILOUS/	כרכר
CAR/	כרכרה
CRIMSON/	כרם
CRIMSON/	כרמיל
GRAIN/KERNEL/	כרמל
CRUSH/	כרס
CRUSH/	כרסם
CAR/CREASE/CROUCH/CURVE/ GYRE/KNEEL(A)/SCORCH/	כרע
CAR/	כרק
CASTRATE/CURT/SCISSORS/SCORE/ SECRET/SKIRT/	כרת
GRAZE/OVIS/	כשב
ARITHMETIC/CATHARTIC(A)/ COPACETIC/	כשר
CATHARTIC(A)/	כשרות
CUT/	כת
BID/TUB(A)/	כתב
SAUCE/	כתוש
SAUCE/	כתות
CUT/	כתיבה
TIARA/	כתית
DIKE/	כתל
TIARA/	כתם
COTTON/	כתן
COTTON/	כתנה
COTTON/	כתנת
CLEAVER/SCABBLE/	כתף
CZAR/KAISER/SIR/TAG/TIARA/	כתר
ILLEGAL(A)/NO/SLUDGE/	לא
LATE/	לאות
LATE/LID/	לאט
ANGEL(A)/	לאך
ASHAMED/	לאשמת
LATE/	לאת
LOBO/LOVE/MEEK/VOLUNTEER(A)/	לב
LOVE/	לבב
LOVE/	לבבתני
BIT/DIVIDED/	לבד
LAVA/LOVE/PILE/	לבה
VEST/	לבוש
ABASH/VEST/	לבש
LEOPARD/LOBO/	לביא
PILE/	לבלב
ALBINO/BONNY(A)/DILUTE/ LAVA/LUNAR(A)/MILK/PENGUIN/	לבן
ALBINO/BEAM(A)/CLEAVE/ LUNAR(A)/	לבנה
VEST/	לבש
ARITHMETIC/GILL(A)/LIQUID/	לנ
DIALECT/LAUGH/	לנלנ
LAD/	לד
LAD/	לדה

MAT/	מט
MACABRE/MAT/NETHER(A)/	מטה
MAT/	מטה
DIVINE/	מטיב
METAL(A)/	מטיל
METAL(A)/	מטל
TELEVISION/	מטלטלת
TILE/	מטלית
DAMP(A)/DRIP/EMISSARY/WET/	מטר
MARINE/	מי
MAMA/MARINE/	מיא
NUMBER/	מיון
MARBLE(A)/	מילה
MILL/	מילת
MARINE/OCEAN(A)/WET/	מים
MURMUR(A)/	מימר
EXIT/MAN/MANNER/MONEY/	מין
BAR/	מינן
MITE/	מיעוט
MITE/	מיעט
DAMP(A)/MASS/MUSK/	מיץ
MEEK/	מך
MEEK/	מך
KNOCK/MACABRE/	מכה
MACHINE/	מכונה
MACHINE/	מכונה
MEEK/	מכך
CULL(A)/	מכלה
CULL(A)/	מכללה
CENSUS/	מכם
COUPLE/	מכפלה
MARK/MARKET/SHIRE/	מכר
MANY/MOLE(A)/	מלא
ANGEL(A)/	מלאך
ANGEL(A)/LEX/	מלאך
ANGEL(A)/	מלאכות
MELODRAMA/	מלה
MOLE(A)/	מלוא
CLIMATE/	מלונה
MOLE(A)/	מלוא
WARLOCK(A)/	מלחש
CLOT/MORTAR/	מלט
MARBLE(A)/	מלטש
MILL/	מלילה
MELODRAMA/	מליץ
MELODRAMA/	מליצה
LEX/REICH/	מלך
MARBLE(A)/MELODRAMA/MILK/ MILL/MOLAR/MOLE(A)/MORTAR/	מלל
MURMUR(A)/	מלמל
MARBLE(A)/	מלץ
MILK/	מלק
MATHEMATICS(A)/	ממד
MONEY/	ממון
MURMUR(A)/	ממירים
MURMUR(A)/	ממר
NOUS(A)/	ממש
MANY/MINISTER/MINUS/MUNIFICEN- T(A)/	מן
MONEY/	מנא
NOD/	מנד
MAN/MANY/MEANING/MONEY/ MOON/MUNIFICENT(A)/NUMBER/ SUMMON/	מנה
HEGEMONY/	מנהיג
MUNIFICENT(A)/	מנחה
MUNIFICENT(A)/	מני
MONEY/MOON/NUMBER/	מנין
MUNIFICENT(A)/	מנע

MISANTHROPE/	מאס
PALL/	מאפל
ARCHIPELAGO/BLOAT/WELT/	מבול
TOWER/	מבצר
BURST/	מברץ
BRUSH/	מברשת
MAGIC/MEEK/	מג
MUSK/	מגד
GRAIN/	מגורה
SAW/	מגן
SAW/	מגרד
CARVE/SCRAPER/	מגרפה
GRASS/	מגרש
MATHEMATICS(A)/METER/MODE/	מד
BARRIO/FEROCIOUS(A)/	מדבו
MATHEMATICS(A)/METER/	מדר
METER/MODE/TIME/	מדה
SEDUCE/	מדוחים
SEDUCE/	מדיח
DAMN/MADONNA/	מדינה
ORTHODOX/	מדע
TACTICIAN/	מדקדק
GRADE/	מדרגה
MORTAR/	מהט
CAR/HURRY/SHIRE/	מהר
MAIM/	מום
MOCK/	מוק
MISS/	מוש
MEEK/	מונג
MOAT/NOD/	מוט
METAL(A)/	מוטה
MACHINE/	מוכן
MACHINE/	מוכני
MARKET/	מוכר
MOLE(A)/	מול
LAD/	מולדת
MAIM/	מום
MOON/	מונה
MEET/	מועד
MEET/	מועדה
PHOSPHORUS/TOPAZ/	מופז
MOCK/	מוק
CAUTERIZE/	מוקד
MOCK/	מוקיון
CATCH/	מוקש
MYRTLE/	מור
MISS/	מוש
CHECKMATE/CZAR/MASCULINE/	מות
MOAT/	מוט
MOON/	מונה
MEET/	מועד
MOTHER(A)/	מותר
MIX/	מכנ
CHECKMATE/	מזה
MEZZANINE(A)/	מזוזה
EMISSARY/	מזלות
RISE/	מזרח
MOUCHOIR(A)/	מחה
CHORUS/	מחול
HULA/	מחולה
MOUCHOIR(A)/	מחט
HOLLOW/	מחילה
MARKET/SHIRE/	מחיר
CLEMENCY(A)/	מחל
HAUNT/INN(A)/	מחנה
HOUSE/MAGAZINE/	מחסה
MAGAZINE/	מחסן
HURRY/	מחר
HEARSE/	מחרשה

RUM/	מרא
MIRROR/	מראה
PAD/	מרבד
ROTATE/	מרוץ
MARBLE(A)/	מרח
WEAK/	מרי
RIVALRY/	מריבה
MARINE/	מרים
MARINE/	מרירי
WEAK/	מרך
CORE/	מרכז
MARBLE(A)/MULLIGAN(A)/	מרק
MARJORAM(A)/	מרקח
MARJORAM(A)/	מרקחת
NOUS(A)/	משש
MISS/	מש
MASS/	משא
MISS/	משה
SAW/	משור
MEASURE/	משורה
SOAK/	משח
STAITH(A)/	משטח
SATRAP/SIDEREAL/	משטר
MUSCLE/	משך
MUSCLE/	משך
MOSAIC(A)/	משכית
SIMULATION/	משל
SOLE/	משעול
MASS/	משרה
MISS/NOUS(A)/	משש
MEASURE/	משורה
SAW/	משור
CHECKMATE/ETYMOLOGY/ MASCULINE/TIME/	מת
DELICACY(A)/MUSK/SOUND/	מתוק
MUSK/	מתוק
MASCULINE/TIME/	מתי
MUSK/	מתיקה
ENDOW/	מתן
NOW/	נא
BONNY(A)/SKUNK/	נאוה
AMENABLE/	נאמן
NYMPHET(A)/	נאף
NYMPHET(A)/	נאפת
NUTS/	נאץ
NUTS/	נאצה
NECK/	נאק
NAG/	נאקה
FUNGUS/NEW/PHONETICS/	נב
PHONETICS/	נבא
BOTANY/FUNGUS/	נבנ
FUNGUS/	נבנא
BAMBOO(A)/NAVY/OBOE/	נבוב
BONE/	נבון
PHONETICS/VOCALIZE/	נבח
BOTANY/NEW/VATICAN(A)/WEED/	נבט
PHONETICS/	נביא
NAVY/	נבך
NAVY/	נבך
ABLATION(A)/EVIL/VIAL(A)/	נבל
PHONETICS/	נבע
NIB/	נבר
KNOCK/	נגד
GAUDY/IGNITION(A)/LIGHT/	נגה
CHANGE/	נגון
NICK/	נגח
KNOCK/NICK/NOXIOUS/	נגע
CUFF/NICK/NOXIOUS/	נגף
KNOCK/	נגר

MAP/	מנפה
MINUS/	מנת
SOFA/	מסב
SKIRT/	מסגרת
STILL(A)/	מסדרון
EMISSARY/	מסה
MASK/	מסוה
SAW/	מסור
SUPPER/	מסיבה
MIX/	מסך
MASK/MIX/	מסך
MASK/	מסכה
MASK/MIX/	מסכת
EMISSARY/SUN/	מסלה
EMISSARY/	מסלול
SPARE/	מספר
SUPPER/	מספוא
SPARE/	מספר
EMISSARY/	מסר
RAKE/	מסרק
MYSTERY/	מסתר
MYSTERY/	מסתר
FUHRER/	מעביר
FERRY/	מעבר
FERRY/	מעברת
MOAT/	מעד
MITE/	מעט
COTTON/	מעטפה
MAW(A)/	מעי
ORIGIN/	מעין
MALIGN/	מעל
ALLEY/SCALE/	מעלה
MEANING/	מען
CUBE/	מעקב
EUROPE/	מערב
MAP/	מפה
MAP/	מפה
PATRON/	מפזר
FALL/	מפלה
FINICKY/	מפנק
BREACH/	מפרז
BREACH/	מפרץ
PHRASE/PREACH/	מפרש
MASS/SMUT/	מץ
MEET/	מצא
MASTABAH(A)/STABLE/	מצב
MASTABAH(A)/STABLE/	מצבה
CHECKMATE/MASS/	מצה
MASS/	מצוי
MARROW(A)/	מצוע
DESTROY(A)/	מצור
ANTIQUE/MARROW(A)/ MAZARD(A)/	מצח
MEZZANINE(A)/	מציעא
MYSTERY/	מצמץ
SORE/	מצר
SORE/	מצרים
MUCK/	מק
MACABRE/	מקבי
MACABRE/	מקבת
HOOF/	מקוה
CAMERA/	מקום
KEEN/	מקוננות
CORE/GRAIN/	מקור
ACCELERATE/	מקל
CLOT/	מקלט
COIN/	מקנה
CAST/	מקשה
MARINE/MASCULINE/MYRTLE/RAM/ TOMENTUM(A)/	מר

LOVE/	נלוים
NUMB/	נם
NOSTALGIA/SIGN/SIGN(A)/	נם
SWIVEL/	נסב
NUISANCE(A)/	נסה
HONEST(A)/	נסון
NUISANCE(A)/	נסיון
NUISANCE(A)/	נסיון
SACK/	נסך
SUFFICE/	נספח
SAW/	נסר
MYSTERY/	נסתרות
HAUNT/	נע
NEW/	נעורים
AMENABLE/	נעים
TINE/	נעץ
TINE/	נעצץ
ALUMNI/MARRY(A)/MORON/NEW/	נער
MARRY(A)/MORON/	נערה
MARRY(A)/MORON/	נערות
FAN/	נפה
FAN/	נפח
BIG(A)/	נפך
EVIL/FAIL(A)/FALL/SNAP/SPILL/	נפל
SPREAD/	נפלא
COLOSSUS/	נפלים
ASPIRE/FAN/GRAZE/	נפש
STUBBORN/	נצבה
STUBBORN/	נצב
STABLE/STUBBORN/	נצבה
CHRYSANTHEMUM/	נצה
NOTARY/SANGRIA/	נצח
STUBBORN/	נציב
STEAL/	נצל
SYNOD/	נצמד
DAWN/NITROGEN/	נצץ
NOTARY/	נצרת
NOOK/	נק
ALCOVE/CAVITY/HARROW/MACABRE/NOOK/	נקב
CAVITY/NOOK/	נקבה
NICK/	נקד
MOUCHOIR(A)/NAG/	נקה
NOOK/	נקור
MITT/	נקט
KNOCK/	נקיפה
NOOK/	נקיק
KNOCK/	נקישה
CUFF/NICK/	נקף
NOOK/	נקק
NOOK/	נקרה
FIRE/	נר
MIRROR/	נראה
ANIMUS(A)/	נשמה
KISS/	נשקה
ASPIRE/	נשב
NUISANCE(A)/	נשואה
SAG/	נשוג
SNAKE/	נשיכה
SNAKE/	נשך
SHAMBLES/SMASH/	נשם
ANIMUS(A)/	נשמה
ASPIRE/GRAZE/	נשף
KISS/	נשקה
CYCLE/	נשר
DATA(A)/	נתון
SAXON/	נתח
DATA(A)/EMISSARY/THESIS(A)/	נתן
SAG/	ננש
DUNE(A)/NOD/UNDULATION/	נר
EMISSARY/ENDOW/	נרב
ENDOW/	נרבה
DOODLE(A)/NOD/UNDULATION/WANDER/	נרד
DOUCHE(A)/NOD/SEDUCE/	נרח
DUMB/	נרם
UNDULATION/	נרנד
UNDULATION/	נרנדה
MONEY/	נה
AGONY/HEGEMONY/NAG/	נהג
INERT/	נהל
RUMBLE/	נהם
CATSKILL/HURRY/INERT/	נהר
NO/	נוא
NOON(A)/	נון
NO/	נוא
NEW/	נוב
NOD/WANDER/	נוד
NOZZLE/	נוזלת
NOTARY/	נוטר
NOTARY/	נוטריון
NUMB/	נום
NOON(A)/	נון
NOSTALGIA/	נום
MAP/NIP/PANIC/	נוף
NOZZLE/	נוצל
NOTARY/	נוצר
NOTARY/	נוצרי
ANCIENT/	נושן
SENILE/	נושן
ANCIENT/	נושנת
MOTHER(A)/	נותר
NEW/	נוב
WANDER/	נוד
NOTARY/	נוטר
SEETHE/	נזיד
NOZZLE/	נזם
HAUNT/NIGHT(A)/	נח
NAG/	נחה
SNAKE/	נחוש
SNAKE/	נחושת
HASTE/	נחיצה
BROOK/CATSKILL/GILL(A)/INERT/LIQUID/	נחל
KIND(A)/	נחם
HASTE/NAG/	נחץ
KILL/	נחר
GUERRILLA/	נחרה
HEARSE/	נחרץ
GUESS/SNAKE/WARLOCK(A)/	נחש
BRASS/	נחשת
NETHER(A)/NIGHT(A)/QUIET/	נחת
NOD/	נט
EXTEND(A)/MAT/THIN/	נטה
TELEVISION/	נטיל
ATLAS/TELEVISION/	נטל
DUMB/	נטמה
ME/	ני
NIB/NIP/PHONETICS/	ניב
NOD/	ניד
BABY/NOON(A)/SON/	נין
NOXIOUS/	נכא
VANDYKE/	נכד
KNOCK/NOXIOUS/	נכה
MACHINE/	נכון
ACME/	נכמר
MARK/	נכר
MARK/	נכרי

ENSCONCE/MASK/OBSCURE/SHACK/	סכך
SKILL/	סכל
SAXON/	סכנ
SAXON/	סכנה
SELL/	סלא
EXULT(A)/	סלד
SILICON/SOLE/SOLITARY/	סלה
SILICON/SLALOM/	סלול
SLALOM/	סלם
TAIL/	סלסול
SLALOM/	סלסל
CIRRUS(A)/	סלסלה
SILICON/	סלע
SILICON/	סלת
SMELL(A)/	סם
PERSIMMON/SMELL(A)/	סמים
SIMULATION/	סמל
SIMULATION/	סמלון
SUMAC/	סמק
HONEST(A)/	סן
SANDAL/	סנדל
SANDAL/	סנדלר
SYNDICATE/	סנדק
TINE/	סנה
HONEST(A)/	סנות
UMBRELLA(A)/	סנורים
HONEST(A)/	סנות
SLOUGH/	סניף
SNAP/	סנפיר
PARASITE(A)/SATISFY/SCADS(A)/	סעד
SATISFY/	סעדה
SKEPTIC/SKILL/	סעף
SCOUR/SHOWER/SOW/SQUALL/SURF/	סער
HAVEN(A)/SIP/SUPPER/SURF/XIPHOID/	סף
SOFA/	ספה
GOSPEL/	ספור
SAMPAN(A)/	ספינה
SAPPHIRE/	ספיר
SOFA/SUPPER/	ספה
FUNGUS/	ספוג
DECIPHER/GOSPEL/	ספור
CRUCIFIX/SUFFICE/	ספח
SCAB/	ספחת
SUPPER/	ספי
SUPPER/	ספיה
SAMPAN(A)/	ספינה
FEROCIOUS(A)/JASPER/SAPPHIRE/	ספיר
SPHERES/	ספירות
SPHERES/	ספירות
SIP/	ספל
SALVATION/	ספן
SKEPTIC/SPANK/SUFFICE/	ספק
SKEPTIC/	ספקא
SKEPTIC/	ספקנות
DECIPHER/GOSPEL/SPARE/SPHERES/SPIRAL/	ספר
SPHERES/	ספרה
SILICON/	סקל
GAZE/SCARLET/	סקר
SCARLET/	סקרה
SERF/	סרב
SILO/	סרה
REEK/	סרח
SAW/SCRATCH/SERRATED/STRAND(A)/	סרט
CRAB/SAW/	סרטן
RAKE/	סרק
TAKE/	נתק
MUST(A)/NITROGEN/	נתר
SOUND/	סאון
SANDAL/	סאן
ESPALIER(A)/	סבל
SWIVEL/	סב
SIP/	סבא
SWIVEL/	סבב
FOR/SWIVEL/	סבה
SEEP/	סבון
SAVOIR-FAIRE/	סבורא
SWIVEL/	סביבון
SWIVEL/	סביבון
ESPALIER(A)/EYE/SUFFER/	סבל
SUFFER/	סבלנות
ASPIRE/SAVOIR-FAIRE/SUFFER/	סבר
SKULL/	סגלגל
CHECKMATE/	סגן
GIRDLE/SHACKLE/SIEGE/	סגר
SIDEREAL/	סדור
SIDEREAL/	סדיר
SODIUM/SODOMY/	סדם
STEM/	סדן
STEM/	סדנא
DESTROY(A)/HERD/SATRAP/SET/SIDEREAL/STILL(A)/SULTAN/	סדר
SIDEREAL/	סדרא
SIDEREAL/	סדרה
SLALOM/	סולם
PEGASUS/	סוס
SURF/	סוף
SHEERING/SWERVE/	סור
SUIT/	סות
SLALOM/	סוללה
CLIMATE/SLALOM/	סולם
HOOF/PEGASUS/	סוס
ABYSS(A)/SPHERES/SURF/TOP/XIPHOID/	סוף
ASPIRE/	סופה
SHEERING/SURF/SURPASS/SWERVE/	סור
SWERVE/	סורר
SUIT/	סות
SUFFER/	סובר
SAGA/	סח
SHABBY/	סחב
SHABBY/	סחבה
SAUCE/	סחוט
SACK/SQUAT/	סחיטה
CAR/CYCLE/SCOUR/SCURRILOUS/SELL/	סחר
SCURRILOUS/	סחרחרה
SOT/	סט
SIDE/	סטר
SIEGE/	סיג
SEMANTIC/	סימה
SEMANTIC/	סימן
XIPHOID/	סיף
XIPHOID/	סיפא
SILO/	סיר
SOAK/	סך
ACACIA(A)/MASK/SAGEBRUSH(A)/SHACK/SOAK/	סך
SHACK/	סכה
SEEK/	סכוי
SAXON/	סכין
ENSCONCE/GAZE/HOUSE/SEEK/SHACK/	סכה
SEEK/	סכוי
KEEN/SAXON/SKILL/	סכין

ELM/	ערמון	OOZE/SAUCE/	עסה
CRECHE/CROSS/	ערסל	USE/	עסוק
COLLAR/GARGLE/ROOF/SCARF/ SCRUFF/TROPHY/	ערף	OOZE/SAUCE/	עסים
ROOF/	ערפל	SAUCE/	עסיסי
CREED/CURTSY(A)/HORRID/SCARE/	ערץ	SAUCE/	עסם
CRECHE/	ערש	CAUSE/USE/	עסק
CRECHE/	ערש	AVIATE/JIFFY(A)/PEGASUS/	עף
PARASITE(A)/	עש	AVIATE/BARRIO/METROPOLIS/	עפל
ASSASSIN/CZAR/	עשב	CAPRICORN/COVER/FRUIT/ GRAPHITE/PUERILE/ PULVERIZE(A)/TROPHY/	עפר
CAUSE/GESTURE(A)/USE/	עשה		
CZAR/	עשו		
CAUSE/USE/	עשיה	GRAPHITE/	עפרון
CZAR/SIR/	עשיר	BRASS/GRAVE/	עפרת
ASH/	עשן	ASHTREE/OSTEOMA/STICK/	עץ
CAUSE/COSSACK(A)/SAKE/SEEK/ USE/	עשק	OYSTER/	עצור
		LATE/	עצל
RICHES/SCORE/SURPASS/	עשר	MEZZANINE(A)/OSTEOMA/ OYSTER/STEM/	עצם
USE/	עשש		
SIDEREAL/	עשתרת	CZAR/	עצר
CAUSE/GESTURE(A)/	עשה	ANKLE/	עק
USE/	עשיה	ANKLE/CUBE/HOOF/QUIBBLE(A)/ SABOTAGE/	עקב
COSSACK(A)/	עשק		
ANTIQUE/	עתיק	QUIBBLE(A)/	עקבה
ANTIQUE/AT/OATH/SUN/TIME/ VETERAN/	עת	GATHER/	עקד
		AGONY/	עקה
GOAT/	עתוד	ANKLE/	עקול
VETERAN/	עתון	ANKLE/ENGLISH/KNOCK/	עקל
VETERAN/	עתי	ANKLE/	עקלקל
ANTIQUE/	עתיד	ANKLE/	עקם
ANTIQUE/VETERAN/	עתיק	ANKLE/	עקף
ANTIQUE/	עתיקות	ACACIA(A)/ACME/ACUMEN/ACUTE/ GOAD/STICK/TICKLE/	עקץ
TACK/TAKE/	עתק	AGRICULTURALIST/CORE/GRAIN/	עקר
CAUSE/	עתר	COCKROACH(A)/CRAB/SCARAB/	עקרב
TROPHY/	ף	COCKROACH(A)/	עקרבות
PAD/	פדר	CORE/KARATE/	עקרה
PHOSPHORUS/TOPAZ/	פז	ANKLE/	עקש
PIZAZZ/	פזז	BURN/ORIENTATION/ORIOLE/ TARIFF/URGE/	ער
DIASPORA(A)/	פזר		
PAUCITY/	פחות	OCCUR/	עראי
PIT/	פחת	GARBLE/SCRAMBLE(A)/	ערבל
BUTTON(A)/	פטם	BET/COCKROACH(A)/COIN/CRAB/ CRIB/CROW/CURB/EUROPE/ EVENING/FOR/GARBLE/NEW/ RAVEN/RAVENOUS/REEVE/ RHAPSODY/RIBOFLAVIN/ROOF/ RUG/SCARAB/	ערב
PATRON/POUT/PROTOTYPE/	פטר		
PIVOT/	פיפיה		
PORE/	פיר		
ARCHIPELAGO/PLUG/	פלג		
PLOUGH/	פלח		
PLEA/	פלל	ARBOR/BARRIO/CRIB/ RIBOFLAVIN/	ערבה
PULSE(A)/	פלמא		
PEPPER/	פלפל	ARBOR/	ערבות
PANIC/	פנג	RIBOFLAVIN/	ערבי
PENGUIN/PENULTIMATE/POINT/	פנה	CORAL/GARBLE/SCRAMBLE(A)/	ערבל
PENCHANT/	פניה	RAVENOUS/URGE/	ערג
PANE/PENETRATE/	פנים	URGE/	ערגה
PEDIATRICIAN/	פעוט	GORE/KARATE/	ערה
PALM/	פעם	CURB/EVENING/GUERRILLA/ RHAPSODY/SCRAMBLE(A)/	ערוב
PUTSCH/	פצע		
PETARD/	פצץ	URGE/	ערוה
PESTER/	פצר	ARCHITECT/	ערוך
PEEK/	פקח	CHROME/URGE/	ערום
PACK/	פקיע	URGE/	ערטל
PICK/	פקע	CRECHE/	עריסה
PACKET(A)/	פקעת	ROOF/	עריף
BORAGE(A)/	פר	CURTSY(A)/CZAR/DEMOCRAT/ RAID/	עריץ
PREPARE/	פרא		
SPRIG(A)/	פרג	DEMOCRAT/	עריצות
SPREAD/	פרד	ARCHITECT/REICH/	ערך
FRUIT/	פרות	REACH/	ערכו
PLAZA/	פרזה	GUERRILLA/	ערל
FRUCTIFY/PUERILE/	פרח	GIRL/	ערלה
PART/PLATOON/	פרט	CAMEL/	ערמה

ORIENTATION/	עורר
OGRE/	עוג
AUXILIARY/	עוזר
GIRL/	עולל
CLIMATE/CLIMATE(A)/	עולם
GRAPHITE/	עופרת
CROW/RAVEN/	עורב
AUXILIARY/GOAT/	עז
GAUZE/	עזה
AUSCULATE/	עזניה
AUXILIARY/	עזר
COTTON/MITE/	עט
COTTON/	עטה
COTTON/	עטיפה
COTTON/	עטלף
COTTON/	עטף
TIARA/TIRE/	עטר
TIARA/TIRE/	עטרה
GOAD/	עידוד
COTTON/KITE/	עיט
BET/COIN/EYE/GENIUS/ KENNING(A) KIN/ORIGIN/SIGN/	עין
JIFFY(A)/	עיף
INCARCERATE(A)/ORIENTATION/	עיר
GOPHER/	עכבר
ASP/	עכ
CRAB/	עכבר
ASP/	עכשוב
AIR(A)/ALLEY/COLLAR/	על
DIALECT/	עלג
ADOLESCENT/ALLEY/CULMINATE/ GIRL/ORIENTATION/PATCHOULI/ SCALE/WALK/	עלה
LEECH/	עלוקה
LEECH/	עלוקה
CULL(A)/	עלל
ALUMNI/CLAM(A)/CLIMATE/ CLIMATE(A)/GILL(A)/SLUDGE/	עלם
ALUMNI/	עלמן
CLIMATE/	עלמא
ALUMNI/GILL(A)/GIRL/	עלמה
ALUMNI/	עלמות
CLAM(A)/	עלמים
LICK/	עלע
BY/	עלפי
ADD/AMITY/COMMON/ GENOCIDE(A)/KIN/	עם
MOAT/NOD/	עמד
TOM(A)/	עמוק
CAMERA/	עמיר
AMITY/	עמית
ADMIRAL/AMERICA/CAMEL/	עמל
MASS/	עמם
ADMIRAL/	עמר
GONORRHEA/	עמרה
ANNOYANCE/	ענ
AMBER/	ענבר
HONEY(A)/NEW/	ענב
AMBER/	ענבר
HONEY(A)/	ענג
KEEN/	ענה
ANNOYANCE/	ענות
ANNOYANCE/	ענו
ANNOYANCE/HONEY(A)/	ענוי
ANNOYANCE/	ענות
ANNOYANCE/	עני
KNAVE/NEW/	ענף
HANG/NECK/	ענק
CENSUS/	ענש
SAUCE/	עם

INCITE/	סת
STYMIE/	סתום
STEM/STYMIE/	סתום
STYMIE/	סתומה
STEM/	סתם
STEM/STYMIE/	סתמי
MYSTERY/SIDEREAL/STEAL/	סתר
SIDE/	סתרא
OBESE/	עאב
CAP/EVENING/	עב
EIGHT/OBEDIENCE/OPUS(A)/	עבד
OBEDIENCE/	עבדות
EIGHT/OBEDIENCE/	עבדות
OBESE/	עבה
FOR/	עבור
OPUS(A)/	עבודה
VOCALIZE/	עבוט
AFFIDAVIT/BET/CAPITALISM/ FAITH/VOCALIZE/WED/	עבט
AFFIDAVIT/	עבטיט
ABERRATION/EVIL/	עבירה
ABERRATION/AVERAGE/CURB/ FERRY/ FOR/OVER/PARASITE(A)/ PROTOTYPE/PUERILE/VEER/	עבר
AVERAGE/FERRY/VEER/WRATH/	עברה
ABERRATION/OVER/	עברי
GRAPHITE/OVER/	עברית
OGRE/	עג
CATECHISM(A)/	ענב
CYCLE/	עגול
EGRET/	עגור
CYCLE/	עגול
CURVE/EGRET/	עגור
CYCLE/	עגיל
CAKE/CALF(A)/CYCLE/GYRE/ SKULL/	עגל
CYCLE/	עגלגלת
CAR/CYCLE/	עגלה
AGONY/	עגמה
ANKLE/	ענן
ADD/AT/BET/OATH/SAMURAI/	עד
GADABOUT(A)/GATHER/HERD/ SOVIET/	עדה
HEDONISM/JANUARY/MEAT(A)/	עדן
BET/HEDONISM/	עדנה
ADD/	עדף
CARD/HERD/	ערר
EVENING/	עוב
OGRE/	עוג
CAKE/	עונה
ADD/AT/EACH/TOO/	עוד
EVIL/	עוה
EVIL/	עוון
BET/EVIL/ILLEGAL(A)/SCRUFF/	עול
ALL/EVIL/	עולה
ALLEY/	עולים
ALUMNI/GIRL/	עולל
CLIMATE/CLIMATE(A)/	עולם
EVIL/	עון
AVIATE/CAPON(A)/	עוף
GRAPHITE/	עופרת
CHROME/CREAM/ORIENTATION/ ORIOLE/SWERVE/TARIFF/ UMBRELLA(A)/URGE/	עור
RAVEN/	עורב
ARCHITECT/	עורך
ARCHITECT/	עורך
BROOK/	עורק

ARCHIPELAGO/BROOK/CATSKILL/FLAG/PLUG/	פלג
PLUG/	פלגה
FRACTION/	פלגתא
ARCHIPELAGO/FEAR(A)/FELLAH(A)/FLAKE/PLOUGH/PLUG/PULSE(A)/	פלח/ם
PLOUGH/	פלחה
FELLAH(A)/PLOUGH/	פלחן
FLEET/SHIELD/	פלט
PLUG/	פליג
SHIELD/	פליט
FLEET/	פליטה
PEPPER/	פלך
PLEA/	פלל
BALE(A)/	פלם
PULSE(A)/	פלסא
PEPPER/	פלפל
PEPPER/	פלפלתא
FLUTTER/PSALM/PULSE(A)/	פלץ
FLUTTER/	פלצות
FIN/	פן
PENGUIN/	פנ
VAIN/	פנאי
PANIC/	פננ
BUNTING/	פנדה
FIN/PANE/PANIC/PENCHANT/PENGUIN/PENULTIMATE/PIONEER/POINT/VAIN/WANDER/	פנה
PIONEER/VAIN/	פנוי
PENGUIN/	פנות
PANE/	פני
PENCHANT/	פניה
PANE/PENETRATE/PENULTIMATE/POINT/	פנים
PENETRATE/	פנימה
PENETRATE/	פנימי
PENETRATE/	פנינה
FINICKY/	פנק
PIECE/	פסג
AFTER/	פסד
ABYSS(A)/PATIO/PIECE/	פסה
SPILL/	פסול
PALTER(A)/	פסולת
HADDOCK/PATIO/	פסח
PSALM/	פסנתרין
ABYSS(A)/AFTER/	פסם
BASIS/	פסע
PATIO/	פסק
BASIS/	פסתרגל
VOCALIZE/	פעה
FETUS/PEDIATRICIAN/	פעוט
PORE/	פעור
PAUCITY/FACULTY/PLOUGH/	פעל
PALM/	פעם
PALM/	פעמון
PORE/TROPHY/	פער
PATIO/	פצה
PATIO/	פצח
BASIL/BREACH/PATIO/	פצל
PUTSCH/	פצע
PETARD/	פצץ
BREACH/DISPERSE/PESTER/PIRATE/PRESS/	פצר
PICK/	פקד
PACK/PEEK/PICK/	פקח
PACK/PACKET(A)/	פקיע
FAKER/	פקיר
BEAKER/CRUCIFIX/PACK/PICK/	פקע
PACKET(A)/	פקעים
PACK/PACKET(A)/	פקעת
PACK/	פקק
BERRY/	פרי
PIRATE/	פריץ
BREACH/	פריצה
PROSTITUTE/	פריצות
DISPERSE/PRIZE/	פרס
PERK/	פרע
PYRALIDID(A)/	פרפר
PRESS/	פרץ
BARK(A)/FLICK/PARK/PLUCK/	פרק
PULVERIZE(A)/	פרר
PREACH/	פרש
PACE/	פשע
PITA/	פתה
PATIO/	פתה
PUZZLE/	פתיל
PIECE/	פתית
PYTHON/	פתן
BEAUTY(A)/	פאות
BIG(A)/FAG/FIG/	פג
FIG/PACKET(A)/	פגג
FIG/	פגה
FIG/	פגיה
POKE(A)/	פגיון
FEAGUE(A)/POKE(A)/PUGNACIOUS/	פגע
FAG/FIGURE/VACATE/	פגר
VACATE/	פגרה
FIGURE/	פגרים
PATE/	פדחת
FAT/PAD/	פדר
AFTER/BEAKER/BY/PHONETICS/WHERE(A)/	פה
WHERE(A)/	פו
PHONETICS/	פוח
PHONETICS/	פום
BALL/	פור
BARK(A)/	פורקן
BARK(A)/	פורקת
PHOSPHORUS/TOPAZ/	פז
PIZAZZ/	פזז
PIZAZZ/	פזיז
PSALM/	פזם
PSALM/	פזמה
DIASPORA(A)/SOW/	פזר
PATRON/	פזרן
COP/PIT/	פח
HADDOCK/	פחום
PAUCITY/	פחות
PAUCITY/	פחיתה
PAUCITY/	פחיתות
PAUCITY/PIT/POKE(A)/	פחת
PAUCITY/	פחתת
BUTT/	פטיש
BOTANY/BUTTON(A)/FAT/	פטם
BID/	פטפט
PART/PATRON/POUT/PROTOTYPE/	פטר
BY/	פי
FADE/	פיד
BEAUTY(A)/	פיותא
BID/	פיוט
BEAUTY(A)/	פיותא
SCALE/	פים
PALM/	פימה
XIPHOID/	פינה
PIVOT/	פיפוה
BORE/PORE/	פיר
PORE/	פירא
BEAKER/PIT/VIAL(A)/	פך
PICK/	פכר
ASPHALT/METROPOLIS/	פל
FULFILL/SPREAD/	פלא

PREACH/	פשר
PATE/PIECE/PITA/VENTRICLE/	פת
BID/PACE/PATIO/PIT/PITA/	פתה
PATIO/PIT/	פתח
FATUITY(A)/	פתיות
FATUITY(A)/	פתיות
PALTER(A)/PREACH/PSALM/ PUZZLE/	פתיל
PSALM/PUZZLE/	פתילה
PREACH/PUZZLE/PYTHON/	פתירה
PIECE/	פתית
PALTER(A)/PSALM/PYTHON/	פתל
PALTER(A)/PSALM/PUZZLE/	פתלתל
ASP/PYTHON/	פתן
PIZAZZ/	פתע
SPREAD/	פתר
PREACH/	פתרון
PIECE/	פתת
EXIT/SON/	צא
EXIT/SON/	צאה
MILL/	צאן
EXIT/SON/	צאצא
SEPIA/STUBBORN/	צב
SAMURAI/SEPIA/	צבא
SWELL/	צבה
SPIRE/	צבט
BEAUTY(A)/EL/	צבי
DAUB(A)/SEPIA/	צבע
ASPHALT/SPIRE/SWELL/	צבר
SHOOT/SIDE/STUDY/SYNDICATE/	צד
SIDE/	צדד
DUO/SYNDICATE/	צדק
DESTROY(A)/	צור
STYLE/	צורה
BID/	צו
SAFFRON/SCRUFF/	צואר
STEAL/	צול
SPY/	צופה
TURTLEDOVE/	צוצל
SICK/	צוק
SICK/	צוקה
DESTROY(A)/SILICON/STYLE/ TOWER/	צור
STYLE/	צורה
SERUM/	צורר
SICK/	צוק
SACK/	צח
SACK/	צחה
BIT/CHUCKLE(A)/	צחוק
SACK/	צחח
SACK/	צחיח
SKUNK/SMELL(A)/	צחן
SKUNK/	צחנה
SACK/	צחצח
CHUCKLE(A)/FOR/SHRIEK/ SYNDICATE/	צחק
PARASITE(A)/SATISFY/	ציד
SIGN/	ציון
SEMANTIC/SIGN/	ציון
STYLE/	ציור
SIGN(A)/	צין
SOUTACHE(A)/	ציצה
SOUTACHE(A)/	ציצית
AUXILIARY/STYLE/	ציר
STEAL/	צל
SNAP/	צליפה
TEAL/TOLL/	צלל
SIMULATION/STYLE/TALISMAN/	צלם
SILL/STALK/TIMBER/	צלע
TOLL/	צלצל
CRYOGENICS/MASS/TOM(A)/	צם

PACKET(A)/	פקקת
CAPRICORN/FLAKE/NEW/PART/ SPREAD/	פר
FEROCIOUS(A)/FREE/PREPARE/	פרא
CAPRICORN/FRUCTIFY/FRUIT/ PUERILE/SPRIG(A)/	פרג
BURRO/CYCLE/MARE(A)/PEGASUS/ SPREAD/	פרד
FRUIT/SPREAD/	פרדם
PREPARE/	פרה
FRUIT/	פרו
PART/	פרוד
FRUIT/	פרודה
PILE/PLUCK/	פרוה
PLAZA/PROSTITUTE/	פרוז
DIASPORA(A)/	פרום
BARE/BRIO(A)/	פרוע
PROSTITUTE/	פרוץ
DISPERSE/	פרוק
FLAKE/PART/	פרור
VIAL(A)/	פרור
DIASPORA(A)/	פרוש
FRUIT/	פרות
PLAZA/	פרזה
BRASS/	פרזל
CAPRICORN/CARP/FLAKE/ FRUCTIFY/FRUIT/PERK/PUERILE/ REEK/SPRIG(A)/WRECK/	פרח
FRUIT/PUERILE/	פרחה
PART/PATRON/PLATOON/SPREAD/	פרט
PART/	פרטי
BERRY/FLAKE/FRUCTIFY/FRUIT/ PERSIMMON/PREPARE/	פרי
PART/SPARROW/	פרידה
FRACTION/	פריכה
PATRON/PIRATE/PROTOTYPE/	פריץ
BREACH/	פריצה
PROSTITUTE/	פריצות
FRACTION/PARK/	פריקה
BREACH/	פרישה
PROSTITUTE/	פרישות
WRECK/	פרך
PARK/	פרכת
DISPERSE/PREACH/PRIZE/	פרם
GOSPEL/PROSTITUTE/	פרסום
PREACH/	פרסם
BORAGE(A)/FORAY(A)/FREE/ PARASITE(A)/PERK/PILE/	פרע
BORAGE(A)/FORAY(A)/ PARASITE(A)/PILE/PYRALIDID(A)/	פרעוש
FLUTTER/PYRALIDID(A)/	פרפור
FLUTTER/PYRALIDID(A)/	פרפר
BREACH/BURST/DISPERSE/ PETARD/PIRATE/PLAZA/PRESS/ PROTOTYPE/SPREAD/	פרץ
BARK(A)/CARP/FAKER/FLICK/ FORK(A)/FRACTION/FREE/PARK/ PERK/PLUCK/	פרק
FRACTION/PARK/	פרקה
PLUCK/	פרקת
FRACTION/PULVERIZE(A)/	פרר
DISPERSE/PEGASUS/PHRASE/ PREACH/	פרש
PREACH/	פרשן
FRUIT/	פרת
PATRON/	פרתם
PATIO/	פשה
VEST/	פשט
PATIO/	פשיעה
PREACH/	פשל
ABASH/PACE/	פשע

242

SIREN/STRAND(A)/	צרור
SORE/	צרות
SHRIEK/	צרח
STRAND(A)/	צרט
STRAND(A)/	צרטון
SORE/	צרי
ROOK(A)/	צריח
ESTROGEN(A)/	צריך
CREAK/	צריחה
SERUM/	צרם
ESTROGEN(A)/	צרעה
SORE/	צרעת
SNAP/	צרף
SERUM/	צרציר
SERUM/	צרק
SERIES/STRAND(A)/	צרר
ALCOVE/CAB/CUBBY/	קבה
CUBE/	קביה
CABAL(A)/	קבלה
CUP/	קבעת
CAB/CUBE/	קב
ALCOVE/CAB/CAVITY/CUBBY/ CUBE/VILLA(A)/	קבה
CUP/	קבול
CUBE/	קביה
CABAL(A)/CAVITY/HAVEN(A)/	קבל
CABAL(A)/	קבלה
COVER/CRUCIFIX/	קבע
BEAKER/CUBE/CUP/GOBLET/	קבעת
CUFF/	קבץ
BORE/CAVITY/COVER/CRAB/GRAVE/ OVER/	קבר
CUBE/	קברת
PRECEDE/	קד
CUT/DECAY/HEAD(A)/PRECEDE/	קדד
CUD/HEAD/	קדה
KITTEN/	קדול
CHASTISE(A)/	קדוש
SAXON/	קדושה
CAUTERIZE/	קדח
CAUTERIZE/	קדחת
CAUTERIZE/	קדחתם
ANTIQUE/	קדים
HEAD/PRECEDE/	קדימה
ANTIQUE/HEAD/HEAD(A)/PRECEDE/ SUCCEED/	קדם
ANTIQUE/HEAD/	קדמה
COTTON/	קדקד
CUD/HEAD/HEAD(A)/PRECEDE/ TAG/	קדקד
CALDRON/DARK/GIBBON/	קדר
CALDRON/	קדרא
CADDY/	קדרה
CHASTE/	קדש
CULL(A)/OCHLOCRACY(A)/	קהל
CULL(A)/OCHLOCRACY(A)/	קהלה
CAVITY/CUBE/HEAD/HOOF/	קו
CAP/COIFFURE/	קובע
CAPITALISM/	קוה
BIT/CALL/CRY/LAUGH/SLANG/	קול
CALL/	קולות
ACME/CAMERA/COMB(A)/CREAM/ SCALE/	קום
ACME/COMB(A)/	קומה
COIN/	קונה
GIBBON/	קוף
GAP/	קופא
ACACIA(A)/ACUTE/CATCH/GOAD/ STICK/TACK/	קוץ
CHAETA(A)/	קוצה
RAVEN/	קורא
MASS/	צמא
SEAM/SYNOD/TEAM/	צמד
SEAM/SEAMY/SYNOD/	צמה
SMASH/SUMAC/TOMENTUM(A)/ TUMOR(A)/	צמח
SUMAC/	צמיחה
SUMAC/	צמיקה
TIME/	צמית
MITE/SMASH/SUMAC/	צמצום
CRYOGENICS/MASS/THIN/ TOM(A)/	צמצם
CRYOGENICS/MASS/SMASH/THIN/ TOM(A)/	צמק
CAMEL/TOMENTUM(A)/	צמר
CRYOGENICS/	צמרמרת
SUMMIT/	צמרת
SEAM/SMASH/SMITE/TOM(A)/	צמת
TINE/	צן
TINE/	צנ
SANGFROID/SIGN/SLUDGE/	צנה
THIN/	צנום
EXTEND(A)/SMASH/THIN/	צנום
NOZZLE/SIREN/SNORKEL/SOUND/ STEIN/	צנור
TINE/	צנורה
SEAMY/	צנות
SNORKEL/	צנור
SUMAC/	צנח
TINE/TONIC/	צנין
TOM(A)/	צנם
CRYOGENICS/	צנן
THIN/	צנע
STEIN/	צנצנת
STEIN/	צנתר
PARASITE(A)/STUDY/	צער
STUDY/	צערו
CHUCKLE(A)/	צעצע
CHUCKLE(A)/SHRIEK/SICK/	צעק
SORE/	צער
SPARROW/TOP/	צף
CAPITALISM/SPY/TOP/	צפה
SPARROW/	צפור
ASP/	צפע
SPIRIT/SPY/	צף
ASPIRE/SPARROW/SPY/TOP/ TOP/	צפה
TOP/	צפוי
POINT/SALVATION/SPARROW/TOP/	צפון
CAPRICORN/PYRALIDID(A)/ SPARROW/ SPIRAL/SPIRIT/SPY/	צפור
SPARROW/SPIRAL/	צפורן
SIP/SUPPER/	צפחת
ASPIRE/	צפיה
SUPPER/	צפיחית
CAPRICORN/SPIRAL/	צפיר
SPARROW/SPIRAL/SPIRIT/TOP/	צפירה
ASP/	צפע
ASP/	צפעני
SPARROW/	צפצוף
SPIRIT/	צפצף
SPARROW/SPIRIT/	צפר
SPARROW/	צפרא
SPARROW/SPIRIT/	צפרדע
ASPHALT/SPARROW/TOP/	צפת
SACK/	צקלן
CAST/	צקת
ESTROGEN(A)/SORE/STARE(A)/ STRAND(A)/STYLE/	צר
SERUM/XEROX(A)/	צרב
XEROX(A)/	צרבת
SORE/	צרה
TROPHY/	צרוף

CANDY/CANE/CANOE/CINNAMON/ COIN/GENIUS/GENOCIDE(A)/KEEN/ KIN/ORIGIN/	קנה
KHAN/	קנין
Ipronoun/	קניתי
CINNAMON/	קנמון
CINNAMON/	קנמון
CENSUS/	קנס
CANE/	קנקן
CURVE/	קעור
CURVE/	קעור
ANKLE/CREASE/CRIB/CROSS/ CROUCH/CURB/CURVE/GRAPPLE/ GYRE/	קער
CURVE/CYCLE/	קערה
CAPON(A)/SYNCOPATION/	קפד
OPAQUE/	קפאון
OPAQUE/	קפאון
CAPON(A)/SYNCOPATION/	קפד
SYNCOPATION/	קפדה
CUBBY/	קפה
COP/CUFF/SYNCOPATION/	קפח
COUPLE/SEVEN/	קפל
SYNCOPATION/	קפנדריא
HOOF/KIBITZ/SYNCOPATION/	קפץ
KIBITZ/	קפצן
UNICORN/	קפת
ACACIA(A)/HATE/HEAD/QUIET/	קץ
CASTRATE/CUT/SCABBLE/SYNCOPATI-ON/	קצב
ACUTE/CASSIA(A)/CASTRATE/CUT/ EXIT/HEAD/SAXON/SCABBLE/ XIPHOID/	קצה
CASTRATE/	קצין
CASSIA(A)/	קציעה
CASSIA(A)/CASTRATE/	קציצה
CASTRATE/CUT/SCABBLE/ SCISSORS/	קצע
	קצץ
CASTRATE/CURT/CUT/SCISSORS/ SCORE/	קצר
ALKALI/BROOK/CALL/CHAR/ CHERISH/COAL/CROSS/CRUST/ CRYOGENICS/INCARCERATE(A)/ UNICORN/	קר
CALL/CRY/OCCUR/RAVEN/	קרא
ALGEBRA/CHERISH/CRAB/ CRAW(A)/GUERRILLA/RAVENOUS/ RIVALRY/SCARAB/	קרב
CLEAVE/	קרבה
CARD/CHARACTER/RAKE/ SCRATCH/SERRATED/	קרד
CURT/SCRATCH/	קרדם
CRYOGENICS/INCARCERATE(A)/ OCCUR/	קרה
CHROME/CREAM/	קרום
FOR/	קרוב
CHROME/CREAM/HAREM/	קרום
CAR/	קרון
CHROME/CREAM/UNICORN/	קרוש
COAL/CRUST/CRYOGENICS/ GALYAK(A)/KARATE/SCALP/	קרח
CARAT/	קרט
CRYOGENICS/	קרי
CRUST/	קריד
COURT/INCARCERATE(A)/	קריה
COURT/	קרית
CHROME/CREAM/CRUST/ CRYOGENICS/UNICORN/	קרם
OCCUR/	קורות
COIFFURE/	קובע
COMB(A)/	קומה
ACACIA(A)/CATCH/	קוץ
CATCH/	קח
CHROME/	קחום
CUT/HATE/KITTEN/SUICIDE/	קט
SUICIDE/	קטב
CAUTERIZE/	קטורה
CAUTERIZE/	קטורת
SUICIDE/	קטיעה
CUT/QUIET/SUICIDE/	קטל
GNAW/	קטם
GNAW/KITTEN/SCANTINESS/THIN/	קטן
SCANTINESS/	קטנות
SCANTINESS/	קטנות
SCANTINESS/	קטע
COMB(A)/GIBBON/	קים
CAMERA/	קימור
CANE/KHAN/	קין
CANE/KEEN/	קינה
GIBBON/	קיץ
CASTRATE/	קיצור
CUCUMBER/	קיק
CUCUMBER/	קיקיון
CUCUMBER/	קיקיון
COURT/INCARCERATE(A)/	קיר
CADDY/	קיתון
ACCELERATE/BROOK/CHERISH/ CLOT/HELD/HURRY/	קל
ALKALI/CALDRON/	קלה
CLOT/	קלוט
CLOT/CRUST/	קלוט
CALUMNY/	קלוך
CALIBER/	קליפית
ACCELERATE/BROOK/CALAMUS(A)/ CATSKILL/INERT/	קלח
CALDRON/	קלחת
CLOT/LID/	קלט
ALKALI/CALDRON/CHAR/COAL/ CRYOGENICS/	קלי
SCALLOP/	קליפה
CRAB/SCARAB/	קליפה
CALL/HAIL/	קלל
ACCELERATE/	קללה
CALAMUS(A)/	קלם
CALL/HAIL/	קלם
HAIL/	קלע
CALIBER/CARVE/CHROME/ GLABROUS/PLOUGH/SCALP/ SCURVY/	קלף
CALIBER/SCALP/	קלפה
CALIBER/CARP/SCALLOP/	קלפה
CALIBER/CARP/SCALLOP/	קלפין
ACCELERATE/KILL/	קלקל
CAMERA/MEEK/	קם
ACME/COMB(A)/RICE/	קמה
CAMERA/	קמור
MILL/	קמח
ACME/HEM/KNEEL(A)/MEEK/MITT/	קמט
MILL/MUCK/	קמל
HEM/MITT/QUANTITY(A)/	קמץ
QUINTET/	קמצוץ
CAMEL/CAMERA/	קמר
CELL/ENSCONCE/HAUNT/KIN/ ORIGIN/	קן
COIN/	קנאה
CANE/NIP/	קנב
CANE/	קנבוס

AIR(A)/EUROPE/KARATE/REEK/ ROOM(A)/	רוח
REICH/	רועה
FLEET/	רוץ
RICE/	רן
AMITY/REACH/ROOM(A)/	רחב
ROC/	רחוף
CRACK/	רחוק
ROCK/	רחים
AMITY/CHERISH/CLEMENCY(A)/ ROC/WOMAN/	רחם
ROCK/	רחף
NEW/	רחץ
QUERY/	רחק
DIALECT/RUCKUS/	רחש
RAKE/	רחת
NEW/WET/	רטב
RATTLE/SCARE/	רטט
RAVE/	רטן
RIVALRY/	ריב
AIR(A)/FLAKE/FRUCTIFY/REEK/ REICH/	ריח
ARCHIPELAGO/CATSKILL/CRACK/ HOLLOW/KARATE/SHRIEK/ WREAK(A)/	ריק
KARATE/	ריקא
CHERISH/	ריקה
KARATE/	ריקים
REACH/WEAK/	רך
NEW/WEAK/	כך
BURRO/PEGASUS/ROCK/	רכב
RICHES/	רכוש
RICHES/	רכוש
CORE/	רכות
DIALECT/	רכיל
PEGASUS/	רכש
RAM/RUM/	רם
CRIMSON/NEW/RAM/RUM/WORM/	רמה
PALM/	רמון
SIMULATION/	רמז
RAM/	רמח
RUM/	רמיה
RUM/	רמיסה
CAMEL/MARE(A)/PEGASUS/	רמך
PALM/	רמן
ROAM(A)/RUM/WORM/	רמש
SPARROW/WORM/	רמשא
RUM/	רמת
CORONA/GROUND/	רן
CHERISH/NEW/WRONG/	רע
RAVENOUS/URGE/	רעב
CREED/HORRID/RATTLE/ROCK/ SCARE/	רעד
VOLUNTEER(A)/	רעוא
NEW/	רעלה
GROAN/RUMBLE/	רעם
GRASS/	רען
GRASS/NEW/	רענן
SCARE/	רעץ
RUCKUS/	רעש
HUSH/ROCK/RUCKUS/	רעש
RUCKUS/	רעשן
SCARF/SCRUFF/	רף
THERAPY/TORPID/	רפא
PAD/	רפד
BARON/SNAP/THERAPY/TORPID/	רפה
RHAPSODY/THERAPY/	רפואה
REFUSE/RHAPSODY/	רפס
RHAPSODY/	רפסודה
RHAPSODY/	רפסודה
PYRALIDID(A)/	רפרוף

CAPITAL/COIN/CORNER/CORNET/ CORNUCOPIA/CORONA/CRAB/ CREASE/CRIMSON/CROWN/ DEMOCRAT/RAM/UNICORN/	קרן
UNICORN/	קרנא
CORNER/	קרנות
CREASE/CROSS/CROUCH/ CURTSY(A)/	קרם
CROSS/	קרסל
CRACK/CREASE/CURT/SKIRT/	קרע
CURT/	קרץ
CARD/	קרצף
AGRICULTURALIST/	קרקע
CAP/CAPITAL/HEAD/UNICORN/	קרקפת
CRAB/	קרקפתא
CRY/	קרקר
RUCKUS/	קרקש
CRYOGENICS/	קרר
CRUST/	קרש
CHROME/CROSS/CRUST/ CRYOGENICS/	קרש
COURT/	קרתא
COURT/	קרת
COURT/	קרתא
COURT/	קרתה
CHESS(A)/	קש
CASEFY(A)/	קשה
CAST/	קשת
ASSASSIN/CASEFY(A)/CATCH/ CHESS(A)/	קש
SCAVENGE/	קשב
ASSASSIN/CASEFY(A)/	קשה
CUCUMBER/	קשוא
CUCUMBER/	קשות
CASEFY(A)/	קשי
CASEFY(A)/SEEK/	קשיה
CASEFY(A)/	קשקש
ENCASE/	קשקשת
CAST/ROVE/SHOOT/	קשת
TAKE/	קת
GUT/	קתרום
MIRROR/ORIOLE/	ראה
RAM/	ראם
SIR/	ראש
RIFE/RIVALRY/VERY(A)/	רב
ROVE/	רבב
ROOT/SCARF/	רבד
RIFE/	רבה
RIFE/	רבים
EIGHT/	רביעי
QUARTER/	רבע
IRE/RUCKUS/	רגז
DIRECTION/REGULAR/	רגיל
ALLEY/GALA/HADDOCK/RACK/ REACH/REGULAR/WALK/	רגל
REGULAR/	רגלי
REGULAR/	רגלים
ROCK/	רגם
GROAN/	רגן
ROCK/	רגע
RAID/ROOT/TOWER/	רד
RAID/SULTAN/	רדה
RAID/	רדוי
DORM/DRIP/	רדם
DRIVE/RAID/ROTATE/	רדף
GONORRHEA/	רה
RAVE/	רהב
LATE/NEW/ROTATE/	רהוט
ROVE/	רובה
RAID/	רודן
RIFE/	רוה

SHIELD/	שלט		REFUSE/	רפש
SULTAN/	שלטון		DINOSAUR(A)/INERT/ROTATE/	רץ
SLAM/SOLEMN/	שלם		ROTATE/	רצא
SOLVE/	שלף		NEW/ROTATE/	רצה
ESMERELDA/	שמיר		ROTATE/	רצון
SHAMBLES/	שממה		STRAND(A)/	רצועה
SESAME/	שמן		ROTATE/	רצוף
SMUT/	שמץ		ROTATE/	רצח
CHANGE/INSOMNIA/SUN/	שנה		SURF/	רציף
SNAKE/	שנק		SNAP/STRAND(A)/	רצף
SEIZE/	שסה		CHERISH/	רק
SOLE/	שעל		REEK/	רקב
CHAFE/	שף		ORCHESTRA/	רקד
SPIT/	שפוד		CHORUS/	רקוד
SUPER/	שפיר		REEK/	רקח
SUPPLE/	שפל		RACK/	רקיע
ASPHALT/	שפלה		CAKE/	רקיק
SCOOT/	שקד		RACK/REACH/	רקע
SCALE/	שקל		ARITHMETIC/	רשום
SYCAMORE/	שקמה		RESUME/	רשימה
SCAVENGE/SCOPE/	שקף		PHRASE/RICHES/SIR/	רש
STARE(A)/	שר		LOOSE(A)/	רשול
SHRIEK/	שריקה		ARITHMETIC/	רשום
DINOSAUR(A)/	שרץ		LOOSE(A)/	רשות
SASH/SIX/	שש		RESUME/	רשימה
INSTALL/	שתל		LOOSE(A)/	רשיש
SEAT/SET/	שת		LOOSE(A)/	רשל
STOMACH/	שתום		LOOSE(A)/	רשלן
SEEP/SIP/SOB/	שאב		RESUME/	רשם
SHRIEK/	שאג		AFTER/	רתב
SILO/	שאול		IRE/RATTLE/	רתח
SOUND/	שאון		IRE/	רתחה
CONSULT/	שאל		IRE/	רתחן
CONSULT/	שאלה		RATTLE/	רתת
CONSULT/	שאלתה		SOB/	שאב
SOUND/	שאן		SILO/	שאול
INSOMNIA/SOUND/	שאנן		SOUND/	שאון
ASPIRE/	שאף		CONSULT/	שאלתה
BUTCHER(A)/RESIDUE/SARCASTIC/SURPASS/TAURUS/	שאר		SARCASTIC/	שאר
RESIDUE/	שארית		SPELT/	שבלת
SABOTAGE/	שבוט		BASTE(A)/	שבץ
SALVATION/SEVEN/SOFA/SWALLOW/SWIVEL/	שב		SPACE/	שבת
SALVATION/	שבה		SEPT/SWITCH/	שבט
BOOT(A)/SABOTAGE/	שבוט		SEVEN/	שבענה
SABOTAGE/	שבוטא		SHIVER/	שבר
BASIS/SPELT/	שבלת		SHADE/	שד
SEVEN/	שבע		SHOOT/	שוט
BAT/SEPT/SPIT/SWITCH/	שבט		SILL/	שול
GOSPEL/SWALLOW/SWERVE/	שביל		ASSUME/SOME/	שום
SPILL/	שבלת		JACKAL/	שועל
SEVEN/SUFFICE/SWASTIKA/	שבע		SERIES/	שורה
SEVEN/	שבענה		SAVANNA/	שויון
BASTE(A)/	שבץ		TAURUS/	שור
ASPIRE/SHIVER/SPELT/SPILL/SUFFER/	שבר		SATRAP/	שוטר
SEVEN/SPACE/	שבת		SAMURAI/	שומר
SAG/	שנא		SHANK/	שוק
SAG/	שנה		SAG/	שח
GAZE/	שנח		SCADS(A)/	שחד
SAGA/	שנר		SCAUP/	שחף
SAGEBRUSH(A)/	שנשנ		SCOUR/	שחר
SATISFY/SCATHING/SHADE/	שד		SCATHING/	שחת
SOD/	שדה		STAITH(A)/	שטח
SHADE/	שדוד		SPATE/	שטף
SATRAP/SIDEREAL/	שדרה		SIREN/	שיר
OVIS/	שה		SCAB/	שכבה
BET/	שהד		SUCCUBUS/	שכבת
HESITANT/	שהה		SUMMER(A)/	שכם
SAXON/	שהין		ENSCONCE/	שכן
			SLUDGE/	שלנ
			LOOSE(A)/	שלה
			SELL/SLOUGH/	שלח

SHIRE/	שכיר
SCORE/	שכירות
SAG/	שכך
SACK/SAXON/SCALE/SKILL/	שכל
SKILL/	שכלות
ASHAMED/SHAMBLES/ SUMMER(A)/	שכם
SUMMER(A)/	שכמה
ENSCONCE/	שכן
SAKE/SCORE/SHIRE/	שכר
SEISMIC(A)/	שכשוך
LOOSE(A)/SALVATION/SOLITARY/	של
LOOSE(A)/SLOUGH/	שלב
ARITHMETIC/CRYOGENICS/ GLISSADE/SANGFROID/ SLUDGE/	שלג
SACK/SHIELD/	שלד
SLOUGH/	שלה
SWALLOW/	שלו
SALVATION/	שלוה
SLAM/SOLEMN/	שלום
CONSULT/LOOSE(A)/SELL/ SLOUGH/	שלח
SHIELD/SIDEREAL/SULTAN/	שלט
SATRAP/SULTAN/	שלטון
LOOSE(A)/	שליבה
CONSULT/	שליח
SULTAN/	שליט
CONSULT/LOOSE(A)/SELL/	שלל
SALVATION/SELL/SLAM/SOLEMN/ TALISMAN/TELIC/TERM/VAIN/	שלם
GRAZE/SIMULATION/	שלמה
LOOSE(A)/SLOUGH/SOLVE/	שלף
SLOUGH/	שלש
TERZA/	שלשה
ARITHMETIC/	שלשים
LOOSE(A)/	שלשל
LOOSE(A)/	שלשלת
ASHAMED/ASSUME/SEMANTIC/ SIMULATION/SOME/SOUND/ SUMMON/TERZA/	שם
ASSUME/	שמא
SMITE/	שמד
SMUG/	שמה
SEVEN/	שמונה
SAMURAI/	שמור
SAMURAI/	שמורה
ASHAMED/	שמו
SMUG/	שמח
EMISSARY/	שמט
SUMMIT/	שמים
ESMERELDA/SESAME/SMILAX(A)/ SUN/	שמיר
GRAZE/SIMULATION/	שמלה
SESAME/	שמם
SHAMBLES/TIMID/	שממה
SESAME/	שממית
MILL/SESAME/	שמן
SESAME/	שמנמן
SESAME/	שמנת
AUSCULATE/SOUND/SUMMON/	שמע
ASHAMED/SMUT/	שמץ
SMUT/	שמצה
CHANGE/SAMURAI/SMILAX(A)/	שמר
SOUTH/SUMMER(A)/SUMMIT/ SUN/	שמש
SESAME/	שמשם
ANCIENT/CHANGE/GNAW/SNAKE/ TINE/	שן
XENOPHOBIA/	שנא
CHANGE/	שנאה
SUN/	שהם
SOFA/	שובה
SHADE/	שור
SAVANNA/SNORKEL/	שוה
SHOOT/SWITCH/	שוט
SOT/	שוטה
SATRAP/	שוטר
SAVANNA/	שוי
SAVANNA/	שויון
SILL/	שול
ASSUME/SOME/	שום
ASSUME/	שומא
ASSUME/	שומה
SAMURAI/	שומר
MISANTHROPE/XENOPHOBIA/	שונא
SENILE/SIMULATION/SIN/	שונה
SOUND/	שונרא
CHECKMATE/SHRIEK/VOCALIZE/	שוע
JACKAL/	שועל
SOFA/	שופי
SUPER/	שופרא
SHANK/	שוק
QUINTET/SERIES/SWERVE/TAURUS/	שור
JURISDICTION/SERIES/SHEER/ SORGHUM/STARE(A)/SWERVE/ TAURUS/TIER/	שורה
WRESTLE(A)/	שזר
SAG/SAXON/	שח
SCADS(A)/	שחד
SCAUP/	שחה
SQUAT/	שחוח
SQUAT/	שחוק
OBSCURE/SCORCH/SWERVE/	שחור
SHANK/	שחח
SAUCE/SAXON/SCATHING/SQUAT/	שחט
SAGEBRUSH(A)/	שחיף
SCAUP/SCAVENGE/	שחף
OBSCURE/	שחקים
OBSCURE/QUERY/RISE/SUN/	שחר
SAG/SAGEBRUSH(A)/SCATHING/ SHADE/	שחת
SOT/TOSS/	שט
SOT/	שטה
SOT/	שטוף
SOT/	שטות
STAITH(A)/	שטח
SOT/	שטיא
SOT/STYMIE/	שטן
SHOOT/SPATE/	שטף
SATRAP/	שטר
SOD/	שיד
ACACIA(A)/SAGA/SAGEBRUSH(A)/ SHAGGY/	שיח
SAGA/	שיחה
CHECKMATE/	שיך
SHRIEK/SIREN/	שיר
SUIT/	שית
ACACIA(A)/SAGEBRUSH(A)/SAXON/ SHACK/SHOOT/SIEGE/TACK/	שך
QUIET/SAG/SHAMBLES/SOFA/ SUCCUBUS/	שכב
SAXON/SCAB/	שכבה
SUCCUBUS/	שכבת
SAXON/	שכה
ENSCONCE/	שכון
ENSCONCE/SKUNK/	שכונה
OBSCURE/SOAK/	שכור
SAXON/	שכח
OBSCURE/	שכחה
SAXON/	שכים
SAXON/	שכין

CZAR/SHIRE/SIR/SIREN/STARE(A)/WRESTLE(A)/	שר
SEAR/SYRUP/XEROX(A)/	שרב
BAT/ROOT/	שרביט
RESIDUE/SURPASS/	שרד
SLOUGH/	שרול
STRAND(A)/	שרוך
SAW/SCRATCH/SERRATED/	שרט
CIRRUS(A)/SPRIG(A)/	שריג
RESIDUE/SURPASS/	שריד
RAKE/	שריק
CREAK/SHRIEK/	שריקה
SERIES/SHEERING/WRESTLE(A)/	שרך
SAFFRON/SEAR/SERF/SERPENT/SYRUP/	שרף
SAFFRON/	שרפה
SERPENT/	שרפים
SERF/	שרפרף
DINOSAUR(A)/	שרץ
SCARLET/	שרק
SIR/	שרר
SIR/	שררה
SERF/SIR/SULTAN/	שרת
SASH/SHISHKEBAB/SIX/	שש
SIX/	ששון
INSTALL/SEAT/SET/SOUTH/	שת
SOT/	שתהכ
SOT/	שתוי
STOMACH/STYMIE/	שתום
INSTALL/SHOOT/	שתיל
SOT/	שתין
INSTALL/STALK/	שתל
STEM/STOMACH/	שתם
SHOOT/SOT/	שתן
QUIET/	שתק
QUIET/	שתקנות
SET/	שתת
SWASTIKA/	שבע
ASPIRE/	שבר
SOD/	שדה
XENOPHOBIA/	שונא
SQUAT/	שחט
SOT/	שט
SAGA/	שיח
SHIRE/	שכיר
SKILL/	שכל
SCORE/	שכר
SWALLOW/	שלו
SALVATION/	שלוה
BALSAM/	שם
SMUG/	שמח
SORGHUM/	שעורה
SHOWER/	שעיר
SCARE/	שער
SIP/	שפה
SACK/	שק
CZAR/SIR/	שר
CIRRUS(A)/	שריג
RESIDUE/	שריד
RAKE/	שריק
SAFFRON/SEAR/SERF/SERPENT/SYRUP/	שרף
DOE/	תאו
TEAM/	תאום
TAG/	תג
ADD/TOO/	תו
TOUCAN/	תוכי
TOUR/	תור
ADD/TAB/	תו
TABOO/	תועבה
TAURUS/TIRE/TURN/TURTLEDOVE/	תור
CHANGE/	שנאי
ARITHMETIC/CHANGE/INSOMNIA/SENILE/SUN/SYNCOPATION/XENOPHOBIA/	שנה
CHANGE/XENOPHOBIA/	שנואה
CHANGE/	שנוי
CHANGE/DUO/SYNCOPATION/SYNOD/XENOPHOBIA/	שני
CHANGE/	שניות
CHANGE/	שנים
TINE/	שנינה
CHANGE/	שניתי
NECK/SNAKE/	שנק
SEIZE/	שסה
SEIZE/	שסם
SKILL/	שסע
SCHIZOPOD(A)/	שסעת
JACKAL/	שעול
SORGHUM/	שעורה
CZAR/SCARE/SEROW(A)/SHOWER/	שעיר
SQUALL/	שעירים
SOLE/	שעל
SAVOIR-FAIRE/	שעף
CIRRUS(A)/CZAR/SCALE/SCARE/SCORE/SELL/SHAGGY/	שער
CHUCKLE(A)/	שעשע
ALKALI/CHAFE/	שף
ASP/	שפ
ASPHALT/GOSPEL/KISS/SIP/SOFA/SPILL/SURF/	שפה
SPIT/	שפוד
SPIT/	שפודא
ASPHALT/	שפולים
SPILL/	שפוע
SUPER/	שפור
ASPHALT/SPILL/SUPER/	שפי
ASPHALT/	שפיע
ASP/	שפיפון
SUPER/	שפיר
ASPHALT/SEEP/SPILL/	שפך
ASPHALT/SAPPHIRE/SOFA/SPILL/SUPER/SUPPLE/	שפל
ASPHALT/	שפלה
SPILL/	שפלות
ASPHALT/SEEP/SPILL/SUFFICE/	שפע
SUFFICE/	שפק
SAPPHIRE/SUPER/	שפר
SAPPHIRE/	שפרא
SUPER/	שפרה
SUPER/	שפריר
CHAFE/	שפשוף
SCHIZOPOD(A)/	שצע
SPATE/	שצף
ARITHMETIC/QUIET/SACK/	שק
SCOOT/SEEK/SHOOT/	שקד
SCOOT/	שקדים
KISS/SHOWER/SOAK/	שקה
SOAK/	שקוי
QUIET/SCOOT/	שקט
QUIET/SCOOT/	שקידה
SCOPE/	שקיפות
SCALE/SKILL/	שקל
SICK/	שקם
SYCAMORE/	שקמה
SAG/SOAK/	שקע
CUFF/SCAUP/SCAVENGE/SCOPE/SEEK/SPY/	שקף
SEEK/	שקק
SEEK/	שקר
QUIET/	שקשק
SOAK/	שקת

aardvark/BURRO/EARTH
aardwolf/EARTH/LOBO
ab-/OF(A)
abacedarian/ALPHABET
abacus/ALPHABET
abaddon/OBITUARY
abasement/BASIS
abash, -ed, -ment/ABASH/VEST
abate/BUTT/VETO
abba/ABBOT
abbacy/ABBOT
abbe/ABBOT
abbess/ABBOT
abbey/ABBOT
abbot/ABBOT/OF(A)/VIVID
abc/ALPHABET
abdomen/VENTRICLE
abduct/SEDUCE
aberration/ABERRATION/OVER/ROTATE/SIN/VEER
abet/BET/BIT/PIECE
abh/ABBOT
abhor/HORRID
abide/FAITH
abject/JET
abjure/JURISDICTION
ablation/ABLATION(A)/ATLAS/DEVOUR
able/GIVE(A)
abnegate/INSOMNIA
abnormal/KENNING(A)
abode/BASIS/FAITH
abolish/ALUMNI
abort/ORIENTATION
abound/UNDULATION/ABOUT(A)/EXIT
above/AVIATE
abracadabra/ABRACADABRA
abrade/GRADE
abrasion, -ive/GRADE
abroad/SPREAD
abrogate/RACK/URGE
abrosia/DEVOUR
abrupt/TROPHY
abscess/PRECEDE
abscise/SCISSORS
abscond/ENSCONCE
absent/IS
absolute/LOOSE(A)
absolve/LOOSE(A)/SOLVE
absorb/SYRUP
abstain/EXTEND(A)
abundance/BOTULISM(A)
abuse/USE
abut/BUTT/BUTTON(A)
abysmal/ABYSS(A)
abyss/ABYSS(A)
acacia/ACACIA(A)/ACUTE/CATCH/HASTATE/
    SAGEBRUSH(A)/STICK/XIPHOID
acanthus/ACUTE
accede/PRECEDE
accelerate/ACCELERATE/CAR/HELD/HURRY
accent/KEEN
accept/CABAL(A)/CAVITY/HAVEN(A)
accident/DECAY
acclaim/CALL
acclivity/SLALOM
accolade/COLLAR
accomodate/METER
accomplish/FULFILL
accord/CORE
accouter/ACCOUTERMENTS

accouterment/SEAM/ACCOUTERMENTS/
    CHAETA(A)
accoutre/ACCOUTERMENTS
accumbent/SUCCUBUS
accumulate/CAMERA
accusation/CASEFY(A)
acerbate/CARP
acetate/ACUTE
ache/AGONY
acholia/GALL/HALO
acid/ACUTE
acme/ACME/CAMERA
acne/ACME
acorn/UNICORN
acoustic/SCAVENGE
acquaint/KENNING(A)
acquire/QUERY
acre/AGRICULTURALIST
acropolis/METROPOLIS
acrospire/SPIRE
across/CROSS
act/HEGEMONY
acuity/ACUTE
acumen/ACUMEN/COG(A)/HOKUM/KEEN
acute/ACACIA(A)/ACUTE/CATECHISM(A)/CUD/
    CUT/HADDOCK/STICK
ad infinitum/AT
ad-/AT
ad/DURUM(A)
adam/HUMUS(A)
adamant/MADONNA
add/ADD/AT/DATA(A)/DURUM(A)/ENDOW/TOO
addict/SYNDICATE
addition/ADD
address/DIRECTION
adduce/SEDUCE
adele/ADORE
adeps/FAT
adept/AT
adhere/AT
adieu/DIVINE
adjacent/JET
adjective/JET
adjoining/JUXTAPOSE
adjudicate/JURISDICTION
adjure/JURISDICTION
adjust/ASH
adjust/JUXTAPOSE
administer/MEANING
admiral/ADMIRAL
admire/MIRROR
admit/EMISSARY
admix/MIX
admonish/MOON
ado/AT
adolescence, -ent/ADOLESCENT/
    ADOLESCENT/ALUMNI
adolf/ADORE
adolph/ADOLPH(A)/LOBO
adonic/ADONIS
adonis/ADOLPH(A)/ADONIS/DAMN/MADONNA
adopt/OPINION(A)
adoration/ADORE
adore/ADOLPH(A)/ADORE
adorn/ADORE/ARITHMETIC/ARITHMETIC
adsorb/SYRUP
adulation/ADORE
adult/ADOLESCENT/ALUMNI
adumbrate/UMBRELLA(A)

advance/ANTIQUE/MAZARD(A)/PANE
advantage/PANE
advocate/VOCALIZE
aegis/GOAT
aeon/AGONY
aerial/AIR(A)
aero-/AIR(A)
aerobic/HYGIENE(A)/VIVID
aeronaut/NAVY
aestas/GIBBON
aestival/CAUTERIZE
affection/FACULTY
affidavit/AFFIDAVIT/BET/CAPITALISM/FAITH/
    VOCALIZE/WED
affiliate/PUERILE
affix/CRUCIFIX
affluent/BLOAT
affricate/FRACTION
aft/AFTER
after/AFTER/OF(A)
again/COMMON
agenda/HEGEMONY
agent/HEGEMONY
agglomerate/CONGLOMERATE
aggravate/BRIO(A)/GRAVE
aghast/HATE
agile/ACCELERATE/HEGEMONY
agitate/HEGEMONY
agnate/ORIGIN
agni/IGNITION(A)
agony/AGONY/HEGEMONY/SEVEN
agora/CULL(A)
agraffe/CURVE/GRAPPLE
agrapha/SCRAPER
agricultural, -ist, -ure/AGRICULTURALIST
agro/AGRICULTURALIST
ahead/HEAD/HEAD(A)
ahriman/MOON
ailing/HEALTH
air/AIR(A)
akin/COMMON/KIN
al-/ALKALI
al/ALLEY
alamo-/ELM
alarm/ARITHMETIC
alas/LATE
albacore/BUCKAROO
albatross/CADDY/CUD/KIT
albino/ALBINO/BLEAK/BONNY(A)/DAUB(A)/
    DILUTE/GALAXY/LAVA/LUNAR(A)/MILK/
    PALL/PENGUIN
album, -in/ALBINO/ALBINO
alcaide/HEAD
alcalde/HEAD
alcohol/ALCOHOL(A)/COAL
alcove/ALCOVE/CAB/CABAL(A)/CAVITY/CUBBY/
    VILLA(A)
alder/ELM
alderman/LAD
alfalfa/FAT
alfred/ALBINO
algebra/ALGEBRA/CABLE
algum/ELM
alhambra/MAROON
alibi/BY
aliment/ALUMNI
alimony/ALUMNI
aliphatic/LIVER
alkali/ALKALI/CALDRON/CHAR/COAL

alkaloid/ALKALI
all/ALL
all/CULL(A)/HAIL/HEALTH
allah/ALL
allege/ELECT/HEGEMONY
allegory/CULL(A)
allergy/ORGAN
alleviate/ACCELERATE
alley/ALLEY/ORIENTATION/WALK
alm/ALUMNI
alme/ALUMNI
almighty/ALL
almug/ELM
aloes/ALOES(A)
alone/UNIQUE(A)
along/ANTIQUE
alopecia/LOBO
alpaca/BUCKAROO
alpha, -rays/ALPHABET
alphabet/ALPHABET/BOTH
alpine/ALBINO
also/ALL/SAVANNA
altair/SPARROW
altar/ALLEY
altitude/ALLEY/ALUMNI/TALL
alto/TALL
alumna, -i, -us/ALUMNI/ALUMNI/GILL(A)/
    GIRL/ALUMNI
alvah/ALBINO
alveolus/HOLLOW
always/CONVEY/VIA
am/IS
amah/AMAH(A)/MAMA
amaranth/MILL
amass/MASS
amateur/AMITY
amative/AMITY
amatory/AMITY
amber/AMBER
ambi-/MAZARD(A)
ambidextrous/DEXTROUS(A)/MAZARD(A)
ambience/MAZARD(A)
ambiguous/HEGEMONY/MAZARD(A)
ambition/MAZARD(A)
ambivalence/MAZARD(A)
amelia/AMERICA
amen, -able, -ity/AMENABLE/JUBILANT/
    MONEY/OMEN
amend/MAIM
amenorrhea/MOON
america/ADMIRAL/AMERICA
amethyst/MUSK
amiable/AMITY
amicable/AMITY
amice/JET
amid/MEZZANINE(A)
amie/AMITY
amigo/AMITY
amiss/MISS
amity/AMAH(A)/AMITY/CALM/GIBBON/MAMA
ammon/OMEN
amnesia/AMENABLE/MOON
amnesty/AMENABLE/MOON
amniocentesis/QUANT(A)
amorous/AMITY
amount/MONEY
amour/MAMA
amphi-, -bian, -bious/MAZARD(A)/
    HYGIENE(A)/VIVID

amphitheater/MAZARD(A)
amphora/FERRY
amputate/MAZARD(A)
an-/ANEMIC/INSOMNIA
anaconda/SNAKE
analogy/DIALECT/ELECT
analysis/LOOSE(A)
anarchy/ANEMIC
anasarca/SARCASTIC
anastomosis/STOMACH
-ance/ANNOYANCE
ancestor/PRECEDE
anchor/ANKLE
ancient/ANCIENT/ANTIQUE/MAZARD(A)/SENILE
ancillary/AUXILIARY/COLLAR
ancon/ANKLE
ancylostomiasis/STOMACH
and/ADD
andante/WANDER
andes/DUNE(A)
anecdote/DATA(A)/ENDOW
anemic/AMITY/ANEMIC/SANGRIA/UNIQUE(A)
anemo-/ANIMUS(A)
anfractuous/FRACTION
angara/CATSKILL
angel/ANGEL(A)
anger/GROAN/HANG
angle/ANKLE/ENGLISH
angst/HANG
anguilliform/SNAKE
anguine/SNAKE
anguish/HANG
anilingus/LICK
anim-, -ism, -osity, -us/ANIMUS(A)
ankle/ANKLE/ENGLISH/HOOF/KNEEL(A)
annals/SUN
anneal/CAUTERIZE
annihilate/INSOMNIA
anniversary/SUN
annotate/KENNING(A)
annoy, -ance/ANNOYANCE
annual/SUN
annuity/SUN
annul/INSOMNIA
anodyne/HEDONISM
anomalous/ANEMIC
anomaly/COMMON
anon/ANON(A)/UNIQUE(A)
anonymous/ANEMIC
anorectic/RACK
anorexia/RACK
ansate/AUSCULATE
answer/GOSPEL
ant/MITE
ante-/ANTIQUE
ante/ANTIQUE/MAZARD(A)
antecede/PRECEDE
antefix/CRUCIFIX
anterior/ANTIQUE/MAZARD(A)
anthem/PHONETICS
anther/CHRYSANTHEMUM
anthology/CHRYSANTHEMUM
-anthous/CHRYSANTHEMUM
anthozoan/CHRYSANTHEMUM
anthro-/MASCULINE
anthropo-/MASCULINE
anthropology/MASCULINE
anti-/ANTIQUE/MAZARD(A)

antiseptic/ASP
antic/MAZARD(A)
antidote/DATA(A)/ENDOW
antique/ANTIQUE/MAZARD(A)/VETERAN
antiquity, -ies/ANTIQUE
anvil/PULSE(A)
anxiety/HANG
any/UNIQUE(A)
aorta/AIR(A)
apart/PART/SPREAD
ape/GIBBON
aperture/BORE
apian/AVIATE
apical/AVIATE
apodosis/ENDOW
apollyon/FALL
apology/DIALECT
apology/ELECT
apomixis/MIX
apostle/INSTALL/STILL(A)
appall/COLOSSUS/PALL
appar-, -atus, -el/PREPARE
appe-, -al, -late/PLEA/PULSE(A)
appease/CRUCIFIX
append-, -age, -ix/PENGUIN
apple/BAUBLE/FRUIT
apply/COUPLE
apposite/AFTER
appr-, -aise, -ise/PRIZE
appro-, -ach, -ximate/FOR
apri-, -cot, -il/FRUIT/PERSIMMON
apron/MAP
apt/DIVINE
aquanaut/NAVY
arab, -ia/CRIB/RIBOFLAVIN
arable/HARROW
arachnid/ARACHNID(A)/ARCHITECT
ararat/OROLOGY
arbor, -etum/ARBOR
arc/CURVE/DRAG
arcade/DRAG
arcaeology/CARRACK(A)
arcane/ARK
-arch, archao-/ARCHITECT
arch/CURVE/DRAG
archaic/CARRACK(A)
archbishop/ARCHITECT
archery/DRAG
archetype/CARRACK(A)
archipelago/ARCHIPELAGO/BARK(A)/BLOAT/
    BROOK/FLAKE
architect/ARCHITECT/ORGAN
arch-, -ive, -ist, -on/ARCHITECT
arctics/ORCHESTRA
arcturus/ORIENTATION
ard-, -ent, -or/ASH
are/IS/ORIENTATION
area/AREA/EARTH
argo/ARK
argon/ORGAN
argonaut/NAVY
argyle/ARACHNID(A)
aria/AIR(A)
arid/ASH
ari-, -el, -es/ARIES(A)
arise/RISE
aristocracy/ARITHMATIC
aristocrat/CURTSY(A)

arithmetic/ARITHMETIC/CATHARTIC(A)
ark/ARK/CARRACK(A)
arm/ARITHMETIC/ARM
arouse/RISE
arrive/RIFE/TROPHY
arrog-, -ant, -ate/RACK/URGE
arrow/DRAG
arsenal/ARSENAL
arson/ASH
art/ORIENTATION
artery/AIR(A)
arthro-/ARITHMETIC
artifact/FACULTY
artifice/FACULTY
aryan/ARYAN
as/BALE(A)/IS/SIGN(A)
asagai/HASTATE
asbestos/KIBOSH
ascribe/SAXON
ascuso/SACK
ash/ASH/ASHTREE/ASIA
ashamed/ASHAMED/SEMANTIC/SIN
asher/ASH TREE
ashes/ASH
ashmodai/SMITE
ashtree/ASHTREE
asia/ASIA/DAWN/EUROPE
asinine/ASININE/TONIC
ask, -ing/SEEK
asmodeus/SMITE
asp/ASP/PYTHON/SNAKE
asparagus/SPRIG(A)
aspect/SCOPE
asphalt/ASPHALT/SAPPHIRE/SOFA
aspic/SPIRE
aspire, -ant, -ation/ASPIRE/SPIRE/SPIRIT
aspirin/GRAPHITE
ass/ASININE
assassin, -s/ASSASSIN
assembled/SIMULATION
assert/SERIES
assess/SEAT
asset/SATISFY
assiduous/SEAT
assign/SIGN(A)
assimilate/SIMULATION
assinine/BURRO
assist/AUXILIARY
associate/SHAG
assonance/SOUND
assort/SERIES
assuage/HEDONISM
assume, -s, -ptions/ASSUME
aster-, -isk, -oid/SIDEREAL
astigmatism/TACK
astr-, -al, -o/SIDEREAL
astronaut/NAVY/SIDEREAL
astronomy/SIDEREAL
astrophysics/SIDEREAL
asunder/CHANGE
at/ANKLE/AT/DATA(A)
atavism/ABBOT
ataxia/TACTICIAN
atla-, -nta, -tic, -s, -mts./ATLAS/TELEVISION
atone/UNIQUE(A)
atrocious/GIBBON
atrophy/TROPHY

attach, -ed, -ing/STICK/TACK
attack, -s/STICK/TACK/TAKE
attenuate/EXTEND(A)
attest/TERZA
attic, -a, -ism/ANTIQUE
attitude/ADOLESCENT
attract/DRAG/DRAW
auburn/ALBINO
audible, -ility/AUSCULATE
audience/AUSCULATE
audio/AUSCULATE
auditorium/AUSCULATE
aunt/AMAH(A)/MAMA/TITTIE
aur/ORIOLE
aura/AIR(A)
aureate/ORIOLE
aureole/ORIOLE
aurora/ORIOLE
ausculate/AUSCULATE/SOUND
auslander/EXIT
auspice/SCOPE
austere/SEAR
autarky/ARK
auto/SUICIDE
autocracy/DEMOCRAT
autocrat/CURTSY(A)
automatic/MOON
autopsy/SPY
autumn/DAWN
auxiliary/AUXILIARY
avant-garde/PANE
avarice/AVARICE
avast/ACCELERATE
avaunt/PANE
aver/VERY(A)
average/AVERAGE
avia-, -ry, -te, -tion, -tor/AFTER/AVIATE/CAPON(A)/
     JIFFY(A)/OF(A)/PEGASUS/SUPER
avid/AVARICE
avifauna/AVIATE
avocation/VOCALIZE
avoid/VACATE
aware, -ness/SWERVE/TARIFF/
     UMBRELLA(A)/ORIENTATION
away/CONVEY/VIA
aw(e), -ful/NEW/EVIL
awkward/OF(A)
ax/CASTRATE
ax-, -illa, -le/AUXILIARY
azalea/ASH
azimuth/SUMMIT
babble/BABBLE
babble/BALL
babble/CRIB
babel/BABBLE
baby/ABBOT
baby/BABY
baby/BAUBLE
baccalaureate/BUCKAROO
bachelor/BUCKAROO
back/GIBBON
bad/BAD
bad/DIVIDED
bad/FAITH
bad/OBITUARY
bad/VETO
bafel/BABBLE
baffle/BABBLE

bag/BEAKER
bag/BUCKET
bag/VACATE
bagel/CYCLE
bagel/GIBBON
baggy/GIBBON
bahamas/BEHEMOTH
bailiff/PLEA
bairn/FERRY
bairn/FRUIT
bait/BID
bait/BIT
bait/PIECE
bake/FIRE
bake/JINX
bake/OVEN(A)
baksheesh/FAKER
balance/BALE(A)
bald/ALBINO
bale/BALE(A)
bale/BALEFUL(A)
bale/BALL
bale/BOULDER
bale/EVIL
baleen/BALL
baleful/BALEFUL(A)
ball/ALLEY
ball/BABBLE
ball/BALE(A)
ball/BALL
ball/BLOAT
ball/BOULDER
ball/BULLETIN(A)
ball/LIVER
ball/WALK
ball/WALLOW
ballast/BALE(A)
ballast/VEST
balled up/BALL
ballet/BALL
balloon/BALLOON(A)
ballot/BALL
ballots/BALL
balm/BALSAM
balm/PERSIMMON
baloon/BALL
baloon/BOULDER
balooning/BLOAT
balsam/BALSAM
balsam/PERSIMMON
balsamic/BALSAM
bamboo/BAMBOO(A)
bamboo/BIBLE
bamboo/OBOE
banana/BUNTING
band/BUNTING
bandage/BUNTING
banian/PENCHANT
banish/PHONETICS
bankrupt/TROPHY
banners/PANIC
banshee/NOOK/SHADE
bar-/DEVOUR
bar/BAR
barb/BURR(A)/DEVOUR
barbarians/BALL
barbaric/BABBLE
barbecue/BURN
barber/BRUSH
bard/BRUSH

bare/ABASH/BAR/BARE/VEST
bared/BARE
barge/BARK(A)
bario/FEROCIOUS(A)
baritone/BRIO(A)/GRAVE
barium/BRIO(A)
bark/BARK(A)/CARP
barkeeper/BAR
barkentine/BARK(A)
barley/AMBER/BARLEY/FRUIT
barm/BARLEY
barmy/BURN
barn/BARLEY
baro-/DEVOUR
barometer/BRIO(A)/DEVOUR
baron/BARON/BULLY/SPRIG(A)/VIRILE
baronial/BARON
barrage/BAR
barrel/BAR
barren/FERRY
barrette/BAR
barricade/BAR
barrio/AMBER/BAR/BARRIO/BRIO(A)/
      DELTA/METROPOLIS
barrister/BAR
barroom/BAR
barrow/BARRIO/BORE
bars-/BAR
bas-relief/BASIS
base/ABASH/ABYSS(A)/BASIS
baseball/BASIS
bashful/ABASH/VEST
basic/BASIS
basil/BASIL
basin/BUCKET
basinet/BUCKET
basis/BASIS/PACE
bass/BRUSH
basset/BASIS
basso/BASIS
bast/BATISTE(A)
baste/BASTE(A)
bastion/BASTE(A)
bastlille/BASTE(A)
bat/BAT/BIT/BOTANY/BOTH/BUTT/WEED
bateau/BIT/PIECE
bathrobe/VEST
bathyscape/SCABBLE
batiste/BATISTE(A)/WEED
baton/BAT
batten/BAT/DIVINE
batter/BUTT
battery/BUTT
bauble/BAUBLE
bawd/BOULDER
bazooka/BAZOOKA(A)
be- /BE
be- /MAZARD(A)
be/BE/IS
beadle/BID
beak/BEAKER
beaker/BEAKER/BUCKET/CUP/PIT/VACATE
beam/BEAM(A)
bean/BONE
bear/BEAR(A)/FERRY/FRUIT/SUFFER
beard/BRUSH/BURR(A)
bearing/FERRY
beat/BAT/BUTT/BUTTON(A)
beatific/DIVINE
beatify/DIVINE

beauty/BEAUTY(A)/DIVINE
beaver/BEAR(A)
beck, -on, -ing./FAKER/FAKER/FAKER
bedazzle/MAZARD(A)
bedeck/MAZARD(A)
bedlam/BASIS
bee/BY
beef/BUCKAROO
beer-sheba/SEVEN
beer/BARLEY
beetle/BIT/BLOAT/BOTANY/PIECE
befall/FALL
before/FOR/OVER
befuddle/FATUITY(A)
beg, -gar, -gary, -ing, -hard/FAKER
behemoth/BEHEMOTH
behest/FAKER/INCITE
behind/HERE
bejewel/MAZARD(A)
belfry/BARRIO
belie/DIALECT/WARLOCK(A)
belief/LOVE
believe/LOVE
belligerent/GESTURE(A)
belonephobia/KILL
belt/APPENDIX B/BUNTING
bema/BEMA
bemoan/MEANING
ben/NEW/PENETRATE/PENGUIN
bend/BUNTING/POINT
beneath/BE/MAT/NETHER(A)
benediction/SYNDICATE
benevolent/VOLUNTEER(A)
benign/KIND(A)/ORIGIN
berbers/BALL
bereave/TROPHY
berry/BERRY/FRUIT/PEPPER/PERSIMMON
berseem/BARLEY
beseech/FAKER/SEEK
beset/MAZARD(A)
besmirch/SMUT
best/DIVINE
bestow/BESTOW(A)
bet/AFFIDAVIT/BET/FAITH/VOCALIZE/WED
beta/ALPHABET/BETA/BOTH
beth israel/BASIS
bethel/BOTH
bethlehem/BASIS
betray/DATA(A)/ENDOW
better/DIVINE
between/BE/TEAM
bi-/BETA/BOTH
bialy/ALBINO
biannual/BETA
bias/BOTH
bible/BAMBOO(A)/BIBLE/OBOE
bibleot/BAUBLE
bibles/BIBLE
biblical/BIBLE
bibliography/BIBLE
bibliophile/BIBLE
bicameral/CAMERA
biceps/CAPITAL
bicker/BICKER(A)
bid/BID/PHONETICS
bide/BAD/FAITH
bier/FERRY
biforate/BORE
bifurcation/FORK(A)

big/BIG(A)
bigamy/BETA
bilateral/BOTH
bill/BULLETIN(A)
bimonthly/BETA
bin/PENETRATE
binary/BOTH
bindings/BUNTING
binds/BUNTING
binnacle/GIVE(A)
bio-/HYGIENE(A)/VIVID
biotic/HYGIENE(A)
bipartite/PART
bird/SPARROW
birth/FERRY/FRUIT
bis/BETA/BOTH
biscuit/PITA
bisected/BOTH
bishop/SCOPE
bison/BISON/OOZE/PITCH/SEEP
bistle/BRUSH
bistort/BOTH
bit/BIT/DIVIDED/PIECE
bite/BIT/DIVIDED/PIECE
bites/BIT
bits/BIT/PIECE
bitt/BAT/BIT
bitter/BIT/PIECE
bitumen/PITCH
bituminous/PITCH
bivouac/MAZARD(A)
black/BLEAK/FIRE
bladder/BLOAT
blade/TROPHY
blame/BLAME/CULPABLE/STYMIE
blanch/ALBINO
bland/ALBINO
blank/ALBINO/FIRE
blasphemy/BLAME
blast/BURST
blasto-/BURST
blatant/BLOAT
blaze/BURST/FIRE/PILE/SERPENT
bleak/BLEAK
bleed/BLOAT/FLEET/RED
blend/ALBINO
blind/ALBINO
blini/MILL
blink/ALBINO/FLICK
blintz/MILL/PLAZA
blister/BLISTER/BLOAT
blite/MILL
blitzkrieg/GRAVE
bloat, -ed/BALL/BALLOON(A)/BLISTER/BLOAT/
    BULLETIN(A)/BLOAT
block/FLAG/PLUG
blond/ALBINO
blood/BLOAT/FLEET/RED
bloom/PILE
blossom/PILE
blot/BLOAT/BOULDER/LEOPARD/VETO
blotch/BRIT(A)/LEOPARD
blue/FIRE
blush/FIRE
boar/BURRO
board/BAR
boat/BAT/BIT/PIECE/SABOTAGE
boatswain/PIECE
bob/BOBBY

bobbery/HUBBUB
bobbin/BOBBY
bobby/BOBBY
bode/BID
body/VAT
bohemian/HAUNT
boil/BULLETIN(A)
bold/BLOAT
bole/BOULDER
boll/BALL
bolshevik/BOLSHEVIK(A)
bolt/ABLATION(A)/BAR/BLOAT
bolus/BALL
bon bon/MILK
bona fide/BONNY(A)
bonanza/BONNY(A)/MILK
bonbon/BONNY(A)
bond/BUNTING
bone/BONE/MILK/OSTEOMA
boning up/BONE
bonny clabber/MILK
bonny/BONNY(A)/MILK
bonus/BONNY(A)/MILK
boob/OBOE
bool/BALL
boon/PHONETICS
boor/BOOR(A)
boot/BOOT(A)/BOOTY(A)/DIVINE/SABOTAGE
booth/BASIS
booty/BOOTY(A)/BUZZARD/EMBEZZLE
boracite/BORAX(A)
borage/BORAGE(A)
borate/BORAX(A)
borax/BORAX(A)/SIX/SPRIG(A)
bore, -dom, -er/BOOR(A)/BORE/FERRY/FRUIT/
   PORE/BOOR(A)/BORE
boric acid/BORAX(A)
boride/BORAX(A)
boring/BOOR(A)
born/FRUIT
borne/SUFFER
boron/BORAX(A)
borough/BARRIO
borro/BURRO
borscht/BRUSH
borzoi/BURST
botany/BOTANY/BUTTON(A)/FETUS/
   FUNGUS/WEED
both/BETA/BOTH/QUINTET/SOUTH
bother/BUCKAROO
bottle/VAT
botul/dIT
botulism/APPEND.B/BOTULISM(A)/FAT
bough/GIBBON
bouillon/BULLETIN(A)
boulder/BALL/BLISTER/BOULDER
boulevard/BALL/ORGAN/BOULDER
bound/POINT
bourg/BARRIO
bourgeois/BARRIO
bourn/BURN
bourse/BURSAR(A)
bovine/BUCKAROO/NEW
bowel/BOTULISM(A)
bowl/BALL/BULLETIN(A)
bowled/BALL
bowsprit/DIASPORA(A)/SPIT
box, -ing/BEAKER/BUCKET/CUFF/PIT/
   VACATE/CUFF

brach/REEK
brad/BRUSH/BURR(A)
brahma, -ism/FELLAH(A)/FELLAH(A)
braise/BURN
bramble/BURR(A)
branches/ARM
brand, -ish, -y/BURN/BURN/BURN
brash/BREACH/PROSTITUTE
brasil/BRASS
brass, -y/BRASS/BRASS
brat/BROOD(A)
brats/PART
bratwurst/BURN
brawn/BURN
braze/BURN
brazen, -ier/BRASS/PROSTITUTE/BRASS/BURN
breach/BREACH/BURST/PETARD/PORE/
   PRESS/PROTOTYPE
bread/BURN
break out/FRUCTIFY
break/ARCHIPELAGO/BARK(A)/BREACH/BROOK/
   DISPERSE/FELLAH(A)/FLAG/FLAKE/FORK(A)/
   FRACTION/FREAK/FRUCTIFY/
   PARK/PLOUGH/PLUCK/PLUG/
   WRECK/WRONG
breast/BURST
breed/BROOD(A)/SPREAD
breeze/BURN
brew/BURN
brewis/BURN
briar/BURR(A)
bridegroom/HUMUS(A)
brier/BURR(A)
brigade/FLAG
bright/ALBINO/ESMERELDA
brim, -stone/BURR(A)/BURN
brindled/BURN
bring/FERRY
brio/BRIO(A)
brisance/FRACTION
brisket/BURST
bristle/BRUSH/BURR(A)/STARE(A)
brit/BRIT(A)
brittle/SPREAD
broach, -ed/BREACH/BRUSH/PROTOTYPE
broad/PLAZA/SPREAD
broken/BROOK
bronchitis/DEVOUR
bronze/BEAR(A)/BRASS
brooch/BRUSH
brood/BROOD(A)/FRUIT
brook/ARCHIPELAGO/BROOK/FRUCTIFY/FRUIT
broom/BURR(A)
broth/BURN
brothel/SPREAD
brother/PART
brownie/BEAR(A)
browse/BURST
bruin/BEAR(A)
bruise/BURST
brunet/BEAR(A)
brunhild/GUERRILLA
brush/BRUSH/BURR(A)/BURST/CYPRESS/
   ELMHURST/STARE(A)
brutal/PIRATE
brute/BRIO(A)/GRAVE
bubble/BUBBLE
bubo,-es/BUBBLE/BUBBLE
bubonic/BUBBLE

buccal/BUCKET
bucephalus/BUCKAROO
buck/BUTT/POKE(A)
buckaroo/BUCKAROO
bucket/BEAKER/BUCKET/POKE(A)/VACATE
bucolic/BUCKAROO
bud/BOTANY/FAT/FETUS
buddha/BID
buddy/FETUS
buffalo/BUCKAROO
bug/BOTANY
bugle/BUCKAROO
build/APPEND.B
bulge/BLOAT
bulimia/BALLOON(A)
bulk/BALL/BOULDER
bull/BALL/BOULDER/BULLETIN(A)/BULLY/NEW
bulla/BULLETIN(A)
bullet, -in, -s/BULLETIN(A)/BALL
bullrushes/RUCKUS
bully/BULLETIN(A)/BULLY
bulwark/BALL/ORGAN
bund/BUNTING
bundle, -s/BUNTING
bung/PACK/PUGNACIOUS
bunge/PLUG
bunt, -ing, -line/BUNTING/BUTT
burden/FERRY
burg, -er, -lar/BARRIO
burgomaster/SATRAP
burial/BORE
burin/BORE
burn/BROOD(A)/BURN/FIRE/FROST/LAVA/
        PYRALIDID(A)/WRATH
burnish/BEAR(A)/BORAX(A)
burr/BURR(A)
burro/BURRO
burrow/BORE
bursa/BURSAR(A)
bursar/BURSAR(A)/BUTCHER(A)
bursitis/BURSAR(A)
burst, -
        ing/BREACH/BURST/DEBRIS/FLEET/PETARD/
        PROTOTYPE
bury/BORE
bush/BRUSH
business/USE
buss/KISS
bustard/AVIATE
busy/USE
but/BETA/BIT/DIVIDED/EXIT/SPARE/WEED
butcher/BUTCHER(A)/PREACH/SARCASTIC
butt/BOTANY/BUNTING/BUTT/BUTTON(A)/FAT
butter/BUCKAROO/FAT
buttock, -s/BUTTON(A)/FAT
button/BOTANY/BUTTON(A)/FAT
buttress/BUTTON(A)
buzz/GOSPEL
buzzard/BOOTY(A)/BUZZARD/EMBEZZLE
by/BE/BY/CONVEY/VIA
byssus/BATISTE(A)
cab/CAB/CAVITY/COVER/CUBBY
cabal/CABAL(A)
caballero/BARON/VIRILE
cabana/CAB
cabane/CAB
cabaret/CAB/CAMERA
caber/CAPRICORN
cabezon/CAPITAL

cabin, -et/CAB
cable/ALGEBRA/CABAL(A)/CABLE/COUPLE
cabobs/SHISHKEBAB
caboose/CAB
cabrilla/CAPRICORN
cabriolet/CAPRICORN
cacophony/PHONETICS
cadaver/DECAY
caddis/CHAETA(A)
caddy/CADDY/CALDRON/CUD/KIT
cadelle/KITTEN
cadence/DECAY
cadent/DECAY
cadet/CAPITAL
cadre/GATHER/QUARTER
caesar, -arean, -ura/CZAR/SCISSORS
caftan/COTTON
cahier/QUARTER
cain/COIN
cairn/CULMINATE
caisson/ENCASE
cake/CAKE/CYCLE
calabash/CALIBER
calaber/CALIBER
calamity/AMERICA/HARM
calamus/CALAMUS(A)
calash/CYCLE
calcar/HOOF
calculate, -us/CORAL
caldron/ALKALI/CADDY/CALDRON
caleb/CLEAVE
calendar/CALL/CYCLE
calenture/ALKALI
calf/CALF(A)
caliber/CALIBER/CARP
calibration/CALIBER
calibur/SCALE/SCURVY
calipash/CALIBER
calipee/CALIBER/CRAB/SCALLOP/SCALP/
        SCURVY/SKULL
caliper/CALIBER
calix/CHALICE(A)
calk/HOOF
call, ing/CALL/CRY/HAIL/LAUGH
calliope/VOCALIZE
callose/UNICORN
callous/CHROME/UNICORN
callow/GALYAK(A)/GLABROUS/SCALP
callus/UNICORN
calm/CALM
calorie/ALKALI
calumet, -niate, -ny/CALAMUS(A)/CALUMNY
calvarium, -y/GLABROUS/SCALP
calvinism, -ist/SCALP/GLABROUS
calvities/GLABROUS
calyptra/SCALP
calyx/CHALICE(A)
camarilla/CAMERA
camber/CAMERA
came/COMB(A)
camel,-back, -hair, -leopard, -oid, -s/CAMEL/
        CAMERA/CORAL/RAM
camera/ACME/AMITY/CAMEL/CAMERA/CHANGE/
        KYPHOS
camion, -isado, -ise, -isole, -let, -ouflage/CAMEL
camphire/CAMPHOR(A)/CYPRESS
camphor ball/CAMPHOR(A)
camphor/CAMPHOR(A)/GRAPHITE

can-can/CANE
can/CANE/EYE/KENNING(A)/OCEAN(A)
canal/CANE
canape/CANE
canary/CANE
canasta/CANE
cancel/CANE/INCARCERATE(A)
cancer/CRAB/UNICORN
candent/CAUTERIZE
candid/CAUTERIZE
candle/CAUTERIZE
candor/CAUTERIZE
candy/CANDY/CANE
cane sugar/CANE
cane/CALAMUS(A)/CANDY/CANE/CANOE/KEEN/
    OCEAN(A)/SOUND
canephoros/CANE
canister/CANE/OCEAN(A)
canker/UNICORN
cannelon/CANE
cannibal/SLUDGE
cannikin/CANE
cannon/CANE
cannula/CANE
canny/EYE
canoe/CANE/CANOE
canon-/CANE
canonization/CANE
canopicurn/CANE
canopy/CANE/CANOPY(A)
canorous/CANE
cant hook/CANE
cant/ACUTE/CANE/KEEN
cantata/CANE
canteen/ACUTE/CADDY/CANE
cantharis/GNAW
canthus/CANE
canticle/CANE/KEEN
cantilate/KEEN
cantilever/CANE
cantina/CANE
cantle/CANE
canto/CANE/KEEN
canton/ACUTE/CANE
cantor, -ial/KEEN/CANE
cantus/CANE
canvas/CANE
canyon/CANE
canzone/KEEN
canzonet/CANE
cap/CAP/CAVITY/COIFFURE/COVER
capable/COP
capacious/COP
capacity/COP
cape/CAP/CAPITAL
capella/CAPRICORN
capercaille/AVIATE
capital, -ism/CAP/CAPITAL/CAPITALISM/HEAD/
    UNICORN/CAPITALISM
capitate/CAPITAL
capitol/CAPITAL
capitulate/CAPITAL
capitulum/CAPITAL
capo/CAPITAL
capon/AVIATE/CAPON(A)/SCABBLE/SYNCOPATION
caprice/CAPITAL
capricorn/CAPRICORN/FEROCIOUS(A)/
    PUERILE/TROPHY/UNICORN
caprifig/CAPRICORN

capriole/CAPRICORN
capstan/CAPITAL
capsule/CUP/HAVEN(A)
captain/CAPITAL
caption/CAPITAL
captivate/COP
captive/COP
capture, -ing/CABLE/COP/CUFF/FIN/CUFF
car/ACCELERATE/BROOK/CAR/CURVE/
    CYCLE/SCOUR
carabao/UNICORN
caramel/CALAMUS(A)
carapace/CALIBER/CARP/CRAB
carat/CARAT/UNICORN
caraway/GRAIN
carbine/SCARAB
carbon/CHAR/GRAPHITE
carbuncle/CHAR
carcanet/COLLAR
carcass/CHROME
carcinogen/UNICORN
card/CARD/CARVE/CHARACTER
cardiac/CORE
carding/CARD
cardio-/CORE
cardoon/CARD
care/CHERISH/CRY
careen/CYCLE/UNICORN
career/ACCELERATE/CAR
caress/CHERISH
caret/CHASTE
cargo/ACCELERATE/CAR
carib/LOBO
caribbean/BEHEMOTH/SLUDGE
caribou/UNICORN
caricature/ACCELERATE/CAR
carillon/QUARTER
carina/UNICORN
cariole/CAR
carl/GUERRILLA
carminative/CARD
carmine/CRIMSON
carnage/CHROME
carnal/CHROME
carnatin/CHROME
carnation/CHROME/CORONA
carnet/QUARTER
carnival/ACCELERATE/CHROME
carnivore, -ous/DEVOUR/CHROME
carob/CARP/CRAB
carol/CHORUS/HOLLOW
carouse/EXIT
carp/CALIBER/CARP/CRAB/CURVE
carpenter/ACCELERATE
carpet/CARP/RUG
carpology/CARP
carrack/CARRACK(A)
carriage, -es/CAR/CAR
carrion/CHROME
carrot/CHAR/UNICORN
carry/ACCELERATE/BARON/CAR
cart/CAR/CURVE
carte-blanche/CARD
cartel/CARD
carthage/COURT
cartiridge/CARD
cartogram/CARD
cartograph/CARD
carton/CARD

cartoon/CARD
carve, -er/CARVE/SCALP/SCRAPER/CLEAVER/
    CRAB/HARROW
caryo-/GRAIN
caryopsis/GRAIN
caryote/UNICORN
cascade/DECAY
cascara/ENCASE
case, -es, -ing, -ment,/CASEFY(A)/COSSACK(A)/
    DECAY/ENCASE/SACK
caseation/CASEFY(A)
casefy/CASEFY(A)
casein/CASEFY(A)
cashier/CHASTE/SCISSORS
casino/HOUSE
cask/ENCASE
casket/ENCASE
casque/ENCASE
cassava/ASSASSIN
cassette/ENCASE
cassia/CASSIA(A)
cassock/ENCASE
cast iron/CAST
cast/CAST
castanets/ENCASE
caste/CASTRATE/CHASTE/SCISSORS
caster/CAST
castigate/CASTRATE/CHASTE/SCISSORS
casting/CAST
castle/CHASTE/ENCASE/SCISSORS
castoff/CAST
castrate/CASTRATE/CHASTE/CURT/
    SAXON/SCISSORS
cat/CHAETA(A)/KITTEN
cata-/DECAY
cata-/DOXY(A)
catabolic/DECAY
cataclysm/DECAY
catacomb/SOUTH
catalogue/ELECT
catapult/FLUTTER/HEAD/PSALM
cataract/DOXY(A)/HEAD
catarrh/SERUM
catch/CATCH/MITT/SEEK
catchpole/PAUCITY
catechism/CATECHISM(A)
category/CULL(A)
caterpillar/CHAETA(A)/PILE
catgut/GUT
catharsis/CATHARTIC(A)
cathartic/ARITHMETIC/CATHARTIC(A)
cathedral/CHAISE/HEAD
catherine/CATHARTIC(A)
catheter/JET
cathode/DECAY
catholic/ALL/DECAY/SLAM
catskill/BROOK/CATSKILL/GAP/GILL(A)/INERT
cattle/CAPITAL/HERD
caudad/HEAD
caudal/HEAD
caudate/HEAD
caudillo/HEAD/HEAD(A)/HERE/PRECEDE/
    SEDUCE/TAG
caudle/ALKALI
cauldron/CALDRON
caulk/CUFF/HOOF/SABOTAGE
causality/CAUSE
causation/CAUSE
cause celebre/CAUSE

cause/CAUSE/COSSACK(A)
causerie/CAUSE
causes/CASEFY(A)
caustic/CAUTERIZE
cauterize -y/CAUTERIZE/CRYOGENICS
cavalier/BARON/VIRILE
cave/CAB/CAP/CAVITY/PIT
cavern/CAVITY
cavil/QUIBBLE(A)
cavity/ALCOVE/BORE/BUCKET/CAVITY/CUP/
    GAP/GOPHER/GRAVE/HAVEN(A)/
    OVEN(A)/SCOOP/VACATE
ceasar/CZAR
cease/PRECEDE
cebula/BASIL
cede/PRECEDE
ceiling/HOLLOW/RACK
-cele/HOLLOW
celebrate/ACCELERATE
celebrity/ACCELERATE
celerity/ACCELERATE
celibate/ALL/HEALTH
cell/APPEND.B/CELL/HOLLOW/INCARCERATE(A)
cellar/HOLLOW
cemetery/HAUNT
cenobite/COMMON/HYGIENE(A)
censor/CENSUS
censure/CENSUS
census/CENSUS
cent/MITT
centavo/MITT
centenary/MITT
centennial/MITT
center/QUANT(A)
centi-/MITT
centrifugal/AVIATE
century/MITT
ceramic/CERAMIC(A)/CHAR/HUMUS(A)
cerebellum/UNICORN
cerebral/UNICORN
certain/GARBLE/SAXON/SECRET
cervix/UNICORN
cession/PRECEDE
cesspool/SPIRIT
cetacean/HADDOCK
chaeta/ACCOUTERMENTS/CHAETA(A)/GUT
chaetognath/CHIN
chafe, -er, -ing/ALKALI/CHAFE
chair/CHAISE
chaise lounge/CHAISE
chaise/CHAISE/SEAT
chalaza/CRYOGENICS/HAIL
chalazion/HAIL
chalice/CHALICE(A)
challenge/CALUMNY
chamber/CAMERA
chameleon/CERAMIC(A)/HUMUS(A)
chamomile/CERAMIC(A)/HUMUS(A)
chance/DECAY
chancel/INCARCERATE(A)
chancellor/INCARCERATE(A)
chancre/UNICORN
change/CHANGE/INSOMNIA/SENILE/
    SIMULATION/SIN/TIME/ XENOPHOBIA
channel/CANE
chant/KEEN/SOUND
chantage/CANE
chanteuse chanting/CANE
chanticleer/CANE

chaos/HAZE
chap/CAPITALISM
chapel/ALCOVE/CAP
chaperone/CAP
chaplain/CAP
chapman/CAPITALISM
chaps/CAP
chapter/CAPITAL
char/ALKALI/CERAMIC(A)/CHAR/COAL/
    CRYOGENICS/FIRE/HOARSE/IRE/
    SCAR/SCORCH
character, -s/CARD/CHARACTER/GRADE/
    HEARSE/SCRATCH
charade/SIREN
charcoal/CHAR
chard/CARD
chare/SHIRE
charge/ACCELERATE
chariot/ACCELERATE/CAR
charity/CHERISH
charm/KEEN
charnel/CHROME
charring/CHAR
chart/CARD
charwoman/SHIRE
chase/SEEK
chasm/GAP
chaste/CHASTE/CHASTISE(A)
chasten/CHASTE/CHASTISE(A)
chastise/CHASTE/CHASTISE(A)
chauffeur/CHAFE
chautauqua/KITTEN
cheap/CAPITALISM
check up/CHECKMATE
check, -ing, -mate/CHECKMATE/CZAR/MAT/OR
cheder/CHAISE
cheer/SIREN
cheese/CASEFY(A)
chef/CAPITAL
chemise/ASHAMED/CAMEL
cherish, -ed/CHERISH
cherokee/HOLLOW
chess/CHECKMATE/CHESS(A)
chest/ENCASE
chevron/CAPRICORN
chew/CHAFE
chieftain/CAPITAL
child/LAD
chill/CRYOGENICS
chilopod/GILL(A)
chin/CHIN
chip/SYNCOPATION
chiro-/GRAPPLE
chiropractor/GRAPPLE/REACH
chirp/SPARROW
chit/KITTEN
chiton/COTTON
chitterlings/GUT
chivalry/BARON
chive/BASIL
chloasma/HALO
chloro-/HALO
choir/CHORUS/GIRDLE
choke/HANG/NECK
chole-/GALL/HALO
cholera/GALL/HALO/HEALTH
cholinergic/ORGAN
cholla/COAL/SKULL
chop/CAPON(A)

choral/GIRDLE
chorale/GIRDLE
chord/CRAW(A)
chorea/CHORUS/HULA
choreographer/CHORUS
chores/SHIRE
chorus/CHORUS/COURT/CYCLE/GIRDLE/HULA/
    SCURRILOUS
chowder/ALKALI/CALDRON
chrome/CHROME/ORIENTATION
chromosome/TUMOR(A)
chrysalis/CHRYSANTHEMUM
chrysanthemum/CHRYSANTHEMUM
chrysolite/CHRYSANTHEMUM
chuck/CHUCKLE(A)
chuckle/CHUCKLE(A)
chuddar/HEAD(A)
chum/AMITY
churl/GUERRILLA
chute/DECAY
ciborium/CUP
-cide/SUICIDE
cider/SAKE
cigarette/GIRDLE
cimex/GNAW
cinch/CINCTURE(A)
cinchona/CINNAMON
cincture/CINCTURE(A)/HANG/NECK
cinder/GNAW
cinnamon/CANE/CINNAMON
cinque/FIN/QUINTET
cipher/DECIPHER
cipolla/BASIL
circle/CAKE/CURVE/CYCLE
circuit/CYCLE
circulation/CYCLE
circum-/CURVE
circumcise/SCISSORS
circumference/CURVE
circumscribe/SAXON
circumspect/SCOPE
circumstance/CYCLE
circumvent/CYCLE
circus/CYCLE
cirripeds/CIRRUS(A)
cirro-cumulus/CIRRUS(A)
cirrus/CIRRUS(A)/DUO
cist/ENCASE
cistern/ENCASE
cite/INCITE
cithara/GUT
cither/GUT
citra/SIDE
clabber/GALAXY
claim/CALL
clairvoyance/CALL
claive/CLEAVER
clam/CLAM(A)/CLIMATE(A)/CONGLOMERATE
clamber/CONGLOMERATE
clammy/CERAMIC(A)/CLEAVE
clamor/CALL
clamp/CONGLOMERATE/GRAPPLE
clamshell/CLAM(A)
clan/PLAZA
clasp/CROSS
class/CALL
clatter/CALL
claw/CARVE
clay/CLEAVE/CONGLOMERATE

claymore/RUM
clean/CYCLE
clear/CALL
cleat/CLOT/CONGLOMERATE
cleave, -er/CARVE/CLEAVE/CLEAVER/HARROW
cleft/CLEAVER
clemency/CLEMENCY(A)/WOMAN
clement/CLEMENCY(A)
clench/CONGLOMERATE
clergy/CORAL
clergymen/CORAL
cleric/CORAL
clerk, -s/CORAL
clever/CLEAVER
clevis/CLEAVE/CLEAVER
clew/CONGLOMERATE
client/SLALOM
climate/CLIMATE/CLIMATE(A)/SLALOM
climax/CLIMATE/SLALOM
climb/CLIMATE/CONGLOMERATE/CULMINATE
climbing/ALLEY/SLALOM
clime/CLIMATE
clinch/CONGLOMERATE
cling/CONGLOMERATE
clinic/SLALOM
-clino/SLALOM
clip/CLEAVER/GRAPPLE/SCALP
cloaca/CATSKILL
clod/CLOT/CONGLOMERATE
cloister/CLOT
close/CLOT
closet/CLOT
clot, -ing/CLOT/CONGLOMERATE/CRUST/
    CRYOGENICS/HELD/LID
cloud/APPEND.B/CLOT
clout/CLOT
clove/CLEAVE/CLEAVER
clover/CLEAVE
clown/CONGLOMERATE
club/CONGLOMERATE
clue/CONGLOMERATE
clump/CONGLOMERATE/GRAPPLE
clutch/CLOT/CONGLOMERATE
co-/COMMON
co-opt/OPINION(A)
coal/ALCOHOL(A)/CHAR/COAL/HALO
coalesce/ALUMNI
coat/COTTON
coati/CLIMATE(A)
cobble/GIBBON
cobra/CRAB
cockaigne/CAKE
cockchafer/CHAFE
cockney/AVIATE
cockroach/COCKROACH(A)
cod/HADDOCK
coda kd/HEAD/HEAD/HEAD(A)
code/SAMURAI
-coel/HOLLOW
-coele/HOLLOW
coeno-/COMMON
coenocyte/COMMON
coerce/ARK
coffer/CUBBY
coffin/CUBBY
coffle/CABLE
cog/ACUMEN/COG(A)/HOOK
cogent/HEGEMONY

cognate/ORIGIN
cognition/KENNING(A)
cognizance/KENNING(A)
cogon/COG(A)
cohabit/GIVE(A)
cohort/COURT/GIRDLE
cohosh/ASSASSIN
coif/CAP/COIFFURE
coiffeur/COIFFURE
coin/COIN
coinage/COIN
coir/CURVE
coitus/GATHER
coke/CYCLE
col/COLLAR
cold/CRYOGENICS
colet/COLLAR
coleus/HOLLOW
collapse/SNAP
collar/COLLAR/GARGLE
collate/ATLAS
colleague/ELECT
collect/ELECT
colleen/COLLEEN(A)
college/ELECT
collet/COLLAR
collie/COAL
collier/COAL
collossus/COLOSSUS
colonel/CULMINATE
colonnade/CULMINATE
colony/GYRE
colophon/CULMINATE
coloseum/COLOSSUS
colossal/COLOSSUS
colossus/COLOSSUS
column/CULMINATE
com-/COMMON
coma/HAUNT/INSOMNIA
comb/COMB(A)
combine, -ing/GOVERN/COMMON
combustion/ASH/ASIA
come/COMB(A)
comedy/BID
comfort/BARRIO
command/MAN/MOON
commend/MAN
commensurate/METER
comment/MOON
commerce/MARKET
commit/EMISSARY
commix/MIX
commode/METER
common/COIN/COMMON/MUNIFICENT(A)
commotion/NOD
commune/MUNIFICENT(A)
communicate/MUNIFICENT(A)
communism/MUNIFICENT(A)
community/COMMON
compact/CRUCIFIX
companion/COMMON
company/COMMON
compartment/PART
compel/PULSE(A)
compete/COMMON
complacent/FLAKE
complete/FULFILL

completely comparable/COMMON
complex/COMMON/COUPLE
complicate/COUPLE
compliment/FULFILL
comply/FULFILL
component/AFTER/GOVERN
comport/FERRY
compose/AFTER
compound/AFTER/GOVERN/MITT/OF(A)
compress/PRESS
compunction/PUGNACIOUS
compute/GOVERN/MITT
computer/MITT
computing/MITT
comrade/AMITY/CAMERA
con-/COMMON
con/COMMON/KENNING(A)
conan/EYE
concave, -ity/CAVITY/GIBBON
concede/PRECEDE
concern/GARBLE/SECRET
concession/PRECEDE
concierge/SERF
conciliate/CALL
concise/SCISSORS
concourse/ACCELERATE
concubine/SUCCUBUS
concur/ACCELERATE
condemn/DAMN
condense/DENSE(A)
condominium/MADONNA
condone/DATA(A)/ENDOW
condor/KITE
conduce/SEDUCE
conduct/DOUCHE(A)/HEAD/SEDUCE
confer/FERRY
confess/BID
confide/AFFIDAVIT
confidence/FAITH
conflagration/FIRE
confluent/BLOAT
congeal/CRYOGENICS
congenial/ORIGIN
congenital/ORIGIN
congest/GESTURE(A)
conglomerate/CLAM(A)/CLOT/CONGLOMERATE/
    CULMINATE/GRAPPLE
conglomeration/CONGLOMERATE
congregation/CULL(A)
conidium/GNAW
conjecture/JET
conjoin/JUXTAPOSE
conjugal/JUXTAPOSE
conjugate/JUXTAPOSE
conjunction/JUXTAPOSE
conjure/JURISDICTION
connate/ORIGIN

connoisseur/KENNING(A)/EYE
connote/EYE/KENNING(A)
connubial/NYMPHET(A)
conquer/QUERY
conquest/VICTOR(A)
conscience/SAXON/SCHIZOPOD(A)/SKILL
conscious/SAXON/SKILL
conscript/SAXON
consecrate/SAXON
consequent/SHAG
consider/SIDEREAL
considerations/SIDEREAL

consign/SIGN(A)
consolidate/SALVATION/SLAM
consonant/SOUND
consort/SERIES
conspicuous/SCOPE
conspire/SPIRIT
consternate/SOW
construct/DESTROY(A)/SOW
consul/CONSULT
consular/CONSULT
consulate/CONSULT
consult/CONSULT
consultation/CONSULT
contain/EXTEND(A)
contaminate/CONTAMINATE(A)
contend/EXTEND(A)
contest/TERZA
context/TECHNICAL
continue/EXTEND(A)
contort/PUZZLE
contour/TURN
contra-/COMMON
contradict/SYNDICATE
contrary/COMMON
control/ROTATE
convex/CONVEY
convex/GIBBON/VIA
convey/CONVEY/WEIGHTY(A)
convince/KIBOSH/VICTOR(A)
convivial/VIVID
convoke/VOCALIZE
cooky/CAKE
cool/CRYOGENICS
coomb/COMB(A)
coop/CAB/HAVEN(A)
cooperate/OPUS(A)
cop/COP/CUFF
copacetic/COPACETIC
cope/ALCOVE/CUFF
copepod/SCOOP
copious/OPUS(A)
copper/BRASS
copping/COP
copulate/COUPLE
coracle/CHROME
coral/CORAL
corbel/RAVEN
corbina/RAVEN
cordate/CORE
cordial/CORE
cordon/CRAW(A)
core/CORE/GRAIN
corf/CRIB
coriaceous/CHROME
corium/CHROME
cormorant/CRY
corn/CORN/GRAIN/UNICORN
cornea/CORONA
corner/CORNER/CORONA/CREASE/UNICORN
cornet/CORNET
cornice/CORNER
corniculate/CORNER
cornona/UNICORN
cornucopia/CORNUCOPIA/OPUS(A)
corolla/CORONA
corona/CORNER/CORONA/CROWN
coronacrown/CORONA
coronal/CROWN
coronary/CROWN

coronation/CROWN
coroner/CROWN
coronet, -s/CROWN/CORONA
corporal/CRAW(A)
corporate/CRAW(A)
corpse/CRAW(A)
corpus/CZAR
corpuscle/CRAW(A)
corral/CURVE
correct/RACK
corridor/ACCELERATE/CAR
corrie/CURVE
corroborate/RED
corrode/GRADE
corrosion/GRADE
corrosive/GRADE
corrupt/TROPHY
corset/CRAW(A)
cortege/GIRDLE
cortex/SAXON
corum/CHROME
corvee/RACK
corvette/CRAB
corvine/CROW/RAVEN
corvus/RAVEN
cosmetics/COSMOS(A)
cosmo-/COSMOS(A)
cosmonaut/NAVY
cosmopolitan/BARRIO/METROPOLIS
cosmos/COSMOS(A)
cossack/COSSACK(A)/SAKE
cotta/COTTON
cotton/COTTON
cougar/CAPRICORN
could/COULD
coulee/CATSKILL/INERT
council/CALL
counsel/SELL
counselor ii/SELL/CONSULT
count/HEAD/MITT
counter/COMMON/MITT
countermand/MAN
counting knt/QUINTET/MITT
country/COMMON
coup/CUFF
coupe/CAPON(A)/SYNCOPATION
couple, -es, -ling, -lings/CABLE/COUPLE/CUFF/
    SUCCUBUS/ SUPPLE
coupon/CAPON(A)/SYNCOPATION
courage/CORE
courier/CAR
course/ACCELERATE/CAR
court/COURT/CURTSY(A)/CURTSY(A)/GIRDLE/
    INCARCERATE(A)
courteous/COURT/GIRDLE
courtesan/GIRDLE
courtesy/GIRDLE
courtier/GIRDLE
courtly/COURT
couture/ACCOUTERMENTS/SEAM
couturiere/ACCOUTERMENTS
couvade/SUCCUBUS
cove/ALCOVEBARON/CAVITY/HAVEN(A)
cover/COVER/EVENING/HAVEN(A)/HOOF/VAT
covet/CAPITALISM
covey/CUP/SUCCUBUS
cow tow/HEAD
cow/BUCKAROO/CROUCH/REGRET/VICTOR(A)
coward/CREED/CROUCH/CURVE/REGRET

cower/CROUCH/REGRET
cowhage/GIBBON
cowherd/HERD
cowl/VAT
crab/CALIBER/CARP/CARVE/
    COCKROACH(A)/CRAB/GRAVE/SCARAB/
    SCRAPER/SERPENT
crabby/CARP
crack/CRACK/SCORE
cracker/CAKE
cradle/CURVE
craft/CRIB/RAVEN
cram/CULL(A)/RAM
cramble/SCRAMBLE(A)
cramp/CRIB/CURVE/GRAPPLE
cranberry/CORONA/CRIMSON/GROAN
crane, -ing/CRY/GROAN
cranium/CROWN/UNICORN
crank/CURVE
cravat/SCARF/SCRUFF
crave/CROW/RAVENOUS
craw/CRAB/CRAW(A)/DEVOUR/SERPENT
crawl/CARVE/CRAB/SCRAPER
crayfish/CARVE/CRAB/SCRAPER
creak/CRACK/CREAK
cream/CHROME/CREAM/CRUST/HARM/UNICORN
crease/CREASE/CROSS/CURTSY(A)
creatine/CHROME
creche/CRECHE/CURVE
credence/CORE/CREED
credentials/CREED
credible/CORE
credit/CORE/CREED
credo/CORE/CREED
credulous/CORE
creed/CREED
creek/CROUCH/CURVE
creep/CURVE/SERPENT
creepy/CRAB
cremate/CHAR
crepe/CALIBER/SCALP
crescent/CROSS
cress/GRASS
crest/UNICORN
crib/CRIB/CURVE/GARBLE/REEVE
cribbage/CRIB
cribiform/CRIB
cribwork/CRIB
crick/CROUCH
cricket/CREAK/CROUCH
crier/CRY
crime/SECRET
criminal/GARBLE
crimp/CRIB
crimson/CRIMSON/MAROON/WORM
cringe/CURVE
crinkle/CURVE
cripple/CRIB/CURVE
crisis/GARBLE/SAXON/SECRET
crisp/CROSS
criss-cross/CROSS
criterion/SECRET
critic/GARBLE/SAXON/SECRET
crkr/SCARLET
croak/CRY
crochet crooked/CROUCH
crochety/CROSS
crock/CURVE
crocodile/CORAL

crocus/CROCUS(A)
croft/CRIB/CURVE
crofter/BARRIO
cromlech/CAMERA/SILICON
crone/CHROME
crook/ANKLE/CURVE
croon/CRY/GROAN
crop, -s/CALIBER/CLEAVER/CRAB/CRAW(A)/
    CURVE/GRAPPLE/SCRUFF
croquet/CROUCH
cross-wise/CROSS
cross/CREASE/CROSS/CROUCH/CRUCIFIX/
    CURVE
crotch/CROSS
crouch/CROSS/CROUCH/CURVE/GYRE
croup/CURVE
crouton/CRUST
crow/CROW/CRY/RAVEN/ROC/SHRIEK
crowd/HERD
crown, -s/CORONA/CROWN/
    DEMOCRAT/UNICORN
crows/RAVEN
crucifix/CROSS/CRUCIFIX/SUFFICE
crucifixion/CRUCIFIX
crucify/CROSS/CRUCIFIX
crud/CRUST
cruise/CROSS
crum/CREAM
crumb/GRAIN
crumpet/CRIB/CURVE
crumple/CRIB/CURVE
crunch/CRUSH
crusade/CROSS
crusado/CROSS
cruse/CURVE
crush/CRUSH/GRIST/SAUCE
crust/CRUST/CRYOGENICS
crustacean/CRUST
crustaceous/CRUST
crusting/CRYOGENICS
crux/CROSS
cry/CALL/CRACK/CRY
cryo-/CRUST
cryogenics/COAL/CRUST/CRYOGENICS
crystalizing/CRYOGENICS
crystalline/CRUST
cub/CAPRICORN/CUBBY
cubby/ALCOVE/CAB/CUBBY/HAVEN(A)
cubbyhole/CUBBY
cube/CUBE
cubic/CUBE
cubicle/SUCCUBUS
cubit/KYPHOS
cucumber/CUCUMBER
cud/CUD
cuddy/CUD
cudgel/CUD
cudweed/CUD
cuff/CAVITY/CUFF/CUP/ENCASE/HAVEN(A)/
    HOOF/PUGNACIOUS
cuisse/SHANK
culapability/CULPABLE
culex/APPEND.B
cull/ALL/CULL(A)/ELECT/OCHLOCRACY(A)
culminate/CULMINATE
culpa/CULPABLE
culpable/CULPABLE
cultivate/GYRE
culvert/CATSKILL

cum laude/COMMON
cum/COMMON
cummerbund/BUNTING/CAMERA
cumulus/CAMERA
cunctation/HOOK
cunning/KENNING(A)
cup/CAVITY/CUBE/CUP/GIBBON/GOBLET/SCOOP
cupboard/CUP
cupel/CUP
cupola/ALCOVE/CUP
cupule/CUP
cur/CRY/GROAN
curb/CURB/CURVE
curcuma/CROCUS(A)
curd/CRUST
cure/HEALTH
curio/QUERY
curiosity/QUERY
curl/CURVE
current/ACCELERATE/CAR
currier/CHROME
curry kr/RAKE
curry/CARD/CHARACTER
currycomb/CARD
curse/CALL
cursive/ACCELERATE
curt/CURT/CUT/SAXON/SCAR/SCORE/
    SECRET/SKIRT
curtail/CURT
curtain/COURT
curtal/CURT
curtate/CURT
curtel ax/CURT
curtsy/COURT/CREASE/CURTSY(A)/GIRDLE
curvature/CURVE
curve/CORONA/CROSS/CROUCH/CURB/
    CURVE/CYCLE/GRAPPLE
cut/ACACIA(A)/ACUTE/CASTRATE/CHASTE/CURT/
    CUT/GOAD/KITTEN/SAXON/SCANTINESS/
    SCISSORS/SUICIDE/SYNCOPATION
cute/ACUTE/CUT
cuticle/CUT
cutlass/CURT/SUICIDE
cutlery/CURT
cutlet/CURT
cutting/TIME
cuture/GYRE
cycle hurry/CAR/COLLAR/CURVE/CYCLE/
    GYRE/CHORUS
cylinder/CYCLE
cymar/SIMULATION
cyme/CAMERA
cymograph/COMB(A)
cynosure/TAIL
cypress/CYPRESS/GOPHER
cypsela/CUP/SCOOP
cyst/SACK
-cyte/CUD/KIT
cyto-/CUD/KIT
czar/CREAM/CZAR/DASH/KAISER/SHIRE/SIR
dab/DAUB(A)/DIVE/DIVINE
dabble/DIVE/DRIP
dabbling/DIVE
dabster/DIVINE
dace/HADDOCK
dacha/ENDOW
dachshund/TECHNICAL
dactyl/TIMBER
dad/TOOTS

daddy/TOOTS
dado/ENDOW
daff/FATUITY(A)

daffy/DIVE/FATUITY(A)
daft/DIVE/DIVIDED/FATUITY(A)
dagger/HADDOCK/HASTATE
dais/DAIS(A)
dally/ATLAS
dam/MADONNAdam/STEM

damage/DAMN
dame/MADONNA
damn/ADONIS/DAMN/MADONNA
damp/DAMP(A)
dan/MADONNA
dance/DANCE(A)
dandle/ATLAS
dangle/ATLAS
danish/DEMOCRAT
dap/DIVE
dapple, -ling/DAUB(A)/DIVE
darah/DRAG
dark/DARK
darling/ADORE
dart/TELEVISION
dash/DASH/TOSS
dasheen/SOD
dashing off/DASH
dasyure/DENSE(A)/SOD
data/DATA(A)/ENDOW/THESIS(A)
date/DATA(A)/ENDOW/TIMBER
dative/ENDOW
datum/DATA(A)/ENDOW
daub/DAUB(A)/DIVE
daughter/GOAT/TEAT/TOOTS
daunt/MADONNA
dauphin/DIVE
dawdle/ATLAS/DOODLE(A)
dawn/ASIA/DAWN/SANGRIA/SUN
dead/SHADE
deaf/DIVE/FATUITY(A)/THYME
deal/EARTH
dean/MADONNA
dear/ADORE
debark/BARK(A)
debase/ABASH
debit/BET/GIVE(A)
debouche/BEAKER
debrief/DEBRIS
debris/DEBRIS/DIRECTION/FRACTION
debt/GIVE(A)
debtor/BET
decadence/DECAY
decalogue/DIALECT/ELECT
decapitation/CAPITAL
decay/DECAY/PRECEDE
decease/PRECEDE
deceive/DEBRIS
december/MITT
decide/DEBRIS
deciduous/DECAY
decimal/MITT
decimate/MITT
decipher, -ed, -ing/DECIPHER/GOSPEL/SPHERES
deck/TILE
declaim/CALL
declare/CALL/DEBRIS
decline/SLALOM
decoy/CAVITY

decree/GARBLE/SECRET
decumbent/SUCCUBUS
decuple/COUPLE
deduce/SEDUCE
deduct/SEDUCE
deem/DAMN
deemster/DAMN
deep/DIVE/FATUITY(A)
deer/THYME
defame/PHONETICS
defeat/FADE
defence/POINT
defend/POINT
defense/PENETRATE
defer/FERRY
degage/FAITH/WED
degenerate/ORIGIN
degrade/CHARACTER/GRADE
degree/CHARACTER/GRADE
deicide/CUT/DIVINE/SUICIDE
deity/DIVINE
deject/JET
delay/ATLAS
delegate/ELECT/LEX
delicacy/DELICACY(A)
delicateessen/DELICACY(A)
delicious/DELICACY(A)
delight/DELICACY(A)
delilah/DILUTE
delta/BARRIO/DELTA
deltoid/DELTA
demagogue/AGONY/DEMOCRAT
demand/MAN/MOON
demarcation/MARK
deme/DEMOCRAT
demean/DAMN/MUNIFICENT(A)
demented/MOON
demerit/AMERICA
demiurge/ORGAN
democracy/DEMOCRAT/UNICORN
democrat/DEMOCRAT
demolish/MOLE(A)
demon/DAMN/DUMMY/MADONNA
demonstrate/MOON
demotic/DEMOCRAT
demur/WEAK
den/DEMOCRAT
denarius/MITT
dense/DENSE(A)/SESAME
density/DENSE(A)
dental/GNAW/TINE
dentist/TINE
dentrifice/FRACTION
deny/INSOMNIA
depart, -ing/PART
depilate/PILE
deploy/COUPLE
deport/FERRY
deposit/AFTER
depress/PRESS
derogate/RACK/URGE
dervish/TRACK
describe/SAXON
desert/SERIES
deserve/SERF
desiccate/SACK
design/SIGN(A)
desire/SIDEREAL

desk/DAIS(A)
desolate/SOLITARY/SUICIDE
despair/ASPIRE
despicable/SCOPE
despise/SCOPE
despite/SCOPE
despoil/SPILL
destroy/DESTROY(A)/SOW
detain/EXTEND(A)
detect/TILE
deter/SCARE
determine/TERM
determining terminus/TERM
detest/TERZA
detour and/TURN
deuce/DUO
deuteronomy/DUO
deutschland/TOOTS
deva/DIVINE
devest/VEST
device/DIVIDED
devil/EVIL
devious/CONVEY/VIA
devise/DIVIDED
devoid/VACATE
devoir/GIVE(A)
devolve/WALLOW
devote/FAITH/VOCALIZE
devour/ABLATION(A)/DEVOUR/SWALLOW
devout/FAITH/VOCALIZE
dew/DIVE
dewan/DIVAN(A)
dexedrine/DEXTROUS(A)
dexterity/DEXTROUS(A)
dextrous/DEXTROUS(A)
dhole/APPEND.B
dia-/DIALECT
di-/DUO
dia-/DUO
diacritical/SECRET
diagnosis/KENNING(A)
diagram/CARVE/SCRAPER
diakha/CATECHISM(A)
dial/DIVINE
dialect/DIALECT/ELECT
dialogue/DIALECT/ELECT
dialysis/LOOSE(A)
diameter/METER
diamond/MADONNA
diaper/GRAPHITE
diaphonous/PANE
diaphragm/PARK
diarrhea/SERUM
diary/DIVINE
diaspora/DIASPORA(A)/DISPERSE/SPREAD
diastole/INSTALL
dicast/DUO/SYNDICATE
dichotomy/DUO
dictate/CATECHISM(A)/SYNDICATE
diction/SYNDICATE
dictum/SYNDICATE
didactic/CATECHISM(A)
diesis/JET
diet/DIVINE
differ/FERRY
difficult/FACULTY
dig/DIKE
digest/GESTURE(A)
digit/CATECHISM(A)/TIMBER
dik-dik/DIK-DIK(A)

dike/DIKE
dilate/DILUTE
dilatory/ATLAS
dilemma/DILEMMA(A)
diligent/ELECT
dilly-dally/TAIL
dilute/DILUTE/LOUT(A)
dim/DUMB
dime/MITT
dimension/METER
diminish/MINISTER
dimple/DIVE
din/DUMB
dingo/DINGO(A)
dinosaur/DINOSAUR(A)/DUO
dinothere/DUO
dip, -ping/DIVE/DRIP
diploid/COUPLE
diploma/DUO
dire/DUO
direct, -ed/DIRECTION/RACK
direction/CARRACK(A)/DIRECTION/LEX/RACK/
    REACH/REGULAR/REICH/TIER/TRACK/
    TREK/TRUDGE/TURTLEDOVE/WALK
dirge/DIRECTION
dis-/DUO/SHADE
dis/SHADE
disburse/BURSAR(A)
discern/GARBLE/SAXON/SECRET
discourse/ACCELERATE/CAR
discriminate/GARBLE/SECRET
discus/DAIS(A)
disembark/BARK(A)
dish/DAIS(A)
disk/DAIS(A)
dismal/DIVINE/MALIGN
dismay/MACHINE
dismiss/EMISSARY
disparate/PREPARE
dispel/PULSE(A)
disperse/DIASPORA(A)/DISPERSE
display/COUPLE
dispose/AFTER
disrobe/VEST
disrupt/TROPHY
dissect/SAXON
dissertation/SERIES
dissident/SEAT
dissolve/LOOSE(A)/SOLVE
dissonant/SOUND
dissuade/HEDONISM
distend/EXTEND(A)
distill/DRIP
distinguish/TACK
distort/PUZZLE
distress/SORE
ditch/DIKE
divan/DIVAN(A)
dive/DAUB(A)/DIVE/FATUITY(A)/TOWEL
dives/DIVINE
divide/DIVIDED
divided/BETA/DIVIDED/PIECE/WEED
divine/BONNY(A)/DIVIDED/DIVINE/JOVIAL
docent/CATECHISM(A)/ORTHODOX
docile/CATECHISM(A)/ORTHODOX
dock/DOUCHE(A)/SEDUCE/THYME
doctor/CATECHISM(A)/ORTHODOX
doctrine/CATECHISM(A)/ORTHODOX
document/CATECHISM(A)/ORTHODOX
dodder/DOODLE(A)

doe/DOE
dog/DIKE
doge/SEDUCE
dogmatic/ORTHODOX
dolak/ADOLESCENT
dolce/DELICACY(A)
doldrums/DILUTE
doll-eh/DOLL
doll/DOLL
dollar/ATLAS
dolphin/DIVE
dolt/DILUTE/THYME
domain/MADONNA
dome/TIMBER
domestic/TIMBER
domesticate/MADONNA
domicile/TIMBER
dominant/MADONNA
dominate/DAMN
dominion/MADONNA
don juan/MADONNA
don/MADONNA
donate/DATA(A)/ENDOW
donation/ENDOW
donor/DATA(A)/ENDOW
doodle/DOODLE(A)
doody/TOOTS
doom/DAMN
door/DELTA
doormouse/DORM
dope/DIVE/FATUITY(A)
dopey/DIVE
doppess/DIVE/FATUITY(A)
dorm/DORM/DRIP/INSOMNIA
dormant/DORM
dormitory/DORM
dormy/DORM
dot/TEAT
dote/DOODLE(A)
double/DUO
doublet/DUO
doubloon/DUO
doubt/DUO
douceur/MUSK
douche/DOUCHE(A)/SEDUCE
douglas/DARK
dourah/DURUM(A)
douse/DASH
dove/DIVE/NEW/THYME
dowager/ENDOW
down/NETHER(A)/THYME/UNDULATION
downfall/FALL
downs/UNDULATION
dowry/DATA(A)/ENDOW
doxy/DOXY(A)
dozen/DUO/MITT
drab/DARK/DRIP
draft/DRAG/DRAW/TOLL
drag/DRAG/DRAW/DRUDGERY/GRADE/TOLL/
    TRACK/TREK/TRUDGE
dragons/DRAG
drama/DRUDGERY/TOIL(A)
drastic/DRUDGERY/TOIL(A)
draw/DRAG/DRAW/TOLL
dray/DRAG/DRAW/TOLL
dread/CREED/SCARE
dream/DORM
dreary/DRIP
dregs/DARK

drench/DRAG/TOLL
dress/DIRECTION
driad/ARBOR
drib/DRIP
dribble/DRIP
drift/DRIVE
drink/DRAG/TOLL
drip/DRIP
drive/DRIVE
drivel/DARK/DRIP
drizzle/DRIP
dromedary/TRACK
droop/DRIP/TORPID
drop/DRIP
dropsy/WET
dross/DARK
drove/DRIVE
drown/DRAG/TOLL
drowse/DORM/DRIP
drub/DRIVE
drudge/DRUDGERY
drudgery/DRAG/DRUDGERY
drums/THYME
dsylexia/ELECT
duad/DUO
dubious/DUO
ducal/SEDUCE
ducat/SEDUCE
duchess/HEAD/SEDUCE
duchy/SEDUCE
duck, -ing/CUD
duckpins/CUD
ductile/SEDUCE
due/GIVE(A)
duffer/DIVE/FATUITY(A)
dugong/HADDOCK
duke/SEDUCE
dulcify/DELICACY(A)
dulcimer/DELICACY(A)
dulet/DELICACY(A)
dull/DILUTE/DRIP/LOUT(A)/THYME
dumb/DAMN/DUMB/STEM/THYME
dummy/DUMB/DUMMY/MODE
dump/DIVE
dun/DAMN
dunce/DUMB
dunderhead/DUMB
dune/DUNE(A)/UNDULATION
dunk/SOAK
duo/BOTH
duo/DIALECT/DILEMMA(A)/DUO/TOO/TWIST
duodecimal/MITT
duologue dialogue/DUO
duplex/COUPLE/DUO
duplicate/COUPLE/DUO
durbar/DELTA
durian/DURIAN(A)
durra/DURUM(A)
durum/DURUM(A)
dusk/THYME
dutch/TOOTS
duty/GIVE(A)
dwell/SWERVE/THYME
dye/DYE
dynasty/MADONNA
dys-/SHADE
dysentery/SHADE
dysfunction/SHADE
dysgenic/SHADE

each/EACH/UNIQUE(A)
eagle/CYCLE
earnest/ORIENTATION
earth/AREA/EARTH
earwig/CONVEY
ease/JET
east/ASIA
easter/ASIA
eaves/AVIATE
ebony/EBONY
eccentric/QUANT(A)
ecclesia/APPEND.B
ecclesiastes/CALL
echelon/SCALE
echida/SNAKE
echino-/SNAKE
echinoderm/SNAKE
echinus/SNAKE
echo/CATECHISM(A)
eclair/CALL
eclat/CALL
eclectic/ELECT
ecto-/EXIT
eddy/DURUM(A)
edge/ACUTE
edifice/CAUTERIZE
edify/CAUTERIZE
edition/DATA(A)/ENDOW
educate/SEDUCE
effect/FACULTY
effervesce/BURN
effete/FETUS
effigy/FIGURE
efflugent/FLICK
effort/BARRIO
effulgence/EFFULGENT(A)
effulgent/EFFULGENT(A)
effulgent/FIRE
egg/AVIATE
ego/I
egregrious/CULL(A)
egret/EGRET
eight/EIGHT/NOON(A)
eighth/EIGHT
either/WHO
ejaculate/JET
eject/JET
el/EL
eland/EL
elapid/SCALLOP
elapse/SNAP
elate/ATLAS
elder/ALUMNI/ELM/LAD
elect/ALL/CULL(A)/DIALECT/ELECT/LEECH/LEX
electric/LIGHT
electuary/LICK
elephant/ALPHABET
elevate/ACCELERATE
eleven/ALPHABET/UNIQUE(A)
elf/ALBINO
eligible/ELECT
elixir/SAKE/XEROX(A)
elk/ARIES(A)/EL
elm/ELM/ELMHURST
elmhurst/ELMHURST/STARE(A)
elocution/DIALECT
eloquent/DIALECT
elucidate/LIGHT
emancipate/MAN/MOON

emasculate/MASCULINE
embark/BARK(A)
embarrass/ABASH
embarrassment/CHECKMATE
ember/ASH
embezzle/BUZZARD/EMBEZZLE
embher/UMBRELLA(A)
embroider/BRUSH
embryo/FERRY
emerald/ESMERELDA
emeritus/AMERICA
emery/AMERICA/ESMERELDA
emily/AMERICA
emissary, -s/EMISSARY
emission/EMISSARY
emit/EMISSARY
emmet/MITE
emollient/MILL
emotion/NOD
emperor/PREPARE
emphasis/PANE
emphysema/FAN
empire/PIRATE
emporium/FERRY
empty/METER
empyreal/FIRE
emulate/AMERICA
emulsion/MILK
emunctory/MEEK
enamel/MILL
enamor/AMITY
enate/ORIGIN
encase/CASSIA(A)/CAST/ENCASE/MAGAZINE
enchanted/KEEN
encounter/COMMON
encyclopedia/PAUCITY
end/ANTIQUE
endearment/ADORE
endeavor/GIVE(A)
endemic/DEMOCRAT
endocrine/GARBLE
endosteum/OSTEOMA
endow/DATA(A)/EMISSARY/ENDOW/EXTEND(A)/
     THESIS(A)
enema/JET
enemy/AMITY
energy/ORGAN
enforce/BARRIO
engage/FAITH/WED
engender/ORIGIN
engine/GENIUS/KIN/ORIGIN
england/ANKLE/ENGLISH
english/ANKLE/ENGLISH
engrave/CARVE/GRAVE
enhance/ALUMNI
enjoin/JUXTAPOSE
enjoy/GAUDY
ennead/NOON(A)
enormous/KENNING(A)
enough/COMMON/NICK
ensconce, -ed/ENSCONCE/HOUSE/SHACK
ensemble/SIMULATION
ensiform/SAXON
ensue/SHAG
entelechy/TELIC
entertain/EXTEND(A)
enthymene/THYME
entice/INCITE
entity/IS

entranced/DORM
enumerate/MONEY
environment/VEER
environs/VEER
envoy/CONVEY/VIA
eohippus/HOOF
eosine/ASIA
epee/XIPHOID
ephebus/GIBBON
ephemeral/BY
ephor/ORIENTATION
-epi/BY
epic/VOCALIZE
epidemic/DEMOCRAT
epidermis/BY
epidote/ENDOW
epigone/ORIGIN
epigram/SCRAPER
epigraph/SCRAPER
epiphany/PANE
episcopal/SCOPE
epistle/BY/INSTALL/STILL(A)
epoch/SHAG
epos/VOCALIZE
epsilon/CHAFE
equal/HOOF
equation/HOOF
equator/HOOF
equestrian/HOOF
equi-/HOOF
equinox/NIGHT(A)
equity/HOOF
equivocal/VOCALIZE
-er/SANDAL
eradicate/ROOT
erase/GRADE
erect/RACK
erets/EARTH
erev/EVENING
erie/LEOPARD
erode/GRADE
eroticism/ESTROGEN(A)
err/ROTATE
errand/DIRECTION
errant/DIRECTION
erratic/ROTATE
erratum/ROTATE
erroneous/ROTATE
error/ROTATE
ersatz/EXIT/SEAT
eruct/REEK
erupt/TROPHY
erythema/RED
escalate/ALLEY/SCALE
escalator/SCALE
escapades/KIBITZ
escheat/DECAY
escrow/SAXON
-ese/GRAPHITE
esmeralda/ESMERELDA/ESMERELDA
esoteric/MYSTERY
espalier/ESPALIER(A)
esparto/SPIRAL
especial/SCOPE
esperance/ASPIRE
esperanto/ASPIRE
espionage/SCOPE/SPY
espy/SCOPE/SPY
esquire/SAXON/SCHIZOPOD(A)

essay/CAUSE/HEGEMONY
essence/IS/MEZZANINE(A)
establish/STABLE
esther/SIDEREAL
estrogen/ESTROGEN(A)
estrus/ESTROGEN(A)
estuary/CAUTERIZE
et cetera/DURUM(A)/HERE
-et/NYMPHET(A)
etesian/ANTIQUE/VETERAN
ether/CAUTERIZE
ethnic/SUICIDE
ethos/SUICIDE
etiquette/TACK
etm/ETYMOLOGY
etymology/ETYMOLOGY
etymon/ETYMOLOGY
eumenides/MOON
eunuch/SHAG
euphemism/PHONETICS
euphony/PHONETICS
euphoria/FERRY
europa/EUROPE
europe/ASIA/EUROPE
eurus/ASH
eury-/EUROPE
eurydice/SYNDICATE
eutectic/TABES(A)
euxenite/XENOPHOBIA
excrete/SECRET
excursion/ACCELERATE/CAR
execrate/SAXON
execute/SHAG
exedra/CHAISE
exegesis/HEGEMONY/SEEK
exercise/ARK
exergue/ORGAN
exhibit/GIVE(A)
exhume/HUMUS(A)
exigent/HEGEMONY
exile/EXIT
exit/CHAISE/COTTON/EXIT
exo-/EXIT
exoergic/ORGAN
exonerate/MASS
expand/PATIO
expatriate/PATRON
expect/SCOPE
expel/PULSE(A)
expelled/EXIT
experience/PIRATE
experiment/PIRATE
expert/PIRATE/SERIES
expire/SPIRIT
expletive/FULFILL
exponent/GOVERN
export/FERRY
expound/AFTER/GOVERN
express/PRESS
expurgate/BORAX(A)
exquisite/QUERY
evacuate, -tion/BUCKET/VACATE
evangelical/ANGEL(A)
evaporate/EVENING
eve/EVENING
even though/IF/
even/EVENING/IF
evening/COVER/EVENING
ever/CHROME

evict/KIBOSH/VICTOR(A)
evil/BALEFUL(A)/EVIL
evoke/VOCALIZE
evolve/WALLOW
ewe/OVIS
ex-/EXIT
exacerbate/CARP
exalt/ADOLESCENT
examine/HEGEMONY
excalibur/UNICORN
excavate, -ed/CAVITY/GOPHER
exceed/PRECEDE
excel/CULMINATE
excellent/CULMINATE
except/EXIT
excise/SCISSORS
excite/INCITE
exclaim/CALL
exclude/EXIT
excoriate/CHROME
excrement/EXIT/GARBLE/SECRET
exsiccate/SACK
extend/EXTEND(A)/EXTEND(A)/THIN/TONIC
extension/EXTEND(A)
exterminate/TERM
extinguish/TACK
extol/ATLAS
extort/PUZZLE
extremity/EXIT
exult/EXULT(A)
exume/CERAMIC(A)
eye/EYE
eyelet/EYE
fabric/DIVIDED
facile/FACULTY
faction/FACULTY
factory/FACULTY
faculty/FACULTY
fade/FADE
fag/FAG
fail/FAIL(A)/FALL
faineant/VAIN
faiot/FETUS
fair/BORAX(A)/SUPER
faith/AFFIDAVIT/ANTIQUE/BAD/BET/FAITH/
     VOCALIZE/WED
faitor/FAITH/BAD
fake fakir/FAKER
fake, -er/FAKER
fakir/FAKER
falafel/PEPPER
falah/FEAR(A)
falcon/PALL
fall, -en/ASPHALT/COLOSSUS/FAIL(A)/FALL/
     SNAP/SPILL
fallow deer/PALL
fan/FAN/PANIC/POINT
fang/CRUCIFIX/NIB/PENGUIN
fantasy/PANE
faqir/FAKER
far/EUROPE/FERRY/SPREAD/VEER
farce/PARK
farci farcy/PARK
fare/FERRY
farfel/FLAKE
fargiosh/FORAY(A)
farina/BARLEY/PULVERIZE(A)
farinaceous/PULVERIZE(A)
farm/BARRIO

farrago/BARLEY
farrakhan/BARK(A)
farrier/BRASS
farrow/CAPRICORN
farthing/QUARTER
fast/BURST/PIZAZZ
fastidious/BRUSH
fat/BUTTON(A)/FAT/OBESE/PAD/POUT
fate/BID
father/PART/PATRON
fathom/PATIO
fatuity/FATUITY(A)
fatuous/DIVE/FATUITY(A)
fault/FAIL(A)/FALL
faulty/BAD
fawn/FETUS
faze/DIASPORA(A)
feague/FEAGUE(A)/POKE(A)
fealty/FAITH
fear/FEAR(A)/PIRATE/PYRALIDID(A)
federal/AFFIDAVIT
fee/BUCKAROO
feed/FAT
feel/FLUTTER
felicitation/FRUCTIFY
felicitous/FRUCTIFY
felicity/FRUCTIFY
feline/LEOPARD
fell/FALL
fellah/FELLAH(A)/PLOUGH
fellow/BUCKAROO/FELLAH(A)
felon/HALO
felt/PILE/PULSE(A)
felucca/BARK(A)
fen/FENWAY(A)/PENETRATE
fence/PENETRATE/POINT
fencing/PENETRATE
fend/POINT
fender/PENETRATE
fenny/FENWAY(A)
fenway/FENWAY(A)
-fer/FERRY
feral/FEROCIOUS(A)
fere/FERRY
ferine/FEROCIOUS(A)
ferment/BURN
fern/FERRY
ferocious/FEROCIOUS(A)
ferret/FERRY
ferri-/BRASS
-ferrous/BRASS
ferruginous/BRASS
ferry/ABERRATION/ABLATION(A)/AVERAGE/
     BARON/FERRY/FUHRER/OVER/PIRATE/
     PROTOTYPE/SUFFER/VEER
fertile/FERRY/FRUIT
fertility/FRUIT
fertive/FERRY
fervent/BURN
fervid/BURN
fervor/BURN
festinate/BURST
fetid/BISON
fettle/VAT
fetus/BOTANY/FETUS
feudal/BUCKAROO
few/PAUCITY/SPARE
fiance/FAITH
fibula/CRUCIFIX

fichu/CRUCIFIX
fickle/FICKLE/HAVOC
fid/BAT
-fid/BIT
-fid/PIECE
fiddle/BAT/PIECE
fidelity/BAD/FAITH
field/BARRIO
fieldfare/ORIENTATION
fierce/FEROCIOUS(A)
fiery/FIRE
fife/BAMBOO(A)/BIBLE/OBOE
fifteen/FIN
fifty/FIN
fig/FIG/SKULL/SYCAMORE
fight/FEAGUE(A)
figure/FACULTY/FIGURE
figurine/FIGURE
filament/PILE
filigree/GRAIN
filium/PILE
fill/BLOAT/FULFILL
filly/BURRO/PAUCITY/PUERILE
film/PLUCK
fils/PUERILE
filter/PILE/PULSE(A)
filthy/PALL
fin/FIN/PENGUIN/QUINTET/VAIN
finagle/KNAVE/VAIN
finance/VAIN
finch/NIB/PENGUIN
find/POINT
fine/BONNY(A)
finger/FIN/PENGUIN/QUINTET
finical/FINICKY
finicky/FINICKY
finish/VAIN
fiord/SPREAD
fir/BRUSH/BURR(A)
fire/BURN/FIRE/FROST/LIGHT
firkin/QUARTER
firn/OVER
first/FOR/OVER/PROTOTYPE
firth/FERRY
fish/HADDOCK
fissi-/PIECE
fissile/PIECE
fission/BIT/PATIO/PIECE
fissure/BIT/PATIO/PIECE
fist/FIN/QUINTET
fisticuffs/CUFF
fistula/PATIO
fit/DIVINE
fitayoos/FATUITY(A)
fitzroy/FETUS
five/FIN
fix/CRUCIFIX
fixate/CRUCIFIX
fixity/CRUCIFIX
fixture/CRUCIFIX
fjord/FERRY/SPREAD
flag/FAG/FLAG/FLAKE/PLUG
flagrant/FIRE
flagstone/FLAG
flair/FRUCTIFY/REEK
flake/FLAG/FLAKE/PLUG
flame/FIRE
flamingo/FIRE
flan/PLAZA

flannel/CABLE
flap/PYRALIDID(A)
flat/PLAZA
flatter/PLAZA
flavin/FIRE
flax/COUPLE
flay/PLUCK
flea-i/PILE
flea/BORAGE(A)/PARASITE(A)
fleck/FLICK
fleck, -ed/PLUCK
flee/FLEET
fleece/PILE/PLUCK
fleet/ARCHIPELAGO/FLEET
flesh/PLUCK
flick, -ed, -er, -ing/FLICK/PLUCK/EFFULGENT(A)
flight flg/WRECK/ARCHIPELAGO/FLEET
fling/FLICK
flit/FLEET
flitch/BARK(A)/PLUCK
float/ARCHIPELAGO/FLEET
flock/PLUG
flood/ARCHIPELAGO/FLEET
flotsam/ARCHIPELAGO
flounder/PLAZA
flow/ARCHIPELAGO/BLOAT
fluctuate/ARCHIPELAGO/BLOAT
fluet/BLOAT
flugelhorn/PLUG
fluid/BLOAT
fluke/FLAKE/PLUG
fluoride/BLOAT
flush/BLOAT
fluster/FLEET
flutter/FLEET/FLUTTER/PULSE(A)
fluvial/BLOAT
flux/BLOAT
fly/ARCHIPELAGO/FLEET
fng/FUNGUS
foal/BURRO/PAUCITY/PUERILE
fodder/FAT/OBESE
fog/EVENING
foist/FIN
fold/COUPLE
folio/TROPHY
folk/FELLAH(A)/PLUG
folkmote/MEET
follicle/BALL
food/OBESE
fool/BOULDER
for/FOR
forag/FORAY(A)
forage/FORAY(A)
foramen/BORE
foray/FORAY(A)
force/BARRIO
forceps/BURN
ford/FERRY
fore-/FOR/OVER
fore/FOR
forebear/FERRY
forebearance/SUFFER
forecast/CAST
forefather/PATRON
foreign/DELTA
foremost/FOR/OVER
forensic/DELTA
forest/BRUSH/DELTA/ELMHURST
forestall/INSTALL

forge/DIVIDED
forgive/GIVE(A)
fork, -ed/FORK(A)PLUG
former/FOR/OVER
fornicate/BURN
forsake/SEEK
fort/BARRIO
forte/BARRIO
fortify/BARRIO
fortitude/BARRIO
fortress/BARRIO
forty/QUARTER
forum/DELTA
forward/FOR
foster/OBESE
foul/PALL
four/QUARTER
fourteen/QUARTER
fox/JACKAL
foy/CONVEY/VIA
fracas/FLAG/FRACTION
fracted/FRACTION
fraction, -s/FRACTION
fragile/FRACTION
fragment/FRACTION
fragrance/FRUCTIFY
fragrant/FRUCTIFY/REEK
frail/FRACTION
fraternity/PART
fray/FRACTION
freak out/FREAK
freak/FORAY(A)/FREAK/PERK/WRONG
freckle/DISPERSE
free/ARCHIPELAGO/FEROCIOUS(A)/FORAY(A)/
    FREAK/FREE/PERK
freeze/FROST/SERPENT
frequent/PARK
fress/DEVOUR
friable/FLAKE/FRACTION
fricative/FRACTION
friendship/SCABBLE
frigate/BARK(A)
frigid, -ity/SANGFROID
fritter/PART/VAT
frock/PLUCK
from/FOR
frond/TROPHY
frontspiece/SCOPE
frost/CRYOGENICS/FROST/SANGFROID
frozen/FROST
fructify/FRUCTIFY/FRUIT/REEK/SPRIG(A)
fructose/FRUCTIFY/FRUIT
frugal/FRUCTIFY/FRUIT
fruit/BERRY/FREE/FRUCTIFY/FRUIT/MUSK/
    PERSIMMON/PREPARE
fruition/FRUIT
frumenty/FRUIT
frustule/BURST
fry/FIRE/FRUIT
fuddle/FATUITY(A)
fuddy-duddy/FATUITY(A)
fudge/BAD
fuel/FIRE
fugitive/AVIATE/WRECK
fugue/AVIATE
fuhrer/FERRY/FUHRER
fulfill/FULFILL
full/BLOAT/FULFILL/RIFE
fully/BLOAT

fume/THYME
fumigate/HEGEMONY
fund/BUNTING
fungus/BOTANY/FUNGUS
fur/PILE/PLUCK
furcate/FORK(A)
furculum/FORK(A)
furfur/FLAKE
furlough/LOVE
furnace/BURN
furrier/PLUCK
furrow/BORE
furry/PLUCK
further/AFTER/VEER
fury/FIRE/WRATH
furze/BARLEY
fuse/PREACH/PSALM/PUZZLE
gab/HALO
gabion/CAB/CAVITY
gable/GIBBON
gabro/GLABROUS
gad/GADABOUT(A)/HASTATE
gadabout/GADABOUT(A)
gadfly/GOAD
gadoid/HADDOCK
gag/GAG
gage/FAITH/WED
gain/COIN
gainly/MACHINE
gal/GILL(A)/GIRL
gala/GALA/LAUGH
galactic/MILK
galactose/GALAXY
galalith/GALAXY
galaxy/GALAXY/LIVER/MILK
galbanum/CLEAVE/GALBANUM/GALL/LIVER
gale/CLEAVE/CULMINATE
galeon/CULMINATE
gall/GALL/HEALTH
gallant/GALA
gallery/HOLLOW/CULMINATE
galliard/COULD
gallon/ARITHMETIC
gallop/VOLUNTEER(A)
galoshes/GLISSADE
galyak/CHROME/GALYAK(A)/GLABROUS/SCALP
gam-/COMMON
gambit/KYPHOS
gambol/KYPHOS
gamete/COMMON
gamma/CAMEL
gammon/KYPHOS
gander/EYE
ganoid/GAUDY
gantry/ASININE
gaol/CELL
gap/CAVITY/GAP
gape/GAP
garad/GRADE
garage/GIRDLE
garbage/CRAW(A)
garble, -ed/BABBLE/CRIB/GARBLE/SCRAMBLE(A)/
    GARBLE
garcle/COLLAR
garden/GIRDLE
garfish/HASTATE
garganey/GARGLE
gargle/GARGLE/GROAN
gargoyle/GARGLE

garlic/HASTATE
garlic/LOCK(A)
garner/GRAIN
garret/GIRDLE
garrotte/GIRDLE
garrulous/CRY
garter/GIRDLE
garth/GIRDLE
gas/HAZE
gash/HEARSE
gasket/URGE
gasp/ASPIRE
gate/GATHER
gather/GATHER/GOOD
gaudiness/GAUDY
gaudy/GAUDY
gaunt/ANNOYANCE
gaur/BUCKAROO
gauze/GAUZE/GESTURE(A)/GONORRHEA
gavel/GIVE(A)
gayal/BUCKAROO
gaze/GAZE
gazebo/GAZE
gazehound/GAZE
gelatin/CRYOGENICS
gelid/CRYOGENICS
gelt/CHRYSANTHEMUM
gemini/COMMON
gemot/MEET
gen-/KIN
-gen/ORIGIN
gender/ORIGIN
genealogy/GENOCIDE(A)/ORIGIN
general/ORIGIN
generate, -ting, -tion, -tive/ORIGIN
generic generous/ORIGIN
genesis/ORIGIN
-genesis/ORIGIN
genetive/ORIGIN
genette/KITTEN
genial/CHIN
genie/GENIUS
genital/ORIGIN
genitor/ORIGIN
genius/GENIUS/KIN/ORIGIN
genocide/GENOCIDE(A)/ORIGIN
genotype/ORIGIN
genre/ORIGIN
gent/ORIGIN
genteel/GENOCIDE(A)
gentile/GENOCIDE(A)
gentle/KIND(A)
genuflect/COUPLE/KNEEL(A)
genus/ORIGIN
-geny/KIN/ORIGIN
geometry/METER
georgic/ORGAN
geranium/CORONA/CRY/GROAN
gerbial/GARBLE
gerbil/RABBIT(A)
germ/GERM/ORIGIN
german/KIN/ORIGIN
germander/CERAMIC(A)/HUMUS(A)
germane/ORIGIN
germinal/GERM/ORIGIN
germinate, -ting/ORIGIN/GERM
gerund/GESTURE(A)
gestalt/INSTALL/STILL(A)

gestation/GESTURE(A)
geste/GESTURE(A)
gesticulate/GESTURE(A)
gesture/GESTURE(A)
get/GHERKKIN(A)
gherkin/GHERKKIN(A)
gherkkin/GHERKKIN(A)
ghetto/GATHER
ghost/HATE
ghyll/CATSKILL/GILL(A)/INERT
giader/HERD
giant/OGRE
giaour/GIAOUR(A)
gibben/VACATE
gibberish/GARBLE
gibbon/CUP/GIBBON/KYPHOS
gibbose/GIBBON
gibbous/GIBBON
giblet/CRAW(A)
gibosity/GIBBON
giddy/GOAT
gift/GIVE(A)
gigantic/OGRE
gila monster/GILL(A)
gild/CHRYSANTHEMUM
gill/ARITHMETIC/CATSKILL/GAP/GILL(A)/
    GIRL/INERT
gilliam/GILL(A)
gillie/GILL(A)/GIRL
gilly/GIRL
gillyflower/UNICORN
gimel/CAMEL
gin/GENIUS
gingerly/ORIGIN
giopheret/GRAPHITE
gipon/GIPON(A)
giraffe/COLLAR/GARGLE/SAFFRON/
    SCARF/SCRUFF
gird/GIRDLE
girder/GIRDLE
girdle/CINCTURE(A)/COURT/CURTSY(A)/
    GIRDLE/HUG(A)
girl/GIRL
girth/GIRDLE
gist/JET
gittern/GUT
give/GIVE(A)/HALO
glabella/GLABROUS
glabrous/CARVE/GALYAK(A)/GLABROUS
glace/CRYOGENICS
glacier/CRYOGENICS/GLISSADE
glacis/GLISSADE
glad/HALO
glaive/CLEAVER
glance/CORONA
glaze/GLISSADE
gleam/CORONA/HALO
glee/GALA/HALO
gleet/CLOT/CONGLOMERATE
gley/CONGLOMERATE
glib/GALBANUM
glide/GLISSADE
glimpse/CORONA
glissade/CRYOGENICS/GLISSADE/QUARTER/
    SLUDGE
glisten/HALO
glitch/GLISSADE
glitsh/GLISSADE

gloaming/HALO
globe/CONGLOMERATE
globule/CONGLOMERATE
gloss/GLISSADE
glow/HALO
glucose/DELICACY(A)
glue/CLEAVE/CONGLOMERATE
gluteus/CLOT
glutinous/CLOT/CONGLOMERATE
glutton/GARGLE
glyph/CARVE/CLEAVER/SCALP
gnash/GNAW
gnat/GNAW
gnathic/CHIN/GNAW
-gnathous/CHIN
gnaw/CANOPY(A)/CHIN/GNAW/NAG/
    TALCUM/TINE
gnome/KENNING(A)
gnosis/KENNING(A)
goad/ACUTE/GOAD/HASTATE
goat/GOAT/KITTEN
goblet/CAVITY/CUP/GOBLET
god/GOOD
gold/CHRYSANTHEMUM/HALO
golf/CUFF
golgotha/SCALP/SKULL
goliard/GARGLE
gomar/GERM
gonad/KIN/ORIGIN
gono-/ORIGIN
gonorrhea/GAUZE/GESTURE(A)/GONORRHEA
good/DIVINE/GATHER/GOOD
gopher/CAVITY/GOPHER/GRAVE/SCOOP/
    SCRAPER/GRAPHITE
goral/BUCKAROO
gore/CORNER/CRUST/GORE/HASTATE/UNICORN
gorge/GARGLE
gorgeous/GARGLE
gorhen/GORE
gorial/GUERRILLA
gorilla/GUERRILLA
goriness/GORE
gory/CRUST/GORE
gospel/DECIPHER/GOSPEL/SPARE/SPHERES/SEPT
gossip/SUICIDE
gourd/CUCUMBER

govern/GOVERN
grab/GRAPPLE/KNAVE/RAVEN
graben/GRAVE
grade/CARD/CHARACTER/GRADE/GRAIN/
    GRAVE/GRAZE/GROUND/
    SCRAPER/SCRATCH
graffitti/SCRAPER
grain/CORE/CORN/GRAIN/GRIST/GROUND/
    KERNEL/MARBLE(A)/MARINE
gram/CARVE/GRAIN/KERNEL/SCRAPER
-gram/SCRAPER
grammar/SCRAPER
granadilla/GRAIN
granary/GRAIN
grand slam/SLAM
grange/GRAIN
granite/GRAIN
granola/GRAIN
grant/CORE
granular/GRAIN
granule/GRAIN
grape/CURVE/GRAIN
graph/CARVE/SCRAPER

-graph/CARVE
graphics/GRAPHITE
graphite/CARVE/GRAPHITE/SCRAPER
grapline/GRAPPLE
grapnel/GRAPPLE
grapple/CURVE/GRAIN/GRAPPLE
grappling hook/GRAPPLE
grasp/GRAPPLE
grass widow/GRASS
grass/GRASS/GRAZE
grate/CHARACTER/GRADE/SCRATCH
grave/BORE/BRIO(A)/CARVE/CAVITY/GOPHER/
    GRADE/GRAPHITE/GRAVE/SCURVY
gravel/CORAL
gravity/BRIO(A)/GRAVE/WEIGHTY(A)
gravure/GRAVE
gray/CORONA
graze/CURT/GRASS/GRAZE
greaves/GRAVE
green/CORONA/GRASS
greet/CRY
gregarious/CULL(A)
gregorian/ORIENTATION
gregory/ORIENTATION
grenadfe/GRAIN
gribble/CRAB
grief/BRIO(A)/GRAVE
grieve/BRIO(A)/GRAVE
griffe/GARBLE
griffin/GARBLE
grim/GROAN/IRE
grimace/GROAN/IRE
grin/GRIST/GROAN
grind/GRAIN
grip/GRAPPLE
gripe/GRAPPLE
grippe/GRAPPLE
grisle/CRUSH
grist/CRUSH/GRAIN/GRIST
grit/GRIST
grits/GRIST
groan/CRY/GARGLE/GROAN/NECK
groats/GRIST
groin/CORNER
gromwell/GRIST
groove/GRAVE
grope/GRAPPLE
ground/GRAIN/GROUND
group/GRAPPLE
grow/GRASS
grub/CRAB/GRAVE/SCARAB
grubby/CRAB
gruff/CARP
grumble/GROAN/IRE
grunt/GROAN
guanaco/CAMEL
guard/ORIENTATION
guerdon/ENDOW
guerilla/GUERRILLA
guerrilla/GUERRILLA/SKULL
guess/GHERKKIN(A)/GUESS
guest/HOUSE
guilder/HALO
guilt/REGRET
guinevere/NOOK
guitar, -s/GUT
gulch/CATSKILL
gulden/CHRYSANTHEMUM/HALO
gull/CULMINATE/GYRE
gullet/GARGLE

gully/CATSKILL/INERT
gulp/GARGLE
gum/GENOCIDE(A)
guph/PEGASUS
gurgle/GARGLE
guru/BRIO(A)/GRAVE
gush/SAGA
gusies/SAUCE
gut, -s/ACCOUTERMENTS/CHAETA(A)/GUT
guzzle/GUZZLE(A)
gynecology/NOOK
gyping/COP
gyrate/GYRE
gyrating helix/CYCLE
gyrations/GYRE
gyre/CYCLE/GYRE/OGRE
gyrfalcon/HASTATE
gyro-/GYRE
gyve/CABLE
habit/GIVE(A)
hack/HOOK/KNOCK
haddock/GOAD/HADDOCK/SQUAT
hagio-/HAGIOGRAPHA
hagiographa/HAGIOGRAPHA
hail/ALL/CALL/CRYOGENICS/HAIL/
    HALO/HEALTH
hailstones/HAIL
hake/HOOK
hald/CLEAVER
hale/ALL/CALL/HEALTH
half/CLEAVER
halibut/BUTTON(A)
hall/HOLLOW
hallelujah/CALL/HAIL/HALO/ULULATION
halloo/CALL/HAIL
hallow/HAIL
hallowed holy/ALL
hallucination/DORM
halo/HALO
halt/ACCELERATE/GRADE/HELD
halter/HELD
halting/HELD
halve/CLEAVER
ham/SHANK
hamadryad/SIMULATION
hame/HAUNT
hamlet/HAUNT
hamster/HAMSTER
hand/HEAD/MITT/QUINTET
handsel/CONSULT/SELL
handsome/HANDSOME(A)
hang, -ing/CINCTURE(A)/GROAN/HANG/HEM/
    HOOK/NECK/SNAKE
hangman/HANG
hangnail/HANG
hanker/CINCTURE(A)/HOOK
hanuman/CHIN
haploid/SIMULATION
harangue/GUERRILLA
harbinger/GUERRILLA
harbor/GUERRILLA
hard/SLALOM/UNICORN
hardy/UNICORN
hare/HURRY
harem/HAREM/TABOO
hari-kari/CRAW(A)
harm/CREAM/HARM
harness/NOSTALGIA
harp/CURVE

harpoon/CARVE/GRAPPLE
harquebus/HOOK
harrow/CARVE/CLEAVER/HARROW/HEARSE
harry/GUERRILLA
harsh hr/HARROW/HEARSE
hart/UNICORN
hartal/CHRYSANTHEMUM
hartiov/CORE
haruspex/CRAW(A)
has/IS
hasenpfeffer/HASTE
hash/ASSASSIN
hashish/ASSASSIN
haslet/HASTATE
hasp/KYPHOS
hassock/ASSASSIN
hastate/CAST/GOAD/HASTATE/HASTE/SCOOT/
    XIPHOID
haste/CAST/HASTE/HESITANT
hasten/HASTE
hasty/HASTE
hat/CAP/COTTON/HEAD/HEAD(A)
hatch/HATCH(A)
hate/HATE/HEAD
hatred/HATE
haughty/ALUMNI
haulm/CALAMUS(A)
haunt/ENSCONCE/HAUNT/INN(A)
hauteur/CHASTE
have/CAPITALISM/GIVE(A)
haven/CAVITY/GIVE(A)/GOVERN/HAVEN(A)
havoc/FICKLE/HAVOC
hawker/CUP
haze/HAZE
hazy/HAZE
he/HE/HERE/WHO
head for/HEAD
head off/HEAD
head/CAPITAL/COTTON/HEAD/HEAD(A)/HEM
heads/HEAD
headway/HEAD
heal/HEALTH
health/ALL/GALL/HAIL/HEALTH/LEECH
heap/CUP/GIBBON
hear/SCAVENGE
hearken/SCAVENGE
hearse/CHARACTER/HARROW/HEARSE
heart/CORE
hearth/CHAR/SCAR
heat/CAUTERIZE/HEAD
heave/CONVEY/HAVOC/VIA
heaven/ACME/CAMERA/HAVEN(A)
hebdomad/SEVEN
heckle/CHERISH/HOOK
hectic/SHAG
hecto-/MITT
heddle/CABLE
hedonism/BET/HEDONISM/RAVEN
hedonist/HEDONISM
heed/COTTON/HEAD/HEAD(A)
hegemony/HEGEMONY/NAG/SEEK
heifer/BULLY/CAPRICORN
heinous/HATE
hekhereets/CURTSY(A)
held/CLOT/HELD
helicon/CYCLE
helicopter/CYCLE
heliocentric/HORUS
helium/HORUS/SUN

helix/CYCLE/WALLOW
hell/HOLLOW
hello/CALL/HAIL
hem/GIBBON/HEM
hematein/SANGRIA
hematic/ANEMIC
hematocrit/SECRET
hemoglobin/SANGRIA
hemophilia/AMITY
hemophilliac/ANEMIC
hemorrhage/AMITY
hemorrhoid/AMITY/SERUM
hemp/CANE/HEAD
hence/HERE
henna/ANEMIC
henotheism/SIMULATION
hepta-/SEVEN
heptad/SEVEN
her/HERE
herald/GUERRILLA
herb/TROPHY
herd/HERD
herdsman/HERD
here/HERE
heresy/HERESY
heretic/HERESY
heriot/GUERRILLA
hernia/CRAW(A)
heron/GROAN
herpes/SERPENT
herpetology/SERPENT
hesitant/HESITANT
hesitate/HASTE/HESITANT
hesitation/HESITANT
heterodox/ORTHODOX
heterogeneous/ORIGIN
hevel/CABLE
hexa-/SIX
hexad/SIX
hide/COTTON/HOARD
hieroglyphic/CLEAVER
hierophant/PANE
high/CUP/GIBBON/OGRE
hilda/GUERRILLA
hildebrand/GUERRILLA
hildegarde/GUERRILLA
hill/CULMINATE/GIBBON/OROLOGY
hillock/CULMINATE
hind/HEAD/HERE/SCANTINESS
hinder/HERE
hinge/HOOK
hinterland/HERE
hippo-/KIBITZ
hippopotamus/HOOF
hire/SHIRE
hiss/HUSH
hitch/CATCH
hither/HERE
hive/ALCOVE/CAB/GIBBON
hoard, -ing/CHAISE/HOARD
hoarse/HOARSE
hobble/CABLE
hock/ANKLE
hockey/KNOCK
hog/GIRDLE/HUG(A)/HYOSCYAMINE(A)
hoity-toity/HOOT/HOOT(A)
hokum/HOKUM
hold, -ing/ACCELERATE/CLOT/CLOT/HELD
hole/HOLLOW
holiday/ALL

holler/CALL/HAIL
hollow, -s/CALAMUS(A)/CELL/CULMINATE/GAP/
   HERESY/HOLLOW/KILL/LOCK(A)/CELL
holm/CULMINATE
holo-/SLAM
holocaust/ALL/CAUTERIZE/SLAM
holophrastic/PHRASE
holster/HOLLOW
holt/ELMHURST
holy/HAIL
holz/ELMHURST
homage/CERAMIC(A)/HUMUS(A)
hombre/CERAMIC(A)/HUMUS(A)
home/HAUNT
homeo-/SIMULATION
homeopath/COMMON
homicide/CERAMIC(A)/CUT/SUICIDE
homily/SIMULATION
hominid/CERAMIC(A)/HUMUS(A)
homo-/COMMON/SIMULATION
homo/HUMUS(A)
homogeneous/COMMON
homographs/COMMON
homologous/ELECT
homonyms and/COMMON
homophones/COMMON
honest/HONEST(A)
honey/HONEY(A)/OGRE
honor/HONEST(A)
hood/COTTON/HEAD/HEAD(A)
hoof/HOOF
hook/HANG/HOOK
hooker/HOOK
hoop/CUP/GIBBON
hoot owl/HOOT(A)
hoot/HOOT/HOOT(A)
hootenanny/HOOT/HOOT(A)
hop/KIBITZ
hope/CAPITALISM
hopper/CUP/VAT
hopple/CABLE
hora/HULA
horn/CORNET/HEAD/RAM/UNICORN
hornet/UNICORN
horny/UNICORN
horology/HORUS
horoscope/HORUS/SCOPE
horrendus/HORRID
horrible/HORRID
horrid/HORRID
horrific, -y/HORRID/HORRID
horror/HORRID
horse/CZAR/PEGASUS
horst/ELMHURST
horticulture/COURT/GIRDLE
horus/HORUS/HURRY/SUN
hose/HOUSE
hospice/HOUSE
hospital, -ity/HOUSE
host/HOUSE
hostage/HOUSE/SEAT
hostel/HOUSE
hostile/HOUSE
hostler/HOUSE
hot/CAUTERIZE
hound/CLIMATE(A)
hour/HORUS/HURRY
house/HOUSE/MAGAZINE/SHACK

hovel/CUBBY/HAVEN(A)/VILLA(A)
how/HOW(A)/WHO
howl/ULULATION/WAIL
hub/GIBBON
hubbub/HUBBUB
hubris/EXIT
huckster/CUP
huddle/HERD/HOARD
hug/GIRDLE/HUG(A)
huge/OGRE
hula/CHORUS/HULA/SCURRILOUS
hull/HOLLOW
human/CERAMIC(A)/HUMUS(A)/
    MAN/MASCULINE
humane/HUMUS(A)
humble/CERAMIC(A)/HUMUS(A)
humid/AMITY
humiliate/CERAMIC(A)/HUMUS(A)
humus/CERAMIC(A)/HUMUS(A)
hundred/MITT
hunger/CINCTURE(A)
hunker/CUP
hunt/CLIMATE(A)
hurdle/HOARD
hurl/HURRY
hurry/HORUS/HURRY/SCURRILOUS
hurst/ELMHURST
hush, -ed/HESITANT/HUSH
hussar/ACCELERATE/CAR
hustle/HASTE
hut/CHAISE/HEAD
hutch/HOUSE
hydathode/WET
hydra/WET
hydrant/WET
hydraulic/HOLLOW
hydro-/WET
hydrous/WET
hyena/HYOSCYAMINE(A)
hygiene/HYGIENE(A)
hylozoism/ELMHURST
hymen/SEAM
hyoscyamine/HYOSCYAMINE(A)
hyosine/HYOSCYAMINE(A)
hyper-/GIBBON/SUPER
hypno-/SOFA
hypnosis/INSOMNIA/SOFA
hypocrisy/GARBLE/SECRET
hypotaxis/TACTICIAN
hypothecate/BET
hypothermia/BURN
hypso-/GIBBON
hyssop/HYSSOP/SEEP
hysterectomy/STYLE
hysteria/STYLE
hysterical/STYLE
hystero-/STYLE
i/I
ibis/IBIS
iceberg/BARRIO
ichthy-/HADDOCK
icon/COIN
iconography/SCRAPER
idea/IDEA
idiom/SUICIDE
idiot/SUICIDE
if/IF
igloo/HOLLOW
igneous/IGNITION(A)

ignite/IGNITION(A)
ignition/IGNITION(A)
ignitron/IGNITION(A)
ignorant/EYE/KENNING(A)
ignore/EYE/KENNING(A)
il-/ILLEGAL(A)
ilang-ilang/ELM
ill-/ILLEGAL(A)/HEALTH
illation/ATLAS
illegal/ILLEGAL(A)
illicit/ILLEGAL(A)
illuminate/LIGHT
illustrate/LIGHT
im-/ANEMIC
imbrue/BURN
imitate/DUMMY
immense/METER
immix/MIX
immoderate/METER
immodest/METER
immolate/MILL
immune/MUNIFICENT(A)
impart/PART
impel/PULSE(A)
imperative/PREPARE
imperial/PREPARE
impinge/CRUCIFIX
implacable/FLAKE
implement/FULFILL
importune/FERRY
impose/AFTER
impound/PENETRATE
impress/PRESS
imprint/PRESS
improve/IS
impugn/PUGNACIOUS
in use/USE
in-/ANEMIC/ILLEGAL(A)/INERT
-in/INSOMNIA
in/PENETRATE
incandescent/CAUTERIZE
incantation/KEEN
incarcerate/CELL/COURT/INCARCERATE(A)
incarnate/CHROME
incendiary/CAUTERIZE
incense/CAUTERIZE
incentive/KEEN
incertitude/SECRET
incest/CASTRATE/CHASTE/SCISSORS
inch/EACH/UNIQUE(A)
incident/DECAY
incinerate/GNAW
incise/SCISSORS
incite/INCITE
inclement/CLEMENCY(A)
incline/CLIMATE/SLALOM
incredible/CREED
incredulous/CREED
incubate/SUCCUBUS
inculcate/HOOF
incumbent/SUCCUBUS
incunabula/HAUNT
incur/ACCELERATE/CAR
indemnify/DAMN
indemnity/DAMN
indent/TINE
indict/SYNDICATE
indigenous/ORIGIN
indomitable predominance/MADONNA

induce, -ed/SEDUCE
inert/ARITHMETIC/INERT
inertia/INERT
infamous/PHONETICS
infarct/PARK
infelicity/FRUCTIFY
infer/FERRY/MAT
infernal/MAT
inferno/MAT
infidelity/FAITH
infix/CRUCIFIX
inflate/BLOAT
inflection/COUPLE
influence/BLOAT
infra-/MAT
ingenious/ORIGIN
ingenius/GENIUS
ingenuity/GENIUS
ingenuous/ORIGIN
inhabit/GIVE(A)
inhibit/GIVE(A)
inimical/AMITY
inject/JET
injest/GESTURE(A)
injunction/JUXTAPOSE
injury/JURISDICTION
inn/INN(A)
innate/ORIGIN
innocent/NICK/NOXIOUS
innocuous/NICK/NOXIOUS
innovate/NEW
innuendo/NOD
inquire/QUERY
inquiry/QUERY
inquisition/QUERY
insect/SAXON
insert/SERIES/SOW
insignia/SIGN(A)
insinuate/SIN
insinuous/SIN
insomnia/ILLEGAL(A)/INSOMNIA/NO/
    NUMB/SENILE
inspect/SCOPE
inspire/SPIRIT
install/INSTALL/SEAT/STILL(A)
installment/INSTALL
instigate/TACK
instinct/TACK
instruct/DESTROY(A)/SOW
insuperable/SUPER
integer/GATHER
integrate/GATHER
intellectually/ELECT
intelligent/ELECT
intend/EXTEND(A)
intercede/PRECEDE
intercourse/ACCELERATE/CAR
interest/IS
intergalactic/GALAXY
interject/JET
intermediate/MEZZANINE(A)
internecine/NOXIOUS
interogative/RACK
interpolate/PULSE(A)
interpret/SPREAD
interrogate/URGE
interrogative/URGE
interrupt/TROPHY
intersect/SAXON

intersperse/DIASPORA(A)
intransigent/HEGEMONY
intrepid/SCARE
intricate/DRUDGERY
intrinsic/SHAG
introduce/SEDUCE
introspect/SCOPE
inundate/DURUM(A)/UNDULATION
inure/OPUS(A)
inveigh/CONVEY/VIA
invest/VEST
inveterate/VETERAN
invincible/KIBOSH/VICTOR(A)
invoke/VOCALIZE
involve/WALLOW
iota/IDEA/IOTA/IS/JINX
irascibility/IRE
irate/IRE/RATTLE
ire/CHAR/IRE/ORIOLE
ireland/OBESE
irma/RUM
irrigate/LIQUID
irrupt/TROPHY
is/IS
ischium/ENSCONCE
islam/SLAM
island/ISLAND(A)/BRIO(A)/GRAVE
isometric/METER
-ite/GRAPHITE
item/ADD
iterate/ADD
-itious/GRAPHITE
itty/MITE
-ize/CAUSE
jabiru/IBIS
jacal/HOLLOW
jack/JACK
jackdaws/JACK
jackpot/JACK
jackrabbits/JACK
jade/SYNDICATE
jaguar/CAPRICORN/JUNGLE
jam/COMMON
jamb/KYPHOS
janitor/JANUARY
january/JANUARY
jar/JASPER
jasmine/JASPER
jasper super/SAPPHIRE/JASPER
jerboa/RABBIT(A)
jereed/ROOT
jerek/GHERKKIN(A)
jerk, -ed/JERK/JET
jerky/CHAR
jerusalem/SALVATION
jeshurun/JURISDICTION
jet plane/JET/JERK/JET/KARATE
jetsam/JET
jettison/JET
jetty/JET
jews/JURISDICTION
jib/JIB(A)
jiff/JIFFY(A)
jiffy/JIFFY(A)
jill/GILL(A)
jinni/GENIUS
jinx/IOTA/JINX/JUBILANT
jockey/JACK

jocular/CHUCKLE(A)/JACK
john/JINX
join/COMMON/JUXTAPOSE
joint/JOINT(A)
jointly/JOINT(A)
joke/CHUCKLE(A)/SYNDICATE
jolly/GALA
jonah/JINX
jot/IOTA
journal/DIVINE
journey/DIVINE
joust/JUXTAPOSE
jove/DIVINE/JOVIAL
jovial, -ity/DIVINE/JOVIAL
jowl/GARGLE
joy/GAUDY
jubal/JUBILANT
jubilance/JUBILANT
jubilant/JINX/JOVIAL
jubilant/JUBILANT/JUBILANT
jubilation/JUBILANT
jubilee/JUBILANT
judah/ADORE/JURISDICTION
judaism/ADORE
judge/JURISDICTION/SYNDICATE
judicial/SYNDICATE
judicious/SYNDICATE
juggling/JACK
jugular/JUXTAPOSE
jugum/JUXTAPOSE
juice/SAUCE/SQUAT
juicy/SAUCE
jujitsu/STYLE
julep/RED
julien/GILL(A)
july/DIVINE/JOVIAL
jumble/CONGLOMERATE
junction/JUXTAPOSE
juncture/JUXTAPOSE
jungle/JUNGLE
junta/JUXTAPOSE
jupiter/DIVINE/JOVIAL
jural/JURISDICTION
juridical/JURISDICTION/SYNDICATE
jurisdiction/JURISDICTION/SYNDICATE
jurisprudence/JURISDICTION
jurist/JURISDICTION
jury/JURISDICTION
just/JURISDICTION
justice/SYNDICATE
jut/JET
jutes/JET
juxtapose/GATHER/JOINT(A)/JUXTAPOSE
juxtaposition/JUXTAPOSE
kaaba/CUBE
kaftan/COTTON
kaisar/CZAR/KAISER/SCISSORS
kama sutra/AMITY/AMITY/QUANTITY(A)
kamasutra/SEAM
kame/COMB(A)
kamekaze/HAZE
kamikaze/AMITY
kantar/QUINTET
karate/KARATE/RAKE
karoo/UNICORN
karyo-/GRAIN/UNICORN
karyotin/GRAIN
kasha/ASSASSIN
kate/CATHARTIC(A)

kathleen/CATHARTIC(A)
keel/GARGLE
keen, -ing/CANE/KEEN/SAXON
keep/CABAL(A)/HAVEN(A)
ken/EYE/KENNING(A)
kennel/CANE/CELL/HAUNT
kenning/KENNING(A)
keno/FIN/QUINTET
keratin/UNICORN
kerato-/UNICORN
kerchief/CAPITAL
keren/COIN/CORNER
kerf/CARVE
kermes/WORM
kernel/GRAIN/KERNEL/UNICORN
ketser/CZAR
kettle/CALDRON/KIT
khan/KHAN
khanate/KHAN
kibitz, -ing/KIBITZ/PEGASUS
kibosh/KIBOSH/QUASH/VICTOR(A)
kid/GOAT/KIT/KITTEN
kill/HARM/KILL
killick/SILICON
kin/GENIUS/GENOCIDE(A)/KIN/ORIGIN
kind/KIN/KIND(A)/ORIGIN
kindergarten/GIRDLE/KITTEN/ORIGIN
kindle/CAUTERIZE
kindred/KIN/ORIGIN
kine/COIN
kinetic/COIN
kinfolk/KIN
king/COIN/KHAN/KIN/ORIGIN
kingdom/DAMN/MADONNA
kirtle/CURT
kishke/OBSCURE
kiss/KISS/SAG
kit/CADDY/CALDRON/KIT
kite/KITE
kith/KENNING(A)
kitten/KITTEN/SCANTINESS/TACTICIAN/TALCUM
kittle/TEAT
kitty/CATHARTIC(A)
kiwi/AVIATE
klephto-/APPEND.B
kleptomaniac/KNAVE
kloof/CLEAVER
klotz/CLOT
klutz/CLOT
knacker/HEM/NECK
knapsack/SACK
knave/JANUARY/KNAVE
knee/KNEEL(A)
kneel/KNEEL(A)
knife/CLEAVER/HARROW
knight/HANG/KNAVE
knit/HANG
knock, -ing/KNOCK/NICK
knot/HANG
know/EYE/KENNING(A)
knuckle/ANKLE/KNEEL(A)/KNOCK
kopeck/SYNCOPATION
kosher/COPACETIC
kow tow/DECAY
kowtow/PRECEDE
kreplach/CALIBER
kringle/ORIGIN
kriss/ORIGIN
kudos/HEAD

kugel/CAKE/CYCLE
kummel/APPEND.B
kylix/CHALICE(A)
kyparissos/CYPRESS
kyphos/GIBBON/KYPHOS
labdanum/LOTUS
label/SNAP
labellum/LIVER

labial/LIVER
labile/FALL
labium/LIVER
labret/LIVER
labrum/LIVER
lac/LAQUER(A)
lack/CATSKILL
lackey/HEAD
lacrosse/CROSS
lactate/MILK
lactic/MILK
lacto-/MILK
lacuna/CATSKILL
lad/BROOD(A)/LAD/LOUT(A)
ladanum/LOTUS
ladder/ALLEY
ladt/LID
lagoon/CATSKILL/HOLLOW
lake/CATSKILL/HOLLOW/LOCK(A)
lamb/TOMENTUM(A)
land/EARTH
landscaper/SCABBLE
landsman/MAN
language/DIALECT/LICK/SLANG
lanolin/CAMEL/MILL/TOMENTUM(A)
lapse/SPILL
lapwing/PYRALIDID(A)
laquer/LAQUER(A)
lark/LAUGH
lassitude/LATE
lasso/LOOSE(A)
last(ing)/APPEND.B
last-/LATE
late/LATE
late/LOOSE(A)
latent/LID
latex/WET
lathes/THESIS(A)
latter/LATE
laud/EXULT(A)
laudanium/LOTUS
laugh/LAUGH
laundry/ALBINO/LUNAR(A)
lava/ALBINO/LAVA
lavatory/ALBINO
lave/ALBINO
lavender/ALBINO/CLEAVE
laver/ALBINO
lavish/ALBINO
lax/LOOSE(A)
laxative/LOOSE(A)
lay siege/SIEGE
lazy/LOOSE(A)
leader/SULTAN
leaf/TROPHY
leak/CATSKILL/LIQUID
lean-to/CLIMATE
lean/CLIMATE/SLALOM
lease sl/CONSULT
lease/CONSULT/LOOSE(A)
leash/LOOSE(A)

leather/LEATHER(A)
leave/LIVER/LOVE
leaven/ACCELERATE
lecher/LICK
lechery/NEW
lectern/ELECT
lecture/DIALECT/ELECT
lee/ALKALI/HOLLOW
leech/LEECH/LIQUID
leek/LOCK(A)
leeward/HOLLOW
left/EUROPE
leg/REACH/REGULAR/WALK
legal/ELECT/LEX
legend/ELECT
legible/ELECT
legion/ELECT
legislate/ELECT
legislator/ATLAS/LEX
legitimate/ELECT/LEX
leitmotif/SULTAN
lema/DILEMMA(A)
lemon/PALM
length/REACH
lenient/LATE
leo/LEOPARD
leopard/BRIT(A)/LEOPARD/LOBO/RUMBLE
leper/CALIBER/SCALP
lepido/SCALP
lepoorid/RABBIT(A)
leprechaun/ACCELERATE/CRAW(A)
leprosy/CALIBER/SCALP
lepus/RABBIT(A)
less/IS/LESS(A)
-less/LESS(A)/LOOSE(A)
lessie/LESS(A)
lesson/ELECT
let-/LATE
lethargy/LID
lettuce/MILK
lever/ACCELERATE
levigate/HEGEMONY
leviticus/BICKER(A)
levity/ACCELERATE
levo-/EUROPE
levoduction/EUROPE
lex legislate/LEX
lex/ELECT/LEX/LIQUID
lexical/DIALECT
lexicographer/DIALECT
libido/LOVE
lick/LAQUER(A)/LICK/LIQUID/SLANG
licorice/DELICACY(A)
lid/CLOT/FLEET/LEATHER(A)/LID/SHIELD
lie/DIALECT/WARLOCK(A)
lief/LOVE
liege/LATE
lieutenant/EXTEND(A)
life/LIVER
light out/FLEET/SHIELD/
light/ACCELERATE/ADOLESCENT/DARK/FIRE/
    LIGHT/LUNAR(A)/ORIOLE
lighten/ACCELERATE
lighter/ACCELERATE
ligneous/ELECT
ligule/APPEND.B
lilac/LILAC

lilith/LILAC
lime/ELM
linden/ELM
lingo/DIALECT
linguist/LICK
linguistics/DIALECT/SLANG
lion/LEOPARD/RUMBLE
lip/LIVER
lipo-/LIVER
liquid/ACCELERATE/GILL(A)/LICK/LIQUID
liquify/LIQUID
liquor/LIQUID
liteeth ian/THESIS(A)
litigate/HEGEMONY
litmus/MARINE
litter/LAD
little/LAD/LOUT(A)
liturgy/ORGAN
live/APPEND.B
lively/LIVER
liver/CLEAVE/GALAXY/GALBANUM/LIVER
liverwurst/GUERRILLA
lizard/DINOSAUR(A)
llama/CAMEL
lobe/LIVER
lobo/LOBO
lobster/LOCUST(A)
loch/CATSKILL/HOLLOW/LOCK(A)
lock/LOCK(A)
locket/LOCK(A)
locust/LOCUST(A)
log-/ARITHMETIC
logarithm/ARITHMETIC/DIALECT/ELECT
logic/DIALECT
loiter/LOUT(A)
lonely/UNIQUE(A)
long/REACH
look/EYE
loose/LATE/LESS(A)/LOOSE(A)/SOLVE
loot/RAID/TROPHY
loquacious/DIALECT
lord/SULTAN
los angeles/ANGEL(A)
lose/LOOSE(A)
loss/LESS(A)
lotus/LOTUS
lounge/CLIMATE
loup-garou/LOBO/VIRILE
louse/PARASITE(A)
lout/LOUT(A)
louvre/LOBO
love/LAVA/LIVER/LOVE/VOLUNTEER(A)
low/CALL
loyal/ELECT/LEX
lozenge/SLANG
lubricate/LIVER
lubrication/LIVER
lucid/LIGHT
lucifer/LIGHT/LUNAR(A)
luck/LUCK(A)
lukewarm/ALKALI
luminary/LIGHT
luminous/LIGHT/LUNAR(A)
luna/LUNAR(A)
lunar caustic/LUNAR(A)/ALBINO/LUNAR(A)
lunate/LUNAR(A)
lunatic/LIGHT/LUNAR(A)

lung/ACCELERATE
lupine/LOBO
lust/ESTROGEN(A)/ROTATE
luster/LIGHT/LUNAR(A)
lute/BAT
lycanthorpe/LOBO
lynx/LUNAR(A)
lysis/LOOSE(A)
lyso-/LOOSE(A)
-lyte/LOOSE(A)
-lytic/LOOSE(A)
ma/MAMA
mac/VANDYKE
macabre/MACABRE
mace/MACABRE/MATTOCK(A)
macerate/MASS
maceration/MASS
machete/MACABRE/MATTOCK(A)
machicolate/COLLAR/MACABRE
machine/MACHINE/MIGHT
macho/MASCULINE
macro-/MEGALOMANIAC(A)
mad/MITE
mada/NETHER(A)
madame domineers/MADONNA
madonna/ADONIS/DAMN/MADONNA/TIMBER
maelstrom/MILL/SERUM
maestro/MEGALOMANIAC(A)/SATRAP
magazine/ENCASE/HOUSE/MAGAZINE
maggot/MITE
magi/MAGIC
magic/GUESS/MAGIC
magisterial/MEGALOMANIAC(A)
magistrate/MEGALOMANIAC(A)/SATRAP
magnanimous/MEGALOMANIAC(A)
magnate/MEGALOMANIAC(A)
magnificent/MEGALOMANIAC(A)
magnify/MEGALOMANIAC(A)
magniloquent/MEGALOMANIAC(A)
magnitude/MEGALOMANIAC(A)
magnum/MEGALOMANIAC(A)
maharajah/MEGALOMANIAC(A)/RACK
maharani/RACK
mahatma/MEGALOMANIAC(A)
mahout/METER
mail/MEET
maim/MAIM
main/MACHINE/MIGHT
maintain/EXTEND(A)/MAN/MOON
majesty/SATRAP
major/MEGALOMANIAC(A)
mal-/MALIGN
malady/MALIGN
malaria/AIR(A)
male/MARRY(A)/MASCULINE
malediction/MALIGN
malefactor/MALIGN
malevolent/MALIGN/VOLUNTEER(A)
malice/MALIGN
malicious/MALIGN
malign/MALIGN/ORIGIN
malleable/MILL
mallemuck/MALIGN
mallet/MILL
malleus/MILL
malm/MILL
malt/MILL
maltha/MILL
mama/ABBOT/AMAH(A)/MAMA

mammalia/MAMA
mammon/MONEY
mammy/AMAH(A)
man/AMENABLE/MAN/MANNER/MASCULINE/
    MOON/NUMBER
manacle/MAN/MOON
manage/MAN/MOON
-mancy/MOON
mandarin/MOON
mandate/MAN/MONEY/MOON
maneuver/MAN/MOON/OPUS(A)
mangle/MAIM
mania/MOON
maniac/MOON
manicure/MAN/MOON
manifest/MAN/MOON
manifold/COUPLE
manikin/KITTEN/MAN
manilla/MALIGN
manipulate/MAN/MOON
mankind/MAN
mannequin/MAN
manner/MAN/MANNER/MONEY/MOON
mantic/MOON
manticore/MILL
mantis/MOON
mantra/MOON
manual/MAN/MOON
manufacture/FACULTY/MAN/MOON
manure/MAN/MOON/OPUS(A)
manuscript/MAN/MOON
many/MANY/MUNIFICENT(A)
map/MAP
mar/MARBLE(A)
maraschino/MARINE
marasmus/MILL
marble/MARBLE(A)
march/MARK/MAROON
marchioness/MARK
mare/MARE(A)/MARINE/PEGASUS
margaret/MARINE
margaric/GRAIN
margarine/GRAIN/MARBLE(A)/MARINE
margarite/GRAIN/MARBLE(A)
margin/MARK
marguerite/MARINE
marigold/MARINE
marina/MARINE
marinade/MARINE
marinara/MARINE
marinate/MARINE
marine/GRAIN/MARBLE(A)/MARINE/RAM
marionette/MARINE
marital/MAROON/MARRY(A)/MORON
maritime/MARINE
marjoram/MARJORAM(A)
mark/MARK
market/MARKET
marking/MARK
markka/MARK
maroon/CRIMSON/MAROON
marquee/MARK
marquis/MARK
marrow/MARROW(A)
marry/MARRY(A)/MORON
mars/MAROON
marsh/MARINE
marshal/MARE(A)
mart/MARKET
martian/MAROON

marvel/MIRROR
mary/MARINE
mascara/MASK
mascot/MASK
masculine/MASCULINE/MOON
mash/MIX/SMASH
mashie/MATTOCK(A)
mashy/MATTOCK(A)
mask/MASK
mason/MATTOCK(A)
masque/MASK
masquerade/MASK
mass/EMISSARY/MASS
massachusett/MASS/AT
massacre/MATTOCK(A)
massage/MASS
masseter/MASS
massif/MASS
massive/MASS
mast/MUSK
mastaba/STABLE
mastabah/MASTABAH(A)
master/MEGALOMANIAC(A)/SATRAP
masterbate/MASS
mastic/MASS
masticate/MASS
mastie/MATTOCK(A)
mastiff/MOON
mastodon/MASS
mastoidectomy/MASS
mat/CHECKMATE/MAT/NETHER(A)/
    UNDULATION
mata/MATHEMATICS(A)
matador/CHECKMATE
match/MEEK
mate/MEAT(A)
material/MAMA
maternal/MAMA
mathematics/MATHEMATICS(A)/MOON
matin/DAWN/SANGRIA
matinee/DAWN/SANGRIA
matrass/MATTOCK(A)
matrix/MAMA
matted matte/MAT
matter/MAMA
mattock/MATTOCK(A)
mattress/MAT
maul/MILL
maumee/OCEAN(A)
maund/MONEY
maw/MAW(A)
maximum/MEGALOMANIAC(A)
may/MACHINE/MAMA/MEGALOMANIAC(A)/
    MIGHT
maybe/MACHINE
mayhem/MAIM
mayst/MACHINE
mazaedium/MASS
mazard/MAZARD(A)
me/I/ME/UNIQUE(A)
mead/DAMP(A)/MUSK
meager/MEEK
meal/METER/MILL
mealie/MILL
mealies/MILL
mean/MANY/MEANING/MEZZANINE(A)/
    MUNIFICENT(A)
meaning/MEANING/MINISTER
means/NAVY
measles/SESAME

measure/MEASURE
meat/MEAT(A)/MUSK
mechanic/MACHINE
mechanical/MACHINE
mechanism/MACHINE
mechano-/MACHINE
meddle/MIX
media/VIA
medial/MEZZANINE(A)
median/MEZZANINE(A)
mediate/METER/MEZZANINE(A)
medical/METER
medicate/METER
medicine/METER
medico/METER
medieval/MEZZANINE(A)
mediocre/MEZZANINE(A)
meditate/METER
mediterranean/MEZZANINE(A)
medium/MEZZANINE(A)
mediurge/DEMOCRAT
medley/MIX
meech/MEEK
meek/MEEK/MUCK
meekness/MEEK
meerschaum/MARINE
meet/MEET
mega-/MEGALOMANIAC(A)
megalo-/MEGALOMANIAC(A)
megalomaniac/CAMEL/MEGALOMANIAC(A)
megalopolis/METROPOLIS
meiosis/MINISTER
melancholy/GALL/HALO
melange/MIX
meld/MELODRAMA
melee/MILL
melic/MELODRAMA
melisma/MELODRAMA
mellifluous/BLOAT/MELODRAMA
melodrama/MEET/MELODRAMA
melodramatic/MELODRAMA
melody/BID/MELODRAMA
melon/PALM
melt/MILL
memento/MEANING/MOON
memorialize/SAMURAI
memory/SAMURAI
men/MAN
menarch/MOON
menopause/METER/MOON
menses/MOON
menshevik/MINISTER
menstruate/MOON
mental/MATHEMATICS(A)/MOON
mention/MOON
mentor/MOON
menu/MINISTER
mercantile/MARKET
mercenary/MARKET
mercer/MARKET
merchant/MARKET
mercury/MARKET
mercy/CLEMENCY(A)/MARKET
mere/MARINE
meridian/DIVINE/MEZZANINE(A)
merit/AMERICA
mermaid/MARINE
mescaline/MUSK
mesh/MIX

meso-/MEZZANINE(A)
mesolithic/MEZZANINE(A)
mesosphere/MEZZANINE(A)
mesquite/MUSK
mess/EMISSARY
message/EMISSARY
messiah/SOAK
mestizo/MIX
metal/METAL(A)
metallurgy/ORGAN
metaphor/FERRY/SUFFER
metaphrase/PHRASE
metatarsus/MEZZANINE(A)
metathesis/MEZZANINE(A)
mete/MATTOCK(A)/METER/MODE
meter/MATHEMATICS(A)/MEASURE/METER
-meter/METER
meter/MEZZANINE(A)
metheglin/METER
methylene/ELMHURST/MUSK
metro-/MAMA
metronome/METER
metropolis/AVIATE/BARRIO/METROPOLIS/
      VILLA(A)
-metry/METER
mezuzah/MEZZANINE(A)
mezzanine/MEZZANINE(A)
mezzo-/MEZZANINE(A)
miami/OCEAN(A)/WET
mianus/OCEAN(A)
mickle/MEGALOMANIAC(A)
microbe/HYGIENE(A)/VIVID
microfiche/CRUCIFIX
middle/MEZZANINE(A)
midge/MITE
midriff/CRAW(A)
miesa/EMISSARY
migee/MAW(A)
might/MACHINE/MIGHT
migrain/UNICORN
milch/MILK
milchig/MILK
mild/MILL
milieu/MEZZANINE(A)
milium/MILL
milk, -ing/BONNY(A)/GALAXY/MILK
mill/MARBLE(A)/MILL/MOLAR/TALCUM
millennium/MANY/SUN
millet/MILL
millicent/AMERICA
millimeters/MANY
milling/MILL
million/MANY
millstones/MOLAR
milt/MILL
mince/MINISTER/MUNIFICENT(A)
mind/MATHEMATICS(A)/MEANING/MOON
minerva/MOON
minestrone/MINISTER
mini-/MINUS
minimum/MINUS
minister/MEANING/MINISTER/MINUS
ministry/MINISTER
minor/MINUS
minotaur/TAURUS
mint/MONEY/MOON
minus/MANY/MINISTER/MINUS/MUNIFICENT(A)
minusclue/MINUS
minute/MINISTER/MINUS
miosis/MYSTERY

miot/MASCULINE
miothar/MOTHER(A)

miracle/MIRROR
mirage/MIRROR
mire/MARINE
mirror/MIRROR
mis-/MINUS/MISS
misanthrope/MISANTHROPE
miscegenation/MIX/ORIGIN
miscellaneous/MIX
mischief/CAPITAL
miscreant/CORE
mishmash/MIX
misogamist/MISANTHROPE
misogynist/MISANTHROPE/NOOK
misoneism/NEW
misraq/RISE
miss, -ed/MISS
missile/EMISSARY
mission/EMISSARY
missive/EMISSARY
mistake/MISS
mister/MEGALOMANIAC(A)/SATRAP
mistress/SATRAP
mite/MITE
mitia/MASCULINE
mitt/GOVERN/MITT/MOON/QUANTITY(A)/
    QUINTET/RAKE
mitten/MEZZANINE(A)/MITT
mix/MIX
mixture/MIX
mizzen/MEZZANINE(A)
mizzenmast/MEZZANINE(A)
mnemonic/MOON
moan/MEANING
moat/MOAT/TUMOR(A)
moby dick/HADDOCK
moccasin/MAGAZINE
mock/MOCK
modal/METER
mode/METER/MODE
model/DUMMY/METER/MODE
modern/METER
modest/METER
modicum/METER
modify/METER
modiolus/METER
modulate/METER
module/METER
mohave/AVIATE
moil/MILL
moist/MASS/MEEK/MUSK
moke/MARE(A)
molar/MILL/MOLAR
mold-/METER
mold/MILL
molder/MILL
mole-/MILL
mole/MOLE(A)
molecule/MOLE(A)
molest/MOLE(A)
mollify/MILL
mollusk/MILL

molotov cocktail/OF(A)
mom/MAMA
momentous/NOD
momentum/NOD
momma/MAMA

mommy/MAMA
monad/MINISTER
monarchy/ARCHITECT/REICH
monastery/MINISTER
monetary/MONEY
money/MANY/MEANING/METER/MINUS/
    MONEY/MOON/NUMBER/SUMMON
monitor/MOON
monk/MINISTER
monkey/MAN
mono-/MINISTER
monocle/EYE
monseignior/SENILE
monster/MONEY/MOON
month/METER/MOON
monument/MOON
mood-/METER
mookat/MITE
moon/MAN/MEASURE/METER/MONEY/
    MOON/NUMBER
moor/MARINE
moot/MEET
mop/MAP
moraine/RUM
moratorium/WEAK
moratory/WEAK
morbid/MARBLE(A)
mordant/MILL
more/RUM
morello/MARINE
morgen/MARBLE(A)
moribund/MILL
morning/MARBLE(A)
moron/MARRY(A)/MORON/NEW
morro/RUM
morrow/MARBLE(A)
morsel/MARBLE(A)/MILL
mortal/CHECKMATE/CZAR/MARBLE(A)/MILL
mortar/MARBLE(A)/MILL/MORTAR
mortgage/CHECKMATE/FAITH/WED
mortician/CHECKMATE
mortify/CHECKMATE
mortuary/CHECKMATE
morula/MARINE
mosaic/MOON/MOSAIC(A)
moschatel/MUSK
moslem/SLAM
moss/MARINE
mote-/METER
mote/MUST(A)
moth/MITE
mother/MAMA/MOTHER(A)
motif/NOD
motion/NOD
motive/NOD
motley/TILE
motor/NOD
motte/DUNE(A)
mottled/TILE
mouchoir/MOUCHOIR(A)
moulin/MILL
mourn/SAMURAI
mousse/MUSK
moustache/MASS
mouth/MASS
much/MEGALOMANIAC(A)
mucilage/MEEK
muck/MEEK/MUCK
muco-/MEEK

mucus/MEEK/MUCK
mud/DEMOCRAT
muggy/MEEK
mulberry/MARINE
mulch/MILL
mule/PEGASUS
mull/MILL
muller/MILL
mulligan/MULLIGAN(A)
mullion/MOLE(A)
multiple/COUPLE
multiplication/MANY
multiply/COUPLE
multitude/MANY
municipal/MUNIFICENT(A)
munificence/MUNIFICENT(A)
munificent/MUNIFICENT(A)
mural/MOLE(A)
murder/CHECKMATE/MARBLE(A)/MILL
murky/MARBLE(A)
murmur/MURMUR(A)
murrain/MILL
murrey/MARINE
musaceous/MUSK
muscadel/MUSK
muscadine/MUSK
muscat/MUSK
muscatel/MUSK
muscle/MUSCLE/MUSK
muscovado/MUSK
muse/MOON
museum/MOON
mushy/MUSK
music/MIX/MOON/MUSK/SOUND
musk deer/MUSK
musk melon/MUSK
musk ox/MUSK
musk rose/MUSK
musk/MUSK/SYCAMORE
muskeg/MUSK
muskrat/MUSK
musky/MUSK
muslim/SLAM
musquash/MUSK
must/MARINE/METER/MUST(A)
mustaba/STUBBORN
mustabah/MASTABAH(A)
mustang/MIX
mustard/MARINE
muster/MONEY/MOON
musty/MEEK
mutchkin/METER
mute/DUMB/STEM
mutt/DINGO(A)
mutter/DUMB
mutton/MILL
muzhik/MASCULINE
-mycete/MEEK
myco-/MEEK
mylonite/MILL
myna/MEAT(A)
myopia/MYSTERY/SPY
myron/MYRTLE
myrrh/MARINE/MYRTLE
myrtaceous/MYRTLE
myrtle/MYRTLE
mystery/MINISTER/MYSTERY/STEAL
nacelle/NAVY
nadir/MAT

nag/AGONY/NAG
nail/SAXON
naive/ORIGIN
name/MEANING/MONEY
nanna/MAMA
nanny/MAMA
nap/HEM/NIP
napery/MAP
napkin/MAP
nappe/MAP
narrate/KENNING(A)
nasal/NOZZLE
nascent/ORIGIN
naso-/NOZZLE
nasty/TINE
natal/ORIGIN
natation/NOD
nathan/THESIS(A)
nation/GENOCIDE(A)/ORIGIN
native/ORIGIN
natron/NITROGEN
nature/ORIGIN
naught/INSOMNIA
nausea/NAVY
nautical/NAVY
nautilus/NAVY
naval/NAVY
nave/NAVY
navel orange/NAVY
navel/NAVY
navicular/NAVY
navigate/HEGEMONY/NAVY
navy/NAVY
nay/INSOMNIA
nebula/FALL/PALL
nebulous/PALL
necessary/PRECEDE
neck/CINCTURE(A)/GROAN/HANG/HEM/
    NECK/SCRUFF
necro-/NOXIOUS
necromancy/NOXIOUS
necropolis/METROPOLIS
nectar/NOXIOUS
nectarine/NOXIOUS
nee/ORIGIN
need/CHECKMATE
needle/TINE
nefarious/INSOMNIA
neglect/ELECT/INSOMNIA
negligent/INSOMNIA
negotiate/INSOMNIA
neither/INSOMNIA/WHO
nekton/NOD
neo-/NEW
neon/NEW
neoteric/NEW
nest/MAT/NETHER(A)/NOSTALGIA
nether/MAT/NETHER(A)
netherlands/NETHER(A)
netherworld/NETHER(A)
nettle/TINE
neuter/INSOMNIA
never/INSOMNIA
new/MORON/NEW/NOW
newel/HEM/NECK
niagara/CATSKILL
nib/NIB/NIP/PENGUIN/RABBIT(A)
nibble/CANE/HEM/NIB
nice/SAXON/SCHIZOPOD(A)

niche/NETHER(A)/NOOK
nick/HANG/NICK/NOXIOUS
nickel/BRASS
nicking/NOOK
nidus/NETHER(A)
niece/VANDYKE
niegoon/CHANGE
night/NIGHT(A)
nightinggale/CRY
nightmare/MARBLE(A)/MILL
nihilism/INSOMNIA
nike/SANGRIA
nil/INSOMNIA
nile/INERT
nimiety/INSOMNIA
nine/NOON(A)
niothar/MOTHER(A)
nip/HEM/NIB/NIP/PENGUIN
nipa/NIP
nipper/NIP
nipple/NIB/NIP
nippy/NIP
nisi/SNORKEL
nisus/NUISANCE(A)
niter/NITROGEN
niton/NITROGEN
nitrates/NITROGEN
nitric/NITROGEN
nitro-/NITROGEN
nitrogen/NITROGEN
nitrous/NITROGEN
no/ANEMIC
no/INSOMNIA/NO/SLUDGE
noble/KENNING(A)
nock/HEM/NECK
nocti-/NIGHT(A)
nocturnal/NIGHT(A)
nod/NOD/WANDER
node/DUNE(A)
noel/ORIGIN
noesis/NOUS(A)
noise/NAVY/SOUND
nomenclature/CALL
non-/INSOMNIA
nona-/NOON(A)
nonchalant/ALKALI
none/INSOMNIA/UNIQUE(A)
noo/NOW
nook/HEM/NECK/NOOK
noon/NOON(A)
nor/INSOMNIA
normal/KENNING(A)
nose/NOZZLE
nosh/GNAW
nostalgia/NOSTALGIA
nostril/NOZZLE
not/INSOMNIA
notar/MUST(A)
notary public/NOTARY/NOTARY
notch/SAXON
note/KENNING(A)/NOTARY
nothing/INSOMNIA
notice/NOTARY
notify/KENNING(A)
notion/KENNING(A)
notorious/KENNING(A)
notornis/MAT/NETHER(A)
notun/EMISSARY
nougat/HEM/NECK

noumenon/NOUS(A)
nous/NOUS(A)
nova/NEW
novation/NEW
novel/NEW
novelty/NEW
november/NOON(A)
novena/NOON(A)
novice/NEW
now/NEW/NOW
noxious/NICK/NOXIOUS/NUISANCE(A)
noyade/NOXIOUS
nozzle/NOZZLE/SNAP
nubile/NYMPHET(A)
nucellus/NECK
nucleus/HEM/NECK
nuisance/NICK/NOXIOUS/NUISANCE(A)
nullify/INSOMNIA
numb/INSOMNIA/NUMB
number/MANY/MONEY/MOON/NUMBER
numen/NOD
nun/MAMA
nuptial/NYMPHET(A)
nut/HEM
nutation/NOD
nutria/WET
nuts/BOTANY/NUTS/NUTS
nuzzle/NOZZLE
nymph/NYMPHET(A)
nymphet/NYMPHET(A)
nymphomania/NYMPHET(A)
nyx/NIGHT(A)
oath/OATH/SOUTH
obeah/OBI
obedience/OBEDIENCE/OPUS(A)
obese/FAT/OBESE
obi/OBI
obit/OBITUARY
obituary/OBITUARY/VIVID
object/JET
oblate/ATLAS
obnoxious/NICK/NOXIOUS
oboe/BAMBOO(A)/BIBLE/OBOE
obscure/OBSCURE/SCORCH
obsequious/SHAG
obsession/SEAT
obstreperous/SPARROW
obstruct/DESTROY(A)/SOW
obtain/EXTEND(A)
obtest/TERZA
obvious/CONVEY/VIA
obvolute/WALLOW
ocarina/AVIATE
occasion/DECAY
occult/CLOT
occur/ACCELERATE/CAR/OCCUR
occurances/OCCUR
ocean/CANE/OCEAN(A)
ochlocracy/OCHLOCRACY(A)
ochlocrat/OCHLOCRACY(A)
ochlophobia/OCHLOCRACY(A)
octave/EIGHT
october/EIGHT
octogenarian/EIGHT/MITT
octogon/EIGHT
octopus/BOOT(A)/EIGHT
octuple/COUPLE
ocular/EYE
oculist/EYE

ode/ADORE/BID/RHAPSODY
odin/ADONIS
odious/HATE
-odon/TINE
odor/CAUTERIZE
of/OF(A)
-of/OF(A)
off/AFTER/AVIATE/OF(A)
-off/OF(A)
offal/FALL/OF(A)/PALL
offend/POINT
offense/POINT
offer/FERRY
ogee/GIBBON
ogive/GIBBON
ogle/EYE/SIGN
ogre/COLOSSUS/OGRE
oil/SESAME
oken/OCEAN(A)
old/ALUMNI/LAD
olfactory/REEK
olive/APPEND.B
oliver/ALBINO
ombudsman/BID/MAZARD(A)
omega/MEGALOMANIAC(A)
omen/AMENABLE/OMEN/SEMANTIC
omer/CERAMIC(A)
omit/EMISSARY
omniscient/SAXON
onager/ASININE
once/UNIQUE(A)
oncology/NICK
one/EACH/I/UNIQUE(A)
onerous/MASS
-ont/IS
onto-/IS
onus/MASS
oology/AVIATE
ooze/BISON/OOZE/SAUCE/SQUAT
opaque/OPAQUE
opera/OPUS(A)
operate/OPUS(A)
ophite/PYTHON
ophitic/PYTHON
-opia/SPY
opine/BONE/OPINION(A)
opinion,-s/OPINION(A)/BONE
opportune/FERRY
opportunity/PORE
oppose/AFTER
oppress/PRESS
-opsis/SPY
-opsy/SPY
opt/CAPITALISM/OPINION(A)
opthalmic/SPY
opthalmology/SPY
optic/SPY
optimum/OPUS(A)
option/CAPITALISM
optmistic/CAPITALISM
optometry/SPY
opulent/OPUS(A)
opus/OPUS(A)
or/OR
oracle/ORIOLE
orange/PALM
orbit/CHROME
orc/ORCHESTRA
orchard/COURT/GIRDLE

orchestra/ORCHESTRA/SCURRILOUS
orchestrate/ORCHESTRA
orchid/ORCHESTRA
order/HERD
orees/BORAX(A)
orestes/OROLOGY
organ/ARACHNID(A)/ARCHITECT/ORGAN
organization/ORGAN
organized/ORGAN
organon/ORGAN
orgy/ORGAN
ori/ORIGIN
orient/ORIENTATION
oriental, -s/ORIENTATION/ORIENTATION
orientation/ORIENTATION/ORIGIN/UMBRELLA(A)
origin/GENIUS/GERM/KIN/ORIENTATION/ORIGIN
original/ORIENTATION
originating/ORIGIN
oriode/ORIOLE
oriole/ORIOLE
ormer/MARINE
oro-/OROLOGY
orogenesis/OROLOGY
orogeny/OROLOGY
orography/OROLOGY
orology/CULMINATE/OROLOGY
orometer/OROLOGY
orphan/TROPHY
ort/EXIT
orthodox/IDEA/ORTHODOX/TACTICIAN
os/OSTEOMA
osar/MOTHER(A)
oscine/KEEN
osmatic/SMELL(A)
osmium/SMELL(A)
osprey/AVIATE/OSTEOMA
ossein/OSTEOMA
ossifrage/OSTEOMA
ossify/OSTEOMA
ossis/OSTEOMA
ossuary/OSTEOMA
ost/OSTEOMA
ostensible/EXTEND(A)
osteoma/MEZZANINE(A)/OSTEOMA/OYSTER
osteon is/OSTEOMA
osteotomy/OSTEOMA
ostracize/OSTEOMA
ostrich/AVIATE
other/OR
otology/AUSCULATE
otter/WET
ounce/LUNAR(A)/UNIQUE(A)
-ous/FATUITY(A)
oust/EXIT
out/EXIT
outcast/CAST
outlaw/EXIT
outskirts/SKIRT
-ov/OF(A)
ova/OF(A)
oval/AVIATE
ovary/AVIATE/OF(A)
oven/OVEN(A)
over/ABERRATION/AVERAGE/CURB/FERRY/FOR/
    OVER/PARASITE(A)/PROTOTYPE/SUMMIT/
    SUPER/VEER
overriding/RAID
ovibos/OVIS
ovine/OVIS

ovis/OVIS
ovule/AVIATE
ovum/AVIATE
-ow/OF(A)
owe/GIVE(A)
owl/ULULATION/WAIL
owlet/ULULATION
owlish/ULULATION
oxygen/ACME
oxymoron/MORON
oyster/OSTEOMA/OYSTER
ozone/SMELL(A)
pa/ABBOT/MAMA/OF(A)
pace/BASIS/CRUCIFIX/PACE/PATIO
pacific/CRUCIFIX
pacify/CRUCIFIX
pack/PACK/PACKET(A)
package/PACKET(A)
packet/PACK/PACKET(A)
pad/FAT/PAD
padre/PATRON
pagan/CRUCIFIX
page/CRUCIFIX/PAUCITY
pageant/CRUCIFIX
pail/VIAL(A)
paillasse/PULVERIZE(A)
pain/PENGUIN
paint/PANE
pale/PALL
palea/PULVERIZE(A)
pall-mall/BOULDER/MILL
pall/PALL
pallor/PALL
palm/PALM
palomino/PALL
palpable/FLUTTER/PSALM
palpebral/FLUTTER/PSALM
palpitate/FLUTTER/PSALM/PYRALIDID(A)
palter/PALTER(A)
paltry/PALTER(A)
palynology/PULVERIZE(A)
pam/LOVE
pamper/OBESE
pan-/POINT
pan-american/POINT
pan/PANE/PANIC/PATIO/PENETRATE
panache/PANIC
pandemic/DEMOCRAT
pane/PANE/PANIC/PENETRATE/
    PENULTIMATE/POINT
panegyric/CULL(A)
panel/PANE
pang/PENGUIN
pangolin/GYRE
panic/PANE/PANIC/POINT
panicle/FIN/PANE/PANIC
panocha/PANIC
panoche/PANIC
panorama/ORIENTATION/PANE
pant/PANE
panther/BRIT(A)/LEOPARD
papa/ABBOT
papaw/BAUBLE
papaya/BAUBLE
paper/BIBLE
papillon/FLUTTER/PYRALIDID(A)
paprika/PEPPER
papyrus/BIBLE
para-/FOR/PARASITE(A)/FRUIT/PREPARE

parachute/PREPARE
paradise/FOR/FRUIT/SPREAD/VEER
paradox/ORTHODOX
paraffin/PAUCITY
paragraph/CARVE/SCRAPER
paralysis/LOOSE(A)
paramount/FOR
paramour/FOR
paranoia/NOUS(A)
paraphernalia/FERRY
paraphrase/PHRASE
parasite/ABERRATION/PARASITE(A)/SATISFY
parasol/PREPARE
parataxis/TACTICIAN
parcel/DISPERSE/PARK
parchment/SCALP
pard/LEOPARD
pardon/DATA(A)/ENDOW
pare/BARK(A)
parent/FRUIT/PREPARE
paresis/JET
parg iosh/BORAGE(A)
parget/JET
park/PARK/SPREAD
parka/PLUCK
parking/PARK
parody/BID
-parous/FRUIT
-parous/PREPARE
parquet/PARK
parr/PUERILE
parrot/SPARROW
part/BROOD(A)/DISPERSE/PART/PATRON/
    PLATOON/POUT/SPREAD
particle/PART
particular/PART
pas/PATIO
pass/PATIO
passerline/SPARROW
passion/ASPIRE
pasta/PITA
paste/PITA
pastel/PITA
pastor/FAT/OBESE
pasture/FAT
patch/BASTE(A)/PUTSCH
patches/PIECE
patchouli/PATCHOULI
pate/PATE
patella/PATIO
paten/PATIO
patent/PATIO
path/PATIO
patina/PATIO
patio/PACE/PATIO
patois/BID
patriarch/PATRON
patriarchal/PART
patrician/PATRON
patricide/PATRON
patrilineal/PATRON
patrimony/PATRON
patriot/PATRON
patron/PART/PATRON/POUT
patronize/PATRON
patronymic/PATRON
patroon/PATRON
patulous/PATIO
paucity/PAUCITY/PEDIATRICIAN/PUERILE

pauper/PAUCITY
pause/PATIO
pawn/AFFIDAVIT/PIONEER
pay/CRUCIFIX
peace/CRUCIFIX
peach/MUSK
peacock/AVIATE
pear/FRUIT
pearl/MARBLE(A)
peasant/CRUCIFIX
peck/BEAKER/PACK/PACKET(A)/PICK/POKE(A)
pectin/CRUCIFIX
peculate/BUCKAROO
peculiar/BUCKAROO
pecuniary/BUCKAROO
ped/PEDIATRICIAN
pedagogue/AGONY
pedagogue/HEGEMONY/PEDIATRICIAN
pedantic/PEDIATRICIAN
pederast/PEDIATRICIAN
pedestal/INSTALL/STALK/STILL(A)
pediatrician/BOTANY/FETUS/PEDIATRICIAN
pedo-/PAUCITY
peek/PEEK
peel/BARK(A)/SCALP
peepul/PEPPER
pegasus/AVIATE/PEGASUS
pelage/PILE
pelagic/ARCHIPELAGO/FLAKE
pelago/FLAG
pelican/ARCHIPELAGO
pellet, -s/BALL
pellmell/MIX
pellucid/LIGHT
pelops/PALL
pelt/PILE/PLUCK
peltast/SHIELD
peltate/SHIELD
pelted/BALL
pelvis/PLAZA
pen-/PENULTIMATE
pen/NIB/PENETRATE/PENGUIN
penates/PENETRATE
penchant/PENCHANT/POINT
pencil/PENGUIN
pendragon/PENGUIN
penetrate/PENETRATE/POINT
penetration/PANE
penguin/FIN/NIB/PENGUIN/POINT
penis/PENGUIN
penitus/PENETRATE
pennants/PANIC
penninsula/PENULTIMATE
penny/SCALE
pent/PENETRATE
penta-/FIN
pentateuch/FIN
pentecost/FIN
pentecostal/MITT
penultimate/PENULTIMATE
penumbra/PENULTIMATE
penurious/FIN
peon/PIONEER
pepper/PEPPER
peppercorn/PEPPER
per cent/MITT
per se/SUICIDE
per-/FOR/VEER/VERY(A)
per/FOR

pera/BORAGE(A)
peragh/BORAGE(A)
percentage/MITT
perdition/DATA(A)/ENDOW
pere-ah/PILE
perennial/SUN
peretz/PROTOTYPE
perez/BREACH
perfect/FACULTY
perfidy/BAD/FAITH
perfume/THYME
peri-/VEER
pericardium/CORE
peril/FEAR(A)/PIRATE
periostem/OSTEOMA
periphery/FERRY
periphrasis/PHRASE
peristalsis/INSTALL
perjury/JURISDICTION
perk/FREAK/PERK
perky/PERK
permit/EMISSARY
pernicious/NOXIOUS
peroneal/FERRY
perorate/BORE
perplex/COUPLE
perquisite/QUERY
persecute/SHAG
persevere/VERY(A)
persimmon/PERSIMMON
perspective/SCOPE
perspire/SPIRIT
persuade/HEDONISM
pertain/EXTEND(A)
pesen/PYTHON
pester/PESTER/PRESS
pet/PEDIATRICIAN
petal/PATIO/SPREAD
petard/BREACH/PETARD
petch/PUTSCH
peten/PYTHON
peter/PART
petite/BIT/PEDIATRICIAN
petrel/SPARROW
petrify/PART
petro-/PART
petticoat/PEDIATRICIAN
pettifoy/PEDIATRICIAN
petty/BIT/PEDIATRICIAN
pewter/PEWTER(A)
phallus/BALL/BOULDER
phanak/FINICKY
phanerogam/PANE
phantasm/PANE
phantasmagoria/PANE
phantom/PANE
pharoor/VIAL(A)
pharynx/BORE
phase/PANE
-phasia/PHONETICS
phelogen/BOULDER
pheno-/PANE
phenomenon/PANE
pheromone/FERRY
phial/VIAL(A)
philately/ATLAS
-phile/LOVE
-philia/LOVE
philosemite/LOVE

philosophy/LOVE/SPY/SAVOIR-FAIRE
-philous/LOVE
philter/LOVE
phlegm/FIRE
phloem/BLOAT
phlox/FIRE
phobia/AVIATE
phoneme/PHONETICS
phonetic, -s/PHONETICS
phono-/PHONETICS
phonograph/PHONETICS
-phony/PHONETICS
phore/FERRY
phosphate/PHOSPHORUS
phosphene/PANE
phosphorescent/PHOSPHORUS
phosphorus/PHOSPHORUS/TOPAZ
photo-/PHOSPHORUS
photoelectric/PHOSPHORUS
photography/PHOSPHORUS
phrase/PHRASE/PREACH
phreatic/BURN
phyll/TROPHY
phylloxera/XEROX(A)
physiognamy/KENNING(A)
physo-/FAN
piazza/PLAZA
pica/PAUCITY
picayune/PAUCITY

piccolo/PAUCITY
pick/BEAKER/PICK/POKE(A)
pickax/PICK
picking out/PICK
picot/PAUCITY
pie/OVEN(A)
piece/BIT/DIVIDED/PIECE
piecemeal/METER
pig/FIG
pigeon/JINX
pilar/PILE
pile/PILE/PLUCK
pileate/PILE
pileus/PILE
piliferous/PILE
piliform/PILE
pillage/FORAY(A)/PILE/SCALP
pillion/PILE
pillow/PILE
pilocarpine/PILE
pilose/PILE
pilosity/PILE
pilot/BAT
pilus/PILE
pimpernel/PEPPER
pin/NIP
pince-nez/NOZZLE
pincer/PENGUIN
pinch/FIN
pine/PENGUIN
pineapple/PENGUIN
pinehurst/ELMHURST
pinfold/PENETRATE
pinion/PENGUIN
pink/FINICKY
pinkie/FINICKY
pinnate/PENGUIN
pinnule/PENGUIN
pioneer/PIONEER
pip/OBESE

pipe/BAMBOO(A)/OBOE
piracy/PIRATE
piragua/BARK(A)
piranha/TINE
pirate/PIRATE/PROSTITUTE/PROTOTYPE
pirogue/BARK(A)
pisces/HADDOCK
pit /PIT/BUCKET/PIT/POKE(A)/POUT
pita/PITA/PITCH
pitaron/PREACH
pitch/BISON/PITA/PITCH
pitcher/BEAKER
pitfall/PIT
pithiera/PYTHON
pitiel/PUZZLE
pitman/PIT
pitted/PIT
pituitary/OBESE
pivot/PIVOT
pizazz/PIZAZZ
pizza/PITA
pizzle/PUZZLE
placate/FLAKE
place/PLAZA
placebo/FLAKE
placenta/FLAKE
placid/FLAKE
plagiarize/PLUCK
plagiary/FLAKE
plague/FRUCTIFY
plan/PLAZA
planchet/FLAKE
plane/PLAZA
plank/FLAKE
plant/PLAZA
plantain/PLAZA
plantar/PLAZA
plantigrade/PLAZA
plate/PLAZA
plateau/PLAZA
platform/PLAZA
platitude/PLAZA
platoon/PLATOON
platter/PLAZA
platy/PLAZA
platypus/PLAZA
platz/BURST
plaza/BURST/PLAZA
plea/PLEA
plead/FLAKE/PLEA
pleasant/FLAKE
please/FLAKE
plexus/COUPLE
pliant/COUPLE
-ploid/COUPLE
plotz/BURST
plough/ARCHIPELAGO/FELLAH(A)/FLAG/
    FLAKE/PLOUGH
ploughman/FELLAH(A)
plow/PLOUGH
plowboy/PLOUGH
ploy, -s/PLEA
pluck, -ed/BARK(A)/PILE/PLUCK
plug/FLAG/PLOUGH/PLUG
plum/FRUIT
plume/PLUCK
plush/PILE
pluto/ARCHIPELAGO
pluvial/ARCHIPELAGO

pneuma/FAN
pneumonia/ARCHIPELAGO/FAN
pock/PIT/POKE(A)
pocket/BUCKET/PICK/PIT/VACATE
pockmark/PICK
poco/PAUCITY
poetry/BID/GROAN/IRE/OF(A)
poignant/PENGUIN
point/NIP/PANIC/PENCHANT/PENETRATE/
　　PENGUIN/POINT/WANDER
pointing/PANE
poke/BUCKET/PIT/POKE(A)
pokey/POKE(A)/VACATE
poland/BARRIO
pole/CRUCIFIX
policlinic/METROPOLIS
policy/METROPOLIS
polis/METROPOLIS
politics/METROPOLIS
polity/METROPOLIS
pollen/PULVERIZE(A)
pollex/BLOAT/FLUTTER
pollu/PILE
poltergeist/HATE
poly-/RIFE
polygyny/NOOK
pom pom/PALM
pom/PALM
pomace/PALM
pomade/PALM
pome/PALM
pomegranite/GRAIN
pommel/PALM
pompon/PALM
pond/PENETRATE
pone/PANIC
poniard/PENGUIN/PUGNACIOUS
pontiff/PENGUIN
pony/PAUCITY/PUERILE
pool/PAUCITY
poolkhan/FELLAH(A)
poor/PAUCITY
pope/ABBOT
poppet/BAUBLE
poppycock/OBESE
porch/PORE
porcupine/BURRO/PENGUIN/SPIRE
pore/BORE/PORE/TROPHY
pork/BURRO
porous/PORE
porpoise/BURRO
port/BREACH/FERRY/PORE
portable/FERRY
portage/FERRY
portal/BREACH
portcullis/BREACH
portecochere/BREACH
porter/FERRY
portfolio/FERRY
porthole/BREACH
portiere/BREACH
portray/DRAG/DRAW
posed/PREACH
position/AFTER/OF(A)
positive/AFTER
possess/SEAT
post-/AFTER
post/AFTER
posture/AFTER

pot/VAT
potato/BOTANY
pouch/PIT/POKE(A)
poultice/PULVERIZE(A)
pounce/PUGNACIOUS
pound/PENETRATE
pout/POUT
pouting/POUT
poverty/PAUCITY
powder/PULVERIZE(A)
pox/BUCKET/PIT
praedial/FAITH/WED
prairie/BARRIO
pray/PLEA
prayer/PLEA
pre-/FOR
preach/PHRASE/PREACH
preacher/FLAKE/PREACH
precede/HEAD/PRECEDE
precedence/PRECEDE
precedent/PRECEDE
preceding/OVER
precinct/CINCTURE(A)
precipitate/CAPITAL
precise/SCISSORS
precursor/ACCELERATE/CAR
predator/PIRATE
predatory/PIRATE/TROPHY
predatroy pirates/PIRATE
predecessor/PRECEDE
predicate/SYNDICATE
preface/BID
prefer/FERRY
prefix/CRUCIFIX
pregnant/PRESS
prejudice/JURISDICTION/SYNDICATE
prelate/ATLAS
premier/OVER
premise/EMISSARY
premonition/MOON
preparatory/PREPARE
prepare/PREPARE
preposterous/OF(A)
preppy/PREPARE
prepuce/FAN
prerogative/RACK/URGE
presage/SEEK
prescient/SAXON
preside/SEAT
press/PRESS/PROSTITUTE
pressure/PRESS
presto/BURST
presuming/ASSUME
presumption/ASSUME
presumptuously/ASSUME
pretend/EXTEND(A)
pretext/TECHNICAL
prevail/BARON
previoius/CONVEY/VIA
prey/FORAY(A)
priceless/LESS(A)
primal/OVER
prime/OVER
primitive/OVER
primogeniture/ORIGIN
primordial/OVER
prince/PIRATE/PROTOTYPE
princes/PIRATE
print/PRESS

prior/FOR
privilege/ELECT/LEX
prize/PRIZE
pro-/FOR/FRUIT
pro/FOR
proceed/PRECEDE
proclaim/CALL
proclivity/SLALOM
procumbent/SUCCUBUS
prodigal/HEGEMONY
produce/SEDUCE
profess/BID
proffer/FERRY
progenitor/ORIGIN
progeny/FRUIT/ORIGIN
prognosis/KENNING(A)
program/CARVE/SCRAPER
prohibit/GIVE(A)
project/JET
prolan/FRUIT
prolate/ATLAS
proletarian/FRUIT
prolicide/FRUIT
proliferate/FRUIT
prolific/ALUMNI/FRUIT
prologue/DIALECT/ELECT
promiscuous/MIX
promise/EMISSARY
promote/NOD
propel/PULSE(A)
prophet/PHONETICS
prosecute/SHAG
prospect/SCOPE
prosper/ASPIRE/SUFFICE
prostitute/PROSTITUTE
prot-/PROTOTYPE
protagonist/HEGEMONY/PROTOTYPE
protect/TILE
protein/FOR/PROTOTYPE
protest/TERZA
proto-/FOR/PROTOTYPE
protocol/PROTOTYPE
protoerozoic/FOR
proton/FOR/PROTOTYPE
protoplasm/PROTOTYPE
prototype/PATRON/PROTOTYPE
protozoa/PROTOTYPE
protuberance/BOTANY
proud/IS
provender/GIVE(A)
provoke/VOCALIZE
provost/AFTER
prow/FOR/OVER
proximity/FOR
prune/FRUIT/ROTATE
pry/PORE
psalm/FLUTTER/PSALM/SOUND
psaltery/FLUTTER/PSALM
pseudepigrapha/SCRAPER
psittacosis/TOUCAN
psoriasis/SEAR/SORE
psorosis/SORE
psyche/ASPIRE
psychic/ASPIRE
psycho-/ASPIRE
psychosomatic/SEMANTIC/TUMOR(A)
psylla/PARASITE(A)
pterodactyl/SPREAD
pudendum/VENTRICLE

pudgy/VENTRICLE
puerile/PUERILE
puerperal/PUERILE
pug/FIG/PUGNACIOUS
pugil stick/PUGNACIOUS
pugilism/PUGNACIOUS
pugilist/POKE(A)
pugnacious/PUGNACIOUS/QUINTET
pullet/FRUIT/PAUCITY/PUERILE
pulmonary/ARCHIPELAGO
pulsate/PULSE(A)
pulse/FLUTTER/PULSE(A)/PULVERIZE(A)
pulverize/PULVERIZE(A)
pump/OBOE
punch/FIN/PUGNACIOUS
puncheon/PUGNACIOUS
punctual/PENGUIN
punctuate/PUGNACIOUS
puncture/PENGUIN
pund/PENETRATE
punish/FIN
punjab/FIN
punk/FIN
punkah/FIN
punt/BUTT
puny/ORIGIN
pupil/BAUBLE
puppet/BAUBLE
pure/BARE/BORAX(A)
purge/BORAX(A)
puritan/BORAX(A)
purlieu velt/BARRIO
purport/FERRY
purse/BURSAR(A)
purser/BURSAR(A)
pursue/SHAG
pus/BISON
push/PULSE(A)
pusilaimous/ANIMUS(A)
pusillanimous/PAUCITY
pustule/FAN
putrid/BISON
putsch/PUTSCH
puzzle/PUZZLE/PYTHON
puzzles/PREACH
pygmy/PUGNACIOUS
pylon/PORE
pyralidid/PYRALIDID(A)
pyralioid/SPARROW
pyre/FIRE
pyrene/BARLEY
pyretic/FIRE
pyrites/FIRE
pyromaniac/FIRE
pyroxene/XENOPHOBIA
python/ASP/PYTHON
qnt/QUINTET
qua/WHERE(A)
quadrant/QUARTER
quadrate/QUARTER
quadrille/QUARTER
quadroon/QUARTER
quadruple/COUPLE
quaestor/QUERY
quail/CRY/CURVE
quaint/KENNING(A)
qualm/HARM
quandry/QUANTITY(A)
quant/QUANT(A)

quantitative/QUANTITY(A)
quantity/MITT/QUANTITY(A)
quantum/QUANTITY(A)
quarantine/QUARTER
quarrel/GUERRILLA/QUARTER
quarry/QUARTER/QUERY
quart/QUARTER
quarter/EIGHT/QUARTER
quarto/QUARTER
quartz/SIREN
quash/CASTRATE/CHASTE/KIBOSH/QUASH/
    SCISSORS/VICTOR(A)
quasi/SNORKEL
quatrain/QUARTER
quean/NOOK
queen/NOOK
quell/KILL
querist/QUERY
quern/GRAVE
query/CASEFY(A)/QUERY/SCOUR
quest/QUERY
question/CASEFY(A)/QUERY
quetzal/HEAD
queu/HEAD
quibble/QUIBBLE(A)/WHERE(A)
quiche/CAKE
quick/HYGIENE(A)
quiet/QUIET
quinate/QUINTET
quindecennial/QUINTET
quinine/CINNAMON
quinquagenarian/QUINTET
quinsy/HANG
quint/QUINTET
quintain/QUINTET
quintessence/IS/QUINTET
quintet/FIN/GOVERN/MITT/QUANTITY(A)/
    QUINTET/RAKE
quintile/QUINTET
quintillion/QUINTET
quintuple/COUPLE
quintuplet/QUINTET
quirk/CURVE
quiver/CUBBY
quoin/COIN/CORNER
quorum/WHERE(A)
rabbit/RABBIT(A)
raccoon/CHARACTER/RAKE
race/ROOT/ROTATE
rack/RACK/RAKE/REACH/REGULAR/REICH/URGE
racket/RUCKUS
radical/ROOT
radish/ROOT
radix/ROOT
radula/GRADE
raft/RHAPSODY/RIFE
rafter/RHAPSODY
rag/LAUGH/RUG
rage/IRE
ragnarok/REICH
rahaw/ROOM(A)
raid, -ing/RAID
rail/RACK
raise/RISE
rajah/RACK
rajput/FETUS/PEDIATRICIAN
rake, -ing/CHARACTER/KARATE/RACK/RAKE
ralph/LOBO
ram/RAM/RUM/TOMENTUM(A)

rama/RUM
ramble/ROAM(A)
rambunctious/RED
ramekin/CREAM
ramp/ROAM(A)/RUM
rampage/ROAM(A)/RUM
rampant/RUM
rampart/PREPARE
ramses/RUM
rancid/RAM/REEK
rancor/RAM/REEK
range/REACH
rani/RACK
rank/GRADE/RACK/RAM/REEK
ransack/SEEK
rant/RAVE
rapacious/TROPHY
rape/ROVE/TROPHY
raphe/TROPHY
rapid rapine/TROPHY/PYRALIDID(A)/TROPHY
rapport/FERRY
rapt/TROPHY
rash/GRADE
raskhan irascible/IRE
raspberries/RUCKUS
raspberry/RUCKUS
rasping rustle/RUCKUS
rat/GRADE/SERRATED
ratchet/RUG
rationale/ROTATE
rationalization/ROTATE
rattle/RATTLE/SCARE
rattlesnake/RATTLE
rave/RAVE
raven/CROW/RAVEN/RAVENOUS/ROOF/ROVE/
    SHRIEK/TROPHY
ravenous/CROW/RAVEN/RAVENOUS/
    TROPHY/URGE
ravens/RAVEN
ravine/PORE
raving/RAVE
ravish/TROPHY
raw/RIVALRY
razz/RAZZ(A)/RUCKUS
reach/DIRECTION/RACK/REACH/REGULAR
read/ROOT
ready/RAID
real/RACK
realm/CLIMATE/RACK
reap/RIFE/TROPHY
rearward/ORIENTATION
reason/ROTATE
reave/TROPHY
rebuttal/BUTTON(A)
recalescence/ALKALI
recant/KEEN
recede/PRECEDE
receipt/CAVITY
receive/CABAL(A)/CAVITY
recension/CENSUS
recidivism/DECAY
recision/SCISSORS
reck/RACK
reckless/RACK
reckon/RACK
reclaim/CALL
recognize/KENNING(A)
recommend/MAN
record/CORE

recourse/CAR
recreant/CORE
rectangle/RACK
rectify/RACK
rectitude/RACK
rector/RACK
rectum/RACK
recumbent/SUCCUBUS
recur/ACCELERATE/CAR
red/RED/SANGRIA/SCARLET
redeem/DAMN
redemption/DAMN
redoubt/SEDUCE
redound/UNDULATION
reduce/SEDUCE
redundant/UNDULATION
reed/ROOT
reef/RHAPSODY
reek/FRUCTIFY/REEK
reeve/REEVE/RHAPSODY/ROVE/RUG/
    SOW/WRESTLE(A)
refer/FERRY
refrigerator/SANGFROID
refugee/AVIATE
refurbish/BORAX(A)
refuse/REFUSE/RHAPSODY
refute/BUTTON(A)
regal/ARCHITECT/RACK
regale/GALA
regel/BASIS/HADDOCK
regent/RACK
regicide/RACK/SUICIDE
regime/RACK
regiment/RACK
region/RACK
register/GESTURE(A)
regret/REGRET
regular/DIRECTION/LEX/RACK/REGULAR
regularities/REGULAR
regularly/REGULAR
regulars/REGULAR
regulate/RACK
regulations/REGULAR
regurgitate/DEVOUR
reich/ARCHITECT/DIRECTION/REICH/RICHES
reign/RACK
reimburse/BURSAR(A)
reindeer/RAM/UNICORN
reinforce/BARRIO
reject/JET
rejoice/GAUDY
relapse/SNAP
relate/ATLAS
relax/LOOSE(A)
relegate/ELECT/LEX
relieve/ACCELERATE
remand/MAN
remark/MARK
remedy/METER
reminiscence/AMENABLE
reminiscent/MOON
remission/EMISSARY
remit/EMISSARY
remora/WEAK
remorse/MILL
remote/NOD
remunerate/MUNIFICENT(A)
renaissance/ORIGIN
rend/TROPHY
render/DATA(A)/ENDOW

renege/GROAN/INSOMNIA
renovate/NEW
rent/DATA(A)
reoccur/OCCUR
repair/PREPARE
repast/OBESE
repertory/FRUIT/PREPARE
replete/FULFILL
replicate/COUPLE
report/FERRY
reposit/AFTER
represent/IS
repress/PRESS
reprimand/PRESS
repugnant/PUGNACIOUS
require/QUERY
resemble/SIMULATION
reside/RESIDUE/SEAT
residence/RESIDUE
residency/RESIDUE
residential/RESIDUE
residual/RESIDUE
residuary/RESIDUE
residue/RESIDUE
residuum/RESIDUE
resolve/LOOSE(A)
resolved/SOLVE
resorb/SYRUP
resound/SOUND
respect/SCOPE
respiration/SPIRIT
respite/SCOPE
resplendent/SAPPHIRE
rest, -ing/RESIDUE
restive/RESIDUE
restless/RESIDUE
resume/RESUME
resuscitate/INCITE
retain/EXTEND(A)
retaliate/ATLAS
retch/SHRIEK
retroactive/HEGEMONY
retrocede/PRECEDE
retrospect/SCOPE
return/TURN
revere/ORIENTATION
revest/VEST
revive/HYGIENE(A)/VIVID
revoke/VOCALIZE
revolve/WALLOW
rewah/ROOM(A)
reward/ORIENTATION
rex/ARCHITECT
rhapsody/BID/REEVE/RHAPSODY/RIVALRY/ROOF
rheo-/SERUM
rhine/INERT
rhinoceros/UNICORN
rhoda/RED
rhododendron/RED
rhone/INERT
rhyme/SERUM
rhyolite/SERUM
rhythm/SERUM
rib/RHAPSODY
riband/RHAPSODY
ribbon/RHAPSODY
riboflavin/RIBOFLAVIN
ribose/RIBOFLAVIN
rice/RICE
rich, -es/RACK/RICHES

rid/RAID/ROOT
riddance/RAID
ridden/SULTAN
riddle/GARBLE/SECRET
ride, -ing/RAID/SULTAN
rife/QUARTER/RIFE/VERY(A)
riffle/PYRALIDID(A)
rifle/ROVE
rift/PORE/RIFE/RIVALRY/TROPHY
rigatoni/RIFE
right/RACK
rigid/REACH
rigor/REACH
rim/RUM
rimose/RIFE
rind/TROPHY
rindepest/UNICORN
ring/SHRIEK
ringhals/BET
rip-off/TROPHY
rip/PORE/TROPHY
riparian/RIFE/TROPHY
ripe/RIFE/TROPHY
ripping/TROPHY
ripple/RIFE/TROPHY
rise, -es/RISE
risk/SAXON
rite/ARITHMETIC
rivage/TROPHY
rival/RIVALRY
rivalry/GUERRILLA/RIVALRY/WRESTLE(A)
rive/RIFE/TROPHY
river/RIFE/TROPHY
road/RAID
roam/ROAM(A)/RUM
rob/ROVE/TROPHY
robe/TROPHY/VEST
robot/OPUS(A)
robus/RED
robust/RED
roc/ROC
rocambole/RUG
rochet/ROCHET(A)/RUG
rock/ORCHESTRA/ROCK/ROOK(A)/SILICON
rocket/ORCHESTRA/RUG
rockettes/ORCHESTRA
rod/ROOT
rodent/GRADE/SERRATED
rodeo/ROTATE
roll/ROTATE
rome/RUM
romp, -ing/RUM
rood/ROOT
roof/RHAPSODY/ROOF
roofs/RHAPSODY
rook/ROOK(A)
rookery/ROC
rooks/ROC
room/ROOM(A)
root/RAID/ROOT/SCORE
roots/BIT/CAPITAL/CRIB/CROW/CRUCIFIX/
    CULMINATE/CULPABLE/DURUM(A)/
    GRAPHITE/ IOTA/JASPER/JET/MATTOCK(A)/
    OVEN(A)/PEGASUS/POKE(A)/RABBIT(A)/
    ROOT/WHERE(A)
rope/RIFE/TROPHY
rostrum/GRADE
rooster/RISE/PEGASUS/POKE(A)/RABBIT(A)/ROOT/
    WHERE(A)

rope/RIFE/TROPHY
rostrum/GRADE
rota/ROTATE
rotary/ROTATE
rotate/INERT/ROTATE/TIRE
rotiform/ROTATE
rotogravure/ROTATE
rotor/ROTATE
rotund/ROTATE
rotunda/ROTATE
rouge/RED/SCARLET
roughage/TROPHY
roulette/ROTATE
round/ROTATE
roust/RISE
rout/RAID/SULTAN
route/DIRECTION
routed/RAID
routine/DIRECTION
rove/EUROPE/REEVE/ROVE
rover/ROVE/TROPHY
row/RIVALRY
rowel/ROTATE
rowen/RED
royal/RACK
-rrhea/SERUM
rubbish/REFUSE
rubella/RED
rubric/RED
ruby/RED
ruckus/RUCKUS
ruction/RUCKUS
ruddy/RED
ruffle/PYRALIDID(A)
rug/ARACHNID(A)/RUG/WRONG
rule/RACK
rum/CREAM/RUM/WORM
rumble/RUMBLE
rummage/ROOM(A)
rummer/RUM
rung/GRADE
runnels/INERT
runt/RAM/UNICORN
rupture/TROPHY
rural/ROOM(A)
ruse/SWERVE
rush/ROTATE
russet/RED
rust/GRADE/RED
rustic/ELMHURST/ROOM(A)
rut/DIRECTION/ESTROGEN(A)
rutabaga/ROOT
ruth/BLAME/SODOMY
ruthless/BABBLE/OGRE
rye/RACK
sabadilla/SPELT
sabbath/SEVEN/SPACE
sabbatical/SPACE
sabot/SABOTAGE
sabotage/BOOT(A)/SABOTAGE
saboteur/SABOTAGE
sabra/SPIRE
sabulous/CHAFE
sac/SACK
sacaton/ASSASSIN
saccharin/MUSK
saccule/SACK
sachem/CHECKMATE
sachet/SACK

sack/CASEFY(A)/ENCASE/SACK/SHIELD/SKUNK
sackbut/BUTTON(A)
sackcloth/SACK
sacks/SACK
sacque/SACK
sacred/SAXON
sacrifice/FACULTY
sacrilege/ELECT
sacrosanct/SAXON
sad/SATISFY
saddle/SEAT
safari/FERRY
safe/SALVATION/SLAM
saffron/SAFFRON/SERPENT
sag/KISS/SAG/SQUAT/SUCCUBUS
saga/SAGA
sagacious/SEEK
sagamore/CHECKMATE
sagas/SAGA
sage/SAGA/SAGEBRUSH(A)/SALVATION/
    SAVOIR-FAIRE
sagebrush/ACACIA(A)/SAGEBRUSH(A)
sagittarius/HASTATE
saguaro/SAGEBRUSH(A)
saint/SAXON
sake/SAKE/SEEK/SEIZE
salaam/SLAM
sale/CONSULT/SELL
salience/EXULT(A)
salient/EXULT(A)
sally/EXULT(A)
salmon/EXULT(A)
salome/SLAM
salon/SOLE/SOLEMN
saloon/SOLE/SOLEMN
salsa/SAUCE
salt/SILICON
saltant/EXULT(A)
saltarello/EXULT(A)
saltatory/EXULT(A)
saltigrade/EXULT(A)
salubrious/SALVATION/SLAM
salutary/EXULT(A)
salutation/SLAM
salute/EXULT(A)/SALVATION/SLAM
salutory/SALVATION
salvador/SALVATION
salvage/SALVATION/SLAM
salvation/SALVATION/SLAM
salvo/SALVATION
same/SIMULATION
sameness/SIMULATION
samizdat/DATA(A)/ENDOW
samovar/BURN/FIRE
sampan/SAMPAN(A)
samsara/SERUM/SIMULATION
samurai/AMENABLE/CHANGE/SAMURAI/
    SMILAX(A)
sanctity/SAXON
sand/CHAFE/SMUT
sandal/SANDAL
sandalwood/CAUTERIZE/SANDAL
sang-froid/SANGRIA
sangfroid/FROST/SANGFROID
sangria/ANEMIC/DAWN/SANGFROID/SANGRIA
sanguine/SANGRIA
sanhedrin/CHAISE
sanskrit/SIMULATION

sap/OOZE/SEEP
sapid/SAVOIR-FAIRE
sapient/SAVOIR-FAIRE
saponate/SEEP
saponite/SEEP
sapor/SAVOIR-FAIRE
sapphira/SAPPHIRE
sapphire/SAPPHIRE/SUPER
sapsago/SCABBLE
saraband/SIR
sarcasm/SARCASTIC
sarcastic/BUTCHER(A)/SARCASTIC
sarcoma/SARCASTIC
sarcophagus/SARCASTIC
sarcoptic mange/SYNCOPATION
sash/SASH
satchel/SACK
sated/SATISFY
satem/MITT
satiate/SATISFY
satire/SATISFY
satisfy/PARASITE(A)/SATISFY
satrap/SATRAP/SIDEREAL/STARE(A)/SULTAN
saturate/SATISFY
sauce/OOZE/SAUCE
saucer/SAUCE
sauerbraten/BURN
savanna/SAVANNA
savant/SAVOIR-FAIRE
save/SALVATION/SLAM
saving/SALVATION
savior/SALVATION
savoir-faire/SAGA/SAVOIR-FAIRE
savor/SAVOIR-FAIRE
savvy/SAVOIR-FAIRE
saw/NEW/SAGA/SAW/SAXON/SHIVER
sawra/SOW
saxatile/SILICON
saxon/CASTRATE/CUT/SAW/SAXON/
    SCHIZOPOD(A)/SCISSORS/ SHIVER/SKILL
say/SAGA
scab/SCURVY
scabble/SCABBLE/SHABBY/SYNCOPATION
scabbord/SAXON
scabrous/SCABBLE
scads/SCADS(A)
scald/ALKALI
scale/ALLEY/SCALE/SCALLOP/SKILL
scall/SCALE/SCALP
scallion/SCALLION
scallop/CALIBER/SCALLOP/SCALP
scalp/CALIBER/CARP/SCALLOP/SCALP/SKULL
scalpel/CLEAVER/SCALP
scam/ASHAMED
scamble/SCRAMBLE(A)
scamper/SCALE
scan navia/SKUNK
scandal/ASHAMED/SKUNK
scandinavia/SKUNK
scant/KITTEN/SCANTINESS
scantily/SCANTINESS
scantiness/SCANTINESS
scantling/SCANTINESS
scanty/SCANTINESS
scaphoid/SCABBLE
scapula/CLEAVER/SCABBLE/SCOOP
scar/CHAR/SAXON/SCAR/SCORCH/SCORE/
    SILICON
scarab/COCKROACH(A)/CRAB/SCARAB
scare/RATTLE/SCARE/SCURRILOUS

scared/CREED/HORRID/SCARE
scarf/COLLAR/SCARF/SCRUFF
scarlet/SCARLET
scat/SCADS(A)/SCOOT/SHOOT
scathe/SCATHING
scathing/SCATHING
scato-/SAXON
scatter/HASTATE
scaup/SCAUP/SCAVENGE
scavenge/SCAVENGE/SCOPE
scavenger/SCAUP/SCAVENGE
scavengers/SCAVENGE
scenario/ENSCONCE
scene/ENSCONCE
scene/HOUSE/SHACK
scenery/ENSCONCE
scepter/SWITCH
schadenfrude/SCATHING
schedule/SAXON
scheme/SHAG
schism/SAXON/SCHIZOPOD(A)/SCISSORS
schist/SCHIZOPOD(A)
schizo-/SCHIZOPOD(A)
schizo/SAXON
schizoid/SCHIZOPOD(A)
schizophrenia/SCHIZOPOD(A)/SCISSORS
schizopod/SCHIZOPOD(A)
schmaltz/APPEND.B/MILL
schmeer/SESAME
schmuck/MEEK
schnorrer/SNORKEL
scholar/SKILL
scholarship/SKILL
scholastic/SHAG
school/SHAG/SKILL
schuss/HASTATE/SHOOT
science/SAXON/SCHIZOPOD(A)/SKILL
scimitar/SMITE
scimiter/SMITE
scintillate/CAUTERIZE
sciolism/SKILL
scion/SUMAC
scire facias/SCHIZOPOD(A)
scissors/SCHIZOPOD(A)/SCISSORS
scoff/CHUCKLE(A)/FOR
scold/SAGA/CENSUS
sconce/ENSCONCE/SCAVENGE
scoop/CAVITY/CUFF/CUP/GOBLET/
    SCABBLE/SCOOP
scoot/SCOOT/SHOOT
scop/CHUCKLE(A)
scope/FOR/SCAVENGE/SCOPE/SEEK/SKEPTIC/SPY
-scopy/SCOPE
scorch/CHAR/SCAR/SCORCH
score/CRACK/SAXON/SCORE/SCRAPER
scorn/UNICORN
scorpion/CALIBER/COCKROACH(A)/SERPENT
scot/HASTATE/SCADS(A)/SHOOT
scotia/SHADE
scotoma/SHADE
scour/QUERY/SCOUR/SCURRILOUS/SHOWER
scout/HASTATE/SHOOT
scrabble/SAXON
scraggly/SHAGGY
scramble/SCRAMBLE(A)
scrap/RIVALRY
scrape/CHARACTER/SAXON
scraper/CARVE/CHARACTER/CRAB/GRAPHITE/
    SCRAPER/SCURVY
scrapping/SCARAB

scratch/CARD/CHARACTER/GRADE/SCRATCH
scrawl/CARVE
screak/CREAK/SHRIEK
scream/SHRIEK
screech/SHRIEK
screed/SCRATCH
screen/SAMURAI/SAXON
screw/SAXON
scribble/SAXON
scribe/SAXON
scrible/CARVE
scrimmage/SAMURAI
script/CARVE
scripture/CARVE/SAXON
scrivener/CARVE
scrobiculate/CARVE
scrofula/SCRUFF
scroll/SAXON
scrotum/SCRATCH
scrub/CARVE/SAXON
scruff/SCARF/SCRUFF
scrutiny/SCRATCH
scrutinys/SCRATCH
scud/HEAD
scuffle/CHAFE/SCOOP
scullery/CHALICE(A)/GILL(A)/SCULLERY
scullion/SCULLERY
sculpt/CARVE
sculpture/CARVE/SCALP
scum/SESAME
scummy/SESAME
scupper/SCOOP
scurf/SCURVY
scurfy/SCURVY
scurrility/SCURRILOUS
scurrilous/CHORUS/SCARE/SCURRILOUS
scurry/HULA/SCURRILOUS
scurvy/GRAVE/SCURVY
scut/HEAD
scuttle/HASTATE/KIT
scythe/CUT/SAXON
sea/OCEAN(A)
seal/JACKAL/TEAL
seam/ACCOUTERMENTS/SEAM/SEAMY
seamstress/SEAM
seamy/SEAM/SEAMY
seance/SEAT
sear/SEAR/SERIES/SYRUP
search/SCOUR
season/SOW
seat/INSTALL/SEAT/SET
secco/SACK
secede/PRECEDE/SUICIDE
seclude/SUICIDE
second/SHAG
secret/GARBLE/GIRDLE/SECRET/SUICIDE
secrete/SECRET
sect/SHAG
section/SAXON
sector/SAXON
secure/GIRDLE/SHACKLE/SIEGE/SKIRT/SUICIDE
sedate/SEAT
sedentary/SEAT
sedge/SAXON
sedilia/SEAT
sediment/SEAT
seduce/DOUCHE(A)/SEDUCE
see/GAZE/SCOPE/SEAT/SEE(A)
seecatch/SEE(A)
seeisa/SEISMIC(A)

seek/SAKE/SCOPE/SCOUR/SEEK
seem/SEMANTIC/SIMULATION
seeming/SIMULATION
seemly/SIMULATION
seep/ASPHALT/BISON/HYSSOP/SEEP/SIP/SOB
seepage/SEEP
seer/SHEERING
seet/SEETHE
seethe/SEETHE
seething/SEETHE
segment/SAXON
segregate/SUICIDE
segue/SHAG
seguidilla/SHAG
seicento/SIX
seise/SEIZE
seisin/SEIZE
seism/SEISMIC(A)
seismic/SEISMIC(A)
seismo-/SEISMIC(A)
seize/SEEK/SEIZE
seized/SEIZE
seizin/SEIZE
seizure/SEISMIC(A)/SEIZE
select/ELECT/SUICIDE
self/SUICIDE
sell/CONSULT/SELL
semantic/OMEN/SEMANTIC
semantics/SEMANTIC/SIGN/SIMULATION
semaphore/SEMANTIC
sematic/SEMANTIC
semen/SESAME
semester/METER/MOON/SIX
seminal/SESAME
seminar/SESAME
seminarians/SESAME
seminary/SESAME
semiology/SEMANTIC
semiotic/SEMANTIC
semites/ASHAMED
semitic/SEMANTIC
senate/SENILE
senator/SENILE
senectitude/SENILE
senescent/SENILE
senile/ANCIENT/SENILE/SIR/SUN
senility/SENILE
senior/SENILE
sennet/SEMANTIC
senopia/SENILE
senses/SIMULATION
sentient/SIMULATION
sentry/SATRAP
separate/PART/PREPARE/SPREAD/SUICIDE
separated/SPREAD
separation/PART
sepia/SEPIA
sepoy/SEPIA
seps/ASP
sepsis/ASP
sept/SEPT/SWITCH
september/SEVEN
septennial/SEVEN
septentrion/SEVEN
septet/SEVEN
septi-/SEVEN
septic tank/ASP
septuagint/MITT/SEVEN
septuple/COUPLE/SEVEN

sequacious/SHAG
sequel/SHAG
sequence/SHAG
serac/SERUM
seraph/SEAR
serapis/SERPENT
sere/SEAR
sered/CIRRUS(A)
serenade/SIREN
serene/SLAM/XEROX(A)
serf/SERF/SHEERING/SHIRE/SIR
sergeant/SERF
serial/SERIES
seriate/SERIES
series/JURISDICTION/SERIES/SHEERING/SWERVE
serin/SIREN
sermon/SERIES
serow/SEROW(A)
serpent/ASP/SAFFRON/SERPENT/SNAKE
serpentne/SERPENT
serpigo/SERPENT
serrated/SAW/SCRATCH/SERRATED
serried/SERIES
serum/SERUM/XEROX(A)
servant/SERF
serve/SERF
server/SERF
service/SERF
servile/SERF
servitude/SERF
sesame/PATCHOULI/SESAME/SHAMBLES/SMITE
session/SEAT
sester/SIX
sestina/SIX
set/INSTALL/SEAT/SET
settle/INSTALL/SEAT/SET
sevel/SEEP
seven/SEVEN/SIX/SUFFICE/SWASTIKA
sever/PREPARE/SHIVER
several/PREPARE
severe/SHIVER/VERY(A)
severity/SHIVER
sew/SEAM
sewan/SAVANNA
sewer/SEAT/SEEP
sex-/SIX
sextan/SIX
sextant/SIX
sextile/SIX
sextodecimo/SIX
sextuple/COUPLE
shabby/SCABBLE/SHABBY
shack/ENSCONCE/HOUSE/SHACK/SHOWER
shackle/SHACKLE
shad/HADDOCK
shade/SHADE/SHED
shadow/SHADE
shady/SHADE
shaft/SCABBLE
shag/MITT/SEEK/SEISMIC(A)/SHAG/SHAGGY/SIGN
shaggy/SAGEBRUSH(A)/SHAGGY
shake/SEISMIC(A)
shale/SCALLOP/SILICON
shallot/SCALLION
shalom/SLAM
sham/ASHAMED/SIMULATION
shamanism/SIMULATION
shambles/SHAMBLES
shame/ASHAMED

shamo/SHAMBLES
shank/SHANK
shanty/SENILE
shape/SCABBLE/SYNCOPATION
shaping/SCABBLE
shard/SAXON
share/SAXON/SCORE
sharif/SHIRE
sharp/CHARACTER/SAXON
shatter/SAXON
shave/SCABBLE
shaving/SCABBLE
shaw/SAGEBRUSH(A)
she/HE
shear/SAXON/SCORE
sheath/SCHIZOPOD(A)
sheave/SHIVER
shed/SCHIZOPOD(A)/SHED
sheen/SCAVENGE
sheep/OVIS
sheer/SHEER/SHEERING
sheering/SHEERING/SWERVE
sheet/HASTATE/SHOOT
sheik/CHECKMATE
shekel, -s/SCALE
shelf/SHIVER
shell/SCALE/SCALLOP
shellac/LAQUER(A)
shenanigan/CHANGE
shepherd/HERD
sherbet/SYRUP
sheriff/SERF/SHIRE
shibboleth/SPELT/SPILL
shiek/CHECKMATE
shield/SACK/SCALLOP/SHIELD/SIGN
shilling/SCALE
shimmer/SUN
shin/SAXON/SCHIZOPOD(A)/SHANK
shine/SUN
shingle/SAXON
shingles/CINCTURE(A)
ship/SCABBLE
-ship/SYNCOPATION
shipshape/SCABBLE
shire/CZAR/SERF/SHIRE
shirr/SERIES
shirt/CURT/SAXON/SKIRT
shishkebab/SHISHKEBAB
shive/SHIVER
shiver/SAW/SHIVER
shmata/SMITE
shock/SEISMIC(A)
shogun/CHECKMATE
shoot/HASTATE/SCOOT/SHOOT
shore/SERIES
short/CASTRATE/CURT/SAXON/SCORE
shot/HASTATE/SHOOT
shout/HOOT(A)
shove/SCOOP
shovel/SCOOP
show/SCAVENGE
shower/SCOUR/SHOWER/SOAK/SQUALL
shred/SAXON
shred/SCRATCH
shreik/CREAK
shrew/SAXON/SCRATCH
shriek/SHRIEK
shrike/SHRIEK
shrivel/SAXON

shroud/SAXON
shrub/SYRUP
shtick/STUDY/TILE
shuffle/SCOOP
shut/HASTATE/STEM
shuttle/HASTATE/SHOOT
siath/SOUTH
sib/SEPT
sibling/SEPT/SUICIDE
siccative/SACK
sick/SHAG/SICK
sickle/APPEND.B/SAXON
side/SIDE
sidereal/HERD/SATRAP/SIDEREAL/SULTAN
siege wall/SIEGE/SEAT/SIEGE
sieve/SEEP
sift/SEEP
sight/GAZE/SCOPE
sigmund/SANGRIA
sign/SEMANTIC/SHAG/SIGN/SIGN(A)
signet/SIGN
signify/SIGN
signory/SENILE
silence/SLAM
silex/SILICON
silica/SILICON
silicate/SILICON
siliceous/SILICON
siliciferous/SILICON
silicon/ROOK(A)/SCAR/SHIELD/SILICON
silk/WORM
sill/SILL
silly/SILLY(A)
silo/SILO
silos/SILO
silt/SILICON
silvicolous/GYRE
simar/SIMULATION
simian/SIMULATION
similar/SIMULATION
similarity/SIMULATION
simile/CHANGE/SIMULATION
simple/SIMULATION
simplicity/SIMULATION
simulate/SIMULATION
simulation/SEMANTIC/SIGN(A)/
SIMULATION/SOME
simulations/SIMULATION
simultaneous/SIMULATION
sin/CHANGE/IS/SEAMY/SIN
sine/SIN
sinecure/CHANGE
sinful/SIN
singapore/BARRIO/METROPOLIS
singing/SOUND
single/SIMULATION
sinister/CHANGE/SIN
sink/SAG
sinus/SIN
sion/SIGN
sip/SEEP/SIP/SOB/SUPPER
siphon/SIP/SOB
sipuli/BASIL
sir/CZAR/RICHES/SENILE/SERF/SHIRE/SIR
sirdar/SIR
sire/SENILE/SIR
siren/SIREN
sirocco/RISE
sirup/SYRUP

sisal/SASH
sistrum/SEISMIC(A)
sit/SEAT/SET
sitar/EXTEND(A)/TERZA
sitzbath/SEAT
six/SIX
skean/SAXON
skeet/HASTATE/SHOOT
skel/SCALLOP
skeleton/SACK
skeptic/SCOPE/SKEPTIC
skeptical/SKEPTIC
skepticism/SKEPTIC
sketch/SHOOT
skidaddle/SCOOT/SHOOT
skidoo/SHOOT
skiff/SCABBLE
skill/SAXON/SKILL
skilling/SCALE
skim/SMASH
skin/ENSCONCE/SAXON
skip/KIBITZ/PATIO
skipper/SCABBLE
skirmish/SAMURAI/SAXON
skirt/CURT/SAXON/SKIRT
skivvies/SUCCUBUS
skoal/SCALLOP
skotia/SCATHING
skull/CYCLE/SCALP/SKULL
skullduggery/SKILL
skunk/SKUNK
sky/OBSCURE
slack/LOOSE(A)
slalom/SLALOM
slam/SALVATION/SLALOM/SLAM/SOD/SOLEMN/
    TALISMAN/TELIC
slander/SLANG
slang/LICK/SLANG
slant/SLALOM
slap/SNAP
slat/SERRATED
slate/SHIELD/SILICON
slattern/LOOSE(A)
slave/SERF/SUFFER
slaver/SNAP
slavs/SWALLOW
sledge/QUARTER
sleep/SPILL
sleet/SLUDGE
sleeve/SLOUGH
sleigh/QUARTER/SLUDGE
slice/SLOUGH
slime/SESAME
sling/SLOUGH
slip/SLOUGH
slipcase/ENCASE
slipper/SLOUGH
slippery/ASPHALT/SLOUGH
slit/SERRATED
slob/ASPHALT
slog/GLISSADE/QUARTER/SLUDGE
slogan/CRY
slope/ASPHALT
sloppy/ASPHALT
sloth/LOOSE(A)
slouch/LOOSE(A)
slough/LOOSE(A)/SLOUGH
sludge/GLISSADE/SLUDGE
slug/SLUDGE
sluggard/SLUDGE

slumber/APPEND.B/INSOMNIA/NUMB
slung/SLOUGH
slurp/SYRUP
slush/SLUDGE
slut/LOOSE(A)
small/CRYOGENICS/SMASH/TOM(A)
smart/MILL
smash/SMASH/SMITE/SUMAC/THIN/TOM(A)/
    VENTRICLE
smear/SESAME
smell/SIMULATION/SMELL(A)
smellie/SMELL(A)
smelt/MILL
smidge/SMUT
smilax/SMILAX(A)
smile/SMUG
smirk/MIRROR/SMUG
smirtch/SMUT
smit/SMITE
smite/SESAME/SMASH/SMITE
smith/SEEK/SMITE
smithereens/SMITE
smiths/SMITE
smock/MEEK
smolder/SMELL(A)
smudge/SMUT
smug/MEEK/SMUG
smuggle/MEEK
smut/ASHAMED/SMUT
smutch/SMUT
snag/TINE
snaggletooth/TINE
snail/SNAKE
snake/SNAKE
snakes/NECK
snap/SNAP/SPANK
snapper/SNAP
snarl/SNORKEL
sneak/MASK/SNAKE/SNEAK
sneer/SNORKEL
sneeze/NOZZLE
sniff/SMELL(A)
sniggle/SNAKE
snigs/SNAKE
snip/SNAP
snipping/SNAP
snore/SNORKEL
snorkel/NOZZLE/SIREN/SMELL(A)/SNORKEL/
    SOUND/STEIN
snorkelbreakbreak/SNORKEL
snort/SNORKEL
snow/SANGFROID/SLUDGE
snub/SNAP
snuff/SNAP
so long/SLAM
so/SOVIET/THIS
soak/SACK/SAKE/SAUCE/SHOWER/SOAK/SQUALL
soap/HYSSOP/SEEP
sob/SOB
sober/SUICIDE
social/SHAG
socket/SAG
socks/SACK
sod/SEETHE/SOD/SODIUM
soda/SOD/SODIUM
sodden/SOD
sodium/SODIUM/SODOMY
sodomite/SODOMY
sodomy/SODIUM/SODOMY
sofa bed/SOFA/ASPHALT/SOFA/SUPPLE

sofas/SOFA
soggy/SOAK
soil/SEAT
sol/SUN
solar/SUN
sole/SOLE/SOLEMN/SOLITARY/SUICIDE
solemn/SALVATION/SLAM/SOLE/SOLEMN
solicit/INCITE
solicitous/SLAM
solid/SALVATION/SLAM
soliloquy/DIALECT/SOLITARY/SUICIDE
solipsism/SUICIDE
solitaire/SOLITARY
solitary and/SOLITARY/SOLE/SOLITARY/SUICIDE
solitude/SOLITARY
solo/SOLITARY
solomon/SLAM
soloveitchik/SWALLOW
soluble/LOOSE(A)
solum/SOLE
solution/LOOSE(A)/SOLVE
solve/LOOSE(A)/SOLVE
soma/SMUG/TUMOR(A)
somato-/TUMOR(A)
some/SOME
-some/TUMOR(A)
somnambulent/INSOMNIA
somni-/INSOMNIA
somnolent/INSOMNIA
somnus/INSOMNIA
son/SON
sonant/SOUND
sonata/SOUND
sone/SOUND
song/PSALM/SOUND
sonic/SOUND
sonnet/PSALM/SOUND
sonorous sonata/PSALM
sonorous/SOUND
soos/HOOF
soot/SEAT
sooth/IS
soothe/IS
sop/SOB
sophism/SAVOIR-FAIRE/SPY
sophisticated/SAVOIR-FAIRE
sophistication/SPY
sophistry/SAVOIR-FAIRE
sophomore/SAVOIR-FAIRE
-sophy/SAVOIR-FAIRE
sopor/SOFA
soporific/INSOMNIA/SOFA
soprano/SUPER
sorcerer/SERIES
sordid/OBSCURE
sore/SORE
sorghum/SORGHUM
sorrel/SEAR
sorry/SORE
sot/SHED/SOD/SOT
soubrette/SUPER
sound/AUSCULATE/OSTEOMA/PSALM/
    SEMANTIC/SLANG/SOUND
soup/SIP
soutache/SOUTACHE(A)
soutane/SOUTH
south/SOUTH/SUN
southern/SOUTH
sovat/BESTOW(A)
sovereign/SUPER

soviet/SIMULATION/SOVIET
sow/HYOSCYAMINE(A)/NEW/SOW/STRIKE
space/SPACE
spade/SPIT/XIPHOID
spahee/SEPIA
spahi/SEPIA
spank/SNAP/SPANK
spare/SPARE
spark/SPARK(A)
sparkie/SPARK(A)
sparkle/SPARK(A)
sparling/SPIRE
sparrow/CAPRICORN/FREE/SPARROW/SPIRIT
sparse/DIASPORA(A)/SPARE
spate/SCOPE/SPATE/SPIT
spatter/SPATE
spatula/SPIT
species/SCOPE
specimen/SCOPE
specious/SCOPE
spectacle/SCOPE
spectrum/SCOPE
speculate/SCOPE
speed/SPATE
spell/DECIPHER/GOSPEL/SPHERES
spelling/GOSPEL
spelt/SPELT/SPILL
sperm/DIASPORA(A)
sphere/DECIPHER/SPARE/SPHERES
spheres/SPHERES/SPIRAL
spherical/SPHERES
spheroid/SPHERES
sphinx/HANG
spica/SPIRE
spiculum/SPIRE
spider/SWIVEL
spiel/DECIPHER/GOSPEL
spike/SPIRE
spile/ASPHALT/SPIRE
spill/ASPHALT/SPELT/SPILL/SPIRE/SUPER
spillway/ASPHALT/SPILL
spin/SWIVEL
spindle/SWIVEL
spine/PENGUIN
spine/SPIRE
spinel/SPIRE
spinnaker/SNAP
spinney/SPIRE
spiracle/SPIRIT
spiraea/SPIRAL
spiral/SPHERES/SPIRAL
spiraling/SPIRAL
spirants/SPIRIT
spire/SPIRAL/SPIRE/SPIT
spirea/SPIRAL
spirit/ASPIRE/SPIRIT
spit/DIASPORA(A)/SPATE/SPIRE/SPIT
spiteful spat/SPATE
spitz/SPIRE
splendid/SAPPHIRE
spoil/SPILL
spoiled/SPILL
spoke/SPIRE
sponge/FUNGUS
sporadic/DIASPORA(A)
spore/DIASPORA(A)/SPREAD
sport/FERRY
sportsmanship/SCABBLE
spout/SHOOT/SPATE
spouting/ASPHALT

sprawl/DIASPORA(A)
spray/DIASPORA(A)
spread/DIASPORA(A)/FLAKE/FREE/SPREAD
spreading/SPREAD
sprig/FRUIT/SPRIG(A)
sprit/SPIT
sprout/DIASPORA(A)/FRUIT/SPREAD
spry/DIASPORA(A)
spud/SPIT
spudder/SPIT
spurran/BURSAR(A)
spurt/DIASPORA(A)/SPATE
spy/SCOPE/SPY
squad/GATHER/QUARTER
squall/SHOWER/SOAK/SQUALL
square/QUARTER
squash/CUCUMBER/SAUCE/SQUAT
squat/HEGEMONY/SQUAT
squaw/SUCCUBUS
squawk/CREAK
squeal/SHRIEK
squeeze/SAUCE/SQUAT
squish/SAUCE
squirrel/SUN
stab/SPIRE
stabilizing/STABLE
stable/MASTABAH(A)/PROSTITUTE/SATRAP/
    STABLE/STUBBORN
stack/QUARTER/STICK/TACK
staff/STUBBORN/SWITCH
stag/STICK/TACK
stage/TACK
stagger/STICK
staith/STAITH(A)
stake/STICK/TACK
staking/TACK
stalactite/DRIP
stalk/INSTALL/STALK/STEAL/STICK/STILL(A)
stall/INSTALL/STABLE
stallion/INSTALL/STILL(A)
stammer/DUMB/STEM
stamp/TAP
stamped/TAP
stampede/TAP
standard/UNICORN
star/SIDEREAL/STARE(A)
stare/STARE(A)
stars steer/SIDEREAL
stave/SWITCH
steak/CASSIA(A)/CASTRATE/TACK
steal/STEAL
stealth/STEAL
steam/THYME
steeple/STABLE
steer/SATRAP/STARE(A)/TAURUS
steering/SATRAP
stein/STEIN
stele/INSTALL/STALK/STILL(A)
stellar/SATRAP/SIDEREAL
stem/DUMB/OSTEOMA/STEM/STOMACH/STYMIE
stench/SKUNK
stern/SATRAP
sternum/SOW
steward/ORIENTATION
stick/ACACIA(A)/HASTATE/STICK
stickleback/TACK
stiff/STUBBORN
stigma/TACK
stileto/STYLE

still/INSTALL/STILL(A)
stilo/STYLE
stilt/INSTALL/STALK/STILL(A)
sting/STICK/TACK/TINE
stink/SKUNK
stitch/TACK/TECHNICAL
stochastic/STICK/TACK
stockade/STICK/TACK
stole/INSTALL/STILL(A)
stolid/STALK/STILL(A)
stollen/INSTALL/STALK
stolon/INSTALL/STALK
stomach/STEM/STOMACH/STYMIE/TUMOR(A)
stomato-/STOMACH
stomatous/STOMACH
-stomy/STOMACH
stone/STEIN
stoor/DESTROY(A)
stop/SEVEN/SPACE
store/OYSTER/STYLE
stout/INSTALL/STILL(A)
strafe/SNAP
strain/SOW
strait/SORE/STRAND(A)
strand/STRAND(A)
strap/SNAP/STRAND(A)
stratagem/HEGEMONY/SOW
strath/SOW
straw/SOW
stream/INERT/SERUM
street/SATRAP/STILL(A)/STRAND(A)
streptomycin/MEEK
stress/SORE/SWERVE
stretch/SHEER
strew/SOW
strife/RIVALRY
strike/STRIKE
striking/STRIKE
string/STRAND(A)
strip/STRAND(A)
stripe/SNAP/STRAND(A)
strive/RIVALRY
stroma/SOW
structure/DESTROY(A)
strudel/SERUM
stub/STUBBORN
stubble/STUBBORN
stubborn/MASTABAH(A)/STABLE/STUBBORN
stubbornly/STUBBORN
stucco/TILE
stuck/TACK
student/STUDY
study/SHOOT/STUDY
stultify/INSTALL/STALK/STILL(A)
stum/STEM/STYMIE
stumble/STEM/STYMIE
stump/STEM/STUBBORN/STYMIE
stun/DUMB/STYMIE
stupa/TOP
stupid/DIVE/FATUITY(A)/STUDY
style/DESTROY(A)/SILICON/STYLE
stylish/STYLE
stylus/STYLE
stymie, ied/STOMACH/STYMIE
suave/HEDONISM
sub-/SOFA
sub/ASPHALT
subduction/SEDUCE
subdue/SEDUCE

subjacent/JET
subject/JET
sublunary/LUNAR(A)
submarine/MARINE
submit/EMISSARY
subrogate/RACK/URGE
subsequent/SHAG
subside/SEAT
subsidy/SEAT
substratum/SOW
subterfuge/AVIATE
subtle/TECHNICAL
succeed/PRECEDE/SUCCEED
success/SUCCEED
successor/SUCCEED
succinct/CINCTURE(A)/SUCCEED
succor/ACCELERATE/AUXILIARY/CAR/SUCCEED
succubus/SAG/SOFA/SUCCUBUS
succulent/SAUCE/SOAK
succumb/SUCCUBUS
such/SNORKEL
suck/SOAK
suction/SOAK
suds/SEETHE
sue/SHAG
suffer/FERRY/SUFFER
suffice/SUPPER/SEVEN/SUFFICE/SWASTIKA
sufficiency/SUFFICE
sufficient/SUFFICE
suffix/CRUCIFIX/SUFFICE
suffrage/SUPER
sugar/MUSK
sugery/GRAPPLE
suggest/GESTURE(A)
suicide/CUT/SUICIDE
suit/SUIT
suitor/SHAG
sulfur/SERPENT
sullen/SOLITARY
sullun/SUICIDE
sulphur/SERPENT
sultan/SATRAP/SIDEREAL/SULTAN
sum/SUMMIT
sumac/SUMAC/SUMMIT/SYCAMORE/TUMOR(A)/
    VENTRICLE
summer/SUMMER(A)/SUN
summit/SUMAC/SUMMIT
summon/MOON/SESAME/SUMMON
summons/SUMMON
sumpter/SUMMER(A)
sun/SOUTH/SUMMER(A)/SUN/TIME
sundry/CHANGE
sunken/SAG
sup/SIP/SOB/SUPPER
super-/SUPER
super/ASPHALT/SPILL/SUPER/SURPASS
superb/SUPER
supercede/SEAT
supererogate/URGE
superfluous/BLOAT
superior/SUPER
superiority/SUPER
superlative/ATLAS
supernal/SUPER
supine/ASPHALT/SOFA
supper/SIP/SUPPER
supplant/PLAZA
supple/COUPLE/SOFA/SUPPLE
supplement/SUFFICE

supplicate/COUPLE
supply/FULFILL/SUFFICE
support/FERRY
suppress/PRESS
supra-/SUPER
supremacy/SUPER
supreme/SUPER
supremo/SUPER
sur-/SURPASS
surcease/SURPASS
surcharge/SURPASS
surf/SURF
surfeit/SURPASS
surge/RACK
surgeon/GRAPPLE
surgery/ORGAN/REACH
surly/SENILE/SIR
surmise/EMISSARY
surmullet/SEAR
surname/SURPASS
surpass/SURPASS/USE
surplus/SURPASS
surrender/DATA(A)/ENDOW
surreptitious/TROPHY
surround/DURUM(A)/UNDULATION
survive/HYGIENE(A)/VIVID
survivor/SURPASS
sus-/SUCCEED
sus/SOUTH
susceptible/SOUTH
suspect/SCOPE/SOUTH/SUCCEED
suspend/SOUTH
suspense/SOUTH
suspire/SOUTH/SPIRIT
sussex/SOUTH
sustain/EXTEND(A)
sutra/SIDEREAL
suttee/IS
suture/SEAM/SIDEREAL
swag/SWIVEL
swain/SUICIDE
swallow/DEVOUR/SWALLOW
swami/SUICIDE
swan/SOUND
swank/SWIVEL
swap/SWIVEL
swarm/SLALOM
swarthy/OBSCURE/SWERVE
swastika/IS/SEVEN/SUFFICE/SWASTIKA
swat/SEPT/SWITCH
sway/SWIVEL
swear/GOSPEL
sweat/SEEP
sweep/SWIVEL
sweet/HEDONISM/QUARTER
swell/BLOAT/SWELL
swerve/SERIES/SHEERING/SWERVE/SWIVEL
swift/SWIVEL
swill/DEVOUR/SEEP
swim/SWIVEL
swine/HYOSCYAMINE(A)
swineherd/HERD
swing/SWIVEL
swirl/SWIVEL
switch/SEPT/SPIT/SWITCH/SWIVEL
swivel/SWERVE/SWIVEL
swoop/SWIVEL
swoor/SWERVE
sword/SHIVER

sycamine/SYCAMORE
sycamore/SUMAC/SYCAMORE
syce/PEGASUS
sycee/SASH
syconium/SYCAMORE
sycophant/PANE/SYCAMORE
sycosis/SYCAMORE
syllable/GOSPEL
syllabus/GOSPEL
syllogism/ELECT
sym-/SIMULATION/SYNCOPATION/SYNOD
symbiosis/HYGIENE(A)
symbol/SIMULATION/SYNOD
symmetry/SYNOD
sympathy/SYNOD
sympatric/PATRON
symphony/PHONETICS/SYNOD
sympton/SIMULATION
syn-/SIMULATION/SYNCOPATION/SYNOD
synagogue/AGONY/HEGEMONY/SYNOD
synalepha/LIVER
syncopation/SCABBLE/SYNCOPATION
syndic/SYNDICATE
syndicate/SYNDICATE
syndication/SYNDICATE
synergism/ORGAN
synesis/JET
synizesis/SEAT
synkaron/UNICORN
synod/SIMULATION/SYNCOPATION/
        SYNOD/TEAM
synonym/SYNOD
synonymous/CHANGE
synonyms/SIMULATION
synopsis/SPY
syntax/TACTICIAN
synthesis/SYNOD
syphilis/SEEP/SPILL
syrphus fly/SERPENT
syrup/SEAR/SYRUP
tab /TAB
taboo /TABOO
tabor/TAP
tabret/TAP
tach/TACK
tack/ACACIA(A)/DIKE/STICK/TACK/TAG/TAKE
tact/TACTICIAN
tactful/TACTICIAN
tactic/TACTICIAN
tactician/TACTICIAN
tactics/TACTICIAN
tactitian/CATECHISM(A)/TACTICIAN/TECHNICAL
tael/ATLAS
taffeta/TOWEL/TWIST
tag/TACK/TAG
tahiti/SOUTH
tail/TACK/TAG/TAIL
tailor/TILE
taint/SOAK
taj/TAG
take/TACK/TAKE
takhat/DOXY(A)
talc/CHIN/TACTICIAN/TALCUM
talcum powder/TALCUM
talcum/DIK-DIK(A)/TACTICIAN/TALCUM
talent/ATLAS
talion/ATLAS
talipes/TILE
talipot/TROPHY

talisman/SIMULATION/TALISMAN/TELIC
tall/DILUTE/TALL/TOWER
tallow/DRIP
talon/TILE
talus/EARTH/TILE
tamarack/TIMBER
tamarin/TIMBER
tamarind/TIMBER
tamarisk/ASHTREE/TIMBER
tambourine/TAP
tambrel/TAP
tame/MADONNA/TIMBER
tandem/TEAM
tang/GNAW/TINE
tantalize/ATLAS
tantalus/ATLAS
tap/TAP/TOP
tapa/TOWEL/TWIST
tape/TOWEL/TWIST
tapestry/TOWEL
tapis tapestry/TWIST
taps/TAP
tariff/ORIENTATION/TARIFF
tarsus/DASH/TRACK
tassel/SOUTACHE(A)
taunt/TINE
taurine/TAURUS
tauro/TAURUS
taurus/QUINTET/STARE(A)/TAURUS/TERZA/TINE
tava/TWIST
taw/TOWEL
tax/TACTICIAN
taxis/TACTICIAN
taxo-/TACTICIAN
teach k-dt/CATECHISM(A)
teal/TEAL
team/SEDUCE/SYNCOPATION/TEAM
teammate/TEAM
teamster/TEAM
teamwork/TEAM
tear/TROPHY
teardrop/DRIP
teat/TEAT/TICKLE/TOOTS
technical/TACTICIAN/TECHNICAL
technician/TECHNICAL
technology/TECHNICAL
tectonic/TECHNICAL
teem/SEDUCE
teensy/TOM(A)
teeter/DOODLE(A)/TRACK
telamon/ATLAS/TELEVISION
tele-/TELEVISION
telecast/TELEVISION
telegraph/TELEVISION
teleology/TELIC
teleost/OSTEOMA/TELIC
telephone/PHONETICS/TELEVISION
telescope/SCOPE
television/TELEVISION
telic/TELIC/TERM
telium/TELIC
telo-/TELIC
telophase/TELIC
teluric/EARTH
temed/MUSK
temerity/DUMB
tempo/TIME
ten/MITT
tenable/EXTEND(A)

tenacious/EXTEND(A)
tenacity/TINE/TONIC
tenaculum/TINE
tenant/EXTEND(A)/TONIC
tend/TONIC
tendency/TONIC
tender/EXTEND(A)
tendril/EXTEND(A)
tenement/EXTEND(A)
tenet/EXTEND(A)
tennis/TONIC
tenon/EXTEND(A)/TINE/TONIC
tenor/EXTEND(A)/TONIC
tentacle/TINE/TONIC
tenuous/EXTEND(A)
tenure/EXTEND(A)/TONIC
tephrite/GRAPHITE
teqhnique/TECHNICAL
term/TELIC/TERM/TIME
terminate/TERM
terms/TERM
terrain/EARTH
terre-verte/WET
terrestial/EARTH
terrible/SCARE
terrific/SCARE
territory/EARTH
terror/RATTLE/SCARE
terza rima/TAURUS/TERZA
terza/TERZA
terzarima/BAD
testament/TERZA
testify/TERZA
testimony/TERZA
tetragrammaton/CARVE/SCRAPER
teuton/TOOTS
teutonic/TOOTS
tevet/DIVINE
text/TECHNICAL
textile/TECHNICAL
-th/EIGHT
thanatophobia/CHECKMATE
thanatos/ARITHMETIC
thane/KITTEN
thank/ORTHODOX
thatch/TILE
thaumatology/SMUG
thaumaturge/ORGAN
thaw/TABES(A)
thebromine/DEVOUR
theca/ARITHMETIC
thee/THOU
them/HE/THEM
theodily/SYNDICATE
theophany/PANE
theorum/THEORY(A)
theory/THEORY(A)
therapeutics/THERAPY
therapy/THERAPY/TORPID
therm/CHAR
thermal/CHAR
thermometer/BURN/CHAR
thermy/BURN
thesis/THESIS(A)
theta/EIGHT
thick/CATECHISM(A)
thiemiar/THYME
thimble/TUMOR(A)
thin/EXTEND(A)/THIN

thine/THOU
think/ORTHODOX
thionine/THYME
third/TERZA
thirteen/TERZA
thirty/TERZA
this/HERE/SNORKEL/THIS
thistle/STICK
thole/ATLAS
thomas/TEAM
thorn/DURIAN(A)
thou/SOUTH/THEM/THOU
thought/ORTHODOX
thrash/DASH/TRACK
three/TERZA
thresh/DASH
threshold/DASH/TRACK
thrice/TERZA
through/CHECKMATE
throw/SOW/TELEVISION
thrum/TERM
thug/TILE
thumb/TUMOR(A)
thus/THIS
thy/THOU
thyme/DUMB/THYME
thyroid/DELTA
tiara/TIARA/TIER/TIRE
tick/TACK
ticket/TACK
tickle/TEAT/TICKLE/TOUCH
tie/SEDUCE/TWIST
tier/TIARA/TIER/TIRE/TOUR/TOWER/TURN
tiffany/PANE
tiger/TACK
tile/CLOT/LID/TILE
tiles/TILE
tiller/TECHNICAL
timber/TIMBER
timberland/TIMBER
timberline/TIMBER
timberwolf/TIMBER
time/TIME
timid/TIMID
timorous/TIMID
tin/TIN
tinct/SOAK
tine/TINE/TUNA
tinge/SOAK
tinker/TECHNICAL
tint/SOAK
tiny/TOM(A)
tip/DIVE/TOP
tippler/DIVE
tipsy/DIVE
tire/ROTATE/TIARA/TIRE/TOIL(A)
tired/TOIL(A)
titillate/TEAT/TITILLATE
titillation/TOOTS
title/EARTH
titmouse/TEAT
tittie/TITTIE
tittle/TEAT
titty/TITTIE
to/AT/TOO
tobacco/TOBACCO
tochis/SUCCEED
toddle/DOODLE(A)
toga/COTTON/TILE

together/GATHER/GOOD
toil/TECHNICAL/TILE/TOIL/TOIL(A)
toilet/TILE
tokay/MUSK
tolerate/ATLAS
toll/ATLAS/TOLL
tollhouse/ATLAS
tom thumb/TOM(A)/TUMOR(A)
tom/TOM(A)
tomahawk/KNOCK
tomato/SUMAC/TUMOR(A)
tomb/TUMOR(A)
tomboy/TEAM
tomcat/TEAM
tomentose/TOMENTUM(A)
tomentum/TOMENTUM(A)
tomfool/DUMB
tommyrot/DUMB
tomtit/TOM(A)
ton/TON/TUNA
tone/ASININE/TONIC
tongs/GNAW/TINE
tongue/SLANG
tonic/TONIC
tonnage/TON
too/ADD/TOO
tool/TOWEL
tooth/TINE
toots/TEAT/TITILLATE/TITTIE/TOOTS
tootsy/TOOTS
top/PATE/SEPIA/TOP
topaz/PHOSPHORUS/TOPAZ
topmost/AVIATE
topography/SCRAPER
topping/TOP
topple/FALL
tops/TOP
toque kt/HEAD(A)
toque/HEAD
torch/ADOLESCENT
tore/TROPHY
toreador/TAURUS
torn/TROPHY
torpedo/TORPID
torpid/THERAPY/TORPID
torpor/TORPID
torsion/PUZZLE
tort/PUZZLE
tortoise/PUZZLE
tortuous/PUZZLE
torture/PUZZLE
tory/ROTATE
toss/DASH/TOSS
tot/DOODLE(A)/TEAT
tote/TOTE(A)
totem/DUMMY
totter/DOODLE(A)
toucan/TOUCAN
touch/TICKLE/TOUCH
touching off/TOUCH
tough/GNAW
toupee/TOP
tour/STARE(A)/THEORY(A)/TOUR/
        TURN/TURTLEDOVE
tourist/TOUR
tow/TOWEL/TWIST
towel/TOWEL/TWIST
tower/TIER/TOWER
toxic/HASTATE

toy/CHUCKLE(A)
trace/TRACK
trachea/DARK
track/DIRECTION/DRAG/TRACK
tract/DRAG/DRAW
trade/TRACK
tradition/DATA(A)/ENDOW
traduce/SEDUCE
tragedy/BID
trail/DRAG/DRAW
train/DRAG/DRAW
traipse/TRACK
traitor/DATA(A)/ENDOW
trajectory/JET
tram/TRAMMEL
trammel/TERZA/TRAMMEL
trampoline/TRACK
tramroad/TRAMMEL
tramway/TRAMMEL
trance/DORM
transducer/SEDUCE
transfer/FERRY/SUFFER
transfix/CRUCIFIX
translate/ATLAS
translucent/LIGHT
transmit/EMISSARY
transpire/SPIRIT
transport/FERRY
trap/TRACK
travail/TOIL(A)
travel/CRUCIFIX/TOIL(A)
travesty/VEST
tray/ARBOR
tread/TRACK
treason/ENDOW
treasure/DATA(A)
treat/DRAG
trecento/TERZA
tree/ARBOR
trek/TREK
trembling/SCARE
tremendous/SCARE
tremor/SCARE
tremulous/SCARE
trephine/TERZA
trepidation/SCARE
tresspass/PATIO
tri-/TERZA
triad/TERZA
triceps/CAPITAL
triceratops/UNICORN
trichotomy/TERZA
triclinium/TERZA
tricolor/TERZA
tridactyl/TERZA
trierarch/TERZA
trimester/METER/MOON
trimurti/TERZA
trine/TERZA
trinity/TERZA
trio/TERZA
triple/COUPLE/TERZA
tritium/TERZA
tritone/TERZA
triumvirate/TERZA/VIRILE
triune/UNIQUE(A)
trivia/CONVEY/VIA
trocar/TERZA
troche/DRAG

troika/TERZA
trophy/FRUIT/GRASS/PATCHOULI/PORE/
    RAVENOUS/RIFE/TROPHY
trot/TRACK
trough/ARBOR
trounce/DASH/TRACK
trout/TROUT(A)
truck/DRAG
trudge/TRACK/TRUDGE
true/ETYMOLOGY
truffle/BOTANY
tsar/CZAR
tsetse/TOSS
tsibele/BASIL
tub/TUB(A)/VAT
tuber/BOTANY
tuchis/SUCCEED
tucket/TUCKET
tuesday/DIVINE
tuft/TOP
tug/HEAD/SEDUCE
tukhus/SUCCEED
tumefaction/VENTRICLE
tumefy/TUMOR(A)/VENTRICLE
tumescence/VENTRICLE
tumid/TUMOR(A)/VENTRICLE
tumidity/VENTRICLE
tummy/TUMOR(A)/VENTRICLE
tumor/TOMENTUM(A)/TUMOR(A)/VENTRICLE
tumult/TUMOR(A)
tumulus/TUMOR(A)
tun/TON
tuna/DINOSAUR(A)/TON/TUNA
tunic/COTTON
tunicle/COTTON
tunny/TON/TUNA
tup/TAP
turf/TWIST
turkey/CZAR/TOUCAN
turn/TOUR
turn/TURN/TURTLEDOVE
turret/TOWER
turtle/PUZZLE/TOWER
turtledove/TURTLEDOVE
tusk/GNAW/TINE
tussock/SOD
tut/SUCCEED
twain/DUO/TEAM
tweed/TOWEL/TWIST
twelve/DUO
twenty/DUO
twice/DUO
twiddle/TOWELtwiddle/TWIST
twig/DUO
twilight/DUO
twill/DUO/TOWEL/TWIST
twin/BOTH/TEAM
twine/DUO/TWIST
twirl/TOWEL/TWIST
twist/DUO/TOWEL/TWIST
two/BOTH/DUO/NEW/TEAM/TOO
tycoon/KHAN
tyke/GOAT
tympan/TAP
tympanic/TAP
tympany/TAP
type/TAP
typhus/THYME
typical/TAP

typing/TAP
typography/TAP
typology/TAP
tyrant/SULTAN
tyre/TOWER
ubiquitous/BY
udder/TEAT
-uity/FATUITY(A)
ulcer/ULCER(A)
ulm/ELM
ulmaceous/ELM
ululant/ULULATION
ululate/ULULATION
ululation/ULULATION/WAIL
umbel/UMBRELLA(A)
umbrage/UMBRELLA(A)
umbrella/UMBRELLA(A)
umlaut/MAZARD(A)
un-/INSOMNIA
unanimous/ANIMUS(A)/UNIQUE(A)
uncle/OF(A)
under/MAT/NETHER(A)
underneath/MAT/NETHER(A)
undine/UNDULATION
undulate/DUNE(A)/DURUM(A)/MAT/
    NOD/UNDULATION
undulation/UNDULATION
uni-/UNIQUE(A)
unicom/UNIQUE(A)
unicorn/CAPITAL/CORNER/CORNET/
    CORNUCOPIA/CORONA/CRAB/CREAM/
    CROWN/RAM/SKULL/UNICORN
union/UNIQUE(A)
unique/UNIQUE(A)
unison/SOUND
unit/EACH
unite/EACH/UNIQUE(A)
unity/UNIQUE(A)
universe/UNIQUE(A)
univocal/VOCALIZE
unique/UNIQUE
unravel/GARBLE
until/MAZARD(A)
up/AVIATE/OF(A)
upo/AVIATE
uppermost/AVIATE
upsilon/CHAFE
ur-/CARRACK(A)
uraeus/CARRACK(A)
uranium/ORIOLE
urban/BARRIO
uredo/ASH
urge/RAVENOUS/URGE/WREAK(A)/WRECK
urgency/URGE
urgent/URGE
urine/CARRACK(A)
urn/ASH/ORIOLE
uro-/CARRACK(A)
urology/CARRACK(A)
ursprache/GOSPEL
usable/USE
usage/USE
usages/USE
usance/USE
use up/USE
use/USE
useful/USE
useless/LESS(A)
user/USE

usually/USE
usufruct/USE
usurious/USE
usurp/USE
usury/USE
uterus/STYLE
utmost/EXIT
utter/BID/EXIT
vacancies/BUCKET
vacant/VACATE
vacate/BUCKET/CAVITY/EMBEZZLE/FAG/GIBBON/
    PICK/VACATE/VAIN
vacating/VACATE
vacation/VACATE
vacca/BUCKAROO
vaccination/BUCKAROO
vaccine/BUCKAROO
vacuity/VACATE
vacuous/VACATE
vacuum/BEAKER/VACATE
vacuums/BUCKET
vagabond/BUCKET/VACATE
vagary/VACATE
vagina/BUCKET
vaginate/VACATE
vagrancy/VACATE
vagrant/BUCKET
vague/VACATE
vain/PIONEER/VACATE
vain/VAIN
valedictorian/BARON
valence/BARON
valentine/BARON
valhalla/HOLLOW
valiant/BARON
valid/BARON
valise/BURSAR(A)
valley/ASPHALT/WALLOW
value/BARON
valve/WALLOW
vamoose/VAIN
vamp/PANE
van/VANDYKE
vandal/POINT/WANDER
vandyke/VANDYKE
vane/PANE/POINT
vang/CRUCIFIX
vanguard/PANE
vanish/PANE/VACATE/VAIN
vanity/VACATE/VAIN
vanquish/KIBOSH/VICTOR(A)
vapid/EVENING
vapor/EVENING
var/VERY(A)
vase/SIP
vat/VAT
vatic/VATICAN(A)/VETERAN/
    VATICAN(A)/VETERAN
vault/BALL/BLISTER/BLOAT/BOULDER/WALLOW
vaulted/BLOAT
vaunt/VACATE
veal/VETERAN
vector/CONVEY/VIA
veda/IDEA
vedanta/MAZARD(A)
veer/ABERRATION/PARASITE(A)/VEER
veering/VEER
vehicle/CONVEY/FERRY/VIA
veil/NEW/PALL

vein/FERRY
veliger/GESTURE(A)
vend/DATA(A)/ENDOW
veneer/PANE
venerate/PENCHANT
venereal/PENCHANT
venery/PENCHANT
venom/PENCHANT
vent/BOTULISM(A)
venter/VENTRICLE
ventilate/FAN
ventral/VENTRICLE
ventricle/BOTULISM(A)/SUMAC/TUMOR(A)/
    VENTRICLE/WOMAN
ventricose/VENTRICLE
ventriloquism/DIALECT/TUMOR(A)/VENTRICLE
venus/PENCHANT
verboten/BID
verdant/FRUIT/WET
verdict/SYNDICATE/VERY(A)
verdigris/WET
verditer/WET
verdure/WET
verify/VERY(A)
verisimilar/VERY(A)
verity/VERY(A)
vermeil/WORM
vermi/WORM
vermillion/CRIMSON
vermin/WORM
vert/WET
very/RIFE/VERY(A)
vessel/SIP
vest/ABASH/SUIT/VEST
vested/VEST
vestee/VEST
vestiary/VEST
vestibule/VEST
vesting/VEST
vestment/VEST
vestments/ABASH
vestry/VEST
vesture/VEST
vetch/WEAK
veten/VENTRICLE
veteran/VETERAN
veterinary/VETERAN
veto/VETO/VOCALIZE
vex/CONVEY/VIA
via/CONVEY/VIA
viable/HYGIENE(A)/VIVID
viaduct/CONVEY
vial/VIAL(A)
viand/HYGIENE(A)/VIVID
viator/VIA
vicar/WEAK
vicarious/WEAK
vice/BAD/WEAK
viceroy/RACK
vicissitude/WEAK
victor/KIBOSH/QUASH/VICTOR(A)
victory/VICTOR(A)
victual/HYGIENE(A)/VIVID
vicuna/BUCKAROO
video/BOTANY/TELEVISION/VATICAN(A)
vigor/BARON
vile/BALEFUL(A)/EVIL
villa/METROPOLIS/VILLA(A)
village/BARRIO/METROPOLIS

villain/EVIL/METROPOLIS
vindicate/SYNDICATE
vinegar/ACME
violet/PALL
viper/FRUIT
virago/SPRIG(A)/VIRILE
virescent/WET
virgate/SPRIG(A)
virgin/FRUIT/SPRIG(A)
virgo/SPRIG(A)
virgulate/SPRIG(A)
virgule/SPRIG(A)
virid/WET
virile/BARON/VIRILE
virility/BARON
virtue/BARON/VIRILE
virtuoso/VIRILE
virus/BISON
viscid/BISON
viscous/BISON
vision/TELEVISION
vital/HYGIENE(A)/VIVID
vitality/NEW
vitamin/VIVID
vitellus/VETERAN
vitiate/BAD/VETO
viva/HYGIENE(A)/VIVID
vivacious/HYGIENE(A)/VIVID
vivi/VIVID
vivian/VIVID
vivid/HYGIENE(A)/VIVID
vivification/VIVID
vocable/VOCALIZE
vocal/VOCALIZE
vocalize/VOCALIZE
vocalizing/VOCALIZE
vocation/VOCALIZE
vociferate/FERRY
vodka/WET
vogue/CONVEY/VIA
voice/VOCALIZE
void/FAITH/VACATE/VETO
volant/AVIATE
volary/AVIATE
volatile/AVIATE
volcano/AVIATE
volition/VOLUNTEER(A)
volley/AVIATE
volt/WALLOW
voluble/WALLOW
volume/WALLOW
volunteer/VOLUNTEER(A)
voluptuous/VOLUNTEER(A)
volute/WALLOW
volutin/WALLOW
volvox/WALLOW
voracious/DEVOUR
votary/VOCALIZE
vote/AFFIDAVIT/BET/FAITH/VETO/
    VOCALIZE/WED
votive/FAITH/VOCALIZE
vouch/VOCALIZE
voussoir/WALLOW
vow/VOCALIZE
vowel/VOCALIZE
voyage/CONVEY/VIA
vulgar/FELLAH(A)
vulpine/LOBO
waddy/BAT

wadset/AFFIDAVIT
wafer/GOPHER
waffle/GOPHER
wag/CONVEY/ROCK/VIA
wage/FAITH/WED
wager/FAITH/WED
wagon/CONVEY/VIA
wail/ULULATION/WAIL/WOE
wain/CONVEY/VIA
wake/BUCKET/VACATE
wale/VOLUNTEER(A)
walk/ALLEY/WALK/WALLOW
wallop/VOLUNTEER(A)
wallow/ASPHALT/BALL/WALLOW
waltz/WALLOW
wand/WANDER
wander/NOD/POINT/WANDER
wanderer/WANDER
wanderlust/POINT/WANDER
wane/POINT/VACATE/VAIN
want/NEW/VACATE
wanting/POINT
wanton/SEDUCE
wapentake/TAKE
wapiti/EL
war/GUERRILLA/RIVALRY
ward/ORIENTATION
warden/ORIENTATION
warder/ORIENTATION
wardrobe/ORIENTATION
ware/ORIENTATION
warlock/DIALECT/WARLOCK(A)
warm/BURN
warp/GARBLE/REEVE
wart/BLISTER
wary/ORIENTATION
was/BE/IS
wash/NEW/WASH(A)/WET
waste/BUZZARD/EMBEZZLE/VACATE
wastefulness/EMBEZZLE
water/DAMP(A)/WET
watershed/SHED
wattle/WEED
wave/CONVEY/VIA
way/CONVEY/DIRECTION/VIA
wayfarer/FERRY
we/I
weak/NEW/WEAK
weakfish/WEAK
wealth/VOLUNTEER(A)
wear/ABASH/VEST
weasel/BISON
weave/COIN
weaving/REEVE
web/REEVE/RUG
webster/REEVE
wed/AFFIDAVIT/FAITH/VOCALIZE/WED
wedding/AFFIDAVIT/FAITH/WED
wedlock/FAITH/LAUGH/WED
wednesday/ADONIS
wee/CONVEY
weed out/WEED/BOTANY/WEED
week/SEVEN/WEAK
weep/HUBBUB
weft/COIN/NEW/REEVE
weigh/CONVEY/VIA/WEIGHTY(A)
weight/BOTULISM(A)/CONVEY/WEIGHTY(A)
weighty/WEIGHTY(A)

weir/BAR/BARRIO
welfare/FERRY
well/BLOAT/BURN/VOLUNTEER(A)/WALLOW
wellaway/WAIL/WOE
welling/SWELL
welt/ARCHIPELAGO/BLISTER/BLOAT/
    BOULDER/SWELL/WELT
welter/WALLOW
wen/BUBBLE
wend/POINT/WANDER
went/POINT/WANDER
wentletrap/POINT/WANDER
werewolf/BARON/VIRILE
wergeld/VIRILE
wet/NEW/WASH(A)/WET
wharf/REEVE
wharp/REEVE
wharve/REEVE
what/WHO
wheat/WHEAT
wheel/GYRE
wheelbarrow/FERRY
whelp/ALL/LOBO
when/WHEN/WHO
whence/WHO
where/WHERE(A)/WHO
whet/ACUTE
whether/WHO
whir/PYRALIDID(A)
whisky/SAKE
whisper/ASPIRE/GOSPEL
white/WHEAT
whither/WHO
whiting/WHEAT
who/WHEN/WHO
whole/ALL
wholesome/ALL/HAIL
whom/WHO
whose/WHO
wicker/WEAK
widow/BIT/DIVIDED
wiggle/CONVEY/VIA/WALK
wight/KIBOSH
wild/BARRIO/FEROCIOUS(A)
will/VOLUNTEER(A)
willing/VOLUNTEER(A)
win/PENCHANT
wince/POINT
wind/FAN/POINT/WANDER
winding/PANE/WANDER
windlass/POINT/WANDER
winds/PANE/POINT
winnow/FAN
winter/WET
wisent/BISON
wish/NEW
witenagemot/MEET
with/BE/BY
wizen/WIZEN(A)
wizened/WIZEN(A)
woe/HUBBUB/WAIL/WAIL/WOE
woes/WOE
wok/BEAKER
wolf/LOBO
wolfram/LOBO
wolverine/LOBO
woman/NEW/VENTRICLE/WOMAN
womb/WOMAN
wont/PENCHANT

wood/BAT
woof/COIN/REEVE
wool/CABLE/PILE
work/ORGAN/PLOUGH
world/VIRILE
worm/CRIMSON/NEW/WORM
worse/GUERRILLA
worst/GUERRILLA
wound/BUBBLE
wrack/URGE/WREAK(A)/WRECK
wrath/WRATH
wreak/URGE/WREAK(A)/WRECK/URGE/WREAK(A)
wreck/WRECK
wrestle/WRESTLE(A)
wretch/URGE/WRECK
wright/ORGAN
wrong/NEW/WRONG
wroth/WRATH
wrought/ORGAN
wurst/GUERRILLA
wych elm/WEAK
xeno-/XENOPHOBIA
xenon/XENOPHOBIA
xenophobia/XENOPHOBIA
xero-/XEROX(A)
xeroderma/SEAR
xerosis/SEAR
xerox/XEROX(A)
xiphoid/XIPHOID
xiphosuran/XIPHOID
yankee/ANKLE
yard/GIRDLE/HASTATE
yare/ORIENTATION
yarn/CRAW(A)
yawn/GAP
yell/CRY/ULULATION
yellow/HALO
yelp/CRY
yen/COIN
yerk/JERK
yes/IS
yesterday/EXIT
yiddishkeit/ADORE
yiewood/WED
yoga/JUXTAPOSE
yohanon/MADONNA
yoke/JUXTAPOSE
yolk/GHERKKIN(A)
zacaton/ASSASSIN
zamindar/HUMUS(A)
zany/CHANGE/SIN
zax/SAXON
zee/OCEAN(A)
zemstvo/HUMUS(A)
zen/SEMANTIC
zenana/NOOK
zenith/SUMMIT
zero/DECIPHER
zest/SIDE
zeugma/JUXTAPOSE
zinc/GNAW/TINE
zion/SIGN
zloty/CHRYSANTHEMUM/HALO
zoo/HYGIENE(A)/SEISMIC(A)
zoom/SOUND
zwieback/DUO
zwiebel/BASIL
zygote/JUXTAPOSE
-zygous/JUXTAPOSE
zyme/MASS

SELECT BIBLIOGRAPHY

Ayres, Donald M. *English Words from Latin and Greek Elements.* The University of Arizona Press, Tucson Arizona, 1982.

Ben-Yehuda, Ehud, *Ben-Yehuda's English—Hebrew, Hebrew—English Dictionary.* Pocket Books, New York 1964.

Bergman, Peter M. *The Concise Dictionary of 26 Languages.* Signet Book/New American Library, New York, 1968.

A Concise Chinese—English Dictionary. Kong Ching Publishing Co., Hong Kong, 1982.

Dinh-Hoa, Nguyen. *Two Hundred and One Vietnamese Verbs.* Southern Illinois University at Carbondale, 1979.

Eidelberg, Joseph. *The Japanese and the Ten Lost Tribes of Israel.* The Sycamore Press, Givatayim, Israel, 1980.

Español-Euskara (Spanish-Basque). Editorial Cantabrica, Bilbao, Spain, 1984.

Even-Shoshan, Avraham, *Melon Hadash (The New Hebrew Dictionary).* Kiryat Sefer, Jerusalem, Israel, 1965.

Glazerson, Rabbi Matityahu, *Lashon HaKodesh Shoresh HaLishonot. (Hebrew as the Source of Languages).* Shaarei Yoseph Press, Bnai Brak, Israel, 1983.

Grossman, Rueben Avinoam, *Compendious Hebrew-English Dictionary.* Ovir Publishing Co., Tel Aviv Israel, 1968.

Hall, Arthur. *Hebrew Unveiled.* Asher & Co. London, 1894.

Hall, Harold A. *A Partial Vocabulary of the Ngalooma Aboriginal Tribe.* Australian Institute of Aboriginal Studies, Canberra, 1971.

Hebrew—English Lexicon of the Bible. Schocken Books, New York, 1975.

The Holy Scriptures: According to the Masoretic Text. The Jewish Publication Society of America, Philadelphia, 1917—1 volume; 1962, 1978, and 1982—3 volumes.

Jastrow, Marcus, *A Dictionary of the Targumim, The Talmud Babli and Yerushalmi, and the Midrashic Literature.* Traditional Press, Inc. Brooklyn, NY, 2 volumes, 1903.

Klein, Ernest. *A Comprehensive Etymological Dictionary of the Hebrew Language.* MacMillan, NY, 1987.

Kwee, John B. *Indonesian.* The English Universities Press Ltd., London, 1965.

Langacker, Ronald W. *Language and Its Structure.* Harcourt Brace Janovich, New York, 1967.

Mandelkern, Solomon. *Concordantiae Hebraicae Atqye Chaldaicae.* Schocken Publishers, Jerusalem, Israel, 1921.

Perlman, Simon. *English Words of Hebrew Origin.* Narod Press, London, 1947.

Pukui, Mary K. and Elbert, Samuel H. *Hawaiian—English, English—Hawaiian Dictionary.* University of Hawaii Press, Honolulu, 1971.

Robertson, Richard G. *Robertson's Practical English—Thai Dictionary.* Charles E. Tuttle Co., Tokyo, 1985.

Schutz, A.J. *Say it in Fijian.* Pacific Publications, Sydney, Australia, 1979.

Shipley, Joseph T. *Dictionary of Word Origins.* Philosophical Library, 2nd edition, New York, 1945.

_____. *The Origins of English Words: A Discursive Dictionary of Indo-European Roots.* Johns Hopkins University Press, 1984.

Simpson, D.P. *Cassell's New Latin Dictionary.* Funk & Wagnalls Co., New York, 1960.

Thorlin, Eldora S. and Brannen, Noah S. *Everyday Japanese.* Weatherhill, Tokyo, Japan, 1984.

Thorlin, Eldora S., and Henthorn, Taesoon. *Everyday Korean.* Weatherhill, Tokyo, Japan, 1984.

Tozzer, Alfred M. *A Maya Grammar.* Dover Publications, Inc., New York, 1977.

Wallace, Alfred Russel. *The Malay Archipelago.* Dover Publications, Inc., New York, 1962.

Watkins, Calvert. *The American Heritage Dictionary of Indo-European Roots.* Houghton-Mifflin Co., Boston, 1985.

Webster's New World Dictionary, College Edition, Nelson, Foster and Scott Ltd., Toronto, 1966.

Whitney, Arthur H. *Finnish.* Hodder and Stoughton, London, 1977.

Resources

Lists of "1,000 Identicals" for English and words in French, German, Hebrew, Italian, Japanese, Russian and Spanish may be obtained by writing Ruth Freedman/Words, Ltd/1503 Punahou, #3C/Honolulu, Hawaii/96872. Not based on historical principles, these word pairs are valuable for language acquisition.

Those interested in Anglo-Saxon vocabulary and possible historical links between Hebrew and English should get *The Tribes: The Israelite Origins of Western Nations* (Russell-Davis Publishing Co., Hebron, 1993). This 480-page book linking Goths to Gad and Celts to Gilliad is available from the author, Yair Davidy, Susia, 90401, Israel for $25.

The best book on language superfamilies is Merrit Ruhlen's *The Origin of Language: Tracing the Evolution of the Mother Tongue* (John Wiley & Sons, New York, 1994).

Magazine articles recapping the work of the Nostraticists include Philip E. Ross, "Hard Words," *Scientific American,* April 1991, and Robert Wright, "Quest for the Mother Tongue," *The Atlantic Monthly,* April 1991.

About the Author

Isaac Mozeson has taught English at Touro College, Yeshiva College, and New York University. He is on the staff of *Kirkus Reviews*. His recent books, coauthored with Lois Stavsky, include *A 2 Z: A Dictionary of Slang* and *Jerusalem Mosaic*. He has also published books of Jewish poetry and history. As the founder of Emetology, he has lectured on Hebrew as the mother tongue to a wide variety of audiences from his home bases in the New York area and German Colony, Jerusalem.